A DICTIONARY OF
TWENTIETH-CENTURY COMPOSERS
(1911-1971)

A
DICTIONARY
OF
TWENTIETH-CENTURY
COMPOSERS
(1911-1971)

Kenneth Thompson

FABER & FABER

LONDON

First published in 1973
by Faber and Faber Limited
3 Queen Square, London
Printed in Great Britain
by Ebenezer Baylis and Son Ltd.
The Trinity Press, Worcester, and London
All rights reserved

ISBN 0 571 09002 8

Lovingly dedicated to
my wife
VIVIEN

Contents

Introduction	*page* 9
Béla Bartók	17
Alban Berg	41
Ernest Bloch	53
Ferruccio Busoni	62
Claude Debussy	77
Frederick Delius	116
Edward Elgar	131
Manuel de Falla	139
Gabriel Fauré	167
Paul Hindemith	181
Gustav Holst	209
Arthur Honegger	226
Charles Ives	251
Leoš Janáček	264
Zoltán Kodály	281
Gustav Mahler	295
Bohuslav Martinů	313
Carl Nielsen	338
Francis Poulenc	353
Sergei Prokofiev	371

Contents

Giacomo Puccini   *page* 395

Sergei Rachmaninov   405

Maurice Ravel   419

Albert Roussel   440

Erik Satie   456

Arnold Schoenberg   466

Jean Sibelius   494

Richard Strauss   521

Igor Stravinsky   566

Edgar Varèse   606

Ralph Vaughan Williams   610

Anton Webern   646

Addenda   659

Introduction

The origins of this dictionary lie in long-term investigation begun in 1948 and continued sporadically for over a decade. When this sorting stage was eventually completed in the mid-sixties, the result was tested when, in the summer of 1966, *The Musical Times* commissioned a catalogue and bibliography of the music of Sir Arthur Bliss, required within a few weeks for an issue celebrating the composer's seventy-fifth birthday. The layout of material which evolved appeared to be satisfactory and led to a more precise direction for consolidating research and thereby to the production of two similar catalogues, awkwardly too long for periodical publication, too short for book presentation. A solution was forthcoming in September 1967 when Donald Mitchell suggested a collection of some thirty such catalogues for a reference book and consequently commissioned the present volume.

The initial problem was the selection of the composers of international stature to be represented in a selective and necessarily single-volume dictionary. Although the original scheme was to cover both modern and contemporary music, selection in these terms proved almost impossibly difficult and was soon abandoned in favour of a suggestion that its scope be confined to twentieth-century composers now dead and whose body of work is accordingly complete. This idea had much to commend it: not only did it make selection considerably easier but it also afforded the prospect of comparatively uncomplicated future revision. It was then proposed to tackle the unequivocally major composers in complete form, the more subsidiary figures in condensed style. The procedure appeared attractive enough in theory, but in practice it was difficult to find a really satisfactory formula for abbreviated treatment; finally it was decided to deal comprehensively with all composers selected for inclusion.

A dictionary of which the content is almost entirely a series of catalogues and bibliographies necessarily departs from—and in effect completely reverses—the normal procedure in which a biographical and critical essay is the principal feature, checklist of compositions and short bibliography the supplementary material. Here the content is completely factual, precluding critical opinion of any sort; in addition it reduces biographical accounts to a skeleton note in the form of an introductory paragraph. This approach is not so eccentric as it might appear, since plentiful critical and biographical material exists in easily accessible form, whereas a proportion of the principal content of the present Dictionary is not so readily accessible: the presentation in handy reference form of data hitherto difficult of access is its principal *raison d'être*.

In common with any encyclopaedia-style compilation, much has necessarily been copied from information made available by the researches of various writers and scholars, in particular from detailed studies by authorities on individual composers. My debt in this direction is enormous, and some specific sources which have been used as a basis for my own catalogues are gratefully acknowledged. None the less, the present compilation is not confined to copying existing data from a variety of sources but has been the subject of considerable cross-checking and new research. Clarity of presentation and general usefulness have been the chief aims and have always taken preference in any clash with the doubtful desirability of completely inflexible consistency. Although I evolved some general rules to govern the style of the compilation, I have not hesitated to break them if there seemed good reason.

Liberal use has been made of the interrogative point, denoting not that the questioned information is necessarily incorrect but that in my view it is open to some suspicion and should be approached with caution. Ideally it would have been preferable to employ a second or even third point of interrogation to denote degrees of such suspicion, but in view of the wide field covered such a procedure would have entailed almost impossible nicety of judgment.

Arrangement is chronological and information is given in the following order: catalogue number, title, opus number, authorship of song texts, composition date or particulars, authorship of texts of large works, dedication, duration, instrumentation, first performance(s), publication, bibliography.

Titles Titles of French, German and Italian works are listed in the original language without translation. Czech, Hungarian and Danish works are listed by English titles, normally those of published editions but with variants noted in instances where these can frequently be found, followed by original titles in parentheses. Russian works are listed in English. No English titles have been coined for this dictionary; consequently foreign works with no accepted English translation are given in the original language only.

The language problem in relation to titles is a vexed question to which there seems to be no single solution. Original titles are surely imperative for reference purposes and English translations confined to less widely read languages might be considered an acceptable solution despite the element of inconsistency involved and consequent departure from a strictly correct indexing procedure which would not find, say, *Padmâvatî* followed by an English 'translation' (Padmavati) absurd. Little guidance is to be had from common usage which is tending to become increasingly varied. British concerts and broadcasting programmes were once inclined to adhere to original titles rather than the vernacular favoured in many other countries, but for some considerable time translated titles have been increasingly used, if without much consistency. For instance the formerly encountered original title *Ma Mère l'Oye* has almost entirely succumbed to the English version *Mother Goose*, but *Valses nobles et sentimentales* almost invariably remains untranslated: were both works included in a Ravel programme, one title in French and the other in English would be unblinkingly accepted. The disappearance of French titles for non-French works, usually occasioned by publication considerations, is more complete so that the once familiar *Le Sacre du Printemps* is no longer much used in this country; nevertheless there are plentiful exceptions, and in cases such as Martinů's *La Revue de Cuisine*, still more frequently encountered than *The Kitchen Revue*, I have not hesitated to use the French titles. Perhaps apology is due to those who find language admixture abhorrent; but 'Sad Waltz' from *Death* appears decidedly quaint in contrast with the familiar language blend of 'Valse triste' from *Kuolema*. I can but hope that the consistent sort of inconsistency which I have preferred to adopt over such matters will not offend too many.

Composition dates   Normally these may be taken as completion dates, but more specific information is given where such data is printed in the score or is available from a reliable source.

Durations   Though often viewed by me with distrust, timings arc given only if printed in the score, specified by the composer, or available from a reliable authority. On occasion, even seemingly dependable sources differ, in which event a timing appears thus: Dur. 17–19′.

Instrumentation   Orchestration details are listed from overall standpoint without regard to doubling and the number of players actually required. No attempt has been made to standardize those instruments, notably in the percussion department, known by various names. The exceptions are 'GC' for bass drum on account of the easy abbreviation, and 'side drum' in cases where this avoids an untidy-looking abbreviation of the German 'kleine Trommel'. The abbreviations are sufficiently standard not to require listing: less common instruments are given in full.

First performances   Some effort has been made to prise out information locked between the covers of old periodicals, although only research concerned with the post-1875 period has been of use for the present purpose. For want of a short-cut, this operation was a matter of toothcombing methods to dredge up as many pertinent facts as possible, although to date only English and French sources have been tackled and much work yet remains to be done along these lines. However, I believe it to have yielded a significant amount of data not otherwise available in reference form. I am convinced that in the late nineteenth century the term 'first performance in London' is, as often as not, synonymous with 'first performance in England', but unless concrete evidence to the contrary was found it was obviously safer to adhere to the form used during that period. At the other extreme I learned to view with considerable suspicion the legend 'première audition' in pre-war French periodicals and concert announcements; Parisian musical circles were at times inclined to be shameless in making first performance claims irrespective of whether a work had been performed elsewhere in the world, elsewhere in France or even on a previous occasion in Paris: often the truth of such claims amounts merely to 'first performance at these concerts'.

The following abbreviations have been used:

fp	..	..	first perfomance
fbp	..	..	first broadcast perfomance
fAp	..	..	first perfomance in the United States

fCp	..	..	first performance in Czechoslovakia
fDp	..	..	first performance in Denmark
fEp	..	..	first performance in England
fFp	..	..	first performance in France
fGp	..	..	first performance in Germany
fGBp	..	..	first performance in Great Britain
fHp	..	..	first performance in Hungary
fIp	..	..	first performance in Italy
fRp	..	..	first performance in Russia

Periodicals   Names of periodicals have normally been given in full, but some extensively-used musical journals have been abbreviated as follows: *AMZ* (Allgemeine Musik Zeitung), *Anbruch* (Musikblätter des Anbruch), *M&L* (Music and Letters), *M&M* (Music and Musicians), *MMR* (Monthly Musical Record), *MN&H* (Musical News and Herald), *MO* (Musical Opinion), *MQ* (Musical Quarterly), *MR* (Music Review), *MS* (Musical Standard), *MT* (Musical Times), *NMZ* (Neue Musik Zeitung), *NZfM* (Neue Zeitschrift für Musik), *ÖM* (Österreichische Musikzeitschrift), *P(R)MA* (Proceedings of the [Royal] Musical Association), *RM* (Revue Musicale), *SM* (Schweizerische Musikzeitung).

First broadcast performances   Although to some minds the one type of première worth consideration is the first live performance, many now consider broadcast performances equally and sometimes possibly more important. Particularly in respect of modern and contemporary music there does seem sound sense in the view that a work broadcast for the first time will reach a larger audience than if it were performed in a concert hall every night for a year. But again most of the relevant data is not easily accessible and required another toothcomb type of investigation. This line of research was somewhat arduous so far as the pre-war period was concerned but became progressively less intricate after the war when first broadcast information became more consistently and comprehensively noted in the *Radio Times*. I should make it clear that the responsibility for the accuracy of the broadcast information in this dictionary is entirely mine, and no blame whatever for any shortcomings can be laid at the door of the British Broadcasting Corporation: it was clearly impractical to approach the Corporation with a list of many hundreds of broadcasts for confirmation that transmissions took place as advertised in every particular. In addition, only a fraction of the performances listed here as radio premières of some kind were in fact announced as such by the BBC. Some margin of error must be allowed since it is inconceivable that, in studying something to the order of 15,000 days of broadcast programmes, some works, especially songs and shorter pieces, have not slipped through the net. Such an operation is for safety purposes better done more than once but is rather too formidable an undertaking to repeat entirely, though part of it at least was done twice so that I have some reason to hope that the degree of inaccuracy might not be too considerable. Perhaps it should be defined that the term 'first broadcast performance' signifies the first broadcast since detailed daily programmes were listed with the inauguration of the *Radio Times* in September 1923.

Publication Publication details have been treated more selectively than material under previous headings. Publication date and original publisher have been given as a matter of course wherever possible. Changes in publisher or new editions are noted provided I have seen corresponding scores—inclusion has largely depended on whether a copy is deposited with the British Museum. Arrangements other than the composer's own have been approached in decidedly selective fashion, and only important reductions or arrangements have been noted.

Bibliography The bibliographies are necessarily selective but have been compiled with a view to reasonable comprehensiveness. Perhaps some further explanation is advisable in light of a suggestion, received as it happened at rather too late a stage in the book's preparation to act upon, which nevertheless might reflect a body of opinion on the subject. Essentially this pleaded that the bibliography should be compiled to some rigidly set terms of reference, e.g. only articles published in specifically musical journals should be considered, or alternatively that inclusion or otherwise should be determined on a basis of an arbitrarily chosen minimum length, or possibly even on a basis of informed authorship. Such inflexibility would have been alien to my approach in the catalogue sections, but apart from this I felt such proposals to be open to serious objections. If non-musical journals were automatically to be denied consideration, much useful material would certainly have remained unlisted: it is by no means always the case that valuable articles are confined to musical journals. Much the same objection can be levelled at length as the determining factor: if a length of 1,000 words were chosen as that determining inclusion or rejection, a useful reference condensed into 800 words would be precluded, one of doubtful value running to 1,200 words would make the grade. The principle of confining a bibliography to reputable authors and recognised authorities has much to commend it for the compilation of brief bibliographies, but for the more comprehensive references attempted here it would have demanded judgments which I would not care to have been called upon to make. And so I can only offer apologies to readers who would have preferred a more rigid scheme or more rigorous weeding-out of the deadwood which inevitable must have found its way into the listings. The aim, however much a rainbow-chasing one, has rather been not to miss references which might be found useful. With few exceptions, newspaper articles apart from a number in *The Times* and the *New York Times* have not been included, nor have reviews and articles relating to gramophone recordings in respects other than discographies.

K. T.

ACKNOWLEDGEMENTS

I owe grateful thanks on a personal level to helpful people who have been kind enough to respond to requests for information: Christopher Calthrop, Charles Ford, Elspeth Grant, James Harding, Diana McVeagh, Norman Del Mar, and Lionel Salter. I would like to express special thanks to Eric Fenby, who was kind enough to look through my Delius catalogue in draft and answer a number of queries besides supplying instrumentation details of unpublished works. My debt to Imogen Holst for her generous, friendly and painstaking help and advice in preparing the Holst catalogue is enormous, and to her I offer my warmest thanks.

I owe a special debt to a number of authorities who have been kind enough to give me the benefit of their specialised knowledge of individual composers by reading page-proofs and making corrections, additions and suggestions. In this respect I would like to express my warm appreciation and grateful thanks to John Weissmann (Bartók); Colin Matthews (Berg); Ronald Stevenson (Busoni); Bill Hopkins (Debussy); Dr. Norman Suckling (Fauré); Ian Kemp (Hindemith); Dr. Hans Hollander (Janáček); Dr. Percy Young (Kodály); Donald Mitchell (Mahler); Dr. Robert Simpson (Nielsen); James Harding (Poulenc & Satie); Mosco Carner (Puccini); Israel Nestyev (Prokofiev); Patrick Piggott (Prokofiev & Rachmaninov); Felix Aprahamian (Ravel); Professor Basil Deane (Roussel); David Matthews (Schoenberg); Robert Layton (Sibelius); Norman Del Mar (Strauss); Eric Walter White (Stravinsky) and Michael Kennedy (Vaughan Williams). I am particularly indebted to the following published works: *The Life and Works of Béla Bartók* by Halsey Stevens; *Letters of Edward Elgar* edited by Percy M. Young; various writings on Honegger by Willy Tappolet; *Leoš Janáček: his Life and Works* by Jaroslav Vogel; *Gustav Mahler: the Early Years* by Donald Mitchell; various writings on Martinů by Miloš Safránek; *Sergei Rachmaninov* by Sergei Bertensson and Jay Leyda; *Albert Roussel: a study* by Norman Demuth; *The Works of Arnold Schoenberg* by Josef Rufer; *Richard Strauss: a critical commentary on his life and works* by Norman Del Mar; *Stravinsky* by Eric Walter White; various writings on Vaughan Williams by Michael Kennedy, particularly *The Works of Ralph Vaughan Williams*.

So far as is practicable at page-proof stage, such material has been incorporated into the main body of the text or set out in the form of an appendix of additions and corrections. Since this book was written in 1968–69, much additional information has become available, and it is already apparent that some catalogues (notably Hindemith and Strauss) could well benefit from further revision; and some of the late revisions made to the text, particularly in respect of early and unpublished works, have had to be incorporated in less than ideal placement resulting in departures from the generally adopted chronological sequence.

The addenda, however, could form the nucleus of a subsequent revised edition, for which purpose further supplementary information would be gratefully received. And possibly, depending on reaction, some major changes might be considered. For example, I have virtually omitted Russian bibliography and the vast Hungarian bibliography of Bartók as too specialist as well as space-consuming for a 'general purpose' volume. Perhaps the listing of percussion instruments could benefit from a more systematic presentation: I have been content to follow listings by publishers or on scores, or, where neither is available, to adopt their 'order of appearance' in a score. Again, my selective approach to publication history and basis of copyright rather than imprint might possibly prove more confusing than helpful, judging by pre-publication comments. It is hoped that practical use will reveal whether any such changes are desirable in future revision.

BÉLA BARTÓK (1881–1945)

Bartók was born on 25 March 1881, in what was then Nagyszentmiklós (Hungary) and is now Sînnicolaul-Mare (Romania). His father, the director of an agricultural school, died when Bartók was eight, but his mother—to whom he was deeply attached—lived for another fifty years. Though given a chance of advanced musical training in Vienna, he chose instead to go to Budapest, studying at the Royal Academy of Music there from 1899 to 1903. He studied composition with Hans Koessler, but concentrated most of his energies on the piano, only turning seriously to creative work in his last year at the Academy. In 1905 he began to transcribe Magyar peasant songs and much of the next fourteen years was spent in ethno-musicological fieldwork on Magyar, Slovak, Romanian and (in 1913) North African folk-song, often in collaboration with his friend Zoltán Kodály. Bartók also toured as a concert pianist until 1912 and from 1907 taught the piano—though never composition—at the Budapest Academy. After a crisis at the Academy in 1919 reflecting the political and economic crises in Hungary as a whole (during which Bartók contemplated emigrating to Transylvania), his non-composing career entered a new phase: classification and publication of his earlier fieldwork in folk-music alternating with much more extensive concert tours abroad, including visits to the USA in 1927–8 and the USSR in 1929. In 1923 he divorced his first wife, Márta Ziegler (whom he had married in 1909) and married Ditta Pásztory, with whom he was later to give many two-piano recitals. Though becoming an international figure and contributing much to the activities of the ISCM, Bartók continued to live in Budapest. He resigned from his teaching post at the Academy in 1934 so as to concentrate on ethno-musicology, making field-trips to Egypt in 1932 and Turkey in 1936; but with the Nazi seizure of power in Austria (March 1938) he again contemplated emigration. He used a second concert tour of the United States as a stepping-stone to more permanent work there, crossing to New York in the spring of 1940. After returning briefly to Hungary the same summer, Bartók spent the rest of his life in America. He lived mainly in New York, researching at Columbia University and giving concerts: but he was dogged by grave financial worries and increasing ill-health until his death from leukaemia in September 1945.

CATALOGUE OF WORKS

1. (**Juvenilia**). Unpub.
   a. *A Budapesti tornaverseny* (Gymnastics Contest in Budapest).
   b. *Gyorspolka* (Fast Polka).
   c. *'Béla' Polka*.
   d. *'Katinka' Gyorspolka*.
   e. *'Jolán' Polka*.
   f. *Nefelejts* (Forget-me-not).

2. **The Danube River** (A Duna folyása). For piano. ?1890, Nagyszöllös.
   fp: 1 May 1892, Nagyszöllös, Béla Bartók. Unpub.

3. **Introduction and Allegro.** For piano. 189?. Unpub.

4. **Scherzo.** For piano. 1897. Ded. Gabriella Lator. Unpub.

5. **Three Pieces.** For piano. 1894. Ded. Gabriella Lator.
   1. *Spring Song* (Tavaszi dal).
   2. *Valse*.
   3. *In Wallachian style* (Oláhos). (?)
   Unpub.

6. **Three Pieces.** For piano. 1897. Pozsony. Ded. Gabriella Lator.
   1. *Adagio—Presto*; 2. (Untitled—no tempo indication); 3. *Adagio, sehr düster*.
   Unpub.

7. **Piano Sonata.** 1897. Unpub.

8. Piano Quartet. 1898.
fp: 1898, Pozsony.
Unpub.

9. Three Songs (Drei Lieder). For voice and piano. August 1898, Pozsony. Ded. Countess Matilde von Wenckheim.
　1. *Im wunderschönen Monat Mai* (Heinrich Heine).
　2. *Nacht am Rheine* (Karl Siebel).
　3. *Ein Lied.*
Unpub. Facsimile of No. 1 in *Lev.* 1, p. 204.

10. String Quartet. 1899, Pozsony. Unpub.

11. Quintet. 1899, Budapest. ?Unfinished. Unpub.

12. Love Songs (Liebeslieder) (Friedrich Rückert). For voice and piano. 1900, Budapest.
　1. *Diese Rose pflück ich hier.*
　2. *Ich fühle deinen Odem.*

13. Minuet. For piano. 1901. Unpub.

14. Four Songs (Négy dal) (Lajos Pósa). For voice and piano. 1902.
　1. *Autumn breeze* (Őszi szellő).
　2. *The girls of Szeged scorn me* (Még azt vetik a szememre).
　3. *There is no such sorrow* (Nincs olyan bú).
　4. *Well, well!* (Ejnye! Ejnye!).

15. Symphony. 1902. Pub. in piano reduction only. Two movements orchestrated by Denijs Dille.
fp: 28 September 1961, Orchestra of Hungarian Radio, cond. György Lehel.

16. Scherzo. For orchestra. 1902. Part of preceding.
fp: 29 February 1904, Budapest Opera Orchestra, cond. István Kerner.
Unpub.

17. Evening (Est). For voice and piano (Kálmán Harsányi). 1903 (?April).

17a. Evening (Est). For four-part male chorus (Kálmán Harsányi). April 1903. Pub. 1964, in *Documenta Bartókiana*, I.

18. Four Songs. For voice and piano. 1903 (?June). Unpub. Lost.

19. Violin Sonata. 1903.
fp (3rd movement only): 8 June 1903, Sándor Köszegi and Béla Bartók.
fp (complete): 25 January 1904, Jenö Hubay and Béla Bartók.

20. Kossuth. Symphonic Poem in ten tableaux for large orchestra. 2 April–18 August 1903. Dur. 28′.
　3 fl, pic, 3 ob, ca, E-flat cl, 2 cl, bcl, 3 bsn, cbsn; 8 hn, 4 tpt, 3 tmb, 2 ten tuba, tuba; 3 timp, cym, tgle, tamb pic, GC, tamtam; 2 hp, strings (16-16-12-10-18).
fp: 13 January 1904, Budapest, Philharmonic Society, cond. István Kerner.
fEp: 18 February 1904, Manchester, Hallé Orchestra, cond. Hans Richter.
fLondon p: 6 December 1966, Royal Festival Hall, New Philharmonia Orchestra, cond. Norman Del Mar.
Pub. 1963, Editions Musica (Budapest), Boosey & Hawkes (London), ed. D. Dille.

BIBLIOGRAPHY:
David Clegg: Bartók's Kossuth Symphony, *MR*, August 1962, p. 215.

20a. Funeral March (Gyászinduló). For piano. 1903. From 'Kossuth'. Pub. Charles Rozsnyai.

21. Four Pieces. For piano. 1903.
　1. *Study for the left hand.* Dated; January 1903, Budapest. Ded. István Thomán.
fp: 13 April 1903, Nagyszentmiklós, Béla Bartók.
　2. *Fantasy I* (Ábránd). Dated: 8 February 1903, Budapest. Ded. Emma Gruber.
fp: 27 March 1903, Budapest, Béla Bartók.
　3. *Fantasy II* (Ábránd). Dated: 12 October 1903, Berlin. Ded. Emsy and Irmy Jurkovics.
　4. *Scherzo.* Dated: June–September 1903, Budapest–Gmunden. Ded. Ernö Dohnányi.
fp: 25 November 1903, Budapest, Béla Bartók.
Pub. 1953, Zerboni; 1956, Zenemükiadó Vállalat.

22. Piano Quintet. 1904.
fp: 21 November 1904, Vienna, Béla Bartók and the Prill Quartet.
Pub. 1970, Zenemükiadó Vállalat.

23. Three Songs (Három népies müdal). For voice and piano. ?1904.
1. *Evening song* (Esti dal) (Sándor Peres).
2. *The benefactors* (A jótevök) (István Havas).
3. *Bell sound* (Harangszó) (Béla Sztankó). Pub. in Énekiskola (Ödön Geszler).

24. Two Songs. For mixed chorus. ?1904.
1. *My hen is lost* (Elveszett a tyúkom).
2. *If I go in* (Ha bemegyek).
Unpub.

25. Rhapsody Op. 1. For piano solo. November 1904. Ded. Emma (Gruber).
fp: 4 November 1906, Pozsony, Béla Bartók.
fEbp: 16 October 1961, Thomas Rajna.
Pub. 1908, Rózsavölgyi.

25a. Rhapsody Op. 1. Version for piano and orchestra. November 1904. Ded. Emma Gruber.
2 fl, pic, 2 ob, 2 cl, bcl, 2 bsn; 4 hn, 2 tpt, 3 tmb; timp, tamtam, GC, tamb pic, tgle; strings.
fp: 15 November 1909, Budapest, Béla Bartók and the Orchestra of the Academy of Music, cond. Jenö Hubay.
fEp: 15 October 1921, Queen's Hall, Promenade Concert, Auriol Jones and the New Queen's Hall Orchestra, cond. Sir Henry Wood.
fEbp: 4 March 1932, Béla Bartók and the BBC Orchestra, cond. Sir Henry Wood.
Pub. 1910, Rózsavölgyi: score, parts, and reduction for two pianos four hands by Béla Bartók.
Revised version. Dur. 17′.
2 fl, pic, 2 ob, 2 cl, bcl, 2 bsn; 4 hn, 2 tpt, 3 tmb; timp, tgle, tamb pic, cym, GC, tamtam; strings.
fEp: 3 March 1953, Royal Festival Hall, Andor Földes and the Royal Philharmonic Orchestra, cond. Walter Susskind.
Pub. 1954, Zenemükiadó Vállalat.

25b. Rhapsody Op. 1. Version for two pianos. November 1904.

BIBLIOGRAPHY:
J. Carmichael: Bartók's First Op. 1, *M&M*, February 1964, p. 41.

26. Scherzo Op. 2. For piano and orchestra. 1904.
3 fl, pic, 2 ob, ca, E-flat cl, 3 cl, 3 bsn, cbsn; 4 hn, 3 tpt, 3 tmb, tuba; timp, cym, GC, tgle, campanella, tamb pic, tamburo, tamtam; 2 hp, strings.
fp: 28 September 1961, Budapest, E. Tusa and Orchestra of Hungarian Radio, cond. György Lehel.
Pub. 1961, Zenemükiadó Vállalat (Budapest).

BIBLIOGRAPHY:
D. Dille: Preface to the first edition of Bartók's Scherzo for piano and orchestra, *Musical Events*, January 1961, p. 10.
John S. Weissmann: A new-old Bartók, *Musical Events*, February 1963, p. 8.

27. Székely Folksong (Székely népdal). For voice and piano. 1904.
Pub. 1905, in Supplement to *Magyar Lant*.

28. Hungarian Folksongs (Magyar népdalok). For voice and piano. 1905 (First series), 1906 (Second series). Only the following were published:
Set I:
1. *They have mown the meadow* (Lekaszálták már a rétet).
Set II:
4. *If I go to the inn* (Ha bemegyek a csárdába).
6. *I drank the red wine from the glass* (Megittam a piros bort).
7. *Maiden stringing pearls* (Ez a kislány gyöngyöt füz).
8. *Hey, when they take me for a soldier* (Sej, mikor engem katonának visznek).

29. Suite No. 1 Op. 3. For large orchestra. 1905, Vienna.
1. *Allegro vivace*; 2. *Poco adagio*; 3. *Presto*; 4. *Moderato*; 5. *Molto vivace*.
3 fl, pic, 2 ob, ca, 3 cl, bcl, 3 bsn, cbsn; 4 hn, 3 tpt, 3 tmb, bs tuba; timp, cinelli, tgle, tamb, campanella; 2 hp, strings.
fp (three movements only): 29 November 1905, Vienna, Gesellschaftkonzerte, cond. Ferdinand Löwe.
fEp: 1 September 1914, Queen's Hall, Promenade Concert, Queen's Hall Orchestra, cond. Sir Henry Wood.

fEbp: 4 March 1932, BBC Orchestra, cond. Sir Henry Wood.

Pub. 1912, Rózsavölgyi.

30. To the little 'Slovak' (A kicsi 'tót'-nak.) Five songs for a child. Dated: 20 December 1905, Vienna. Unpub.: No. 3 in facsimile in *Lev.* 1, p. 207.

31. Twenty Hungarian folksongs. For voice and piano. December 1906, rev. 1938. Nos. 1–10 by Bartók, others by Kodály.
    1. *I set out for my fair homeland* (Elindultam szép hazámbul).
    2. *I would cross the Tisza in a boat* (Általmennek én a Tiszán ladikon).
    3. *László Fehér stole a horse* (Fehér László lovat lopott).
    4. *In the Gyula garden* (A gyulai kert alatt).
    5. *I walked in the Kertmeg garden* (A kertmegi kert alatt sétáltam).
    6. *In my window shone the moonlight* (Ablakomba, ablakomba besütött a holdvilág).
    7. *From the withered branch no rose blooms* (Száraz ágtól messze virít a rózsa).
    8. *I walked to the end of the great street in Tárkány* (Végig mentem a tárkányi sej, haj, nagy uccán).
    9. *Not far from here is Kismargitta* (Nem messze van ide Kis Margitta).
    10. *My sweetheart is ploughing, jingle, clatter* (Szánt a babám csireg, csörög).

Pub. 1907, Rozsnyai Károly.

31a. The street is on fire (Ucca, ucca, ég az ucca). For voice and piano. 1906. Deleted, as not an authentic folksong, from the 1938 revision of No. 31.

31b. On my mother's rosebush (Edesanyám rózsafája). For voice and piano. ?1906. Intended for inclusion in No. 31.

32. Suite No. 2 Op. 4. For small orchestra. November 1905, Vienna—1 September 1907, Rákospalota.
    1. *Comodo*; 2. *Allegro scherzando*; 3. *Andante*; 4. *Comodo*.
fp (No. 2 only): 2 January 1909, Berlin, cond. Béla Bartók.
fp (complete): 22 November 1909, Budapest, Philharmonic Society, cond. István erner.

32a. Suite No. 2 Op. 4. For orchestra. Revised version, 1920. Dur. 25'.
2 fl, pic, 2 ob, ca, 2 cl, E-flat cl, bcl, 2 bsn, cbsn; 3 hn, 2 tpt; 3 timp, GC, small dm, tgle, tamtam, cym, tamb; 2 hp, strings.
Pub. 1921, Universal-Edition; 1939, Hawkes.

32b. Suite No. 2 Op. 4. Revised version, 1943.
Instrumentation as for No. 32a.
fEp (broadcast): 16 December 1953, BBC broadcast, Goldsborough Orchestra, cond. Charles Mackerras.
fEp (concert): 6 October 1959, Royal Festival Hall, London Philharmonic Orchestra, cond. Samuel Rosenheim.
Pub. 1948, Hawkes; also arr. by Béla Bartók for two pianos, 1943.

33. Three Hungarian folksongs from the Csík district. For piano. 1907. Pub. Rozsnyai. Also arr. by János Szebenyi for flute and piano, and by György Balassa for clarinet and piano.

34. Violin Concerto No. 1. 1 July 1907, Jászberény–5 February 1908, Budapest. Ded. Stefi Geyer. Dur. 21'.
    1. *Andante sostenuto*; 2. *Allegro giocoso*.
2 fl, pic, 2 ob, ca, 2 cl, bcl, 2 bsn; 4 hn, 2 (3) tpt, 2 tmb, tuba; timp, tgle, GC; 2 hp, strings.
fp: 30 May 1958, Basle, Hans-Heinz Schneeberger and the Basle Chamber Orchestra, cond. Paul Sacher.
f London p: 21 January 1960, Yehudi Menuhin and the London Philharmonic Orchestra, cond. Jaroslav Krombholc.
Pub. 1958 (reduction), 1959 (score), Boosey & Hawkes. Reduction by Hans-Heinz Schneeberger.

BIBLIOGRAPHY:
Colin Mason: Bartók's early Violin Concerto, *Tempo* No. 49, autumn 1958.
Peter Stadlen: Bartók's early Violin Concerto, *Musical Events*, April 1960, p. 47.

35. Two Portraits Op. 5. For violin and orchestra. 1907–8.
2 fl, pic, 2 ob, ca, 2 cl, bcl, 2 bsn; 4 hn, 2 tpt, 2 tmb, bs tmb; tgle, timp, tamb pic, cinelli, GC, tamtam; 2 hp, strings.
fp: 1909, Budapest, Imre Waldbauer and

the Budapest Symphony Orchestra, cond. László Kún.

fEp: 11 May 1914, Aeolian Hall, Queen's Hall Orchestra, cond. Sir Henry Wood.

Pub. 1912, Rozsnyai Károly (Budapest).

36. Fourteen Bagatelles Op. 6. For piano. May 1908, Budapest.

1. *Molto sostenuto*; 2. *Allegro giocoso*; 3. *Andante*; 4. *Grave*; 5. *Vivo*; 6. *Lento*; 7. *Allegretto molto capriccioso*; 8. *Andante sostenuto*; 9. *Allegretto grazioso*; 10. *Allegro*; 11. *Allegretto molto rubato*; 12. *Rubato*; 13. *'Elle est morte': Lento funebre*; 14. *Valse* ('Ma mie qui danse'): *Presto*.

fp: 29 June 1908, Berlin (for Busoni's piano class).

fEbp (Nos. 2–5, 7, 10 & 12): 24 November 1930, Béla Bartók.

37. Ten Easy Pieces. For piano. June 1908, Budapest.

Dedication (Ajánlás): 1. *Peasant song* (Paraszt-dal); 2. *Frustration* (Lassú vergödés); 3. *Slovakian boys' dance* (Tót legények tánca); 4. *Sostenuto*; 5. *Evening with the Széklers* (Este a Székelyeknél); 6. *Hungarian folksong* (Magyar népdal); 7. *Dawn* (Hajnal); 8. *Folksong* (Azt mondják, nem adnak); 9. *Five-finger exercise* (Gyakorlat); 10. *Bear dance* (Medvetánc).

Pub. Rozsnyai. Nos. 5 & 10 transcribed for orchestra as first two movements of 'Hungarian Sketches', 1931. No. 5 arr. by József Pécsi for wind orchestra, 1949.

38. String Quartet No. 1 Op. 7. Dated: 27 January 1909.

1. *Lento*; 2. *Allegretto*; 3. *Allegro vivace*.

fp: 19 March 1910, Budapest, Waldbauer-Kerpely Quartet.

fEp: 9 May 1922, Grafton Galleries, London Chamber Concert, Hungarian Quartet.

fEbp: 7 May 1928, Amar-Hindemith Quartet.

Pub. 1911, Rózsavölgyi; 1957, Zene-mükiadó Vállalat.

39. Erlkönig. Beethoven, orch. Béla Bartók. *c.* 1904–11.

BIBLIOGRAPHY:
Denijs Dille: Ein unbekanntes Bartók-Manuskript, *ÖM*, May 1967, p. 283.

40. Two Elegies Op. 8b. For piano. 1908–9.
1. *Grave*. Dated: February 1908.
2. *Molto adagio sempre rubato*. Dated: December 1909.

fEp: 11 March 1914, Aeolian Hall, Franz Liebich.

Pub. 1910, Rozsnyai Károly.

41. For Children (A gyermekeknek; Pro dêti). For piano. 1908–9, rev. January 1945. 85 pieces in 4 vols. (original version), 79 pieces in 2 vols. (revised version).

Vol. 1. *Based on Hungarian folktunes.*
Vol. 2. *Based on Slovakian folktunes.*

fEp (8 pieces from Vol. 2): 7 May 1923, London Contemporary Music Centre–British Music Society meeting, Béla Bartók.

Pub. Rózsavölgyi; 1947, Boosey & Hawkes. Arrangements: *Swinherd's dance* (Kanásztánc) orch. by Béla Bartók as finale of 'Hungarian Sketches', 1931. Ten pieces transcribed by Leó Weiner for orchestra, 1952.

42. Seven Sketches Op. 9. For piano. 1908–1910, rev. 19 January 1945.

1. *Portrait of a girl* (Leányi arckép). 1908. Ded. Márta (Bartók). Dur. 1′ 40″.
2. *See saw, dickory-daw* (Hinta palinta . . .). Dur. 52″.
3. *Lento*. August 1910. Ded. Emma and Zoltán (Kodály). Dur. 1′ 50″.
4. *Non troppo lento*. Dur. 3′ 40″.
5. *Rumanian folksong* (Román népdal). Dur. 1′ 10″.
6. *In Walachian style* (Oláhos). Dur. 33″.
7. *Poco lento*. Dur. 1′ 45″.

Pub. Rozsnyai Károly; revised edition 1950, Edward B. Marks (USA), Augener.

43. Two Rumanian Dances (Két román tánc) Op. 8a. For piano. 1909–10. Dated: March 1910.

1. *Allegro vivace* (C minor).
2. *Poco allegro* (G major).

fp: 12 March 1910, Paris, Béla Bartók.

fEbp (No. 1): 15 March 1927, Béla Bartók.

Pub. 1910, Rózsavölgyi (as Op. 8, revised by Frederick Delius).

43a. Two Rumanian Dances. Orch. Leó Weiner. Dur. 9′ 30″.

2 fl, pic, 2 ob, 2 cl, 2 bsn; 4 hn, 2 tpt, 3 tmb;

timp, cym, GC, tgle, tamb pic, tamb basque, tamtam; hp, strings.
Pub. ?1939, Rózsavölgyi.

44. Four Dirges (Négy siratóének) (Quatre nénies). For piano. 1910, Budapest; rev. ?1945.
1. *Adagio*. Dur. 2 12".
2. *Andante*. Dur. 2' 16".
3. *Poco lento*. Dur. 2' 18".
4. *Assai andante*. Dur. 2' 55".
fp (incomplete): 17 October 1917, Budapest, Ernö Dohnányi.
fEp (two only): ?11 May 1923, Wigmore Street, George Woodhouse's studio, Béla Bartók.
Pub. 1912, Rózsavölgyi (as Op. 8b); revised version, 1945, Delkas (Los Angeles).

45. Two Pictures (Deux Images) Op. 10. For Orchestra. August 1910, Budapest. Dur. 16'.
1. *In full flower* (Virágzás).
2. *Village dance* (A falu tánca).
3 fl, pic, 2 ob, ca, 3 cl, bcl, 3 bsn, cbsn; 4 hn, 4 tpt, 3 tmb, tuba; timp, cym, GC, campane; celesta, 2 hp, strings.
fp: 25 February 1913, Budapest, Philharmonic Society, cond. István Kerner.
f New York p: 11 April 1919, Carnegie Hall, New Symphony Orchestra of the Musician's New Orchestra Society, cond. Edgar Varèse.
?fEp: 18 June 1928, Queen's Hall, Budapest Orchestra, cond. Ernö Dohnányi.
Pub. 1912, Rózsavölgyi; 1953, Zenemükiadó Vállalat.

46. Three Burlesques Op. 8c. For piano. 1908–11.
1. *Quarrel* (Perpatvar). November 1908. Ded. Márta (Bartók).
2. *A bit drunk* (Kicsit ázottan). May 1911.
3. *Molto vivo, capriccioso*. 1910.
fp (Nos. 1 & 2): 17 October 1917, Budapest, Ernö Dohnányi.
?fEp: 7 May 1923, London Contemporary Music Centre meeting, Béla Bartók.
fEbp (No. 2): 15 March 1927, Béla Bartók.
Pub. 1912, Rózsavölgyi.

47. Duke Bluebeard's Castle (A kéksza-

kállú herceg vára) Op. 11. Opera in one act. September 1911, Rákoskeresztúr. Libretto: Béla Balázs. Ded. Márta (Bartók).
4 fl, 2 pic, 2 ob, ca, 3 cl, bcl, 4 bsn, cbsn; 4 hn, 4 tpt, 4 tmb, bs tuba; timp, GC, tamb pic, tamtam, cym, susp cym, xyl a tastiera, tgle; 2 hp, celesta, organ, strings. Stage music: 4 tpt, 4 alto tmb.
fp: 24 May 1918, Budapest, cond. Egisto Tango; with Olga Haselbeck (Judith), Oszkár Kálmán (Bluebeard).
fEbp: 17 April 1937, BBC broadcast relayed from Royal Opera House, Budapest, cond. Sergio Failoni; with Mihály Székely (Bluebeard), Ella Némethy (Judith).
Pub. 1922 (vocal score), 1925 (full score), Universal-Edition; 1952, Boosey & Hawkes.

BIBLIOGRAPHY:
Béla Balázs: Vorspruch und Randbemerkungen, *Blätter der Staatsoper* (Berlin), December (No. 14) 1928, p. 6.
M.-D. Calvocoressi: Three Bluebeard operas, *MMR*, 1923, p. 232.
— Bartók's Duke Bluebeard's Castle, *MMR*, 1924, p. 35.
Max Chop: Die Burg des Blaubart, Ballade von BB, *Signale*, 1929, No. 4, p. 108.
Edward J. Dent: A Hungarian Bluebeard, *National & Athenaeum*, 3 June 1922, p. 354.
Erich Doflein: Herzog Blaubarts Burg, *NZfM*, December 1961.
Gyorgy Kroó: Duke Bluebeard's Castle, *Studia musicologica*, 1961, No. 3–4, p. 251.
E. Latzko: BBs Herzog Blaubarts Burg, *Anbruch*, June 1925.
L. Knessl: Mysterium und Legende, *Opern Welt*, No. 2, February 1967, p. 28.
Michael Marcus: Castle of Blood, *Records & Recordings*, June 1963, p. 16.
Edwin von der Nüll: Stilelemente in Bartóks Oper Herzog Blaubarts Burg, *Melos*, 1929.
Willi Tappolet: Le château du duc de Barbe-Bleu de BB, *SM*, 1950.
Sándor Torday: Bartóks Hertog Blauwbaard en de Wonderlijke Madarijn, *Mens en melodie*, April 1948, p. 115.
Sándor Veress: Bluebeard's Castle, *Tempo*, No. 13, autumn 1949, p. 32, No. 14, winter 1949–50, p. 25.

48. Allegro barbaro. For piano. 1911.
fp: 27 February 1921, Budapest, Béla Bartók.
Ebp: 15 March 1927, Béla Bartók.
Pub. 1918, Universal-Edition; 1939, Hawkes.

49. Four Pieces Op. 12. For orchestra. 1912, orch. 1921.
1. *Preludio*; 2. *Scherzo*; 3. *Intermezzo*; 4. *Marcia funebre.*
4 fl, 3 ob, ca, 3 cl, bcl, 4 bsn, cbsn; 4 hn, 4 tpt, 4 tmb, tuba; timp, tgle, cinelli, GC, tamb pic, tamtam, campanella, xyl; hp, piano, strings.
fp: 9 January 1922, Budapest, Philharmonic Society, cond. Ernö Dohnányi.
fFp: 1 May 1923, Paris, cond. Walter Straram.
fEp: 15 March 1936, BBC broadcast, BBC Orchestra, cond. Sir Adrian Boult.
Pub. 1923, Universal-Edition.

50. Four old Hungarian folksongs. For four-part male chorus (TTBB) a cappella. 1912.
1. *Long ago I told you* (Rég megmondtam); 2. *Oh God, why am I waiting?* (Jaj istenem! kire várok); 3. *In my sister-in-law's garden* (Ángyomasszony kertje); 4. *Farmboy, load the cart well* (Béreslegény, jól megrakd a szekeret).
Pub. 1928, Universal-Edition; German version by R. St. Hoffmann.

51. The first term at the piano (Kezdök zongoramuzsikája). For piano. 1913. Eighteen elementary pieces for the piano method of Sándor Reschofsky. Pub. 1929, Rózsavölgyi.

52. Danse orientale. For piano. ?1913.
?fp: 23 October 1954, Bakersfield (California), Halsey Stevens.
Pub. 1913, Christmas issue of *Pressburger Zeitung.*

53. Sonatina. For piano. 1915. Based on Rumanian folktunes.
1. *Bagpipers* (Dudások); 2. *Bear dance* (Medvetánc); 3. *Finale: Allegro vivace.*
fEbp: 19 September 1926, Gordon Bryan.
Pub. 1919, Rózsavölgyi. Arrangements: by André Gertler for violin and piano, 1931; by György Balassa for clarinet and piano, 1955.

53a. Transylvanian Dances (Erdélyi táncok). Version for orchestra by the composer of No. 53. 1931. Dur. 4'.
1. *Allegretto*; 2. *Moderato*; 3. *Allegro vivace.*
2 fl, pic, 2 ob, 2 cl, bcl, 2 bsn; 2 hn, 2 tpt, 2 tmb, bs tuba; timp, tgle; hp (or piano), strings.
fEbp: 11 January 1933, BBC Orchestra, cond. Edward Clark.
Pub. 1932, Rózsavölgyi.

54. Rumanian folkdances from Hungary. For piano. 1915. Ded. Professor Ion Busitia. Dur. 4' 15".
1. *Stick dance* (Joc cu bâta); 2. *Sash dance* (Brâul); 3. *In one spot* (Pe loc); 4. *Horn dance* (Buciumeana); 5. *Rumanian polka* (Poarga romaneasca); 6. *Fast dance* (Maruntel); 7. *Fast dance* (Maruntel).
Pub. 1918, Universal-Edition; 1945, Boosey & Hawkes.

54a. Rumanian folkdances from Hungary. Version for small orchestra. 1917.
2 fl, pic, 2 cl, 2 bsn; 2 hn; strings.
fEp: 13 January 1925, Chelsea Town Hall, Chelsea Music Club concert, cond. (Sir) Eugene Goossens.
Pub. 1922, Universal-Edition.

54b. Rumanian folkdances from Hungary. Version by Arthur Willner for string orchestra. Pub. 1929, Universal-Edition.

BIBLIOGRAPHY:
Harold Rawlinson: Some famous works for string orchestra, No. 23—Rumanian folkdances, BB, *Strad*, February 1951, p. 354.

54c. Rumanian folkdances from Hungary. Version by Zoltán Székely for violin and piano.
fEp: 4 March 1929, Arts Theatre Club, Zoltán Székely and Béla Bartók.

55. Rumanian Christmas songs (Colinde). For piano. 1915. Two series of ten each. Pub. 1918, Universal-Edition.

56. Nine Rumanian songs. For voice and piano. 1915. Unpub.

57. Two Rumanian folksongs. For four-part women's chorus. 1915. Unpub.

58. Four Slovakian folksongs. For voice and piano. ?1907 (Nos. 1 3), 1916 (No. 4).
   1. *Near the borders of Bistrita* (V tej bystrickej bráne); 2. *Mourning song* (Phrební pisen); 3. *Message* (Priletel pták); 4. *Tono whits the spindle* (Krutí Tono vretana).

59. The Wooden Prince (A fából faragott királyfi) Op. 13. Ballet in one act. 1914–16, Rákoskeresztur. Libretto: Béla Balázs. Ded. Egisto Tango.
   fp: 12 May 1917, Budapest, Hungarian State Opera House, cond. Egisto Tango; design, Miklós Bánffy.
   Pub. 1921, Universal-Edition (piano score).

BIBLIOGRAPHY:
Alexander Jemnitz: Der holzgeschnitzte Prinz, *Signale*, 1917, Nos. 22–23 (6 June), p. 434.
Hellmuth Christian Wolff: BBs holzgeschnitzter Prinz und seine Beziehungen zu Igor Strawinsky, *Musik der Zeit*.

59a. The Wooden Prince: Suite. For orchestra. 1931.
   fp: 23 November 1931, Budapest, Philharmonic Society, cond. Ernö Dohnányi.

60. Suite Op. 14. For piano. February 1916, Rákoskeresztúr.
   1. *Allegretto.* Dur. 2'.
   2. *Scherzo.* Dur. 1' 50".
   3. *Allegro molto.* Dur. 2' 5".
   4. *Sostenuto.* Dur. 2' 35".
   fp: 21 April 1919, Budapest, Béla Bartók.
   fEp: 1923, Wigmore Street, George Woodhouse's studio, Béla Bartók.
   fEbp: 4 March 1929, Béla Bartók.
   Pub. 1918, 1945, Universal-Edition.

BIBLIOGRAPHY:
János Liebner: Une œuvre oubliée de Bartók, *SM*, November–December 1960, p. 357.
Gerd Sannemüller: BBs Suite Op. 14, *SM*, January–February 1965, p. 10.

61. Five Songs Op. 15. For voice and piano. Words: by unknown writers, but Nos. 4–5 said to be by Béla Balázs.
   1. *My love* (As én szerelmem); 2. *Summer* (Nyár); 3. *Night of desire* (A vágyak éjjele); 4. *In vivid dreams* (Színes álomban); 5. *In the valley* (Itt lent a völgyben).
   fEp: 17 November 1961, 4 St. James's Square, Philip Lewtas (baritone), acc. Alan Bush.
   Pub. 1958, Béla Bartók Archives (New York), Pallas Gallery (London); English versions by Peter Bartók and Howard Sachler; 1961, Universal-Edition: English versions by Eric Smith, German versions by Ernst Hartmann.

BIBLIOGRAPHY:
Pál Jardányi: Mensch und Natur in Bartóks Geisteswelt—Noch einmal Bartóks Op. 15, *ÖM*, December 1961.

61a. Five Songs Op. 15. Version orch. Zoltán Kodály. 1961.
   3 fl, 2 ob, 2 cl, 2 bsn; 4 hn; piano, strings.
   Pub. 1962, Universal-Edition: English versions by Eric Smith, German versions by Ernst Hartmann.

62. Five Songs (Endre Ady) Op. 16. For voice and piano. February–April 1916, Rákoskeresztúr. Ded. Béla Reinitz.
   1. *Three autumn tears* (Három öszi könnycsepp).
   2. *Sounds of autumn* (Az öszi lárma).
   3. *My bed calls me* (Az ágyam hívogat).
   4. *Alone with the sea* (Egyedül a tengerrel).
   5. *I cannot come to you* (Nem mehetek hozzád).
   fp: 21 April 1919, Budapest, Ilona Durigó, acc. Béla Bartók.
   fEbp: 15 March 1927, Mária Basilides.
   Pub. 1923, Universal-Edition.

63. Eight Hungarian folksongs. For voice and piano. 1907–17.
   1. *Black is the earth* (Fekete föd).
   2. *My God, my God, make the river swell* (Istenem, istenem, áraszd meg a vizet).
   3. *Wives, let me be one of your company* (Asszonyok, asszonyok).
   4. *So much sorrow lies on my heart* (Annyi bánat az szüvemen).
   5. *If I climb yonder hill* (Ha kimegyek arr'a magos tetöre).
   6. *They are mending the great forest highway* (Töltik a nagy erdö útját).
   7. *Up to now my work was ploughing in springtime* (Eddig való dolgom a tavaszi szántás).
   8. *The snow is melting* (Olvad a hó).

fEbp (Nos. 1, 5 & 8): 5 October 1926, Grotrian Hall, Mária Basilides; (No. 2): 16 June 1929, Mária Basilides; (Nos. 3 & 4): 20 March 1932, Mária Basilides.

Pub. 1922, Universal-Edition; 1939, Hawkes; 1955, with English versions by Nancy Bush, Hawkes.

64. Fifteen Hungarian peasant songs. For piano. 1914–17.

1. *Rubato*; 2. *Andante*; 3. *Poco rubato—Sostenuto*; 4. *Andante*; 5. *Scherzo: Allegro*; 6. *Ballade* (*tema con variazioni*); 7. *Allegro*; 8. *Allegretto*; 9. *Allegretto*; 10. *L'istesso tempo*; 11. *Assai moderato*; 12. *Allegretto*; 13. *Poco più vivo—Allegretto*; 14. *Allegro*; 15. *Allegro*.

fEbp: 5 March 1929, Béla Bartók.
Pub. 1920, Universal-Edition.

64a. Hungarian peasant songs. Version for orchestra, 1933. Dur. 9'.

2 fl, pic, 2 ob, ca, 2 cl, 2 bsn; 2 hn, 2 tpt, 2 tmb, bs tuba; timp, GC; hp, strings.

fp: 18 March 1934, Szombathely, cond. Gyula Baranyai.

fEp: 26 September 1935, Queen's Hall, Promenade Concert, BBC Symphony Orchestra, cond. Sir Henry Wood. (*N.B.*: fEp originally announced for 28 January 1934, Berlin Philharmonic Orchestra, cond. Wilhelm Furtwängler).

Pub. 1933, Universal-Edition.

Note: The above version consists of Nos. 6–12 and 14–15 of the original Nos. 7–15 were transcribed by Tibor Polgár as Old Hungarian Dances, 1927. There is also a transcription for flute and piano by Paul Arma (dur. 13' 30"), pub. 1956, Boosey & Hawkes.

65. Three Hungarian folktunes. For piano. 1914–17.

Pub. 1942, in *Homage to Paderewski*. An earlier version of No. 1 pub. in *Periscop* (Arad, Rumania), June–July 1925. No. 3 orch. Tibor Serly as Prelude to Suite from 'Mikrokosmos'.

66. String Quartet No. 2 Op. 17. 1915–October 1917, Rákoskeresztúr. Ded. Hungarian Quartet (Waldbauer, Temesváry, Kornstein and Kerpely).

1. *Moderato*; 2. *Allegro molto capriccioso*; 3. *Lento*.

fp: 3 March 1918, Budapest, Waldbauer–Kerpely Quartet (Hungarian Quartet).

fEp: 9 May 1922, Grafton Galleries, London Chamber Concert, Hungarian Quartet.

fEbp: 19 February 1926, Hungarian Quartet.

Pub. 1920, Universal-Edition.

67. Five Slovak folksongs. For four-part male chorus (TTBB). 1917.

1. *Hey, my dear, kind comrades* (Ej, posluchajte málo).

2. *If I must go to the war* (Ked' ja smutny pojdem).

3. *Let us go, comrades* (Kamarádi mojí).

4. *Hey, if soon I fall* (Ej, a ked' mna zabiju).

5. *To battle I went forth* (Ked' som siou na vojnu).

Pub. 1918, Universal-Edition, 1939, 1955, Hawkes: English versions, Nancy Bush; German versions, Mirko Jelusich; Hungarian versions, Wanda Gleiman.

68. Four Slovak folksongs. For four-part mixed chorus and piano. 1917.

1. *Thus sent the mother* (Zadala mamka).

2. *In alpine pastures* (Na holi, na holi).

3. *Food and drink's your only pleasure* (Rada pila, rada jedla).

4. *Let the bagpipe sound* (Gajdujte, gajdence).

?fp: 5 January 1917, Budapest, cond. Emil Lichtenberg.

fEbp: 21 March 1936, BBC Singers, cond. Trevor Harvey.

Pub. 1924, Universal-Edition. Arrangement: orch. by Endre Szervánszky, 1950.

69. Three Studies Op. 18. For piano. 1918, Rákoskeresztúr.

1. *Allegro molto*; 2. *Andante sostenuto*; 3. *Rubato, tempo giusto, capriccioso*.

fp: 21 April 1919, Budapest, Béla Bartók.
Pub. 1920, Universal-Edition.

70. The Miraculous Mandarin Op. 19. Pantomime in one act. October 1918–May 1919, Rákoskeresztúr. Libretto: Menyhért Lengyel.

3 fl, pic, 3 ob, ca, 3 cl, bcl, 3 bsn, cbsn; 4 hn, 3 tpt, 3 tmb, bs tuba; timp, tamb, tamb pic, cinelli, tgle, tamtam, xyl; celesta, piano, organ, hp, strings.

Bartók, Béla

fp: 27 November 1926, Cologne, cond. Jenö Szenkár.

Pub. 1925 (reduction for piano, four hands), 1927 (full score), Universal-Edition.

BIBLIOGRAPHY:

Piero Coppola: Le mandarin merveilleux de BB, in *Dix-sept ans de musique à Paris*, Libr. F. Rouge (Lausanne) 1944, p. 173.

Edward Crankshaw: Bartók's pantomime, *Radio Times*, 24 February 1933, p. 454.

A. L. Haskell: The miraculous mandarin, *London Musical Events*, October 1956, p. 27.

J. Holcman: Bartók à la Chinese torture, *Saturday Review*, 13 October 1956, p. 38.

Alexander Jemnitz: Der wunderbare Mandarin, *Melos*, 1931.

Ernö Lendvai: Der wunderbare Mandarin, *Sudia musicologica*, 1961, Nos. 3–4, p. 363.

Günter Lossau: Bartóks Pantomime Der wunderbare Mandarin, *Melos*, June 1966, p. 173.

Colin Mason: The Miraculous Mandarin, in *Decca Book of Ballets*, Muller, (London) 1958, p. 65.

A. Nirschy: Varianten zu Bartóks Pantomime Der wunderbare Mandarin, *Studia musicologica*, 1962, No. 14, p. 189.

B. Pociej & N. Karaskiewicz: Mandaryn na wybrzezu, *Ruch Muzyczny*, 1 May 1960, p. 12.

Bence Szabolcsi: Le Mandarin miraculeux, *Studia musicologica*, 1961, Nos. 3–4, p. 341.

Sándor Torday: Bartóks Hertog Blauwbaard en de Wonderlijke Mandarijn, *Mens en melodie*, April 1948, p. 115.

Hermann Unger: Der wunderbare Mandarin in Köln, *Der Auftakt*, 1926, Nos. 11–12, p. 230.

John Vinton: The case of The Miraculous Mandarin, *MQ*, January 1964, p. 1.

70a. The Miraculous Mandarin: Suite. For orchestra.

fp: 15 October 1928, Budapest, Philharmonic Society, cond. Ernö Dohnányi.

fEp: 14 February 1930, Queen's Hall, BBC Symphony Orchestra, cond. Sir Henry Wood.

fFp: 29 October 1933, Paris, l'Orchestre Symphonique de Paris, cond. Piero Coppola.

71. Eight Improvisations on Hungarian peasant songs Op. 20. For piano. 1902,

Budapest. No. 7 ded. to the memory of Claude Debussy.

1. *Molto moderato*; 2. *Molto capriccioso*; 3. *Lento, rubato*; 4. *Allegretto scherzando*; 5. *Allegro molto*; 6. *Allegro moderato, molto capriccioso*; 7. *Sostenuto, rubato*; 8. *Allegro*.

fp (No. 7): 24 January 1921, Paris, Salle des Agriculteurs, Société Musicale Indépendante concert, Ernest Lévy.

fp (complete): 27 February 1921, Budapest, Béla Bartók.

fEp: 24 March 1922, Aeolian Hall, Béla Bartók.

Pub. 1921, Universal-Edition. No. 7 orig. pub. 1920, in *Le Tombeau de Claude Debussy*.

BIBLIOGRAPHY:

Stuart Thyne: Bartók's Improvisations, an essay in technical analysis, *M&L*, 1950.

72. Violin Sonata No. 1. October–12 December 1921, Budapest. Ded. Jelly d'Aranyi.

1. *Allegro appassionato*; 2. *Adagio*; 3. *Allegro*.

fp: 24 March 1922, London, Aeolian Hall, Jelly d'Arányi and Béla Bartók.

?fEbp: 4 February 1937, Zoltán Székely and Béla Bartók.

Pub. 1923, Universal-Edition.

73. Violin Sonata No. 2. July–November 1922. Ded. Jelly d'Aranyi.

1. *Molto moderato*; 2. *Allegretto*.

fp: 7 May 1923, London, Queen's Square, London Contemporary Music Centre concert, Jelly d'Arányi and Béla Bartók.

fEbp: 6 January 1930, Arts Theatre Club, Joseph Szigeti and Béla Bartók.

Pub. 1923, Universal-Edition.

74. Dance Suite (Táncszvit). For orchestra. August 1923, Radvány. Composed for the fiftieth anniversary of the merging of Pest, Buda and Obuda into the city of Budapest. Dur. 17–20′

1. *Moderato*; 2. *Allegro molto*; 3. *Allegro vivace*; 4. *Molto tranquillo*; 5. *Comodo*; 6. *Finale: Allegro*.

2 fl, 2 pic, 2 ob, ca, 2 cl, bcl, 2 bsn, dbsn; 4 hn, 2 tpt, 2 tmb, tuba; timp, tgle, little bell, 2 tamb (large & small), GC, cym, tamtam; celesta, hp, piano, strings.

fp: 19 November 1923, Budapest, Philharmonic Society, cond. Ernö Dohnányi.

fEp: 20 August 1925, Queen's Hall, Promenade Concert, New Queen's Orchestra, cond. Sir Henry Wood.

fEbp: 2 March 1926, Birmingham Town Hall, City of Birmingham Orchestra, cond. (Sir) Adrian Boult.

Pub. 1924 (score), 1925 (piano score), Universal-Edition; 1939, Boosey & Hawkes.

75. Five Village Scenes (Falun, népdalok). For voice and piano. December 1924, Budapest. Slovak folksongs from the Zólyom district. Ded. Ditta (Pásztory Bartók).

1. *Szénagyüjtéskor*(Heuernte); 2. *A menyasz-szonynál* (Bei der Braut); 3. *Lakodalom* (Hochzeit); 4. *Bölcsödal* (Wiegenlied); 5. *Legénytánc* (Burschentanz).

fp: 8 December 1926, Budapest, Mária Basilides, acc. Béla Bartók.

Pub. 1927, Universal-Edition; German text, Bence Szabolcsi.

75a. Village Scenes. Version for 4 or 8 women's voices and chamber orchestra. Commissioned by the League of Composers, New York.

1. *Lakodalom* (Wedding); 2. *Bölcsödal* (Lullaby); 3. *Legénytánc* (Lads' dance).

fl, pic, ob, ca, E-flat cl, 2 cl, also sax, bsn; hn, tpt, ten tmb, bs tmb; side dm (with snares), side dm (without snares), GC, cym, 3 bells; piano, hp, string quintet.

Pub. 1954, Boosey & Hawkes; English text, Martin Lindsay.

76. Piano Sonata. June 1926, Budapest. Ded. Ditta (Pásztory Bartók).

1. *Allegro moderato*; 2. *Sostenuto e pesante*; 3. *Allegro molto*.

fp 8 December 1926, Budapest, Béla Bartók.

fEbp: 15 March 1927, Béla Bartók.

Pub. 1927, Universal-Edition; 1955, Boosey & Hawkes.

77. Out of Doors (Szabadban). For piano. June–August 1926, Budapest. No. 4 ded. Ditta (Bartók).

1. *With drums and pipes* (Síppal, dobbal); 2. *Barcarolla*; 3. *Musettes*; 4. *The night's music* (Az éjszaka zenéje); 5. *The chase* (Hajsza).

fp (Nos. 1 & 4): 8 December 1926, Budapest, Béla Bartók.

fEbp (No. 4): 3 February 1937, Béla Bartók.

Pub. 1927, Universal-Edition.

78. Nine Little Piano Pieces. Dated: 31 October 1926.

1–4. *Dialogues*; 5. *Menuetto*; 6. *Air*; 7. *Marcia delle bestie*; 8. *Tambourine*; 9. *Preludio, all'ungherese*.

fp (omitting one Dialogue): 8 December 1926, Budapest, Béla Bartók.

Pub. 1927, Universal-Edition.

79. Piano Concerto No. 1. August–12 November 1926, Budapest. Dur. 23′.

1. *Allegro moderato*; 2. *Andante*; 3. *Allegro molto*.

2 fl, pic, 2 ob, ca, 2 cl, bcl, 2 bsn; 4 hn, 2 tpt, 3 tmb; timp, 2 small dms (with & without snares), tgle, 4 cym, GC, tamtam; strings.

fp: 1 July 1927, Frankfurt a. M., International Society for Contemporary Music Festival, Béla Bartók, cond. Wilhelm Furtwängler.

fEp: 10 October 1927, BBC broadcast, Béla Bartók and the Wireless Symphony Orchestra, cond. Edward Clark.

fEp (concert): 14 February 1930, Queen's Hall, Béla Bartók, cond. Sir Henry Wood.

Pub. 1927, Universal-Edition: incl. reduction for two pianos.

BIBLIOGRAPHY:

Antal Molnár: BB, Koncezt für Klavier und Orchester, *Analyse* (Vienna) 1929.

Aladár Tóth: Das neue Klavierkonzert von BB, *Pult und Taktstock*, May–June 1927.

Ivan F. Walbauer: Bartók's First Piano Concerto, a publication history, *MQ*, April 1965, p. 336.

80. Three Rondos on folktunes. For piano. 1916–27.

1. *Andante—Allegro molto*. 1916. Dur. 2′ 50″.
2. *Vivacissimo—Allegro*. 1927. Dur. 2′ 34″.
3. *Allegro molto*. 1927. Dur. 2′ 35″.

fEp: 4 March 1929, Arts Theatre Club, BBC broadcast, Béla Bartók.

Pub. 1930, Universal-Edition. Arrangement: by Pál Bodon, for orchestra, 1938.

81. String Quartet No. 3. September 1927, Budapest. Ded. Musical Fund Society of Philadelphia.

1. *Moderato*; 2. *Allegro*; 3. *Recapitulation of 1*; 4. *Coda: Allegro molto.*

fp: 12 February 1929, BBC broadcast, Hungarian Quartet.

fp (public): 19 February 1929, Wigmore Hall, Hungarian Quartet.

Pub. 1929, Universal-Edition; 1939, Boosey & Hawkes.

82. Rhapsody No. 1. For violin and piano. 1928. Ded. Joseph Szigeti.

1. *Lassú*; 2. *Friss.*

?fp: 4 March 1929, Arts Theatre Club, BBC broadcast, Zoltán Székely and Béla Bartók.

Pub. 1929, Universal-Edition; also version for cello and piano.

82a. Rhapsody No. 1. Version for violin and orchestra. Dur. 4′ 30″ (first part), 5′ 45″ (second part with first ending), 5′ (second part with second ending). Ded. Joseph Szigeti.

2 fl, pic, 2 ob, 2 cl, bcl, 2 bsn; 4 hn, 2 tpt, tmb, bs tuba; cimbalom, strings.

fEp: 28 November 1929, Queen's Hall, Royal Philharmonic Society concert, Joseph Szigeti and the London Philharmonic Orchestra, cond. Hermann Scherchen.

Pub. 1931, Universal-Edition; 1939, Hawkes.

83. Rhapsody No. 2. For violin and piano. 1928, rev. 1945. Ded. Zoltán Székely.

1. *Lassú*; 2. *Friss.*

fp: 19 November 1928, Amsterdam, Zoltán Székely and Béla Bartók.

fEp: 4 March 1929, Arts Theatre Club, BBC broadcast, Zoltán Székely and Béla Bartók.

fEp ('new version'): 6 January 1930, Arts Theatre Club, BBC broadcast, Joseph Szigeti and Béla Bartók.

Pub. 1929, Universal-Edition; 1947, Boosey & Hawkes.

83a. Rhapsody No. 2. Version for violin and orchestra. ?1928, rev. 1944. Dur. 12′. Ded. Zoltán Székely.

2 fl, pic, 2 ob, ca, 2 cl, bcl, 2 bsn; 2 hn, 2 tpt, tmb, bs tuba; timp, side dm (without snares), tgle, cym, GC; piano, celesta, hp, strings.

fp: 24 January 1932, Amsterdam, Zoltán Székely and the Concertgebouw Orchestra, cond. Pierre Monteux.

Pub. 1931, Universal-Edition; 1939, Hawkes; 1949 (revised version), Hawkes.

84. String Quartet No. 4. July–September 1928, Budapest. Ded. Pro Arte Quartet.

1. *Allegro*; 2. *Prestissimo, con sordino*; 3. *Non troppo lento*; 4. *Allegretto pizzicato*; 5. *Allegro molto.*

?fp: 22 February 1929, BBC broadcast, Hungarian Quartet.

fp (concert): 20 March 1929, Budapest, Hungarian (Waldbauer–Kerpely) Quartet.

fEp (concert): 19 January 1930, Aeolian Hall, Gerald Cooper concert, Hungarian Quartet.

fFp: 12 December 1932, Paris, Société Musicale Indépendante concert, Pro Arte Quartet.

Pub. 1929, Universal-Edition.

BIBLIOGRAPHY:

Colin Mason: An essay in tonality, symmetry, and latent serialism in Bartók's Fourth Quartet, *MR*, 1947.

A. Mihály: Metrika Bartók, IV. vonósnégyesének, II. tételében, *Muzsika*, December 1967, p. 35.

Raymond Monelle: Notes on Bartók's fourth quartet, *MR*, May 1968, p. 123.

Leo Treitler: Harmonic procedure in the Fourth Quartet of Bartók, *Journal of Music Theory*, November 1959, p. 292.

85. Twenty Hungarian folksongs. For voice and piano. 1929.

1. *In prison* (A tömlöcben) (Dur. 3′ 33″); 2. *Ancient grief* (Régi keserves) (Dur. 2′ 35″); 3. *The fugitive* (Bujdosó-ének) (Dur. 1′ 46″); 4. *Herdsman's song* (Pásztornóta) (Dur. 1′ 52″); 5. *Székely 'lassú'* (Dur. 2′ 5″); 6. *Székely 'friss'* (Dur. 1′ 15″); 7. *Swineherd's dance* (Kanásztánc) (Dur. 1′ 37″); 8. *Six-florin dance* ('Hatforintos' nóta) (Dur. 1′ 53″); 9. *The shepherd* (Juhászcsúfoló) (Dur. 1′ 50″); 10. *Joking song* (Tréfás nóta) (Dur. 1′ 30″); 11. *Nuptial serenade* (Párosító I) (Dur. 1′ 45″); 12. *Humorous song* (Párosító II) (Dur. 1′ 21″); 13. *Dialogue song* (Pár-ének) (Dur. 3′ 30″); 14. *Complaint* (Panasz) (Dur. 1′ 21″); 15. *Drinking song*

(Bordal) (Dur. 1' 13"); 16. *Oh, my dear mother* (Hej, édes anyám) (Dur. 1' 50"); 17. *Ripening cherries* (Érik a ropogós cseresznye) (Dur. 27"); 18. *Long ago at Dobos fell the snow* (Már Dobozon régen leesett a hó) (Dur. 1' 45"); 19. *Yellow cornstalk* (Sárga kukoricaszál) (Dur. 28"); 20. *Wheat, wheat* (Buza, buza) (Dur. 2' 19").

?fp (four only): 6 January 1930, Arts Theatre Club, Mária Basilides.

fp: 30 January 1930, Budapest, Mária Basilides, acc. Béla Bartók.

Pub. 1932, Universal-Edition; German versions by Bence Szabolcsi & R. St. Hoffmann.

85a. Hungarian folksongs. For voice and orchestra. 1933. Nos. 1, 2, 10, 11, 14 of preceding.

fp: 23 October 1933, Budapest, Mária Basilides, Philharmonic Society Orchestra, cond. Ernö Dohnányi.

fEp: 26 September 1935, Queen's Hall, Promenade Concert, BBC Symphony Orchestra, cond. Sir Henry Wood.

86. Four Hungarian folksongs. For mixed chorus a cappella. May 1930, Budapest.

1. *The prisoner* (A rab); 2. *The rover* (The wanderer) (A bujdosó); 3. *The marriageable girl* (Finding a husband) (Az eladó lány); 4. *Song* (Love song) (Dal).

Pub. 1932, Universal-Edition, 1939, 1956, Hawkes; English versions, Nancy Bush; German versions, R. St. Hoffmann.

87. Cantata Profana (The Nine Enchanted Stags). For double mixed chorus, tenor and baritone soloists, and orchestra. Dated: 8 September 1930, Budapest. Dur. 16–17'.

1. *Molto moderato*; 2. *Andante*; 3. *Moderato*.

3 fl, pic, 3 ob, 3 cl, bcl, 3 bsn, cbsn; 4 hn, 2 tpt, 3 tmb, bs tuba; timp, tamb pic, GC, cym, tamtam; hp, strings.

fp: 25 May 1934, BBC broadcast, Trefor Jones, Frank Phillips, Wireless Chorus and the BBC Symphony Orchestra, cond. Aylmer Buesst.

fEp (concert): 25 March 1936, Queen's Hall, Henry Wendon, Arnold Matters, BBC Choral Society and Symphony Orchestra, cond. Sir Adrian Boult.

Pub. 1934, Universal-Edition: German text, Benedikt Szabolcsi; 1951, Universal-Edition: English version by M.-D. Calvocoressi as 'The Giant Stags'.

BIBLIOGRAPHY:
Alexander Jemnitz: Bartók's Cantata Profana, Erstaufführung in Budapest, *SM*, 1937.
Karl Kerényi: Über Bartóks Cantata profana, *SM*, 1946, Nos. 8–9.
Antal Molnár: Bedeutung der Cantata profana von BB, Pester Lloyd (Budapest) 1936.
I. Sipos: Csak tiszta forrásból, *Muzsika*, December 1967, p. 4.

88. Piano Concerto No. 2. October 1930–September/October 1931, Budapest. Dur. 24' 30"–25'.

1. *Allegro*; 2. *Adagio—Prestissimo*; 3. *Allegro molto*.

2 fl, pic, 2 ob, 2 cl, 3 bsn, cbsn; 4 hn, 3 tpt, 3 tmb, bs tuba; timp, tamb pic, tgle, cym, GC; strings.

fp: 23 January 1933, Frankfurt a. M., Béla Bartók and the Frankfurt Radio Symphony Orchestra, cond. Hans Rosbaud.

fEp: 8 November 1933, Queen's Hall, Béla Bartók and the BBC Symphony Orchestra, cond. Sir Adrian Boult.

Pub. 1932, Universal-Edition.

BIBLIOGRAPHY:
Jack Holgate: Bartók's Second Piano Concerto, *Halle*, March 1948, p. 9.
R.-Aloys Mooser: Bartók, 2me Concerto pour piano, in *Aspects de la musique contemporaine*, Editions Labor et Fidès (Geneva) 1957, p. 199.
Edmund Rubbra: Bartók's Second Piano Concerto, *MMR*, 1933, p. 199.

89. Forty-Four Duos. For two violins. 1931.

fp (incomplete): 20 January 1932, Budapest, Imre Waldbauer and György Hannover.

fEbp (12 duos): 20 January 1938, Frederick Grinke and David Martin.

Pub. 1933, Universal-Edition.

BIBLIOGRAPHY:
Erich Doflein: A propos des 44 Duos pour deux violons de Bartók, *RM*, May 1955, p. 110.

Bartók, Béla

Sister M. Genovefa: The pedagogical significance of the Bartók Duos, *American String Teacher*, 1962, No. 3, p. 22.

89a. Petite Suite. Transcriptions for piano of six numbers from preceding. 1936.
fEbp: 4 February 1937, Béla Bartók.

90. Hungarian Sketches. For orchestra. August 1931, Mondsee. Transcriptions of Nos. 5 & 10 from Ten Easy Pieces, No. 2 of Four Dirges, No. 2 of Three Burlesques, and No. 40 of For Children Vol. 1.
2 fl, pic, 2 ob, 2 cl, bcl, 2 bsn, cbsn; 2 hn, 2 tpt, 2 tmb, bs tuba; timp, tgle, 2 tamb pic (alto & bass), xyl, GC; hp, strings.
1. *An evening in the village* (Dur. 2′ 43″); 2. *Bear dance* (Dur. 1′ 43″); 3. *Melody* (Dur. 2′ 5″); 4. *Slightly tipsy* (Dur. 2′ 62″); 5. *Swineherd's dance* (Dur. 1′ 45″).
fp: 26 November 1934, Budapest Philharmonic Society, cond. Heinrich Laber.
Pub. 1932, Rozsnyai & Rózsavölgyi.

91. Szekely songs. For male chorus a cappella. November 1932, Budapest.
1. *How often I've regretted* (Hej, de sokszor megbántottál); 2. *My God, my life* (Istenem, életem); 3. & 5. *Slender thread, hard seed* (Vékony cérna, kemény mag); 4. *In Kilyénfalva girls are gathering* (Kilyénfalvi középtizbe); 6. *Do a dance, priest* (Járjad pap a táncot).
Pub. 1938, Magyar Kórus.

92. String Quartet No. 5 6 August–6 September 1934, Budapest. Ded. Mrs. Elizabeth Sprague Coolidge. Dur. 27′ 39″.
1. *Allegro* (Dur. 7′ 4½″); 2. *Adagio molto* (Dur. 5′ 19½″); 3. *Scherzo: alla bulgarese* (Dur. 4′ 36″); 4. *Andante* (Dur. 4′ 17½″); 5. *Finale: Allegro vivace* (Dur. 6′ 21½″).
f public p: 8 April 1935, Washington, Kolisch Quartet.
fEbp: 5 December 1935, Kolisch Quartet.
Pub. 1936, Universal-Edition.

BIBLIOGRAPHY:
Roger E. Chapman: The Fifth Quartet of BB, *MR*, 1951, p. 296.
Alexander Jemnitz: BB, V. Streichquartett, *Musica Viva*, April 1936.

93. Twenty-seven choruses. For 2-part and 3-part children's or women's voices. 1935.
1. *Don't leave me* (Ne menj el) (Dur. 1′ 36″,

orig. 1′ 30″); 2. *Hussar* (Huszárnóta) (Dur. 1′ 45″, orig. 1′ 36″); 3. *Letter to those at home* (Levél az otthoniakhoz) (Dur. 2′ 4″); 4. *Play song* (Játék) (Dur. 41″); 5. *I've no one in the world* (Senkim a világon) (Dur. 1′ 17″); 6. *Alas, alas* (Héjja, héjja) (Dur. 45″); 7. *Breadbaking* (Cipósütés) (Dur. 2′ 10″, orig. 2′); 8. *I have a ring* (Van egy gyürüm) (Dur. 1′ 2″); 9. *Girls' teasing song* (Lánycsúfoló) (Dur. 1′ 25″); 10. *Don't leave her* (Ne hagyj itt!) (Dur. 1′ 50″); 11. *Loafers' song* (Resteknek nótája) (Dur. 40″, orig. 39″); 12. *Wandering* (Bolyongás) (Dur. 1′ 40″); 13. *Courting* (Leánynézö) (Dur. 1′ 37″, orig. 1′ 7″); 14. *Enchanting song* (Jószág-igézö) (Dur. 1′ 15″); 15. *Suitor* (Leánykérö) (Dur. 1′ 37″); 16. *Spring* (Tavasz) (Dur. 2′, orig. 2′ 2″); 17. *Boys' teasing song* (Legénycsúfoló) (Dur. 57″); 18. *Had I not seen you* (Ne láttalak volna) (Dur. 2′ 17″); 19. *Grief* (Keserves) (Dur. 1′ 47″); 20. *Regret* (Bánat) (Dur. 1′ 30″); 21. *The bird flew away* (Elment a madárka) (Dur. 1′ 20″); 22. *Bird song* (Madárdal) (Dur. 1′ 24″); 23. *Jeering* (Csujogató) (Dur. 1′ 15″); 24. *Pillow dance* (Párnás táncdal) (Dur. 2′ 57″); 25. *Michaelmas congratulation* (Mihálynapi köszöntö) (Dur. 2′ 55″); 26. *God be with you* (Isten veled!) (Dur. 2′ 34″); 27. *Canon: I'm dying for Csurgó* (Kanon: Meghalok Csurgóért) (Dur. 55″).
fp (Nos. 1–17 & 25): 7 May 1937, Budapest, cond. Paula Radnai, László Preisinger (Perényi), Mme Ferenc Barth, Benjamin Rajeczky, Adrienne Stojanovics.
Pub. 1937, Magyar Kórus; Boosey & Hawkes, with English versions by Elizabeth Herzog or Nancy Bush, German versions by Ernst Roth. Nos. 1, 2, 7, 11, 12 with orch. acc. pub. 1937, Magyar Kórus.

94. From olden times (Elmult idökböl). For 3-part male chorus a cappella. 1935. After old Hungarian folk and art song texts.
1. *No one's more unhappy than the peasant* (Nincs boldogtalanabb) (Dur. 5′ 6″); 2. *One, two, three, four* (Egy, kettö, három, négy) (Dur. 2′ 30″); 3. *No one is happier than the peasant* (Nincsen szerencsésebb) (Dur. 5′ 30″).
fp: 7 May 1937, Budapest, Béla Endre Chamber Chorus, cond. Béla Endre.
Pub. 1937, Magyar Kórus.

95. Music for strings, percussion and celesta. Dated: 7 September 1936, Budapest. Commissioned for the tenth anniversary of the Basle Chamber Orchestra.

1. *Andante tranquillo* (Dur. 6′ 30″); 2. *Allegro* (Dur. 6′ 55″); 3. *Adagio* (Dur. 6′ 35″); 4. *Allegro molto* (Dur. 5′ 40″).

fp: 21 January 1937, Basle, Basle Chamber Orchestra, cond. Paul Sacher.

fEp: 7 January 1938, BBC invitation concert of contemporary music, BBC Orchestra, cond. Hermann Scherchen.

fEp (concert): 30 March 1938, Queen's Hall, Royal Philharmonic Society concert, cond. Sir Thomas Beecham.

Pub. 1937, Universal-Edition.

BIBLIOGRAPHY:

Everett Helm: Bartóks Musik für Saiteninstrumente, *Melos*, September 1953, p. 245.

Robert Smith: BB's Music for strings, percussion and celesta, *MR*, August–November 1959, p. 264.

96. Sonata for two pianos and percussion. July–August 1937, Budapest. Dur. 24′ 30″.

1. *Assai lento—Allegro molto*; 2. *Lento, ma non troppo*; 3. *Allegro non troppo*.

fp: 16 January 1938, Basle, tenth anniversary concert of the Basle Group of the Swiss section of the International Society for Contemporary Music, Béla and Ditta Bartók, Fritz Schiesser and Philipp Rühlig.

f Paris p: 27 February 1939, Société Philharmonique de Paris concert, Béla and Ditta Bartók, cond. Hermann Scherchen.

Pub. 1942, Hawkes.

96a. Concerto for two pianos and orchestra. Transcription of preceding. December 1940.

2 fl, pic, 2 ob, ca, 2 cl, 2 bsn, dbsn; 4 hn, 2 tpt, 3 tmb; pcssn; celesta, strings.

fp: 14 November 1942, Royal Albert Hall, Royal Philharmonic Society concert, Louis Kentner and Ilona Kabos, cond. Sir Adrian Boult, with E. Gillegin and F. Bradshaw (percussion).

fAp: 21 January 1943, New York, Béla and Ditta Bartók, cond. Fritz Reiner.

Pub. 1970, Boosey & Hawkes.

97. Contrasts. For violin, clarinet and piano. Dated: 24 September 1938, Budapest. Ded. Benny Goodman and Joseph Szigeti.

1. *Recruiting dance* (Verbunkos); 2. *Relaxation* (Pihenö); 3. *Fast dance* (Sebes).

fp: 9 January 1939, New York, Joseph Szigeti, Benny Goodman and Endre Petri.

Pub. 1942, Hawkes.

98. Violin Concerto No. 2. August 1937–31 December 1938, Budapest. Ded. Zoltán Székely. Dur. 32′.

1. *Allegro non troppo* (Dur. 12′ 16″); 2. *Andante tranquillo* (Dur. 9′ 37″); 3. *Allegro molto* (Dur. 9′ 40″).

2 fl, pic, 2 ob, ca, 2 cl, bcl, 2 bsn, cbsn; 4 hn, 2 tpt, 3 tmb; timp, 2 side dm, GC, 2 cym, tgle, tamtam; celesta, hp, strings.

fp: 23 March 1939, Amsterdam, Zoltán Székely and the Concertgebouw Orchestra, cond. Willem Mengelberg.

fEp: 20 September 1944, BBC broadcast, Yehudi Menuhin and the BBC Symphony Orchestra, cond. Sir Adrian Boult.

f London p (concert): 28 November 1945, Royal Albert Hall, Yehudi Menuhin and the BBC Symphony Orchestra, cond. Sir Adrian Boult.

Pub. 1941, 1946 (score), Hawkes: incl. reduction by the composer.

BIBLIOGRAPHY:

Henry Cowell: Bartók and his Violin Concerto, *Tempo*, No. 8, September 1944.

S. Edvi-Illés: Bartók's Violin Concerto, an analysis with special regard to its Magyar characteristics, *Canon*, October 1957, p. 64.

Herbert Eimert: Das Violinkonzert von Bartók, *Melos*, October 1947, p. 335; *Musik der Zeit*, 1954, No. 9, p. 50.

Julian Herbage: Bartók's Violin Concerto, *MR*, May 1945.

Dyneley Hussey: Bartók's Violin Concerto, *Spectator*, 7 December 1945, p. 539.

99. Mikrokosmos. 153 progressive pieces for piano. 1926–39. Vols. 1 & 2 ded. Peter Bartók; Nos. 148–53 (Six Dances in Bulgarian rhythm) ded. Harriet Cohen.

fEp (twenty pieces): 20 January 1938, BBC broadcast, Béla Bartók.

Pub. 1940, Hawkes.

31

Bartók, Béla

BIBLIOGRAPHY:

Sylvia van Ameringen: Teaching with Bartók's Mikrokosmos, *Tempo*, No. 21, autumn 1951.

Peter Benary: Der zweistimmige Kontrapunkt in Bartók's Mikrokosmos, *Archiv für Musikwissenschaft*, 1958, No. 3, p. 198.

W. D. Dustin: Two voiced textures in the Mikrokosmos of BB, *Dissertation Abstracts*, March 1960, p. 3768.

R. Elkin: Mikrokosmos, an analysis of three pieces by Bartók, *Music in Education*, No. 308 (1964), p. 167.

Hans Ulrich Engelmann: Chromatische Ausstufung in BBs Mikrokosmos, *Melos*, May 1951, p. 138.

— BBs Mikrokosmos, Versuch einer Typologie 'Neuer Musik', Konrad Triltsch Verlag (Würzburg), 1953.

Ferenc Farkas: Bartók Mikrokosmosa, *A Zene*, 1940.

Massimo Mila: BB e il suo Mikrokosmos, *Il Diapason*, January 1950.

Ylda Novik: Teaching with Mikrokosmos, *Tempo*, winter 1967–8, p. 12.

Benjamin Suchoff: BB and a guide to Mikrokosmos, *Dissertation Abstracts*, April 1957, p. 867.

— History of BB's Mikrokosmos, *Journal of Research in Musical Education*, 1959, No. 2, p. 185.

Jürgen Uhde: Leben und Ordnung, BBs Mikrokosmos, *NZfM*, February 1954, p. 85.

Hellmuth Christian Wolff: Der Mikrokosmos von BB, *Musica*, 1951, No. 4, p. 134.

Anon: BB's Mikrokosmos, *Tempo*, No. 2 (American edition), April 1940.

99a. Seven Pieces from Mikrokosmos. Transcribed by the composer for two pianos. Nos. 113, 69, 135, 123, 127, 145, 146. Pub. 1947, Boosey & Hawkes. Note also: 23 progressive duos transcribed by Benjamin Suchoff, 1961, Boosey & Hawkes.

99b. Suite from Mikrokosmos. Arr. & orch. Tibor Serly. Nos. 139, 137, 117, 142, 102, 151 & 153, with No. 3 from 'Three Hungarian Folk Tunes' as prelude. Dur. 16–17'.

3 fl, 2 ob, 2 cl, 2 bsn; 4 hn, 3 tpt, 3 tmb, tuba; timp, pcssn; celesta, hp, strings.
Pub. 1943, Hawkes.

99c. Five Pieces from Mikrokosmos. Arr. by Tibor Serly for string orchestra. Nos. 139, 102, 108, 116, 142.

100. Divertimento. For string orchestra. Dated: 2–17 August 1939, Saanen. Ded. Basle Chamber Orchestra. Dur. 22' 13".

1. *Allegro non troppo* (Dur. 8' 16"); 2. *Molto adagio* (Dur. 7' 27"); 3. *Allegro assai* (Dur. 6' 32").

fp: 11 June 1940, Basle, Basle Chamber Orchestra, cond. Paul Sacher.

fEp: 2 October 1940, Liverpool, Philharmonic Hall, Louis Cohen's Merseyside Chamber Orchestra.

f London p: 22 May 1941, Cambridge Theatre (London), Jacques Orchestra, cond. Reginald Jacques. (*N.B.*: f London p originally announced for a Savoy Theatre concert by the Sidney Beer Symphony Orchestra.)

Pub. 1940, Hawkes.

BIBLIOGRAPHY:

Henry Pleasants: BB's Divertimento, *Tempo*, No. 3 (American edition), September 1940.

Constantin Regamey: Le Divertimento pour orchestre à cordes de BB, *Revue musicale de Suisse Romande*, December 1965.

101. String Quartet No. 6. August–November 1939, Saanen, Budapest. Ded. Kolisch Quartet. Dur. 26' 10".

1. *Mesto—Vivace* (Dur. 6' 46"); 2. *Mesto—Marcia* (Dur. 7'); 3. *Mesto—Burletta* (Dur. 6' 44"); 4. *Mesto—Molto tranquillo* (Dur. 5' 40").

fp: 20 January 1941, New York, Kolisch Quartet.

Pub. 1941, Hawkes.

BIBLIOGRAPHY:

Gerald Abraham: Bartók, String Quartet No. 6, *MR*, 1942.

Benjamin Suchoff: Structure and concept in Bartók's Sixth Quartet, *Tempo*, winter 1967–8, p. 3.

John Vinton: New light on Bartók's Sixth Quartet, *MR*, August 1964, p. 224.

102. Concerto for orchestra. 15 August–

8 October 1943, Saranac Lake. Composed for the Koussevitzky Music Foundation in memory of Natalie Koussevitzky. Dur. 37'.

1. *Introduzione*; 2. *Giuoco delle coppie*; 3. *Elegia*; 4. *Intermezzo interrotto*; 5. *Finale*.

3 fl, pic, 3 ob, ca, 3 cl, bcl, 3 bsn, dbsn; 4 hn, 3 (4) tpt, 2 ten tmb, bs tmb, tuba; timp, side dm, GC, tamtam, cym, tgle; 2 hp, strings.

fp: 1 December 1944, Boston, Boston Symphony Orchestra, cond. Serge Koussevitzky.

f New York p: 10 January 1945, Carnegie Hall, Boston Symphony Orchestra, cond. Serge Koussevitzky.

f Ep: 16 October 1945, Liverpool, Liverpool Philharmonic Orchestra, cond. (Sir) Malcolm Sargent.

f London p: 6 March 1946, BBC concert, BBC Symphony Orchestra, cond. Sir Adrian Boult.

f Scottish p: 26 August 1948, Edinburgh Festival, Concertgebouw Orchestra, cond. Eduard van Beinum.

Pub. 1946, Hawkes.

BIBLIOGRAPHY:

William Austin: Bartók's Concerto for orchestra, *MR*, February 1957, p. 21.
Gilbert G. French: Continuity and discontinuity in Bartók's Concerto for orchestra, *MR*, May 1967, p. 122.
George F. Linstead: Bartók's Concerto for orchestra, *Halle*, January 1950, p. 3.
J. Volek: Über einige interessante Beziehungen zwischen thematischer Arbeit und Instrumentation in Bartóks Werk: Concerto für Orchester, *Studia musicologica*, 1964, No. 1–4, p. 557.
Anon: Le Concerto pour orchestre de BB, *Dissonances*, March–April 1946.

103. Sonata for unaccompanied violin. Dated: 14 March 1944, Asheville. Ded. Yehudi Menuhin. Dur. 23' 35".

1. *Tempo di ciaccona* (Dur. 8' 45"); 2. *Fuga* (Dur. 3' 50"); 3. *Melodia* (Dur. 6' 22"); 4. *Presto* (Dur. 4' 35").

fp: 26 November 1944, New York, Yehudi Menuhin.

Pub. 1947, Hawkes: ed. Yehudi Menuhin.

104. The husband's grief (A férj keserve).

Ukrainian folksong for voice and piano. February 1945. Ded. Pál Kecskeméti. Unpub.

105. Piano Concerto No. 3. Summer 1945. Unfinished; completed by Tibor Serly (last 17 bars).

1. *Allegretto*; 2. *Adagio religioso*; 3. (*Allegro vivace*).

2 fl, 2 ob, 2 cl, 2 bsn; 4 hn, 2 tpt, 3 tmb, tuba; timp, xyl, tgle, tamb pic, cym, GC, tamtam; strings.

fp: 8 February 1946, György Sándor and the Philadelphia Orchestra, cond. Eugene Ormandy.

f Ep: 27 November 1946, Royal Festival Hall, BBC concert, Louis Kentner and the BBC Symphony Orchestra, cond. Sir Adrian Boult.

Pub. 1947, Boosey & Hawkes: incl. reduction by Mátyás Seiber for two pianos.

BIBLIOGRAPHY:

Mosco Carner: Piano Concerto No. 3, in *The Concerto*, Pelican Books (London) 1952, p. 343.

106. Viola Concerto. 1945. Unfinished; reconstructed and orch. Tibor Serly. Composed for William Primrose. Dur. 20' 30".

1. *Moderato*; 2. *Adagio religioso*; 3. *Allegro vivace*.

2 fl, pic, 2 ob, 2 cl, 2 bsn; 3 hn, 2 tpt, 2 tmb, tuba; timp, pcssn; strings.

fp: 2 December 1949, William Primrose and the Minneapolis Symphony Orchestra, cond. Antal Dorati.

f Ep: 2 September 1950, Edinburgh Festival, William Primrose and the Halle Orchestra, cond. Sir John Barbirolli.

f London p: 5 September 1950, Royal Albert Hall, Promenade Concert, William Primrose and the London Philharmonic Orchestra, cond. Basil Cameron.

Pub. 1949, Boosey & Hawkes: incl. reduction.

BIBLIOGRAPHY:

Mosco Carner: Bartók's Viola Concerto, *MT*, August 1950, p. 301.
— Bartók's Viola Concerto, in *The Concerto*, Pelican Books (London) 1952, p. 350.
Tibor Serly: Notiz zu Bartóks Bratschenkonzert, *Musik der Zeit*, No. 9 (1954), p. 53.

Bartók, Béla

Denis Stevens: A note on Bartók's Viola Concerto, *Music Survey*, 1950.

107. Cadenzas for Mozart's Concerto in E flat K.482.

BARTÓK'S WRITINGS:
See: BB, Essays (ed. Benjamin Suchoff), Faber (London) 1972.

GENERAL BIBLIOGRAPHY:
Gerald Abraham: The Bartók of the quartets, *M&L*, 1945; in *Slavonic and Romantic Music*, Faber (London) 1968, p. 339.
— Bartók in England, *Studia musicologica*, 1964, Nos. 1–4, p. 339.
Philippe Arthuys: BB, expression du phénomène contemporain, *RM*, May 1955, p. 117.
Milton Babbitt: The string quartets of Bartók, *MQ*, July 1949, p. 377.
Ernö Balogh: BB, *Pro Musica*, March 1928.
— Bartók's last years, *Tempo*, No. 36, summer 1955.
János Bartók: Bartók, pionnier de la musicologie (transl. Paule de Rotalier), *RM*, May 1955, p. 41.
Joseph Baruzi: Festival BB, *Le Ménestrel*, 22 March 1929, p. 137.
Victor Bátor: Bartók's executor speaks, *Musical Courier*, 1951.
— The BB Archives, history and catalogue, Bartók Archives (New York) 1963.
J. Batel: Nezname listy Belu Bartoka, *Slovenska Hudba*, January 1958, p. 15.
Harry Cassin Becker: BB and his credo, *Musical America*, 1927.
Gregor Berger: Motivische Gestaltung des Quintraumes bei Bartók, *Musik im Unterricht*, 1954.
Oskar Bie: Brief an BB, *Anbruch*, 1921.
Eric Blom: The string quartets of BB, *MO*, May 1922, p. 696.
— Bartók's third period, *Tempo*, No. 5, August 1941.
G. Bodnar: Bartók et le mouvement 'Nyugat', *Studia musicologica*, 1964, Nos. 1–4, p. 347.
Ferenc Bónis: Quotations in Bartók's music— a contribution to Bartók's psychology of composition, *Studia musicologica*, 1964, Nos.

1–4, p. 355; Zitate in Bartóks Musik, *ÖM*, September 1965.
André Boucourechliev: Les disques—six quatuors de Bartók, *Nouvelle revue française*, No. 55 (1957), p. 159.
Henry Boys: BB, *MT*, November 1945, p. 329.
Constantin Brailoiu: BB folkloriste, *SM*, March 1948.
Gisèle Brelet: BB, musique savante et musique populaire, *Contrepoints*, 1946, No. 3 (March–April), p. 38.
— L'esthétique de BB, *RM*, May 1955, p. 21.
Robert Breuer: Ein Requiem für BB, *SM*, June 1958, p. 252.
S. Brichta: BB und Wagner, *Signale*, 1931, Nos. 27–28, p. 694.
Arthur G. Browne: BB, *M&L*, January 1931, p. 35.
Eyvind H. Bull: BB replies to Percy Grainger, *Music News* (Chicago), 1934.
Storm Bull: Bartók the teacher, *Musical Facts* (Chicago), 1941.
— Bartók's teaching pieces, *Repertoire*, October 1951, p. 1.
— The piano music of BB, *Repertoire*, November 1951, p. 70.
L. Burlas: Neuerertum und Tradition in Bartóks Formenwelt, *Studia musicologica*, 1964, Nos. 1–4, p. 383.
M.-D. Calvocoressi: BB, an introduction, *MMR*, March 1922.
— BB, notes on his musical career, *MN&H*, March 1922, p. 306.
— More about Bartók and Kodály, *MMR*, August 1922.
— BB and his piano concertos, *The Listener*, 8 November 1933, p. 714.
Mosco Carner: BB, *The Listener*, 1945.
Alfredo Casella: In memoriam di BB, *Janus Pannonius* (Rome), 1947.
Ernest Chapman: BB, an estimate and appreciation, *Tempo*, No. 13, December 1945.
Frank Choisy: Les chansons populaires hongroises recueillies par Bartók et Kodály, *Revue des Etudes Hongroises et Finno-Oogriennes*, Vol. 2, No. 2, 1925.
Pierre Citron: Bartók, Editions du Seuil (Paris) 1963.

Arthur Clyne: BB and Magyar music, *Bookman*, June 1922, p. 145.

André Coeuroy: BB et les Balkans, in *Panorama de la musique contemporaine*, Simon Kra (Paris) 1928; Eng. transl., *Eolus*, January 1929.

F.F.C. & G.J.C.: The works of BB on records, *Tempo*, No. 13, autumn 1949, p. 39; No. 14, winter 1949–50, p. 36.

Paul Collaer: Hommage à BB, *Aspects*, No. 2, December 1954, p. 41.

Adrian Collins: Bartók, Schoenberg and some songs, *M&L*, April 1929.

Geoffrey Crankshaw: Bartók and the string quartet, *MO*, December 1951, p. 145.

— Bartók quartets, II, *M&M*, January 1968, p. 58.

Anthony Cross: Portrait of Debussy, 2: Debussy and Bartók, *MT*, February 1967, p. 125.

Suzanne Demarquez: Souvenirs et réflexions, *RM*, May 1955, p. 91.

J. Demény: BBs Stellung in der Musikgeschichte des 20. Jahrhunderts, *Studia musicologica*, 1964, Nos. 1–4, p. 403.

A. Demo: Zodkazu Belu Bartóka, *Slovenska Hudba*, July–August 1961, p. 330.

Norman Demuth: BB, in *Musical Trends in the 20th Century*, Rockliff (London) 1952, p. 265.

Edward J. Dent: BB, *Athenaeum*, 1 April 1922, p. 30.

Denijs Dille: BB, *La Sirène*, March 1937.

— BB, N.V. Standaard-Boekhandel (Antwerp) 1939.

— BB, National Instituut voor Radio-Omroep (Brussels) 1947.

— The life of BB, *Tempo*, No. 13, autumn 1949, p. 3.

— Probleme der Bartók-Forschnung, *ÖM*, December 1961.

— BB und Wien, *ÖM*, November 1964.

— Les problèmes des recherches sur Bartók, *Studia musicologica*, 1964, Nos. 1–4, p. 415.

— Vier unbekannte Briefe von BB, *ÖM*, September 1965.

Denijs Dille (ed.): Documenta Bartókiana I, Akadémiai Kiadó (Budapest), Schott (Mainz) 1964–70.

Erich Doflein: BB, *Melos*, May–June 1949, p. 129.

— Bartók und die Musikpädagogik, *Musik der Zeit*, 1952.

— BBs Kompositionen für die Musikpädagogik, *Musik im Unterricht*, October 1955.

— BB, *SM*, October 1955, p. 377.

R. L. Donahue: A comparative analysis of phrase structure in selected movements of the string quartets of BB and Walter Piston, *Dissertation Abstracts*, February 1968, p. 3207A.

J. W. Downey: La musique populaire dans l'œuvre de BB, *Dissertation Abstracts*, June 1963, p. 4650; Centre de documentation universitaire (Paris) 1967.

Imre Fábián: Das Bartók-Archiv in Budapest, *ÖM*, December 1961.

— BB und die Wiener Schule, *ÖM*, May–June 1964.

— Bartók-Literatur, *ÖM*, September 1965.

— Ungarische Musik nach Bartók, *ÖM*, November 1966, p. 620.

Chao Feno: Bartók and Chinese music culture, *Studia musicologica*, 1964, Nos. 1–4, p. 393.

Helmut A. Fiechtner: BB, *ÖM*, May 1957.

Gerold Fierz: Bartók records, *SM*, March–April 1963, p. 99.

M. Fleuret: Lorsque BB découvrait Paris, *Musica* (Chaix), No. 109, April 1963, p. 4.

Andor Foldes: My first meeting with Bartók, *Etude*, March 1955, p. 12; *Canon*, July 1955, p. 453.

— Bartók as pianist, *Juilliard Review*, fall 1955.

— BB, *Tempo*, No. 43, spring 1957.

— Souvenirs sur BB, *Feuilles musicales*, November–December 1957.

Hubert J. Foss: An approach to Bartók, *MO*, April 1944, p. 218.

Alan Frank: BB, in *The Heritage of Music*, Vol. 3, O.U.P. (London) 1951, p. 172.

A. Frankenstein: Exploring the piano with BB, *High Fidelity*, August 1956, p. 41.

Géza Frid: Ter herdenking van BB, *Mens en melodie*, 1946.

— Pleidooi voor de piano composities van Bartók, *Mens en melodie*, November 1947, p. 342.

Hans Gal (ed.): BB, in *The Musicians World* (Great Composers in their Letters), Thames & Hudson (London) 1965, p. 434.

Edith Gerson-Kiwi: BB, scholar in folk music, *M&L*, April 1957.

Gianandrea Gavazzeni: BB, *La Rassegna musicale*, 1939, p. 1.

Bernard Gavoty: Die letzten Werke von BB, *Melos*, October 1947.

Jean Gergely: Les chœurs à cappella de BB, *RM*, May 1955, p. 127.

André Gertler: Souvenirs sur BB, *RM*, May 1955, p. 99.

Scott Goddard: Perspective about BB, *The Listener*, 1948.

Ottó Gombosi: BBs neueste Werke, *Melos*, January 1928.

— BB, *Ungarische Jahrbücher* (Berlin), 1931.

— BB, *MQ*, January 1946, p. 1.

M. Gorczycka: Folklor w tworczosci Beli Bartóka, *Muzyka*, 1961, No. 3, p. 111.

— Nowatororstwo kwartetow Bartóka, *Muzyka*, 1962, No. 2, p. 47.

— BB, *Ruch Muzyczny*, 1960, 1 April, p. 30: 15 April, p. 8.

— Krytyka systemu Lendvai'a, *Ruch Muzyczny*, 1 October 1960, p. 6.

— Neue Merkmale der Klangtechnik in Bartóks Streichquartetten, *Studia musicologica*, 1964, Nos. 1–4, p. 425.

F. Lopez Graça: Evocation de BB, *RM*, May 1955, p. 112.

— Stravinsky e BB, *Gazeta musical*, 1959, July–August, p. 329; September, p. 361.

Cecil Gray: BB, *Sackbut*, November 1920, p. 301.

— BB, *Anbruch*, 1921, No. 5, p. 90.

— BB, in *A Survey in Contemporary Music*, O.U.P. (London) 1927, p. 194.

M. Guiomar & M. Marnat: BB, *Disques*, No. 126, January 1962, p. 40.

A. Gwynn-Browne: Beginning Bartók, *Disc*, winter 1951, p. 158.

Maurice Halperson: BB explains himself, *Musical America*, 1928.

Günter Händel: Bartók und die Wiener Klassik, *Melos*, April 1955, p. 103.

Gyula Harangozó: Erinnerungen an BB, *ÖM*, May 1967, p. 258.

Emil Haraszti: La musique de chambre de BB, *RM*, August–September 1930.

— BB, Kortársaink (Budapest), 1930.

— BB, his life and works, Lyrebird Press (Paris), 1938.

Ralph Hawkes: BB, a recollection by his publisher, *Tempo*, No. 13, autumn 1949, p. 10.

Robin Hawthorne: The fugal technique of BB, *MR*, 1949, p. 277.

J. von Hecker: Bartóks Streichquartette, *Musica Schallplatte*, No. 6 (1958), p. 81.

G. Heerup: BB, *Dansk Musiktidsskrift*, February 1929.

Hans Heinsheimer: Erinnerungen an BB, *NZfM*, 1951.

Everett Helm: Bartóks Kindheit und Jugend, *Melos*, May 1965, p. 145.

— Bartók on stage, *High Fidelity*, November 1964, p. 74.

Leigh Henry: BB, *MO*, October 1920, p. 53.

— BB, *Chesterian*, No. 22, April 1922.

Lajos Hernádi: BB, le pianiste, le pédagogue, l'homme, *RM*, May 1955, p. 77.

Philip Heseltine: Modern Hungarian composers, *MT*, March 1922, p. 164.

H. A. Horn: Idiomatic writing of the piano music of BB, *Dissertation Abstracts*, June 1964, p. 5451.

Z. Hrabussay: Nevydane listy Belu Bartóka v Archive mesta Bratislavy, *Slovenska Hudba*, October 1958, p. 446.

— BBa Bratislava, *Slovenska Hudba*, March 1961, p. 127.

Dyneley Hussey: BB and the Hungarian folksong, *The Listener*, 1946.

Bernard Jacobson: Bartók for piano, *R&R*, February 1964, p. 17.

P. Jardanyi: Bartók und die Ordnung der Volkslieder, *Studia musicologica*, 1964, Nos. 1–4, p. 435.

Alexander Jemnitz: BB, eine westöstliche Geburtstagbetrachtung, *Anbruch*, 1931, No. 4, p. 77.

— Asien und Europa (Bartók Studie), *Melos*, 1931.

— BB, *MQ*, July 1933, p. 260.

— Bartók-Fest in Kecskemet, *Der Auftakt*, 1937, Nos. 7–8.

— BB, his life and music, Hungarian Reference Library (New York), 1940.

A. Kárász: BB et la musique hongroise, *La Revue européenne*, 1930.

Erich Katz: BB, *Anbruch*, December 1927, p. 416.

G. Kerenyi & B. Rajeczky: Über Bartóks

Volksliedaufzeichnungen, *Studia musicologica*, 1964, Nos. 1–4, p. 441.

Sigmund Klein: BB, a portrait, *Pro Musica*, 1925.

W. Klinkenberg: Het Bartók-Seminarie te Boedapest, *Mens en melodie*, 7 December 1967, p. 365.

Zoltán Kodály: BB elsö operája, *Nyugat* (Budapest), 1918; Bartók Weg und Werk; Bartók, sa vie et son œuvre.

— Bartóks Kinderstücke, *Anbruch*, 1920.

— BB, *RM*, March 1921, p. 205.

— Les sonates de BB, *RM*, 1923.

— New music for old, *Modern Music*, 1925.

— Bartók le folkloriste, *RM*, 1952, p. 31 (orig. pub. in *Uj Zenei Szemle*, Budapest, 1950).

— Ungarische Jugend bei Bartók im Schuld, *Musik der Zeit*, 1952.

— Hungary's Bartók, *M&M*, January 1957, p. 17.

— Bartók als Folklorist, *Musik der Zeit*, No. 9, 1954, p. 33.

— Opening address, *Studia musicologica*, 1964, Nos. 1–4, p. 9

Stefan Krehl: Die Dissonanz als musikalisches Ausdrucksmittel, *Zeitschrift für Musikwissenschaft*, 1919.

L. E. Kreter: Motivic and textual delineation of the formal design in the first three Bartók quartets, *Dissertation Abstracts*, April 1962, p. 3692.

J. Kroo: Monothematik und Dramaturgie in Bartóks Bühnenwerken, *Studia musicologica*, 1964, Nos. 1–4, p. 449.

V. Kucera: Podivuhodny umelec, *Hudebni Rozhledy*, 1961, No. 7, p. 282.

René Leibowitz: BB, *L'Arche* (Paris), 1946–7.

— BB, ou la possibilité de compromis dans la musique contemporaine, *Les Temps modernes*, 1947; Eng. transl. *Transition*, 1948.

— BB und die Volksmusik, *Musikblätter*, 1948, No. 9, p. 6.

Hugo Leichtentritt: Bartók and the Hungarian folksong, *Modern Music*, March–April 1933.

— On the art of BB, *Modern Music*, March–April 1929.

Ernö Lendvai: Bartók und die Zahl, *Melos*, November 1960.

— Duality and synthesis in the music of BB, *New Hungarian Quarterly*, 1962.

— Bartók und der goldene Schnitt, *ÖM*, November 1966, p. 607.

— Bartók vonosnegyesei, *Muzsika*, December 1967, p. 26; January 1968, p. 34; February 1968, p. 16.

Lajos Lesznai: BB, *Melos*, 1949, Nos. 5–6, p. 146 (abridged from *Zenei Szemle*, 1948).

— Realistische Ausdrucksmittel in der Musik Bartóks, *Studia musicologica*, 1964, Nos. 1–4, p. 469; *Musik und Gesellschaft*, December 1961, p. 722.

Heinrich Lindlar: Schicksalskomponenten, *Musica*, 1958, No. 1, p. 9.

Robert Lorenz: Trial by Bartók, *British Musician*, March 1934, p. 56.

Jan Löwenbach: BB, *Tempo* (Prague), 1946.

Watson Lyle: BB, a personal impression, *MN&H*, 19 May 1923, p. 495.

— BB, a sketch, *Bookman*, April 1932, p. 67.

Joseph Machlis: BB, in *Introduction to Contemporary Music*, Norton (USA), 1961, Dent (London), p. 183.

— Three works by Bartók, in *-do-*, p. 191.

Colin Mason: BB, *British Musician*, February 1949, p. 32.

— Bartók's Rhapsodies, *M&L*, 1949.

— Bartók through his quartets, *MMR*, 1950, p. 3.

— BB and folksong, *MR*, 1950, p. 292.

— BB, in *Decca Book of Ballets*, Muller (London) 1958, p. 63.

— Bartók and the piano concerto, *The Listener*, 10 September 1959, p. 412.

— Bartók revival and a discovery, *Guardian*, 7 October 1961, p. 6.

— Bartók and folksong, *The Listener*, 4 October 1962, p. 541.

— Pianist composer, *Guardian*, 22 August 1963, p. 6.

Ludwig K. Mayer: BB, *Blätter der Staatsoper* (Berlin), December (No. 14) 1928, p. 1.

Jacques de Menasce: Berg and Bartók, *Modern Music*, 1944.

— The classicism of BB, *Modern Music*, 1946.

Yehudi Menuhin: BB, the solitary composer, in *Music Magazine*, Rockliff (London) 1953, p. 18; *The Listener*, 10 September 1959, p. 412; in *Essays on Music*, Cassell (London) 1967, p. 32.

Yehudi Menuhin: Begegnung mit Bartók, *Musik der Zeit*, No. 9 (1954), p. 54.

Agathe Messe-Albrecht: Erinnerungen an BBs Jugendjahre, *SM*, October 1955, p. 377.

E. Michelsen: En bedre verden . . . indtryk fra Bartók-festivalen i Budapest, *Dansk Musiktidsskrift*, November, 1956, p. 93.

Paul Mies: Volksliedsätze von Bartók, *Musik der Zeit*, No. 9 (1954), p. 38.

Massimo Mila: BB, il musicista della libertà, *L'Italia socialista*, 1948.

— La natura e il mistero nell'arte di BB, *La Rassegna musicale*, 1948, p. 95; *Chigiana*, 1965.

Donald Mitchell: Bartók, Stravinsky and Schoenberg, *Chesterian*, No. 175, July 1953.

Raymond Monelle: Bartók's imagination in the later quartets, *MR*, February 1970, p. 81.

Douglas Moore: Homage to Bartók, *Modern Music*, 1946.

Serge Moreux: *BB*, Paris, 1949; Ger. transl. by Ursula Müller, Zürich/Freiburg, 1950.

Roberto García Morillo: Sobra una sonata de BB, *El Momento musical*, September 1937.

Dorothy Moulton Mayer: Bartók, *Crescendo*, No. 114, October 1961, p. 8; No. 122, October 1962, p. 33; No. 132, February 1964, p. 1.

H.N.: BB's visit to Wales, *MN&H*, 25 March 1922, p. 377.

I. Nest'ev: BB v Rossii, *Studia musicologica*, 1964, Nos. 1–4, p. 481.

Ernest Newman: The Bartók quartets, in *More Essays from the World of Music*, Calder (London) 1958, p. 38.

O. Nordwall: BB and modern music, *Studia musicologica*, 1967, Nos. 3–4, p. 265.

Edwin von der Nüll: Zur Kompositionstechnik Bartóks, *Anrubch*, November–December 1928.

— BB, *Anbruch*, 1929.

— BB, ein Beitrag zur Morphologie der neuen Musik (Halle), 1930.

— BB, Geist und Stil, *Melos*, March (No. 4) 1933, p. 135.

Antonio Odiozola: BB (discography), *Musica* (Madrid), 1953, Nos. 3–4, p. 225.

— La bibliografia sobre BB y el reciente libro de Halsey Stevens, *Musica* (Madrid), 1953, No. 5, p. 20.

Hans Oesch: Um Bartóks Nachlass, *ÖM*, February 1959.

Gustáv Oláh: Bartók and the theatre, *Tempo*, No. 14, winter 1949–50, p. 4.

A. Otvös: Magyar explorers, *League of Composers Review*, April 1925.

I. B. Palotay: BB, composer, teacher and person, *Music of the West Magazine*, November 1960, p. 6.

Domenico De Paoli: Los cuartetos de BB, *Musica* (Madrid), 1953, No. 5, p. 37.

Anthony Payne: The static and dynamic in Bartók, *The Listener*, 2 April 1964, p. 570.

George Perle: Symmetrical formations in the string quartets of BB, *MR*, November 1955, p. 300.

J. M. Pernecky: The historical and musico-ethnological approach to the instrumental compositions of BB, *Dissertation Abstracts*, December 1956, p. 2476.

K. W. Peterson: Apropos Bartók's klaverskole, *Dansk Musiktidsskrift*, 1954, Nos. 2–3, p. 37.

Coriolan Petranu: BB et la musique roumaine, *Revue de Transylvanie*, 1937.

— Observations en marge des réponses de M. BB, *Revue de Transylvanie*, 1937.

— Epilogue de la discussion avec M. BB sur la musique roumaine, *Revue de Transylvanie*, 1939.

Felix Petyrek: BBs Klavierwerke, *Anbruch*, 1921.

Paul A. Pisk: Bartók und Kodály, *Berliner Börsen-Zeitung*, 9 June 1926.

Henry Pleasants & Tibor Serly: Bartók's historic contribution, *Modern Music*, 1940.

László (Ladislaus) Pollatsek: BB, *Der Auftakt*, October 1928 (No. 9), p. 205.

— Der Weg BBs, *SM*, 1929.

— BB, der Fünfzigjährige, *AMZ*, 20 March 1931, p. 203.

— BB and his work, *MT*, 1931, May, p. 411; June, p. 506; July, p. 560; August, p. 697.

— Bartóks neuere Werke, *Der Auftakt*, 1931, No. 4, p. 108.

Josef Polnauer: Noch einmal—Bartók und Wien, *ÖM*, September 1965.

J. Racek: Leoš Janáčeks und BBs Bedeutung in der Weltmusik, *Studia musicologica*, 1964, Nos. 1–4, p. 501.

Bernard Rands: The use of canon in Bartók's quartets, *MR*, August 1957, p. 183.

Othmar Reich: Petranu contra Bartók, *SM*, 1 April 1938.

Willi Reich: In memoriam BB, *SM*, 1945.

— BB, eigene Schriften und Erinnerungen der Freunde, Benno Schwabe (Stuttgart) 1958.

G. Révész: BB en Zoltán Kodály, *Mens en melodie*, May 1953, p. 148.

D. Richards: Bartók Quartets, I, *M&M*, January 1968, p. 49.

Reimar Riefling: Pedagogiske refleksjoner, *Nordisk Musikkultur*, February 1954.

Hector Manuel Romero: La herencia musical de Bartók, *Orientation musical*, 1947.

Claude Rostand: BB, chemins et contrastes du musicien, *Contrepoints*, No. 3 (March–April), 1946, p. 31.

W. Rudzinski: System zlotej proporcji u Bartoka, *Ruch Muzyczny*, 1 October 1960, p. 6.

Robert Sabin: Revolution and tradition in the music of Bartók, *Musical America*, 1949.

Paul Sacher: BB, *ÖM*, May 1953.

— BB zum Gedächtnis, *SM*, 1945.

Adolfo Salazar: BB, in *Música y músicos de hoy*, Editorial Mundo Latino (Madrid), 1928, p. 327.

Lazare Saminsky: Bartók and the graphic current in music, *MQ*, July 1924, p. 400.

— Schoenberg and Bartók, pathbreakers, *Modern Music*, February 1924.

A. Adnan Saygun: Bartók in Turkey, *MQ*, January 1951, p. 5.

Boris de Schloezer: Nota su BB, *La Rassegna musicale*, 1945, p. 106.

— A propos de BB, Fontaine (Paris) 1947.

— BB, history v. esthetica, *Transition*, 1948.

— BB i Manuel de Falla, *Ruch Muzyczny*, 1947.

Ernst Schoen: Bartók and musical folklore, *Radio Times*, 9 February 1934, p. 372.

Willi Schuh: Bartóks Basler Auftragswerke, *Musik der Zeit*, No. 9 (1954), p. 45.

Erwin Schulhoff: Das neue Klavierspiel: BB der bedeutendste der jungungarischen-rumänischen Richtung, *Der Auftakt*, 1924.

Irmgard Seefried: Meine Wege zu Hindemith und Bartók, *ÖM*, 1954.

Mátyás Seiber: BB, *MMR*, 1945, p. 195.

— The string quartets of BB, Boosey & Hawkes (London) 1945.

— Bartók's chamber music, *Tempo*, No. 13, autumn 1949, p. 19.

Gisella Selden-Goth: Ein Bartók-Gedenkblatt, *SM*, October 1955, p. 378.

— 'I shall never forget' . . . a vignette of BB, *Musical Courier*, October 1955, p. 14.

Tibor Serly: Bartók tribute, *New York Times*, 25 September 1955, Section 2, p. 9.

Desmond Shawe-Taylor: Bartók quartets, *New Statesman*, 17 November 1945, p. 333.

Gábor Steinberger: BB, *Revista musical Chilena*, 1946.

Halsey Stevens: The life and music of BB, O.U.P. (New York) 1953; rev. edition, 1964.

— A Bartók bibliography, *Tempo*, 1949–50.

— Some 'unknown' works of Bartók, *MQ*, January 1966, p. 37.

Heinrich Strobel: Bartóks neueste Werke, *Melos*, January 1928.

H. H. Stuckenschmidt: BB, *Die Sendung*, 1930.

— Urbanität und Volksliedgeist: Über BB, *Der Monat*, 1953.

— BB, in *Schöpfer der neuen Musik*, Suhrkamp-Verlag (Frankfurt a. M.), 1958, p. 98.

Benjamin Suchoff: BB's contributions to music education, *Journal of Research in Music Education*, 1961, No. 1, p. 3.

— Computer applications to Bartók's Serbo-Croatian material, *Tempo*, No. 80, spring 1967, p. 15.

Bence Szabolcsi: Liszt and Bartók, *New Hungarian Quarterly*, 1961.

— BB, Leben und Werk, Verlag Philipp Reclam Jun. (Leipzig) 1961.

— Man and nature in Bartók's world, *New Hungarian Quarterly*, 1961; Ger. transl. in *Studia musicologica*, 1964, Nos. 1–4, p. 525.

Bence Szabolcsi & Ferenc Bónis: BB, his life in pictures, Boosey & Hawkes (London), Corvina Press (Budapest), 1964.

Joseph Szigeti: A tribute to Bartók, *Tempo*, No. 10, winter 1948–9.

— Bekenntnis zu Bartók, *Musik der Zeit*, No. 9 (1954), p. 55.

Joseph Szigeti: Working with Bartók, *M&M*, April 1963, p. 8.

Jenö v. Takács: BB, Unbekannt biographisches, *Melos*, May (No. 3) 1951, p. 65.

— Aus Bartóks Briefen, *Melos*, April 1956, p. 103.

— BB in Österreich, *ÖM*, February 1957.

— BBs Kinderjahre, *ÖM*, September 1965.

E. Tanzberger: Jean Sibelius und BB, *Sibelius-Mitteilungen*, No. 5, December 1961, p. 4.

Winthrop P. Tryon: How Bartók composes, *Christian Science Monitor*, 1927.

J. Ujfalussy: Einige inhaltliche Fragen der Brückensymmetrie in Bartóks Werken, *Studia musicologica*, 1964, Nos. 1–4, p. 541.

Z. Vancea: Einige Beiträge über das erste Manuskript der Colinda-Sammlung von BB und über seine einschlägigen Briefe an Constantin Brailoiu, *Studia musicologica*, 1964, Nos. 1–4, p. 549.

L. Vargyas: Bartók's melodies in the style of folk-songs, *Journal of the Internatianal Folk Music Council*, Vol. 16 (1964), p. 30.

G. Vasarhelyi: BB, *Dansk Musiktidsskrift*, November 1955, p. 86.

J. Vyslouzil: Tri Bartokova jevistni dila, *Hudebni Rozhledy*, 1961, No. 2, p. 74.

Sándor Veress: Erinnerungen an BB, *SM*, 1950.

— Indførelse i BBs strygekvartetter, *Dansk Musiktidsskrift*, 1951.

— Eröffnungsrede zum Bartók-Festival in Basel, *SM*, December 1958, p. 460.

I. Volly: Bartók és Serly, *Muzsika*, January 1964, p. 15.

Bernard Wagenaar: Bartók's quartets, *New York Times*, 1949.

M. F. Walker: Thematic, formal and tonal structure of the Bartók string quartets, *Dissertation Abstracts*, December 1955, p. 2543.

Nis L. Wallin: Analysproblem i BBs stråkkvartetter, *Prisma*, No. 1 (1950), p. 34.

J. Weber: Konkurs im Bartoka dla dzieci, *Ruch Muzyczny*, 1 September 1960, p. 16.

John S. Weissmann: BB and folk music, *Keynote*, 1946; BB und die Volksmusik, *Melos*, 1949, Nos. 5–6, p. 149.

— Bartók's music, *Hallé*, March 1948, p. 9.

— Bartók festival in Budapest, *MR*, 1949, p. 36.

— Bartók's piano music, *Tempo*, No. 14, winter 1949–50, p. 8; Bartóks Klaviermusik, *Melos*, 1953, March, p. 75; April, p. 104.

— La musique de piano de Bartók—l'évolution d'une écriture, *RM*, May 1955, p. 171.

— Notes concerning Bartók's solo vocal music, *Tempo*, No. 36, summer 1955; No. 38, winter 1955–6; No. 40, summer 1956.

— Bartók and folk music, *MMR*, 1957, p. 92.

— Bartókiana, *Tempo*, Nos. 55–56, autumn–winter 1960.

— Bartók and the orchestra, *The Listener*, 30 May 1963, p. 941.

— On some problems of Bartók research in connection with Bartók's biography, *Studia musicologica*, 1964, Nos. 1–4, p. 587.

Egon Wellesz: Die Streichquartette von BB, *Anbruch*, 1920.

— Un rénovateur de la musique hongroise: BB, *Les Cahiers d'aujourd'hui*, 1922, No. 8, p. 79.

Kurt Westphal: BB und die moderne ungarische Musik, *Die Musik*, December (No. 3), 1927, p. 188.

Frank Whitaker: A visit to BB, *MT*, March 1926, p. 220.

— The most original mind in modern music, *Radio Times*, 26 February 1932, p. 504.

Ole Willumsen: Om Bartóks klaverskole, *Nordisk Musikkultur*, February 1954.

Charles Wilson: Bartók and Hungarian folk music, *MMR*, 1947, p. 150.

Hellmuth Christian Wolff: BB und die Musik der Gegenwart, *Melos*, August 1952, p. 209.

George Woodhouse: BB, *MN&H*, 1 December 1925, p. 474.

David Woolridge: Bartók in Beirut, *The Composer*, No. 13, spring 1964, p. 18.

Jos Wouters: De contrapunttechnik van BB, *Mens en melodie*, February 1958.

P. Yates: BB, *Partisan Review*, June 1949, p. 643.

Kurt Zimmerreimer: Der Stil BBs, *Musica*, 1947, Nos. 5–6, p. 261.

Various contributors: Hommage à BB, *RM*, May 1955, p. 7 (incl. contributions by Claude Delvincourt, Roger Delage, Louis Durey, Geza Frid, Tibor Harsanyi, Jacques

Ibert, Joseph Kosma, Darius Milhaud and Francis Poulenc).

MISCELLANEOUS OR UNSIGNED:
BB, *Literature* (Budapest), November 1925.
BB, modern master, *Tempo*, No. 4, January 1941.
BBs Werk (chronologie), *Melos*, 1949, Nos. 5–6, p. 153.
Drei Briefe von BB, *Melos*, May–June 1949, p. 138.
Some early letters, *Tempo*, No. 13, autumn 1949, p. 8.
Bartók's style, *The Times*, 19 March 1954, p. 8.
Deux lettres de BB, *RM*, May 1955, p. 65.
BB *Disques*, No. 71, April 1955, p. 372.

ALBAN BERG (1885–1935)

Berg was born into a well-to-do Viennese family on 9 February 1885 and lived in Vienna for the greater part of his life. His early interests and ambitions were literary and it was not until he was fifteen that he began to compose. At first he was self-taught, but when he was nineteen he met Arnold Schoenberg, who was to be his teacher for the next six years (1904–10). The didactic influence of Schoenberg was as profound and lasting as the friendship between the two men. Anton Webern, another brilliant pupil of Schoenberg's, also became a close friend. From 1904 to 1906 Berg worked as an accountant in the Austrian civil service, but thereafter devoted himself entirely to music. He made his début as a composer in 1907, married the singer Helene Nahowski in 1911 and in 1913 was present at the formidable riot which greeted the first performance of two of his Orchestral Songs (Op. 4) in a concert conducted by Schoenberg. Berg served in the Austrian Army from 1915 to 1918 and after the War until 1921 helped Schoenberg to run the Society for Private Musical Performances in Vienna. His first great success with the public came in 1924 with the première in Frankfurt under Hermann Scherchen of the Three Fragments from the completed but at that time unperformed opera *Wozzeck*. Berg's life after 1918 was externally uneventful, being mainly divided between composing and private teaching—also between Vienna in the winter and the Carinthian lakes (the Ossiachersee and Wörthersee) in the summer. He made several visits to other parts of Europe in the 1920s and '30s to attend performances of his own works (notably the Leningrad *Wozzeck* in 1927) and to serve on various musical juries; but suffering as he did from perennial ill-health, especially (after 1908) from asthma, he very rarely appeared in public as a pianist and never as a conductor. He died in Vienna in December 1935 from blood-poisoning brought on by an insect bite, having completed all but the Third-Act orchestration of his second opera, *Lulu*.

CATALOGUE OF WORKS

1. Schliesse mir die Augen beide (Storm). For voice and piano. 1900. Pub. 1930, in *Die Musik* (Vol. XXII, No. 5); 1955, Universal-Edition (ed. Hans F. Redlich).

2. Early Songs. For voice and piano. Unpub.
   1. *Heilige Himmel* (F. Evers). 1900.
   2. *Herbstgefühl* (Siegfried Fleischer). *c.* 1902.
   3. *Unter der Linden* (Walther von der Vogelweide). 1900.
   4. *Spielleute* (Ibsen). *c.* 1902.
   5. *Wo der Goldregen steht* (Lorenz). *c.* 1902.
   6. *Lied des Schiffermädels* (O. J. Bierbaum). *c.* 1902.
   7. *Abschied* (Monsterberg). *c.* 1902.
   8. *Liebeslied* (Dolorosa). *c.* 1902.
   9. *Über meinen Nächten* (Dolorosa). *c.* 1902.
   10. *Sehnsucht I* (Hohenberg). *c.* 1902.
   11. *Sternenfall* (Wilhelm). *c.* 1902.
   12. *Er klagt, dass der Frühling so kortz blüht* (Arno Holz). *c.* 1902.
   13. *Ich und du* (Busse). *c.* 1902.
   14. *Über Nacht* (Rognetti). *c.* 1902.
   15. *Verlassen* (Bohemian folksong). *c.* 1902.
   16. *Traurigkeit* (Peter Altenberg). *c.* 1902.
   17. *Hoffnung* (Peter Altenberg). *c.* 1902.
   18. *Flötenspielerin* (Peter Altenberg). *c.* 1902.
   19. *Spaziergang* (Mombert). *c.* 1902.
   20. *Soldatenbraut* (Mörike). *c.* 1902.
   21. *So regnet es sich langsam ein* (Caesar Flaischlen). *c.* 1902.
   22. *Grenzen der Menschheit* (Goethe). *c.* 1902.

23. *Ballade des äusseren Lebens* (Hofmanns-thal). Duet. *c.* 1902.
24. *Im Walde* (Björnson). *c.* 1902.
25. *Viel Träume* (Amerling). Duet. *c.* 1902.
26. *Tiefe Sehnsucht* (Liliencron). Duet. 1904 or 1905.
27. *Über den Berg* (Busse). *c.* 1902.
28. *Am Strande* (G. Scherer). *c.* 1902.
29. *Reiselied* (Hofmannsthal). *c.* 1902.
30. *Spuk* (Hebbel). *c.* 1902.
31. *Aus Pfingsten* (Evers). *c.* 1902.
32. *Winter* (J. Schlaf). *c.* 1902.
33. *O wär' mein Lieb ein Röslein rot* (Burns). *c.* 1902.
34. *Sehnsucht II* (Hohenberg). *c.* 1902.
35. *Ich liebe dich* (Grabbe). *c.* 1904–5.
36. *Ferne Lieder* (Rückert). *c.* 1904–5.
37. *Ich will die Fluren meiden* (Rückert). *c.* 1904–5.
38. *Geliebte Schöne* (Heine). *c.* 1904–5.
39. *Schattenleben* (Graf). *c.* 1904–5.
40. *Am Abend* (Geibel). *c.* 1904–5.
41. *Wenn Gespenster auferstehn* (Felix Dör-mann). *c.* 1904–5.
42. *Vom Ende* (Marie Madeleine). *c.* 1904–5.
43. *Vorüber* (Wiesbacher). *c.* 1904–5.
44. *Scheidelied* (Baumbach). *c.* 1904–5.
45. *Eure Weisheit* (Fischer). *c.* 1904–5.
46. *Schlummerlose Nacht* (Greif). *c.* 1904–5.
47. *Nachtgesang* (O. J. Bierbaum). *c.* 1904–5.
48. *Es wandelt, was wir schauen* (Eichen-dorff). *c.* 1904–5.
49. *Liebe* (Rilke). *c.* 1904–5.
50. *Wandert, ihr Wolken* (Avenarius). *c.* 1904–5.
51. *Im Morgengrauen* (Stieler). *c.* 1904–5.
52. *Grabschrift* (Jakobowski). *c.* 1904–5.
53. *Traum* (Semmler). *c.* 1904–5.
54. *Furcht* (Palma). *c.* 1904–5.
55. *Augenblicke* (Hamerling). *c.* 1904–5.
56. *Trinklied* (Rückl). *c.* 1904–5.
57. *Fromm* (Gustav Falke). *c.* 1904–5.
58. *Leben* (Evers). *c.* 1904–5.
59. *Näherin* (Rilke). *c.* 1904–5.
60. *Erster Verlust* (Goethe). *c.* 1904–5.
61. *Süss sind mir die Schollen des Tales* (Knodt). *c.* 1904–5.
62. *Der milde Herbst anno 45* (Max Mell). *c.* 1904–5.
63. *Menschenherz* (delle Grazie). *c.* 1904–5.
64. *Holophan* (Wallpach). *c.* 1904–5.

65. *Mignon* (Goethe). *c.* 1904–5.
66. *Läuterung* (Hohenberg). *c.* 1904–5.
67. *Die Sorglichen* (Falke). *c.* 1904–5.
68. *Das stille Königreich* (Busse). *c.* 1904–5.
69. *Trinklied* (Henckell). *c.* 1904–5.
70. *An Leukon* (Gleim). Spring 1908. Pub. 1937, in Willi Reich's *Alban Berg*.

3. Seven Early Songs. For voice and piano. 1905–8. Ded. Helene Berg.
1. *Im Zimmer* (Johannes Schlaf). Summer 1905.
2. *Die Nachtigall* (Th. Storm). Winter 1905–6 (?Spring 1907).
3. *Liebesode* (O. E. Hartleben). Summer (?Autumn) 1906.
4. *Traumgekrönt* (R. M. Rilke). August 1907.
5. *Sommertage* (Paul Hohenberg). Spring (?Summer) 1908.
6. *Nacht* (Karl Hauptmann). Spring 1908.
7. *Schilflied* (Lenau). Spring 1908.
fp (Nos. 2, 3, 4): 7 November 1907, Vienna, Wiener Kaufmannschaft (Saal des Gremiums), concert by Schoenberg's pupils, Elsa Pazeller, acc. Karl Horwitz.
Pub. 1928, Universal-Edition (revised version).

3a. Seven Early Songs. Version for voice and orchestra.
fp: 6 November 1928, Vienna.
fEp: 15 September 1931, BBC broadcast, Margot Hinnenberg Lefebre and the BBC Orchestra, cond. Sir Henry Wood.
Pub. Universal-Edition.

BIBLIOGRAPHY:
Theodor Wiesengrund-Adorno: ABs frühe Lieder, *Anbruch*, February 1929, p. 90.

4. Fugue. For string quintet and piano. Summer 1907.
fp: 7 November 1907, Vienna, Wiener Kaufmannschaft (Saal des Gremiums), concert by Schoenberg's pupils, with Alban Berg (piano).
Unpub. Lost.

5. Compositions for 6/8-part chorus. Summer 1907. Unpub. Lost.

6. Variations on an original theme. For piano. 1908.
fp: 8 November 1908, Vienna, Musik-

verein, concert by Schoenberg's pupils, Irene Bien.
Pub. 1957, in Hans F. Redlich's *Alban Berg*.

7. Piano Sonata Op. 1. Summer 1907–summer 1908.
fp: 24 April 1911, Vienna, Ehrbarsaal, Viennese Society for Art and Culture concert, Etta Werndorf.
f Paris p: 10 May 1921, Léo-Pol Morin.
fEp: 24 October 1928, BBC broadcast, Ernst Bachrich.
fEp (concert): 27 May 1931, Wigmore Hall, John Hunt.
Pub. 1910, Robert Lienau; revised version, 1920, C. Haslinger; 1927, Universal-Edition.

8. Four Songs Op. 2. For voice and piano. Early 1909–spring 1910.
  1. *Schlafen, schlafen* (Hebbel).
  2. *Schlafend trägt man mich* (Mombert).
  3. *Nun ich der Riesen Stärksten* (Mombert).
  4. *Warm die Lüfte* (Mombert).
fp: untraced.
?fFp: March 1928, Paris, Mme René Dubost concert, Ružena Herlinger acc. Alban Berg.
fEbp (two only): 1 February 1932, Emmy Heim.
Pub. 1910, Robert Lienau; revised version, 1920, C. Haslinger; 1927, Universal-Edition. Version orch. René Leibowitz, unpub.

9. String Quartet Op. 3. Spring 1910, Vienna. Ded. to the composer's wife (Helene Berg).
  1. *Langsam*; 2. *Mässige Viertel*.
fp: 24 April 1911, Vienna, Ehrbarsaal, Viennese Society for Art and Culture concert.
fFp: 15 January 1924, Concerts Wiéner, Pro Arte Quartet.
fEbp: 19 November 1937, Shadwick Quartet.
Pub. 1920, Robert Lienau; 1924, Universal-Edition.

10. Five songs (picture postcard texts by Peter Altenberg) Op. 4. For voice and orchestra. August 1912.
  1. *Seele wie bist du schöner*; 2. *Sahst du nach dem Gewitterregen*; 3. *Über die Grenzen des All*; 4. *Nichts ist gekommen*; 5. *Hier ist Friede*.

fp: 31 March 1913, Vienna, Musikverein (uncompleted).
fp (complete): 1952, Rome, cond. Jascha Horenstein.
fEp: 4 May 1953, Bernard Demigny and l'Orchestre National de la Radiodiffusion Française, cond. Jascha Horenstein.
fEp (concert): 1960, Royal Albert Hall, Promenade Concert, Pamela Bowden and London Symphony Orchestra, cond. Basil Cameron.
Pub. 1953, Universal-Edition (vocal score, ed. H. E. Apostel). No. 5 orig. pub. 1921, in *Menschen* (Dresden), No. 5, repr. October 1948 in *MQ* (ed. René Leibowitz).

BIBLIOGRAPHY:
Ernst Krenek: Fünf Orchesterlieder nach Ansichtskartentexten von Peter Altenberg Op. 4, in *Alban Berg* by Willi Reich, Vienna, 1937, p. 43.
René Leibowitz: AB's five orchestral songs Op. 4, *MQ*, October 1948, p. 487.
Hans F. Redlich: AB's Altenberg Songs Op. 4, *MR*, February 1970, p. 43.
Mark De Voto: Some notes on the unknown Altenberg Lieder, *PNM*, fall–winter 1966.
— AB's picture postcard songs, *Dissertation Abstracts*, November 1967, p. 1836A.

11. Four Pieces (Vier Stücke) Op. 5. For clarinet and piano. Summer 1913. Ded. Arnold Schoenberg.
  1. *Mässig—Langsam*; 2. *Sehr langsam*; 3. *Sehr rasch*; 4. *Langsam*.
fp: 17 October 1919, Vienna, concert of Schoenberg's Verein für musikalische Privataufführungen.
fFp: 2 June 1921, Paris, Société Musicale Indépandante concert, Suzie Welty and J. Guyot.
fEbp: 22 August 1926, Newcastle station, Robert Baulks.
Pub. 1920, C. Haslinger; 1924, Universal-Edition.

12. Three Pieces (Drei Orchesterstücke) Op. 6. For large orchestra. 1914–15, rev. 1929. Ded. Arnold Schoenberg on his fortieth birthday.
  1. *Präludium*. Dated: 8 September 1914.
  2. *Reigen*. Dated: August 1915.

3. *Marsch.* Dated: 23 August 1914.

4 fl, pic, 4 ob, ca, 4 cl (incl. D cl & E-flat cl), bcl, 3 bsn, cbsn; 6 hn, 4 tpt, 4 tmb, cbs tuba; GC, side dm, cym, susp cym, 2 tamtams (low & high), 2 timp, tenor dm, tgle, large hammer, glock, xyl; 2 hp, celesta, strings.

fp (Nos. 1 & 2): 5 June 1923, Berlin, cond. Anton Webern.

fp (complete): 14 April 1930, Oldenburg, cond. Johannes Schüler.

fEp: 8 April 1938, BBC concert of contemporary music, BBC Orchestra, cond. Sir Adrian Boult.

Pub. 1923, Universal-Edition; revised version, 1954, Universal-Edition.

BIBLIOGRAPHY:

R.-A. Mooser: 3 Orchesterstücke Op. 6, in *Aspects de la musique contemporaine*, Editions Labor et Fidès (Geneva), 1957, p. 166.

Hans F. Redlich: Der Symphoniker AB, *ÖM*, May 1954.

13. **Wozzeck** Op. 7. Opera in three acts, fifteen scenes. 1917–April 1922. Ded. Alma Maria Mahler.

4 fl, 4 pic, 4 ob, ca, 2 E-flat cl, 4 cl, bcl, 3 bsn, cbsn; 4 hn, 4 tpt, 4 tmb, cbs tuba; timp, cym, susp cym, GC, Rute, several side dms, 2 tamtams (low & high), tgle; xyl, celesta, hp, strings. *On stage:* pic, 2 fl, 2 ob, 2 E-flat cl, 2 bsn, 2 hn, 2 tpt, 3 tmb, cbs tuba; GC, cym, small dm, tgle; 2 fiddles, cl, accordeon, guitar, bombardon (or bs tuba), out-of-tune piano; fl, pic, ob, ca, E-flat cl, bcl, bsn, cbsn, 2 hn, string quintet.

fp: 14 December 1925, Berlin, Staatsoper, cond. Erich Kleiber; with Leo Schützendorf (Wozzeck), Sigrid Johanson (Marie), Waldemar Henke (Hauptmann), Fritz Soot (Tambourmajor), Gerhard Witting (Andres), Martin Abendroth (Doktor), Jessyka Koettrik (Margret).

Pub. 1930, 1958, Universal-Edition. Vocal score by Fritz Heinrich Klein.

BIBLIOGRAPHY:

Hilda Andrews: Berg's Wozzeck, *MMR*, 1930, p. 331.

Lothar Band: AB, Wozzeck—Uraufführung in der Berliner Staatsoper, *NMZ*, 1926, No. 8, p. 171.

L. Berio: Invita a Wozzeck, *Il Diapason* (Milan), March–April 1952.

Kurt Blaukopf: New light on Wozzeck, *Saturday Review*, 26 September 1953, p. 62.

— Autobiographische Elemente in ABs Wozzeck, *ÖM*, May 1954.

Eric Blom: The tragedy of a soldier, *Radio Times*, 3 March 1933, p. 517.

Robert Boas: Wozzeck, a preview, *Music*, December 1951, p. 27.

P. Brown: Berg and Wozzeck, *Choir*, October 1964, p. 193.

Donald Chittum: The triple fugue in Berg's Wozzeck, *MR*, 1967, p. 52.

Max Chop: Wozzeck, *Signale*, 1925, Nos. 51–52, p. 1954.

J. J. Cochofel: Wozzeck d'AB, *Gazeta de todas as artes* (Lisbon), No. 96, 1959.

Herbert Connor: ABs Wozzeck, *Signale*, 1926, No. 30, p. 1131.

Edward Crankshaw: Wozzeck, *Bookman*, May 1934, p. 103.

K. H. David: Wozzeck in Zürich, *SM*, 1 November 1931.

Edward Downes: Wozzeck, *Portfolio*, 1959, No. 1, p. 40.

Alfred Einstein: Berg's Wozzeck, *MMR*, 1934, p. 49.

— ABs Wozzeck, in *Von Schütz bei Hindemith*, Pan Verlag (Zürich) 1957, p. 142.

Edwin Evans: Wozzeck the underdog, *Radio Times*, 9 March 1934, p. 712.

Hans Georg Fellmann: ABs Wozzeck im Essener Opernhaus, *Der Auftakt*, 1930, No. 2, p. 57.

H. A. Fiechtner: Wozzeck und die Wiener, *Melos*, 1952, Nos. 6–7, p. 192.

Dietrich Fischer-Dieskau: ABs Wozzeck, *NZfM*, 1960, No. 10, p. 342.

Erich Forneberg: Das Volkslied als expressionistisches Symbol in ABs Wozzeck, *NZfM*, 1959, No. 5, p. 261.

— ABs Passacaglia aus der Oper Wozzeck, *Musik im Unterricht*, 1962, No. 4, p. 100.

— Wozzeck von AB, Robert Lienau (Berlin) 1963.

Martin Friedland: Zur Ästhetik des Wozzeck, *AMZ*, January 1926.

Roberto Gerhard: Berg's Wozzeck, *Foyer*, No. 2, winter 1951–2, p. 16.

Igor Glebow & Simon Ginsburg: Wozzeck, *Triton* (Leningrad), 1927.

Tito Gobbi: An impression of Wozzeck, *London Musical Events,* July 1952, p. 30.

B. Goldschmidt: Wozzeck in London, *Melos*, 1952, No. 3, p. 89.

Antoine Golea: Apropos du Wozzeck d'AB, *La Vie musicale*, 1951, No. 5, p. 10.

Iain Hamilton: Wozzeck and the muse of musical imagery, *The Listener*, 7 January 1960, p. 44.

Hans Heinsheimer: Wozzeck in Prag, *Anbruch*, 1926, No. 10, p. 417.

Gerh. Hellmers: Wozzeck, *Signale*, 1926, No. 18, p. 693.

Erich Hermann: Stuttgart spielt zum erstenmal Bergs Wozzeck, *Melos*, 1957, No. 1, p. 16.

W. Hirschberg: ABs Wozzeck, *Signale*, 7 December 1932.

B. Holmqvist: AB och Wozzeck, *Operans programhäfte*, April 1957.

Arthur Jacobs & Stanley Sadie: Wozzeck, in *The Opera Guide*, Hamish Hamilton (London) 1964, p. 341.

Bernard Jacobson: The soldier's tale, *M&M*, October 1964, p. 22.

D. Jaksic: Muzicki i scenski prikaz opere Wozzeck Albana Berga, *Zvuk*, 1961, No. 51, p. 11.

Pierre Jean Jouve: Wozzeck d'AB, *RM* (L'Oeuvre du XXe siècle), April 1952, p. 87.

— Wozzeck, argument, *RM* (Les Carnets critiques), May 1952.

— Matière musicale de Wozzeck, *Preuves*, No. 15, May 1952, p. 2.

Pierre Jean Jouve & Michel Fano: Wozzeck ou le nouvel opéra, Librairie Plon (Paris) 1953.

Julius Kapp: Wozzeck, Inhaltsangabe der Oper, *Blätter der Staatsoper* (Berlin), December 1925, p. 8.

Hans Keller: The eclecticism of Wozzeck, *MR*, May 1952, p. 133.

Joseph Kerman: Wozzeck and The Rake's Progress, in *Opera as Drama*, O.U.P. (London) 1957, p. 219.

István Kertesz: A Wozzeck masik szereposztasa, *Muzsika*, May 1964, p. 36.

Fritz Heinrich Klein: ABs Wozzeck, *Anbruch*, October 1923, p. 216.

John W. Klein: Some reflections on Wozzeck, *MO*, May 1952, p. 465.

— Wozzeck, a summing-up, *M&L*, April 1963, p. 132.

Edward Lockspeiser: Wozzeck given first English production in London, *Musical America*, March 1952, p. 6.

Sylvia Loeb: Wozzeck, *MO*, March 1934, p. 524.

Wolf Eberhard von Lewinski: Wieland Wagners Wozzeck unter Pierre Boulez in Frankfurt, *Melos*, June 1966, p. 186.

Melanie Lüders: Wozzeck, ein Fragment, *Blätter der Staatsoper* (Berlin), December 1925, p. 4.

H. von Lüttwitz: Bergs Wozzeck (Aufführung in Dortmund), *Musica*, 1961, No. 3, p. 131.

Fritz Mahler: Zu ABs Oper Wozzeck, Universal-Edition (Vienna), 1957; (incl. 'Wozzeck, Bermerkungen' by Alban Berg).

Marcel Marnat: Wozzeck à l'Opéra, *Preuves*, No. 156, February 1964, p. 68.

Frederick Marshall: AB's Wozzeck, *R.C.M. Magazine*, 1949, No. 2, p. 43.

R.-A. Mooser: Wozzeck d'AB, *Dissonances*, March 1934.

Ernest Newman: Wozzeck, in *Opera Nights*, Putnam (London) 1943, p. 559.

— Wozzeck, in *From the World of Music*, John Calder (London) 1956, pp. 148, 150, 163.

— Wozzeck, on the first production in England, in –do–, p. 155.

— Wozzeck—this 'Sprechgesang', in –do–, p. 160.

Jeremy Noble: Wozzeck in Paris, *The Gramophone*, February 1967, p. 416.

Arthur Notcutt: Wozzeck, *Halle*, March 1952, p. 10.

— Wozzeck makes London stage debut, *Musical Courier*, 15 February 1952, p. 12.

A. Parente: Attualità del Wozzeck, *La Scala*, 15 February 1950.

George Perle: Wozzeck—Ein zweiter Blick auf das Libretto, *NZfM*, May 1968.

András Pernye: AB, Wozzeck, *Muzsika*, 1962, March, p. 7; April, p. 17.

Willem Pijper: AB's Wozzeck, *De Muziek*, October 1930.

Gerd Ploebsch: Die Stimme in der Oper—Zu ABs Wozzeck, *NZfM*, November 1965.

Berg, Alban

Malcolm Rayment: Berg's unheroic hero, *Records & Recording*, October 1965, p. 16.

H. F. Redlich: Wozzeck, *Musica*, 1956, No. 2, p. 120.

Willi Reich: Wozzeck—a guide to the words and music of the opera by AB, *Modern Music*, No. 2 of a series of monographs, The League of Composers (New York) 1931; reprinted in *MQ*, January 1952, p. 1 (transl. A. Weiss; postscript by Alban Berg).

— AB, Wozzeck, in *Musik der Zeit*, Vol. 6 (Oper in XX. Jahrhundert), Boosey & Hawkes (Bonn) 1954, p. 27.

— H. Rosbaud dirigiert Wozzeck in Zürich, *Melos*, 1956, No. 4, p. 117.

— Wozzeck—Reminiszenzen aus seiner Urzeit, *Musik und Szene*, 1962-3, No. 10, p. 1.

Charles Reid: How Kleiber brought Wozzeck to the stage, *M&M*, January 1958, p. 13.

C. Rostand: Wozzeck d'AB, in *Musique contemporaine*, 1951.

Robert Sabin: AB's Wozzeck, *Musical America*, April 1951, p. 6.

— Wozzeck, sung in English, staged by City Opera, *Musical America*, 15 April 1952, p. 5.

— The wonder of Wozzeck, *American Record Guide*, February 1959, p. 372.

Paul Sanders: Wozzeck, *De Muziek*, October 1930.

Gunter Schaab: ABs Wozzeck—20 Jahre später, *Melos*, August–September (No. 9) 1948, p. 240.

Rudolf Schaefke: AB's opera Wozzeck, *Melos*, 1926, pp. 267 & 283.

Reinhold Scharnke: Wozzeck, Kleiber und die Berliner Staatsoper, *Das Orchester* (Berlin), January 1926.

Ferdinand Scherber: Wozzeck in Wien, *Signale*, 1930, No. 16, p. 514.

Ernst Schoen: London—AB Wozzeck, *Anbruch*, March 1934, p. 52.

Walter Schrenk: Manfred Gurlitt—Wozzeck, *Anbruch*, May 1926, p. 228.

Johannes Schüler: Das Märchen von den unüberwindlichen Schwierigkeiten des Wozzeck, *Pult und Taktstock*, March–April 1929.

Humphrey Searle: Wozzeck, *World Review*, March 1952, p. 133.

Geoffrey Sharp: Wozzeck, *MR*, Vol. XIII, No. 1, p. 52.

Desmond Shawe-Taylor: Wozzeck, *New Statesman*, 26 January 1952, p. 96.

Henry W. Simon: Wozzeck, in *Festival of Opera*, W. H. Allen (London) 1957, p. 534.

Charlotte Spitz: Season in London—Wozzeck, *Der Auftakt*, 1934, No. 9, p. 152.

Paul Stefan: Wozzeck, *Anbruch*, January 1926, p. 4.

— Wozzeck, an atonal opera, *Modern Music*, April 1926.

— Wozzeck in Prag, *Anbruch*, December 1926, p. 416.

— Wozzeck und Wien, *Anbruch*, April–May 1930, p. 176.

Erwin Stein: Berg's Wozzeck, *Ballet*, May 1949, p. 29.

— Wozzeck, *Opera*, January 1952.

— Wozzeck, in *Orpheus in New Guises*, Rockliff (London) 1953, p. 103.

Erich Steinhard: AB—Nach der Wozzeck-Uraufführung an der Berliner Staatsoper, *Der Auftakt*, 1926, No. 1, p. 10.

— Bergs Wozzeck in Prag, *NMZ*, 1927, No. 8, p. 16.

G. Steinhard: AB's Wozzeck, *De Muziek*, January 1927.

G. Strück: Wozzeck in Kassel, *Musica*, 1955, No. 5, p. 216.

H. H. Stuckenschmidt: Bergs Wozzeck und die Berliner Aufführung, *Pult und Taktstock*, January 1926.

— ABs Wozzeck, Berliner Staatsoper 1925, in *Oper in dieser Zeit*, Friedrich Verlag (Hannover) 1964, p. 7.

— Wozzeck-Bahn gebrochen, *Melos*, 1956, No. 2, p. 46.

Deems Taylor: Ein Meisterwerk—Wozzeck, *ÖM*, February 1946, p. 50.

Martin Tegen: Analysen, 3: Wozzeck, *Musik*, 1963, No. 3, p. 3.

G. A. Trumff: Bergs Wozzeck in Maizer Repertoire, *NZfM*, 1959, No. 12, p. 619.

Ernst Viebig: Berg's Wozzeck—Ein Beitrag zum Opernproblem, *Die Musik*, April 1923, p. 506.

— Zur Einführung in den Stil der Wozzeck-Musik, *Blätter der Staatsoper* (Berlin), December 1925, p. 12.

Nevile Wallis: Wozzeck, *Spectator*, 13 November 1964, p. 637.

Karl Westermayer: Nochmals—Wozzeck, *Signale*, 1927, No. 4, p. 107.

Th. W. Werner: ABs Wozzeck in Oldenburg, *Anbruch*, April 1929, p. 164.

J. Weterings: Wozzeck d'AB, *Les Cahiers de la musique*, September–October 1937.

Theodor Wiesengrund-Adorno: AB—zur Uraufführung des Wozzeck, *Anbruch*, December 1925, p. 531.

K. H. Wörner: Die musikalischen Formen im Wozzeck, *NZfM*, 1956, No. 10, p. 539.

Otto Zoff: Bergs Wozzeck in der Metropolitan Opera, *Melos*, 1959, No. 5, p. 155.

UNSIGNED:

Wozzeck—Bemerkungen von AB, *Anbruch*, February 1930, p. 52.

ABs Wozzeck in der Wiener Oper, *Der Auftakt*, 1930, No. 4, p. 118

Wozzeck, *The Times*, 25 June 1932, p. 10.

Wozzeck produced, *The Times*, 8 September 1930, p. 10.

Wozzeck d'AB, *Dissonances*, November 1931.

Wozzeck discussed, *The Times*, 11 March 1949, p. 6.

Wozzeck, performance, *The Times*, 17 March 1949, p. 8.

Wozzeck reviewed, *The Times*, 23 January 1952, p. 7.

Wozzeck, *Opera News*, 9 March 1959, 8 April 1961.

Wozzeck, *The Times*, 14 September 1961.

BERG'S OWN WRITINGS:

A word about Wozzeck, *Modern Music*, November 1927.

Die musikalischen Formen in meiner Oper Wozzeck, *Die Musik*, February 1924; reprinted in *Alban Berg* by Willi Reich, Vienna, 1937.

Praktische Anweisungen zur Einstudierung des Wozzeck, 1930; in *Alban Berg* by Willi Reich, Vienna, 1937.

13a. Wozzeck: Three Fragments (Drei Bruckstücke) Op. 7.

4 fl, 4 pic, 4 ob, ca, 4 cl, 2 E-flat cl, bcl, 3 bsn, cbsn; 4 hn, 4 tpt, 4 tmb, cbs tuba; timp, cym, susp cym, GC, Rute, side dm, 2 tamtams (low & high), tgle, xyl; celesta, hp, strings.

fp: June 1924, Frankfurt a. M., cond. Hermann Scherchen.

fEp: 15 September 1931, Queen's Hall, Promenade Concert, Margot Hinnenberg-Lefebre and the BBC Symphony Orchestra, cond. Sir Henry Wood.

Pub. 1924, Universal-Edition.

BIBLIOGRAPHY:

J. Diether: Berg—Wozzeck excerpts, *American Record Guide*, October 1964, p. 120.

Armand Machabey: AB—Wozzeck (Suite d'orchestre, avec chant, extraits de l'opéra), *RM*, April 1931, p. 444.

14. Chamber Concerto (Kammerkonzert). For piano, violin and wind. 1923–5. Dated: 23 July 1925. Ded. Arnold Schoenberg on his fiftieth birthday.

1. *Thema con variazioni*. For piano and wind.

2. *Adagio*. For violin and wind.

3. *Rondo ritmico con Introduzione* ('Kadenz'). For piano, violin and wind.

2 fl, pic, ob, ca, E-flat cl, cl, bcl, bsn, cbsn; tpt, 2 hn, tmb.

fp: 27 March 1927, Berlin, Steffi Geyer (violin), Walter Grey (piano), cond. Hermann Scherchen.

f Paris p: March 1928, Salle Pleyel, cond. Walter Straram.

fEbp: 21 April 1933, Eduard Steuermann, Rudolf Kolisch, and members of the BBC Orchestra, cond. Anton Webern.

Pub. 1925, Universal-Edition; 1955, Universal-Edition.

BIBLIOGRAPHY:

M. Deutsch: Le Concerto de chambre d'AB, *SM*, September 1949, p. 328.

14a. Adagio. From Chamber Concerto, arr. by Alban Berg for violin, clarinet and piano. 1935.

fp: 1936, Vienna.

Pub. 1956, Universal-Edition.

14b. Adagio. Version for violin and piano.

fp: 30 November 1935, BBC broadcast, Dea Gombrich.

15. Schliesse mir dir Augen beide (Storm). For voice and piano. Summer 1925. Second setting.

Pub. February 1930, in *Die Musik*; 1955, Universal-Edition (ed. Hans F. Redlich).

16. Lyric Suite (Lyrische Suite). For string quartet. October 1925–October 1926. Ded. Alexander von Zemlinsky.

1. *Allegretto giovale*; 2. *Andante amoroso*; 3. *Allegro misterioso—Trio estatico*; 4. *Adagio appassionato*; 5. *Presto delirando—Tenebroso*; 6. *Largo desolato*.

fp: 8 January 1927, Vienna, Kolisch (New Vienna) Quartet.

fEp: 13 February 1928, BBC concert of contemporary music, Vienna Quartet.

f Paris p: March 1928, Mme René Dubost concert, Vienna Quartet.

Pub. 1927, Universal-Edition.

BIBLIOGRAPHY:
Eric Blom: AB, Lyric Suite for strings, *Music Teacher*, April 1933, p. 171.
Fritz Bouquet: ABs Lyrische Suite, *Melos*, August–September 1948, p. 227.
Reginald Smith-Brindle: The symbolism in Berg's Lyric Suite, *The Score*, No. 21, October 1957, p. 60.
Erwin Stein: Analyse der Lyrischen Suite, Philharmonia Score No. 173, Universal-Edition, 1927.

16a. Three Movements from the Lyric Suite. Version for string orchestra. 1928.

1. *Andante amoroso*; 2. *Allegro misterioso—Trio estatico*; 3. *Adagio appassionato*.

fp: 31 January 1929, Berlin, cond. Jascha Horenstein.

fEp: 21 April 1933, BBC invitation concert, BBC Orchestra, cond. Anton Webern.

fEp (concert): 23 October 1935, BBC Symphony Orchestra, cond. Sir Adrian Boult.

Pub. 1928, Universal-Edition.

17. Der Wein. Concert Aria for voice and orchestra. May–23 July 1929; full score completed: 23 August 1929. Poem: Baudelaire, transl. Stefan George. Ded. Ružena Herlinger.

2 fl, 2 pic, 2 ob, ca, alto sax, 2 cl, bcl, 2 bsn, cbsn; 4 hn, 2 tpt, 2 tmb, tuba; timp, cym, GC, tgle, tamtam (high), ten dm, gong, susp cym, glock; piano, hp, strings.

fp: 4 June 1930, Königsberg, Ružena Herlinger, cond. Hermann Scherchen.

?fEp: 10 February 1934, BBC broadcast, Ružena Herlinger and the BBC Orchestra, cond. Robert Heger.

Pub. 1930 (vocal score, by Erwin Stein), 1931 (full score), Universal-Edition.

BIBLIOGRAPHY:
Jaromír Pacít: Berg wünschte einen Tenor für die Weinarie, *Melos*, April 1966, p. 114.
Hans F. Redlich: Bergs Konzertarie Der Wein, *ÖM*, 1966, Nos. 5–6 (May–June), p. 284.
Willi Reich: Der Wein, een niew Werk van AB, *De Muziek*, February 1930.
— AB und Anton Webern in ihren neuen Werken—Bergs Konzertarie Der Wein, *Der Auftakt*, 1930, Nos. 5–6, p. 32.
Humphrey Searle: Berg and Der Wein, *The Listener*, 17 October 1963, p. 630.

18. Four-Part Canon ('Alban Berg an das Frankfurter Opernhaus'). Summer 1930. Words: Alban Berg. Composed for the celebration of the fiftieth anniversary of the Frankfurt Opera House.

fEbp: 13 April 1947, BBC Singers, cond. Leslie Woodgate.

Pub. 1937, USA.

19. Lulu. Opera in three acts. 1929–35. Libretto: Alban Berg, after 'Erdgeist' and 'Büchse der Pandora', by Franz Wedekind. Ded. Arnold Schoenberg on his sixtieth birthday. Unfinished.

fp: 2 June 1937, Zürich, cond. Robert F. Denzler, with Nuri Hadzic (Lulu), Maria Bernhard, Frieda Kurz, Erika Feichtinger, Karl Melzer, Paul Feher, Asger Stig, Peter Baxevanos, Albert Emmerich, Fritz Honisch, Oscar Mörwald, Walter Frank, Peter Pöschl.

fEp: 10 October 1962, Sadler's Wells, Hamburg State Opera, cond. Leopold Ludwig; with Helga Pilarczyk (Lulu), Toni Blankenheim (Dr. Schön), Kurt Ruesche (Alwa), Gisela Litz (Countess Geschwitz), Ratko Delorko (The Painter); producer, Gunther Rennert; set, Teo Otto.

BIBLIOGRAPHY:
A. Berger: AB's Lulu on records, *Saturday Review*, 25 October 1952, p. 60.
Martin Cooper: Berg's new work Lulu, *London Mercury*, May 1935, p. 59.
K. H. David: Lulu von AB, *SM*, I July 1937, p. 397.

E.: Deutsche Erstaufführung in Essen—ABs Lulu, *Melos*, April 1953, p. 116.

Torsten Ekbom: Tillvarons grymma menageri, *Nutida musik*, Vol. 5 (1961–2), No. 2, p. 1.

R. S. Hill: Berg's Lulu, *MQ*, January 1953, p. 134.

Hans Keller: Lulu, *MR*, 1953, p. 302.

Kurt List: Lulu, after the première, *Modern Music*, November–December 1937.

Otto Mayer: Lulu, la nova ópera d'AB, *Mirador* (Barcelona), 14 February 1935.

Donald Mitchell: The character of Lulu, *MR*, November 1954, p. 268.

George Perle: The music of Lulu—a new analysis, *Journal of the American Musicological Society*, 1959, Nos. 2–3, p. 185.

— Lulu—the formal design, *Journal of the American Musicological Society*, 1964, p. 179.

— A note on act III of Lulu, *PNM*, spring–summer 1964, p. 8.

— The character of Lulu, *MR*, November 1964, p. 311.

— The score of Lulu, *PNM*, spring–summer 1965, p. 127.

— Lulu—thematic material and pitch organisation, *MR*, November 1965, p. 127.

— Erwiderung auf Willi Reichs Aufsatz 'Drei Notizblätter zu ABs Lulu', *SM*, 1967, No. 3 (May–June), p. 163.

— Die Reihe als Symbol in Bergs Lulu, *ÖM*, October 1967, p. 589.

— Die Personen in Bergs Lulu, *Archiv für Musikwissenschaft*, 1967, No. 4, p. 283.

Willi Reich: ABs Lulu, *Der Auftakt*, 1934, Nos. 11–12, p. 202.

— Lulu—the text and music, *Modern Music*, April 1935.

— AB's Lulu, *MQ*, October 1936, p. 383.

— ABs' Lulu (Zur Zürcher Uraufführung der Oper), *SM*, 1 June 1937.

— Berg's Lulu has première in Zurich, *Musical America*, July 1937.

— ABs Oper Lulu, *Melos*, December 1952, p. 337.

— Zur deutschen Erstaufführung von ABs Lulu, *Blätter der Essener Stadt. Bühnen*, 1952–1953, No. 13.

— Drei Notizblätter zu ABs Oper Lulu, *SM*, 1966, No. 6 (November–December), p. 336.

Stanley Sadie: Berg at Sadler's Wells, *Musical Events*, November 1962, p. 21.

G. Schab: Lulu im Essener Opernhaus, *Musikleben*, April 1953, p. 135.

H. C. Schonberg: Lulu, Berg's 'Freudian opera', *New York Times*, 28 September 1952, Sect. 2, p. 11.

Rudolf Stephan: ABs Lulu, *NZfM*, July–August 1961.

Erwin Stein: Berg's opera Lulu in Zurich, in *Orpheus in New Guises*, Rockliff (London) 1953, p. 108.

H. H. Stuckenschmidt: AB Lulu, Städtische Bühnen, Essen, 1953, in *Oper in dieser Zeit*, Friedrich Verlag (Hannover) 1964, p. 8.

Emile Vuillermoz: Lulu, *Revue hommes et mondes*, August 1953, p. 296.

H. Weinstock: Lulu in Italy, *Saturday Review*, 28 November 1959, p. 70.

John S. Weissmann: Jack the Ripper on the stage, *Musical Events*, October 1962, p. 9.

Gerard Werker: AB en zijn opera Lulu, *Mens en melodie*, May 1953, p. 167.

J. Weterings: Une création à Zurich, Loulou, d'AB, *RM*, October 1937, p. 277.

A. Young: Lulu arrives—American stage première, *Musical America*, September 1963, p. 30.

MISCELLANEOUS OR UNSIGNED:

ABs nachgelassene Oper, *Anbruch*, June 1937, p. 174.

Lulu, broadcast performance, *The Times*, 22 August 1949, p. 8.

Lulu, Netherlands Festival performance, *The Times*, 10 July 1953, p. 5.

Lulu—actress engaged for scream in score, *The Times*, 10 February 1959, p. 4.

19a. Lulu-Symphonie. Summer 1934. Dur. 30'.

1. *Rondo* (Andante & Hymne).

2. *Ostinato* (Allegro).

3. *Lied der Lulu* (Comodo). Ded. Anton Webern on his fiftieth birthday. Pub. 1935, Universal-Edition. Dur. 3'. Reduction by Erwin Stein.

4. *Variationen*.

5. *Adagio*.

3 fl, pic, 3 ob, ca, alto sax, 2 E-flat cl, 3 cl, 2 bsn, cbsn; 4 hn, 3 tpt, 3 tmb, bs (or cbs) tuba; 4 timp, GC, ten dm, tamtam (low), small tamtam (gong), tgle; vib, piano, hp, strings; also high soprano voice (in No. 3).

Berg, Alban

fp: 30 November 1934, Berlin, Berlin Symphony Orchestra, cond. Erich Kleiber.

fEp: 20 March 1935, Queen's Hall, May Blyth and the BBC Symphony Orchestra, cond. Sir Adrian Boult.

Pub. 1935 (full score), Universal-Edition.

BIBLIOGRAPHY:

Theodor W. Adorno: Bergs Lulu-Sinfonie, *Melos*, February 1960.

Alfred Burgatz: ABs Lulu-Musik—Uraufführung im Berliner Staatsopernkonzert, *Die Musik*, January 1935, p. 263.

P. Collaer & J. Weterings: Une nouvelle œuvre d'AB, Loulou, *RM*, March 1935, p. 169.

Scott Goddard: An erotic opera, *Radio Times*, 15 March 1935, p. 14.

D. Hussey: Suite from the opera Lulu, *Spectator*, 29 March 1935, p. 530.

A. Pernye: AB, Lulu-Szimfonia, *Muzsika*, May 1964, p. 29.

Willi Reich: ABs Lulu-Symphonie, *Anbruch*, November–December 1934, p. 190.

— ABs Lulu-Symphonie, *Neue Zürcher Zeitung*, March 1936.

H. Rottweiler: Zur Lulu-Symphonie—Erinnerungen an den Lebenden, '*23*', 1936, Nos. 24–26.

20. Violin Concerto ('To the memory of an angel'). Dated: 11 August 1935. Ded. Louis Krasner. Dur. 25–30'.

1. *Andante—Allegretto*; 2. *Allegro—Adagio*.

2 fl, 2 pic, 2 ob, ca, alto sax, 3 cl, bcl, 2 bsn, cbsn; 4 hn, 2 tpt, ten tmb, bs tmb, bs tuba; timp, GC, cym, ten dm, tamtam (low), gong (high), tgle; hp, strings.

fp: 19 April 1936, Barcelona, ISCM Festival, Louis Krasner, cond. Hermann Scherchen.

fEp: 1 May 1936, BBC invitation concert, Louis Krasner and the BBC Orchestra, cond. Anton Webern.

fEp (public): 9 December 1936, Queen's Hall, BBC concert, Louis Krasner and the BBC Symphony Orchestra, cond. Sir Henry Wood.

Pub. 1936 (full score), 1938 (reduction by R. Kurzmann, rev. Alban Berg), Universal-Edition.

BIBLIOGRAPHY:

Mosco Carner: AB, Violin Concerto, in *The Concerto* (ed. Ralph Hill), Pelican Books (London) 1952, p. 362.

Marcel Baesberg: Le style atonal et le Concerto pour violon d'AB, *Les Cahiers de la musique*, March 1937.

Franz Blasl: Das Violinkonzert von AB, *Musikerziehung*, November 1965.

Erich Forneberg: Der Bach-Choral in ABs Violinkonzert, *Melos*, September 1956, p. 247.

Pierre Jean Jouve: A la mémoire d'un ange, *La Nouvelle revue française*, January 1937.

Rudolf Kastner: AB och hans violinkonsert, *Musikrevy*, Vol. XIV (1959), p. 230.

Michael Kennedy: Berg's Violin Concerto, *Halle*, April 1954, p. 3.

Henri Martelli: AB, Concerto pour violon et orchestre, *RM*, December 1936, p. 443.

Andrew Porter: AB's Violin Concerto, *London Musical Events*, March 1954, p. 37; January 1959, p. 16.

Willi Reich: Le Concerto pour violon d'AB, *Beaux-Arts*, 24 January 1938.

Max Rostal & Hans Keller: Berg's Violin Concerto—a revision, *MT*, February 1954, p. 87.

Claude Rostand: ABs Violinkonzert, *Melos*, December 1957.

Anon: Zur Entstehung des Violinkonzertes von AB, *Anbruch*, October 1936, p. 196.

WRITINGS BY BERG

Ecrits choisis, traduits et commentés par Henri Pousseur, Editions du Rocher (Monaco) 1957.

Various articles, reprinted in *Alban Berg* by Willi Reich, Vienna, 1937; and in *The Life and Work of Alban Berg* by Willi Reich, Atlantis-Verlag (Zürich) 1963, Thames & Hudson (London) 1965.

List of Berg's writings, in *Alban Berg—The Man and his Music* by Hans F. Redlich, John Calder (London) 1957.

Briefe an seine Frau, Langen-Müller (Munich, Vienna) 1965.

AB, Letters to his wife (ed. Bernard Grun), Faber (London), 1971.

GENERAL BIBLIOGRAPHY

Helene Berg: Ein Nachtrag zu 'Bergs Briefe an seine Frau', *ÖM*, December 1966, p. 727.

M. Bernheimer: AB, an upbeat, *Saturday Review*, 12 September 1964.

J. Binet: A propos d'un article d'AB, *SM*, 1945.

Pierre Boulez: AB heute gesehen, *Melos*, February 1960.

A. J. Broekema: A stylistic analysis and comparison of the solo vocal works of Arnold Schoenberg, AB and Anton Webern, *Dissertation Abstracts*, November 1962, p. 1730.

Sten Broman: 50-årsdagen, *Sydsvenska Dagbladet*, 7 February 1935.

Barclay Brown: Music of AB—recordings, *PNM*, spring 1963, p. 170.

A. Burgatz: Nekrolog auf AB, *Die Musik-Woche*, 1936, No. 2, p. 12.

A.D.C.: La morte di AB, *Musica d'oggi*, 1936, p. 7.

Mosco Carner: The Berg Affair, Venice 1934, *MT*, November 1969, p. 1129

A. Cohn: Feast of AB, *American Record Guide*, February 1962, p. 450.

E. Conrath: Einführung in die Musik von AB, *Musikerziehung*, 1963, No. 4, p. 182.

Paul Collaer: Arnold Schoenberg, Anton Webern, Alban Berg, in *La Musique moderne*, Elsevier (Paris), 1955, p. 35.

Martin Cooper: Modern trio, *London Mercury*, March 1939, p. 532.

John Culshaw: A tonal achievement—AB, in *A Century of Music*, Dobson (London) 1952, p. 178.

O. Daniel: Berg in duplicate, *Saturday Review*, 10 February 1962, p. 51.

Christian Darnton: AB's operas, *The Listener*, 9 February 1939, p. 333.

Norman Demuth: AB, in *Musical Trends in the 20th Century*, Rockliff (London) 1952, p. 239.

B. F. Dolbin: Last portrait of AB, *Modern Music*, March–April 1936.

Misha Donat: Mathematical mysticism, *The Listener*, 2 April 1970, p. 458.

David Drew: Berg on record, *New Statesman*, 24 August 1962, p. 238.

Allen Edwards III: Willi Reich's Alban Berg, some biographical and critical considerations, *PNM*, spring–summer 1966, p. 157.

Herbert Eimert: AB, *Blätter der Städt. Bühnen Essen*, 1952–3, No. 13.

— Leben und Werk von AB, *Melos*, September 1964.

Edwin Evans: AB, pioneer of modern music, *Radio Times*, 10 January 1936, p. 8.

Peter Evans: Berg's operatic forms, *The Listener*, 20 September 1962, p. 453.

Johannes B. Falkner: AB—tjugofem år efter hans död, *Musikrevy*, 1961, No. 8, p. 258.

Michel Fano: Pouvoirs transmis, in *La Musique et ses problèmes contemporaines* (Cahiers de la Compagnie Madeleine Renaud—Jean-Louis Barrault No. 3), Julliard (Paris) 1954, p. 38.

A. Frankenstein: Bandwagon for AB?, *High Fidelity*, February 1962, p. 64.

A. de G.: AB, *Le Monde musical*, 1936, p. 21.

Noël Goodwin: Wozzeck, Lulu, and after, *M&M*, September 1962, p. 28.

M. Gorczycka: AB, *Ruch Muzyczny*, 1961, No. 19, p. 7.

Ethel Glenn Hier: To AB, a tribute, *Musicology* (Middlebary, Vt.), 1947, Vol. 1, No. 3.

André Hodeir: AB, in *Since Debussy* (transl. Noel Burch), Secker & Warburg (London) 1961, p. 57.

Hans Holländer: AB, *MQ*, October 1936, p. 375.

Herbert Hübner: AB, in *MGG*, Vol. 1 (1949–1951), p. 1682.

Heinrich Jalowetz: AB, *Der Auftakt*, 1935, Nos. 7–8, p. 117.

Hans Keller: AB and the C major triad, *MR*, November 1952, p. 332.

Dieter Kerner: ABs Ende, *Melos*, April 1962.

M. Kernochan: Shackled muse, *Outlook*, 11 November 1931, p. 349.

René Leibowitz: AB et l'essence de l'opéra, *L'Arche*, No. 13, 1946.

— Innovation and tradition in contemporary music, III: AB, or the seduction to Truth, *Horizon*, No. 8, 1947.

— Schoenberg et son école, Editions Janin (Paris), 1947; transl. Dika Newlin, USA, 1949.

Wolf Eberhard von Lewinski: Der Zwölfton-Klassiker—Zum Todestag ABs, *Musica*, 1960, No. 12, p. 806.

Heinrich Lindlar: 'Mir fehlt die grosse Freunde . . .', *Musica*, 1955, No. 12, p. 594.

Armand Machabey: Notes sur la musique allemande contemporaine, III: AB, *Le*

Ménestrel, 1930, 11 July, p. 309; 18 July, p. 321; 25 July, p. 329.

A. Mantelli: Note su AB, *La Rassegna musicale*, April 1936, pp. 117, 163.

Joseph Machlis: AB, in *Introduction to Contemporary Music*, Norton (USA), Dent (London), 1961, p. 366.

Leonard Marker: Portrait of AB, *Musical Courier*, 1 December 1955, p. 11.

John Maycock: AB, a revaluation, *Halle*, June 1950, p. 18.

Otto Mayer: Esbozo sobre la produccion de AB, *Revista de Arte*, November 1937.

— Apuntes sobre AB, *Revista Musical Catalana*, April 1936.

Donald Mitchell: The emancipation of the dissonance, *Hinrichsen Year Book*, 1952, p. 142.

Robert U. Nelson: Form and fancy in the variations of Berg, *MR*, February 1970, p. 54.

Moses Pergament: AB, *Svenska Dagbladet*, 8 January 1936.

George Perle: *Serial composition and atonality*, Faber (London) 1962.

András Pernye: AB, *Muzsika*, February 1960, p. 38.

Willem Pijper: AB, *De Muziek* (Amsterdam), December 1935, p. 106; transl. Herbert Antcliffe, *MT*, May 1936, p. 414.

Hans F. Redlich: AB—Versuch einer Würdigung, Universal-Edition (Vienna) 1957.

— AB—The Man and his Music, John Calder (London) 1957.

— Alle guten Dinge, *Melos*, February 1955, p. 39.

— Significato del dramma musicale di AB (transl. Bruno Voccia), *La Rassegna musicale*, 1962, p. 217.

— AB and posterity, *MR*, November 1964, p. 320.

— Bergs Briefe an seine Frau, *ÖM*, July 1966, p. 338.

Willi Reich: AB, Herbert Reichner (Vienna) 1937.

— AB—Bildnis im Wort, Peter Schiffert—Verlags AG, 'Die Arche' (Zürich) 1959.

— AB, Leben und Werk, Atlantis Verlag (Zürich) 1963; transl. Cornelius Cardew as *The Life and Work of Alban Berg*, Thames & Hudson (London) 1965.

— AB, *Die Musik*, February 1930, p. 347.

— Les dernières œuvres d'AB, *RM*, February 1931, p. 148.

— AB, *MMR*, 1935, p. 34.

— Zur Biographie AB, '23' (Vienna), 15 September 1937.

— Erinnerungen an AB, *SM*, January 1951, p. 1.

— Aus unbekannten Briefen von AB an Anton Webern, *SM*, February 1953, p. 49.

— Aus ABs Jugendzeit, *Melos*, February 1955, p. 33.

— AB als Apologet Arnold Schoenbergs, *SM*, December 1955, p. 475.

— Erich Kleiber und AB, *SM*, October 1958, p. 374.

— Ein unbekannter Brief von Arnold Schoenberg an AB, *ÖM*, January 1959.

— Scherzzeichnungen von AB, *ÖM*, January 1960.

— An der Seite von AB, *Melos*, February 1960.

— Persönliches von AB, *ÖM*, June–July 1961.

— Anton Webern über AB, *NZfM*, April 1963.

— Zwei verschollene Porträts von Arnold Schoenberg und Alban Berg, *SM*, July–August 1963, p. 186.

— Vom Wiener 'Schoenberg-Verein'—Mit unbekannten Briefen von AB, *SM*, November–December 1965, p. 340.

— Berg und Webern schreiben an Hermann Scherchen, *Melos*, July–August 1966, p. 225.

Rolf Urs Ringger: AB, *Musica*, 1963, No. 4, p. 158.

L. Rognoni: Espressionismo e dodecafonia, Giulio Einaudi (Turin) 1966.

E. Rudolph: AB zum 25. Todestag, *Musik und Gesellschaft*, December 1960, p. 720.

Josef Rufer: Dokumente einer Freundschaft (AB's letters to Schoenberg), *Melos*, February 1955, p. 42.

— Der Mensch und der Künstler, *Das Musikleben*, June & July–August 1955, pp. 205 and 251.

Daniel Ruyneman: AB, *La Revue musicale belge*, Vol. 12 (1936), No. 4, p. 2.

Friedrich Saathen: Rede auf AB, *NZfM*, July–August 1961.

Helmut Schmidt-Garre: Berg als Lehrer, *Melos*, February 1955, p. 40.

Bloch, Ernest

Arnold Schoenberg: Über AB, *SM*, June 1959, p. 221.

Humphrey Searle: Berg's operas, *London Magazine*, October 1962, p. 71.

— Berg's two operas, in *Opera 66*, Alan Ross (London) 1966, p. 143.

J. Smolik: AB, *Hudebni Rozhledy*, 1960, No. 4, p. 137.

W. Sorell: Magic formula, *Opera News*, 8 April 1961, p. 22.

P. Suvchinsky: AB, *L'Arc* (Aix-en-Provence), No. 27 (L'opéra), 1965.

Paul Stefan: Festspruch auf AB, *Anbruch*, January 1935, p. 8.

Erwin Stein: AB—Anton von Webern, *Anbruch*, January 1923, No. 1, p. 13; *Chesterian*, No. 26, October 1922, p. 33.

— Berg und Schoenberg, *Tempo*, No. 44, summer 1957, p. 4.

Erich Steinhard: AB, *Der Auftakt*, January 1926.

— In memoriam AB, *Der Auftakt*, 1936, Nos. 1–2, p. 4.

Charles Stuart: AB, another view, *Halle*, June 1950, p. 21.

H. H. Stuckenschmidt: Memorial to Berg, *Modern Music*, November–December 1937.

— AB—Finale: Requiem, *Modern Music*, March–April 1936.

— AB, in *Schöpfer der neuen Musik*, Suhrkamp Verlag (Frankfurt a.M.) 1958, p. 180.

— Debussy or Berg? The mystery of a chord progression, *MQ*, July 1965, p. 453.

Oscar Thompson: AB, composer of Wozzeck is dead, *Musical America*, 1936, No. 1, p. 8.

Viktor Ullmann: AB, *Anbruch*, February 1930, p. 50.

Konrad Vogelsang: AB, Leben und Werken, Max Hesses Verlag (Berlin), 1959.

Mark De Voto: Reich contra Berg, *PNM*, spring–summer 1966, p. 150.

Margareta Weimann: ABs Handschrift, *Melos*, December 1960.

Ulrich Weisstein (ed.): AB, in *The Essence of Opera*, Free Press & Glencoe (New York) 1964, p. 313.

Egon Wellesz: AB, *MMR*, 1936, p. 27.

— An AB manuscript at Oxford, *Tempo*, No. 15, June 1946.

Fritz Werle: Zwei Künstlerhoroskope, *Anbruch*, April 1927, p. 163.

Theodor Wiesengrund-Adorno: Berg and Webern—Schoenberg's heirs, *Modern Music*, January–February 1931.

— AB, in *Klangfiguren*, Shurkamp-Verlag (Berlin) 1959, p. 121.

Friedrich Wildgans: AB zum 75. Geburtstag, *ÖM*, January 1960.

Franz Willnauer: AB über Musik und Musiker, *Neue Zeitung*, April 1966, p. 128.

MISCELLANEOUS OR UNSIGNED

Worte aus dem Ausland über AB, *Anbruch*, January–February 1936, p. 9.

AB, work discussed, *The Times*, 15 December 1950, p. 8.

AB, *Röster i Radio*, 1952, No. 39, p. 8.

Berg by Totenberg, *Saturday Review*, 15 November 1952, p. 32.

AB, biography, *The Times*, 15 February 1957, p. 3.

75th anniversary celebrations, *The Times*, 13 December 1960, p. 15.

Opera on records: Wozzeck, Lulu, *Opera News*, 8 April 1961, p. 33.

Operas by AB, *The Times*, 5 October 1962, p. 18.

AB in seinen Briefen, *ÖM*, February 1965.

ERNEST BLOCH (1880–1959)

Bloch was born of Swiss-Jewish parents on 24 July 1880 in Geneva where his father ran a clock business. Although the home was not particularly musical, he had composed an 'Oriental Symphony' by the time he was fifteen. From 1897 to 1899 he attended the Brussels Conservatoire, taking violin lessons from Eugène Ysaÿe, then at the turn of the century studied for a year apiece at the Frankfurt and Munich Conservatoires, where his composition teachers were respectively Iwan Knorr and Ludwig Thuille. Bloch next moved to Paris but came to believe that he could not make a career of composing, and so returned to work in his father's Geneva business in 1904, the year of his marriage. However, he still composed in his spare time, conducted subscription concerts in Lausanne and Neuchâtel (1909–10) and lectured on the aesthetics of music at the Geneva Conservatoire in the years immediately preceding the

53

First World War. In these years the French novelist and critic Romain Rolland was an ardent champion of his works. In 1916 Bloch visited the USA for the first time to be conductor for an extended tour by the Maud Allen dance troupe. The troupe went bankrupt on his arrival, however, and the stranded Bloch decided to settle in New York. He soon began to make his mark in America as a composer, notably by winning the Elizabeth Sprague Coolidge prize in 1919 for his Viola Suite; but his life at this time was dominated by teaching: at the David Mannes School of Music in New York (1917–19), as Director of the Cleveland Institute of Music from 1920 until internal politics forced him to resign in 1925, and as Director of the San Francisco Conservatoire from 1925 to 1930. His composition-pupils included Randall Thompson, Quincy Porter and Roger Sessions. He became an American citizen in 1924 and in 1930 a San Francisco patron endowed a ten-year pension so that Bloch might be able to devote himself exclusively to composition. He spent much of the 1930s in Europe, especially at Roveredo Capriasca in Switzerland, but in 1938 returned to the United States and taught for a while at Berkeley in California. From 1943 onwards he lived on the Pacific coast at Agate Beach in Oregon, but began to succumb in the mid-1950s to the cancer from which he died at Portland (Oregon) in July 1959.

CATALOGUE OF WORKS

1. Symphonie orientale. c. 1895–6. Unpub.

2. String Quartet. c. 1895–6. Unpub.

3. Orientale. For orchestra. c. 1896–9. Unpub.

4. Violin Concerto. c. 1896–9. Unpub.

5. Cello Sonata. c. 1896–9. Unpub.

6. Vivre–Aimer. Symphonic Poem for orchestra. 1900. Unpub.

7. Symphony in C-sharp minor. 1901–2. Ded. Robert Godet.
   1. *Lento—Allegro agitato ma molto energico*; 2. *Andante molto moderato*; 3. *Vivace*; 4. *Allegro energico e molto marcato*.
   4 fl, 2 pic, 3 ob, ca, 3 cl, bcl, 2 bsn, cbsn; 4 hn, 4 tpt, 3 tmb, 2 tuba; 3 timp; GC, tgle, cym, tamtam, tamb, campanelle, glock; 2 hp, strings.
   ?fEp: 9 February 1952, BBC broadcast, BBC Symphony Orchestra, cond. Clarence Raybould.
   Pub. 1925, Leuckart (Leipzig).

8. Historiettes au crépuscule (Camille Mauclair). For voice and piano. 1903.
   1. *Légende*. Ded. Jan Reder.
   2. *Les fleurs*. Ded. Nina Faliero-Dalcroze.
   3. *Ronde*. Ded. Mme Jean d'Udine.
   4. *Complainte*. Ded. to the composer's sister.
   Pub. c. 1930, Eschig.

9. Hiver–Printemps. Two Symphonic Poems for orchestra. 1904–5.
   fEp: 12 February 1934, Queen's Hall, London Philharmonic Orchestra, cond. Ernest Bloch.
   ?Unpub.

10. Macbeth. Lyric Drama in seven scenes (prologue and three acts). 1903–9. Libretto: Edmond Fleg, after Shakespeare. Ded. Lucienne Bréval.
   fp: 1910, Paris, Opéra-Comique, cond. Fr. Ruhlmann; with Henri Albers (Macbeth), Vieuille (Macduff), Lucienne Bréval (Lady Macbeth), Mme L. Vauthrin (Lady Macduff), Jean Laure (Banquo), Feodoroff (Duncan), Mario (Malcolm), Vaurs (Lennox), Mmes. Duvernay, Brohly and Charbonnel (Three Witches), Mme Carrière (Macduff's son); producer, Carbonne; décors, Jusseaume.
   Pub. 1910, G. Astruc (Paris), vocal score; 1951, Edizioni Suvini Zerboni (Milan), vocal score: Eng. version by Alex Cohen & Ernest Bloch.

BIBLIOGRAPHY:
Alex. Cohen: EB's Macbeth, *M&L*, April 1938, p. 143.
Judith Gartier: M. Bloch's Macbeth at the Parish Opéra-Comique, *MS*, 10 December 1910, p. 373 (reprinted from *Excelsior*, Paris).
Guido M. Gatti: Due Macbeth, *La Cultura musicale* (Bologna) 1922, No. 4; The two Macbeths, *Sackbut*, January 1923, p. 164; *MQ*, January 1926, p. 22.

R. Hall: The Macbeth of Bloch, *Modern Music*, May–June 1938.

R. Mariani: Bloch e il suo Macbeth, *La Scala*, February 1953.

Alfredo Parente: Macbeth d'EB, *La Rassegna musicale*, March 1938.

V. Raeli: Shakespeare e Bloch in Macbeth, *Rivista nazionale di musica*, May 1934.

G. Roncaglia: Rileggendo il Macbeth di Bloch, *Rivista musicale italiana*, July–September 1950, No. 3.

Franz Walter: Macbeth d'EB à La Scala Milan, *SM*, March–April 1960, p. 110.

10a. Macbeth: Two Interludes. For orchestra. Dur. $11\frac{1}{2}'$.

1. *Interlude, Act I.* Dur. 5'.
2. *Interlude, Act III.* Dur. $6\frac{1}{2}'$.

3 fl, pic, 2 ob, ca, 3 cl, bcl, 2 bsn, cbsn; 4 hn, 3 tpt, 3 tmb, bs tuba; timp, tgle, cym, GC, tamb, tamtam; hp, strings.

fEp: March 1939, Bournemouth Festival. Pub. 1945, Edizioni Suivini Zerboni (Milan).

11. Poèmes d'automne (Béatrix Rodès). For voice and piano (or orchestra). 1906.

1. *La vagabonde*; 2. *Le déclin* (The waning); 3. *L'abri* (The Shelter).

Pub. 1918. Eng. version, Sigmund Spaeth.

12. Deux Psaumes. For soprano and orchestra. 1912, Geneva. Poems adapted from the Hebrew by Edmond Fleg, Eng. transl. Waldo Frank. Ded. Edmond and Madeleine Fleg.

4 fl, 2 pic, 3 ob, ca, 3 cl, bcl, 3 bsn, dbsn; 6 hn, 4 tpt, 3 tmb, tuba; timp, GC, cym, snare dm, gong; celesta, 2 hp, strings.

?fp: 24 January 1922, Paris, Salle des Agriculteurs, Vera Janacopulos.

fEpb: 11 April 1931, Tatiana Makushina.

fEp (concert): 12 February 1934, Queen's Hall, Tatiana Makushina and the London Philharmonic Orchestra, cond. Ernest Bloch.

Pub. 1921, Schirmer.

13. Trois Poèmes juifs. For orchestra. Dated: August–September 1913, Satigny, nr. Geneva. Ded. to the memory of the composer's father.

1. *Danse*; 2. *Rite*; 3. *Cortège funèbre*.

fp: 23 March 1917, Boston, Boston Symphony Orchestra, cond. Ernest Bloch.

fEp: 13 January 1923, Queen's Hall, New Queen's Hall Orchestra, cond. Sir Henry Wood.

Pub. 1918, Schirmer.

14. Psaume 22. For baritone and orchestra. 1914. Poems adapted from the Hebrew by Edmond Fleg, Eng. transl. Waldo Frank. Ded. Romain Rolland.

4 fl, 2 pic, 3 ob, ca, 3 cl, E-flat cl, bcl, 3 bsn, dbsn; 6 hn, 4 tpt, 3 tmb, tuba; timp, GC, tgle, cym, snare dm, gong; celesta, 2 hp, strings.

Pub. 1921, Schirmer.

15. Schelomo. Hebrew Rhapsody for cello and orchestra. Dated: January–February 1916, Geneva. Ded. Alexander and Catherine Barjansky.

3 fl, pic, 2 ob, ca, 2 cl, bcl, 2 bsn, cbsn; 4 hn, 3 tpt, 3 tmb, tuba; timp, tamburo, tamburo basco, GC, cym, tamtam; celesta, 2 hp, strings.

fp: 3 May 1916, New York, Carnegie Hall, Bloch concert given by the Society of Friends of Music, with Hans Kindler (cello).

fFp: 28 November 1921, Paris, Théâtre du Châtelet, A. Hekking and Orchestre Colonne, cond. Gabriel Pierné.

fEp: 11 October 1922, Queen's Hall, Promenade Concert, May Mukle and the New Queen's Hall Orchestra, cond. Sir Henry Wood.

Pub. 1918, 1945, Schirmer.

16. String Quartet No. 1. Dated: June 1916, Geneva—September 1916, New York. Ded. Flonzaley Quartet.

1. *Andante moderato*; 2. *Allegro frenetico*; 3. *Andante molto moderato* (Pastorale); 4. *Finale* (Vivace).

fFp: 10 February 1923, Théâtre du Vieux Colombier, Revue Musicale concert, Rosé Quartet.

Pub. 1919, Schirmer.

BIBLIOGRAPHY:

Alex. Cohen: A note on the String Quartet of EB, *MT*, November 1937, p. 945.

17. Israel Symphony. For two sopranos, two contraltos, bass and orchestra. 1912–16, Geneva. Ded. Mrs. J. F. D. Lanier.

4 fl, 2 pic, 3 ob, ca, 3 cl, bcl, 3 bsn, cbsn; 6 hn, 4 tpt, 3 tmb, tuba; 3 or 4 timp, GC, cym, side dm, tgle, tamtam (low); 2 hp, celesta, strings.

fp: 3 May 1916, New York, Carnegie Hall, Bloch concert given by the Society of Friends of Music, cond. Ernest Bloch.

fFp: 24 October 1926, Paris, Théâtre du Châtelet, Mmes Lalande, Marilliet, Mahieu, Cernay, M. Peyre, Orchestre Colonne, cond. Gabriel Pierné.

fEp: 28 April 1928, Queen's Hall, BBC concert, National Symphony Orchestra, cond. Sir Henry Wood.

Pub. 1925, Schirmer.

17a. Adonaï Elohim. From the Symphony 'Israel'. For SSAAB and piano. Pub. 1924, Schirmer.

18. Jézabel. Opera, 1918. Unfinished.

19. Suite. For viola and orchestra. 1918–19.

fEp: 29 June 1923, Aeolian Hall, Lionel Tertis, cond. Eugene Goossens.

fFp: 25 October 1924, Paris, Théâtre du Châtelet, Lefranc (viola) and Orchestre Colonne, cond. Gabriel Pierné.

Pub. 1920.

19a. Suite. Version for viola and piano. 1919. New York. Ded. Mrs. E. S. Coolidge, Awarded first prize, Berkshire Chamber Music Festival Competition, September 1919.

1. *Lento—Allegro—Moderato*; 2. *Allegro ironico*; 3. *Lento*; 4. *Molto vivo*.

fp: 27 September 1919, Pittsfield (Mass.), Louis Bailly and Harold Bauer.

fEbp: 24 July 1933, Lionel Tertis and Solomon.

20. Violin Sonata. 1920. Ded. Paul Rosenfeld.

1. *Agitato*; 2. *Molto quieto*; 3. *Moderato*.

fEp: 17 October 1922, St. John's Institute (Westminster), Music Society concert, Jelly d'Aranyi and Yvonne Arnaud.

fEbp: 24 October 1938, Eda Kersey and John Wills.

Pub. 1922, Schirmer.

BIBLIOGRAPHY:

H. Berkley: The EB Sonata, a descriptive analysis, *Etude*, October 1954, p. 25.

21. In the night. A Love Poem for piano. Dated: 22 July 1922, Cleveland.

Pub. 1923, Schirmer.

22. Piano Quintet. 1921–3. Dated: 27 March 1923, Cleveland. Ded. Harold Bauer and the Lenox Quartet.

1. *Agitato*; 2. *Andante mistico*; 3. *Allegro energico*.

fp: 11 November 1923, New York City, Klaw Theatre, League of Composers concert, Harold Bauer and the Lenox Quartet.

fEbp: 11 June 1926, Music Room of Seaford House (Belgrave Square), British Music Society, Kathleen Long, Marjorie Haywood, Stella Pattenden, Rebecca Clarke and May Mukle.

Pub. 1924, Schirmer.

BIBLIOGRAPHY:

Alex. Cohen: A note on the Piano Quintet of EB, *MO*, December 1937, p. 213.

Ernest Newman: The Bloch Quintet, in *More Essays from the World of Music*, Calder (London) 1958, p. 46.

23. Enfantines (Ten pieces for children). For piano. 1923.

1. *Lullaby*. Ded. Suzanne Bloch.
2. *The joyous party*. Ded. Mrs. F. B. Kortheuer.
3. *With mother*. Ded. Lucienne Bloch.
4. *Elves*. Ded. Ruth Edwards.
5. *Joyous march*. Ded. Beryl Rubinstein.
6. *Melody*. Ded. Dorothy Price.
7. *Pastorale*. Ded. Eleanor Foster.
8. *Rainy day*. Ded. Nathan Fryer.
9. *Teasing*. Ded. M. Edith Martin.
10. *Dream*. Ded. Anita Frank.

Pub. 1924, Fischer.

24. Baal Shem. Three Pictures of Chassidic Life for violin and piano. 1923. Ded. to the memory of the composer's mother.

1. *Vidui* (Contrition); 2. *Nigun* (Improvisation); 3. *Simchas Torah* (Rejoicing).

?fEp: 19 November 1927, Wigmore Hall, Isolde Menges.

Pub. 1924, Fischer.

24a. Baal Shem. Version for violin and orchestra. Dated: August 1939.

2 fl, pic, 2 ob, 2 cl, 2 bsn; 4 hn, 3 tpt; 3 timp, tgle, cym; hp, celesta, strings.

fp: 19 October 1941, New York, Joseph Szigeti and the WPA Orchestra.

fEp: 16 August 1950, BBC broadcast, Yfrah Neaman and the BBC Scottish Orchestra, cond. Ian Whyte.

Pub. 1940, Fischer.

25. Mélodie. For violin and piano. 1923. Ded. André de Ribaupierre. Pub. 1924, Fischer.

26. Nirvana. Poem for piano. Dated: 14 April 1923, Cleveland. Ded. Povla Frijsh.

fEbp: 13 March 1934, Harriet Cohen.

Pub. 1924, Schirmer.

27. Five Sketches in Sepia. For piano. Dated: July 1923, New York. Ded. Marguerite Fischel.

1. *Prélude*; 2. *Fumées sur la ville*; 3. *Lucioles*; 4. *Incertitude*; 5. *Epilogue*.

Pub. 1924, Schirmer.

28. Poems of the Sea. A cycle of three pieces for piano. Dated: 2–11 July 1923, Cleveland.

1. *Waves*; 2. *Chanty*; 3. *At sea*.

fEbp: 25 April 1926, Birmingham station, Gordon Bryan.

Pub. 1923, Schirmer.

28a. Poems of the Sea. Version for orchestra.

fEp: 22 October 1937, BBC broadcast, BBC Orchestra, cond. Clarence Raybould.

?Unpub.

29. From Jewish Life. Three Sketches for cello and piano. 1924. Ded. Hans Kindler. Pub. 1925, Fischer.

30. Night. For string quartet. 1924. Ded. Roger Sessions.

fEp: 26 April (?3 May) 1924, Wigmore Hall, Flonzaley Quartet.

Pub. 1925, Fischer.

31. Nuit exotique. For violin and piano. 1924. Ded. Joseph Szigeti.

Pub. 1925, Fischer.

32. Three Nocturnes. For violin, cello and piano. 1924. Ded. The New York Trio.

1. *Andante*; 2. *Andante quieto*; 3. *Tempestoso*.

?fEp: 20 January 1928, London, Budapest Trio.

fEbp: 15 September 1935, Grinke Trio (Frederick Grinke, Florence Hooton and Dorothy Manley).

Pub. 1925, Fischer.

33. Paysages (Landscapes). For string quartet. 1924. Ded. Carl Engel.

1.*North*; 2. *Alpestre*; 3. *Tongataboo*.

fEp: 26 April (?3 May) 1924, Wigmore Hall, Flonzaley Quartet.

Pub. 1925, Fischer.

34. Poème mystique (Violin Sonata No. 2). 1924. Ded. André de Ribaupierre and Beryl Rubinstein.

?fEp: 10 December 1937, Aeolian Hall, Bloch Society concert, Max Rostal and Franz Osborn.

Pub. 1925, Leuckart (Leipzig).

BIBLIOGRAPHY:

Alex. Cohen: Bloch's Poème mystique, *Strad*, May 1938, p. 7.

35. In the Mountains (Haute Savoie). Two Sketches for string quartet. 1924. Ded. to the composer's cousin Léon Goetschel.

1. *Dusk*; 2. *Rustic dance*.

Pub. 1925, Fischer.

36. Meditation hebraïque. For cello and piano. 1924. Ded. Pablo Casals. Pub. 1925, Fischer.

37. Prelude (Recueillement). For string quarter. 1925. Pub. 1929, Fischer.

38. Concerto grosso. For string orchestra with piano obbligato. 1924–5.

1. *Prelude* (*Allegro energico e pesante*); 2. *Dirge* (*Andante moderato*); 3. *Pastorale and Rustic Dances* (*Assai lento—Allegro*); 4. *Fugue* (*Allegro*).

?fp: 19 February 1925, Queen's Hall, Myra Hess and the New Queen's Hall Orchestra, cond. Sir Henry Wood.

Pub. 1925, Birchard.

39. Four Episodes. For chamber orchestra. Dated: May 1926, San Francisco. Dur. 14′.

1. *Humoresque macabre*. Dur. 3′.
2. *Obsession*. Dur. 3′.
3. *Calm*. Dur. 4′.
4. *Chinese*. Dur. 4′.

Piano, string quintet, fl, ob, cl, bsn, hn.

fEp: 7 October 1933, Wigmore Hall,

Dorothy Hesse (piano) and the London String Players (augmented).

fEbp: 7 February 1936, BBC Midland Orchestra, cond. Leslie Heward.

Pub. 1929, Birchard.

40. America. An Epic Rhapsody in three parts for orchestra. 1926, San Francisco. Ded. 'to the memory of Abraham Lincoln and Walt Whitman whose vision has upheld its inspiration'.

1. ... 1620. *The Soil—The Indians—(England)—The Mayflower—The Landing of the Pilgrims.*

2. ... 1861–1865. *Hours of Joy—Hours of Sorrow.*

3. 1926 ... *The Present—The Future.*

3 fl, pic, 2 ob, ca, 2 cl, bcl, 2 bsn, cbsn; 4 hn, 3 tpt, 3 tmb, tuba; 4 timp, tamb, tamb basco, 2 GC, cym, tamtam, tgle, wood block, Indian dm, campanelle (glock), campana, 2 anvils, steel plate, automobile horn (ad lib); 2 hp, celesta, organ (ad lib); strings.

Pub. 1928, Birchard.

BIBLIOGRAPHY:

Ernest Fowles: America, *The Dominant*, March–April 1927, p. 15.

41. Helvetia (The Land of Mountains and its People). Symphonic Fresco for orchestra. Dated: 1900, Munich—1929, San Francisco. Dur. 23–25′.

4 fl, 2 pic, 3 ob, ca, 3 cl, bcl, 3 bsn, cbsn; 6 hn, 4 tpt, 3 tmb, tuba; 8 timp, tamburo, GC, cym, tamtam; 2 hp, celesta, strings.

fEp: 12 February 1934, Queen's Hall, London Philharmonic Orchestra, cond. Ernest Bloch.

Pub. 1931, Birchard.

42. Abodah (God's Worship). A Yom Kippur melody for violin and piano. 1929. Ded. Yehudi Menuhin. Pub. 1929, Fischer.

43. Avodath Hakodesh (Sacred Service). For baritone, mixed chorus and orchestra. Dated: May 1933. Ded. Gerald Warburg. Dur. 49′.

1. *Meditation* (*Mah Tovu*); 2. *Kedushah* (*Sanctification*); 3. *Silent Devotion*; 4. *Returning the Scroll to the Ark*; 5. *Vaanachnu. Benediction* (Dated: 7 June 1933).

fp: February 1934, Turin, cond. Ernest Bloch.

fFp: 26 January 1937, Paris, Temple israélite de la rue de la Victoire, Concert Spirituel, Joseph Blumberg (cantor), la chorale Amicitia, la chorale Mizmor, and l'Orchestre Colonne, cond. Ernest Bloch.

fEp: 26 March 1938, Birmingham, Roy Henderson and the City of Birmingham Choir and Orchestra, cond. G. D. Cunningham.

f London p: 13 October 1949, Royal Albert Hall, London Philharmonic Choir and Orchestra, cond. Ernest Bloch.

Pub. 1934, Birchard. English text, Denis Stevens.

BIBLIOGRAPHY:

A. W. Binder: EB's Avodath Hakodesh, *American Guild of Organists Quarterly*, January 1957, p. 7.

Ernest Newman: Bloch's Sacred Service, a work Jewish at heart, in *From the World of Music*, Calder (London) 1956, p. 138.

Henry Prunières: Avodath Hakodech, d'EB, *RM*, February 1937, p. 127.

Lazare Saminsky: Apropos of Bloch's Sabbath Service, *Menorah Journal*, October 1934, p. 172.

44. Piano Sonata. Dated: March–October 1935, Paris-Châtel. Ded. Guido Agosti.

1. *Maestoso ed energico*; 2. *Pastorale: Andante*; 3. *Moderato alla marcia.*

fEbp: 25 September 1936, Charles Lynch.

Pub. 1948, Carisch (Milan).

BIBLIOGRAPHY:

Alan Frank: Bloch's Sonata, *Radio Times*, 18 September 1936, p. 15.

45. Voice in the Wilderness. Symphonic Poem for orchestra with cello obbligato. 1934–6. Dated: 26 January 1936, Châtel, Haute Savoie. Dur. 25′.

1. *Moderato*; 2. *Poco lento*; 3. *Moderato*; 4. *Adagio piacevole*; 5. *Poco agitato—Cadenza—Calmo*; 6. *Allegro.*

3 fl, pic, 2 ob, ca, 2 cl, bcl, 2 bsn, cbsn; 4 hn, 3 tpt, 3 tmb, tuba; 4 timp, GC, tamtam, cym, tamburo, tgle; 2 hp, celesta, strings.

fp: 21 January 1937, Los Angeles, Los Angeles Philharmonic.

fFp: 17 October 1937, Paris, Salle Pleyel, Charles Baretsch and l'Orchestre Symphonique de Paris, cond. Pierre Monteux.
Pub. 1936, Schirmer.

45a. Voice in the Wilderness. Version for cello and piano. 1936.
fGBp: 10 November 1937, Glasgow, Luigi Gasparini and Erik Chisholm.
Pub. 1937, Schirmer.

45b. Visions et prophéties. Version of 'Voice in the Wilderness' for piano.
1. *Moderato*; 2. *Poco lento*; 3. *Moderato*; 4. *Adagio, piacevole*; 5. *Poco agitato*.
Pub. 1940, Schirmer.

46. Evocations. Symphonic Suite for orchestra. Dated: May 1937, Châtel, Haute Savoie. Dur. 16–17′.
1. *Contemplation*; 2. *Houang Ti* (God of War); 3. *Renouveau*.
3 fl, pic, 2 ob, ca, 2 cl, 2 bsn; 4 hn, 2 tpt, 3 tmb, tuba; 3 timp, tamburo, tamtam, cym, GC, tgle, glock; celesta, piano, hp, strings.
fp: San Francisco.
f European p: 10 March 1938, Birmingham, City of Birmingham Orchestra, cond. Leslie Heward.
Pub. 1937, Schirmer.

BIBLIOGRAPHY:
Anon: EB's Evocations, *Strad*, April 1938, p. 550.

47. Violin Concerto. 1937–8. Dur. 34½′.
1. *Allegro deciso*; 2. *Andante*; 3. *Deciso*.
3 fl, pic, 2 ob, ca, 2 cl, bcl, 2 bsn, cbsn; 4 hn, 3 tpt, 3 tmb, tuba; timp, pcssn; celesta, hp, strings.
fp: 15 December 1938, Cleveland (Ohio), Joseph Szigeti and the Cleveland Orchestra, cond. Dimitri Mitropoulos.
Pub. 1938, Hawkes; incl. reduction by Ernest Bloch.

BIBLIOGRAPHY:
Ernest Chapman: Violin Concerto, in *The Concerto*, Pelican Books (London) 1952, p. 317.
Alan Frank: EB's Violin Concerto, *Strad*, April 1939, p. 535.
R.-A. Mooser: Le Concerto récent d'EB, *Dissonances*, November 1939.

Geoffrey Sharp: EB's Violin Concerto, *MR*, No. 1, 1940.
Anon: Bloch's Concerto: the map and the country, *The Times*, 11 March 1939, p. 10.

48. Suite Symphonique. For orchestra. 1944. Dur. 20′.
1. *Overture*; 2. *Passacaglia*; 3. *Finale*.
3 fl, pic, 2 ob, ca, 2 cl, bcl, 2 bsn, cbsn; 4 hn, 3 tpt, 3 tmb, tuba; timp, cym, GC; strings.
fEp: 23 August 1946, Royal Albert Hall, Promenade Concert, London Symphony Orchestra, cond. Basil Cameron.
Pub. 1947, Hawkes.

49. String Quartet No. 2. 1945. Ded. Alex Cohen. Dur. 33′.
1. *Moderato*. Dur. 5½′.
2. *Presto*. Dur. 7½–8′.
3. *Andante*. Dur. 7½′.
4. *Allegro molto*. Dur. 12½′.
Pub. 1947, Boosey & Hawkes.

BIBLIOGRAPHY:
Frederick Rimmer: Bloch's Second String Quartet, *Tempo*, No. 52, autumn 1959.

50. Concerto Symphonique. For piano and orchestra. 1946–8. Ded. Mary Tibaldi Chiesa. Dur. 38′.
1. *Pesante*; 2. *Allegro vivace*; 3. *Allegro deciso*.
3 fl, pic, 2 ob, ca, 2 cl, bcl, 2 bsn, cbsn; 4 hn, 3 tpt, 3 tmb, tuba; timp, GC, cym, tamb mil, tamtam, celesta; strings.
fp: 3 September 1949, Edinburgh Festival, Corinne Lacomble and the Scottish Orchestra, cond. Ernest Bloch.
f London p: 6 September 1949, Royal Albert Hall, Promenade Concert, Corinne Lacomble and the London Philharmonic Orchestra, cond. Ernest Bloch.
Pub. 1950, Hawkes; incl. reduction by Ernest Bloch for two pianos.

BIBLIOGRAPHY:
Ernest Chapman: Concerto symphonique, in *The Concerto*, Pelican Books (London) 1952, p. 322.

51. Scherzo fantasque. For piano and orchestra. Dated: 23 December 1948, Agate Beach, Oregon. Ded. A. E. and Corinne Lacomble.
fp: December 1950, Chicago, Bloch Festival, Idah Fren, cond. Ernest Bloch.

fEp: 10 September 1951, Royal Albert Hall, Promenade Concert, Iris Loveridge and the London Philharmonic Orchestra, cond. Basil Cameron.

Pub. 1950, Schirmer; incl. reduction by Ernest Bloch for two pianos.

52. Six Preludes. For organ. 1946–50.
1. *Andante.* Ded. Dr. John Stark Evans.
2. *Poco lento.* Ded. Tracy Y. Cannon.
3. *Andante.* Ded. Alexander Schreiner.
4. *Grave.* Ded. Charles H. Marsh.
5. *Un poco animato.* Ded. Frank W. Asper.
6. *Processional* (*Moderato*). Ded. Marcel Tyrrel.
Pub. 1950, Schirmer.

53. Concertino. For flute, viola (or clarinet) and string orchestra (or piano). 1950.
1. *Allegro comodo*; 2. *Allegro* (*Fuga*).
fEp: 9 January 1953, BBC broadcast, Geoffrey Gilbert (flute), William Primrose (viola) and the London Chamber Orchestra, cond. Anthony Bernard.
Pub. 1951, Schirmer; incl. reduction.

54. Deux Pièces. For string quartet. 1938–1950. Ded. Griller String Quartet.
1. *Andante moderato.* 1938.
2. *Allegro molto.* 1950.
Pub. 1952, Joseph Williams.

55. Four Wedding Marches. For organ. 1946–50.
1. *Moderato*; 2. *Maestoso*; 3. *Moderato*; 4. *Moderato.*

56. Suite hebraïque. For violin or viola and piano. 1951. Ded. Covenant Club of Illinois.
1. *Rapsodie*; 2. *Processional*; 3. *Affirmation.*
Pub. 1953, Schirmer.

56a. Suite hebraïque. For orchestra. Dur. 11½'.
1. *Rapsodie.* Dur. 5' 30".
2. *Processional.* Dur. 2' 15".
3. *Affirmation.* Dur. 3' 45".
2 fl, 2 ob, 2 cl, 2 bsn; 4 hn, 3 tpt; timp, tamburo, cym, tamtam; hp, strings.
fEp: 24 September 1954, BBC broadcast, Maurice Loban and the BBC Midland Orchestra, cond. Leo Wurmser.
Pub. 1953, 1957, Schirmer; 1957, Chappell.

57. String Quartet No. 3. 1951–2. Ded. The Griller Quartet.
1. *Allegro deciso*; 2. *Adagio non troppo*; 3. *Allegro molto*; 4. *Allegro-Fuga.*
fEbp: 14 June 1953, Griller Quartet.
Pub. 1953, Schirmer.

58. Sinfonia breve. For orchestra. 1952.
1. *Moderato—Allegro*; 2. *Andante*; 3. *Allegro molto*; 4. *Allegro deciso.*
2 fl, pic, 2 ob, ca, 2 cl, bcl, 2 bsn, cbsn; 4 hn, 3 tpt, 2 tmb, tuba; timp, snare dm, GC, cym, tamtam; celesta, hp, strings.
fp: 11 April 1953, BBC broadcast, BBC Symphony Orchestra, cond. Sir Malcolm Sargent.
Pub. 1955, Schirmer.

59. Concerto grosso No. 2. For string quartet and string orchestra. Dated: April–July 1952, Agate Beach, Oregon.
1. *Maestoso*; 2. *Andante*; 3. *Allegro*; 4. *Tranquillo—Allegro.*
fp: 11 April 1953, BBC broadcast, BBC Symphony Orchestra, cond. Sir Malcolm Sargent.
Pub. 1953, Schirmer.

60. String Quartet No. 4. Dated: 10 July–5 November 1953, Agate Beach, Oregon. Ded. Ernest Chapman. Dur. 26'.
1. *Tranquillo—Allegro energico.* Dur. 7'.
2. *Andante.* Dur. 6'.
3. *Presto—Moderato.* Dur. 5'.
4. *Calmo—Allegro deciso.* Dur. 8'.
fp: 18 July 1954, London, Griller Quartet.
Pub. 1956, Schirmer.

61. Meditation and Processional. For viola and piano. Ded. Milton Preves. Pub. Schirmer.

62. Symphony in E-flat major. For trombone and orchestra. 1954–5. Ded. Davis Shuman. Dur. 16½'.
1. *Maestoso*; 2. *Agitato*; 3. *Allegro deciso.*
2 fl, pic, 2 ob, ca, 2 cl, bcl, 2 bsn, cbsn; 4 hn, 3 tpt, 3 tmb, tuba; timp (timp pic), GC, cym, snare dm, tamtam; celesta, hp, strings.
fp: 15 February 1956, London, Royal Festival Hall, Royal Philharmonic Society concert, Royal Philharmonic Orchestra, cond. Efrem Kurtz.

fbp: 26 September 1956, BBC Scottish Orchestra, cond. Ian Whyte.
Pub. 1956, Broude Brothers.

BIBLIOGRAPHY:
S. Williams: Bloch's new symphony, *New York Times*, 6 May 1956, Sect. 2, p. 7.

63. Proclamation. For trumpet and orchestra. 1955.
fEp (broadcast): 25 January 1958, William Overton and the BBC Symphony Orchestra, cond. Sir Malcolm Sargent.
Pub. 1956, Broude Brothers.

64. String Quartet No. 5. 1956. Ded. to the composer's daughter, Suzanne Bloch-Smith. Dur. 30–31'.
1. *Grave—Allegro*; 2. *Calmo*; 3. *Presto*; 4. *Allegro deciso*.
Pub. 1961, 1966, Broude Brothers.

BIBLIOGRAPHY:
K. Kirchbcrg: Ein Streichquartett von EB, *Musica*, December 1956, p. 859.

65. Three Suites. For unacc. cello. 1956–7.
fEp (No. 1): 28 May 1957, BBC broadcast, Zara Nelsova.
fp (No. 2): 20 October 1957, BBC broadcast, Zara Nelsova.

66. Two Suites. For unacc. violin. 1956.
Suite No. 1. Ded. Zara Nelsova. Dated: 1956. Dur. 10'.
1. *Prelude*; 2. *Allegro*; 3. *Canzona*; 4. *Allegro*.
fEp: 6 August 1960, BBC broadcast, Yfrah Neaman.
Pub. 1957, Broude Brothers.
Suite No. 2.
f London p: 8 December 1961, 4 St. James's Square, Paul Collins.

67. Piano Quintet No. 2. 1957. Dur. *c*. 19½'.
1. *Animato*; 2. *Andante*; 3. *Allegro*.
Pub. 1962, 1966, Broude Brothers.

68. Suite modale. For flute and string orchestra. 1957. Ded. Elaine Shaffer. Dur. 12'.
1. *Moderato*; 2. *L'istesso tempo*; 3. *Allegro giocoso*; 4. *Adagio*.
Pub. 1959, Broude Brothers.

68a. Suite modale. For flute and piano.
fEbp: 22 April 1958, Elaine Shaffer and Bela Siki.
Pub. 1957, Broude Brothers.

PRINCIPAL WRITINGS BY BLOCH
The future of the harp, *Eolian Review*, No. 1, 1922.
Mahler, Strauss, Bruckner, *Die Musik*, June 1923, p. 664.
Zu Fidelio, *Blätter der Staatsoper* (Berlin), No. 8, November 1927, p. 1.
Don Giovanni, *Blätter der Staatsoper* (Berlin), No. 13, 1928, p. 1.
Man and music, MQ, October 1933, p. 374.
Gruss an Otto Klemperer als Conductor der Meister, *Schallplatte und Kirche*, 1967, No. 3, p. 55.

GENERAL BIBLIOGRAPHY
W. R. Anderson: Tipping a winner, *MM&F*, October 1932, p. 13.
Edmond Appia: Hommage à EB, *SM*, October 1959, p. 350.
Felix Aprahamian: Bloch in London, *MO*, April 1934, p. 601.
S. Bloch: A father's souvenirs, *New York Times*, 6 December 1959, Sect. 2, p. 13.
Ernest Chapman: EB, *MT*, February 1934, p. 121.
— EB, *Philharmonic Post*, September–October 1949, p. 3.
— EB at 75, *Tempo*, No. 35, spring 1955.
Joan Chissell: Style in Bloch's chamber music, *M&L*, January 1943.
— The Jewish EB, *The Listener*, 15 January 1959, p. 145.
— The chamber music of EB, *The Listener*, 19 September 1963, p. 445.
A. Della Corte: EB, *La Nazione* (Florence), 20 July 1933.
Henry Cowell: Current chronicle, *MQ*, 1954, p. 235.
Carl Engel: Bloch and the Library of Congress, *Musical America*, 10 November 1928, p. 6.
David Ewen: EB, *Disques*, May 1932.
— EB, *MMR*, 1934, p. 25.
— Music of EB, *Menorah Journal*, January 1938, p. 35.
Gajanus: Il volto biblico di EB, *Il Resto del Carlino* (Bologna), 16 September 1933.
Guido M. Gatti: EB, *MQ*, 1921, p. 20; transl. Paul Stefan, *Anbruch*, May 1922, p. 133.
Julius Hartt: EB, *RM*, April 1923, p. 218.

J. Hastings: EB and modern music, *Menorah Journal*, 1948, p. 196.

Leigh Henry: Two Hebrew composers, *MS*, 8 August 1925, p. 40.

William M. Jones: EB's five string quartets, *MR*, May 1967, p. 112.

— The music of EB, *Dissertation Abstracts*, June 1964, p. 5451.

Edward William Morgan: EB, *Scottish Musical Magazine*, March 1930, p. 79.

Dika Newlin: The later works of EB, *MQ*, October 1947, p. 443.

D. Hugh Ottaway: Looking again at EB, *MT*, June 1950, p. 234.

— EB and Edmund Rubbra, *MO*, November 1949, p. 72.

Guido Pannain: EB, *La Rassegna musicale*, February 1929, p. 77.

Ildebrando Pizzetti: EB, in *Musicisti contemporanei*, Fratelli Treves (Milan) 1914, p. 191.

Andrew Porter: EB, in *Chamber Music*, Penguin Books (London) 1957, p. 215.

M. Rinaldi: Arte e umanità in EB, *Rivista nazionale di musica*, May 1933.

Paul Rosenfeld: EB, *Anbruch*, 1921, No. 7 (April), p. 135.

Fred Service: EB and his chamber music, *Music Parade*, 1951, No. 6, p. 7.

Roger Sessions: EB, *Modern Music*, December 1927.

Desmond Shawe-Taylor: Prophet and kapellmeister, *New Statesman*, 22 October 1949, p. 452.

Mary Tibaldi Chiesa: EB, *Bollettino bibliografico musicale*, November 1931, p. 5.

— EB, *RM*, February 1934, p. 123.

— Notes sur EB, *L'Art musical*, 15 October 1937.

Franz Walter: EB, musicien Suisse?, *SM*, July 1953, p. 293.

Karl H. Wörner: Die Musik in der Philosophie EBs, *SM*, July–August 1965, p. 201.

Anon: Bibliography of works by EB, *The Dominant*, March 1928, p. 34.

Anon: EB, his ancestral instincts and chassidic consciousness, *British Musician*, July 1932, p. 143.

Anon: EB, in *Musik der Zeit*, Vol. 10 (Schweizer Komponisten), Boosey & Hawkes (Bonn) 1955, p. 56.

FERRUCCIO BUSONI (1866–1924)

Busoni's parents were both professional musicians, his father a clarinettist, his mother a pianist. He was born in the Tuscan town of Empoli on 1 April 1866; but much of his early childhood was spent in Trieste while his parents were on concert tours. It was with his parents that he made his first public appearance as a pianist at the age of seven. Two years later he was playing his own compositions in Vienna and in the next few years became known in Austria and Italy as a child prodigy. Busoni studied composition with Wilhelm Mayer at Graz (1880–1) and in 1886 broke away from parental domination by leaving for Leipzig, where he stayed for two years. From 1888 to 1889 he taught the piano at the Conservatoire of Helsinki in Finland. There he met Gerda Sjöstrand, the daughter of a Swedish sculptor, whom he married in 1890 while in Russia teaching at the Moscow Conservatoire. In 1891 he paid the first of several visits to the USA, teaching at Boston for a year and then spending two years based in New York as a touring virtuoso pianist. In 1894 he returned to Europe and—though retaining his Italian nationality—settled in Berlin, which he used until the outbreak of the First World War as the base for his continual concert-touring of Europe. He also gave master-classes in piano at Weimar (1900–1), Vienna (1907–8) and Basle (1910), as well as conducting a remarkable series of concerts of modern music in Berlin between 1902 and 1909. From the turn of the century onwards, composition came more and more to be Busoni's predominant activity, though it had to be largely a summer activity. In 1913 he became director of the Liceo Rossini in Bologna, but was replaced in 1915 during his final concert tour of the USA. He lived in Zürich from 1915 to 1920, refusing to perform in any country involved in the war and beginning to suffer from the kidney disease which eventually caused his death. In 1920 he returned to Berlin to direct a master-class in composition at the Prussian Academy of Arts, where his pupils included Stefan Wolpe and Kurt Weill; but he died in July 1924, leaving unfinished the final scene of his *magnum opus*, the opera *Doktor Faust*.

CATALOGUE OF WORKS

1. Ave Maria Op. 1. For voice and piano. 1877. Ded. Angelo Masini. Pub. 1878, Cranz.

2. Cinq Pièces Op. 3. For piano. 1877.
1. *Preludio*; 2. *Menuetto*; 3. *Gavotta*; 4. *Etude*; 5. *Giga*.
Pub. 1877, Spina (Vienna).

3. Trois Morceaux Op. 4–6. For piano. 1877. Ded. Mme de Preleuthner.
1. *Scherzo* Op. 4.
2. *Preludio e fuga* Op. 5.
3. *Scena di ballo* Op. 6.
Pub. 1884, Wetzler (Vienna).

4. Scherzo Op. 8. From a sonata for piano. 1877. Ded. Filippo Dr. Filippi. Pub. 1880, Lucca (Milan).

5. Ave Maria Op. 2. For voice and piano. 1878. Ded. Princess Maria Stcherbatoff. Pub. 1879, Cranz.

6. Racconti fantastici Op. 12. Three Characteristic Pieces for piano. 1878. Ded. S. Golinelli.
1. *Duello*; 2. *Klein Zaches*; 3. *La caverna di Steenfoll*.
Pub. 1882, Trebbi (Bologna).

7. Minuetto Op. 14. For piano. 1878. Ded. Paula Flamm. Pub. 1880, Lucca (Milan).

8. Preludo e Fuga in stile libero (in C minor) Op. 21. For piano. Ded. L. F. Casamorata. Pub. 1880, Lucca (Milan).

9. Gavotta Op. 25. For piano. 1878. Ded. Paula Flamm. Pub. 1880, Lucca (Milan).

10. Lied der Klage (Sons of the Morning, Op. 38 (O. von Kapff). For voice and piano, 1878. Ded. E. Polko. Pub. 1879, Spina.

11. Una Festa di Villaggio Op. 9. Six Characteristic Pieces for piano. Ded. Angelo and Fanny Speckel.
1. *Preparazioni alla Festa*; 2. *Marcia trionfale*; 3. *In chiesa*; 4. *La fiera*; 5. *Danza*; 6. *Notte*.
Pub. 1882, Lucca (Milan).

12. Tre pezzi nello stile antico Op. 10. For piano.
1. *Minuetto*. Ded. Ernesto Colombani.
2. *Sonatina*. Ded. G. Gaiani.

3. *Gigue*. Ded. Alessandro Busi. Pub. 1882, Lucca (Milan).

13. Danze antiche Op. 11. For piano.
1. *Minuetto*. Ded. Riccardo Eckhel.
2. *Gavotta*. Ded. Giulio Fumagalli.
3. *Gigue*. Ded. Giuseppe Sinico.
Pub. 1882, Lucca (Milan).

14. Danza notturna Op. 13. For piano. Pub. 1882, Trebbi (Bologna).

15. Zwei hebräische Melodien Op. 15 (Byron). For voice and piano. Ded. C. Gomperz-Bettelheim.
1. *Ich sah die Thräne* (I saw thee weep); 2. *An Babylons Wassern* (The waters of Babylon).
Pub. 1884, Gutmann; Universal-Edition.

16. Zwei Gesänge Op. 24. For low voice and piano. 1879.
1. *Lied des Monmouth: Es zieht sich eine blut'ge Spur* (Th. Fontane).
2. *Es ist bestimmt in Gottes Rath* (E. von Feuchtensleben). Ded. Melanie Mayer.
Pub. 1887, Kahnt (Leipzig).

17. Preludio e Fuga Op. 36. For piano. Ded. Alfredo Catalani.
1. *Prelude (Allegro)*; 2. *Fuga (Allegro maestoso)*.
Pub. 1882, Lucca (Milan).

18. Menuetto capriccioso Op. 61. For piano. 1879. Ded. Josefine von Wetheimstein. Pub. 1880, Spina (Vienna).

19. Gavotte Op. 70. For piano. 1880. Ded. Baroness Sophie von Todesco. Pub. 1880, Kranz.

20. Prelude and Fugue Op. 7. For organ. 1881. Ded. W. Mayer.
fEbp: 16 March 1936, Fernando Germani, organ of Concert Hall, Broadcasting House.
Pub. 1881, Cranz.

21. String Quartet No. 1 in C major Op. 19. 1880–1. Ded. Julius Heller.
1. *Allegro moderato, patetico*; 2. *Andante*; 3. *Leggiero e grazioso*; 3. *Finale: Andante con moto, alla Marcia*.
Pub. 1886, Kistner (Leipzig).

22. Zweite Balletszene Op. 20. For piano. Ded. Anna Weiss-Busoni. Pub. 1885, Breitkopf & Härtel.

23. Preludes Op. 37. For piano. 1879–81. Dated: November 1881, Milan.

1. Moderato (C major); 2. *Andantino sostenuto (A minor);* 3. *Andante con moto (G major);* 4. *Allegretto (E minor);* 5. *Vivace assai quasi presto (D major);* 6. *Moderato (B minor);* 7. *Allegro vivace (A major);* 8. *Allegro moderato (F-sharp minor);* 9. *Allegretto vivace e con brio (E major);* 10. *Vivace ed energico (C-sharp minor);* 11. *Allegretto piacevole 'alla danza' (B major);* 12. *Andantino (G-sharp minor);* 13. *Allegretto scherzando (F-sharp major);* 14. *Lento funebre (E-flat minor);* 15. *Andantino sostenuto (D-flat major);* 16. *Maestoso ed energico (B-flat minor);* 17. *Allegretto vivace (A-flat major);* 18. *Allegretto con moto (F minor);* 19. *Allegro vivo (E-flat major);* 20 *Allegro moderato (C minor);* 21. *Andantino sostenuto (B-flat major);* 22. *Vivace e scherzoso (G minor);* 23. *Allegro vivace (F major);* 24. *Presto (D minor).*

Pub. 1882, Lucca (Milan); 1928, repr. 1949, Ricordi.

24. Six Etudes Op. 16. For piano. 1883. Ded. J. Brahms. Pub. 1883, Gutmann (Vienna).

25. Etude (en forme d'Adagio d'une Sonate). For piano. ?1883. Intended for Op. 16. Ded. Gussy Cottlow. Unpub.

26. Two Etudes. For piano. 1883. Intended for Op. 16.

1. Etude (Nocturne in B minor); 2. *Etude in F minor.*

?Unpub.

27. Piano Sonata in F minor. 1883. Ded. Anton Rubinstein. Unpub.

28. Etude in Form von Variationen Op. 17. For piano. Ded. Johannes Brahms. Pub. 1884, Gutmann; Schirmer; Breitkopf & Härtel.

29. Zwei altdeutsche Lieder Op. 18. For voice and piano. Ded. Pie von Sicherer.

1. Wohlauf! Der Kühle Winter ist vergangen (Neidhard von Reuenthal).

2. Unter der Linden (Walter von der Vogelweide).

Pub. 1885, Kistner & Siegel.

30. Variationen und Fuge Op. 22. For piano. 1884. Ded. Carl Reinecke. In free form, on Chopin's C-minor Prelude Op. 28 No. 20.

Pub. 1885, Breitkopf & Härtel. For revised version see No. 92.

31. Two songs. For voice and piano.

1. Wer hat das erste Lied erdacht? (V. Blüthgen). 1880.

2. Bin ein fahrender Gesell (R. Baumbach). ?1884.

Pub. 1884, Vicentini (Trieste).

32. Album vocale Op. 30. For voice and piano. 1884.

1. Il fiore del pensiero (Ferdinand Busoni).

2. L'ultimo sonno (Michele Buono).

3. Un organetto suona per la via (Lorenzo Stecchetti).

4. Ballatella (Arrigo Boito).

Pub. 1884, Vicentini (Trieste); ?1890, Carlo Schmidl (Trieste).

33. Marcia di paesani e contadine Op. 32. For piano. Composed as an additional number for Op. 9. Pub. 1883, Lucca.

34. Macchiette medioevali Op. 33. For piano.

1. Dama (Moderato); 2. *Cavaliere (Veloce);* 3. *Paggio (Vivace);* 4. *Guerriero (Tempo di marcia);* 5. *Astrologo (Sostenuto);* 6. *Trovatore (Moderato).*

Pub. 1883, Trebbi (Bologna).

35. Serenata Op. 34. For cello and piano. 1882. Ded. Francesco Serato. Pub. Lucca (Milan).

36. Ave Maria Op. 35. For baritone and orchestra or piano. 1882. Ded. Nicola Bezzi.

2 fl, 2 ob, 2 cl, 2 bsn; 4 hn, 2 tpt; strings.

Pub. Lucca (Milan).

37. Fantasie über Motive aus 'Der Barbier von Bagdad', komische Oper von Peter Cornelius. For piano. Pub. 1887, Kahnt (Leipzig).

38. Kleine Suite Op. 23. For cello and piano. 1886. Ded. Alwin Schroeder.

1. Moderato, ma energico; 2. *Andantino con grazia;* 3. *Sostenuto ed espressivo;* 4. *Allegro moderato, ma con brio.*

?fEp: 7 October 1907, Manchester, James Richardson.

Pub. 1886, Breitkopf & Härtel.

39. Symphonisches Suite Op. 25. For orchestra. 1888. Ded. Hans Richter.

1. *Praeludium*; 2. *Gavotte*; 3. *Gigue*; 4. *Langsames Intermezzo*; 5. *Alla breve* (*Allegro fugato*).

3 fl, pic, 3 ob, ca, 3 cl, bcl, 3 bsn; 4 hn, 3 tpt, 3 tmb, bs tuba; 2 timp, cym, tgle; strings.

Pub. 1888, Kahnt (Leipzig).

40. String Quartet No. 2 in D minor Op. 26. 1889. Ded. Henri Petri.

1. *Allegro energico*; 2. *Andante con moto*; 3. *Vivace assai*; 4. *Andantino*.

fEp announced for spring 1901, Jan Mulder concert in Salle Erard, but cancelled.

Pub. 1889, Breitkopf & Härtel.

41. Finnländische Volksweisen Op. 27. For piano, four hands. Ded. Anna Lindelöf.

1. *Andante molto espressivo—Allegretto moderato* (*Alla marcia*); 2. *Andantino—Tranquillo—Vivace*.

Pub. 1889, Peters (Leipzig); 1953, Peters.

42. Bagatellen Op. 28. For violin and piano. Ded. Egon Petri.

1. *Aus der Zopfzeit*; 2. *Kleiner Mohrentanz*; 3. *Wiener Tanzweise*; 4. *Kosakenritt*.

Pub. 1888, Peters (Leipzig).

43. Violin Sonata in E minor Op. 29. 1890. Ded. Adolf Brodsky.

1. *Allegro deciso*; 2. *Molto sostenuto*; 3. *Allegro molto e deciso*.

fEp: 28 November 1903, St. James's Hall, Saturday Popular Concert, Johann Kruse and Egon Petri.

fEbp: 15 September 1932, Sascha Lasserson and Lonie Basche.

Pub. 1891, Rahter (Leipzig); ?1921, Breitkopf & Härtel.

44. Zwei Klavierstücke Op. 30. 1890.

1. *Kontrapunktisches Tanzstück*; 2. *Kleine Ballet—Scene III*.

Pub. Rahter.

44a. Zwei Tanzstücke Op. 30a. For piano. ?1914.

1. *Waffentanz*; 2. *Friedenstanz*.

fEbp: 29 November 1936, Egon Petri.

Pub. Rahter.

45. Konzertstück (Introduction & Allegro) Op. 31a. For piano and orchestra. Ded. Anton Rubinstein.

2 fl, 2 ob, 2 cl, 2 bsn; 4 hn, 2 tpt, 3 tmb; timp; strings.

fEbp: 3 November 1935, BBC broadcast, Egon Petri and the BBC Orchestra, cond. Sir Henry Wood.

Pub. 1892, Breitkopf & Härtel.

46. Kultaselle. Ten Variations on a Finnish folksong for cello and piano. *c.* 1891. Ded. Professor Alfred von Glehn, Moscow.

?fEp: 9 January 1908, Julius Klengel and Egon Petri.

Pub. ?1891, Dietrich (Leipzig); Breitkopf & Härtel.

47. Symphonisches Tongedicht Op. 32a. For orchestra. 1888-9, rev. 1893. Ded. Artur Nikisch.

1. *Sostenuto—Allegro con fuoco*; 2. *Allegro moderato, ma deciso*; 3. *Moderato, un poco alla Marcia*.

3 fl, pic, 2 ob, ca, 2 cl, bcl, 2 bsn, cbsn; 4 hn, 3 tpt, 3 tmb, tuba; 3 timp, cym, tgle, side dm, GC, glock; hp, strings (16-16-12-10-8).

Pub. 1892, Breitkopf & Härtel.

48. Vierte Ballet Szene in Form eines Concert-Walzers Op. 33. For piano. 1892. Ded. Carl Stasny.

48a. Vierte Ballett-Szene (Walzer und Galopp) Op. 33a. For piano. Revised version of preceding. Ded. Carl Stasny. Pub. 1913, Breitkopf & Härtel.

49. Stücke Op. 33b. For piano. Ded. Max Reger (Nos. 1-3), Mrs. Isabella S. Gardner, Boston (Nos. 4-6).

1. *Schwermuth*; 2. *Frohsinn*; 3. *Scherzino*; 4. *Fantasia in modo antico*; 5. *Finnische Ballade*; 6. '*Exeunt omnes*'.

fEbp (No. 4): 29 November 1936, Egon Petri.

Pub. 1896, Peters (Leipzig).

50. Violin Concerto in D major Op. 35a. 1896-7. Ded. Henri Petri.

3 fl, pic, 2 ob, 2 cl, 2 bsn; 4 hn, 2 tpt, 3 tmb, tuba; 3 timp, tgle, GC & cym; strings.

fEp: 24 September 1913, Queen's Hall, Promenade Concert, Arthur Catterall and the Queen's Hall Orchestra, cond. Sir Henry Wood.

Busoni, Ferruccio

fEbp: 22 January 1932, Joseph Szigeti and BBC Orchestra, cond. Sir Adrian Boult.
Pub. 1899, Breitkopf & Härtel.

BIBLIOGRAPHY:
Gerald Abraham: Busoni's Violin Concerto, *Radio Times*, 17 November 1933, p. 480.

51. Violin Sonata No. 2 in E minor Op. 36a. 1898. Ded. Ottokar Nováček.
fEp: February 1902, London, Adolf Brodsky and W. H. Dayas.
fEbp: 1 February 1938, Arthur Catterall and R. J. Forbes.
Pub. 1901, Breitkopf & Härtel.

52. Zweite-Orchestersuite (Geharnischte Suite) Op. 34a. 1895, rev. 1903. Ded. Den 'Leskowiten' in Helsingfors (1897).
 1. *Vorspiel.* Ded. Jean Sibelius.
 2. *Kriegstanz.* Ded. Adolf Paul.
 3. *Grabdenkmal.* Ded. Armas Järnefelt.
 4. *Ansturm.* Ded. Eero Järnefelt.
2 fl, 2 ob, ca, 2 cl, bcl, 2 bsn; 4 hn, 3 tpt, 3 tmb, tuba; 3 timp, side dm, cym; strings.
Pub. 1905 (full score), Breitkopf & Härtel.

53. Lustspielouvertüre (Comedy Overture) Op. 38. For orchestra. 1897, rev. 1904.
2 fl, pic, 2 ob, 2 cl, 2 bsn; 4 hn, 2 tpt; 2 timp, GC & cym, tgle; strings.
fEp: 20 October 1906, Queen's Hall, Promenade Concert, Queen's Hall Orchestra, cond. Sir Henry Wood.
fEbp: 22 January 1932, BBC Orchestra, cond. Sir Adrian Boult.
Pub. 1904, Breitkopf & Härtel.

54. Piano Concerto Op. 39. 1903-4. Dated: 3 August 1904.
 1. *Prologo e Introito* (Allegro, dolce e solenne).
 2. *Pezzo giocoso* (Vivacemente, ma senza fretta).
 3. *Pezzo serioso* (Introductio: Andante sostenuto, pensoso—Prima pars: Andante, quasi Adagio—Alters pars: Sommessamente—Ultimo pars: A tempo, Andante idillico.
 4. *All'Italiana* (Vivace).
 5. *Cantico* (Largamente—Allegro con fuoco).
3 fl, 2 pic, 3 ob, ca, 3 cl, bcl, 3 bsn; 4 hn, 3 tpt, 3 tmb, bs tuba; 3 timp, tamb mil, GC,

tamb, tgle, cym, glock, tamtam; strings (12-10-8-8-8); men's chorus of 48 voices.
fp: 10 November 1904, Berlin, Ferruccio Busoni, cond. Karl Muck.
fEp: 22 October 1909, Newcastle Festival, Egon Petri and the London Symphony Orchestra, cond. Ferruccio Busoni.
f London p: 8 June 1910, Queen's Hall, Mark Hambourg and the New Symphony Orchestra with the Edward Mason Choir, cond. Ferruccio Busoni.
fEbp: 21 February 1934, Egon Petri, Wireless Chorus and BBC Symphony Orchestra, cond. Sir Adrian Boult.
Pub. 1906, Breitkopf & Härtel; reduction for two pianos by Egon Petri pub. 1909, Breitkopf & Härtel.

BIBLIOGRAPHY:
Havergal Brian: Busoni's Piano Concerto, *Radio Times*, 15 February 1934, p. 450.
Donald Mitchell: An enigmatic piano concerto, *The Listener*, 2 June 1960, p. 993.
Denis Stevens: Piano Concerto, in *The Concerto*, Pelican Books (London) 1952, p. 286.
Francis B. Westbrooke: Busoni's Concerto in C, *Choir*, July 1935, p. 150.

55. Turandot Suite Op. 41. For orchestra. 1904.
 1. *Die Hinrichtung, Das Stadttor, Der Abschied.*
 2. *Truffaldino* (Introduzione e marcia grotesca).
 3. *Altoum* (March).
 4. *Turandot* (March).
 5. *Das Frauengemach.*
 6. *Tanz und Gesang.*
 7. *Nächtlicher Walzer.*
 8. *In modo di Marcia funebre & Finale alla Turca.*
3 fl, pic, 3 ob, ca, 3 cl, bcl, 3 bsn, cbsn; 4 hn, 4 tpt, 3 tmb, tuba; 2 pic timp, 3 timp, tamtam, GC & cym, campanelli, tgle, tamb, tamburo; hp, strings.
fp: 21 October 1905, Berlin, Beethoven-Saal, cond. Ferruccio Busoni.
fEp: 21 August 1906, Queen's Hall, Promenade Concert, Queen's Hall Orchestra, cond. Sir Henry Wood.
fEbp: 14 September 1925, Newcastle

Station Symphony Orchestra, cond. Edward Clark.

Pub. 1906 (full score), Breitkopf & Härtel.

55a. Turandot. Incidental music for version by Karl Vollmöller of the play by Gozzi.

fp: 27 October 1911, Berlin, Deutsches Theater; producer, Max Reinhardt.

55b. Turandot. Opera in two acts. 1917. Libretto: Ferruccio Busoni, after C. Gozzi. Ded. Arturo Toscanini.

fp: 11 May 1917, Zürich.

f Ebp: 12 January 1947, NWDR (Hamburg) recording, NWDR Symphony Orchestra, cond. Jarnach; with Klara Ebers (Turandot), Wilhelm Lückert (Kalaf), Theo Herman (Altoum), Gustav Neidlinger (Barak).

Pub. 1919 (vocal score), Breitkopf & Härtel.

BIBLIOGRAPHY:

Giovanni Carli Ballola: La Turandot di FB, *La Rassegna musicale*, 1962, p. 133.

G. Guerrini: La Turandot di FB, *Il Musicista* (Rome), March–April 1940.

— La Turandot di G. Puccini e quella di FB, *Illustrazione Toscana e dell'Etruria*, April 1940.

Fernando Previtali: Turandot, *La Rassegna musicale*, 1940, p. 38.

E.S.: Turandot, Princess of China, *MMR*, 1913, p. 40.

Ronald Stevenson: Busoni's Turandot, *The Listener*, 14 April 1966, p. 556.

56. Elegien (7 Klavierstücke). 1907.

1. *Nach der Wendung* (Recueillement). Ded. Gottfried Galston.

2. *All'Italia!* (In modo napolitano). Ded. Egon Petri.

3. *'Meine Seele bangt und hofft zu Dir . . .'* (Choralvorspiel). Ded. Gregor Beklemischeff.

4. *Turandots Frauengemach* (Intermezzo). Ded. Michael von Zadora.

5. *Die Nächtlichen* (Walzer). Ded. O'Neil Phillips.

6. *Erscheinung* (Notturno). Ded. Leo Kestenberg.

7. *Berceuse.* Ded. Johan Wijsman (Wysman).

f London p: 1 February 1912, Bechstein Hall, Ursula Newton.

f Ebp (No. 4): 16 October 1927, Arthur Rubinstein.

f Ebp (omitting one): 7 January 1929, Eduard Steuermann.

Pub. 1908–9, Breitkopf & Härtel.

57. Nuit de Noël (Esquisse). For piano. 1908. Ded. Frida Kindler.

f Ebp: 8 August 1935, Frida Kindler.

Pub. 1909, Durand.

58. An die Jugend. For piano. 1909 (? 1908).

1. *Preludietto, Fughetta ed Esercizio.* Ded. Josef Turczynski.

2. *Preludio, Fuga e Fuga figurata* (Studie nach J. S. Bach's Wohltemperiertem Klavier). Ded. Louis Theodor Grünberg.

3. *Giga, Bolero e Variazione* (Studie nach Mozart). Ded. Leo Sirota.

4. (i) *Introduzione e Capriccio* (Paganinesco). Ded. Louis Closson.

(ii) *Epilogo.* Ded. Emile R. Blanchet.

f Ebp (No. 3): 17 April 1934, Philip Lèvi.

f Ebp (No. 4(i)): 28 September 1937, Philip Lèvi.

f Ebp (No. 1): 4 December 1936, Egon Petri.

Pub. 1909, Zimmermann (Leipzig).

59. Fantasia (nach Sebastian Bach). For piano. 1909. Ded. to the memory of the composer's father, Ferdinando Busoni.

?f Ep: 4 October 1912, Liverpool, Philharmonic Hall, Ferruccio Busoni.

f Ebp: 7 November 1938, Eiluned Davies.

Pub. 1909, Breitkopf & Härtel.

60. Berceuse élégiaque Op. 42. 'Des Mannes Wiegenlied am Sarge seiner Mutter' —Poesie for orchestra. October 1909, London. Ded. 'In memoriam Anna Busoni, N. Weiss, M.3.Oct. MCMIX'.

3 fl, ob, 2 cl, bcl; 4 hn; gong; celesta, hp, strings.

f Ep: 5 June 1912, Queen's Hall, Queen's Hall Orchestra, cond. Ferruccio Busoni.

Pub. 1910, Breitkopf & Härtel.

61. Grosse Fugue (Kontrapunktische Fantasie über J. S. Bachs letztes unvollendetes Werk). For piano. Dated: New Year 1910, aboard the steamship *Barbarossa*—1 March 1910, New Orleans. Ded. Wilhelm Middelschulte.

Fuga I (Tempo giusto)—Fuga II—Fuga III—Intermezzo—Variazione 1—Variazione 2—Variazione 3—Cadenza—Fuga IV—Stretta.
Pub. 1910, Schirmer. Limited edition.

61a. Fantasia contrappuntistica. For piano. June 1910. Ded. Wilhelm Middelschulte.

Preludio corale—Fuga I—Fuga II—Fuga III—Intermezzo—Variazione I—Variazione II—Variazione III—Cadenza—Fuga IV—Corale—Stretta.
fEbp: 1 November 1929, Eduard Steuermann.
Pub. 1910, Breitkopf & Härtel.

61b. Preludio al corale e fuga sopra un frammento di Bach (Edizione minore della 'Fantasia contrappuntistica'). For piano. 1912. Ded. Richard Bühlig. Pub. 1912, Breitkopf & Härtel.

61c. Fantasia contrappuntistica. Version for organ by W. Middelschulte (in collab. with Busoni). Pub. 1912, Breitkopf & Härtel.

61d. Fantasia contrappuntistica. Version for two pianos.
fEp: 18 February 1922, Wigmore Hall, Ferruccio Busoni and Egon Petri.

61e. Fantasia contrappuntistica. Version for orchestra.

62. Sonatina No. 1. For piano. 1910. Ded. Rudolph Ganz.
fEbp: 7 May 1928, Eduard Steuermann.
Pub. 1910, Zimmermann (Leipzig).

63. Sonatina seconda. For piano. 1912. Ded. Mark Hambourg.
fEbp: 7 May 1928, Eduard Steuermann.
Pub. 1912, Breitkopf & Härtel.

64. Nocturne symphonique Op. 43. For orchestra. 1912. Ded. Oskar Fried.
3 fl, ob, ca, 2 cl, bcl, 2 bsn, cbsn; 3 hn; 3 timp, GC & cym, tamtam; celesta, hp, strings (12-10-8-8-6).
Pub. 1914, Breitkopf & Härtel.

65. Die Brautwahl Op. 45. Opera (Musical Fantasy Comedy) in three acts. 1908–11. Ded. Gustave Brecher.
3 fl, pic, 3 ob, ca, 2 cl, bcl, 3 bsn, cbsn; 4 hn, 3 tpt, 3 tmb, tuba; cornet à piston; 4 timp, 2 cym, tamb, GC, tgle, xyl, tamtam, glock; organ, celesta, hp, strings.
fp: 13 April 1912, Hamburg, cond.

Brecher; with Von Scheidt (Leonhard), Lohfing (Manasseh), Wiedemann (Melchior Voswinkel), Marak (Edmund Lehsen), Birrenkoven (Thusman), Fräulein Puritz-Schumann (Albertine); sets, Karl Walser.
Pub. (full score) 1914, Harmonie (Berlin); (vocal score) 1914, Breitkopf & Härtel.

BIBLIOGRAPHY:
Rudolf Cahn-Speyer: Busonis Brautwahl in ihrem stilistischen Verhältnis zur modernen Opernproduktion, *Die Musik*, May 1912, p. 246.
H. W. Draber: FB, Die Brautwahl, *NMZ*, May 1912.
August Spanuth: Die Brautwahl, *Signale*, 1912, No. 16 (17 April), p. 527.
H. H. Stuckenschmidt: Busonis Brautwahl, *SM*, November–December 1962, p. 344.
L. Thurneiser: Die Brautwahl, eine Berlinische Oper Busonis, *Melos*, October 1925.
Karl Westermayer: Busonis Brautwahl, *Signale*, 1926, No. 3, p. 77.

65a. Die Brautwahl: Suite Op. 45. For orchestra. Ded. Curt Sobernheim.
1. *Spukhaftes Stück* (Ghostly music).
2. *Lyrisches Stück* (Lyrical music).
3. *Mystiches Stück* (Mystic music).
4. *Hebräisches Stück* (Hebrew music).
5. *Heiteres Stück* (Joyous music).
3 fl, 3 pic, 3 ob, ca, 2 cl, bcl, 3 bsn, cbsn; 4 hn, 3 tpt, 3 tmb, tuba; timp, glock, xyl, tgle, tamb, GC & cym; celesta, hp, strings.
fEp: 22 June 1920, Queen's Hall, London Symphony Orchestra, cond. Ferruccio Busoni.
Pub. 1917, Breitkopf & Härtel.

66. Indianische Fantasie Op. 44. For piano and orchestra. 1913. Ded. Natalie Curtis.
2 fl, ob, ca, 2 cl, 2 bsn; 3 hn, 2 tpt; timp, glock, tgle, tamtam, tamb mil, GC & cym; hp, strings.
fEp: 22 June 1920, Queen's Hall, Ferruccio Busoni and the London Symphony Orchestra, cond. Julius Harrison.
fEbp: 16 December 1935, Eileen Joyce and BBC Orchestra, cond. Constant Lambert.
Pub. 1915, Breitkopf & Härtel.

67. Rondo Arlecchinesco Op. 46. For orchestra. 1915. Ded. Frederick Stock.

2 fl, 2 pic, ob, 2 cl, 2 bsn; 3 hn, 2 tpt, 3 tmb; 3 timp, glock, tgle, tamb, tamburo, cym; tenor voice; strings.

fEp: 14 March 1921, Queen's Hall, New Queen's Hall Orchestra, cond. Sir Henry Wood.

Pub. 1917, Breitkopf & Härtel.

68. Indianisches Tagebuch Op. 47. Erstes Buch: Vier Klavierstudien über Motive der Rothäute Amerikas. For piano. 1915. Ded. Helen Luise Birch.

1. *Allegretto affettuoso, un poco agitato*; 2. *Vivace*; 3. *Andante*; 4. *Maestoso ma andando*.

fEbp: 17 April 1934, Philip Lèvi.

Pub. 1916, Breitkopf & Härtel.

68a. Indianisches Tagebuch Op. 47. Zweites Buch: Gesang vom Reigen der Geister. For orchestra. 1915. Ded. Charles Martin Loeffler.

fl, ob, cl, bsn; tpt, tmb; timp; strings.

fEbp: 11 July 1926, Newcastle Station Symphony Orchestra, cond. Edward Clark.

Pub. 1916, Breitkopf & Härtel.

69. Improvisation über das Bachsche Chorallied 'Wie wohl ist mir'. For two pianos. Dated: June 1916, S. Remigio—August 1916, Zürich. Ded. S. Della Valle di Casanova. Pub. 1917, Breitkopf & Härtel.

70. Sonatina (ad usum infantis Madeline Mx Americanae). For piano. ?1916.

1. *Molto tranquillo*; 2. *Andantino melancolico*; 3. *Vivace (alla Marcia)*; 4. *Molto tranquillo*; 5. *Polonaise*.

?fEp: 8 July 1921, Wigmore Hall, Francesco Ticciati.

fEbp: 3 December 1936, Egon Petri.

Pub. 1916, Breitkopf & Härtel.

71. Sechs Klavierübungen und Präludien (Der Klavierübung, I. Teil). For piano. Dated: 10 October 1917, Zürich. Pub. 1918, 1925, Breitkopf & Härtel.

72. Zwei Kontrapunkt-Studien (nach Joh. Seb. Bach). For piano.

1. *Fantasia and Fugue in A minor*; 2. *Variations and Fugue on a theme of Frederick the Great*.

Pub. 1917, Breitkopf & Härtel.

73. Albumblatt. For flute or muted violin and piano. ?1917. Ded. Albert Biolley. Pub. 1917, Breitkopf & Härtel.

74. Sonatina (in Diem Nativitatis Christi MCMXVII). For piano. Dated: 22 December 1917. Ded. Benvenuto (Busoni).

?fEp: 8 December 1926, LCMC concert, Francesco Ticciati.

fEbp: 7 August 1936, Frida Kindler.

Pub. 1918, Breitkopf & Härtel.

75. Arlecchino Opera ('Theatrical Capriccio') in one act. Libretto: Ferruccio Busoni. Ded. Arthur Bodanzky.

I. Satz:

1. *Einleitung, Szene und Liedchen* (Introduction, scena and canzonetta).

2. *Duet*.

3. *Trio*.

II. Satz:

4. *March and Scena*.

III. Satz:

5. *Scene & Aria, and Arietta*.

6. (a) *Romanza*; (b) *Dialogue*; (c) *Duettino*; (d) *Dialogue*; (e) *Cavatina, Stretta & Scena*.

IV. Satz:

7. *Scena, Quartet & Melodrama*.

8. *Monologue*.

9. *Procession & Final Scene*.

fl, pic, ob, ca, 2 cl, 2 bsn; 3 hn, 2 tpt, 3 tmb; 3 timp, tgle, tamb, tamb mil, cym; strings.

fp: 11 May 1917, Zürich.

fEp: 27 January 1939, BBC broadcast, BBC Orchestra, cond. Clarence Raybould; with William Parsons (Ser Matteo del Sarto), Dennis Noble (Abbate Cospicuo), Norman Allin (Dottor Bombasto), Steuart Wilson (Arlecchino), Jan van der Gucht (Leandro), Olive Groves (Colombina).

Pub. 1917 (vocal score by Philipp Jarnach), 1918 (full score), Breitkopf & Härtel.

BIBLIOGRAPHY:

Mosco Carner: The satirical harlequin, *Radio Times*, 20 January 1939, p. 13.

F. Grunfeld: Busoni and Arlecchino, *Saturday Review*, 31 March 1956, p. 44.

Vittorio Gui: Arlecchino, *La Rassegna musicale*, 1940, p. 30.

Ronald Stevenson: Busoni's Arlecchino, *MT*, June 1954, p. 307.

— FB's Arlecchino, *MO*, August 1954, p. 637.

Busoni, Ferruccio

76. Clarinet Concerto Op. 48. For clarinet and small orchestra Ded. Edmondo Allegra.
2 ob, 2 bsn; 2 hn; tgle; strings.
Pub. 1918, Breitkopf & Härtel; incl. reduction by Otto Taubman.

77. Zwei Gedichte Op. 49. For male voice and orchestra.
1 *Altoums Gebet* (from 'Turandot').
2 fl, ob, ca, 2 bsn; timp; strings (without violins).
2 *Lied des Mephistopheles* (Goethe).
2 ob, 2 cl; tpt, 2 timp; strings.
Pub. 1919, Breitkopf & Härtel.

78. Zwei Gedichte von Goethe. For voice and piano. Ded. Augustus Milner.
1 *Lied des Unmuts* (Kleinen Reimer wird man finden).
2 *Lied des Mephistopheles* (Es war einmal ein König).
fEp: 26 October 1920, London, Augustus Milner, acc. George O'Connor Morris.
Pub. 1919, Breitkopf & Härtel.

79. Drei Klavierübungen und Präludien (Der Klavierübung, II. Teil). For piano. 1917–1918. Pub. 1919, Breitkopf & Härtel.

80. Duetto Concertante. After the finale of Pinao Concerto in F major by Mozart. For two pianos. 1919.
fEbp: 18 October 1925, Charles Kelly and Lucy Pierce.
Pub. 1921, Breitkopf & Härtel.

81. Sonatina brevis (in Signo Joannis Sebastiani Magni). For piano. ?1919. Ded. Philipp Jarnach. Pub. 1919, Breitkopf & Härtel.

82. Sarabande und Cortège (Zwei Studien zu 'Doktor Faust') Op. 51. For orchestra. 1918–19 Ded. Volkmar Andreae.
1. *Sarabande.*
3 fl, ob, 2 ca, cbsn; 3 tmb; 3 timp, tamtam, GC; celesta, hp, strings.
2. *Cortège.*
3 fl, pic, 2 ob, 2 cl, bcl, 2 bsn, cbsn; 4 hn, 3 tpt, 3 tmb, tuba; 4 timp, tgle, tamburo, GC, cym; celesta, 2 hp, strings.
fEp: 22 November 1919, Queen's Hall, cond. Ferruccio Busoni.

fEbp: 15 January 1935, London Philharmonic Orchestra, cond. Leslie Heward.
Pub. 1922, Breitkopf & Härtel.

83. Lo Staccato (Der Klavierübung, III. Teil). For piano. Dated: July 1920, Zürich. Ded. Basel Musikschule & Konservatorium.
Pub. 1921, Breitkopf & Härtel.

84. Elegie. For clarinet and piano. 1920, London, Zürich. Ded. Edmondo Allegra.
Pub. 1921, Breitkopf & Härtel.

85. Kammer-Fantasie über Carmen (Sonatina No. 6). For piano. 1920. Ded. Monsieur L. Tauber.
fEbp: 29 November 1936, Egon Petri.
Pub. 1921, Breitkopf & Härtel.

86. Divertimento Op. 52. For flute and small orchestra. Ded. 'Mr. le Professeur Gaubert'.
2 ob, 2 cl, 2 bsn; 2 hn, 2 tpt; timp, tgle; strings.
Pub. 1922, Breitkopf & Härtel; incl. reduction for flute and piano by Kurt Weill.

87. Tanz-Walzer Op. 53. For orchestra. 1920. Ded. 'Dem Andenken Johann Strauss'.
fl, pic, 2 ob, 2 cl, 2 bsn; 4 hn, 2 tpt, 3 tmb; timp, glock, side dm, tgle, GC, cym; strings.
fEbp: 4 July 1926, Newcastle Station Symphony Orchestra, cond. Edward Clark.
Pub. 1921 (piano reduction by Michael von Zadora), 1922 (full score), Breitkopf & Härtel.

88. Romanza e Scherzoso (Concertino) Op. 54. For piano and orchestra. Ded. Alfredo Casella. Pub. 1922, Breitkopf & Härtel.

89. Drei Albumblätter. For piano. 1917–21.
1. (*Zürich*). 1917. Ded. Albert Biolley.
2. (*Rome*). 1921. Ded. Francesco Ticciati.
3. (*Berlin*). 1921. Ded. Felice Boghen.
f London p (No. 2): 14 December 1921, Wigmore Hall, Francesco Ticciati.
fEbp (complete): 28 November 1936, Egon Petri.
Pub. 1921, Breitkopf & Härtel.

90. Toccata (Preludio, Fantasia, Ciacona). For piano. ?1921. Ded. I. Philipp.
fEp: 19 February 1921, Wigmore Hall, Ferruccio Busoni.

fEbp: 5 September 1935, Philip Lèvi.
Pub. 1921, Universal-Edition; 1922, Breitkopf & Härtel.

91. Die Bekehrte (Goethe). For voice and piano. 1921. Ded. Frl. Artôt de Padilla. Unpub.

92. Variationen, Perpetuum mobile und Tonleitern (Der Klavierübung, V. Teil). For piano. ?1922.
 1. *Zehn Variationen über ein Präludium von Chopin*. Ded. Gino Tagliapietra.
 2. *Sechs Variationen zu Etüden und Präludien von Chopin*.
 3. *Perpetuum mobile (nach des Concertino II. Satze)*. Ded. Cella Delavrancea.
 4. *Tonleitern*.
Pub. 1922, Breitkopf & Härtel.

93. Fünf kunze Stücke zur Pflege des polyphonen Spiels. For piano. Ded. Edwin Fischer. Pub. 1923, Breitkopf & Härtel. Also pub. as Book 9 of *Der Klavierübung*, 2nd edn.

94. Zigeunerlied Op. 55 No. 2. Ballade for baritone and orchestra (Goethe). 1923.
 2 fl, 2 ob, 2 cl, 2 bsn; 2 hn; cym; strings.
fEbp: 25 March 1934, Jean Morel, with piano acc.
Pub. May 1923, in *Die Musik*; 1924 (full score), Breitkopf & Härtel.

95. Grausige geschichte vom Münzjuden Lippold. For voice and orch. 1923. Unpub.

96. Prélude & Etude (en arpèges). For piano. 1923. Pub. 1923, Heugel.

97. Schlechter Trost (Goethe). For voice and piano. 1924. Pub. 1924, in Navigare necesse est (Leipzig).

98. Doktor Faust. Unfinished opera. 1916–1924. Preface dated: 23 July 1922. Completed by Philipp Jarnach.
 1. *Symphonia* (Oster-Vesper und Frühlings-Keimen).
 2. *Vorspiel I*.
 3. *Vorspiel II*.
 4. *Intermezzo*.
 5. *Hauptspiel* (Erstes Bild).
 6. *Symphonisches Intermezzo* (Sarabande).
 7. *Zweites Bild*.
 8. *Letzter Bild*.
fp: 21 May 1925, Dresden, cond. Fritz

Busch; with Robert Burg (Doktor Faust), Theo Strack (Mephistopheles).
 fEp: 17 March 1937, Queen's Hall, BBC Choral Society and BBC Symphony Orchestra, cond. Sir Adrian Boult; with Dennis Noble (Doktor Faust), Parry Jones (Mephistopheles), Foster Richardson (Wagner), Henry Wendon (Duke), May Blyth (Duchess).
 Pub. 1926, Breitkopf & Härtel: piano score, with text, by Egon Petri and Michael von Zadora.

BIBLIOGRAPHY:
Ferruccio Busoni: Dell'Opera—Saggio d'una prefazione al Dottore Faust, *Il Pianoforte*, April 1922.
— Über die Partitur des Doktor Faust, *Blätter der Staatsoper* (Berlin), October (No. 6) 1927, p. 8; *Musik und Szene*, 1961–2, No. 9, p. 101.
Max Chop: FBs Doktor Faust in der Berliner Staatsoper (27. Oktober 1927), *Signale*, 1927, No. 44, p. 1518.
Ernst Closson: Un nouveau Faust, *La Revue belge*, 1 July 1925.
Edward Dent: Busoni a Berlino e il Dottor Faust, *Il Pianoforte*, Vol. 2, No. 6.
G. Selden Goth: Il Dottor Faust di Busoni nelle lettere a un'amica, *La Scala*, March 1954.
G. Guerrini: Intorno al Dottor Faust di FB, *Il Musicista*, September 1941.
G. Guerrini & P. Fragapane: Il Dottor Faust, Monsalvato (Florence), 1942.
Hermann Gurtler: Doktor Faust de Busoni, *RM*, 1 July 1925, p. 77.
Julius Kapp: Einführung in das Werk, *Blätter der Staatsoper* (Berlin), October (No. 6) 1927, p. 13.
E. Kerntler: Busoni, Doktor Faust, *Crescendo*, August–September 1927.
Guido Pannain: Il Dottor Faust, *La Rassegna musicale*, 1940, p. 20.
H. Platzbecker: FB, Doktor Faust—Uraufführung in der Dresdner Staatsoper, *NMZ*, 1925, No. 20, p. 476.
E. Schmitz: Busonis Doktor Faust, *Die Musik*, July 1925, p. 760.
Paul Stefan: Doktor Faust von Busoni, *Anbruch*, June–July 1925, p. 323.
H. H. Stuckenschmidt: FB, Doktor Faust,

Busoni, Ferruccio

Städtische Oper Berlin 1954, in *Oper in dieser Zeit*, Friedrich Verlag (Hannover) 1964, p. 17.

— Rede über Busonis Doktor Faust, *SM*, January 1956, p. 3.

Harold Truscott: Busoni and Doktor Faust, *The Listener*, 5 November 1959, p. 800.

Max Unger: FB, Doktor Faust, Uraufführung in der Dresdner Staatsoper, *Der Auftakt*, 1925, No. 7, p. 214.

Wladimir Vogel: Über Busonis Doktor Faust, *SM*, 1966, No. 2 (March–April), p. 66.

Kurt Weill: Busonis Faust und die Erneuerung der Opernform, *Anbruch*, January–February 1927, p. 12.

BUSONI'S ARRANGEMENTS

Several checklists of Busoni's numerous arrangements, cadenzas, transcriptions and editions exist in various standard reference works, and that in G. Guerrini's 'Busoni' (1944) also lists a number of unpublished arrangements.

BUSONI'S WRITINGS

Über Instrumentationslehre, *Die Musik*, November (1) 1905, p. 168.

Entwurf einer neuen Ästhetik der Tonkunst, Schmidl (Trieste) 1907; 2nd (enlarged) edition, Leipzig, 1910; Eng. transl. by Theodore Baker as 'Sketch of a New Esthetic of Music', New York, 1911; repr. in 'Three Classics in the Aesthetic of Music', New York, 1962.

Der mächtige Zauberer. Libretto, after Gobineau. Ded. Gerda Busoni. Pub. 1905, Schmidl (Trieste).

Lehre von der Übertragung von Orgelwerken auf das Klavier, n.d.

Versuch einer organischen Klavier-Notenschrift, Breitkopf & Härtel, 1910.

Ce que doit être une grand pianiste, *La Vie musicale*, Vol. III, No. 15.

Die Brautwahl. Libretto. Schmidl (Trieste), 1907; Berlin, 1913; Breitkopf & Härtel, 1920.

Turandot. Libretto. 1918. Breitkopf & Härtel.

Arlecchino, oder Die Fenster. 1917 (?1919), Breitkopf & Härtel.

Der Arlecchineide Fortsetzung und Ende. Unpub.

Doktor Faust: Dichtung für Musik. Dated: 30 July 1919, Zürich. Ded. Faculty of Philosophy, Zürich University. Pub. 1920, Gustav Kiepenheuer (Potsdam).

Das Wandbild (Eine Szene und eine Pantomime), Breitkopf & Härtel, 1920.

Doktor Faust. Libretto. 1920, Breitkopf & Härtel.

Gesammelte Aufsätze (Von der Einheit der Musik), Max Hesse Verlag, 1922.

Sketches and leaves from a diary, *Sackbut*, June 1921, p. 33.

An open letter, *Melos*, August 1922.

Drittltonmusik, *Melos*, 1922, Nos. 4–5, p. 198. (With English translation by H. Leichtentritt.)

Offener Musikbrief an Fritz Windisch, *Melos*, 1922, No. 2.

Was gab uns Beethoven?, *Die Musik*, October 1922, p. 19.

Aufzeichnungen und Tagebuchblätter, *Anbruch*, January 1921, p. 19.

Pensieri sull'arte e sulla musica, *Il Pianoforte*, Vol. 2, No. 6.

Mozart, *Blätter der Staatsoper* (Berlin), January 1922, p. 1.

L'insegnamento di Beethoven, *Il Pianoforte*, May 1923.

Zeitwelle, *Berliner Börsen-Courier*, 1 April 1923.

Mozarts Don Giovanni und Liszts Don Juan Fantasie, *Rheinische Musik- und Theaterzeitung*, 14 April 1923.

Das Geheimnis. Libretto, after Villier de l'Isle-Adam. Pub. November 1924 in *Blätter der Staatsoper* (Berlin).

Die Götterbraut. Libretto after L. T. Gruenberg, n.d.

Vom Wesen der Musik, *Melos*, August 1924, February 1930.

Franz Liszts Vorrede zur ersten Kollektivausgabe von Fields Nocturnes, *Die Musik*, February 1924, p. 309.

Schnitzel und Späne, *NZfM*, December 1932, p. 1059.

Briefe an seiner Frau, Rotapfel-Verlag (Erlenbach–Zürich) 1935, ed. Friedrich Schnapp with foreword by Willi Schuh; Eng. transl. as 'Letters to his Wife' by Rosamond Ley, E. Arnold (London) 1938.

Fünfundzwanzig Busoni-Briefe, Hubert

Reichner (Vienna) 1937, ed. Gisella Selden-Goth.

Die Naechtlichen, *Musica Viva* (Rhode St. Genése), No. 1, April 1936.

Briefe Busonis an Hans Huber, Hug & Co. (Zürich–Leipzig) 1939, ed. Edgar Refardt.

Anmerkungen zum 'Wohltemperierten Klavier', *SM*, February 1952, p. 49.

Wesen und Einheit der Musik, Max Hesses Verlag, 1956 (revised and edited by Joachim Herrmann).

On the nature of music, *MR*, November 1956, p. 282.

Der innere Klang, *NZfM*, September 1957.

Drei Essays, *Melos*, July–August 1958.

Scritti e pensieri sulla musica, Felice le Monnier (Florence) 1941; ed. Luigi Dallapiccola & Guido M. Gatti, with an introduction by Massimo Bontempelli.

GENERAL BIBLIOGRAPHY

D. Alderighi: FB, nei ricordi Bolignesi di un discopolo, *Il Musicista*, June 1938.

R. De Angelis: Il dualismo FB, *Rivista nazionale di musica*, 27 March 1925.

P. Baglioni: Ricordo di FB a Siena, *Bollettino dell'Accademia Musicale*, Chigiana, December 1949.

Lothar Band: FB, *NMZ*, 1925, No. 3, p. 62.

Rodolfo Barbacci: Musica pianística moderna, *America Musical* (Argentina), 20 May 1937.

Willy Bardas: Bemerkungen zu Busonis Frage: was gab uns Beethoven, *Die Musik*, December 1922, p. 203.

Paul Bekker: FB, in *Neue Musik*, 1919.

— Busoni, *Anbruch*, 1924, No. 10 (October), p. 402.

Francesco Berger: Busoni, *MMR*, 1924, p. 257.

F. Boghen: L'italianità di FB, *Rivista nazionale di musica*, September 1924.

Helge Böhmer: Busonis Zukunftsglaube, *Melos*, December 1951, p. 337.

A. Bonaccorsi: Bibliografica di FB, *Rivista nazionale di musica*, March 1932.

M. Bontempelli: Busoni teorico, *La Rassegna musicale*, 1940, p. 3.

A. Brent-Smith: FB, *MT*, February 1934, p. 113.

Andres Briner: Freiheit und Bindung im Denken von FB, *SM*, January 1956, p. 9.

A. Brugnoli: La cerebralità e il paradorsale nell'arte di FB, *Il Pianoforte*, Vol. 2, No. 6.

Gerda Busoni: Erinnerungen an FB, Afas-Musik-Verlag (Berlin) 1958.

— Il mio incontro con FB, *Musica d'oggi*, January 1960.

G. Sjöstrand Busoni: Ricordi su FB, *Bollettino Storico Empolese*, 1958, No. 4.

Alfredo Casella: Busoni pianista, *Il Pianoforte*, Vol. 2, No. 6; *La Rassegna musicale*, 1940, p. 7.

Jean Chantavoine: Chronique musicale—FB, *Revue hebdomadaire*, 17 April 1920, p. 369.

— FB, *Anbruch*, January 1921, p. 1.

— Busoni, *MQ*, 1921, p. 331.

— Busoni, écrivain, *Le Courrier musical*, 15 May 1923.

— FB, *Le Ménestrel*, 8 August 1924, p. 347.

— FB, *RM*, October 1924, p. 235.

David Chesterman: Boult remembers Busoni, *M&M*, April 1966, p. 25.

Herbert Connor: Busoni, *Signale*, 1926, No. 16, p. 629.

Johannes Conze: Offener Brief an FB, *AMZ*, 1912, No. 6.

Deryck Cooke: Busoni, classic romantic, *The Listener*, 27 April 1961, p. 757.

M. Corti: Ricordi di FB, *La Rassegna musicale*, 1940, p. 16.

U. Creighton: Reminiscences of Busoni, *Recorded Sound*, No. 8 (1962), p. 249.

Luigi Dallapiccola: Pensieri su Busoni, *La Rassegna musicale*, 1940, p. 47.

Edward J. Dent: Busoni and the pianoforte, *Athenaeum*, 24 October 1919, p. 1072.

— Busoni as composer, *Athenaeum*, 5 December 1919, p. 1294.

— The return of Busoni, *Athenaeum*, 17 December 1920, p. 844.

— Busoni und das Klavier, *Anbruch*, January 1921, p. 27.

— Busoni als Komponist, in –do–, p. 30.

— Busoni, father of the moderns, *Radio Times*, 15 January 1932, p. 120.

— FB 'italiano', *La Rassegna musicale*, 1940, p. 44.

— FB, a biography, London, 1933.

— Busoni, *The Listener*, 16 October 1935, p. 685.

— Busoni and his operas, *Opera*, July 1954, p. 391.

Busoni, Ferruccio

Max Dessoir: FB, *Vossische Zeitung*, 16 May 1925.
— Il morte di FB, *Il Pianoforte*, October 1924.
H. W. Draber: Busoni in Weimar, *Anbruch*, January 1921, p. 39.
David Drew: FB, *Music*, December 1952, p. 18.
H. Eimert: Vollender und Wegbereiter, *Musik und Szene*, 1961–2, No. 9, p. 97.
Alfred Einstein: Busoni als Briefschreiber, in *Von Schütz bei Hindemith*, Pan-Verlag (Zürich–Stuttgart) 1957, p. 134.
Richard Engländer: FB, *Nutida musik*, Vol. 6 (1962–3), No. 2, p. 23.
Erhart Ermatinger: Busoni, Briefe an seine Frau, *Neue Schweizer Rundschau*, Vol. 3 (1935–6), p. 571.
— Busoni und wir, *SM*, 1950.
Paul Ertel: FB, *NMZ*, 1908, No. 11.
E. Fischer: Busoni and Philipp, *Recorded Sound*, No. 8 (1962), p. 242.
Arthur Friedheim: Busoni und Liszt-Interpretation, *Signale*, 1909, No. 6 (10 February), p. 202.
Herbert Fryer: Recollections of Busoni, *RCM Magazine*, 1936, No. 1, p. 3.
G. M. Gatti: In memoria di FB, *Rivista musicale italiana*, December 1924.
— Busoni the magician, *MQ*, April 1925.
— FB operista, *Scenario*, October 1933, p. 519; *Ricordiana*, December 1956.
— The stage works of FB, *MQ*, 1934, p. 267.
— Operkomponist FB, *Melos*, June 1958.
Herbert Gerigk: Bemerkungen über Busoni, *Die Musik*, August 1934, p. 907.
— Neue Bemerkungen über Busoni, *Die Musik*, December 1934, p. 189.
Terence White Gervais: Busoni's continued significance, *Chesterian*, No. 173, January 1953, p. 63.
— Busoni's possible influence, *Chesterian*, No. 175, July 1953, p. 1.
— Busoni as a contemporary figure, *Chesterian*, No. 201, winter 1960.
Jan van Gilse: Busoni, herinneringen, *Caecilia en het Muziekcollege*, September 1926.
Franzpeter Goebels: Deutung und Bedeutung der Bach-Ausgaben FBs, *Die Musikforschung*, September 1964.
Siegfried Golisch: Das Wandbild, *Musica*, 1957, No. 6, p. 322.

Cecil Gray: FB, in *A Survey of Contemporary Music*, O.U.P. (London) 1927, p. 210.
— Busoni and Liszt, *Radio Times*, 27 August 1937, p. 14.
Guido Guerrini: FB, maestro, *La Rassegna musicale*, 1940, p. 51.
— FB, la vita, la figure, l'opera, Monsalvato (Florence) 1944.
— FB, *Studium*, April 1953.
— FB nei ricordi bolognesi di un discepolo, *Rassegna dell'Istruzione artistica*, 1935, Nos. 1–3; *Santa Cecilia*, March–April 1954.
A. M. Henderson: Memories of great artists, III: FB, *MM&F*, February 1932, p. 40.
— Busoni as artist and teacher, *Music Teacher*, November 1956, p. 515.
Albert K. Henschel: FB, *Schallkiste*, November 1927.
Alfred Heuss: FB, *NZfM*, 1924, p. 435.
Leopold Hirschberg: FB, *Berliner Tageblatt*, 28 July 1924.
Karl Holl: Auf Busonis Tod, *Frankfurter Zeitung*, No. 707, 21 September 1924.
— Erinnerung an Busoni, *Der Auftakt*, 1934, No. 10, p. 165.
R. Hove: Apokryfferne II, *Dansk Musiktidsskrift*, 1961, No. 4, p. 155; No. 6, p. 231.
Philipp Jarnach: Das Stilproblem der neuen Klassizität im Werker Busonis, *Anbruch*, January 1921, p. 16.
— FB, *Berliner Börsen-Courier*, No. 153, 1 April 1926.
— FB, Rede, geh, anlässlich der Busoni-Feier in Köln, *NZfM*, December 1932, p. 1050.
— In memoria di FB, *La Rassegna musicale*, 1940, p. 59.
H. Jelmoli: FBs Zürcherjahre, Zürich, 1929.
G. Kinsky: Das Bühnenschaften FBs, *SM*, 1 August 1933.
Hans Kleemann: Busoni und der Kritiker, *Signale*, 1926, No. 15, p. 538.
E. Kollin: Busoni, *Literature* (Budapest), January 1928.
Heinrich Kosnick: Busoni in der Geschichte des Klavierspiels, *AMZ*, 1934, p. 429.
— Busoni als Interpret, *SM*, February 1954, p. 59; *NZfM*, 1954, p. 403.
E.L.: FB, *Rytmus*, November 1936.
Hugo Leichtentritt: Busoni und Bach, *Anbruch*, January 1921, p. 12.
— FB, Leipzig, 1916.

Jón Leifs: Busoni, Südländer oder nord-länder?, *NMZ*, 15 November 1924 (No. 4), p. 91.
— Busonis Rasse, *Auftakt*, 1926, No. 1, p. 16.
F. Liuzzi: Busoni e la sua visione dell'arte, *L'Esame*, 1924, No. 1.
Francis Lombriser: FB, *Musikalische Rundschau der Schweiz*, June 1955.
A. Longo: FB, *L'Arte pianistica*, August–September 1924.
Laura Luzzatto: Lettere di FB, *La Rassegna musicale*, December 1936, p. 367.
Wilson G. Lyle: FB, *MO*, April 1941, p. 296.
Joseph Machlis: FB, in *Introduction to Contemporary Music*, Norton (USA) 1961, Dent (London), p. 239.
Basil Maine: Some Busoni recollections, *MO*, April 1937, p. 586.
André Mangeot: FB, William Carl, *Le Monde musical*, August 1924.
Michael Marcus: Busoni revisited, *M&M*, July 1962, p. 42.
Jean Matter: Busoni et l'art de la transcription, *Revue musicale de Suisse Romande*, June 1966, p. 3.
Wilfrid Mellers: The problem of Busoni, *M&L*, July 1937, p. 240 (Supplement to an article by the same author in *Scrutiny*, December 1936).
H. Mersmann, H. Schultze-Ritter and Heinrich Strobel: FB, *Melos*, October 1930.
Adolf Mirus: Die Meisterschule von Busoni in Weimar, *NZfM*, 1901.
Hans Joachim Moser: FB, *Berliner Börsen-Zeitung*, 31 July 1924.
E. Müller: Busoni und die Wiener Philharmoniker, *AMZ*, 1934, No. 41.
Siegfried F. Nadel: FB, Breitkopf & Härtel (Leipzig) 1931.
W. Nagel: FB als Aesthetiker, *NMZ*, 1917, No. 15, p. 239; No. 16, p. 253.
Ernest Newman: Busoni and the opera, *Sunday Times*, September 1922.
— Busoni and the opera, in *More Essays from the World of Music*, Calder (London) 1958, pp. 61, 65.
Guido Pannain: Busoni, *La Rassegna musicale*, June 1928, p. 352.
D. C. Parker: FB as pioneer, *MMR*, 1917, p. 177.

— Busoni, a personality in modern music, *MS*, 17 July 1920, p. 24.
Adolf Paul: Busoni-Erinnerungen, *Berliner Lokalanzeiger*, 25 July 1926.
Carl Johann Perl: Gedanken über FB, *Die Premiere* (Berlin), 1925, No. 3.
H. E. Pfitzner: Futuristengefahr, Bei Gelegenheit von Busonis Ästhetik, 1917.
I. Philipp: Qualche ricordo di Busoni, *L'Arte pianistica*, June–July 1925.
Paul A. Pisk: FBs Offener Musikbrief, *Anbruch*, April (Nos. 7–8) 1922, p. 104.
Lazare Ponnelle: FB, in *A Munich*, Fischbacher (Paris) 1913, p. 87.
R. Prechtel: Zweig auf Busonis Grab, *Melos*, September 1924.
Melanie Prelinger: Erinnerungen und Briefe aus FBs Jugendheit, *NMZ*, 1926, No. 1, p. 6; No. 2, p. 37; Ricordi e lettere giovanili di FB, *Il Pianoforte*, December 1926.
R. Proctor-Gregg: Busoni, pianist and composer, *Sackbut*, July 1920, p. 101.
P. Rattalino: Scritti giovanili di FB, *Musica d'oggi*, 1959, March, p. 105; April, p. 152.
E. Refardt: Briefe Busonis an Hans Huber, Zürich/Leipzig, 1939.
Willi Reich: Busoni-Briefe, *Der Auftakt*, 1936, Nos. 1–2, p. 16.
— Busoni in England, *MT*, October 1936, p. 890.
C. Righini: Un aspetto di FB, *Il Pensiero musicale*, March 1923.
Waldemar Rosen: Zu Busonis 70. Geburtstag: Schöpfertum zwischen zwei Nationen, *AMZ*, 1936, p. 269.
Edward Sackville-West: A latter-day Faust, in *Essays on Music* (an anthology of *The Listener*), Cassell (London) 1967, p. 69.
Siegfried Salomon: FB, *Die Musikwelt*, 1 August 1924.
C. Sartori: Adolescenza ardente di FB e un suo primo ignorato progretto di opera lirica, *La Rassegna musicale*, 1940, p. 183.
Adolfo Salazar: FB, in *Música y músicos de hoy*, Editorial Mundo Latino (Madrid) 1928, p. 313.
Arnolfo Santelli: Busoni, Rome, 1939.
P. Saul: Busoniana (incl. discography), *Recorded Sound*, No. 8 (1962), p. 256.
Hermann Schildberger: FB, *Oberschlesisches*

Busoni, Ferrucio

Abendblatt (Gleiwitz), No. 179, 4 August 1924.

Leopold Schmidt: Busoni als Komponist, *Der Kunstwart*, May (2) 1914, p. 254.

Friedrich Schnapp: FB, zwei autobiographische Fragmente, *Die Musik*, October 1929, p. 1.

— Busonis persönliche Beziehungen zu Anton Rubinstein, *NZfM*, December 1932, p. 1053; Busoni's personal relations to Anton Rubinstein (transl. Robert Lorenz), *MM&F*, March 1933, p. 175.

— Busonis musikalisches Schaffen, *NZfM*, December 1932, p. 1045.

— FB e Antonio Rubinstein, *La Rassegna musicale*, 1940, p. 63.

Harold C. Schonberg: Recalling Busoni— Mitropoulos remembers teacher with affection, *New York Times*, 7 October 1951.

R. Schulz-Dornburg: FB, *Das Musikleben*, October 1950.

P. Schwers: FB, *AMZ*, 8 August 1924.

Gisella Selden-Goth: FB, E. P. Tal & Co. (Leipzig, Vienna) 1922.

— Das Goethesche in Busoni, *Anbruch*, January 1921, p. 37.

— FB, *Pan* (Milan), 1934, Fasc. I, p. 76.

— Fünf und zwanzig Busoni-Briefe, Vienna, 1937.

— FB, un profilo, Leo S. Olschki (Florence) 1934.

James Simon: Der musikalische Stil, *Anbruch*, January 1921, p. 32.

— FB, *Ur Nutidens Musikliv*, April 1924.

Larry Sitsky: FB's 'Attempt at an organic notation for the Pianoforte' and a practical adaptation of it, *MR*, February 1968, p. 27.

August Spanuth: Der verdächtigte Busoni, *Signale*, 1911, No. 9 (1 March), p. 327.

— Zur Busoni-Biographie, *Signale*, 1916, No. 43 (25 October), p. 723.

Paul Stefan: Busoni, *Der Auftakt*, September 1925, p. 241.

— Bildnis Busonis, *Anbruch*, April–May 1933, p. 49.

Ronald Stevenson: Busoni and Mozart, *The Score*, No. 13, September 1955, p. 25.

— Busoni, the legend of a prodigal, *The Score*, No. 15, March 1956, p. 15.

— Busoni e la Gran Bretagna, *Bollettino Storico Empolese*, No. 4, 1958.

E. van der Straeten: Obituary, FB, *Strad*, September 1924, p. 256.

Heinrich Strobel: Busonis Briefe an seine Frau, *Neues Musikblatt*, 1936, No. 13, p. 4.

H. H. Stuckenschmidt: FB, in *Schöpfer der neuen Musik*, Suhrkamp Verlag (Frankfurt a.M.) 1958, p. 9.

— FB als Komponist, *SM*, 1967, No. 4 (July–August), p. 191.

— FB, Zeittafel eines Europäers, Atlantis Verlag (Zürich) 1967; FB, Chronicle of a European (transl. Sandra Morris), Calder & Boyars (London) 1970.

M. H. S. Sulzberger: FB nel ricordo di un discepolo, *La Rassegna musicale*, 1940, p. 67.

Joseph Szigeti: Some personal memories of Busoni, *Radio Times*, 27 August 1937, p. 15.

G. Tagliapietra: FB trascrittore e revisore, *La Rassegna musicale*, 1940, p. 12.

Karl Thiessen: Busoni als Erfinder einer neuen Notenschrift, *Signale*, 1910, No. 45 (9 November), p. 1685.

Ernst Tobler: FB, *Neue Zürcher Zeitung*, 29–30 July 1924.

Harold Truscott: Busoni the composer, *The Listener*, 10 May 1962, p. 829.

F. Vatielli: FB a Bologna, *La Rassegna musicale*, 1938, p. 417.

Roman Vlad: Busoni's destiny, *The Score*, No. 7, December 1952, p. 3; Destino di Busoni, *La Rassegna musicale*, April 1953, p. 122.

Vladimir Vogel: Aus der Zeit Meisterklasse Busoni, *SM*, May–June 1964, p. 165.

John C. G. Waterhouse: Busoni into focus, *M&M*, April 1966, p. 24.

Marga Weigert: Busoni at Weimar in 1901, *MR*, February 1954, p. 47.

Adolf Weissmann: FB, *Die Musik*, 1924, No. 12 (September), p. 887.

Militza von Witt: Aus Briefen Busonis, *Deutsche Allgemeine Zeitung*, 8 May 1931.

Kurt von Wolfurt: FB, *Berliner Börsen-Zeitung*, 27 October 1927.

Michael Zadora: Erlebnisse mit Busoni, *Vossische Zeitung*, 11 January 1933.

Reinhold Zimmermann: Zu FBs Volkstum, *NMZ*, 1925, No. 8 (15 January), p. 186.

Paul Zschorlich: Busonis Briefe an seine Frau, *AMZ*, 1936, p. 271.

MISCELLANEOUS OR UNSIGNED

Busoni spricht, *Signale*, 1909, No. 4 (27 January), p. 125.

Busoni über Amerika, *Signale*, 1910, No. 45 (9 November), p. 1685.

Offener Musikbrief von FB in den Herausgeber, *Melos*, 1922, No. 2.

FB Werk-Verzeichnis, Breitkopf & Härtel (Leipzig) 1924.

FB, *AMZ*, 1924, Nos. 31–32, p. 574.

Briefe und Zeichnungen Busonis, *Vossische Zeitung Musikbeilage*, No. 6, 11 October 1924.

Zeitwelle—Musikalische Betrachtungen von FB, *Blätter der Staatsoper* (Berlin), October 1924, p. 6.

Busoni, by one of his pupils, *The Gramophone* (Player-Piano Supplement), November 1924, p. 3.

FB, *Der Fränkische Bund*, January 1925.

Unveröffentlichte Briefe Busonis an seine Frau, *Deutsche Allg. Zeitung*, April 1925.

Bibliothek FB—Auktion 96, am 30. und 31. März 1925, Max Perl, Antiquariat (Berlin) 1925.

Aus einem Briefwechsel Busonis mit Hans Reinhardt, *Individualitet*, October 1926.

Aus unveröffentlichten Briefen, *Blätter der Staatsoper* (Berlin), October (No. 6) 1927, p. 1.

Busoni Briefe, *NMZ*, 1928, No. 2, p. 46.

FB, cennibiografici bibliografica, *Bollettino bibliografico musicale*, April 1928, p. 1.

Brief an Giuseppe Verdi, *NZfM*, December 1932, p. 1057.

Brief an Marcel Remy, *–do–*, p. 1058.

Anekdoten um Busoni, *–do–*, p. 1094.

Über Busoni, *Melos*, 1934, No. 708, p. 224.

Um das Erbe Busonis—Offener Brief an Herrn Herbert Gerigk, *Die Musik*, December 1934, p. 187.

FB schreibt an seine Frau, *Anbruch*, October 1936, p. 194.

Neue Briefe von Busoni, *Anbruch*, 1936, No. 7, p. 195.

Wie Busoni Liszt feierte, *Anbruch*, 1936, Nos. 9–10, p. 249.

Aus Busonis Briefen an seiner Frau, *Schweizerische Musikpädagogische Blätter*, 1936, p.85.

Zwei unbekannte Briefe Busonis, *Der Auftakt*, 1936, Nos. 11–12, p. 180.

Stefan Zweig über FB, *Das Musikleben*, July–August 1954, p. 280.

Briefe und Widmungen an Othmar Schoeck, *SM*, 1966, No. 3 (May–June), p. 132.

CLAUDE DEBUSSY (1862–1918)

Achille-Claude Debussy—he reversed the order of his Christian names in the early 1890s—was born on 22 August 1862 at Saint-Germain-en-Laye, where his parents kept a china shop; but in 1867 he moved with them the short distance to Paris and lived there for the rest of his life, except for holidays, study in Rome and professional engagements abroad (including seven visits to London). He attended the Paris Conservatoire from 1872 until 1884, when he won the Grand Prix de Rome (at the third attempt) with *l'Enfant Prodigue*. His first compositions were premièred in the early 1880s and at the same time he was employed during the summer vacations as pianist in attendance on Nadejda von Meck, Tchaikovsky's patroness, making two trips to Moscow in her entourage. After spending part of 1885–7 in Rome at the Villa Medici, Debussy settled again in Paris, forming a liaison (1889–98) with Gabrielle Dupont and meeting three men who were to have a considerable influence on his work: Stéphane Mallarmé (1887), Erik Satie (1891) and Pierre Louÿs (1893). In 1899 he married Rosalie Texier, but deserted her five years later for Emma Bardac. Chouchou, his daughter by Emma, was born in 1905, the year in which he and Rosalie were divorced. Debussy married Emma in 1908. The scandals resulting and the controversy over the première of *Pelléas et Mélisande* in 1902 made a celebrity of Debussy, as did the music criticism he contributed to several Parisian journals from 1901 onwards. He was nonetheless an extremely retiring man, only rarely making professional public appearances as pianist and conductor. During the First World War, Debussy—self-styled *musicien français*—helped the war-effort by compiling non-German editions of works by Bach and Chopin; but the rectal cancer which had first shown itself in 1909 and later necessitated two serious operations brought about his death six months before the War ended.

CATALOGUE OF WORKS

1. Nuit d'étoiles (Th. de Banville). For voice and paino. 1876.
fEbp: 19 March 1924, Beatrice Paramor.
Pub. 1882, Société d'éditions, d'estampes et de musique; 1918, Coutarel.

2. Ballade à la lune (Alfred de Musset). For voice and piano. ?1876. Unpub.

3. Fleur des eaux (Maurice Boucher). For voice and piano. ?1876. Unpub.

4. Fleur des blés (André Girod). For voice and piano. ?1877. Pub. 1891, Girod; 1919, Leduc.

5. Beau soir (Paul Bourget). For voice and piano. ?1878. Pub. 1891, Girod; Fromont.

6. Piano Trio in G. ?1880. Ded. Emile Durand.
1. *Andantino con moto allegro*; 2. *Intermezzo*; 3. *Finale: Appassionato.*
Unpub.

7. Symphonie en si. ?1880. Exists only in piano duet version, pub. 1933, Moscow.
fp: 27 January 1937, Paris, Le Triptyque concert.

BIBLIOGRAPHY:
R.-A. Mooser: Sur une prétendue 'Symphonie' de Debussy, *Dissonances*, December 1932.

8. Hymnis. Cantata. Words: Théodore de Banville. Unfinished.

9. Danse bohémienne. For piano. ?1880.
fEbp: 9 June 1932, Frank Mannheimer.
Pub. 1932, Eschig.

10. Andante. For piano. *c.* 1880. Unpub.

11. Intermezzo. For cello and piano. Unknown date.

12. L'Archet (Charles Cros). For voice and piano. *c.* 1880. Unpub.

13. Rondel chinois. For voice and piano. *c.* 1880–1. Ded. Mme Vasnier. Unpub.

14. Pierrot (Th. de Banville). For voice and piano. *c.* 1880–2. Ded. Mme Vasnier.

fEp: 4 January 1927, Grotrian Hall, BBC chamber concert, Dora Stevens, acc. Harold Craxton.
Pub. May 1926, *La Revue musicale*.

15. Aimons-nous (Th. de Banville). For voice and piano. *c.* 1880–4. Unpub.

16. Caprice (Th. de Banville). For voice and piano. *c.* 1880–4. Unpub.

17. O floraison divine des lilas (Th. de Banville). For voice and piano. *c.* 1880–4.
fEp: 23 September 1938, BBC broadcast, Claire Croiza.
Unpub.

18. Souhait (Th. de Banville). For voice and piano. *c.* 1880–4.
fEp: 23 September 1938, BBC broadcast, Claire Croiza.
Unpub.

19. Sérénade (Th. de Banville). For voice and piano. *c.* 1880–4.
fEp: 23 September 1938, BBC broadcast, Claire Croiza.
Unpub.

20. Zéphir (Th. de Banville). For voice and piano. 1881.
fEp: 9 June 1932, BBC broadcast, Anne Thursfield.
Pub. 1 September 1890, *Revue musicale*; 1932, Eschig.

21. Fête galante (Th. de Banville). For voice and piano. *c.* 1880–4. Unpub.

22. La Fille aux cheveux de lin (Leconte de Lisle). For voice and piano. *c.* 1880–4. Unpub.

23. Eglogue (Leconte de Lisle). Duo for soprano and tenor. *c.* 1882. Unpub.

24. Jane (Leconte de Lisle). For voice and piano. *c.* 1880–4.
fEp: 23 September 1938, BBC broadcast, Claire Croiza.
Unpub.

25. Triomphe de Bacchus. Divertissement for orchestra. 1882. Orchestral version not known to exist; version for two pianos by the composer.

25a. Triomphe de Bacchus. Orchestrated by Marius François Gaillard. November 1927, Paris. Dur. 3′ 45″.

2 fl, pic, 2 ob, ca, 2 cl, 3 bsn; 4 hn, 3 tpt, 3 tmb, tuba; timp, GC, cym; 2 hp, strings.
Pub. 1928, Choudens; also piano reduction.

26. Scherzo. For cello and piano. 1882. Unpub.

27. Scherzo. For violin and orchestra. Unknown date.

28. Intermezzo. For orchestra. 1882. Unpub. Reduction for piano four hands by the composer dated 21 June 1882.

29. Flots, palmes, sables (Armand Renaud). For voice and piano. 2 June 1882. Unpub.

30. Rondeau (Alfred de Musset). For voice and piano. 1882. Ded. Alexander von Meck.
fEp: 9 June 1932, BBC broadcast, Anne Thursfield.
Pub. 1935, Eschig.

31. Le Printemps (Comte de Ségur). Chorus for women's voices and orchestra. Dur. 4′ 5″.
2 fl, pic, 2 ob, 2 cl, 2 bsn; 3 hn, tpt; 2 hp, strings.
Pub. (as 'Salut printemps') 1928, Choudens, in reduction by M. F. Gaillard.

32. Daniel (Emile Cécile). Cantata for three voices. c. 1880–4. Unpub.

33. Il dort encore (Th. de Banville: 'Hymnis'). For voice and piano. c. 1880–4. Unpub.

34. Coquetterie posthume (Th. Gautier). For voice and piano. Dated: 31 March 1883.

35. Chanson espagnole. Duo for two equal voices. c. 1880–4. Unpub.

36. Séguidille (J. L. Vauthier). For voice and piano. c. 1880–4. ?Unpub.

37. Invocation (Lamartine). Chorus for four male voices and orchestra. 1883. Composed for the Concours de Rome. Dur. 5′–5′ 10″.
2 fl, pic, 2 ob, 2 cl, 2 bsn; 4 hn, 2 tpt, 3 tmb; 2 hp, strings.
Pub. 1957, Choudens.

38. Le Gladiateur (Emile Moreau). Cantata.

1883. Composed for the Concours de Rome.
fp: 22 June 1883, with Gabrielle Krauss, Taskin and Muratet as soloists.
Unpub.

39. Romance (Paul Bourget). For voice and piano. September 1883. First version. See also No. 43.

40. Silence ineffable (Paul Bourget). For voice and piano. September 1883.

41. Paysage sentimental (Paul Bourget). For voice and piano. November 1883. Pub. 1902, Société Nouvelle d'éditions musicales; La Sirène musicale.

42. Suite No. 1. For orchestra. 1883–4.
1. *Fête*; 2. *Ballet*; 3. *Rêve*; 4. *Bacchanale*.
Unpub. Also reduction for two pianos, unpub.

43. Romance (Paul Bourget). For voice and piano. January 1884. Second version. Pub. 1902, Société Nouvelle d'éditions musicales; La Sirène musicale; Durand & Schoenewerk.

44. Le Romance d'Ariel (Paul Bourget). For voice and piano. February 1884. Unpub.

45. Regret (Paul Bourget). For voice and piano. February 1884. Unpub.

46. Musique (Paul Bourget). For voice and piano. ?1884. Unpub.

47. Printemps (Jules Barbier). Chorus for four voices. 1884. Unpub.

48. Apparition (Stéphane Mallarmé). For voice and piano. 8 February 1884, Ville-d'Avray. Ded. Mme Vasnier.
fEp: 4 January 1927, Grotrian Hall, BBC chamber concert, Dora Stevens, acc. Harold Craxton.
Pub. May 1926, *La Revue musicale*.

49. Fêtes galantes (P. Verlaine). For voice and piano. 1880–4. First version (unpub. as a set). See also Nos. 74 & 91.
1. *Pantomime*. 1882–4. Pub. May 1926, *La Revue musicale*.
2. *En sourdine*. 16 September 1882, Vienna.
3. *Mandoline*. 1880–3. Ded. Mme Vasnier. Pub. 1 September 1890, *Revue illustrée*; 1890, Durand & Schoenewerk; 1905, Durand.
4. *Clair de lune*. 1882–4. Pub. May 1929, *La Revue musicale*.

Debussy, Claude

5. *Fantoches.* ?8 January 1882.
fEp (Nos. 1 & 4): 4 January 1927, Grotrian Hall, BBC chamber concert, Dora Stevens, acc. Harold Craxton.
fEp (No. 3): 13 February 1905, Aeolian Hall, Blanche Marchesi.
fEbp (No. 3): 21 July 1924, Kate Winter.

BIBLIOGRAPHY:
Edward Lockspeiser: Debussy's symbolism, *M&L*, 1968, No. 1, p. 100.
Roger Nichols: Debussy's two settings of Clair de lune, *M&L*, July 1967, p. 229.

49a. Mandoline. Version orch. Louis Beydts. Dur. 1′ 30″.
2 fl, ob, 2 cl, 2 bsn; 3 hn, tpt; timp, tgle, cym, susp cym; hp, celesta, strings.
fp: 12 January 1929, Paris, Concerts Lamoureux.
Pub. 1930, Durand.

50. L'Enfant prodigue (Edouard Guinand). Lyric Scene for three solo voices and orchestra. 1884, reorchestrated 1905, 1908. Composed for the Concours de Rome. Dur. 45′. Ded. Ernest Guiraud.
3 fl, pic, 2 ob, ca, 2 cl, 2 bsn; 4 hn, 2 tpt, 3 tmb, tuba; timp, cym, tamb de basque; 2 hp, strings.
fp: 27 June 1884, Paris, Rose Caron (Lia), Van Dyck (Azäel) and Taskin (Siméon), with piano acc. by Claude Debussy and René Chansarel.
fEp: 8 October 1908, Sheffield Festival, in a version revised and rescored for the occasion, Agnes Nicholls, Felix Senius and Herbert Witherspoon, cond. Sir Henry Wood.
fGBbp: 31 August 1925, 5WA Choir and Cardiff Station Symphony Orchestra, cond. Warwick Braithwaite, with Miriam Licette (Lia), Tudor Davies (Azäel) and Harry Brindle (Siméon).
Pub. 1884, Durand; 1908, full score.

BIBLIOGRAPHY:
Albert Vanderlinden: L'Enfant prodigue de Debussy au Théâtre Royal de la Monnaie en 1913, *Revue belge de musicologie*, 1962, p. 97.

51. Diane au bois (Th. de Banville). Lyric fragments. *c.* 1885.

fEbp: 9 November 1968, Elizabeth Simon and Ian Partridge, with Paul Hamburger and Viola Tunnard (pianos).
Unfinished. Unpub.

52. Zuleima (George Boyer, after Heine's 'Almanzor'). Symphonic Ode. 1886. Unpub.

53. Printemps. Symphonic Suite for orchestra and chorus. 1887. Pub. 1904, *La Revue musicale*, reduction for voices and piano four hands; Durand.

53a. Printemps. Definitive version reorchestrated by Henri Büsser. 1913 (?1908). Ded. to the memory of Auguste Durand. Dur. 17′.
2 fl, pic, ob, ca, 2 cl, 2 bsn; 4 hn, 2 tpt, 3 tmb; timp, cym, tgle, tambour; hp, piano four hands, strings.
fp: 18 April 1913, Paris, Salle Gaveau, Société Nationale de Musique concert, cond. Rhené-Baton.
fEp: 13 June 1913, Queen's Hall, Beecham Symphony Orchestra, cond. Thomas Beecham.
fEbp: 31 August 1925, Newcastle Station Symphony Orchestra, cond. Edward Clark.
Pub. 1913, Durand; full score, min. score, parts, reductions for piano four hands and for two pianos four hands.

BIBLIOGRAPHY:
N. van der Elst: Printemps, een jeugdwerk van CD, *Mens en melodie*, April 1964, p. 110.
Louis Laloy: Printemps, in *La Musique retrouvée*, Librairie Plon (Paris) 1928, p. 125.

54. La Damoiselle élue (D. G. Rossetti, transl. Gabriel Sarrazin). Lyric Poem for soprano, mezzo-soprano, female chorus and orchestra. 1887–8. Ded. Paul Dukas. Dur. 21′.
3 fl, 2 ob, ca, 3 cl, bcl, 3 bsn; 4 hn, 3 tpt, 3 tmb; 2 hp, strings.
fp: 8 April 1893, Paris, Salle Erard, Société Nationale de Musique, Julia Robert, Thérèse Robert, cond. Gabriel Marie.
f London p: 29 February 1908, Queen's Hall, Leeds Choral Union, Perceval Allen, Elsie Nicholl, Queen's Hall Orchestra, cond. (Sir) Henry Wood.
fGBbp: 27 March 1927, Sara Fischer, Sybil Maden, Cardiff Station Choir and Symphony Orchestra (? cond. Warwick Braithwaite).

Pub. 1893, Librairie de l'Art Indépendant, de luxe limited edition; 1902, Durand.

BIBLIOGRAPHY:
René de Castera: La Damoiselle élue, *L'Occident*, January 1903.
Louis Laloy: La Damoiselle élue, *RM*, 1903.

55. Ariettes oubliées (P. Verlaine). For voice and piano. 1887–8. Ded. Mary Garden.
Ariettes oubliées:
  1. *C'est l'extase.*
  2. *Il pleure dans mon cœur.*
  3. *L'ombre des arbres.*
Paysages belges:
  4. *Chevaux de bois.*
Aquarelles:
  5. *Green.*
  6. *Spleen.*
fp (two only): 2 February 1889, Paris, Salle Pleyel, Société Nationale de Musique, Bagès (tenor).
fEp: 13 February 1905, Aeolian Hall, Blanche Marchesi.
fEbp (incomplete): 25 November 1923, Kate Winter.
Pub. 1888, Girod, as 'Ariettes, paysages belges, aquarelles'; 1903, Fromont, as 'Ariettes oubliées', ded. Mary Garden, English version by M.-D. Calvocoressi; Nos. 1 & 5 orch. André Caplet; No. 4 orch. Manuel Rosenthal, pub. Jobert.

56. Deux arabesques. For piano. 1888.
  1. *E major*; 2. *G major.* Dur. 3' 30" and 2' 40".
fEbp: 23 March 1924, Birmingham Station, Frank Edwards.
Pub. 1891, Durand.

57. Cinq Poèmes de Charles Baudelaire. For voice and piano. 1887–9. Ded. Etienne Dupin.
  1. *Le Balcon.* January 1888.
  2. *Harmonie du Soir.* January 1889.
  3. *Le Jet d'eau.* March 1889.
  4. *Recueillement.* Undated.
  5. *La Mort des amants.* December 1887.
fEp (No. 1): 25 February 1906, Aeolian Hall, Carlos Ronzevalle, acc. Mary Cracroft.
?fEp (Nos. 4 & 5): 16 February 1908, Aeolian Hall, Franz Liebich concert, Mme Le Mar.

Pub. 1890, Librairie de l'Art Indépendant (limited edition); 1902, Durand.

57a. Le Balcon. Version orch. Louis Aubert. Dur. 6' 30".
2 fl, ob, ca, 2 cl, 2 bsn; 4 hn, 2 tpt, 3 tmb; timp; hp, strings.
Pub. Durand.

57b. Le Jet d'eau. Version orch. by the composer. January 1907.
3 fl, 2 ob, 2 cl, 2 bsn; 4 hn, 2 tpt; celesta, hp, strings.
fp: 24 February 1907, Paris, Concerts Colonne.
Pub. 1907, Durand.

58. Petite Suite. For piano four hands. 1889. Dur. 13'.
  1. *En bateau* (Dur. 3'); 2. *Cortège* (Dur. 3'); 3. *Menuet* (Dur. 3'); 4. *Ballet* (Dur. 4').
Pub. February 1889, Durand; arr. for piano solo by Jacques Durand, pub. 1906.

58a. Petite Suite. Orch. Henri Büsser. Dur. 13'.
2 fl, pic, 2 ob, 2 cl, 2 bsn; 2 hn, 2 tpt; timp, tgle, cym, tamb de basque; hp, strings.
fEp: 17 February 1908, Manchester, Gentleman's Concert, cond. (Sir) Granville Bantock.
f London p: 11 March 1908, Queen's Hall, New Symphony Orchestra, cond. (Sir) Thomas Beecham.
fEbp: 9 April 1924, Central Hall (Westminster), Royal Philharmonic Orchestra, cond. Sir Hamilton Harty.
Pub. 1907, Durand. Also transcr. for small orch. by H. Mouton, 1909.

59. Fantaisie. For piano and orchestra. October 1889 – April 1890. Ded. René Chansarel. Dur. 22'.
3 fl, 2 ob, ca, 2 cl, 3 bsn, bcl; 4 hn, 3 tpt, 3 tmb; GC, timp, piano; 2 hp, strings.
fp: 20 November 1919, London, Royal Philharmonic Society concert, Alfred Cortot, cond. Albert Coates.
fFp: 7 December 1919, Paris, Concerts Lamoureux, Marguerite Long; Lyon, Grands Concerts, Alfred Cortot.
Pub. 1919, Jobert.

60. Gymnopédies. Erik Satie, orch. Claude Debussy.

Debussy, Claude

fp: 20 February 1897, Paris, Salle Erard, Société Nationale de Musique.
fGBbp: 10 February 1925, Glasgow studio, Scottish Orchestra.

61. Rêverie. For piano. 1890. Dur. 3′ 30″. Pub. 1890, Choudens; 1905, Fromont; Jobert.

62. Ballade slave (Ballade). For piano. 1890. Dur. 6′.
Pub. 1890, Choudens, as 'Ballade slave'; 1903, Fromont, as 'Ballade'; Jobert.

BIBLIOGRAPHY:
Maurice Dumesnil: Debussy's Ballade, *Etude*, February 1948, p. 68.

63. Tarantelle styrienne (Danse). For piano. 1890. Dur. 4′ 35″.
fp: 10 March 1900, Paris, Société Nationale de Musique concert, Wurmser.
fEp: 8 July 1908, Steinway Hall, H. Brewster-Jones.
Pub. 1890, Choudens, as 'Tarantelle styrienne'; 1903, Fromont, as 'Danse'; Jobert.

63a. Danse. Orch. Maurice Ravel.
2 fl, 2 ob, 2 cl, 2 bsn; 2 hn, 2 tpt; timp, tgle, tamb de basque, tambour, cym, GC, crotales; hp, strings.
fp: 18 March 1923, Paris, Salle Gaveau, Orchestre Lamoureux, cond. Paul Paray.
Pub. 1923, Jobert.

64. Valse romantique. For piano. 1890. Ded. Rose Depecker. Dur. 3′. Pub. 1890, Choudens; 1903, Fromont; Jobert.

65. Nocturne. For piano. 1890. Dur. 5′ 35″.
fEbp: 7 September 1925, Birmingham studio, Alice Couchman.
Pub. 1890, *Le Figaro musical*; January 1903, La Sirène musicale; 1907, Société d'éditions musicales; 1907, Eschig.

66. La Belle au bois dormant (V.-E. Hyspa). For voice and piano. July 1890. Pub. 1902, Société nouvelle d'éditions musicales; 1907, Eschig.

67. Suite bergamasque. For piano. 1890. Dur. 15′ 15″.
1. *Prélude*. Dur. 3′ 30″.
2. *Menuet*. Dur. 3′ 15″.
3. *Clair de lune*. Dur. 5′.

4. *Passepied*. Dur. 3′ 30″.
fGBbp (complete): 24 July 1925, Aberdeen studio, Julien Rosetti.
Pub. 1905, Fromont.

BIBLIOGRAPHY:
Daniel Ericourt: Master class—a lesson on Debussy's Clair de lune, *Piano Teacher*, 1962, No. 6, p. 2.

67a. Suite bergamasque. Version for orchestra. Nos. 1, 2 & 4 orch. G. Cloez; No. 3 orch. André Caplet. Dur. 17′.
2 fl, ob, ca, 2 cl, 2 bsn; 2 hn, 2 tpt, 2 tmb; timp, pcssn; hp, strings.
fEbp: 16 October 1925, Newcastle Station Symphony Orchestra, cond. Edward Clark.
Pub. Jobert.

68. Les Angélus (Grégoire Le Roy). For voice and piano. 1891. Pub. 1891, Hamelle.

69. Dans le jardin (Paul Gravolet). For voice and piano. 1891. Pub. 1905, Hamelle.

70. Trois mélodies (Paul Verlaine). For voice and piano. December 1891.
1. *La mer est plus belle*. Ded. Ernest Chausson.
2. *Le son du cor s'afflige*. Ded. Robert Godet.
3. *L'échelonnement des haies*. Ded. Robert Godet.
?fEbp (No. 3): 20 October 1935, Ninon Vallin.
Pub. 1901, Hamelle; 1907, Nos. 2 & 3 only, Fromont.

71. Deux Romances sur des poèmes de Paul Bourget. For voice and piano. 1891.
1. *Romance* (*L'âme évaporée*); 2. *Les cloches*.
?fEp: 14 June 1906, Bechstein Hall, John Coates, acc. Haddon Squire.
fEbp (No. 2): 21 July 1924, Kate Winter.
Pub. 1891, Durand; 1907, Eschig.

72. Mazurka. For piano. 1891. Dur. 2′ 10″. Pub. 1904, Hamelle; 1905, Fromont.

73. Marche écossaise (sur un thème populaire). For piano four hands. 1891. Dur. 4′ 20″.
Pub. 1891, Choudens, as 'Marche des anciens comtes de Ross, dédiée à leur descendant le général Meredith Reid, Grande Croix de l'Ordre Royal du Rédempteur'; 1903, Fromont, as 'Marche écossaise'; 1914, Durand, for piano solo.

73a. Marche écossaise. Version for orchestra by Claude Debussy. Dur. 6′ 30″.

2 fl, pic, 2 ob, ca, 2 cl, 2 bsn; 4 hn, 2 tpt, 3 tmb; timp, cym, tambour; hp, strings.

fp: 22 October 1913, Paris, Théâtre des Champs-Elysées, cond. D.-E. Inghelbrecht.

fEbp: 5 April 1925, Wireless Orchestra, cond. (Sir) Dan Godfrey.

Pub. Jobert.

74. Fêtes galantes (P. Verlaine). Set One. For voice and piano. 1892 (?1891).

  1. *En sourdine.* Ded. Mme Robert Godet.

  2. *Fantoches.*

fEp: 14 June 1906, Bechstein Hall, John Coates, acc. Haddon Squire.

  3. *Clair de lune.*

fEp (complete): 11 May 1908, Bechstein Hall, Mme Le Mar.

Pub. 1903, Fromont; Jobert. English version by M.-D. Calvocoressi.

75. Rodrigue et Chimène. Opera (unfinished) in three acts. Libretto: Catulle Mendès. 1890–2. Ded. Gabrielle Dupont.

BIBLIOGRAPHY:

Alfred Cortot: Une drame lyrique de CD, in *Inédits sur CD*, Collection Comoedia-Charpentier, 1942, p. 12.

76. Proses lyriques. For voice and piano. 1893.

  1. *De rêve.* Ded. V. Hocquet.

  2. *De grève.* Ded. Raymond Bonheur.

  3. *De fleurs.* Ded. Mme E. Chausson.

  4. *De soir.* Ded. Henry Lerolle.

fp (Nos. 3 & 4): 17 February 1894, Paris, Société Nationale de Musique, Thérèse Roger, acc. Claude Debussy.

fEp (No. 4): 25 February 1906, Aeolian Hall, Carlos Ronzevalle, acc. Mary Cracroft.

Pub. 1895, Fromont.

76a. Proses lyriques. Version orch. Roger-Ducasse. Dur. 23′.

3 fl, 2 ob, ca, 2 cl, 3 bsn; 4 hn, 3 tpt; timp, cym, celesta; 2 hp, strings.

fp: 8 March 1924, Paris, Salle Gaveau, Mlle Balguerie, Orchestre Lamoureux, cond. Paul Paray.

BIBLIOGRAPHY:

Boîte à Musique: Sur les Proses lyriques de M. CD, *Le Courrier musical*, 15 December 1900.

77. String Quartet. 1893. Ded. Ysaÿe Quartet. Dur. 23′ 30″.

  1. *Animé et très décidé*; 2. *Assez vif et bien rythmé*; 3. *Andantino, doucement expressif*; 4. *Très modéré.*

fp: 29 December 1893, Paris, Salle Pleyel, Société Nationale de Musique concert, Ysaÿe Quartet (Ysaÿe, Gückboom, Van Hout, Joseph Jacob).

?fEp: 3 December 1907, Newcastle, Parisian Quartet.

f London p: 7 December 1907, Queen's Hall, Parisian Quartet.

fEbp: 21 July 1924, Snow Quartet (Jessie Snow, Kenneth Skeaping, Ernest Tomlinson, Edward Robinson).

Pub. 1894, Durand; new edition ed. L. Garban, 1929; reduction for piano four hands, 1904.

78. Prélude à l'après-midi d'un faune. For orchestra. September 1894. Ded. Raymond Bonheur. Dur. 10′.

3 fl, 2 ob, ca, 2 cl, 2 bsn; 4 hn; 2 hp, antique cym; strings.

fp: 22 December 1894, Paris, Salle d'Harcourt, Société Nationale de Musique concert, cond. Gustave Doret; repeated, 23 December.

fEp: 20 August 1904, Queen's Hall, Promenade Concert, Queen's Hall Orchestra (with Albert Fransella, flute), cond. (Sir) Henry Wood; repeated 26 November.

fEbp: 25 November 1923, cond. A. Corbett-Smith.

f stage p: 29 May 1912, Paris, Théâtre du Châtelet, Diaghilev's Ballets Russes, with choreography by Nijinsky.

Pub. 1895, Fromont; reduction for two pianos by the composer; reduction for piano four hands by Maurice Ravel.

BIBLIOGRAPHY:

Luis Pedro Mondino: Prélude à l'après-midi d'un faune (82 pp. programme note), Amante (Buenos Aires) 1946.

Thomas Munro: 'The Afternoon of a Faun' and the interrelation of the Arts, *Journal of Aesthetics and Art Criticism*, 1951, p. 95; in *Toward Science in Aesthetics* (New York), 1956, p. 342.

Léon Vallas: Le Prélude à l'après-midi d'un

faune, *Revue musicale de Lyon*, 4 February 1906.

79. Trois Chansons de Bilitis (Pierre Louÿs). For voice and piano. 1892–8. Ded. Mme M. V. Peter.

1. *La flûte de Pan.*
2. *La chevelure.*

Pub. October 1897, Image; ded. Mme Alice Peter.

3. *Le tombeau des Naïades.*

fp: 17 March 1900, Paris, Salle Pleyel, Société Nationale de Musique concert, Blanche Marot.

fEbp: 7 July 1931, Anne Thursfield.

Pub. 1899, Fromont.

BIBLIOGRAPHY: Paule de Lestang: Les chansons de Bilitis, *Revue musicale de Lyon*, 2 December 1906.

79a. Trois Chansons de Bilitis. Version orch. Maurice Delage. Dur. 7'.

2 fl, 2 ob, ca, 2 cl, 2 bsn; 4 hn, 2 tpt; timp, cym; celesta, hp, strings.

fp: 20 February 1926, Paris, Théâtre du Châtelet, Vera Janacopulos and l'Orchestre Colonne, cond. Gabriel Pierné.

Pub. Jobert.

80. Nocturnes. Symphonic Triptych for orchestra and (in No. 3) women's chorus. 1898–9. Ded. Georges Hartmann.

1. *Nuages.* Dur. 7'.

2 fl, 2 ob, ca, 2 cl, 3 bsn; 4 hn; timp; hp, strings.

2. *Fêtes.* Dur. 6' 30".

3 fl, 2 ob, ca, 2 cl, 3 bsn; 4 hn, 3 tpt, 3 tmb, tuba; timp, cym, tamb mil; 2 hp, strings.

3. *Sirènes.* Dur. 10'.

3 fl, 2 ob, ca, 2 cl, 3 bsn; 4 hn, 3 tpt; female chorus; 2 hp, strings.

fp (Nos. 1 & 2 only): 9 December 1900, Paris, l'Orchestre Lamoureux, cond. Camille Chevillard.

fp (complete): 27 October 1901, Paris, L'Orchestre Lamoureux, cond. Camille Chevillard.

fEp: 27 February 1909, Queen's Hall, Queen's Hall Orchestra with women's voices from the Smallwood Metcalf Choir, cond. Claude Debussy.

fEbp (Nos. 1 & 2): 3 March 1927, Royal Albert Hall, National Orchestra, cond. Sir Landon Ronald.

fGBbp (complete): 27 March 1927, female chorus and Cardiff Station Symphony Orchestra (? cond. Warwick Braithwaite).

Pub. 1900, Fromont; new definitive edition reorch. by the composer, October 1930, Jobert; reduction for two pianos four hands by Maurice Ravel, 1909, Fromont.

BIBLIOGRAPHY:

Eric Blom: Three Nocturnes, *Music Student*, November 1932, p. 559.

Paul Dukas: Les Nocturnes, *Revue hebdomadaire*, 9 February 1901.

Constant Lambert: Three aspects of Nature, *Radio Times*, 3 March 1939, p. 12.

Jean Marnold: Les Nocturnes, *Le Courrier musicale*, 1 and 15 March 1902, 15 December 1902, 15 January 1903, 15 February 1903.

81. Berceuse (sur une vieille chanson poitevine). April 1899. Composed for a song in 'La Tragédie de la Mort' by René Peter, intended for the Théâtre Libre but unperformed. Unpub.

82. Chansons de Bilitis. Incidental music. 1900.

2 fl, 2 hp, celesta.

fp: 7 February 1901, organized by *Le Journal*.

82a. Chansons de Bilitis. Incidental music. Arr. Pierre Boulez for reciter, two harps, two flutes and celesta.

fEp: 23 March 1965, Wigmore Hall Madeleine de la Vaivre (reciter), Susan Bradshaw (celesta), cond. John Carewe.

83. Lindaraja. For two pianos four hands. April 1901. Dur. 4' 40".

fp: 28 October 1926, Paris, Société Musicale Indépendante concert.

fEbp: 28 May 1930, Ethel Bartlett and Rae Robertson.

Pub. October 1926, Jobert; also reduction for piano solo.

84. Pour le piano. 1896–1901. Dur. 12' 50".

1. *Prélude.* Dur. 4'. Ded. Mlle W. de Romilly.

2. *Sarabande.* Dur. 4' 30". Ded. Mme E. Rouart (née Lerolle). Pub. 17 February 1896, Le Grand Journal.

3. *Toccata*. Dur. 4' 20". Ded. N.-G. Coromo.

fp: 11 January 1902, Paris, Salle Erard, Société Nationale de Musique concert, Ricardo Viñes.

fEp: 19 November 1903, St. James's Hall, Broadwood concert, Evelyn Suart.

fGBbp: 24 July 1924, Aberdeen studio, Maurice Cole.

Pub. 1901, Fromont; Jobert.

84a. Sarabande. Orchestrated by Maurice Ravel. 1920.

2 fl, ob, ca, 2 cl, 2 bsn; 2 hn, tpt; cym, tam-tam; hp, strings.

fp: 18 March 1923, Paris, Salle Gaveau, Orchestre Lamoureux, cond. Paul Paray.

Pub. 1923, Jobert.

85. Pelléas et Mélisande. Lyric Drama in five acts. Text: Maurice Maeterlinck. 1892–1902. Dur. 3 hrs. Ded. André Messager; to the memory of Georges Hartmann.

3 fl, ob, ca, 2 cl, 3 bsn; 4 hn, 3 tpt, 3 tmb, tuba; cym, tgle, glock, bell; 2 hp, strings.

fp: 30 April 1902, Théâtre National de l'Opéra-Comique, with Mary Garden (Mélisande), Jean Périer (Pelléas), Hector Dufranne (Golaud), Félix Vieuille (Arkel), Mme Gerville-Réache (Geneviève), Blondin (Yniold), Vigué (Un médecin), cond. André Messager; chorus master, Henri Büsser; décors, Jusseaume & Ronsin; costumes, Bianchini.

f New York p: 19 February 1908, Manhattan Opera House, with Mary Garden (Mélisande), Jean Périer (Pelléas), Hector Dufranne (Golaud), Arimondi (Arkel), Mme Gerville-Réache (Geneviève), Mlle Sigrist (Yniold), Crabbé (Un médecin), cond. Cleofonte Campanini.

fEp: 21 May 1909, Covent Garden, with Rose Féart (Mélisande), Edmond Warnery (Pelléas), Bourbon (Golaud), Vanni Marcoux (Arkel), Jane Bourgeois (Geneviève), Emma Trentini (Yniold), Crabbé (Un médecin), cond. Cleofonte Campanini.

fEbp: 18 November 1930, with Maggie Teyte (Mélisande), Tudor Davies (Pelléas), Kenneth Ellis (Golaud), Foster Richardson (Arkel), Evelyn Arden (Geneviève), Bernard

Ross (Un médecin), Wireless Chorus and BBC Symphony Orchestra, cond. Percy Pitt.

Pub. 1902, Fromont; full score, 1904; 1907, Durand. Reduction of Interludes for piano solo by Gustave Samazeuilh, 1905, Durand.

BIBLIOGRAPHY:

Jules van Ackere: Pelléas et Mélisande, ou le rencontre miraculeux d'une poésie et d'une musique, Brussels, 1952.

Georges Auric: Reprise de Pelléas et Mélisande, *Nouvelle revue française*, January 1940, No. 322, p. 102.

Valdo Barbey: Projet de mise en scène pour Pelléas, *RM*, December 1926, p. 136.

Camille Bellaigue: Pelléas et Mélisande, *Revue des deux mondes*, 15 May 1902.

Julien Benda: A propos de Pelléas et Mélisande, *Revue blanche*, 1 July 1902.

Lennox Berkeley: Pelléas et Mélisande, *Ballet*, September 1949, p. 48.

André Boll: Pelléas et sa présentation décorative, *RM*, November 1927, p. 94.

— La mise en scène de Pelléas et Mélisande, *RM*, April 1964, p. 61.

Abel Bonnard: Pelléas et Mélisande, *L'Information musicale*, 20 February 1942, p. 763.

Hans Georg Bonte: Fünfzig Jahre Pelléas, *NZfM*, 1952, p. 280.

Roger Boss: Pelléas et Mélisande, *Pages musicales* (Neuchâtel), November 1962.

Alfred Bruneau: Debussy und Maeterlinck, *Blätter der Staatsoper* (Berlin), November (No. 7) 1927, p. 9.

Robert Brussel: Pelléas et Mélisande, La Damoiselle élue, Cinq poèmes de Charles Baudelaire, *Revue d'art dramatique*, 15 February 1903, p. 450.

José Bruyr: Pelléas et ses décors, *SM*, November–December 1962, p. 340.

Henri Büsser: A propos de Pelléas et Mélisande, *Revue des deux mondes*, 1 April 1952.

Antonio Capri: Appendice il Pelléas et Mélisande di Debussy, in *La musica da camera*, Giuseppe Laterza & Figli, 1925, p. 253.

— Attualità del Pelléas, *La Scala* (Milan) May 1953.

M.-D. Calvocoressi: Pelléas et Mélisande, *L'Art moderne*, 15 May 1902.

— Pelléas et Mélisande 1902–1922, *MMR*, July 1922.

Debussy, Claude

Neville Cardus: Debussy and Pelléas et Mélisande, *Halle*, November 1948, p. 1.

Jacques Chailley: Le symbolisme des thèmes dans Pelléas et Mélisande, *L'Information musicale*, 1942, No. 6.

Max Chop: CD—Pelléas et Mélisande, *Signale*, 1927, No. 47, p. 1609.

André Coeuroy: Pelléas et Mélisande en disques, *Nouvelle revue française*, No. 344, p. 510.

Ernest Closson: Pelléas und Mélisande, *Signale*, 1907, Nos. 15–16 (20 February), p. 241.

A. Damerini: 'Metadramma' non 'Dramma musicale'—Nota al Pelléas di CD, *Il Pianoforte*, November 1921.

Etienne Destranges: Pelléas et Mélisande, *Revue musicale de Lyon*, 13, 20 and 27 November 1910.

Antun Dubronic: Debussy et Pelléas à Zagreb, *RM*, 1 July 1924, p. 90.

Paul Dukas: Pelléas et Mélisande, *Chronique des Arts*, 10 May 1902.

René Dumesnil & Martin Cooper: Pelléas 1902, Pelléas 1952, *Saturday Review*, 26 April 1952, p. 46.

Maurice Emmanuel: Pelléas et Mélisande, Mellottée (Paris) 1926.

Oswald d'Estrade-Guerra: Les manuscrits de Pelléas et Mélisande, *RM* (Les Carnets Critiques), 1957.

André Espiau de la Muaestre: Debussys Deklamationstechnik in Pelléas et Mélisande im Lichte des Briefwechsels von Richard Strauss und Romain Rolland, *ÖM*, January 1962.

Edwin Evans: Pelléas et Mélisande, *MS*, 5 June 1909, p. 361; Fr. transl., *Revue musicale de Lyon*, 1 January 1910. (Text of a lecture given before the Concertgoers' Club, the Play-Goers' Club and the Society of British Composers, in association with the Société des Concerts Français, at the Royal Academy of Music on 25 May 1909.)

— Pelléas et Mélisande, *Radio Times*, 26 October 1928, p. 248.

Marg. Falk: Pelléas et Mélisande 1902–1952, *Mens en melodie*, December 1952, p. 377.

Guy Ferchault: A propos de Pelléas et Mélisande, *L'Information musicale*, 7 March 1942, p. 819.

Th. Ferneuil: Pelléas et Mélisande, *Revue philomatique de Bordeaux*, 1 August 1902, p. 337.

Jacques Feschotte: Pelléas a 50 ans, *La Vie musicale*, April 1952, p. 9.

R. de Flers: Pelléas et Mélisande (interview with Claude Debussy), *Le Figaro*, 16 May 1902.

J. W. Freeman: On records, Pelléas et Mélisande, *Opera News*, 29 December 1962, p. 36.

Othmar Fries: Pelléas et Mélisande in Zürich, *Melos*, March 1950, p. 114.

Bennitt Gardiner: Debussy, Maeterlinck and Pelléas, *Musical Events*, March 1962, p. 18.

H. Gaubert: Pelléas, une venue au monde... plutôt mouvementée, *Musica* (Chaix), No. 70, January 1960, p. 30.

— La bataille de Pelléas, *Musica* (Chaix), No. 71, February 1960, p. 2.

— Pelléas, le déchaînement de la critique, *Musica* (Chaix), No. 72, March 1960, p. 13.

Lawrence Gilman: Debussy's Pelléas et Mélisande: a guide to the opera, Schirmer (New York), 1907.

— Debussy's Pelléas et Mélisande, *Nation*, 26 December 1907, p. 595.

— Pelléas et Mélisande as an opera, *Harper's Weekly*, 21 March 1908, p. 25.

Mateusz Glinski: Pelléas et Mélisande, fragments de l'histoire de l'impressionisme, *Muzyka*, May 1928.

H. Glass: As never before: London's Pelléas et Mélisande, *American Record Guide*, April 1965, p. 694.

Robert Godet: Pelléas et Mélisande, *La musique en suisse*, 1 June 1902, p. 219.

Antoine Goléa: Pelléas et Mélisande, analyse poétique et musicale, Paris, 1952.

Vittorio Gui: Il ritorno di Pelléas et Mélisande, *La Rassegna musicale*, 1962, p. 117.

André Hallays: Pelléas et Mélisande, *Revue de Paris*, 15 May 1902, p. 411.

Edward Burlingame Hill: Debussy's Pelléas et Mélisande, an inquiry, *MS*, 1908, 6 June, p. 359; 13 June, p. 371.

Vincent d'Indy: A propos de Pelléas et Mélisande, essai de psychologie du critique d'art, *Occident*, June 1902.

Arthur Jacobs & Stanley Sadie: Pelléas et

Mélisande, in *The Opera Guide*, Hamish Hamilton (London) 1964, p. 236.

Pierre Jaquillard: A propos de Mélisande, *SM*, March 1955, p. 103.

Robert Jardillier: La vérité de Pelléas, *RM*, March 1927, p. 199.

— Pelléas, C. Aveline (Paris) 1927.

Iván Kertész: Pelléas és Mélisande, *Muzsika* (Budapest), July 1963, p. 7.

Paul Ladmirault: Pelléas et Mélisande, *Ouest-Artiste*, May 1902.

Louis Laloy: Opéra-Comique—reprise de Pelléas et Mélisande, *Revue S.I.M.*, 15 July 1908, p. 792.

— Pelléas et Mélisande, in *Essays on Music* (an anthology of *The Listener*, ed. Felix Aprahamian), Cassell (London) 1967, p. 74.

Pierre Lalo: La bataille de Pelléas et Mélisande *Dissonances*, May–June 1942 (repr. from *Le Temps*); in *De Rameau à Ravel* (Portraits et Souvenirs), Editions Albin Michel (Paris) 1947, p. 367.

— Pelléas et Mélisande à l'Opéra-Comique (mai 1902), in *De Rameau à Ravel*, p. 383.

René Leibowitz: Pelléas et Mélisande ou le No Man's Land de l'art lyrique, *Critique*, 1957, p. 22; in *Histoire de l'Opéra*, Paris, 1957, p. 297.

Mrs. Franz (Louise S.) Liebich: Debussy's Pelléas et Mélisande, *MS*, 12 January 1907, p. 20.

— A few thoughts on Pelléas et Mélisande, *MS*, 29 May 1909, p. 340.

G. Lilley: Debussy's Pelléas et Mélisande, *Contemporary Review*, January 1911, p. 61; *Living Age*, 25 February 1911, p. 475.

Jean Lorrain: Pelléastres, Paris, 1910.

Herbert McCullagh: The immolation of Maeterlinck, *MS*, 26 June 1909, p. 406.

R. Malipiero: Pelléas et Mélisande, Milan, 1949.

André Mangeot: Pelléas et Mélisande, *Le Monde musical*, 15 May 1902.

Jean Marnold: Pelléas et Mélisande, *Mercure de France*, June 1902, December 1902, May 1905.

— Pelléas et Mélisande, in *Musique d'autrefois et d'aujourd'hui*, Dorbon-Ainé (Paris) 1912, pp. 71, 193.

Camille Mauclair: Pelléas et Mélisande, in *Revue universelle*, tome II, p. 331.

Octave Maus: Pelléas et Mélisande, 20 May 1902.

André Messager: Les premières representations de Pelléas, *RM*, April 1964, p. 57.

Edward Mitchell: A Debussy revival, *MN&H*, 31 July 1920, p. 99.

M. Modrakowska: Wspomnienia 'Melizandy', *Ruch Muzyczny*, 1963, No. 16, p. 9.

Pierre Mollet: Quelques réflexions sur Pelléas et Mélisande, *Feuilles musicales*, November 1959.

— Pelléas et Mélisande, *SM*, November–December 1962, p. 338.

Ernst Newman: Pelléas et Mélisande, in *Opera Nights*, Putnam (London) 1943, p. 431.

C. L. Osborne, Pelléas in stereo, with Ansermet in brilliant form, *High Fidelity*, April 1965, p. 72.

Guido Pannain: Pelléas et Mélisande, in *L'opera e le opere*, Naples.

Domenico de Paoli: Monteverdi's Orfeo and Debussy's Pelléas et Mélisande, *M&L*, October 1939, p. 381.

H. Pfeilschmidt: Pelléas et Mélisande, *Die Musik*, May 1907.

Constantin Photiadès: CD et la centième de Pelléas et Mélisande, *Revue de Paris*, 1 April 1913, p. 513.

G. Pioch: Pelléas et Mélisande, *Musica*, 1908, p. 115.

René Peter: Ce que fut la 'générale' de Pelléas et Mélisande, in *Inédits sur CD*, Collection Comoedia-Charpentier, 1942, p. 3.

Ildebrando Pizzetti: Pelléas et Mélisande, in *Musicisti contemporanei*, Milan, 1914.

Lucien Rebatet: L'enregistrement de Pelléas et Mélisande, *L'Information musicale*, 7 March 1942, p. 819.

William Ritter: Pelléas et Mélisande à Munich, *Le Courrier musical*, 1 November 1908.

Romain Rolland: Pelléas et Mélisande, *Morgen*, 29 November 1907.

— Die Bedeutung des Werkers, *Blätter der Staatsoper* (Berlin), November 1927, p. 14.

L. Ronga: I cinquant'anni del Pelléas et Mélisande, in *Arte et gusto nella musica*, Naples, 1956.

K. M. Roof: Borderland art: the opera of Debussy and Maeterlinck, *Craftsman*, November 1908, p. 130.

Debussy, Claude

Joseph Ryelandt: Pelléas et Mélisande, *Durendal*, February 1907.

Paul Rosenfeld: Pelléas et Mélisande, *Dial*, 8 February 1919, p. 138.

Gustave Samazeuilh: Le quarantenaire de Pelléas, in *Musiciens de mon temps*, Editions Marcel Daubin (Paris) 1947, p. 114.

Paul F. Sanders: Pelléas et Mélisande à Amsterdam, *RM*, January 1928, p. 276.

Gerd Sievers: Pelléas und Mélisande, *Musica*, 1961, No. 4, p. 171.

Henry W. Simon: Pelléas et Mélisande, in *Festival of Opera*, W. H. Allen (London) 1957, p. 351.

Pierre Souday: Pelléas et Mélisande, *La Revue*, 15 May 1902, p. 481.

Gérard Souzay: Who is Mélisande?, *Music Journal*, March 1963, p. 32.

August Spanuth: Debussy's Pelléas und Mélisande, *Signale*, 1908, No. 46 (11 November), p. 1433.

Madeau Stewart: The first Mélisande, *R.C.M. Magazine*, 1965, No. 1, p. 8.

Maggie Teyte: Reflections on Pelléas, *Music Magazine*, August 1962, p. 14.

Anette Vaillant: Deux fois cent ans: Maeterlinck et Debussy, *Preuves*, No. 141, November 1962, p. 76.

Léopold Wallner: Pelléas und Mélisande—Musikdrama von Debussy. Erstaufführung in Théâtre de la Monnaie am 9. Januar, *NZfM* (Musikalisches Wochenblatt), 1907, No. 5 (31 January), p. 114.

John S. Weissmann: Le centenaire de Debussy en Angleterre: Un Pelléas sensationnel à Glyndebourne, *Feuilles musicales*, November 1962, p. 156.

— Pelléas et Mélisande at Glyndebourne, *Musical Events*, July 1962, p. 12.

Alfred Westarp: Pelléas et Mélisande à Munich, *Revue S.I.M.*, 15 December 1908, p. 1307.

Kurt Westphal: Pelléas et Mélisande in der Berliner Staatsoper, *Melos*, March 1950, p. 114.

Jos Wouters: Debussy over de Pelléas et Mélisande, *Mens en melodie*, December 1953, p. 379.

MISCELLANEOUS OR UNSIGNED ARTICLES:

Pelléas et Mélisande, *L'Approdo musicale*, 1959, Nos. 7–8.

Pelléas et Mélisande, *Opera*, No. 11, November 1923, p. 26.

Les premières représentations de Pelléas, *RM*, May 1926, p. 110.

Musical significance of Pelléas et Mélisande, *Current Literature*, April 1908, p. 426.

Pelléas et Mélisande—drama of decoration, *Outlook*, 28 March 1908, p. 673.

A reflection on Debussy, *The Times*, 15 July 1911, p. 11.

Pelléas et Mélisande, *Opera News*, 16 January 1960; 29 December 1962.

86. Estampes. For piano. July 1903. Dur. 12′ 20″.

1. *Pagodes.* Ded. J.-E. Blanche. Dur. 4′.

fEp: 15 November 1905, Bechstein Hall, Percy Grainger.

2. *Soirée dans Grenade.* Ded. Pierre Louÿs. Dur. 4′ 10″.

fEp: 25 February 1906, Aeolian Hall, Mary Cracroft.

3. *Jardins sous la pluie.* Dur. 4′ 10″.

fEp: 25 February 1906, Aeolian Hall, Mary Cracroft.

fp (complete): 9 January 1904, Paris, Salle Erard, Société Nationale de Musique, Ricardo Viñes.

fEp (complete): 2 June 1908, Aeolian Hall, Richard Buhlig.

fEbp (No. 3): 23 March 1924, Birmingham studio, Frank Edwards.

fEbp (No. 1): 21 May 1925, Manchester studio, Marcelle Meyer.

Pub. 1903, Durand.

86a. Pagodes. Orch. André Caplet. Dur. 4′.

2 fl, pic, 2 ob, 2 cl, 2 bsn; 4 hn, 3 tpt, 3 tmb, tuba; timp, tgle, cym, gong; celesta, 2 hp, strings.

fp: 31 May 1924, Paris, Théâtre Gaîté-Lyrique, Concerts Grassi, danced by Mado Minty, cond. E.-C. Grassi.

Pub. Durand.

86b. Soirée dans Grenade. Orch. Henri Büsser. Dur. 5′.

2 fl, ob, ca, 2 cl, 2 bsn; 2 hn, 2 tpt; timp, cym, tgle, cast; celesta, hp, strings.

Pub. Durand.

87. D'un cahier d'esquisses (orig. 'Esquisses'). For piano. 1903. Dur. 4′ 30″.

fp: 20 April 1910, Paris, Salle Gaveau, Société Musicale Indépendante, Maurice Ravel.

Pub. March 1904, Paris-Illustré (L'Album de musique); 1904, Schott Frères (Brussels). Also arr. for violin and piano, for piano four hands.

88. Rapsodie. For alto saxophone and orchestra. 1903–5. Uncompleted; orch. 1919 by Roger-Ducasse. Ded. Elise Hall. Dur. 10′.

3 fl, 2 ob, ca, 2 cl, 2 bsn; 4 hn, 2 tpt, 3 tmb, tuba; timp, tgle, tamb de basque, cym; hp, strings.

fp: 14 May 1919, Paris, Salle Gaveau, Société Nationale de Musique, Mayeur (sax), cond. André Caplet.

fEp: 11 January 1931, Bradford, Bradford Philharmonic Society concert, Harry Watson (sax), cond. Sir Hamilton Harty.

Pub. 1919, Durand; score, parts, reduction for saxophone and piano; arr. for piano four hands.

89. Le Diable dans le beffroi. Opera (unfinished) after Edgar Allan Poe. 1902–3.

90. Danses. For harp and string orchestra. 1903. Ded. A. Gustave Lyon. Dur. 9′.

1. *Danse sacrée*; 2. *Danse profane*.

fp (chromatic harp): 6 November 1904, Paris, Concerts Colonne, with Mme Wurmser as soloist.

fEp: 25 February 1909, Leeds, Albert Hall, with Mme L. Wurmser-Delcourt as soloist.

f London p: 26 February 1909, Bechstein Hall, with Mme L. Wurmser-Delcourt as soloist.

fp (pedal harp): 1 February 1910, Paris, Salle Erard, with Henriette Renié as soloist.

fEbp: 25 November 1923, cond. A. Corbett-Smith.

Pub. 1904, Durand; reduction for two pianos four hands by the composer.

91. Fêtes galantes (P. Verlaine). Set Two. For voice and piano. 1904.

1. *Les ingénus*; 2. *Le faune*; 3. *Colloque sentimental*.

Pub. 1904, Durand.

91a. Le faune. Orch. Roland-Manuel. Dur. 1′ 50″.

2 fl, 2 cl, 2 bsn; 2 hn, 2 tpt; timp, tamb de basque, caisse-claire (or tamb); hp, strings.

fp: 27 January 1924, Paris, Concerts Colonne.

Pub. 1929, Durand.

91b. Colloque sentimental. Orch. Louis Beydts. Dur. 3′.

2 fl, 2 ob, ca, 2 cl, bcl, 2 bsn; 3 hn, tpt; 3 timp, tgle, cym, GC, susp cym; celesta, hp, strings.

fp: 12 January 1929, Concerts Lamoureux.

Pub. 1929, Durand.

92. Trois Chansons de France. For voice and piano. 1904. Ded. Mme S. Bardac.

1. *Rondel* (Le temps a laissié son manteau) (Charles d'Orléans).

2. *La grotte* (Tristan Lhermite).

fEp: 25 February 1906, Aeolian Hall, Carlos Ronzevalle, acc. Mary Cracroft.

3. *Rondel* (Pour ce que Plaisance est morte) (Charles d'Orléans).

Pub. 1904, Durand.

93. Masques. For piano. July 1904. Dur. 4′.

fp: 18 February 1905, Paris, Salle Pleyel, Société Nationale de Musique, Ricardo Viñes.

Pub. 1904, Durand.

94. L'Isle joyeuse. For piano. Dated: September 1904. Dur. 4′ 45″.

fp: 18 February 1905, Paris, Société Nationale de Musique, Ricardo Viñes.

fEp: 6 June 1906, Bechstein Hall, Harold Bauer.★

fGBbp: 2 June 1924, Cardiff station, Maurice Cole.

Pub. 1904, Durand.

94a. L'Isle joyeuse. Orch. Bernadino Molinari. Dur. 7′.

3 fl, pic, 2 ob, ca, 3 cl, bcl, 3 bsn, cbsn; 4 hn, 4 tpt, 3 tmb, 3 tuba; 4 timp, xyl, cym, tgle, tamb de basque; celesta, 2 hp, strings.

fp: 1 November 1923, Amsterdam, Concertgebouw Orchestra, cond. Gabriel Perné.

fFp: 11 November 1923, Paris, Concerts

★ A performance a year later (13 June 1907) by Percy Grainger was so widely reported in press reviews as the first in London that it was probably, though wrongly, claimed as such.

Debussy, Claude

Colonne, Théâtre du Châtelet, cond. Gabriel Pierné.
Pub. 1923, Durand.

95. Musiques pour 'Le Roi Lear'. Incidental music (Shakespeare) for orchestra. 1904.
1. *Fanfare.* Dur. 1' 40".
3 tpt, 4 hn; 3 timp, tambour; 2 hp.
2. *Le sommeil de Lear.* Dur. 2' 40".
2 fl, 4 hn; timp; hp, strings.
fp: 30 October 1926, Paris, Théâtre-Mogador, Orchestre Pasdeloup, cond. Albert Wolff.
Pub. Jobert; also arr. for piano solo.

96. Images. Set One. For piano. 1905. Dur. 15' 20".
1. *Reflets dans l'eau.* Dur. 5'.
2. *Hommage à Rameau.* Dur. 7'.
3. *Mouvement.* Dur. 3' 20".
fp: 3 March 1906, Paris, Société Nationale de Musique concert, Ricardo Viñes.
Pub. 1905, Durand.

BIBLIOGRAPHY:
T. P. Currier: Debussy's Reflets dans l'eau, *Musician*, April 1912, p. 278.
Maurice Dumesnil: Dripping dew drops: interpretation of Reflections in the water, *Etude*, May 1949, p. 282.
— Reflections in the water: details concerning tone production and pedaling, *Etude*, August 1949, p. 462.

97. La Mer. Three Symphonic Sketches for orchestra. 1903–5. Dated: 5 March 1905. Ded. Jacques Durand. Dur. 21'.
1. *De l'aube à midi sur la mer*; 2. *Jeux de vagues*; 3. *Dialogue du vent et de la mer.*
2 fl, pic, 2 ob, ca, 2 cl, 3 bsn, cbsn; 4 hn, 3 tpt, 2 cornets à pistons, 3 tmb, tuba; 3 timp, cym, tamtam, GC, tgle, glock (or celesta); 2 hp, strings.
fp: 15 October 1905, Paris, Concerts Lamoureux, cond. Camille Chevillard.
fEp: 1 February 1908, Queen's Hall Saturday Concert, Queen's Hall Orchestra, cond. Claude Debussy.
fEbp: 28 April 1928, Wireless Symphony Orchestra, cond. Ernest Ansermet.
Pub. 1905, Durand; score, parts, min. score; reduction for piano four hands by the composer; reduction for two pianos four hands.

BIBLIOGRAPHY:
A. Chipman: LP overview of Debussy's seascape La Mer, *American Record Guide*, January 1964, p. 390.
Lawrence Gilman: Debussy's The Sea, *Harper's Weekly*, 23 March 1907, p. 438.
Louis Laloy: La Mer, trois esquisses symphoniques de CD, *Le Mercure musical*, August 1905, p. 233.
— La Mer, in *La Musique retrouvée*, Librairie Plon (Paris) 1928, p. 139.
Henri Lesbroussart: La Mer, *L'Art moderne*, 10 December 1905.
Fausto Magnani: Sur La Mer, poème symphonique de CD, *L'Art musical*, 19 November 1937; *Le Courrier musical*, May 1939.
Jean Marnold: La Mer, *Mercure de France*, 1 November 1905.
Octave Maus: La Mer, *L'Art moderne*, 5 November 1905.
Hugh Ottaway: Debussy's orchestral masterpiece, *Halle*, May 1956, p. 5.
Dr. Petit de la Villéon: CD sur la Côte d'Emeraude—Le poème pour orchestre La Mer, *Annales de la Société d'Histoire et d'Archéologie*, Saint-Malo, 1959.

98. Images. Set Two. For piano. October 1907–8. Dur. 12' 40".
1. *Cloches à travers les feuilles.* Dur. 4' 15".
2. *Et la lune descend sur le temple qui fut.* Dur. 4' 45".
3. *Poissons d'or.* Dur. 3' 40".
fp: 21 February 1908, Paris, Cercle Musical, Ricardo Viñes.
Pub. 1908, Durand.

99. Trois Chansons de Charles d'Orléans. For SATB unacc. 1898–1908.
1. *Dieu! qu'il la fait bon regarder!*; 2. *Quand j'ai ouy le tabourin*; 3. *Yver, vous n'estes qu'un villain.*
fp: 9 April 1909, Paris, Concerts Colonne, cond. Claude Debussy.
Pub. 1908, Durand.

BIBLIOGRAPHY:
G. Boulay: Trois Chansons de Charles d'Orléans, *Le Monde musical*, 15 April 1909.
Louis Laloy: Trois Chansons de Charles d'Orléans, *Grande Revue*, 15 April 1909.

100. Children's Corner. For piano. 1906–8.

Ded. composer's daughter Chouchou. Dur. 14' 40".

1. *Doctor Gradus ad Parnassum.* Dur. 2'.

2. *Jimbo's lullaby* (Berceuse des éléphants). Dur. 3' 10".

3. *Serenade for the doll* (Sérénade à la poupée). Dur. 2' 50". Pub. 1906.

4. *Snow is dancing* (La neige danse). Dur. 2'.

5. *The little shepherd* (Le petit berger). Dur. 2'.

6. *Golliwog's cake-walk.* Dur. 2'40".

fp: 18 December 1908, Paris, Cercle Musical, Harold Bauer.

fEbp: 30 August 1925, Harold Samuel.

Pub. 1908, Durand.

BIBLIOGRAPHY:
Harold Bauer: Children's Corner, *New York Times*, 21 December 1930.

100a. Children's Corner. Orch. André Caplet. Dur. 15'.

2 fl, pic, 2 ob, 2 cl, 2 bsn; 4 hn, 2 tpt; tgle, cym, GC, tambour; hp, strings.

fp: 1910, New York.

fFp: 25 March 1911, Paris, Cercle Musical, cond. Claude Debussy.

fEp: 12 September 1911, Queen's Hall, Promenade Concert, Queen's Hall Orchestra, cond. Sir Henry Wood.

Pub. 1911, Durand.

101. The Little Nigar (Le petit nègre). For piano. 1909. Dur. 1' 20".

fEbp: 17 October 1947, Yvonne Lefébure.

Pub. 1934, Leduc.

BIBLIOGRAPHY:
Maurice Dumesnil: Little Nigar: story connected with its publication, *Etude*, June 1949, p. 348.

102. Hommage à Haydn. For piano. 1909. Dur. 1' 30".

fp: 11 March 1911, Paris, Salle Pleyel, Société Nationale de Musique, Trillat.

Pub. January 1910, Revue S.I.M.; 1911, Durand.

103. Première Rapsodie. For clarinet and piano. December 1909–January 1910. Ded. P. Mimart. Dur. 8'.

fp: 16 January 1911, Paris, Société Musicale Indépendante concert.

fEp: 8 April 1911, Steinway Hall, Charles Draper and Elsie Hall.

fEbp: 23 November 1938, Reginald Kell and John Willis.

Pub. 1910, Durand.

103a. Première Rapsodie. For orchestra with principal clarinet. Orch. Claude Debussy. October 1910.

3 fl, 2 ob, ca, 2 cl, 3 bsn; 4 hn, 2 tpt; cym, tgle; 2 hp, strings.

Pub. 1911, Durand.

104. Petite Pièce. For clarinet and piano. 1910. Dur. 1'. Pub. 1910, Durand; also transcr. for violin and piano and for piano solo. ? Also version orch. by the composer.

105. Douze Préludes. Book One. For piano. December 1909–February 1910. Dur. 32' 30".

1. *Danseuses de Delphes.* 7 December 1909. Dur. 2' 40".

fp: 25 May 1910, Paris, Société Musicale Indépendante, Claude Debussy.

2. *Voiles.* 12 December 1909. Dur. 2' 50". fp as No. 1.

3. *Le Vent dans la plaine.* 11 December 1909. Dur. 2' 10".

fEp: 2 June 1910, Bechstein Hall, Franz Liebich.

4. *Les Sons et les parfums tournent dans l'air du soir.* 1 January 1910. Dur. 2' 45".

5. *Les Collines d'Anacapri.* 26 December 1909. Dur. 2' 40".

fp: 14 January 1911, Paris, Société Nationale de Musique, Ricardo Viñes.

?fEp: 3 May 1912, Bechstein Hall, Frank Merrick.

6. *Des Pas sur la neige.* 27 December 1909. Dur. 2' 50".

7. *Ce qu'a vu le vent d'Ouest.* n.d. Dur. 3' 15".

8. *La Fille aux cheveux de lin.* 15–16 January 1910. Dur. 1' 45".

fEp: 2 June 1910, Bechstein Hall, Franz Liebich.★

9. *La Sérénade interrompue.* n.d. Dur. 2' 15".

fp: 14 January 1911, Paris, Société Nationale de Musique, Ricardo Viñes.

★ It seems possible that Liebich's was the first public performance: it antedates by several months Ricardo Viñes's performance in Paris (14 January 1911, Société Nationale) held by some authorities to have been the première.

Debussy, Claude

10. *La Cathédrale engloutie.* n.d. Dur. 4′ 50″.
fp: 25 May 1910, Paris, Société Musicale Indépendante, Claude Debussy.
fEp: 2 June 1910, Bechstein Hall, Franz Liebich.

11. *La Danse de Puck.* 4 February 1910. Dur. 2′ 30″.
fp as No. 10.
fEp as No. 10.

12. *Minstrels.* 5 January 1910. Dur. 2′.
Pub. 1910, Durand.

BIBLIOGRAPHY:

Maurice Dumesnil: From an old legend: La cathédrale engloutie, *Etude*, July 1947, p. 368.
— Puzzling notation in Maid with the flaxen hair, *Etude*, August 1955, p. 23.
A. Gabeaud: Préludes pour piano, *L'Education musicale*, No. 36, 1957.
J. Matthews: Debussy's Preludes, *MO*, September 1910, p. 833.
L. M. Peppercorn: The piano style in Debussy's Preludes, *MO*, August 1937, p. 952.
L. Perracchio: Il libro dei preludi di Debussy, *Il Pianoforte*, 1920.
Peter Hugh Reed: Debussy's Piano Preludes, *American Music Lover*, August 1938.

105a. La Cathédrale engloutie. Orch. Henri Büsser. Dur. 4′ 30″.
2 fl, 2 ob, 2 cl, 2 bsn; 4 hn, 2 tpt, 3 tmb, tuba; timp, GC, cym, tamtam, tgle; 2 hp, strings.
fp: 28 April 1927, Paris, Concerts Straram.
Pub. Durand.

106. La Plus que lente. For piano. August 1910. Dur. 3′ 20″.
fEp: 26 November 1910, Aeolian Hall, Cernikoff.
fEbp: 5 May 1924, Bournemouth station, H. Austin Dewdney.
Pub. 1910, Durand.

BIBLIOGRAPHY:

Maurice Dumesnil: Puzzling meter: La Plus que lente, *Etude*, June 1952, p. 23.

106a. La Plus que lente. Version for orchestra by the composer. Dur. 4′ 15″.
fl, cl, cymbalom, piano, strings.
Pub. 1912, Durand.

107. Le Promenoir des deux amants
(Tristan Lhermite). For voice and piano. 1910.
1. *Auprès de cette grotte sombre* (orig. 'La Grotte' in Trois Chansons de France, 1904).
2. *Crois mon conseil, chère Climène.*
3. *Je tremble en voyant ton visage.*
fp: 14 January 1911, Paris, Salle Erard, Société Nationale de Musique, Jane Bathori, acc. Ricardo Viñes.
fEp: 8 June 1922, London, Anne Thursfield.
fEbp: 20 October 1930, Claire Croiza.
Pub. 1910, Durand.

BIBLIOGRAPHY:

Hennie Schouten: Debussy's Le Promenoir des deux amants, *Mens en melodie*, November 1948, p. 335.

107a. Le Promenoir des deux amants. Orch. Louis Beydts. Dur. 4′ 30″.
2 fl, ob, ca, 2 cl, bcl, 2 bsn; 4 hn, tpt; timp, cym, celesta; 2 hp, strings.
fp: 15 October 1927, Paris, Concerts Pasdeloup.
Pub. Durand.

108. Trois Ballades de François Villon. For voice and piano. May 1910.
1. *Ballade de Villon à s'amye*; 2. *Ballade que feit Villon à la requeste de sa mère pour prier Nostre-Dame*; 3. *Ballade des femmes de Paris.*
fEp (No. 3 only): 18 November 1910, Aeolian Hall, Maggie Teyte, acc. C. Stoeger.
fp (complete): 5 February 1911, Paris, Paule de l'Estang.
fEp (complete): 27 February 1918, Wigmore Hall, Muriel Foster, acc. Anthony Bernard.
Pub. 1910, Durand. English words by Nita Cox.

108a. Trois Ballades de François Villon. Version with orchestra by the composer. Dur. 7′.
3 fl, pic, 2 ob, ca, 2 cl, 3 bsn; 4 hn, 2 tpt; hp, strings.
fp: 5 March 1911, Paris, Concerts Sechiari, Charles W. Clark, cond. Claude Debussy.
fGBbp (No. 3 only): 27 March 1927, Sara Fischer and Cardiff Station Symphony Orchestra.
fEp: 10 October 1947, BBC broadcast, Camille Maurane and the Paris Conservatoire Orchestra, cond. André Cluytens.
Pub. 1911, Durand.

109. Le Martyre de Saint-Sébastien.
'Mystère' in five acts (Gabriele d'Annunzio).
1911. For soloists, chorus and orchestra.

2 fl, 2 pic, ob, ca, 3 cl, bcl, 3 bsn, cbsn; 6 hn, 4 tpt, 3 tmb, tuba; timp, hmnm, cym, GC, tamtam; celesta, 3 hp, strings.

fp: 22 May 1911, Paris, Théâtre du Châtelet, cond. André Caplet; with Ida Rubinstein (Le Saint), Mlle A. Dudlay (La Mère douloureuse), Véra Sergine (La Fille malade des fièvres), Desjardins (L'Empereur)—sung roles: Rose Féart, Mlle E. Vallin, Mme Courso, Chadeigne; chorus master, D.-E. Inghel-brecht; producer, Armand Bour; décor and costumes, Léon Bakst; choreography, Michel Fokine.

fEp: 18 January 1929, BBC concert, Queen's Hall, Kate Winter, Theresa Ambrose, Linda Seymour and Rispah Goodacre, National Chorus and Orchestra, cond. Ernest Ansermet.

Pub. 1911, Durand; also reduction by André Caplet; also Fanfares.

109a. Le Martyre de Saint-Sébastien.
Symphonic Fragments. Dur. 20'.
1. *Prelude, Act I*; 2. *Danse extatique & Finale, Act I*; 3. *La Passion*; 4. *Le Bon Pasteur*.

2 fl, pic, 2 ob, ca, 3 cl, bcl, 3 bsn, cbsn; 6 hn, 4 tpt, 3 tmb, tuba; timp, cym, GC, tamtam; celesta, 3 hp, strings.

fEp: 24 August 1915, Queen's Hall, Promenade Concert, Queen's Hall Orchestra, cond. Sir Henry Wood.

Pub. 1912, Durand.

BIBLIOGRAPHY:

Robert Bernard: Autour du Martyre de Saint-Sébastien, *L'Information musicale*, 20 June 1941, p. 663.

José Bruyr: Le Martyre de Saint-Sébastien, *Schweizerische Musikpädagogische Blätter*, April 1957.

André Coeuroy: Musiques françaises, *Revue universelle*, 15 July 1922, p. 248.

Gustave Cohen: Gabriele d'Annunzio et le Martyre de Saint-Sébastien, *RM*, 1957, p. 29.

— Souvenirs sur Gabriele d'Annunzio et sur le Martyre de Saint-Sébastien, *L'Opéra de Paris*, XIV, 1957.

R. Cuttoli: Le Martyre de Saint-Sébastien, création et reprises, *RM*, No. 234, 1957, p. 9.

H. Devillez: L'adaptation du poème, *RM*, No. 234, 1957.

Arthur Farwell: The Debussy of St. Sebastian, *Musical America*, 24 February 1912, p. 21; *MS*, 6 April 1912, p. 213.

G. Hirsch: A l'Opéra, *RM*, No. 234, 1957.

G. Inghelbrecht: Le Martyre de Saint-Sébastien, mystère de G. Annunzio, musique de CD, Paris, 1948.

M. Jacquemont: Notes sur la mise en scène, *RM*, No. 234, 1957.

F. Labisse: J'ai voulu garder l'esprit de l'œuvre, *L'Opéra de Paris*, XIV, 1957.

Louis Laloy: Le Martyre de Saint-Sébastien, *Comoedia*, 5 June 1922.

Serge Lifar, Ludmila Tcherina, F. Labisse and L. Fourestier: Témoignages, *RM*, No. 234, 1957.

Edward Lockspeiser: The authenticity of Le Martyre, *The Listener*, 5 May 1966, p. 662.

Jean Marnold: Le Martyre de Saint-Sébastien de M. Gabriel d'Annunzio, musique de CD, *Mercure de France*, No. 583, 1 October 1922, p. 234.

R.-A. Mooser: Debussy et d'Annunzio, *Dissonances*, March 1938.

Arthur Pougin: Le Martyre de Saint-Sébastien, *Le Ménestrel*, 3 June 1911, p. 171.

Alec Robertson: The Martyrdom of Saint Sebastian, *The Gramophone*, July 1935, p. 57.

V. Seroff, Towards Debussy's Bayreuth: Martyrdom of Saint-Sébastian, *Saturday Review*, 15 October 1960, p. 72.

P. Saegel: Opéra—Le Martyre de Saint-Sébastien, *Le Ménestrel*, 23 June 1922, p. 274.

Boris de Schloezer: Le Martyre de Saint-Sébastien à l'Opéra, *Nouvelle revue française*, No. 107, 1922, p. 243.

Pasteur Valléry-Radot: Présentation du Martyre de Saint-Sébastien, *RM*, April 1964, p. 75.

Emile Vuillermoz: Autour du Martyre de Saint-Sébastien, *RM*, December 1920, p. 155.

— Le Martyre de Saint-Sébastien, *L'Opéra de Paris*, XIII, 1956.

Le Martyre de Saint-Sébastien (interview with Claude Debussy), *Excelsior*, 11 February 1911.

Debussy, Claude

110. Images. For orchestra, 1906–12.

1. *Gigues.* Orig. 'Gigues tristes'. 4 January 1909 – 10 October 1912. Orchestration completed by André Caplet. Dur. 7′.

2 fl, 2 pic, 2 ob, ob d'amore, ca, 3 cl, bcl, 3 bsn, cbsn; 4 hn, 4 tpt, 3 tmb; timp, cym, tambour, xyl, celesta; 2 hp, strings.

fp: 26 January 1913, Paris, Concerts Colonne, cond. Gabriel Pierné (in a complete performance of the triptych).

Pub. 1913, Durand.

2. *Ibéria.* 25 December 1908. Dur. 20′.

1. *Par les rues et par les chemins*; 2. *Les parums de la nuit*; 3. *Le matin d'un jour de fête.*

3 fl, pic, 2 ob, ca, 3 cl, 3 bsn, cbsn; 4 hn, 3 tpt, 3 tmb, tuba; timp, tamb de basque, tamb mil, cast, xyl, cym, 3 bells; celesta, 2 hp, strings.

fp: 20 February 1910, Paris, Concerts Colonne, cond. Gabriel Pierné.

fEp: 18 September 1913, Queen's Hall, Promenade Concert, Queen's Hall Orchestra, cond. Sir Henry Wood.

Pub. 1910, Durand.

3. *Rondes de printemps.* Ded. Emma Claude Debussy. Dur. 9′.

3 fl, pic, 2 ob, ca, 3 cl, 3 bsn, cbsn; 4 hn; 2 timp, tgle, tambour, cym; celesta, 2 hp, strings.

fp: 2 March 1910, Paris, Salle Gaveau, Concerts Durand, cond. Claude Debussy.

fEp: 23 May 1911, Queen's Hall, London Musical Festival, Queen's Hall Orchestra, cond. Sir Henry Wood.

fEbp (No. 3): 4 March 1926, Manchester, Free Trade Hall, Halle Orchestra, cond. Sir Hamilton Harty.

fEbp (No. 1): 28 April 1928, Wireless Symphony Orchestra, cond. Ernest Ansermet.

Pub. 1909, Durand.

BIBLIOGRAPHY:

Louis Laloy: Rondes de printemps, *Grande Revue*, 15 March 1910.

— Ibéria, *Grande Revue*, 10 March 1910.

— Ibéria, in *La Musique retrouvée*, Librairie Plon (Paris), p. 174.

Maurice Ravel: L'art et les hommes—A propos des Images de Claude Debussy, *Cahiers d'aujourd'hui*, No. 3, February 1913, p. 135.

Kurt Westphal: Debussys Ibéria-Suite für Orchester, *Melos*, March 1950, p. 107.

111. Jeux. 'Poème dansée' for orchestra. August–September 1912. Ded. Jacques Durand. Dur. 20′.

2 fl, 2 pic, 3 ob, ca, 3 cl, bcl, 3 bsn, sarrusophone; 4 hn, 4 tpt, 3 tmb, tuba; timp, tamb de basque, tgle, cym, xyl; celesta, 2 hp, strings.

fp: 15 May 1913, Paris, Théâtre des Champs-Elysées, Diaghilev's Ballets Russes, with Tamar Karsavina, Ludmila Schollar and Nijinsky, cond. Pierre Monteux; choreography, Nijinsky; décors and costumes, Léon Bakst.

fEp: 25 June 1913, Drury Lane, cond. Pierre Monteux; with Tamar Karsavina (First Girl), Ludmilla Schollar (Second Girl), Nijinsky (The Youth).

f concert p: 1 March 1914, Paris, Théâtre du Châtelet, Concerts Colonne, cond. Gabriel Pierné.

Pub. 1912, Durand; also reduction for piano solo by the composer, for piano four hands by Léon Roques.

BIBLIOGRAPHY:

Georges Auric: Jeux de CD, *Nouvelle revue française*, 1921, No. 88, p. 101.

Herbert Eimert: Debussy's Jeux, *Die Reihe*, No. 5, 1959; English edition 1961, p. 3.

Edward Lockspeiser: Jeux, in *Decca Book of Ballet*, Muller (London), 1958, p. 117.

André Mangeot: Jeux, *Le Monde musical*, 30 May 1913.

R.-A. Mooser: Jeux, poème dansée de CD, *Dissonances*, 1943.

B. Schäffer: 'Jeux' Debussy'ego, *Ruch Muzyczny*, 1962, No. 16, p. 14.

Anon.: M. Debussy's new ballet: Dance of lawn-tennis players, *The Times*, 23 May 1913, p. 10.

Anon.: M. Debussy's new ballet: production of Jeux at Drury Lane, *The Times*, 26 June 1913, p. 6.

112. Khamma. Ballet-pantomime in three scenes ('Légende dansée'). 1912. Orchestrated by Charles Koechlin. Scenario: W. L. Courtney and Maud Allan. Dur. 22′.

3 fl, pic, 3 ob, ca, 3 cl, bcl, 3 bsn, cbsn; 4 hn, 3 tpt, 3 tmb, tuba; timp, GC, cym, antique cym, tgle, tamtam, jeux de timbres, gong; piano, celesta, 2 hp, strings.

fp: 15 November 1924, Paris, Théâtre du

Châtelet, Orchestre Colonne, cond. Gabriel Pierné.

f stage p: 26 March 1947, Paris, Opéra-Comique.

Pub. 1912, Durand; reduction for piano solo by the composer, for piano four hands by Lucien Garban.

113. Douze Préludes. Book Two. ?1913. Dur. 32′ 40″.

1. *Brouillards.* Dur. 2′ 40″.
2. *Feuilles mortes.* Dur. 2′ 55″.
3. *La Puerta del Vino.* Dur. 2′ 45″.
4. *Les Fées sont d'exquises danseuses.* Dur. 2′ 40″.
5. *Bruyères.* Dur. 2′ 30″.
6. *General Lavine—eccentric.* Dur. 2′ 20″.
7. *La Terrasse des audiences du clair de lune.* Dur. 3′ 45″.
8. *Ondine.* Dur. 2′ 45″.
9. *Hommage à S. Pickwick, Esq., P.P.M.P.C.* Dur. 2′.
10. *Canope.* Dur. 2′ 35″.
11. *Les Tierces alternées.* Dur. 2′ 25″.
12. *Feux d'artifice.* Dur. 3′ 20″.

fp (Nos. 4, 7 & 12): 5 April 1913, Paris, Salle Pleyel, Société Nationale de Musique, Ricardo Viñes.

fEp (No. 6): 3 June 1913, Aeolian Hall, Fanny Davies; note also: 9 June 1913, Aeolian Hall, Robert Chignell.

fEp (No. 9): 3 June 1913, Aeolian Hall, Fanny Davies.

fEp (complete): 12 June 1913, Aeolian Hall, Walter Morse Rummel.

Pub. 1913, Durand.

BIBLIOGRAPHY:

Dieter Schnebel: Brouillards—Tendencies in Debussy, in *Die Reihe*, No. 6, 1960, Universal-Edition; English edition 1964, Theodore Preiser (Pennsylvania).

Anon.: Some pianoforte music: new Preludes by Debussy, *The Times*, 13 May 1913, p. 9.

See also bibliography following No. 105.

114. Trois Poèmes de Stéphane Mallarmé. For voice and piano. Summer 1913.

1. *Soupir*; 2. *Placet futile*; 3. *Eventail.*

fp: 21 March 1914, Paris, Ninon Vallin.

Pub. 1913, Durand.

115. Syrinx. For solo flute. 1913. Ded. Louis Fleury. Dur. 1′ 40″.

fp: 1 December 1913, residence of Louis Mors, Louis Fleury (offstage in a performance of 'Psyché' by Gabriel Mourey).

fEp: 30 June 1922, London, reception given by Mme Alvar for Maurice Ravel, Louis Fleury.

Pub. 1913, Jobert.

116. La Boîte à joujoux. Ballet in three tableaux for children. For piano. October 1913. Scenario: André Hellé. Dur. 30′.

fp: 10 December 1919, Paris, Théâtre du Vaudeville, cond. D.-E. Inghelbrecht; with Mlle Sakhy and R. Quinault; choreography and production, R. Quinault.

fEp: November 1922, London, Court Theatre, Ballets suédois de Rolf de Maré, cond. D.-E. Inghelbrecht; producer, Jean Borlin.

Pub. 1913, Durand.

BIBLIOGRAPHY:

Claude Debussy: La Boîte à joujoux, *Comoedia*, 1 February 1914.

Edward Lockspeiser: La Boîte à joujoux, in *Decca Book of Ballet*, Muller (London) 1958, p. 114.

Anon.: Toys and tales in music—a ballet for children, *The Times*, 6 January 1914, p. 8.

116a. La Boîte à joujoux. Version for orchestra. Sketched: spring 1914; orchestration completed after Debussy's death by André Caplet.

2 fl, 2 ob, ca, 2 cl, 2 bsn; 2 hn, 2 tpt; timp, tgle, tambour, cym, GC, crecelle; piano, celesta, hp, strings.

fp: 17 February 1923, Paris, Théâtre du Châtelet, Orchestre Colonne, cond. Gabriel Pierné.

fEbp: 20 June 1926, Newcastle Station Symphony Orchestra, cond. Edward Clark (arr. H. Mouton).

Pub. 1920, Durand.

117. Berceuse héroïque (pour rendre hommage à S.M. le Roi Albert I de Belgique et à ses soldats). For piano. November 1914. Dur. 4′ 20″.

fEp: 11 May 1915, Bechstein Hall, William Murdoch.

Pub. 1914, in King Albert's Book.

117a. Berceuse héroïque. Version for orchestra. December 1914.

2 fl, 2 ob, ca, 3 cl, 3 bsn; 4 hn, 2 tpt, 3 tmb, tuba; timp; 2 hp, strings.

fp: 26 October 1915, Paris, cond. Camille Chevillard.

Pub. 1915, Durand.

118. Six Epigraphes antiques. For piano four hands. 1914. Dur. 14' 25".

1. *Pour invoquer Pan, dieu du vent d'été* (Dur. 2' 20"); 2. *Pour un tombeau sans nom* (Dur. 3'); 3. *Pour que la nuit soit propice* (Dur. 2' 15"); 4. *Pour la danseuse aux crotales* (Dur. 2'); 5. *Pour l'Egyptienne* (Dur. 2' 40"); 6. *Pour remercier la pluie au matin* (Dur. 2' 10").

Pub. 1915, Durand. Reduction for piano solo by the composer (fEbp: 17 February 1938, Edmund Rubbra.)

118a. Six Epigraphes antiques. Orch. Ernest Ansermet. Dur. 18'.

3 fl, pic, 2 ob, ca (ob d'amore, ad lib), 3 cl, bcl, 2 bsn, cbsn; 4 hn, 3 tpt, 3 tmb; timp, GC, cym, tgle, tamtam, glock, crotales, xyl; 2 hp, strings.

?fp: 13 November 1932, BBC Orchestra, cond. Ernest Ansermet.

?fp (concert): 31 May 1935, Paris, Salle Rameau, Société Philharmonique de Paris, cond. Ernest Ansermet.

Pub. 1939, Durand.

119. Cello Sonata. Late July–early August 1915. Ded. Emma Claude Debussy. Dur. 10' 30".

1. *Prologue*; 2. *Sérénade*; 3. *Finale.*

fEp: 4 March 1916, Aeolian Hall, C. Warwick Evans and Mrs. Alfred Hobday.*

fEbp: 4 April 1926, Newcastle studio, John Barbirolli and Ethel Bartlett.

Pub. 1916, Durand.

120. En Blanc et Noir. Three pieces for two pianos. Summer 1915. Dur. 16'.

1. *Avec emportement.* Ded. Serge Koussevitzky.

2. *Lent, sombre.* Ded. Lt. Jacques Charlot.

3. *Scherzando.* Ded. Igor Stravinsky.

---

* The actual première remains in doubt. The suggestion that the first performance was given in Paris on 24 March 1917 by Joseph Salmon and Claude Debussy must be discounted in view of this London performance of over a year earlier.

fp: 21 December 1916, Paris, war charity concert, Claude Debussy and Roger-Ducasse.

fEbp: 31 October 1927, Ethel Bartlett and Rae Robertson.

Pub. 1915, Durand.

121. Douze Etudes. For piano. 27 September 1915. Dur. 38' 40".

Book I:

1. *Pour les cinq doigts.* Dur. 2' 45".
2. *Pour les tierces.* Dur. 3' 20".
3. *Pour les quartes.* Dur. 4'.
4. *Pour les sixtes.* Dur. 3' 15".
5. *Pour les octaves.* Dur. 2' 15".
6. *Pour les huit doigts.* Dur. 1' 30".

Book II:

7. *Pour les degrés chromatiques.* Dur. 2'.
8. *Pour les agréments.* Dur. 4'.
9. *Pour les notes répétées.* Dur. 3'.
10. *Pour les sonorités opposées.* Dur. 4' 35".
11. *Pour les arpèges composés.* Dur. 3'.
12. *Pour les accords.* Dur. 5'.

fp: 14 December 1916, Walter Morse Rummel.

Pub. 1916, Durand.

BIBLIOGRAPHY:

Richard Bryceson: Debussy's Piano Studies, *Gramophone Record*, September 1934, p. 3.

Maurice Dumesnil: Debussy Etudes: correct approach as to pedaling, phrasing and tonal colours, *Etude*, October 1947, p. 552.

122. Sonata for flute, viola and harp. September–October 1915. Ded. Emma Claude Debussy. Dur. 16'.

fp (private): 10 December 1916, Paris, at the home of Durand.

fEp: 2 February 1917, Aeolian Hall, concert of the London String Quartet, Albert Fransella (fl), H. Waldo Warner (va) and Miriam Timothy (hp).

fFp (public): 9 March 1917, Paris, charity concert; then: 21 April 1917, Société Musicale Indépendante concert, Manouvrier (fl), Jarecki (va), Pierre Jamet (hp).

fEbp (incomplete): 1 October 1925, Joseph Slater, Rebecca Clarke and Gordon Bryan (piano).

fEbp (complete): 2 January 1928, Robert Murchie, Ernest Tomlinson and John Cockerill.

Pub. 1916, Durand.

123. La Chute de la Maison Usher. Opera after Edgar Allan Poe. Unfinished.

124. Noël des enfants qui n'ont plus de maison (Claude Debussy). For voice and piano. December 1915.
   fp: 9 April 1916, Paris, Jane Monjovet.
   fEbp: 6 July 1927, Sara Fischer.
   Pub. 1916, Durand. Version for children's voices unpub.

124a. Noël des enfants qui n'ont plus de maison. Orch. D.-E. Inghelbrecht. Dur. 2′ 30″.
   ca, 2 cl, bsn; hn, tpt; timp; hp, strings.
   Pub. 1949, Durand.

125. Violin Sonata. Winter 1916–March 1917. Ded. Emma Claude Debussy. Dur. 11′ 40″.
   1. *Allegro vivo*; 2. *Intermède (fantasque et leger)*; 3. *Finale.*
   fp: 5 May 1917, Paris, Salle Gaveau, Gaston Poulet and Claude Debussy.
   fEp: 13 July 1917, Wigmore Hall, Albert Sammons and William Murdoch.
   fGBbp: 9 July 1925, Glasgow studio, William Primrose and Gordon Bryan.
   Pub. 1917, Durand.

126. Ode à la France (Louis Laloy). For soloists, chorus and orchestra. 1916–17. Unfinished. Completed and orchestrated by Marius François Gaillard. Dur. 10′ 45″.
   3 fl, 2 ob, ca, 3 cl, bcl, 3 bsn, cbsn; 4 hn, 4 tpt, 3 tmb, tuba; timp, cym, tamtam, GC, 2 tamb; strings.
   fp: 2 April 1928, Paris, Salle Pleyel.
   Pub. 1954, Choudens.

BIBLIOGRAPHY:
Louis Laloy: La dernière œuvre de CD— l'Ode à la France, *Musique*, No. 6, 15 March 1928, p. 245.
Henry Prunières: L'Ode à la France et quelques œuvres de jeunesse de CD, *RM*, May 1928, p. 199.

TRANSCRIPTIONS BY DEBUSSY
Humoresque en forme de valse. Raff, arr. for piano solo.
Caprice (on airs from the ballet 'Alceste' by Gluck). Saint-Saëns, arr. for piano four hands. Pub. Durand.

Etienne Marcel: Excerpts from the ballet music. Saint-Saëns, arr. for two pianos four hands, also for piano solo. Pub. Durand.
Introduction and Rondo capriccioso. Saint-Saëns, arr. for two pianos. Pub. Durand.
Symphony No. 2. Saint-Saëns, arr. for two pianos. Pub. Durand.
Am Springbrunnen (A la fontaine). Schumann (Op. 85 No. 9), arr. for two pianos and for piano solo. Pub. 1895, Fromont.
Stüdien für den Pedal-Flugel (Six studies in canon form). Schumann (Op. 56), arr. for two pianos. Pub. *c.* 1890, Durand.
   fEbp: 9 November 1924, Manchester station, Harry Greenwood and Eric Fogg.
Swan Lake: Three Dances. Tchaikovsky, arr. for piano solo.
The Flying Dutchman: Overture. Wagner, arr. for two painos. Pub. Durand.
Die Götterdämerung: Chorus of Gibichungs. Wagner, arr. for orchestra.
   fEp: 21 June 1935, BBC broadcast, BBC Orchestra, cond. (Sir) Eugene Goossens.
Gymnopédies. Erik Satie, arr. for orchestra. See No. 60.

WRITINGS BY DEBUSSY
Musique, *Revue blanche*, 1 April 1901.
Le Chambre d'enfants de Moussorgski, *Revue blanche*, 15 April 1901.
Une sonate pour piano de M. P. Dukas, *Revue blanche*, 15 April 1901.
Concerts symphoniques du Vaudeville, *Revue blanche*, 15 April 1901.
Bach, Beethoven, *Revue blanche*, 1 May 1901.
Le Roi de Paris de M. G. Hüe & Concerts Nikisch, *Revue blanche*, 15 May 1901.
L'Ouragon de M. A. Bruneau, *Revue blanche*, 15 May 1901.
La Musique de plein air & Concerts Nikisch, *Revue blanche*, 1 June 1901.
L'Entretien avec M. Croche, *Revue blanche*, 1 July 1901.
De quelques superstitions et d'un opéra (les Barbares, de C. Saint-Saëns), *Revue blanche*, 15 November 1901.
Grisélidis, de Massenet, *Revue blanche*, 1 December 1901.
Réponse à l'enquête sur l'orientation musicale, *Musica*, October 1902.
Réponse à l'enquête sur l'influence allemande, *Mercure de France*, January 1903.

G

L'Etranger, de M. V. d'Indy, *Gil Blas*, 12 January 1903.

Considérations sur la musique de plein air, *Gil Blas*, 19 January 1903.

Titania, de M. G. Hüe, *Gil Blas*, 21 and 26 January 1903.

Castor et Pollux, de Rameau, à la Schola Cantorum, *Gil Blas*, 2 February 1903.

M. Weingartner, *Gil Blas*, 16 February 1903.

Reprise de la Traviata, de Verdi, *Gil Blas*, 16 February 1903.

Lettre ouverte à M. le Chevalier Gluck, *Gil Blas*, 23 February 1903.

Pour le peuple, *Gil Blas*, 2 March 1903.

M. Siegfried Wagner aux Concerts Lamoureux, *Gil Blas*, 2 March 1903.

De l'Opéra et de ses rapports avec la musique, *Gil Blas*, 9 March 1903.

Aux Concerts Colonne: Parysatis, de C. Saint-Saëns, *Gil Blas*, 16 March 1903.

Muguette, de E. Missa, *Gil Blas*, 19 March 1903.

A propos de Muguette, *Gil Blas*, 23 March 1903.

Penthésilée, de M. A. Bruneau, *Gil Blas*, 23 March 1903.

Le Mozart de Saint-Maur, *Gil Blas*, 30 March 1903.

Richard Strauss, *Gil Blas*, 30 March 1903.

Parsifal et la Société des Grandes Auditions de France, *Gil Blas*, 6 April 1903.

Les Béatitudes, de C. Franck, *Gil Blas*, 13 April 1903.

Grieg, *Gil Blas*, 20 April 1903.

Reprise de Werther, de Massenet, *Gil Blas*, 27 April 1903.

Une renaissance de l'opéra-bouffe: le Sire de Vergy, de Claude Terrasse, *Gil Blas*, 27 April 1903.

Considérations sur le Prix de Rome au point de vue musical, *Musica*, May 1903.

La Tétralogie, de R. Wagner—lettre de Londres, *Gil Blas*, 15 May 1903.

Berlioz et M. Günzbourg, *Gil Blas*, 18 May 1903.

Henri VIII, de Saint-Saëns, *Gil Blas*, 19 May 1903.

Impressions sur la Tétralogie, à Londres, *Gil Blas*, 1 June 1903.

La Petite Maison (W. Chaumet), *Gil Blas*, 6 June 1903.

Les Impressions d'un prix de Rome, *Gil Blas*, 10 June 1903.

Le Bilan musical en 1903, *Gil Blas*, 28 June 1903.

Réponse à l'enquête sur l'état actuel de la musique française par M. P. Landormy, *Revue bleue*, 26 March and 2 April 1904.

A propos de Gounod, *Musica*, July 1906.

Mary Garden, *Musica*, January 1908.

A propos d'Hippolyte et Aricie, *Le Figaro*, 8 May 1908.

Que faire au Conservatoire?, *Le Figaro*, 4 February 1909.

La musique d'aujourd'hui et de demain, *Comoedia*, 4 November 1909.

Réponse à l'enquête sur la musique moderne italienne par L. Borgex, *Comoedia*, 31 January 1910.

Une renaissance de l'idéal classique, *Paris-Journal*, 8 May 1910.

Décentralisation musicale, *Comoedia*, 26 January 1911.

La musique russe et les compositeurs français, *Excelsior*, 9 March 1911.

Réponse à l'enquête sur les rapports du vers et de la musique, *Musica*, March 1911.

Concerts Colonne: Les Concerts du mois de novembre, *Revue S.I.M.*, November 1912.

Du respect dans l'art, *Revue S.I.M.*, December 1912.

Les concerts du mois, *Revue S.I.M.*, December 1912.

Fin d'année: Notes sur les concerts, *Revue S.I.M.*, 15 January 1913.

Du goût, *Revue S.I.M.*, 15 February 1913.

Du Précurseur, *Revue S.I.M.*, 15 March 1913.

Concerts Colonne: Fanelli, *Revue S.I.M.*, 15 March 1913.

Les concerts, *Revue S.I.M.*, 15 May, 1 Nov., 1913.

Concerts Colonne—Société des Nouveaux Concerts, *Revue S.I.M.*, 1 December 1913.

Lettre de Russie, *Revue S.I.M.*, 1 January 1914.

Sur deux chefs-d'œuvre—Les Concerts: l'Etrangère, de M. Max d'Ollone, *Revue S.I.M.*, 1 February 1914.

La Boîte à joujoux, *Comoedia*, 1 Feb. 1914.

Concerts Colonne, *Revue S.I.M.*, 1 March 1914.

Préface à l'édition des œuvres complètes de Chopin, Durand (Paris) 1915.

Preface to 'Pour la musique française', Crès (Paris) 1917.

Monsieur Croche antidilettante, Paris, 1921.

GENERAL BIBLIOGRAPHY

Gerald Abraham: Debussy as a critic, *MS*, 19 November 1927, p. 178.

Julia d'Almendra: Les Modes grégoriens dans l'œuvre de CD, G. Enault (Paris) 1947–8.

— Debussy e o movimento modal na musica do seculo xx., *Arte musical*, 1962, No. 18, p. 12;

— Debussy et le mouvement modal dans la musique du XXe siècle, *Le Lutrin* (Geneva), January 1963.

— Debussy e a sua obra, *Broténa* (Lisbon), No. 2, 1962.

Hidenotu Amano: CD and G. F. Malipiero, Yokohama, 1927 (Japanese text).

Francis Ambrière: La vie romaine de CD, *RM*, January 1934, p. 20.

— Lettres à Emile Baron, *RM*, January 1934.

Hendrik Andriessen: Debussy en het Kind, *Mens en melodie*, April 1948, p. 97.

Ernest Ansermet: Le langage de Debussy, *Feuilles musicales*, June–July 1962, p. 63.

— An inner unity (conversations with Peter Heyworth), *High Fidelity*, September 1962, p. 56.

A. Antoine: Mes souvenirs sur le Théâtre Antoine et sur l'Odéon, Paris, 1928.

M. Arconada: En torno a Debussy, Espasa-Calpe (Madrid) 1926.

Rodolfo Arizaga: Debussy y España, *Ars* (Buenos Aires) No. 82, 1958, p. 101.

Gabriel Astruc: Le pavillon des fantômes—souvenirs, Paris, 1937.

William W. Austin: The adventure and achievement of Debussy, in *Music in the 20th Century*, W. W. Norton (New York) 1966, p. 1.

— Debussy's 20th-century music: History in the service of 'recruiting unknown friends', in –*do*–, p. 42.

Ursula Bäcker: Frankreichs Moderne von CD bei Pierre Boulez, Gustav Bosse Verlag (Regensburg) 1962.

F. Baldensperger: Causerie sur CD, *Le Courrier musical*, March 1903.

D. Baldwin: Debussy, an appreciation—with some reference to Mr. D. C. Parker, *MS*, 19 December 1914, p. 419.

Jürgen Balzer: CD, Jespersen og Pios Forlag (Copenhagen) 1949. (Includes discography.)

Jean-Joël Barbier: Notes sur Debussy, *RM*, April 1964, p. 99.

Raoul Bardac: Dans l'intimité de CD, *Terres latines* (Brussels), March 1936, p. 71.

G. Barini: CD, *Nuova Antologia*, 1918.

Jean Barraqué: Debussy, Editions du Seuil (Paris) 1962.

M. Baschet: Portrait de CD à 23 ans, *Le Monde musical*, April 1919.

Jane Bathori: Sur l'interprétation des mélodies de CD, Editions Ouvrières (Paris) 1953.

— Les musiciens que j'ai connu, 2: Debussy, *Recorded Sound*, spring 1962, p. 174.

Richard Batka: Debussy und kein Ende!, *Der Kunstwart*, 1911, No. 17 (1 July), p. 35.

Harold Bauer: Recollections of Debussy, *Musician*, February 1931, p. 21.

William Behrend: CD, Tilskveren (Copenhagen) 1918.

Camille Bellaigue: A short sketch of the student, in *Great Composers Through the Eyes of their Contemporaries*, Dutton (New York) 1951, p. 400.

Ralph H. Bellairs: Debussy and Sibelius (A paper read at Worcester on 16 May 1908), *Journal of Incorporated Society of Musicians*, June 1908; *MO*, July 1908, p. 748.

Peter Benary: Debussy und das impressionistische Raumgefühl, *SM*, July–August 1962, p. 204.

Frank J. Benedict: Debussy's harmonies and how to study them, *The Musician*, September 1910, p. 618; *MS*, 17 September 1910, p. 181.

P. Bertrand: A la gloire de Debussy, *Le Ménestrel*, 24 June 1932.

Marc Blancpain: Le centenaire de Debussy et l'alliance française, *RM*, April 1964, p. 153.

Jacques-Emile Blanche: Souvenirs sur Manet et sur Debussy, *Le Figaro*, 22 June 1932.

Helga Böhmer: Alchimie der Töne—Die Mallarmé-Vertonungen von Debussy und Ravel, *Musica*, 1968, No. 2 (March–April).

Sylvain Bonmariage: CD, Pierre Louÿs, P.-J. Toulet, in *Catherine et ses amis*, Ophrys (Gap), n.d.

Raymond Bonheur: Souvenirs et impressions

d'un compagnon de jeunesse, *RM*, May
1926.
Henri Borgeaud: Correspondance de CD et
Pierre Louÿs, Librairie José Corti (Paris)
1945.
Charles Du Bos: Pages de journal: Debussy,
Revue de Paris, March 1946.
Adolphe Boschot: Debussy et ses boutades, in
Portraits de musiciens, Vol. 2, Librairie Plon
(Paris), 1947, p. 103.
Roger Boss: CD et le piano, *SM*, November–
December 1962, p. 331.
Maurice Boucher: CD—Essai pour la con-
naissance du devenir, Editions Rieder
(Paris) 1930.
Pierre Boulez: La corruption dans les encen-
soirs, *Melos*, 1956, p. 276; Korruptionen i
rökelsekaren, *Nutida musik*, Vol. 3 (1959–
60), No. 1, p. 10.
— General Debussy—eccentric, *Melos*
November 1962.
Constantin Brailoiu: CD: coup d'œil histori-
que, CD: Textes et Documents inédits,
Revue de musicologie, 1962.
— Patru muzicanti francezi, Bucarest, 1935.
— Pentatonismes chez Debussy, in *Studia
Memoriae Belae Bartók Sacra*, (Budapest)
1956, p. 375; Pentatony in Debussy's music,
in 3rd (English) edition, 1959, p. 377.
Gustav Bret: Debussy and the public,
Weekly Critical Review, 5 November 1903.
Maurice Brillant: Maurice Denis et CD,
Cahiers de la nouvelle journée, No. 2, 1925.
Donald Brook: Debussy, in *Five Great Com-
posers*, Rockliff (London) 1946, p. 129.
A. R. Brugeot: CD, 1862–1918, *Les Arts
français*, No. 16, 1918, p. 77.
Robert Brussel: CD livré aux bêtes, *Revue
d'art dramatique*, May 1902.
— CD, *Le Monde musical*, April 1919.
— CD et Paul Dukas, *RM*, May 1926, p. 92.
José Bruyr: CD, *Disques*, No. 126, January
1962, p. 38.
C. L. Buchanan: Debussy, *Bookman*, May
1918, p. 330.
J. Burk: Estimating Debussy, *New Music
Review* (New York), 1918.
Edward Burlingame Hill: (Debussy's piano
works), *The Musician* (Boston), August
1906; L'œuvre de piano de CD, *Le Mercure
musical*, 15 October 1906.

Henri Büsser: Souvenirs de jeunesse sur CD, in
CD, Chronologie de sa vie et de ses œuvres,
Catalogue de l'Exhibition, 1942.
Rudolf Cahn-Speyer: Debussy—Eine kritisch-
ästhetische Studie von Giacomo Setaccioli,
Die Musik, August 1912, p. 233.
Charles-Francis Caillard & José de Berys: Le
cas Debussy, Bibliothèque du Temps Pré-
sent, Librairie Henri Falque (Paris) 1910.
Julien Cain: L'exposition Debussy à Lisbonne,
RM, April 1964, p. 133.
M.-D. Calvocoressi: CD, critique, *Renais-
sance latine*, 15 December 1902.
— A few remarks on modern French piano
music, *MMR*, June 1906.
— CD, *MT*, February 1908, p. 81.
— Les tendances de la musique française con-
temporaine, *Apollon* (Petrograd), February
1911.
— Tragedy of CD, *19th Century*, February
1933, p. 220.
— Debussy and the leitmotive, *MT*, August
1925, p. 695.
— Debussy and his time, *MMR*, 1933, p. 33.
— Pierre Louÿs and Debussy, in *Musicians
Gallery*, Faber & Faber (London) 1933,
Chapter III.
— CD, in *Musicians Gallery*, Faber & Faber
(London) 1933, p. 118.
— CD, Novello (London) 1944.
Antonio Capri: Debussy, in *La musica da
camera*, Gius. Laterza & Figli, 1925.
— Le origini dell'impressionismo musicale,
La Rassegna musicale, January 1928.
— Debussy a vent'anni della morte, *Bollettino
mensile di vita e cultura musicale*, February
1938.
— CD, in *Musica e musicisti d'Europa*, Ulrico
Hoepli (Milan), 2nd edn. 1939, p. 173.
Mosco Carner: Portrait of Debussy, 4: De-
bussy and Puccini, *MT*, June 1967, p. 502.
Gaston Carraud: Théâtre-Lyrique—Trois
ouvrages de CD: L'Enfant prodigue, La
Damoiselle élue, La Boîte à joujoux, *Le
Ménestrel*, 19 December 1919, p. 91.
Alfredo Casella: CD, *Ars nova* (Rome), April
1918.
— Debussy et la jeune école italienne, *RM*,
December 1920, p. 213.
— CD, *MMR*, January 1933, p. 1.
J. Chailley: Malentendus sur la 'révolution'

harmonique de Debussy, *Revue musicale de Suisse Romande*, 30 April 1963, p. 13.

René Chalupt: CD et les affinités littéraires de sa musique, *L'Echo musical*, 1919, p. 22.

Claude Chamfray: Debussy, impressioniste ou expressioniste?, *Le Ménestrel*, 31 May 1935, p. 181.

— Debussy dans l'art actuel, *Feuilles musicales*, June–July 1962, p. 80.

Jean Chantavoine: Debussy démodé, *La Revue musicale de Lyon*, 15 April 1911.

— CD, sa place et son rôle dans l'art français, *L'Echo musical*, 1919, p. 6.

— M. CD, *L'Echo musical*, March 1914; in *De Couperin à Debussy*, Alcan (Paris) 1921.

— Les écrits de Debussy, *Le Ménestrel*, 7 January 1927, p. 1.

— Debussy et son temps, *Le Ménestrel*, 13 January 1933, p. 9.

— Debussy et nous, *Terres latines* (Brussels), March 1936, p. 68.

D. Chennevière: CD et son œuvre, A. Durand (Paris) 1913.

Frank Choisy: CD, *La Fédération artistique* (Brussels), Vol. 37, No. 14.

M. Chesneau: Debussy och symbolisterna, *Musikrevy*, 1962, Nos. 6–7, p. 187.

Claes M. Cnattingius: Notes sur les œuvres de jeunesse de CD, *Svensk tidskrift för musikforskning* (Uppsala), 1962, p. 31.

— Generationerna efter Debussy, *Musikrevy*, 1962, Nos. 6–7, p. 190.

— Debussy och Rameau, *Musikrevy*, 1964, No. 5, p. 291.

Jean Cocteau: Hommage à CD, in *CD, Chronologie de sa vie et de ses œuvres,* Catalogue de l'Exposition (Paris) 1942.

André Coeuroy: Debussy et l'harmonie romantique, *RM*, May 1921, p. 117.

— D'Annunzio musicien et Loyse Baccaris, *RM*, June 1925, p. 296.

— La jeunesse de Debussy, *Revue universelle*, 1 July 1926, p. 115.

— Alas, poor Debussy, *RM*, 1 January 1927, p. 92.

— Appels d'Orphée, Paris, 1928.

— CD, Paris, 1930.

— Le CD de Stroebel, *La Chronique de Paris*, July 1944, p. 62.

Alexander Cohen: Debussy's poets translated, *M&L*, April 1937, p. 158.

Ed. Combe: Le Debussysme, *Semaine littéraire de Genève*, December 1906.

Deryck Cooke: Delius, Debussy and pure creation, *The Listener*, 1 February 1962, p. 853.

James Francis Cooke: CAD—a short biography, The Etude Musical Booklet Library, Theodore Preisser (Philadelphia) 1930.

G. Copeland: Debussy, the man I knew, *Atlantic Monthly*, January 1955, p. 34.

Aaron Copland: The Impressionism of Debussy, in *The New Music*, McGraw-Hill (1941), Macdonald (1968, revised and enlarged edition, p. 28).

Raphaël Cor & Charles Francis Caillard: CD et le snobisme contemporain, *Revue du temps présent*, 1909, 2 October, p. 193, 2 November, p. 275, 2 December, p. 323; in *Essais sur la sensibilité contemporaine*, Henri Falque (Paris) 1912, p. 145.

Alfred Cortot: La musique pour piano de Debussy, *RM*, December 1920, p. 127.

— The piano music of Debussy (transl. Violet Edgell), Chester (London) 1922.

— The piano music of Debussy, in *French Piano Music*, O.U.P. (London) 1932, p. 1.

— CD; Conférence, Université des Annales (Paris) 1933.

— Sur le génie de Debussy, *Feuilles musicales*, June–July 1962, p. 74.

Anthony Cross: Portrait of Debussy, 2: Debussy and Bartók, *MT*, February 1967, p. 125.

T. P. Currier: Debussy's piano music, *Musician*, 1910, October, p. 702; November, p. 776.

G. Courty: Dernières années de Debussy: Lettres inédites, *Revue des deux mondes*, October 1958.

L. Crowder: Debussy and subtraction, *Clavier*, 1962, No. 4, p. 10.

John Culshaw: Impressionist achievement: Debussy, in *A Century of Music*, Dennis Dobson (London) 1952, p. 82.

Gerald Cumberland: Studies in musical psychology, No. 3—CD, *MO*, April 1911, p. 480.

— CD, *MO*, November 1908, p. 100.

William H. Daly: Debussy—a study in

modern music, Methuen Simpson (Edinburgh) 1908.

Werner Danckert: CD, W. de Gruyter (Berlin) 1950.

Laurence Davies: CD, hedonist and voluptuary, in *The Gallic Muse*, J. M. Dent (London) 1967, p. 57.

Ernst Decsey: CD—Biographie, Leykam-Verlag (Graz/Vienna) 1936; 2 vols. 1949.

Georges Delaquys: An interview with Debussy (transl. Richard Capell), *MS*, 28 January 1911, p. 57.

Célestin Deliège: La relation forme-contenu dans l'œuvre de Debussy, *Revue belge de musicologie*, 1962, p. 71.

Jörg Demus: CD, *Musikrevy*, 1962, Nos. 6–7, p. 179.

Norman Demuth: CD, in *Musical Trends in the 20th Century*, Rockliff (London) 1952, p. 34.

Henry Dérieux: La poétique de Pierre Louÿs, *Mercure de France*, No. 649, 1 July 1925, p. 34.

Dershelbe: Les idées de CD, musicien français, Les Editions musicales de la librairie de France, 1927.

Marcel Dietschy: The family and childhood of Debussy, *MQ*, July 1960, p. 301 (transl. Edward Lockspeiser).

— Debussy et Wagner, *Feuilles musicales*, June–July 1962, p. 87.

— La Passion de CD, Editions La Baconnière (Neuchâtel) 1962.

— CD et André Suarès, *Revue musicale de Suisse Romande*, 1963, 30 June p. 14, 31 August p. 14.

— L'éblouissement d'amour dans l'œuvre de Debussy, *Revue musicale de Suisse Romande*, 30 March 1963, p. 16.

Denijs Dille: Debussy et ses derniers biographes, *Syrinx*, December 1937, January 1938, March 1938.

— Inleiding tot het vormbegrip bij Debussy, in *Mélanges* ('Hommage à Charles van den Borren'), Antwerp, 1945, p. 175.

R. Dionisi: Aspetti technici e sviluppo storico del sistema 'escordale' da Debussy e poi, *Rivista italiana di musicologia*, 1966, No. 1.

Gustave Doret: Lettres et billets inédits de C. A. Debussy, *Lettres romandes* (Geneva), 23 November 1934.

— Erik Satie et Debussy, *Le Monde musical*, November 1938.

P. Douliez: CD, Haarlem, 1954.

Norbert Dufourcq: Debussy, in *La Musique française*, Librairie Larousse (Paris) 1949, p. 287.

Leonard Duck: Debussy and Ravel, *Halle*, No. 118, 1961–2, p. 26.

Paul Dukas: CD, *Gaceta musical*, May 1928.

L. Dunton-Green: L'Anglais et Debussy, *RM*, December 1920, p. 210.

Maurice Dumesnil: Conferences with CD, *Etude*, February–March 1933, pp. 81, 155.

— Personal conferences with CD, *Etude*, January 1935, p. 5.

— CD's American born teacher, *Etude*, November 1937, p. 707.

— Debussy principles in pianoforte playing, *Etude*, March 1938, p. 153.

— How to play and teach Debussy ('Endorsed by Mme Claude Debussy'), Schroeder & Gunther (New York) 1932.

— New insights to the mastery of Debussy, *Etude*, May 1940, p. 294.

— Debussy, master of dreams, New York, 1940.

— CD, French patriot, *Etude*, September 1943, p. 559.

— Debussy's influence on piano writing and playing, *Proceedings of Music Teachers' National Association*, 1945, p. 39.

— CD as a music critic, *Etude*, April 1946, p. 203.

— Spineless Debussy?, *Etude*, May 1946, p. 246.

— Coaching with Debussy, *Piano Teacher*, 1962, No. 1, p. 10.

— Debussy, the life, *Music Magazine* (Evanston, Ill.), August 1962, p. 10.

René Dumesnil: CD, in *Portraits de musiciens français*, Librairie Plon (Paris) 1938, p. 24.

— Den musikaliska impressionismens källor—CD, *Musikrevy*, 1955, p. 31.

— Du nouveau sur CD, *Le Monde*, 27 May 1957.

— El centenario de Debussy, *Buenos Aires Musical*, No. 277 (1962), p. 4; O centenario do nascimento de CD, *Gazeta musical*, No. 137 (1962), p. 101.

Jacques Durand: Quelques souvenirs d'un éditeur de musique, 2 vols., Paris, 1924–5.

— Lettres de CD à son éditeur, Durand (Paris) 1927.

A. Eaglefield-Hull: Debussy and Musorgsky, *MMR*, 1918, p. 149.

J. Eisenburg: Debussy and the pedals, *Etude*, January 1942, p. 20.

Maurice Emmanuel: Les ambitions de Claude Achille, *RM*, May 1926, p. 43; April 1964, p. 33; Las ambiciones de Claudio Aquiles Debussy, *Ars* (Buenos Aires), 1958, No. 82, p. 43.

— Debussy inconnu, *Revue Pleyel*, April 1927.

Daniel Ericourt: Debussy, the person, *Music Magazine* (Evanston, Ill.), August 1962, p. 12.

Rudolf Escher: Toscanini en Debussy, magie der werkelijkeid, Rotterdam, 1938.

Edwin Evans Sr.: Debussy's harmonies, *MO*, August 1909, p. 786.

Edwin Evans: CD (obituary article), *Fortnightly Review*, May 1918, p. 755.

— Debussy for singers, *Sackbut*, November 1921, p. 8.

— Great song writers, II: CD, *MM&F*, February 1931, p. 47.

Imre Fábián: Debussy und der ungarischen Musik, *ÖM*, January 1963.

László Fabian: CD und sein Werk, mit besonderer Rücksicht auf den musikalischen Impressionismus, Drei Masken Verlag (Munich) 1923.

— Debussy élete, kora és müvészete, *Zenemükiadó Vállalat* (Budapest), 1957.

L. Fait: CD Prix de Rome, *Studi romani*, 1962, No. 5.

Manuel de Falla: L'Espagne dans l'œuvre de Debussy, *RM*, December 1920, p. 206.

— CD and Spain, *Chesterian*, No. 12, January 1921.

— Hommage à Debussy, *Gaceta musical*, April 1928.

— Escritos sobre musica y musicos, Debussy, Wagner, el 'Canto jondo', Buenos Aires, 1950.

Georges Favre: CD, *Bulletin mensuel de l'Union Française des Oeuvres Laïques d'Education Artistique*, March 1950.

Guy Ferchault: CD, musicien français, *La Colombe* (Paris), 1948.

Jacques Feschotte: A Claude-Achille-Debussy, *Feuilles musicales*, June–July 1962, p. 69.

Helmut A. Fiechtner: Debussy und sein 'Parsifal', *ÖM*, June 1953.

Paul Le Flem: CD et la révolution de l'art français, *Les Heures de Paris*, 30 March 1938.

— Souvenirs debussystes, *Musica* (Chaix), No. 104, November 1962, p. 4.

Maurice Fleuret: Debussy speaks of Stravinsky, Stravinsky speaks of Debussy (transl. F. Harling-Comyns), *MO*, January 1963, p. 211.

Floresztán: A zenei impresszionizmusról, *A Zene*, No. 13, 15 April 1928, p. 253.

Jean de Foville: CD, *Les Essais*, April 1904, p. 16.

Alfred Frankenstein: Debussy: orchestral and vocal works, *High Fidelity*, January 1958, p. 79.

Juan Pedro Franze: Debussy, músico de cámara, *Ars* (Buenos Aires), 1958, No. 82, p. 111.

Frigyes Frideczky: Debussy, *Muzsika*, August 1962, p. 5.

Gaianus: Strauss, Debussy e compagnia bella, Bongiovanni (Bologna) 1913.

Hans Gal (ed.): CD, in *The Musicians World* (Great Composers in their Letters), Thames & Hudson (London) 1965, p. 401.

G. L. Garnier: Correspondance de CD et P.-J. Toulet, *Le Ménestrel*, 2 August 1929, p. 345.

Guido M. Gatti: L'opera pianistica di CD, *Rivista musicale italiana*, March 1920, p. 139; The piano works of Debussy, *MQ*, 1921, p. 418.

— Gli scritti di Debussy, *Il Pianoforte* (Turin), April 1927.

G. Gatti-Cassazza: Debussy, *New York Times*, 15 March 1925.

André Gauthier: Debussy, documents iconographiques, Pierre Cailler (Geneva) 1952.

François Gervais: Etude parallèle des langages harmoniques de Fauré et de Debussy, Paris, 1951, 2 vols. roneo.

— La notion d'arabesque chez Debussy, *RM*, No. 241, 1958, p. 3.

— Structures Debussystes, *RM*, April 1964, p. 77.

— Debussy et la tonalité, in *Debussy et l'évolution* (ed. E. Weber), Paris, 1965, p. 97.

Lawrence Gilman: Poet and dreamer, *Harper's Weekly*, 31 March 1906, p. 452; *North*

American Review, 2 November 1906, p. 877.

Lawrence Gilman: The music of CD, *Musician* (Boston), 1907.

— Debussy and nature painting, *Harper's Weekly*, 22 January 1910, p. 28.

— Debussy of today, *Harper's Weekly*, 3 December 1910, p. 25.

— Wagner and Debussy, *MS*, 1908, 28 November, p. 347; 5 December, p. 363; reprinted from *The Musician*.

— Geography and landscape in music, *Harper's Weekly*, 4 February 1911, p. 26.

— CD (obituary article), *Century Magazine*, August 1918, p. 465.

— Debussy and his legend, *New Republic*, 15 June 1921, p. 75.

— Debussy reconsidered, *North American Review*, April 1922, p. 556.

Alberto Ginastera: Evolución de la armonía en la obra de Debussy, *Ars* (Buenos Aires), No. 82, 1958, p. 59.

Scott Goddard: Baudelaire, Ravel, Debussy, *MN&H*, 4 June 1921, p. 717.

Robert Godet: CD, *La Semaine littéraire de Genève*, 13, 20 and 27 April 1918; *Le Monde musical*, August 1919.

— Le lyrisme intime de Debussy, *RM*, December 1920, p. 167, January 1921, p. 43.

— En marge de la marge, *RM*, May 1926, p. 51.

— Weber and Debussy, *Chesterian*, No. 55, June 1926.

— CD, souvenirs, *L'Information musicale*, 26 March 1943, p. 257.

Percy Godfrey: CD, a biography by Jules Lépine epitomized by Percy Godfrey, *MO*, January 1932, p. 308.

Fred Goldbeck: Blick auf Debussy, *Anbruch*, February 1929, p. 58.

— Heritage of Debussy, *High Fidelity*, September 1962, p. 51.

Harris Goldsmith & Conrad L. Osborne: Debussy on microgroove, *High Fidelity*, 1962, September, p. 66; October, p. 98; November, p. 84.

Antoine Goléa: Debussy und die Freiheit, *NZfM*, July–August 1962.

Sir E. W. Gosse: French profiles, London, 1905.

Cecil Gray: CD, in *A Survey of Contemporary Music*, O.U.P., 1927, p. 95.

Hans Gregor: Besuch bei Debussy, *Skizzen*, 1936, No. 2, p. 9.

Fernand Gregh: Etude sur Victor Hugo, suivi de pages sur . . . Debussy, Paris, 1905.

J. C. Griggs: Debussy's music, *Yale Review*, April 1912, p. 484.

Vittorio Gui: Debussy en Italia, *Revista de musica*, 1929, No. 8; Debussy in Italia, *Musica d'oggi*, December 1932, p. 463; Debussy in Italy, *MO*, 1939, January p. 305, February p. 404, March p. 498.

— Le due muse di CD, *Il Ponto* (Florence), 1962, No. 11.

P. Guillet: CD, *Göteborgs Handels- och sjöfartstidning*, 17 October 1934.

Fritz Gysi: CD, Allgemeinen Musikgesellschaft in Zürich—Hug & Co. (Zürich) 1926.

H. Halbreich: CD, *Phonoprisma*, 1964, No. 2, p. 34.

Victor Hallut: CD, in *De Bach à Debussy*, Editions L'Amphore (Paris) 1929, p. 323.

Bengt Hambraeus: Debussy—hans sista verk och eftervärlden, *Musikrevy*, 1962, Nos. 6–7, p. 183.

D. Handman: La psychologie dans la musique de Debussy, *SM*, July 1949; Psychology in Debussy's music, *Musicology* (New York), 1949, p. 243.

J. Handschin: CD, *SM*, 1–15 October, 1932.

Erwin Hardeck: Untersuchungen zu den Klavierliedern CDs, Gustave Boss (Regensburg) 1967.

Mary Hargrave: CD by Louis Laloy, *MMR*, 1910, p. 102.

Arthur Hartmann: CD as I knew him, *Musical Courier*, 23 May 1918; *Canadian Journal of Music*, April–May (No. 10), 1919, p. 151.

H. B. Harvey: Claude de France: the story of Debussy, New York, 1948.

Winifred Heath: Debussy, poet of tone, *Musical Courier*, 18 April 1936.

F. Heinlein: Debussy critico, *Revista musical chilena*, No. 80 (1962), p. 66.

Hans W. Heinsheimer: Debussy, *NZfM*, March 1968.

Robert Henderson: Portrait of Debussy, 3: Debussy and Schoenberg, *MT*, March 1967, p. 222.

Henry-Jacques: CD, Maurice Ravel, Gabriel Fauré et le disque, Saint Quentin, *c.* 1939.

Hermann Heyer: CDs musikalische Ästhetik: Versuch einer Analyse, *Deutsche Jahrbuch der Musikwissenschaft*, 1963, p. 36.

Ralph Hill: The gramophile's favourite composers, No. 5—CD, *Musical Mirror*, 1930, July, p. 187; August, p. 220.

Leopold Hirschberg: CD, *Signale*, 1912, No. 34 (21 August), p. 1107, No. 35 (28 August), p. 1132.

Vital Hocquet: Souvenirs confiés à Marius Richard, *La Liberté*, 11–13 December 1931.

André Hodeir: Young French music (transl. D. Noakes), *Saturday Review*, 25 May 1957, p. 41.

Leslie Hodgson: Debussy, a portrait and an analysis, *Musical America*, 10 December 1937.

Arthur Hoérée: Entretiens inédits d'E. Guiraud et de CD notés par M. Emmanuel (1889 90), in *Inédits sur CD*, Collections Comoedia-Charpentier, 1942, p. 25.

Karl Holl: CD, *Neues Musikblatt*, March 1938.

J. Hollman: Debussy on disc, *Saturday Review*, 25 August 1962, p. 34.

Richard Holt: CD, *The Gramophone*, September 1931, p. 115.

V. Holzknecht: Claude de France, *Hudebni Rozhledy*, 1962, No. 15, p. 629.

K. Hoover: Quiet voluptuary, *Opera News*, 29 December 1962, p. 8.

J. M. Howard: The musical affinity of Mozart and Debussy, *American Music Lover*, February 1937.

Gervase Hughes: Debussy, in *The Handbook of Great Composers*, Arthur Barker (London) 1965, p. 210.

C. van Hulse; Debussy, *Etude*, March 1927, p. 175.

Jean Huré: 'C'est du Debussy', *Le Monde musical*, 15 September 1905.

Paul Huvelin: Symbolistes et impressionistes, in *Pour la musique française*, Georges Crès (Paris) 1917, p. 299.

D.-E. Inghelbrecht: Souvenirs, *RM*, December 1920, p. 165.

Germaine & D.-E. Inghelbrecht: CD, Costard (Paris) 1953.

David Irvine: Wagner and Debussy, a reply, *MS*, 19 December 1908, p. 392; 2 January 1909, p. 6; 12 June 1909, p. 379.

Albert Jakobik: Die assoziative Harmonik in den Klavierwerken CDs, Würzburg, 1940.

— Zur Einheit der neuen Musik, Würzburg, 1957.

Vladimir Jankélévitch: Debussy et le Mystère, Editions La Baconnière (Neuchâtel) 1949.

— L'immédiat chez Debussy, *RM*, April 1964, p. 89.

Robert Jardillier: CD, de Pelléas aux dernières sonates, *La Revue de Bourgogne* (Dijon), 12 February and 15 May 1922.

Stefan Jarocinski: Debussy i Strauss, *Ruch Muzyczny*, 1960, No. 9 (15 May), p. 8.

— Podroze muzyczne Debussy'ego w latach, 1908–1914, *Ruch Muzyczny*, 1960, 15 February, p. 20; 1 March, p. 16.

— Debussy odnowiciel, *Ruch Muzyczny*, 1962, No. 16, p. 1.

G. Jean-Aubry: CD, *La Vie musicale* (Lausanne), 15 September 1908.

— CD et la musique française moderne en Angleterre, *Revue S.I.M.*, 15 March 1909, p. 262.

— CD, *Revue des idées*, 15 February 1910; *Revue de Hongroie*, 15 November 1910, p. 507.

— A propos d'un ouvrage sur CD, in *La musique française d'aujourd'hui*, Perrin (Paris) 1916, p. 101; CD, in same, p. 82.

— CD, *Ladies' Field*, 5 May 1917.

— CD, *MQ*, October 1918, p. 542.

— CD (obituary article), *MO*, May 1918, p. 441.

— Some recollections of Debussy, *MT*, May 1918.

— CD, *Music Student*, May 1918, p. 352.

— L'œuvre critique de Debussy, *RM*, December 1920, p. 191; La obra critica de CD, *Ars* (Buenos Aires), No. 82, 1958, p. 119.

— CD, musicien français, in *La Musique et les nations*, La Sirène (Paris) 1922, p. 39.

— Victor Segalen et CD, *Cahiers du Sud*, No. 288, 1948.

Annie Joly-Segalen & André Schaeffner: Segalen et Debussy, documents recueillis, Editions du Rocher (Monaco) 1962.

J. De Jong: Debussy als criticus, *Nieuwe Gids*, November 1918, p. 704.

Franz M. Junghanns: CD, Gestalt und Wandlung, *Phono* (Vienna), winter 1957.

Adele T. Katz: Debussy, in *A Challenge to*

Musical Tradition (A new concept of tonality), Putnam, 1945 (USA), 1947 (GB), p. 248.

István Kecskeméti: 'CD, musicien français'—his last sonatas, *Revue Belge de musicologie* (Brussels), 1962, p. 117.

A. E. Keeton: Debussy—his science and his music, *19th Century & After*, September 1909, p. 492; *Living Age*, 30 October 1909, p. 270.

Dieter Kerner: CDs Frankheit, *NZfM*, July–August 1962.

Dallas Kenmare: Debussy and Fiona Macleod, *British Musician*, May 1929, p. 208.

Piet Ketting: Claude-Achille Debussy, Becht (Amsterdam) 1941; transl. W. A. G. Deyk-Davidson, Symphonia Books, Sidgwick & Jackson (London).

John W. Klein: Debussy as a musical dramatist, *MR*, August 1962, p. 208.

— Debussy, the music, *Music Magazine*, August 1962, p. 15.

Otto Kleinpeter: Mozart und Debussy, *Der Merker*, December (1) 1914, p. 651.

Tristan Klingsor: Les musiciens et les poètes contemporains, *Mercure de France*, November 1900.

Gaston Knosp: CD, *NZfM*, 27 September 1905 (No. 40), p. 755.

Charles Koechlin: Le contrepoint chez Debussy, *Cahiers d'art*, No. 9, 1926.

— Quelques anciennes mélodies inédites de Debussy, *RM*, May 1926, p. 115.

— Debussy, H. Laurens (Paris), 1927, 1941, 1956.

— La leçon de Debussy, *RM*, January 1934, p. 1.

— Souvenirs sur Debussy, la Schola et la S.M.I., *Revue de musicologie*, November 1934.

— Sur l'évolution de la musique française avant et après Debussy, *RM*, April 1935.

— Debussy et le Debussysme dans l'époque, *RM*, 1952, p. 55.

Hans Friedrich Kölsch: Der Impressionismus bei Debussy, Nolte (Düsseldorf) 1937.

Ré Koster: Brieven van Debussy aan André Caplet, *Mens en melodie*, November 1957.

Serge Koussevitzky: Debussy, the resurrected Pan, *Atlantic Monthly*, June 1942, p. 741.

P. Krummreich: Claude Achille Debussy, a study in experience and reflection, *General Magazine and Historical Chronicle* (Camden, New York), 1930.

Karl Lahm: Erinnerungen an CD, *Melos*, November 1954, p. 314.

Pierre Lalo: CD, in *De Rameau à Ravel*, Editions Albin Michel (Paris) 1947, p. 158.

Louis Laloy: Musique moderne: MM. CD et Paul Dukas, *RM*, 1902.

— CD—La simplicité en musique, *RM*, 15 February 1904, p. 106.

— Le drame musical moderne, 4: CD, *Le Mercure musical*, August 1905, p. 233.

— Paroles sur CD, *Le Mercure musical*, March 1906, p. 193.

— Les partis musicaux en France, *Grande Revue*, 25 December 1907.

— La nouvelle manière de CD, *Grande Revue*, 10 February 1908, p. 530.

— CD, Bibliophiles fantaisistes (Paris) 1909; 2nd edn. 1944.

—CD et le Debussysme, *La Revue S.I.M.*, August 1910, p. 507; CD und der Debussysmus, *Der Merker*, May (2) 1911, p. 675.

— Le théâtre de CD, *RM*, December 1920, p. 151; El teatro de CD, *Ars* (Buenos Aires), No. 82, 1952, p. 85.

— L'amitié de CD, in *La Musique retrouvée*, Librairie Plon (Paris) 1928, p. 119; also: Debussystes, p. 129; Claude de France, p. 194.

— Debussy, *Revue des deux mondes*, 15 July 1932.

— Souvenir de CD, *RM*, April–May 1938.

Paul Landormy: CD et le progrès de l'art musical, *Le Courrier musical*, 15 June 1903.

— Debussy et l'avenir de la musique française, *Le Courrier musical*, 1 February 1910.

— Debussy est-il un impressioniste?, *Le Ménestrel*, 28 January 1927, p. 23; Is Debussy an Impressionist?, *MO*, July 1927, p. 981.

— Debussy inconnu, *Revue Pleyel*, No. 41, February 1927.

Enrico Larroque: Debussy y la canción de cámera, *Ars* (Buenos Aires), No. 82, 1958, p. 91.

Lionel de Le Laurencie: Notes sur l'art de Debussy, *Durendal* (Brussels), October 1903, p. 614; revised version, *Le Courrier musical*, March 1904, p. 141.

Thérèse Lavauden: Humour in the work of Debussy, *Chesterian*, No. 69, March 1928; L'humeur dans l'œuvre de Debussy, *Revue de musicologie*, April–June 1928; *RM*, February 1930, p. 97.

— Plainsong and Debussy, *Commonweal*, 4 March 1931, p. 485.

G. Leblanc: Souvenirs, Paris, 1931.

— Maeterlinck and I (transl. Janet Flanner), London, 1932.

Tristan Leclère: Les musiciens de Verlaine, *Revue Belge*, 14 November 1903.

Ton de Leeuw: Debussy en de exotische Muziek, *Mens en melodie*, December 1954, p. 395.

Paul Léon: Debussy, in *L'Art français— esquisses et portraits*, Fasquelle (Paris) 1933.

Sergio Leoni: L'arte pianistica in Martucci . . . Debussy, Padova, 1915.

Richard Anthony Leonard: Debussy, in *The Stream of Music*, Hutchinson (London) 1945 (rev. 1961, 1967), p. 327.

A. Leonardi: Claude Achille Debussy, *Corriere musicale dei piccoli*, August 1927.

Charles Leirens: Debussy vu par Suarès, *Revue internationale de musique*, May–June 1938, p. 321.

Jean Lépine: La vie de CD, Albin Michel (Paris) 1930.

Henri Lesbroussart: Debussy et la Belgique, *RM*, December 1920, p. 205.

Ogier de Lesseps: 'Quatre Préludes' et une 'Image' de CD, *Le Monde musical*, October 1938.

François Lesure: Debussy e Strawinski, *Musica d'oggi*, June 1959, p. 242.

— Correspondance de CD et de Louis Laloy, *Revue de musicologie*, 1962.

— Bibliographie debussyste, *Revue de musicologie*, 1962, p. 129.

— Lettres inédites de Debussy, *Candide*, 21 June 1962.

— CD, Catalogue de l'Exposition, Paris, 1962.

— Debussy et le XVIᵉ siècle, in *Hans Albrecht in Memoriam*, Kassel, 1962, p. 242.

— CD after his centenary, *MQ*, July 1963, p. 277.

— 'L'affaire' Debussy–Ravel: Lettres inédites, in *Festschrift Friedrich Blume zum 70. Geburtstag*, Kassel, 1963, p. 231.

— Les expositions consacrées à Debussy en 1962, *RM*, April 1964, p. 137.

— Debussy et Edgard Varèse, in *Debussy et l'évolution*, Paris, 1965, p. 333.

R. Leydi: Discografia delle opere di CD, *L'Approdo musicale*, 1959, Nos. 7–8.

Mrs. Franz (Louise Shirley) Liebich: CD and his music of legend and dream, *MS*, 20 February 1904, p. 119.

— Symbolism and Impressionism—Stéphane Mallarmé and CD, *MS*, 3 December 1904, p. 357.

— Claude-Achille Debussy, John Lane The Bodley Head (London) 1908, 1925.

— Debussy and nationality in music, *MS*, 26 November 1910, p. 337.

— An Englishwoman's memories of Debussy, *MT*, June 1918, p. 250.

Andreas Liess: CD und seine Zeit, *Anbruch*, April–May (Nos. 4–5) 1930, p. 148.

— L'harmonie dans les œuvres de CD, *RM*, January 1931, p. 37.

— Debussys musikgeschichtliche Bedeutung, *Die Musik*, April 1931 (No. 7), p. 487.

— CD, das Werk im Zeitbild, Heitz (Strassburg), 2 vols., 1936.

— Debussy, Dukas, Maeterlinck, *Anbruch*, June–July 1935, p. 186.

— CD, *Die Musik*, September 1937, p. 823.

— CD und das deutsche Musikschaffen, Konrad Triltsch Verlag (Würzburg) 1939.

— CD im Briefe, *Das Musikleben*, June 1951, p. 165.

— Die Stimme des Orients, *Musica*, 1960, p. 769.

— CD, der wegweisender Klassiker der modernen Musik, *Universitas*, 1962, p. 1209.

— Die okzidentale Gegenwartsmusik und der Einbruch der antiabendländischen Welt: ein Entwurf, *NZfM*, 1962, p. 315.

— CD und die 'Fünf', *NZfM*, February 1967, p. 69.

Emirto de Lima: Debussy, *Revista Brasileira de Musica* (Buenos Aires), 1934, Nos. 3–4.

— Debussy, suas obras e seus intérpretes, *Revista Brasileira de Musica* (Buenos Aires), 1937, Nos. 3–4, p. 125.

Albert Van Der Linden: Debussy, Octave Maus et Paul Gilson, *Revue belge de musicologie* (Brussels), 1962, p. 107.

Stefania Lobaczewska: O harmonice Klaud-jusza Achillesa Debussy'ego w pierwszym okresie jego twórczosci, *Kwartalnik Muzyczny* (Warsaw), 1930.

— Les ouvrages critiques de Debussy, *Musyka*, 1928 (Polish text).

Edward Lockspeiser: Debussy and Wagner, *MMR*, pp. 81, 113.

— Some projects of Debussy, *Chesterian*, No. 123, September–October 1935.

— Debussy and Shakespeare, *MT*, October 1935, p. 887.

— Debussy, Tchaikovsky et Mme von Meck, *RM*, November 1935, p. 245; *MQ*, January 1936, p. 38.

— Debussy, Dent (London) 1936; 3rd edition, 1951.

— A new study of Debussy, *MMR*, 1936, p. 106.

— CD and the Symbolists, *The Listener*, 12 August 1936, p. 323.

— Les Symbolistes et CD, *Le Ménestrel*, 7 and 14 August 1936, p. 241.

— Maggie Teyte and Debussy, *The Gramophone*, February 1937, p. 371.

— CD in the correspondence of Tchaikovsky and Mme Von Meck, *MO*, May 1937, p. 691; CD dans la correspondance de Mme Von Meck, *RM*, October 1937, p. 217.

— Mussorgsky and Debussy, *MQ*, October 1937, p. 421.

— Debussy during the last war, *MO*, November 1940, p. 59.

— Debussy, *Philharmonic Post*, November–December 1948, p. 8.

— New letters of Debussy, *MT*, August 1956, p. 404.

— Lettres inédites à André Caplet, Editions du Rocher (Monaco) 1957.

— Debussy and Swinburne, *MMR*, February 1959.

— CD, in *Decca Book of Ballets*, Muller (London) 1958, p. 110.

— New literature on Debussy, *M&L*, April 1959, p. 140.

— The mind of Debussy, *The Listener*, 17 May 1962, p. 853.

— The significance of Debussy, *M&M*, August 1962, p. 14.

— Debussy et Edgar Poë—Documents inédits, Editions du Rocher (Monaco) 1961.

— Debussy and Edgar Allan Poe, *The Listener*, 18 October 1962, p. 609.

— Debussy's concept of the dream, *PRMA*, 1962–3, p. 49.

— Debussy, his life and mind, 2 vols., London, 1962–5.

— Music and painting: Chabrier, Debussy and the Impressionists, *Apollo*, January 1966, p. 10.

Francis Lombriser: L'expression de la nature dans la musique de CD, *Schweizerische Pädagogische Blätter* (Zürich), July 1954.

Marguerite Long: Souvenirs sur CD, *L'Art musical*, 24 December 1937.

— Conseils de Debussy, *Revue internationale de musique*, April 1939, p. 889.

— Au piano avec CD, Julliard (Paris) 1960.

George Lowe: The piano works of Debussy, *MO*, June 1910, p. 625.

— The songs of Debussy, *MO*, August 1910, p. 765.

Adriano Lualdi: CD, la sua arte e la sua parabola, *Rivista musicale italiana*, 1918, p. 271; revised version, *La Critica musicale*, 1919.

C. Lucas: Debussy and the pedal blur, *Etude*, March 1935, p. 145.

Joseph Machlis: CD, in *Introduction to Contemporary Music*, Norton (USA), Dent (London) 1961, p. 123.

R. McMullen: Respectable Claude, the irreverent Achille, *High Fidelity*, September 1962, p. 63.

G. E. Magnat: Debussy ou le paysage enchanté, in *Portraits de quelques musiciens*, Foetisch-Frères (Lausanne) 1948, p. 85.

Charles Malherbe: CD, *Revue S.I.M.*, August 1910.

H. Malherbe: Debussy, *Le Temps*, 14 February 1923.

O. Mancini: Richard Strauss, Debussy ed il modernismo musicale, *Rivista nazionale di musica* (Rome), Nos. 307–8, April–May 1933; also August 1933.

Alberto Mantelli: CD, *L'Approdo musicale*, July–December 1959 (Nos. 7–8), p. 5.

G. A. Mantelli: Debussy e Mallarmé, *Rivista musicale italiana*, October–December 1932, p. 545.

André Mangeot: CD, *Le Monde musical*, 15 May 1903.

— Les faux Debussy, *Le Monde musical*, 31 July 1932.

— Le 20ᵉ anniversaire de CD, *Le Monde musical*, March 1938.

G. Marek: Master of the whisper, *Good Housekeeping*, October 1950, p. 114.

Lionel Markson: Debussy on disc, *Records & Recording*, August 1962, p. 15.

— Debussy's distillation of dreams, *Records & Recording*, January 1965, p. 12.

Jean Marnold: M. Debussy, *Mercure de France*, 1 April 1908.

Auguste Martin: CD, chronologie de sa vie et de ses œuvres, Catalogue de l'Exposition, H.M.V. (Paris) 1942.

Henri Martineau (ed.): Correspondance de CD et Paul-Jean Toulet, Paris, 1929.

Martin-Guis: L'inspiration musicale de Debussy, *Bulletin des Séances de l'Académie de Nîmes*, 1961.

Jean Matter: Sibelius et Debussy, *SM*, March–April 1965, p. 82.

Camille Mauclair: La 'Debussyte', *Le Courrier musical*, 1905.

John Maycock: Debussy, poetry and painting, *MO*, April 1953, p. 403.

W. H. Mellers: The later works of CD, *M&L*, April 1939, p. 168; revised in *Studies in Contemporary Music*, 1948, p. 43.

— Debussy and Ravel, in *Man and his Music*, Barrie & Rockliff (London) 1962, p. 935.

Pierre Meylan: Colloque sentimental, *Feuilles musicales*, June–July 1962, p. 86.

Paul Mies: Widmungsstücke mit Buchstaben —Motto bei Debussy und Ravel, *Studien zur Musikwissenschaft*, 1962, p. 363.

Massimo Mila: Musica e letteratura in Debussy, *La Rassegna musicale*, 1930, p. 474.

— Debussy nella recente critica tedesca, in *Cent'anni di musica moderna*, Milan, 1944, p. 169.

Darius Milhaud: Reminiscences of Debussy and Ravel, *The Listener*, 29 May 1958, p. 896.

Jean Mistler: Le centenaire de CD, *Revue de Paris*, August 1962, p. 82.

Denyse Molié: A propos of the interpretation of CD, *Eolus* (New York), January 1929; Interpretación de Debussy, *Musicalia* (Havana), January–February 1929.

Guy Mollat du Jourdin: L'année Debussy, *RM*, April 1964, p. 11.

Henri Mondor: Mallarmé et Debussy, *Les Cahiers de marottes et violons d'Ingres*, September–October 1954.

Gabriel Mourey: Memories of CD, *MN&H*, 11 June 1921, p. 747.

Rollo H. Myers: Debussy, Duckworth (London) 1948.

— The unknown Debussy, *The Listener*, 8 May 1958, p. 774.

— CD and Russian music, *M&L*, October 1958, p. 336.

Wilibald Nagel: CD, *NMZ*, 1918, No. 14, p. 210.

Arthur Neisser: CD, *NMZ*, 1907, No. 17.

J. Nenadovic: CD, *Zvuk*, 1963, No. 56, p. 25.

Gérard Neuhaus: Debussy et la France, *Le Démocrate*, 4 April 1938.

Ernest Newman: A note on Debussy, *MT*, May 1910, p. 293.

— Debussy on nationality in music, *MT*, November 1910, p. 700.

— The development of Debussy, *MT*, 1918, May, p. 199; August, p. 343.

— Debussy as a critic, *MO*, March 1922, p. 509.

— Wagner, Debussy and musical form, in *Testament of Music* (ed. Herbert Van Thal), Putnam 1962, p. 196; also: Debussy, p. 277.

Rosa Newmarch: CD (obituary article), *Contemporary Review*, May 1918, p. 538.

Walter Niemann: Der französische Impressionismus; CDs malerische Stimmungsmusik—seine Jünger und Zeitgenossen, *Die Musik*, September (2) 1913, p. 323.

Jeremy Noble: Portrait of Debussy, 1: Debussy and Stravinsky, *MT*, January 1967, p. 22.

Z. Novacek: CD a impresionizmus, *Slovenska Hudba*, September 1962, p. 200.

V. Ocampo: CD, *Clave*, No. 50, October–December 1962, p. 2.

Léon Oleggini: Au cœur de CD, Rene Julliard (Paris) 1947.

Poul Rovsing Olsen: Debussy og de nordiske lande, *Nutida musik*, Vol. 6 (1962–3), No. 5, p. 54.

Frank Onnen: Debussy als criticus en essayist, The Hague, 1946.

— Debussy et l'esprit du temps, *RM*, 1952, p. 65.

— Over Debussy's onbekende Werken, *Mens en melodie*, March 1948, p. 67.

Giacomo Orefice: In memoria di CD, *Rivista d'Italia*, 1918.

(D.) Hugh Ottaway: Debussy as an 'Old Master', *Halle*, January 1951, p. 13.

Charles Oulmont: Deux Amis—CD et Ernest Chausson: documents inédits, *Mercure de France*, 1 December 1934, p. 248.

Wouter Paap: Debussy en het Impressionisme, *Mens en melodie*, March 1948, p. 65.

G. Paglia: Strauss, Debussy e compagnia bella —Saggio di critica semplicista e spregiudicata per il gran publico, Bologne, 1914; 2nd edition, 1919.

John G. Palache: Debussy as critic, *MQ*, July 1924, p. 361.

Guido Pannain: La musiche di Pizzetti e Debussy, *Scenario* (Rome), D'Annunzio number, April 1934.

Rodolfo Paoli: Debussy, Sansoni (Florence) 1947; 2nd edition 1951 (includes six letters of CD to D'Annunzio, Vittorio Gui, B. Molinari, Alfredo Casella and Marquis de Casafuerte).

D. C. Parker: Debussy, *MS*, 27 April 1918, p. 254.

A. J. Patry: Du nouveau sur Debussy, *SM*, 1957, July, p. 291; September, p. 354.

Henri Pellerin: CD et le pays d'Auge, *Pays d'Auge*, 7ᵉ année, May–June (Nos. 5–6) 1957.

Edm. Pendleton: An interview with Debussy's sister, *Musical America*, 27 March–1 April 1938.

András Pernye: Debussy és Shaw, *Muzsika*, November 1960, p. 45.

L. Perrachio: Claude Achille Debussy, *Bollettino bibliografico musicale*, May 1927, p. 1.

— L'opera pianistica di CD, Milan, 1924.

René Peter: Du temps 'Achille', *RM*, December 1920, p. 159.

— CD, vue prises de son intimité, Gallimard (Paris), 1931; enlarged edition with unpublished letters, 1944.

G. Petrocchi: Le correnti ideali impressionistiche de l'arte di CD, *Rivista harmonica*, 1914.

C. H. Phillips: The symbolism of Debussy, *M&L*, July 1932.

Gabriel Pierné: Souvenirs d'Achille Debussy, *RM*, May 1926, p. 10.

— Debussy in his teens, in *Great Composers through the Eyes of their Contemporaries*, Dutton (New York) 1951, p. 401.

M. Pincherle: CD, écrivain, *L'Echo musical*, 1919, p. 36.

Peter J. Pirie: Debussy and Delius, *MO*, July 1963, p. 593.

— Portrait of Debussy, 5—Debussy and English music, *MT*, July 1967, p. 599.

Ildebrando Pizzetti: CD, in *Musicisti contemporanei*, Fratelli Treves (Milan) 1914, p. 107.

D. Ch. Planchet: CD, *Le Censeur*, 25 January 1908.

A. Porebowiczowa: Krytyka muzyczna we Francji i 'Monsieur Croche' Debussy'ego, *Ruch Muzyczny*, 1962, No. 16, p. 16.

Jean Poueigh: En souvenir de CD, *Revue hommes et mondes*, No. 21, April 1948, p. 702.

Francis Poulenc: La leçon de CD, in *CD, Chronologie de sa vie et de ses œuvres*, Paris, 1942.

H. Powischer: Studien zur Harmonik Debussys, Prague, 1931.

Margit Prahács: Debussy és az Impreszionizmus, *A Zene*, 27 March 1943, p. 132.

Gustavo Presenti: Debussy, musicista aristocratico, Dalmazzo (Bertello) 1951.

Gwilym Price-Jones: New light on Debussy, *M&M*, August 1962, p. 19.

J. G. Prod'homme: CD, *Revue de Paris*, 1 June 1918, p. 509.

— C-AD, *MQ*, October 1918, p. 555.

— An intolerant critic, in *Great Composers through the Eyes of their Contemporaries*, Dutton (New York) 1951, p. 408.

Henry Prunières: A la Villa Médici, *RM*, May 1926, p. 23.

— The youth of Debussy, *Sackbut*, October 1926, p. 58.

— Les tendances actuelles de la musique, *RM*, January 1936.

— Autour de Debussy, *RM*, 1934, May, p. 349, June, p. 21; Réponse de M. Léon Vallas, September–October, p. 189.

M. Puig: Le choix de Debussy, *L'Arc* (Aix-en-Provence), No. 27 ('L'opéra'), 1965.

Muñoz de Quedo: Debussy el antigüo y Ravel el moderno, *Mercurio Musical* (Buenos Aires), 1936, No. 61, p. 8.

Virginia Raad: CD, Anglophile, *Musical Courier*, March 1961, p. 8.

— Musical quotations in CD, *American Music Teacher*, 1968, No. 3, p. 22.

Henri Rambaud: Un musicien et un poète: Debussy et Pierre Louÿs, *Contrepoints*, No. 4, May–June 1946, p. 13.

C.-F. Ramuz: Sur Debussy, la littérature française et la musique, *RM*, 1952, p. 31.

H. Rebois: Les Grands Prix de Rome de musique, Paris, 1932.

Henri de Regnier: Souvenirs sur Debussy, *RM*, May 1926, p. 89; Memories of Debussy, *Living Age*, 19 June 1926, p. 644.

Willi Reich: Neue Wegweiser zu Debussy, *Der Auftakt*, 1906, Nos. 7–8, p. 128.

H. D. Reynaud: Hommage de la Bourgogne à CD, *Beaux-Arts* (Paris), No. 177, 6 August 1948.

— Les origincs auxoises de CD, XXᵉ Congrès de l'A.B.S.S. (Semur), 1949.

G. A. Rimsky-Korsakov: Debussy w rodzinie Meck (transl. Z. Pytowska), *Muzyka*, 1960, No. 1, p. 48.

M. Rinaldi: Dukas altre Debussy, Chigiana, 1965.

P. Ipuche Riva: CD y sus melodias de camara, *Clave*, No. 50, October–December 1962, p. 6.

Jacques Rivière: Les poèmes d'orchestre de CD, *Etudes*, 1911.

Roland-Manuel: Notre Debussy, *Musique*, No. 6, 15 March 1928, p. 249.

— Notes sur Debussy, in *Vigile* (2ᵉ cahier), Desclée, de Brouwer et Cie (Paris) 1931.

— Debussy und die deutsche Musik, *Melos*, March 1950, p. 99.

M. Robertazzi: Musica e parole nell'estetica di CD, *Il Convegno* (Milan), 1933, Nos. 3, 4 & 5.

Luigi Ronga: The meeting of poetry and music, New York, 1956.

Kajsa Rootzén: CD, Wählstrom & Widstrand (Stockholm) 1948.

— CD, in *Fransk musik* (?Stockholm), 1957, p. 40.

Charles Rosen: Where Ravel ends and Debussy begins, *High Fidelity*, May 1959, p. 42.

Claude Rostand: Debussy gestern—Debussy heute, *Melos*, November 1962.

Albert Roussel: CD et l'école moderne, *L'Echo musical*, 1919, p. 17.

Jean Roy: Trois lettres inédites de CD, *RM*, April 1964, p. 117.

Edmund Rubbra: Debussy, an introduction, *MMR*, 1933, pp. 82, 170.

— Edward Lockspeiser's 'Debussy', *MMR*, 1936, p. 199.

Dane Rudhyar (i.e. Daniel Chennevière): CD et son œuvre, Paris, 1913.

H. Rutz: CD, Dokumente seines Lebens und Schaffens, Munich, 1954.

Nicholas Ruwet: Note sur les duplications dans l'œuvre de CD, *Revue belge de musicologie*, 1962, p. 57.

J. S. S.: Debussy, *MMR*, 1918, p. 97.

Leonid Sabaneev: CD, Moscow, 1922 (Russian text).

— CD, *M&L*, January 1929.

— The Debussy period, *MO*, February 1941, p. 197.

Pedro Sáenz: La obra pianistica de CD, *Ars* (Buenos Aires), No. 82, 1958, p. 77.

Jacques Salève: Pour Debussy, E. Figuière (Paris) 1926.

Rient van Sant: CD, Kruseman ('s-Gravenhage) 1926; 2nd edition, 1947.

V. Salas Viu: La formacion estética de Debussy, *Cuadernos hispano-americanos* (Madrid), 1962.

Adolfo Salazar: CD, in *Música y músicos de hoy*, Editorial Mundo Latino (Madrid), 1928, p. 167.

Gustave Samazeuilh: Sur deux ouvrages inédits de Chausson et Debussy, *Le Temps*, 25 December 1933; in *Musiciens de mon temps*, Editions Marcel Daubin (Paris), 1947, p. 126.

— La musique d'orchestre de CD, *L'Echo musical*, 1919, p. 30.

Lazare Saminsky: Debussy à Petrograd, *RM*, December 1920, p. 216.

F. Santoliquido: Il dopo-Wagner: CD e Richard Strauss, Rome, 1909.

Henri Sauguet: CD, *Musikrevy*, 1962, Nos. 6–7, p. 175.

Richard Saville: Debussy and the French public, *MS*, 7 November 1908, p. 296.

André Schaeffner: Debussy et ses rapports avec la musique russe, in *Un Siècle de la musique russe*, Vol. 1, Paris, 1953, p. 95.

— CD e Victor Segalen: *La Rassegna musicale*, September 1959, p. 205.

André Schaeffner: CD, in *Histoire de la musique* (ed. Roland-Manuel), Pléiade (Paris), 1963, Vol. 2, p. 909.

— CD et ses projets shakespeariens, *Revue d'histoire du théâtre*, 1964, No. 4, p. 446.

— Debussy et ses rapports avec la peinture, in *Debussy et l'évolution*, Paris, 1965, p. 151.

Georg Schaeffner: CD und das Poetische, A. Francke (Bern), 1943.

E. W. Schallenberg: Moessorgskij en Debussy, *De Wereld der Muziek*, November 1938.

— CDs titel musicien français, *Mens en melodie*, 1965, p. 108.

Helmut Schmidt-Garre: Die Klangstruktur Debussys in ihrer Beziehung zu Mehrstimmigkeit des Mittelalters, *Melos*, 1950, No. 4, p. 104.

— Rimbaud-Mallarmé-Debussy — Parallelen zwischen Dichtung und Musik, *NZfM*, July–August 1964, p. 290.

Florent Schmitt: CD, *L'Echo musical*, 1919.

Elie Robert Schmitz: What Debussy and Ravel told me about their piano music, *Proceedings of Music Teachers National Association* (Pittsburgh), 1949.

— The piano works of CD, Duell, Sloane and Pearce (New York), 1950.

Robert Schmitz: A plea for the real Debussy, *Etude* (Philadelphia), December 1937.

Dieter Schnebel: Tendenzen bei Debussy, *Die Reihe*, No. 6, 1960.

Edouard Schneider: Claude Achille Debussy, *Musica*, September 1910, p. 134.

L. Schneider: CD, *RM*, 1902.

Percy Scholes: A lesson on Debussy, *School Music Review*, April 1922, p. 164.

H. C. Schonberg: Still ecstatic about Debussy, *New York Times* (Magazine), 19 August 1962, p. 20.

Willi Schuh: Debussy, Yvonne Lerolle, Renoir, *Neue Zürcher Zeitung*, 19 August 1962.

— Neue Debussy-Literatur, *SM*, March–April 1963, p. 100; *Melos*, June 1963.

Friederike Schwarz: Debussy als espressiver Gestalter, *Der Auftakt*, January–February 1933, p. 6.

Hellmut Seraphin: Debussys Kammermusikwerke der mittleren Schaffenszeit: analytische und historische Untersuchungen im Rahmen des Gesamtschaffens, Munich, 1962.

V. Seroff: Debussy, musician of France, Putnam (New York), 1956.

— Footnote on Debussy's Gaby, *Saturday Review*, 25 January 1958, p. 44.

Georges Servières: Lieder français: CD, *Guide musical*, 15 September 1895, also 1913, pp. 293, 316, 338.

Giacomo Setaccioli: Debussy è un innovatore?, Edizione Musica (Rome), 1910; Ger. transl. by F. Spiro as Debussy, Eine kritische-ästhetische Studie, Leipzig, 1911.

Frank H. Shera: Debussy and Ravel, London, 1925.

Ernst Silz: Debussy und Ravel als Wegbereiter der neuen Musik, *Musikerziehung* (Vienna), September 1965.

Roger Smalley: Debussy and Messiaen, *MT*, February 1968, p. 128.

Eileen Souffrin: Debussy lecteur de Banville, *Revue de musicologie*, December 1960, p. 200.

André Souris: Debussy et la nouvelle conception du timbre, *Cahiers musicaux*, 1956, No. 6.

— Debussy et Stravinsky, *Revue belge de musicologie* (Brussels), 1962, p. 145.

Robert de Souza: Maurice Maeterlinck and CD (Lecture to Maison d'Arts, 16 November 1907), *Revue S.I.M.*, 15 December 1907, p. 1270.

August Spanuth: Achille Claude Debussy, *Signale*, 1918, Nos. 14–15 (10 April), p. 288.

Friedrich Spigl: Wagner et Debussy, *Revue blanche*, 1 December 1902.

E. Staempfli: Militär, Radio und CD, *SM*, 1943.

May Stanley: Debussy the man as Maggie Teyte knew him, *Musical America*, 13 April 1918, p. 5.

Paul-Stefan: Der Schriftsteller Debussy, *Anbruch*, 1922, Nos. 19–20, p. 292; *Berliner Börsen-Courier*, No. 597, 21 December 1922.

Paul de Stoecklin: M. CD et l'avenir de la musique française, *Le Courrier musical*, 1910, No. 3.

Heinrich Strobel: Hommage à Debussy, *Melos*, March 1950, p. 97.

— CD, Atlantis Verlag (Zürich), 1940, 5th edition 1961; Fr. transl. by André Coeuroy, Editions Balzac (Paris), 1943; new edition, Plon (Paris), 1952.

— Madame CD, née Bardac, *Melos*, November 1961.

— CD, Persönlichkeit und Werk, *Melos*, November 1962.

— Reflexionen über Debussy, *Melos*, November 1966, p. 349.

H. H. Stuckenschmidt: CD, in *Schöpfer der neuen Musik*, Suhrkamp Verlag (Frankfurt a.M.), 1958, p. 28.

— Debussy or Berg? The mystery of a chord progression, *MQ*, July 1965, p. 453.

André Suarès: Debussy, *RM*, December 1920, p. 98.

— Debussy, Emile-Paul frères (Paris), 1922; new editions, 1936, 1949.

Arthur Symons: The Symbolist movement in literature, London, 1899.

— CD, *Saturday Review*, 8 February 1908.

Magda Tagliaferro: Debussy et Ravel, *Le Monde musical*, July 1936.

Alexander Tansman: CD, *Blok* (Warsaw), 1924, No. 6.

Otto Taubman: Debussy, *AMZ*, 5 April 1918.

Eric Taylor: Debussy, the early years. *Month*, 29 January 1963, p. 30.

Andrew de Ternant: Debussy and Brahms, *MT*, July 1924, p. 608.

— Debussy and some Italian musicians, *MT*, September 1924, p. 812.

— Debussy and others on Sullivan, *MT*, December 1924, p. 1089.

V. Terenzio: Debussy e Mallarmé, *La Rassegna musicale*, 1944, p. 132.

Maggie Teyte: Star on the door, London, 1958.

— Memories of Debussy, *M&M*, August 1962, p. 16.

Louise Thomas: CD (A propos du livre de Louis Laloy), in *Vingt Portraits*, Messein (Paris), 1911, p. 37.

Oscar Thompson: Debussy, man and artist, Dodd, Mead (New York), 1937.

C. Thoresby: Claude's letters to Emma: a myth exposed, *Musical America*, February 1958, p. 24.

Yvonne Tiénot & O. D'Estrade-Guerra: Debussy et Erik Satie, *Feuilles musicales*, June–July 1962, p. 86.

— Debussy, l'homme, son œuvre, son milieu, H. Lemoine (Paris), 1962.

Julien Tiersot: CD, *Le Courrier musical*, 15 April 1918.

— CD, in *Un demi-siècle de musique française*, Felix Alcan (Paris), 1918, p. 207.

— Oeuvres de première jeunesse de Berlioz et de Debussy, *Le Ménestrel*, 6 January 1933, p. 1.

— Promenades à l'exposition universelle, *Le Ménestrel*, 1889, 26 May, 30 June, 14 July.

V. Tomasini: CD et l'impressionismo nelle musica, *Rivista musicale italiana*, 1907.

Guy de Tosi (ed.): CD et Gabriele d'Annunzio —Correspondance inédite, Paris, 1948.

Maurice Touchard: CD, *La Nouvelle revue*, 15 October 1919.

J. Ujfalussy: Debussy, Budapest, 1959.

Jorge d'Urbano: La orquesta de Debussy, *Ars* (Buenos Aires), No. 82, 1958, p. 67.

Léon Vallas: Le nouveau style pianistique: CD, *Revue musicale de Lyon*, 14–21 October 1906.

— A propos de Debussy, *Revue musicale de Lyon*, 15 October 1905.

— Un livre sur CD, *Revue française de musique*, 10 November 1913.

— Beethoven et Debussy, *Nouvelle revue musicale* (Lyons), July 1925.

— Debussy (1862–1918), Librairie Plon (Paris), 3rd edition, 1926.

— Les idées de CD, Librairie de France (Paris), 1927; transl. M. O'Brien as The theories of Debussy, musicien français, O.U.P. (London), 1929.

— Achille Debussy, élève du Conservatoire, devant la critique, *Revue Pleyel*, No. 48, September 1927.

— En feuillant les manuscrits de Debussy, *Musique*, No. 2, November 1927.

— Le Nationalisme de Verdi, Wagner, Debussy, *Nouvelle revue musicale* (Lyon), August–September 1924.

— Debussy, l'essentiel de la vie demeurée jusqu'à présent un peu mysterieuse du grand musicien français, Librairie Plon (Paris), 1927.

— CD et son temps, Felix Alcan (Paris), 1932; new edition, Albin Michel (Paris), 1958; transl. Maire and Grace O'Brien as CD, his life and works, O.U.P. (London), 1933.

— Achille Claude Debussy, Paris, 1944.

— Autour de Debussy, *Musique*, November 1928.

— Achille Debussy, jugé par ses professeurs du

H

Conservatoire, *Revue de musicologie*, Nos. 101–2, July 1952, p. 46.

Léon Vallas: Une renaissance de Bilitis, *Domaine musical*, No. 1, 1954.

Pasteur Valléry-Radot: CD, souvenirs, *Revue des deux mondes*, 15 May 1938, p. 390.

— Le Maître toujours insatisfait, in *Great Composers Through the Eyes of their Contemporaries*, E. P. Dutton (New York), 1951, p. 410.

— Tel était CD, Rene Julliard (Paris).

— Lettres de CD à sa femme Emma, Flammarion (Paris), 1957.

— Amours de Debussy, *Marottes et violons d'Ingres*, 1961.

— CD et le culte de l'amitié, *RM*, April 1964, p. 107.

Ninon Vallin: CD, *Sovetskaya Muzika*, January 1936.

Marguerite Vasnier: Debussy à dix-huit ans, *RM*, May 1926, p. 17; The eighteen-year-old, in *Great Composers Through the Eyes of their Contemporaries*, Dutton (New York), 1951, p. 400.

Ary Verhaar: Het leven van CD, The Hague, 1951.

Mathilde Verlaine: Mémoires de ma vie, 1935.

Marcos Victoria: Debussy y nuestra sensibilidad, *Crótalos* (Buenos Aires), December 1935–April 1936.

Paul Vidal: Souvenirs d'Achille Debussy, *RM*, May 1926, p. 11.

Emile Vuillermoz: Debussy et les Debussystes, *Nouvelle presse*, 26 February 1907.

— CD, *Le Ménestrel*, 1920, 11 June, p. 241; 18 June, p. 249.

— CD et la pensée contemporaine, *Grande Revue*, 25 July 1913.

— CD, the man, *Christian Science Monitor*, 11 March 1936, p. 3.

— CD, *La Revue Rhénane*, June 1921.

— CD, Kister (Geneva), 1957; 2nd edition, Flammarion (Paris), 1962.

Franz Walter: Debussy le dernier poète, *SM*, November–December 1962, p. 330.

P. Warren: Debussy, *New Republic*, 6 April 1918, p. 294.

Edith Weber: Debussy et l'évolution de la musique au XXe siècle, *RM*, April 1964, p. 123; Editions du Centre National de la Recherche Scientifique (Paris), 1965.

H. Weinstock: On singing Debussy, *Saturday Review*, 29 January 1955, p. 52.

Adolf Weissmann: Debussy und seine Nachahmer, *Blätter der Staatsoper* (Berlin), November 1927, p. 5.

— Debussy und seine historische Bedeutung, *Die Musikwelt*, 15 October 1922.

Egon Wellesz: Die letzten Werke CDs, *Melos*, 1920, No. 7, p. 166.

— Der Stil der letzten Werke Debussys, *Anbruch*, February (No. 3) 1921, p. 50.

Constant van Wessem: CD, Hollandia-Drukkerij, 1920.

Kurt Westphal: Die moderne Musik im Lichte Debussys, *Die Musik*, June 1928 (No. 9), p. 633.

— CD und die neue Musik, *Musikblätter*, 1948, No. 6, p. 1.

J. A. Westrup: Debussy as a critic, *MMR*, 1929, p. 163.

Eric Walter White: Stravinsky and Debussy, *Tempo*, spring–summer 1962, p. 2.

W. G. Whittaker: The music of Debussy, 1. Instrumental works, *Music Student*, February 1910, p. 81; 2. Vocal works, chamber and instrumental music, *Music Student*, March 1910, p. 108.

Hellmuth Christian Wolff: Melodische Urform und Gestaltvariation bei Debussy, in *Deutsches Jahrbuch der Musikwissenschaft für 1966*, Edition Peters (Leipzig), 1967, p. 95.

Klaus Wolters: Die Bedeutung Debussys im Klavierunterricht, *SM*, July–August 1962, p. 208.

H. Woollett: CD, *Le Monde musical*, Vol. 31, Nos. 17-18.

Russell Woollen: Episodic compositional techniques in late Debussy, *Journal of the American Musicological Society*, 1958, p. 79.

Ralph W. Wood: Debussy and the minor second, *MO*, March 1942, p. 193.

L. E. Wyckoff: Steps to piano mastery—interpretative attitudes towards the music of CD, *Musician*, June 1926, p. 15.

I. Xenakis: Debussy a sformalizowanie muzyki, *Ruch Muzyczny*, 1962, No. 16, p. 7.

E. Ysaÿe: Lettres inédites de CD à Eugène Ysaÿe, *Les Annales politiques et littéraires* (Paris), 25 August 1933.

H. Zagwijn: Debussy, Kruseman (Hague), 1940.

Jean Zay: CD, *RM*, April–May 1938, p. 241.

A. Zelling: CD, Van Eck & Zoon (Hague), 1918.

J. Zukerman: Debussy, *American Scholar*, 1945, No. 3, p. 335.

MISCELLANEOUS OR UNSIGNED ARTICLES

Work of Debussy, *Harper's Weekly*, 4 March 1905, p. 337.

Debussy and the music of tomorrow, *Current Literature*, August 1907, p. 198.

La nouvelle manière de CD, *Grande revue*, 10 February 1908.

Debussy, *MS* 1909, repr. from *Musical America*.

Comments and opinions, an interesting interview with Debussy, *MS*, 27 August 1920, p. 127.

The concert season in Paris: M. Debussy as conductor, *The Times*, 22 October 1913, p. 11.

CD, what he thinks of modern music, including his own, *Current Opinion*, July 1914, p. 28.

CD on works of Walter Morse Rummel, *MMR*, 1914, p. 147.

Le style pianistique de Debussy et de Ravel, *Dissonances*, December 1932.

Debussy's hatred of Wagner, *Literary Digest*, 4 May 1918, p. 33.

Debussy's music: its achievements and limitations, *The Times*, 6 April 1918, p. 9.

Passing of France's foremost musician, *Current Opinion*, May 1918, p. 327.

Student Debussy, *Musician*, July 1918, p. 467.

Debussy as a music critic, *MT*, 1918, July p. 295, August p. 348, November p. 498; 1919, August p. 410, November p. 605.

CD, *Musical News*, 6 April 1918, p. 123.

Death of CD, *Musical Herald*, May 1918, p. 135.

Deux lettres de Debussy à M. J. Durand, *Le Monde musical*, April 1919.

Quelques fragments de lettres de CD, *Le Monde musical*, May 1919.

Lettre, *Le Monde musical*, November 1919.

Lettre inédite de Debussy, *Le Monde musical*, 15 and 30 January (Nos. 1-2) 1920.

Correspondance inédite de Chausson et Debussy, *RM*, December 1920.

Lettre inédite, *Dissonances*, December 1923.

Debussy exotique?, *Nouvelle revue musicale* (Lyon), October–November 1924.

Debussy et l'Espagne, *Nouvelle revue musicale* (Lyon), December 1924.

Debussy critique musical, *Nouvelle revue musicale* (Lyon), 1925.

Bach et Debussy, *Nouvelle revue musicale* (Lyon), 1925.

Debussy et les Russes, *Nouvelle revue musicale* (Lyon), 1925.

Debussy et Puccini, *Nouvelle reve musicale* (Lyon), 1925.

Lettres à Monsieur Vasnier, *RM*, May 1926.

Deux lettres à Chausson, *RM*, May 1926, p. 87.

Debussy en Ravel, *De Muziekbode*, October and November 1927.

Lettre de Pierre Louÿs à CAD, *Le Rouge et le Noir*, May–June 1928.

Debussy's mind, *The Times*, 20 April 1929, p. 10.

Correspondance de CD et P. J. Toulet, *Le Divan* (Paris), Collection Saint-Germain-des-Prés, No. 10., 1929.

Correspondance inédite de Pierre Louÿs et de CD, *L'Esprit français*, No. 55, January 1931.

Rameau jugé par Debussy . . . et par Rameau, *Dissonances*, October 1930.

Parsifal jugé par CD, *Dissonances*, August 1932.

Opinions de CD, *Dissonances*, January 1933.

Lettres inédite de CD à Eugène Ysaÿe, *Annales politiques et littéraires*, 25 August 1933.

Zwei Wiener Bücker über CD, *Anbruch*, May 1936, p. 73.

L'art de J.-S. Bach vu par Debussy, *Dissonances*, July–August 1938.

Un enregistrement de CD, *Dissonances*, 1936, p. 166.

Lauriers funèbres à la mémoire de Claude Achille Debussy et Paul Verlaine, Impr. des Dernières Nouvelles de Strasbourg, 1936.

Lettres à deux amis, Robert Godet et G. Jean-Aubry, Paris, 1942.

Propos et opinions de CD, *Dissonances*, January–February 1943.

Gounod consideré par Debussy, *Dissonances*, October 1943.

Mystery of a Debussy title unveiled by a critic, *Musician*, July 1945, p. 133.

L'opinion de Debussy sur 'Louise' (Lettre à Pierre Louÿs), *Dissonances*, May–June 1946.

7 Kritiker schreiben über Debussy, *Melos*, February 1948, p. 44.

Busy Debussy, *Etude*, April 1950, p. 54.

Debussy soirée, recordings, *Musical America*, 15 November 1953, p. 17.

Lettres de CD à sa femme Emma, Flammarion (Paris), 1957.

CD: Textes et documents inédits, *Revue de musicologie*, July–December 1962:
Correspondance de Debussy et Louis Laloy, p. 3.; Trois textes de Debussy, p. 41; Dix lettres d'Ernest Chausson à CD, p. 49; Neuf lettres de Pierre Louÿs à Debussy, p. 61; Trois lettres d'Erik Satie à Debussy, p. 71; Deux lettres de Gabriel Fauré à CD, p. 75; Cinq lettres de Robert Godet à CD, p. 77; Notes et documents, p. 96.

Music of mystery, *Times Literary Supplement*, 17 August 1962, p. 617.

Mary Garden on Debussy, Debussy on Mary Garden, *Opera*, May 1962, p. 305.

CD Briefe an Igor Stravinsky, *Melos*, November 1962.

Hommage de la Revue Musicale à CD, *RM*, April 1964, p. 157.

FREDERICK DELIUS (1862–1934)

Delius was born on 29 January 1862, in Bradford, the fourth of the fourteen children of a prosperous wool merchant who had emigrated to Yorkshire from his native Germany in the 1850s. There was much music in the Delius household, but it was seen as a leisure activity only, and the future composer was firmly apprenticed to the wool trade in 1880. He made several trips to Europe, officially to study the trade, but managed to escape from his apprenticeship in 1884 by persuading his father to set him up as an orange planter in the United States. He crossed to Solano Grove on the St. John's River in Florida, but soon he was taking composition lessons from Thomas Ward (an

organist he met downstream at Jacksonville), handing his plantation over to his brother and earning his living as an organist and music teacher in Jacksonville, Danville (Virginia) and New York. He returned to Europe in 1886 to study at the Leipzig Conservatoire, staying there for eighteen months and—as a facet of his life-long enthusiasm for Norwegian life and art—forming a significant friendship with Edvard Grieg. Having largely broken with his parents, Delius moved to Paris where he stayed until 1896, living most of the time on Montrouge. Here his friends included Strindberg and Gauguin and here he met the painter Jelka Rosen. From 1897 onwards he lived mainly at her house in Grez-sur-Loing, near Fontainebleau, marrying her in 1903. Apart from being obliged to return to England for most of the First World War, Delius lived at Grez for the rest of his life. Lacking major financial worries, he was able in his maturity to be exclusively a composer, never teaching and very rarely conducting. His conductor *par excellence* from 1907 onwards was Sir Thomas Beecham, whose advocacy of his art reached its climax in 1929 with a festival of six concerts of Delius's works in London, which the composer attended. By this time, however, Delius had been totally blind and was paralysed for four years, as a result of the recurrence of syphilis contacted in the 1890s. From 1928 until the year before Delius's death (at Grez in June 1934), the devoted help of a young Yorkshireman, Eric Fenby, enabled him to produce several works in spite of his physical state.

CATALOGUE OF WORKS

1. Zwei bräune Augen (Hans Andersen). For voice and piano. 1885. Unpub.

2. Over the mountain high (Björnstjerne Björnsen). For voice and piano. 1885. Unpub.

3. Zum Carnival. Polka for piano. Pub. 1886, Campbell (Jacksonville, Florida).

4. Florida. Suite for orchestra. 1886–7. Ded. to the people of Florida. Dur. $33\frac{1}{2}'$.
  1. *Daybreak*. Dur. 10'.
  2. *By the river*. Dur. $6\frac{1}{2}'$.
  3. *Sunset*. Dur. 8'.

4. *At night.* Dur. 9'.
3 fl, pic, 2 ob, ca, 2 cl, bcl, 2 bsn; 4 hn, 2 tpt, 3 tmb; timp, tamb, tgle, cym, GC; hp, strings.
fp (private): 1888, Leipzig.
fp (public): 1 April 1937, Queen's Hall, Royal Philharmonic Society concert, cond. Sir Thomas Beecham.
Pub. 1963, Hawkes (ed. Sir Thomas Beecham).

5. Hiawatha. Tone poem for orchestra. 1888.
2 fl, 2 ob, 2 cl, 2 bsn; 4 hn, 2 tpt, 3 tmb, tuba; timp, hp, strings.
Unpub.

6. Paa Vidderne. Melodrama (Ibsen): recitation with orchestra. October 1888. Ded. Edvard Grieg.
2 fl, pic, 2 ob, ca, 2 cl, 2 bsn; 4 hn, 2 tpt, 3 tmb, tuba; timp, glock; strings.
Unpub.

BIBLIOGRAPHY:
Rachel Lowe: Delius's first performance?, *MT*, March 1965, p. 190.

7. Pastorale. For violin and orchestra. September 1888, St. Malo.
3 fl, 2 ob, 2 cl, 2 bsn; 4 hn, 2 tpt, 3 tmb, tuba; timp; strings.
Pub. Joseph Williams.

8. Rhapsodie Variations. For orchestra. 1888. Unfinished.
2 fl, pic, 2 ob, 2 cl, 3 bsn; 4 hn, 2 tpt, 2 cornets, 3 tmb, tuba; timp, tgle, cym; strings.

9. Five Songs from the Norwegian. For voice and piano. 1888.
　1. *Slumber song* (Björnsen).
　2. *The nightingale* (Welhaven).
　3. *Summer eve* (J. Paulsen).
　4. *Longing* (Th. Kjerulf).
　5. *Sunset* (A. Munck).
Pub. 1892, Augener; English words, W. Grist.

10. Sakuntala (Holger Drachmann). For tenor and orchestra. 1889.
3 fl, 2 ob, ca, 2 cl, bcl, 2 bsn; 4 hn; timp; 2 hp, strings.
Unpub.

11. Petite Suite d'Orchestre. 1889.

1. *March*; 2. *Berceuse*; 3. *Scherzo*; 4. *Theme and variations.*
2 fl, pic, 2 ob, 2 cl, 2 bsn; 4 hn, 2 tpt, 3 tmb, tuba; timp; strings.
Unpub.

12. Aus dem Volksleben. Humoresk No. 2: Norwegian Wedding Procession Passing By, Grieg, orch. Frederick Delius. 2 December 1889.
2 fl, pic, 2 ob, 2 cl, 2 bsn; 4 hn, 2 tpt, 2 cornets, 3 tmb, tuba; timp; strings.
Unpub.

13. Two Pieces. For piano. 1889–90. Unpub.

14. Seven Songs from the Norwegian. For voice and piano. 1889–90.
　1. *Cradle song* (Ibsen). Ded. Nina Grieg.
　2. *The homeward journey* (A. O. Vinje).
　3. *Evening voices* (Björnsen).
　fp: 13 March 1899, Queen's (Small) Hall, Albert Fransella chamber concert, Minna Fischer.
　4. *Venevil* (Björnsen).
　fp: as No. 3.
　5. *Minstrels* (Ibsen).
　6. *Secret love* (Björnsen).
　7. *The bird's story* (Ibsen).
Pub. 1892, Augener; 1899, Concorde Concert Control (as *Seven German Songs*); c. 1905, Breitkopf & Härtel; 1910, Tischer & Jagenberg; 1949, O.U.P. English words: William Archer (No. 1), W. Grist (Nos. 2, 3, 4, 5, 6), F. S. Copeland (No. 7). No. 3 also pub. 1930, O.U.P., as *Twilight fancies* with English words by F. S. Copeland.

15. Sagen (Legends). For piano and orchestra. 1890. Unfinished.

16. Summer Evening. For orchestra. 1890. Dur. 6'.
3 fl, pic, 2 ob, 2 cl, 2 bsn; 4 hn, 2 tpt, 3 tmb, tuba; timp; strings.
fp: 2 January 1949, BBC broadcast, Royal Philharmonic Orchestra, cond. Sir Thomas Beecham.
Pub. 1951, Joseph Williams (ed. & arr. Sir Thomas Beecham).

17. Maud (Tennyson). Song cycle for voice and orchestra. 1891.
　1. *Come into the garden*; 2. *Go not, happy day*;

Delius, Frederick

3. *I was walking a mile*; 4. *Birds in the high-hall garden*; 5. *Rivulet crossing my ground.*
3 fl, 2 ob, ca, 2 cl, 2 bsn; 4 hn, 2 tpt; timp; hp, strings.

18. Three English Songs (Shelley). For voice and piano. 1891.
   1. *Indian love song.*
   2. *Love's philosophy.*
   3. *To the queen of my heart.*
Pub. 1894, Augener; 1899, Concorde Concert Control; 1910, Tischer & Jagenberg (Cologne).

19. Two Pieces. For orchestra.
   1. *Marche Caprice.* 1888.
2 fl, pic, 2 ob, 2 cl, 2 bsn; 4 hn, 2 tpt, 2 ten tmb, bs tmb, tuba; timp, GC, tgle, cym; strings.
fp: 18 November 1946, Central Hall (Westminster), Delius Festival concert, Royal Philharmonic Orchestra, cond. Sir Thomas Beecham.
Pub. 1951, Joseph Williams (ed. & arr. Sir Thomas Beecham).
   2. *Schlittenfahrt.* 1890.
Unpub.

20. Paa Vidderne (Sur les cimes). Concert Overture after Ibsen, for orchestra. 1890, rev. 1892.
2 fl, pic, 2 ob, 2 cl, bcl, 2 bsn; 4 hn, 2 tpt, 2 cornets, 3 tmb, tuba; timp; hp, strings.
fp: 10 October 1891, Christiana Music Society, cond. Iver Holter.
fEp: 8 November 1946, Royal Albert Hall, Delius Festival concert, Royal Philharmonic Orchestra, cond. Sir Thomas Beecham.
Unpub.

21. Irmelin. Opera in three acts. 1890-2. Libretto: Frederick Delius.
3 fl, 2 ob, ca, 2 cl, bcl, 3 bsn; 4 hn, 3 tpt, 3 tmb, tuba; timp, pcssn; hp, strings.
fp: 4 May 1953, Oxford, New Theatre, Royal Philharmonic Orchestra, cond. Sir Thomas Beecham; with Edna Graham (Irmelin), Thomas Round (Nils); producer, Dennis Arundell.
fbp: 22 November 1953, BBC Chorus and Royal Philharmonic Orchestra, cond. Sir Thomas Beecham; with Joan Stuart (Irmelin),

Arthur Copley (The King), Thomas Round (Nils), George Hancock (Rolf).
Pub. 1953, Hawkes: vocal score by Dennis Arundell.

BIBLIOGRAPHY:
R. Gelatt: Irmelin at Oxford, *Saturday Review*, 30 May 1953, p. 32.
Andrew Porter: Irmelin first performance, *MT*, June 1953, p. 275.
Desmond Shawe-Taylor: Irmelin first performance, *New Statesman*, 9 May 1953, p. 546.

21a. Irmelin: Prelude. For orchestra. Dur. 4'.
2 fl, ob, ca, 2 cl, bcl, 2 bsn; 2 hn; hp, strings.
Pub. 1938, Hawkes. Arrs. for piano and organ by Eric Fenby.

21b. Irmelin: Suite, Act II. For orchestra. Ed. and arr. Sir Thomas Beecham. Dur. 15½'.
3 fl, pic, 2 ob, ca, 2 cl, bcl, 3 bsn; 4 hn, 2 cornets, 2 tpt, 3 tmb, tuba; timp, tgle, cym, glock; hp, strings.
Pub. 1955, Hawkes.

22. Violin Sonata. 1892. Unpub.

23. String Quartet. 1893. Unpub.

24. The Magic Fountain. Opera in three acts. 1893. Libretto: Frederick Delius.
3 fl, 2 ob, ca, 3 cl, bcl, 3 bsn, dbsn; 4 hn, 3 tpt, 3 tmb, tuba; timp; 2 hp, strings.
Unpub. Vocal score, Eric Fenby.

25. Legende. For violin and orchestra. 1893.
2 fl, 2 cl, 2 ob, 2 bsn; 4 hn; timp; hp, strings.
fp: 30 May 1899, St. James's Hall, Delius concert, John Dunn, cond. Alfred Hertz.
fbp: 5 November 1924, Alfred Wall and Newcastle Augmented Station Orchestra, cond. Edward Clark.
Pub. 1916 (reduction), Forsyth.

26. Two Songs (Verlaine). For voice and piano. 1895.
   1. *Il pleure dans mon cœur.*
?fp: 22 February 1911, Aeolian Hall, Joseph Holbrooke chamber concert, Jean Waterston, acc. Louie Heathe.
   2. *Le ciel est par dessus la toit.*
Pub. 1910, Tischer & Jagenberg (Cologne).

26a. Il pleure dans mon cœur. Version with orch. acc.

fp: 25 January 1915, Grafton Galleries, Music Club concert, Jean Waterston, orchestra cond. Sir Thomas Beecham.

Unpub.

27. Over the Hills and Far Away. Tone Poem for orchestra. 1895.

3 fl, pic, 2 ob, 2 cl, 3 bsn; 4 hn, 2 tpt, 3 tmb, tuba; timp, sd dm, cym; strings.

fp: 30 May 1899. St. James's Hall, Delius concert, cond. Alfred Hertz.

revival: 16 May 1908, Queen's Hall, Mischa Elman concert, New Symphony Orchestra, cond. Sir Thomas Beecham.

Pub. 1950, Schirmer (ed. Sir Thomas Beecham).

28. Plus vite mon cheval. For voice and piano. 1895. Unpub. Withdrawn.

29. Romance. For cello and piano. 1896. Composed for Joseph Hollmann. Unpub.

30. Romance. For violin and piano. 1896. Unpub.

31. Koanga. Opera in three acts with prologue and epilogue. 1895–7. Libretto: C. F. Keary, after G. W. Cable's novel 'The Grandissimes'.

3 fl, 3 ob, ca, 3 cl, bcl, 3 bsn, dbsn; 4 hn, 3 tpt, 3 tmb, tuba; timp, tgle, tamb; hp, strings.

fp (excerpts only): 30 May 1899, St. James's Hall, Delius concert, with Ella Russell, Tilly Koenen, Vanderbeeck, William Llewellyn and Andrew Black.

fp (stage): 30 March 1904, Elberfeld, Stadttheater, with Clarence Whitehill in the title role, cond. Fritz Cassirer.

fEp & fbp: 23 September 1935, Covent Garden, with John Brownlee (Koanga), Oda Slobodskaya (Palmyra), Frank Sale (Simon Perez), Leyland White (Martinez), Constance Willis (Clothilda), London Philharmonic Orchestra, cond. Sir Thomas Beecham.

Pub. 1935 (vocal score by Eric Fenby), Winthrop Rogers/Boosey & Hawkes: libretto revised by Sir Thomas Beecham and E. Agate.

BIBLIOGRAPHY:

Eric Fenby: The story of Koanga, *Radio Times*, 20 September 1935, p. 11.

D. Hussey: Koanga, *Spectator*, 27 September 1935, p. 463.

W. J. Turner: Koanga, *New Statesman*, 5 October 1935, p. 446.

31a. La Calinda. From Koanga, for orchestra. Arr. Eric Fenby. Dur. 3½'.

fl, pic, ob, 2 cl, bsn; 4 hn, 2 tpt, 3 tmb, tuba (ad lib); timp, tamb, tgle; hp, strings.

Pub. 1938, Hawkes. Arr. for piano solo by Harold Perry, 1949; for two pianos by Joan Trumble, 1947.

32. Piano Concerto. First version, in three movements, 1897.

fp: 1904, Elberfeld, with Julius Buths as soloist, cond. Hans Haym.

Unpub.

32a. Piano Concerto. Revised version, in one movement, 1906. Ded. Théodor Szantó. Dur. 30'.

3 fl, 2 ob, ca, 2 cl, 3 bsn; 4 hn, 2 tpt, 3 tmb, bs tuba; timp, cym, GC; strings.

fp: 22 October 1907, Queen's Hall, Promenade Concert, Théodor Szantó and the Queen's Hall Orchestra, cond. (Sir) Henry Wood.

fbp: 14 April 1924, Desirée McEwen and Augmented Wireless Orchestra, cond. (Sir) Dan Godfrey.

Pub. 1907, Harmonie (Berlin); 1943, 1951 (revised edition), Hawkes. Reduction for two pianos by Otto Singer, with solo part revised by Théodor Szantó, 1908.

BIBLIOGRAPHY:

Arthur Hutchings: Piano Concerto, in *The Concerto*, Pelican Books (London) 1952, p. 263.

33. Folkeraadet (Parliament). Incidental music to a satirical play by Gunnar Heiberg. 1897.

3 fl, 3 ob, 3 cl, 3 bsn; 4 hn, 3 tpt, 3 tmb, tuba; timp; strings.

fp: October 1897, Christiania, cond. Frederick Delius.

fEp: 30 May 1899, St. James's Hall, Delius concert, cond. Alfred Herz (third and fourth movements only).

March perf: 29 January 1917, Royal Philharmonic Society concert, cond. Sir Thomas Beecham.

Prelude Act III, fEp: November 1946, Central Hall, Westminster, Delius Festival.

34. Seven Danish Songs. For voice and piano (or orchestra). 1897.
1. *On the seashore* (Holger Drachmann).
2. *Through long, long years* (J. P. Jacobsen).
3. *Wine roses* (J. P. Jacobsen).
4. *Let springtime come* (J. P. Jacobsen).
5. *Irmelin rose* (J. P. Jacobsen).
fp (Nos. 1–5): 30 May 1899, St. James's Hall, Delius concert, Christianna Andray.
6. *In the seraglio garden* (J. P. Jacobsen).
fp: 1901, Paris, Société Nationale de Musique concert, Christianna Andray, with orchestra cond. Vincent d'Indy.
?fEp: 29 October 1906, Bechstein Hall, Muriel Foster acc. Kate Eadie.
7. *Silken shoes* (J. P. Jacobsen).
Nos. 1–3 unpub. No. 5 pub. 1906, Harmonie (Berlin) as *Irmelin*. No. 4 pub. 1915, Tischer & Jagenberg (Cologne). Nos. 6–7 pub. Universal-Edition.

35. Five Songs. For voice and piano. 1898.
1. *Der Wandrer und sein Schatten* (Nietzsche).
2. *Der Einsame* (Nietzsche).
3. *Der Wandrer* (Nietzsche).
4. *Nacht neuen Meeren* (Nietzsche).
5. *Im Glück wir lachend Gingen* (Holger Drachmann).
Pub. 1910, Tischer & Jagenberg (Cologne); 1924, Universal-Edition (Nos. 1–4, as *Lieder nach Gedichten von Friedrich Nietzsche*, No. 5 then being withdrawn.)

36. Mitternachtslied (Nietzsche). For baritone, male voice choir and orchestra. 1898. Unpub.
3 fl, 3 ob, ca, 3 cl, bcl, 3 bsn, dbsn; 4 hn, 3 tpt, 3 tmb, tuba; timp, glock, tamtam; 2 hp, strings.

37. La Ronde se deroule. Tone Poem after Hilge Rode's drama 'Dansen Gaar', for orchestra. 1899, rev. 1901 as *Life's Dance*.
fp (original version): 30 May 1899, St. James's Hall, Delius concert, cond. Alfred Herz.
fp (revised version): February 1904, Düsseldorf, cond. Julius Buths.

fEp (as *Dance of Life*): 19 January 1908, Royal Albert Hall, London Symphony Orchestra, cond. Arbós.
Unpub.

37a. Life's Dance. Tone Poem for orchestra. 1912. Final revision and published version of preceding. Ded. Oskar Fried.
3 fl, pic, 3 ob, ca, 3 cl, bcl, 3 bsn, dbsn; 4 hn, 3 tpt, 3 ten tmb, bs tuba; timp, GC, cym, tgle, glock; hp (or several hps), strings.
fp: 1912, Berlin, cond. Oskar Fried.
fEp: 25 February 1913, Queen's Hall, Balfour Gardiner concert, New Symphony Orchestra.
Pub. 1912, Tischer & Jagenberg (Cologne).

38. Paris: The Song of a Great City. Nocturne for orchestra. 1898. Ded. Hans Haym.
2 fl, pic, 3 ob, ca, 3 cl, bcl, 3 bsn, cbsn; 6 hn, 3 tpt, 3 ten tmb, bs tuba; timp, glock, tgle, tamb, cast, GC, cym; 2 hp, strings.
fp: 1901, Elberfeld, cond. Hans Haym.
Note also: 15 November 1902, Berlin, Beethoven-Saal, cond. Ferruccio Busoni.
fEp: 11 January 1908, Liverpool, New Symphony Orchestra, cond. Sir Thomas Beecham. (NB: fEp originally announced for the 1905 season of Promenade Concerts.)
f London p: 26 February 1908, Queen's Hall, New Symphony Orchestra, cond. Sir Thomas Beecham.
fbp: 13 December 1927, Liverpool (Philharmonic Hall), Liverpool Philharmonic Orchestra, cond. Paul von Klenau.
Pub. 1909, Leuckart (Leipzig).

BIBLIOGRAPHY:
Sydney Grew: Delius's Paris, the Song of a Great City, *MO*, March 1911, p. 408.

39. Two Songs. For voice and piano. 1900.
1. *The violet* (Ludwig Holstein).
2. *Autumn* (J. P. Jacobsen).
Pub. 1906, Harmonie (Berlin).

40. Black roses (J. P. Jacobsen). For voice and piano. 1901. Pub. 1915, Tischer & Jagenberg (Cologne).

41. A Village Romeo and Juliet. Opera. Libretto: C. F. Keary, from a novel by Gottfried Keller. 1900–1, Grez-sur-Loing.

3 fl, pic, 3 ob, ca, 3 cl, bcl, 3 bsn, cbsn; 6 hn, 3 tpt, 3 tmb, bs tuba; 2 timp, xyl, tamtam, bells, cym; 2 hp, strings. On stage: solo v, 6 hn, 2 cornets, 2 alto tmb, Wirbeltrommel, Stahlplatten, church bells, organ.

fp: 21 February 1907, Berlin, Komisches Oper, cond. Fritz Cassirer.

fEp: 22 February 1910, Covent Garden, cond. Sir Thomas Beecham, with Ruth Vincent (Vrenchen), Walter Hyde (Sali) and Robert Maitland (The Dark Fiddler).

Revival: 19 March 1920, Covent Garden, cond. Sir Thomas Beecham, with Miriam Licette (Vrenchen), Walter Hyde (Sali) and Percy Heming (The Dark Fiddler).

fbp: 20 May 1932, BBC, with Dora Labbette (Vrenchen), Jan van der Gucht (Sali) and Dennis Noble (The Dark Fiddler), Wireless Chorus and BBC Orchestra, cond. Sir Thomas Beecham.

Pub. 1910, Harmonie (Berlin); vocal score by Otto Lindemann.

BIBLIOGRAPHY:

Deryck Cooke: Delius's operatic masterpiece, *Opera*, April 1962, p. 226.

Edward J. Dent: A Village Romeo and Juliet, *Athenaeum*, 26 March 1920, p. 422.

Tom Hammond: A Village Romeo and Juliet, *M&M*, April 1962, p. 21.

Robert d'Humières: Une première à l'Opéra-Comique de Berlin, *Bulletin de la S.I.M.,* 1907, p. 324.

Karl Holl: FD, Romeo und Julia auf dem Dorfe, *Anbruch*, January 1928, p. 20.

D. Hussey: A Village Romeo and Juliet, *Spectator*, 6 July 1934, p. 15.

John W. Klein: 'The loveliest of operas', *MT*, April 1962, p. 227.

— Delius's neglected masterpiece, *Music Magazine*, January 1962, p. 18.

William Mann: A Village Romeo and Juliet, *The Listener*, 5 April 1962, p. 617.

R. H. Myers: A Village Romeo and Juliet, *Canon*, June 1962, p. 18.

A. Sch.: Romeo und Julia auf dem Dorfe, dramatisches Idyll von FD—Uraufführung in der Komischer Oper am 21. Februar, *NZfM* (Musikalisches Wochenblatt), 1907, No. 10 (7 March), p. 243.

Norman Tucker: A Village Romeo and Juliet, *Centenary Festival Souvenir Programme*, p. 12.

Anon.: A Village Romeo and Juliet—the story of FD's opera, *Music Teacher*, May 1932, p. 245.

41a. Walk to the Paradise Garden. Intermezzo for orchestra from 'A Village Romeo and Juliet'. Dur. 8'.

2 fl, 2 ob, ca, 2 cl, 2 bsn; 4 hn, 2 tpt, 2 tmb, bs tmb; timp; hp, strings.

Pub. 1934, Universal-Edition (arr. Keith Douglas); 1940, Hawkes (arr. Sir Thomas Beecham). Arr. for piano solo by Harold Perry, 1950.

41b. A Village Romeo and Juliet. Suite for orchestra, arr. Eric Fenby.

2 fl, 2 ob, ca, 2 cl, 2 bsn; 4 hn, 2 tpt, 3 tmb, bs tuba; timp; hp, strings.

Score and material: 1948, Boosey & Hawkes.

42. Summer landscape (Holger Drachmann). For voice and piano. 1902. Pub. 1952, O.U.P.

43. The nightingale has a lyre of gold (W. E. Henley). For voice and piano. 1910. Pub. 1915, Tischer & Jagenberg (Cologne).

44. La lune blanche (Verlaine). For voice and piano. 1910. Pub. 1910, Tischer & Jagenberg (Cologne).

44a. La lune blanche (Verlaine). Version with orchestra.

fp: 25 January 1915, Grafton Galleries, Music Club concert, Jean Waterston with orchestra, cond. Sir Thomas Beecham.

Unpub.

45. Chanson d'automne (Verlaine). For voice and piano. 1911. Pub. 1915, Tischer & Jagenberg (Cologne).

46. I-Brasil (Fiona Macleod). For voice and piano. 1913. Pub. 1915, Tischer & Jagenberg (Cologne).

47. Margot La Rouge. Opera in one act. 1902. Libretto: Mme Rosenval. Lithographed but unpublished: *c.* 1905: vocal score by Maurice Ravel.

48. Appalachia. Variations for orchestra and

Delius, Frederick

chorus. 1898–1902. Ded. Julius Buths. Dur. 45'.

3 fl, 3 pic, 3 ob, ca, E-flat cl, 2 cl, bcl, 3 bsn, dbsn; 6 hn, 3 tpt, 3 tmb, tuba; timp, tgle, sd dm, GC, tamtam; 2 hp, strings.

fp: 1904, Elberfeld, cond. Hans Haym.

fEp: 22 November 1907, Queen's Hall, New Symphony Orchestra with the Sunday League Choir, cond. Fritz Cassirer.

Revised version:

fp: 10 March 1921, Queen's Hall, Royal Philharmonic Society concert with the Philharmonic Choir, cond. Albert Coates.

Pub. 1906, Harmonie (Berlin), incl. piano score by Otto Singer, 1907; 1921, Universal-Edition; revised edition (ed. Sir Thomas Beecham) 1951, Hawkes.

49. Sea Drift. For baritone, chorus and orchestra. 1903. Text: Walt Whitman. Ded. Max Schillings. Dur. 30'.

3 fl, 3 ob, ca, 3 cl, bcl, 3 bsn, cbsn; 6 hn, 3 tpt, 3 tmb, tuba; timp, GC; 2 hp, strings.

fp: 24 May 1906, Essen, Tonkünstlerfest, Josef Loritz, Essen Musikverein, cond. George Witte.

fEp: 7 October 1908, Sheffield Festival, Frederic Austin, Festival Chorus and the Queen's Hall Orchestra, cond. (Sir) Henry Wood.

f London p: 22 February 1909, Queen's Hall, Frederic Austin, North Staffordshire Choral Society and New Symphony Orchestra, cond. (Sir) Thomas Beecham.

fbp: 3 February 1925, Glasgow, Scottish Choir and Orchestra, cond. Wilfred Senior.

Pub. 1906, Harmonie (Berlin), incl. vocal score by S. Fall; 1928, Universal-Edition; 1939, Hawkes; revised edition (ed. Sir Thomas Beecham) 1951, Hawkes.

BIBLIOGRAPHY:
Constant Lambert: Delius and Sea Drift, *Radio Times*, 27 January 1933, p. 188.

50. A Mass of Life. For soprano, alto, tenor and baritone soloists, chorus and orchestra. 1904–5. Words selected by Fritz Cassirer from Nietzsche's 'Also sprach Zarathustra'. Ded. Fritz Cassirer.

3 fl, pic, 3 ob, bs ob, ca, 3 cl, bcl, 3 bsn, cbsn; 6 hn, 4 tpt, 3 ten tmb, bs tuba; timp,

GC, ten dm, cym, tgle, glock, tamtam, 2 bells; strings.

fp (second part only): 1908, Munich, Tonkünstlerfest.

fp (complete): 7 June 1909, Queen's Hall, Beecham symphony concerts, Cicely Gleeson-White, Grainger Kerr, Charles W. Clark, Webster Millar and Stanley Adams, North Staffordshire Choral Society and the Beecham Orchestra, cond. (Sir) Thomas Beecham; given in an English translation by William Wallace.

Pub. 1907, Harmonie (Berlin), with English translation by John Bernhoff.

BIBLIOGRAPHY:
Adrian Collins: Delius's Mass of Life, *Chesterian*, No. 77, March 1929.
Edwin Evans: A Delius-Nietzsche Mass, *Radio Times*, 19 October 1934, p. 185.
Hans Haym: Thematische Analyse, Universal-Edition (Vienna) 1913, Eng. transl. 1925.
D. Hussey: Mass of Life, *Saturday Review*, 11 April 1925, p. 385.
Edgar Istel: A Mass of Life, first performance at Munich, *MMR*, 1913, p. 62.
Adolf Keller: Uraufführung von FDs Lebensmesse, Elberfeld, den 12. Dezember 1909, *Signale*, 1909, No. 50 (15 December), p. 1827.
H. Oehlerking: FD, Eine Messe des Lebens, *NZfM*, 23 December 1909, p. 565.
E. Sackville-West: Mass of Life, *Spectator*, 11 April 1925, p. 589.
Walter Schrenk: Deliuss Messe des Lebens in Berlin, *Anbruch*, December 1927, p. 434.
Anon.: A Mass of Life, *British Musician*, April 1933, p. 74.

51. Cynara. For baritone and orchestra. 1907. Words: Ernest Dowson. Ded. to the memory of Philip Heseltine.

3 fl, pic, 2 ob, ca, 3 cl, bcl, 3 bsn, dbsn; 4 hn, 3 tpt, 3 ten tmb, bs tuba; timp, xyl, tgle, cym; hp, strings.

fp: 18 October 1929, Queen's Hall, Delius Festival, John Goss and the BBC Orchestra, cond. Sir Thomas Beecham.

Pub. 1931, Winthrop Rogers/Hawkes: piano score by Philip Heseltine; German text, Jelka Delius.

52. Brigg Fair. An English Rhapsody for orchestra. 1907. Ded. Percy Grainger.

3 fl, 2 ob, ca, 3 cl, bcl, 3 bsn, cbsn; 6 hn, 3 tpt, 3 ten tmb, bs tuba; 3 timp, GC, tgle, tub bells; hp, strings (16-16-12-12-12).

fp: 1907, Basle, Tonkünstlerfest, cond. Hermann Suter.

fEp: 18 January 1908, Liverpool, Liverpool Orchestral Society, cond. (Sir) Granville Bantock.

2Ep: 19 February 1908, Birmingham Orchestral Society concert, Halle Orchestra, cond. (Sir) Landon Ronald.

f London p: 31 March 1908, Queen's Hall, New Symphony Orchestra, cond. (Sir) Thomas Beecham.

?fAp: 28 October 1910, New York, New York Symphony Orchestra, cond. Walter Damrosch.

fbp: 12 August 1924, Wireless Symphony Orchestra, cond. (Sir) Dan Godfrey.

Pub. 1910, Leuckart (Leipzig); *c.* 1924, 1951, Universal-Edition. Also arr. for piano four hands.

53. On Craig Dhu (Arthur Symons). An Impression of Nature for SATTBB and piano. December 1907.

fp: Blackpool, Competition Festival.

Pub. 1910, Harmonie (Berlin).

54. Midsummer Song. Chorus for SSAA, TTBB and piano. 1908.

fp: December 1910, Whitley Bay and District Choral Society, cond. W. G. Whittaker.

Pub. 1910, Harmonie (Berlin).

55. Wanderer's Song (Arthur Symons). For TTBB and piano. 1908. Pub. 1910, Harmonie (Berlin); 1939, Hawkes.

56. Songs of Sunset (Ernest Dowson). For mezzo-soprano and baritone soloists, chorus and orchestra. 1906-8. Ded. Elberfeld Gesangverein.

3 fl, ob, ca, bs ob, 3 cl, 3 bsn, sarrusophone (or cbsn); 4 hn, 2 tpt, 3 ten tmb, bs tuba; timp, GC, tgle; hp, strings.

fp: 16 June 1911, Queen's Hall, Julia Culp and Thorpe Bates, Edward Mason Choir and Beecham Orchestra, cond. Sir Thomas Beecham.

Pub. 1911, Leuckart (Leipzig); German words, Jelka Rosen.

57. In a Summer Garden. Rhapsody for orchestra. Spring 1908, Grez-sur-Loing. Ded. composer's wife (Jelka).

3 fl, 2 ob, ca, 2 cl, bcl, 3 bsn; 4 hn, 2 tpt, 3 ten tmb, bs tuba; 3 timp, glock, tgle; hp, strings (16-16-12-12-12).

fp: 11 December 1909, Queen's Hall, Philharmonic Society of London, cond. Frederick Delius.

Revised version:

fp: 1913, Edinburgh, Scottish Orchestra, cond. Emil Mlynarski.

f London p: 27 March 1914, Queen's Hall, F. B. Ellis concert, Queen's Hall Orchestra, cond. Geoffrey Toye.

fbp: 17 May 1925, Newcastle Station Symphony Orchestra, cond. Edward Clark.

Pub. 1911, Leuckart (Leipzig).

58. Dance Rhapsody No. 1. For orchestra. 1908. Ded. Hermann Suter.

3 fl, pic, ob, ca, bs ob, 3 cl, bcl, 3 bsn, sarrusophone (or cbsn); 6 hn, 3 tpt, 3 ten tmb, bs tuba; timp, tamb, tgle, cym; hp, strings.

fp: 8 September 1909, Hereford, Shire Hall, Three Choirs Festival, London Symphony Orchestra, cond. Frederick Delius.

f London p: June 1911, Beecham concert of Delius's music.

fbp: 30 January 1927, Wireless Symphony Orchestra, cond. Geoffrey Toye.

Pub. 1910, Leuckart (Leipzig).

59. Fennimore and Gerda. Opera: two episodes in the life of Niels Lyhne in eleven pictures after the novel by J. P. Jacobsen. 1908-10. Ded. Sir Thomas Beecham.

3 fl, pic, 2 ob, ca, bs ob, 3 cl, bcl, 3 bsn, sarrusophone (or cbsn); 4 hn, 3 tpt, 3 tmb, tuba; timp, campanelle (or glock), tgle, cym; 2 hp, strings.

fp: October 1919, Frankfurt a. M., Opernhaus.

fEp: 27 March 1962, BBC broadcast, Sybil Michelow (Fennimore), Jeanette Sinclair (Gerda), John Cameron (Niels Lyhne), Max Worthley (Erik), Ambrosian Singers and BBC Symphony Orchestra, cond. Stanford Robinson.

Delius, Frederick

Pub. 1919, Universal-Edition, vocal score by Otto Lindemann; 1926, full score. English version by Philip Heseltine.

59a. Intermezzo. For orchestra, from Fennimore and Gerda. Dur. 3'.
2 fl, ob, ca, 2cl, 2 bsn; 2 hn, tpt; strings.
Pub. 1945, Hawkes.

60. Arabesk (J. P. Jacobsen). For baritone, chorus and orchestra. 1911. Ded. Halfdan Jebe.
3 fl, pic, 2 ob, ca, bs ob, 3 cl, clarone, 3 bsn, sarrusophone; 4 hn, 3 tpt, 3 ten tmb, tuba; timp; celesta, hp, strings.
fp: 1920, Newport.
f London p: 18 October 1929, Queen's Hall, Delius Festival, John Goss, London Select Choir and the BBC Orchestra, cond. Sir Thomas Beecham.
Pub. 1914 (piano score by Heinrich Hartmann), 1920 (full score), Universal-Edition. English version, Philip Heseltine.

61. The Song of the High Hills. For chorus and orchestra. 1911.
3 fl, 2 ob, ca, 3 cl, bcl, 3 bsn, sarrusophone (or cbsn); 4 hn, 3 tpt, 3 ten tmb, tuba; 4 timp, GC, cym, glock; celesta, 2 hp, strings.
fp: 26 February 1920, Queen's Hall, Royal Philharmonic Society concert, Philharmonic Choir (first appearance), cond. Albert Coates.
Pub. 1915, Leuckart (Leipzig); 1923, Universal-Edition.

BIBLIOGRAPHY:
Michael Kennedy: The Song of the High Hills, *Halle*, December 1954, p. 1.

62. Two Pieces for small orchestra. 1911–1912. Ded. H. Balfour Gardiner.
1. *On hearing the first cuckoo in spring.* 1912. fl, ob, 2 cl, 2 bsn; 2 hn; strings.
2. *Summer night on the river.* 1911.
2 fl, ob, 2 cl, 2 bsn; 2 hn; strings.
fp: 2 October 1913, Leipzig.
f Ep: 20 January 1913, Queen's Hall, Royal Philharmonic Society concert, cond. Willem Mengelberg.
fbp: 26 November 1923, Augmented Orchestra, cond. Percy Pitt.
Pub. 1914, Tischer & Jagenberg (Cologne); 1930, O.U.P. Arrs. incl. for piano solo by Gerard Bunk, 1914; for piano duet by Peter

Warlock, 1931. No. 1 arr. for organ by Eric Fenby.

63. Two Songs for a children's album. 1913.
1. *What does the little birdie say?* (Tennyson). Unison.
2. *The streamlet's slumber song.* Two-part.
Pub. 1924, O.U.P.

64. Violin Sonata No. 1. *c.* 1905–14.
fp: 1915, Manchester, Arthur Catterall and R. J. Forbes.
f London p: 16 June 1915, Aeolian Hall, May Harrison and (Sir) Hamilton Harty.
Pub. 1917, Forsyth; violin part revised and fingered by Arthur Catterall, piano part edited and revised by R. J. Forbes.

BIBLIOGRAPHY:
Frederick Bye: The two violin sonatas of FD, No. 1, *Strad*, January 1930, p. 484.

65. North Country Sketches. For orchestra. 1913–14. Ded. Albert Coates.
1. *Autumn* (The wind soughs in the trees).
2. *Winter landscape.*
3. *Dance.*
4. *The march of Spring* (Woodlands, meadows, and silent moors).
2 fl, 2 ob, ca, 2cl, 2 bsn; 4 hn, 2 tpt, 3 ten tmb, bs tuba; timp, tgle, tamb; strings.
fp: 10 May 1915, Queen's Hall, London Symphony Orchestra, cond. Sir Thomas Beecham.
fbp: 5 December 1926, Newcastle Station Symphony Orchestra, cond. Edward Clark.
Pub. 1922 (piano duet score by Philip Heseltine), 1923 (full score), Augener.

BIBLIOGRAPHY:
A. E. Hull: North Country Sketches, *MMR*, April 1922.

66. Air and Dance. For string orchestra. 1915. Ded. (1931) The National Institute for the Blind.
fp (private): 1915, home of Lady Cunard, cond. Sir Thomas Beecham.
fp (public): 16 October 1929, Queen's Hall, Delius Festival, cond. Sir Thomas Beecham.
Pub. 1931, Winthrop Rogers; also arr. for piano solo by Eric Fenby.

BIBLIOGRAPHY:
Harold Rawlinson: Famous Works for String Quartet, No. 18: Air and Dance, *Strad*, 1949, September p. 142, October p. 176.

67. Double Concerto. For violin, cello and orchestra. 1915. Ded. May and Beatrice Harrison.

2 fl, ob, ca, 2 cl, 2 bsn; 4 hn, 2 tpt, 3 tmb, tuba; timp; hp, strings.

fp: 21 February 1920, Queen's Hall, Royal Philharmonic Society concert, May and Beatrice Harrison and the New Queen's Hall Orchestra, cond. Sir Henry Wood.

Pub. 1922, Augener; also piano reduction by Philip Heseltine.

BIBLIOGRAPHY:
Arthur Hutchings: Concerto for violin, cello and orchestra, in *The Concerto*, Pelican Books (London) 1952, p. 267.

67a. Double Concerto. Version for violin, viola and orchestra by Lionel Tertis.

fp: 3 March 1935, BBC broadcast, May Harrison and Lionel Tertis and the BBC Orchestra, cond. Sir Adrian Boult.

Pub. 1935, Augener.

68. Four Old English Lyrics. For voice and piano. 1915–16.

1. *Spring, the sweet Spring* (Thomas Nashe). Dated: February 1915.
2. *To Daffodils* (Herrick). Dated: March 1915.
3. *So white, so soft, so sweet is she* (Ben Jonson). Dated: March 1915.
4. *It was a lover and his lass* (Shakespeare). 1916.

fp (Nos. 1–3): ?1915, ?Grafton Galleries, Music Club concert.*

fbp: 5 November 1924, Newcastle station, Ethel M. Stanley (Nos. 1 & 2), William Heseltine (No. 3).

Pub. 1919, Winthrop Rogers.

69. Requiem. For soprano, baritone, double chorus and orchestra. 1914–16. Text: Frederick Delius, after Nietzsche. Ded. 'to the

memory of all young artists fallen in the war'.

3 fl, pic, 2 ob, ca, bs ob, 3 cl, bcl, 3 bsn, cbsn (or sarrusophone); 6 hn, 3 tpt, 3 tmb, tuba; timp, GC, cym, tamb pic, tgle, campanelle; celesta, hp, strings.

fp: 23 March 1922, Queen's Hall, Royal Philharmonic Society concert, Amy Evans, Norman Williams, Philharmonic Choir, cond. Albert Coates.

Pub. 1921 (vocal score), 1922 (full score), Universal-Edition 1952, Boosey & Hawkes. English version, Philip Heseltine.

BIBLIOGRAPHY:
Anthony Payne: Delius's Requiem, *Tempo*, No. 76, spring 1966, p. 12.
John Rippin: Delius Requiem, *MO*, May 1966, p. 465.
Percy A. Scholes: The new Delius Requiem, *Observer*, 19 March 1922.

70. Violin Concerto. 1916. Ded. Albert Sammons. Dur. 26'.

2 fl, ob, ca, 2 cl, 2 bsn; 4 hn, 2 tpt, 3 tmb, bs tuba; timp; hp, strings.

fp: 30 January 1919, Queen's Hall, Royal Philharmonic Society concert, Albert Sammons, cond. (Sir) Adrian Boult.

fbp: 30 January 1927, Albert Sammons and Wireless Symphony Orchestra, cond. Geoffrey Toye.

Pub. 1919 (reduction by Philip Heseltine), 1921 (full score), Augener.

BIBLIOGRAPHY:
Eric Blom: Delius, Concerto for violin and orchestra, *Music Teacher*, August 1932, p. 375.
Arthur Hutchings: Violin Concerto, in *The Concerto*, Pelican Books (London) 1952, p. 270.
Donald F. Tovey: Violin Concerto, in *Essays in Musical Analysis*, Vol. 3, O.U.P. (London) 1936, p. 203.

71. Dance Rhapsody No. 2. For orchestra. 1916. Ded. Norman O'Neill.

2 fl, pic, 2 ob, ca, 2 cl, 2 bsn; 4 hn, 2 tpt, 3 tmb, bs tuba; timp, glock, tgle, celesta, tamb, GC, mil dm; hp, strings.

?fEp: 8 February 1929, BBC broadcast from Kingsway Hall, cond. Sir Thomas Beecham. (NB: Sir Thomas himself

---

* According to Warlock; but when on 17 November 1918 Muriel Foster sang Nos. 2 & 3, reviews of her recital (at Wigmore Hall) treated her performances as the first.

announced this as 'probably' the first performance in England.)

Pub. 1922 (reduction for piano duet by Philip Heseltine), 1923 (full score), Augener.

72. String Quartet No. 2. 1916.

1. *With animation*; 2. *Quickly and lightly*; 3. *Late Swallows* (slow and wistfully); 4. *Very quickly and vigorously.*

fp: 1 February 1919, Aeolian Hall, London String Quartet.

fbp: 19 February 1925, Kutcher Quartet (Samuel Kutcher, George Whitaker, Leonard Rubenstein and John Barbirolli).

Pub. 1921, Augener.

72a. Late Swallows. Third movement from String Quartet No. 2, arr. for string orchestra by Eric Fenby.

fp: October 1963, Houston (Texas), Houston Symphony Orchestra, cond. Sir John Barbirolli.

Pub. 1963, Galliard.

73. Cello Sonata. 1916.

fp: 11 January 1919, Wigmore Hall, Beatrice Harrison and (Sir) Hamilton Harty.

Pub. 1919, Winthrop Rogers.

BIBLIOGRAPHY:

Frederick Bye: FD, Sonata for cello and piano, *Strad*, November 1929, p. 343.

74. Eventyr (One Upon a Time). Ballad for orchestra, after Asbjörnsen's fairy tales. 1917. Ded. Sir Henry J. Wood.

2 fl, pic, 2 ob, ca, 2 cl, bcl, 3 bsn, sarrusophone; 4 hn, 3 tpt, 3 tmb, bs tuba; timp, cym, tgle, glock, xyl; celesta, hp, strings.

fp: 11 January 1919, Queen's Hall, Queen's Hall Orchestra, cond. Sir Henry Wood.

Pub. 1921, Augener; also reduction for piano duet by B. J. Dale.

75. To be sung of a summer night on the water. Two choruses for SATTBB a cappella. 1917.

fp: 28 June 1920, London, Oriana Madrigal Society, cond. Charles Kennedy Scott.

Pub. 1920, Winthrop Rogers.

75a. Two Aquarelles. Arr. from the above choruses for string orchestra by Eric Fenby. Dur. 2' each. Pub. 1938, Hawkes. Also arr. for organ by Dom Gregory Murray, 1938.

76. A Song Before Sunrise. For small orchestra. 1918. Ded. Philip Heseltine.

2 fl, ob, 2 cl, 2 bsn; 2 hn; strings.

?fp: 25 November 1931, Bournemouth, Municipal Orchestra, cond. Sir Dan Godfrey.

Pub. 1922, Augener; also reduction for piano duet by Philip Heseltine, 1922.

77. A Poem of Life and Love. For orchestra. 1918. Unfinished. Lost. Some material from this work was later used in 'A Song of Summer' (No. 89).

78. Avant que tu ne t'en ailles (Verlaine). For voice and piano. 1919. Pub. 1932, Boosey & Hawkes.

79. A Dance for harpsichord. 1919. Ded. Mrs. Gordon Woodhouse.

?fp: January 1922, Paris, Salle des Agriculteurs, Evlyn Howard-Jones (piano).

fbp: 5 September 1924, BBC broadcast, Evlyn Howard-Jones (piano).

fEp (concert): 8 November 1924, London, chamber concert of Delius's music, Evlny Howard-Jones (piano).

Pub. 1919, *Music & Letters* (Vol. I, No. 1) supplement; 1922, Universal-Edition.

80. Hassan, or The Golden Journey to Samarkand. Incidental music (James Elroy Flecker). 1920.

fl, pic, ob, ca, cl, bsn; 2 hn, tpt, tmb, bs tuba; 6 v, 2 va, 2 c, db; hp, piano, timp, xyl, cym. On stage: pavillon chinois.

fp: 20 September 1923, His Majesty's Theatre, with Henry Ainley (Hassan), Basil Gill (Rafi), Frank Cochrane (Jafar), Cathleen Nesbitt (Yasmin), Leon Quartermaine (Ishak), Malcolm Keen (The Caliph), Laura Cowie (Pervaneh); arr. for the stage and produced by Basil Dean; ballets arr. by Michel Fokine.

fbp: 8 November 1925, 2LO broadcast, with substantially the same cast, cond. Percy Fletcher; presented by Donald Calthrop and R. E. Jeffrey.

Pub. 1923, Universal-Edition; Hawkes. German text, R. S. Hoffmann.

80a. Intermezzo and Serenade. From 'Hassan', arr. Sir Thomas Beecham.

1. *Intermezzo.* Dur. 2'.

fl, ob, ca, cl, bsn; 2 hn, tpt; timp; hp, strings.

2. *Serenade*, Dur. 2'.
hp, strings.
Pub. 1940, Hawkes. *Serenade* also arranged: for piano solo, 1923, Universal-Edition, 1939, Hawkes; for cello and piano by Eric Fenby, 1931; for organ by Eric Fenby, 1934, Universal-Edition, 1939, Hawkes; for violin and piano by Lionel Tertis, 1939.

80b. Hassan: Suite. Arr. Eric Fenby.
1. *Desert scene*; 2. *Procession of Protracted Death*; 3. *Serenade*; 4. *Ballet:* (i) *Dance of the beggars*, (ii) *Chorus of women*, (iii) *Chorus of women*, (iv) *General dance*.
2 fl, ob, ca, 2 cl, 2 bsn; 4 hn, 2 tpt, 3 tmb, tuba; timp, camel-bells; hp, strings.
fp: 1 August 1933, BBC broadcast, BBC Orchestra, cond. Victor Hely-Hutchinson.

BIBLIOGRAPHY:
Julia Chatterton: Delius and the music to Hassan, *MS*, 20 October 1923, p. 166.
Dynley Hussey: Hassan—the figure in the carpet, *M&L*, January 1924.
F. Gilbert Webb: The music of Hassan, *MN&H*, 6 October 1923, p. 278.

81. Cello Concerto. 1921.
2 fl, 2 ob, ca, 2 cl, 2 bsn; 4 hn, 2 tpt, 3 tmb, tuba; timp; hp, strings.
fp: 30 January 1921, Frankfurt, with Alexandre Barjansky as soloist.
fEp: 3 July 1923, Queen's Hall, concert in aid of the Great Ormond Street Hospital for Sick Children, Beatrice Harrison and the Goossens Orchestra, cond. (Sir) Eugene Goossens.
fbp: 7 September 1927, Hereford (Shire Hall), Three Choirs Festival, Beatrice Harrison.
Pub. 1922 (full score), 1923 (reduction by Philip Heseltine), Universal-Edition.

BIBLIOGRAPHY:
J. R. Bennett: Delius and the Cello Concerto, *Halle*, November 1953, p. 7.
Beatrice Harrison: From the performer's point of view—Delius's Cello Concerto, *Music Bulletin*, August 1927.
Arthur Hutchings: Concerto for cello and orchestra, in *The Concerto*, Pelican Books (London) 1952, p. 272.

82. The splendour falls on castle walls (Tennyson). Chorus. ?1923.
fp: 17 June 1924, Aeolian Hall, Oriana Madrigal Society, cond. Charles Kennedy Scott.
Pub. 1924, O.U.P.

83. Three Preludes. For piano. ?1923. Ded. Evlyn Howard-Jones.
fp: 4 September 1924, BBC broadcast, Evlyn Howard-Jones.
fFp: 9 February 1925, Paris, Evlyn Howard-Jones.
Pub. 1923, Anglo-French; O.U.P.

84. Five Pieces. For piano. 1923. Ded. Evlyn Howard-Jones.
1. *Mazurka and waltz* (for a little girl); 2. *Waltz*; 3. *Waltz*; 4. *Lullaby for a modern baby*; 5. *Toccata*.
?fp: 8 November 1924, Evlyn Howard-Jones.
Pub. 1925, Universal-Edition.

85. Violin Sonata No. 2. ?1923.
fp: 7 October 1924, Westminster, Music Society concert, Albert Sammons and Evlyn Howard-Jones.
fbp: 2 April 1925, Albert Sammons and Evlyn Howard-Jones.
Pub. 1924, Hawkes (ed. Albert Sammons and Evlyn Howard-Jones); also adapted and ed. for viola by Lionel Tertis.

BIBLIOGRAPHY:
Frederick Bye: The two violin sonatas of FD, No. 2, *Strad*, February 1930, p. 538.
E. van der Straeten: Modern violin solos— FD, Sonata No. 2, *Strad*, November 1926, p. 403.

86. A Late Lark (W. E. Henley). For voice and orchestra. 1925.
fl, ob, ca, 2 cl, 2 bsn; 2 hn, tpt, 3 ten tmb; strings.
Pub. 1931, Hawkes; incl. reduction by Eric Fenby. German text, Jelka Delius.

87. Violin Sonata No. 3. Spring 1930. Ded. May Harrison.
1. *Slow*; 2. *Andante scherzando*; 3. *Lento— Con moto*.
fp: 6 November 1930, Wigmore Hall, May Harrison and (Sir) Arnold Bax.

Delius, Frederick

fbp: 2 October 1931, Elsie Owen and Kathleen Thomson.

Pub. 1931, Boosey & Hawkes (phrased and ed. May Harrison and Eric Fenby). Also adapted and ed. for viola by Lionel Tertis.

88. Songs of Farewell (Walt Whitman). For double chorus and orchestra. 1930. Ded. to the composer's wife (Jelka).

2 fl, 2 ob, ca, 2 cl, bcl, 3 bsn, dbsn; 4 hn, 3 tpt, 3 ten tmb, bs tuba; timp; hp, strings.

fp: 21 March 1932, Queen's Hall, Philharmonic Choir and the London Symphony Orchestra, cond. (Sir) Malcolm Sargent.

Pub. 1931, Winthrop Rogers; incl. vocal score by Eric Fenby. German words, Jelka Delius.

89. A Song of Summer. For orchestra. 1930. Dur. 7′.

3 fl, pic, 2 ob, ca, 3 cl, bcl, 3 bsn, dbsn; 4 hn, 3 tpt, 3 tmb, tuba; timp; hp, strings.

fp: 17 September 1932, Queen's Hall, Promenade Concert, BBC Orchestra, cond. Sir Henry Wood.

Pub. 1931, Winthrop Rogers.

90. Caprice and Elegy. For cello and chamber orchestra. 1930. Arr. Eric Fenby. Ded. Beatrice Harrison. Dur. 6½′.

fl, ob, ca, cl, bsn; 2 hn; hp, strings.

Pub. 1931, Hawkes.

90a. Caprice and Elegy. Version for cello and piano.

fEp: 23 April 1931, Wigmore Hall, Beatrice Harrison and Vera de Villiers.

Pub. 1931, Hawkes. Also adapted for viola and piano by Lionel Tertis.

91. Fantastic Dance. For orchestra. 1931. Ded. Eric Fenby. Dur. 3–4′.

2 fl, 2 ob, ca, 2 cl, 2 bsn; 4 hn, 2 tpt, 3 tmb, bs tuba; timp, cym, glock, GC; strings.

fp: 12 January 1934, Queen's Hall, BBC Symphony Orchestra, cond. Sir Adrian Boult.

Pub. 1933, Boosey & Hawkes. Also arr. for two pianos four hands by Ethel Bartlett and Rae Robertson, 1936.

92. Idyll: Once I passed through a populous city (Walt Whitman). For soprano, baritone and orchestra. 1930–2:

portions of the opera 'Margot La Rouge' re-worked and adapted to the Whitman text.

2 fl, 2 ob, ca, 2 cl, 2 bsn; 4 hn, 2 tpt, 3 tmb, tuba; timp; hp, strings.

fp: 3 October 1933, Queen's Hall, Promenade Concert, Roy Henderson and Dora Labbette, cond. Sir Henry Wood.

Pub. 1933, Boosey & Hawkes; German text, Jelka Delius.

BIBLIOGRAPHY:

Eric Fenby: Idyll, *Radio Times*, 29 September 1933, p. 736.

GENERAL BIBLIOGRAPHY

Gerald Abraham: Delius and his music, *Music Teacher*, February 1926, p. 97.
— Delius and his literary sources, *M&L*, April 1929; in *Slavonic and Romantic Music*, Faber (London) 1968.
Hilda Andrews: FD, *Music Teacher*, June 1928, p. 367.
Herbert Antcliffe: The system of FD, *MN&H*, 28 January 1922, p. 121.
Sir Thomas Armstrong: Delius today, *Centenary Festival Souvenir Programme*, p. 16.
C. Arnold: A singer's memories of Delius, *Music Teacher*, April 1950, p. 165.
Sir Thomas Beecham: FD, *Tempo*, winter No. 26, 1952–3, p. 6; repr. from 'A Mingled Chime'.
— Early days with Delius, *Saturday Review*, 25 June 1960, p. 41.
Paul Bekker: Delius, *Frankfurter Zeitung*, 30 January 1927.
Leland J. Berry: FD, *MS*, 11 August 1928, p. 40.
Eric Blom: Delius and America, *MQ*, July 1929, p. 438.
G. Bourke: The genius of Delius, *Music Magazine*, January 1962, p. 15.
L. V. Brant: Delius in America, *Etude*, August 1950, p. 7.
Havergal Brian: The art of FD, *MO*, 1924, March p. 598, April p. 700, May p. 799, June p. 906, July p. 1002, August p. 1098, September p. 1194, October p. 49.
Norman Cameron: The Delius Society, 1933, p. 183.
— Delius, *The Gramophone*, March 1933, p. 389.

Richard Capell: The Delius Festival, *MMR*, 1929, pp. 332, 364.

Julia Chatterton: The morning and afternoon of Delius, *Sackbut*, October 1929, p. 77.

W. A. Chislett: Neglected composers, IV: FD, *The Gramophone*, April 1927, p. 450.

Max Chop: FD, eine biographische Studie (mit Bildbeilage), *NZfM* (Musikalisches Wochenblatt), 1907, Nos. 35–36 (29 August) p. 705, No. 37 (12 September) p. 731.

— FD, Harmonie (Berlin) 1907.

— Tonsetzer des Gegenwart, *NMZ*, 1910, Nos. 15–16.

— FD, *Signale*, 1927, No. 39, p. 1315.

Deryck Cooke: Delius, a centenary evaluation, *The Listener*, 25 January 1962, p. 195; in *Essays on Music*, Cassell (London) 1967, p. 84.

— Delius, Debussy and pure creation, *The Listener*, 1 February 1962, p. 233.

— Delius and form—a vindication, *MT*, 1962, June p. 392, July p. 460, August p. 653.

— Delius the unknown, *PRMA*, 1962–3, p. 17.

Martin Cooper: Delius, *Spectator*, 15 June 1951, p. 781; see also 22 June, p. 817.

I. A. Copley: A Delius Miniature and some memories, *M&L*, January 1962, p. 4.

Gerald Cumberland: Pen portraits of musicians, IV—FD, *MO*, July 1909, p. 700.

Clare Delius: FD, memories of my brother, Ivor Nicholson & Watson (London) 1935.

Frederick Delius: At the crossroads, *Sackbut*, September 1920, p. 205.

— Recollections of Strindberg, *Sackbut*, December 1920, p. 353.

— Musik in England im Kriege, *Anbruch*, November 1919, p. 18.

Suzanne Demarquez: Alfred Bruneau, Gustav Holst, Frederick Delius, *RM*, July 1934, p. 158.

Norman Demuth: FD, in *Musical Trends in the 20th Century*, Rockliff (London) 1952, p. 128.

John Dene: Delius, *Music in New Zealand*, April 1931.

Bernard van Dieren: Delius, *MMR*, 1934, p. 121.

— FD, *MT*, July 1934, p. 598.

Keith Douglas: The Delius Society, *The Gramophone*, September 1933, p. 132.

Sir Edward Elgar: My visit to Delius, *British Musician*, May 1933, p. 102.

Edwin Evans: Delius, *Sackbut*, December 1929, p. 118.

— FD, *Chesterian*, No. 117, September–October 1934.

Eric Fenby: Delius's last years, *MT*, July 1934, p. 604.

— Delius as I knew him, Bell (London) 1936, repr. 1949 Quality Press, 1966 Icon Books.

— Delius after twenty years, *M&M*, June 1954, p. 13.

— FD, *Canon*, January–February 1962, p. 4.

— Delius, no drooping dreams, *M&M*, March 1962, p. 17.

— FD, *Crescendo*, No. 122, October 1962, p. 27.

— Revisiting Solano Grove—Delius in Florida, *Composer*, No. 21, autumn 1966, p. 5.

— FD, in *Composers and their Times*, Garnet Miller (London) 1969.

— Delius, Faber (London) 1971.

Hubert Foss: Profile—FD, *Crescendo*, No. 30, October 1950, p. 5; No. 40, June 1951, p. 339.

— The instrumental music of FD, *Tempo*, No. 26, winter 1952–3, p. 30.

Percy Grainger: Das Genie Delius, *Anbruch*, January 1923, p. 23.

Cecil Gray: FD, in *A Survey of Contemporary Music*, O.U.P. (London) 1927, p. 58.

— Delius and Beecham—a Delius festival, *Nation*, 16 November 1929, p. 251.

Sydney Grew: FD, *Sackbut*, October 1922, p. 67.

— Delius, *Midland Musician*, March 1926, p. 91.

May Harrison: The music of Delius, *PRMA*, 1944–5, p. 43.

— Delius, *R.C.M. Magazine*, 1937, No. 2, p. 47.

Philip Heseltine: FD, *Musik* (Copenhagen), February 1923.

— FD, Lane (London) 1923.

— FD, *Music Bulletin*, May 1923.

— Some notes on Delius and his music, *MT*, March 1915, p. 137.

— Musik in England, II: FD (transl. Rose Hoffmann), *Anbruch*, March 1922, p. 81.

— The Yorkshire genius of Friday's concert, *Radio Times*, 1 February 1929, p. 259.

— Delius, *Radio Times*, 4 October 1929, p. 7.

Delius, Frederick

Ralph Hill: The gramophile's favourite composers, No. 1: FD, *Musical Mirror*, October 1929, p. 261.
— A few notes on Delius, *Strad*, December 1929, p. 438.
Basil Hogarth: FD, a critical estimate, *English Review*, August 1934, p. 154.
Joseph Holbrooke: Musical impressions, XIII: Of Fritz Delius, *MS*, 13 April 1907, p. 233.
A. Holde: FD, *AMZ*, 20–27 January 1933.
A. K. Holland: The songs of Delius, *MO*, 1936, October p. 19, November p. 118; 1937, January p. 306, February p. 403, April p. 592, May p. 695, June p. 783.
— The songs of Delius, O.U.P. (London) 1951.
— Delius as a song writer, *Tempo*, No. 26, winter 1952–3, p. 18.
H. Hughes: Mystery of Delius, *Saturday Review*, 16 June 1934, p. 708.
Robert H. Hull: The quintessence of Delius, *MT*, June 1927, p. 497.
— Delius, Leonard & Virginia Woolf at the Hogarth Press (London) 1928.
Robin Hull: The range of Delius, *Disc*, autumn 1950, p. 100.
— Three British composers: Elgar, Delius and Holst, *MT*, July 1959, p. 380.
D. Hussey: FD, *Spectator*, 15 June 1934, p. 921.
Arthur Hutchings: The chamber works of Delius, *MT*, 1935, January p. 17, March p. 214, April p. 310, May p. 401.
— Delius, Macmillan (London) 1948.
— Delius's operas, *Tempo*, No. 26, winter 1952–3, p. 22.
A.J.: Bradford Delius Festival, *Opera*, May 1962, p. 347.
Michael Kennedy: Elgar, Delius and Holst, *Halle*, April 1959, p. 8.
John W. Klein: Delius as a musical dramatist, *MR*, November 1961, p. 294.
— Delius's advance to mastery, *Tempo*, winter 1961–2, p. 2.
Gustav Klemm: Delius in America, *Tempo*, Vol. II, No. 2 (American edition), February 1942.
Paul Klenau: The approach to Delius, *Music Teacher*, January 1927, p. 19.
Constant Lambert: The intimate appeal of Delius, *Radio Times*, 22 June 1934, p. 899.

'Lieder': Songs worth singing—Coleridge-Taylor and Delius, *MO*, July 1914, p. 801.
Edward Lockspeiser: Schoenberg, Nietzsche and Delius, *The Listener*, 9 March 1961, p. 463.
George Lowe: Two modern song writers—Sibelius and Delius, *MS*, 9 July 1910, p. 25.
Robert Lyle: Delius and the philosophy of romanticism, *M&L*, April 1948.
Joseph Machlis: FD, in *Introduction to Contemporary Music*, Norton (USA), Dent (London) 1961, p. 144.
Joseph Marx: FD, *Anbruch*, November 1919, p. 49.
Wilfrid Mellers: Delius, Sibelius and Nature, in *Man and his Music*, Barrie & Rockliff (London) 1962, p. 923.
Donald Mitchell: Delius—the choral music, *Tempo*, No. 26, winter 1952–3, p. 8.
— The private world of FD, *MO*, April 1953, p. 405.
— Delius and opera, *The Listener*, 23 January 1958, p. 177.
— Delius twenty years after, *The Listener*, 12 June 1958, p. 993.
Frederick P. Nathan: Delius, some recollections, *Halle*, March 1951, p. 18.
Ernest Newman: A note on Delius, in *From the World of Music* (ed. Felix Aprahamian), Calder (London) 1956, p. 105.
— Delius, the end of a chapter on music, in –*do*–, p. 114.
— Delius and the opera—a quest for the impossible?, in –*do*–, p. 122.
Robert Nichols: The power of music, *London Mercury*, 1937, p. 270.
— Delius as I knew him, in *Music Magazine* (ed. Anna Instone and Julian Herbage), Rockliff (London) 1953, p. 5.
C. W. Orr: FD, some personal recollections, *MO*, August 1934, p. 944.
— Delius versus the rest: a study in musical egotism, *Making Music*, No. 28, summer 1955, p. 5.
H. Ould: Songs of FD, *English Review*, November 1928, p. 603.
D. C. Parker: The Delius Festival—some reflections, *MS*, 28 December 1929, p. 211.
Anthony Payne: Delius's stylistic development, *Tempo*, winter 1961–2, p. 6.

Christopher Palmer: Delius and poetic realism, *M&L*, October 1970, p. 81.
— Delius and folksong, *MT*, January 1971, p. 24.
D. E. Pike: The future of Delius, *Chesterian*, No. 50, November 1925.
Peter J. Pirie: Debussy and Delius, *MO*, July 1963, p. 593.
A. Pryce-Jones: Delius festival, *London Mercury*, December 1929, p. 172.
Robert Ralph: Delius, *MO*, October 1913, p. 16.
Henry Raynor: 'A supreme and complete egoist', *MO*, April 1954, p. 401.
Hans F. Redlich: FD, in *MGG*, Vol. 3 (1954), p. 134.
Peter Hugh Reed: Delius, the musical sunset of the romanticists, *MS*, 23 March 1929, p. 93.
C. B. Rees: The Delius centenary, *Musical Events*, April 1962, p. 4.
Eduard Reeser: FD, *Caecilia en de Muziek*, August–September 1934.
Charles Reid & Ernest Bradbury: Two views on Delius, *M&M*, May 1962, pp. 14, 15.
G. N. Sharp: Delius, *British Musician*, 1938, August p. 176, September p. 204, October p. 230.
Derek Shepherd: Delius and the Norwegian fairy tales, *Crescendo*, No. 69, October 1955, p. 6.
Heinrich Simon: Jelka Delius, *MMR*, 1935, p. 219.
— FD, *MO*, 1935, February p. 406, March p. 503.
— Für Delius, *Frankfurter Zeitung*, 30 January 1927.
— FD—Zum 60. Geburtstag am 29. Jänner 1923, *Anbruch*, 1923, January p. 1, February p. 45.
— Delius Festival in London, *Anbruch*, November–December 1929, p. 349.
W. H. Haddon Squire: Delius and Nietzsche, *Tempo*, No. 7, spring 1948.
— Delius and Warlock, *Tempo*, No. 26, winter 1952–3, p. 37.
Katharine Phyllis Stanley: FD, *MO*, September 1935, p. 1004.
Reid Stewart: The string music of Delius, *Strad*, 1935, September p. 216, October p. 266.

Dennis Stoll: FD, *London Philharmonic Post*, May 1941, p. 8.
Norman Suckling: Delius after a generation, *MMR*, 1949, p. 255.
Paul Stefan: Ein Wort für Delius, *Anbruch*, February–March 1932, p. 48.
—Delius, *Anbruch*, June 1934, p. 118.
Stainton de B. Taylor: Great song writers, X: FD, *MM&F*, November 1931, p. 309.
G. Tetley: Delius as a teacher in Virginia, *Musical America*, 15 February 1955, p. 7.
Robert Thralfall: Delius in Eric Fenby's MSS, *Composer*, spring 1969, p. 19.
W. J. Turner: Delius and Sibelius, *New Statesman*, 17 November 1934, p. 718.
Bruno Weigl: FD, *NZfM*, 16 May 1910, p. 79.
Terence White: Delius, *British Musician*, August 1936, p. 180.
Perry M. Young: FD, in *A History of British Music*, Ernest Benn (London) 1967, p. 534.

MISCELLANEOUS OR UNSIGNED

FD, *MT*, March 1915, p. 137.
FD, *Musical Herald*, November 1919, p. 359.
Gramophone records of the music of Delius, *Midland Musician*, 1926, March p. 94, April p. 130.
A letter in facsimile and portrait, *British Musician*, April 1927, p. 300.
Delius, *British Musician*, July 1933, p. 146.
Delius, the nostalgic fallacy, *British Musician*, October 1936, p. 222.
FD, Bradford City Art Gallery and Museums, 1962.
Two promising young men: Elgar and Delius, *Music Teacher*, December 1950, p. 583 (repr. from *The Gazette*, 1899).

EDWARD ELGAR (1857–1934)
Elgar's father and uncle kept a music shop in Worcester, and it was at Broadheath, near Worcester, that Elgar himself was born on 2 June 1857. From 1873 he deputized for his father as organist at a Roman Catholic church in Worcester (succeeding him in 1885) and from 1879 was bandmaster at the county lunatic asylum. He took advanced violin lessons with Adolph Pollitzer, with the aim (abandoned in 1884) of becoming a profes-

sional soloist; but he had no formal training in composition, lacking the funds to fulfil his long-held ambition of studying in Leipzig. Until the end of the century Elgar's career as performer and composer was largely confined to his native county and the world of the English provincial choral festival, especially—though Elgar himself was a Catholic—the Anglican cathedral festivals of the 'Three Choirs' at Gloucester, Worcester and Hereford. Two people who influenced his life profoundly in these years were Caroline Alice Roberts, whom he married in 1889, and August Jaeger (1860–1909) who worked for his publishers, Novello & Co. After his marriage, Elgar's principal homes were in Malvern (1891–1904), Hereford (1904–11) and London (1912–20). With the new century, the provincial figure became a national one. Recognition of this included a knighthood (and a three-day festival of his music at Covent Garden) in 1904, the Order of Merit in 1911, the Mastership of the King's Musick in 1924 and a baronetcy in 1931. In his maturity, Elgar was exclusively a composer, conducting little music but his own, taking no private pupils and—except for three years as an unconventional professor at Birmingham University (1905–8)—keeping aloof from the academic world. His wife died in 1920, and this was a blow from which he never fully recovered. Retiring for over ten years from ambitious composition, Elgar lived a rootless life before settling again in Worcester (1929), where he died from the effects of a malignant tumour in February 1934. Sketches for an opera and a symphony left at his death suggest that his creativity was returning during the last two years of his life.

CATALOGUE OF WORKS
1. The Wand of Youth. Music for Elgar children's play. *c.* 1867. Revised at various times, notably 1879–81 and *c.* 1902.

1a. The Wand of Youth: Suite No. 1 Op. 1a. For orchestra. 1907. Ded. C. Lee Williams.
   1. *Overture*; 2. *Serenade*; 3. *Minuet*; 4. *Sun Dance*; 5. *Fairy pipers*; 6. *Slumber scene*; 7. *Fairies and giants*.

2 fl, pic, 2 ob, 2 cl, 2 bsn, cbsn (ad lib); 4 hn, 2 tpt, 3 tmb, tuba; timp, tgle, GC, cym, tamb pic (ad lib); hp, strings.
   fp: 14 December 1907, Queen's Hall, Queen's Hall Orchestra, cond. (Sir) Henry Wood.
   Pub. 1908, Novello.

1b. The Wand of Youth: Suite No. 2 Op. 1b. For orchestra. 1908. Ded. Hubert A. Leicester.
   1. *March*; 2. *The little bells*; 3. *Moths and butterflies*; 4. *Fountain dance*; 5. *The tame bear*; 6. *The wild bears*.
   2 fl, pic, 2 ob, 2 cl, 2 bsn; 4 hn, 2 tpt, 3 tmb, tuba; timp, xyl (ad lib), tamb, tamb pic, tgle, GC, cym; hp, strings.
   fp: 9 September 1908, Worcester, Public Hall, Three Choirs Festival. cond. Edward Elgar.
   f London p: 17 October 1908, Queen's Hall, Saturday afternoon concert, Queen's Hall Orchestra, cond. Edward Elgar.
   f bp: 20 February 1924, Birmingham Studio Orchestra.
   Pub. 1908, Novello.

2. Fugue in G minor. For organ. *c.* 1870. Unfinished.

3. The language of flowers (Percival). For voice and piano. 1872. Ded. 'to my sister Lucy on her birthday'. Unpub.

4. Chantant. For piano. 1872.

5. Anthem. Arr. for strings with original introduction. 1874.
   ?fp: 1874, Worcester, All Saints Church.

6. Five well-known pieces. Arr. Elgar as studies for the violin. 1877.
   1. *Larghetto* (Mozart); 2. *Cavatina* (Raff); 3. *Romance* (de Bériot); 4. *Romance* (Vieuxtemps); 5. *Gigue* (Ries).
   Pub. 1877, Schott.

7. Study for strengthening the third finger. For violin. 1877. Recopied 1920 and ded. Jascha Heifetz.

8. Adeste fidelis. Arr. for orchestra. 1878 Unpub.

9. Finale of Violin Sonata. Beethoven (Op. 23), arr. Elgar for wind quintet. 1878. Unpub.

10. Concerto. Corelli, arr. for wind quintet. 1878.

11. Ariodante: Overture. Handel, arr. for small orchestra. 1878.

12. Oberon: 'O 'tis a glorious sight'. Weber, arr. 'for Mr. F. J. Pedley'.

13. Fantasia. For violin and piano. 1878. Unfinished.

14. String Quartet in D minor. 1878. Unfinished.

15. String Quartet in B flat. 1878. Unfinished.

16. String Trio in C. 1878. Unfinished.

17. Trio. For two violins and piano. 1878. Unfinished.

18. Promenades. For wind quintet (two flutes, oboe, clarinet and bassoon). 1878.
1. *Moderato e molto maestoso*; 2. *Moderato* ('*Madame Tussaud's*'); 3. *Presto*; 4. *Andante*; 5. *Allegro molto*; 6. *Allegro maestoso* ('*Hell and Tommy*').

19. Allegro. For oboe, violin, viola and cello. 1878. Unfinished.

20. Romance Op. 1. For violin and piano. 1878. Ded. Oswin Grainger.
fp: 20 October 1885, Worcester.
Pub. 1885, Schott.

21. Menuetto (Scherzo). For orchestra. 1878. Recopied 1930. Unpub.

22. Symphony in G minor (after Mozart). 1878.

23. Introductory Overture for Christy Minstrels. For orchestra. 1878.
fp: 12 June 1878, Worcester, Public Hall, cond. Edward Elgar.
Unpub.

24. Salve Regina (orig. Op. 1). 1878.
fp: 6 June 1880, Worcester, St. George's Church.

25. Domine Salvam Fac. 1878.
fp: 29 June 1879, Worcester, St. George's Church.

26. Tantum Ergo. (orig. Op. 2). 1878.

fp: 29 June 1879, Worcester, St. George's Church.

27. Brother, for thee He died. Easter anthem. 1878.

28. Hymn tune in G major. 1878.

29. Hymn tune in F major. 1878. Pub. 1898, 1912, in Westminster Hymnal (as Drakes Broughton).

30. If she loves me (Temple Bar Rondeau). Song. 1878.

31. Two Polonaises. For violin and piano. 1879. Ded. 'For J.K. with esteem'. Unfinished.

32. Harmony music. For wind quintet. 1879.
1. *Allegro molto*.
2. *Allegro non tanto*. Ded. W. B. Leicester.
3. *Allegro*. Unfinished.
4. *Allegro molto* (*The farmyard*).
5. *Allegro moderato* (*The mission*), Minuet: *Andante* (*Noah's ark*), *Allegro*.
6. *Allegro molto, andante arioso*.
7. *Allegro, Scherzo: Allegro giusto*. 1881.

33. Intermezzos. For wind quintet. 1879.
1. *Allegro molto*; 2. *Adagio*; 3. *Allegretto* (*Nancy*); 4. *Andante con moto*; 5. *Allegretto*.

34. Menuetto (Allegretto). For wind quintet. 1879.

35. Gavotte (The Alphonsa). For wind quintet. 1879.

36. Sarabande (Largo). For wind quintet. 1879. Recopied for 'The Spanish Lady'.

37. Gigue (Allegro). For wind quintet. 1879.

38. Andante con variazioni ('Evesham andante'). For wind quintet. 1879. Ded. H. A. L. (Hubert Leicester).

39. Adagio cantabile. For wind quintet. 1879.

40. Minuet (Grazioso). For orchestra. 1879. MS lost or destroyed.
?fp: 22 January 1879, Worcester.

41. 'Asylum music'. 1879. Written for Worcester City and County Pauper Lunatic Asylum, Powick.

Elgar, Edward

1. *Five Quadrilles, La Brunette.* Ded. Geo. Jenkins.
   2. *Five Quadrilles or Caledonians, Die junge Kokette.* Ded. Miss J. Holloway.
   3. *Five Quadrilles, L'Assomoir.*
   pic, fl, cl, 2 cornets, euphonium, 2 v, va, c, db, piano.

42. Adagio solenne. For organ. 1879. Pub. 1913, Novello.

42a. Cantique Op. 3. Version of preceding for small orchestra. 1912. Ded. Hugh Blair.
   fp: 15 December 1912, Royal Albert Hall. Pub. 1913, Novello.

43. Allegro. From Mozart's Violin Sonata in F (K.547) arr. as Gloria for St. George's Church, Worcester. *c.* 1880.

44. Credo. Themes from Beethoven's 5th, 7th and 9th Symphonies arr. for St. George's Church, Worcester, by 'Bernhard Pappenheim' (i.e. Edward Elgar). *c.* 1880.

45. Scherzo. From Schumann's Overture, Scherzo and Finale (Op. 52) arr. for piano solo. *c.* 1880.

46. Music for Powick. For orchestra. ?1880.
   1. *Polka (Maud).*
   2. *Five Quadrilles, Paris:* (a) *Chatelet,* (b) *L'Hippodrome,* (c) *Alcazar d'Eté (Champs-Elysées),* (d) *La! Suzanne!,* 5. *Café des Ambassadeurs: La femme d'emballeur.* Ded. Miss J. Holloway.
   3. *Five Lancers (The Valentine).*

47. O Salutaris Hostia. For 4-part chorus. 1880. Pub. 1888, Cary.

48. Credo in E minor (orig. Op. 3). 1880. Unpub.

49. Fantasia on Irish airs. For violin and piano. 1881. Unfinished.

50. Fugue in F sharp minor. 1881. Unfinished. Incorporated into 'The Spanish Lady'.

51. Polka (Nelly). For orchestra. 1881. Composed for the Powick band.

52. Air de ballet—Pastorale. For orchestra. 1882.
   fp: 14 March 1882, Worcester.

52a. March—Pas redoublé. For orchestra. As preceding. March incorporated in Suite in D (see No. 56) and in 'The Spanish Lady'.

53. Air de ballet. For orchestra. 1882. Lost.
   fp: August 1882, Worcester.

54. Polka (La Blonde). For orchestra. 1882. Composed for the Powick band.

55. Rosemary. For piano. Dated: 4 September 1882, Settle. Pub. 1915, Elkin.

55a. Rosemary. Version for small orchestra. 1882. Unpub.

56. Suite in D. For small orchestra. 1882–3.
   1. *Mazurka;* 2. *Intermezzo: Sérénade Mauresque;* 3. *Fantasia gavotte;* 4. *March—pas redoublé.*
   fp (No. 2): 13 December (?23 February) 1883, Birmingham, cond. W. C. Stockley.
   fp (No. 4): 14 March 1882, Worcester.
   fp (complete): 1 March 1888, Birmingham, cond. W. C. Stockley.

56a. Three Characteristic Pieces Op. 10. Revised version of preceding. 23–24 January 1889. Ded. Lady Mary Lygon.
   1. *Mazurka;* 2. *Sérénade Mauresque;* 3. *Contrasts: The Gavotte A.D. 1700 and 1900.*
   2 fl, pic, 2 ob, 2 cl, 2 bsn; 4 hn, 2 tpt, 3 tmb, tuba; timp, GC & cym, tgle; strings.
   fp: 16 July 1899, New Brighton Tower, Sunday afternoon concert, cond. Edward Elgar.
   fbp: 11 April 1925, Bournemouth Wireless Augmented Orchestra, cond. Capt. W. A. Featherstone.
   Pub. 1899, Novello.

57. O Salutaris Hostia. For bass solo. 1882.

58. Four Litanies for the Blessed Virgin Mary. For a cappella choir. Ded. Fr. T. Knight, S.J., Worcester. Pub. 1888, Cary.

59. Tannhäuser: Entry of the minstrels. Wagner, arr. for piano. 1883.

60. Une Idylle Op. 4 No. 1. 'Esquisse facile' for violin and piano. 1883. Ded. E.E., Inverness. Pub. 1885, Beare; 1910, Ashdown (ed. William Henley): numerous arrangements exist.

61. Pastourelle Op. 4 No. 2. For violin and piano. 1883. Ded. Miss Hilda Fitton, Malvern. Pub. 1906, Swan; 1912, Novello.

62. Virelai Op. 4 No. 3. For violin and piano. 1883. Ded. Frank W. Webb. Pub. 1906, Swan; 1912, Novello.

63. Fugue in D minor. For oboe and violin. 1883.

64. Polka (Helcia). For orchestra. 1883. Composed for the Powick band.

65. Polka (Blumine). For orchestra. 1884. Composed for the Powick band.

66. Sevillana Op. 7. 'Scène espagnole' for orchestra. 1884, rev. 1889 (?1887). Ded. W. C. Stockley.
  fl, pic, 2 cl, 2 bsn; 2 cornets, 2 hn, 3 tmb, tuba; side dm, tamb, GC, cym, tgle; strings.
  fp: 1 May 1884, Worcester, Philharmonic Society, cond. Dr. W. Done.
  f London p: 9 July 1884, Crystal Palace, cond. August Manns.
  Pub. 1884, Tuckwood; 1895 (revised version), Ascherberg.

67. A soldier's song Op. 5 (C. Flavell Hayward). For male voices. 1884. Ded. F.G.P., Worcester.
  fp: 17 March 1884, Worcester Glee Club. Pub. 1890, Magazine of Music.

67a. A war song. Retitled version of preceding.
  fp: 1 October 1903, Royal Albert Hall. Pub. 1903, Boosey.

68. Absent and present. Maud Valérie White, arr. for cello obbligato. 1885.

68a. Out on the rocks. C. H. Dolby, arr. for cello obbligato. 1885.

68b. Melody. C. W. Buck, arr. for piano acc. 1885.

69. Gavotte. For violin and piano. 1885. Ded. Dr. C. W. Buck. Pub. 1886, Schott.

70. Allegretto on G-E-D-G-E. For violin and piano. 1885. Ded. The Misses Gedge, Malvern. Pub. 1889, Schott.

71. The Lakes. Overture for orchestra. 1885. Lost.

72. Scottish Overture. For orchestra. 1885. Lost.

73. Through the long days (John Hay). For voice and piano. August 1885, Settle. Ded. Rev. E. Vine Hall.
  fp: 25 February 1897. St. James's Hall.
  Pub. 1887, Stanley Lucas, Weber; 1890, Ascherberg; 1907, Ascherberg (in Seven Lieder of Edward Elgar, Op. 16 No. 2).

74. Piano Trio. 1886. Fragment only. Recopied 21 September 1920.

75. Is she not passing fair? (Charles Duc d'Orléans, transl. Louisa Stuart Costello). 1886. Pub. 1908, Boosey.

76. String Quartet Op. 8. 1887. Destroyed.

77. Violin Sonata Op. 9, 1887. Destroyed.

78. Ave, Verum Corpus (Jesu, Word of God Incarnate) Op. 2 No. 1. 1887. Ded. 'In memoriam W.H.'. Pub. 1902, 1907, Novello; also arr. for SSC, 1930.

79. Ave Maria (Jesu, Lord of Life and Glory) Op. 2 No. 2. 1887. Ded. Mrs. H. A. Leicester. Pub. 1907, Novello.

80. Ave Maris Stella (Jesu, Meek and Lowly) Op. 2 No. 3. 1887. Ded. Rev. Canon Dolman, O.S.B., Hereford. Pub. 1907, Novello.

81. String Quartet in D. 1888. Unfinished. *Intermezzo* (3rd movement) used as No. 3 of Eleven Vesper Voluntaries, 1889.

82. Three Pieces. For string orchestra. 1888. Lost. ?Revised as Serenade in E minor.
  1. *Spring song* (*Allegro*); 2. *Elegy* (*Adagio*); 3. *Finale* (*Presto*).
  fp: 7 May 1888, Worcestershire Musical Union.

83. Salut d'amour (Liebesgruss) Op. 12. For piano. 1888. Ded. 'A Carice'. Pub. 1901, Schott.

83a. Salut d'amour Op. 12. 'Morceau mignon' for orchestra. Version of preceding.
  fl, 2 ob, 2 cl, 2 bsn; 2 hn; strings.
  fp: 11 November 1889, Crystal Palace, cond. August Manns.
  Pub. 1889, Schott.

84. Ecce Sacerdos Magnus. For chorus and organ. 1888. Ded. Hubert Leicester.
fp: 9 October 1888, Worcester, St. George's Church.
Pub. 1888, Cary.

85. As I laye a-thynkynge (Richard Barham, 'Thomas Ingoldsby'). For voice and piano. 1888. Pub. 1888, Beare.

86. The wind at dawn (C. Alice Roberts). For voice and piano. Ded. (1907), Dr. Ludwig Wüllner. Pub. 1888, Magazine of Music; 1907, Boosey.

87. Liebesahnung. For violin and piano. 1889. Ded. Alice.

88. Mot d'amour Op. 13 No. 1. For violin and piano. 1889. Pub. ?1889, Orsborn & Tuckwood; 1890, Ascherberg (incl. various arrs.).

89. Bizarrerie Op. 13 No. 2. For violin and piano. 1889. Pub. ?1889, Orsborn & Tuckwood; 1890, Ascherberg; 1920, Ashdown.

90. Eleven Vesper Voluntaries Op. 14. For organ. 1889–90. Dated: January 1890. Ded. Mrs. W. A. Raikes. Pub. 1891, Orsborn & Tuckwood/Ascherberg. Arr. as *Suite* for organ by Reginald Goss Custard, pub. 1911, Ascherberg.

91. Queen Mary's song (Tennyson). For voice and piano. 1889. Ded. J. H. Meredith. Pub. 1889, Orsborn & Tuckwood; 1892, Ascherberg; 1907, Ascherberg (in 'Seven Lieder of Edward Elgar').

92. Violin Concerto. ?1890. Destroyed.

93. Froissart Op. 19. Concert Overture for orchestra. Dated: 6 April–July 1890, West Kensington.
2 fl, pic, 2 ob, 2 cl, 2 bsn, cbsn (ad lib); 4 hn, 2 tpt, 3 tmb; timp, cym; strings.
fp: 9 September 1890, Worcester, Shire Hall, Three Choirs Festival, cond. Edward Elgar.
f London p: 16 November 1900, St. James's Hall, cond. Henry Such.
fbp: 3 August 1924, Manchester station, 2ZY Symphony Orchestra, cond. Sir Dan Godfrey.
Pub. 1890, 1901 (full score), Novello.

94. O happy eyes Op. 18 No. 1 (C. Alice Elgar). Partsong for SATB. January 1890. Pub. 1896, Novello.

95. Love Op. 18 No. 2 (Arthur Maquarie). Partsong for SATB. January 1890, rev. 2 June 1907. Pub. 1907, Novello.

96. My love dwelt in a northern land Op. 18 No. 3 (Andrew Lang). Partsong for SATB. January 1890. Ded. Rev. J. Hampton, M.A., Warden of St. Michael's College, Tenbury.
fp: 13 November 1890, Tenbury Musical Society.
Pub. 1890, Novello.

97. Clapham Town end. Folksong arrangement for voice and piano. 1890.

98. La Capricieuse Op. 17. 'Morceau de genre' for violin and piano. 24 December 1891. Ded. Fred Ward. Pub. 1893, Breitkopf & Härtel; 1941, British & Continental.

99. Spanish Serenade (Stars of the summer night) Op. 23. Partsong for SATB. 10 November 1891.

99a. Spanish Serenade Op. 23. Version with orchestra. 12 June 1892.
fp: 7 April 1893, Herefordshire Philharmonic Society.
Pub. 1892, Novello.

100. Very melodious exercises in the first position Op. 22. For solo violin. Ded. May Grafton. 1892. Pub. 1892, Chanot; 1927, Laudy.

101. Etudes caractéristiques Op. 24. For solo violin. 1892. Ded. Adolphe Pollitzer. Pub. 1892, Chanot.

102. Serenade in E minor Op. 20. For string orchestra. 1892. Ded. W. H. Winfield.
1. *Allegro piacevole*; 2. *Larghetto*; 3. *Allegretto*.
fp (No. 2 only): 7 April 1893, Hereford.
f London p (No. 2 only): 19 June 1894, St. Andrew's Hall.
fp (complete): 23 July 1896, Antwerp.
fEp (complete): 16 July 1899, New Brighton.
f London p (complete): 5 March 1905, Bechstein Hall, cond. Edward Elgar.

fFp: December 1906, Paris, Théâtre Sarah Bernhardt, Concerts Lamoureux, cond. Camille Chevillard.

fbp: 10 April 1924, Wireless String Orchestra, cond. Capt. W. A. Featherstone.

Pub. 1893, Breitkopf & Härtel.

BIBLIOGRAPHY:

Harold Rawlinson: Some famous works for string orchestra, No. 2: Serenade for strings (E minor) Op. 20, *Strad*, May 1946, p. 9.

103. The Black Knight Op. 25. Cantata for chorus and orchestra. September 1892. Poem: Uhland, transl. H. W. Longfellow. Ded. Hugh Blair. Dur. 35′.

2 fl, pic, 2 ob, 2 cl, bcl, 2 bsn; 4 hn, 2 tpt, 3 tmb, tuba; timp, GC, cym, tgle, tamb pic, tamb; organ, strings.

fp: 18 April 1893, Worcester Festival Choral Society, cond. Edward Elgar.

Pub. 1893, 1898 (vocal score, 2nd edition, 1905 (full score), Novello.

104. A spear, a sword. Song. 1892.

105. Like to the damask rose (Simon Wastell). For voice and piano. 1892.

fp: 25 February 1897, St. James's Hall.

Pub. 1893, Tuckwood, Ascherberg; 1907, Ascherberg (in 'Seven Lieder of Edward Elgar').

106. The poet's life (Alice Burroughs). For voice and piano. 1892. Pub. 1907, Ascherberg (in 'Seven Lieder of Edward Elgar').

107. A song of autumn (Adam Lindsay Gordon). For voice and piano. 1892. Ded. Miss Marshall. Pub. 1892, Orsborn & Tuckwood/Ascherberg; 1907, Ascherberg (in 'Seven Lieder of Edward Elgar').

108. Shepherd's song Op. 16 No. 1 (Barry Pain). For voice and piano. 22 August 1892. Pub. 1895, Tuckwood; 1896, Ascherberg; 1907, Ascherberg (in 'Seven Lieder of Edward Elgar').

109. Parsifal: Good Friday music. Wagner, arr. Elgar for small orchestra. 1894.

fp: 13 June 1894, Worcester High School. Unpub.

110. Sursum Corda (Elévation) Op. 11. For strings, brass and organ. 1 April 1894. Ded. H. Dyke Acland.

2 tpt, 4 hn, 3 tmb, tuba; timp; organ, strings.

fp: 9 April 1894, Worcester Cathedral.

Pub. 1901, Schott.

111. Two partsongs Op. 26 (C. A. Elgar). For SSAA with two violins and piano. 1894. Ded. Mrs. E. B. Fitton, Malvern.

1. *The snow*; 2. *Fly, singing bird*.

Pub. 1895, Novello.

111a. Two partsongs Op. 26. Version for 3-part female chorus, organ and orchestra. 19 December 1903.

fp: 12 March 1904, Queen's Hall, Sunday Concert, Smallwood Metcalfe's Choir, Percy Pitt (organ), Queen's Hall Orchestra, cond. (Sir) Henry Wood.

112. The wave. For voice and piano. 1894.

113. Muleteer's song. For voice and piano. 1894.

114. Rondel Op. 16 No. 3 (Longfellow: 'Froissart'). For voice and piano. 4 January 1894.

fp: ?7 December (?25 February) 1897, St. James's Hall.

Pub. 1896, Ascherberg; 1907, Ascherberg (in 'Seven Lieder of Edward Elgar').

115. Sonata in G Op. 28. For organ. ?1894 (?completed 3 July 1895). Ded. C. Swinnerton Heap.

1. *Allegro maestoso*; 2. *Allegretto*; 3. *Andante espressivo*; 4. *Presto (comodo)*.

fp: 8 July 1895, Worcester Cathedral, Hugh Blair.

Pub. 1896, Breitkopf & Härtel.

116. From the Bavarian Highlands Op. 27. Six Choral Songs with piano. 1895. Bavarian folksongs adapted by C. Alice Elgar. Ded. Mr. and Mrs. Henry Slingsby Bethell, Garmisch.

1. *The dance*; 2. *False love*; 3. *Lullaby*; 4. *Aspiration*; 5. *On the Alm*; 6. *The marksman*.

fp: 21 April 1896, Worcester Festival Choral Society, cond. Edward Elgar.

Pub. 1896, Joseph Williams.

116a. From the Bavarian Highlands Op.

27. Version with orchestra. 1896. Pub. 1907, Novello.

116b. Three Bavarian Dances. For orchestra. Nos. 1, 3 & 6 of preceding.

1. *Allegretto giocoso*; 2. *Moderato*; 3. *Allegro vivace*.

fp: 23 October 1897, Crystal Palace, cond. August Manns.

fbp: 12 October 1924, Birmingham Station Symphony Orchestra, cond. Joseph Lewis.

Pub. 1901 (full score), Joseph Williams.

117. After Op. 31 No. 1 (Philip Bourke Marston). For voice and piano. 21 June 1895.

fp: 2 March 1900, St. James's Hall.

Pub. 1900, Boosey.

118. A song of flight Op. 31 No. 2 (Christina Rossetti). For voice and piano. Date unknown.

fp: 2 March 1900, St. James's Hall.

Pub. 1900, Boosey.

119. The Light of Life (Lux Christi) Op. 29. Short Oratorio for soprano, contralto, tenor and bass soloists, chorus and orchestra. January–June 1896. Words adapted from the Scriptures by Rev. E. Capel-Cure. Ded. C. Swinnerton Heap.

2 fl, pic, 2 ob, 2 cl, 2 bsn, cbsn (ad lib); 4(2) hn, 2 tpt, 3 tmb, tuba; timp, cym; hp, organ, strings.

fp: 10 September 1896, Worcester, Three Choirs Festival, Anna Williams, Jessie King, Edward Lloyd and Watkin Mills, cond. Edward Elgar.

f London p: 16 October 1896, Queen's Hall, National Sunday League concert, Anna Williams, Hannah Jones, Iver McKay and Bantock Pierpoint.

Pub. 1896, 1908 (full score), Novello.

120. Scenes from the Saga of King Olaf Op. 30. Cantata for soprano, tenor, bass soloists, chorus and orchestra. 15 July 1894–August 1896. Words: Longfellow and H. A. Acworth. Dur. 100′.

1. *Introduction*; 2. *The challenge of Thor*; 3. *King Olaf's return*; 4. *The conversion*; 5. *Gudrun*; 6. *The wraith of Odin*; 7. *Sigrid*; 8. *Thyri*; 9. *The death of Olaf*; 10. *Epilogue*.

2 fl, pic, 2 ob, ca, 2 cl, bcl, 2 bsn; 4 hn, 3 tpt, 3 tmb, tuba; timp, GC, cym, tgle, tamb pic, tamtam, bell; hp, organ, strings.

fp: 30 October 1896, Hanley, Victoria Hall, North Staffs. Festival, Medora Henson, Edward Lloyd and Ffrangcon Davies, cond. Edward Elgar.

f London p: 3 April 1897, Crystal Palace Choir and Orchestra, Medora Henson, Edward Lloyd and Andrew Black, cond. Edward Elgar.

fbp: 25 March 1925, Newcastle, Town Hall, Newcastle and Gateshead Choral Union and Newcastle Philharmonic Orchestra, with Elsie Suddaby, J. Adams and E. J. Potts, cond. W. G. Whittaker.

Pub. 1896, 1905 (full score), Novello.

BIBLIOGRAPHY:

Joseph Bennett: Scenes from the Legend of King Olaf, analytical note, Novello (London) 1896.

Francis Bonavia: King Olaf, *Radio Times*, 19 November 1937, p. 13.

120a. As torrents in summer. Partsong for SATB. Extracted from preceding.

121. Minuet. For piano solo. 1897. Ded. Paul Kilburn. Pub. 1897, The Dome; Joseph Williams.

121a. Minute Op. 21. Version for orchestra of preceding. 1897.

fp: 16 July 1899, New Brighton, cond. (Sir) Granville Bantock.

Pub. 1899, Joseph Williams.

122. Chanson de matin Op. 15 No. 1 (orig. No. 2). For violin and piano. ?1897 (?earlier). Pub. 1899, Novello.

122a. Chanson de matin Op. 15 No. 1. Version for small orchestra.

fl, ob, cl, bsn; hn; hp or piano (ad lib), strings.

?fp: 14 September 1901, Queen's Hall, Promenade Concert, Queen's Hall Orchestra, cond. (Sir) Henry Wood.

Pub. 1901, Novello. Also numerous arrangements.

123. Chanson de nuit Op. 15 No. 2 (orig. No. 1). For violin and piano. ?1897 (?earlier). Ded. F. Ehrke. Pub. 1897, Novello.

123a. Chanson de nuit Op. 15 No. 2. Version for small orchestra. Instrumentation and performance as No. 122a. Pub. 1899, Novello. Also numerous arrangements.

124. Imperial March Op. 32. For orchestra. 6 February 1897.
fp: 19 April 1897, Crystal Palace, cond. August Manns. Also: 25 April 1897, Queen's Hall, Sunday Concert, Queen's Hall Orchestra, cond. Alberto Randegger.
Pub. 1897, 1902, Novello.

125. The Banner of St. George Op. 33. Ballad for chorus and orchestra. January–March 1897 (?reworked from an earlier version). Text: Shapcott Wensley.
2(1) fl, pic, 2(1) ob, 2(1) cl, 2(1) bsn; 4(2) hn, cornets, 2(1) tmb, bs tmb, tuba (ad lib); timp, GC & cym (ad lib), tamb pic (ad lib); strings.
fp: 18 May 1897, Kensington, St. Cuthbert's Hall Choral Society, cond. Cyril Miller.
fbp: 23 April 1925, Birmingham, Station Repertory Chorus and Symphony Orchestra, cond. Joseph Lewis.
Pub. 1897 (vocal score and parts), 1905 (full score), Novello.

126. Te Deum & Benedictus Op. 34. For chorus and organ. 31 July 1897. Ded. G. R. Sinclair.
fp: 12 September 1897, Hereford, Three Choirs Festival.
Pub. 1897, Novello.

127. Grete Malverne on a rock. 1897. Private Christmas card.

127a. Lo, Christ the Lord is born. Carol for SATB. 1897. Published version of preceding. Pub. 1909.

128. Rondel (The little eyes that never knew) (Swinburne). For voice and piano. 1897 (?1887).
fp: 26 April 1897, Worcester Musical Union, Gertrude Walker, acc. Edward Elgar.
Unpub.

129. Love alone will stay (Lute song) (C. Alice Elgar). For voice and piano. 30 May 1897. Pub. 1898, The Dome. Later became No. 2 of 'Sea Pictures'.

130. The holly and the ivy. Arranged for chorus and orchestra. 1898. For the Worcestershire Philharmonic Society, 9 January 1899.

131. Festival March in C. For orchestra. ?1898.
fp: 14 October 1898, Crystal Palace, cond. August Manns.
Unpub. Lost, apart from fragment.

132. Caractacus Op. 35. Cantata for soprano, tenor, baritone and bass soloists, chorus and orchestra. 1897–8. Dated: 21 August 1898. Text: H. A. Acworth. Ded. H. M. Queen Victoria. Dur. 105'.
2 fl, pic, 2 ob, 2 cl, 2 bsn, cbsn; 4 hn, 4 tpt, 3 tmb, tuba; timp, GC, cym, tgle, tamb pic, gong, small gong, glock, side dms; hp, organ, strings.
fp: 5 October 1898, Leeds Festival, Medora Henson, Edward Lloyd, Andrew Black, John Browning, cond. Edward Elgar.
f London p (*March* only): 15 October 1898, Crystal Palace, cond. Edward Elgar.
f London p (complete): 29 November 1898, Highbury Philharmonic Society, Medora Henson, Edward Lloyd, Andrew Black, Charles Copland, cond. G. H. Betjemann.
Pub. 1898, 1905 (full score), Novello.

BIBLIOGRAPHY:
Herbert Thompson: Caractacus, analytical note, Novello (London) 1898.

132a. The sword song (Leap, leap to the light). Partsong for SATB. Extracted from preceding.

133. Variations on an original theme ('Enigma') Op. 36. For orchestra. 1898–9, Malvern. Ded. 'to my friends pictured within'.
1. *Andante.* Ded. C.A.E.
2. *Allegro.* Ded. H.D.S.-P. (Hew David Steuart-Powell).
3. *Allegretto.* Ded. R.B.T. (Richard Baxter Townshend).
4. *Allegro di molto.* Ded. W.M.B. (W. M. Baker).
5. *Moderato.* Ded. R.P.A. (Richard P. Arnold).
6. *Andantino.* Ded. Ysobel (Isabel Fitton).
7. *Presto.* Ded. Troyte (Troyte Griffith).
8. *Allegretto.* Ded. W.N. (Winifred Norbury).
9. *Adagio.* Ded. Nimrod (A. J. Jaeger).

10. *Intermezzo: Allegretto.* Ded. Dorabella (Dora Penny).

11. *Allegro di molto.* Ded. G.R.S. (George Robertson Sinclair).

12. *Andante.* Ded. B.G.N. (Basil G. Nevinson).

13. *Romanza: Moderato.* Ded. x x x (Lady Mary Lygon).

14. *Allegro.* Ded. E.D.U.

2 fl, pic, 2 ob, 2 cl, 2 bsn, cbsn; 4 hn, 3 tpt, 3 tmb, tuba; timp, tamb pic, tgle, GC & cym; organ (ad lib), strings.

fp: 19 June 1899, St. James's Hall, cond. Hans Richter.

fGp: 7 February 1901, Düsseldorf, cond. Julius Buths.

fFp: 12 February 1905, Paris, Concerts Lamoureux.

fbp: 24 October 1923, Manchester station, Augmented 2ZY Orchestra, cond. (Sir) Dan Godfrey.

Pub. 1899, Novello.

BIBLIOGRAPHY:

Ivor Atkins: Elgar's Enigma Variations, *MT*, 1934, April p. 328, May p. 411.

Cecil Barber: Enigma Variations, *M&L*, April 1935, p. 137.

R. Elkin: The Enigma Variations, *Music in Education*, 15 July 1962, p. 95.

J. H. Elliot: The Enigma Variations, *Halle*, October 1950, p. 10.

Roger Fiske: The Enigma, a solution, *MT*, November 1969, p. 1124.

I. Kolodin: What is the enigma?, *Saturday Review*, 28 February 1953, p. 53.

— Winners of the enigma contest, *Saturday Review*, 30 May 1953, p. 48.

Robert Lorenz: Enigma Variations—a different approach, *MO*, December 1934, p. 212, January 1935, p. 311.

Jerrold N. Moore: An approach to Elgar's Enigma, *MR*, February 1959, p. 38.

Ernest Newman: Elgar and his Enigma, *Sunday Times*, 1929, 16/23/30 April, 7 May.

R. C. Powell: Elgar's Enigma, *M&L*, July 1934, p. 203.

Eric Sams: Elgar's cypher letter to Dorabella, *MT*, February 1970, p. 151.

— Variations on an original theme (Enigma), *MT*, March 1970, p. 258.

— Elgar's Enigmas, a past script and a post script, *MT*, July 1970, p. 692.

J. A. Westrup: Elgar's Enigma, *PRMA*, 1959–1960, p. 79.

R. T. White: Elgar's Enigma Variations, *Music Student*, May 1924, p. 296.

MISCELLANEOUS OR UNSIGNED:

AudioGraphic music rolls: Elgar explains the Enigma Variations, *British Musician*, January 1930, p. 16.

Elgar's Enigma theme, *The Times*, 14 July 1934, p. 10.

Enigma Variations, *The Times*, 19 June 1944, p. 6.

'To my friends pictured within' (illustrated feature), *M&M*, June 1957, p. 19.

134. O Salutaris Hostia (in Tozer's Benediction Manual). 1898. Pub. 1898, Cary.

135. To her beneath whose steadfast star (Frederick W. H. Myers). For SATB. 7 February 1899.

fp: 24 May 1899, Windsor Castle, before Queen Victoria.

Pub. 1899, Macmillan.

136. Sérénade lyrique. 'Melodie' for small orchestra. June 1899. Ded. Ivan Caryll's Orchestra.

2 fl, 2 ob, 2 cl, 2 bsn; 2 hn; timp; hp, strings.

fp: 27 November 1900, St. James's Hall.

Pub. 1899, Chappell; also for piano or violin and piano.

137. Dry thou fair, those crystal eyes (Henry King). For voice and piano. 1899.

fp: 21 June 1899, Royal Albert Hall.

Pub. 1899, Souvenir of Charing Cross Hospital Bazaar.

138. The Dream of Gerontius Op. 38. Oratorio for mezzo-soprano, tenor and bass soloists, chorus and orchestra. 1899–1900. Dated: 3 August 1900, Birchwood. Text: John Henry Newman. Ded. A.M.D.G. Dur. 100'.

2 fl, pic, 2 ob, ca, 2 cl, bcl, 2 bsn, cbsn; 4 hn, 3 tpt, 3 tmb, tuba; timp, GC, cym, tgle, tamb pic, tamtam, bells, glock; 2(1) hp, organ, strings.

fp: 3 October 1900, Birmingham Festival, Marie Brema, Edward Lloyd, H. Plunket Greene, cond. Hans Richter.

f London p (*Prelude* only): 10 November 1900, Crystal Palace, cond. August Manns.

f London p (*Prelude & Angel's Farewell* only): 20 February 1901, Queen's Hall, Kirkby Lunn and the Queen's Hall Orchestra, cond. (Sir) Henry Wood.

fGp: December 1901, Düsseldorf, Antonie Beel, Ludwig Wüllner, Willy Metzmacher, cond. Julius Buths.

fAp: 23 March 1903, Chicago, Apollo Musical Club, cond. Theodore Thomas.

f New York p: 26 March 1903, Carnegie Hall, Ada Crossley, Ellison Van Hoose, David Bispham, cond. Frank Damrosch.

f London p (complete): 6 June 1903, Westminster Cathedral, Muriel Foster, Ludwig Wüllner, Ffrangcon-Davies, North Staffordshire Choral Society, cond. Edward Elgar.

fFp: 25 May 1906, Paris, Salle du Trocadero, Concerts Lamoureux, Claire Croiza, Plamondon, Louis Fröhlich, cond. Camille Chevillard.

fbp: 20 April 1924, Rachel Hunt, John Perry, Lee Thistlethwaite, 2ZY Opera Chorus and Augmented Orchestra, cond. Sir Dan Godfrey.

Pub. 1900, 1902 (full score), Novello. German version, Julius Buths.

BIBLIOGRAPHY:

Sir John Barbirolli: The Dream of Gerontius, a personal note, *The Gramophone*, October 1965, p. 193.

William Bennett: Gerontius: the first performance, *MMR*, 1933, p. 34.

Sir Walford Davies: Elgar's Gerontius, *Radio Times*, 16 March 1934, p. 792.

Edgar Day: Interpreting 'Gerontius', *MT*, June 1969, p. 607.

Victor Debay: Le songe de Gérontius, *Le Courrier musical*, 1906.

A. J. Jaeger: The Dream of Gerontius, analytical note, Novello (London) 1900.

— Mr. Elgar's setting of The Dream of Gerontius, *MT*, October 1900, p. 663.

Basil Maine: Gerontius: an excerpt, *MMR*, 1932, p. 225.

— A note on Elgar's Gerontius, *Halle*, February–March 1947, p. 12.

M. Maxwell: The Dream of Gerontius, *American Record Guide*, May 1966, p. 796.

Mrs. Richard Powell: The first performance of Gerontius, *MT*, February 1959, p. 78.

'Rubato': Elgar's Gerontius at Westminster Cathedral, *The Vocalist*, July 1903, p. 98.

J. R. Talbot: A note on Gerontius, *Halle*, March 1955, p. 10.

Gerard Werker: The Dream of Gerontius, *Mens en melodie*, March 1947, p. 85.

Francis B. Westbrook: The Dream of Gerontius, Hinrichson Edition (London), No. 12, n.d.

139. Pipes of Pan (Adrian Ross). For voice and piano. 1899 (?1900).

fp: 31 March 1900, Queen's Hall, London Ballad Concert, Andrew Black.

Pub. 1900, Boosey.

140. Sea Pictures Op. 37. Five songs for contralto and orchestra. 1897–9. Dated: July 1899, Birchwood; orch. 18 August 1899.

1. *Sea slumber song* (Hon. Roden Noel).

2 fl, 2 ob, 2 cl, 2 bsn; 4 hn, 2 tpt, 3 tmb, tuba; timp, GC, gong; hp, strings.

2. *In haven* (C. Alice Elgar). Orig. comp. 1897.

2 fl, 2 ob, 2 cl, 2 bsn; 2 hn; hp, strings.

3. *Sabbath morning at sea* (Elizabeth Barrett Browning).

2 fl, 2 ob, 2 cl, 2 bsn; 4 hn, 2 tpt, 3 tmb, tuba; timp; hp, organ, strings.

4. *Where corals lie* (Richard Garnett).

2 fl, 2 ob, 2 cl, 2 bsn; 2 hn; timp; hp, strings.

5. *The swimmer* (Adam Lindsay Gordon).

2 fl, 2 ob, 2 cl, 2 bsn, dbsn; 4 hn, 2 tpt, 3 tmb, tuba; timp, GC, gong; hp, organ (ad lib), strings.

fp: 5 October 1899, Norwich Festival, Clara Butt, cond. Edward Elgar.

fbp: 3 April 1924, Muriel Sotham.

Pub. 1900, Boosey.

141. Always and everywhere (Krasinski, transl. F. E. Forty). For voice and piano. Date unknown. Pub. 1901, Boosey.

142. May song. For piano. 2 March 1901. Pub. 1901, W. H. Broome; 1901, Morrice.

Elgar, Edward

142a. May song. Version for orchestra. Pub. 1928, Elkin.

143. Cockaigne (In London Town) Op. 40. Overture for orchestra. 24 March 1901. Ded. 'To my friends the members of British orchestras'.

2 fl, pic, 2 ob, 2 cl, 2 bsn, cbsn; 4 hn, 2 tpt, 2 cornets, 3 tmb, tuba; timp, GC, cym, tgle, tamb, bells, side dm; organ, strings.

fp: 20 June 1901, Queen's Hall, Philharmonic Society, cond. Edward Elgar.

fbp: 27 March 1924, Manchester station, Augmented 2ZY Orchestra, cond. Sir Dan Godfrey.

Pub. 1901, Boosey: incl. reductions for piano solo or piano duet by O. Singer, 1901. Min. score: 1942, Hawkes.

144. Concert Allegro. For piano. 21 November 1901. Composed for Fanny Davies.

fp: 2 December 1901, St. James's Hall, Fanny Davies.

Unpub.

BIBLIOGRAPHY:
Diana McVeagh: Elgar's Concert Allegro, *MT*, February 1969, p. 135.

145. Pomp and Circumstance March No. 1 in D Major Op. 39 No. 1. For orchestra. July 1901, Birchwood.

2 fl, 2(1) pic, 2 ob, 2 cl, bcl, 2 bsn, cbsn; 4 hn, 2 tpt, 2 cornets, 3 tmb, tuba; timp, GC & cym, tgle, tamb pic, jingles; 2 hp, organ, strings.

fp: 19 October 1901, Liverpool, Liverpool Orchestral Society, cond. A. E. Rodewald.

f London p: 21 October 1901, Queen's Hall, Promenade Concert, Queen's Hall Orchestra, cond. (Sir) Henry Wood.

Pub. 1902, Boosey; also various arrs.

146. Pomp and Circumstance March No. 2 in A minor Op. 39 No. 2. For orchestra. 13 August 1901. Ded. Granville Bantock.

2 fl, pic, 2 ob, 2 cl, bcl, 2 bsn, cbsn; 4 hn, 2 tpt, 2 cornets, 3 tmb, tuba; timp, 2(1) tamb pic, tgle, bell, jingles, GC & cym; strings.

fp and f London p: as No. 145.

Pub. 1902, Boosey.

147. Grania and Diarmid Op. 42. Inci-

dental music (George Moore and W. B. Yeats). 4 October 1901. Ded. Henry J. Wood.

fp: October 1901, Dublin, Gaiety Theatre. Pub. 1902, Novello.

147a. Funeral March. From preceding.

2 fl, 2 ob, ca, 2 cl, bcl, 2 bsn, cbsn; 4 hn, 2 tpt, 3 tmb, tuba; timp, GC, cym, gong (ad lib); hp, strings.

fp: 18 January 1902, Queen's Hall, Queen's Hall Orchestra, cond. (Sir) Henry Wood.

fbp: 8 December 1924, Bournemouth, Winter Gardens, Bournemouth Municipal Orchestra, cond. Sir Dan Godfrey.

Pub. 1902, Novello.

147b. They are seven that pull the thread. Song from preceding (W. B. Yeats).

fl, cl, bsn; hn; hp, strings.

Pub. 1902, Novello.

148. Emmaus. A. Herbert Brewer, orch. Edward Elgar. 1901. Pub. 1901, Novello.

149. Come, gentle night (Clifton Bingham). For voice and piano. ?1901.

fp: 12 October 1901, Queen's Hall, Clara Butt.

Pub. 1901, Boosey.

150. Two songs Op. 41 (A. BC. enson). For voice and piano. Date unknown.

1. *In the dawn.*

2. *Speak, music.* Ded. Mrs. E. Speyer Ridgehurst.

fp (No. 1): 26 October 1901, Queen's Hall. Pub. 1901, Boosey.

151. God Save the King. Arr. for soprano, chorus and orchestra. 1902. Pub. 1902, Novello.

152. Dream Children Op. 43. Two pieces for small orchestra. 14 January 1902.

1. *Andante*; 2. *Allegretto piacevole.*

2 fl, 2 ob, 2 cl, 2 bsn; 4 hn; timp; hp, strings.

?fp: 4 September 1902, Queen's Hall, Queen's Hall Orchestra, cond. (Sir) Henry Wood.

Pub. 1902, Joseph Williams; 1913, Schott. Also for piano solo and various arrs.

153. Coronation Ode Op. 44. For soprano,

contralto, tenor and bass soloists, and chorus orchestra. 1901–2. Dated: 21 February 1902. Rev. 1911. Composed for the Grand Opera Syndicate for the state performance at Covent Garden. Ded. H.M. King Edward VII.

1. *Crown the King with Life.*
1a. *The Queen* (chorus). Added 1911.
2. *The daughter of ancient kings.* Chorus.
3. *Britain, ask of thyself.* Solo and male chorus.
4. (i) *Hark upon the hallowed air.* Tenor and soprano solo. (ii) *Only let the heart be pure.* Quartet.
5. *Peace, gentle peace.* Unacc. quartet and chorus.
6. *Finale: Land of hope and glory.* Contralto and tutti.

2 fl, pic, 2 ob, 2 cl, bcl, 2 bsn, dbsn; 4 hn, 3 tpt, 3 tmb, tuba; timp, GC & cym, side dm; organ, hp, strings; and military band.

fp: 2 October 1902, Sheffield Festival, Agnes Nicholls, Muriel Foster, John Coates, Frangcon-Davies, cond. Edward Elgar.

f London p: 26 October 1902, Queen's Hall, Agnes Nicholls, Edna Thornton, Lloyd Chandos, Ffrangcon-Davies, Queen's Hall Choral Society and Queen's Hall Orchestra, cond. Edward Elgar.

fbp: 4 June 1925, Aberdeen, Maud Pennington, Lena Dunn, Alex. Leitch, Robert Watson, 2BD Choir and Wireless Orchestra, cond. Arthur Collingwood.

Pub. 1902, 1911, Boosey. Arr. for female voices (SC) by Alec Rowley, 1937, Boosey; shortened version, 1953.

153a. Land of hope and glory. Song from preceding.
fp: 21 June 1902, Emma Albani's Coronation Concert, Clara Butt.
Pub. 1902, Boosey.

BIBLIOGRAPHY:
'A tune that will go round the world' said the King, *M&M*, June 1957, p. 9.

154. O mightiest of the mighty (Rev. S. Childs Clarke). Hymn. 1901. Ded. H.R.H. The Prince of Wales.
fp: 9 August 1902, Coronation of Edward VII.
Pub. 1902, Novello.

155. Weary wind of the west (T. E. Brown). Partsong for SATB a cappella. November 1902.
fp: 2 May 1903, Morecambe Musical Festival.
Pub. 1903, Novello.

156. Speak, my heart (A. C. Benson). For voice and piano. 1902. Pub. 1903, Boosey.

157. Five partsongs from the Greek Anthology Op. 45. For TTBB. 11 November 1902, Longdon Marsh. Ded. Sir Walter Parratt.

1. *Yea, cast me from the heights* (Anon., transl. Alma Strettell).
2. *Whether I find thee* (Anon., transl. Andrew Lang).
3. *After many a dusty mile* (Anon., transl. Edmund Gosse).
4. *It's oh, to be a wild wind* (Anon., transl. William M. Hardinge).
5. *Feasting I watch* (Marcus Argentarius, transl. Richard Garnett).

fp: 25 April 1904, Royal Albert Hall.
Pub. 1903.

158. Skizze. For piano. *c.* 1902–3. Ded. Julius Buths. Pub. 1903, Musik-Beilag zur neuen Musikzeitung (Stuttgart/Leipzig).

159. Offertoire (Andante religioso). For violin and piano. Date unknown. Ded. Serge Derval, Antwerp. Pub. 1903, Boosey.

160. The Apostles Op. 49. Oratorio for soprano, contralto, tenor and three bass soloists, chorus and orchestra. 1902–3, Longdon Marsh. Dated: 17 August 1903. Words compiled from the Scriptures by the composer. Ded. A.M.D.G. Dur. 75' (Part I) + 55' (Part II).

Part I: 1. *Prologue*; 2. *The Calling of the Apostles*; 3. *By the wayside*; 4. *By the Sea of Galilee.* Part II: 5. *Introduction*; 6. *The betrayal*; 7. *Golgotha*; 8. *At the sepulchre*; 9. *The Ascension.*

2 fl, pic, 2 ob, ca, 2 cl, bcl, 2 bsn, cbsn; 4 hn, 3 tpt (also extra tpt representing the Shofar), 3 tmb, tuba; timp, GC, side dm, cym, tgle, tamb, tamtam, small gong, antique cym, glock; 2(1) hp, organ, strings.

fp: 14 October 1903, Birmingham Festival, Emma Albani, Muriel Foster, John Coates,

Elgar, Edward

Kennerley Rumford, Andrew Black, Ffrang-con-Davies, cond. Edward Elgar.

fAp: 9 February 1904, New York, Carnegie Hall, New York Oratorio Society, cond. Frank Damrosch.

f London p: 15 March 1904, Elgar Festival, Agnes Nicholls, Kirkby Lunn, John Coates, Kennerley Rumford, Andrew Black, Ffrang-con-Davies, Halle Orchestra, cond. Hans Richter.

fGp: 22 May 1904, Cologne, Lower Rhine Festival, cond. Fritz Steinbach.

fbp: 10 March 1927, Newport, Central Hall, Newport Choral Society, Ida Cooper, Gladys Palmer, Sidney Pointer, Walter Saull, Frederick Woodhouse, Herbert Heyner, special orchestra, cond. Arthur E. Sims.

Pub. 1903, 1904 (full score), Novello.

BIBLIOGRAPHY:

Canon C. V. Gorton: Dr. Elgar's oratorio The Apostles, *MT*, October 1903, p. 656.
— An interpretation of the libretto, Novello (London) 1903.
A. J. Jaeger: The Apostles, analytical note, Novello (London) 1903.
Michael Kennedy: The Apostles, *Halle*, March 1957, p. 10.
Anthony Payne: Gerontius apart, *M&M*, December 1964, p. 25.
Mrs. Richard Powell: The words of The Apostles and The Kingdom, *MT*, July 1948, p. 201, May 1949, p. 149.
— The first performances of The Apostles and The Kingdom, *MT*, January 1960, p. 21.
Otto Reissel: Die Apostel, *Signale*, 1904, No. 38 (15 June), p. 676.

MISCELLANEOUS OR UNSIGNED:

Elgar's new oratorio The Apostles, *MS*, 4 April 1903, p. 215.
Dr. Elgar's new oratorio The Apostles, *MT*, April 1903, p. 228.
The Apostles, *MT*, July 1903, p. 449.
The Apostles, *The Vocalist*, November 1903, p. 228.

161. In the South ('Alassio') Op. 50. Overture for orchestra. 1903–4. Dated: 21 February 1904. Ded. Leo F. Schuster.

3 fl, pic, 2 ob, ca, 2 cl, bcl, 2 bsn, cbsn; 4 hn, 3 tpt, 3 tmb, tuba; timp, GC, cym, tamb pic, tgle, glock; hp, strings.

fp: 16 March 1904, Covent Garden, Elgar Festival, Halle Orchestra, cond. Edward Elgar.

fbp: 29 June 1924, Cardiff Station Symphony Orchestra, cond. Warwick Braithwaite.

Pub. 1904, Novello.

161a. In moonlight (Canto popolare). For small orchestra. Extracted from preceding. Pub. Novello, incl. various arrs.

162. Pomp and Circumstance March No. 3 in C minor Op. 39 No. 3. For orchestra. November 1904. Ded. Ivor Atkins.

2 fl, pic, 2 ob, ca, 2 cl, bcl, 3 bsn, cbsn; 4 hn, 2 tpt, 2 cornets, 3 tmb, tuba; timp, tamb tenore, tamb pic, GC & cym; strings.

fp: 8 March 1905, Queen's Hall, London Symphony Orchestra, cond. Sir Edward Elgar.

Pub. 1905, Boosey. Also various arrs.

163. Introduction and Allegro Op. 47. For string quartet and string orchestra. 1904–5. Dated: 13 February 1905. Ded. Prof. S. S. Sandford, Yale University.

fp: 8 March 1905, Queen's Hall, A. W. Payne, W. H. Eaynes, A. Hobday and B. Patterson Parker, London Symphony Orchestra, cond. Sir Edward Elgar.

fbp: 19 July 1925, 2LO String Orchestra, cond. Sir Dan Godfrey.

Pub. 1905, Novello.

BIBLIOGRAPHY:

Harold Rawlinson: Famous works for string orchestra, No. 13: Introduction and Allegro, *Strad*, June 1948, p. 27.
W. R. Anderson: Introduction and Allegro for strings, *The Gramophone*, September 1932, p. 132.

164. In Smyrna. For piano. 1905. Pub. 1905, Daily Mail Queen's Xmas Carol Book.

165. Evening scene (Coventry Patmore). For SATB a cappella. 25 August 1905.

fp: 12 May 1906, Morecambe Competitive Festival.

Pub. 1906, Novello.

166. Piece for organ. 1906. 'For Dot's nuns.'

167. The Kingdom Op. 51. Oratorio for

soprano, contralto, tenor and bass soloists, chorus and orchestra. 1905–6. Dated: August 1906. Words compiled from the Scriptures by the composer. Ded. A.M.D.G. Dur. 111′.

1. *Prelude*; 2. *In the upper room*; 3. *At the beautiful gate*; 4. *Pentecost*: (a) *In the upper room*, (b) *In Solomon's porch*; 5. *The sign of healing*: (a) *At the beautiful gate*, (b) *The arrest*; 6. *The upper room*: (a) *In fellowship*, (b) *The breaking of bread*, (c) *The prayers*.

3 fl, pic, 2 ob, ca, 2 cl, bcl, 2 bsn, cbsn; 4 hn, 3 tpt, 3 tmb, tuba; timp, GC, cym, side dm; 2 hp, organ, strings.

fp: 3 October 1906, Birmingham Festival, Agnes Nicholls, Muriel Foster, John Coates, William Higley, Festival Chorus and Halle Orchestra, cond. Sir Edward Elgar.

f London p: 17 November 1906, Alexandra Palace Choral and Orchestral Society, Cicely Gleeson-White, Edna Thornton, John Coates, Dalton Baker, cond. Allen Gill.

Pub. 1906, 1907 (full score), Novello. German version, Julius Buths.

BIBLIOGRAPHY:
W. R. Anderson: The Kingdom, *Radio Times*, 9 December 1932, p. 744.
F. Bonavia: Elgar's The Kingdom, *MT*, April 1945, p. 111.
Rev. Canon C. V. Gorton: An interpretation of the libretto, Novello (London) 1906.
A. J. Jaeger: The Kingdom, analytical note, Novello (London) 1906.
Anthony Payne: Gerontius apart, *M&M*, December 1964, p. 25.
Anon.: The Kingdom, Sir Edward Elgar's new oratorio, *MT*, October 1906, p. 675.

168. Berceuse (Petite Reine). Victor Berard, arr. Elgar for violin and piano. Early (?*c*. 1880). Pub. 1907, Ashdown.

169. Andantino. For violin, mandolin and guitar. 1907. Unfinished.

170. Pomp and Circumstance March No. 4 in G major Op. 39 No. 4. For orchestra. 7 June 1907. Ded. G. R. Sinclair.

3 fl, pic, 2 ob, ca, 2 cl, bcl, 2 bsn, cbsn; 4 hn, 3 tpt, 3 tmb, tuba; timp, tamb pic, GC & cym; hp, strings.

fp: 24 August 1907, Queen's Hall, Promenade Concert, Queen's Hall Orchestra, cond. Sir Edward Elgar.

Pub. 1907, Boosey. Also numerous arrs.

171. Two single chants for Venite. May 1907.
1. *D major*; 2. *G major*.
Pub. 1909, New Cathedral Psalter; Novello.

172. Two double chants in D (for Psalms 68 & 75). May 1907. Pub. 1909, Novello.

173. How calmly the evening (T. E. Lynch). For SATB a cappella. ?1907. Pub. 1907, Novello (in *MT*).

174. A Christmas greeting Op. 52. Carol for two sopranos, male chorus (ad lib), two violins and piano. 8 December 1907. Words: C. Alice Elgar. Ded. G. A. Sinclair and Hereford Cathedral Choir.

fp: 1 January 1908, Hereford Cathedral.
Pub. 1907, Novello.

175. Four Partsongs Op. 53. For SATB a cappella. 1907, Rome.
1. *There is sweet music* (Tennyson). Dated: February 1907, Rome. Ded. Canon Gorton.
2. *Deep in my soul* (Byron). Ded. Julia H. Worthington.
3. *O wild west wind* (Shelley). Ded. W. G. McNaught.
4. *Owls, an epitaph* (Edward Elgar). Ded. 'Pietro d'Alba'.
Pub. 1908, Novello.

176. The reveille Op. 54 (Bret Harte). For TTBB. 26 December 1907, Rome. Ded. Henry C. Embleton.

fp: 17 October 1908, Blackpool Festival.
Pub. 1908, Novello.

177. Pleading Op. 48 (Arthur Salmon). For voice and piano. Date unknown. Ded. Lady Maud Warrender. Pub. 1908, Novello.

177a. Pleading Op. 48. Version with orchestra. Dated: 23 November 1908.

178. Follow the colours (Capt. de Courcy Stretton). Marching Song for SATB. Date unknown.

fp: 24 May 1908, Royal Albert Hall, Empire Day Concert, Royal Choral Society.
Pub. 1908, Novello.

178a. Follow the colours. Version for male chorus. 1914.

fp: 10 October 1914, Royal Albert Hall. Pub. 1914, Novello.

179. Symphony No. 1 in A flat major Op. 55. For orchestra. June 1907–September 1908. Ded. Hans Richter.

1. *Andante: Nobilmente e semplice—Allegro*; 2. *Allegro molto*; 3. *Adagio*; 4. *Lento—Allegro*.

3 fl, pic, 2 ob, ca, 2 cl, bcl, 2 bsn, cbsn; 4 hn, 3 tpt, 3 tmb, tuba; timp, GC, cym, tamb pic; 2 hp, strings.

fp: 3 December 1908, Manchester, Free Trade Hall, Halle Orchestra, cond. Hans Richter.

f London p: 7 December 1908, Queen's Hall, London Symphony Orchestra, cond. Hans Richter.

f European p: 20 January 1909, Vienna, Konzertverein, cond. Ferdinand Löwe.

fGp: 11 February 1909, Leipzig, Gewandhaus, cond. Artur Nikisch.

fbp: 8 September 1927, Queen's Hall, Promenade Concert, Wood Symphony Orchestra, cond. Sir Henry Wood.

Pub. 1908, Novello.

BIBLIOGRAPHY:

W. R. Anderson: The chivalry of Elgar's First Symphony, *Radio Times*, 5 September 1930, p. 475.

Francis Bonavia: Symphony No. 1 in A flat, in *The Symphony*, Pelican Books (London) 1949, p. 318.

William Henry Caunt: Elgar's First Symphony—production at Manchester, *MS*, 12 December 1908, p. 374.

C.L.G.: Sir Edward Elgar's Symphony, *MO*, February 1909, p. 336; repr. from *The Spectator*.

'Musicus': Sir Edward Elgar's Symphony, *MO*, January 1909, p. 256; repr. from *The Daily Telegraph*.

Hugh Ottaway: Elgar and his First Symphony, *Halle*, May 1955, p. 1.

Anon.: Sir Edward Elgar's Symphony, *MT*, December 1908, p. 778.

180. Angelus (Tuscany) Op. 56. For SATB. Words adapted from the Tuscan. Date unknown. Ded. Mrs. Charles Stuart Wortley.

fp: 8 December 1910, Queen's Hall, London Choral Society, cond. Arthur Fagge. Pub. 1909, Novello.

181. Go, song of mine Op. 57 (Guido Cavalcanti, transl. D. G. Rossetti). Partsong for SSAATB a cappella. May 1909, Carreggi. Ded. Alfred H. Littleton.

fp: 9 September 1909, Three Choirs Festival, cond. G. R. Sinclair.

Pub. 1909, Novello.

182. They are at rest (John Henry Newman). Elegy for SATB a cappella. 1909.

fp: 22 January 1910, Royal Mausoleum, on anniversary of Queen Victoria's death. Pub. 1910, Novello.

183. Elegy Op. 58. For string orchestra. 5 July 1909. Ded. Worshipful Company of Musicians, in memory of Rev. R. H. Hadden, late Junior Warden.

fp: 13 July 1909, London, Mansion House memorial concert of the Worshipful Company of Musicians.

Pub. 1910, Novello.

184. A child asleep (E. B. Browning). For voice and piano. December 1909. Ded. Anthony Goetz. Pub. 1910, Novello.

185. The Kingsway (C. Alice Elgar). For voice and piano. 25–27 December 1909.

fp: 15 January 1910, Alexandra Palace. Pub. 1910, Boosey.

186. Song cycle Op. 59 (Gilbert Parker). For voice and orchestra. December 1909–January 1910. Nos. 1, 2 & 4 never composed.

3. *Oh, soft was the song*; 5. *Was it some golden star?*; 6. *Twilight*.

fp: 24 January 1910, Queen's Hall, Jaeger memorial concert, Muriel Foster, cond. Sir Edward Elgar.

Pub. 1910, Novello.

187. Two songs Op. 60. For voice and piano or orchestra. 1909–10. Words: Folksongs of Eastern Europe, paraphrased by Elgar and 'Pietro d'Alba'. Ded. Yvonne.

1. *The torch.* 23 December 1909. Orchestral version: 26 July 1912.

2. *The river.* 18 February 1910. Orchestral version: July 1912.

fp: 11 September 1912, Hereford, Three Choirs Festival.

Pub. 1910, Novello.

188. Violin Concerto Op. 61. 1909–10.
Dated: 5 August 1910. Ded. Fritz Kreisler.

1. *Allegro*; 2. *Andante*; 3. *Allegro molto—Molto maestoso*.

2 fl, 2 ob, 2 cl, 2 bsn, cbsn (ad lib); 4 hn, 2 tpt, 3 tmb, tuba (ad lib); timp; strings.

fp: 10 November 1910, Queen's Hall, Philharmonic Society, Fritz Kreisler, cond. Sir Edward Elgar.

f European p: 13 January 1911, Amsterdam, Fritz Kreisler and the Concertgebouw Orchestra, cond. Willem Mengelberg.

f Berlin p: 21 October 1911, Emil Telmanyi.

fAp: 9 December 1911, Chicago, Albert Spalding and the Theodore Thomas Orchestra.

fbp: 15 January 1925, Albert Sammons, orchestra cond. Ernest Ansermet.

Pub. 1910, Novello: incl. full score, reduction by the composer, min. score.

BIBLIOGRAPHY:

Herbert Byard: Violin Concerto in B minor, in *The Concerto*, Pelican Books (London) 1952, p. 254.

Jack Diether: Menuhin's Elgar: intimacy and bravura, *American Record Guide*, September 1966, p. 38.

Sydney Grew: Elgar's Concerto for violin and orchestra, *MO*, 1911, July p. 685, August p. 761, September p. 832.

B. Jacobson: Elgar's Violin Concerto as played by Menuhin today and by Menuhin yesterday, *High Fidelity*, September 1966, p. 86.

Charles Karlyle: Elgar's Violinkonzert, *Signale*, 1910, No. 46 (16 November), p. 1732.

Ernest Newman: Elgar's Violin Concerto, *MT*, October 1910, p. 631.

D. Hugh Ottaway: Elgar's Violin Concerto, *Halle*, April 1951, p. 3.

W. H. Reed: The Violin Concerto, *M&L*, January 1935, p. 30.

— Elgar and his Violin Concerto, in *Essays on Music*, Cassell (London) 1967, p. 97.

C. B. Rees: Menuhin and Elgar's Violin Concerto, *Musical Events*, November 1961, p. 8.

Donald F. Tovey: Violin Concerto in B minor, in *EMA*, Vol. 3, O.U.P. (London) 1936, p. 152.

R. T. White: Elgar's Violin Concerto, *Music Student*, January 1925, p. 51.

Anon.: M. Ysaÿe and the Elgar Violin Concerto, *MT*, January 1913, p. 19.

— Sir Edward Elgar's new Violin Concerto, *MMR*, 1910, p. 270.

189. Romance Op. 62. For bassoon and orchestra. January 1910. Ded. Edwin F. James.

2 fl, 2 ob, 2 cl, 2(1) bsn; 3 hn, 3 tmb (ad lib); timp; strings.

fp: 16 February 1911, Herefordshire Orchestral Society, Edwin F. James, cond. G. R. Sinclair.

Pub. 1910 (reduction), 1912 (full score), Novello.

190. Symphony No. 2 in E flat major Op. 63, 1910–11, Venice and Tintagel. Ded. to the memory of Edward VII. Dur. 51′.

1. *Allegro vivace e nobilmente*; 2. *Larghetto*; 3. *Rondo: Presto*; 4. *Moderato e maestoso*.

3 fl, pic, 2 ob, ca, E-flat cl, 2 cl, bcl, 2 bsn, cbsn; 4 hn, 3 tpt, 3 tmb, tuba; timp, GC, tamb pic, cym, tamburino (ad lib); 2 hp, strings.

fp: 24 May 1911, Queen's Hall, London Musical Festival, Queen's Hall Orchestra, cond. Sir Edward Elgar.

fAp: 24 November 1911, Cincinnati, cond. Leopold Stokowski.

f New York p: 10 December 1911, Century Theatre, New York Symphony Orchestra, cond. Walter Damrosch.

Pub. 1911, Novello; also reduction for piano or piano duet by Sigfrid Karg-Elert, 1912.

BIBLIOGRAPHY:

Neville Cardus: Second Symphony—Elgar, *Halle*, October 1946, p. 4.

F. Bonavia: Symphony No. 2 in E flat, in *The Symphony*, Pelican Books (London) 1949, p. 321.

Sydney Grew: Elgar's Second Symphony, *MO*, 1914, January p. 247, February p. 328.

W. McNaught: A note on Elgar's Second Symphony, *MT*, February 1915, p. 57.

Ernest Newman: Elgar's Second Symphony, *MT*, May 1911, p. 295.

Donald F. Tovey: Symphony in E flat No. 2, in *EMA*, Vol. 2, O.U.P. (London) 1935, p. 114.

Elgar, Edward

R. T. White: Elgar's Second Symphony, *Music Student*, March 1924, p. 159.

Anon.: Elgar's Second Symphony in America, *The Times*, 3 January 1912, p. 7.

191. O hearken thou Op. 64. Offertory for chorus and orchestra. 1911.

fp: 22 June 1911, Coronation of King George V.

Pub. 1911, Novello; also published as *Intende voci orationis meae*.

192. Coronation March Op. 65. For orchestra. May 1911.

3 fl, pic, 2 ob, ca, 2 cl, bcl, 2 bsn, cbsn; 4 hn, 3 tpt, 3 tmb, tuba; timp, tamb pic, tamb tenore, GC & cym; 2 hp, organ (ad lib), strings.

fp: 22 June 1911, Coronation of King George V.

Pub. 1911, 1912 (full score), Novello. Also various arrs.

193. St. Matthew Passion: Two Chorales. Bach, orch. Elgar.

3 tpt, 4 hn, 3 tmb, tuba.

fp: 14 September 1911, Worcester, Three Choirs Festival.

194. St. Matthew Passion. Bach, performing edition by Edward Elgar and Ivor Atkins. Pub. 1911, Novello.

195. The Crown of India Op. 66. Imperial Masque in two tableaux for soloists, chorus and orchestra. 1911–12. Dated: February 1912. Text: Henry Hamilton.

1. *Introduction and sacred measure*; 2. *Dance of Nautch girls*; 3. *Hail, immortal Indi*; 4. *March of Mogul emperors*; 5. *Entrance of John Company*; 6. *Rule of England*; 7. *Interlude*; 8. *Warriors' dance*; 9. *Cities of India*; 10. *Crown of India March*; 11. *Crowning of Delhi*; 12. *Ave Imperator*.

fp: 11 March 1912, Coliseum, cond. Sir Edward Elgar; with Marion Bealey (Agra), Harry Dearth (St. George), Nancy Price (India), May Leslie-Stuart (Delhi), Evelyn Kerry (Calcutta), Sybil Etherington (Benares); producer, Oswald Stoll; costumes and scenery, Percy Anderson.

Pub. 1912, Enoch: piano reduction by Hugh Blair.

BIBLIOGRAPHY:

Crown of India performed, *The Times*, 12 March 1912, p. 8.

195a. The Crown of India: Concert Suite. For orchestra.

1. *Introduction and Dance of Nautch girls*; 2. *Minuet*; 3. *The warriors' dance*; 4. *Interlude*; 5. *March of the Mogul emperors*.

2 fl, pic, 2 ob, 2 cl, bcl (ad lib), 2 bsn, dbsn (ad lib); 4 hn, 3(2) tpt, 2 tmb, bs tuba; timp, tgle, glock tamtam, jingles, big gong, GC, cym, gong, tomtoms, tamb, side dm; hp, strings.

fp: 11 September 1912, Hereford, Shire Hall, Three Choirs Festival, London Symphony Orchestra, cond. Sir Edward Elgar.

f London p: 17 September 1912, Queen's Hall, Promenade Concert, Queen's Hall Orchestra, cond. Sir Henry Wood.

fbp: 28 January 1925, Bournemouth Wireless Orchestra, cond. Capt. W. A. Featherstone.

196. Great is the Lord Op. 67. Anthem for 4-part chorus. 24 August 1910–March 1912. Ded. Dean of Wells, J. Armitage Robinson.

fp: 16 July 1912, Westminster Abbey.

Pub. 1912, Novello.

197. The Music Makers Op. 69. Ode for contralto, chorus and orchestra. 21 August 1912. Text: Arthur O'Shaughnessy. Ded. Nicholas Kilburn.

fp: 1 October 1912, Birmingham Festival, Muriel Foster, cond. Sir Edward Elgar.

f London p: 28 November 1912, Royal Albert Hall, Muriel Foster, Royal Choral Society, cond. Sir Frederick Bridge.

fbp: 2 June 1927, Murial Brunskill, Wireless Chorus and Symphony Orchestra, cond. Sir Edward Elgar.

Pub. 1912, Novello.

198. Falstaff Op. 68. Symphonic Study for orchestra. 1913. Ded. Landon Ronald. Dur. 30'.

2 fl, pic, 2 ob, ca, 2 cl, bcl, 2 bsn, cbsn; 4 hn, 3 tpt, 3 tmb, tuba; timp, GC, cym, tamb pic, tamb, tgle, tabor (or tamb pic without snares); 2 hp, strings.

fp: 1 October 1913, Leeds Festival, London Symphony Orchestra, cond. Sir Edward Elgar.

f London p: 3 November 1913, Queen's Hall, New Symphony Orchestra, cond. (Sir) Landon Ronald.

fbp: 25 November 1926, Royal Albert Hall, National Orchestra, cond. Sir Edward Elgar.

Pub. 1913, Novello.

BIBLIOGRAPHY:

Eric Blom: Elgar's Falstaff, *MO*, December 1921, p. 225.
— The Listener's Repertoire: Elgar (Op. 68) Falstaff, Symphonic Study, *Music Student*, September 1930, p. 505.
V. C. Clinton-Baddeley: The Shakespearean background to Elgar's Falstaff, in *Music Magazine*, Rockliff (London) 1953, p. 46.
Sir Edward Elgar: Falstaff, *MT*, September 1913, p. 575.
— Falstaff, analytical note, Novello (London) 1933.
Constant Lambert: Elgar at his most English, *Radio Times*, 14 October 1938, p. 14.
Robert Lorenz: An amateur's study of Elgar's Falstaff, *MT*, November 1932, p. 989.
Peter J. Pirie: A fat knight and his music, *High Fidelity*, January 1963, p. 46.
Anon.: Elgar's Falstaff: 'Passetyme with good cumpanie', *The Times*, 19 February 1927, p. 10.

198a. Falstaff: Two Interludes. Arr. for piano by the composer. Pub. 1914, Novello.

199. Carissima. For small orchestra. 1913. Ded. Winifred Stephens.

2(1) fl, 2 cl, 2 cornets, 2 ob, 2 bsn; 2 hn, 2(1) tmb; timp; hp (ad lib), strings.

fp: 21 January 1914, Hayes (Middlesex), Gramophone Co. recording session.

f public p: 15 February 1914, Royal Albert Hall.

Pub. 1914, Elkin; also for full orchestra, and numerous arrs.

200. Sospiri Op. 70. For strings, harp and organ. 1914. Ded. W. H. Reed.

fp: 15 August 1914, Queen's Hall, Promenade Concert (opening night), Queen's Hall Orchestra, cond. Sir Henry Wood.

Pub. 1914, Breitkopf & Härtel.

201. Fear not, O land. Harvest anthem for 4-part chorus. January 1914. Pub. 1914, Novello.

202. Arabian serenade (Margery Lawrence). For voice and piano. Date unknown. Pub. 1914, Boosey.

203. Chariots of the Lord (John Brownlie). For voice and piano. January 1914. Ded. Fight for Right movement.

fp: 28 June 1914, Royal Albert Hall.

Pub. 1914, Boosey.

204. The birthright (George A. Stocks). Marching Song for boys with acc. for bugles and drums. Date unknown. Pub. 1914, Novello: also version for SATB.

205. Two Partsongs Op. 71 (Henry Vaughan). For SATB.

1. *The shower.* 1914, Mill Hill. Ded. Miss Frances Smart, Malvern.

2. *The fountain.* 1914, Totteridge. Ded. W. Mann Dyson, Worcester. Pub. 1914, Novello.

206. Death on the hills Op. 72 (Maikov, transl. Rosa Newmarch). For SATB. January 1914. Ded. Lady Colvin. Pub. 1914, Novello.

207. Two Partsongs Op. 73 (Maikov, transl. Rosa Newmarch). For SATB. January 1914.

1. *Love's tempest.* Ded. C. Sanford Terry.

2. *Serenade.* Ded. Percy C. Hull.

Pub. 1914, Novello.

208. Give unto the Lord Op. 74. Anthem for 4-part chorus, organ and orchestra. January–March 1914. Ded. Sir George Martin.

fp: 30 April 1914, St. Paul's Cathedral, Festival of the Sons of the Clergy.

Pub. 1914, Novello.

209. Soldier's song (Begbie). For voice and paino. 6 September 1914. Withdrawn.

210. Carillon Op. 75. Recitation with orchestra. November 1914. Poem: Emile Cammaerts.

fp: 7 December 1914, Queen's Hall, Tita Brand (reciter) and the London Symphony Orchestra, cond. Henri Verbrugghen.

fbp: 27 March 1925, J. P. K. Groves (reciter), Bournemouth Augmented Orchestra, cond. Capt. W. A. Featherstone.

Pub. 1914, Elkin; English version, Tita Brand Cammaerts. Various arrs.

Elgar, Edward

BIBLIOGRAPHY:
Carillon produced, *The Times*, 8 December 1914, p. 7.

210a. Carillon. New version. Poem: Laurence Binyon. Pub. 1942, Elkin.

211. Rosemary ('That's for remembrance'). For orchestra. 1915.
2 fl, 2 ob, 2 cl, 2 cornets, 2 bsn; 2 hn, 3 tmb; timp, tgle (ad lib), hp or piano (ad lib), strings.
Pub. 1915, Elkin: incl. various arrs.

212. Polonia Op. 76. Symphonic Prelude for orchestra. 1 June 1915. Ded. I. J. Paderewski.
2 fl, pic, 2 ob, ca, 2 cl, bcl, 2 bsn, cbsn; 4 hn, 3 tpt, 3 tmb, tuba; timp, tamb pic, tgle, tamb, GC, cym; 2 hp, organ, strings.
fp: 6 July 1915, London, Polish Victims' Relief Fund concert, London Symphony Orchestra, cond. Sir Edward Elgar.
fbp: 31 March 1925, Wireless Symphony Orchestra, cond. Sir Edward Elgar.
Pub. 1915, Elkin.

BIBLIOGRAPHY:
'Other nationalism' in music: Sir Edward Elgar's new work, *The Times*, 10 July 1915, p. 9.

213. Une voix dans le désert Op. 77. Recitation with orchestra. July 1915. Poem: Emile Cammaerts. Ded. Sir Claude Phillips.
fp: 29 January 1916, London, Shaftesbury Theatre, Carlo Liten (reciter), Olga Lynn (soloist), cond. Sir Edward Elgar.
Pub. 1916, Elkin: reduction. English version, Tita Brand Cammaerts.

214. The Starlight Express Op. 78. Incidental music for a play by Violet Pearn adapted from 'A Prisoner from Fairyland' by Algernon Blackwood. November–December 1915.
Unpub.

214a. The Starlight Express: Suite.
1. *To the children* (*Organ-grinder's 1st song*); 2. *Come little winds & Wind dance*; 3. *Curfew song* (*Orion*); 4. *The Laugher's song*; 5. *The Blue-Eyes Fairy* (*Organ-grinder's 2nd song*); 6. *Tears and laughter—Sunrise song*; 7. *My old tunes* (*Organ-grinder's 3rd song*); 8. *Hearts must be soft-shiny dressed* (*Duet*); 9. *Finale*.

fp: 29 December 1915, Kingsway Theatre, cond. Julius Harrison; with Clytie Hine (soprano) and Charles Mott (bass).
Pub. 1916, Elkin. The Organ-grinder's songs (Nos. 1, 5 & 7) arr. voice and piano by Julius Harrison.

BIBLIOGRAPHY:
A. E. Keeton: Elgar's music for The Starlight Express, *M&L*, 1945, No. 1.
Anon.: Starlight Express: Sir Edward Elgar's music, *The Times*, 30 December 1915, p. 11.

215. Fight for the Right (William Morris). For voice and piano. 1916. Ded. Members of the Fight for the Right movement. Pub. 1916, Elkin.

216. Le Drapau belge Op. 79. Recitation with orchestra. 1917. Poem: Emile Cammaerts.
fp: 14 April 1917, Queen's Hall, Carlo Liten (reciter), cond. (Sir) Hamilton Harty.
Pub. 1917, Elkin.

217. The Spirit of England Op. 80. For soprano or tenor, chorus and orchestra. 1915–1917. Text: Laurence Binyon, from 'The Winnowing Fan'. Ded. 'to the memory of our glorious men, with a special thought for the Worcesters'.
1. *The Fourth of August*. May 1917.
fp: 4 October 1917, Birmingham, Rosina Buckman and the Appleby Matthews Chorus.
Pub. 1917, Novello.
2. *To Women*. 1915. (?1916.)
fp: 8 May 1916, Queen's Hall, part of a week of concerts organized by Clara Butt in aid of Red Cross funds, Agnes Nicholls and John Booth with the Leeds Choral Union and London Symphony Orchestra, cond. Sir Edward Elgar.
Pub. 1916, Novello.
3. *For the Fallen*. 1915 (?1916).
fp: as No. 2.
Pub. 1916, Novello.
fp (complete): 24 November 1917, Royal Albert Hall, Agnes Nicholls and Gervase Elwes, Royal Choral Society, cond. Sir Edward Elgar.
Pub. (complete), 1917, Novello.

BIBLIOGRAPHY:
Sydney Grew: The Fourth of August, *MO*, July 1917, p. 651.

Ernest Newman: The Spirit of England—
Edward Elgar's new choral work, *MT*.
May 1916, p. 235.
— Elgar's Fourth of August, *MT*, July 1917,
p. 295.

218. The fringes of the Fleet (Rudyard
Kipling). Four songs for four baritones.
March–May 1917. No. 1 ded. Admiral Lord
Beresford.
    1. *The Lowestoft Boat*; 2. *Fate's discourtesy*;
3. *Submarines*; 4. *The sweepers*.
    fp: 11 June 1917, London Coliseum,
Charles Mott, Henry Barratt, Frederick
Henry and Frederick Stewart, cond. Sir
Edward Elgar.
    Pub. 1917, Enoch.

BIBLIOGRAPHY:
W. Wright Roberts: Elgar's Fringes of the
Fleet, *MO*, February 1918, p. 278.
Anon.: Rudyard Kipling and Edward Elgar:
songs from 'Sea Warfare' sung at London
Coliseum, *The Times*, 12 June 1917, p. 3.

218a. Inside the bar (Gilbert Parker). Song
for four baritones. 1917. Ded. 'the four
singers'.
    fp: 25 June 1917, otherwise as preceding.
    Pub. 1917, Enoch.

219. The Sanguine Fan Op. 81. Ballet
based on a fan by Charles Condor. February–
March 1917.
    fp: 20 March 1917, Chelsea Palace Theatre,
cond. Sir Edward Elgar.
    Unpub.

219a. Echo's Dance. From preceding. For
piano. Pub. 1917, Elkin.

220. Ozymandias (Shelley). For voice and
piano. 12 July 1917. ?Unpub.

221. Violin Sonata in E minor Op. 82.
September 1918, Brinkwells. Ded. Marie
Joshua.
    1. *Allegro*; 2. *Romance: Andante*; 3. *Allegro
non troppo*.
    fp: 13 March 1919, British Music Society
meeting, W. H. Reed and Anthony Bernard.
    f public p: 21 March 1919, Aeolian Hall,
W. H. Reed and (Sir) Landon Ronald.
    fbp: 3 April 1924, Cardiff station, Daisy
Kennedy and Maurice Cole.
    Pub. 1919, Novello.

BIBLIOGRAPHY:
Anon.: Elgar's Violin Sonata, *MT*, April
1919, p. 162.

222. String Quartet in E minor Op. 83.
25 March–24 December 1918. Ded. Brodsky
Quartet.
    1. *Allegro moderato*; 2. *Piacevole (poco
andante)*; 3. *Finale: Allegro moderato*.
    fp (private): 3 May 1919, home of Leo
Schuster.
    fp (public): 21 May 1919, Wigmore Hall,
Albert Sammons, W. H. Reed, Raymond
Jeremy and Felix Salmond.
    fbp: 17 July 1924, Birmingham Station
Quartet (Frank Cantell, Elsie Stell, Arthur
Kennedy and Leonard Dennis).
    Pub. 1919, Novello.

BIBLIOGRAPHY:
Anon.: Elgar's String Quartet, *MT*, July 1919,
p. 337.

223. Piano Quintet in A minor Op. 84.
Summer 1918–April 1919. Ded. Ernest
Newman.
    1. *Moderato—Allegro*; 2. *Adagio*; 3. *Andante
—Allegro*.
    fp (private): 3 May 1919, home of Leo
Schuster.
    fp (public): 21 May 1919, Wigmore Hall,
William Murdoch, Albert Sammons, W. H.
Reed, Raymond Jeremy and Felix Salmond.
    Pub. 1919, Novello.

BIBLIOGRAPHY:
Richard Bryceson: Elgar's Piano Quintet,
Gramophone Record, May 1934, p. 6.
H. C. Colles: Elgar's Quintet for piano and
strings, *MT*, November 1919, p. 596.

224. Cello Concerto in E minor Op. 85.
August 1919, Brinkwells. Ded. Sidney and
Frances Colvin.
    1. *Adagio—Moderato*; 2. *Lento—Allegro
molto*; 3. *Adagio*; 4. *Allegro—Moderato—
Allegro non troppo*.
    2 fl, pic (ad lib), 2 ob, 2 cl, 2 bsn; 4 hn, 2 tpt,
3 tmb, tuba (ad lib); timp; strings.
    fp: 27 October 1919, Queen's Hall, Felix
Salmond and the London Symphony Orches-
tra, cond. Sir Edward Elgar.
    fbp: 2 May 1924, Central Hall, Beatrice
Harrison and Royal Philharmonic Orchestra,
cond. Sir Edward Elgar.

Elgar, Edward

Pub. 1919 (reduction by the composer), 1921 (score), Novello.

BIBLIOGRAPHY:
Eric Blom: Elgar, Concerto in E minor for violoncello and orchestra, *Music Student*, November 1933, p. 575.
Herbert Byard: Violoncello Concerto in E minor, in *The Concerto*, Pelican Books (London) 1952, p. 258.
H. C. Colles: Elgar's Violoncello Concerto, *MT*, February 1920, p. 85.
R. Elkin: Elgar's Cello Concerto, an analysis, *Music in Education*, No. 308 (1964), p. 167.
Donald F. Tovey: Violoncello Concerto in E minor, in *EMA*, Vol. 3, O.U.P. (London) 1936, p. 200.
Francis Toye: Elgar's Cello Concerto, *Nation*, 15 November 1919, p. 236.
Anon.: Elgar's Cello Concerto, *British Musician*, February 1929, p. 36.
Anon.: Cello Concerto—Casals playing, *The Times*, 23 January 1937, p. 10.

224a. Cello Concerto Op. 85. Version arr. for viola by Lionel Tertis.
fp: 21 March 1930, Queen's Hall, Lionel Tertis and the BBC Symphony Orchestra, cond. Sir Edward Elgar.
Pub. 1929, Novello.

225. Fantasy and Fugue in C minor Op. 86. Bach, orch. Elgar. 1921–2.
2 fl, pic, 2 ob, ca, 2 cl, bcl, 2 bsn, cbsn; 4 hn, 3 tpt, 3 tmb, tuba; timp, GC, tamb pic, tamb, tgle, cym; glock, 2 hp, strings.
fp (Fugue only): 27 October 1921, Queen's Hall, Goossens Orchestra, cond. (Sir) Eugene Goossens.
fp (complete): 7 September 1922, Gloucester, Three Choirs Festival, London Symphony Orchestra, cond. Sir Edward Elgar.
fFp: 30 October 1923, Paris, cond. Piero Coppola.
fbp: 25 January 1925, Bournemouth Wireless Orchestra, cond. Capt. W. A. Featherstone.
Pub. 1921 (Fugue), 1922 (Fantasia), Novello.

BIBLIOGRAPHY:
Harvey Grace: The Bach–Elgar Fugue, *MT*, January 1922, p. 21.

226. Jerusalem. Parry, orch. Elgar.
fp: 1922, Leeds Festival.

227. Overture in D minor. Handel, arr. Elgar for full orchestra. 1923.
2 fl, pic, 2 ob, ca, 2 cl, bcl, 2 bsn, cbsn; 4 hn, 3 tpt, 3 tmb, tuba; timp, tamb pic, GC & cym; strings, organ (ad lib).
fp: 2 September 1923, Worcester, Three Choirs Festival, London Symphony Orchestra, cond. Sir Edward Elgar.
fbp: 31 March 1925, Wireless Symphony Orchestra, cond. Sir Edward Elgar.
Pub. 1923, Novello.

228. O Lord, look down from heaven. Motet by Battishill, orch. Elgar. 1923.
fp: 6 September 1923, Worcester, Three Choirs Festival.

229. Let us lift up our hearts. Motet by S. S. Wesley, orch. Elgar. 1923.
fp: 6 September 1923, Worcester, Three Choirs Festival.

229. King Arthur. Incidental music to a play by Laurence Binyon. 1922–3.
fp: 12 March 1923, Old Vic, cond. Charles Corri.
Unpub.

230. Memoriam chimes for a carillon. 1923.
fp: 22 July 1923, opening of the Loughborough War Memorial Carillon.
Unpub.

231. The wanderer (Anon., adapted from 'Wit and Drollery', 1661). For TTBB. ?1923. Pub. 1923, Novello.

232. Zut, zut, zut (Richard Marden). For TTBB. ?1923. Pub. 1923, Novello.

233. Empire March. For orchestra. 1924.
fp: 23 April 1924, Wembley, opening ceremony of the British Empire Exhibition, cond. Sir Edward Elgar.
Pub. 1924, Enoch.

234. March. For violin, cello and piano. 1924. Composed for the Grafton family. Unpub.

235. Military March. 1924. Pub. 1956, Boosey (orch. & ed. Percy M. Young).

236. Pageant of Empire (Alfred Noyes). Songs for solo or chorus. 1924.

1. *Shakespeare's kingdom*; 2. *The islands*; 3. *The blue mountains*; 4. *The heart of Canada*; 5. *Sailing westward*; 6. *Merchant adventurers*; 7. *The immortal legions*; 8. *A Song of Union* (for SATB).

fp: April 1924, Wembley, British Empire Exhibition; also *c*. October 1924, Central Hall, Enoch concert, Empire Pageant Choir and British Women's Symphony Orchestra.

fbp: 7 November 1924, Arthur J. Williams and Cardiff Station Orchestra, cond. Warwick Braithwaite.

Pub. 1924, Enoch. Also Nos. 5 & 7 arr. for SATB.

237. The herald (Alexander Smith). For SATB. ?1925. Pub. 1925, Novello.

238. The Prince of Sleep (Walter de la Mare). For SATB. 1925. Pub. 1925, Elkin.

239. Civic fanfare. 1927. Ded. Percy C. Hull.

fp: 4 September 1927, Hereford Festival, at the Mayoral Procession.

Unpub.

240. Beau Brummel. Incidental music for a play by Bertram Matthews.

fp: 5 November 1928, Birmingham, Theatre Royal.

Unpub.

240a. Minuet. From Beau Brummel. For orchestra.

2 fl, 2 ob, 2 cl, 2 bsn; 2 tpt or cornets, 2 hn, 3 tmb; timp, tamb, GC & cym; strings.

Pub. 1929, Elkin: incl. various arrs.

241. I sing the birth (Ben Jonson). Carol for SATB. ?1928. Ded. Rev. Harcourt B. S. Fowler. Pub. 1928, Novello.

242. Jehova, quam multi sunt hostes mei. Motet by Purcell, orch. Elgar. 1929.

fp: 10 September 1929, Worcester, Three Choirs Festival.

243. Goodmorrow (George Gascoigne). Carol for the King's recovery, for SATB. 1929.

fp: 9 December 1929, Windsor, Albert Institute, annual concert of St. George's Chapel Choir, cond. Sir Edward Elgar.

Pub. 1929, Novello.

244. It isnae me (Sally Holmes). For voice and piano. 1929. Ded. Joan Elwes.

fp: October 1930, Dumfries, Joan Elwes. Pub. 1931, Prowse.

245. Severn Suite Op. 87. For brass band. April 1930. Ded. G. Bernard Shaw.

1. *Introduction* (*Worcester Castle*); 2. *Toccata* (*Tournament*); 3. *Fugue* (*Cathedral*); 4. *Minuet* (*Commandery*); 5. *Coda*.

fp: 27 September 1930, Crystal Palace Brass Band Festival.

Pub. 1930, R. Smith.

245a. Severn Suite Op. 87a. Version for orchestra. 1932.

fp: 23 June 1932, HMV recording studios at Abbey Road, London Symphony Orchestra, cond. Sir Edward Elgar.

f public p: 7 September 1932, Worcester, Three Choirs Festival, London Symphony Orchestra, cond. Sir Edward Elgar.

Pub. 1932, Prowse.

245b. Severn Suite Op. 87a. Arr. as *Organ Sonata No. 2* by Ivor Atkins.

fp: 1933, London, Organ Music Society. Pub. 1933, Prowse.

246. Pomp and Circumstance March No. 5 in C major Op. 39 No. 5. ?1930.

fp: 20 September 1930, Queen's Hall, Promenade Concert, BBC Symphony Orchestra, cond. Sir Henry Wood.

Pub. 1930, Boosey: incl. piano reduction by Victor Hely-Hutchinson and various arrs.

247. Nursery Suite. For orchestra. 1931. Ded. T.R.H. Princesses Elizabeth and Margaret Rose.

1. *Aubade*; 2. *The serious doll*; 3. *Busy-ness*; 4. *The sad doll*; 5. *The waggon* (*passes*); 6. *The mercy doll*; 7. *Dreaming*; 8. *'Envoi'*.

fp: 4 June (?23 May) 1931, Kingsway Hall, HMV recording session, London Symphony Orchestra, cond. Sir Edward Elgar.

f concert p: 20 August 1931, Queen's Hall, Promenade Concert, BBC Symphony Orchestra, cond. Sir Edward Elgar.

Elgar, Edward

Pub. 1931, Prowse: piano reduction by Charles Woodhouse.

BIBLIOGRAPHY:
Ralph Hill: Elgar's Nursery Suite, *MM&F*, October 1931, p. 293.

248. The rapid stream (Charles Mackay). Unison song. Pub. 1931, Prowse.

249. When swallows fly (Charles Mackay). Unison song. Pub. 1931, Prowse.

250. So many true princesses who have gone (John Masefield). Ode for chorus. 1932.
fp: 9 June 1932, Marlborough House, unveiling of Queen Alexandra memorial.
Unpub.

251. Sonatina. For piano. Ded. May Grafton. Pub. 1931, Prowse.

252. Funeral March from Sonata in B flat minor. Chopin, arr. Elgar. 1933.
fp: 25 February 1934, Queen's Hall, Royal Philharmonic Society memorial concert.
Pub. 1933, Prowse.

253. Adieu. For piano. Pub. 1932, Prowse.

254. Serenade. For piano. Ded. John Austin. Pub. 1933, Prowse.

255. The woodland stream (Charles Mackay). 1933. Ded. Stephen S. Moore, Worcester.
fp: 18 May 1933, Worcester City Schools Music Festival.
Pub. 1933, Prowse.

256. Mina. For small orchestra. 1933. Recorded: 8 February 1934 and (in arr. by Haydn Wood) 7 January 1935. Pub. 1934, Prowse.

257. Soliloquy. For oboe. 1930, orch. 1967 by Gordon Jacob.
fp: 11 June 1967, BBC Television, Leon Goossens, cond. Neils Gron.

258. The Spanish Lady. Opera in two acts. Libretto: Elgar and Sir Barry Jackson, from Ben Jonson's 'The Devil is an Ass'. Incomplete.
Pub. 1955, Elkin (*Songs*, ed. Percy M. Young); 1956, Elkin (*Suite* for string orchestra, ed. Percy M. Young).

BIBLIOGRAPHY:
Sir Barry Jackson: Elgar's Spanish Lady, *M&L*, January 1943.

259. Symphony No. 3 Op. 88. Sketches only.

BIBLIOGRAPHY:
W. H. Reed: Elgar's Third Symphony, *The Listener*, 28 August 1935.

260. Piano Concerto Op. 90. Unfinished.
fp: 1956, Harriet Cohen and the Boyd Neel Orchestra, cond. Walter Goehr.

WRITINGS BY ELGAR
Programme notes for Worcestershire Philharmonic Society, 1898–1904.
Preface to 'The Singing of the Future' (by David Ffrangcon-Davies), 1904.
Prospects of English music, *MO*, February 1906, p. 355.
Falstaff, *MT*, September 1913; repr. in pamphlet form, Novello (London).
Gray, Walpole, West and Ashton, the Quadruple Alliance, *Times Literary Supplement*, 4 September 1919.
Musical notation, *MT*, August 1920, p. 513.
Scott and Shakespeare, *Times Literary Supplement*, 21 July 1921.
Contribution to 'Opinions', *Chesterian*, No. 68, January–February 1928.
Foreword to 'Forgotten Worcester' (by H. A. Leicester), 1920.
My Friends Pictures Within, Novello (London). Originally written (?1913) as descriptive notes for pianola rolls.
An essay on the gramophone, *Recorded Sound*, January 1963, p. iv.
A future for English music and other lectures by Edward Elgar (ed. Percy M. Young), Dobson (London) 1968.

GENERAL BIBLIOGRAPHY
Gerald Abraham: The mentality of Elgar, *Scottish Musical Magazine*, May 1930, p. 118.
— Pomp and poetry—a look at Sir EE across a century, *High Fidelity*, June 1957, p. 44.
P. Affelder: A guide to Elgar on records, *High Fidelity*, June 1957, p. 46.
W. R. Anderson: Some beauties of Elgar, *The Gramophone*, August 1930, p. 121.
— Introduction to the music of Elgar, London, 1949.

H. Orsmond Anderton: A modern Muraeus, *MO*, January 1921, p. 327.
— Elgar, and the way of the world, *MO*, August 1931, p. 943.
Herbert Antcliffe: Elgar and Strauss, *MMR*, 1905, p. 84.
— Elgar and MacDowell, *MO*, September 1908, p. 897.
— A study of Elgar, *Music Student*, June 1911, p. 169.
Wulstan Atkins: Music in the Provinces: The Elgar-Atkins letters, *PRMA*, 1957–8, p. 27.
C. Barber: Estimate of Elgar, *Dublin Review*, January 1911, p. 24.
Sir John Barbirolli: Elgar, the man, *Halle*, May 1957, p. 1.
Friedrich Baser: EE zum Gedächtnis, *Die Musik*, April 1934, p. 519.
Stanley Bayliss: Elgar in his letters, *M&L*, April 1957.
Carice Elgar Blake: My memories of my father, *M&M*, June 1957, p. 11.
— Re-opening of Elgar birthplace, *Music* (Oxford), 1967, No. 1, p. 46.
Eric Blom: Elgar, *Chesterian*, No. 24, June 1922.
F. Bonavia: Three aspects of Elgar's art, *Radio Times*, 8 November 1935, p. 16.
— Elgar after half a century, *Radio Times*, 27 May 1949, p. 3.
Rutland Boughton: The genius of Elgar, *Yorkshire Observer*, 1 November 1909; *Music Student*, December 1909, p. 60.
A. E. Brent-Smith: The humour of Elgar, *M&L*, January 1935, p. 20.
Alexander Brent-Smith: Profile, EE, *Crescendo*, No. 40, June 1951, p. 329.
Havergal Brian: The Elgar manuscripts, *MO*, September 1934, p. 1029.
Richard Bryceson: The music of Elgar, *Gramophone Record*, 1934, January p. 7, February p. 8.
R. J. Buckley: Sir EE, London, 1905.
Richard Capell: Elgar and the English, *MS*, 7 January 1911, p. 5.
— A new book about Elgar, *Music Student*, September 1921, p. 680.
— Elgar and Vaughan Williams, *Sackbut*, September 1924, p. 40.

Neville Cardus: Elgar, in *Ten Composers*, London, 1945.
— Elgar and Mahler, more than nationalists, *Radio Times*, 1 May 1931, p. 259.
W. A. Chislett: Sir EE, O.M., *Halle*, February 1959, p. 10.
Alex. Cohen: Two Elgar problems, *MO*, August 1934, p. 948.
— Elgar, poetic visions and patriotic vigour, *Radio Times*, 2 December 1932, p. 669.
Martin Cooper: Modern trio, *London Mercury*, March 1939, p. 532.
— Elgar in retrospect, *Spectator*, 17 June 1949, p. 812.
Rupert de Cordova: Dr. Elgar, an interview, *Strand Magazine*, May 1904.
David Cox: Elgar, in *The Symphony*, Vol. 2, Penguin Books (London) 1967, p. 15.
John Culshaw: Elgar and British music, in *A Century of Music*, Dobson (London) 1952, p. 92.
Gerald Cumberland: A study of Sir EE, *MS*, 20 October 1906, p. 246; reprinted from *The Etude*.
— The work of Sir EE, *MO*, December 1908, p. 175.
— Pen portraits of musicians, 1: Sir EE, *MO*, April 1909, p. 481.
— Elgar, in *Set Down in Malice*, London, 1919.
Mary G. Dann: Elgar's use of sequence, *M&L*, July 1938, p. 255.
Suzanne Demarquez: Sir EE et la renaissance musicale en Angleterre, *RM*, April 1934, p. 334.
A. E. F. Dickinson: The drama behind Elgar's music, *M&L*, April 1942.
Leonard Duck: The influence of Elgar, *Halle*, May 1957, p. 9.
Thomas Dunhill: Elgar, London, 1938.
J. H. Elliot: Elgar and England, *Sackbut*, October 1931, p. 11.
— Elgar and the bands, *Halle*, May 1957, p. 4.
Edwin Evans: The Elgar Festival, *MS*, 19 March 1904, p. 179.
— EE, *Anbruch*, March 1934, p. 47.
P. d'Exideuil: Sir EE, *L'Europe nouvelle*, 17 June 1933, p. 581.
W. J. Finn: Sir EE, *Catholic World*, May 1934, p. 138.
Stuart Fletcher: Elgar the Enigma, *Sackbut*, May 1933, p. 157.

H. J. Foss: Elgar and his age, *M&L*, January 1935, p. 5.

A. H. Fox Strangways: Elgar, *M&L*, April 1934, p. 109.

Hans Gal (ed.): EE, in *The Musicians World— Great Composers in their Letters*, Thames & Hudson (London) 1965, p. 417.

G. M. Gatti: Ricordo di Sir EE, *Pan*, 1934, p. 746.

Peter Garvie: Falstaff and the King: Reflections on Elgar, *Canadian Musical Journal*, autumn 1957, p. 26.

Stanley Goodman: The Elgars of Dover, *MT*, July 1949, p. 245.

Harvey Grace: Elgar's new partsongs, *MO*, May 1914, p. 632.

H. G. & W. McN.: EE, *MT*, April 1934, p. 319.

Cecil Gray: EE, in *A Survey of Contemporary Music*, O.U.P. (London) 1927, p. 78.

M. Gray: A man and his music, *Strad*, May 1957, p. 16.

Robin Gregory: Elgar's use of 'Nobilmente', *MMR*, 1948, p. 208.

Sydney Grew: Sir EE, O.M., in *Our Favourite Musicians*, London, 1924.

Sydney Grew: Elgar, *Midland Musician*, February 1926, p. 49.

— Elgar's quotations, *Midland Musician*, March 1926, p. 90.

— EE, *British Musician*, April 1934, p. 77.

Robert A. Hall Jr.: Elgar and the intonation of British English, *The Gramophone*, June 1953, p. 6.

Julius Harrison: Letters of EE, *MT*, January 1957, p. 20.

Norman Harvey: Elgar and the modern audience, *MO*, May 1949, p. 398.

Max Hehemann: EE, *Die Musik*, 1903, No. 7, p. 15.

— EE, *NZfM*, 1905, No. 40 (27 September), p. 760.

Everett Helm: The Elgar case: ruminations pro and contra, *MR*, May 1957, p. 101.

Ralph Hill: Elgar and his instrumental works, *Musical Mirror*, 1929, January p. 9, February p. 42.

— When Elgar played for £2.12.6, *Radio Times*, 19 November 1937, p. 15.

Basil Hogarth: EE, the noble romantic, *English Review*, April 1934, p. 428.

Hans Hollander: Elgar in der Gegenwart, *NZfM*, November 1959.

John Horton: Two possible Elgar allusions, *MT*, August 1960, p. 490.

Frank Howes: The two Elgars, *M&L*, January 1935, p. 26.

— EE, in *The Heritage of Music*, Vol. 3, O.U.P. (London) 1951, p. 138.

Gervase Hughes: Elgar, in *The Handbook of Great Composers*, Arthur Barker (London) 1965, p. 192.

P. Hull: Some personal memories of Elgar, *Making Music*, No. 34, summer 1957, p. 5.

Robert H. Hull: Sir EE, *English Review*, February 1931, p. 226.

— Sir EE, *Chesterian*, No. 114, March–April 1934.

Robin Hull: Three British Composers: Elgar, Delius and Holst, *MT*, July 1959, p. 300.

Reginald Hunt: Elgar and the common touch, *MO*, April 1945, p. 200.

Michael Hurd: Elgar, Faber (London) 1969.

Arthur Jacobs: Elgar's solo songs, *MT*, August 1949, p. 267.

Everard Jose and Heath Cranston: The significance of Elgar, 1934.

Percy Judd: Elgar's partsongs, *MT*, January 1938, p. 24.

Charles Karlyle: Das Londoner Elgarfest, *Signale*, 1904, No. 29 (20 April), p. 475.

Hans Keller: Elgar—'the first of the new', *M&M*, June 1957, p. 17.

— Elgar the progressive, *MR*, November 1957, p. 294.

— Elgar, *The Listener*, 7 March 1963, p. 441.

Michael Kennedy: Elgar, the dreamer of dreams, *Halle*, September 1952, p. 14.

— Elgar's chamber music, *Halle*, May 1957, p. 6.

— Elgar, Delius and Holst, *Halle*, April 1959, p. 8.

— Portrait of Elgar, O.U.P. (London) 1968.

Herman Klein: Cowen and Elgar, *The Gramophone*, March 1932, p. 415.

H. E. Krehbiel: Cincinnati Musical Festival and Sir EE, *MT*, June 1906, p. 396.

Herbert Lambert: Modern British Composers, 17 Portraits, London, 1923.

Emmie Bowman Leaver: Some impressions of Sir Edward, *MO*, 1934, June p. 770, July p. 869.

Edward Lockspeiser: Elgar festival, *Musical America*, July 1949, p. 6.

Robert Lorenz: This 'nobilmente' business, *MO*, May 1934, p. 692.

Alan Loveday: Elgar in Moscow, *RCM Magazine*, 1954, No. 3, p. 76.

George Lowe: Elgar's new chamber works, *MS*, 3 January 1920, p. 10.

Charles Mackerras: The Elgar centenary, *Canon*, July 1957, p. 385.

Basil Maine: Elgar and Sibelius, *Spectator*, 30 January 1932, p. 140.

— Elgar, last of the great Edwardians, *Radio Times*, 8 April 1932, p. 67.

— Elgar celebrations, *Spectator*, 23 December 1932, p. 890.

— Elgar, some early influences, *MO*, March 1933, p. 504.

— Shaw and Elgar, *The Rotunda*, September 1933.

— Elgar, *MMR*, 1934, p. 73.

— Elgar, his life and works, Bell (London) 1933 (2 vols.).

— Elgar, early Malvern days, *MM&F*, March 1933, p. 168.

— Elgar, an appraisement, *19th Century and After*, April 1934, p. 466.

— Elgar's place in European music, *Spectator* 2 March 1934, p. 316.

— Elgar's sketches in relation to musicology, *MO*, 1936, February p. 397, March p. 492.

— Once an Elgar lover, *Radio Times*, 28 May 1948, p. 6.

— Elgar and youth, in *Music Magazine*, Rockcliff (London) 1953, p. 46.

— Passing on the secret of Elgar, *Radio Times*, 31 May 1957, p. 3.

Daniel Gregory Mason: Elgar, in *Contemporary Composers*, New York, 1918.

— Story of Elgar, *Etude*, November 1934, p. 645.

Wilfried Mellers: Elgar and Vaughan Williams, in *Man and his Music*, Barrie & Rockliff (London) 1962, p. 966.

Donald Mitchell: Some thoughts on Elgar, *M&L*, April 1957.

Jerrold N. Moore: Elgar as a University professor, *MT*, 1960, October p. 630, November p. 690.

— An Elgar discography, *Recorded Sound*, No. 9, January 1963, p. 1.

Dorothy Moulton-Mayer: Elgar, *Crescendo*, No. 9, November 1947, p. 13.

— EE, *Crescendo*, No. 40, June 1951, p. 329; No. 76, October 1956, p. 6.

M. McNaught: Elgar's birthplace, *MT*, June 1947, p. 185.

Diana McVeagh: EE, his life and music, Dent (London) 1955.

— Elgar's post-war passport, *RCM Magazine*, 1957, No. 2, p. 34.

— Elgar's birthplace, *MT*, June 1957, p. 308.

Boyd Neel: EE, *Canadian Musical Journal*, summer 1957, p. 27.

Ernest Newman: The new school of British music, No. 2: EE, *The Speaker*, 22 December 1901.

— EE, *The Musician*, 1906.

— Elgar, London, 1904.

— Elgar's chamber music, *The Musician*, September 1919, p. 13.

— Famous contemporary sums up Elgar, *Musical America*, February 1957, p. 3.

— Elgar, in *Testament of Music*, Putnam (London) 1962, p. 268.

— 'Stately sorrow', in *Essays on Music*, Cassell (London) 1967, p. 101.

Arthur Notcutt: Recollections of some early Elgar performances, *MO*, October 1950, p. 9.

C. W. Orr: Elgar and the public, *MT*, January 1931, p. 17.

— Elgar's popularity, *MMR*, 1931, pp. 71, 109.

— The lesser Elgar, *MO*, April 1935, p. 596.

D. Hugh Ottaway: Elgar in 1950, *Halle*, August 1950, p. 22.

— The Malvern Elgar Festival, *MO*, November–December 1950, p. 167, July 1951, p. 521.

— Elgar and a new generation, *MO*, October 1952, p. 17.

— Elgar reconsidered, *Halle*, February 1956, p. 12.

H. Ould: Songs of Sir EE, *English Review*, September 1928, p. 355.

D. C. Parker: Sir EE, *MS*, 8 July 1916, p. 313.

— EE, *MS*, June 1932, p. 99.

Claude W. Parnell: Elgar in perspective, *MMR*, 1924, p. 132.

Ian Parrott: Was Elgar's orchestration impeccable?, *Chesterian*, No. 191, summer 1957, p. 20.

Anthony Payne: A new look at Elgar, *The Listener*, 29 October 1964, p. 694.

Peter J. Pirie: Crippled splendour: Elgar and Mahler, *MT*, February 1956, p. 70.

John F. Porte: Elgar, London, 1921.

— The other Elgar, *MN&H*, 10 May 1923, p. 449.

— Byrd and Elgar, *Chesterian*, No. 49, September–October 1925.

— Elgar, *Disques*, April 1931.

— Elgar and his music, an appreciative study, Pitman (London) 1933.

Mrs. Richard Powell: Memories of a variation, London, 1937, 2nd edn. 1947.

Harold Rawlinson: EE, violinist, *Strad*, 1954, May p. 8, June p. 44, July p. 76, August p. 110, October p. 176, November p. 220.

— Elgar and Romberg's violin duets, *Strad*, July 1957, p. 88.

Henry B. Raynor: Elgar and Englishness, *MO*, June 1957, p. 527.

Hans F. Redlich: EE, in *MGG*, Vol. 3 (1954), p. 1274.

W. H. Reed: Elgar as I knew him, Gollancz (London) 1936.

— Edward Elgar, an intimate picture, *Radio Times*, 23 April 1937, p. 13.

— Elgar, Dent (London) 1939.

C. B. Rees: Elgar, *London Musical Events*, May 1957, p. 21.

Godfrey Ridout: Elgar the Angular Saxon, *Canadian Musical Journal*, summer 1957, p. 33.

Harold Rutland: Elgarian notes and comments, *MT*, June 1957, p. 310.

Sir Malcolm Sargent: Elgar as I knew him, *M&M*, June 1957, p. 13.

H. A. Scott: Elgar, the man and his music, *Contemporary Review*, April 1934, p. 464.

Geoffrey Sharp: A note on Elgar's music, *MR*, May 1957, p. 106.

A. T. Shaw: Elgar's birthplace reopened, *MT*, July 1967, p. 607.

George Bernard Shaw: Sir EE, *M&L*, January 1920, p. 7.

A. J. Sheldon: On Elgar, *MO*, 1925, December p. 261; 1926, January p. 373, February p. 487, March p. 599, April p. 711, May p. 823, June p. 927, July p. 1007, August p. 1098, September p. 1200.

— EE (introduction by Havergal Brian), *Musical Opinion* (London), 1932.

F. H. Shera: Elgar, instrumental works, O.U.P. (London) 1931.

Patric Stevenson: A visit to Elgar's birthplace, *MT*, October 1942, p. 297.

Dennis Stóll: EE, *London Philharmonic Post*, November 1941, p. 4.

Irving J. Stone: EE, *Musical Record*, 1933, No. 4.

R. A. Streatfeild: Un musicista inglese, EE, *Rivista d'Italia*, October 1912.

Donald F. Tovey: Elgar, master of music, *M&L*, January 1935, p. 1.

E. O. Turner: Tempo variation, with examples from Elgar, *M&L*, July 1938, p. 308.

W. J. Turner: Sir EE, *New Statesman*, 5 December 1925, p. 236.

— Handel and Elgar, *New Statesman*, 7 January 1933, p. 12.

— Saint-Saëns and Elgar, *New Statesman*, 21 September 1935, p. 374.

M. G. Urch: Landon Ronald and the Elgar symphonies, *MS*, 30 June 1917, p. 435.

Ralph Vaughan Williams: What have we learnt from Elgar?, *M&L*, January 1935, p. 13.

Walther Volbach: EE and Fritz Volbach, *MO*, July 1937, p. 870.

John Warrack: Elgar and after, *The Listener*, 26 December 1963, p. 1084.

A. W. B. Webb: The Elgar recordings, *The Gramophone*, May 1937, p. 513.

W. Wells-Harrison: Some notable British music, X: EE, settings of Cammaerts' poems, *MS*, 28 October 1916, p. 313.

C. Whitaker Wilson: Elgar, composer and conductor, *MO*, February 1911, p. 327.

Arnold Whittall: Elgar's last judgment, *MR*, February 1965, p. 23.

S. Williams: The Elgar centenary, *New York Times*, 2 June 1957, Section 2, p. 7.

N. F. Wright: Sir EE, *Catholic Choirmaster*, fall 1957, p. 109.

Percy M. Young: Elgar O.M.—A study of a musician, Collins (London) 1955.

— EE, in *A History of British Music*, Ernest Benn (London) 1967, p. 524.

Percy M. Young (ed.): Letters of EE and other writings, London, 1956.

— Letters to Nimrod from EE, London, 1965.

MISCELLANEOUS OR UNSIGNED

EE, *MT*, October 1900, p. 641.

Dr. EE at home, *MS*, 14 December 1901, p. 370.

EE's hobbies, *MS*, 13 October 1900.

Dr. EE at Malvern, *The World*, 11 December 1901.

Sir EE and conductors, *MS*, 30 July 1904, p. 70.

The Elgar Festival, *MT*, April 1904, p. 241.

Elgar in London, *Pall Mall Gazette*, 21 March 1904.

Sir EE, *MS*, 9 December 1905, p. 370.

Elgar and representative music, *MO*, September 1907, p. 891; repr. from *Saturday Review*.

Sir EE, O.M., *The World*, 22 October 1912.

Elgar's chamber works: music of yesterday and today, *The Times*, 24 May 1919, p. 15.

Diverse paths of symphony: Brahms and Elgar, *The Times*, 13 December 1924, p. 10.

Pre-war symphonists: Elgar and Mahler, *The Times*, 1 February 1930, p. 10.

Sir EE—Musicians protest against Professor E. J. Dent's alleged injustice, *MO*, March 1931, p. 504.

Bibliografica delle opere musicali di Sir EE, *Bollettino bibliografico musicale*, 1931, No. 10, p. 5.

Elgar's life and career, *MT*, April 1934, p. 314.

Some of Elgar's friends, *MT*, April 1934, p. 319.

Tribute and commentary (various authors), *MT*, April 1934, p. 320.

Elgar's quotations, *The Times*, 8 August 1947, p. 7.

Elgar's symphonies, *The Times*, 23 April 1948, p. 7.

Elgar's oratorios, *The Times*, 23 July 1948, p. 7.

Two promising young men—Elgar and Delius, *Music Teacher*, December 1950, repr. from *The Gazette*, 1899.

Elgar in perspective: a new analysis of his style, *The Times*, 9 September 1955, p. 7.

Another Elgar enigma: the Cambridge telegram, *The Times*, 30 September 1955, p. 3.

Elgar today: a symposium, *MT*, June 1957, p. 302.

Musical Kipling, *Time*, 10 June 1957, p. 72.

Sir Edward's dream, *Time*, 2 February 1959, p. 46.

MANUEL DE FALLA (1876–1946)

Manuel de Falla y Metheu was born in Cadiz on 23 November 1876. He played the piano from an early age but did not decide until his late teens that music was his vocation. After studying the piano with José Tragó at the Madrid Conservatoire in the mid-1890s and then trying without success to gain a reputation as a composer of light operas, he took a crucial step in 1901 by apprenticing himself for three years to Filippe Pedrell, the influential composition-teacher and folklorist. Falla supported himself by giving piano lessons in Madrid until the opportunity came in 1907 to fulfil his long-held ambition to visit Paris. He lived there frugally for seven years, gaining much from the friendship of Debussy, Ravel and (especially) Dukas. At the start of the First World War Falla returned to Spain, living first in Madrid and then (from 1920) in Granada, where he helped organize a festival of *cante jondo* in 1922. He remained in Granada, apart from two lengthy visits to Palma in Majorca, until he left Europe in 1939. Until the mid-1930s Falla (an extremely self-effacing man and a life-long bachelor) travelled often in western Europe as concert pianist and latterly as conductor. In 1938 Franco's régime offered him the Presidency of the newly founded Instituto de España, which he refused. Ill-health had begun to undermine his career in 1936, and it was a combination of medical advice and increasing unhappiness at the Spanish political situation which drove Falla to Argentina in 1939. He conducted a series of concerts of Spanish music in Buenos Aires that year, but then retreated four hundred miles up country to the Sierras de Córdoba, where he lived with his sister María del Carmen in semi-invalid semi-retirement at Alta Gracia until his death in November 1946. His last and most ambitious work, the *Atlántida*, which was begun in 1928, remained unfinished at his death.

Falla, Manuel de

CATALOGUE OF WORKS

1. Lied. For cello and piano. *c.* 1888–9. Lost.

2. Piano Quartet (Andante and Scherzo only). *c.* 1888–9. Lost.

3. Fantasía. For flute, violin, viola, cello and piano. Unknown date. Lost.

4. Serenata Andaluza. For piano. Unknown date.
fEbp: 4 September 1924, Newcastle station, Gladys Willis.
Pub. Faustino Fuentes (Madrid); 1940, Union Musicale Espagnole.

5. Valse Capricho. For piano. *c.* 1900. Pub. Faustino Fuentes (Madrid); 1940, Union Musicale Espagnole.

6. Nocturno. For piano. *c.* 1900. Pub. 1940, Union Musicale Espagnole.

7. Chanson. For piano. 1900.
fp: untraced date, Gerardo Diego.
Unpub.

8. Tus Ojillos Negros (Cristobal de Castro). Andalusian song for voice and piano. Ded. Marquis and Marquise de Alta Villa. Pub. Faustino Fuentes (Madrid); Union Musicale Espagnole.

9. Allegro de Concierto. For piano. *c.* 1900–2.
fp: 1903, Madrid Conservatory; also: 4 May 1905, Madrid, Athénée, Manuel de Falla.
Unpub.

10. La Casa de Tócame Roque. Zarzuela. Unperf. Unpub.

11. Limosna de Amor. Zarzuela. Unperf. Unpub.

12. El Corneta de Órdenes. Zarzuela in three acts. Unperf. Unpub.

13. La Cruz de Malta. Zarzuela. Unperf. Unpub.

14. Los Amores de la Inés. Zarzuela in one act, two scenes. *c.* 1902. Libretto: Emilio Dugi.
fp: 12 April 1902, Teatro Cómico, Loreta Prado and Enrique Chicote company.
Unpub.

15. La Vida Breve. Lyric drama in two acts, four scenes. 1904–5. Dated: 31 March 1905. Libretto: Carlos Fernandez-Shaw (French text by Paul Milliet). Composed in memory of Carlos Fernandez-Shaw. Ded. Mme Adiny-Milliet and Paul Milliet.
fp: 1 April 1913, Nice, Casino Municipal, with Lillian Grenville (Salud), David Devries (Paco), Mlle Fanty (La Grand'Mère), Mlle Gerday (Carmela), Cotreuil (L'Oncle Sarvaor), Raynal (Le chanteur), Rouziery (Manuel), cond. J. Miranne.
f Paris p: 7 January 1914, Opéra-Comique, with Marguerite Carré (Salud), Fernand Francell (Paco), Mme Brohly (La Grand'Mère), Mme Syril (Carmela), Vieuille (L'Oncle Sarvaor), Vigneau (Le chanteur), Vaurs (Manuel), cond. Franz Ruhlmann.
fEp (excerpts): 8 May 1927, broadcast, Aksarova and Wireless Symphony Orchestra, cond. Edward Clark.
Pub. 1913, Max Eschig.

BIBLIOGRAPHY:

M.-D. Calvocoressi: M de F and his first opera, in *Musicians Gallery*, Faber & Faber (London) 1933, p. 64.

Jean Chantavoine: La Vie Brève à l'Opéra-Comique, *Le Ménestrel*, 16 March 1928, p. 119.

Rudolf Hartmann: Ein kurzes Leben, *Signale*, 1926, No. 48, p. 1723.

P. L. Miller: La vida breve—Victoria de los Angeles, *American Record Guide*, November 1966, p. 206.

J. B. Trend: Falla and La Vida Breve, *MMR*, September 1929, p. 265.

Max Unger: Ein kurzes Leben, *Der Auftakt*, 1926, Nos. 11–12, p. 231.

16. Cuatro Piezas Españolas. For piano. 1907–8, Madrid, Paris. Ded. Isaac Albeniz.
1. *Andaluza*; 2. *Cubaña*; 3. *Aragonesa*; 4. *Montañesca*.
fp: November 1908, Paris, Société Nationale de Musique concert, Ricardo Viñes.
Pub. 1908, Durand; Union Musical Española.

17. Trois Mélodies (Théophile Gautier). For voice and piano. 1909.
1. *Les Colombes.* Ded. Mme Adiny-Milliet.
2. *Chinoiserie.* Ded. Mme R. Brooks.

3. *Seguidille.* Ded. Mme Claude Debussy.
fp: late 1910, Paris, Société Musicale Indépendante, Mme A. Adiny-Milliet, acc. Manuel de Falla.
Pub. 1910, Rouart-Lerolle.

18. Oración de las Madres que tienen a sus hijos en Brazos (Gregorio Martinez Sierra). For voice and piano. December 1914.
fp: 8 February 1915, Madrid, Sociedad Nacional de Musica, Josefina Revillo, acc. Manuel de Falla.
Unpub.

19. Siete Canciones Populares Españolas. For voice and piano. 1914. Ded. Mme Ida Godbebska.
1. *El Paño moruno*; 2. *Seguidilla marciana*; 3. *Asturiana*; 4. *Jota*; 5. *Nana*; 6. *Canción*; 7. *Polo.*
fp: 14 January 1915, Madrid, Ateneo, Luisa Vela, acc. Manuel de Falla.
?f Paris p: 29 May 1920, Société Nationale de Musique concert, Madeleine Greslé, acc. Manuel de Falla.
fEp (No. 4): 12 March 1924, Wigmore Hall, Dorothea Webb.
fEp (complete): 31 March 1924, Wigmore Hall, Alice Mandeville.
fGBbp (Nos. 1, 2 & 3): 19 February 1925, Glasgow station, Roy Henderson.
fEbp (Nos. 1–5): 12 June 1925, F. H. Etcheverria.
fEbp (complete): 3 October 1927, Sara Fischer.
Pub. 1922, Max Eschig; French adaptation, Paul Milliet.

19a. Siete Canciones Populares Españolas (Sept Chansons populaires espagnoles). Version orchestrated by Ernesto Halffter. Dur. 12′ 3″.
1. *El Paño moruno* (Le drap mauresque). Dur. 1′ 20″.
2 fl, ob, cl, bcl, bsn; hn; hp, strings.
2. *Seguidilla marciana* (Seguidille murcienne). Dur. 1′ 23″.
2 fl, ob, 2 cl, 2 bsn; 2 hn; hp; 2 timp, tamb; strings.
3. *Asturiana* (Asturienne). Dur. 2′ 55″.
fl, cl, 2 bsn; 2 hn; hp, strings.
4. *Jota.* Dur. 3′ 20″.

2 fl, ob, ca, cl, bcl, 2 bsn; 2 hn; 2 timp, cast; hp, strings.
5. *Nana* (Berceuse). Dur. 1′ 50″.
2 fl, bcl; hn; hp, strings.
6. *Canción* (Chanson). Dur. 1′ 10″.
2 fl, ob, 2 cl, 2 bsn; 2 hn; 2 timp; hp, strings.
7. *Polo.* Dur. 1′ 25″.
2 fl, ob, ca, 2 cl, 2 bsn; 2 hn; 2 timp; hp, strings.

19b. Suite Populaire Espagnole. Version of Siete Canciones Populares Españolas for violin and piano. Ded. Mme Ida Godebska and Paul Kochanski.
fEbp: 22 March 1926, Birmingham station, William Primrose (violin).
Pub. 1925, Max Eschig; adapted and fingered by Paul Kochanski. Also for cello and piano, transcribed and fingered by Maurice Maréchal.

20. Noches en los Jardines de España. Symphonic Impressions for piano and orchestra. 1909–15. Ded. Ricardo Viñes.
1. *En el Generalife* (Allegretto tranquillo e misterioso).
2. *Danza lejana* (Allegretto giusto).
3. *En los jardines de la Sierra de Córdoba.*
2 fl, pic, 2 ob, ca, 2 cl, 2 bsn; 4 hn, 2 tpt, 3 tmb, tuba; 3 timp; hp, strings.
fp: 9 April 1916, Madrid, Teatro Real, José Cubiles and Madrid Symphony Orchestra, cond. Enrique Fernandez Arbós.
fFp: January 1920, Opéra, Joaquin Nin (piano), cond. Enrique Fernandez Arbós.
fEp: 20 May 1921, Queen's Hall, Manuel de Falla (piano), cond. Edward Clark.
fEbp: 4 October 1925, Marcelle Meyer and the London Chamber Orchestra, cond. Anthony Bernard.
Pub. 1922, 1923, Max Eschig; reduction by Gustave Samazeuilh.

BIBLIOGRAPHY:
Eric Blom: M de F, Nights in the Gardens of Spain, *Music Teacher*, April 1932, p. 196.

21. El Amor Brujo. Ballet in one act. 1915.
Libretto: Gregorio Martinez Sierra.
fl, pic, ob, 2 cl, bsn; 2 hn, 2 tpt; timp; piano, strings.

Falla, Manuel de

fp (original version): 15 April 1915, Madrid, Teatro Lara, with Pastora Imperio.

fp (definitive version): 28 March 1916, Madrid, Madrid Philharmonic Orchestra, cond. Bartolome Perez Casas.

fEp: 23 November 1921, Queen's Hall, cond. Eugene Goossens.

fFp: 28 January 1923, Paris, Théâtre du Châtelet, Yvonne Courso and Orchestre Colonne, conducted by Enrique Fernandez Arbós.

fEbp (complete): 9 February 1925, Elsie Treweek and Newcastle Station Symphony Orchestra, cond. Edward Clark.

fEp (complete): 5 July 1928, Arts Theatre Club, Sara Fischer and chamber orchestra, cond. Edward Clark.

Pub. 1924, Chester.

BIBLIOGRAPHY:

Eric Blom: M de F's El Amor Brujo, *Music Teacher*, August 1931, p. 423.

H.J.: El Amor Brujo, *Disques*, June 1951.

Lionel Salter: El Amor Brujo, in *Decca Book of Ballet*, Muller (London) 1958, p. 146.

F. G. Youens: Love the Magician, *The Gramophone*, May 1939, p. 508.

22. Otelo. Incidental music (Shakespeare). May–June 1915.

fp: 1915, Barcelona, Teatro Novedades.

Unpub.

23. El Sombrero de tres Picos. Ballet. 1917–19. Libretto: Martinez Sierra, after 'El Corregidor y la Molinera' by Alarcon. Dur. 30'.

2 fl, pic, 2 ob, ca, 2 cl, 2 bsn; 4 hn, 3 tpt, 3 tmb, tuba; hp, celesta, piano; timp, cast, xyl, 2 cym, campanelle, GC, tgle, tamb, tamtam; strings.

fp: 22 July 1919, London, Alhambra, Diaghilev's Ballets Russes, with Léonide Massine (The Miller), Thamar Karsavina (The Miller's Wife), Leon Woisikovsky (The Corregidor), Mlle Grantzeva (The Corregidor's Wife), Stanislas Idzikovsky (The Dandy); cond. Ernest Ansermet; décor, Pablo Picasso.

fEbp: 24 April 1931, Olga Lynn and BBC Orchestra, cond. Pedro Morales.

fEp (with narration): 25 May 1965, Wimbledon Town Hall, Sarah Lawson (speaker) and Wimbledon Symphony Orchestra, cond. Kenneth V. Jones.

Pub. 1921, Chester.

BIBLIOGRAPHY:

Edwin Evans: The Three Cornered Hat, *Chesterian*, May 1921, p. 453.

Leigh Henry: The Three Cornered Hat, *MT*, November 1919, p. 122.

Lionel Salter: The Three Cornered Hat, in *Decca Book of Ballet*, Muller (London) 1958, p. 147.

J. B. Trend: Falla and the ballet, *Criterion*, April 1929, p. 480.

23a. El Sombrero de tres Picos. Suite from Part One.

1. *Introduction*; 2. *Afternoon*; 3. *Dance of the Miller's Wife* (Fandango); 4. *The Grapes*.

Pub. Chester.

23b. El Sombrero de tres Picos. Suite from Part Two.

1. *The Neighbour's Dance* (Seguidillas); 2. *Dance of the Miller*; 3. *The Corregidor's Dance*; 4. *Final Dance*.

fEbp: 13 October 1924, Bournemouth Municipal Orchestra, cond. (Sir) Dan Godfrey.

Pub. Chester.

24. Fuego Fatuo. Opera in three acts after Chopin. May–September 1918. Libretto: G. Martinez Sierra. Unperf.

25. Fantasía Bética (Fantasia Baetica). For piano. January–May 1919. Commissioned by and ded. Arthur Rubinstein.

fp: 1920, New York, Arthur Rubinstein.

fEp: 18 December 1920, Wigmore Hall, Arthur Rubinstein.

fFp: 7 December 1922, Paris, Salle Pleyel, Société Musicale Indépendante concert, Mme Grovlez.

fEbp: 20 December 1930, Henri Gil-Marchex.

Pub. 1922, Chester.

BIBLIOGRAPHY:

Roberto García Morillo: M de F y la Fantasía Baetica, *Boletino Latino-americo de Música* (Montevideo), No. 5, October 1941, p. 585.

26. Homenaje a Debussy. For guitar. December 1920.

fp: 24 January 1921, Paris, Salle des Agriculteurs, Société Musicale Indépendante concert in memory of Debussy, Mme M.-L. Casadesus (arpa-laud).

fp (guitar): 2 December 1922, E. Pujol.

fEp: 7 December 1926, Aeolian Hall, Andres Segovia.

Pub. 1 December 1920, La Revue musicale; 1921, Chester. Also transcription by the composer for piano.

27. El Retablo de Maese Pedro. Chamber opera. 1919–June 1922, Madrid, Granada. Musical and scenic adaptation of an episode from 'El Ingenioso Cavallero Don Quixote de la Mancha' by Miguel de Cervantes; French version by G. Jean-Aubry; English version by J. B. Trend, based on Shelton's 'Don Quixote' of 1620. Composed in hommage to Miguel de Cervantes. Ded. Mme La Princesse Edmond de Polignac.

fl, pic, 2 ob, ca, cl, bsn; 2 hn, 2 tpt; 2 timp, tenor dm with wooden rim, xyl, 2 rattles, large tamb without bells, tamtam, small bell; harpsichord, arpa-laud or pedal-harp; strings.

fp (concert form): 23 March 1923, Sevilla, Sociedad Sevillana de Conciertos, with Lledó (Don Quijote), Segura (Maese Pedro), Nino F. Redondo (Trujamán), Orquesta Bética de Cámara, cond. Manuel de Falla.

fp: 23 June 1923, Paris, privately at the salon of Princesse Edmond de Polignac, with Hector Dufranne (Don Quijote), Thomas Salignac (Maese Pedro), Manuel Garcia y Amparito Peris (Trujamán); Wanda Landowska (harpsichord), Mme Henri Casadesus (arpa-laud), Orchestre des Concerts Golschmann, cond. Vladimir Golschmann.

f Paris p (public): 15 November 1923, Concerts Wiéner, with Hector Dufranne (Don Quijote), Salignac (Maese Pedro), A. Peris (Trujamán), Société moderne d'instruments à vent (augmented), cond. Manuel de Falla.

fEp (public): 14 October 1924, Bristol, Victoria Rooms, Avonmouth and Shirehampton Choral Society, with Tom Goodey, Muriel Tannahill, Arthur Cranmer, T. Squire and W. Powell, cond. (Sir) Malcolm Sargent; five performances were given, two conducted by (Sir) Adrian Boult.

fEbp (Final Scene): 26 June 1926, Arthur Cranmer and Newcastle Station Orchestra, cond. Edward Clark.

fEbp (complete): 24 June 1931, BBC Orchestra, cond. Manuel de Falla; with Roy Henderson (Don Quijote), Frank Titterton (Maese Pedro), Mary Hamlin (Trujamán).

Pub. 1923, Max Eschig/Chester.

BIBLIOGRAPHY:

Henry W. Simon: Master Peter's Puppet Show, in Festival of Opera, W. H. Allen (London) 1957, p. 287.

E. Torres: El retablo de Maese Pedro, Vida Musical (Madrid), April 1923.

28. Concerto. For harpsichord or piano and chamber ensemble. 1923–6, Granada. Ded. Wanda Landowska.

1. Allegro; 2. Lento; 3. Vivace.

fl, ob, cl, v, c.

fp: 4 November 1926, Barcelona, Asociación de Música de Cámara, Wanda Landowska and Casals Orchestra, cond. Casals.

f Paris p: early 1927, Salle Pleyel, with Manuel de Falla as soloist.

fEp: 22 June 1927, Aeolian Hall, Manuel de Falla (piano) and the London Chamber Orchestra, cond. Anthony Bernard.

fEbp: 24 June 1931, Manuel de Falla and BBC Orchestra, cond. Sir Henry Wood.

Pub. 1928, Max Eschig.

BIBLIOGRAPHY:

G. Clarence: L'enregistrement du Concerto de Manuel de Falla, Cahiers d'Art, 1928, No. 10.

F. Lliurat: El Concerto de Manuel de Falla, Revista Musical Catalana, May 1929.

L. de Pablo: El Concerto para Clavicembalo y Cinco Instrumentos de Manuel de Falla, Buenos Aires Musical, No. 372 (1967), p. 5.

Henry Prunières: Le Concerto pour clavecin et instruments de M de F, RM, 1 July 1927, p. 54.

Adolfo Salazar: Le Concerto de M de F— Langage et style, classicisme et modernisme, Cahiers d'Art, 1927, No. 10, p. 352.

— El Concerto de M de F, in Sinfonía y ballet, Editorial Mundo Latino (Madrid) 1929, p. 232.

Terpander: M de F's Concerto, The Gramophone, October 1934, p. 174.

Juan M. Thomas: Falla's Concerto, Chesterian, December 1926, p. 92.

Rogelio Villar: Falla y su Concierto de Cámara—Conferencia leida el 21 de diciembre de 1931, in el Teatro Maria Guerrero, con motivo del Centenario de la fundacion del Conservatorio, Publicaciones de 'Ritmo' (Madrid) 1932.

29. Psyche (G. Jean-Aubry). For voice, flute, harp, violin, viola and cello. ?1924.

fp: December 1924, Barcelona, Concepción Badia.

fFp: 2 December 1925, Paris, Salle Erard, Société Musicale Indépendante concert.

fEbp: 25 July 1932, Anne Thursfield, Robert Murchie, Sidonie Goossens, André Mangeot, Eric Bray and Jack Shinebourne.

Pub. 1927, Chester.

30. Soneto a Córdoba. For soprano and harp. October 1926–April 1927. Composed at the request of Gerardo Diego and Federico Garcia Lorca for the tricentenary of the death of Córdoba. Words: Luis de Gongota.

fp: 14 May 1927, Paris, Salle Pleyel, Madeleine Greslé.

fEbp: 14 June 1938, Tatiana Makushina and Maria Korchinska.

Pub. 1932, Max Eschig/O.U.P.; 1956, Chester.

31. Fanfare (sobre el nombre E. F. Arbós). For instrumental ensemble. December 1933–April 1934. Composed for the seventieth birthday of Arbós.

fp: April 1934, Madrid, Teatro Calderon, Madrid Symphony Orchestra, cond. Enrique Fernandez Arbós.

See also No. 35.

32. Balada de Mallorca. For a cappella chorus. 1933. See also No. 35.

33. Pour le tombeau de Paul Dukas. For piano. December 1935. Pub. May–June 1936, La Revue musicale. See also No. 35.

34. Pedrelliana. For orchestra. 1938. See No. 35.

35. Homenajes. For orchestra. 1938. Dur. 18'.

1. *Fanfare, sobre el nombre E. F. Arbós.* Orch 1938.

2. *A C. Debussy* (Elegía de la guitarra). Orch. 1938.

3. *A P. Dukas* (Spes vitae). Orch. 1938.

4. *Pedrelliana.*

2 fl, pic, 2 ob, ca, 2 cl, bcl, 2 bsn, cbsn; 4 hn, 3 tpt, 3 tmb, bs tuba; timp, tamb basco, tamb mil, tamburo, tgle, cym, tamtam, GC; celesta, hp, strings.

fp: 18 November 1939, Buenos Aires, Teatro Colón, cond. Manuel de Falla.

fEp (concert): 14 November 1953, Royal Festival Hall, Philharmonia Orchestra, cond. Norman Del Mar.

Pub. 1953, Chester/Ricordi.

36. Atlàntida. Cantata Scenica in prologue and three parts. 1926–45. Poem: Jacinto Verdaguer, adapted by Manuel de Falla. Posthumous work, completed by Ernesto Halffter.

fp (concert): 24 October 1961, Barcelona, Lyceum, with Victoria de los Angeles and Raimondo Torres, cond. Eduardo Toldrá.

fp (stage): 18 June 1962, Milan, La Scala, with Lino Puglisi (Il Corifeo), Antonino di Minno (Il Ragazzo), Giuletta Simionato (Pierene), Teresa Stratas (Isabelle), cond. Thomas Schippers; producer, Margherita Wallmann.

f British p: 24 August 1962, Edinburgh Festival, with Teresa Berganza and Raimundo Torres, London Symphony Orchestra, cond. Igor Markevitch.

Pub. 1962, Ricordi (vocal score).

BIBLIOGRAPHY:

Ernest Ansermet: Falla's Atlantida, *Opera News*, 29 September 1962, p. 8.

A. Fernandez Cid: L'incognita dell'Atlantida di de Falla, *La Scala* (Milan), May 1955.

Martin Cooper: Falla's last work, *The Listener*, 16 August 1962.

Suzanne Demarquez: Une première mondiale à Barcelone, L'Atlantida de M de F, *Musica* (Chaix), No. 95, February 1962, p. 55.

René Dumesnil: A Atlàntida na Opèra de Paris, *Gazeta de todas as artes* (Lisbon), 1959, No. 96.

G. Fieni: Atlantida di M de F al Teatro Colon di Buenos Aires, *Musica e dischi*, October 1962, p. 62.

Enrique Franco: Estreno triunfal de Atlantida de Falla en Barcelona y Cadiz, *Buenos Aires Musical*, 1961, No. 268, p. 1.

— La grande avventura di Atlantida, *Musica d'oggi*, July–October 1962.

J. de Freitas Branco: A Atlantida de M de F, *Arte musical*, 1961, No. 15, p. 515.

F. Grunfeld: M de F and the 'Lost Continent', *Hi Fi/Stereo Review*, January 1962, p. 39

P. Heyworth: Atlantyda Manuel de Falli, *Ruch Muzyczny*, 1962, No. 5, p. 17.

A. Inglesias: Falla's posthumous La Atlantida to be premièred at Cadiz in 1956, *Musical America*, 1 January 1955, p. 34.

J. Knepler: Argentine Atlantis, *Opera News*, 28 September 1963, p. 27.

I. Kolodin: Falla's Atlantida—presentation at Philharmonic Hall, *Saturday Review*, 13 October 1962, p. 39.

F. L. Lunghi: Atlantida, opera postuma di M de F, *Santa Cecilia*, August 1962, p. 9.

Massimo Mila: Valori dell'Atlantida, *Musica d'oggi*, July–October 1962.

Gwynn Morris: Atlantis regained, *Ricordiana*, July 1962, p. 4.

N. Nabokov: L'Atlantida, Preuves (Paris) No. 15, 1952.

Jaime Pahissa: Origine dell'Atlantida, *Musica d'oggi*, July–October 1962.

C. Rostand: Atlantida di Falla eseguita a Barcellona: un capolavora, *Musica d'oggi*, 1961, No. 6, p. 263 (repr. from *Le Figaro*).

Martin Ruhoff: M de F's Atlantida, *SM*, September–October 1962, p. 300.

W. Sandalewski: Atlantyda Manuel de Falli, *Ruch Muzyczny*, 1962, No. 17, p. 14.

Claudio Sartori: Atlántida reaches the stage, *Opera*, September 1962, p. 599.

W. Starkie: M de F's La Atlantida, *Saturday Review*, 11 November 1961, p. 64.

Desmond Shawe-Taylor: Falla and La Atlántida, *Ricordiana*, January 1962, p. 1.

E. Valenti Ferro: La Atlantida o el noble Falla, *Buenos Aires Musical*, 1963, No. 290, p. 1.

Anon.: Falla's finale, *Newsweek*, 4 December 1961, p. 54.

Anon.: Falla's last dream, *Time*, 29 June 1962, p. 49.

WRITINGS BY FALLA

Preface to G. Jean-Aubry's *La Musique française d'aujourd'hui*, Perrin (Paris) 1916.

Preface to Joaquín Turina's *Enciclopedia abreviada de musica*, 1917.

Nuestre musica, *Musica* (Madrid), June 1917.

L'Espagne dans l'œuvre de Debussy, *RM*, December 1920, p. 206.

El Cante jondo—Sus origenes, sus valores, su influencia en el arte europeo, *anonymous publication*, 1922, on the occasion of the first festival of cante jondo, Granada, 13–14 June 1922; *Midland Musician*, 1926, May–June p. 185, July p. 234; *RM*, October 1938.

Felipe Pedrell, *RM*, February 1923, p. 1; *Revista Catalana de Musica*, May 1923.

Dichiarazioni, *Excelsior*, 1925; *RM*, July 1925.

Hommage à Debussy, *Gaceta Musical*, April 1928.

Risposta a un'inchiesta, *Musique* (Paris), May 1929.

Richard Wagner, *Cruz y Raya* (Madrid), September 1933; *RM*, 1961, No. 3; Nota sobre Wagner, *Nuestra Musica* (Mexico), No. 5, 1947.

Notas sobre Ravel, *Isla* (Jerez de la Frontera), September 1939; Manuel de Falla et Ravel, *Le Monde musical*, June–July 1939.

GENERAL BIBLIOGRAPHY

Edward Allam: M de F (obituary article), *Bulletin of Spanish Studies*, January 1947, p. 58.

M. De Almagro San Martin: Silhueta de Falla, *ABC* (Madrid).

J.-P. Altermann: M de F, *RM*, June 1921, p. 202.

Fedele D'Amico: Conoscere Manuel de Falla, *Musica d'Oggi*, July–October 1962.

J. Bal y Gay: M de F, *Nestra Musica* (Mexico), No. 5, 1947.

Leland J. Berry: M de F, *MS*, 26 January 1929, p. 22.

— M de F, Spanish composer, *Calcutta Review*, November–December 1932, p. 257.

Paul Bertrand: M de F, *Le Ménestrel*, 23 May 1930, p. 233.

R. Capell: M de F at home, *MMR*, September 1929, p. 266.

M. Castelnuovo-Tedesco: M de F, *Il Piano-forte*, January 1923.

Gilbert Chase: Falla's music for piano solo, *Chesterian*, No. 148, January–March 1940.

— M de F, in *The Music of Spain*, 1941; 2nd edition, Dover Publications, 1959, p. 182.

André Coeuroy: A l'Opéra-Comique—La

Falla, Manuel de

Vida Breve, L'Amour Sorcier, Le Trétaux de Maître Pierre, de M de F, *RM*, 1 April 1928, p. 252.
— F. Pedrell, Falla et l'ibérisme, in *Panorama de la musique contemporaine*, Simon Kra (Paris) 1928.
Harriet Cohen: My friend de Falla, *Crescendo*, No. 139, February 1965, p. 89.
Henri Collet: M de F, in *L'Essor de la musique espagnole*, Editions Max Eschig (Paris) 1929, p. 67.
— M de F, *RM*, January 1947, p. 27.
Edward J. Dent: M de F, *Nation*, 28 May 1921, p. 335.
R. Forrer: M de F, sa vie et son œuvre, *L'Orient musical*, June 1928.
A. Fraser: M de F, *Chesterian*, December 1927, p. 69.
Frigyes Frideczky: M de F, *Muzsika*, December 1961, p. 38.
Sydney Grew: Falla, *Midland Musician*, May–June 1926, p. 183.
Leigh Henry: M de F, *MO*, 1921, July p. 847, August p. 929.
Basil Hogarth: M de F, the Voltaire of the Ballet, *The Gramophone*, July 1935, p. 55.
Edgar Istel: M de F, *MQ*, October 1926, p. 497.
G. Jean-Aubry: M de F, *MT*, April 1917, p. 151.
— Glory of M de F, *Chesterian*, June 1928, p. 214.
Joseph Machlis: M de F, in *Introduction to Contemporary Music*, Norton (USA) 1961, Dent (London), p. 258.
A. Mantelli: M de F, *La Rassegna musicale*, 1944, p. 199.
E. Markham Lee: M de F, *MO*, June 1929, p. 814.
M. García Matos: Folklore en Falla, *Musica* (Madrid), 1953, Nos. 3–4, p. 41 and No. 6, p. 33.
Otto Mayer-Serra: Falla's musical nationalism, *MQ*, January 1943, p. 1.
O. de Mendoza: M de F, *Cultura Musical* (Cadiz), 31 January 1923.
Antonio Odiozola: M de F, discography, *Musica* (Madrid), 1953, Nos. 3–4, p. 222.
Kurt Pahlen: M de F und die Musik in Spanien, *ÖM*, March 1957.
Guido Pannain: M de F, *La Rassegna musicale*,

November 1930, p. 461; Ger. transl. by Viktor Joss, *Der Auftakt*, 1932, Nos. 7–8, p. 169.
Mathilde Pomès: A Grenade, avec M de F, *RM*, April 1934, p. 257.
Jean Poueigh: La musique, *Revue hommes et mondes*, January 1947, p. 199.
Henry Prunières: M de F et la musique espagnole, *Conferencia*, 15 October 1926.
— M de F, *New York Times*, 8 April 1928.
A. Quevedo: M de F en Paris, *Musicalia*, No. 1, May–June 1928.
Roland-Manuel: M de F, *Musique*, 15 April 1928.
— Falla, *Gaceta Musical*, May 1928.
— Les debuts de M de F, *Musique*, Nos. 11–12, 1928.
— M de F, ses derniers ouvrages, *Musique*, September 1929.
— M de F, Editions Cahiers d'Art (Paris) 1929.
Wouter Paap: Werken van M de F op het Holland Festival, *Mens en melodie*, May 1953, p. 179.
Adolfo Salazar: La jeune musique—Falla et Halffter, *RM*, 1 October 1924, p. 254.
Lionel Salter: M de F, in *Decca Book of Ballet*, Muller (London) 1958, p. 144.
Gustave Samazeuilh: M de F, in *Musiciens de mon temps*, Editions Marcel Daubin (Paris) 1947, p. 334.
Irving Schwerké: Hommage to M de F, in *Views and Interviews* (Paris), 1936, p. 39.
Tomás Andrade De Silva: El piano de M de F, *Música* (Madrid), 1953, Nos. 3–4, p. 69.
Federico Sopena: Souvenir de M de F, *La Vie musicale*, February 1952, p. 3.
Walter Starkie: M de F's music, *Fortnightly*, February 1947, p. 138.
H. H. Stuckenschmidt: M de F, in *Schöpfer der neuen Musik*, Suhrkamp Verlag (Frankfurt am Main) 1958, p. 115.
Juan Maria Thomas: M de F in the Island, *Chesterian*, No. 153, January 1948.
J. B. Trend: Falla in Arabia, *M&L*, April 1922, p. 133.
— Recollections of Falla, *MT*, January 1947, p. 15.
— Two books on Falla, *Chesterian*, July 1948.
— M de F and Spanish music, Knopf (New York) 1929; new edition, 1935.

J. Turina: M de F, *Chesterian*, May 1920.

C. Van Vechten: M de F, *Etude*, August 1927, p. 580.

Rogelio De Villar: M de F, *La Revista de Musica*, October 1927.

— M de F, *Mundo musical* (Buenos Aires), July 1929.

— M de F, *Musica d'oggi*, November 1929, p. 448.

Arnold Walter: Versuch ûber de Falla, *Anbruch*, August 1935, p. 217.

M. H. Wiborg: Foremost composer of Spain today, *Arts and Decoration*, December 1925, p. 50.

Karl H. Wörner: M de F, *Musica*, 1947, No. 1, p. 28.

Helmuth Wirth: M de F, in *MGG*, Vol. 3 (1954), p. 1747.

MISCELLANEOUS OR UNSIGNED

M de F, *British Musician*, July 1928, p. 127.

M de F, cenni biografici, *Bollettino bibliografico musicale*, March 1929, p. 1.

M de F, 1876–1946, *Newsweek*, 25 November 1946, p. 93.

Zum Tod von M de F & Letzter Besuch bei de Falla, *Melos*, December 1946, p. 45.

GABRIEL FAURÉ (1845–1924)

Gabriel Urbain Fauré, the sixth child of parents with no great musical interests, was born on 12 May 1845 at Pamiers in the French Pyrenean *département* of Ariège and brought up by foster-parents until he was four. He showed his musical gifts early, and it was to develop these that Louis Niedermeyer awarded him a free place at his music school in Paris. Fauré studied at the Ecole Niedermeyer from 1855 to 1865, being befriended in 1860 by the young Saint-Saëns, who had just started teaching piano there. From 1886 to 1870 Fauré was a church organist at Rennes in Brittany, and after spending part of 1870 in the French infantry during the Franco-Prussian War, worked for many years as an organist in Paris, being *inter alia* assistant to Widor at Saint-Sulpice and to Dubois and Saint-Saëns at the Madeleine. In 1877 he was engaged to Marianne Viardot, daughter of the opera singer Pauline Viardot, but the engagement was broken off and in 1883 he married Marie Fremiet, daughter of the sculptor Emmanuel Fremiet. He had begun to teach at the Ecole Niedermeyer in 1872 and in 1896 was appointed both principal organist at the Madeleine and Professor of Composition at the Conservatoire, where his pupils were to include Maurice Ravel, Florent Schmitt, Charles Koechlin and Nadia Boulanger. Several visits to Germany in the late 1870s and trips to Venice and London (1890, 1898) represent the sum of Fauré's travels. From 1903 to 1914 he was music critic for *Le Figaro* and from 1905 to 1920 Director of the Conservatoire, replacing Theodore Dubois who had resigned over the affair of Ravel and the Prix de Rome. From 1909 onwards, Fauré was much concerned with the activities of the new *Société Musicale Independente*, of which he was president; but increasing deafness eventually forced him to retire from all administrative work. He died in November 1924.

CATALOGUE OF WORKS

1. **Le Papillon et la fleur** Op. 1 No. 1 (Victor Hugo). For voice and piano. 1860. Ded. Mme Miolan-Carvalho. Pub. 1869, Choudens; Hamelle.

2. **Mai** Op. 1 No. 2 (Victor Hugo). For voice and piano. *c.* 1865. Ded. Mme Henri Garnier. Pub. 1878, Choudens; Hamelle.

3. **Dans les ruines d'une abbaye** Op. 2 No. 1 (Victor Hugo). For voice and piano. 1869. Ded. Mme Henriette Escalier. Pub. 1870, Choudens; Hamelle.

4. **Les Matelots** Op. 2 No. 2 (Théophile Gautier). For voice and piano. *c.* 1865. Ded. Mme Edouard Lalo. Pub. 1871, Hartmann; 1876, Choudens; Hamelle.

5. **Seule!** Op. 3 No. 1 (Théophile Gautier). For voice and piano. *c.* 1865. Ded. E. Fernier. Pub. 1879, Choudens; Hamelle.

6. **Sérénade toscane** Op. 3 No. 2 (Romain Bussine). For voice and piano. *c.* 1865. Ded. Mme la Baronne de Montagnac (née de Rosalès). Pub. 1879, Choudens; Hamelle.

7. **Chanson du pêcheur** (Lamento) Op. 4 No. 1 (Théophile Gautier). For voice and piano. *c.* 1865. Ded. Pauline Viardot.

Fauré, Gabriel

?fp: 22 April 1876, Paris, Pauline Viardot. Pub. ?1878, Choudens; 1896, Metzler (Eng. version, A.S.).

8. Lydia Op. 4 No. 2 (Leconte de Lisle). For voice and piano. *c. 1865.* Ded. Mme Marie Trélat. Pub. 1878, Choudens; Hamelle.

9. Chant d'automne Op. 5 No. 1 (Charles Baudelaire). For voice and piano. *c. 1865.* Ded. Mme M. Camille Clerc. Pub. 1879, Choudens; Hamelle.

10. Rêve d'amour Op. 5 No. 2 (Victor Hugo). For voice and piano. *c. 1865.* Ded. Mme C. de Gomiecourt. Pub. 1875, Choudans; Hamelle.

11. L'Absent Op. 5 No. 3 (Victor Hugo). For voice and piano. Dated: 3 April 1871. Ded. Romain Bussine. Pub. 1875, Choudens; Hamelle.

12. Aubade Op. 6 No. 1 (Louis Pomey). For voice and piano. *c. 1865.* Ded. Mme Amélie Duez. Pub. ?1879, Choudens; Hamelle.

13. Tristesse Op. 6 No. 2 (Théophile Gautier). For voice and piano. *c. 1865.* Ded. Mme Edouard Lalo. Pub. 1876, Choudens; Hamelle.

14. Sylvie Op. 7 No. 1 (Paul de Choudens). For voice and piano. *c. 1865.* Ded. Mme la Vicomtesse de Gironde. Pub. *c.* 1880, Choudens (as Op. 6 No. 3); Hamelle.

15. Après un rêve Op. 7 No. 2 (Romain Bussine). For voice and piano. *c. 1865.* Ded. Mme Marguerite Baugnies. Pub. 1877, Choudens; 1912, Thurwanger (Eng. version, N. H. Dole). Free arr. for piano solo by Percy Grainger, 1939, Schirmer.

15a. Après un rêve Op. 7 No. 2. Version orch. Henri Büsser.
fp: 4 January 1925, Paris, Théâtre du Châtelet, Yvonne Gall and l'Orchestre Colonne, cond. Gabriel Pierné.

16. Hymne Op. 7 No. 3 (Charles Baudelaire). For voice and piano. *c. 1865.* Ded. Félix Lévy. Pub. 1878, Choudens; *c.* 1910, Hamelle.

17. Barcarolle Op. 7 No. 4 (Marc Monnier).

For voice and piano. *c. 1865.* Ded. Mme Pauline Viardot.
?fp: 20 March 1875, Paris, Mme de Grandval.
Pub. 1878, Choudens; *c.* 1910, Hamelle.

18. Au bord de l'eau Op. 8 No. 1 (Sully Prudhomme). For voice and piano. *c. 1865.* Ded. Mme Claudie Chamerot.
?fp: 19 January 1878, Paris, Mlle de Miramont-Tréogate.
Pub. 1878, Choudens; Hamelle.

19. La Rançon Op. 8 No. 2 (Charles Baudelaire). For voice and piano. *c. 1865.* Ded. Henri Duparc. Pub. 1878, Choudens; Hamelle.

20. Ici-bas Op. 8 No. 3 (Sully Prudhomme). For voice and piano. *c. 1865.* Ded. Mme Georges Lecoq (née Mac-Brid).
?fp: 2 December 1874, Paris, Marguerite Baron.
Pub. 1878, Choudens; Hamelle.

21. L'Aurore (Victor Hugo). For voice and piano. ?Date. Ded. Anna Dufresne. Pub. 1958, in *Das Musikwerk*, Heft. 16: Das ausserdeutsche Sololied 1500–1900.

22. Cadenza. For Beethoven's piano concerto in C minor. 1869. Pub. 1927, Magasin Musical.

23. Duets Op. 10. For two sopranos (or soprano and tenor) with piano. *c.* 1870.
1. *Puisqu'ici-bas toute âme* (Victor Hugo). Ded. Mmes Georges Chamerot and Alphonse Duvernoy.
2. *Tarantelle* (Marc Monnier). Ded. Mme Claudie Chamerot and Mlle Marianne Viardot.
fp (Nos. 1 & 2): 10 April 1875, Paris, Mme Claudie Chamerot and Mlle Marianne Viardot.
Pub. ?1897, Choudens; Hamelle.

24. Symphonie (Suite). 1872–3.
1. *Allegro*; 2. *Andante*; 3. *Gavotte*; 4. *Finale.*
fp: 8 February 1873, Paris, Camille Saint-Saëns and Gabriel Fauré (pianos).
fp with orchestra: 16 (?12) May 1874, Paris, Salle Herz, Société Nationale de Musique, cond. Edouard Colonne.
Note: The evidently later title of *Suite* was designated Op. 20.

Unpub. (except for first movement: see No. 24a).

24a. Allegro symphonique Op. 68. For orchestra. First movement of preceding. Pub. Hamelle; also arr. for piano four hands by L. Boellmann, 1929, Hamelle.

25. Cantique de Racine Op. 11. For mixed voices with harmonium and string quintet, or solo voice with organ or piano. ?1864. Ded. César Franck. Pub. 1876, Schoen; 1903, Hamelle.

26. Ave Maria. For male voices (TTB) and organ. August 1871. Pub. 1957, Heugel.

27. Les Djinns Op. 12 (Victor Hugo). For mixed voices and orchestra or piano. *c.* 1875 (?earlier). Pub. Hamelle.

28. Violin Sonata in A Op. 13. 1876. Ded· Paul Viardot.

1. *Allegro molto*; 2. *Andante*; 3. *Allegro vivace*; 4. *Allegro quasi presto*.

fp: 27 January 1877, Paris, Marie Tayau and Gabriel Fauré.

fEp: 1 June 1880, Steinway Hall, Ovide Musin and Camille Saint-Saëns.

fEbp: 6 July 1928, Amina Lucchesi and Margery Cunningham.

Pub. 1878, Breitkopf & Härtel.

29. Violin Concerto Op. 14. 1878. Unpub.

30. Piano Quartet No. 1 in C minor Op. 15. 1879. Ded. H. Léonard.

1. *Allegro molto moderato*; 2. *Scherzo: Allegro vivo*; 3. *Adagio*; 4. *Allegro molto*.

fp: 14 February 1880, Paris, Société Nationale de Musique, Gabriel Fauré, Ovide Musin, Van Waefelghem and Mariotti.

fEp: 1896, David Bispham concert, Gabriel Fauré, Brodsky, Hobday and Squire.

fEbp: 8 January 1925, Richard H. Walthew, Charles Woodhouse, Ernest Yonge and Charles A. Crabbe.

Pub. Hamelle.

31. Berceuse Op. 16. For piano and violin. 1879. Ded. Camille Saint-Saëns.

?fp: 18 February 1881, Paris, Société Nationale de Musique, Ovide Musin.

Pub. 1879, Hamelle. Also arr. for piano solo by A. Benfeld.

31a. Berceuse Op. 16. Version for violin or cello and orchestra.

fl, cl; strings.

Pub. Hamelle.

32. Trois Romances sans Paroles Op. 17. 1863.

1. *A flat. Andante, quasi Allegretto*. Ded. Mme Félix Lévy.

2. *A minor. Allegro molto*. Ded. Mlle Laure de Leyritz.

3. *A flat. Andante moderato*. Ded. Mme Florent Saglio.

?fp (two only): 25 February 1881, Paris, Société Nationale de Musique, Pauline Roger.

Pub. Hamelle; incl. various arrangements.

32a. Romance Op. 17 No. 3. Version for cello or violin and small orchestra.

fl, ob, cl, bsn; hp, strings.

Pub. *c.* 1900, Hamelle.

33. Messe Basse. For female voices (soloists and chorus) and organ or harmonium. Early work: date unknown.

1. *Kyrie*; 2. *Sanctus*; 3. *Benedictus*; 4. *Agnus Dei*.

Pub. 1907, 1934, Heugel.

34. Souvenirs de Bayreuth. Fantaisie en forme de quadrille ('sur les thèmes favoris de l'Anneau du Nibelung de Richard Wagner') for piano four hands. ?Date. Composed with André Messager. Pub. 1930, Editions Costallat; also arr. for piano solo by Gustave Samazeuilh.

35. Arrangements. Reductions by Gabriel Fauré of works by Saint-Saëns. *c.* 1880–1. (i) *La Princesse jaune* (overture), for piano four hands; (ii) *Piano Concerto No. 4*, for two pianos; (iii) *Suite for orchestra*, for two pianos eight hands; (iv) *Suite Algérienne*, for piano four hands; (v) *Septet*, for piano four hands. Pub. Durand.

36. Nell Op. 18 No. 1 (Leconte de Lisle). For voice and piano. 1880. Ded. Mme. Camille Saint-Saëns.

fp: 29 January 1881, Paris, Société Nationale de Musique, Henriette Fuchs.

Pub. ?1880, Hamelle.

37. Le Voyageur Op. 18 No. 2 (Armand Silvestre). For voice and piano. 1880. Ded. Emmanuel Jadin.

Fauré, Gabriel

fp: 7 May 1881, Paris, Société Nationale de Musique, Félix Lévy.
Pub. ?1880, Hamelle.

38. Automne Op. 18 No. 3 (Armand Silvestre). For voice and piano. 1880.
fp: 29 January 1881, Paris, Société Nationale de Musique, Henriette Fuchs.
Pub. ?1880, Hamelle.

38a. Automne Op. 18 No. 3. Version with orchestra. Orch. Henri Büsser.
fp: 4 January 1925, Paris, Théâtre du Châtelet, Yvonne Gall and l'Orchestre Colonne, cond. Gabriel Pierné.

39. Ballade Op. 19. For piano and orchestra (orig. for piano solo). 1881. Ded. Camille Saint-Saëns.
2 fl, 2 ob, 2 cl, 2 bsn; 2 hn; strings.
fp: 23 April 1881, Paris, Société Nationale de Musique, Gabriel Fauré.
fEp: 23 October 1913, Queen's Hall, Promenade Concert, Emilienne Bompard and the Queen's Hall Orchestra, cond. Sir Henry Wood.
fEbp: 20 September 1932, Maurice Reeve and BBC Orchestra, cond. B. Walton O'Donnell.
Pub. 1881, Hamelle: incl. reduction for two pianos.

BIBLIOGRAPHY:
Marguerite Long: La Ballade de GF, *L'Art musical*, 5 May 1939.

40. Poème d'un jour Op. 21 (Charles Grandmougin). For voice and piano. 1880. Ded. Mme la Comtesse de Grandville.
1. *Rencontre*; 2. *Toujours*; 3. *Adieu*.
fp: 29 January 1881, Paris, Société Nationale de Musique, Mazalbert.
Pub. 1881, Durand; 1897, Metzler (Eng. version, Paul England).

41. Le Ruisseau Op. 22. Chorus for mezzo-soprano and 2-part (SC) female chorus and piano. 1881. Ded. Mme Pauline Roger.
?fp: 14 January 1882, Paris, Société Nationale de Musique.
Pub. Hamelle.

41a. Le Ruisseau Op. 22. Version with acc. of two flutes and string quintet.

?fp: 2 April 1887, Paris, Société Nationale de Musique.

42. Les Berceaux Op. 23 No. 1 (Sully Prudhomme). For voice and piano. 1882. Ded. Mlle Alice Boissonnet. Pub. Hamelle; 1912, Thurwanger (Eng. version, J. H. Brewer).

43. Notre Amour Op. 23 No. 2 (Armand Silvestre). For voice and piano. 1882. Ded. Mme A. Castillon. Pub. *c.* 1885, Hamelle; 1897, Metzler (Eng. version, A.S.).

43a. Notre Amour Op. 23 No. 2. Version orch. Henri Büsser.
fp: 4 January 1925, Paris, Théâtre du Châtelet, Yvonne Gall and l'Orchestre Colonne, cond. Gabriel Pierné.

44. Le Secret Op. 23 No. 3 (Armand Silvestre). For voice and piano. 1882. Ded. Mlle Alice Boissonnet.
?fp: 6 January 1883, Paris, Société Nationale de Musique, Quirot.
Pub. Hamelle.

45. Elégie Op. 24. For piano and cello. 1883.
?fp: 15 December 1883, Paris, Société Nationale de Musique, Loëb.
Pub. 1883, Hamelle.

45a. Elégie Op. 24. Version for cello and orchestra.
2 fl, 2 ob, 2 cl, 2 bsn; 4 hn; strings.
Pub. Hamelle.

46. Impromptu No. 1 in E flat Op. 25 1882. *Allegro ma non troppo.*
fp: 9 December 1882, Paris, Société Nationale de Musique, Camille Saint-Saëns.
Pub. Hamelle.

47. Barcarolle No. 1 in A minor Op. 26. 1882. *Allegretto moderato.* Pub. ?1883, Hamelle.

48. Deux mélodies Op. 27 (Armand Silvestre). For voice and piano. 1883.
1. *Chanson d'amour.* Ded. Mlle Jane Huré.
2. *La Fée aux chansons.* Ded. Mme Edmond Fuchs.
Pub. Hamelle.

49. Romance Op. 28. For violin and piano (?or orchestra). 1882. Ded. Mlle Arma Harkness.

fp: 3 February 1883, Paris, Arma Harkness. Pub. Hamelle.

50. La Naissance de Vénus Op. 29. Mythological Scene for soloists, chorus and orchestra. 1882. Text: Paul Collin. Ded. Sigismond Bardac.

fp: 3 April 1886, Paris, Société Nationale de Musique, with Mme Castillon, Mme Storm, Auguez and Dupas as soloists.

fEp: October 1898, Leeds Festival, cond. Sir Arthur Sullivan.

?fEbp: 24 January 1954, Ena Mitchell, Betty Bannerman, Alexander Young, Francis Loring, Covent Garden Opera Chorus and Royal Opera House Orchestra, cond. Douglas Robinson.

Pub. Hamelle: incl. reduction by the composer.

51. Valse-Caprice No. 1 in A Op. 30. For piano. 1883. *Allegro molto.* Pub. Hamelle.

52. Impromptu No. 2 in F minor Op. 31. For piano. 1883. *Allegro molto.* Pub. Hamelle.

53. Mazurka in B flat Op. 32. For piano. 1883. Pub. Hamelle.

54. Trois Nocturnes Op. 33. For piano. 1883.

1. *E flat minor. Lento.* Ded. Mme M. Baugnies.

2. *B major. Andantino espressivo.* Ded. Mme Félix Guyon.

3. *A flat. Andante con moto.* Ded. Mme A. Bohomoletz. Pub. Hamelle.

55. Impromptu No. 3 in A flat Op. 34. For piano. 1883. *Allegro.* Pub. Hamelle.

56. Madrigal Op. 35 (Armand Silvestre). For SATB quartet or chorus and piano. 1884. Ded. André Messager.

fp: 12 January 1884, Paris, Société Nationale de Musique.

Pub. Hamelle.

57. Nocturne No. 4 in E flat Op. 36. For piano. 1884. *Andante molto moderato.* Ded. Mme la Comtesse de Mercy-Argenteau. Pub. Hamelle.

58. Nocturne No. 5 in B flat Op. 37. For piano. 1884. *Andante quasi allegretto.* Ded. Mme Marie P. Christofle. Pub. Hamelle.

59. Valse-Caprice No. 2 in D flat Op. 38. For piano. 1884. *Allegretto moderato.* Ded. Mme André Messager. Pub. Hamelle.

60. Aurore Op. 39 No. 1 (Armand Silvestre). For voice and piano. 1884. Ded. Mme H. Roger-Jourdain.

fp: 16 October 1884, Paris, Société Nationale de Musique, Mme Mauvernay.

Pub. Hamelle.

61. Fleur jetée Op. 39 No. 2 (Armand Silvestre). For voice and piano. 1884. Ded. Mme Jules Gouin.

fp: 16 October 1884, Paris, Société Nationale de Musique, Mme Mauvernay.

Pub. Hamelle.

62. Le Pays des rêves Op. 39 No. 3 (Armand Silvestre). For voice and piano. 1884. Ded. Mlle Thérèse Guyon.

fp: 27 December 1884, Paris, Société Nationale de Musique, Thérèse Guyon.

Pub. Hamelle.

63. Les Roses d'Ispahan Op. 39 No. 4 (Leconte de Lisle). For voice and piano. 1884. Ded. Mlle Louise Collinet.

fp: 27 December 1884, Paris, Société Nationale de Musique, Thérèse Guyon.

Pub. Hamelle; 1896, Metzler (Eng. version, Adela Maddison).

64. Symphony in D minor Op. 40. 1884.

fp: 15 March 1885, Paris, cond. Edouard Colonne.

Unpub.

65. Barcarolle No. 2 in G major Op. 41. For piano. 1885. *Allegretto quasi allegro.* Pub. Hamelle.

66. Barcarolle No. 3 in G flat Op. 42. For piano. 1885. *Allegretto.* Pub. Hamelle.

67. Noël Op. 43 No. 1 (Victor Wilder). For voice and piano. 1886. Pub. Hamelle.

68. Nocturne Op. 43 No. 2 (Villiers de l'Isle Adam). For voice and piano. Ded. Mme H. Roger-Jourdain. Pub. Hamelle.

69. Barcarolle No. 4 in A flat Op. 44. For piano. 1886. *Allegretto.* Ded. Mme Ernest Chausson. Pub. Hamelle.

70. Piano Quartet No. 2 in G minor Op. 45. 1886. Ded. Hans von Bülow.

Fauré, Gabriel

1. *Allegro molto moderato*; 2. *Allegro molto*; 3. *Adagio non troppo*; 4. *Allegro molto*.

fp: 22 January 1887, Paris, Gabriel Fauré, Rémy, Van Waefelghem and Delsart.

fEp: 9 November 1887, St. James's Hall, Monday Popular Concert, Schonberger, Ysaÿe, Straus and Whitehouse.

Pub. 1886, Hamelle.

71. Les Présents Op. 46 No. 1 (Villiers de l'Isle Adam). For voice and piano. 1887. Ded. Comte Robert de Montesquiou Fezensac. Pub. Hamelle.

72. Clair de lune (Menuet) Op. 46 No. 2 (Paul Verlaine). For voice and piano. 1887. Ded. Emmanuel Jadin.

?fp: 28 April 1888, Paris, Société Nationale de Musique, Maurice Bagès.

Pub. Hamelle.

73. O Salutaris Op. 47 No. 1. For solo voice with organ or piano. 1887. Ded. J. Faure. Pub. 1887, Hamelle.

74. Maria, Mater Gratiae Op. 47 No. 2. Duet for soprano (or tenor) and mezzo-soprano (or baritone) with organ or piano and solo violin (or string trio). ?1887 (?1888). Pub. Hamelle.

75. Requiem Op. 48. For soprano and baritone soloists, chorus, organ and orchestra. 1887–8.

1. *Introit et Kyrie*; 2. *Offertoire*; 3. *Sanctus*; 4. *Pie Jesu*; 5. *Agnus Dei*; 6. *Libera me*; 7. *In Paradisum*.

2 fl, 3 cl, 2 bsn; 4 hn, 2 tpt, 3 tmb; timp; hps, organ, strings.

fp: January 1888, Paris, Madeleine.

Pub. 1900, Hamelle.

BIBLIOGRAPHY:

Camille Benoît: La Messe de Requiem de GF, *Le Guide musical*, Nos. 32–33 (9–16 August), 1888, p. 195.

Malcolm Boyd: Fauré's Requiem, a reappraisal, *MT*, June 1963, p. 408.

Pierre Lalo: Le Requiem, *Le Temps*, 27 January 1906.

Marguerite Long: Sur le Requiem de GF, *Le Courrier musical*, 1 April 1930.

P. J.-M. Plum: En entendant le Requiem de Fauré, *Musica Sacra* (Bruges), Vol. XLIII (1936), p. 42.

Roland-Manuel: Le Requiem de Fauré, *La Vie Catholique*, 22 November 1924.

76. Petite Pièce Op. 49. For cello and piano. 1889. Unpub.

77. Pavane Op. 50. For orchestra with (ad lib) SATB chorus. 1887. Ded. Mme la Comtesse Greffulhe.

2 fl, 2 ob, 2 cl, 2 bsn; 2 hn; strings.

fp: 28 April 1888, Paris, Société Nationale de Musique (with chorus).

Pub. Hamelle: incl. reduction for piano solo.

78. Larmes Op. 51 No. 1 (Jean Richepin). For voice and piano. 1889. Ded. Mme la Princesse Wynaretta de Scey-Montbéliard. Pub. 1891, Hamelle.

79. Au cimetière Op. 51 No. 2 (Jean Richepin). For voice and piano. 1889. Ded. Mme. Maurice Sulzbach.

fp: 2 February 1889, Paris, Société Nationale de Musique, Maurice Bagès.

Pub. 1891, Hamelle; 1896, Metzler (Eng. version, A.S.).

80. Spleen Op. 51 No. 3 (Verlaine). For voice and piano. 1889. Ded. Mme Henri Cochin. Pub. 1891, Hamelle.

81. La Rose Op. 51 No. 4 (Leconte de Lisle). For voice and piano. 1889. Ded. Maurice Bagès. Pub. 1891, Hamelle.

82. Caligula Op. 52. Incidental music to a tragedy by Alexandre Dumas. 1888.

1. *Prologue* (*Fanfares, Marche et Chœurs*); 2. *Chœur*; 3. *Air de danse*; 4. *Mélodrame et Chœur*; 5. *Mélodrame et Chœur*.

2 fl, pic, 2 ob, 2 cl, 2 bsn; 4 hn, 3 tpt, 3 tmb; timp, tgle, tamb de basque, cym antiques, tamb mil; 2 hp, strings.

fp: 8 November 1888, Paris, Théâtre National de l'Odéon.

Pub. Hamelle: incl. vocal score.

83. En prière (Stéphane Bordèse). For voice and piano. 1890. Ded. Mme Leroux-Ribeyre. Pub. 1890, Durand (in *Contes mystiques*); 1897, Metzler (Eng. version, Elizabeth Bennett).

84. La Passion. Prelude to the poem by Edmond Hauracourt. For orchestra. 1890.

fp: 21 April 1890, Paris, Société Nationale de Musique.
Unpub.

85. Ecce Fidelis Servus Op. 54. Motet for soprano, tenor and baritone with organ and double bass (or organ pedal). *c.* 1890. Ded. M. l'Abbé A. Vantroys. Pub. 1894, Hamelle.

86. Tantum Ergo Op. 55. For tenor or soprano and 4-part chorus with organ, harp, (or piano) and double bass. *c.* 1890. Pub. 1894 Hamelle.

86a. Tantum Ergo. Version for soprano or tenor and mixed voice chorus. November 1904. Pub. 1905, Durand.

86b. Tantum Ergo. Version for mezzo-soprano or baritone with (ad lib) unison chorus. ?1905. Pub. 1905, Durand.

87. Dolly Op. 56. Six Pieces for piano duet. 1893–6. Ded. Mlle Hélène Bardac.
   1. *Berceuse*; 2. *Mi-a-ou*; 3. *Dolly's garden* (*Le Jardin de Dolly*); 4. *Kitty-Valse*; 5. *Tenderness* (*Tendresse*); 6. *Spanish dance* (*Le pas espagnol*).
?fp: 30 April 1898, Paris, Edouard Risler and Alfred Cortot.
Pub. 1897, Metzler; 1925, Hamelle. Orig. misprinted as Op. 36. Various arrs. incl. for piano solo by Alfred Cortot.

87a. Dolly Op. 56. Suite for orchestra. Orch. Henri Rabaud. *c.* 1912.
fp: 1912, Paris.
fp (as a ballet): 23 January 1913, Paris, Théâtre des Arts.
fEbp: 24 November 1925, Newcastle Station Symphony Orchestra, cond. Edward Clark.

88. Shylock Op. 57. Incidental music to a verse drama by Edmond Haraucourt, after Shakespeare. 1889. Ded. Paul Porel.
   1. *Chanson.*
fl, cl; hn; 2 hp, strings; tenor voice.
   2. *Entr'acte.*
2 fl, 2 ob, 2 cl, 2 bsn; 4 hn, 2 tpt; timp; hps. strings.
   3. *Madrigal.*
2 cl, bsn; hn; hp, strings; solo voice.
   4. *Epithalame.*
2 fl, 2 ob, 2 cl, 2 bsn; 4 hn, 2 tpt; timp; hp, strings.

   5. *Nocturne.*
strings.
   6. *Final.*
2 fl, 2 ob, 2 cl, 2 bsn; 4 hn, 2 tpt; timp, tgle; hp, strings.
fp: 17 December 1889, Paris, Odéon.
?f concert p: 3 March 1895, Paris, Concerts Lamoureux.
fEbp: 1 September 1936, Edward Reach (tenor), BBC Orchestra, cond. Constant Lambert.
Pub. Hamelle. No. 3 pub. 1897, Metzler (Eng. version by A.S.).

89. Cinq mélodies Op. 58 (Paul Verlaine). For voice and piano. 1891. Ded. Princesse Edmond de Polignac.
   1. *Mandoline*; 2. *En sourdine*; 3. *Green*; 4. *A Clymène*; 5. *C'est l'extase . . .*
fp: 2 April 1892, Paris, Société Nationale de Musique, Maurice Bagès.
Pub. 1891, Hamelle; 1896 (?No. 1 only), Metzler (Eng. version, Adela Maddison).

90. Valse-Caprice No. 3 in G flat Op. 59. For piano. 1891. *Allegro molto.* Ded. Mme Philippe Dieterlen. Pub. Hamelle.

91. La bonne chanson Op. 61. Song cycle for voice and piano (Paul Verlaine). 1892–3. Ded. Mme Sigismond Bardac.
   1. *Une Sainte en son auréole*; 2. *Puisque l'aube grandit*; 3. *La lune blanche luit dans les bois*; 4. *J'allais par des chemins perfides*; 5. *J'ai presque peur, en vérité*; 6. *Avant que tu ne t'en ailles*; 7. *Donc, ce sera par un clair jour d'été*; 8. *N'est-ce pas?*; 9. *L'hiver a cessé.*
fp: 20 April 1895, Paris, Jeanne Remacle.
?fEp: 10 November 1915, Aeolian Hall, Classical Concerts Society, Jean Waterston.
Pub. Hamelle.

BIBLIOGRAPHY:
Paul Ladmirault: Sur la Bonne Chanson, *Le Courrier musical*, 31 March–7 April 1900.
J. Méraly: GF et la Bonne Chanson, *RM*, 15 November 1903.
Georges Servières: La Bonne Chanson, *Guide musical*, 24 December 1894.

91a. La bonne chanson Op. 61. Version for voice, string orchestra and piano.
fEp (Nos. 1–5 only): 22 January 1928,

Fauré, Gabriel

Odette de Foras and the London Chamber Orchestra, cond. Anthony Bernard.

fbp (complete): 9 January 1953, BBC broadcast, Richard Lewis and the London Chamber Orchestra, cond. Anthony Bernard.

92. Sérénade du Bourgeois Gentilhomme. For voice and piano. 1893. Pub. 1957, Heugel (Engl. version, Rollo Myers).

93. Valse-Caprice No. 4 in A flat Op. 62. For piano. 1894. *Molto moderato, quasi lento.* Ded. Mme Max Lyon. Pub. Hamelle.

94. Nocturne No. 6 in D flat Op. 63. For piano. 1894. *Adagio.* Ded. Eugène d'Eichthal. Pub. Hamelle.

95. Hymn to Apollo Op. 64. Greek Chant (11th century B.C.): text reconstituted by H. Weil, transcribed by Th. Reinach; accompaniment by Gabriel Fauré. 1894.

fp: 1894, Paris, l'Ecole des Hautes Etudes. Pub. 1894, Bornemann; Novello.

96. Ave Verum Op. 65 No. 1. Chorus for two female voices *or* duet for tenor and baritone with organ. *c.* 1894. Pub. Hamelle.

97. Tantum Ergo Op. 65 No. 2. Chorus for three female voices (with soli) and organ. *c.* 1894. Pub. Hamelle.

98. Barcarolle No. 5 in F sharp minor Op. 66. For piano. 18 September 1894. *Allegretto moderato.* Ded. Mme Vincent d'Indy.

fEp: 10 December 1896, St. James's Hall, Léon Delafosse.

Pub. Hamelle.

99. Salve Regina Op. 67 No. 1. For mezzo-soprano or baritone and organ or piano. *c.* 1895. Pub. 1895, L'Illustration (supplement); 1932, Hamelle.

100. Ave Maria Op. 67 No. 2. For mezzo-soprano or baritone and organ or piano. *c.* 1895. Pub. 1937, Hamelle.

101. Prison Op. 83 (orig. 68) No. 1 (Verlaine). For voice and piano. *c.* 1895.

fp: 3 April 1897, Paris, Thérèse Roger. Pub. 1896, Fromont; 1897, Metzler (Eng. version, Paul England); Hamelle (as Op. 83).

102. Soir Op. 83 (orig. 68) No. 2 (A. Samain). For voice and piano. *c.* 1895.

fp: 3 April 1897, Paris, Thérèse Roger. Pub. 1896, Fromont; 1897, Metzler (Eng. version, Adela Maddison); Hamelle (as Op. 83).

103. Romance in A Op. 69. For cello and piano. 1894. Pub. 1894, Hamelle.

104. Barcarolle No. 6 in E flat Op. 70. For piano. 1895. *Allegretto vivo.*

fp: 3 April 1897, Paris, Edouard Risler. Pub. 1896, Metzler; Hamelle.

105. Pleurs d'or Op. 72 (Albert Samain). Duet for mezzo-soprano and baritone with piano. *c.* 1896. Ded. Camilla Landi and David Bispham (Eng. edn.). Pub. 1896, Metzler (Eng. version, Paul England); Hamelle. One edition gives Op. no. as 71.

106. Thème et variations Op. 73 (orig. 71). For piano. 1896. Ded. Mlle Thérèse Roger.

fEp: 10 December 1896, St. James's Hall, Léon Delafosse.

fEbp: 5 October 1931, Marguerite de Pachmann.

Pub. 1897, Metzler.

106a. Thème et variations Op. 73. Version orch. D.-E. Inghelbrecht. Pub. 1955, Hamelle.

107. Nocturne No. 7 in C sharp minor Op. 74. 1897. *Molto lento.* Ded. Mme Adéla Maddison.

?fp: 20 March 1901, Paris, Alfred Cortot. Pub. ?1898, Hamelle.

108. Andante Op. 75. For piano and violin. 1894. Ded. Johannes Wolff.

fp: 22 January 1898, Paris, Société Nationale de Musique, A. Parent.

fEp: 10 June 1904, Aeolian Hall, Johannes Wolff and Camille Saint-Saëns.

Pub. 1897, Metzler; Hamelle.

109. Le Parfum impérissable Op. 76 No. 1 (Leconte de Lisle). For voice and piano. 1897. Ded. Paolo Tosti.

fp: 30 April 1898, Paris, Thérèse Roger. Pub. 1897, Hamelle; 1897, Metzler (Eng. version, Adela Maddison).

109a. Le Parfum impérissable Op. 76 No. 1. Version orch. Henri Büsser.

fp: 4 January 1925, Paris, Théâtre du Châtelet, Yvonne Gall and l'Orchestre Colonne, cond. Gabriel Pierné.

110. Arpège Op. 76 No. 2 (A. Samain). For voice and piano. 1897. Ded. Mme Charles Dettelbach.

fp: 30 April 1898, Paris, Thérèse Roger.

Pub. 1897, Hamelle; 1897, Metzler (Eng. version, Adela Maddison).

111. Papillon Op. 77. Pièce for cello and piano. 1897. Pub. 1898, Hamelle; also arr. for string quintet or violin and piano.

112. Sicilienne Op. 78. For cello and piano. March 1893. Pub. 1896, Metzler; Hamelle.

113. Fantaisie Op. 79. For flute and piano. 1898. Composed for examinations at the Paris Conservatoire. Ded. Paul Taffanel.

f public p: 5 January 1901, Paris, Philippe Gaubert, acc. Alfredo Casella.

?fEp: 30 November 1908, Manchester, Louis Fleury and Gabriel Fauré.

f London p: 5 December 1908, Louis Fleury.

Pub. 1898, Hamelle.

113a. Fantaisie Op. 79. Version orch. Louis Aubert. Pub. 1958, Hamelle.

114. Pelléas et Mélisande Op. 80. Incidental music for the play by Maurice Maeterlinck. 1898.

fp: 21 June 1898, London, Prince of Wales' Theatre, cond. Gabriel Fauré; with Mrs. Patrick Campbell (Mélisande), Forbes Robertson (Golaud), Martin Harvey (Pelléas), Georgina Thomas (Yniold), James Hearn (Arkel), Alexes Leighton (Queen); given in Eng. transl. by J. W. Mackail.

Unpub.

114a. Mélisande's song. From preceding. Dated: 31 May 1898. Pub. 1937, Hamelle.

114b. Pelléas et Mélisande: Suite Op. 80. Ded. Mme la Princesse Edmond de Polignac.

1. *Prélude*; 2. *La Fileuse*; 3. *Sicilienne*; 4. *La Mort de Mélisande*.

2 fl, 2 ob, 2 cl, 2 bsn; 4 hn, 2 tpt; timp; hps; strings.

fp: 3 February 1901, Paris, Concerts Lamoureux, cond. Camille Chevillard.

fEp: 18 September 1902, Queen's Hall, Promenade Concert, Queen's Hall Orchestra, cond. (Sir) Henry Wood.

fEbp: 1 July 1928, Cardiff, National Orchestra of Wales, cond. Warwick Braithwaite.

Pub. 1900, Hamelle: incl. reduction for piano solo or piano four hands. Various other arrangements exist, including some published in 1898–9 by Metzler, and a transcription of La Fileuse by Alfred Cortot which is designated in some lists as (Fauré's) Op. 81.

115. Prométhée Op. 82. Lyric Tragedy in three acts. 1900. Text: Jean Lorrain and A. Ferdinand Hérold. Ded. Castelbon de Beauxhostes.

fp: 26–27 August 1900, Béziers (Arènes); with Mme Fierens-Peters (Bia), Rose Feldy (Gaïa), Mlle Torrès (Aenoë), Valentin Duc (Kratos), Vallier (Héphaistos), Rousselière (Andros); spoken roles: Cora Laparcerie (Pandore), Odette de Fehl (Hermès), de Max (Prométhée).

Pub. Hamelle.

BIBLIOGRAPHY:

Paul Dukas: Prométhée, *Revue hebdomadaire*, 31 October 1900.

Charles Koechlin: Prométhée, *Mercure de France*, September 1901.

Jean Marnold: Prométhée, *Mercure de France*, 16 July 1917, p. 336.

115a. Les Préludes de Prométhée Op. 82. For orchestra, rev. D.-E. Inghelbrecht. Pub. 1955, Hamelle.

116. Pièces brèves Op. 84. For piano. 1898–1902. Ded. Mme Jean-Léonard Koechlin.

1. *Capriccio in E flat*; 2. *Fantaisie in A flat*; 3. *Fugue in A minor*; 4. *Adagietto in E minor*; 5. *Improvisation in C sharp minor*; 6. *Fugue in E minor*; 7. *Allégresse in C major*; 8. *Nocturne in D flat*.

Pub. Hamelle.

117. Cadenza. For Mozart's Piano Concerto K.491. Dated: 15 April 1902. Written for Mme Marguerite Hasselmans. Pub. Pierre Schneider.

118. Trois mélodies Op. 85. For voice and piano. 1902.

Fauré, Gabriel

1. *Dans la forêt de Septembre* (Catulle Mendès). Ded. Mlle Lydia Eustis.
2. *La fleur qui va sur l'eau* (Catulle Mendès). Ded. Mlle Pauline Segond.
3. *Accompagnement* (A. Samain). Ded. Mme Edouard Risler.
Pub. 1903, Hamelle.

119. Impromptu Op. 86. For harp. 1904. Ded. Alphonse Hasselmans.
fp: 7 January 1905, Paris, Micheline Kahn.
Pub. 1904, Durand.

119a. Impromptu No. 6 Op. 86 bis. For piano, after the Impromptu for harp. 1913.
Pub. 1913, Durand.

120. Le plus doux chemin Op. 87 No. 1 (Armand Silvestre). For voice and piano. 1904. Ded. Mme Edouard Risler. Pub. 1907, Hamelle.

121. Le Ramier Op. 87 No. 2 (Armand Silvestre). For voice and piano. 1904. Ded. Mlle Claudie Segond. Pub. 1904, Gramophone Co. (Italy) Ltd.; 1907, Hamelle.

122. Le Voile du bonheur Op. 88. Incidental music to a play by G. Clémenceau. 1901.
fp: 4 November 1901, Paris, Théâtre de la Renaissance.
Unpub.

123. Piano Quintet No. 1 in D minor Op. 89. 1903–6. Ded. Eugène Ysaÿe.
1. *Molto moderato*; 2. *Adagio*; 3. *Allegretto moderato*.
fEp: 21 March 1907, Aeolian Hall, Broadwood concert, Marguerite Long and the Capet Quartet.
Pub. 1907, Schirmer.

124. Barcarolle No. 7 in D minor Op. 90. For piano. August 1905. *Allegro moderato*. Ded. Mme I. Philipp. Pub. 1906, Heugel.

125. Impromptu No. 4 in D flat Op. 91. For piano. 1905. *Allegro non troppo*. Ded. Mme de Marliave (Marguerite Long). Pub. 1906, 1933, Heugel.

126. Le Don silencieux Op. 92 (Jean Dominique). For voice and piano. August 1906. Pub. 1906, Heugel.

127. Ave Maria Op. 93. Duet for two sopranos. 1876, rev. August 1906. Pub. 1906, Heugel.

128. Chanson Op. 94 (Henri de Régnier). For voice and piano. 1907. Pub. 1907, Heugel.

129. Vocalise. For voice (wordless) and piano. 1907. Pub. 1907, Heugel.

130. La Chanson d'Eve Op. 95 (Charles Van Lerberghe). Song cycle for voice and piano. 1906–10. Ded. Mme Jeanne Raunay.
1. *Paradis*; 2. *Prima verba*; 3. *Roses ardentes*; 4. *Comme Dieu rayonne*; 5. *L'aube blanche*; 6. *Eau vivante*; 7. *Veilles-tu, ma senteur de soleil?*; 8. *Dans un parfum de roses blanches*; 9. *Crépuscule*; 10. *O Mort, poussière d'étoiles.*
fEbp: 28 November 1935, Sophie Wyss.
Pub. 1907–10, Heugel.

BIBLIOGRAPHY:
Pierre Lalo: La Chanson d'Eve, *Le Temps*, 31 August 1910.

131. Barcarolle No. 8 in D flat Op. 96. For piano. 1908. *Allegretto moderato*. Ded. Mlle Suzanne Alfred-Bruneau. Pub. 1908, Heugel.

132. Nocturne No. 9 in B minor Op. 97. For piano. 1908. *Quasi adagio*. Ded. Mme Alfred Cortot. Pub. 1908, Heugel.

133. Sérénade Op. 98. For cello and piano. 1908. Ded. Pablo Casals. Pub. 1908, Heugel.

134. Nocturne No. 10 in E minor Op. 99. For piano. 1908. *Quasi adagio*. Ded. Mme Brunet-Lecomte. Pub. 1909, Heugel.

135. Barcarolle No. 9 in A minor Op. 101. For piano. 1910. *Andante moderato*. Ded. Mme Charles Neef. Pub. 1909. Transcription for cello and piano by Gustave Samazeuilh pub. 1948, Heugel.

136. Impromptu No. 5 in F sharp minor Op. 102. For piano. 1909. *Allegro vivo*. Ded. Mlle Cella Delavrancea. Pub. 1909, Heugel.

137. Neuf Préludes Op. 103. For piano. 1910. Ded. Mlle Elisabeth de Lallemand.
1. *Andante molto moderato* (D flat); 2. *Allegro* (C sharp minor); 3. *Andante* (G minor); 4. *Allegretto moderato* (F major); 5. *Allegro* (D minor); 6. *Andante* (E flat minor); 7. *Andante moderato* (A major); 8. *Allegro* (C minor); 9. *Adagio* (E minor).
Pub. 1910–11, Heugel.

138. Pénélope. Lyric Drama in three acts. 1913. Text: René Fauchois.

fp: 4 March 1913, Monte-Carlo, Opéra, cond. Léon Jehin; with Rousselière (Ulysse), Bourbon (Eumée), Ch. Delmas (Antinoüs), Allard (Eurymaque), Lucienne Bréval (Pénélope), Mme Raveau (Euryclée); décors, Visconti; costumes, Zamperoni.

fFp: 10 May 1913, Paris, Théâtre des Champs-Elysées, cond. Louis Hasselmans; with Muratore (Ulysse), P. Blancard (Eumée), Tirmont (Antinoüs), Dangès (Eurymaque), Lucienne Bréval (Pénélope), Cécile Thévenet (Euryclée); décors, X.-K. Roussel; costumes, H.-G. Ibels.

Pub. 1913, Heugel. *Prelude* arr. for piano, 1913, Durand.

BIBLIOGRAPHY:

Claude Avenaz: Pénélope, *Bulletin de la Semaine*, 14 May 1913.

Camille Bellaigue: A travers le répertoire lyrique: Pénélope, *Revue universelle*, 15 December 1928, p. 699.

Nadia Boulanger: Opéra de Monte-Carlo: Pénélope, *Le Ménestrel*, 15 March 1913, p. 82.

Claire Croiza: Pénélope de GF, *Le Monde musical*, 30 June 1934.

Philippe Fauré-Fremiet: La genèse de Pénélope, *RM*, May–June 1929, p. 53.

Armand Machebey: La Pénélope de GF à l'Opéra, *L'Information musicale*, 16 April 1943, p. 285.

Arthur Niesser: Pénélope, *Signale*, 1913, No. 11 (12 March), p. 399.

— Neue Opern in Monte Carlo, *NZfM*, 20 March 1913, p. 174.

Arthur Pougin: Théâtre des Champs-Elysées: Pénélope, *Le Ménestrel*, 17 May 1913, p. 154.

139. Nocturne No. 11 in F sharp minor Op. 104 No. 1. For piano. 1913. *Molto moderato*. Ded. in memory of Noémi Lalo. Pub. 1913, Durand.

140. Barcarolle No. 10 in A minor Op. 104 No. 2. For piano. 1913. *Allegretto moderato*. Ded. Mme Léon Blum. Pub. 1913, Durand.

141. Deux Barcarolles Op. 105. For piano. 1914–15.

1. *Barcarolle No. 11 in G. minor*. *Allegretto moderato*. Ded. Mlle Laura Albeniz.

2. *Barcarolle No. 12 in E flat* (orig. Op. 106 bis). *Allegretto giocoso*. Ded. Louis Diémer. Pub. 1914 (No. 1), 1916 (No. 2), Durand.

142. Le Jardin clos Op. 106 (Van Lerberghe). Song cycle for voice and piano. 1914–15.

1. *Exaucement*. Ded. Mme Albert Mockel.

2. *Quand tu plonges tes yeux dans mes yeux*. Ded. Mlle Germaine Sanderson.

3. *La messagère*. Ded. Mme Gabrielle Gills.

4. *Je me poserai sur ton cœur*. Ded. Mme. Louis Vuillemin.

5. *Dans la nymphée*. Ded. Mme Croiza.

6. *Dans la pénombre*. Ded. Mme Houben-Kufferath.

7. *Il m'est cher, amour*. Ded. Mme Faliero-Dalcroze.

8. *Inscription sur le sable*. Ded. Mme Durand-Texte.

fEbp: 29 November 1935, Sophie Wyss. Pub. 1915, Durand.

143. Nocturne No. 12 in E minor Op. 107. For piano. 1915. *Andante moderato*. Ded. Robert Lortat. Pub. 1916, Durand.

144. Violin Sonata No. 2 in E minor Op. 108. 1916.

1. *Allegro non troppo*; 2. *Andante*; 3. *Final: Allegro non troppo*.

Pub. 1917, Durand.

145. Cello Sonata No. 1 in D minor Op. 109. 1917. Ded. Louis Hasselmans.

1. *Allegro*; 2. *Andante*; 3. *Final: Allegro commodo*.

Pub. 1918, Durand.

146. Une Chatelaine en sa tour Op. 110. For harp. 1918. Ded. Micheline Kahn. Pub. 1918, Durand; also transcribed by Jacques Durand for piano solo.

147. Fantaisie in G major Op. 111. For piano and orchestra. 1919. Ded. Alfred Cortot.

2 fl, 2 ob, 2 cl, 2 bsn; 4 hn, tpt; timp; hp, strings.

fEp: 2 September 1920, Queen's Hall, Promenade Concert, Emma Barnett and the New Queen's Hall Orchestra, cond. Sir Henry Wood.

Pub. 1919, Durand.

148. Masques et Bergamasques. Divertissement. February–March 1919. Scenario: R. Fauchois.

Fauré, Gabriel

fp: April 1919, Monte Carlo, Opéra.
fFp: 4 March 1920, Paris, Opéra-Comique;
with Yvonne Brothier, Creus and Baugé.

148a. Masques et Bergamasques: Suite
Op. 112. For orchestra. Ded. Nicole and
Huguette Réveillac.
 1. *Ouverture*; 2. *Menuet*; 3. *Gavotte*;
4. *Pastorale*.
 2 fl, 2 ob, 2 cl, 2 bsn; 2 hn, 2 tpt; timp; hp,
strings.
 fp: 16 November 1919, Paris, Paris Conservatoire Orchestra, cond. Philippe Gaubert.
 fEp: 7 October 1920, Queen's Hall,
Promenade Concert, New Queen's Hall
Orchestra, cond. Sir Henry Wood.
 Pub. 1919, Durand.

149. Mirages Op. 113 (Baronne de Brimont).
Song cycle for voice and piano, July–August
1919. Ded. Mme Gabriel Hanotaux.
 1. *Cygne sur l'eau*; 2. *Reflets dans l'eau*;
3. *Jardin nocturne*; 4. *Danseuse*.
 fEbp: 29 November 1935, Sophie Wyss.
 Pub. 1919, Durand.

150. C'est la paix! Op. 114 (Mlle Georgette
Debladis). For voice and piano. December
1919. Pub. 1920, Durand.

151. Chant funéraire. Military music for
the centenary of the death of Napoleon.
February–March 1921.
 fp: 5 May 1921, Paris, Invalides.
 Unpub.

152. Piano Quintet No. 2 Op. 115. 1919–21.
Ded. Paul Dukas.
 1. *Allegro moderato*; 2. *Allegro vivo*;
3. *Andante moderato*; 4. *Allegro molto*.
 fp: 21 May 1921, Paris, Salle du Conservatoire, Société Nationale de Musique, Robert
Lortat, Tourret, Gentil, Vieux and Gérard
Hekking.
 fEp: 2 November 1921, Wigmore Hall,
Classical Concerts Society, Alfred Cortot and
the Allied String Quartet.
 Pub. 1921, Durand.

153. Barcarolle No. 13 in C major Op. 116.
For piano. February 1921. *Allegretto*. Ded.
Mme A. Soon Gumaelius. Pub. 1921, Durand.

154. Cello Sonata No. 2 in G minor Op.
117. 1921. Ded. Charles Martin Loeffler.
 1. *Allegro*; 2. *Andante*; 3. *Allegro vivo*.
 fp: 13 May 1922, Paris, Salle ancien Conservatoire, Société Nationale de Musique,
Gérard Hekking and Alfred Cortot.
 Pub. 1922, Durand.

155. L'Horizon chimérique Op. 118 (Jean
de la Ville de Mirmont). Song cycle. 1921.
Ded. Charles Panzéra.
 1. *La mer est infinie*; 2. *Je me suis embarqué*;
3. *Diane, Séléné*; 4. *Vaisseaux, nous vous aurons
aimés*.
 fp: 13 May 1922, Paris, Salle ancien
Conservatoire, Société Nationale de Musique,
Charles Panzéra.
 fEbp: 27 August 1933, Charles Panzéra.
 Pub. 1922, Durand.

156. Nocturne No. 13 in B minor Op. 119.
For piano. December 1921. *Andante*. Ded.
Mme Fernand Maillot. Pub. 1922, Durand.

157. Deux Noëls d'enfants. 'Cantiques
populaires' for solo voice and chorus with
organ or piano, harmonized by Gabriel
Fauré. ?Date.
 1. *Il est né, le divin Enfant*; 2. *Les Anges dans
les campagnes*.
 Pub. 1923, Hamelle.

158. Piano Trio Op. 120. 1922–3. Ded. Mme
Maurice Rouvier.
 1. *Allegro ma non troppo*; 2. *Andantino*;
3. *Allegro vivo*.
 fp: 12 May 1923, Paris, Société Nationale
de Musique, Tatiana Sanzewitch (piano),
Krettly and Patte.
 fEp: ?December 1923, St. John's Institute
(Westminster), Music Society concert.
 fEbp: 9 August 1927, Edgar L. Bainton,
Alfred M. Wall and Carl Fuchs.
 Pub. 1923, Durand.

159. String Quartet Op. 121. 1923–4.
Annecy-le-Vieux.
 1. *Molto moderato*; 2. *(unmarked)*; 3. *Allegro*.
 fp: June 1925, Paris, Vieille Salle du Conservatoire, Jacques Thibaud, Robert Krettly,
Maurice Vieux and André Hekking.
 fEp: 20 October 1925, Westminster, Music
Society concert, Mangeot String Quartet.

fEbp: 5 November 1928, Arts Theatre Club, Pro Arte Quartet.

Pub. 1925, Durand (fascimile of autograph).

BIBLIOGRAPHY:

Jean Chantavoine: Première audition de Quatuor à cordes posthume de GF, *Le Ménestrel*, 19 June 1925, p. 267.

E. Cools: Le Quatuor à cordes de GF, *Le Monde musical*, June 1925.

Alfred Cortot: La musique de chambre: Le Quatuor en sol de GF et le Concerto de Chausson, *Le Monde musical*, July 1938.

André Mangeot: Les Fantaisies d'Henry Purcell et le Quatuor de GF, *Le Monde musical*, October 1925.

WRITINGS BY FAURÉ

Lettre à propos de la réforme de la musique religieuse, *Le Monde musical*, 15 December 1903.

Critical writings, *Le Figaro*, 1903–14.

Joachim, *Musica*, April 1906.

Lucienne Bréval, Jeanne Raunay, *Musica*, January 1908.

Edouard Lalo, *Le Courrier musical*, 15 April 1908.

André Messager, *Musica*, September 1908.

Preface to 'Dogmes musicaux' by J. Huré, Editions du Monde musical (Paris) 1909.

Réponse à l'enquête sur la musique moderne italienne de L. Borgex, *Comoedia*, 31 January 1910.

Preface to 'Nouvelle Edition des œuvres classiques pour piano', Ricordi (Milan) 1910.

Preface to 'Décentralisation musicale' by Henri Auriol, *Comoedia*, 26 December 1912.

Preface to 'La Musique française d'aujourd'hui' by G. Jean-Aubry, Perrin (Paris) 1916.

Ariane et Barbe-Bleue, *Le Figaro*, 4 May 1921.

Les Troyens, *Le Figaro*, 9 June 1921.

Camille Saint-Saëns, *RM*, 1 February 1922.

Souvenirs, *RM*, 1 October 1922.

Hommage à Eugène Gigout, Floury (Paris) 1923.

Preface to 'Musique d'aujourd'hui' by E. Vuillermoz, Crès (Paris) 1923.

Preface to 'Les Quatuors de Beethoven' by J. De Marliave, Alcan (Paris) 1925.

Opinions musicales (ed. P. B. Gheusi), Rieder (Paris) 1930.

Lettres à une fiancée (1877) (ed. Camille Bellaigue), *Revue des deux mondes*, 15 August 1928.

Lettres intimes (1885–1924) (ed. Ph. Fauré-Fremiet), La Colombe (Paris) 1951.

GENERAL BIBLIOGRAPHY

L. Aguettant: Les mélodies de GF, *Le Courrier musical*, 1 February 1903.

— GF, Lyon, 1924.

Alex van Amerongen: Brieven van GF, *Mens en melodie*, April 1951, p. 115.

Felix Aprahamian: The chamber music of GF, *The Listener*, 18 April 1963, p. 692.

Louis Aubert: GF et ses mélodies, *Radio Magazine*, 22 May 1938.

— Fauré, in *Les Musiciens célèbres*, Editions d'Art Lucien Mazenod (Geneva) 1948, p. 274.

Jane Bathori: Les musiciens que j'ai connu, 1: Roussel, Fauré, Hahn, Chabrier, Ravel, *Recorded Sound*, winter 1961–2, p. 144.

Camille Bellaigue: GF, *Revue hebdomadaire*, 7 March 1925.

— Lettres à une fiancée: GF et Marianne Viardot, *Revue des deux mondes*, August 1928.

Walter Bertschinger: GF, *SM*, September 1954, p. 363.

Maurice Bex: GF, *Revue hebdomadaire*, 15 November 1924, p. 351.

Adolphe Boschot: GF, compositions pour piano, *Le Ménestrel*, 11 April 1924, p. 167.

— Figures de musiciens: GF, *Revue politique et littéraire* (Revue bleue), 1924, p. 808.

Nadia Boulanger: La musique religieuse, *RM*, October 1922, p. 296.

Alfred Bruneau: La vie et les œuvres de GF, Paris, 1925.

José Bruyr: En parlant de GF avec son fils, *Le Guide du Concert*, 11, 18 and 25 March and 1, 8 and 22 April 1938.

M.-D. Calvocoressi: GF, in *Musicians Gallery*, Faber (London) 1933, p. 132.

Gaston Carraud: GF, *Le Ménestrel*, 9 April 1920, p. 149.

Alfredo Casella: GF, *Il Pianoforte*, December 1924.

Jean Chantavoine: L'hommage national à GF, *Le Ménestrel*, 16 June 1922, p. 265.

— GF, *Le Ménestrel*, 14 November 1924, p. 469.

Fauré, Gabriel

André Coeuroy: GF, in *La Musique française moderne*, Librairie Delagrave (Paris) 1922, p. 21.

— GF, *Revue universelle*, 1 December 1924, p. 631.

— GF (transl. Rita Boetticher), *Die Musik*, January 1925, p. 363.

— GF, *Muzika* (Riga), January 1925.

— Fauré–Caplet–Satie, *Anbruch*, 1925, No. 7, p. 430.

— GF, *Sackbut*, March 1925, p. 235.

— GF, *Larousse mensuel*, February 1925.

Martin Cooper: Some aspects of Fauré's technique, *MMR*, May 1945, p. 75.

— The operas of GF, *MMR*, 1947, p. 32.

Aaron Copland: GF, a neglected master, *MQ*, October 1924, p. 573.

A. della Corte: Le vacanze di Fauré, *La Scala*, May 1957.

Alfred Cortot: La musique de piano, *RM*, October 1922, p. 272.

— The piano music of GF, in *French Piano Music*, O.U.P. (London) 1932, p. 109.

F. Crucy: GF, *Le Petit Parisien*, 28 April 1922.

Laurence Davies: GF, Orpheus of French song, in *The Gallic Muse*, Dent (London) 1967, p. 1.

Norman Demuth: GF, *MO*, February 1948, p. 165.

Leonard Duck: Fauré, the gentle revolutionary, *Halle*, November 1956, p. 1.

Norbert Dufourcq: GF, in *La Musique française*, Librairie Larousse (Paris) 1949, p. 277.

René Dumesnil: GF, in *Portraits de musiciens français*, Librairie Plon (Paris) 1938, p. 77.

Philippe Fauré-Fremiet: GF, Les Editions Rieder (Paris) 1929.

— GF, *Le Monde musical*, May 1929.

— La musique de chambre de GF, *Le Monde musical*, 30 June 1930.

— GF, in *MGG*, Vol. 3 (1954), p. 1868.

Georges Favre: GF, *Bulletin mensuel de l'Union Française des Oeuvres Laïques d'Education Artistique* (Paris), January 1950.

Max Favre: GFs Kammermusik, Max Niehans Verlag (Zürich), 1949.

Hans Gal (ed.): GF, in *Great Composers in their Letters*, Thames & Hudson (London) 1965, p. 397.

André George: GF *Les Nouvelles littéraires*, 7 May 1938.

P. B. Gheusi: Les quatre printemps de GF, *Le Figaro*, 12 May 1924.

Hugues Imbert: GF, *L'Indépendance musicale et dramatique*, September–October 1887.

— GF, in *Profils du musiciens*, Fischbacher (Paris) 1888.

Vladimir Jankélevitch: GF et ses mélodies, Librairie Plon (Paris) 1938.

Robert Jardillier: La jeunesse de GF, *L'Art musical*, 5 May 1939.

G. Jean-Aubry: GF, in *La Musique française d'aujourd'hui*, Perrin (Paris) 1916, p. 72.

Tristan Klingsor: Musiciens et poètes contemporains, *Mercure de France*, November 1900.

Charles Koechlin: GF, *Le Ménestrel*, 1921, 27 May p. 221, 3 June p. 233.

— Le Théâtre, *RM*, October 1922, p. 226.

— GF, Félix Alcan (Paris) 1927.

Pierre Lalo: Le théâtre lyrique de GF, in *De Rameau à Ravel*, Editions Albin Michel (Paris) 1947, p. 350.

Paul Landormy: GF, *MQ*, July 1931, p. 293.

— GF et ses mélodies, *Le Ménestrel*, 1938, 10–17 June p. 161, 24 June p. 169.

— GF, in *La Musique française après Debussy*, Gallimard (Paris) 1943, p. 11.

W.-L. Landowski: Frédéric Chopin et GF, Richard-Masse (Paris) 1946.

Tristan Leclère: Les musiciens de Verlaine, *Revue bleue*, 14 November 1908.

Edward Lockspeiser: Fauré and the Song, *MMR*, May 1945, p. 79.

— GF et Marcel Proust, *The Listener*, 1 June 1961, p. 985; in *Essays on Music*, Cassell (London) 1967, p. 107.

Marguerite Long: Au piano avec GF, René Julliard (Paris) 1963.

André Mangeot: Hommage à Fauré, *Le Monde musical*, November 1924.

Jean Marnold: GF, *Mercure de France*, No. 635, 1 December 1924, p. 499.

Jean Matter: Brahms et Fauré, *SM*, February 1959, p. 58.

Wilfrid Mellers: Two traditionalists: Fauré and Strauss, in *Man and his Music*, Barrie & Rockliff (London) 1962, p. 952.

— The later work of GF, in *Studies in*

Contemporary Music, Dobson (London) 1947, p. 56.

Darius Milhaud: Hommage à Fauré, *Intentions*, January 1923.

Philip Miller: The importance of GF, *American Music Lover*, December 1936.

Bayan Northcott: Fauré our contemporary, *M&M*, April 1970, p. 32.

Leslie Orrey: GF, the songs, *MO*, April 1945, p. 197.

— GF, the chamber music, *MO*, May 1945, p. 229.

— The songs of GF, *MR*, May 1945.

— GF, *MT*, May 1945, p. 137.

D. C. Parker: GF, a contemporary study, *MMR*, 1918, p. 225.

J. C. Piguet: Brahms et Fauré, *Revue belge de musicologie*, 1951, No. 4 (April), p. 143.

Maurice Ravel: Les mélodies de GF, *RM*, October 1922, p. 214.

Roger-Ducasse: La musique de chambre, *RM*, October 1922, p. 252.

Roland-Manuel: L'heritage de GF, *Revue Pleyel*, November 1924.

Fred Rothwell: GF, *MO*, December 1924, p. 280.

Claude Rostand: L'œuvre de GF, Paris, 1947; also in Ger. transl. by Alfred Brockhaus as GF und sein Werk.

Alec Rowley: The pianoforte music of GF, *Chesterian*, No. 96, July 1931,

Gustave Samazeuilh: La leçon de l'art de GF, in *Musiciens de mon temps*, Editions Marcel Daubin (Paris) 1947, p. 56.

J. P. Sarraute: Reflexões sobre a arte GF, *Gazeta de todas as artes*, No. 93, December 1958.

Georges Servières: Les mélodies récentes de GF, in *Guide musical*, 28 January 1898.

— Lieder français: GF, *Guide musical*, 3–10 August 1913.

— GF, Henri Laurens (Paris) 1930.

Florent Schmitt: Les œuvres d'orchestre, *RM*, October 1922, p. 242.

— GF, *Chesterian*, No. 43, December 1924.

Speculum: Fauré, *La Rassegna musicale*, 1938, p. 293.

Alexander Spitzmüller-Harmersbach: Streit um Fauré, *Anbruch*, September–October 1935, p. 255.

H. H. Stuckenschmidt: GF, *Melos*, 1947, No. 12 (October), p. 326.

Norman Suckling: Homage to GF, *MMR*, 1944, p. 124.

— The songs of Fauré, *The Listener*, 15 March 1945.

— Fauré the unknown, *MMR*, May 1945, p. 84.

— GF, classic of modern times, *MR*, May 1945.

— Fauré in the theatre, in *Essays on Music*, Cassell (London) 1967, p. 107.

R. D. Symes: An introduction to GF, *MM&F*, September 1932.

A. Tanner: Remarques sur Fauré à propos de ses deux sonates de violon, *Schweizer. Musikpäd. Blätter*, 1937, pp. 203, 219, 235.

Lotte Taube: GF, ein französischer Musikpoet, *Deutsche Rundschau*, 1947, No. 4, p. 25.

Louis Thomas: Images d'enfants par GF, *Bulletin de la S.I.M.*, 1909, No. 5.

Julien Tiersot: GF et l'école de Saint-Saëns, in *Un demi-siècle de musique française*, Felix Alcan (Paris) 1918.

Mac Ulpem: GF, *Gaceta musical*, September 1928.

L. Vuillermin: GF, sa vie et son œuvre, Durand (Paris) 1914.

Emile Vuillermoz: GF, *Revue illustrée*, 1 July 1905.

— GF, *Le Courrier musical*, 1 June 1906.

— GF, *Excelsior*, November 1924.

— GF, *Revue Rhénane*, December 1924.

— GF, Flammarion (Paris) 1960.

E. Wieniawski: GF, *Mouzyka*, No. 1, 1924.

MISCELLANEOUS OR UNSIGNED

GF, critique musical, *Le Monde musical*, November 1924.

GF, *Nouvelle revue musicale*, October–November 1924.

GF, *Bollettino bibliografico musicale*, March 1930, p. 5.

PAUL HINDEMITH (1895–1963)

Of Silesian blood, Paul Hindemith was born on 16 November 1895 at Hanau, near Frankfurt am Main. He showed his gifts and his independence early, leaving home at the age of eleven because his parents objected to his musical ambitions and supporting himself for several years as a performer in dance-bands and musical-comedy orchestras while he studied violin, conducting and composition at the Hoch Conservatory in Frankfurt. He was leader of the Frankfurt Opera Orchestra from 1915 to 1923 (apart from a year in the German Army, 1917–18) and in 1924 married Gertrud Rottenberg, the daughter of the orchestra's conductor. He also played second violin and later viola in the Rebner Quartet (1915–21) and in 1922, with his Hungarian friend Licco Amar, founded the Amar Quartet, playing the viola with this group until 1929 and touring Europe extensively with programmes which placed a special emphasis on modern music. From 1921 until 1930 he was involved in the running of the contemporary music festivals at Donaueschingen, Baden-Baden and Berlin and was also closely associated with the early festivals of the ISCM. In 1927 he settled in Berlin, where he had been appointed Professor of Composition at the Staatliche Musikhochschule; but his work there was hindered in the mid-1930s when, in spite of protests from the influential conductor Wilhelm Furtwängler, the Nazis banned his music as 'cultural Bolshevism'. Hindemith's ideas about teaching and the organization of musical life were more welcome in Turkey, and he visited Ankara several times between 1934 and 1937 at the request of the Turkish Government to put them into effect. He was also active as a soloist on viola and viola d'amore throughout the thirties, making three tours in the USA between 1937 and 1939. He left Berlin in 1938 and, after living for a while at Sion in Switzerland, made a new home in America in the spring of 1940, teaching that summer at the Berkshire Music Centre (Tanglewood, Mass.) and then going to Yale University as Professor of the Theory of Music, a post which he held until 1953. He became an American citizen in 1946 and gave the Charles Eliot Norton lectures (*A Composer's World*) at Harvard University in 1949–1950. In the late 1940s he conducted several concerts in Europe, including one in Berlin in February 1949 which marked the end of his musical exile. In 1953 he returned to Europe permanently, living in Zürich (where he

joined the faculty of the University) and increasing his activities as an orchestral conductor. He died of a disease of the circulation at Frankfurt in December 1963.

CATALOGUE OF WORKS

1. Andante and Scherzo Op. 1. For clarinet, horn and piano. 1914. Unpub.

2. String Quartet in C major Op. 2. 1915. Unpub.

3. Cello Concerto in E flat Op. 3. 1916. Unpub.

4. Lustige Sinfonietta Op. 4. For small orchestra. 1916. Unpub.

5. Lieder in Aargauer Mundart Op. 5. For voice and piano. 1916. Unpub.

6. Sieben Walzer Op. 6. For piano four hands. 1916. Unpub.

7. Piano Quintet in E minor Op. 7. 1917. Unpub.

8. Drei Stücke Op. 8. For cello and piano. Pub. 1917, Breitkopf & Härtel.

9. Drei Lieder Op. 9. For soprano and large orchestra. 1917. Unpub.

10. String Quartet No. 1 in F minor Op. 10. 1919 (?1918). Ded. Rudolf and Emma Ronnefeldt. Dur. 28½′.

1. *Sehr lebhaft, straff im Rhythmus*; 2. *Thema mit Variationen*; 3. *Finale: Sehr lebhaft*.

fp: 2 June 1919, Frankfurt a.M., Rebner Quartet.

fEbp: 28 October 1930, Weis Quartet.

Pub. 1919, Schott; incl. study score.

11. Violin Sonata in E flat Op. 11 No. 1. 1918. Dur. 9′.

1. *Frisch*; 2. *Im Zeitmass eines langsamen, feierlichen Tanzes*.

fp: 2 June 1919, Frankfurt a.M., Paul Hindemith and Emma Lübbecke-Job.

fEbp: 31 May 1930, Adila Fachiri and Donald F. Tovey.

Pub. 1920, Schott.

12. Violin Sonata in D Op. 11 No. 2. 1918. Ded. Abdul and Olly Linder. Dur. 17–18′.

1. *Lebhaft*; 2. *Ruhig und gemessen*; 3. *Im Zeitmass und Charakter eines geschwinden Tanzes*.

fp: 10 April 1920, Frankfurt a.M., Max Strub and Eduard Zuckmayer.

fEp: 29 June 1923, Steinway Hall, Jessie Munro and Erna Schulz.

fEbp: 5 August 1931, Adila Fachiri and Kathleen Long.
Pub. 1920, Schott.

13. Cello Sonata Op. 11 No. 3. 1919. Dur. 22'.
1. *Mässig schnelle Viertel—Lebhaft*; 2. *Langsam—Sehr lebhaft*.
fp: 27 October 1919, Frankfurt a.M., Maurits Frank and Emma Lübbecke-Job.
fFp: 29 November 1922, Paris, Alexanian (cello) and Andrée Vaurabourg.
Pub. 1922, Schott.

14. Viola Sonata in F Op. 11 No. 4. 1919. Dur. 16'.
1. *Fantasie (Ruhig)*; 2. *Thema mit Variationen*; 3. *Finale (mit Variationen)*.
fp: 2 June 1919, Frankfurt a.M., Paul Hindemith and Emma Lübbecke-Job.
Pub. 1922, Schott.

15. Sonata for unaccompanied viola Op. 11 No. 5. 1919. Ded. Karl Schmidt. Dur. 13'.
1. *Lebhaft, aber nicht geeilt*; 2. *Mässig schnell, mit viel Wärme vortragen*; 3. *Scherzo (schnell)*; 4. *In Form und Zeitmass einer Passacaglia*.
fp: 14 November 1920, Friedburg, Paul Hindemith.
fEbp: 7 January 1957, Kenneth Essex.
Pub. 1923, Schott.

16. Mörder, Hoffnung der Frauen Op. 12. Opera in one act. 1919. Libretto: Oskar Kokoschka. Dur. 21'.
3 fl, pic, 2 ob, ca, 2 cl, bcl, 2 bsn, cbsn; 6 hn, 4 tpt, 3 tmb, bs tuba; timp, side dm, parade dm, tgle, tamtam, cym, GC; strings.
fp: 4 June 1921, Stuttgart, Landestheater, cond. Fritz Busch.
Pub. 1921, Schott: piano score by Hermann Uhticke.

BIBLIOGRAPHY:
W. Nagel: PH—Mörder, Hoffnung der Frauen—Das Nusch-Nuschi—Zwei Opern-Einakter, *NMZ*, 1921, No. 19, p. 300.

17. Lieder (Acht Lieder nach verschiedenen Dichten) Op. 18. For soprano and piano. 1920. Ded. Nora Pisling-Boas.
1. *Die trunkene Tänzerin* (Curt Bock). Dur. 1½'.

2. *Wie Sankt Franciscus schweb'ich in der Luft* (Christian Morgenstern). Dur. 1¼'.
3. *Traum* ('Der Schlaf entführte mich') (Else Lasker-Schüler). Dur. 2½'.
4. *Auf der Treppe sitzen meine Öhrchen* (Christian Morgenstern). Dur. ¾'.
5. *Vor dir schein' ich aufgewacht* (Christian Morgenstern). Dur. 1'.
6. *Du machst mich traurig—hör'* ('Bin so müde') (Else Lasker-Schüler). Dur. 2'.
7. *Durch die abendlichen Gärten* (Heinar Schilling). Dur. 2'.
8. *Trompeten* ('Unter verschnittenen Weiden') (Georg Trakl). Dur. 3'.
fp: 25 January 1922, Berlin, Nora Pisling-Boas, acc. Felix Petyrek.
fEbp (Nos. 2, 3, 5 & 8): 23 March 1930, John Armstrong.
Pub. 1922, Schott.

18. Das Nusch-Nuschi Op. 20. Play for Burmese marionettes in one act. 1920. Libretto: Franz Blei. Dur. 30'.
2 fl, 2 pic, 2 ob, ca, E-flat cl, 2 cl, bcl, 2 bsn, cbsn; 2 hn, 2 tpt, 3 tmb, bs tuba; hp, celesta, mandoline, 2 timp, side dm, parade dm, GC & cym, cym, large gong, tgle, tamb, Ratsche, Rute, xyl, glock, bells; strings.
fp: 4 June 1921, Stuttgart, Landestheater, cond. Fritz Busch.
Pub. 1921, Schott; incl. full score (autograph facsimile) and piano score by Reinhold Ewald.

18a. Das Nusch-Nuschi Op. 20. Dance Suite for orchestra. Dur. 8½'.
2 fl, 2 pic, 2 ob, ca, E-flat cl, 2 cl, bcl, 2 bsn, cbsn; 2 hn, 2 tpt, 3 tmb, bs tuba; 3 pcssn; hp, celesta, strings.
fEp: 13 October 1923, Queen's Hall, New Queen's Hall Orchestra, cond. Sir Henry Wood.
Pub. Schott; also for piano four hands by Reinhold Merten.

19. String Quartet No. 2 in C major Op. 16. 1921. Ded. to the composer's brother Rudolf. Dur. 26'.
1. *Lebhaft und sehr energisch*; 2. *Sehr langsam*; 3. *Finale (Ausserst lebhaft)*.
fp: 1 August 1921, Donaueschingen, Amar Quartet.
fEp: March 1923, London (6 Queen

Hindemith, Paul

Square), British Music Society concert, Mandeville Quartet.

Pub. 1922, Schott.

20. Sancta Susanna Op. 21. Opera in one act. 1921. Libretto: August Stramm. Dur. 40'.

3 fl, 3 pic, 2 ob, ca, E-flat cl, 2 cl, bcl, 2 bsn, cbsn; 4 hn, 2 tpt, 3 tmb, bs tuba; timp, tgle, side dm, cym, GC, gong, xyl, glock; hp, celesta, organ, strings.

fp: 26 March 1922, Frankfurt a.M., Opernhaus, cond. Ludwig Rottenberg.

Pub. 1921, Schott: piano score and study score.

BIBLIOGRAPHY:

S. Günther: PH's Sancta Susanna, *Melos*, December 1924, p. 250.

Hans F. Schaub: Hindemiths Sancta Susanna in Hamburg, *AMZ*, 1923, Nos. 22–23, p. 385.

21. Kammermusik No. 1 Op. 24 No. 1. For small orchestra. 1921. Ded. Prince von Fürstenberg. Dur. 14$\frac{1}{2}$'.

1. *Sehr schnell und wild*; 2. *Mässig schnelle Halbe*; 3. *Quartett: Sehr langsam und mit Ausdruck*; 4. *Finale: 1921 (Äusserst lebhaft)*.

fl, cl, bsn; tpt, xyl, side dm, wooden dm, small cym, tamb, tgle, tin sheet & sand, siren, glock; hmnm, piano, string quintet.

fp: 31 July 1922, Donaueschingen, cond. Hermann Scherchen.

fEbp: 30 May 1933, BBC Orchestra, cond. Edward Clark.

Pub. 1922, Schott: study score.

22. Tanzstücke Op. 19. For piano. 1922. Dur. 12'.

1. *Mässig schnell*; 2. *Sehr lebhaft*; 3. *Mässig schnell*; 4. *Pantomime*; 5. *Sehr lebhaft*.

fp: 22 September 1924, Dresden, Paul Aron.

Pub. 1928, Schott.

23. String Quartet No. 3 Op. 22. 1922. Dur. 22–24$\frac{1}{2}$'.

1. *Fugato (Sehr langsame Viertel)*; 2. *Schnelle Achtel, sehr energisch*; 3. *Ruhige Viertel, stets fliessend*; 4. *Mässig schnelle Viertel*; 5. *Rondo (Gemächlich und mit Grazie)*.

fp: 4 November 1922, Donaueschingen, Amar Quartet.

fEp: 7 December 1926, Grotrian Hall, BBC chamber concert, Amar Quartet.

fParis p: 12 December 1932, Société Musicale Indépendante concert, Pro Arte Quartet.

Pub. 1923, Schott: study score and parts.

24. Tuttifäntchen. Christmas Fairytale in three scenes, with song and dance. 1922. Text: Hedwig Michel and Franziska Becker.

fl, ob, cl, bsn; hn, tpt; timp, pcssn; strings.

fp: 13 December 1922, Darmstadt, cond. Walter Beck.

Pub. ?1922, Schott. Also 'Tanz der Holzpuppen' ('Dance of the wooden dolls'), Foxtrot for piano, pub. 1922.

25. Des Todes Tod Op. 23a. Three songs for female voice, two violas and two cellos. 1922. Text: Eduard Reinacher. Dur. 16'.

1. *Gesicht von Tod und Elend*; 2. *Gottes Tod*; 3. *Des Todes Tod*.

Pub. 1953, Schott: score, and reduction by Paul Hindemith for voice and piano.

26. Die junge Magd Op. 23 No. 2 (Georg Trakl). Six songs for alto voice, flute, clarinet and string quartet. 1922. Dur. 20'.

1. *Oft am Brunnen*; 2. *Stille schafft sie in der Kammer*; 3. *Nächtens übern kahlen Anger*; 4. *In der Schmiede dröhnt der Hammer*; 5. *Schmächtig hingestreckt im Bette*; 6. *Abends schweben blutige Linnen*.

fp: 31 July 1922, Donaueschingen, Tini Debüser.

fEp: 14 April 1945, Wigmore Hall, Hilda Alexander with John Francis (fl), Eileen Tranmare (cl) and string quartet led by Susan Rozsa.

Pub. 1922, Schott: score, and reduction by Paul Hindemith.

27. Kleine Kammermusik Op. 24 No. 2. For flute, oboe, clarinet, horn and bassoon. 1922. Ded. Die Frankfurter Bläser-Kammermusikvereinigung. Dur. 11$\frac{1}{2}$'.

1. *Lustig, mässig schnelle Viertel*; 2. *Walzer (Durchweg sehr leise)*; 3. *Ruhig und einfach, Achtel*; 4. *Schnelle Viertel*; 5. *Sehr lebhaft*.

fp: 12 July 1922, Frankfurt a.M., Bläser-Kammermusikvereinigung.

fEbp: 6 November 1925, Newcastle station, E. J. Bell, Alfred Smith, Robert Baulks, William Boyce and Stanley Styles.

Pub. Schott: study score and parts.

28. Sonata for unaccompanied viola Op. 25 No. 1. 1922. Ded. Ladislav Černy. Dur. 10'.
1. *Breite Viertel*; 2. *Sehr frisch und straff*; 3. *Sehr langsam*; 4. *Rasendes Zeitmass, wild, Tonschönheit ist Niebensache*; 5. *Langsam, mit viel Ausdruck*.
fp: 18 March 1922, Cologne, Paul Hindemith.
fEp: 3 April 1929, Arts Theatre Club, BBC concert of modern chamber music, Paul Hindemith.
Pub. Schott.

29. Suite: '1922' Op. 26. For piano. 1922. Dur. 14'.
1. *Marsch*; 2. *Shimmy*; 3. *Nachstück*; 4. *Boston*; 5. *Ragtime*.
Pub. 1922, Schott.

30. Kleine Sonate Op. 25 No. 2. For viola d'amore and piano. 1923. Dur. 12'.
1. *Mässig schnell, lustig*; 2. *Sehr langsam*; 3. *Sehr lebhaft*.
fp: June 1922, Heidelberg, Paul Hindemith and Emma Lübbecke-Job.
fEp: 7 October 1929, Arts Theatre Club, BBC concert of modern chamber music, Paul Hindemith and Emma Lübbecke-Job.
Pub. 1929, Schott.

31. Sonata for unaccompanied cello Op. 25 No. 3. 1923. Ded. Maurits Frank. Dur. 7½'.
1. *Lebhaft, sehr markiert*; 2. *Mässig schnell, gemächlich*; 3. *Langsam*; 4. *Lebhafte Viertel*; 5. *Mässig schnell*.
fp: 1923, Freiburg, Maurits Frank.
Pub. 1923, Schott.

32. Das Marienleben Op. 27 (Rainer Maria Rilke). For soprano and piano. 1922–3. Dur. 60–63'.
I. a. *Geburt Mariä*; b. *Die Darstellung Mariä im Tempel*; c. *Mariä Verkündigung*; d. *Mariä Heimsuchung*.
II. a. *Argwohn Josephs*; b. *Verkündigung über die Hirten*; c. *Geburt Christi*; d. *Rast auf der Flucht nach Ägypten*.
III. a. *Vor der Hochzeit zu Kana*; b. *Von der Passion*; c. *Pietà*; d. *Stillung Mariä mit dem Auferstandenen*.
IV. a. *Vom Tode Mariä I*; b. *Vom Tode Mariä II* (*Thema mit Variationen*); c. *Vom Tode Mariä III*.
fp: 15 October 1923, Frankfurt a.M., Beatrice Lauer-Kottlar, acc. Emma Lübbecke-Job.
f Paris p: 22 February 1933, Société Musicale Indépendante concert, Mme Modrakowska.
Pub. 1924, Schott.

32a. Das Marienleben Op. 27. New version. 1936–48. Foreword dated: June 1948, New Haven, Conn. Dur. 69'.
Titles renumbered 1–15; otherwise as in original version except for the following minor revisions: 6. *Verkündigung über den Hirten*; 8. *Rast auf der Flucht in Ägypten*.
fp: 3 November 1948, Hannover, Annelies Kupper, acc. Carl Seemann.
fGBp: 31 August 1950, Edinburgh Festival, Freemasons' Hall, Jennie Tourel, acc. George Reeves.
Pub. 1948, Schott.

32b. Das Marienleben Op. 27. Revised version for soprano and orchestra. 1938–48. Dur. 22–23'.
1. *Geburt Mariä*; 2. *Argwohn Josephs*; 3. *Geburt Christi*; 4. *Rast auf der Flucht in Ägypten*; 5. *Vor der Passion*; 6. *Vom Tode Mariä III*.
2 fl, 2 ob, 3 cl, 2 bsn; 2 hn, 2 tpt, 2 tmb; timp, pcssn; strings.
fp (Nos. 1–4): 13 August 1939, Scheveningen, Henrietta Sala.
fp (Nos. 5–6): 21 September 1959, Copenhagen, Bonna Söndberg.
Pub. Schott; incl. reduction by Paul Hindemith for voice and piano.

BIBLIOGRAPHY:
A. Berger: Spotlight on the moderns: revision of Marienleben, *Saturday Review of Literature*, 27 January 1951, p. 56.
Hans-Werner Henze: Das neue Marienleben, *Melos*, March 1949, p. 75.
Paul Hindemith: Das Marienleben, *Melos*, December 1948, p. 321.
Rudolf Klein: Von Hindemith zu Hindemith —Bemerkungen zu den beiden Fassungen des Marienlebens, *ÖM*, February 1964.
Erich Limmert: Neufassung des Marienlebens in Hannover, *Melos*, December 1948, p. 340.
Wouter Paap: Das Marienleben van PH, *Mens en melodie*, June–July 1949, p. 177.

Hindemith, Paul

Franz Reizenstein: Hindemith's Marienleben, *The Listener*, 17 September 1964, p. 445.

Hans Ludwig Schilling: Hindemith's Passacagliathemen in den beiden Marienleben, *Melos*, April 1956, p. 106.

Rudolf Stepan: Hindemiths Marienleben, *MR*, November 1954, p. 275.

G. Turchi: Breve storia segreta di Das Marienleben, *Rivista musicale italiana*, 1955, No. 2.

33. Der Dämon Op. 28. Dance-pantomime in two scenes by Max Krell. 1922. Dur. 34'.

I. 1. *Tanz des Dämons*; 2. *Tanz der bunten Bänder*; 3. *Tanz der geängsteten Schwalben*; 4. *Tanz des Giftes*; 5. *Tanz der Schmerzen*; 6. *Tanz des Dämons (Passacaglia)*; 7. *Tanz der Trauer und der Sehnsucht*.

II. 1. *Einleitung*; 2. *Vier Tänze des Werbens*; 3. *Tanz der Brutalität*; 4. *Tanz des geschlagenen Tieres*; 5. *Finale: Tanz des Dämons*.

fl, pic, cl, hn; tpt; piano, string quintet.

fp: 1 December 1923, Darmstadt, Landestheater, cond. Josef Rosenstock.

Pub. 1924, Schott: piano score by Hermann Uhticke.

33a. Der Dämon Op. 28. Concert Suite for small orchestra. Dur. 25'.

fl, cl; hn, tpt; piano, string quintet.

Pub. Schott: piano score.

34. Clarinet Quintet Op. 30. 1923. Ded· Werner Reinhart. Dur. 18'.

1. *Sehr lebhaft*; 2. *Ruhig*; 3. *Schneller Ländler*; 4. *Arioso: sehr ruhig*; 5. *Sehr lebhaft*.

fp: 7 August 1923, Salzburg, Philipp Dreisbach and the Amar Quartet.

fEbp: 22 March 1956, Jack Brymer and the Hirsch Quartet.

Pub. 1955, Schott: study score and parts.

35. String Quartet No. 4 Op. 32. 1923. Ded. Beatrice Sutter-Kottlar. Dur. 23–24'.

1. *Lebhafte Halbe*; 2. *Sehr langsam, aber immer fliessend*; 3. *Kleiner Marsch* (*Vivace, sempre crescendo*); 4. *Passacaglia*.

fp: 5 November 1923, Vienna, Amar Quartet.

f London p (?fEp): 4 December 1928, Wigmore Hall, Pro Arte Quartet.

Pub. 1924, Schott.

36. Lieder nach alten Texten Op. 33. For mixed chorus a cappella. 1923.

1. *Vom Hausregiment* (Martin Luther). SSATBarB. Dur. $1\frac{1}{2}$–$1\frac{3}{4}'$.

2. *Frauenklage* (Burggraf zu Regensburg). SSATB. Dur $1\frac{1}{2}'$.

3. *Art lässt nicht von Art* (Spervogel). SATB. Dur. $\frac{3}{4}'$.

4. *Der Liebe Schrein* (Heinrich von Morungen). SSATB. Dur. $\frac{1}{2}$–$\frac{3}{4}'$.

5. *Heimliches Glück* (Reinmar). SSATBarB. Dur. $1\frac{1}{2}'$.

6. *Landesknecktstrinklied*. SSATBarB. Dur. $1\frac{1}{2}'$.

fp: 26 July 1925, Donaueschingen, Stuttgarter Madrigalvereinigung.

?fEbp: 23 September 1951, Wiener Akademie-Kammerchor, cond. Ferdinand Grossmann.

Pub. 1925, Schott, as Liederbuch für mehrere Singstimmen (Book 1).

37. Sonata for unaccompanied violin Op. 31 No. 1. 1924. Ded. Licco Amar. Dur. 10'.

1. *Sehr lebhafte Achtel*; 2. *Sehr langsame Viertel*; 3. *Sehr lebhafte Viertel*; 4. *Intermezzo: Lied*; 5. *Prestissimo*.

fp: 18 May 1924, Donaueschingen, Licco Amar.

Pub. Schott.

38. Sonata for unaccompanied violin Op. 31 No. 2. 1924. Ded. Walter Caspar. Dur. 7'.

1. *Leicht bewegte Viertel*; 2. *Ruhig bewegte Achtel*; 3. *Gemächliche Viertel* (*pizzicato*); 4. *Fünf Variationen über das Lied 'Komm, lieber Mai' von Mozart*.

Pub. Schott.

39. Kanonische Sonatine Op. 31 No. 3. For two flutes. 1924. Ded. Paul Hagemann.

1. *Munter*; 2. *Capriccio*; 3. *Presto*.

Pub. 1924, Schott.

40. Kammermusik No. 2 (Piano Concerto) Op. 36 No. 1. For obbligato piano and twelve instruments. Ded. Emma Lübbecke-Job. Dur. 20'.

1. *Sehr lebhafte Achtel*; 2. *Sehr langsame Achtel*; 3. *Kleines Potpourri*; 4. *Finale: Schnelle Viertel*.

fl/pic, ob, cl, bcl, bsn; hn, tpt, tmb; v, va, c, db.

fp: 31 October 1924, Frankfurt a. M., Emma

Lübbecke-Job and ensemble, cond. Clemens Krauss.

?fFp: 25 March 1926, Paris, Concerts Straram, Andrée Vaurabourg and ensemble, cond. Walter Straram.

fEp: 3 September 1927, Queen's Hall, Promenade Concert, Gerda Nette and members of the New Queen's Hall Orchestra, cond. Sir Henry Wood.*

Pub. 1924, Schott: study score, and reduction by Paul Hindemith for two pianos four hands.

BIBLIOGRAPHY:
Heinrich Strobel: PH, Klavierkonzert, *Anbruch*, August–September 1925, p. 424.

41. String Trio No. 1 Op. 34. For violin, viola and cello. 1924. Ded. Alois Hába. Dur. 15′.
  1. *Toccata: Schnelle Halbe*; 2. *Langsam und mit grosser Ruhe (Achtel)*; 3. *Mässig schnelle Viertel (pizzicato)*; 4. *Fugue: Sehr lebhafte Halbe*.
  fp: 6 August 1924, Salzburg, Licco Amar, Paul Hindemith and Maurits Frank.
  fEbp: 7 May 1928, Licco Amar, Paul Hindemith and Maurits Frank.
  Pub. 1924, Schott: Study score and parts.

42. Die Serenaden Op. 35. Little cantata from Romantic texts for soprano, oboe, viola and cello. 1925. Ded. Gertrud Hindemith. Dur. 20′.
  I:
  1. *Barcarole* (Adolf Licht). For voice, oboe and cello.
  2. *An Phyllis* (J. L. W. Gleim). Toccata for cello, Corrente for voice and cello.
  3. *Nur Mut* (Ludwig Tieck).
  II:
  5. *Duet*. For viola and cello.
  6. *Der Abend: Schweig der Menschen laute hust* (J. von Eichendorff). For voice and oboe.
  7. *Der Wurm am Meer: Wie dies Gewürm* (J. W. Meinhold). For voice, oboe, viola and cello.
  III:
  8. *Trio*. For oboe, viola and cello.
  9. *Gute Nacht* (S. Aug. Mahlmann). For voice and viola.

---

*Emma Lübbecke-Job was soloist at a Promenade Concert performance on 18 August 1931

fp: 15 April 1925, Winterthur, Gertrud Hindemith.

f Paris p: 25 January 1927, Revue Musicale concert, Ružena Herlinger with Bonneau (ob), Ginot (va) and Bloch (c).

fEp: 15 October 1928, Arts Theatre Club, BBC concert, Margot Hinnenberg-Lefevre, Léon Goossens, Eugen Lechner and Benar Heifetz.

Pub. 1925, Schott.

43. Kammermusik No. 3 (Cello Concerto) Op. 36 No. 2. For cello and ten instruments. 1925. Ded. Elsa and Willi Hof. Dur. 16′.
  1. *Majestätisch, und stark, mässig schnelle Achtel*; 2. *Lebhaft und lustig*; 3. *Sehr ruhige und gemessen schreitende Viertel*; 4. *Mässig bewegte Halbe, Munter, aber immer gemächlich*.
  fl/pic, ob, cl/E-flat cl, bsn; hn, tpt, tmb; v, c, db.
  fp: 30 April 1925, Bochum, Rudolf Hindemith (cello), cond. Paul Hindemith.
  fEp: 10 October 1931; BBC broadcast, Sheridan Russell and the BBC Orchestra, cond. Edward Clark.
  Pub. 1925, Schott: study score, and reduction by Paul Hindemith.

44. Kammermusik No. 4 Op. 36 No. 3. For violin and large chamber orchestra. 1925. Dur. 22–23′.
  1. *Signal (Breite, majestätische Halbe)*; 2. *Sehr lebhaft*; 3. *Nachtstück (Mässig schnelle Achtel)*; 4. *Lebhafte Viertel*; 5. *So schnell wie möglich*.
  2 pic, E-flat cl, cl, bcl, 2 bsn, cbsn; cornet à piston, tmb, bs tuba; 4 dm; strings (0-0-4-4-4).
  fp: 25 September 1925, Dessau, Licco Amar (violin), cond. Franz von Hoesslin.
  fEp: 7 January 1937, BBC broadcast, Antonio Brosa and the BBC Orchestra, cond. Warwick Braithwaite.
  f London p: 1 March 1965, Friends' House (Euston Road), English Chamber Orchestra, cond. Norman Del Mar.
  Pub. 1925, Schott: study score, and reduction by Otto Singer.

45. Klaviermüsik Op. 37. For piano. 1925–7.
  1. *Übung in drei Stücken*. 1925. Ded. Ludwig Rottenberg. Dur. 10′.
  fp: November 1925, Berlin, Walter Gieseking.

2. *Reihe kleiner Stücke.* 1927. Dur. 21'.
fp: April 1927, Dessau, Paul Aron.
fEp: 5 November 1928, Arts Theatre Club, BBC concert, Walter Gieseking.
Pub. 1925, 1927, Schott.

46. Konzert für Orchester Op. 38. 1925. Ded. Franz and Margitchen Ernst. Dur. 17'.
1. *Mit Kraft, mässig schnelle Viertel*; 2. *Sehr schnelle Halbe*; 3. *Marsch für Holzbläser (Nicht zu langsame Viertel)*; 4. *Basso ostinato (Schnelle Viertel)*.
2 fl, pic, 2 ob, E-flat cl, cl, bcl, 2 bsn, cbsn; 3 hn, 2 tpt, 2 tmb, tuba; 2 timp, side dm, medium dm, GC & cym, tamb, tgle, wooden dm, wood clapper; strings.
fp: 25 July 1925, Duisberg, cond. Paul Scheinpflug.
fFp: 12 June 1926, Paris, Concerts Koussevitzky.
fEp: 14 September 1926, Queen's Hall, Promenade Concert, New Queen's Hall Orchestra, cond. Sir Henry Wood.
Pub. Schott: study score.

47. Drei Stücke. For five instruments. 1925. Dur. 6'.
1. *Scherzando*; 2. *Langsame Achtel*; 3. *Lebhafte Halbe*.
cl, tpt, v, db, p.
Pub. 1934, Schott: score and parts.

47a. Rondo. For three guitars. 1925.
fp: 1930, Berlin, on the 'Music in the Home' Day of a five-day festival of new music.
Pub. 1969, Schott.

48. Konzertmusik Op. 41. For wind orchestra. 1926. Ded. Hermann Scherchen. Dur. 14-15'.
1. *Konzertante Ouvertüre*; 2. *Sechs Variationen über das Lied 'Prinz Eugen, der edle Ritter'*; 3. *Marsch*.
fl, pic, ob, E-flat cl, 3 cl, 2 flugelhorns *or* 2 sop sax (*or* sop sax & alto sax), 2 Waldhörner, 2 ten hn *or* ten tuba *or* 2 ten sax; baryton *or* bcl; 3 tpt, 3 tmb, 2–3 basses (bs tuba & cbs tuba); side dm, GC with cym.
fp: July 1926, Donaueschingen, cond. Hermann Scherchen.
Pub. Schott.

49. Cardillac Op. 39. Opera in three acts.
1926. Libretto: Ferdinand Lion, after E. T. A. Hoffmann's 'Das Fräulein von Scuderi'.
fl, pic, ob, ca, E-flat cl, cl, bcl, ten sax, 2 bsn, cbsn; hn, 2 tpt, 2 tmb, bs tuba; 2 timp, tgle, zymbeln, side dm, tamb, parade dm, 4 jazz dm, cym, GC, gong, tamtam, 2 bells, glock; piano, strings. Stage music: ob, 2 hn, tpt, tmb, va, 2 db.
fp: 9 November 1926, Dresden, Staatsoper, cond. Fritz Busch; with Robert Burg, Cläre Born, Grete Rikisch, Max Hirzel; producer, Raffaelo Busoni; costumes, Leonhard Fanto.
fEp (Aria and Pantomime only): 3 April 1930, Queen's Hall, Royal Philharmonic Society concert, Dorothy Silk, cond. Oskar Fried.
fEp (complete, concert form): 18 December 1936, BBC Chorus and Symphony Orchestra, cond. Clarence Raybould; with Arthur Fear, Noel Eadie, Frank Mullings, Norman Walker, John McKenna, Miriam Licette and Dennis Noble.
Pub. 1926, Schott: incl. piano score by Otto Singer.

BIBLIOGRAPHY:
Ronald Chrichton: The first Cardillac, *Opera*, March 1970, p. 193.
Edwin Evans: Cardillac, *Radio Times*, 11 December 1936, p. 13.
Albert Henneberg: Märklig operapremiär i Wien: PHs Cardillac, den första atonala operan på Wiens Staatsoper, *Scenen* (Stockholm), Vol. 13 (1927), p. 274.
Walther Hirschberg: PHs Cardillac, *Signale*, 1928, No. 28, p. 869.
Ian Kemp: Hindemith's Cardillac (1926), *The Listener*, 21 April 1966, p. 592.
— Hindemith's Cardillac, *MT*, March 1970, p. 268.
Hans Mersman: PHs Oper Cardillac—Uraufführung, *Melos*, Vol. 5 (1925–6), p. 383.
Walter Petzet: Hindemiths Cardillac, *Signale*, 1926, No. 46, p. 1649.
— Cardillac—Uraufführung Dresden 9. XI. 1926, *AMZ*, 1926, p.956.
Eugen Schmitz: Hindemiths Cardillac—Zur Uraufführung in Dresdener Opernhaus am 9. November 1926, *Die Musik*, January 1927, p. 269.
Paul Stefan: Cardillac, *Anbruch*, December 1926, p. 235.

Erich Steinhard: Hindemiths Cardillac—Deutsches Theater in Prag, *Der Auftakt*, 1927, No. 3, p. 76.

Karl Westermayer: Hindemith's Cardillac, *Signale*, 1926, No. 46, p. 1647.

Kurt Westphal: Cardillac, ein steigender Opernerfolg, *Melos*, May–June 1949, p. 158.

Anon.: An atonal opera—Cardillac, *The Times*, 23 April 1927, p. 8.

49a. Cardillac. Opera in four acts. Revised version, 1952. Libretto: Paul Hindemith, after Ferdinand Lion.

2 fl, pic, ob, ca, E-flat cl, cl, bcl, ten sax, 2 bsn, cbsn; hn, 2 tpt, 2 tmb, bs tuba; timp, pcssn; piano, strings (6-4-4-4). Stage music: fl, ob, bsn, hp, hpschd, v, va, c, db.

fp: 20 June 1952, Zürich, Stadttheater, cond. Victor Reinshagen.

Pub. 1952, Schott: incl. piano score by Paul Hindemith.

BIBLIOGRAPHY:

Willi Reich: Cardillac in neuer Fassung, *Musikleben*, September 1952, p. 257.

K. H. Ruppel, Fritz Brust & Josef Marein: PH, Cardillac II, in *Musik der Zeit*, Vol. 6 (Opera in XX. Jahrhundert), Boosey & Hawkes (Bonn) 1954, p. 65.

T. Staar: Der neue Cardillac als deutscher Erstaufführung, *Musikleben*, April 1953, p. 134.

H. H. Stuckenschmidt: PH, Cardillac, neue Fassung, Städtische Bühnen Frankfurt 1953, in *Oper in dieser Zeit*, Friedrich Verlag (Hannover) 1964, p. 21.

Joseph Wechsberg: Cardillac in Vienna, *Opera*, April 1964, p. 240.

50. Spielmusik Op. 43 No. 1. For string orchestra, two flutes and two oboes. 1927. Dur. 7′.

1. *Mässig bewegte Halbe*; 2. *Langsam schreitende Viertel*; 3. *Schnelle Halbe*.

Pub. 1927, 1955, Schott.

51. Lieder für Singkreise Op. 43 No. 2. For three-part mixed chorus a cappella. 1927.

1. *Ein jedes Band* (August von Platen). Dur. 1′.

2. *O Herr, gib jedem seinen eignen Tod* (Rainer Maria Rilke). Dur. ½′.

3. *Man weiss oft grade denn am meisten* (Matthias Claudius). Dur. ½′.

4. *Was meinst du, Kunz, wie gross die Sonne sei?* (Matthias Claudius). Dur. ¾′.

Pub. 1927, Schott.

52. Schulwerk für Instrumental-Zusammenspiel Op. 44. 1927.

1. *Neun Stücke*. For two violins.

2. *Acht Kanons*. For three violins and viola.

3. *Ach Stücke*. For two violins, viola, cello and double bass.

1. *Mässig schnell*; 2. *Schnell*; 3. *Mässig schnell*; 4. *Lustig, mässig schnell*; 5. *Schnell*; 6. *Mässig schnell*; 7. *Lebhaft*; 8. *Mässig schnell, munter*.

4. *Fünf Stücke*. For string orchestra.

1. *Langsam*; 2. *Langsam—schnell*; 3. *Lebhaft*; 4. *Sehr langsam*; 5. *Lebhaft*.

fEbp (six pieces): 7 May 1928, Amar-Hindemith Quartet.

fEbp (No. 4): 17 March 1934, Boyd Neel String Orchestra, cond. Boyd Neel.

Pub. 1927, Schott.

53. Sing- und Spielmusiken für Liebhaber und Musikfreunde Op. 45. 1928–9.

1. *Frau Musica*. 1928. For mezzo-soprano and baritone soloists, mixed chorus and string orchestra (with ad lib wind). Text: Martin Luther. Dur. 6–7′.

fEp: 28 April 1953, BBC broadcast, Edith Osler, Raymond Nilsson, Dorian Singers and the Goldsbrough Orchestra, cond. Matyas Seiber.

Pub. 1928, Schott. Rev. version, 1943.

2. *Acht Kanons*. 1928. For two-part chorus with (ad lib) two violins, viola and cello. Dur. 6½′.

1. *Hie kann nit sein ein böser Mut* (Old Saying).

2. *Wer sich die Musik erkiest* (Martin Luther).

3. *Die wir dem Licht in Liebe dienen* (Reinhard Goering).

4. *Auf a folgt b* (Christian Morgenstern).

5. *Niemals wieder will ich eines Menschen Antlitz verlachen* (Franz Werfel).

6. *Das weiss ich und hab' ich erlebt* (Jakob Kneip).

7. *Mund und Augen wissen ihre Pflicht* (Hermann Claudius).

8. *Erde, die uns dies gebracht* (Christian Morgenstern).

Hindemith, Paul

Pub. 1928, Schott.

3. *Ein Jäger aus Kurpfalz, der reitet durch den grünen Wald.* 1928. For strings and wind. Dur. 5'.

1. *Breit, majestätisch*; 2. *Munter.*

Pub. 1928, Schott.

4. *Kleine Klaviermusik* (Leichte Fünftonstücke). 1929. Dur. 5'.

1. *Mässig schnell*; 2. *Ruhig bewegt*; 3. *Munter, schnelle Viertel*; 4. *Lebhaft, sehr markiert*; 5. *Schnell, ganze Takte*; 6. *Gemächlich*; 7. *Schnell und wild*; 8. *Mässig schnell*; 9. *Langsam, ruhig schreitend*; 10. *Munter, ziemlich lebhaft*; 11. *Mässig schnell*; 12. *Bewegt.*

Pub. 1930, Schott.

5. *Martinslied.* 1929. For solo voice or chorus and three instruments (strings or wind). Text: Johannes Olorinus. Dur. 3½'.

Pub. 1931, Schott.

54. Hin und zurück (There and Back) Op. 45a. Sketch in one act. 1927. Text: Marcellus Schiffer. Dur. 12'.

fl, cl, alto sax, bsn; tpt, tmb; piano four hands.

fp: 15 July 1927, Baden-Baden, cond. Ernst Mehlich.

fFp: 11 December 1935, Paris, Salle Chopin, Le Triton concert.

Pub. 1927, Schott: piano score by Paul Hindemith.

55. Lügenlied. For two female and one male voices with (ad lib) strings and wind. 1928. Dur. ½'. Pub. 1950, Schott.

56. Kammermusik No. 5 (Viola Concerto) Op. 36 No. 4. For solo viola and large chamber orchestra. 1927. Ded. Arnold Mendelssohn. Dur. 17'.

1. *Schnelle Halbe*; 2. *Langsam*; 3. *Mässig schnell*; 4. *Variante eines Militärmarsches.*

fl, pic, ob, E-flat cl, cl, bcl, 2 bsn, cbsn; hn, 2 tpt, 2 tmb, bs tuba; 4 c, 4 db.

fp: 3 November 1927, Berlin, Paul Hindemith, cond. Otto Klemperer.

fEp: 22 November 1929, Queen's Hall, Paul Hindemith and BBC Symphony Orchestra, cond. Sir Henry Wood.

Pub. 1928, Schott: study score, and reduction by Franz Willms.

57. Kammermusik No. 6 Op. 46 No. 1. For viola d'amore and chamber orchestra. 1927. Dur. 16'.

fl, ob, cl, bcl, bsn; hn, tpt, tmb; strings (0-0-0-3-2).

fp: 29 March 1928, Cologne, Paul Hindemith, cond. Ludwig Rottenberg.

Pub. 1930, Schott.

58. Kammermusik No. 7 (Concerto for organ and chamber orchestra) Op. 46 No. 2. 1927. Ded. Frankfurter Sender. Dur. 17'.

1. *Nicht zu schnell*; 2. *Sehr langsam und ganzruhig*; 3. (*quaver = 184*).

fl, pic, ob, cl, bcl, 2 bsn, cbsn; hn, tpt, tmb; strings (0-0-0-2-1).

fp: 8 January 1928, Frankfurt a.M., Reinhold Merten (organ).

fFp: 10 April 1930, Paris, Marcel Dupré, cond. Walter Straram.

fEp: 5 May 1930, Central Hall, BBC broadcast, Quentin Maclean, cond. Hermann Scherchen.

Pub. 1928, Schott.

59. Acht Stücke. For solo flute. 1927. Dur. 7'.

1. *Gemächlich, leicht bewegt*; 2. *Scherzando*; 3. *Sehr langsam*; 4. *Gemächlich*; 5. *Sehr lebhaft*; 6. *Lied, leicht bewegt*; 7. *Rezitativ*; 8. *Finale.*

Pub. 1958, Schott.

60. Trio Op. 47. For piano, viola and heckelphone (or tenor saxophone). 1928. Dur. 12–13'.

1. *Solo, Arioso, Duett*; 2. *Potpourri.*

fp: 15 March 1928, Wiesbaden, Emma Lübbecke-Job, Paul Hindemith and Dieckmann.

fEp: 7 October 1929, Arts Theatre Club, BBC concert of modern chamber music, Emma Lübbecke-Job, Paul Hindemith and Frederick Waterhouse.

Pub. 1929, Schott.

61. Spruch eines Fahrenden. For women's or children's voices. 1928. Text: fourteenth century. Dur. 1¼'. Pub. 1950, Schott.

62. Neues vom Tage. Comic opera in three parts. 1928–9. Libretto: Marcellus Schiffer.

2 fl/pic, ob, ca, E-flat cl, cl, bcl, alto sax, 2 bsn, cbsn; hn, 2 tpt, 2 tmb, bs tuba; GC, side dm, tomtom, cym, gong; hp, mandoline, banjo, piano, piano four hands, strings (6 v, 4 va, 4 c, 4 db).

fp: 8 June 1929, Berlin, Berliner Festspiele, Kroll Opera, cond. Otto Klemperer.

Pub. 1929, Schott: piano score by Franz Willms.

BIBLIOGRAPHY:

Wilhelm Altmann: Hindemith's Neues vom Tage, *Sackbut*, July 1929, p. 399.

Walther Hirschberg: PHs Neues vom Tage, *Signale*, 1929, No. 25, p. 758.

Ernst Maschke: Hindemiths Neues vom Tage —Erstaufführung am Königsberger Opernhaus, *Signale*, 1932, No. 4, p. 65.

Henry Prunières: Neues vom Tage, opéra comique de PH, *RM*, July 1929, p. 170.

P. Schwers: Hindemiths Neues vom Tage, *AMZ*, 7–14 June 1929.

Erich Steinhard: PH—Neues vom Tage: Uraufführung in der Berliner Staatsoper, *Der Auftakt*, 1929, Nos. 7–8, p. 181.

Franz Willms: Neues vom Tage—Zu Hindemiths lustiger Oper, *Blätter der Staatsoper* (Berlin), June (No. 29) 1929, p. 5.

62a. Neues vom Tage: Overture (concert version). 1929. Dur. 8'.

2 fl, pic, ob, ca, E-flat cl, cl, bcl, alto sax, 2 bsn, cbsn; hn, 2 tpt, 2 tmb, bs tuba; GC, side dm, tomtom, cym, small cym, tgle; strings (6 v, 4 va, 4 c, 4 db).

fp: January 1930, Nürnberg, cond. Bertil Wetzelsberger.

fEp: 9 November 1930, BBC broadcast, BBC Symphony Orchestra, cond. Sir Henry Wood.

Pub. 1930, Schott.

62b. Neues vom Tage. Opera in two acts. Revised version, 1953.

2 fl, pic, ob, ca, E-flat cl, cl, bcl, alto sax, 2 bsn, cbsn; hn, 2 tpt, 2 tmb, tuba; GC, side dm, tomtom, cym, gong, zymbel, tgle, glock, xyl, 3 electric bells; piano, piano four hands, hp, mandoline, banjo, strings (6 v, 4 va, 4 c, 4 db).

Pub. 1954; Schott: piano score by Franz Willms.

63. Lehrstück. For soloists, chorus and orchestra. 1929. Text: Bert Brecht. Dur. 50'.

1. *Bericht vom Fliegen*; 2. *Untersuchung: Ob der Mensch dem Menschen hilft*; 3. *Der Chor spricht zum Abgestürzten*; 4. *Betrachtet den Tod*;

5. *Belehrung*; 6. *Zweite Untersuchung: Ob der Mensch dem Menschen hilft (Szene für Clowns)*; 7. *Examen.*

fp: 28 July 1929, Baden-Baden, Josef Witt, Oskar Kálmán, Gerda Müller-Scherchen (speaker), Theo Lingen, Karl Paulsen & Benno Carlé (Three Clowns), Hugo Holles Madrigalvereinigung, Musiker und Musikliebhaber (orchestra), Musikvereinhichtental (wind orchestra), cond. Alfons Dressel & Ernst Wolff.

fEp: 24 March 1933, BBC invitation concert at Broadcasting House, Tudor Davies, Arthur Cranmer, Wireless Chorus, section of Wireless Military Band and BBC Orchestra, cond. Sir Adrian Boult.

Pub. 1929, Schott: piano score by Paul Hindemith.

BIBLIOGRAPHY:

Hans-Oscar Hiege: Lehrstück, *Signale*, 1930, No. 22, p. 714.

64. Zwei Männerchöre. For unacc. TTBB. 1929.

1. *Über das Frühjahr* (Bert Brecht). Dur. 2'.

2. *Eine lichte Mitternacht* (Walt Whitman, transl. Johannes Schlaf). Dur. 2'.

Pub. 1930, Schott.

65. Zwei kanonische Duette. For two violins. 1929. Dur. 10'. Pub. Schott.

66. Der Lindberghflug. Composed in collaboration with Kurt Weill. For soloists and orchestra. 1929.

fEbp: March 1930, Betty Mergler, Erik Wirl, Herbert Janssen and the Berlin Funkorchester, cond. Hermann Scherchen.

Withdrawn.

67. Du musst dir alles geben (Gottfried Benn). For unacc. TTBB. 1930. Dur. $1\frac{3}{4}'$.

fp: May 1931, Vienna, cond. Hans Wagner-Schönkirch.

Pub. Schott.

67a. Fürst Kraft (Gottfried Benn). For unacc. TTBB. 1930. Dur. $2\frac{1}{4}'$.

fp: as preceding.

Pub. c. 1950, Schott.

68. Vision des Mannes (Gottfried Benn). For unacc. TTBB. 1930. Dur. $2\frac{1}{2}'$. Pub. ?1930, Schott.

Hindemith, Paul

69. Konzertmusik Op. 48. For viola and large chamber orchestra. 1930. Ded. Darius and Madeleine Milhaud. Dur. 20'.
   1. *Lebhafte, bewegte Halbe*; 2. *Ruhig gehend*; 3. *Lebhaft*; 4. *Leicht bewegt*; 5. *Sehr lebhaft*.
fl, pic, ob, ca, cl, bcl, 2 bsn, cbsn; 3 hn, 2 tpt, tmb, bs tuba; strings (0-0-0-4-4).
fp: 28 March 1930, Hamburg, Paul Hindemith (viola), cond. Wilhelm Furtwängler.
?fEp: 19 March 1933, BBC broadcast, Paul Hindemith and the BBC Orchestra, cond. Sir Henry Wood.
fFp: 31 May 1935, Paris, Salle Rameau, Paul Hindemith and Société Philharmonique, cond. Ernest Ansermet.
Pub. 1930, Schott: study score; also reduction by Franz Willms, 1931.

70. Konzertmusik Op. 49. For piano, brass and two harps. 1930. Ded. Elizabeth Sprague Coolidge. Dur. 21'.
4 hn, 3 tpt, 2 tmb, bs tuba; 2 hp.
fp: 12 October 1930, Chicago, Emma Lübbecke-Job (piano), cond. Hugo Kortschak.
fEp: 6 March 1931, BBC broadcast, Emma Lübbecke-Job and the BBC Orchestra, cond. Frank Bridge.
fEp (concert): 8 February 1932, Queen's Hall, Courtauld-Sargent concert, Beveridge Webster (piano) and the London Symphony Orchestra, cond. Otto Klemperer. (NB: fEp originally announced for 18 August 1931, Promenade Concert.)
Pub. 1930, Schott.

BIBLIOGRAPHY:
H. Schultze-Ritter: Hindemiths neues Klavierkonzert, *Melos*, July 1931.

71. Konzertmusik Op. 50. For strings and wind. 1930. Composed for the fiftieth anniversary of the Boston Symphony Orchestra. Dur. 18–19'.
   1. *Mässig schnell, mit Kraft—Sehr breit, aber stets fliessend*; 2. *Lebhaft—Langsam—Im ersten Zeitmass*.
fp: 3 April 1931, Boston, Boston Symphony Orchestra, cond. Serge Koussevitzky.
fEp: 17 February 1932, Queen's Hall, BBC Symphony Orchestra, cond. Sir Henry Wood.
Pub. 1931, Schott: incl. study score.

72. Wir bauen eine Stadt. Play for children. 1930. Text: Robert Seitz. Dur. 15'.
fp: 21 June 1930, Berlin, cond. Alexander Curth.
fEp: 25 July 1931, Oxford, Holywell music room, cond. Ronald Biggs.
Pub. 1930, Schott: incl, piano score by Paul Hindemith.

72a. Wir bauen eine Stadt. Piano pieces for children. 1931. Ded. Olga Strecker. Dur. 4'.
   1. *Marsch*; 2. *Lied: Wir bauen eine Stadt*; 3. *Musikstück: Man zeigt neu ankommen—den Leuten die Stadt*; 4. *Lied: Ich bin ein Schaffner*; 5. *Man spielt 'Besuch'*; 6. *Die Diebe kommen in der Nacht*.
Pub. 1931, Schott.

73. Chorlieder für Knaben (Karl Schnog). 1930. Dur. 7½'.
   1. *Bastellied*; 2. *Lied des Musterknaben*; 3. *Angst vorm Schwimmunterricht*; 4. *Schundromane lesen*.
Pub. 1930, Schott.

74. Das Unaufhörliche. Oratorio in three parts for soprano, tenor, baritone and bass soloists, mixed chorus, children's chorus and orchestra. 1931. Text: Gottfried Benn. Dur. 85'.
2 fl, pic, 2 ob, 2 cl, 2 bsn; 3 hn, 2 tpt, 2 tmb, bs tuba; timp, pcssn; strings.
fp: 21 November 1931, Berlin, cond. Otto Klemperer.
fEp: 22 March 1933, Queen's Hall, Mrs. Cranmer, Adelheid Armhold, Parry Jones, Harold Williams, BBC Chorus, boys of St. Margaret's Westminster and of St. Mark's North Audley Street, BBC Symphony Orchestra, cond. Sir Henry Wood: performed in an English translation by Rose and Cyril Scott as 'The Perpetual'.
Pub. 1931, Schott; incl. reduction by Paul Hindemith.

BIBLIOGRAPHY:
Gerald Abraham: Hindemith's Das Unaufhörliche, *MM&F*, March 1933, p. 171.
Walter Berten: PHs Oratorium Das Unaufhörliche, *NZfM*, June 1932, p. 475.

Alfred Einstein: Hindemith's oratorio, *Radio Times*, 4 May 1934, p. 342.

Hanns Gutman: Da Unaufhörliche, Hindemith-Uraufführung, *Der Auftakt*, 1931, Nos. 11–12, p. 276.

R.-A. Mooser: Das Unaufhörliche de PM, *Dissonances*, August 1932.

Edmund Rubbra: Hindemith's oratorio Das Unaufhörliche, *MMR*, 1933, p. 54.

75. Vierzehn leichte Stücke. For two violins (first position). 1931. Dur. 11–12'. Pub. Schott.

76. Der Tod (Friedrich Hölderlein). For unacc. TTBB. 1932. Dur. 2'.

fEp: 23 December 1932, Broadcasting House (invited audience), BBC Chorus, cond. Cyril Dalmaine.

Pub. Schott.

77. Philharmonisches Konzert (Philharmonic Concerto). Variations for orchestra. 1932. Composed for Wilhelm Furtwängler and the Berlin Philharmonic on its fiftieth anniversary. Dur. 20–21'.

3 fl, pic, 2 ob, ca, 2 cl, bcl, 2 bsn, cbsn; 4 hn, 3 tpt, 3 tmb, bs tuba; timp, cym, side dm, GC, small cym, tgle; strings.

fp: 14 April 1932, Berlin, Berlin Philharmonic Orchestra, cond. Wilhelm Furtwängler.

fEp: 2 January 1933, Queen's Hall, Winter Promenade Concert, BBC Symphony Orchestra, cond. Sir Henry Wood.

2Ep: 15 February 1933, Queen's Hall, Berlin Philharmonic Orchestra, cond. Wilhelm Furtwängler.

Pub. 1932, Schott.

78. Plöner Musiktag. 1932.
A. Morgenmusik. Dur. 10'.
2 tpt (flugelhorns), 2 tmb (hn), tuba (ad lib).
B. Tafelmusik. Dur. 15'.
1. *Marsch*; 2. *Intermezzo*; 3. *Trio*; 4. *Walzer*.
fl, tpt (cl), string trio.
C. Kantate ('Mahnung an die Jugend, sich der Musik zu befleissigen'). For children's chorus, solo voices, speaker, string orchestra with ad lib wind and percussion. Words: Martin Agricola. Dur. 35'.
1. *Marsch*; 2. *Vier Chöre*; 3. *Arie*; 4. *Kanon*; 5. *Melodram*; 6. *Schlusschor.*
D. Abendkonzert.

1. *Einleitungsstück* (Introduction). For orchestra. Dur. 8'.
2. *Flötensolo mit Streichern.* Dur. 6'.
3. *Zwei Duette für Violine und Klarinette.* Dur. 4'.
4. *Variationen für Klarinette und Streicher.* Dur. 3–3½'.
5. *Trio für Blockflöten.* Dur. 7–8'.
6. *Quodlibet.* For orchestra. Dated: June 1932, Berlin. Dur. 4½'.
fp: June 1932, Plön, State School Music Festival.

Pub. 1932, Schott.

79. String Trio No. 2. 1933. Dur. 22½'.
1. *Mässig schnell*; 2. *Lebhaft*; 3. *Langsam.*
fp: 17 March 1933, Antwerp, Szymon Goldberg, Paul Hindemith and Emanuel Feuermann.

fEbp: 19 January 1934, Szymon Goldberg, Paul Hindemith and Emanuel Feuermann.

Pub. 1934, Schott; incl. study score.

80. Duett. For viola and cello. 1934. Dur. 4'.
Pub. 1957, Schott.

81. Mathis der Maler. Symphony for orchestra. 1934. Dur. 26'.
1. *Engelkonzert*; 2. *Grablegung*; 3. *Versuchung des heiligen Antonius.*
2 fl, pic, 2 ob, 2 cl, 2 bsn; 4 hn, 2 tpt, 3 tmb, bs tuba; timp, glock small cym, cym, tgle, side dm, GC; strings.

fp: 12 March 1934, Berlin, Berlin Philharmonic Orchestra, cond. Wilhelm Furtwängler.

fEp: 21 December 1934, BBC broadcast, BBC Orchestra, cond. Paul Hindemith.

fEp (concert): 10 February 1936, Queen's Hall, Courtauld-Sargent concert, London Philharmonic Orchestra, cond. Fritz Stiedry.

fFp: 31 May 1935, Paris, Salle Rameau, Société Philharmonique, cond. Ernest Ansermet.

Pub. 1934, Schott; incl. study score, and reduction for piano four hands by Paul Hindemith.

BIBLIOGRAPHY:

H. Boettger: Symph. Mathis der Maler, *Die Musikpflege*, V, 1934.

Alfred Brasch: Musik zum Isenheimer Altar—PH, Symph. Mathis der Maler, *NZfM*, December 1934, p. 1203.

Hindemith, Paul

H. Daviel: Mathis der Maler, *SM*, 1 June 1934.
Otto Mayer: La sinfonia Mathis el Pintor de PH, *Revista musical Catalan* (Barcelona), May 1935.
R.-A. Mooser: Mathis der Maler, *Dissonances*, June 1934.
A. von Reck: Konstruktive Dichte in Hindemith's Mathis-Sinfonie, *SM*, 1950.
Erich Steinhard: PH, Symphonie Mathis der Maler, in der Tschechischen Philharmonie, *Der Auftakt*, 1934, No. 10, p. 188.
Heinrich Strobel: Hindemiths Neue Sinfonie, *Melos*, April 1934.
Anon.: Mathis der Maler, *NZfM*, January 1935, p. 65.

82. Mathis der Maler. Opera in seven scenes. 1934–5. Text: Paul Hindemith.
2 fl/pic, 2 ob, 2 cl, 2 bsn; 4 hn, 2 tpt, 3 tmb, tuba; timp, 2 pcssn; strings. Stage music: 3 tpt.
fp: 28 May 1938, Zürich, Stadttheater, cond. Robert F. Denzler; with Asger Stig (Mathis), Peter Baxevanos (Kardinal Albrecht), Hans Schwalb (Ernst Mosbacher), Albert Emmerich (Riedinger), Simon Bermani (Rat Capito), Judith Hellwig, Ursula Riedinger, Leni Funk, Georgine von Milinkovic.
fEp (Two Fragments): 24 June 1938, Queen's Hall, ISCM concert, cond. Clarence Raybould.
fEp: 15 March 1939, Queen's Hall, Philharmonic Choir and BBC Symphony Orchestra, cond. Clarence Raybould; with Dennis Noble (Mathis), Parry Jones (Albrecht), Stiles Allen (Ursula), Muriel Brunskill (Countess Helfenstein), John McKenna (Capito), Noel Eadie (Regina), Norman Walker (Lorenz von Pommersfelden).
Pub. 1937, Schott: incl. study score, and vocal score by the composer.

BIBLIOGRAPHY:
Michael Bell: Hindemith's Mathis der Maler, *MMR*, 1939, p. 77.
an L. Broeckx: Mathis der Maler en de moderne Opera, *Mens en melodie*, August 1947, p. 251.
Hans Carrodi: Zürich—Mathis le Peintre, opéra de PH, *RM*, June 1938, p. 403.
Roman Clemens: Decors for Hindemith's

Mathis der Maler, *Modern Music*, May–June 1938.
Martin Cooper: Mathis the painter, *Radio Times*, 10 March 1939, p. 13.
Richard Engländer: Mathis der Maler in Stockholm, *Melos*, April 1950, p. 119.
Karl Geiringer: Mathis the painter, *The Listener*, 9 March 1939, p. 545.
Antoine Golea: A Strasbourg, Théâtre Municipal, Mathis le Peintre et PH, *La Vie musicale*, 1951, No. 8 (July–August), p. 16.
Karl Holl: Zu Hindemiths Mathis der Maler, *Das Musikleben*, 1954, No. 7 (September).
A. Huth: Mathis der Maler af Hindemith, *Dansk Musiktidsskrift*, August 1938.
Armando Plebe: Il problema del linguaggio melodrammatico nel Mathis di Hindemith, *La Rassegna musicale*, 1962, p. 224.
Willi Reich: Hindemith's Mathis der Maler produced in Zürich, *Musical America*, July 1938.
Edward Sackville-West: Mathis der Maler, *Opera*, September 1952, p. 536.
Roger Sessions: Hindemith's Mathis der Maler, *Modern Music*, November–December 1934.
Heinrich Strobel: Mathis der Maler, *Melos*, January 1947, p. 65.
H. H. Stuckenschmidt: PH Mathis der Maler, Stadttheater Zürich 1938, in *Oper in dieser Zeit*, Friedrich Verlag (Hannover) 1964, p. 19.
— PH Mathis der Maler, Städtische Oper Berlin 1957, in –do–, p. 25.
G. Turchi: Mathis der Maler, *L'Approdo musicale*, 1958, No. 3.
Anon.: Mathis der Maler, *MO*, February 1939, p. 402.

83. Sechs Lieder (Friedrich Hölderlin). For tenor and piano. 1933–5.
1. *An die Parzen.* 1935.
2. *Sonnenuntergang.* 1935.
3. *Ehmals und jetzt.* 1935.
4. *Des Morgens.* 1935.
5. *Fragment.* 1933.
6. *Abendphantasie.* 1933.
fp (except No. 4): 4 November 1964, Frankfurt a.M., Ernst Haefliger and Hans Petermandl.
Pub. Schott.

84. Violin Sonata in E. 1935. Dur. 9'.
1. *Ruhig bewegt*; 2. *Langsam—Sehr lebhaft.*
fp: February 1936, Geneva, Stefan Frankel and Mme Orloff.
Pub. 1935, Schott.

85. Der Schwanendreher. Concerto after folksongs for viola and small orchestra. October 1935. Dur. 24–25'.
1. *'Zwischen Berg und tiefem Tal' (Langsam— Mässig bewegt).*
2. *'Nun laube, Lindlein, laube!' (Sehr ruhig)*; Fugato: *'Der Gutzgauch auf dem Zaune sass'.*
3. *Variationen: 'Seid ihr nicht der Schwanendreher' (Mässig schnell).*
2 fl, ob, 2 cl, 2 bsn; 3 hn, tpt, tmb; timp; hp, strings.
fp: 14 November 1935, Amsterdam, Paul Hindemith and the Concertgebouw Orchestra, cond. Willem Mengelberg.
fEp: 22 January 1936, BBC broadcast, Paul Hindemith and BBC Symphony Orchestra, cond. Sir Adrian Boult.
fAp: 11 April 1937, Washington D.C., Paul Hindemith, cond. Carlos Chavez.
fEp (concert): 6 December 1937, Queen's Hall, Courtauld-Sargent concert, Paul Hindemith and the London Philharmonic Orchestra, cond. Erich Kleiber.
Pub. 1936, Schott; incl. study score, and reduction by Paul Hindemith for viola and piano, 1937.

BIBLIOGRAPHY:
Franz Reizenstein: New viola concerto, *Radio Times*, 17 January 1936, p. 13.

86. Trauermusik. For viola (or violin, or cello) and string orchestra. Dated: 21 January 1936. 'Zum Tode König Georgs V. von England'. Dur. 9'.
1. *Langsam*; 2. *Ruhig bewegt*; 3. *Lebhaft*; 4. *Choral: 'Vor deinen Thron tret ich hiermit'.*
fp: 22 January 1936, London, Paul Hindemith, cond. Sir Adrian Boult.
Pub. 1936, Schott; incl. score, and reduction by Franz Willms.

87. Five Songs on Old Texts. For mixed chorus (SSATB). 1936. Includes new versions of numbers from Op. 33.
1. *True love (Wahre Liebe)* (Heinrich von Veldeke). Dur. 1½'.

2. *Lady's lament (Frauenklage)* (Burggraf zu Regensburg). Dur. 1½–2'.
3. *Of household rule (Vom Hausregiment)* (Martin Luther). Dur. 1½–1¾'.
4. *Trooper's drinking song (Landsknechtstrinkleid)* (Anon.). Dur. 1½'.
5. *The Devil a monk would be (Art lässt nicht von Art).* Dur. ¾'.
Pub. 1943, Schott. English versions by Arthur Mendel (No. 1) and W. Strunk Jr. (Nos. 2–5).

88. Wahre Liebe (Tristan musste ohne Dank) (Heinrich v. Veldecke). For SSATB. 1936. Dur. 1¼–1½'. Pub. Schott.

89. Piano Sonata No. 1 in A (Der Main). 1936. Dur. 21'.
1. *Ruhig bewegte Viertel*; 2. *Im Zeitmass eines sehr langsamen Marsches*; 3. *Lebhaft*; 4. *Ruhig bewegte Viertel*; 5. *Lebhaft.*
Pub. 1936, Schott.

90. Piano Sonata No. 2 in G. 1936. Dur. 10'.
1. *Mässig schnell*; 2. *Lebhaft*; 3. *Sehr langsam.*
Pub. 1936, Schott.

BIBLIOGRAPHY:
Friedrich Metzler: Hindemiths zweite Klaviersonate, *Melos*, December 1954, p. 342.

91. Piano Sonata No. 3 in B flat. 1936. Dur. 20'.
1. *Ruhig bewegt*; 2. *Sehr lebhaft*; 3. *Mässig schnell*; 4. *Fugue (Lebhaft).*
fbp: 7 September 1938, BBC broadcast, Franz Reizenstein.
Pub. 1936, Schott.

92. Flute Sonata. 1936. Dur. 13–14'.
1. *Heiter bewegt*; 2. *Sehr langsam*; 3. *Sehr lebhaft*; 4. *Marsch.*
fp: 9 April 1937, Washington D.C., Georges Barrère and Jesús Maria Sanromá.
fEbp: 27 December 1937, John Francis and Millicent Silver.
Pub. 1937, Schott.

93. Symphonische Tanze (Symphonic Dances). For orchestra. 1937. Dur. 32'.
1. *Langsam*; 2. *Lebhaft*; 3. *Sehr langsam*; 4. *Mässig bewegt—Lebhaft.*
2 fl, 2 ob, 2 cl, 2 bsn; 4 hn, 2 tpt, 3 tmb, tuba;

timp, GC, side dm, tamb, cym, small cym, tgle, glock; strings.

fp: 5 December 1937, BBC broadcast, BBC Orchestra, cond. Paul Hindemith.

fEp (concert): January 1938, Newcastle, City Hall, BBC Symphony Orchestra, cond. Sir Adrian Boult.

f London p (concert): 12 January 1938, BBC Symphony Orchestra, cond. Sir Adrian Boult.

Pub. 1938, Schott; incl. study score, and reduction by H. G. Schnell for piano four hands.

94. Organ Sonata No. 1. 1937. Dur. $17\frac{1}{2}'$.
1. *Mässig schnell—Lebhaft*; 2. *Sehr langsam—Phantasie, frei—Ruhig bewegt.*

fp: 18 January 1938, West London Synagogue, London Contemporary Music Centre/Organ Music Society recital, Ralph Downes.

fEbp: 10 May 1938, Ralph Downes, organ of Broadcasting House.

Pub. 1937, Schott.

95. Organ Sonata No. 2. 1937. Dur. $10\frac{1}{2}'$
1. *Lebhaft*; 2. *Ruhig bewegt*; 3. *Fugue* (*Mässig bewegt, heiter*).

fp: as for No. 94.

fbp: 27 October 1938, C. H. Trevor, organ of Broadcasting House.

Pub. 1937, Schott.

96. Sonata. For piano four hands. 1938. Dur. 13′.
1. *Mässig bewegt*; 2. *Lebhaft*; 3. *Ruhig bewegt.*
Pub. 1939, Schott.

97. Drei leichte Stücke. For cello and piano. 1938. Dur. 7–8′.
1. *Mässig schnell, munter*; 2. *Langsam*; 3. *Lebhaft.*
Pub. 1938, Schott.

98. Bassoon Sonata. 1938. Dur. 9′.
1. *Leicht bewegt*; 2. *Langsam, Marsch, Pastorale.*

fp: 6 November 1938, Zürich.

fEbp: 10 September 1948, Norman Fawcett and Walter Bergmann.

Pub. 1939, Schott.

99. Quartet. For clarinet, violin, cello and piano. 1938. Dur. 24′.

1. *Mässig bewegt*; 2. *Sehr langsam*; 3. *Mässig bewegt—Lebhaft.*

fEbp: 10 September 1948, Frederick Thurston, Marie Wilson, John Shinebourne and Franz Reizenstein.

Pub. 1939, Schott; incl. score, and reduction by Paul Hindemith for two pianos four hands.

100. Oboe Sonata. 1938. Dur. $11\frac{1}{2}'$.
1. *Munter*; 2. *Sehr langsam, lebhaft.*

fp: 28 March 1938, BBC broadcast, Leon Goossens and Harriet Cohen.

Pub. 1939, Schott.

101. Nobilissima Visione. Dance Legend in six scenes by Paul Hindemith and Léonide Massine. 1938. Dur. 35′.
1. *Einleitung und Lied des Troubadours*; 2. *Tuchkäufer und Bettler*; 3. *Der Ritter*; 4. *Marsch*; 5. *Erscheinung der drei Frauen*; 6. *Festmusik*; 7. *Schluss des Festes*; 8. *Meditation*; 9. *Geigenspiel, Der Wolf*; 10. *Kärgliche Hochzeit*; 11. *Incipiunt laudes creaturarum.*

fl, ob, 2 cl, bsn; 2 hn, 2 tpt, tmb; timp, GC, side dm, small cym, tgle, big dm, glock; strings.

fp: 21 July 1938, Royal Opera House, Covent Garden, Ballet de Monte Carlo, cond. Paul Hindemith; given under the title 'St. Francis'.

fAp: 14 October 1938, New York, Metropolitan Opera House, cond. Paul Hindemith.

Pub. 1938, Schott; incl. piano score by Paul Hindemith.

BIBLIOGRAPHY:
Iain Hamilton: Nobilissima Visione, in *Decca Book of Ballet*, Muller (London) 1958, p. 167.
R.-A. Mooser: Nobilissima Visione de PH, *Dissonances*, November 1938.

101a. Nobilissima Visione. Revised orchestration, for full orchestra. 1939.
fl, 2 ob, 2 cl, 2 bsn; 4 hn, 2 tpt, 3 tmb, tuba; timp, pcssn; strings.

101b. Nobilissima Visione: Suite. 1938. Dur. 20–23′.
1. *Einleitung und Rondo*; 2. *Marsch und Pastorale*; 3. *Passacaglia.*
2 fl, 2 ob, 2 cl, 2 bsn; 4 hn, 2 tpt, 3 tmb,

tuba; timp, tgle, small cym, GC, cym, side dm, glock, big dm; strings.

fp: 13 September 1938, Venice.

fEp: 10 February 1939, BBC broadcast, BBC Orchestra, cond. Ernest Ansermet.

fAp: 23 March 1939, Los Angeles, Los Angeles Philharmonic Orchestra, cond. Paul Hindemith.

Pub. 1940, Schott; incl. study score.

101c. Meditation (from 'Nobilissima Visione'). For violin (or viola, or cello) and piano. Pub. 1938, Schott.

102. Horn Sonata. 1939. Dur. 16'.
1. *Mässig bewegt*; 2. *Ruhig bewegt*; 3. *Lebhaft*.
Pub. 1940, Schott.

103. Trumpet Sonata. 1939. Dur. 12'.
1. *Forceful*; 2. *Moderately fast—Lively*; 3. *Music of Mourning (Very slow)—Chorale* (*'Alle Menschen müssen sterben'*).
Pub. 1940, Schott.

104. Harp Sonata. 1939. Dur. 9'. Ded. Clelia Gatti-Aldrovandi.
1. *Mässig schnell*; 2. *Lebhaft*; 3. *Lied (Sehr langsam)*.
fEbp: 26 July 1948, Maria Korchinska.
Pub. 1940, Schott.

105. Violin Sonata in C. 1939. Dur. 11–12'.
1. *Lebhaft*; 2. *Langsam—Lebhaft*; 3. *Fugue (Ruhig bewegt)*.
Pub. 1940, Schott.

BIBLIOGRAPHY:
Günter Kehr: Wir studieren ein Hindemith-Violin Sonate, *Melos*, February 1947, p. 109.

106. Viola Sonata in C. 1939. Dur. 24'.
1. *Breit, mit Kraft—Ruhig—Lebhaft*; 2. *Sehr lebhaft*; 3. *Phantasie (sehr langsam, frei)*; 4. *Finale (mit 2 Variationen)*.
fbp: 20 January 1950, Herbert Downes and Noël Mewton Wood.
Pub. 1940, Schott.

107. Clarinet Sonata. 1939. Dur. 16–17½'.
1. *Mässig bewegt*; 2. *Lebhaft*; 3. *Sehr langsam*; 4. *Kleines Rondo: gemächlich*.
Pub. 1940, Schott.

108. Violin Concerto. 1939. Dur. 24'.
1. *Mässig bewegte Halbe*; 2. *Langsam*; 3. *Lebhaft*.

2 fl, pic, 2 ob, 2 cl, bcl, 2 bsn; 4 hn, 3 tpt, 3 tmb, tuba; timp, GC, side dm, cym, tgle, tamb, gong; strings.

fp: 14 March 1940, Amsterdam, Ferdinand Helmann and the Concertgebouw Orchestra, cond. Willem Mengelberg.

fEp: 6 June 1950, London, Denis East and the Chelsea Symphony Orchestra, cond. Norman Del Mar.

Pub. 1939, Schott; incl. study score, and reduction by Horst-Günther Schnell.

109. Six Chansons. For unacc. mixed chorus (SATB). 1939. Texts: Rainer Maria Rilke, English transl. Elaine de Sinçay. Dur. 7–8'.
1. *La Biche (The doe)*; 2. *Un Cygne (A swan)*; 3. *Puisque tout passe (Since all is passing)*; 4. *Printemps (Springtime)*; 5. *En Hiver (In winter)*; 6. *Verger (Orchard)*.
fbp: 27 June 1950, BBC broadcast, Dorian Singers, cond. Matyas Seiber.
Pub. 1939, Schott.

BIBLIOGRAPHY:
August Vörding: De Six Chansons van PH, *Mens en melodie*, June 1954, p. 177.

110. Drei Chöre. For male chorus (TTBB). Dated: 28 May 1939.
1. *Das verflüchte Geld* (old text). Dur. 1'.
2. *Nun da der Tag des Tages müde ward* (Nietzsche). Dur. 1¾'.
3. *Die Stiefmutter* (old text). Dur. 1½'.
fp: August 1939, Ostend, Haghe Zanghers.
Pub. 1939, Schott.

111. Erster Schnee (Gottfried Keller). For male chorus (TTBB). 1939. Dur. 3'. Pub. Schott.

112. Variationen über ein altes Tanzlied ('Das jung und auch das alte'). For male chorus (TTBB). 1939. Dur. 5¼'. Pub. Schott.

113. The Demon of the Gibbet (Das Galgenritt) (Fritz James O'Brien). For male chorus (TBB). 1939. Ded. Marshall Bartholomew and the Yale Glee Club. Dur. 3'. Pub. Schott; German text by Paul Hindemith.

114. Organ Sonata No. 3 (über alte Volkslieder). 1940. Dur. 11'.
1. *Oh Lord, to whom should I complain*

Hindemith, Paul

(*Moderato*); 2. *Awake, my treasure* (*Very slow*); 3. *I bid her then* (*Quietly, agitated*).
fp: 31 July 1940, Tanglewood (Mass.), E. Power Biggs.
Pub. 1940, Schott.

115. Old Irish Air ('The harp that once thro' Tara's halls'). For mixed chorus (SATB) and piano (or harp and strings). 1940. Dur. 3'.
Pub. 1958, Schott: vocal score and orchestral parts.

116. Theme and Variations: 'The Four Temperaments'. For string orchestra and solo piano. 1940. Dur. 27–28'.
1. *Theme*; 2. *Melancholy*; 3. *Sanguine*; 4. *Phlegmatic*; 5. *Choleric*.
fp: 3 September 1940, Boston, Lukas Foss and strings of the Boston Symphony Orchestra, cond. Richard Burgin.
fEp: 7 January 1947, Wigmore Hall, Kathleen Riddick String Orchestra.
Pub. 1949, Schott; incl. reduction by K. Hammer for two pianos four hands.

BIBLIOGRAPHY:
R.-A. Mooser: Thema mit 4 Variationen de PH, *Dissonances*, March–April 1944.
Harry Olt: Menniskan är skapt aff fyra elementer—Om Hindemiths Tema med fyra variationer för piano och stråkorkester, *Nutida musik*, Vol. 5 (1961–2), No. 3, p. 29.
G. Schab: Getanzter Hindemith, *Musikleben*, November 1952, p. 340.

117. Cello Concerto. 1940. Dur. 28'.
1. *Allegro moderato*; 2. *Andante con moto*; 3. *March* (*Allegro marciale*).
2 fl, 2 ob, 2 cl, bcl, 2 bsn; 4 hn, 2 tpt, 3 tmb, tuba; timp, side dm, cym, GC, tgle, tamb, big dm; celesta, strings.
fp: 7 February 1941, Boston, Gregor Piatigorsky.
Pub. 1940, Schott; incl. study score, and reduction by Paul Hindemith (1941), by H. G. Schnell (1943).

BIBLIOGRAPHY:
Ernst Laaf: Hindemiths neues Cello-Konzert (1940), *Melos*, May–June 1947, p. 212.

118. Symphony in E flat. 1940. Dur. 31–33'.
1. *Sehr lebhaft*; 2. *Sehr langsam*; 3. *Lebhaft*; 4. *Mässig schnelle Halbe*.

2 fl, pic, 2 ob, ca, 2 cl, bcl, 2 bsn, cbsn; 4 hn, 3 tpt, 3 tmb, tuba; timp, side dm, glock, tamb, Rute, tgle, GC, cym; strings.
fp: 21 November 1941, Minneapolis, Minneapolis Symphony Orchestra, cond. Dimitri Mitropulos.
f New York p: 25 December 1941, New York Philharmonic-Symphony, cond. Otto Klemperer.
fEp: 20 February 1944, BBC broadcast, BBC Symphony Orchestra, cond. Clarence Raybould.
Pub. 1940, Schott; incl. study score, and reduction by H. G. Schnell for piano four hands.

BIBLIOGRAPHY:
R.O.: Hindemiths neue Symphonie, *SM*, 1943.
Anon.: La Symphonie de PH, *Dissonances*, January–February 1943.

119. A frog he went a-courting. Variations on an old English nursery song for cello and piano. 1941. Dur. 4½'.
fbp: 8 June 1947, Zara Nelsova and Phyllis Spurr.
Pub. 1951, Schott.

120. Cor Anglais Sonata. 1941. Dated: 27 August 1941. Dur. 10½'.
1. *Slow*; 2. *Allegro pesante*; 3. *Moderato*; 4. *Scherzo* (*fast*); 5. *Moderato*; 6. *Allegro pesante*.
fp: January 1942, New York, Louis Speyer and Jesús Maria Sanromá.
fbp: 5 July 1948, BBC broadcast, John Cruft and Franz Reizenstein.
Pub. 1942, Schott.

121. Trombone Sonata. October 19. Dur. 10½–12'.
1. *Allegro moderato maestoso*. 2. *Allegretto grazioso*; 3. *Swashbuckler's Song: Allegro pesante—Allegro moderato maestoso*.
Pub. 1942, Schott.

122. A Song of Music (George Tyler). For female chorus (SSA) and piano or string orchestra. 1942. Dur. 2'. Pub. Schott; German version by Paul Hindemith.

123. Ludus Tonalis. Studies in counterpoint,

tonal organization and piano playing. October 1942. Dur. 48'.

fp: 15 February 1943, Chicago, Willard McGregor.

?fEp: early 1945, Morley College, Noël Mewton-Wood; also 26 March 1945, National Gallery, Noël Mewton-Wood.

BIBLIOGRAPHY:
F. Fleischer: Il Ludus Tonalis di Hindemith, *Il Diapason*, January 1950.
D. Hussey: Ludus Tonalis, *Spectator*, 6 April 1945, p. 311.
G. Maier: Hindemith's Ludus Tonalis, *Etude*, October 1953, p. 21.
Alf Thoor: Hindemith, Ludus Tonalis, *Dansk Musiktidsskrift*, 1952, No. 2.
— Hindemith, Ludus Tonalis och intellektualismen, *Musikrevy*, 1952, No. 2, p. 63.
Louis Saguer: Ludus Tonalis de PH, *Contrepoints*, No. 4, May–June 1946, p. 20.
Hans Tischler: Hindemith's Ludus Tonalis and Bach's Well-Tempered Clavier, a comparison, *MR*, August–November 1959, p. 217.
Michael Tippett: Ludus Tonalis, *New Statesman*, 24 March 1945, p. 188.
G. Werker: Ludus Tonalis van Hindemith, *Mens en melodie*, January 1968, p. 21.

124. Sonata. For two pianos four hands. August 1942. Dur. 16'.

1. *Chimes*; 2. *Allegro*; 3. *Canon*; 4. *Recitative: 'This World's Joy'*; 5. *Fugue: moderate*.

fp: 20 November 1942, New York, Dougherty and Ruzitska.

fEbp: 9 June 1947, Peter Stadlen and Noël Mewton-Wood.

Pub. 1942, Schott.

BIBLIOGRAPHY:
Ernst Laaff: Das Rezitativ in Hindemiths Sonate für 2 Klaviere, *Melos*, April 1948, p. 103.

125. La Belle Dame Sans Merci (Keats). For voice and piano. 1942. Dur. 5'. Pub. Schott.

126. Orfeo. Claudio Monteverdi, realization by Paul Hindemith. 1943. Dur. 60'.

fp: 3 June 1954, Vienna, cond. Paul Hindemith.

Pub. Schott.

127. Cupid and Psyche. Ballet Overture for orchestra. July 1943. Dur. 6'.

fl, pic, 2 ob, 2 cl, 2 bsn; 2 hn, 2 tpt, 2 tmb; timp, tgle, cym, glock; strings.

fp: 29 October 1943, Philadelphia, Philadelphia Orchestra, cond. Eugene Ormandy.

fEp: 3 August 1945, Royal Albert Hall, Promenade Concert, London Symphony Orchestra, cond. Constant Lambert.

Pub. 1944, Schott.

128. String Quartet No. 5 in E flat. May 1943. Ded. Budapest String Quartet. Dur. 26'.

1. *Sehr ruhig und ausdrucksvoll*; 2. *Lebhaft und sehr energisch*; 3. *Ruhig, Variationen*; 4. *Breit und energisch*.

fp: 7 November 1943, Washington, Budapest Quartet.

fEbp: 9 June 1947, Aeolian Quartet.

Pub. 1944, Schott: study score and parts.

BIBLIOGRAPHY:
W. Kolneder: Hindemiths Streichquartett V in Es, *SM*, 1950.

129. Symphonic Metamorphosis on Themes of Carl Maria von Weber. For large orchestra. August 1943. Dur. 18'.

1. *Allegro*; 2. *Turandot Scherzo*; 3. *Andantino*; 4. *Marsch*.

2 fl, pic, 2 ob, ca, 2 cl, bcl, 2 bsn, cbsn; 4 hn, 2 tpt, 3 tmb, tuba; 4 timp, GC, side dm, parade dm, tomtom, tamb, tgle, cym, small cym, small gong, bells, glock; strings.

fp: 20 January 1944, New York, New York Philharmonic-Symphony, cond. Artur Rodzinsky.

fEp: 3 September 1946, Royal Albert Hall, Promenade Concert, BBC Symphony Orchestra, cond. Constant Lambert.

Pub. 1945, Schott; incl. study score, and reduction by Jon Thorarinsson for two pianos four hands (1952).

BIBLIOGRAPHY:
Wilfried Brennecke: Die Metamorphosen-Werke von Richard Strauss und PH, *SM*, 1962, May–June p. 129, July–August p. 199.
Anon.: Metamorphoses symphoniques de PH, *Dissonances*, July–August 1946.

130. Saxophone Sonata. For alto saxophone (or alto horn, or French horn) and piano. 1943. Dur. 11'.

Hindemith, Paul

1. *Ruhig bewegt*; 2. *Lebhaft*; 3. *Sehr langsam*;
4. *Das Posthorn (Zwiegespräch)—Lebhaft*.
Pub. 1956, Schott.

131. Nine English Songs. For soprano (or
mezzo-soprano) and piano. 1942–4.
  1. *Echo* (Thomas Moore). 1942. Dur. 1'.
  2. *Envoy* (Francis Thompson). 1942. Dur.
4'.
  3. *The moon* (Shelley). 1942. Dur. 3'.
  4. *On a fly drinking out of his cup* (William
Oldys). 1942. Dur. 2'.
  5. *On hearing 'The Last Rose of Summer'*
(Charles Wolfe). 1942. Dur. 3'.
  6. *The wild flower's song* (William Blake).
1942. Dur. 2'.
  7. *The whistlin' thief* (Samuel Lover). 1942.
Dur. 3'.
  8. *Sing on there in the swamp* (Walt Whitman). 1943. Dur. 2$\frac{1}{2}$'.
  9. *To music, to becalm his fever* (Herrick).
1944. Dur. 4'.
  Pub. 1944–5, Schott.

132. Hérodiade. Orchestra Recitation. 1944.
Poem: Stéphane Mallarmé. Dur. 22'.
fl, ob, cl, bsn; hn; piano, strings.
fp: 30 October 1944, Washington D.C.,
Martha Graham dance recital.
fEp: 11 June 1947, BBC broadcast, New
London Orchestra, cond. Paul Hindemith.
Pub. Schott: reduction by Paul Hindemith.

133. String Quartet No. 6. 1945, New
Haven, Conn. Dur. 15'.
  1. *Fast*; 2. *Quiet, scherzando*; 3. *Slow*;
4. *Canon: moderately fast, gay*.
fp: 21 March 1946, Washington D.C.,
Budapest Quartet.
fEp: 28 March 1950, BBC broadcast,
Amadeus Quartet.
Pub. 1949, Schott: study score and parts.

134. Piano Concerto. Dated: 29 November
1945, New Haven, Conn. Ded. Jesús Maria
Sanromá. Dur. 26–30'.
  1. *Moderately fast*; 2. *Slow*; 3. *Medley, 'Tre
Fontane'* (*Canzona, March, Valse lente, Caprice,
'Tre Fontane'—medieval dance*).
fl, pic, 2 ob, 2 cl, bcl, 2 bsn; 2 hn, 2 tpt, 2
tmb, tuba; 3 timp, 2 pcssn; strings.
fp: 27 February 1947, Cleveland (Ohio),

Jesús Maria Sanromá and the Cleveland
Orchestra, cond. George Szell.
fEp: 1 April 1950, BBC broadcast, Noël
Mewton-Wood and the BBC Symphony
Orchestra, cond. Sir Adrian Boult.
Pub. 1948, Schott: score, and reduction by
Paul Hindemith for two pianos four hands.

**135. When Lilacs Last in the Door-Yard
Bloom'd.** Requiem 'For Those We Love'.
For mezzo-soprano, baritone, mixed chorus
and orchestra. Dated: 20 April 1946, New
Haven, Conn. Text: Walt Whitman; German
version by Paul Hindemith. Dur. 63–65'.
fl, pic, ob, ca, cl, bcl, bsn, cbsn; 3 hn, 2 tpt, 2
tmb, tuba; timp, GC, cym, gong, glock, tgle,
snare dm, parade dm, chimes; organ, army
bugle; strings.
fp: 5 May 1946, New York, Collegiate
Chorale, cond. Robert Shaw.
fEbp: 1 June 1950, Eugenia Zareska, Jean
Claverie, Chorus of Radiodiffusion Français
and l'Orchestre National, cond. Manuel
Rosenthal.
fEp: December 1950, BBC broadcast,
Nancy Evans, Arthur Reckless, BBC Chorus,
BBC Orchestra, cond. Paul Sacher.
f London p (concert): 17 April 1962, Royal
Festival Hall, Janet Baker, Thomas Hemsley,
London Philharmonic Choir and Orchestra,
cond. Paul Hindemith.
Pub. 1948, Schott; incl. vocal score by the
composer.

BIBLIOGRAPHY:
D. Fuller: Hindemith's Lilacs, *Modern Music*,
July 1946, p. 202.
Hugo Puetter: PHs Requiem, *Melos*, Decem-
ber 1948, p. 341.
R. Sabin: Requiem, by and for, PH, *American
Record Guide*, May 1964, p. 756.
August Vördning: Het Requiem van Hinde-
mith, *Mens en melodie*, February 1949, p. 47.
Edith Weber: Première audition à Strasbourg
du Requiem de Hindemith en sa version
allemande, *La Vie musicale*, 1952, No. 12,
p. 12.

135a. Requiem: Prelude. Dur. 5'. Same
orchestration. Pub. Schott.

136. Symphonia Serena. For orchestra,

1946. Ded. Dallas Symphony Orchestra. Dur. 25–30'.

1. *Moderately fast*; 2. *Rather fast* (*for wind instruments only*); 3. *Colloquy* (*for string orchestra in two sections*)—*Quiet*; 4. *Finale: Gay*.

2 fl, pic, 2 ob, ca, 2 cl, bcl, 2 bsn, cbsn; 4 hn, 2 tpt, 2 tmb, tuba; 2 timp, GC, cym, tgle, wood blocks, glock, snare dm, tamb; celesta, solo violin, solo viola, strings.

fp: 1 February 1947, Dallas, Dallas Symphony Orchestra, cond. Antal Dorati.

fEp: 14 June 1947, BBC broadcast, London Philharmonic Orchestra, cond. Paul Hindemith.

fEp (concert): 13 March 1957, Royal Philharmonic Orchestra, cond. Rudolf Kempe.

Pub. 1947, Schott; incl. study score.

BIBLIOGRAPHY:
Ernst Laaff: Hindemiths Symphonia serena, *Melos*, December 1948, p. 328.

137. Apparebit repentina dies. For mixed chorus and wind instruments. Text: Latin, 700. 1947. Ded. 'For the Symposium on Music Criticism, Harvard University'. Dur. 16–17'.

1. *Apparebit repentina dies*; 2. *Hujus omnes ad electi colligentur dexteram*; 3. *Retro ruent tunc injusti ignes in perpetuos*; 4. *Ydri fraudes ergo cave*.

4 hn, 2 tpt, 3 tmb, bs tuba.

fp: May 1947, Cambridge (Mass.), cond. Robert Shaw.

fEbp: 14 June 1948, Chorus and Orchestra of NWDR, cond. Hans Schmidt-Isserstedt.

Pub. Schott: vocal score by Paul Hindemith.

138. Clarinet Concerto. 1947. Ded. Benny Goodman. Dur. 21'.

1. *Rather fast*; 2. *Ostinato*; 3. *Quiet*; 4. *Gay*.

2 fl, pic, 2 ob, 2 bsn; 2 hn, 2 tpt, 2 tmb; timp, pcssn; strings.

fp: December 1950, Philadelphia, Benny Goodman and the Philadelphia Orchestra, cond. Eugene Ormandy.

fEp: 17 August 1951, Royal Albert Hall, Promenade Concert, Frederick Thurston and the London Symphony Orchestra, cond. Basil Cameron.

Pub. 1950, Schott; incl. reduction by Paul Hindemith.

139. Wind Septet. 1948. Dur. 15'.

1. *Lebhaft*; 2. *Intermezzo* (*Sehr langsam, frei*);

3. *Variationen* (*Mässig schnell*); 4. *Intermezzo* (*Sehr langsam*); 5. *Fugue: Alter Berner Marsch* (*Schnell*).

fp: 30 December 1948, Milan, wind group from the Teatro Nuovo orchestra.

fEbp: 9 September 1955, Marsyas Wind Ensemble.

Pub. 1949, Schott: study score and parts.

140. Cello Sonata. 1948. Dated: 8 March 1948, New Haven, Conn. Dur. 20'.

1. *Pastorale*; 2. *Moderately fast—Slow*; 3. *Passacaglia*.

fp: 1 November 1948, BBC broadcast, Zara Nelsova and Wilfrid Parry.

Pub. 1948, Schott.

141. Concerto for woodwind, harp and orchestra. 1949. Ded. Alice M. Ditson Fund.

1. *Moderately fast*; 2. *Grazioso*; 3. *Rondo* (*Rather fast*).

Solo instruments: fl, ob, cl, bsn, hp. Orchestra: 2 hn, 2 tpt, tmb; strings.

fp: 15 May 1949, New York, cond. Thor Johnson.

Pub. 1950, Schott; incl. study score.

142. Concerto for trumpet and bassoon with string orchestra. 1949. Ded. Connecticut Academy of Arts and Sciences. Dur. 16–17'.

1. *Allegro spiritoso*; 2. *Molto adagio*; 3. *Vivace*.

fp: 4 November 1949, New Haven (Conn.), cond. Keith Wilson.

Pub. 1954, Schott.

143. Sinfonietta in E. For orchestra. 1949. Ded. Louisville Symphony Orchestra. Dur. 21'.

1. *Fast*; 2. *Adagio and Fugato*; 3. *Intermezzo ostinato* (*Presto*); 4. *Recitative and Rondo*.

fl, pic, 2 ob, 2 cl, 2 bsn; 3 hn, tpt, 2 tmb, tuba; 3 timp, cym, glock; celesta, strings.

fp: 1 March 1950, Louisville (Kentucky), Louisville Symphony Orchestra, cond. Paul Hindemith.

fEp: 6 April 1951, Royal Albert Hall, London Symphony Orchestra, cond. Hans Schmidt-Isserstedt.

Pub. Schott; incl. study score.

144. Double Bass Sonata. 1949. Dur. 14–15'.

Hindemith, Paul

1. *Allegretto*; 2. *Scherzo (Allegro assai)*; 3. *Molto adagio—Allegretto grazioso (Lied)*.

fp: 26 April 1950, Vienna, Otto Rühm and Gerhard Rühm.

Pub. 1950, Schott.

145. Vier Kanons. For women's chorus a cappella. 1928–49. Dur. 2½'.

1. *Sine musica nulla disciplina* (Hrabanus Maurus). 1946.

2. *Musica divinas laudes* (Old Proverb). 1949. Ded. Elizabeth Sprague Coolidge. Pub. 1950.

3. *Hie kann nit sein böser Mut* (Old Proverb). 1928.

4. *Wer sich die Musik erkiest* (Martin Luther). 1928.

Pub. 1951, Schott.

146. Horn Concerto. 1949. Dur. 15'.

1. *Moderately fast*; 2. *Very fast*; 3. *Very slow—Moderately fast*.

fl, pic, 2 ob, 2 cl, 2 bsn; timp; strings.

fp: 8 June 1950, Baden-Baden, Dennis Brain, cond. Paul Hindemith.

Pub. 1950, Schott.

147. Symphony in B flat. For concert band. 1951. Dur. 19'.

1. *Moderately fast, with vigor*; 2. *Andantino grazioso*; 3. *Fugue (Rather broad—Fast, energetic)*.

2 fl, pic, 2 ob, E-flat cl, solo cl, 3 cl, alto cl, bcl, 2 bsn, 2 alto sax, ten sax, bar sax; solo cornet, 3 cornets, 2 tpt, 4 hn, 3 tmb, baritone, 2 basses; timp, snare dm, GC, glock, tamb, tgle, cym.

fp: 5 April 1951, Washington D.C., cond. Paul Hindemith.

fEp (broadcast): 8 May 1953, BBC, Band of the Irish Guards, cond. Capt. C. H. Jaeger.

Pub. 1951, Schott; incl. study score.

148. Symphonie: Die Harmonie der Welt. For orchestra. 1951. Ded. Paul Sacher and the Basle Chamber Orchestra on its twenty-fifth anniversary. Dur. 32–34'.

1. *Musica Instrumentalis*; 2. *Musica Humana*; 3. *Musica Mundana*.

2 fl, pic, 2 ob, 2 cl, bcl, 2 bsn, cbsn; 4 hn, 2 tpt, 3 tmb, tuba; timp, snare dm, cym, GC, parade dm, glock, tgle, small cym, tamb; strings.

fp: 24 January 1952, Basle, Basle Chamber Orchestra, cond. Paul Sacher.

fGBp: 1953, Edinburgh Festival, Vienna Philharmonic Orchestra, cond. Wilhelm Furtwängler.

f London p: 16 March 1955, Royal Festival Hall, Royal Philharmonic Society concert, Royal Philharmonic Orchestra, cond. Paul Hindemith.

Pub. 1952, Schott; incl. study score.

BIBLIOGRAPHY:

Walther Krüger: Die Harmonie der Welt—Geschichtliche Betrachtungen zu PHs neue sinfonie, *Musica*, 1952, Nos. 7–8, p. 289.

Willi Reich: Hindemiths Sinfonie Die Harmonie der Welt in Basel uraufgeführt, *Musikleben*, March 1952, p. 87.

149. Sonata for four horns. 1952. Dur. 8'.

1. *Fugato (Sehr langsam)*; 2. *Lebhaft*; 3. *Variationen über 'Ich schell mein Horn'*.

fp: June 1953, Vienna, members of the Vienna Symphony Orchestra (Wiener Symphoniker).

fEbp: 5 January 1956, Dennis Brain, Neill Sanders, Edmund Chapman and Alfred Cursue.

Pub. 1953, Schott: study score and parts.

150. Ite, angeli veloces. Cantata in three parts. 1953–5. Text: Paul Claudel. Ded. UNESCO. Dur. 45'.

1. *Chant de triomphe du roi David*. For alto, tenor, mixed chorus, audience, orchestra and wind orchestra. 1955.

2 fl, 3 ob, 3 cl, 3 bsn; 4 hn, 2 tpt, 3 tmb, tuba; timp, pcssn; piano, strings. Secondary group: fl, ob, cl, bsn; hn, tpt, tmb; strings. Wind orchestra: tpt, hn, tmb.

fp: 4 June 1955, Wuppertal, cond. Paul Hindemith.

Pub. 1955, Schott: vocal score.

2. *Custos quid de nocte*. For tenor, mixed chorus and orchestra. 1955.

fl, ob, cl, bsn; hn, tpt, tmb, tuba; piano, strings.

fp: 4 June 1955, Wuppertal, cond. Paul Hindemith.

Pub. 1955, Schott.

3. *Cantique de l'espérance* (Canticle to Hope). For mezzo-soprano, mixed chorus, audience, orchestra and wind orchestra. 1953.

Orchestration as No. 1.

fp: 9 July 1953, Brussels, United Nations Day concert, cond. Paul Hindemith.

Pub. 1953, Schott: vocal score, German and English texts by Paul Hindemith.

BIBLIOGRAPHY:
Martin Stephen: Hindemiths Kantaten-Trilogie, *Das Musikleben*, July–August 1955, p. 269.
Karl H. Wörner: Hindemiths Claudel-Kantate—Zu Hindemiths 60. Geburtstag am 16. November, *NZfM*, November 1955, p. 67.

151. Tuba Sonata. For bass tuba and piano. 1955. Dur. 11'.

1. *Allegro pesante*; 2. *Allegro assai*; 3. *Variationen*.

Pub. 1957, Schott.

152. Two Songs. For soprano or tenor and piano. 1955. Words: Oscar Cox. Ded. Oscar and Louise.

1. *Image*. Dur. $1\frac{1}{4}$–$1\frac{1}{2}$'.
2. *Beauty touch me*. Dur. $1\frac{1}{4}$–$1\frac{1}{2}$'.

Pub. Schott.

153. Die Harmonie der Welt. Opera in five acts. 1956–7. Text: Paul Hindemith.

2 fl, pic, 2 ob, ca, 2 cl, bcl, 2 bsn, cbsn; 4 hn, 2 tpt, 3 tmb, tuba; timp, pcssn; hp, strings. Stage music: fl, 2 pic, ob, 2 cl, bsn; hn, 3 tmb; pcssn; va, c, db.

fp: 11 August 1957, Munich, Prinzregentheater, cond. Paul Hindemith; with Liselotte Fölser, Hertha Töpper, Keith Engen, Josef Metternich, Richard Holm, Kurt Wehofschnitz, Marcel Cordes; producer Rudolf Hartmann. Relayed by BBC.

Pub. Schott; incl. full score facsimile of autograph, vocal score by the composer.

BIBLIOGRAPHY:
Andres Briner: Eine Bekenntnisoper PHs, *SM*, 1959, January p. 1, February p. 50.
G. M. Gatti: L'Armonia del mondo di PH, *Nuova antologia di lettere, arte e scienze*, November 1957.
Everett Helm: Hindemith's Harmony of the World, *MR*, November 1957, p. 320.
Paul Hindemith: Die Harmonie der Welt, Proben von Dichtung und Musik, *Melos*, June 1957.
Guido Pannain: Die Harmonie der Welt e l'ultimo Hindemith, *La Rassegna musicale*, September 1957, p. 193.
Eduard Reeser: Die Harmonie der Welt van Hindemith, *Mens en melodie*, November 1957.
H. H. Stuckenschmidt: PH, Die Harmonie der Welt, Staatsoper München, in *Oper in dieser Zeit*, Friedrich Verlag (Hannover) 1964, p. 22.

154. Octet. For clarinet, bassoon, horn, violin, 2 violas, cello and double bass. 1957–8. Ded. Kammermusikvereinigung der Berliner Philharmoniker.

1. *Breit*; 2. *Varianten* (*Mässig bewegt*); 3. *Langsam*; 4. *Sehr lebhaft*; 5. *Fuge und drei altmodische Tänze* (*Walzer, Polka, Galopp*).

fp: 23 September 1958, Berlin Festival, Berlin Philharmonic Chamber Music Group, with Paul Hindemith (viola).

fEp: 1 November 1958, BBC broadcast, Prometheus Ensemble.

Pub. 1958, Schott: score and parts.

BIBLIOGRAPHY:
Karl H. Wörner: Hindemiths neue Oktett, *Melos*, November 1958.

155. Suite französischer Tänze. For small orchestra. 1958. From 'Livres de Danceries' (1547–57) by Claude Gervaise and Estienne du Tertre. Dur. 8'.

1. *Pavane und Gaillarde* (Estienne du Tertre); 2. *Tourdion* ('C'est grand plaisir'); 3. *Bransle simple*; 4. *Bransle de Bourgongne* (Claude Gervaise); 5. *Bransle simple* (Claude Gervaise); 6. *Bransle d'Escosse* (Estienne du Tertre)—*Pavane*.

fl, pic, ob, ca, bsn; tpt, lute; strings.

Pub. 1958, Schott.

156. Pittsburgh Symphony. For orchestra. Dated: 13 November 1958, Bloney. Composed for the Bicentennial of the City of Pittsburgh. Dur. 25–26'.

1. *Molto energico*; 2. *Slow march* (*Moderato*); 3. *Ostinato* (*Allegro molto*).

2 fl, pic, 2 ob, ca, 2 cl, bcl, 2 bsn, cbsn; 4 hn, 2 tpt, 3 tmb, tuba; 4 timp, tgle, glock, cast, wood block, tomtom, 2 snare dm, small cym, cym, GC; strings.

fp: 31 January 1959, Pittsburgh, cond. Paul Hindemith.

Pub. 1959, Schott; incl. study score.

BIBLIOGRAPHY:

Andres Briner: Hindemiths Pittsburgh Symphony, *Melos*, September 1959.

157. Zwölf Madrigale (Josef Weinheber). For 5-part mixed chorus (SSATB) a cappella. 1958. Ded. Hedi Straumann.

1. *Mitwelt.* Dur. 1'.
2. *Eines Narren, eines Künstlers Leben.* Dur. 2'.
3. *Tauche deine Furcht in schwarzen Wein.* Dur. 2½'.
4. *Trink aus!* Dur. 1½'.
5. *An eine Tote.* Dur. 7'.
6. *Frühling.* Dur. 1'.
7. *An einen Schmetterling.* Dur. 1¾'.
8. *Judaskuss.* Dur. 3'.
9. *Magisches Rezept.* Dur. 2½'.
10. *Es bleibt wohl, was gesagt wird.* Dur. 1¼'.
11. *Kraft fand zu Form.*
12. *Du Zweifel an dem Sinn der Welt.* Dur. 2¼'.

fp: 18 October 1958, Vienna, Wiener Kammerchor, cond. Paul Hindemith.

Pub. 1958, Schott.

158. 13 Motetten. For soprano or tenor and paino. 1941–60.

1. *Exiit edictum.* 1960. Dur. 6'. Pub. 1960.
2. *Pastores loquebantur.* 1944. Dur. 3½'. Pub. 1952.
3. *Dicebat Jesus scribis et pharisaeis.* 1959. Dur. 5'. Pub. 1959.
4. *Dixit Jesus Petro.* 1959. Dur. 3½'. Pub. 1959.
5. *Angelus Domini apparuit.* 1958. Dur. 4½'. Pub. 1959.
6. *Erat Joseph et Maria.* 1959. Dur. 4'. Pub. 1959.
7. *Defuncto Herode.* 1958. Dur. 3'. Pub. 1959.
8. *Cum natus esset.* 1941. Dur. 5'. Pub. 1952.
9. *Cum factus esset Jesus.* 1959. Dur. 3½'. Pub. 1960.
10 *Vidit Joannes Jesum.* 1959. Dur. 4'. Pub. 1960.
11. *Nuptiae factae sunt.* 1944. Dur. 4'. Pub. 1952.
12. *Cum descendisset Jesus.* 1960. Pub. 1960.

13. *Ascendente Jesu in naviculam.* 1943. Dur. 3½'. Pub. 1959.

fp (Nos. 1, 4, 6, 10, 12): 13 April 1961, Venice Festival, Magda Laszlo, acc. Eugenio Magnoli.

fp (Nos. 2, 8, 11): 2 April 1951, Vienna Festival, Irmgard Seefried, acc. Erik Werba.

f London p: March 1952, Irmgard Seefried, acc. Gerald Moore.

fEbp: 8 September 1952, Irmgard Seefried, acc. Gerald Moore.

fp (Nos. 3, 5, 9, 13): 2 October 1960, Berlin Festival, Ernst Haefliger, acc. Hertha Klust.

fEp: 23 February 1961, BBC broadcast, Max Worthley, acc. Ernest Lush.

Pub. Schott.

BIBLIOGRAPHY:

Erik Werba: Hindemiths Motetten für sopran, *Musikerziehung*, December 1954.

159. The Long Christmas Dinner. Opera in one act. 1961. Text: Thornton Wilder; German version by Paul Hindemith. Dur. 60'.

2 fl, pic, ob, cl, bcl, 2 bsn, cbsn; 2 tpt, 2 tmb, tuba; snare dm, tamb, glock, bells, GC; hpschd, strings.

fp: 17 December 1961, Mannheim, Nationaltheater, cond. Paul Hindemith; with Elisabeth Thoma, Eva-Maria Molner, Gertrud Schretter-Petersik, Petrina Kruss, Erika Ahsbahs, Thomas Tipton, Jean Cox, Frederick Dalberg, Georg Völker; producer, Hans Schüler.

Pub. Schott.

BIBLIOGRAPHY:

Richard Engländer: En ny Hindemith-opera—The long Christmas dinner, *Musik*, 1962, No. 4, p. 18.

Willi Schuh: PH–Thornton Wilder—Das lange Weihnachtsmal, *SM*, January–February 1962, p. 36.

160. Mainzer Umzug. For soprano, tenor, baritone, mixed chorus and orchestra. 1962. Dur. 38'.

2 fl, 2 ob, 2 cl, 2 bsn; 2 hn, 2 tpt, 2 tmb; GC, snare dm, parade dm, cym, tomtom, tgle, glock, bells (2 players); strings.

fp: 23 June 1962, Mainz, Städtisches Theater, Anny Schlemm, Josef Traxel,

Hubert Hofmann, chorus and orchestra of Städtisches Theater, cond. Paul Hindemith. Pub. Schott.

161. Organ Concerto. 1962. Composed for the New York Philharmonic for the opening of the Lincoln Center for the Performing Arts. Dur. 25′.
2 fl, 2 ob, 2 cl, 3 bsn; 2 hn, 2 tpt, 3 tmb, tuba; timp, small dm, GC, cym, glock; celesta, strings.
fp: 25 April 1963, New York, Anton Heiller and the New York Philharmonic, cond. Paul Hindemith.
Pub. Schott; incl. study score.

162. Messe. For mixed chorus a cappella. 1963. Dur. 20′.
fp: 12 November 1963, Vienna, Wiener Kammerchor, cond. Paul Hindemith.
fGp: 17 January 1964, Berlin Philharmonic concert, RIAS Kammerchor, cond. Günther Arndt.
Pub. 1963, Schott.

BIBLIOGRAPHY:
Clytus Gottwald: Hindemiths Messe a cappella, *Melos*, November 1965, p. 386.
Anon.: PHs Messe, *SM*, September–October 1965, p. 294.

WRITINGS BY PAUL HINDEMITH
Unterweisung im Tonsatz, Mainz, 1937; transl. as The Craft of Musical Composition, Associated Music Publishers (New York) 1941–42.
A Concentrated Course in Traditional Harmony, Associated Music Publishers (New York) Book 1, 1943, 1953: Book 2, Schott (London).
Elementary Training for Musicians, 1946, Schott (1948).
How music happens, *Saturday Review*, 29 December 1951, p. 29.
J. S. Bach: Heritage and Obligation, Yale University Press (New Haven) 1952.
A Composer's World: Horizons and Limitations, Harvard University Press (Cambridge, Mass.) 1952; Ger. transl. by the author as Komponist in seiner Welt, Mainz, 1959.

GENERAL BIBLIOGRAPHY
Walter Abendroth: PHs Sendung in unserer Zeit, *Musica*, 1964, No. 2, p. 49.

Gerald Abraham: Hindemith is as bracing as Skegness, *Radio Times*, 17 March 1933, p. 660.
Jean Absil: Hommage à Hindemith, *Bulletin de la classe des beaux-arts* (Académie royale de Belgique), 1964, Nos. 2–3.
Liko Amar: Freundschaft mit PH, *Melos*, November 1955, p. 314.
C. O. Andberg: PH och musikutvecklingen, *Musikern*, No. 6, June 1960, p. 13.
M. Anderson: Hindemiths tonesprog, teori og praksis, *Dansk Musiktidsskrift*, November 1955, p. 89.
Paul Bekker: Hindemith, *Anbruch*, February 1925, p. 57.
Erich Benninghoven: Der Geist im Werke Hindemiths, *Die Musik*, July 1929, p. 718.
W. Berten: PH und die deutsch Musik, *NZfM*, June 1933, p. 537.
Howard Boatwright: PH as teacher, *MQ*, July 1954, p. 279.
Richard Bobbitt: Hindemith's twelve-tone scale, *MR*, May 1965, p. 104.
Alfred Brasch: Kulturpolitische Reaktion um PH, *NZfM*, December 1934, p. 1271.
Andres Briner: Hindemith und der Fortschritt des Jahrhunderts, *Melos*, July–August 1966, p. 216.
Arthur G. Browne: PH and neo-classic music, *M&L*, January 1932, p. 42.
Fritz Büchtger: Hindemiths Schulwerk, *Münchner Neueste Nachrichten*, 25 March 1928; *Der Auftakt*, 1929, No. 11, p. 285.
Sas Bunge: Ein belangrijk boek van Hindemith, *Mens en melodie*, May 1954, p. 150.
K. Burke: Hindemith does his part, *Nation*, 24 October 1934, p. 487.
E. T. Canby: Music for use, *Saturday Review of Literature*, 30 August 1947, supplement, p. 6.
Norman Cazden: Hindemith and nature, *American Musicological Society Journal*, summer 1954, p. 288; *MR*, November 1954, p. 288.
M. J. Colucci: A comparative study of contemporary musical theories in selected writings of Piston, Krenek and Hindemith, *Dissertation Abstracts*, November 1957, p. 2628.
Arnold Cooke: PH, *Music Survey*, 1949, No. 1 p. 8, No. 2 p. 80.

Hindemith, Paul

N. Costarelli: PH, *Santa Cecilia*, June 1957.
John Culshaw: Hindemith and utility music, in *A Century of Music*, Dobson (London) 1952, p. 144.
Luigi Dallapiccola: PH, *Musica d'oggi*, 1964, No. 1, p. 10.
O. Daniel: Hindemith, 1895–1963, *Musical America*, January 1964, p. 58.
Norman Demuth: Gebrauchmusik, in *Musical Trends in the 20th Century*, Rockliff (London) 1952, p. 192.
Marteen Dijk: PHs Unterweisung im Tonsatz, *De Wereld der Muziek*, January and February 1938.
Denijs Dille: un grand ouvrage de PH sur la composition, *Revue internationale de musique*, No. 7, January 1940, p. 38.
Walter Dirks: PH und dieser Stunde, *Frankfurter Hefte*, 1946, No. 4, p. 28.
Erich Doflein: Choral works by Hindemith, *Anbruch*, November–December 1929.
— Die sechs Streichquartette von PH, *SM*, November 1955, p. 413.
Hans Ehinger: PH und die Schweiz, *NZfM*, February 1964.
Alfred Einstein: PHs Unterweisung im Tonsatz, in *Von Schütz bei Hindemith*, Pan-Verlag (Zürich/Stuttgart) 1957, p. 147.
— PH, *Modern Music*, April 1926.
Hans Eppstein: Hindemith och traditionen, *Nutida musik*, Vol. 3 (1959–60), No. 1, p. 6.
Peter Epstein: PHs Theatermusik, *Die Musik*, May 1931, p. 583.
Peter Evans: Hindemith's piano music, *MT*, November 1956, p. 572.
R. Evett: Hindemith early and late, *New Republic*, 6 April 1963, p. 26.
David Ewen: PH, *American Music Lover*, May 1937.
Kurt von Fischer: PH—Musica humana, *SM*, 1966, No. 3 (May–June), p. 147.
J. V. Forsman: PH, et musikalisk Portraet, *Tidsskrift f. d. folkl. musiklevet*, 1952, p. 78.
E. Franco: Hindemith y Dallapiccola en Madrid, *Musica* (Madrid), October–December 1954, p. 104.
A. A. Fraser: PH, *M&L*, April 1929, p. 167.
Peter Racine Fricker: Two song cycles, *The Listener*, 24 January 1963, p. 185.
Wilhelm Furtwängler: Il caso Hindemith, *Musica d'oggi*, December 1958.

Herm. Rud. Gail: PH als Lyriker, *Stuttgarter Neues Tagblatt*, 4 September 1926.
Wolfram Gerbracht: Begegnung mit Hindemith, *Musica*, 1948, No. 6, p. 314.
Georg Gregor: Hindemiths pädagogisches Werk, *Musik im Unterricht*, November 1960.
Berta Gressmar: Der Fall Hindemith, *Musica*, 1948, Nos. 1–2, p. 40.
A. Hallenberg: PH och den nya musiken, *Kyrkosångsförb*, 1952, p. 31.
Iain Hamilton: PH, in *Decca Book of Ballet*, Muller (London) 1958, p. 165.
Josef Häusler: Der Klassiker PH, *Melos*, January 1964, p. 5.
Howard Hartog: A man for his season, *M&M*, February 1964, p. 12.
Everett Helm: Hindemith's successful visit to Germany, *Musical America*, July 1949, p. 20.
— Universal musician, *High Fidelity*, May 1964, p. 36.
Friedrich W. Herzog: Der Fall Hindemith-Furtwängler, *Die Musik*, January 1935, p. 241.
Martin Huerlimann: PH, die letzten Jahre (Ein Zeugnis in Bildern), Schott (Mainz)/Atlantis-Verlag (Zürich) 1965.
William Hymanson: Hindemith's variations, a comparison of early and recent works, *MR*, February 1952, p. 20.
Albert Jakobik: PH, in *Zur Einheit der neuen Musik*, Konrad Triltsch Verlag (Würzburg) 1957, p. 70.
Ian Kemp: PH, *MT*, March 1964, p. 184.
— Hindemith, O.U.P. (London) 1970.
Silvia Kind: Mein Lehrer Hindemith, *SM*, January–February 1964, p. 43; *Melos*, November 1965, p. 392.
Rudolf Klein: Literatur um PH, *ÖM*, February 1964.
Günter Kleinen: Zu Hindemiths Tonleiterversuch, *Die Musikforschung*, January–March 1965.
I. Kolodin: Hindemith at the New Friends, *Saturday Review*, 20 December 1952, p. 29.
— Hindemith returns, *Saturday Review*, 28 February 1959, p. 27.
Ernst Laaff: PH, Zum 65. Geburtstag, *NZfM*, November 1960.
Victor Landau: PH, a case study in theory and practice, *MR*, February 1960, p. 38.

— The harmonic theories of PH in relation to his practice as a composer of chamber music, *Dissertation Abstracts*, March 1957, p. 1062.

— Hindemith the system builder—a critique of his theory of harmony, *MR*, May 1961, p. 136.

Gerald Larner: PH, *Records and Recording*, February 1964, p. 17.

René Leibowitz: PH, *L'Arche*, No. 21, November 1946.

Walter Leigh: The music of PH, in *Essays on Music* (ed. Felix Aprahamian), Cassell (London) 1967, p. 127.

Andreas Liess: A travers l'œuvre de PH, *RM*, July–August 1933, p. 93.

H. Lindlar: PH, *Musikhandel*, February 1964, p. 33.

J. Löwenbach: Zu PH, *Der Auftakt*, 1922, No. 2.

Watson Lyle: PH (interview), *Bookman*, June 1933, p. 158.

Armand Machabey: PH, musicien allemand, *RM*, October 1930, p. 193.

— Notes sur la musique contemporaine, PH, *Le Ménestrel*, 17 October 1930.

— Esquisse de PH, *Le Ménestrel*, 13 February 1931, p. 65.

Joseph Machlis: PH, in *Introduction to Contemporary Music*, Norton (USA) 1961, Dent (London), p. 198.

Marina Magaldi: Due aspetti di Hindemith, *Rassegna musicale curci* (Milan), June 1965.

Wilhelm Maler: Die Tragik um den späten Hindemith, *Musik im Unterricht*, July–August 1964.

A. Mantelli: L'ultimo Hindemith, *La Rassegna musicale*, February 1937, p. 53.

Gertrud Marbach: Schlemmers Begegnungen mit Schoenberg, Scherchen und Hindemith, *NZfM*, December 1962.

James McKay Martin: PH, *Halle*, October 1951, p. 7.

Colin Mason: Hindemiths Kammermusik, *Melos*, 1957, June and September.

— Some aspects of Hindemith's chamber music, *M&L*, April 1960, p. 150.

— PH, *The Composer*, No. 13, spring 1964, p. 8.

Wilfried (W. H.) Mellers: Hindemith today, *Chesterian*, No. 152, September 1947.

— Schoenberg and Hindemith, in *Man and his Music*, Barrie & Rockliff (London) 1962, p. 982.

Darius Milhaud: PH, *Les Nouvelles littéraires*, 11 June 1938.

Donald Mitchell: The world of PH, *Chesterian*, No. 176, October 1953, No. 177, January 1954.

Frani B. Muser: The recent work of PH, *MQ*, January 1944, p. 29.

D. Newlin: Case of Hindemith, *Partisan Review*, April 1949, p. 412.

E. J. O'Connor: A recital and a study of PH's style in his compositions for solo French horn, *Dissertation Abstracts*, October 1967, p. 1460A.

Antonio Odriozola: PH, discography, *Musica* (Madrid), 1953, Nos. 3–4, p. 245.

Wouter Paap: PH, *Mens en melodie*, February 1964, p. 44.

Guido Pannain: Compositori del nestro tempo: PH, *La Rassegna musicale*, February 1928, p. 94.

— PH, *Mundo musical* (Buenos Aires), 1929, Nos. 4–5.

— Taccuino del critico, III: Pensiero su Hindemith, *Gazzetta musicale di Napoli*, 1956, Nos. 1–2.

D. C. Parker: PH, *MS*, 29 June 1929, p. 213.

R. Parland: Den nya saklighetens tonsättare, *Röster i Radio*, 1951, No. 11, p. 4.

P. Patera: En lagbunden musik, *Ung höger*, 1952, No. 6, p. 7.

L. Pestalozza: Le Kammermusiken di Hindemith, *La Rassegna musicale*, March 1958, p. 16.

B. Pociej: PH, *Ruch Muzyczny*, 1964, No. 5, p. 3.

A. Porfeyte: PH, *Muzyca*, March 1964, p. 31.

V. Pospisil: Monolog Paula Hindemitha o soudobosti v opere, *Hudebni Rozhledy*, 1961, No. 17, p. 722.

Mel Powell, Lukas Foss, Easley Blackwood: In memorian PH, *PNM*, spring–summer 1964, p. 1.

Eberhard Preussner: PH in Salzburg *ÖM*, 1947, No. 10, p. 272.

— Hindemith als Musikerzieher, *Melos*, December 1948, p. 334.

— David-Orff-Hindemith—De tre från 1895, *Musikrevy*, 1955, p. 352.

— PH, in *MGG*, Vol. 6 (1957), p. 439.

Hugo Puetter: PH, *Melos*, December 1948, p. 338.

H.R.: PH über die 'Probleme eines heutigen Komponisten', *SM*, January 1949, p. 13.

Edgar Rabsch: Von den Beziehungen Hindemiths zur gegenwärtigen Musikerziehung, *NZfM*, 1951, p. 70.

L. Raver: PH, *American Organist*, February 1964, p. 13.

Hans F. Redlich: PH, a reassessment, *MR*, August 1964, p. 241.

Willi Reich: PH, *Chesterian*, No. 82, November 1929, p. 33.

— PH, *MQ*, October 1931, p. 486.

— Hindemith wirkt in der Schweiz, *Musikleben*, March 1952, p. 86.

— Die Welt eines Komponisten, *Neue Schweizer Rundschau*, 1953–4, p. 546.

Kurt Reinhard: Hindemith, ein Hörproblem?, *Musikblätter*, 1948, No. 9, p. 11.

Franz Reizenstein: Hindemith, some aspersions answered, *The Composer*, No. 15, spring 1965, p. 7.

— PH, *The Listener*, 19 March 1964, p. 498; in *Essays on Music*, Cassell (London) 1967, p. 132.

— Composer and string player, *The Listener*, 2 March 1967, p. 304.

— PH visits London, *London Musical Events*, March 1955, p. 30.

M. Rinaldi: Hindemith il contrappuntista, *La Nuova Italia musicale*, February 1931.

H. Rosenberg: PH teoretikeren, *Dansk Musiktidsskrift*, 1964, No. 1, p. 2.

P. Rosenfeld: Neo-classicism and PH, *New Republic*, 2 April 1930, p. 193.

Edmund Rubbra: PH, *MMR*, September 1933, p. 146.

K. H. Ruppel: PH, Leben und Wirken oder Bild und Denkmal, *Melos*, November 1965, p. 381.

H. Rutz: Hindemith und Bruckners Zukunft, *Musikleben*, July–August 1952, p. 229.

Lionel Salter: PH, *The Gramophone*, February 1964, p. 362.

E. Salzman: PH, master of many trades, *New York Times*, 15 February 1959, Section 2, p. 9.

L. E. Sanner: Hindemith, rationalistisk mystiker, *Tidsskrift f. d. folkl. musiklevet*, 1952, p. 78.

G. Schab: Hindemith dirigierte Hindemith, *Musikleben*, May 1952, p. 143.

H. Schaefer: PH gestorben, *Musik und Gesellschaft*, February 1964, p. 94.

Hans Ludwig Schilling: PH, *SM*, January–February 1964, p. 2.

— Melodischer Sequenzbau im Werke PHs, *SM*, November 1956, p. 429.

— Hindemith auf dem Katheder, *Melos*, November 1955, p. 312.

H. Schmidt-Garre: Hindemith als Komponist und Dirigent, *Musikleben*, April 1952, p. 113.

E. Schoen: Hindemith, *Cahiers d'art*, 1926, No. 9.

Heinrich Schole: Hindemiths Unterweisung im Tonsatz, *Die Musik*, May 1938, p. 528.

Robert Schollum: Metamorphosen über das Thema Hindemith, *Musica*, 1955, No. 11, p. 533.

H. C. Schonberg: PH, *New York Times*, 5 January 1964, Section 2, p. 9.

Leo Schrade: Hindemith in der Neuen Welt, *Melos*, November 1955, p. 315.

Marion M. Scott: PH, his music and its characteristics, *PRMA*, 1929–30, p. 91.

H. G. Sear: Hindemith and performers, *MO*, January 1954, p. 209.

Arthur Seidl: Von PHs neuer Tonkunst, *Der Auftakt*, 1925, Nos. 11–12, p. 312.

Desmond Shawe-Taylor: Hindemith, *New Statesman*, 21 June 1947, p. 453.

C. M. Smith: Hindemith's Chicago birthday party, *Modern Music*, January 1946, p. 61.

Erich Steinhard: Hindemith und Finke, *Der Auftakt*, 1923, No. 1.

Walter Steinhauer: Max Reger und PH, *Der Auftakt*, 1935, Nos. 1–2, p. 3.

Heinrich Straumann: Die Berufung PHs an die Universität Zürich, *SM*, 1966, No. 6 (November–December), p. 334.

Willy Strecker: Gruss an Hindemith, *Melos*, November 1955, p. 309.

Heinrich Strobel: PH, *Die Musikwelt*, January 1925.

— Neue Kammermusik von Hindemith, *Melos*, July 1925.

— Hindemith, *Der Auftakt*, 1927, Nos. 7–8, p. 145.

— PH, *Musique*, January 1930.

— Hindemiths Unterweisung im Tonsatz,

Melos, 1947, July p. 241, August–September p. 273.

— PH, Schott (Mainz) 1948.

— Wiedersehen mit PH, *Melos*, December 1948, p. 326.

— Meister seiner Epoche, *Melos*, January 1964, p. 1.

H. H. Stuckenschmidt: Le nouveau style de PH, *L'Art musical*, 30 October 1936.

— Hindemiths neuer Stil, *Der Auftakt*, 1936, Nos. 11–12, p. 177.

— Portrait of Hindemith, *Chesterian*, No. 133, May–June 1937, p. 122.

— Hindemith today, *Modern Music*, January–February 1937.

— PH, in *Schöpfer der neuen Musik*, Suhrkamp Verlag (Frankfurt a. M.) 1958, p. 241.

Bruno Stürmer: Offener Brief an Herrn Professor PH, Berlin, *Die Musik*, October 1930, p. 41.

P. Tinel: Hindemith compositeur des opéras, *Bulletin de la classe des beaux-arts* (Académie royale de belgique), 1964, Nos. 2–3.

H. Tischler: Remarks on Hindemith's contrapuntal technique, *Journal of the International Folk Music Council*, Vol. 16 (1964), p. 53.

G. D. Townsend: A stylistic and performance analysis of the clarinet music of PH, *Dissertation Abstracts*, February 1968, p. 3214A.

G. Turchi: PH, *L'Appropodo musicale*, July–September 1958.

W. J. Turner: Stravinsky and Hindemith, *New Statesman*, 22 February 1936, p. 262.

Hermann Wagner: Und Hindemith?, *NZfM*, December 1934, p. 1263.

John Warrack: Hindemith, *Crescendo*, No. 119, March 1962, p. 130.

Adolf Weissmann: PH, *Die Musik*, May 1924, p. 579.

— La jeune musique allemande et PH, *L'Esprit nouveau*, 1924, No. 20.

F. Weler: Hindemith, eine Kulturpolitische Betrachtung, *Die Musik*, March 1934.

Elisabeth Westphal: PH, eine Bibliographie des In- und Auslandes seit 1922 über ihn und sein Werk, Greven Verlag (Cologne) 1957.

Theodor Wiesengrund-Adorno: Kammermusik von PH, *Die Musik*, October 1926, p. 24.

L. Henderson Williams: Hindemith's violin sonatas, *MM&F*, February 1933, p. 141.

Johannes Wolf: Altniederländische Kunst und Chormusik von Krenek und Hindemith, *Der Auftakt*, 1928, Nos. 5–6, p. 114.

Karl H. Wörner: Hindemith's Traditional Harmony, *Melos*, August–September 1947, p. 277.

— Hindemith, Kepler und die Zahl, *Melos*, November 1955, p. 319.

Jos Wouters: PH, *Mens en melodie*, May 1947, p. 143.

— De Variatietechniek bij PH, *Mens en melodie*, November 1955, p. 348.

— PH als leraar, *Mens en melodie*, February 1964, p. 47.

MISCELLANEOUS OR UNSIGNED

PH, *Dissonances*, May 1924.

PH, *Bollettino bibliografico musicale*, February 1930.

Nochmals—Hindemith, ein Kulturpolitischer Fall, *Die Musik*, May 1934, p. 596.

PH, Kulturpolitisch nicht Tragbar, *Die Musik*, November 1934, p. 138.

Furtwängler über Hindemith, *Neues Musikblatt* (Mainz), December 1934, p. 3.

De PH à Wilhelm Furtwängler—Wilhelm Furtwängler pro PH, *Dissonances*, December 1934.

Ein Harmonielehre von Hindemith, *Anbruch*, September 1937, p. 213.

PHs Besuch in Frankfurt—und ein Interview, *Melos*, July 1947, p. 254.

PH, *Röster i Radio*, 1952, No. 8, p. 4; 1954, No. 15, p. 6.

Compleat musician, *Time*, 17 October 1960, p. 77.

GUSTAV HOLST (1874–1934)

Gustav von Holst—he dropped the 'von' in 1918—was descended on his father's side from a family of Swedish musicians who had lived in England for three generations. He was born on 21 September 1874 in Cheltenham, where his father was an organist, conductor and piano-teacher. After a spell as an organist himself, Holst entered the Royal College of Music in London in 1893, eventually studying with C. V. Stanford. A career as pianist was closed to him by neuritis in the right hand, and instead he specialized in the trombone, earning a living as trombonist until the turn of the century in various orchestras (the Scottish Orchestra, the Carl Rosa, the White Viennese Band, etc.). His meeting with Ralph Vaughan Williams in 1895 was the start of a friendship which was to be of immense importance to both men. In 1901 Holst married Isobel Harrison and settled in London until the outbreak of the First World War. From 1903 onwards he divided his life between composing and teaching in London, the latter notably at St. Paul's Girls' School (1905–1934), Morley College for Working Men and Women (1907–24) and the Royal College of Music (1919–24). In addition he developed an absorbing interest in folk-song, in Sanskrit literature and later in the work of the English Madrigalists. In 1916 he inaugurated a series of Whitsun choral festivals (the first at Thaxted in Essex, where he was then living), and in 1918–19 worked in Salonika as musical organizer for the YMCA Army Education Scheme for the Near East. Between 1923 and 1934 Holst's health was rarely good, but he did manage during these years to make two trips to the United States to teach and conduct at Michigan and Harvard Universities. He died in May 1934.

CATALOGUE OF WORKS

1. Lansdown Castle. Operetta. 1892.
fp: 8 February 1893, Cheltenham, Corn Exchange.
Unpub.

2. The Revoke Op. 1. Opera in one act. 1895. Unpub.

3. Three Pieces Op. 2. For oboe and string quartet. 1896, rev. 1910.
1. *March*; 2. *Minuet*; 3. *Scherzo*.
Unpub.

4. Quintet Op. 3. For piano and wind. 1896. Unpub.

5. Light leaves whisper (Fritz B. Hart). Part song for SSATBB. *c.* 1896. Ded. Nina von Holst.
fp: 3 June 1897, St. James's Hall, Magpie Madrigal Society, cond. Lionel Benson.

Pub. Laudy.

6. Clear and cool Op. 5 (Charles Kingsley). For 5-part chorus (SSATB) and orchestra. 1897.
3 fl, 2 ob, 2 cl, 2 bsn; 4 hn, 2 tpt, 3 tmb, tuba; timp; strings.
fp: 26 March 1897, The Athenaeum (Goldhawk Road, Shepherds Bush), The Hammersmith Socialist Choir (with piano acc.), cond. Gustav Holst.
Unpub.

7. A Winter Idyll. For orchestra. 1897.
2 fl, 2 ob, ca, 2 cl, 2 bsn; 4 hn, 2 tpt, 3 tmb, tuba; timp, cym; strings.
Unpub.

8. Four Songs Op. 4. For voice and piano. 1896–8.
1. *Slumber-song* (Soft, soft wind) (Charles Kingsley). Ded. A. E. Newman. Pub. 1897, Laudy, as Two Songs No. 1 (with Dutch translation).
2. *Margaret's cradle song* (Ibsen, transl. William Archer). Ded. A. E. Newman. Pub. 1897, Laudy, as Two Songs No. 2 (with original Norwegian).
3. *Soft and gently* (Heine). Unpub.
4. *Awake, my heart* (Robert Bridges). 1898. Pub. 1908, Arthur P. Schmidt (Boston), as Two Songs No. 2; 1914, Schott; 1927, Enoch.
fp (No. 3 only): 2 December 1904, Bechstein Hall, Ralph Vaughan Williams concert, Edith Clegg, acc. Gustav Holst.

9. Ornulf's Drapa Op. 6. Scena for baritone and orchestra. 1898. Words: transl. William Archer from Ibsen's 'Vikings at Helgeland'.
2 fl, 2 ob, ca, 2 cl, bcl, 2 bsn; 4 hn, 3 tpt, 3 tmb, tuba; timp, cym; hp, strings.
Unpub.

10. The Idea. Operetta for children. 1898. Text: Fritz B. Hart. Ded. Mrs. and Miss Newman and the Pupils of St. Mary's School, Barnes.
fl, ob, cl; hn; strings.
Pub. 1903 (piano score only), Novello.

11. Clouds o'er the summer sky (Fritz B. Hart). Canon for SS and piano. 1898. Pub. 1903, Novello.

12. Walt Whitman Overture Op. 7. For orchestra. 1899.

2 fl, 2 ob, 2 cl, 2 bsn; 4 hn, 3 tpt, 3 tmb, tuba; timp, cym; strings.

Unpub.

13. Suite de Ballet in E flat Op. 10. For orchestra. 1899. Dur. *c.* 18′ 30″.

1. *Danse rustique*; 2. *Valse*; 3. *Scène de nuit*; 4. *Carnival*.

2 fl, pic, 2 ob, 2 cl, 2 bsn; 4 hn, 2 cornets, 3 tmb, tuba; timp, tgle, cym, glock, tamb pic, GC; strings.

fp: 20 May 1904, St. James's Hall, first Patron's Fund concert, cond. Gustav Holst.

Pub. 1914, Novello, for Royal College of Music Patron's Fund.

14. She who is dear to me (Walter E. Grogan). For voice and piano. *c.* 1899–1900. Pub. 1908, Arthur P. Schmidt (Boston), as Two Songs No. 1; *c.* 1908, Enoch.

15. Symphony in F: The Cotswolds Op. 8. For orchestra. 1899–1900.

1. *Allegro con brio*; 2. *Molto Adagio* (*Elegy in memoriam William Morris*); 3. *Presto* (*Scherzo*); 4. *Allegro moderato*.

2 fl, 2 ob, 2 cl, 2 bsn; 2 hn, 2 tpt; timp; strings.

fp: 24 April 1902, Bournemouth, Winter Gardens, Municipal Orchestra, cond. (Sir) Dan Godfrey.

Unpub.

16. Five Partsongs Op. 9a. 1898–1900.

1. *Love is enough* (William Morris). For SATB. 1898. Ded. M. T. von Holst. fp: 1 May 1902, Watford Public Library, Watford Choral Union, cond. E. Howard-Jones. Pub. 1898, Novello.

2. *To Sylvia* (Francis Thompson). For SATB. 1899. Ded. E. I. Harrison. Pub. 1899, Novello.

3. *Autumn Song* (William Morris). For SSAA. 1899. First setting. Ded. Nina von Holst. Unpub.

4. *Come away, death* (Shakespeare). Madrigal for 6 voices (SSATTB). 1900. Unpub.

5. *A love song* (William Morris). For SATB. 1900. Ded. Isobel von Holst. Pub. 1902, Laudy.

17. Ave Maria Op. 9b. For 8-part female chorus (SSAA-SSAA). 1900. Ded. 'To the memory of my mother'. Dur. *c.* 4′.

fp: 23 May 1901. St. James's Hall, Magpie Madrigal Society, cond. Lionel Benson.

Pub. 1900, Laudy.

18. Deux Pièces. For piano. *c.* 1901.

1. *Fancine*. Ded. Nina von Holst.

2. *Lucille*. Ded. Isobel von Holst.

Pub. 1902, Weekes.

19. The Youth's Choice Op. 11. A Musical Idyll in one act. 1902. Libretto: Gustav Holst.

3 fl, pic, 2 ob, ca, 2 cl, 2 bsn; 4 hn, 2 tpt, 3 tmb, tuba; timp, cym; hp, strings.

Unpub.

20. (Instrumental pieces). *c.* 1902–3.

1. *Ländler*. For two violins and piano. Pub. 1903, in *The Vocalist*.

2. *Lied ohne Worte*. For violin and piano. Ded. Frank Forty. Pub. December 1902, in *The Vocalist*, as Six Solos for violin and piano, No. 1.

3. *A Spring Song*. For violin or cello and piano. Pub. 1903, in *The Vocalist*, as Six Solos for violin and piano, No. 2; 1923, Ashdown.

4. *Greeting*. For violin and piano. Ded. Nina von Holst. Pub. 1903, Novello. Also version for orchestra, pub. 1904, Novello.

5. *Maya* (Romance). For violin and piano. Pub. 1904, Novello.

6. *Valse-Etude*. For violin and piano. Pub. in arrangement for piano solo by Henry Geehl, 1926, Ashdown.

21. Partsongs Op. 12. 1902–3.

1. *Dream tryst* (Francis Thompson). For SATB. Ded. Mrs. Ralph Vaughan Williams. ?fp: 11 December 1904, Passmore Edwards Settlement, cond. Gustav Holst.

Pub. 1902, Novello.

2. *Ye little birds* (From 'The Fair Maid of the Exchange', anon. 1607). Pub. 1902, Novello.

3. *Her eyes the glow-worm lend thee* (Herrick). For SATB. 1903. Unpub.

4. *Now is the month of maying* (Anon.). 1903. Ded. Miss May Cameron. Pub. 1903, Novello.

5. *Come to me*. Unpub.

22. Thou did'st delight mine eyes (Robert Bridges). Partsong for SATB. *c.* 1903. Pub. 1904, Novello.

Holst, Gustav

23. Indra Op. 13. Symphonic Poem for orchestra. 1903.
2 fl, pic, 2 ob, ca, 2 cl, bcl, 2 bsn, cbsn; 4 hn, 2 tpt, 2 cornett, 3 tmb, tuba; timp, tgle, cym, tamburo, gong, glock; hp, strings.
Unpub.

24. Wind Quintet Op. 14. 1903. Unpub.

BIBLIOGRAPHY:
Anon.: Holst manuscript discovered: unpublished wind quintet, *The Times*, 3 December 1952, p. 3.

25. Six Songs Op. 15. For baritone and piano. 1902–3.
1. *Invocation to dawn* (transl. Gustav Holst from 'Rig Veda'). 1902. Ded. J. Campbell McInnes.
fp: 22 April 1902, Barnes, Cleveland Hall, J. Campbell McInnes.
Pub. 1903, in *The Vocalist*.
2. *Fain would I change that note* (16th cent. anon.). 1903. Unpub.
3. *The Sergeant's song* (Thomas Hardy).
fp (broadcast): 4 May 1924, Kenneth Ellis.
Pub. 1903, Enoch; 1923, Ashdown.
4. *In a wood* (Thomas Hardy). 1903.
fp: 2 December 1904, Bechstein Hall, Ralph Vaughan Williams concert, Edith Clegg, acc. Gustav Holst.
Unpub.
5. *Between us now* (Thomas Hardy). 1903. Unpub.
6. *I will not let thee go* (Robert Bridges). 1903. Unpub.

26. Six Songs Op. 16. For soprano and piano. 1903–4.
1. *Calm is the morn* (Tennyson). 1903. Unpub.
2. *My true love* (Sidney). 1903. Unpub.
3. *Weep you no more* (Anon.). 1903. Pub. 1907, Stainer & Bell.
4. *Lovely kind and kindly loving* (Nicholas Breton). 1903. Ded. Maja Kjöhler.
?fp: 16 December 1906, Passmore Edwards Settlement, Maja Kjöhler.
Pub. 1923, Chappell.
5. *Cradle song* (Blake). 1904. Unpub.
6. *Peace* (Alfred H. Hyatt). 1904.
fp: 2 December 1904, Bechstein Hall, Edith Clegg, acc. Gustav Holst.
Unpub.

27. Spring song. For voice and piano. Date unknown.
fp: 8 May 1905, Aeolian Hall, Gregory Hast, acc. Mrs. Gregory Hast.
Unpub.

28. Dewy roses (Alfred H. Hyatt). For voice and piano. 1904. Pub. 1904, Chappell.

29. King Estmere Op. 17. Old English Ballad for chorus and orchestra. 1903. Words: Anon. Ded. Sir Charles Villiers Stanford.
2 fl, 2 ob, 2 cl, 2 bsn; 4 hn, 2 tpt, 3 tmb, tuba; timp, GC, cym, tamb, tgle; hp, strings.
fp: 4 April 1908, Queen's Hall, first concert of the Edward Mason Choir, with the New Symphony Orchestra, cond. Edward Mason.
Pub. 1906, Charles Avison Edition/Breitkopf & Härtel; Novello.

30. The Mystic Trumpeter Op. 18 (Walt Whitman). Scena for solo voice and orchestra. 1904, finally revised 1912. Dur. 19'.
3 fl, 2 ob, ca, 2 cl, bcl, 2 bsn; 4 hn, 3 tpt, 3 tmb, tuba; timp, cym, tenor dm, GC; hp, strings.
fp: 29 June 1905, Queen's Hall, Patron's Fund concert, Cicely Gleeson White, combined London Symphony Orchestra and Royal College of Music Orchestra, cond. Gustav Holst.
fp (revised version): 25 February 1913, Queen's Hall, Balfour Gardiner concert, Cicely Gleeson White, cond. Gustav Holst.
Unpub.

31. Song of the night Op. 19 No. 1. For violin and orchestra. 1905.
2 fl, ob, ca, 2 cl, 2 bsn; 2 hn, tpt; timp; strings.
Unpub.

32. Invocation Op. 19 No. 2. For cello and orchestra. 1911.
2 fl, 2 ob, 2 cl, 2 bsn; 2 hn, tpt; pcssn; hp, strings.
fp: 2 May 1911, Queen's Hall, May Mukle and the New Symphony Orchestra, cond. (Sir) Landon Ronald.
Unpub.

33. Songs from 'The Princess' Op. 20a (Tennyson). For female voices (SSAA) a cappella. 1905. Ded. 'The J.A.G.S.' (James Allen Girls' School). Dur. *c.* 10'.

1. *Sweet and low*; 2. *The splendour falls on castle walls*; 3. *Tears, idle tears*; 4. *O swallow, swallow*; 5. *Now sleeps the crimson petal.*

fp: probably privately at the James Allen Girls' School.

f professional p (No. 1 only): 5 June 1907, Royal College of Music concert hall, Magpie Madrigal Society.

Pub. 1907, Novello.

33a. Home they brought her warrior dead. Orig. No. 5 of preceding but not included in the published set.

34. Songs of the West Op. 21a. For orchestra. 1906 (first version).

2 fl, 2 ob, 2 cl, 2 bsn; 4 hn, 2 tpt, 3 tmb; timp, pcssn; strings.

fp: 3 February 1906, City of Bath Pump Room Orchestra, cond. Gustav Holst.

Unpub.

34a. Songs of the West Op. 21a. For orchestra. 1907 (revised version).

fp: 8 October 1909, India, Governor's Band, cond. Edward Behr.

fEp: 11 December 1909, Excelsior Hall (Bethnal Green Road), Oxford House Musical Association, cond. Gustav Holst.

Unpub.

35. A Somerset Rhapsody Op. 21b. For orchestra. 1906, rev. 1907. Ded. Cecil Sharp. Dur. *c.* 8' 40".

2 fl, ob & ob d'amore (or 2 ob), 2 cl, 2 bsn; 4 hn, 2 tpt, tmb, tuba; timp, tamburo, GC, cym; strings.

fp: 6 April 1910, Queen's Hall, concert of the Edward Mason Choir, cond. Edward Mason.

Pub. 1927, Hawkes (as Op. 21).

36. Two Songs Without Words Op. 22. For small orchestra. 1906. Ded. Ralph Vaughan Williams.

1. *Country Songs*. Dur. *c.* 3' 55".
2 fl, pic, 2 cl, 2 bsn; 2 hn; strings.
2. *Marching Song*. Dur. *c.* 4'.
2 fl, pic, 2 cl, 2 bsn; 2 hn, 2 tpt, ten tmb; timp, tamb pic, GC; strings.

fp (Nos. 1 & 2): 19 July 1906, Royal College of Music students' concert, cond. Gustav Holst.

Pub. 1922, Novello; incl. arr. by Gustav Holst for piano solo, 1907.

37. Sita Op. 23. Opera in three acts. *c.* 1899–1906. Libretto by Gustav Holst, founded on 'The Ramayana'. Dur. 160'.

3 fl, 2 ob, ca, 2 cl, bcl, 2 bsn, cbsn; 4 hn, 2 tpt, 2 cornett, 2 ten tmb, bs tmb, cbs tmb; timp; hp, strings.

Unpub. Unperformed.

38. The heart worships (Alice M. Buckton). For voice and piano. 1907. Dur. *c.* 3' 10".

fp: 16 November 1907, Aeolian Hall, Edith Clegg.

Pub. 1910, Stainer & Bell.

39. Seven Scottish Airs. Arr. by Gustav Holst for piano and strings. 1907. Ded. 'H.S.'. Pub. 1908, Novello.

40. Four Old English Carols Op. 20b (Anon.). For chorus and piano (No. 3 is unacc.). 1907.

1. *A Babe is born*; 2. *Now let us sing*; 3. *Jesu, Thou the Virgin-born*; 4. *The Saviour of the World*.

Pub. 1909, Bayley & Ferguson; also arr. for female voices.

41. Hymns from the Rig Veda Op. 24 (Transl. Gustav Holst). For voice and piano. 1907–8.

Group I: 1. *Ushas (Dawn)*; 2. *Varuna I (Sky)*; 3. *Maruts (Stormclouds)*. Group II: 4. *Indra (God of storm and battle)*; 5. *Varuna II (The Waters)*; 6. *Song of the frogs*. Group III: 7. *Vac (Speech)*; 8. *Creation*; 9. *Faith.*

fp (Nos. 1 & 6): 16 November 1907, Aeolian Hall, Edith Clegg.

fp (complete): 28 April 1911, Bechstein Hall, Leila Duart.

fbp (No. 1): 14 April 1924, Gladys Palmer.

fbp (Nos. 1–6): 1 June 1924, Cardiff station, Gustav Holst night, Joseph Farrington.

Pub. 1920, Chester.

42. Savitri Op. 25. Opera di camera in one act: an episode from the Mahabharata. Libretto: Gustav Holst. 1908. Dur. 30'.

2 fl, ca, strings (double string quartet & double-bass).

fp: 5 December 1916, Wellington Hall (St. John's Wood), London School of Opera, cond. Hermann Grunebaum.

f professional p: 23–24 June 1921, Lyric Theatre (Hammersmith), cond. (Sir) Arthur Bliss; with Dorothy Silk (Savitri), Steuart Wilson (Satyavan), Clive Carey (Death); costume design and scenery supervision, C. Lovatt Fraser.

fp (broadcast): 1 June 1924, Cardiff, Gustav Holst night, cond. Warwick Braithwaite; with Dorothy Silk (Savitri), Browning (Satyavan), Joseph Farrington (Death).

Pub. 1923, Goodwin; Curwen.

BIBLIOGRAPHY:

Warwick Braithwaite: Savitri, *Opera*, No. 7, July 1923, p. 17.

R.C.: Holst's Savitri, *MMR*, 1923, p. 236.

Richard Capell: Death comes to Satyavan, *Radio Times*, 18 October 1935, p. 15.

Ian Parrott: Holst's Savitri and bitonality, *MR*, 1967, No. 4, p. 323.

J. B. Trend: Savitri, an opera from the Sanskrit, *M&L*, October 1921.

43. Choral Hymns from the Rig Veda (Set One) (Transl. Gustav Holst) Op. 26 No. 1. For chorus and orchestra. 1908–10.

1. *Battle hymn*. 1908–9.
2. *To the unknown God.* 1910.
3. *Funeral hymn.* 1908.

3 fl, 2 ob, ca, 2 cl, 2 bsn, cbsn; 4 hn, 3 tpt, 3 tumb, tuba; timp; hp, organ, strings.

fp: 6 December 1911, Newcastle, Town Hall, Newcastle on Tyne Musical Union, cond. Edgar L. Bainton.

f London p: 25 March 1912, Queen's Hall, Edward Mason Choir.

Pub. 1911, Stainer & Bell.

44. Choral Hymns from the Rig Veda (Set Two) (Transl. Gustav Holst) Op. 26 No. 2. For female voices and orchestra (or piano and two violins ad lib). 1909. Ded. Edward Mason and his Choir.

1. *To Varuna (Gold of the Waters)*; 2. *To Agni (God of Fire)*; 3. *Funeral chant.*

2 fl, 2 ob, 2 cl, bcl, 2 bsn; 4 hn, 3 tpt, 3 tmb; timp; hp, strings.

fp: 22 March 1911, Queen's Hall, Edward Mason Choir.

Pub. 1912, Stainer & Bell.

45. A Song of London. Unison song. *c.* 1909. Pub. 1909, privately printed.

46. Masque: The Vision of Dame Christian Op. 27. Incidental music 1909. Words: Frances Ralph Gray. Composed for St. Paul's Girls' School.

fp: 22 July 1909, St. Paul's Girls' School, with Morley College Orchestra.

Unpub. Printed for private circulation, for exclusive use at St. Paul's Girls' School.

47. First Suite in E flat Op. 28a. For military band. 1909. Dur. *c.* 8' 55".

1. *Chaconne*; 2. *Intermezzo*; 3. *March.*

fp (private): unestablished date, Military School of Music, Kneller Hall.

fbp: 4 May 1924, Band of H.M. Grenadier Guards.

Pub. 1921, Boosey & Hawkes.

48. Choral Hymns from the Rig Veda (Set Three) (Transl. Gustav Holst) Op. 26 No. 3. For female voices and harp. 1910. Composed for and ded. Frank Duckworth and his Ladies' Choir, Blackburn.

1. *Hymn to the dawn*; 2. *Hymn to the waters*; 3. *Hymn to Vena (The sun rising through the mist)*; 4. *Hymn of the travellers.*

fp: 16 March 1911, Blackburn, Town Hall, Blackburn Ladies' Choir, cond. Frank Duckworth.

f London p: 27 February 1913, Queen's Hall, Edward Mason Choir.

fbp: 14 June 1928, Wireless Chorus, cond. Stanford Robinson.

Pub. 1912, Stainer & Bell.

49. Beni Mora (Oriental Suite in E minor) Op. 29 No. 1. For orchestra. 1910 (No. 1 composed in 1909 as 'Oriental Dance'); rev. 1912. Ded. 'E.E.' (Edwin Evans). Dur. *c.* 14' 40".

1. *First dance*; 2. *Second dance*; 3. *Finale: In the Street of the Ouled Nails.*

2 fl, pic, 2 ob, ca, 2 cl, 2 bsn; 4 hn, 2 tpt, 3 tmb, tuba; timp, cym, tamb, tgle, GC, gong; 2 hp, strings.

fp: 1 May 1912, Queen's Hall, Balfour Gardiner concert, New Symphony Orchestra, cond. Gustav Holst.

fbp: 13 October 1925, Birmingham, Town

Hall, City of Birmingham Symphony Orchestra, cond. Gustav Holst.

Pub. 1921, Goodwin & Tabb; Curwen. Arr. for piano solo, 1925, Curwen.

50. Christmas Day. Choral Fantasia on old carols for chorus and orchestra (or organ). 1910. Ded. students of Morley College.

2 fl, 2 ob, 2 cl, 2 bsn; 2 hn, 2 tpt, 2 tmb (ad lib); timp, glock (ad lib).

Pub. 1910, Novello.

51. Four Partsongs for children (Whittier). With piano acc. 1910.

1. *Song of the shipbuilders*; 2. *Song of the shoemakers*; 3. *Song of the fishermen*; 4. *Song of the drovers*.

Pub. 1911, Novello.

52. The swallow leaves her nest (Thomas Lovell Beddoes). For female voices (SSC) a cappella. *c.* 1910. Dur. *c.* 2' 15". Pub. 1914, Curwen.

53. Pastoral(Anon.). For female voices a cappella. *c.* 1910. Dur. *c.* 1' 30". Pub. 1913, Stainer & Bell.

54. Phantastes. Suite for orchestra. 1911.

fp: 23 July 1912, Queen's Hall, Patron's Fund concert, New Symphony Orchestra, cond. Gustav Holst.

Unpub. Withdrawn.

55. Autumn song (William Morris). Second setting: partsong for SATB. *c.* 1911. Pub. 1912, Stainer & Bell.

56. Two Partsongs. For SATB. *c.* 1911.

1. *In youth is pleasure* (Robert Wever, *c.* 1550).

2. *Now rest thee from all care.*

No. 1. Pub. 1912, Stainer & Bell. No. 2. Unpub.

57. In loyal bonds united (Shapcott Wensley). Unison song. 1911. Pub. 1911, Novello. Re-issued by Novello with altered words as an 'Empire Day song'.

58. O England my country (G. K. Menzies). Unison song with orchestra. *c.* 1909 or 1911.

2 fl, 2 ob, 2 cl, 2 bsn; 2 hn, 2 cornets, tmb; timp; strings.

?fp: 17 December 1912, Eton, School Hall, Music Society concert.

Pub. 1921, Stainer & Bell.

59. Second Suite in F Op. 28b. For military band. 1911. Ded. J. Causley Windram. Dur. 10' 30".

1. *March*; 2. *Song without words*; 3. *Song of the blacksmith*; 4. *Fantasia on the Dargason.*

fp (private): unestablished date, Military School of Music, Kneller Hall.

?fp (public): 30 June 1922, Royal Albert Hall, Band of Royal Military School of Music (Kneller Hall), cond. Lieut. H. E. Adkins.

fbp: 23 March 1924, Manchester station, Radio Military Band, cond. Harry Mortimer.

Pub. 1922, Boosey & Hawkes.

60. Two Eastern Pictures. For female voices and harp or piano. 1911. Words: Kalidasa, transl. by Gustav Holst.

1. *Spring* (Dur. 1' 40"); 2. *Summer* (Dur. 2' 15").

fp: 21 March 1912, Blackburn, Town Hall, Blackburn Ladies Choir, cond. Frank Duckworth.

Pub. 1912, Stainer & Bell.

61. Hecuba's Lament Op. 31 No. 1. For contralto, female chorus and orchestra. 1911. Words: from 'The Trojan Women' of Euripides, transl. Gilbert Murray.

2 fl, 2 ob, 2 cl, 2 bsn; 2 hn, 2 tpt, 3 tmb, tuba; timp, GC, cym; hp, strings.

?fp: *c.* March 1923, London, Clara Serena and the Philharmonic Choir, cond. Charles Kennedy Scott.

Pub. 1921, Stainer & Bell.

62. The Cloud Messenger Op. 30. Ode for chorus and orchestra. 1910, rev. 1912. Text: Gustav Holst, founded on a Sanscrit poem of Kalidasa. Dur. *c.* 38' 05".

3 fl, pic, 2 ob, ca, 2 cl, bcl, 2 bsn, dbsn; 4 hn, 3 tpt, 2 ten tmb, bs tmb, cbs, tmb; timp, pcssn; 2 hp, organ, strings.

fp: 4 March 1913, Queen's Hall Balfour Gardiner concert, London Choral Society and New Symphony Orchestra, cond. Gustav Holst.

Pub. 1912, Stainer & Bell.

63. Choral Hymns from the Rig Veda (Set Four) Op. 26 No. 4. For male voices and orchestra. 1912.

Holst, Gustav

1. *Hymn to Agni* (*The sacrificial fire*); 2. *Hymn to Soma* (*The juice of a sacrificial herb*); 3. *Hymn to Manas* (*The spirit of a dying man*); 4. *Hymn to Indra* (*God of heaven, storm and battle*).

2 tpt, 2 hn, 3 tmb; hp (in No. 1 only), strings.

fp: 27 February 1913, Queen's Hall, Edward Mason Choir and the New Symphony Orchestra.

Pub. 1912, Stainer & Bell.

64. Two Psalms. For chorus, string orchestra and organ. 1912.

1. *Psalm 86: To my humble supplication* (authorized version, with metrical psalm by Joseph Bryan, 1620). Dur. *c.* 7′ 25″.

2. *Psalm 148: Lord, Who hast made us for Thine own* (paraphrase by Frances Ralph Gray). Dur. *c.* 4′ 30″.

fbp: 9 February 1924, Choir and London Symphony Orchestra, relayed from Southwark Cathedral.

Pub. 1920, Augener, No. 2 a₁so arr. for female voices.

65. St. Paul's Suite Op. 29 No. 2. For string orchestra. 1912–13. Dur. *c.* 12′ 30″.

1. *Jig*; 2. *Ostinato*; 3. *Intermezzo*; 4. *Finale: The Dargason*.

fp: 1913, St. Paul's Girls' School.

fbp: 10 April 1924, Wireless String Orchestra, cond. Capt. W. A. Featherstone.

Pub. 1922, Goodwin & Tabb; Curwen. Arr. by Vally Lasker for piano solo, 1923, Goodwin.

BIBLIOGRAPHY:

Harold Rawlinson: Some famous works for string orchestra, No. 3: St. Paul's Suite Op. 29 No. 2, *Strad*, June 1946.

66. Hymn to Dionysus Op. 31 No. 2. For chorus of female voices and orchestra. 1913. Words: from 'The Bacchae' of Euripides, transl. Gilbert Murray. Ded. H.B.G. (H. Balfour Gardiner).

3 fl, 2 ob, ca, 2 cl, bcl, 2 bsn; 4 hn, 3 tpt, 3 tmb, tuba; timp, pcssn; hp, strings.

fp: 10 March 1914, Queen's Hall, Oriana Madrigal Society and Queen's Hall Orchestra, cond. Gustav Holst.

Pub. 1914, Stainer & Bell.

67. The Homecoming (Hardy). For male

voices (TTBB) a cappella. 1913. Composed for the 1914 Morecambe Musical Festival. Pub. 1913, Stainer & Bell.

68. A Dirge for Two Veterans (Walt Whitman). For male voices (TTBB), brass and percussion. 1914. Dur. *c.* 5′ 10″.

3 tpt, 2 bombardons (or tmb & tuba), side dm, GC.

Pub. 1914, Curwen.

69. Nunc Dimittis. For 8-part chorus a cappella. 1915. Written for Westminster Cathedral. Unpub.

70. Japanese Suite. Op. 33. For orchestra. 1915. Ded. 'To the Amanuensis'. Suite composed for the Japanese dancer Michio Ito who supplied all the themes except that of 'Dance of the Marionette'. Dur. *c.* 12′.

Prelude; 1. *Ceremonial dance*; 2. *Dance of the Marionette*; *Interlude*; 3. *Dance under the cherry tree*; 4. *Finale: Dance of the wolves*.

2 fl, pic, ob, ca, 2 cl, 2 bsn; 4 hn, 2 tpt, 3 tmb, tuba; timp, sleigh bells, glock, GC, xyl, gong, cym; strings.

fp: 19 October 1919, Queen's Hall Sunday Concert, Queen's Hall Orchestra, cond. Sir Henry Wood.

fbp: 18 February 1925, Wireless Orchestra, cond. Sir Dan Godfrey.

Pub. 1923, Hawkes.

71. This have I done for my true love Op. 34 (Traditional words). For unacc. chorus. 1916. Ded. Conrad Noel.

fp (private): 19 May 1918, Thaxted Church, Whitsun Festival Singers, cond. Gustav Holst.

fp (professional): 23 December 1919, Aeolian Hall, Oriana Madrigal Society, cond. Charles Kennedy Scott.

Pub. 1919, Augener.

72. Carols. For unacc. chorus. 1916.

1. *Lullay my liking* (Anon.). For solo soprano or tenor and chorus. Dur. *c.* 3′ 15″.

f public p: 19 December 1916, Aeolian Hall, Oriana Madrigal Society, cond. Charles Kennedy Scott.

2. *Bring us in good ale* (Anon.). Ded. Conrad Noel. Dur. *c.* 1′ 10″.

3. *Of one that is so fair* (Anon.). For soli

216

SATB and chorus. *c.* 1916. Pub. 1919, Curwen.

73. Two Carols. For chorus, oboe and cello. 1908–16. Words: Anon.
   1. *A welcome song.* 1908. Dur. *c.* 1′ 50″.
   2. *Terly terlow.* 1916. Dur. *c.* 1′ 50″.
fp: 19 December 1916, Aeolian Hall, Oriana Madrigal Society, cond. Charles Kennedy Scott.
   Pub. 1913 (No. 1), 1916 (No. 2), Stainer & Bell.

74. Three Carols. Arr. for chorus in unison and orchestra. *c.* 1916.
   1. *I saw three ships* (Anon.).
   2. *On this day* (Christmas song) (Transl. from medieval Latin by J. M. Joseph).
   3. *Masters in this hall* (William Morris).
   2 fl, 2 ob, 2 cl, 2 bsn; 2 hn, 2 tpt; timp, tgle, bells; organ (ad lib), strings. (NB: Cued for strings only, or strings plus any combination of above instruments.)
   Pub. 1924, Curwen.

75. Six Choral Folksongs Op. 36. Arr. for SCTB a cappella. 1916.
   1. *I sowed the seeds of love* (Hampshire folksong). Ded. W. G. Whittaker and his singers.
   2. *There was a tree* (Hampshire folksong). Ded. as No. 1.
   3. *Matthew, Mark, Luke and John* (West country folksong). Ded. as No. 1.
   4. *The song of the blacksmith* (Hampshire folksong). Ded. Charles Kennedy Scott and the Oriana Madrigal Society.
   5. *I love my love* (Cornish folksong). Ded. as No. 4.
   6. *Swansea Town* (Hampshire folksong). Ded. as No. 4.
   Pub. 1917, Curwen. Arr. (except No. 2) for TTBB, 1924–5, Curwen.

75a. Diverus and Lazarus. Folksong arr. SATB a cappella. *c.* 1916. Pub. *c.* 1920, Stainer & Bell.

76. Phantasy String Quartet. 1916. Founded on Hampshire folksongs.
   fp: 29 November 1917, Steinway Hall, John Saunders, C. J. Woodhouse, Raymond Jeremy, Arthur Williams.
   Unpub. Withdrawn.

77. Three Festival Choruses. With orchestra. 1916.
   1. *Let all mortal flesh keep silence* (Liturgy of St. James, transl. G. Moultrie) (French traditional melody).
   2 fl, 2 ob, 2 cl, 2 bsn; 2 hn, 2(3) tpt; timp; organ, strings.
   2. *Turn back, O Man* (Clifford Bax) (Old 124th, from the Genevan Psalter).
   2 fl, 2 ob, 2 cl, 2 bsn; 2 hn, 2(3) tpt; timp; organ, strings.
   3. *A Festival Chime* (Clifford Bax) (Welsh melody—'St. Denio').
   2 fl, 2 ob, 2 cl, 2 bsn; 2 hn, 2(3) tpt; timp, bells (or glock); organ (or tuba), strings.
   fp: probably 27 May 1917, Thaxted church.
   Pub. 1919 (Nos. 2 & 3), 1921 (No. 1), Stainer & Bell.

78. The Planets Op. 32. Suite for large orchestra. 1914–16. Dur. *c.* 53′.
   1. *Mars, the bringer of war.* 1914.
   2. *Venus, the bringer of peace.* 1914.
   3. *Mercury, the winged messenger.* 1916.
   4. *Jupiter, the bringer of jollity.* 1914.
   5. *Saturn, the bringer of old age.* 1915.
   6. *Uranus, the magician.* 1915.
   7. *Neptune, the mystic.* 1915.
   4 fl, 2 pic, bs fl, 3 ob, bs ob, ca, 3 cl, bcl, 3 bsn, dbsn; 6 hn, 4 tpt, 3 tmb, ten tuba, bs tuba; 6 timp, tgle, side dm, tamb, cym, GC, gong, bells, glock, celesta, xyl; 2 hp, organ strings; female chorus (in No. 7).
   fp (private): 29 September 1918, New Queen's Hall Orchestra, cond. (Sir) Adrian Boult.
   fp (public, omitting Venus & Neptune): 27 February 1919, Queen's Hall, Royal Philharmonic Society concert, cond. (Sir) Adrian Boult.
   fp (No. 2): 22 November 1919, Queen's Hall, cond. Gustav Holst.
   fp (complete): 15 November 1920, Queen's Hall, London Symphony Orchestra, cond. Albert Coates.
   fbp: 2 April 1924, ladies' choir and 2ZY Orchestra, cond. Sir Dan Godfrey, Manchester station.
   Pub. 1921, Goodwin & Tabb; 1923, Curwen. Arr. by Nora Day & Vally Lasker for piano duet, 1923, Goodwin; arr. by Gustav Holst for two pianos, 1949, Curwen.

Holst, Gustav

BIBLIOGRAPHY:
Eric Blom: Holst's The Planets, *Music Teacher*, February 1931, p. 91.
Sir Adrian Boult: Interpreting the Planets, *MT*, March 1970, p. 263.
Frank Howes: The Planets, *Halle*, January 1948, p. 7.
R. O. Morris: The Planets, *Athenaeum*, 3 December 1920, p. 768.
A. J. Sheldon: GH's The Planets, *MO*, March 1923, p. 551.
Friedrich Wilckens: Planeten—Eine choreographische Fantasie nach der gleichnamigen Symphonie von GH, *Blätter der Staatsoper* (Berlin), May 1931, p. 4.

79. Four Songs Op. 35. For voice and violin. 1916–17. Words: from A Medieval Anthology, ed. Mary Segar. Dur. *c.* 7′ 40″.
  1. *Jesu sweet, now will I sing*; 2. *My soul has nought but fire and ice*; 3. *I sing of a maiden*; 4. *My Leman is so true*.
  fp: 4 May 1918, The Hall, Blackheath (S.E.3), 5 o'Clock Saturday Group concert, Ethel Waddington (sop) and Dr. M. Beddow Bayly.
  fbp (3 songs): 27 January 1924, Carmen Hill and Daisy Kennedy.
  Pub. 1920, Chester.

BIBLIOGRAPHY:
Arthur Newson: A musical experiment, *The Musician*, February 1921, p. 120.

80. Two Partsongs for children (Whittier). For two voices and piano. 1917.
  1. *The corn song*; 2. *Song of the lumberman*.
  Pub. 1918, Arnold.

81. A Dream of Christmas (From: 'A Medieval Anthology', ed. Segar). For female voices (SS) and strings or piano. 1917. Pub. 1919, Curwen.

82. The Hymn of Jesus Op. 37. For two choruses, semi-chorus (SSA) and orchestra. 1917. Words transl. by Gustav Holst from the Apocryphal Acts of St. John. Ded. R.V.W. (Ralph Vaughan Williams). Dur. *c.* 20′ 25″.
  1. *Prelude*; 2. *The Hymn*.
  3 fl, 2 ob, ca, 2 cl, 2 bsn; 4 hn, 2 tpt, 3 tmb; timp, cym; celesta, piano, organ, strings.
  fp: 25 March 1920, Queen's Hall, Royal Philharmonic Society concert with the Philharmonic Choir, cond. Gustav Holst.
  fbp: 9 February 1924, Choir and London Symphony Orchestra, relayed from Southwark Cathedral.
  Pub. 1919, Stainer & Bell, for the Carnegie Collection of British Music.

BIBLIOGRAPHY:
Richard Capell: Introduction to Holst's The Hymn of Jesus, *MMR*, 1927, p. 38.
Edward J. Dent: The Hymn of Jesus, *Athenaeum*, 2 April 1920, p. 455.
Scott Goddard: Holst's Hymn of Jesus, *The Listener*, 8 March 1962, p. 449.
— An original genius, *Radio Times*, 10 April 1936, p. 11.

83. The Sneezing Charm. Ballet music for orchestra. 1918. Composed as incidental music to Clifford Bax's play 'The Sneezing Charm'.
  2 fl, 2 ob, 2 cl, 2 bsn; 2 hn, 2 tpt; timp, pcssn; hp, strings.
  fp (private): 9 June 1918, Court Theatre (Sloane Square), Plough Society.
  Unpub. Later revised as Ballet Music from 'The Perfect Fool' (see No. 88a).

84. Ode to Death (Walt Whitman) Op. 38. For chorus and orchestra. 1919. Dur. *c.* 12′ 20″.
  2 fl, 2 ob, ca, 2 cl, 2 bsn; 4 hn, 2 tpt, 3 tmb; timp; celesta, hp, organ, strings.
  fp: 6 October 1922, Leeds Festival, Festival Chorus and the London Symphony Orchestra, cond. Albert Coates.
  f London p: 19 December 1923, Queen's Hall, Bach Choir, cond. Ralph Vaughan Williams.
  Pub. 1922, Novello.

BIBLIOGRAPHY:
Anon.: A new choral work by Holst, *MT*, October 1922, p. 689.

85. Short Festival Te Deum. For chorus and orchestra. 1919. Ded. Morely College.
  2 fl, 2 ob, 2 cl, 2 bsn; 2 hn, 2 tpt, 3 tmb; timp, GC, cym; strings.
  fp (private): 23 May 1920, Quadrangle of Old College, Dulwich, Whitsun Festival, cond. Gustav Holst.
  Pub. 1920, Stainer & Bell.

86. Seven Choruses from Alcestis (transl.

Gilbert Murray). Incidental music for voices in unison, harp and three flutes. 1920. Ded. Frances Ralph Gray. Pub. 1921, Augener.

87. I vow to thee, my country (Cecil Spring Rice). Unison song with orchestra. 1921. Melody taken from 'Jupiter', No. 4 of 'The Planets'.

2 fl, 2 ob, 2 cl, 2 bsn; 2 hn, 2 tpt, 3 tmb, tuba; timp; organ, piano, strings.

Pub. 1921, Curwen.

88. The Perfect Fool Op. 39. Opera in one act. 1920–2. Ded. Nora Day and Vally Lasker. Dur. *c.* 63′ 30″.

2 fl, pic, 2 ob, ca, bcl, 2 bsn, cbsn; 4 hn, 4 tpt, 3 tmb, tuba; timp, GC, cym, tamtam, tamburino, jingles (sleigh bells), xyl; celesta, hp, string.

fp: 14 May 1923, Covent Garden, British National Opera Company, cond. (Sir) Eugene Goossens; with Robert Parker (The Wizard), Raymond Ellis (The Fool), Edna Thornton (His Mother), Maggie Tyte (The Princess), Walter Hyde (The Troubadour), Frederick Collier (The Traveller), Sydney Russell (The Peasant), Doris Lemon, Gladys Leathwood and Florence Ayre (Three Girls), Philip Bertram, Fred Hitchin, P. G. Travers and Eric Fort (Four Retainers), Lenore Leslie (Spirit of Earth), Eily Gerald (Spirit of Water) and Olive Joyner (Spirit of Fire); producer, Paget Bowman; décor and lighting, Oliver Bernard; ballets designed by Ethel King; the opera prepared musically by Leslie Heward and Herbert Withers.

fbp: 2 July 1924, relayed from His Majesty's Theatre, British National Opera Company.

Pub. 1923, Novello. Vocal score by Vally Lasker.

BIBLIOGRAPHY:

Herbert Antcliffe: The Perfect Fool, *MN&H*, 19 May 1923, p. 494.

Warwick Braithwaite: The Perfect Fool, *Opera*, No. 6, June 1923, p. 26.

M.-D. Calvocoressi: Le Parfait Sot de GH à Covent Garden, *RM*, 1 July 1923, p. 262.

Richard Capell: The Perfect Fool at Covent Garden, *MMR*, 1923, p. 161.

Julia Chatterton: The Perfect Fool, *MS*, 19 May 1923, p. 166.

Alfred Einstein: Holst's The Perfect Fool, *MMR*, 1923, p. 198.

Edwin Evans: The Perfect Fool, *MT*, June 1923, p. 389.

Donald Tovey: The Perfect Fool, or the perfect opera, *MT*, July 1923, p. 464.

R. T. White: The Perfect Fool, *Music Teacher*, July 1924, p. 410.

88a. Ballet Music from 'The Perfect Fool'. 1918. Dur. *c.* 10′ 45″.

Orchestration as for No. 88.

fp: 22 November 1920, Patron's Fund public rehearsal. Note also: 1 December 1921, Queen's Hall, Royal Philharmonic Society concert, cond. Albert Coates.

fbp: 1 June 1924, Cardiff, Gustav Holst night, cond. Warwick Braithwaite.

Pub. 1923, Novello: incl. arr. by Vally Lasker for piano; arr. by Nora Day for piano duet.

89. The Lure. Ballet. 1921. Unpub. Withdrawn.

90. The Gordian Knot Untied: Suite No. 1. Purcell, arr. Gustav Holst.

2 fl, 2 ob, 2 cl, bsn; 2 hn, 2 tpt; timp; strings.

Pub. 1922; Novello.

90a. The Gordian Knot Untied: Suite No. 2. Purcell, arr. Gustav Holst.

2 fl, 2 ob, 2 cl, bsn; 2 hn, 2 tpt; timp; strings.

fbp: September 1924, Cardiff Station Orchestra, cond. Warwick Braithwaite.

Pub. 1922; Novello.

91. A Fugal Overture Op. 40 No. 1. For orchestra. 1922. Ded. 'J.M.J.' (Jane M. Joseph). Dur. *c.* 5′.

2 fl, pic, 2 ob, ca, 2 cl, bcl, 2 bsn, dbsn; 4 hn, 3 tpt, 3 tmb, tuba; timp, jingles (sleigh bells), GC, glock; strings.

fp: 11 October 1923, Queen's Hall, Promenade Concert, New Queen's Hall Orchestra, cond. Gustav Holst.

fbp: 1 June 1924, Cardiff, Gustav Holst night, cond. Warwick Braithwaite.

Pub. 1923, Novello.

BIBLIOGRAPHY:

Donald F. Tovey: Fugal Overture for

orchestra, *EMA*, Vol. 2, O.U.P. (London) 1935, p. 210.

92. Fugal Concerto Op. 40 No. 2. For flute, oboe (or two solo violins) and string orchestra. 1923. Ded. M.R.J. & I.C.H. Dur. *c.* 7′ 50″.

f public p: 11 October 1923, Queen's Hall, Promenade Concert, New Queen's Hall Orchestra, cond. Gustav Holst.

fbp: 2 November 1924, Bournemouth station, Wireless String Orchestra, cond. Capt. W. A. Featherstone.

Pub. 1923, Novello.

BIBLIOGRAPHY:
Donald Tovey: A Fugal Concerto Op. 40 No. 2, in *EMA*, Vol. 2, O.U.P. (London) 1935, p. 208.

93. First Choral Symphony Op. 41. For soprano, chorus and orchestra. 1923–4. Words selected from the poems of John Keats. Composed for the Leeds Festival, 1925. Dur. *c.* 52′.

Prelude: Invocation to Pan; 1. *Song and Bacchanal*; 2. *Ode on a Grecian urn*; 3. *Scherzo: Fancy—Folly's Song*; 4. *Finale*.

3 fl, pic, 2 ob, ca, 2 cl, bcl, 2 bsn, dbsn; 4 hn, 3 tpt, 3 tmb, tuba; timp, tgle, cym, tamb, GC, gong, glock, xyl, bells, jingles (sleigh bells); celesta, hp, strings.

fp: 7 October 1925, Leeds Festival, Dorothy Silk, Festival Chorus and the London Symphony Orchestra, cond. Albert Coates.

f London p: 29 October 1925, Queen's Hall, Royal Philharmonic Society concert, Dorothy Silk, Leeds Festival Choir, cond. Albert Coates.

Pub. 1925, Novello.

BIBLIOGRAPHY:
Harvey Grace: Holst's Choral Symphony, *MT*, October 1925, p. 892.
Frank Howes: Choral Ode, *M&M*, January 1964, p. 22.
Ernest Newman: Holst's choral Symphony, in *From the World of Music*, Calder (London) 1956, pp. 93, 95.
— Words and music, in *More Essays from the World of Music*, Calder (London) 1958, p. 71.
Anon.: Symphonies and poets: the new eclecticism, *The Times*, 3 October 1925, p. 8.

— Two choral compositions: Holst and Vaughan Williams, *The Times*, 17 October 1925, p. 10.

94. At the Boar's Head Op. 42. A Musical Interlude in one act. 1924. Libretto taken from Shakespeare's 'King Henry IV'; music founded on Old English melodies. Ded. 'To my Scribes'. Dur. *c.* 62′.

fl, pic, ob, ca, 2 cl, 2 bsn; 2 hn, 2 tpt, tuba (or euphonium); timp; strings.

fp: 3 April 1925, Manchester, Opera House, British National Opera Company, cond. (Sir) Malcolm Sargent; with Tudor Davies and Norman Allin as principals.

f London p: 20 April 1925, Golders Green Hippodrome, as above.

Pub. 1925, Novello. Vocal score, Vally Lasker.

BIBLIOGRAPHY:
Francis Bonavia: At the Boar's Head, *M&L*, July 1925.
Harvey Grace: At the Boar's Head—Holst' new work, *MT*, April 1925, p. 305.
Ernest Newman: At the Boar's Head, *MT*, May 1925, p. 413.
Sforzando: The first performance of Holst' new opera, *MMR*, 1925, p. 131.

95. Toccata. For piano. 1924. Founded on a Northumbrian pipe tune, 'Newburn Lads'. Dur. *c.* 2′ 10″. Ded. Adine O'Neill and her pupils.

fbp: 20 October 1926, Liverpool station, Joseph Greene.

Pub. 1924, Curwen.

96. Terzetto. For flute, oboe and viola. 1925. Dur. *c.* 9′ 30″.

fp: 2 March 1926, Faculty of Arts Gallery, Albert Fransella, Léon Goossens and Harry Berly.

fbp: 11 June 1926, British Music Society concert from the Music Room of Seaford House (Belgrave Square), Albert Fransella, Léon Goossens and Harry Berly.

Pub. 1944, Chester.

97. The Virtuous Wife. Purcell, arr. Gustav Holst.

2 fl, 2 ob, 2 cl, bsn; 2 hn, 2 tpt; timp; strings.

Pub. 1925; Novello.

98. Two Motets Op. 43. For unacc. 8-part chorus. 1924–5.

1. *The Evening-watch* (Henry Vaughan). 1924. Dur. *c.* 4′.
2. *Sing me the men* (Digby Mackworth Dolben). 1925.

fp (No. 1): 10 September 1925, Gloucester, Three Choirs Festival.

Pub. 1925, Curwen; 1965, Faber Music (No. 1 only).

99. Seven Partsongs Op. 44. For female voices and strings. 1925–6. Words: Robert Bridges. Ded. (Nos. 1, 2, 3) Dr. J. E. Wallace and the Liverpool Bach Choir; (Nos. 4, 5, 6) Harold Brooke; (No. 7) Frank Duckworth.

1. *Say who is this?*; 2. *O Love, I complain*; 3. *Angel spirits of sleep*; 4. *When first we met (A Round)*; 5. *Sorrow and joy*; 6. *Love on my heart from heaven fell*; 7. *Assemble all ye maidens (An Elegy)*.

fp (No. 6): 28 November 1925, Liverpool, Liberty Buildings, cond. Gordon Stutely.

fp (Nos. 1–5): 2 December 1926, Harold Brooke's Choir.

fp (No. 7): 24 May 1927, Dora Labbette and the Bach Choir, cond. Ralph Vaughan Williams.

fbp: 20 December 1928, Harold Brooke's Choir with Elsie Suddaby (six only performed).

Pub. 1926 (Nos. 1–6), 1927 (No. 7), Novello.

100. The Golden Goose Op. 45 No. 1. A Choral Ballet. 1926. Founded on a tale of Grimm. Written and designed by Jane M. Joseph. Ded. Morley College.

2 fl, pic, 2 ob, ca, 2 cl, 2 bsn; 2 hn, 2 tpt, 3 tmb, tuba; timp, tgle, tamb, glock; celesta; strings.

fp (private): 24 May 1926, Brook Green, gardens of Bute House, Whitsun festival, cond. Gustav Holst.

fbp and fp of complete work: 21 September 1926, Wireless Chorus and Symphony Orchestra, cond. Gustav Holst.

fp (concert): 24 February 1930, Cheltenham, P. J. Taylor Choir and the City of Birmingham Orchestra, cond. Gustav Holst.

Pub. 1928, O.U.P.: piano arrangement by Vally Lasker.

101. The Morning of the Year Op. 45 No. 2. A Choral Ballet. 1926–7. Words: Steuart Wilson. Design: Douglas Kennedy. Ded. 'To the E.F.D.S.' (English Folk Dance Society).

2 fl, pic, 2 ob, ca, 2 cl, 2 bsn; 4 hn, 2 tpt, 3 tmb, tuba; timp, cym, glock, organ pedals; strings.

fp: 17 March 1927, Royal Albert Hall, BBC concert, National Chorus and Orchestra, cond. Gustav Holst.

f stage p (private): 1 June 1927, Parry Opera Theatre, Royal College of Music, cond. Gustav Holst.

Pub. 1927, O.U.P.

102. Chrissemas Day in the Morning Op. 46 No. 1. For piano. 1926. Ded. Vally Lasker. Founded on a tune from 'North Countrie Ballads'. Dur. *c.* 2′ 10″.

fbp: 24 December 1934, Betty Humby.

Pub. 1927, O.U.P.

103. Two Folksong Fragments Op. 46 No. 2. For piano. 1927. Ded. Nora Day. Founded on tunes from 'North Countrie Ballads'. Dur. *c.* 3′ 5″.

1. *O I hae seen the roses blaw*; 2. *The Shoemakker.*

Pub. 1928, O.U.P.

104. Man Born to Toil. Anthem for SATB chorus and organ with bells (ad lib). 1927. Words: Robert Bridges. Composed for the Bath and Wells Diocesan Choral Festival, 1928. Pub. 1927, Curwen.

104a. Gird on thy sword. For four voices and organ with bells (ad lib). Final hymn from No. 104, pub. separately, 1927, Curwen.

105. Eternal Father (Robert Bridges). Short anthem for soprano, chorus, organ and (ad lib) bells. 1927. Dur. *c.* 3′. Pub. 1928, Curwen.

106. The Coming of Christ. Music to a Mystery Play for chorus, piano, organ (or string orchestra) and trumpet. 1927. Words: John Masefield.

1. *First song of the host of heaven*; 2. *Song of the four angels*; 3. *Second song of the host of heaven*; 4. *First song of the kings*; 5. *Second song of the kings*; 6. *The Antiphonal*; 7. *The song of the coming of Christ.*

fp: 28 May 1928, Canterbury Cathedral, Choir and Orchestra from Morley College and St. Paul's Girls' School, cond. Gustav Holst.

Pub. 1928, Curwen.

BIBLIOGRAPHY:

R.C.: The Coming of Christ at Canterbury, *MMR*, 1928, p. 204.

107. Egdon Heath Op. 47. Homage to Thomas Hardy, for orchestra. 1927. Composed for the New York Symphony Orchestra. Dur. *c.* 11' 30".

2 fl, 2 ob, ca, 2 cl, 2 bsn, dbsn; 4 hn, 3 tpt, 3 tmb, tuba; strings.

fp: 10 February 1928, New York, New York Symphony Orchestra.

f European p: 13 February 1928, Cheltenham, Town Hall, City of Birmingham Orchestra, cond. Gustav Holst.

f London p: 23 February 1928, Queen's Hall, Royal Philharmonic Society concert, cond. Vaclav Talich.

fFp: 20 October 1929, Paris, Salle Pleyel, l'Orchestre Symphonique de Paris, cond. Pierre Monteux.

Pub. 1928, Novello.

BIBLIOGRAPHY:

Henry Prunières: Egdon Heath, de GH, à l'O.S.P., *RM*, January 1930, p. 66.

108. The Married Beau. Purcell, arr. Gustav Holst.

2 fl, 2 ob, 2 cl, bsn; 2 hn, 2 tpt; timp; strings.

fbp: 25 December 1932, BBC Orchestra, cond. Norman O'Neill.

Pub. 1928, Novello.

109. A Moorside Suite. For brass band. 1928. Dur. *c.* 14' 40".

1. *Scherzo*; 2. *Nocturne*; 3. *March*.

fp: 29 September 1928, Crystal Palace, National Brass Band Festival championship contest.

Pub. *c.* 1928, R. Smith & Co.

110. Fugue à la Gigue. Bach, arr. for orch. by Gustav Holst. 1928.

2 fl, 2 ob, 2 cl, 2 bsn; 2 hn, 2 tpt, 2 ten tmb, tuba; strings.

Pub. 1929, Boosey & Hawkes.

111. Twelve Songs (Humbert Wolfe) Op. 48. For voice and piano. 1929.

1. *A little music.* Dur. *c.* 1' 25".
2. *Betelgeuse.* Dur. *c.* 3' 25".
3. *Envoi.* Dur. *c.* 3' 45".
4. *In the street of lost time.* Dur. *c.* 50".
5. *The thought.* Dur. *c.* 1' 30".
6. *Things lovelier.* Dur. *c.* 1'.
7. *Journey's end.* Dur. *c.* 1' 45".
8. *Now in these fairylands.* Dur. *c.* 1' 20".
9. *Persephone.* Dur. *c.* 1' 20".
10. *Rhyme.* Dur. *c.* 2'.
11. *The Dream city.* Dur. 2' 45".
12. *The floral bandit.* Dur. *c.* 2' 15".

The numbering of these songs is arbitrary.

fp (private): 9 November 1929, Paris, home of Louise Dyer, Dorothy Silk, acc. Vally Lasker; omitting Nos. 2 & 10.

fp (public): 5 February 1930, Wigmore Hall, Dorothy Silk, acc. Kathleen Markwell; omitting No. 5.

fbp: 16 October 1934, Norah Scott Turner: Nos. 6–9 & 12 only.

fbp (complete): 16 September 1948, Elsie Suddaby, acc. Josephine Lee.

Pub. 1930, Augener.

112. Double Concerto Op. 49. For two violins and orchestra. 1929. Ded. Adila Fachiri and Jelly d'Aranyi. Dur. *c.* 14' 25".

1. *Scherzo*; 2. *Lament*; 3. *Variations on a ground.*

2 fl, 2 ob, 2 cl, 2 bsn; 2 hn, 2 tpt; timp; strings.

fp: 3 April 1930, Queen's Hall, Royal Philharmonic Society concert, Adila Fachiri and Jelly d'Aranyi, cond. Oskar Fried.

Pub. 1930, Curwen.

113. The Wandering Scholar Op. 50. Chamber opera in one act. 1929–30. Libretto: Clifford Bax, founded on an incident in Helen Waddell's 'The Wandering Scholars'. Originally called 'The Tale of the Wandering Scholar'. Ded. Helen Waddell. Dur. *c.* 28'.

fl, pic, ob, ca, 2 cl, 2 bsn; 2 hn; strings.

fp: 31 January 1934, Liverpool, David Lewis Theatre, cond. J. E. Wallace; producer, Frederick Wilkinson.

Pub. 1968, Faber Music.

114. Choral Fantasia Op. 51. For soprano (or semichorus), chorus, organ, and instrumental ensemble. 1930. Words: Robert

Bridges. Ded. 'In homage, Robert Bridges'. Dur. *c*. 17′ 5″.

3 tpt, 2 ten tmb, bs tmb, tuba; organ, strings.

fp: 8 September 1931, Gloucester, Three Choirs Festival, Dorothy Silk, cond. Gustav Holst.

Pub. 1931, Curwen.

BIBLIOGRAPHY:

T. L. Martin: Holst's Choral Fantasia, *MMR*, 1931, p. 265.

115. Hammersmith Op. 52. A Prelude and Scherzo for military band. 1930. Ded. to the author of 'The Water Gypsies'. Dur. *c*. 14′ 25″. Pub. Boosey & Hawkes.

115a. Hammersmith Op. 52. Version for orchestra. 1931. Dur. *c*. 14′ 25″.

2 fl, pic, 2 ob, ca, 2 cl, bcl, 2 bsn, dbsn; 4 hn, 3 tpt, 3 tmb, tuba; timp, xyl, tgle, cym, GC, gong; strings.

fp: 25 November 1931, Queen's Hall, BBC Symphony Orchestra, cond. Sir Adrian Boult.

Pub. 1963, Boosey & Hawkes.

BIBLIOGRAPHY:

Robert Cantrick: Hammersmith and the two worlds of GH, *M&L*, July 1956.

116. Nocturne. For piano. 1930. Ded. Imogen (Holst). Dur. *c*. 3′ 50″.

fbp: 29 March 1931, Kathleen Long.

Pub. 1934, Curwen; 1965, Faber Music (with No. 124).

117. Twelve Welsh Folksongs. For mixed chorus a cappella. 1930–1. Words: traditional Welsh, transl. Steuart Wilson.

1. *Lisa Lan*; 2. *Green grass*; 3. *The dove*; 4. *Awake, awake*; 5. *Nightingale and linnet*; 6. *The mother-in-law*; 7. *The first love*; 8. *Monday morning*; 9. *My sweetheart's like Venus*; 10. *White summer rose*; 11. *The lively pair*; 12. *The lover's complaint*. (The numbering of these songs is arbitrary.)

Pub. 1932 and 1933, Curwen.

118. Wassail Song. Folksong arrangement for mixed chorus a cappella. ?1931. Ded. Huddersfield Glee and Madrigal Society. Dur. *c*. 2′ 20″. Pub. 1931, Curwen.

119. Roadways (John Masefield). Unison song. ?1931. Composed for the 'Masque of Guiding'. Pub. 1932, Year Book Press.

120. The Bells. 1931. Music for the Associated Sound Film Industries production, directed by Oscar Werndorff and Harcourt Templeman; with Donald Calthrop as The Burgomaster.

121. Six Choruses Op. 53. For male voices (TTBB) and strings (or organ, or piano). 1931–1932. Words transl. from medieval Latin by Helen Waddell. Dur. *c*. 26′.

1. *Intercession*. Ded. Irving Silverwood and the Holme Valley Choir.

fp (broadcast): 12 March 1932, Huddersfield, Town Hall, Holme Valley Choir.

2. *Good Friday*. Ded. Ernest Bullock and Westminster Abbey Choir.

fp: 13 December 1932, Westminster Abbey.

3. *Drinking song*. Ded. Bernard Naylor and the Winnipeg Male Voice Choir.

fEp: 30 May 1933, Oriana Madrigal Society.

4. *Love song*. A canon for TB. Ded. Archibald T. Davison and the Harvard Glee Club.

5. *How mighty are the Sabbaths*. Ded. as for No. 4.

6. *Before sleep*. A canon for TB. Ded. as for No. 4.

fp: 27 April 1932, Harvard, Harvard Glee Club.

Pub. 1932–3, Hawkes: Winthrop Rogers edition. No. 5 arr. for unison voices and organ or piano.

122. Six Canons. For equal voices a cappella. 1932. Words transl. from medieval Latin by Helen Waddell.

1. *If you love songs*. For 3 voices. Ded. S.P.G.S. Dur. *c*. 54″.

2. *Lovely Venus*. For 3 voices. Ded. Wallace Woodworth and Radcliffe College. Dur. *c*. 52″.

3. *The fields of sorrow*. For 3 voices. Ded. as for No. 2. Dur. *c*. 1′ 9″.

4. *David's Lament for Jonathan*. For 3 voices. Ded. as for No. 1. Dur. 1′ 15″.

5. *O strong of heart*. For 3 choirs, 9 voices. Ded. as for No. 2. Dur. *c*. 1′ 27″.

6. *Truth of all truth*. For 2 choirs, 6 voices. Ded. as for No. 2. Dur. *c*. 3′ 27″.

Holst, Gustav

Pub. 1933, Curwen; 1965, Faber Music with No. 123 as Eight Canons).

123. Two Canons. For 2 equal voices and piano. 1932. Words transl. from medieval Latin by Helen Waddell.

1(7). *Evening on the Moselle.* Ded. Overstone. Dur. *c.* 1′ 15″.

2(8). *If 'twere the time of lilies.* Ded. S.P.G.S. (St. Paul's Girls' School). Dur. *c.* 1′ 5″.

Pub. 1933, Curwen; 1965, Faber Music (with No. 122 as Eight Canons).

124. Jig. For piano. 1932. Ded. Imogen (Holst). Dur. 2′ 45″. Pub. 1934, Curwen; 1965, Faber Music (with No. 116).

125. Capriccio ('Jazz-band piece'). 1932. Edited by Imogen Holst, 1967, as Capriccio for orchestra. Dur. *c.* 6′ 10″.

fl, pic, ob, ca, cl, bcl, 2 bsn; 2 hn, 3 tpt, 2 ten tmb, tuba; timp, side dm, GC, cym, tgle, glock, marimba, tub bells; hp, piano, celesta (ad lib); strings. (NB: The original version had single woodwind, three saxophones and three cornets instead of trumpets.)

fp: 10 January 1968, Queen Elizabeth Hall, English Chamber Orchestra, cond. Imogen Holst.

Pub. 1969, Faber Music.

126. Brook Green Suite. For string orchestra and (ad lib) woodwind. 1933. Ded. St. Paul's Girls' School Junior Orchestra. Dur. *c.* 6′ 40″.

1. *Prelude*; 2. *Air*; 3. *Dance.*

Pub. 1934, Curwen. Also arr. for piano by Vally Lasker, 1935.

127. Lyric Movement. For viola and small orchestra. 1933. Ded. Lionel Tertis. Dur. *c.* 9′ 50″.

fl, ob, cl, bsn; strings.

fp: 18 March 1934, BBC broadcast, Lionel Tertis and the BBC Orchestra, cond. Sir Adrian Boult.

Pub. 1948, O.U.P.

128. Scherzo (from an unfinished symphony). For orchestra. 1933–4. Dur. 5′ 5″.

2 fl, pic, 2 ob, ca, 2 cl, 2 bsn; 4 hn, 3 tpt, 3 tmb, tuba; timp; hp, strings.

fp: 6 February 1935, Queen's Hall, BBC Symphony Orchestra, cond. Sir Adrian Boult.

Pub. 1947, Boosey & Hawkes.

BIBLIOGRAPHY:
Robert Hull: Holst's last Scherzo, *Radio Times*, 1 February 1935, p. 12.
A Payne: Inconsequential Hammersmith, *M&M*, December 1967, p. 47.

WRITINGS BY HOLST
A British school of composers (letter), *Musical Herald*, September 1915, p. 401.
The Mystic, the Philistine and the Artist, in *The Quest*, 1920; repr. in *GH: A biography* (Imogen Holst), O.U.P. (London) 1938.
The tercentenary of Byrd and Weelkes, *P(R)MA*, 1922–3, p. 29.
My favourite Tudor composer, *Midland Musician*, 4 January 1926.
Opinions (contribution), *Chesterian*, No. 68, January–February 1928.
De l'inspiration musicale (contribution), *Le Monde musical*, July 1928.
Henry Purcell, in *The Heritage of Music*, Vol. 1, O.U.P. (London) 1927.
The teaching of Art (1929), in *Heirs and Rebels*, O.U.P. (London) 1959; repr. in *GH: A biography* (2nd edition) (Imogen Holst), O.U.P. (London) 1969.
Haydn (1932), in *Heirs and Rebels*, O.U.P. (London) 1959.

GENERAL BIBLIOGRAPHY
Gerald Abraham: The art of GH, *Music Teacher*, July 1924, p. 387.
Hilda Andrews: GH, *Music Teacher*, July 1928, p. 403.
Clifford Bax: Recollections of GH, *M&L*, January 1939, p. 1.
(Sir) Arthur Bliss: A lonely figure, *Radio Times*, 15 June 1934, p. 819.
X. Marcel Boulestin: Holst (in 'Les Post-Elgarians ou la jeune école anglaise'), *Revue S.I.M.*, 1914, p. 24.
Sir Adrian Boult: The man and his work, *Radio Times*, 15 June 1934, p. 819.
Havergal Brian: GH, an English composer, *MO*, January 1940, p. 154.
E.L.B.: GH, *MO*, March 1911, p. 397.
Richard Capell: GH, *M&L*, 1926–7.
— GH, notes for a biography, *MT*, December 1926 p. 1073, January 1927 p. 17.

G. Confalonieri: GH, *La Critica musicale* (Florence), 1923, Nos. 2–3.

Suzanne Demarquez: GH, *RM*, May 1931, p. 402.

— Alfred Bruneau, GH, Frederick Delius, *RM*, July 1934, p. 158.

Norman Demuth: GH, in *Musical Trends in the 20th Century*, Rockliff (London) 1952, p. 136.

Bernard van Dieren & Richard Capell: GH ('Stereoscopic Views' No. 3), *The Dominant*, December 1928, p. 13.

Edwin Evans: GH, *MT*, 1919, October p. 524, November p. 588, December p. 657.

— GH, *The Dominant*, April 1928, p. 24.

— GH, July 1934, p. 593.

K. Eggar: How they make music at Morley College, *Music Student*, March 1921, p. 359.

Arnold Foster: An appreciation of GH, *MMR*, July–August 1934, p. 126.

Hans Gal (ed.): GH, in *The Musicians World* (Great Composers in their Letters), Thames & Hudson (London) 1965, p. 418.

Harvey Grace: GH, teacher, *MT*, August 1934, p. 689.

Sydney Grew: GvH, *MO*, February 1914, p. 359.

Fritz Hart: Early memories of GH, *RCM Magazine*, 1943, No. 2 p. 43, No. 3 p. 84.

Leslie Heward: GH and a Method, *Opera*, No. 12, December 1923, p. 12.

Leonard Hibbs: GH, *Gramophone Record*, June 1934, p. 8.

Basil Hogarth: GH, *Musical Mirror*, August 1925, p. 149.

Imogen Holst: GH, a biography, O.U.P. (London) 1938; 2nd edition, 1969.

— The music of GH, O.U.P. (London) 1953; 2nd edition, 1968.

Robin Hull: Three British composers: Elgar, Delius and Holst, *MT*, July 1959, p. 380.

Peter Jackson: Do we pay only lip service to Holst?, *M&M*, May 1959, p. 17.

Michael Kennedy: Elgar, Delius and Holst, *Halle*, April 1959, p. 8.

Jeffery Mark: Vaughan Williams and Holst, *Modern Music*, January 1924, p. 24.

Wilfrid Mellers: Holst and the English language, *MR*, August 1941; in *Studies in Contemporary Music*, Dobson (London) 1947, p. 144.

Peter J. Pirie: In defence of GH, *MO*, September 1957, p. 723.

Henry Raynor: The case of Holst, *MMR*, 1954, pp. 31, 70.

Edmund Rubbra: GH as teacher, *MMR*, 1930, p. 199.

— Holst, some technical characteristics, *MMR*, 1932, p. 70.

— GH, *Chesterian*, No. 116, July–August 1934.

— Early manuscripts of GH, *MMR*, July–August 1935, p. 123.

— A life of Holst, *MMR*, 1938, p. 267.

— GH, *Crescendo*, No. 19, January 1949, p. 15.

Adolfo Salazar: Dos ingleses: Vaughan Williams y GvH, in *Sinfonía y ballet*, Editorial Mundo Latino (Madrid) 1929, p. 158.

Michael Tippett: Holst, a figure of our time, *The Listener*, 13 November 1958, p. 800.

Ralph Vaughan Williams: GH, *M&L*, July & October, 1920.

— Introductory talk to Holst memorial concert, BBC, 1934; repr. in *The Orchestra Speaks* (Bernard Shore), Longmans, Green (London) 1938.

— GH, man and musician, *RCM Magazine*, December 1934, p. 78.

— A note on GH, in *GH* (Imogen Holst), O.U.P. (London) 1938, p. vii.

— GH, in *Dictionary of National Biography*, 1931–40, O.U.P. (1949), p. 441.

— GH, an essay and a note (1953), in *National music and other essays*, O.U.P. (London) 1963.

— GH, a great composer, *The Listener*, 3 June 1954, p. 965.

William Vowles: GH with the Army, *MT*, September 1934, p. 794.

Ernest Walker: Holst's harmonic methods, *MMR*, 1930, p. 232.

John Warrack: A new look at Holst, *MT*, February 1963, p. 100.

Ralph W. Wood: The riddle of Holst, *MO*, February 1938, p. 401.

Percy M. Young: Vaughan Williams and Holst, in *History of British Music*, Ernest Benn (London) 1967, p. 547.

MISCELLANEOUS OR UNSIGNED
GvH, *MS*, 16 May 1914, p. 461.

Mr. GvH, *Musical Herald*, July 1918, p. 199.

Mr. GH at University College, London, on Purcell, *The Times*, 10 April 1922, p. 12.

Mr. GH at London Academy of Music, on English music: Byrd and Weelkes, *The Times*, 10 January 1923, p. 8.

Mr. GH, health, *The Times*, 24 March 1924, p. 15.

Mr. GH awarded Howland Memorial Prize, *The Times*, 19 November 1924, p. 13.

Mr. GH to deliver Alsop lectures on music at Liverpool University, *The Times*, 5 February 1925, p. 14.

English music: Mr. GH on past triumphs, *The Times*, 14 November 1927, p. 12.

Private performance of works, *The Times*, 27 May 1926, p. 12.

Memorial broadcast, *The Times*, 23 June 1934, p. 10.

Holst's artistic faith, *The Times*, 2 February 1951, p. 3.

ARTHUR HONEGGER (1892–1955)

Though Swiss by nationality and maintaining many Swiss connections, Honegger lived almost all his life in France. His parents were natives of Zürich but lived in Le Havre, where his father was a coffee-importer, and it was in Le Havre that Honegger was born on 10 March 1892. He showed his musical gifts early, studying at the Zürich Conservatoire for a couple of years while living in Switzerland in 1909–11. Returning to Le Havre he enrolled at the Paris Conservatoire and commuted from the coast to the capital once a week. He moved to Paris in 1913, settled in Montmartre (where he was to live for the rest of his life) and became the close friend of the composer Darius Milhaud and the pianist Andrée Vaurabourg. He stayed on at the Conservatoire, studying the violin under Lucien Capet and composition under Widor, Gedalge and d'Indy. At the start of the First World War he served in the Swiss frontier guard but went back to the Conservatoire in 1916. He associated with *les Nouveaux Jeunes*, a group of composers which came into prominence at the end of the War under the guidance of Erik Satie. In 1920 the critic Henri Collet labelled half a dozen of the group (Milhaud, Poulenc, Auric, Durey, Germaine Tailleferre and Honegger himself) *les Six*; but it was not a label to bind them aesthetically, and Honegger soon showed his independence with his first international success, *Le Roi David* (1921). In the next few years he formed a liaison with the singer Claire Croiza, who bore him a son; but in 1927 he married Andrée Vaurabourg. In 1928–9 Honegger visited the United States for the first time on a concert tour with his pianist wife, and frequently conducted his own music in various parts of Europe during the 1930s. He stayed in Paris during the Second World War, visiting the USA again in 1947 to teach at the Berkshire Music Centre at Tanglewood (Mass.). On this visit, however, he suffered a severe heart attack which rendered him an invalid— though a prolific composer none the less— until his death in Paris in November 1955.

CATALOGUE OF WORKS

1. Trois Pièces. For piano. 1910.
1. *Scherzo.*
2. *Humoresque.*
3. *Adagio espressivo.*
Pub. Desforges (Le Havre).

2. Quatre Poèmes. For piano. 1914–16. Ded. Jane Bathori.
1. (Untitled)(A. Fontainas). Dated: November 1914.
2. (Untitled) (Jules Laforgue). Dated: May 1916, Paris.
3. (Untitled) (Francis Jammes). Dated: July 1915, Zürich.
4. (Untitled) (Archag Tchobanian). Dated: March 1916, Paris.
Pub. 1921, Chester.

3. Toccata et Variations. For piano. Dated: September 1916, Paris. Ded. 'En mémoire de mon Oncle O.H.'.
fp: 15 December 1916, Paris, Andrée Vaurabourg.
fEbp: 29 April 1936, Jehanne Chambard.
Pub. 1921, Mathoy/Salabert.

4. Trois Poèmes (Paul Fort: 'Complaintes et Dits'). For voice and piano.
1. *Le chasseur perdu en forêt.* Dated: August 1916, Paris. Ded. Madeleine Bonnard.
Version with orch. acc. fp: 25 January 1930,

Paris, Théâtre des Champs-Elysées, Lina Falk and Orchestre Pasdeloup, cond. A. van Raalte.

2. *Cloche du soir*. Dated: October 1916, Paris. Ded. Rose Armandie.

3. *Chanson de fol*. Dated: November 1916, Paris. Ded. Elisabeth Vuillémoz.

fEbp (No. 3): 17 February 1931, Sophie Wyss.

Pub. 1922, Senart.

5. Prélude pour 'Aglavaine et Sélysette'. For orchestra, after Maurice Maeterlinck. Dated: 1 January 1917, Paris.

fl, ob, 2 cl, 2 bsn; tpt, 2 hn; strings.

fp: 3 April 1917, Paris Conservatoire orchestral class, cond. Arthur Honegger.

Pub. 1956, Salabert.

6. Six Poèmes (Guillaume Apollinaire: 'Alcools'). For voice and piano. 1916–17. Ded. Fernand Ochsé.

1. *A la 'Santé'*. Dated: May 1916, Paris.
2. *Clotilde*. Dated: March 1916, Paris.
3. *Automne*. Dated: August 1915, Zürich.
4. *Les Saltimbanques*. Dated: March 1917, Paris.
5. *L'Adieu*. Dated: January 1917, Paris.
6. *Les Cloches*. Dated: March 1917, Paris.

fp (Nos. 1–3): 10 July 1916, Mme R. Armandie.

fp (complete): 15 January 1918, Paris, Théâtre du Vieux Colombier, Jane Bathori.

fEbp (Nos. 5 & 6): 4 January 1927, Dora Stevens.

Pub. 1921, Mathoy/Salabert.

Version with orch. acc. Nos. 1 & 4 fp: 25 January 1930, Paris, Théâtre des Champs-Elysées, Lina Falk and Orchestre Pasdeloup, cond. A. van Raalte. ?Unpub.

7. Rhapsodie. For two flutes, clarinet and piano *or* 2 violins, viola and piano. Dated: April 1917, Paris. Ded. Charles M. Widor.

fp: 17 November 1917, Paris, Parthénon, Manouvrier and Leroy (fl), Tournier (cl) and Andrée Vaurabourg (piano).

?fEp: 5 March 1922, Contemporary Chamber Concert.

fEbp: 26 August 1936, Joseph Slater (fl), Jean Pougnet (v), Rebecca Clarke (va) and Angus Morrison (piano).

Pub. 1923, Senart.

8. String Quartet. 1916–17. Ded. Florent Schmitt.

1. *Appassionato* (Violent et tourmenté). Dated: July 1917, Paris.
2. *Adagio* (Très lent). Dated: April 1916, Le Havre.
3. *Allegro* (Rude et rythmique). Dated: October 1917, Paris.

fp: 22 June 1919, Paris, Société Musicale Indépendante, Capelle Quartet.

?fEp: 26 October 1927, L.C.M.C. concert, Brosa Quartet.

fEbp: 23 March 1931, Stratton Quartet.

Pub. 1921, La Sirène; also arr. for piano four hands.

9. Two Pieces. For organ. Dated: September 1917, Paris.

1. *Fugue*. Ded. Robert Charles Martin.
2. *Choral*. Ded. Andrée Vaurabourg.

Pub. 1920, Chester.

10. Le Chant du Nigamon. For orchestra, Dated: December 1917, Paris. Ded. Rhené-Baton.

2 fl, pic, ob, ca, 2 cl, 2 bsn, cbsn; 4 hn, 2 tpt, 3 tmb, tuba; timp, cym, GC, tgle; strings.

fp: 3 January 1920, Paris, Cirque d'Hiver, Orchestre Pasdeloup, cond. Rhené-Baton. Also: March 1921, Paris, Théâtre des Champs-Elysées, Loïe Fuller dance recital.

Pub. 1927, Senart; also min. score and arr. for piano four hands, 1926.

11. Violin Sonata No. 1. 1916–18. Ded. Andrée Vaurabourg.

1. *Andante sostenuto*. Dated: July 1916, Paris.
2. *Presto*. Dated: March 1917, Paris.
3. *Adagio—Allegro assai*. Dated: February 1918, Paris.

fp: 19 March 1918, Paris, Théâtre du Vieux Colombier, Hélène Jourdan-Morhange and Andrée Vaurabourg.

fEp: 30 May 1922, St. John's Institute (Tufton Street), André Mangeot and Yvonne Arnaud.

Pub. 1921, Senart.

12. Le Dit des Jeux du Monde, Incidental music (Paul Méral): ten dances, interludes and epilogue for chamber orchestra. May–November 1918, Paris & Etel. Ded. Fernand Ochsé.

Honegger, Arthur

1. *Le soleil et la fleur*; 2. *La montagne et les pierres*; 3. *L'enfant et la mer*; 4. *L'homme tournant sur le sol*; 5. *L'homme fou* (Interlude 1); 6. *Les hommes et le village*; 7. *Les hommes et la terre*; 8. *L'homme et la femme*; 9. *L'homme qui lutte et conduit* (Interlude 2); 10. *L'homme et l'ombre*; 11. *Le rat et la mort*; 12. *L'homme et la mer*; 13. *Epilogue*.

fl, pic; timp, GC, tambour, bouteillophone; strings.

fp: 3 December 1918, Paris, Théâtre du Vieux Colombier, cond. Walter Straram.

fp (concert): January 1921, Paris, Salle Gaveau, Concerts Golschmann, cond. Vladimire Golschmann.

Pub. 1928, Senart.

13. La Mort de Sainte Alméenne. Incidental music for a Mystery (Max Jacob). December 1918.

Interludes fp (concert): 30 October 1920, Paris. Théâtre du Châtelet, Orchestre Colonne, cond. Gabriel Pierné.

14. Danse de la Chèvre. For solo flute. 1919. Ded. René Le Roy.

fp: May 1919, Paris, concert given by the dancer Lysana, René Le Roy.

Pub. 1932, Senart.

15. La Danse Macabre. Incidental music (Carlos Larronde). 1919.

fp: May 1919, Paris, Odéon.

Unpub.

16. Trois Pièces. For piano. 1915–19.

1. *Prélude.* Dated: May 1919, Paris. Ded. Walter Morse Rummel.

2. *Hommage à Ravel.* Dated: November 1915, Paris.

3. *Danse.* Dated: May 1919, Paris. Ded. Ricardo Viñes.

?fp (No. 2): 10 May 1921, Paris, Léo-Pol Morin.

Pub. 1921, Mathot/Salabert.

17. Entré, Nocturne et Berceuse. For piano and small orchestra. 1919.

fp: 1919, Paris.

Unpub.

18. Sept Pièces Brèves. For piano. Dated: October 1919–January 1920.

1. *Souplement.* October 1919. Ded. Rose Martin-Lafon.

2. *Vif.* November 1919. Ded. Minna Vaurabourg.

3. *Très lent.* January 1920. Ded. Andrée Vaurabourg.

4. *Légèrement.* December 1919. Ded. Marcelle Milhaud.

5. *Lent.* January 1920. Ded. Myty' Fraggi.

6. *Rythmique.* January 1920. Ded. Mme E. Alleaume.

7. *Violent.* January 1920. Ded. Robert Casadessus.

fp: 4 March 1920, Paris, Salle Gaveau, Andrée Vaurabourg.

fEbp: 21 December 1930, Walter Frey.

Pub. 1921, La Sirène musicale.

19. Sarabande. For piano. 1920.

Pub. 1920, Eschig, in 'Album des Six'.

20. Les Pâques à New York. Three Fragments for soprano and string quartet (Blaise Cendrars). 1920.

1. *Grave.* Dated: March 1920, Paris.

2. *Tourmenté.* Dated: March 1920, Aix en Provence.

3. *Modéré.* Dated: July 1920, Zürich.

fp: 20 February 1924, Paris, Salle Erard, Gabrielle Gills and the Pro Arte Quartet.

?fEp (broadcast): 4 February 1929, Arts Theatre Club, BBC concert, Claire Croiza, with piano acc. Victor Hely-Hutchinson.

Pub. 1923, Composer's Music Corporation: reduction for voice and piano by the composer.

BIBLIOGRAPHY:

André George: Les Pâques à New York, *RM*, May 1924, p. 250.

21. Viola Sonata. 1920. Ded. Henri Casadesus.

1. *Andante—Vivace.* Dated: March 1920, Paris.

2. *Allegretto molto moderato.* Dated: January 1920, Paris.

3. *Allegro non troppo.* Dated: February 1920, Paris.

fp: 2 December 1920, Paris, Société Musicale Indépendante, Henri Casadesus and Robert Casadesus.

fEbp: 3 October 1938, Watson Forbes and Myers Foggin.

Pub. 1921, La Sirène.

22. Sonatine. For two violins. 1920. Ded. Darius Milhaud.
1. *Allegro non tanto.* Dated: April 1920, Paris.
2. *Andantino.* Dated: June 1920, Paris.
3. *Allegro moderato.* Dated: May 1920, Paris.
fp: 1920, Paris, Studio des Champs-Elysées, Darius Milhaud and Arthur Honegger.
fEp: 5 May 1922, YMCA (Great Russell Street), British Music Society concert, André Mangeot and Kenneth Skeaping.
fEbp: 7 November 1927, A. Onnou and L. Halleux (of the Pro Arte Quartet).
Pub. 1922, La Sirène.

23. Cello Sonata. 1920. Ded. René Gosselin.
1. *Allegro non troppo.* Dated: September 1920, Zürich.
2. *Andante sostenuto.* Dated: June–July 1920, Paris–Zürich.
3. *Presto.* Dated: September 1920, Zürich.
fp: 23 April 1921, Paris, Salle du Conservatoire, Société Nationale concert, Diran Alexanian and Andrée Vaurabourg.
fEp: 13 May 1927, Wigmore Hall, Beatrice Harrison and Gerald Moore.
Pub. 1922, La Sirène.

BIBLIOGRAPHY:
Josef Rufer: AH, Cellosonate, *Anbruch*, August–September 1925, p. 429.

24. Hymne. For ten strings. Dated: 9 October 1920.
fp: 17 October 1921, Paris, Art et Action concert, Dixtuor Léo Sir.
Unpub.

25. Cadence. For violin and piano. 1920. Composed for the cinema fantasy 'Le Bœuf sur le Toit' by Darius Milhaud.
fp: March 1920, Paris, Théâtre des Champs-Elysées, Spectacle-Concert, Darius Milhaud and Raoul Dufy.
Pub. La Sirène.

BIBLIOGRAPHY:
Gustave Samazeuilh: Théâtre des Champs-Elysées Spectacle Concert, *Le Ménestrel*, 12 March 1920, p. 107.

26. Pastorale d'Eté. 'Poème symphonique' for orchestra. August 1920.

fl, ob, cl, bsn; hn; strings.
fp: 17 February 1921, Paris, Salle Gaveau, Concerts Golschmann, cond. Vladimir Golschmann.
fEp: 27 October 1921, Queen's Hall, Goossens Orchestra, cond. (Sir) Eugene Goossens. (NB: fEp orig. announced for 20 April 1921, Edward Clark concert).
fEbp: 11 October 1925, Newcastle Station Symphony Orchestra, cond. Edward Clark.
Pub. 1922, Senart; also arr. for piano four hands by the composer. Prix Verley, 1921.

27. Vérité-Mensonge. Ballet. 1920.
fp: November 1920, Paris, Salon d'Automne.
Unpub.

28. Horace Victorieux. 'Symphonie mimée' after Tite-Live (Titus Livius) for orchestra. December 1920–February 1921, Paris, orch. 1921. Ded. Serge Koussevitzky.
3 fl, pic, 2 ob, ca, 2 cl, bcl, 2 bsn, cbsn; 4 hn, 3 tpt, 3 tmb, tuba; timp, cym, GC, tamb, tamtam, crécelle; hp, strings.
fp: 2 November 1921, Geneva, L'Orchestre de la Suisse Romande cond. Ernest Ansermet.
fFp: 1 December 1921, Paris, cond. Serge Koussevitzky.
fEp: 16 December 1921, Queen's Hall, Ursula Greville concert, cond. Ernest Ansermet.
Pub. Senart; also arr. piano four hands.

29. Le Roi David. For soloists, chorus and orchestra (René Morax). Dated: 25 February–28 April 1921, Paris & Zürich. Five parts, twenty-eight numbers.
fp (excerpts only): 2 June 1921, Paris, Société Musicale Indépendante concert, Mme Schéridan, with piano acc. M. Schéridan.
fp: 13 June 1921, Mézières, Théâtre du Jorat, cond. Arthur Honegger.
Pub. Foetisch Frères (Lausanne): vocal score.

BIBLIOGRAPHY:
Maurice Bex: Le Roi David, Psaume dramatique en deux parties, musique d'AH, *Revue hebdomadaire*, 15 October 1921, p. 365.
Henri Ghéon: Au théâtre de Jorat—Le Roi

David de René Morax, *Nouvelle revue française*, July–December 1921, p. 362.

Jacques Maritain: Le Roi David au Jorat, *Revue des Jeunes*, 10 August 1921.

Emile Vuillermoz: AH, Le Roi David, *Le Temps*, 30 December 1921.

— AH, Le Roi David, in *Musiques d'aujourd'hui*, Crès (Paris) 1923, p. 131.

Stanley Wise: Letter from Switzerland— René Morax's King David, *MN&H*, 14 May 1921, p. 620.

29a. Le Roi David. Revised, reorchestrated version. 1923. Three parts, twenty-seven numbers.

fl, pic, 2 ob, 2 cl, 2 bsn; 4 hn, 2 tpt, 3 tmb, tuba; timp, GC, cym; hp, strings.

fp: 2 December 1923, Winterthur, Stadthaus, Clara Wirz-Wyss, Carl Seidel and Lisa Zuppenzeller, chorus and Stadtorchester, cond. Ernest Wolters; sung in German.

fFp: 14 March 1924, Salle Gaveau, Jacques Copeau (narrator), Gabrielle Gills, Charles Panzéra and Cellier, La Chorale française and L'Art choral, cond. Robert Siohan.

fEp: 17 March 1927, Royal Albert Hall, BBC National Concert, Robert Loraine (narrator), Elsie Suddaby, Phyllis Archibald, Frank Titterton, National Chorus and Orchestra, cond. Arthur Honegger.

Pub. 1924, Foetisch Frères.

BIBLIOGRAPHY:

Denis Arundell: King David, *The Listener*, 6 January 1966, p. 40.

A. Berger: King David and reforestation, *Saturday Review*, 29 May 1952, p. 33.

Maurice Brillant: Cinq minutes au café après le Roi David, *La Vie Catholique*, 30 January 1925.

Gian Bundi: König David, *Der Bund*, 15 December 1925.

Hans David: Honeggers König David, *Melos*, February 1927, p. 83.

Edwin Evans: The life story of King David, *Radio Times*, 8 February 1935, p. 12.

André George: Le Roi David d'AH, *RM*, 1 April 1924, p. 70.

Arthur Hoérée: Le roi David, psaume dramatique de René Morax, musique d'AH, *Beaux-Arts*, 1 May 1924, p. 140.

— Le Roi David et la révolution, *SM*, June 1931, p. 459.

Arthur Honegger: Honegger om Konung David, *Röster i radio*, 1951, No. 14, p. 4.

I. Kolodin: King David, *Saturday Review*, 3 May 1952, p. 33.

M. Lacloche: Le roi David, *Revue politique et littéraire (Revue bleue)*, 7 February 1925, p. 102.

Louis Meyer: Le Roi David à Rotterdam, *RM*, 1 July 1925, p. 81.

Roland-Manuel: Le Roi David d'AH, *Revue Pleyel*, April 1924; *Dissonances*, April 1925.

J. Samson: Le Roi David et la musique religieuse, *RM*, 1 October 1925, p. 246.

André Schaeffner: Le Roi David, notice bibliographique, Foetisch Frères (Lausanne) 1925.

Florent Schmitt: La Musique—Le Roi David, *Revue de France*, 1 November 1924.

E. Schneider: Le Roi David d'AH, *Le Monde musical*, March 1924.

Willi Tappolet: König David von AH, *Neue Zürcher Zeitung*, 18 February 1925.

— König David, *Der Caecilienbote* (Soleure), October 1929.

— AHs König David, *Solothurner Zeitung*, 22 October 1929.

29b. Le Roi David: Suite. Four pieces for orchestra. Pub. Salabert.

30. Marche Funèbre. For orchestra. June 1921. Composed for 'Les Mariées de la Tour Eiffel', ballet by Jean Cocteau, music by Les Six.

fp: 18 June 1921, Paris, Théâtre des Champs-Elysées, Ballets suédois de Rolf de Marè; with Jean Borlin.

Unpub.

31. Skating Rink. Ballet (Canudo). December 1921.

fp: 20 January 1922, Paris, Théâtre des Champs-Elysées, Ballets suédois, cond. D.-E. Inghelbrecht; curtain, scenery and costumes, Fernand Léger.

Pub. Universal-Edition.

BIBLIOGRAPHY:

Maurice Bex: Skating Rink, poème de Canudo, musique d'AH, rideau, costumes et décor de Fernand Léger, *Revue hebdoma-daire*, 25 February 1922, p. 499.

Pierre de Lapommerage: Skating Rink, *Le Ménestrel*, 27 January 1922, p. 35.

32. Saül. Incidental music (André Gide). May 1922.

fp: 16 June 1922, Paris, Théâtre du Vieux Colombier; with Jacques Copeau (Saul), Pierre Daltour (David), François Vibert (Jonathan), Carmen d'Assilva (La Reine), Blanche Albaine (La Sorcière); direction, Jacques Copeau.

Unpub.

BIBLIOGRAPHY:

Léon Morris: Le Vieux Colombier: Saül, drame en cinq actes d'André Gide, *Le Ménestrel*, 23 June 1922, p. 274.

33. Sonatine in A. For clarinet and piano *or* cello and piano. 1921–2. Ded. Werner Reinhart.

1. *Modéré*. Dated: July 1922, Zürich.
2. *Lent et soutenu*. Dated: October 1921, Zürich.
3. *Vif et rythmique*. Dated: November 1921, Paris.

fp: 5 June 1923, Paris (Salle Pleyel), Concerts Wiéner, Cahuzac (cl) and Jean Wiéner.

fEbp: 19 June 1937, Reginald Kell and Kathleen Cooper.

Pub. 1925, Rouart Lerolle/Salabert.

34. Trois Contrepoints. For piccolo, oboe/cor anglais, violin and cello. November 1922, Paris.

1. *Prélude à 2 voix*. Ded. Maurice Jaubert.
2. *Chorale à 3 voix*. Ded. Jacques Brillouin.
3. *Canon sur basse obstinée à 4 voix*. Ded. Marcel Delannoy.

fp: 16 February 1926, Paris, Salle Erard, Société Musicale Indépendante, Fleury (pic), Gaudard (ob/ca), Krettly (v) and Pierre Fournier (c).

Pub. 1926, Hansen; also reduction for piano four hands.

35. Fantaisie. Ballet (Georges Wague). December 1922. Unpub.

36. Antigone. Incidental music (Jean Cocteau, after Sophocles). For harps and woodwind. December 1922.

fp: 20 December 1922, Paris, Théâtre de l'Atelier; with Genica Atanasiou (Antigone), Charles Dullin (Créon); décor, Pablo Picasso.

Pub. January 1923, Feuilles libres.

BIBLIOGRAPHY:

Paul Bertrand: Au Théâtre du Jorat: Antigone, *Le Ménestrel*, 21 August 1925, p. 355.

37. Chant de Joie. For orchestra. January 1923, Paris. Ded. Maurice Ravel.

2 fl, pic, 2 ob, ca, 2 cl, bcl, 2 bsn, cbsn; 4 hn, 3 tpt, 3 tmb, tuba; cym, GC, celesta; hp, strings.

fp: 7 April 1923, Geneva, L'Orchestre de la Suisse Romande, cond. Ernest Ansermet.

f Paris p: 3 May 1923, cond. Serge Koussevitzky.

f London p: 22 November 1923, Royal Philharmonic Society, cond. Ernest Ansermet.

fEbp: 1 November 1926, Newcastle Station Symphony Orchestra, cond. Edward Clark.

Pub. 1924, Senart; also reduction by the composer for piano four hands.

38. Prélude pour 'La Tempête'. After Shakespeare, for orchestra. February 1923, Paris. Ded. Mme L. Maillot.

fl, pic, ob, ca, cl, bcl, bsn, cbsn; 4 hn, 2 tpt, 3 tmb, tuba; cym, GC, tgle, tamtam; strings.

fp: 1 May 1923, Paris, Théâtre des Champs-Elysées, cond. Walter Straram.

fEp: 8 January 1927, Queen's Hall, New Queen's Hall Orchestra, cond. Sir Henry Wood.

Pub. 1924, Senart; also reduction for piano four hands.

39. Deux Chants d'Ariel (Shakespeare, transl. Guy de Pourtalès). For voice and orchestra. April 1923, Paris.

1. *Modéré*. Ded. Gabrielle Gills.
2. *Un peu animé*. Ded. Joy MacArden.

fp: 18 March 1926, Paris, Opéra, Gabrielle Gills, cond. Arthur Honegger.

Pub. 1925, Senart: reduction.

40. Chanson de Fagus. For voice, string quartet and piano. May 1923.

fp: 24 March 1926, Paris, Salle Gaveau, La

Revue musicale concert, Gabrielle Gills, Nivard Quartet and Andrée Vaurabourg. Unpub.

41. Six Poésies (Jean Cocteau). For voice and piano. 1920–3. Ded. Rose Féart.

1. *Le Nègre*. Dated: May 1920, Paris.
2. *Locutions*. Dated: May 1920, Paris.
3. *Souvenirs d'enfance*. Dated: June 1920, Paris.
4. *Ex-voto*. Dated: June 1923, Paris.
5. *Une danseuse*. Dated: June 1923, Paris.
6. *Madame*. Dated: January 1923, Paris.

fp: 17 November 1924, Paris, Salle Pleyel, Claire Croiza, acc. Arthur Honegger.
f Ebp (No. 3): 4 January 1927, Dora Stevens.
Pub. 1924, Senart.

42. Liluli. Incidental music (Romain Rolland). 1922.

fp: December 1922, Paris, Art et Action. Unpub.

43. Le Cahier romand. Five pieces for piano. July 1921–July 1923.

1. *Calme*. Dated: September 1921, Zürich. Ded. Alice Ecoffey.
2. *Un peu animé*. Dated: July 1923, Paris. Ded. Jacqueline Ansermet.
3. *Calme et doux*. Dated: July 1921, Zürich. Ded. Miquette Wagner-Rieder.
4. *Rythmé*. Dated: June 1923, Paris. Ded. Paul Boepple.
5. *Egal*. Dated: April 1922, Paris. Ded. René Morax.

fp: 30 January 1924, Paris, Salle Erard, Société Musicale Indépendante, Andrée Vaurabourg.
Pub. Senart.

44. La Roue. Music for the film produced by Charles Pathé; director, Abel Gance; assistant, Blaise Cendrars; with Séverin Mars and Ivy Close. 1921. Unpub. 'Pacific 231' (No. 45) was subsequently used.

BIBLIOGRAPHY:
Luigi Pestalozza: Honeggers incontra con Gance in una locomotiva del 1922, *Cinema*, 1951.

45. Pacific 231. 'Mouvement symphonique' for orchestra. 1923, Paris, Winterthur, Zürich. Ded. Ernest Ansermet.

2 fl, pic, 2 ob, ca, 2 cl, bcl, 2 bsn, cbsn; 4 hn, 3 tpt, 3 tmb, tuba; caisse roulante, cym, GC, tamtam; strings.

fp: 8 May 1924, Paris, Opéra, cond. Serge Koussevitzky.
fEp: November 1924, Manchester, Halle Orchestra, cond. Sir Hamilton Harty.
f London p: 29 January 1925, Queen's Hall, Royal Philharmonic Society, cond. (Sir) Eugene Goossens.
fEbp: 26 March 1925, Manchester, Halle Orchestra, cond. Sir Hamilton Harty.
Pub. Senart; also for small orchestra, for piano, for piano four hands.

BIBLIOGRAPHY:
André Coeuroy: Pacific 231, *Art et Décoration*, November 1932.
André George: Pacific 231 d'AH, *RM*, May 1924, p. 246.
Constant Lambert: Railway music, *Nation*, 16 August 1930, p. 620.
Jean Marnold: Concerts Koussevitzky: AH— Pacific (231), *Mercure de France*, No. 625, 1 July 1924, p. 235.
Roberto García Morillo: Pacific 231 de Honegger, *El Momento musical* (Buenos Aires), April 1937.
Anon.: Setting locomotives to music, *Literary Digest*, 25 October 1924, p. 29.
FILM:
Pacific 231. USSR, 1931. Director, M. Tsekhanuski.
Pacific 231. France, 1949. Production, Tadié-Cinema; director, Jean Mitry.

46. Chanson (Ronsard). For voice and piano or flute and string quartet). February 1924.

fp: 10 May 1924, Paris, Théâtre du Vieux-Colombier, Revue musicale concert ('Hommage à Ronsard'), Claire Croiza.
fp (chamber version): 24 January 1925, Paris, Régine de Lormoy with Blanquart (fl) and the Poulet Quartet, cond. Arthur Hoérée.
fEbp (chamber version): 4 February 1929, Arts Theatre Club, Claire Croiza and instrumental ensemble.
Pub. May 1924, Revue musicale/Senart/Salabert.

47. Sous-Marine. Ballet (Carina Ari). September 1924.

fp: June 1925, Paris, Opéra-Comique, with Carina Ari.

f concert p: 8 December 1929, Paris, Theatre de la Gaîté-Lyrique, Concerts Siohan.

48. Concertino. For piano and orchestra. September–November 1924. Ded. Andrée Vaurabourg.

Allegro molto moderato—Larghetto sostenuto—Allegro.

2 fl, 2 ob, 2 cl, 2 bsn; 2 hn, 2 tpt, tmb; strings.

fp: 23 May 1925, Paris, Opéra, Andrée Vaurabourg, cond. Serge Koussevitzky.

fEp: 3 January 1929, Bournemouth, Gordon Bryan and the Bournemouth Municipal Orchestra, cond. Sir Dan Godfrey.

f London p: 24 August 1929, Queen's Hall, Promenade Concert, Elsa Karen and the Wood Symphony Orchestra, cond. Sir Henry Wood.

Pub. 1925, Senart; also reduction for two pianos.

BIBLIOGRAPHY:

Hans David: Concertino pour piano et orchestre d'AH, *Melos*, July 1927, p. 277.

49. Prélude et Blues. For quartet of chromatic harps, arr. Jeanne Daliés. 1925.

fp: 27 January 1925, Paris, Quatuor de harpes Casadesus.

Unpub.

50. Judith. Thirteen pieces for a Biblical drama in three acts (René Morax). 1925, Paris. Ded. Claire Croiza.

Part 1: 1. *Lamentations*; 2. *La Trompe d'alarme*; 3. *Prière*; 4. *Cantique funèbre*; 5. *Invocation*. Part 2: 6. *Fanfare*; 7. *Incantation*; 8. *Scène à la source*; 9. *Musique de fête*; 9a. *La mort d'Holopherne*. Part 3: 10. *Nocturne*; 10a. *Retour de Judith*; 11. *Cantique de la bataille*; 11a. *Interlude*; 12. *Cantique des vierges*; 13. *Cantique de victoire*.

2 fl, pic, 2 ob, 2 cl, bcl, 2 bsn; 4 hn, 2 tpt, 2 tmb; harmonium, 2 pianos, tamtam, GC, cym, tamb; strings.

fp: 11 June 1925, Mézières, Théâtre du Jorat, with Claire Croiza, cond. Arthur Honegger.

Pub. 1925, Senart; also reduction.

BIBLIOGRAPHY:

Paul Bertrand: Judith, *Le Ménestrel*, 21 August 1925, p. 355.

F. Choisy: Judith, *Le Courrier musical*, 1 July 1925.

H. Gagnebin: Judith au Théâtre de Mézières, *Le Monde musical*, August 1925.

Robert Godet: La Judith d'AH, *RM*, 1 August 1925, p. 161.

Arthur Hoérée: Théâtre du Jorat: Judith, drame biblique de René Morax, musique d'AH, *Nouvelle revue française*, 15 November, 1925, p. 312.

Marguerite Scherer: AH's Judith at the Théâtre du Jorat, *Chesterian*, No. 48, July 1925.

Willi Tappolet: Judith in Mézières, *Neue Zürcher Zeitung*, 23 June 1925; *Die Musik*, August 1925, p. 863.

Terpander: Honegger's Judith (1925)—six excerpts, *The Gramophone*, November 1934, p. 211.

See also No. 52.

51. Impératrice aux Rochers (Un Miracle de Notre Dame). Music for a drama in five acts and a prologue (Saint-Georges de Bouhélier). Dated: 6 August–13 November 1925. Ded. Ida Rubinstein.

1. *Prologue*; 2. *Prélude, Act I*; 2b. *La Chasse de l'Empereur* (fanfare); 3. *Interlude*; 4. *La Salle du Conseil*; 5. *Entrée du Pape*; 6. *Sortie de l'Empereur* (with SATB chorus); 7. *Prélude, Act II* (La Neige sur Rome); 8. *Interlude*; 9. *La Tour*; 10. *Postlude*; 11. *Prélude, Act III* (Les Jardins du Palais); 12. *Concert Champêtre*; 13. *Post-Lude*; 14. *Le Retour de l'Empereur*; 15. *Cortège d l'Impératrice*; 16. *L'Orage*; 17. *Prélude, Act IV* (L'Orgie au Palais); 18. *Musique de fête*; 19. (soprano solo); 20. *Le Rocher*; 21. *Apparition* (with soprano); 22. (*Calme*), with soprano; 23. (*Lent*), with soprano; 24. *Prélude, Act V* (Les Ruines du Temple); 25. *Le Parvis de la Cathédrale*; 26. *Chœur final*.

fp: 17/18 February 1927, Paris, Opéra, with Ida Rubinstein, Suzanne Desprès, Hervé, Grétillat and Desjardins, cond. Philippe Gaubert.

Pub. 1926, Senart; also reduction by Andrée Vaurabourg and Arthur Honegger.

Honegger, Arthur

BIBLIOGRAPHY:
A. Jullien: L'impératrice aux rochers, *Journal des Débats*, 4 March 1927.
P. Saegel: L'Impératrice aux Rochers, *Le Ménestrel*, 25 February 1927, p. 85.
G. Rageot: L'impératrice aux rochers, *Revue politique et littéraire (Revue bleue)*, 5 March 1927, p. 152.

51a. Impératrice aux Rochers. Suite for orchestra.
1. *La Chasse de l'Empereur*; 2. *La Neige sur Rome (Prelude, Act II)*; 3. *Orage*; 4. *Le Jardin*; 5. *Orgie*.

2 fl, pic, 2 ob, ca, 2 cl, bcl, 2 bsn, cbsn; 4 hn, 4 tpt, 3 tmb, tuba; celesta, hp; cym, tamtam, GC; strings.

fEbp: 7 November 1929, Bournemouth Pavilion, Bournemouth Symphony Orchestra, cond. Sir Dan Godfrey.
Pub. 1928, Senart; also reduction; No. 2 arr. for piano, 1926.

52. Judith. Opera seria in three acts and five scenes. November–December 1925. Ded. Claire Croiza.
fp: 13 February 1926, Monte Carlo, Opéra, with Mme Bonavia, cond. Arthur Honegger.
fp (as an oratorio): 1926, Rotterdam, with Berthe Serven, cond. Evert Cornélis.
Pub. Senart.

BIBLIOGRAPHY:
Peter Epstein: Judith, *Melos*, November 1929, p. 497.
Arthur Hoérée: Judith, action musicale par AH, *RM*, 1 May 1928, p. 198.
— Salle Pleyel, Première de Judith au Festival Honegger, *Beaux Arts*, 15 July 1928, p. 220.
Maurice Jaubert: Judith, *Revue Pleyel*, March 1926.
Werner Kulz: Judith, *Signale*, 1928, No. 39, p. 1108.
Ernst Latzko: Judith, *Melos*, April 1928, p. 201.
Henry Prunières: Judith d'AH à Monte Carlo, *RM*, 1 March 1926, p. 260.
Paul Riesenfeld: Honegger's Judith im Breslauer Stadttheater, *Signale*, 1929, No. 44, p. 1329.
Roland-Manuel: Judith à la Monnaie de Bruxelles, *RM*, 1 April 1927, p. 208.

53. Phaèdre. Music for a tragedy in three acts (Gabriele d'Annunzio, transl. André Doderet). March 1926, Paris. Ded. André George.
1. *Prélude*; 2. *Cortège des suppliantes*; 3. *Prélude*; 4. *Imprécation de Thésée*; 5. *Prélude*; 6. *Mort de Phaèdre*.

2 fl, ob, ca, 2 cl, 2 bsn; 2 hn, 2 tpt, 3 tmb, tuba; timp, pcssn; strings.
fp: 19 April 1926, Rome, Teatro Costanzi, with Ida Rubinstein, cond. Arthur Honegger.
Pub. 1930, Senart.

54. Trois Chansons de la Petite Sirène (René Morax, after Hans Andersen). For voice and piano (or flute and string quartet, or string orchestra). 1926.
1. *Chanson des Sirènes*; 2. *Berceuse de la Sirène*; 3. *Chanson de la Poire*.

fp (chamber version): 23 March 1927, Paris, Salle Pleyel, Durand concert, Régine de Lormoy, Rémon (fl) and Roth Quartet, cond. Arthur Honegger.
Pub. 1930, Senart.

55. Antigone. Musical Tragedy in three acts (Sophocles-Cocteau). January 1924–February 1927, Paris. Composer's preface dated September 1927, Barrème. Ded. Vaura.
fp: 28 December 1927, Brussels, Théâtre de la Monnaie, with E. Colonne (Creon), Mlle S. Baillard (Antigone), Mlle E. Deulin (Ismène), Mme M. Gerday (Eurydice) and M. Yovanovitch (Tiresias), cond. Corniel de Thoran.
f concert p: 19 May 1931, Chorus and Orchestra of Bayerisches Rundfunks, cond. Hermann Scherchen, with Cl. M. Elshorst (Antigone) and Heinrich Gürtler (Creon).
Pub. 1927, Senart (vocal score).

BIBLIOGRAPHY:
Jean Cocteau: Antigone, *Nouvelle revue française*, 1928.
Paul Collaer: Antigone (Etude), Editions Senart (Paris) 1928.
H. Denizeau: La création en France de l'Antigone d'AH, *Appogiature*, 15 January 1931, p. 11.
André George: AH's Antigone, *Chesterian*, No. 70, April–May 1928.
— Antigone, *Les Nouvelles littéraires*, 21 January 1928.

Arthur Hoérée: Antigone, *Chantecler*, 14 January 1928.

— Antigone, *Beaux Arts*, 1 February 1928, p. 47.

— Antigone à la Monnaie de Bruxelles, *La Revue européenne*, March 1928.

— Antigone, *L'Information musicale*, 3 February 1943, p. 197.

Jean Marnold: Antigone, *Mercure de France*, No. 720, 15 June 1928, p. 703.

Léo Mélitz: L'Antigone d'Honegger, *RM*, October 1927, p. 242.

René Morax: Antigone, *La Gazette de Lausanne*, 5 January 1928.

Hans Müllner: Honeggertage in Essen: Deutsche Uraufführung der Oper Antigone, *Signale*, 1928, No. 6, p. 169.

Mario Pilati: Antigone di Honegger, *Bollettino bibliografico musicale*, February 1928, p. 13.

Henry Prunières: Antigone, tragédie musicale d'AH et Jean Cocteau, au Théâtre de la Monnaie, Bruxelles, *RM*, 1 February 1928, p. 59.

Roland-Manuel: L'Antigone, *Le Ménestrel*, 6 January 1928.

— L'Antigone d'AH, *Musique*, 15 January 1928.

Erik Reger: Antigone von AH zur Essener Première, *Anbruch*, 2 February 1928, p. 62.

R. Schulz Dornburg: Zur Aufführung der Antigone, *Der Scheinwerfer*, January 1928.

Emile Vuillermoz: Antigone, *Excelsior*, 16 January 1928.

Anon.: Antigone—new musical tragedy by M. Honegger, *The Times*, 5 January 1928, p. 10.

56. Napoleon. Music for the film. 1927. Written and directed by Abel Gance; with Albert Dieudonné (Napoleon), Gina Manès (Josephine de Beauharnais), Antonin Artaud (Marat), Alberti (Jean-Jacques Rousseau), Abel Gance (Saint-Just).

57. Rose de Métal. Ballet (Elisabeth Grammont de Clermont-Tonnerre). 1928. Unpub.

58. Rugby. For orchestra. August 1928, Paris. Ded. René Delange.

2 fl, pic, 2 ob, ca, 3 cl, 2 bsn, cbsn; 4 hn, 3 tpt, 3 tmb, tuba; strings.

fp: 19 October 1928, Paris, inaugural concert of l'Orchestre Symphonique de Paris, cond. Ernest Ansermet.

fEp: 7 September 1929, Queen's Hall, Promenade Concert, Wood Symphony Orchestra, cond. Sir Henry Wood.

Pub. 1928, Senart. Version for piano solo by the composer (facsimile of autograph score) with lithographs by Josué Gaboriaud pub. 1929, Senart.

BIBLIOGRAPHY:

Arthur Hoérée: Rugby, Mouvement symphonique par AH, *Beaux Arts*, 1 December 1928, p. 316.

Henry Prunières: Rugby d'AH au premier concert de l'Orchestre Symphonique de Paris, *RM*, 1 November 1928, p. 53.

Anon.: Football in music: AH's Rugby, *British Musician*, February 1931, p. 39.

59. Hommage à Albert Roussel. For piano. 13 December 1928, Paris.

fp: 13 April 1929, Paris, Salle ancien Conservatoire, Festival Roussel, Pierre Maire.

Pub. April 1929, Revue musicale; Senart.

60. Suite. For two pianos. 1928.

fp: 31 March 1930, Paris, Ecole Normale de Musique, Pierre Maire and Arthur Honegger.

Unpub.

61. Vocalise-Etude. 1929. Pub. 1929, Leduc.

62. Amphion. Mélodrame (Paul Valéry). For reciter, baritone solo, four women's voices, chorus and orchestra. 1929, Paris. Ded. Ida Rubinstein.

fp: 23 June 1931, Paris, Opéra, with Ida Rubinstein (Amphion), Charles Panzéra (Apollo), Nelly Martyl, Madeleine Mathieu, Mady Arty and Mlle Kirova (Les Muses), cond. M. Cloez; décor and costumes, Alexandre Benois; choreography, Léonide Massine.

f concert p: 14 January 1932, Université des Annales, with Ida Rubinstein and Henri Fabert, cond. Robert Siohan.

Pub. 1931, Rouart-Lerolle; Salabert.

BIBLIOGRAPHY:

Arthur Hoérée: Amphion, *Candide*, 25 June 1931.

Henry Prunières: Amphion d'AH et Paul Valéry, *RM*, October 1931, p. 239.

Boris de Schloezer: Amphion, mélodrame de Paul Valéry et AH, *Nouvelle revue française*, No. 215, 1931, p. 347.

Willi Tappolet: Amphion, *Journal de Genève*, 1 December 1932.

Paul Valéry: Histoire d'Amphion, *Conferencia*, 1933, No. 16, p. 157.

62a. Prelude, Fugue, Postlude. From Amphion, for orchestra. 1948. Dur. $30\frac{1}{2}'$.

3 fl, ob, ca, 2 cl, bcl; 2 bsn, alto sax; 4 hn, 3 tpt, 3 tmb, tuba; GC, cym; hp, celesta, strings.

fp: 3 November 1948, Geneva, l'Orchestre de la Suisse Romande, cond. Ernest Ansermet.

Pub. 1948, Salabert.

63. Cello Concerto. August 1929, Paris. Ded. Maurice Maréchal.

fp: 17 February 1930, Boston, Maurice Maréchal and Boston Symphony Orchestra, cond. Serge Koussevitzky.

f Paris p: 16 May 1930, Salle Pleyel, Maurice Maréchal and l'Orchestre Symphonique de Paris, cond. Pierre Monteux.

fEbp: 29 July 1935, Anthony Pini and BBC Orchestra, cond. Julian Clifford.

Pub. 1931, Senart; Salabert.

64. Symphony No. 1. December 1929–May 1930, Paris, Mougins. Ded. Boston Symphony Orchestra and Serge Koussevizky.

1. *Allegro marcato*; 2. *Adagio*; 3. *Presto*.

2 fl, pic, 2 ob, ca, 2 cl, bcl, 2 bsn, cbsn; 4 hn, 3 tpt, 3 tmb, tuba; tamtam, GC; strings.

fp: 13 February 1931, Boston, Boston Symphony Orchestra, cond. Serge Koussevitzky.

f Paris p: 2 June 1931, Festival Honegger, Orchestre Straram, cond. Arthur Honegger.

fEbp: 24 January 1932, BBC Orchestra, cond. Ernest Ansermet.

Pub. 1930, Senart; Salabert.

BIBLIOGRAPHY:

Fred. Goldbeck: La Symphonie d'AH, *RM*, October 1931, p. 243.

65. Les Aventures du Roi Pausole. Operette in three acts (Albert Willemetz, from the novel by Pierre Louÿs), 1929–30, Royan, Buenos Aires, Paris. Ded. Fernand Ochsé.

fp: 12 December 1930, Paris, Théâtre des Bouffes-Parisiens, with Dorville (Pausole), Jacqueline Francell (Aline), Koval (Taxis), Meg Lemonnier (Mirabelle), Pasquali (Giglio) and Germaine Duclos (Diane à la Houppe), cond. Bervily.

Pub. 1930, Salabert (vocal score).

BIBLIOGRAPHY:

Tony Aubin: Les Aventures du Roi Pausole, *Le Ménestrel*, 26 December 1930, p. 551.

Henry Prunières: Le Roi Pausole, operette de Willemetz et AH, *RM*, January 1931, p. 60.

Willi Reich: Erotik als Burgerpflicht, *Neue Schweizer Rundschau*, Vol. 21 (1953–4), p. 565.

66. Les Noces d'Amour et Psyche. Arr. by Arthur Honegger from the French Suites of Bach, orch, Arthur Hoérée. 1930.

fp: 1930, Paris, Opéra, Ida Rubinstein.
?Unpub.

66a. Les Noces d'Amour et Psyche. Suite. 1933. Dur. $11\frac{1}{2}'$.

1. *L'Anglaise* (Dur. $2\frac{1}{2}'$); 2. *Sarabande* (Dur. $2\frac{1}{2}'$); 3. *Gavotte* (Dur. $1\frac{1}{2}'$); 4. *Menuet* (Dur. $2'$); 5. *Gigue* (Dur. $3'$).

fl, ob, sop sax, bsn; 2 hn; strings.

fp: 4 February 1934, Paris, Salle Pleyel, l'Orchestre Symphonique de Paris, cond. Pierre Monteux.

Pub. 1933, Universal-Edition.

67. La Belle de Moudon. Operette in five acts (René Morax). 1931.

fp: 30 May 1931, Mézières, Théâtre du Jorat, with Louis Barraud (Moudon) and Lucy Berthrand (Isabelle).

BIBLIOGRAPHY:

Willy Tappolet: La Belle de Moudon à Mézières, *SM*, 1 August 1931, p. 557.

68. Cris du Monde (René Bizet). For soprano, contralto and baritone soloists, chorus and orchestra. March 1931. Ded. Cäcilienverein, Solothurn, and their conductor Erich Schild.

fp: 3 May 1931, Solothurn, Berthe de Vigier, Pauline Hoch and Carl Rehfuss, Cäcilienverein, cond. Erich Schild.

f Paris p: 3 June 1931, Berthe de Vigier, Lina Falk and Charles Panzéra, Solothurn

Cäcilienverein and Orchestre Straram, cond. Erich Schild.

fEp: 22 December 1933, BBC broadcast, Kate Winter, Betty Bannerman and Mark Raphael, Wireless Choir and Orchestra, cond. Sir Adrian Boult; English version, Edward Agate.

Pub. 1931, Senart; Salabert.

BIBLIOGRAPHY:

K. H. David: Der Weltenschrei und das Unaufhörliche, *SM*, 1 December 1932, p. 717.

H. Denizeau: La création des Cris du Monde, *Appogiature*, May 1931, p. 114.

Edmund Rubbra: An oratorio of the modern city, *Radio Times*, 15 December 1933, p. 805.

Dominique Sordet: Cris du monde, *Revue universelle*, 1 July 1931, p. 126.

Ch. Willm: Cris du Monde, d'AH, à Strasbourg, *RM*, July–August 1933, p. 137.

69. Sonatine. For violin and cello. September 1932, Paris. Ded. Albert and Anna Neuburger.

fp: *c.* December 1932, Paris, Ecole Normale de Musique, Roth and Van Dooren.

Pub. 1932, Senart; Salabert.

BIBLIOGRAPHY:

Fred. Goldbeck: AH—Sonatine pour violon et violoncelle, *RM*, January 1933, p. 53.

70. Le Grand Etang (Jean Tranchant). For voice and piano. 1932. Unpub.

71. Mouvement Symphonique No. 3. For orchestra. October 1932, orch. December 1932–January 1933, Paris. Ded. Wilhelm Furtwängler and the Berlin Philharmonic Orchestra.

2 fl, pic, 2 ob, ca, 2 cl, alto sax, 2 bsn, cbsn; 4 hn, 3 tpt, 3 tmb, tuba; cym, tamtam, GC; strings.

fp: 26 March 1933, Berlin, Berlin Philharmonic Orchestra, cond. Wilhelm Furtwängler.

fEp: 16 September 1933, Queen's Hall, Promenade Concert.

fFp: 21 October 1933, Paris, Théâtre des Champs-Elysées, Orchestre Pasdeloup, cond. Arthur Honegger.

Pub. 1933, Senart.

BIBLIOGRAPHY:

R.-A. Mooser: Mouvement Symphonique No. 3, *Dissonances*, November 1933, p. 310.

72. Prélude, Arioso, Fughette (Sur le nom de Bach). For piano. October 1932. Ded. Maurice Senart.

fp: untraced date, Paris, Salle de Géographie, children's concert, Andrée Vaurabourg.

fEp: 10 October 1935, Royal Academy of Music New Music Society, Duke's Hall, Jehanne Chambard.

fEbp: 5 February 1937, Eileen Ralph.

Pub. December 1932, La Revue musicale; 1933, Senart.

72a. Prélude, Arioso, Fughette. Version for string orchestra. ?1936.

fp: 5 December 1936, Paris, Salle Gaveau, Orchestre Féminin de Paris, cond. Jane Evrard.

Pub. 1937, Senart.

BIBLIOGRAPHY:

Arthur Hoérée: Prelude-Arioso-Fughette par AH, *RM*, December 1936, p. 446.

73. Sémiramis. Ballet-Melodrama in three scenes (Paul Valéry). May 1933.

fp: 11 May 1934, Paris, Opéra, Ballets Ida Rubinstein, with Ida Rubinstein (Sémiramis) and Leister (le beau Prisonnier).

Pub. Salabert.

BIBLIOGRAPHY:

Suzanne Demarquez: Sémiramis, d'AH, aux Ballets de Mme Ida Rubinstein, *RM*, June 1934, p. 45.

74. Les 12 Coups de Minuit. Radio-mystère (Carlos Larronde). For chorus and small orchestra. 1933.

fp: 27 December 1933, Paris, Art et Action. Unpub.

75. Rapt. 1933. Music for the film directed by Dimitri Kirsanov from the novel 'La Separation des Races' by C.-F. Ramuz; with Jeanne Marie-Laurent, Auguste Boverio, Nadia Sibirskaia and Lucas Gridoux. Music also composed by Arthur Hoérée. Film first screened in Britain, December 1934, Academy Cinema.

Honegger, Arthur

BIBLIOGRAPHY:
Arthur Honegger & Arthur Hoérée: Particularités sonores du film Rapt, *RM*, December 1934, p. 88.

76. Les Misérables. 1934. Music for a three-part film based on the novel by Victor Hugo. Production, Pathé-Natan; director, Raymond Bernard; with Harry Baur, Charles Vanel, Charles Dullin and Florelle. Only the first part (101 mins.) was released in Britain, 1934.

76a. Les Misérables. Suite Symphonique.
fp: 19 January 1935, Paris, Salle Rameau, Concerts Siohan.

BIBLIOGRAPHY:
Arthur Hoérée: Les Misérables, suite, par AH, *RM*, February 1935, p. 131.

77. L'Idée. 1934. Music for an animated film, written, directed and photographed by Bertold Bartosch, from woodcuts by Franz Masereel. Film first screened in Britain by the London Film Society.

78. Cessez le Feu. 1934. Music for a film directed by Jacques de Baroncelli.

79. Crime et Châtiment. 1934. Music for the Compagnie Générale de Productions Cinématographiques film, directed by Pierre Chenal from the novel by Dostoievsky; with Pierre Blanchar, Harry Baur, Madeleine Ozeray, Alexandre Rignault and Catherine Hessling. Distributed in Britain by the Film Society, 1936.

80. Le Roi de la Camargue. 1934. Music, composed in collaboration with Roland-Manuel, for the film directed by Jacques de Baroncelli; with Simone Bourday and Tela Tchai.

81. Petite Suite. For two (unspecified) instruments. August 1934, Paris. Ded. Yvonne and Peter Stadler. In three movements without titles or tempo indications.
Pub. 1936, Editions Sociales Internationales; Chant du Monde.

82. Jeanne d'Arc au Bûcher. Dramatic Oratorio (Paul Claudel). For speakers, soloists, chorus, Ondes Martenot and orchestra. Vocal score dated: 30 August 1935; full score dated: 24 December 1935, Paris. Dur. 80'.

Prologue; 1. *Les voix du ciel*; 2. *Le livre*; 3. *Les voix de la terre*; 4. *Jeanne livré aux bêtes*; 5. *Jeanne au poteau*; 6. *Les Rois, ou l'invention du jeu de cartes*; 7. *Catherine et Marguerite*; 8. *Le roi qui va-t-a Rheims*; 9. *L'épée de Jeanne*; 10. *Trimazo*; 11. *Jeanne d'Arc en flammes*.

2 fl, pic, 2 ob, E-flat cl, cl, bcl, 3 alto sax, 3 bsn, cbsn; pic tpt, 3 tpt, 3 tmb, bs tmb (or tuba); 2 pianos, timp, tamtam, tambour, caisse claire, GC, cym, celesta, Ondes Martenot; strings.

fp: 12 May 1938, Basle, Ida Rubinstein, Jean Périer, Serge Sandos, Charles Vaucher (speakers), Ginevra Vivante, Berthe de Vigier, Marianne Hirsig-Löw (sopranos), Lina Falk (contralto), Ernest Bauer (tenor), Paul Sandoz (bass), Les Singknaben de l'Eglise évangélique-réformée, Maurice Martenot (Ondes Martenot), chorus and Basle Chamber Orchestra, cond. Paul Sacher.

f Paris p: 13 June 1939, Ida Rubinstein, De Trévi, Fabert, Jean Hervé, Peyron, Solange Delmas, Lina Falk, Josette Barré, Chorale Raugel, Orchestre Philharmonique de Paris, cond. Louis Fourestier.

fEp: 16 April 1947, BBC broadcast, Olive Groves, Nancy Evans, Gladys Ripley, Parry Jones, Bradbridge White, Rene Soames, Norman Walker, Choir of Mary Datchelor School, BBC Chorus and BBC Symphony Orchestra, cond. Basil Cameron.

fEp (concert): 4 February 1948, Royal Albert Hall, BBC concert, Constance Cummings, Olive Groves, Nancy Evans, Gladys Ripley, Valentine Dyall, Parry Jones, Martin Boddey, Rene Soames, Norman Walker, Choir of Mary Datchelor School, BBC Chorus and BBC Symphony Orchestra, cond. Basil Cameron.

Pub. 1939, Senart; 1947, 1954, Salabert.

BIBLIOGRAPHY:
R. Dumesnil: Jeanne d'Arc au bûcher, oratorio dramatique, *Mercure de France*, 1 July 1939, p. 194.
A. Gabeaud: Jeanne d'Arc au bûcher, *L'Education musicale*, 1957, Nos. 37–39.
R.-A. Mooser: Jeanne d'Arc au bûcher, *Dissonances*, May 1938.
Serge Moreux: Jeanne d'Arc au bûcher, oratorio scénique de P. Claudel et AH, *RM*, July 1939, p. 28.

Willi Reich: Honegger-Claudel—Joan of Arc acclaimed, *Musical America*, July 1938.

Gustave Samazeuilh: Jeanne d'Arc au bûcher de P. Claudel et AH, *Les Annales politiques et littéraires*, 25 June 1939, p. 633.

Boris de Schloezer: Jeanne d'Arc au bûcher, de Paul Claudel et AH, *Nouvelle revue française*, No. 310, 1939, p. 153.

L. Trimble: Presentation of Jeanne d'Arc, *Nation*, 10 May 1958, p. 427.

John Warrack: Joan of Arc at the Stake, *M&M*, October 1954, p. 11.

Kurt Westphal: Johanna auf dem Scheiterhaufen—Honegger-Erstauff. in Berlin, *Melos*, January 1948, p. 21.

83. Fièvre Jaune (Nino). For voice and piano. 1935.

Pub. 1935, La Sirène; German transl. Hansi Gosselin; English transl. Yvonne Deneufville.

84. Der Dämon des Himalaya. 1935. Music for the film directed by Andrew Marton in collaboration with Gunther Oskar Dyhrenfurth; with Gustav Diessl, Erika Dannhoff and Jamila Marton.

85. L'Equipage. 1935. Music for the film. Production, Pathé-Natan; director, Anatole Litvak; script, from the novel by Joseph Kessel; with Annabella, Jean Murat, Jean-Pierre Aumont and Charles Vanel. Distributed in Britain by Colmore Distributors; British première, 29 April 1938, Studio One.

86. Mayerling. 1935. Music for the film. Production, Nero-Film; director, Anatole Litvak; script, from the novel by Claude Anet; with Charles Boyer and Danielle Darrieux. Distributed in Britain by Gaumont-British and later re-issued by Exclusive Films; British première, 22 October 1936, Curzon Cinema.

87. Radio-Panoramique. For string quintet, wind, percussion, organ, tenor and soprano soloists, and chorus. January 1935.

fp: 4 March 1935, Geneva, Salle du Conservatoire, with Violette Andréassi (soprano), Ernest Bauer (tenor), Roger Vuataz (organ), J.-M. Pache (piano).

f Paris p: 19 October 1935, Opéra-Comique, with Orchestre Pasdeloup, cond. Albert Wolff.

Pub. Les Oeuvres françaises.

BIBLIOGRAPHY:

Henry Prunières: Radio-panoramique d'AH, *RM*, November 1935, p. 276.

88. Visages de France. 1935. Music for a documentary film by Dimitri Kirsanoff.

89. Nocturne. For orchestra. March 1936. Ded. Hermann Scherchen. Dur. 9'.

2 fl, pic, 2 ob, ca, 2 cl, sax, bcl, 3 bsn; 4 hn, 3 tpt, tuba; timp, tgle, cym, wd blk, caisse claire, rattle, tambour de basque; hp, strings.

fp: 30 April 1936, Brussels, Orchestre Symphonique de Bruxelles, cond. Hermann Scherchen.

fEp: 9 December 1939, Queen's Hall, Courtauld-Sargent concert, London Philharmonic Orchestra, cond. (Sir) Malcolm Sargent. (fEp originally announced for a Promenade Concert, 24 August 1939.)

f Paris p: 9 April 1940, second concert of l'Association de Musique Contemporaine series, cond. Charles Münch.

Pub. March 1939, Universal-Edition; Boosey & Hawkes.

90. Du Whisky pour Jo (Nino). For voice and piano. 1936. Unpub.

91. Les Mutinés de l'Elseneur. 1936. Music for the film. Production, Général-Productions; director, Pierre Chenal; script, from the novel by Jack London; with Jean Murat and Winna Winfried. Distributed in Britain by Associated British Picture Corporation, 1940.

92. L'Aiglon. Opera in five acts (Henri Cain, after Edmond Rostand). Summer 1936. Composed in collaboration with Jacques Ibert. Ded. Raoul Gunsbourg.

1. *Les Ailes qui s'ouvrent*; 2. *Les Ailes qui batte*; 3. *Les Ailes meurtries*; 4. *Les Ailes brisées*; 5. *Les Ailes fermées*.

fp: 10 March 1937, Monte Carlo, Opéra, with Fanny Heldy (Frantz), Vanni Marcoux (Séraphin Flambeau), Mlle Shirman (Fanny Essler), Mlle Braneze (Thérèse de Lorget), Mlle Gadsden (Marie-Louise), Germaine Chellet (La Comtesse Camerata), Endrèze

Honegger, Arthur

(Le Prince de Metternich), Marvini (Le Maréchal Marmont), Fraikin (Frédéric de Gentz).

f Paris p: 1 September 1937, Opéra, with Fanny Heldy (Frantz), Vanni Marcoux (Séraphin Flambeau), Odette Ricquier (Fanny Essler), Jacqueline Courtin (Thérèse de Lorget), Anita Volfer (Marie-Louise), Milly Morère (La Comtesse Camerata), Endrèze (Le Prince de Metternich), Narçon (Le Maréchal Marmont), Nové (Frédéric de Gentz), cond. François Ruhlmann.

Pub. Heugel.

BIBLIOGRAPHY:
Marcel Belvianes: L'Aiglon à l'Opéra, Le Ménestrel, 10 September 1937, p. 241.
Robert Bernard: L'Aiglon, musique de Jacques Ibert et AH, RM, April 1937, p. 218.
Louis Laloy: L'Aiglon, Revue des deux mondes, 15 April 1937, p. 944.

93. String Quartet No. 2. 1934–6. Ded. Pro Arte Quartet. Dur. 18' 45".
1. *Allegro.* Dur. 6' 30".
2. *Adagio.* Dated: 1934–5. Dur. 6' 15".
3. *Allegro marcato.* Dated: June 1936, Paris. Dur. 6'.

fp: 1936, Venice, Pro Arte Quartet.
fFp: 8 March 1937, Paris, Ecole Normale, Le Triton concert.
fEp: 18 April 1937, BBC broadcast, Brosa Quartet.
Pub. 1936, autograph facsimile, Senart; Salabert.

BIBLIOGRAPHY:
Fred. Goldbeck: AH, IIe Quatuor, RM, April 1937, p. 197.

94. 14 Juillet (Marche sur la Bastille). Incidental music (Romain Rolland). 1936.
fp: 14 July 1936, Paris, La Maison de la Culture, cond. Roger Désormière.
Pub. Editions Sociales Internationales.

BIBLIOGRAPHY:
Léon Kochnitzky: Le Quatorze Juillet, action populaire de Romain Rolland, RM, July–August 1936, p. 42.

95. Regain. 1937. Music for a Films Marcel Pagnol production, written and directed by Marcel Pagnol from the novel by Jean Giono; with Gabriel Gabrio, Orane Demazis and Fernandel. Distributed in Britain by Connoisseur Films, 1956; British première, 26 October 1956, Academy Cinema.

96. Nitchevo. 1937. Music for the film. Production, Méga-Film; director, Jacques de Baroncelli; with Harry Baur, Marcelle Chantal and Georges Rignaud. Distributed in Britain by United Artists, 1937; British première, October 1937, Berkeley Cinema, Tottenham Court Road.

BIBLIOGRAPHY:
D.-E. Inghelbrecht: Nitchevo, RM, November–December 1946, p. 11.

96a. De l'Atlantique au Pacifique (J. Féline). Song from 'Nitchevo'.

97. Mademoiselle Docteur. 1937. Music for a Films Trocadéro production; director, G. W. Pabst; with Pierre Blanchar, Dita Parlo, Pierre Fresnay, Louis Jouvet, Jean-Louis Barrault and Viviane Romance.

98. La Citadelle du Silence. 1937. Music, composed in collaboration with Darius Milhaud, for an Impérial-Film production; director, Marcel l'Herbier; with Annabella, Pierre Renoir, Bernard Lancret and Alexandre Rignault.

99. Marthe Richard au Service de la France. 1937. Music for a Paris-Films production; director, Raymond Bernard; with Edwige Feuillère and Erich von Stroheim. Distributed in Britain by Unity Films, 1939.

100. Passeurs d'Hommes. 1937. Music for a film.

101. La Mille et Une Nuits. Cantata for soprano, tenor, chorus and orchestra (Mardrus).
Pub. Salabert.

102. Jeunesse (Paul Vaillant-Couturier). For voice and piano (or orchestra). 1937.
Pub. Chant du Monde.

103. Liberté (Interlude). Incidental music (M. Rostand). 1 May 1937.
fp: 1937, Paris, Théâtre des Champs-Elysées.
Unpub.

104. Un Oiseau blanc s'est envolé. Ballet (Sacha Guitry). 1937.
fp: June 1937, Paris, Salle Pleyel.
Unpub.

105. String Quartet No. 3. Dated: September 1936–June 1937. Ded. Mrs. Elizabeth Sprague Coolidge.
1. *Allegro*; 2. *Adagio*; 3. *Allegro*.
fp: 22 October 1937, Geneva, Salle de la Réformation, Pro Arte Quartet.
f Paris p: 25 April 1938, Le Triton concert, Pro Arte Quartet.
fEp: 4 October 1938, Cowdray Hall, London Contemporary Music Centre concert, New Hungarian Quartet.
fEbp: 7 October 1938, New Hungarian Quartet.
Pub. 1937, facsimile of autograph, Senart; Salabert.

BIBLIOGRAPHY:
Arthur Hoérée: Troisième Quatuor à Cordes par AH, *RM*, July–August 1938, p. 50.

106. Trois Chansons (R. Kerdyk). For voice and piano. 1935–7.
1. *On est heureux*; 2. *Chanson de la route*; 3. *Le naturaliste*.
Pub. (Nos. 1 & 2): Editions Oeuvres Françaises.

107. Scénic-Railway. For piano. 1937. Contribution to 'Parc d'Attractions—Expo 1937' (Hommage à Marguerite Long).
?fp: 28 November 1938, Paris, Salle Gaveau, Nicole Henriot.
Pub. 1938, Eschig.

108. Les Petites Cardinal. Operette in two acts, composed in collaboration with Jacques Ibert. Libretto: Albert Willemetz and Paul Brach, from a novel by Ludovic Halévy.
fp: 12 February 1938, Paris, Théâtre des Bouffes-Parisiens, with Saturnin Fabre (Le Cardinal), Marguerite Pierry (Madame Cardinal), Robert Pizani, Henri Fabert and Bertolasso, cond. Cariven; décor and costumes, Fernand Ochsé.
Pub. Choudens (vocal score).

BIBLIOGRAPHY:
Paul Bertrand: Les Petites Cardinal, *Le Ménestrel*, 18 February 1938, p. 46.

Suzanne Demarquez: Aux Bouffes Parisiens— Les Petites Cardinal, operette en deux actes de Jacques Ibert et AH, *RM*, March 1938, p. 215.

109. Les Gars du Bâtiment. For voice and piano (or orchestra). 1938. Unpub.

110. Miarka. 1938. Music, composed in collaboration with Tibor Harsanyi, for a film directed by Jean Choux.

111. Pygmalion. 1938. Music for the film. Production, Gabriel Pascal; director, Anthony Asquith; script, from the play by George Bernard Shaw; with Leslie Howard, Wendy Hiller and Wilfred Lawson.

112. La Cantique des Cantiques. Ballet in two acts. 1938. 'Poetic argument', Gabriel Boissy; rhythms, Serge Lifar. Ded. Francis and Andrée Winter.
fp: 2 February 1938, Paris Opéra, with Carina Ari (la Sulamite), Serge Lifar (le berger), Paul Goubé (le roi Salomon); singers, Antoinette Duval, Chastenet and Cotta, cond. Philippe Gaubert; décor, Paul Collin; choreography, Serge Lifar.
Pub. 1938, Heugel.

BIBLIOGRAPHY:
Paul Bertrand: La Cantique des Cantiques, *Le Ménestrel*, 11 February 1938, p. 34.
Henry Prunières: La Cantique des Cantiques, ballet biblique en deux actes d'AH, *RM*, February 1938, p. 137.

113. La Danse des Morts. Oratorio for reciter, soloists, chorus, orchestra and organ (Paul Claudel). Dated: 25 October 1938. Ded. Paul Sacher. Dur. 35'.
fl, pic, 2 ob, 2 cl, 2(4) bsn; 2(4) hn, 2 tpt, 2(4) tmb; piano, organ; 4 timp, GC; strings.
fp: 1 March 1940, Basle, William Aguet (speaker), Ginevra Vivante, Lina Falk, Hugues Cuénot and Walter Kägi, Edouard Muller (organ), Basle Chamber Chorus and Orchestra, cond. Paul Sacher; relayed by the BBC.
f Paris p: 26 January 1941, Salle ancien Conservatoire, Jean-Louis Barrault (speaker), Mme Turba-Rabier, Eliette Schenneberg, Charles Panzéra, la Chorale Gouverné, Paris Conservatoire Orchestra, cond. Charles Münch.

fEp: 29 December 1948, BBC concert, Royal Albert Hall, Dennis Arundell (speaker), Isobel Baillie, Anne Wood, Bruce Boyce, Margaret Cobb (organ), BBC Chorus and BBC Symphony Orchestra, cond. Sir Adrian Boult.

Pub. 1939, Senart.

BIBLIOGRAPHY:

Hans Ehinger: AHs Danse des Morts, *Neue Zürcher Zeitung*, 1 April 1940, p. 100; *SM*, No. 80, 1940, p. 100.

Arthur Hoérée: La Danse des Morts, *L'Information musicale*, 7 February 1941, p. 304.

Orjan Lindberger: Dödsdansen, ett oratorium om köttets uppståndelse, *Nutida musik*, Vol. 3 (1959–60), No. 5, p. 4.

Lennart Reimers: Honeggers dödsdansmusik, *Nutida musik*, Vol. 3 (1959–60), No. 5, p. 7.

Heinrich Strobel: AHs Totentanz, *Melos*, May–June 1947, p. 209.

114. Hommage au Travail (Maurice Senart). For voice and piano. Dated: 31 December 1938.

Pub. 1939, Senart/Eschig.

115. L'Or dans la Montagne. 1939. Music for a Clarté-Films production; director, Max Haufler; script, after C.-F. Ramuz; with Jean-Louis Barrault and Suzy Prim. Music also composed by Arthur Hoérée.

116. Le Deserteur. 1939. Music, composed in collaboration with Henry Verdun, for the film. Production, Eclair-Journal; director, Léonide Moguy; with Jean-Pierre Aumont and Corinne Luchaire. Distributed in Britain by G.C.T. Distributors, 1947.

117. Nicolas de Flue. Dramatic Legend in three acts for mixed chorus, children's chorus, speaker and orchestra (Denis de Rougement). 1939.

fp: 1939, Zürich, Exposition Nationale Suisse.

fp (concert): 26 October 1940, Soleure, William Aguet (speaker), Cäcilienverein (Société Saint-Cécile), Orchestre Municipale de Berne, cond. Erich Schild.

Pub. 1939, Foetisch Frères (Lausanne).

BIBLIOGRAPHY:

R. Dumesnil: Nicolas de Flue, *Mercure de France*, March 1953, p. 516.

Charles Faller: Nicolas de Flue de Denis de Rougement et AH, *RM*, July 1939, p. 63.

Arthur Honegger: AH über Nicolas de Flue, *SM*, May–June 1962, p. 155.

R.-A. Mooser: Nicolas de Flue d'AH, *Dissonances*, November–December 1940.

118. Grad'aud. March for military band. 1939.

119. Trois Poèmes (Paul Claudel). For voice and piano. 1939–40. Ded. Pierre Bernac.

1. *La Sieste.* Dated: 31 March 1939.
2. *Le Delphinium.* Dated: 16 January 1940.
3. *Le Rendezvous.* Dated: 18 January 1940.

fp: 15 November 1941, Paris, Salle Gaveau, Pierre Bernac and Francis Poulenc.

Pub. Salabert.

120. La Naissance des Couleurs. Ballet (E. Klausz). 1940. Pub. Salabert.

121. Cavalcade d'Amour. 1940. Music, composed in collaboration with Darius Milhaud and Roger Desormière, for the film. Production, Arnold Pressburger/CIPRA; director, Robert Bernard; script, Jean Aurenche and Jean Anouilh; with Simone Simon, Michel Simon and Corinne Luchaire.

122. Sonata for violin solo. 1940, Totenberg, New York.

1. *Allegro*; 2. *Largo*; 3. *Allegretto grazioso*; 4. *Presto.*

fp: untraced date, Paris, Christian Ferras.

Pub. 1948, Salabert; fingered by Ginette Neveu.

123. Partita for two pianos. 1940.

1. *Largo*; 2. *Vivace-Allegretto*; 3. *Largo*; 4. *Allegro moderato.*

fp: 31 January 1940, Zürich, Franz-Josef Hirt and Arthur Honegger.

f Paris p: 26 March, Monique Haas and Ina Marika.

?Unpub.

124. Christophe Colomb. 'Jeu radiophonique' (William Aguet).

fp: 17 April 1940, Lausanne Radio, chorus and Orchestre de la Suisse Romande, cond. Ernest Ansermet.

Pub. Salabert.

BIBLIOGRAPHY:
R.-A. Mooser: Christophe Colomb d'Aguet-
Honegger, *Dissonances*, April 1940.

125. Trois Psaumes. For voice and piano.
Dated: 28 December 1940–January 1941.
Ded. Eliette Schenneberg.
 1. *Psaume XXIV*; 2. *Psaume CXL*; 3. *Psaume
CXXXVIII*.
 Pub. 1943, Salabert; Fr. versions by
Theodore de Bèze and Clément Marot.

126. Petit Cours de Morale (Jean Giraudoux: from 'Suzanne et le Pacifique'). For
voice and piano. Dated: 12–17 April 1941.
 fp: 1 July 1942, Paris, Salle Gaveau,
Festival Honegger, Pierre Bernac.
 Pub. 1941, Salabert.

127. Le Mangeur de Rêves. Ballet (H.-R.
Lenormand). 1941.
 fp: untraced date, Paris, Salle Pleyel.
 Unpub.

128. Mandragore. Incidental music (Machia-
velli). 1941.
 fp: 18 September 1942, Paris, Théâtre
Fontaine.

129. L'Ombre de la Ravine. Incidental
music (Synge). 1941.
 fp: untraced date, Paris, Théâtre Fontaine.

130. Les Suppliantes. Incidental music
(Aeschylus). 1941.
 fp: 5 July 1941, Paris, Stade Roland-
Garros; performance organized by Le Comité
National des Sports in aid of Secours National
des Sportifs Prisonniers; Chorale Yvonne
Gouverné and Paris Conservatoire Orchestra,
cond. Charles Münch; artistic director, Jean-
Louis Barrault.

131. 800 Mètres. Incidental music to a
'drame sportif' by André Obey. 1941.
 fp: as No. 130.

132. La Ligne d'Horizon. Incidental music
(Serge Roux). 1941.
 fp: October 1941, Paris, Théâtre des
Bouffes-Parisiens.

133. Six Melodies-Minute. For voice and
piano. 1941. ? Unpub.

134. Symphony No. 2. For string orchestra

and (ad lib) trumpet. Dated: October 1941,
Paris. Ded. Paul Sacher. Dur. 25'.
 1. *Molto moderato*; 2. *Adagio mesto*; 3. *Vivace
non troppo*.
 fp: 18 May 1942, Zürich, Collegium
Musicum, cond. Paul Sacher.
 fEp: 26 April 1944, Wigmore Hall, Boyd
Neel Orchestra, cond. Boyd Neel.
 fEp (broadcast): 27 February 1946, BBC
Symphony Orchestra, cond. Ernest Ansermet.
 Pub. 1942, Salabert.

BIBLIOGRAPHY:
Wolfram Gerbracht: Honeggers Zweite Sin-
fonie, *Melos*, May–June 1947, p. 221.
Arthur Honegger: A propos de la symphonie
pour orchestre de cordes, *SM*, 1944.
R.-A. Mooser: La 2e Symphonie d'AH,
Dissonances, November–December 1942.

135. La Boxe en France. ? 1941. Music for a
documentary film. Production, Hermina-
Film; director, Lucien Ganier-Raymond.

136. Le Grand Barrage. 'Image musicale'
for orchestra. 1942. Unpub.

137. Le Journal Tombe à 5 Heures. 1942.
Music for a film. Production, SNEG-
Gaumont; director, Georges Lacombe; script,
O.-P. Gilbert; with Pierre Fresnay, Pierre
Renoir and Marie Déa. Première: 21 May
1942, Paris, Colisée.

138. Huit Hommes dans un Château.
1942. Music for a film, composed in collaboration with Arthur Hoérée. Production, Sirius-
Films; director, Richard Pottier; with René
Dary, Georges Grey and Jacqueline Gautier.

139. O Salutaris. For voice, organ (ad lib)
and piano or harp. 1942. Ded. Ginette
Guillamat.
 fp: 3 October 1943, Eglise Saint-Séverin,
Noémie Pérugia.
 Pub. 1943, Heugel.

140. Chant de la Libération (Bernard
Zimmer). For baritone, chorus and orchestra.
1942.
 fp: 22 October 1944, Paris, Concerts du
Conservatoire, Jacques Rousseau (baritone),
Paris Conservatoire Orchestra, cond. Charles
Münch.
 Unpub.

Honegger, Arthur

141. Saluste du Bartas (P. Bedat de Montlaur). Six melodies for voice and piano. 1942.
1. *Le Château du Bartas*; 2. *Le long de la Baise*; 3. *Le Départ*; 4. *La Promenade*; 5. *Nérac en fête*; 6. *Duo*.
fp: 21 March 1942, Paris, Salle Gaveau, Noémie Péruga acc. I. Aïtoff.

142. Pasiphaé. Music for radio (Henry de Montherland). 1943.

143. Secrets. 1943. Music for a film. Production, Pathé-Cinéma; director, Pierre Blanchar; script, Bernard Zimmer, from Turgenev's 'A Month in the Country'; with Pierre Blanchar, Marie Déa, Suzy Carrier, Gilbert Gil. Première: 17 March 1943, Paris, l'Ermitage & Helder.

144. Un Seul Amour. 1943. Music for a film directed by Pierre Blanchar, adapted from Balzac; with Pierre Blanchar, Julien Bertheau and Micheline Presle.

145. Calliosto, ou la Petite Nymphe de Diane. 1943. Music, composed in collaboration with Roland-Manuel, for an animated film by André Marty.

146. Le Capitaine Fracasse. 1943. Music for a film. Production, Lux-Film; director, Abel Gance; script, after Théophile Gautier; with Fernand Gravey and Assia Noris.

147. Mermoz. 1943. Music for a film. Production, Productions Françaises Cinématographiques; director, Louis Cuny; with Robert Hugues-Lambert and Lucien Nat. Première: 3 November 1943, Paris, Triomphe & la Scala.

147a. Mermoz. Extracts for orchestra.
1. *La Traversée des Andes*; 2. *Le Vol sur l'Atlantique*.
Pub. 1943, Choudens.

148. Les Antiquités de l'Asie Occidentale. 1943. Music for a documentary film produced by l'Office française des films d'art et l'histoire.

149. Le Soulier de Satin. 1943. Incidental music (Paul Claudel).
fp: 27 November 1943, Paris, Comédie-Française; with Jean-Louis Barrault and Marie Bell; producer, Jean-Louis Barrault; sets, Lucien Coutaud.

BIBLIOGRAPHY:
Roland-Manuel: Le Soulier de Satin à la Comédie Française, *L'Information musicale*, 18 February 1944.

150. L'Appel de la Montagne. Ballet (Favre Le Bret). 1943.
fp: 9 July 1945, Paris, Opéra, cond. Louis Fourestier.

150a. Jour de Fête Suisse. Suite for orchestra from 'L'Appel de la Montagne'.
fp: 14 November 1945, Winterthur, cond. Ernest Ansermet.
Pub. Salabert.

151. Deux Esquisses. For piano. 1943–4. Written in Nicolas Obouhow's simplified notation.
1. *Large et rapsodique*. Dated: 9 October 1943, Paris. Ded. Mme Aussenac de Broglio. Pub. January 1944, Durand.
2. *Allegretto malinconio*. Dated: 2 July 1944. Ded. Yvette Grimaud. Pub. July 1944, Durand.

152. Battements du Monde. 'Jeu radiophonique' (William Aguet). 1944.
fp: 18 May 1944, Lausanne Radio, Orchestre de la Suisse Romande, cond. Ernest Ansermet.
Pub. Salabert.

153. Charles Le Téméraire. Incidental music (René Morax). 1944.
fp: 27 May 1944, Mézières, Théâtre du Jorat, with Léopold Biberti (Charles le Téméraire) and Marguerite Cavadski (Anne); women's chorus and Union Chorale de Vevey, cond. Carlo Hemmerling.
Pub. Salabert.

154. Sérénade à Angelique. For small orchestra. Dated: 15 October 1945.
fp: 19 November 1945, Zürich Radio Orchestra, cond. Hermann Scherchen.
f Paris p: 11 December 1946, Paris Radio Orchestra, cond. Tibor Harsanyi.
Pub. Salabert.

155. Un Ami Viendra Ce Soir. 1945–6. Music for the film. Production, Compagnie Générale Cinématographique; director, Raymond Bernard; with Michel Simon, Madeleine Sologne, Paul Bernard and Louis

Salou. Première: 19 February 1946, Paris. Distributed in Britain by Cameo-Polytechnic Distributors; British première, February 1950, Cameo-Poly Cinema.

156. Quatre Chansons pour voix grave.
Dated: 24 February 1944–December 1945.
1. *La douceur de tes yeux* (Archag Tchobanian).
2. *Un grand sommeil noir* (Verlaine).
3. *La terre, l'eau, l'air et le vent* (Ronsard).
4. *Chanson de marin* (William Aguet).
fp: 21 May 1944, Paris, Salle du Conservatoire, Ginette Guillamat, acc. Pierre Sancan.
?fEbp: 19 March 1951, Nancy Evans acc. Ernest Lush.
Pub. Salabert.

157. Chota Roustaveli. Ballet (Serge Lifar). Music by Arthur Honegger (Tableaux 1 & 4), Tcherepnine & Harsanyi.
fp: 1945, Théâtre de Monte-Carlo.
fEp: July 1946, London, New Monte Carlo Ballet; with Yvette Chauviré, Serge Lifar and Janine Charrat; choreography, Serge Lifar.
Pub. Salabert.

158. Symphony No. 3 (Liturgique). 1945–6. Ded. Charles Münch. Dur. 30′.
1. *Dies irae* (Allegro marcato); 2. *De Profundis Clamavi* (Adagio); 3. *Dona Nobis Pacem* (Andante).
3 fl, 2 ob, ca, 2 cl, bcl, 2 bsn, cbsn; 4 hn, 3 tpt, 3 tmb, tuba; piano, GC, tamtam, cym, caisse roulante; strings.
fp: 17 August 1946, Zürich, Orchestre de la Tonhalle et du Théâtre, cond. Charles Münch.
fIp: 3 November 1946, Milan, La Scala Orchestra, cond. Arthur Honegger.
f Paris p: 14 November 1946, cond. Charles Münch.
fEp: 7 December 1946, BBC broadcast, BBC Symphony Orchestra, cond. Charles Münch.
fAp: 23 January 1947, New York Philharmonic Symphony, cond. Charles Münch.
f British p (concert): 23 August 1948, Edinburgh Festival, Concertgebouw Orchestra, cond. Charles Münch.
fEp (concert): 26 August 1949, Royal Albert Hall, Promenade Concert, London Philharmonic Orchestra, cond. Basil Cameron.
Pub. 1946, Salabert.

BIBLIOGRAPHY:
Hector Silver: Honeggers Lithurgische Sinfonie, *Melos*, November 1947, p. 383.

159. Prométhée. Incidental music (Aeschylus, French version by A. Bonnard). 1946.
fp: 5 June 1946, Avenches (Vaud), Open Air Theatre.
Pub. Salabert.

160. Hamlet. Incidental music (Shakespeare, French transl. by André Gide), 1946.
fp: 17 October 1946, Paris, Théâtre Marigny; producer, Jean-Louis Barrault; sets and costumes, André Masson.

161. Sortilèges. For Ondes Martenot. 1946.

162. Symphony No. 4 (Deliciae Basilienses). 1946. Ded. Paul Sacher and the Basle Chamber Orchestra for their 20th anniversary. Dur. 31′ 45″.
1. *Lento e misterioso*; 2. *Larghetto*; 3. *Allegro*.
2 fl, 2 ob, 2 cl, bsn; 2 hn; tpt; glock, cym, piano; strings.
fp: 21 January 1947, Basle, Basle Chamber Orchestra, cond. Paul Sacher.
?fEp: 24 March 1958, Chelsea Town Hall, symphony orchestra, cond. Foster Clark.
Pub. 1947, Salabert.

163. Les Démons de l'Aube. 1946. Music, composed in collaboration with Arthur Hoérée, for a film. Production, Gaumont; director, Yves Allegret; with Georges Marchal, André Valmé, Jacqueline Pierreux and Simone Signoret. Première, 9 April 1946, Paris, Madeleine-Cinema. Pub. 1946, Choudens, piano score: 1. *Les Démons de l'aube générique*; 2. *Attaque nocturne*; 3. *Escalade*; 4. *Plein air* (chant sans parole); remaining five published numbers by Arthur Hoérée.

164. Un Revenant. 1946. Music for a film. Production, Compagnie Franco-Coloniale Cinématographique; director, Christian-Jaque; with Louis Jouvet, Gaby Morlay, François Périer and Ludmaile (Ludmila) Tcherina. Distributed in Britain by Film Traders (Academy Cinema), 1948. Pub. 1947, Choudens, piano score (facsimile): 1. *Un revenant*; 2. *Ballet romantique*; 3. *Andromède et Persée*.

165. Mimaamaquim. For voice and piano. December 1946. Pub. Salabert.

166. Oedipe. Incidental music (Sophocles, French transl, by André Gide). 1947.
fp: ?1947, Paris, Théâtre des Champs-Elysées.
Pub. Salabert.

167. Intrada. For trumpet and piano. Dated: April 1947, Paris. Composed for the Concours International d'Exécution musicale, Geneva, 1947. Pub. 1947, Salabert (facsimile).

168. Le Village Perdu. 1947. Music for a film. Production, Agence Générale Cinématographique; director, Christian Stengel; script, from a novel by Gilbert Dupé; with Gaby Morlay, Alfred Adam and Lucienne Laurence. Première: 21 November 1947, Paris, Empire and Le Français cinemas.

169. Souvenir de Chopin. For piano. 1947. Ded. Jacqueline Potier-Landowski. Pub. 1947, Choudens.

170. Tête d'Or. Radio music (Paul Claudel). 1948. Pub. Salabert.

171. L'Etat de Siège. Incidental music (Albert Camus). 1948.
fp: 27 October 1948, Paris, Théâtre Marigny, Compagnie Madeleine Renaud-Jean-Louis Barrault; with Pierre Bertin (La Peste), Madeleine Renaud (La Secrétaire), Pierre Brasseur (Nada), Maria Casarès (Victoria), Albert Medina (Le Juge), Marie-Hélène Dasté (La Femme du Juge), Jean-Louis Barrault (Diégo); director, Jean-Louis Barrault; décor and costumes, Balthus.

172. Concerto da Camera. For flute, cor anglais and string orchestra. Dated: 28 October 1948, Paris. Ded. Elizabeth Coolidge. Dur. 16' 30".
fp: 6 May 1949, Zürich, André Jaunet (fl), Marcel Saillet (ca), Collegium Musicum, cond. Paul Sacher.
fEp: 10 April 1950, BBC broadcast, Gareth Morris (fl), Terence MacDonagh (ca), Philharmonia Orchestra, cond. Ernest Ansermet.
Pub. 1949, Salabert.

173. Saint François d'Assise. 'Jeu radiophonique' (William Aguet). 1949.
fp: 3 December 1949, Lausanne Radio, chorus and l'Orchestre de la Suisse Romande, cond. Ernest Ansermet.
Pub. Salabert.

174. De la Musique. Ballet (R. Wild). Pub. Salabert.

175. Bourdelle. 1950. Music for a documentary film. Production, DOC; director, René Lucot.

176. Symphony No. 5 (Di tre re). 1950. Composed for the Koussevitzky Music Foundation. Ded. to the memory of Natalie Koussevitzky.
1. *Grave.* Dated: 5 September, orch. October.
2. *Allegretto.* Dated: 1 October, orch. 23 November.
3. *Allegro marcato.* Dated: 10 November, Paris; orch. 3 December.
3 fl, 2 ob, ca, 2 cl, bcl, 3 bsn; 4 hn, 3 tpt, 3 tmb, tuba; timp (ad lib); strings.
fp: 9 March 1951, Boston Symphony Orchestra, cond. Charles Münch.
fEp: 26 May 1952, BBC broadcast, Royal Festival Hall, Boston Symphony Orchestra, cond. Charles Münch.
Pub. 1951, Salabert.

BIBLIOGRAPHY:
André Gauthier: La Ve Symphonie d'AH, *La Revue internationale de musique* (Paris), No. 11, autumn 1951, p. 501.

177. Monopartita. For orchestra. Dated: 26 March 1951, Paris. Ded. Tonhalle-Gesellschaft, Zürich.
2 fl, 2 ob, ca, 2 cl, bcl, 2 bsn; 4 hn, 3 tpt, 3 tmb; timp; strings.
Pub. 1951, Salabert.

BIBLIOGRAPHY:
Hans Rosbaud: Monopartita und 5. Sinfonie, *Melos*, February 1952, p. 43.
Willi Schuh: AHs Monopartita, *SM*, 1 July 1951, p. 308.

178. Paul Claudel. 1951. Music for a documentary film. Production, Atlantic-Film director, André Gillet.

179. Suite Archaïque. For orchestra. Dated: 15 January 1951, Paris. Ded. Louisville Philharmonic Society. Dur. 18' 30".
1. *Largamente*; 2. *Pantomime*; 3. *Ritournelle et Sérénade*; 4. *Processional*.
2 fl, 2 ob, 2 cl, 2 bsn; 2 tpt, 2 tmb; strings.
fp: 28 February 1951, Louisville, Louisville Symphony Orchestra, cond. R. Whitney.
fEp: 7 August 1952, BBC broadcast, Leighton Lucas Orchestra, cond. Leighton Lucas.
Pub. 1951, Salabert.

BIBLIOGRAPHY:
O. Daniel: Louisville special—recording of Suite archaïque, *Saturday Review*, 14 April 1962, p. 31.

180. La Rédemption de François Villon. Radio music (José Bruyr). 1951. Pub. Salabert.

181. On ne badine pas avec l'Amour. Incidental music (Alfred de Musset). 1951.
fp: 13 December 1951, Paris, Théâtre Marigny; director, Jean-Louis Barrault; sets and costumes, Jean-Denis Malclès.
Pub. Salabert.

182. La Tour de Babel. 1951, Music for a documentary film. Production, Films Rony; director, George Rony. Première: 26 December 1951, Paris, Studio de l'Etoile.

183. Toccata (sur un thème de Campra). For orchestra. November 1951, Paris. Contribution to 'Guirlande de Campra'.
2 fl, 2 ob, 2 cl, 2 bsn; 2 hn, 2 tpt; strings.
fp: 31 July 1952, Aix-en-Provence Festival, Paris Conservatoire Orchestra, cond. Hans Rosbaud.
Pub. 1954, Salabert.

184. Oedipe-Roi. Incidental music (Sophocles, French transl. by Th. Maulnier). May 1952.
fp: 1952, Paris, Comédie-Français; producer, Julien Bertheau; sets, Georges Wakhévitch.
Pub. Salabert.

185. Romance. For flute and piano. 1953. Pub. Pierre Noël, in Les Contemporains écrivent pour les instruments à vent, collection Fernand Oubadrous, *La Flûte*, Vol. 1.

186. Une Cantate de Noël. For baritone solo, children's voices, mixed chorus, organ and orchestra. Dated: 25 January 1953, Paris, from sketches dated 24 January 1941. Liturgical and popular texts transl. Fred. Goldbeck and Rollo Myers. Ded. Basle Chamber Orchestra on its twenty-fifth anniversary, and its founder Paul Sacher.
fp: 18 December 1953, Basle, Derrick Olsen (baritone), Basle Chamber Chorus and Orchestra, cond. Paul Sacher.
f London p: 7 October 1959, BBC concert, John Noble (baritone), BBC Chorus, boys from Emanuel School Choir, BBC Symphony Orchestra, cond. Ernest Ansermet.
Pub. 1953, Salabert.

BIBLIOGRAPHY:
R.-Aloys Mooser: Cantate de Noël, in *Aspects de la musique contemporaine*, Editions Labor et Fidès (Geneva) 1957, p. 22.
Willi Schuh: AHs Weihnachtskantate, *SM*, February 1954, p. 61.

WRITINGS BY HONEGGER
Adaptations musicales, *Gazette des Sept Arts*, 25 January 1923.
Le métier du compositeur de musique, *La Revue nouvelle*, 15 December 1924, p. 17.
L'Enfant et les Sortilèges, *Musique et Théâtre*, 15 April 1925.
Opinions, *Dissonances*, April 1925.
Beethoven et nous, *Le Correspondant*, 25 March 1927, p. 861.
Rugby, *Excelsior*, 29 November 1927.
Du cinéma sonore à la musique réelle, *Plans*, 1931; *Appogiature*, May 1931, p. 105.
Pour prendre congé, *Appogiature*, February 1932, p. 36.
La situation sociale du compositeur de musique, *Le Mois*, No. 32, 1933, p. 217.
Particularités sonores du film 'Rapt' (with Arthur Hoérée), *RM*, December 1934, p. 88.
Problems of the professional composer, *The Musician*, May 1932, p. 26.
La situation sociale du compositeur de musique, *Le Mois*, No. 32, 1933, p. 217.
Ravel et le Debussysme, *RM*, December 1938.
Sur Igor Stravinsky, *RM*, May–June 1939.
Franck et Stravinsky, *L'Information musicale*,

Honegger, Arthur

1941, 19 September p. 39, 26 September p. 63.

Contribution to 'Werner Reinhart zum 60. Geburtstag', *SM*, 1944.

La musique à Paris après la libération, *Dissonances*, January–February 1945; reprinted from *Labyrinthe*.

Lettre-préface, in *Regards sur la musique contemporaine* by R.-A. Mooser, Lausanne, 1946, p. 13.

Préface, in *Traité d'harmonie tonale, atonale et totale* by Nicolas Obouhow, Paris, 1946; also *RM*, November–December 1946, p. 15.

Préface, in *Béla Bartók* by Serge Moreux, Paris, 1949.

Souvenirs sur Othmar Schoeck, *SM*, 1946, Nos. 8–9.

Vad kan baletten göra för unga komponisten, *Prisma*, 1946, No. 6, p. 76.

Incantations aux Fossiles, Editions d'Ouchy (Lausanne) 1948.

Über die Musik-Kritiker, *Melos*, April 1948, p. 97.

Die Geschichte der Fossile, *Melos*, January 1950, p. 1.

Souvenirs sur la classe de Vincent d'Indy au Conservatoire, *Revue internationale de musique*, 1951, No. 10, p. 345.

Honegger om Konung David, *Röster i Radio*, 1951, No. 14, p. 4.

Je suis compositeur, Editions du Conquistador, Paris, 1951.

Ich bin ein Komponist, *ÖM*, No. 10, 1951; *Das Musikleben*, February 1952.

An die jungen Musiker!, *Melos*, February 1952, p. 35.

Der Lohn des Komponisten, *Musica*, February 1953.

Mozart, *ÖM*, December 1955.

Collaboration avec Claudel, *Nouvelle nouvelle revue française*, No. 33, 1955, p. 553.

Nachgelassene Schriften (ed. Willi Reich), Arche (Zürich) 1957.

GENERAL BIBLIOGRAPHY

Karl Bachler: An Honeggers Grab, *NZfM*, November 1956.

Samuel Baud-Bovy: AH et la musique religieuse, *Feuilles musicales*, September 1952, p. 200.

P. Bedat de Montlaur: En témoignage de la reconnaissance gasconne à AH, *Bulletin de la Société archéologique, historique, littéraire et scientifique du Gers (Auch)*, Ier Trim., 1956.

Robert Bernard: Une lettre ouverte à AH, *L'Information musicale*, 2 October 1942, p. 46.

Walter Berten: Der Musikdramatiker AH, *NMZ*, 1928, No. 11, p. 348.

René Berthelot: Une lettre ouverte à AH, *L'Information musicale*, 10 October 1941, p. 133.

Maurice Bex: AH, *Revue Rhénane*, October 1922.

A. Boll: AH, *Revue d'histoire du théâtre* (Paris), 1956, No. 1.

Pierre Boulez: AH, *Cahiers de la Compagnie Madeleine Renaud—Jean-Louis Barrault*, 15e cahier, January 1956.

A. G. Browne: AH, *M&L*, October 1929.

Francis Bonavia: The future of music according to Honegger, *MT*, May 1928, p. 413.

José Bruyr: AH, in *L'Ecran des musiciens*, Les Cahiers de France (Paris) 1930.

— Honegger et son œuvre, Editions Corrêa, 1947.

— Dans le souvenir d'AH, *Revue musicale de la Suisse Romande*, 1 June 1964, p. 7.

L. Burkat: Current chronicle—sixtieth anniversary, *MQ*, January 1952, p. 118.

J. Chailley: Honegger et le théâtre, *Revue d'histoire du théâtre* (Paris), 1956, No. 1.

René Chalupt: AH, *RM*, January 1922, p. 42.

Gilbert Chappallaz: AH et la musique du cinéma, *Feuilles musicales*, September 1952, p. 208.

Jean Cocteau: Die Gruppe der Sechs, *Melos*, January 1954, p. 1.

André Coeuroy: AH, *L'Ere nouvelle*, 10 August 1921.

— AH, in *La Musique française moderne*, Librairie Delagrave (Paris) 1922, p. 121.

— AH, in *Panorama de la musique contemporaine*, Simon Kra (Paris) 1928.

Paul Collaer: Les compositeurs issus du groupe des 'Six', in *La Musique moderne*, Elsevier (Paris) 1955, p. 163.

Ermanno Comuzio: Honegger e il cinema, *Cinema*, 1955.

Martin Cooper: Modern trio, *London Mercury*, March 1939, p. 532.

Hans Corrodi: Musikeröpfe der Gegenwart, *Neue Schweizer Rundschau*, Vol. 2 (1934–5), p. 453.

Aldo Damo: AH und die anti-impressionistiche Reaktion, *Neue Schweizer Rundschau*, Vol. 20, 1927, No. 1.

R. Delange: Honegger le constructeur, *France Illustration*, 15 March 1952, p. 258.

Marcel Delannoy: Honegger, Pierre Horay (Paris) 1953.

Norman Demuth: AH, in *Musical Trends in the 20th Century*, Rockliff (London) 1952, p. 96.

— AH, *MO*, February 1956, p. 275.

Jean Douël: Lettre ouverte à AH, *L'Information musicale*, 28 August 1942, p. 2.

Martial Douël: AH, *Chesterian*, No. 58, November 1956.

René Dumesnil: AH, in *La Musique contemporaine en France* (tome II), Lib. Armand Colin (Paris) 1930, p. 14.

Louis Durey: Les Six, *Créer*, June 1922.

Ernst Egli: AHs männliche Ahnen, *SM*, May–June 1962, p. 156.

Rene Elvin: AH, *M&M*, December 1952, p. 7.

Hans Ehinger: AH, *NZfM*, February 1956.

— AH als Musikdramatiker, *NZfM*, November 1962.

M. Favre: AHs Sinfonien, *Der Bund* (Bern), 10 March 1952.

H. Febvre-Longeray: AH et les Six, *Gazette musicale de Lyon*, February 1926.

Jacques Feschotte: Honegger et les explorateurs du ciel, *SM*, 1966, No. 2 (March–April), p. 89.

A. Frankenstein: Mr. Honegger comes to America, *Review of Reviews*, January 1929, p. 158.

L. de Freitas-Branco: Os Seis, *Revista de Conservatorio Nacional* (Lisbon), October 1921.

B. Gavoty: Honegger, de Roi David à Nicolas de Flue, *Le Journal musical français*, 23 October 1952.

— Les opinions d'AH, *Formes et couleurs*, 1948, No. 2.

André George: AH, *Revue de Genève*, December 1924.

— AH, *Le Monde musical*, February 1926.

— AH, Claude Aveline (Paris) 1928.

— AH, *Pro Musica* (New York), June 1928.

Claude Gérard: AH, *Nouvelle revue belge*, 1945.

Fred. Goldbeck: Honegger, oder der Triumph der Naivität, *Die Musik*, November 1932, p. 116.

E. Helm: AH, *Saturday Review*, 31 December 1955, p. 39.

Nicole Hirsch: AH, un romantique contemporaine, *Tout la Danse*, January 1956, p. 24.

Arthur Hoérée: AH, *Eolus* (New York), January 1926.

— Opéra: Festival Honegger, *Beaux Arts*, 15 April 1926, p. 126.

— AH et les locomotives, *Revue Pleyel*, No. 47, August 1927.

— AH, musicien populaire, *RM*, January 1929.

— AH, folk musician, *Sackbut*, November 1929, p. 90.

— Une visite à AH, *Musique*, 15 September 1929; *SM*, 1 September 1929, p. 581.

— AH, l'optimiste, *Candide*, 28 July 1932.

— La vie, l'œuvre, l'homme, Les publications techniques (Paris) 1942.

A. Hughes: Les Six a generation later, *Musical America*, 15 February 1954, p. 12.

— Honegger—death was often his theme, *Musical America*, 1 January 1956, p. 7.

I. Jirko: AH, *Hudebni Rozhledy*, 1960, No. 22, p. 928.

Paul Landormy: AH, *La Victoire*, 28 September 1920.

— La groupe des Six, *Revue de Genève*, September 1921.

— AH, in *La Musique française après Debussy*, Gallimard (Paris) 1947.

Marcel Landowski: Honegger, Editions du Seuil (Paris) 1957.

Heinrich Lindlar: Honegger zwischen 'Pacific' und 'Monopartita', *Melos*, June 1954, p. 165.

— Universalist und Humanist, *Melos*, 1956, No. 2, p. 133.

Edward Lockspeiser: AH, *Chesterian*, No. 185, winter 1956.

A. Machabey: AH et la musique française, *L'Information musicale*, 3 October 1941, p. 98.

Joseph Machlis: AH, in *Introduction to Contemporary Music*, Norton (USA), Dent (London) 1961, p. 225.

André Marot: Le groupe des Six, *Le Carnet critique*, June 1922.

Honegger, Arthur

Léo Melitz: Honegger, *Die Musik*, January 1927, p. 249.
— AH, *Der Scheinwerfer*, January 1928.
— AH, *Anbruch*, April–May 1930, p. 155.
Hans Mersman: Neue Werke von AH, *Melos*, May 1928.
Peter Mieg: Zum Tod von AH, *Schweizerische Musikpädagogische Blätter*, January 1956.
Darius Milhaud: AH, *Chesterian*, No. 19, December 1921.
— Die Sechs, *Anbruch*, May 1922.
Marius Monnikendam: AH, in *Musikale Ommegang* (Amsterdam), 1943, p. 525.
Gösta Nystroem: AH, *Göteborgs Handels- och Sjöfartstidning*, 4 December 1933.
Eberhard Otto: AH, Mensch unter Menschen —Zum 60. Geburtstag, *NZfM*, 1952, p. 155.
Guido Pannain: AH, *La Rassegna musicale*, 1928, p. 467.
Francis Poulenc: A propos d'une lettre d'AH, *SM*, May–June 1962, p. 156.
Fred K. Prieberg: Honeggers elektronisches Experiment, *Melos*, January 1956, p. 20.
Henry Prunières: AH, *Melos*, November 1924.
— AH, *Il Pianoforte* (Turin), April 1925.
Willi Reich: Honeggers Bildnis im eigenen Wort, *Melos*, February 1952, p. 41.
Charles Ribèyre: Du 'Chant du Nigamon' à 'Pacific 231', *L'Orient musical*, 1 October 1924.
K. Riisager: AH, *Dansk Musiktidsskrift*, 1927, No. 4.
— AH à Copenhague, *RM*, 1 December 1927, p. 163.
Jean Rochat: La prosodie dans la musique d'AH, *Feuilles musicales*, January 1957.
L. Rognoni: Due colloqui con AH, *L'Approdo musicale*, 1965, Nos. 19–20.
Roland-Manuel: AH, Senart (Paris) 1925.
— Douze heures avec Honegger, *Revue Pleyel*, January 1925.
— Les cinquante ans d'AH, *Les Publications techniques*, 1942, p. 14.
Kajsa Rootzén: AH some 'biblisk' tondiktare, *Credo*, 1952, p. 148.
Hans Rosbaud: Zwei neue Werke von Honegger—Monopartita und 5. Sinfonie, *Melos*, February 1952, p. 43.
Claude Rostand: AH, ein beispielhafter Humanist, *Melos*, February 1952, p. 36.

Jean Roy: AH, in *Musique française*, Présences contemporarines, Editions Debresse (Paris) 1962, p. 167.
K. H. Ruppel: AH und das musikalische Theater, *Melos*, January 1956, p. 16.
Gustave Samazeuilh: AH, in *Musiciens de mon temps*, Editions Marcel Daubin (Paris) 1947, p. 350.
Erik Satie: Les Six, *Les Feuilles libres*, February 1922.
M. Schild-Muntzinger: Visite au Maître Honegger, *Cæcilienbote* (Soleure), May–July 1930.
Boris de Schloezer: AH, *Nouvelle Revue Française*, 1956, No. 37, p. 164.
Max F. Schneider: Von Nägeli bis Honegger, *Melos*, 1952, p. 233.
Emil Staiger: AH, *SM*, May–June 1962, p. 150.
Paul Stefan: AH, *Living Age*, March 1939, p. 49.
Heinrich Strobel: Gruss an AH, *Melos*, February 1952, p. 33.
— Abschied von Honegger, *Melos*, January 1956, p. 12.
H. H. Stuckenschmidt: AH, *Anbruch*, October 1932, p. 166.
Willy Tappolet: AH, *Annales* (Horgen–Zürich), 1928.
— AH, Editions La Baconnière (Neuchâtel) 1939; German transl. Claude Tappolet, 1959.
— AH, *SM*, 15 December 1933.
— Les récentes œuvres d'AH, *SM*, November 1945, p. 417.
— Honegger and his recent works, *MMR*, 1946, p. 75.
— Quelques récentes œuvres d'AH, *SM*, 1 May 1950, p. 240.
— AH—'Je suis compositeur', *SM*, December 1951, p. 499.
— AH, *SM*, March 1952, p. 85.
— AH, *SM*, January 1956, p. 1.
— AH, in *MGG*, Vol. 6 (1957), p. 683.
— AH et l'oratorio, *SM*, May–June 1962, p. 156.
— Der religiöse Gehalt im Werk AHs, *Neue Zürcher Zeitung*, 18 December 1955.
Emile Vuillermoz: Honegger and his time, *Modern Music*, December 1925.
— AH, *Hommes et mondes* (Paris), January 1956.

Bo Wallner: AH, in *Fransk musik* (Stockholm), 1957, p. 138.
— Oratoriet hos Honegger och Rosenberg, *Prisma*, 1950, Nos. 5–6, p. 83.
Paul Walther: AH dirigierte, *Melos*, July–August 1949, p. 197.
J. Weterings: Honegger, musicien sportif, *Cahiers de Belgique*, December 1928.

SYMPOSIA
Hommage à Honegger, *SM*, March 1952, p. 87.
Hommage à Honegger, *Melos*, January 1956, p. 1. (Includes contributions by Georges Auric, Jean Cocteau, Pierre Boulez, Aaron Copland, Luigi Dallapiccola, Werner Egk, Hans Werner Henze, Frank Martin, G.-F. Malipiero, Carl Orff, Francis Poulenc, Olivier Messiaen, Darius Milhaud, etc.)

ANONYMOUS OR UNSIGNED
AH, *British Musician*, June 1930, p. 154.
AH, *Bollettino bibliografico musicale*, January 1929, p. 1.
Machine music, *Musical Mirror*, March 1925, p. 49.
AH, *Röster i Radio*, 1952, No. 11, p. 14.
La dernière interview d'AH, *L'Opéra de Paris*, 1956.

FILM
Arthur Honegger. 1955, Production, Cinextension; director, Georges Rouquier. A film of the life and work of Honegger, with recollections and narration by the composer. Music selected from Honegger's works and includes the final scene of *Jeanne d'Arc au bûcher*, re-enacted before Rouen Cathedral.

CHARLES IVES (1874–1954)

The son of a U.S. Army bandmaster of remarkable aural imagination, Charles Ives was born into a long-established New England family at Danbury in Connecticut on 20 October 1874. His father gave him music lessons from the age of five and he became a noted figure in Danbury music by the time he was fourteen. Ives was organist successively at Danbury, New Haven (Conn.), Bloomfield (N.J.) and New York City between 1887 and 1902. He studied music under Horatio Parker at Yale (1894–8) but decided after graduation to choose a non-musical career, since he felt that he could not avoid compromising his musical ideals if he made music his profession. He opted instead for life insurance in New York, working first as an actuarial clerk and then going into partnership with his friend Julian Myrick in 1907. The following year he married Harmony Twichell, who—apart from his father and the writings of the New England Transcendentalists, Emerson and Thoreau—was the major influence on his work. Ives spent the rest of his life in New York City, apart from many summers on his farm at West Redding, Connecticut. He was active in directing the prosperous firm of Ives & Myrick—writing a life insurance primer in 1912—until the first of several heart-attacks in 1918. These led eventually to his retirement from business (1930) and rendered him a semi-invalid until his death. His most intense years of composing (an activity for evenings and week-ends) were the two decades after his graduation, these too being brought to an end by the 1918 breakdown. During these years Ives was unable to get his compositions performed publicly or published commercially. After 1918 he gave up all attempts to promote his own music beyond having his 'Concord' Sonata and a collection of 114 songs printed and distributed at his own expense (1919 and 1922). The rare performances of his work which followed—notably two movements from the Fourth symphony in New York (1927)—met with such hostility that Ives largely turned his back on music-making, though he did give much financial help to the promotion of radical American music in his later years. He died in May 1954.

CATALOGUE OF WORKS
The following abbreviations have been used in respect of song publication details:

(114)   Published in 114 Songs, privately printed in 1922, repr. ?1925.
(114/50) Published as above and also in 50 Songs, privately printed in 1923 in a volume actually containing 51 songs.

(7)   Published in 7 Songs by Cos Cob Press, 1932.

(4)   Published in 4 Songs by Mercury, 1950.

(10)   Published in 10 Songs by Peer, 1953.

(12)   Published in 12 Songs by Peer, 1954.

(14)   Published in 14 Songs by Peer, 1955.

(15)   Published in 15 Songs by Peer, 1955.

(9)   Published in 9 Songs by Peer, 1956.

(13)   Published in 13 Songs by Peer, 1958.

1. Slow March (? Harmony T. Ives) (?Charles Ives). For voice and piano. 1888 (?1887). 'To the Children's Faithful Friend.' Pub. (114) No. 114; (10).

2. Hear my prayer, O Lord. ?1888.

3. At parting (Peterson). For voice and piano. 1889. Pub. October 1933, in *New Music* (Vol. 7, No. 1).

4. Turn ye, turn ye. For SATB chorus and piano or organ. 1889. Pub. Mercury.

5. When stars are in the quiet skies (Bulwer-Lytton). For voice and piano. 1891. Pub. (114) No. 113.

6. Variations on 'America'. For organ. 1891.
     fp: 1891, Brewster (New York), Charles Ives, at a recital celebrating the Fourth of July.
     Pub. 1949, Music Press (New York); Mercury.

6a. Variations on 'America'. Orch. William Schuman.
     fp: May 1964, New York Philharmonic.

7. Abide with me (Henry Francis Lyte). For voice and piano. 1891. Pub. (13); also in *Sacred Songs*.

8. A song—for anything (Charles Ives). For voice and piano. 1892. Pub. (114) No. 89 (as *Sentimental Ballads* No. 5); (15).

9. To Edith (Harmony T. Ives). For voice and piano. 1892. Pub. (114) No. 112; (10).

10. The world's highway (Harmony T. Ives). For voice and piano. 1893. Pub. (114) No. 90 (as *Sentimental Ballads* No. 6); (13).

11. Song for harvest season (Stanza from an old hymn). For voice, cornet, trombone and basso, or voice and organ. 1894. Pub. October 1933 in *New Music* (Vol. 7, No. 1).

12. Canon (Thomas Moore). For voice and piano. 1894. Pub. (114) No. 111; October 1935 in *New Music* (Vol. 9, No. 1).

13. The circus band (Charles Ives). For SSATTBB and various instruments. 1894. ?Pub. Peer.

13a. The circus band. Version for voice and piano. 1894. Pub. (114) No. 56 (as *Five Street Songs* No. 5); (10).

14. Kären (Parmo Karl Ploug, transl. Clara Kappey). For voice and piano. 1894. Pub. (114/50) No. 91 (as *Sentimental Ballads* No. 7); (12).

15. A night thought (Moore). For voice and piano. 1895. Pub. (114/50) No. 107; October 1933, in *New Music* (Vol. 7, No. 1).

16. A night song (Moore). For voice and piano. 1894. Pub. (114) No. 88 (as *Sentimental Ballads* No. 4).

17. A son of a gambolier (Anon.). For voice and piano. 1895. Pub. (114) No. 54 (as *Five Street Songs* No. 3); (9).

18. Songs my mother taught me (Transl. and adapted from Heyduk). For voice and piano. 1895. Pub. (114/50) No. 108; (14).

19. Waltz (Charles Ives). For voice and piano. 1895. Pub. (114) No. 109; (12).

20. The world's wanderer (Shelley). For voice and piano. 1895. Pub. (114/50) No. 110; (10).

21. Fugues. For organ and strings. 1892–5.

22. Intercollegiate March. For military band. 1896. Pub. 1896, Pepper (Philadelphia).

23. In the alley (After a session at Poli's) (Charles Ives). For voice and piano. 1896. Pub. (114) No. 53 (as *Five Street Songs* No. 2); (13).

24. An old flame (Charles Ives). For voice and piano. 1896. Pub. (114) No. 87 (as *Sentimental Ballads* No. 3); (13).

25. Marie (R. v. Gottschall). For voice and piano. 1896. Pub. (114/50) No. 92 (as *Sentimental Ballads* No. 8); (14).

26. From 'Amphion' (Tennyson). For voice and piano. 1896. Pub. (114/50) No. 106; (10).

26a. A Scotch Lullaby. For voice and piano. 1896. Pub. December 1896, The Yale Courant.

27. String Quartet No. 1. 1896. 'A Revival Service.'

1. *Andante con moto*; 2. *Allegro*; 3. *Adagio cantabile*; 4. *Allegro marziale*.

Other forms have been quoted as follows:
(a) 1. *Fugue*; 2. *Prelude*; 3. *Offertory*; 4. *Postlude*.
(b) 1. *Prelude: Allegro*; 2. *Offertory: Adagio cantabile* ('from an organ prelude played in 1898'); 3. *Postlude: Allegro marziale—Andante con moto—Allegro marziale*.

f public p: 1957, New York, Museum of Modern Art.

Pub. ?1952, 1961, 1963, Peer.

28. 'Adeste Fidelis' in an organ prelude. 1897 (?1891). Pub. 1949, Music Press (New York); Mercury.

29. For you and me. Partsong for male voices. ?1896. Pub. *c.* 1896, Geo. Molineux (New York).

29a. A Song of Mory's (C. E. Merrill, Jr.). Partsong for TTBB. *c.* 1896. Pub. February 1897, The Yale Courant.

29b. The Bells of Yale. For solo, TTBB and piano. ?1897. Pub. 1963, Th. G. Shepard (New Haven).

30. William Will (S. B. Hill). A McKinley campaign song. 1896. Pub. 1896, Willis Woodward (New York).

31. Dreams (Porteous). For voice and piano. 1897. Pub. (114) No. 85 (as *Sentimental Ballads* No. 1); (9).

32. My native land (Anon.). For voice and piano. 1897. Pub. (114) No. 101; (12).

33. Memories: A, Very Pleasant, B, Very Sad (Charles Ives). For voice and piano. 1897. Pub. (114) No. 102; (10).

34. De la drama: Rosamunde (?Bélanger, from v. Chezy). For voice and piano. 1898. Pub. (114) No. 79; (14).

35. In summer fields (Feldeinsamkeit) (Almers, transl. Chapman). For voice and piano 1897. Pub. (114) No. 82 (as *German Songs* No. 3); October 1935, in *New Music* (Vol. 9, No. 1).

36. Psalm 67. For SATB chorus a cappella. 1898. Pub. 1939, Arrow.

37. The Celestial Country. Cantata. 1898–1899. Pub. 1952, Peer.

37a. Forward into light (Alford, from St. Bernard). Aria for tenor or soprano from 'The Celestial Country'. 1898. Pub. (114) No. 99; (10).

37b. Nought that country needeth (Alford, from St. Bernard). Aria for baritone from 'The Celestial Country'. 1899. Pub. (114/50) No. 98; (14).

38. Symphony No. 1 in D minor. 1896–May 1898.

1. *Allegro moderato*; 2. *Adagio molto*; 3. *Scherzo* (*Vivace*); 4. *Allegro molto*.

Pub. Peer.

39. The South Wind (Charles Ives) (?Harmony T. Ives). For voice and piano. 1899. Orig. composed to 'Die Lotusblume'. Pub. (114/50) No. 97; October 1933, in *New Music* (Vol. 7, No. 1).

40. Ich grolle nicht (I'll not complain) (Heine, transl. John S. Dwight). For voice and piano. 1899. Pub. (114) No. 83 (as *German Songs* No. 4); October 1933, in *New Music* (Vol. 7, No. 1).

41. From 'Night (of) frost in May' (Meredith). For voice and piano. 1899. Pub. (114/50) No. 84; October 1935, in *New Music* (Vol. 9, No. 1).

42. Omens and oracles (Anon.). For voice and piano. ?1900. Pub. (114) No. 66 (as *Sentimental Ballads* No. 2); (10).

43. The old mother (Vinje, transl. Corder). For voice and piano. 1900. Pub. (114) No. 81 (as *German Songs* No. 2); (13).

44. Berceuse (Charles Ives). For voice and piano. 1900. Pub. (114/50) No. 93; (13).

45. Where the eagle (M. P. Turnbull). For voice and piano. 1900. Pub. (114) No. 94; (13).

46. Allegro (Harmony T. Ives). For voice and piano. 1900. Pub. (114) No. 95; (13).

47. A Christmas Carol (Anon.). For voice and piano. Before 1900. Pub. (114/50) No. 100; October 1935, in *New Music* (Vol. 9, No. 1).

48. Romanzo di Central Park (Leigh Hunt). For voice and piano. 1900. Pub. (114) No. 96.

49. Prelude from Pre-First Sonata. For violin and piano. 1900.

50. Largo. For violin, clarinet and piano. 1901.
fEbp: 22 May 1962, Hugh Maguire, Gabor Reeves and Joyce Rathbone. Pub. 1953, Southern.

51. Processional: Let there be Light (John Ellerton). For SATB chorus and piano. 1901.

51a. Let there be Light. Version for male chorus or trombones, organ, and an extra organ player or four violins. 'To the choir of the Central Presbyterian Church, Dec. 1901.' Pub. 1950, Peer.

52. The children's hour (Longfellow). For voice and piano. 1901. Pub. (114/50) No. 74; October 1933, in *New Music* (Vol. 7, No. 1).

53. I travelled among unknown men (Wordsworth). For voice and piano. 1901. Pub. (114/50) No. 75; (10).

54. Qu'il m'irait bien (Anon.). For voice and piano. 1901. Pub. (114) No. 76 (as *French Songs* No. 1); (12).

55. Elegie (Gallet). For voice and piano. 1901. Pub. (114/50) No. 77 (as *French Songs* No. 2); (9).

56. Chanson de Florian (J. P. Claris de Florian). For voice and piano. 1901. Pub. (114) No. 78 (as *French Songs* No. 3); 1950, Mercury.

57. From the steeples (and from the mountains). For bells (chimes) or 2 pianos, trumpet and trombone. 1901. Pub. 1965, Peer.

58. Symphony No. 2. 1897–1901.
1. *Andante moderato*; 2. *Allegro*; 3. *Adagio cantabile*; 4. *Lento maestoso*; 5. *Allegro molto vivace*.
2 fl, pic, 2 ob, 2 cl, 2 bsn, cbsn; 4 hn, 2 tpt, 3 tmb, tuba; timp, snare dm, GC; strings.
fp: 22 February 1951, New York.
fEbp: 25 April 1956, London Symphony Orchestra, cond. Bernard Herrmann.
Pub. 1951, Southern.

BIBLIOGRAPHY:
Henry Cowell: Current chronicle—Symphony No. 2, *MQ*, July 1951, p. 399.
Sydney Robinson Charles: The use of borrowed material in Ives's Second Symphony, *MR*, May 1967, p. 102.

59. Walking (Charles Ives). For voice and piano. 1902. Pub. (114) No. 67.

60. Ilmenau (Over all the treetops) (Goethe, transl. Harmony T. Ives). For voice and piano. 1902. Pub. (114/50) No. 68.

61. Rough wind (Shelley). From Symphony (1898) arr. voice and piano. 1902. Pub. (114) No. 69; October 1933, in *New Music* (Vol. 7, No. 1).

62. Mirage (C. G. Rossetti). For voice and piano. 1902. Pub. (114/50) No. 70; (10).

63. There is a lane (Harmony T. Ives). For voice and piano. 1902. Pub. (114/50) No. 71; (9).

64. Tarrant Moss (Rudyard Kipling). For voice and piano. 1902. Pub. (114) No. 72.

65. Slugging a vampire (Charles Ives). For voice and piano. Version of preceding. Pub. October 1935, in *New Music* (Vol. 9, No. 1).

66. Harpalus: An ancient pastoral (Thomas Percy). For voice and piano. 1902. Pub. (114)

No. 73; October 1933, in *New Music* (Vol. 7, No. 1).

67. Weil' auf mir (Lenau, transl. Westbrook). For voice and piano. 1902. Pub. (114) No. 80 (as *German Songs* No. 1); (14).

68. Spring song (Harmony T. Ives). For voice and piano. 1904. Pub. (114/50) No. 65; (12).

69. The light that is felt (Whittier). For voice and piano. 1904. Pub. (114/50) No. 66; 1950, Mercury.

70. Symphony No. 3. For chamber orchestra. 1901–4, slightly rev. 1911. 'The Camp Meeting.' Dur. 17'.
   1. *Andante maetoso* (Old folks gatherin').
   2. *Allegro* (Children's day).
   3. *Largo* (Communion).
   fl, ob, cl, bsn; 2 hn, tmb; bells (ad lib); strings.
   fp: 5 May 1947, New York.
   Pub. 1947, Arrow; Associated Music Publishers.

71. General Slocum. July 1904. Fragmentary sketches only.

72. Autumn Landscape from Pine Mountain. For strings, woodwind and cornet. 1904. Fragmentary sketches only.

73. Pre-Second String Quartet. 1905.

74. Three-Page Sonata. For piano. August 1905, Saranac Lake. Pub. 1949, Mercury (ed. Henry Cowell).

75. The Pond. For strings, flute and voice, or cor anglais, harp, bells or celesta or piano. 1906. Pub. as No. 2 of *Three Outdoor Scenes*.

76. The Cage (Charles Ives). For voice and piano. 1906. Adapted from No. 1 of *Set* for theatre or chamber orchestra. Pub. (114) No. 63; (14).

77. Central Park in the dark. For chamber orchestra. 1898–1907.
   fl, pic, ob, cl, bsn; tpt, tmb; snare dm, GC; 2 pianos (3 players), strings.
   Pub. 1949, Bomart, as No. 3 of *Three Outdoor Scenes*.

78. Calcium Light Night. For chamber orchestra. 1898–1907.

fl, cl, bsn; 2 tpt, tmb; snare dm, GC, timp, gong (ab lib); piano, strings.
   Pub. 1953, in *New Music* (Vol. 26, No. 4).

79. Space and Duration. For string quartet and mechanical piano. 1907. Sketches only; incomplete.

80. All the way around and back. Scherzo for piano (one or two players), violin (or flute), flute (or clarinet), bugle (or trumpet), bells (or horn). ?1907. Pub. 1953, Peer.

81. Soliloquy, or a study in 7ths and other things (Charles Ives). For voice and piano. 1907. Pub. October 1933, in *New Music* (Vol. 7, No. 1).

82. Those evening bells (Thomas Moore). For voice and piano. 1907. Pub. (114) No. 63; (14).

83. Yale-Princeton Game. August 1907. Sketches only; incomplete.

83a. Giants vs. Cubs. August 1907. Sketches only; incomplete.

84. Autumn (Harmony T. Ives). For voice and piano. 1908. Pub. (114) No. 60; (9).

85. Nature's way (Charles Ives). For voice and piano. 1908. Pub. (114/50) No. 61; (14).

86. The waiting soul (William Cowper). For voice and piano. 1908. Pub. (114) No. 62; (12).

87. Some southpaw pitching. For piano. 1908. Pub. 1949, Mercury (ed. Henry Cowell).

88. The anti-Abolitionist riots in Boston in the 1830s and the 1840s. For piano. 1908–9. Pub. 1949, Mercury (ed. Henry Cowell).

89. The unanswered question. For chamber ensemble or orchestra. 1908. Dur. 8'.
   4 fl (or 2 fl, 3rd fl or ob, 4th fl or cl); tpt (or ca, or ob, or cl); str quartet (or str orchestra).
   fEp: 10 October 1959, Royal Festival Hall, New York Philharmonic, cond. Leonard Bernstein.
   Pub. October 1941, in *Boletín Latino Americano de Musica*, No. 5; 1953, Southern.

90. The innate. For string quartet (basso ad lib) and piano. November 1908.

90a. The innate. Version for voice and piano (or organ). 1916. Pub. (114) No. 40; October 1935, in *New Music* (Vol. 9, No. 1).

91. In re con moto. For string quartet and piano. 1908. Pub. 1953, Peer.

92. Largo Risoluto No. 1 (The Law of Diminishing Returns). For string quartet and piano. ?1908. Pub. 1961.

93. Largo Risoluto No. 2 (A Shadow Made —a Silhouette). For piano and string quartet. ?1908. Pub. 1961.

94. Violin Sonata No. 1. 1903–8 (?1902–1910).
1. *Andante—Allegro vivace*; 2. *Largo cantabile*; 3. *Allegro*.
Pub. 1953, Peer.

95. Allegro sombreoso. For flute, cor anglais (or trumpet, or basset horn), three violins and piano. Before 1910. Pub. 1958, Peer.

96. Like a sick eagle (Keats). Intonation for cor anglais (or basset horn), voices in unison (ad lib), string quintet, flute and piano. 1909.

96a. Like a sick eagle. Version for voice and piano. 1919–20. Pub. (114/50) No. 26; October 1933, in *New Music* (Vol. 7, No. 1).

97. Piano Sonata No. 1. 1902–9.
1. *Adagio con moto*; 2. *Allegro moderato—'In the inn'* (*Allegro*); 3. *Largo—Allegro*; 4. (?) *Andante—Allegro—Presto*; 5. *Andante maestoso—Adagio cantabile—Allegro*.
Pub. 1954, Peer.

98. Violin Sonata No. 2. 1902–10.
1. *Autumn* (Adagio maestoso—Allegro moderato). 1907.
2. *In the barn* (Presto). 1902–7.
3. *The revival* (Largo—Allegretto). 1906, 1909–10.
Pub. 1951, Schirmer.

99. Mists (Harmony T. Ives). For voice and piano. 1910. Pub. (114/50) No. 57; October 1933, in *New Music* (Vol. 7, No. 1).

100. Evidence (Charles Ives). For voice and piano. 1910. Pub. (114) No. 58; (9).

101. Requiem (Robert Louis Stevenson). For voice and piano. November 1911. Pub. October 1935, in *New Music* (Vol. 9, No. 1).

102. Set. Also known as *Theatre Orchestra Set*. For chamber or theatre orchestra. 1904–11.
1. *In the cage* (Andante). 1906.
ob (or fl), ca; timp; piano, strings.
2. *In the inn* (Potpourri) (Allegro). 1904–11.
cl, bsn (or bar sax); timp; piano, violin, viola, cello.
3. *In the night* (Adagio molto).
bells (high and low); harps and violins (or alternative instruments); horn solo, piano (2 players), cellos and basses.
Pub. January 1932, in *New Music* (Vol. 5, No. 2).
For version of *In the cage* as a song see No. 76. For version of *In the inn* as piano solo see No. 97.

103. Tone Roads No. 1. For small orchestra. 1911. Dur. 7–8'.
fl, cl, bsn; strings.
fEbp: 29 October 1960, BBC Symphony Orchestra, cond. Bruno Maderna.
Pub. 1949, Peer.

104. Hallowe'en. For two violins, viola, cello and piano. 1911. Pub. 1949, Bomart, as No. 1 of *Three Outdoor Scenes*.

105. Robert Browning Overture. For large orchestra. 1911. Dur. 24'.
2 fl, pic, 2 ob, ca, 2 cl, 2 bsn, cbsn; 4 hn, 2 tpt, 3 tmb, tuba; timp, snare dm, GC, cym; strings.
fp: 14 October 1956, Symphony of the Air, cond. Leopold Stokowski. (Four missing pages recomposed with the composer's consent by Henry Cowell and Lou Harrison.)
Pub. 1959, Peer.

106. The gong on the hook and ladder, or Firemen's parade on Main Street. For chamber orchestra. Before 1912 (?1911). Dur. 3'.
fl, cl, bsn; 2 tpt, tmb; timp, gong (ad lib), snare dm, tgle; piano, strings.
Pub. 1960, Peer.

107. Ragtime Dances. 'About a dozen, mostly for small theatre orchestra, most used elsewhere.' 1900–11.

108. Piano Trio. 1904–11
1. *Andante moderato*; 2. *Tsiaj: Presto*; 3. *Moderato con moto—Maestoso—Allegro moderato*.
Pub. 1951, Peer.

109. Three harvest home chorales. For SATB and piano or organ and brass. 1898–1912.
1. *Harvest home* (Georges Burgess). 1898.
2. *Lord of the harvest* (John Hampton Gurney).
3. *Harvest home* (Henry ? Alford).
Pub. 1950, Mercury (ed. Henry Cowell).

110. Lincoln, the great commoner. For chorus and large orchestra. 1912. Pub. 1932, *New Music*, repr. January 1953.

110a. Lincoln, the great commoner (Edwin Markham). Version for voice and piano. 1921. Pub. (114) No. 11.

111. '22.' For piano. 1912, Hartsdale, N.Y.
1. *Andante maestoso*; 2. *Allegro vivace (as fast as possible)*.
Pub. October 1947, in *New Music* (Vol. 21, No. 1).

112. The camp meeting (Charlotte Elliott, in part). For voice and piano. 1912. From a movement of *Symphony No. 3*. Pub. (114) No. 47; (13).

113. A Symphony: New England Holidays. 1904–13.
1. *Washington's birthday*. For chamber orchestra. Fall 1909, rescored 1913.
fl, hn, bells (ad lib), strings, pic, Jew's harp.
Pub. October 1936, *New Music*; Associated Music Publishers.
2. *Decoration Day*. For large orchestra. 1912. Pub. Peer.
3. *The Fourth of July*. For large orchestra. 1912–13.
2 fl, pic, 2 ob, 2 cl, 2 bsn, cbsn; 4 hn, 2 tpt, 2 cornets, 3 tmb, tuba; timp, tamb rulante, GC, campana (high and low), cym, xyl, piano, strings.
Pub. 1932, New Music; Associated Music Publishers.
4. *Thanksgiving* (and Forefathers Day). For large orchestra and chorus. August 1904. Ded. Edward Carrington Twichell. Pub. Peer.

BIBLIOGRAPHY:
A. Orga: Anglo-American, *M&M*, December 1967, p. 46.

114. Over the pavements. Scherzo for chamber orchestra. 1906–13. Dur. 11'.
pic, cl, bsn (or sax); tpt, 3 tmb; cym, dm; piano.
fEbp: 29 October 1960, BBC Symphony Orchestra, cond. Bruno Maderna.
Pub. 1954, Peer.

115. December. For unison men's chorus, woodwind and brass. 1912–13. Words: Folgore Da San Geminiano, transl. Rossetti. Dur. 1½'.
pic, 2 cl, 2 hn, 3 tpt, 3 tmb, tuba.
Pub. ? 1952, 1963, Peer.

115a. December. Version for voice and piano. 1920. Pub. (114) No. 37; October 1933, in *New Music* (Vol. 7, No. 1).

116. String Quartet No. 2. 1907–13.
1. *Discussions* (Andante moderato). 1911–1913.
2. *Arguments* (Allegro con spirito). 1907.
3. *The Call of the Mountains* (Adagio). 1911–1913.
Pub. 1954, Peer.

117. Watchman! (John Bowring). For voice and piano. 1913. Adapted from Violin Sonata No. 2. Pub. (114/50) No. 44; (14).

118. His Exaltation (Robert Robinson). For voice and piano. 1913. Adapted from Violin Sonata No. 2. Pub. (114) No. 46; (9).

119. The See'r. Scherzo for cornet, trumpet (or French horn), clarinet, alto horn (or French horn), or trombone (or tenor saxophone), piano and drums. Before May 1913.

119a. The See'r (Charles Ives). Version for voice and piano. 1920. Pub. (114) No. 29.

120. Three Places in New England (Orchestral Set No. 1). 1903–14. Also known as *A New England Symphony*.
1. *The 'St. Gaudens' in Boston Common* (Col. Shaw and his Colored Regiment).
2. *Putnam's Camp, Redding, Connecticut*.
3. *From 'The Housatonic at Stockbridge'*.
fl, pic, ob/ca, cl, bsn; hns, tpts, tmbs, tuba;

S

timp, dms, long snare dm or small timp, GC
& cym; piano, organ, strings.

fp: 10 January 1931, New York, Chamber
Orchestra of Boston, cond. Nicolas Slonimsky.

fEp: 21 March 1960, BBC broadcast,
London Symphony Orchestra, cond. Walter
Goehr.

fEp (concert): 9 September 1960, Royal
Albert Hall, Promenade Concert, London
Symphony Orchestra, cond. Basil Cameron.

Pub. 1935, Birchard; Mercury.

**120a. From 'The Housatonic at Stock-
bridge'** (Robert Underwood Johnson). Version for voice and piano. 1921. Pub. (114) No.
15; (12).

**121. General William Booth enters into
Heaven** (General William Booth's entrance
into Heaven) (Vachel Lindsay). For voice and
piano. 1914.

Pub. October 1935, in *New Music* (Vol. 9,
No. 1).

122. The rainbow (or, So may it be)
(Wordsworth). For voice and chamber
orchestra. 1914.

fl, basset hn (or ca), strings (2-2-2-2-2) and
piano.

Pub. 1959, Peer.

122a. The rainbow. Version for voice and
instruments. 1914.

fl, hp (or piano), celesta and organ.

122b. So may it be. Versio for voice and
piano. 1921. Pub. (114) No. 8.

123. Duty (Emerson). For male chorus and
orchestra. Before 1914.

123a. Duty. Version for voice and piano.
1921. Pub. with *Vita* (114/50) No. 9; October
1933, in *New Music* (Vol. 7, No. 1).

124. (Piano pieces and studies). 1910–14.

125. Three Protests. For piano. 1914.

1. *March time or faster*; 2. *Adagio or allegro or
varied or/and variations, very nice*; 3. *(unmarked)*.

Pub. October 1947, *New Music* (Vol. 21,
No. 1).

126. Violin Sonata No. 3. 1914.

1. *Adagio* (verse 1), *Andante* (verse 2), *Con
moto—Allegretto* (verse 3), *Adagio* (last verse);
2. *Allegro*; 3. *Adagio* (*cantabile*).

fEbp: 6 August 1957, Louis Kaufman and
Frederick Stone. (A gramophone recording
had been broadcast in December 1954.)

Pub. January 1951, *New Music* (Vol. 24,
No. 2) (ed. Sol Babitz and Ingolf Dahl).

127. Set. For string quartet, basso and piano.
1903–14. Three movements that 'may be
played together'.

1. *Hymn*. Largo cantabile for string quartet
and basso (male voice) or solo cello. 1904.

2. *Scherzo*. For string quartet, basso (string
bass) ad lib. 1903 & 1914 (middle section).

3. *The innate*. For string quartet and piano.
1908. (Same as No. 90).

Pub. ?1951, 1958, Peer.

127a. Hymn (Professor Shutter). Version for
voice and piano. 1921. Pub. (114/50) No. 20;
October 1933, in *New Music* (Vol. 7, No. 1).

128. Piano Sonata No. 2 ('Concord, Mass.,
1840–60'). 1909–15.

1. *Emerson*. 1909–summer 1912.

2. *Hawthorne*. Scherzo. 12 October 1915.

3. *The Allcotts*. 1915.

4. *Thoreau*. 1911–15.

f public p (complete): 1949, William
Masselos.

Pub. 1920, privately printed; 1947, Arrow
(ed. John Kirkpatrick).

BIBLIOGRAPHY:

Henry Bellamann: Concord, Mass., 1840–60
—A Piano Sonata by CI, *The Double Dealer*,
October 1921, p. 166.

Lawrence Gilman: A masterpiece of American
music: The Concord Sonata, *New York
Herald Tribune*, 21 January 1939.

Paul Rosenfeld: Ives's Concord Sonata, *Modern
Music*, January–February 1939, p. 109.

128a. Thoreau (Charles Ives). For voice and
piano. 1915. Adapted from themes in Piano
Sonata No. 2. Pub. (114) No. 48; October
1933, in *New Music* (Vol. 7, No. 1).

129. Orchestral Set No. 2. 1912–15.

1. *An Elegy to our Forefathers*; 2. *The Rock-
strewn Hills join in the People's Outdoor Meeting*;
3. *From Hanover Square North at the End of a
Tragic Day* (1915), *the Voice of the People Again
Rose*.

Pub. Peer.

130. Tone Roads No. 3. For chamber orchestra. 1915. Dur. 9′.

fl, cl, tpt, tmb, chimes, piano, strings.

fEbp: 29 October 1960, BBC Symphony Orchestra, cond. Bruno Maderna.

Pub. 1952, Peer.

131. Violin Sonata No. 4 (Children's Day at the Camp Meeting). 1912–15. Dur. 9½′.

1. *Allegro*; 2. *Largo*; 3. *Allegro*.

fEbp: 24 June 1948, Jean Pougnet and Wilfrid Parry.

Pub. 1942, Arrow.

132. On the Antipodes. For two pianos or organ and string orchestra. 1915.

132a. On the Antipodes. For voice and piano four hands. 1923. Pub. October 1935, in *New Music* (Vol. 9, No. 1).

133. Symphony No. 4. 1910–16. Dur. *c.* 30′.

1. *Prelude* (*Maestoso*); 2. *Scherzo* (*Allegretto*); 3. *Fugue* (*Andante moderato*); 4. *Finale* (*Largo maestoso*).

3 fl, 2 pic, 2 ob, 3 cl, 3 sax (ad lib), 3 bsn; 4 hn, 2 cornets, 6 tpt, 3 tmb, tuba; timp, snare dm, mil dm, tomtom, GC, cym, gongs (light & heavy), bells (low & high), tgle; piano 4 hands, piano solo, celesta, organ, theremin (ad lib, later suggestion by the composer); strings plus (distant), 2(4) violins, viola (and/or cl), and hp; 5 violins, 2 hp (4th movement); SATB chorus. 'Battery unit' (4th movement): snare dm, small timp or medium dm, cym & GC, gong.

fp (two movements only): 29 January 1927, New York, Pro Musica concert, orchestra of New York Philharmonic, cond. (Sir) Eugene Goossens.

fEp (two movements only): 6 November 1946, BBC Symphony Orchestra, cond. Bernard Herrmann.

fp (complete): 26 April 1965, New York, American Symphony Orchestra, cond. Leopold Stokowski.

Pub. (first two movements only): January 1929, *New Music* (Vol. 2, No. 2); 1965 (full score). No. 3 arr. for radio orchestra by Bernard Herrmann, for piano by John Kirkpatrick.

BIBLIOGRAPHY:

Arthur Cohn: Divine document—the Ives Fourth, *American Record Guide*, November 1965, p. 220.

David Drew: Fourth Symphony, *New Statesman*, 30 September 1966, p. 489.

R. Franceschini: Postscript on Ives's Fourth, *American Record Guide*, November 1965, p. 223.

A Frankenstein: Ives's Fourth Symphony, an unplayable work gets played, *High Fidelity*, November 1965, p. 83.

Glenn Gould: Ives Fourth, *High Fidelity*, July 1965, p. 96.

I. Kolodin: Music to my ears: Stokowski's performance with the American Symphony Orchestra of CI's Fourth Symphony, *Saturday Review*, 15 May 1965, p. 32.

W. Sargeant: Fourth Symphony performed by American Orchestra, *New Yorker*, 8 May 1965, p. 169.

Kurt Stone: Ives's Fourth Symphony, a review, *MQ*, January 1966, p. 1.

Anon.: Ives's tremendous symphony, *The Times*, 30 April 1965, p. 17.

Anon.: Cantankerous Yankee: world première of Fourth Symphony, *Time*, 7 May 1965, p. 56.

134. Universe Symphony. 1911–16, with subsequent additions. Fragments only.

135. At the river (Robert Lowry). For voice and piano. 1916. Adapted from Violin Sonata No. 4. Pub. (114) No. 45; October 1933, in *New Music* (Vol. 7, No. 1).

136. Serenity (A unison chant) (Whittier). For voice and piano. 1916 (?1919). Pub. (114) No. 42.

137. He is there! ('Here is there!') (Charles Ives). For voice and piano. 30 May 1917. Pub. (114) No. 50 (as *Three Songs of War* No. 2); (9) as *They are there*.

137a. A War Song March: They are there! (Charles Ives). Enlarged version for unison chorus and symphony orchestra. 1917. Dur. 3′.

2 fl, pic, 2 ob, 2 cl, 2 bsn; 4 hn, 3 tpt, 3 tmb, tuba; snare dm, GC, tubular chimes; piano, strings.

Pub. 1952, 1962, Peer (ed. Lou Harrison). Pub. 1961, for unison chorus and piano.

138. Tom sails away (Charles Ives). For voice and piano. 1917. Pub. (114) No. 51 (as *Three Songs of War* No. 3); October 1935, in *New Music* (Vol. 9, No. 1).

139. The things our fathers loved (and the greatest of these was Liberty) (Charles Ives). For voice and piano. 1917. Pub. (114) No. 43; (14).

140. Premonitions (Robert Underwood Johnson). For voice or unison chorus with small orchestra. 1917. From Pieces for basset horn, flute, strings and piano.

140a. Premonitions. Version for voice and piano. Pub. (114) No. 24; October 1933, in *New Music* (Vol. 7, No. 1).

141. Cradle song (A. L. Ives). For voice and piano. 1919. Pub. (114/50) No. 33; October 1935, in *New Music* (Vol. 9, No. 1).

142. Afterglow (James Fenimore Cooper Jr.). For voice and piano. 1919. Pub. (114) No. 39; October 1933, in *New Music* (Vol. 7, No. 1).

143. In Flanders fields (John McCrae). For voice and piano. 1917. Pub. (114) No. 49 (as *Three Songs of War* No. 1); (14).

144. Down East (Charles Ives). For voice and piano. 1919. Pub. (114) No. 55 (as *Five Street Songs* No. 5); (13).

145. Tone Roads No. 2. 1911–19. Unpub.

145a. Chromatimelodtune. For brass quartet and piano. ?1913–?1919.

146. The Celestial Railroad. Fantasy for piano. ?1919. Arr. by the composer from second movement of Symphony No. 4.

147. Old home day (Charles Ives). For voice and piano. 1920. Pub. (114/50) No. 52 (as *Five Street Songs* No. 1); (13).

148. Luck and work (Robert Underwood Johnson). For voice and piano. 1920. From pieces for basset horn, three violins, piano and drum, 1916. Pub. (114) No. 21; October 1933, in *New Music* (Vol. 7, No. 1).

149. Grantchester (with a quotation from Debussy) (Rupert Brooke). For voice and piano. 1920. Pub. (114/50) No. 17; (9).

150. Religion (Root as quoted by Dr. James T. Bixby). For voice and piano. 1920. Pub. (114/50) No. 16; (12).

151. An election (Charles Ives). For male voice or unison chorus and orchestra. 1920. Also known as *It strikes me that* or *November 2, 1920*.

151a. An election. Version for voice and piano. 1921. Pub. October 1935, in *New Music* (Vol. 9, No. 1).

152. August (Folgore da San Geminiano, transl. Rossetti). For voice and piano. 1920. Pub. (114) No. 35; (12).

153. The collection (Stanzas from old hymns). For voice and piano. 1920. Pub. (114) No. 38; (13).

154. La Fède (Ariosto). For voice and piano. 1920. Pub. (114/50) No. 34; October 1935, in *New Music* (Vol. 9, No. 1).

155. Maple leaves (Thomas Bailey Aldrich). For voice and piano. 1920. Pub. (114) No. 23.

156. September (Folgore da San Geminiano, transl. Rossetti). For voice and piano. 1920. Pub. (114) No. 36; October 1933, in *New Music* (Vol. 7, No. 1).

157. On the counter (Charles Ives). For voice and piano. 1920. Pub. (114) No. 28; (14).

158. Set. For instrumental ensemble. 1912–1921.

 1. *The new river.* For trumpet, clarinet, saxophone, piano and four violins (ad lib). 1912. Pub. 1951, Peer.

 2. *The Indians.* For trumpet, oboe, strings and piano. 1921.

 3. *Ann Street.* For trumpet, flute, trombone or baritone horn or baritone saxophone and piano.
 See also Nos. 166 and 167.

159. West London: A Sonnet (Matthew Arnold). For voice and piano. 1921. From an uncompleted overture 'Mathew Arnold' (*sic*), 1912. Pub. (114/50) No. 105; October 1933, in *New Music* (Vol. 7, No. 1).

160. Two little flowers (and dedicated to them) (Harmony T. Ives). For voice and piano. 1921. Pub. (114/50) No. 104; October 1933, in *New Music* (Vol. 7, No. 1).

161. The white gulls (Maurice Morris). For voice and piano. 1921. Pub. (114/50) No. 103; October 1933, in *New Music* (Vol. 7, No. 1).

162. Tolerance (President Hadley). For voice and piano. 1921. Adapted from a piece for orchestra, 1909. Pub. (114) No. 59; October 1933, in *New Music* (Vol. 7, No. 1).

163. Walt Whitman (Whitman). For voice and piano. 1921. Pub. (114/50) No. 31; October 1933, in *New Music* (Vol. 7, No. 1).

164. From 'Paracelsus' (Robert Browning). For voice and piano. 1921. Adapted from instrumental music of 1912. Pub. (114/50) No. 30; October 1935, in *New Music* (Vol. 9, No. 1).

165. From 'The Swimmers' (Louis Untermeyer). For voice and piano. 1915–21. Pub. (114) No. 27; October 1933, in *New Music* (Vol. 7, No. 1).

166. Ann Street (Maurice Morris). For voice and piano. 1921. Pub. (114) No. 25; October 1933, in *New Music* (Vol. 7, No. 1).

167. The Indians (Charles Sprague). For voice and piano. 1921. Adapted from instrumental music of 1912. Pub. (114/50) No. 14.

168. Resolution (Charles Ives). For voice and piano. 1921. Pub. (114/50) No. 13. October 1935, in *New Music* (Vol. 9, No. 1).

169. A sound of a distant horn (? Charles Ives). For voice and piano. Pub. (114) No. 12.

170. Charlie Rutlage (from 'Cowboy Songs' collected by John Lomax). For voice and piano. 1921. Pub. (114/50) No. 10.

171. Vita (Manlius). For voice and piano. 1921. Pub. (with *Duty*) (114/50) No. 9; October 1933, in *New Music* (Vol. 7, No. 1).

172. Disclosure (Charles Ives). For voice and piano. 1921. Pub. (114/50) No. 7; (12).

173. Immortality (Charles Ives). For voice and piano. 1921. Pub. (114/50) No. 5; October 1933, in *New Music* (Vol. 7, No. 1).

174. At sea (Robert Underwood Johnson). For voice and piano. 1921. Pub. (114/50) No. 4; October 1933, in *New Music* (Vol. 7, No. 1).

175. The last reader (Oliver Wendell Holmes). For voice and piano. 1921. Adapted from Pieces for two flutes, cornet, violas and organ, 1911. Pub. (114/50) No. 3; October 1933, in *New Music* (Vol. 7, No. 1).

176. Evening (Milton). For voice and piano. 1921. Pub. (114/50) No. 2.

177. The majority (or, The masses) (Charles Ives). For voice and piano. 1921. Adapted from a chorus with orchestra, 1915. Pub. (114) No. 1; October 1935, in *New Music* (Vol. 9, No. 1).

178. The greatest man (Anne Collins). For voice and piano. 1921. Pub. (114/50) No. 19; October 1933, in *New Music* (Vol. 7, No. 1).

179. From 'The Incantations' (Byron). For voice and piano. 1921. Adapted from a song for cor anglais with violin, flute and piano, before 1910. Pub. (114) No. 18; October 1933, in *New Music* (Vol. 7, No. 1).

180. The side show (Charles Ives). For voice and piano. 1921. Pub. (114) No. 31; (12).

181. Remembrance (Charles Ives). For voice and piano. 1921. Pub. (114/50) No. 12; (12).

182. '1,2,3' (Charles Ives). For voice and piano. 1921. Pub. (114) No. 41; 1950, Mercury.

183. Aeschylus and Sophocles (Landor). For voice and piano. 1922. Pub. October 1935, in *New Music* (Vol. 9, No. 1).

184. Three quarter-tone piano pieces. For piano. 1923–4. Possibly derived from piano pieces of 1903–4.
  1. *Largo*; 2. *Allegro*; 3. *Adagio: chorale*.
  Pub. 1970, Hinrichsen (ed. George Pappastavrou) for two pianos four hands.

185. A farewell to land (Byron). For voice and piano. 1925. Pub. October 1935, in *New Music* (Vol. 9, No. 1).

186. Psalm XXIV. For SATB a cappella. ?Date. Pub. 1955, Mercury.

WRITINGS BY CHARLES IVES
Essays before a sonata, Knickerbocker Press

Ives, Charles

(New York) 1920. Essays before a sonata and other writings (ed. Howard Boatwright), Norton (New York) 1961; (unedited) in *Three Classics in the Aesthetic of Music*, New York, 1962.
Music and its future, in *American Composers on American Music* (ed. Henry Cowell), Stanford University Press, 1933, p. 191.
Children's day at the camp meeting: a program note for the Fourth Violin Sonata, *Modern Music*, January–February 1942.
Memos (ed. John Kirkpatrick), W. W. Norton, 1972.

GENERAL BIBLIOGRAPHY

G. Balanchine: Ivesiana, *Center*, August–September 1954, p. 5.
J. J. Becker: CI, composer with something to say, *Etude*, May 1956, p. 11.
Henry Bellamann: The music of CI, *Pro Musica*, March–April 1927, p. 16.
— CI, the man and his music, *MQ*, January 1933, p. 45.
A. Berger: Ives in retrospect, *Saturday Review*, 31 July 1954, p. 62.
Howard Boatwright: Ives's quarter-tone impressions, *PNM*, spring–summer 1965, p. 22.
Elliott Carter: The case of Mr. Ives, *Modern Music*, March–April 1939, p. 172.
— Ives today, his vision and his challenge, *Modern Music*, May–June 1944, p. 199.
— An American destiny, *Listen*, November 1946, p. 4.
— Shop talk by an American composer, *MQ*, April 1960, p. 198.
Robert Cogan: CI, *Musik och ljudteknik*, 1961, No. 1, p. 4.
Israel Citkowitz: Experiment and necessity, *Modern Music*, January–February 1933, p. 122.
Arthur Cohn: Ives, *American Record Guide*, 1964, p. 761.
Paul Cooper: CI et sa musique, *Zvuk*, No. 68, 1966.
Aaron Copland: One Hundred and Fourteen Songs, *Modern Music*, January–February 1934, p. 59.
— The Ives case, in *Our New Music*, Whittlevey House (New York) 1941, p. 149.

Macdonald (revised and enlarged edition) 1968, p. 109.
Henry Cowell: Four little known modern composers: Chavez, Ives, Slonimsky, Weiss, *Aesthete*, August 1928, pp. 1, 19.
— Three native composers: Ives, Ruggles, Harris, *The New Freeman*, 3 May 1930.
— CI, *Disques*, November 1932, p. 374.
— CI, *Modern Music*, November–December 1932, p. 24.
— CI, in *American Composers on American Music*, Stanford University Press 1933, p. 128.
— Current chronicle: the sonatas, *MQ*, July 1949, p. 458.
— The music and motives of CI, *Center*, August–September 1954, p. 2.
Henry Cowell & Sidney Cowell: CI, *Perspective U.S.A.*, No. 13, 1955, p. 38.
— CI and his music, O.U.P. (New York) 1955.
David Cox: CI, 'the first truly American composer', *The Listener*, 11 March 1965, p. 384.
Peter Crump: Ives, then and now, *Composer*, No. 17, October 1965, p. 12.
Peter Dickinson: CI, *MT*, May 1964, p. 347.
Olin Downes: A lonely American composer, *New York Times*, 29 January 1939.
— CI, *Bulletin of American Composers Alliance*, 1954, No. 1, p. 17.
— Ives memorial: his scores and papers given to Yale, *New York Times*, 5 June 1955, Section 2, p. 9.
— Composer's need, *New York Times*, 6 June 1954, Section 2, p. 7.
R. Evett: Music letter: a post-mortem for Mr. Ives, *Kenyon Review*, 1954, No. 4, p. 628.
T. Chambers Furnas: CI, an essay, in *The Mills of God* (a book of essays and poems), The Whittier Press, Amesbury (Mass.), 1937.
R. Girson: Biographical sketch, *Saturday Review of Literature*, 28 August 1948, p. 45.
Frederic Grunfeld: CI, Yankee Rebel, *Bulletin of American Composers Alliance*, 1955, No. 3, p. 2 (repr. from *High Fidelity*).
Lou Harrison: The music of CI, *Listen*, November 1946.
— On Quotation, *Modern Music*, 1946, No. 3, p. 166.

Ingemar von Heijne: CI eller den största utmaningen, *Nutida musik*, Vol. 6 (1962–3).

Everett Helm: CI, American composer, *MT*, July 1954, p. 356.

— CI, Pionier der modernen Musik, *Melos*, April 1958.

Hans G. Helms: Der Komponist CI—Leben, Werk und Einfluss auf die heutige Generation, *NZfM*, October 1954, p. 425.

— Über statistisches Komponieren bei CI, *NZfM*, March 1966, p. 90.

Bernard Herrmann: CI, *Trend*, September–October 1932, p. 99.

— Four symphonies by CI, *Modern Music*, May–June 1945, p. 215.

Bernard Jacobson: American trail-blazer, *Records & Recording*, December 1964, p. 82.

John Kirkpatrick: A temporary mimeographed catalogue of the music MSS and related materials of CI, New Haven 1960.

— What music meant to CI, *Cornell University Music Review*, 1963, p. 13.

Ernst Krenek: CI, *SM*, April 1955, p. 141.

Paul Henry Lang: CI, hearing things, *Saturday Review of Literature*, 1 June 1946, p. 43.

Bentley Layton: An introduction to the 114 songs of CI (thesis), Harvard University 1963.

Goddard Lieberson: An American innovator, CI, *Musical America*, 10 February 1939.

J. Lyons: A prophet passes, *American Record Guide*, June 1954, p. 313.

John McClure: CI, lonely American giant, *The Gramophone*, April 1957, p. 516.

Wilfrid (W. H.) Mellers: Music in the melting pot—CI and the music of the Americas, *Scrutiny*, March 1939, p. 391.

— American music, an English perspective, *The Kenyon Review*, summer 1943, p. 365.

— CI, in *Music and Society*, Dobson (London) 1946, p. 135.

— CI and the sonata, *The Listener*, 30 November 1961, p. 950.

— Realism and transcendentalism: CI as American hero, in *Music in a New Found Land*, Barrie & Rockliff (London) 1964, p. 38.

— Jottings of CI, in *-do-*, p. 441

Donald Mitchell: A great American composer, *Gramophone Record Review*, July 1959, p. 651.

Paul Moor: On horseback to heaven, CI, *Harper's Magazine*, September 1948, p. 65.

— Two Titans, Schoenberg and Ives, *Theatre Arts*, February 1950, p. 49.

Julian S. Meyrick: What the business owes to CI, *The Eastern Underwriter*, 19 September 1930, p. 18.

F. D. Perkins: On horseback to heaven—a reply, *Harper's Magazine*, December 1948, p. 14.

Paul Rosenfeld: CI, pioneer atonalist, *New Republic*, 20 July 1932, p. 262.

— (CI), in *Discoveries of a music critic*, Harcourt, Brace (New York) 1936, p. 315.

— The advent of American music, *The Kenyon Review*, winter 1939, p. 50.

— The advance of American music, *The Kenyon Review*, spring 1939, p. 187.

— A plea for improvisation, *Modern Music*, November–December 1941, p. 15.

H. G. Sear: CI, song writer, *MMR*, February 1951, p. 34.

L. Schrade: CI, *Yale Review*, June 1955, p. 535.

Charles Seeger: Grass roots for American composers, *Modern Music*, March–April 1939, p. 144.

— CI and Carl Ruggles, *The Magazine of Art*, July 1939, pp. 396, 435.

Nicolas Slonimsky: CI, America's musical prophet, *Musical America*, 15 February 1954, p. 18.

— Bringing Ives alive, *Saturday Review of Literature*, 28 August 1948, p. 45.

— CI, musical rebel, *Américas*, September 1953, p. 6.

H. Taubman: Posterity catches up with CI—an interview, *New York Times Magazine*, 23 October 1949, p. 15.

— Forget posterity, *New York Times*, 23 November 1958, Section 2, p. 11.

Peter Yates: CI, *Arts and Architecture*, September 1944, p. 20.

Gerth van Zanten: CI, Amerikaans Componist, *Mens en melodie*, May 1951, p. 145.

MISCELLANEOUS OR UNSIGNED

Ives and Mayrick to move in May, *National Business Review*, April 1926.

Composer who has clung to his own way: The life and works of the new-found

Charles Ives in Friendly Record, *Boston Transcript*, 3 February 1934.

Insurance man: individual and authentically American U.S. composer, *Time*, 30 January 1939, p. 44.

Double indemnity, *Time*, 23 February 1948, p. 66.

CI, *Life*, October 1949, p. 45.

Yankee music, *Time*, 5 March 1951, p. 72.

CI, American composer, *Vogue*, 1 May 1953, p. 120.

Great innovator, *Musical America*, June 1954, p. 78.

Musical Whitman, *Newsweek*, 31 May 1954, p. 78.

Chronological catalog of the works of the American composer CI, *Boletin de musica y artes visuales*, No. 65, July–August 1953, p. 35.

World of music: complete collection of manuscript works given to Yale university, *Etude*, March 1955, p. 73.

Chronological list of the compositions of CI, *Bulletin of American Composers Alliance*, 1955, No. 3, p. 6.

Radical from Connecticut, *Time*, 22 August 1960, p. 36.

Ives revived, *Newsweek*, 14 October 1963, p. 65.

Transcendentalist, *Newsweek*, 10 May 1965, p. 101.

LEOŠ JANÁČEK (1854–1928)

Janáček was born on 3 July 1854 at Hukvaldy, a Moravian village on the Silesian-Polish border, where he was the tenth of the village school- and choir-master's fourteen children. From the age of eleven until his death, he lived mainly in Brno, the capital of Moravia, though in later life he often spent his summers at Hukvaldy. He sang in the choir and had his basic musical training at the Abbey of St. Augustine in Brno, and then spent five years (1869–74) working for his diploma at the local Teachers Training School. He also studied at the Organ School in Prague (1874–75) and later fitfully at the conservatoires of Leipzig (1879–80) and Vienna (1880). In 1881 he married Zdenka Schulz, the daughter of the director of the Brno Teachers Training

School, where he was employed from 1876. From the mid-1870s to the end of the century, Janáček was much concerned with developing the musical life of Moravia, conducting choirs, founding an organ school at Brno in 1882 and starting a musical journal, *Hudební Listy* (*Musical Letters*), in 1884. From 1888 onwards he was an enthusiastic collector and disseminator of Moravian folk music, often in collaboration with the scholar František Bartoš. He resigned from the Brno Training School in 1904 to concentrate on creative work, and from this time on became increasingly estranged from his wife, both their children having died young (1890, 1903). The final phase of Janáček's life was initiated by three events in the next decade: the great success in 1916 of the first Prague performance of his opera *Jenufa* (which had previously been given only once, at Brno in 1904); the growth during 1917 of a profound love for Kamilla Stössl (nearly forty years his junior) which was to continue until his death; and the establishment in 1918 of the autonomous Czech state. One of the results of the last was the transformation of the Brno Organ School into a conservatoire in 1919, while Janáček himself became head of a master-class in composition at the Prague Conservatoire (1919–25). He remained active to within a week of his death, at Ostrava in August 1928, of a chill caught while on holiday at Hukvaldy.

CATALOGUE OF WORKS

1. Graduale in festo purificationis B.V. Mariae. *c.* 1870. rev. 28 January 1887. Unpub.

2. The unwanted bridegroom (Ženich v nucený). For male choir. 1873. Lost.

fp: 27 April 1873, Brno, Svatopluk Choral Society.

3. Ploughing (Oráni). For male choir. 1873.

fp: 27 April 1873, Brno, Svatopluk Choral Society.

Pub. 1923, 1929, 1948, Hudební Matice.

4. War song (Válečná). For male choir, with piano, trumpet and three trombones. 1873.

fp: 5 July 1873, Brno, Svatopluk Choral Society.
Pub. Hudební Matice.

4a. War song (Válečná). Version for unacc. male choir.

5. Fickle love (Nestálost lásky) (Trad.). For male choir. 1873.
fp: 9 November 1873, Brno, Svatopluk Choral Society.
Unpub.

6. Serbian folksong (Srbská lidová píseň). For mixed choir. *c.* 1873. Lost.
fp: 27 April 1873.

7. Forsaken (Osamělá beztěchy) (Trad.). 1874, rev. 1895 and 1925.
fp: 14 March 1874, Brno, Svatopluk Choral Society.
Unpub.

8. Speciosus Forma. Gradual for male voice choir, quartet of women's voices and organ. 29 December 1874. Unpub.

9. In Nomine Jesu. Introit for mixed choir and organ. 1875. Unpub.

10. Exaudi Deus. First version, for mixed choir and organ. 3 February 1875. ?Unpub.

10a. Exaudi Deus. Second version, for unacc. mixed choir. 10 February 1875. Pub. 1877, in *Cecilie.*

11. Benedictus. For soprano, mixed choir and organ. 17 February 1875. Unpub.

12. Overture. For organ. 19 June 1875. Unpub.

13. Communion. For mixed choir. 20 June 1875. Unpub.

14. Varyto. For organ. 24 June 1875. Unpub.

15. Fidelis servis. For unacc. mixed choir. 20 June 1875. Unpub.

16. Choral Fantasy (Fantasie choralní). For organ. 7 July 1875. Lost.
fp: 22–23 July 1875, examinations at Prague Organ School, Leoš Janáček.

17. Rest in peace (Odpočiň si) (František

Sušil). For male choir. 1875. Pub. 1926, Hudební Matice.

18. Sounds in memory of Förchgott-Tovačovský. For three violins, viola, cello and double-bass. 1875. Unpub.

19. Intrada. For four violins. 23 November 1875, Brno.

20. Intrada in G minor. For four violins. 25 November 1875. Later incorporated into the Scherzo of *Idyll for strings.*

21. If you no longer want me, what is left? (Když mne nechceš, co je víc). 1876.
fp: 23 January 1876, Brno, Svatopluk Choral Society.
Unpub.

22. True love (Láska opravdivá). For male choir. 1876.
fp: 23 January 1876, Brno, Svatopluk Choral Society.
Pub. 1937, Melpa.

23. Choral Elegy (Zpěvná duma) (František Ladislav Čelakovský). Before 23 February 1876. Unpub.

24. Sonnet (Znělky). For violin and string orchestra. *c.* 1876. Lost.

25. In folksong style (Ohlas národních písní). Three Choruses for male choir. 1876. Texts: Traditional.
1. *I wonder at my love* (Divím se milému).
2. *The drowned wreath* (Vínek stonulý).
3. *True love* (Láska opravdivá).
Pub. 1937, Melpa.

26. Festival chorus (Slavnostní sbor). For mixed chorus and piano. Before 29 October 1876. Unpub. fp: 15 July 1899.

27. Death (Smrt) (Lermontov). Melodrama with orchestra. Before 27 March 1876.
fp: 13 November 1876, Brno, Beseda Choral Society.
Unpub.

28. Suite for string orchestra. 1877. Dur. 19′.
1. *Prelude: Moderato*; 2. *Allemande: Adagio*; 3. *Sarabande: Andante con moto*; 4. *Scherzo: Presto—Andante—Presto*; 5. *Air: Adagio*; 6. *Finale: Andante.*

fp: 2 December 1877, Brno, Beseda concert, cond. Leoš Janáček.

fEp: 2 February 1951, Wigmore Hall, Kalmar Chamber Orchestra, cond. Bernard Jacob.

Pub. 1926, Orbis.

29. Exsurge Domine. For mixed choir and organ. *c.* 1878. Unpub.

30. Constitues. Offertory for male choir and organ. *c.* 1878. Unpub.

31. Suscepimus. Gradual for mixed choir and organ. *c.* 1878; final version, 28 January 1887. Unpub.

32. Veni Sancte Spiritus. For male choir. *c.* 1878. Unpub.

33. No escape from Fate (Osudu neujdeš) (Trad.). For male choir. 1878. Unpub.

34. (Composition in the style of a ricercare). For organ. 4 August 1878, Oettingen. Unfinished. Unpub.

35. Idyll for string orchestra. 31 July–24 August 1878. Dur. 29'.

1. *Andante*; 2. *Allegro*; 3. *Moderato*; 4. *Allegro*; 5. *Adagio*; 6. *Scherzo*; 7. *Moderato*.

fp: 15 December 1878, Brno, cond. Leoš Janáček.

fEp: 1 September 1957, BBC broadcast, Harvey Phillips String Orchestra, cond. Harvey Phillips.

Pub. 1951, Orbis. Also for string quintet.

36. Regnum Mundi. For mixed choir and organ. *c.* 1878.

fp: 21 September 1878.

Unpub.

37. Sarabande. For string quintet. *c.* 1878. Lost.

?fp: 8 December 1878.

38. Dumka. For piano. ?1879.

fp: 8 September 1879, Rožnov, Leoš Janáček.

Pub. 1944, Hudební Matice.

39. Piano Sonata No. 1 in E flat. 6 October 1879. Lost.

40. Nokturno. For piano. 16 October 1879, Leipzig. Lost.

41. Die Abendschoppen. For voice and piano. 25 October 1879, Leipzig. Lost.

42. Song (unknown title). For voice and piano. 10 November 1879, Liepzig. Lost.

43. Sanctus. November 1879, Leipzig. Lost.

44. Romances. For violin and piano. 26 October–16 November 1879, Leipzig. Lost, except for No. 4 in E major, pub. 1938, 1949, Hudební Matice.

45. Funeral March (Smuteční pochod). For orchestra. 10 December 1879, Leipzig. Lost. Also for piano solo.

fp: 20 March 1898 as a movement from the cantata *Amarus*.

46. Spring song (Jarní pišne) (Vinzenz Zusner). Song Cycle for voice and piano. 22 April–7 May 1880, rev. 1905. Pub. 1944, Oldřich Pazdírek.

47. Seventeen Fuges. For piano. 9 October–12 January 1880, Liepzig. Lost.

48. Zdenka's minuet (Zdenčin menuet). For piano. 8 January 1880, Leipzig. Lost.

49. Violin Sonata No. 1. 14–18 January 1880, Leipzig. Lost.

50. Theme and variations (Zdenka's variations). For piano. 29 January–22 February 1880, Leipzig.

fEp: 5 May 1952, Liza Fuchsová.

Pub. 1944, Hudební Matice.

51. Rondo. For piano. January 1880. Lost.

52. Piano Sonata No. 2. 10–14 April 1880, Vienna. Lost.

53. Violin Sonata No. 2. 16 (?20) April–12 May 1880, Vienna. Lost.

?fp: 6 January 1881, Brno, Beseda concert.

54. String Quartet (No. O). 25 May–June 1880, Vienna. Lost.

55. Minuet and Scherzo. For clarinet and piano. *c.* 1880. Lost.

?fp (Minuet): 6 January 1881, Brno, Beseda concert.

56. Dumka. For violin and piano. 1880.

fEbp: 7 December 1951, Suzanne Rozsa and Paul Hamburger.

Pub. 1929, 1945, Hudební Matice (also as No. 4 in 'Ten Pieces for violin and piano').

57. Scherzo (for a Symphony). 25 January 1880, Leipzig. Lost.

58. Frühlingslieder. Song cycle. 25 April–7 May 1880, Vienna. Lost.

59. Two pigeons are sitting on a fir tree (Na košatej jedly dva holubi šedˇá). For male choir. *c.* 1880. Unpub.

60. Autumn Song (Písen v jeseni) (Jaroslav Vrchlický). For mixed choir. 18 September 1880.
fp: 12 December 1880, Brno, Beseda Choral Society, cond. Leoš Janáček.
Pub. 1950, Orbis.

61. In the pine tree (Na košatej jedli). For male chorus. 1877–80. Unpub.

62. Ten Czech religious songs (from Lehner's Canzionale). 1881. Pub. 1881–2, 2nd edition 1889, K. Winkler.

63. (Two compositions). For organ. *c.* 1880. Pub. 1884, Benedictine Press.

64. Moravian duets (Moravské dvojzpěvy). Arrangements for mixed choir of six duets by Dvořák. 1877 and 1884. Pub. 1939, Plavec (private print). New edition, 1945.

65. Wild duck (Kačena divoká). For mixed choir. *c.* 1884. Composed for a school song book published in 1885.
?fp: 17 March 1901, Brno, high schools' pupils, cond. Leos Janáček.

66. On the ferry (Na prievoze). For male choir. *c.* 1883–5. Unpub.

67. Four male choruses (Mužské sbory). *c.* June 1885. Ded. Antonin Dvořák.
   1. *Warning* (Výhrůžka) (Trad.).
   2. *Ah, love* (Ó, lásko) (Trad.).
   3. *The soldier's lot* (Ach, vojna vojna) (Trad.). 20 June 1885.
   4. *Your lovely eyes* (Krásné oči tvé) (Jaroslav Tichý).
fp: 1886, Brno, cond. Leoš Janáček.
f Prague p: 1906, Hlahol Society, cond. Adolf Piskáček.
fEp: 8 May 1952, BBC broadcast, London Chamber Singers, cond. Anthony Bernard.

Pub. 1886, Winkler; 1924, 1948, Hudební Matice (as 'Čtveřice mužských sborů').

68. Šárka. Opera in three acts. First version, January–August 1887; second version, completed June 1888; third version, before August 1918; final version, 1925, scoring completed by Osvald Chlubna. Libretto: Julius Zeyer.
fp: 11 November 1925, Brno, cond. František Neumann; producer, Ota Zítek; décor, Vlastislav Hofman.
Unpub.

BIBLIOGRAPHY:
A.K.: Brünn—Eine Jugendoper von Janáček, *Anbruch*, December 1925, p. 555.

69. Jealousy (Žárlivec). For baritone soloist and male choir. 14 May 1888. Unpub.

70. The little queens (Královničky). Ten folksong arrangements. 1889.
fp: 21 February 1889, Brno.
Pub. 1954, State Publishing House.

71. Wallachian-Lachian Dance (Starodávný). For piano. *c.* 1889. Unpub.

72. Lachian Dances (Lašské tance) (orig. Valachian Dances). Six dances for orchestra. 1889–90. Dur. 20′.
   1. *Starodávný*; 2. *Požehnaný*; 3. *Dymák*; 4. *Starodávný II*; 5. *Čeladenský*; 6. *Pilky*.
2 fl, pic, 2 ob, ca, 2 cl, bcl, 2 bsn; 3 hn, 2 tpt, 3 tmb; timp, campane; lyra, hp, organ (ad lib), strings.
fp (Nos. 1 & 6): 21 February 1899, Vesna Choral Society concert of folk music, cond. Leoš Janáček; choreography, Šimůnek.
fp (as ballet): 19 February 1925, Brno, National Theatre, cond. Břetislav Bakala.
fp (concert): 2 May 1925, Písek Philharmonic, cond. Cyril Vymetal.
f Prague p: 21 February 1926, Czech Philharmonic Orchestra, cond. František Neumann.
fEp: 19 August 1930, Queen's Hall, Promenade Concert, BBC Symphony Orchestra, cond. Sir Henry Wood.
Pub. 1890, Bursík & Kohout; 1928, Hudební Matice (with the composer's preface of 1926); 1950, Orbis. Also pub. in a piano arrangement.

73. Hanakian Dances. Ten dances for piano, two and four hands. *c.* 1889–90. Also version for orchestra, or chorus and orchestra. Unpub.

74. Bouquet of Moravian, Slovakian and Czech folksongs (Kytice s národních písní moravských, slovenských i českých). A collection, by František Bartoš and Leoš Janáček, of 195 songs. *c.* 1890. Pub. 1890, 1892, 1901, Scholz; 1929, 1949, Hudební Matice; 1953, State Publishing House.

75. Our song (Naše píseň) (Anon.). For mixed choir. 1890.

76. Three mixed choruses (Tři smíšené sbory). 1880, 1885 and 1890. Words; Jaroslav Vrchlický, Svatopluk Čech, and folk poetry. Pub. 1905, Orbis.

77. Suite (Serenade) Op. 3. For orchestra. January 1891. Dur. 14′.
  1. *Con moto*; 2. *Adagio*; 3. *Allegretto*; 4. *Con moto.*
  2 fl, 2 ob, 2 cl, 2 bsn; 3 hn, 3 tpt; timp, GC, tgle; hp, strings.
  fp: September 1928, Brno, combined Prague and Brno Radio Orchestras, cond. Břetislav Bakala.
  fEp: 13 March 1937, BBC Scottish Orchestra, cond. Guy Warrack.
  Pub. 1958, State Publishing House.

78. Adagio. For orchestra. 1891. ?Unpub.

79. Beginning of a Romance (Počátek románu). Opera in one act. 15 May–2 July 1891. Libretto: Jaroslav Tichý, from a story by Gabriela Preissová. Unpub.

80. Rákocz Rákoczy. Ballet (Scenes from Moravian Slovakia) with dances and songs in one act. May 1891. Scenario: Jan Herben.
  fp: 24 July, Prague, National Theatre; ballet arr. by August Berger.

80a. The Count of Nové Zámky. Version of preceding, revised by Rudolf Walter.
  fp: 14 May 1928, Brno.

80b. Three Choruses from 'Rákocz Rákoczny'. With orchestra. Undated. Unpub.
  1. *When we went to the fair* (Keď jsme šli na hody)*; 2. *The gnats' wedding* (Komáři ženili); 3. *I planted the greens.*

81. Ej, danaj! For piano. 2 April 1892. Unpub.

82. National dances of Moravia (Národní tance na Moravě). For piano and piano duet. *c.* 1891 and 1893. Twenty-three dances collected by Leoš Janáček and others. Pub. 1895, Brno; 1950, Hudební Matice.

83. Moravian dances (Moravské tance). Six dances for orchestra. *c.* 1892. Unpub.

84. I was sowing (Zelené sem sela). For mixed chorus and orchestra. *c.* 1892. Unpub.

85. Our birch tree (Což ta naše bříza) (Eliška Krásnohorská). For male choir. 18 April 1893. Composed for the Svatopluk Choral Society, Brno.
  fEp: 8 May 1952, BBC broadcast, London Chamber Singers, cond. Anthony Bernard.
  Pub. 1929, 1949, Hudební Matice.

86. The wreath (Vínek). For male choir. 1893.
  fEp: as No. 85.
  Pub. 1929, 1948, Hudební Matice.

87. The sun has risen (Už je slunko z tej hory ven). For tenor soloist and male choir. 1893. Words: folk text. ?Unpub.

88. Music for gymnastic exercises (Hudba ke kroužení kužely). For piano. Spring 1893. Composed for the Sokol Gymnastic Association. Pub. 1950, Hudební Matice.

89. (Three Lyrics) (Eliška Krásnohorská). For chorus and piano. 1888–93.
  1. *The jealous one* (Žárlivec). 14 May 1888.
  2. *The dove* (Holubička). 1893.
  3. *Leave-taking* (Loučení). 1893.
  fp (Nos. 2 & 3): 1 September 1956, Moravian Teachers' Choral Society, cond. Jan Šoupal.
  Unpub.

90. Jealousy (Žárlivost). Overture (to 'Jenufa') for orchestra. 31 December 1894.
  f concert p: 10 November 1906, Prague, Czech Orchestral Music Society concert, cond. František Neumann.
  Unpub.

91. Kyrie (Hospodiňe Pomiluj Ny). For

solo quartet, mixed double choir and instrumental ensemble. 1896.

3 tpt, 3 tmb, 2 tubas; organ, hp.

fp: 19 April 1896, Brno, Choir of the Teachers' Training Institute, cond. Leoš Janáček.

Unpub.

92. Folksongs of Moravia, newly collected (Národní písně moravské v nově nasbírané). A collection of 2,057 songs, collected by Leoš Janáček and others with a preface ('The musical aspects of Moravian folksongs') by Janáček. 1897. Pub. 1899 (Vol. 1), 1901 (Vol. 2), Czech Academy, Prague.

93. Festival chorus (Slavnostní sbor) (Vladimír Štastný). For male choir. December 1897. Composed for the St. Joseph Society of Old Brno. ?Unpub.

94. Folk poetry of Hukvaldy in songs (Ukvalská lidová poesie v písních). A collection of thirteen folksongs with piano acc. 1898. Ded. Hukvaldy Folk Song Society. Pub. 1898, Píša; 1929, 1949, Hudební Matice.

95. Amarus. Lyric Cantata for soloists, mixed chorus and orchestra. Spring 1897, rev. 1901 and 1906. Text: Jaroslav Vrchlický. Dur. 27–30′.

1. *Moderato*; 2. *Andante*; 3. *Moderato*; 4. *Adagio*; 5. *Tempo di Marcia funebre* (*Epilogue*).

2 fl, pic, 2 ob, ca, 2 cl, bcl, 2 bsn; 4 hn, 3 tpt, 3 tmb, tuba; timp, tgle, campane, tamtam; hp, strings.

fp: 2 December 1900, Kroměříž, Moravian Choral Society, cond. Leoš Janáček.

Pub. 1938, Hudební Matice; 1957, State Publishing House: vocal score by Otakar Nebuška, rev. K. Šok. English version, Bernard Keeffe.

96. Spring song (Jarní píseň) (Jaroslav Tichý). For high voice and piano. Ded. Vesna Women's Choral Society.

fp: 6 March 1898, Brno.

?Unpub.

97. The hazelbush (Oříšek léskový). Song transcription for piano. 5 March 1899. Lost.

98. Songs. For voice and piano. ?1899. Lost.

fp: 5 March 1899.

99. Russian national dance (Kozáček). For orchestra. 9 December 1899.

fp: 11 February 1900.

Unpub.

100. Serbian national dance (Srbské Kolo). For orchestra. c. 1899.

fp: 11 February 1900.

Unpub. Lost.

101. Folksongs of Hukvaldy (Ukvalské písně). Six songs for mixed choir and piano. 1899. Pub. 1949, Hudební Matice.

102. Veni Sancte Spiritus. For male choir. c. 1900. Unpub.

103. Our Father (Otče náš). For tenor, mixed choir and piano or harmonium. 1901. ?Unpub.

fp: 15 June 1901, Brno Theatre, cond. Leoš Janáček; tableaux vivants directed by Josef Villart.

103a. Our Father (Otče náš). Version with acc. for organ and harp. ?1906.

fEbp: 3 July 1969, BBC Chorus, Martin Neary (organ), John Marson (hp), cond. Peter Gellhorn.

104. Mass. After Liszt's 'Messe pour orgue', arr. Leoš Janáček for mixed choir and organ. 24 September 1901. Unpub.

105. Moravian folk poetry in songs (Moravská lidová poesie v písních). Fifty-three folksongs for voice and piano. 1892 and 1901.

fEbp: 16 April 1953, Ilse Steinová, acc. Liza Fuchsová; 21 May 1953, Otakar Kraus, acc. Liza Fuchsová.

Pub. 1902–3; 1947, Hudební Matice.

106. Saint Wenceslas (Svatý Václave). For choir and organ. c. 1902. Unpub.

107. Elegie (Elegy on the death of Janáček's daughter Olga). Cantata for tenor, mixed chorus and piano. 28 April 1903, rev. 28 March 1904. Russian text: Marii N. Veverica (Vevercová).

fp: 20 December 1930, Brno Radio broadcast.

Pub. 1958, State Publishing House (rev. Theodora Straková). English version, Malcolm Rayment; German version, Kurt Honolka.

108. Constitues. For choir and organ. Before 1903, rev. 15 July 1903. Unpub.

109. When we went to the feast. Highland Dance for mixed choir and orchestra. ?*c.* 1903. Unpub.

110. Jenufa. Moravian Music Drama in three acts. 18 March 1894–18 March 1903, rev. 1906, 1911 and 1916. Libretto: Gabriela Preissová. Ded. to the memory of the composer's daughter Olga.
fp (1903 version): 21 January 1904, Brno Opera Company, cond. Cyril Methodéj Hrazdira; with Leopolda Hanusová-Svobodová (Kostelnička), Marie Kabeláčová (Jenufa), Alois Staněk-Doubravský (Laca), Věra Pivaňková (Burja), Bohdan Procházka (Steva), Karel Beníško (The Miller); producer, Josef Malý; design, Dušan Jurkovič.
fp (final version): 26 May 1916, Prague; with Gabriela Horvátová (Kostelnička), Theodor Schütz (Laca), Věra Pivoňková (Burja).
fEbp: 8 July 1948, Chorus and Orchestra of the Czech Broadcasting Corporation, cond. Karel Nedbal; with Stepanka Jelínková.
fEp (stage): 10 December 1956, Royal Opera House, Covent Garden, cond. Rafael Kubelik; with Sylvia Fisher (Kostelnička), Amy Shuard (Jenufa), John Lanigan (Laca), Edith Coates (Burja), Edgar Evans (Steva), Otakar Kraus (The Miller).
Pub. 1908, Klub přátel umění v Brně; 1917, 1934, 1943, 1949, Hudební Matice; 1917, Universal-Edition (orchestral score and vocal score with German text by Max Brod); 1948, Hudební Matice.

BIBLIOGRAPHY:
Oskar Bie: Janáček, Jenufa in der Staatsoper in Berlin, *Anbruch*, April 1924, p. 160.
S. Brichta: Janáčeks Jenufa auf der deutschen Opernbühne, *Signale*, 1929, No. 36, p. 1052.
Hans Hollander: Drei Briefe LJs zur Wiener Jenufa-Premiere, *ÖM*, November 1964.
Julius Kapp: Einführung in die Oper Jenufa, *Blätter der Staatsoper* (Berlin), April 1924 and 1941–2, No. 5, p. 7.
W. C. M. Kloppenberg: LJ en zijn opera Jenufa, *Mens en melodie*, June 1951, p. 168.
Andrew Porter: Janáček's Jenufa, *London Musical Evens*, December 1956, p. 28.
Ferdinand Scherber: Janufa, Erstaufführung an der Wiener Hofoper am 16. Februar 1918, *Signale*, 1918, No. 8 (20 February), p. 162.
R. Schwers: LJs Jenufa in der Berliner Staatsoper, *AMZ*, 21 March 1924.
Evan Senior: Jenufa comes at last to England, *M&M*, December 1956, p. 8.
Desmond Shawe-Taylor: An introduction to Jenufa, *Opera*, November 1956, p. 660.
— Jenufa at Covent Garden, *Opera*, February 1957, p. 73.
Bohumir Štědron: Die Urfassung von Janáčeks Jenufa, *ÖM*, 1967, No. 4 (April), p. 206.
Paul Stefan: Der Erfolg der Jenufa, *Anbruch*, December 1925, p. 545.
Karl Westermeyer: Jenufa von LJ, *Signale*, 1924, No. 13, p. 394.

111. Moravian Dances (Moravské tance). For piano. 1904. Pub. 1905, Arnošt Píša.

112. Moderato. For orchestra. *c.* 1904. Lost.

113. Ave Maria (Zdrávas Maria). For tenor, mixed choir and organ (also arr. for soprano, violin and organ). ?Before 1904. ?Unpub.

114. Czech religious polyphonic songs from the Přibor cancionale (Církevní zpěvy éské vicehlasné Příborského kancionálu). For 3- and 4-part mixed choirs. *c.* 1904.
  1. *Rejoice and sing* (Slavně budem zpívati).
  2. *The Son of God is born* (Narodil se syn Boží).
  3. *Christ the son of God* (Kristus syn Boží).
  4. *The prophets prophesied* (Prorokovali proroci).
  fp: 7 October 1954, Brno, cond. K. Hradil. ?Unpub.

115. Four Moravian Choruses for male voices (Čtvero muzských sborů moravských). 1904. Words: Ondřej Přikryl and folk poetry. Ded. Moravian Teachers' Choir.
  1. *Now you know* (Dež víš).
  2. *Gnats* (Komáři).
  3. *The evening witch* (Klekánica).

4. *Farewell* (Rozloučení).
Pub. 1906, Urbánek; 1950, Hudební Matice. Nos. 1 & 3 were also pub. with German text in Leipzig, 1908. Nos. 1 and 2 alternatively known in English as 'If you only knew' and 'Mosquitoes'.

116. Fate (Osud). Opera in three scenes. November 1903–May 1904. Libretto: Leoš Janáček and Fedora Bartošová. Unpub.
fp: 18 September 1934, Brno Radio, cond. Břetislav Bakala.
f stage p: 25 October 1958, Brno, Janáckova Opera, cond. František Jílek; with Jindra Pokorna, Jarmila Palivcová, Jaroslav Ulrych, Zdenek Souseki; producer, Václav Veznik.

BIBLIOGRAPHY:
B. Štědron: Janáckova opera Osud, *Slovenská Hudba*, December 1959, p. 532.

117. Piano Sonata 'l.x.1905' ('A Street Scene'—'Z ulice'). 1905.
fEbp: 21 December 1937, Rudolf Firkušný.
Pub. 1924, 1949, Hudební Matice.

118. Spring song. 1905. Composed for Friends of Art Club.
fp: 9 April 1905, Brno, Friends of Art Club.

119. Folk Nocturnes (Lidová Nokturna). Seven Folk Duets (Slovak Nocturnes from Rovné) for women's voices and piano. Before May 1906.
fp: 15 December 1907, Brno, Friends of Art Club concert.
Pub. 1922, 1950, Hudební Matice.

120. Kantor Halfar (Petr Bezruč). For male choir. ?24 October 1906; final version probably 1917.
fp (first version): 27 May 1911, Smetana Choral Society of Plzeň.
fp (final version): 3 August 1918, Luhačovice, Moravian Teachers' Choir.
Pub. 1923, 1947, Hudební Matice.

120a. Maryčka Magdonová (Petr Bezruč). For male choir. Autumn 1906; second version, spring 1907.
fp: 12 April 1908, Prostějov, Moravian Teachers' Choir.
f Paris p: 27 April 1908, Moravian Teachers' Choir.

f Prague p: 26 July 1908, Moravian Teachers' Choir.
?fEbp: 12 March 1958, Moravian Teachers' Choir.
Pub. 1909, Urbánek; 1950, Hudební Matice.

121. On an overgrown path (Po zarostlém Chodníčku). For piano. Nos. 1–7 orig. for harmonium. 1901–11.
Book I:
1. *Our evenings*; 2. *A blown-away leaf*; 3. *Come along with us*; 4. *The Virgin of Frýdek*; 5. *They chattered like swallows*; 6. *One cannot tell* (la parole manqué); 7. *Good-night*; 8. *In anguish*; 9. *In tears*; 10. *The little owl continues screeching.*
Book II:
1(11). *Andante*; 2(12). *Allegretto*; 3(13). *Piu mosso*; 4(14). *Vivo*; 5(15). *Allegro.*
fEbp: 29 January 1935, Michael Mulliner (five pieces only).
fEbp (Book I): 21 May 1953, Liza Fuchsová.
fEbp (Book II): 16 April 1953, Liza Fuchsová.
First complete pub. 1942, Hudební Matice.

122. Piano Trio. Autumn 1908, rev. 1909. Lost.
fp: 2 April 1909, Brno, Friends of Art Club.

123. Mass in E flat major. For mixed choir and organ. 1907–8. Unfinished: Credo completed by Vilém Petrželka.
1. *Kyrie*; 2. *Agnus Dei*; 3. *Credo*.
fp: 7 March 1943, Brno, Church of Saints Cyril and Methodius, cond. Karel Hradil.

123a. Mass in E flat major. Version with orchestra.
fp: 1 March 1946, with Czech Philharmonic Orchestra, cond. Rafael Kubelik.

124. Seventy thousand (Sedmdesát tisíc). For male choir (TTBB). December 1909, rev. 1913. Words: Petr. Bezruč. Ded. Franitšek Spilka.
fp: 4 April, Prague Teachers' Choir, cond. František Spilka.
Pub. 1912, Urbánek; 1923, 1929, Hudební Matice.

125. Six National songs (Šest národních písní). For voice and piano. 1909. 'As sung by Eva Gabel.'

fEbp: 19 September 1952, Ilse Steinová, acc. Clifton Helliwell.

Pub. 1950, Hudební Matice. German version, Max Brod.

126. Presto. For cello and piano. *c.* 1910. Unpub.

127. Fairy tale (Pohádka). For cello and piano. 10 February 1910 (first version); *c.* 1923 (second version). Inspired by the fairy tale 'Czar Berendei' by V. A. Zhukovsky.

fp: 13 March (?10 February), Brno, Rudolf Pavlata (cello) and Ludmila Prokopová.

fp (second version): 21 February 1923, Prague, Mozarteum, Julius Jenek and Růžena Nebušková.

fEp: 6 May 1926, Wigmore Hall, Mannucci and Fanny Davies.

Pub. 1924, 1949, Hudební Matice.

128. There upon the mountains (Čarták on The Soláni) (Na Soláni Čarták). Cantata for male choir and orchestra. February 1911. Text: M. Kurta (Kunert). Ded. Orlice Choral Society, Prostějov. Dur. 6½'.

2 fl, pic, 2 ob, ca, 2 cl, 2 bsn; 4 hn; timp, tgle, carillon; hp, strings.

fp: 13 (?23) March 1912, Orlice Choral Society and military band of Eighth Infantry Regiment stationed in Brno, cond. Vilém Steinman.

Pub. 1958, State Publishing House.

129. Spring song (Jarní píseň). For piano. 1912. Lost.

130. In the mists (V mlhách). For piano. 1912.

1. *Andante*; 2. *Molto adagio*; 3. *Andantino*; 4. *Presto*.

fEbp (Nos. 1 & 4): 20 October 1949, Alfred Kitchin.

Pub. 1929, 1938, 1944, 1950, Hudební Matice.

131. Krajcpolka. Polka for piano. *c.* 1912. Facsimile pub. 17 February 1912 in *Lidové Noviny* Literary Supplement.

132. The Fiddler's Child (Šumařovo dítě). Ballad for orchestra after a poem by Svatopluk Čech. 1912. Dur. 12'.

2 fl, 2 ob, 2 cl, bcl, 2 bsn; 3 hn, 2 tpt, 3 tmb, tuba; timp, tgle, cym, carillon; hp, strings.

fp: 14 November 1917, Prague, Czech Philharmonic Orchestra, cond. Otakar Ostrčil.

fEp: 3 May 1924, Queen's Hall, New Queen's Hall Orchestra, cond. Sir Henry Wood.

fEbp: 3 April 1939, BBC Orchestra, cond. Clarence Raybould.

Pub. 1912, Klub prátel umení (Brno); 1924 (second edition), Hudební Matice.

133. Ballad. For violin and piano. *c.* 1913. Pub. 1915.

134. Violin Sonata No. 3. Early 1914, rev. subsequently to 1921.

1. *Con moto*; 2. *Ballada*; 3. *Allegretto*; 4. *Adagio*.

fp: 1922, Brno, František Kudláček and Jaroslav Kvapil.

fEp: 6 May 1926, Wigmore Hall, Adila Fachiri and Fanny Davies.

Pub. 1922, 1929, 1947, Hudební Matice.

135. The eiderdown (The feather bed) (Peřina). For male choir.

fEp: 8 May 1952, BBC broadcast, London Chamber Singers, cond. Anthony Bernard.

Pub. 1929, 1948, Hudební Matice.

136. Four choruses for male voices (Čtyři lidové mužské sbory). 1873, 1893, 1914. Words: Eliška Krásnohorská and folk poetry. Pub. Hudební Matice.

137. The Everlasting Gospel (Věčné evangelium). A Legend for soprano and tenor soloists, mixed chorus and orchestra. Spring 1914, rev. 1924. Text: Jaroslav Vrchlický. Dur. 21'.

1. *Con moto*; 2. *Adagio*; 3. *Con moto*; 4. *Andante*.

3 fl, pic, 2 ob, ca, 2 cl, bcl, 2 bsn, cbsn; 4 hn, 3 tpt, 3 tmb, tuba; timp, cym, tgle; organ, hp, strings.

fp: 5 February 1917, Prague, Antonín Lebeda and Gabriela Horvátová, Pražský Hlahol Choral Society, cond. Jaroslav Křička.

f Brno p: 1919, Beseda Philharmonic Society, cond. Ferdinand Vach.

fEp: 12 June 1960, Birmingham, Town Hall, invited audience concert, Marian Studholme and William Herbert, City of

Birmingham Choir and Symphony Orchestra, cond. Meredith Davies.

Pub. 1959, State Publishing House (revised by Karl Šok). Vocal score, Břetislav Bakala; English version, Malcolm Rayment; German version, Kurt Honolka.

138. Folk songs of Dětva (Písně detvanské). Eight Songs for voice and piano. 16–19 January 1916. Pub. 1950, Hudební Matice.

139. Ballads of Zbojnice (Zbojnické balady). 1916. Pub. 1950, Hudební Matice.

140. Songs of Hradčany (Hradčanské písničky). Cycle of three songs for female chorus. 1916 (probably 1 February 1916). Words: F. S. Procházka.
  1. *Golden lane* (Zlatá ulička).
  2. *The weeping fountain* (Plačící fontána).
  3. *Belvedere*.
Pub. 1922, Hudební Matice.

141. The wolf track (Vlčí stopa) (Jaroslav Vrchlický). For female chorus and piano. 25 January 1916. Unpub.

142. Kašpar Rucký (František S. Procházka). Ballad for soprano solo and female chorus a cappella. 12 February (? 12 November) 1916.
  fp: 6 April 1921, Prague, Prague Women Teachers' Choir, cond. Method Doležil.
  ?fEbp: 7 July 1956, Cynthia Glover and members of BBC West of England Singers, cond. Reginald Redman.
Pub. 1925, 1938, Hudební Matice. German version, Max Brod.

143. Five folksongs (Pět národních písní). For male chorus and piano or harmonium. 1916–17. Pub. 1950, Hudební Matice.

144. The Excursions of Mr. Brouček (Výlety pana Broučka). Opera in two parts.
  1. *Excursion of Mr. Brouček to the Moon*. Two acts. 1908–17. Libretto: Svatopluk Čech, adapted by Victor Dyk, Karel Mašek, Zikmund Janke, František Gellner, Jiří Mahen and František S. Procházka.
  2. *Excursion of Mr. Brouček to the 15th Century*. Two acts. 1917. Libretto: Svatopluk Čech, adapted by František S. Procházka.
  4 fl, pic, 2 ob, ca, 2 cl, bcl, 2 bsn, cbsn; 4 hn, 4 tpt, 3 tmb, bs tuba; timp, pcssn, celesta, glock, Dudelsack; organ, hp, strings.

fp (both parts): 23 April 1920, Prague, National Theatre, cond. Otakar Ostrčil; with Mirko Štork, Vilém Zítek, Emil Burian, V. Novák, V. Pivoňková, E. Miřiovská and K. Hruška; producer, Gustav Schmoranz; décor, Karel Stapfer.

fEbp: 15 May 1961, Cologne Radio Choir and Symphony Orchestra, cond. Joseph Keilberth; with Lorenz Fehenberger, Fritz Wunderlich, Carlos Alexander, Wilma Lipp, Keith Engen, Antonia Fahberg, Lilian Benningsen, Paul Kuen and Carl Hoppe.

Pub. 1919, Universal-Edition. Vocal score by Roman Vesely.

BIBLIOGRAPHY:
Ludwig Karpath: Die Ausflüge des Herrn Brouček, Oper in zwei Teilen von LJ, Zur Uraufführung im Tschechischen Theater in Prag, *Anbruch*, May (2) 1920, p. 382.
Artuš Rektorys (ed.): Correspondence of LJ with the librettists of The Excursions of Mr. Brouček, Prague, 1950.
Anon.: Janáček's The Excursions of Mr. Brouček, *The Listener*, 11 May 1961, p. 853.

145. Taras Bulba. Rhapsody for orchestra, after Gogol. 1915–29 March 1918. Dur. 22′.
  1. *Smrt Andrijova* (Death of Andrea);
  2. *Smrt Ostapova* (Death of Ostap); 3. *Proroctví a smrt Tarase Bulby* (Capture and death of Taras Bulba).
  2 fl, pic, 2 ob, ca, 2 cl, 2 bsn, cbsn; 4 hn, 2 tpt, 3 tmb, tuba; timp, campani, tgle, tamb pic, cym; organ, hp, strings.

fp: 9 October 1921, Brno, National Theatre Orchestra, cond. František Neumann.
f Prague p: 9 November 1924, Smetana Hall, Czech Philharmonic Orchestra, cond. Václav Talich.
fGp: 1928, Leipzig, Gewandhaus Orchestra, cond. Bruno Walter.
fEp: 16 October 1928, Queen's Hall, concert arranged by the Czech Society of Great Britain, New Queen's Hall Orchestra, cond. Sir Henry Wood.
Pub. 1925 (vocal score), 1927 (full score), 1947, Hudební Matice.

BIBLIOGRAPHY:
Richard Gorer: Janáček and Taras Bulba, *MR*, November 1961, p. 302.

T

146. Songs of Silesia (Slezské písně). Ten folksongs from the collection of Helene Salich, for voice and piano. 1918. Pub. 1920, Svoboda (Brno); 1954, State Publishing House.

147. The Czech Legion (Ceská legie) (Antonín Horák). For male chorus. 18 November 1918. ? Unpub.

148. Diary of a young man who disappeared (Zápisník zmizelého). For tenor and alto soloists, three female voices and piano. September 1917–6 June 1919; final version, 23 November 1921.

fp: 18 April 1921, Brno, Karel Zavřel (tenor) with Břetislav Bakala (piano).

fEp: 27 October 1922, Mischa-Léon (tenor) with Břetislav Bakala.

fFp: 15 December 1922, Mischa-Léon with Břetislav Bakala.

fEbp: 14 March 1951, Richard Lewis, Constance Shacklock, section of BBC Singers.

Pub. 1921 Pazdíred (Brno); 1953, State Publishing House.

BIBLIOGRAPHY:
Karl Holl: Janáček und sein Tagebuch eines Verschollenen, *NZfM*, January 1962.

Basil Maine: A Czecho-Slovak song-cycle, *MN&H*, 22 March 1924, p. 283.

149. The Ballad of Blaník (Balada Blanická). Symphonic Poem for orchestra, after a poem by Jaroslav Vrchický. 1920. Dur. $7\frac{1}{2}'$.

3 fl, pic, 2 ob, 2 cl, bcl, 2 bsn; 3 hn, 3 tpt, 3 tmb, tuba; timp, carillon, celesta, xyl; 2 hp, strings.

Pub. 1958, State Publishing House.

150. Katya Kabanova (K.ta Kabanová). Opera in three acts, after the play 'The Storm' by A. N. Ostrovsky, transl. Vinceno Červinka. November 1919–17 February 1921.

fp: 23 November 1921, Brno, cond. František Neumann; with Rudolf Kaulfus (Dikoj), Zrel Zavřel (Boris), Marie Hladíková (Kabanicha), Pavel Jeral (Tichon), Marie Veselá (Káta), Valentin Sindler (Kudrjáš), Jarmila Pustinská (Varvara), René Milan (Kuligin), Ludmila Šebestlová (Gláša), Ludmila Kvapilová (Fekluša), Václav Šindler (Chodec), Ružena Hoská (Žena); producer, Vladimír Marek; décor, A. V. Hrska.

fEbp: 28 December 1948, Chorus and Orchestra of Brno Opera, cond. Břetislav Bakala; with Emilie Zachardová (Káta), Burja Burian (Tichon), Josef Valka (Boris), Jaroslav Hromadka (Dikoj), Marie Reznicková (Kabanicha), Sona Spurna (Varvara), Antonin Pelc (Kurdjáš), Vlastimil Sima (Kuligin).

fEp: 10 April 1951, Sadler's Wells, cond. Charles Mackerras; with Amy Shuard (Káta), Rowland Jones (Boris), Robert Thomas (Kudrjáš), John Kentish (Tichon), Kate Jackson (Kabanicha), Marion Studholme (Varvara); producer, Dennis Arundell.

Pub. 1922, Universal-Edition. Vocal score by B. Bakala; German version, Max Brod.

BIBLIOGRAPHY:
Max Chop: LJ, Katja Kabanowa, *Signale*, 1926, No. 23, p. 947.

Mária Freuer: Katja Kabanova, *Muzsika*, May 1961, p. 7.

Hans Hollander; LJ's Katya Kabanova (transl. Else Mayer-Lismann), *Opera*, April 1951, p. 227.

John W. Klein: Janáček's 'vile' opera, *Chesterian*, No. 206, spring 1961.

Rafael Kubelik: Katya Kabanova, *Foyer*, No. 1, autumn 1951, p. 18.

Charles Mackerras: Long-lost music for Janáček opera, *M&M*, February 1961, p. 16.

Charles Stuart: Katya Kabanova reconsidered, *MR*, November 1951, p. 289.

H. H. Stuckenschmidt, LJ und Katja Kabanova, *Opera*, April 1951, p. 227.

— LJ und seine Oper Katja Kabanova, in *Musik der Zeit*, Vol. 8 (Tschechische Komponisten), Boosey & Hawkes, 1954, p. 5.

— LJ, Katja Kabanova, Städtische Oper Berlin 1957, in *Oper in dieser Zeit*, Friedrich Verlag (Hannover) 1964, p. 48.

Karl H. Wörner: Katjas Tod, *SM*, March 1959, p. 91.

151. Folksongs of Moravia (Moravské lidové písně). Fifteen pieces for piano. 1922.

fEbp: 16 April 1953, Liza Fuchsová.

Pub. 1950, Hudební Matice.

152. The foolish tramp (The wandering madman) (Potulný šilenec) (Rabindranath Tagore). For male chorus. 1 November 1922.

fp: 21 September 1924, Rosice, Moravian Teachers' Choir, cond. Ferdinand Vach.

Pub. 1925, Hudební Matice.

153. String Quartet No. 1 ('Kreutzer Sonata'). 30 Oct. 1923–7 Nov. 1924. Based on a lost Piano Trio of 1908–9. Dur. 18'.

1. *Adagio con moto*; 2. *Con moto*; 3. *Con moto* (*Vivace–Andante*); 4. *Con moto* (*Adagio*).

fp: 17 September 1924, Prague, Mozarteum, Bohemian Quartet.

fEp: 6 May 1926, Wigmore Hall, Woodhouse Quartet.

fEbp: 8 December 1928, Zika Quartet (Richard Zika, Herbert Berger, Ladislav Cerny and Ladislav Zika).

fFp: 31 Ianuary 1931, Paris, Société Nationale de Musique, Zika Quartet (of Prague).

Pub. 1925, 1948, Hudební Matice.

154. The Cunning Little Vixen (Příhody lišky Bystroušky). Opera in three acts after Rud. Těsnohlídek. 1921–March 1923.

fp: 6 November 1924, Brno; producer, Ota Zítek; décor, Eduard Milén.

fEp: 22 March 1961, Sadler's Wells, cond. Colin Davis; with June Bronhill, Kevin Miller, Neil Easton, Charles Draper, Raymond Nilsson; producer, Colin Grahame; scenery and costumes, Barry Kay.

Pub. 1924, Universal-Edition. Vocal score by Břetislav Bakala; German version, Max Brod.

BIBLIOGRAPHY:

Max Brod: Die Werke des Festes: Das kluge Füchslein von LJ, *Anbruch*, May 1925, p. 285.

K. R. Danler: Janáček's Das schlaue Füchslein, *Musica*, 1967, No. 6, p. 287.

Richard Gorer: Janáček's The Cunning Little Vixen, *The Listener*, 30 March 1961, p. 589.

Alfred Morgenroth: Das schlaue Füchslein, *Signale*, 1927, No. 9, p. 289.

Paul A. Pisk: Eine Janáček-Uraufführung, *Anbruch*, November–December 1924, p. 426.

Andrew Porter, Colin Graham & Barry Kay: The Cunning Little Vixen, *MT*, March 1961, p. 146.

Henry Prunières: Le Ruse petit renard de Janáček, *RM*, August 1925, p. 169.

Hans F. Redlich: Janáček: Das schlaue Füchslein, *Anbruch*, March 1927, p. 136.

Willi Reich: Janáčeks Tieroper, *Musikleben*, April 1955, p. 142.

John Warrack: The Cunning Little Vixen, *Opera*, March 1961, p. 153.

Br. Weigl: Das listige Füchslein—Uraufführung in Brünn, *NMZ*, 1925, No. 12, p. 289.

H. Weinstock: Vixen by Janáček, *Saturday Review*, 24 June 1961, p. 39.

Anon.: The Cunning Little Vixen (synopsis), *The Listener*, 13 August 1959, p. 261.

Anon.: Janáček's opera of humans and animals, *M&M*, March 1961, p. 13.

155. Sanssouci. For flute and piano or harp. 1924. Unfinished.

156. Youth (Mládí). Suite for wind sextet (flute & piccolo, oboe, clarinet, horn, bassoon and bass clarinet). July 1924. Dur. 17'.

1. *Allegro*; 2. *Andante sostenuto*; 3. *Vivace*; 4. *Allegro animato*.

fp: 21 October 1924, Brno, professors of the Brno Conservatoire; also 23 November 1924, Vinohrady Theatre, members of Czech Philharmonic Orchestra.

fEp: 6 May 1926, Wigmore Hall, Robert Murchie, Léon Goossens, Haydn Draper, Aubrey Brain, Paul Draper and R. Newton.

fEbp: 9 October 1927, London Wind Quintet (Robert Murchie, Léon Goossens, Haydn Draper, Fred Wood, Aubrey Brain) and Mendelssohn Draper (bcl).

Pub. 1925, 1947, Hudební Matice.

157. Love songs of Moravia (Moravske písně milostné). 1924. Pub. 1930–6, National Institute for Folksongs, Prague.

158. Nursery Rhymes (Říkadla). Original version: Eight rhymes for three women's voices, clarinet and piano. 1925.

fp: 26 October 1925, Brno.

158a. Nursery Rhymes (Říkadla). Revised version: Nineteen rhymes for solo voice or six to nine voices, piano and eleven instruments (or viola or violin). 1927.

1. *Introduction*; 2. *Turnip's wedding*; 3. *Spring sunshine*; 4. *Mole and hamster*; 5. *Charlie's ride to hell*; 6. *Torn trousers*; 7. *Frank the knacker plays the cello*; 8. *Our doggie*; 9. *A fine sermon*; 10. *Magic*; 11. *How! Now! There's the cows*; 12. *Soup*; 13. *Granny in the bushes*; 14. *Fruit*

Janáček, Leoš

picking; 15. *Farmer Bumpkin*; 16. *Goat lazes in the sun*; 17. *Silly Billy*; 18. *Frankie boy*; 19. *Bear sits down upon a tree trunk.*

2 fl, pic, 2 E-flat cl, 2 bsn, dbsn, ocarina, drum, db, piano.

fp: 25 April 1927.

fEp: 3 December 1928, BBC broadcast from Arts Theatre, chamber chorus and orchestra, cond. Hermann Scherchen; performed in an English version by D. Millar.

Pub. 1928, Universal-Edition. Vocal score by Erwin Stein; English version, Martin Lindsay & Eric Smith; German version, R. St. Hoffmann.

159. Concertino. For piano and clarinet, horn, bassoon, 2 violins and viola. January–29 April 1925. Ded. Janu Heřmanovi. Dur. 19'.

1. *Moderato*; 2. *Più mosso*; 3. *Con moto*; 4. *Allegro.*

fp: 16 February 1926, Brno, Ilona Kurzová-Štěpánová (piano), František Kudláček and Jos. Jedlička (violins), Jos. Trkan (viola), St. Krtička (clarinet), František Jánský (horn) and J. Bříza (bassoon).

fEp: 7 February 1928, Gerald Cooper concert, Angus Morrison (piano), Frederick Thurston (clarinet), Aubrey Brain (horn), M. Newton (bassoon) and members of the International Quartet.

Pub. 1925, 1949, Hudební Matice.

160. The Makropulos Case (Věc Makropulos). Opera in three acts after Karel Čapek. 11 November 1923–12 November 1925.

3 fl, pic, 2 ob, ca, 3 cl, bcl, 2 bsn, cbsn; 4 hn, 4 tpt, 3 tmb, tuba; pcssn; hp, strings. *On stage:* 2 hn, 2 tpt, timp.

fp: 18 December 1926, Brno, cond. František Neumann; with Alexandra Čvánová; producer, Ota Zítek; décor, Josef Čapek.

f Prague p: 1 March 1928, National Theatre, cond. Otakar Ostrčil; with Kejřová, Kubla and Novák; producer, Josef Munclinger; décor, Josef Čapek.

fEp: 12 February 1964, Sadler's Wells, cond. Charles Mackerras; with Stanley Bevan (Vitek), Gregory Dempsey (Gregor), Jenny Hill (Kristina), Eric Schilling (Kolenaty), Marie Collier (Emilia Marty), Raimund

Herincx (Prus), John Chorley (Janek); producer, John Blatchley.

Pub. 1926, Universal-Edition. Vocal score by Ludvík Kundera; German version, Max Brod.

BIBLIOGRAPHY:

J. Bowen, Makropulos matter, *American Record Guide*, November 1961, p. 210.

Peter Burns: The Makropulos Case at Sadlers Wells, *Musical Events*, February 1964, p. 12.

Ernest Chapman: The Makropulos Case, *Musical Events*, March 1964, p. 21.

Winton Dean: The Makropulos Case, *MT*, April 1964, p. 281.

Erwin Felber: Die Sache Makropulos, *Signale*, 1927, No. 1, p. 7.

Hans Hartleb: LJ, Die Sache Makropulos, Uraufführung am Opernhaus Frankfurt a. M., *Signale*, 1929, No. 9, p. 266.

K. B. Jirák: Von Tschechischen Bühnen, 1: Die Oper Sache Makropulos von LJ, *Auftakt*, 1927, No. 2, p. 48.

Ludvík Kundera: The Makropulos Case, *Musical Events*, February 1964, p. 10.

Charles Mackerras: Janáček's Makropulos, *Opera*, February 1964, p. 79.

Colin Mason: The Makropulos Affair, *M&M*, February 1964, p. 13.

Rosa Newmarch: Janáček's latest opera, The Makropulos Affair, *Chesterian*, No. 61, March 1927, p. 161.

Malcolm Rayment: Janáček and The Makropulos Affair, *The Listener*, 20 February 1964, p. 330.

Erich Steinhard: LJ, Die Sache Makropulos, *Auftakt*, 1928, No. 4, p. 96.

Wgd.: Janáček, Sache Makropulos, *Anbruch*, April 1929, p. 167.

161. The Lord Christ is born (Narodil se Kristus Pán). Czech Christmas Carol for piano, with words. Pub. in *Hudební Besídka*, 1926.

162. The Banner (Our flag) (Naše vlajka) (František S. Procházka). 1925–6. Ded. Moravian Teachers' Choir. ?Unpub.

163. Sinfonietta. For orchestra. 1 April 1926.

1. *Allegretto*; 2. *Andante*; 3. *Moderato*; 4. *Allegretto*; 5. *Andante con moto.*

4 fl, pic, 2 ob, ca, 2 cl, E-flat cl, bcl, 2 bsn;

4 hn, 12 tpt, 2 bs tpt, 4 tmb, 2 ten tuba, tuba; timp, cym, campane.

fp: 26 June 1926, Prague, Czech Philharmonic Orchestra, cond. Václav Talich.

fAp: 4 March 1927, New York, New York Symphony Society concert, cond. Otto Klemperer.

fEp: 10 February 1928, Queen's Hall, BBC National concert, cond. Sir Henry Wood.

Pub. 1927, Universal-Edition.

BIBLIOGRAPHY:

M.B.: Eine neue Symphonietta von Janáček, *Anbruch*, September 1926, p. 335.

164. Capriccio. For piano left hand and chamber orchestra. April–30 October 1926. Dur. 17 20'.

1. *Allegro*; 2. *Adagio*; 3. *Allegretto*; 4. *Andante*. fl, pic, 2 tpt, ten tuba, 3 tmb.

fp: 2 March 1928, Prague, Otakar Hollmann and members of the Czech Philharmonic Orchestra, cond. Jaroslav Rídký.

?fEbp: 19 June 1955, Rudolf Firkušný and chamber ensemble, cond. Walter Goehr.

Pub. 1953, State Publishing House.

165. Glagolitic Mass (M'ša Glagolskaja). For soloists, mixed chorus, organ and orchestra. 2 August–15 October 1926. Text: Miloš Weingart. Ded. Dr. Leopoldu Prečanovi.

1. *Úvod*; 2. *Gospodi pomiluj*; 3. *Slava*; 4. *Věruju*; 5. *Svet*; 6. *Agneče Božij*; 7. *Varhany solo*; 8. *Intrada*.

4 fl, 3 pic, 2 ob, ca, 3 cl, bcl, 3 bsn, cbsn; 4 hn, 4 tpt, 3 tmb, tuba; timp, tamb pic, tgle, tamtam, cym, campanelle; 2 hp, celesta, organ, strings.

fp: 5 December 1927, Brno, Philharmonic Society of Brno concert, orchestra and soloists of Brno opera company with Alexandra Čvánová and Stanislas Tauber as guest soloists, cond. Jaroslav Kvapil.

fEp: 23 October 1930, Norwich Festival, Elsie Suddaby, Margaret Balfour, Francis Russell and Frederick Woodhouse, cond. Sir Henry Wood.

fEbp: 28 June 1935, Maida Vale studio before an invited audience, Laelia Finneberg, Doris Owens, Walter Widdop, Stanley Riley, BBC Chorus and Symphony Orchestra, cond. Sir Henry Wood.

Pub. 1928, Universal-Edition. Vocal score,

Ludvik Kundera; English version, Rosa Newmarch; German version, R. St. Hoffmann.

BIBLIOGRAPHY:

Robert Angles: Janáček's Byzantium, *Records & Recording*, March 1964, p. 13.

E.: Janáčeks Fröhliche Messe, *Anbruch,* December 1927, p. 436.

Hans Hollander: Janáček's Glagolitische Messe, *Musica*, 1958, No. 6, p. 329.

Ludvik Kundera: La messe en vieux-slave de Janácek, *Tempo*, February 1928.

P. Rosenfeld: Janáček festival mass, *New Republic*, 3 December 1930, p. 73.

166. Lullaby (Unkolébavka). Piano acc. to J. A. Komensky's 'Lullaby'. 1927–8.

167. Chorus. 1928. Composed for the occasion for the laying of the foundation stone of the Masaryk University, Brno. Text: Antonín Trýb.

fp: 2 April 1928.

168. String Quartet No. 2: 'Intimate Letters' (Listy důvěrné). 29 January – 19 February 1928. Dur. 26'.

1. *Andante—Allegro*; 2. *Adagio—Vivace*; 3. *Moderato—Adagio—Allegro*; 4. *Allegro—Andante—Adagio*.

fp: 11 September 1928, Brno, Moravian Quartet.

fEp: 8 November 1936, BBC broadcast, Prague Quartet.

Pub. 1938, 1949, Hudební Matice.

BIBLIOGRAPHY:

Hans Hollander: Die thematischen Metamorphosen in Janáčeks zweitem Streichquartett, *NZfM*, March 1966, p. 95.

169. Reminiscence (Vzpomínka). For piano. 8 May 1928. Pub. 1928, Muzika (Belgrade); 1936, Melpa.

170. To the dog Čipera. For piano. 8 August 1925–23 April 1928. Unfinished.

171. From the house of the dead (Z mrtvého domu). Opera in three acts after Dostoievsky. February 1927–8 June 1928.

3 pic, 4 fl, 2 ob, ca, 3 cl, 2 E-flat cl, bcl, 3 bsn, cbsn; 4 hn, 3 tpt, bs tpt, ten tuba, 3 tmb, bs tuba; timp, pcssn; hp, celesta, strings.

Janáček, Leoš

fp: 12 April 1930, Brno, National Theatre, cond. Břetislav Bakala; producer, Ota Zítek. fEp (stage): 28 October 1965, Sadler's Wells, cond. Charles Mackerras; with David Bowman, Jon Andrew, Gregory Dempsey, Ronald Dowd, Neil Easton, Margaret Neville, Denis Dowling; producer, Colin Graham; design, Ralph Koltai.

Pub. 1930, Universal-Edition. Vocal score by Břetislav Bakala; German version, Max Brod.

BIBLIOGRAPHY:

Wilhelm Bopp: LJ, Aus einem Totenhaue (Nationaltheater, Mannheim), *Die Musik*, February 1931, p. 357.

Ernest Chapman: Janáček's last opera, *Musical Events*, December 1965, p. 11.

Erwin Felber: Memoiren aus einem Totenhaus—Eine nachgelassene Oper von LJ (Uraufführung am Brünner Nationaltheater), *Der Auftakt*, 1930, Nos. 5–6, p. 150.

— Aus einem Totenhaus, *Signale*, 1930, No. 18. p. 569.

Christopher Grier: Janáček in Siberia, *M&M*, November 1965, p. 18.

Hans Heinsheimer: In jeder Kreatur ein funke Gottes—Janáčeks Oper Aus einem Totenhaus und ihre Entstehunggeschichte, *Anbruch*, November–December 1930, p. 284.

Hans Hollander: Wiederauffindung einer verschollenen Janáček-Oper, *Die Musik*, August 1931, p. 827.

— Janáček's last opera, *MT*, August 1956, p. 407.

Arthur Jacobs: Janáček's From the House of the Dead (synopsis), *The Listener*, 3 September 1964, p. 366.

R. Jones: From the House of the Dead, *American Record Guide*, July 1967, p. 992.

W. C. M. Kloppenberg: Janáček' opera Aus einem Totenhaus, *Mens en melodie*, May 1954, p. 136.

C. L. Osborne: Janáček's House of the Dead—the problems of sung drama, *High Fidelity*, June 1967, p. 75.

Luigi Pestalozza: Da una casa di morti di Janáček, *La Rassegna musicale*, 1962, p. 186.

Adolf Raskin: Janáčeks Totenhaus in Düsseldorf, *Anbruch*, June–July 1931, p. 125.

Paul Stefan: Die nachgelassene Oper von Janáček, *Anbruch*, April–May 1930, p. 174.

Erich Steinhard: Aus einem Totenhaus, Janáček-Premiere im Tschechischen Nationaltheater, *Der Auftakt*, 1931, No. 3, p. 85.

H. H. Stuckenschmidt: LJ, Aus einem Totenhaus, Landestheater Hannover 1958, in *Oper in dieser Zeit*, Friedrich Verlag (Hannover) 1964, p. 51.

Franz Willnauer: Wahrheit des Leidens—Echtheit des Mitleidens: Von Dostojewskijs Roman zu Janáčeks Oper Aus einem Todhaus, *NZfM*, January 1962.

Anon.: Aus einem Totenhaus, *SM*, September–October 1965, p. 292.

172. I wait for you (Čekám Tě). For piano. 5 August 1928. Unfinished.

GENERAL BIBLIOGRAPHY

Gerald Abraham: Janáček without words, *The Listener*, 24 August 1961, p. 293; in *Essays on Music*, Cassell (London) 1967, p. 137.

— Realism in Janáček's operas, in *Slavonic and Romantic Music*, Faber (London) 1968, p. 83.

V. Ambros: LJ ve vzpominkach, *Hudební Vychova*, August 1938.

Hilda Andrews: LJ, neglected modernist of Moravia, *Music Student*, September 1930, p. 513.

P. Bekker: LJs Persönlichkeit, *Anbruch*, June–July 1924.

Vl. Blažek: Vzpominky na dra LJ, *Hudební Výchova*, August 1938.

Helga Böhmer: LJ, *Melos*, October 1953, p. 273.

S. Brichta: LJ, *Signale*, 1928, No. 34, p. 987.

Georg Brieger: Ein Ahnherr der Neuen Musik, LJ, *NZfM*, 1954, p. 403.

Max Brod: LJ, *Anbruch*, February 1922, p. 59.

— LJ, Prague, 1924.

— LJ, *Blätter der Staatsoper* (Berlin), March 1924.

— LJs Persönlichkeit, *Anbruch*, June–July 1924, p. 237.

— Erinnerung an LJ, *Königsberger Hartungsche Zeitung*, 23 August 1928; *Anbruch*, August–September 1928, p. 233.

— Totenmusik für Janáček, *Der Auftakt*, 1929, No. 3, p. 78.

— Sternenhimmel, Kurt Wolff Verlag (Munich) 1933.

— Janáčeks letzte Jahre, in *Musik der Zeit*,

Vol. 8 (Tschechische Komponisten), Boosey & Hawkes 1954, p. 11.
— LJ, Universal-Edition (Vienna) 1956.
Marie Calma: Ze vzpominek na LJ, *Hudební Vychova*, August 1938.
M. Černohorská: Vyznam nápevkov pre Janáckovu opernu tvorbu, *Slovenska Hudba*, December 1958, p. 508.
Erik Chisholm: The operas of LJ, Pergamon Press (London) 1971.
Paul Eckstein: The path of Janáček's operas, in *Opera Annual No. 6*, Calder (London) 1959, p. 103.
R. Ellsworth: Janáček, *American Record Guide*, May 1965, p. 900.
R. Ericson: Janáček remembered by a fellow Czech, *New York Times*, 12 May 1963, Section 2, p. 9.
Erwin Felber: LJ, *RM*, August 1928, p. 98.
Rudolf Felber: LJ als Dramatiker, *Berliner Tageblatt*, 4 August 1927.
— LJ als Opernkomponist, *ÖM*, September 1958.
V. Fellegara: Prospetto cronologico della vita e delle opere di LJ, *L'Approdo musicale*, 1959, No. 10.
Jacques Fescholte: Grandeur de Janáček, *Feuilles musicales*, February 1962, p. 7.
Leoš Firkušný: LJ kritikem brněnské opery, Brno, 1935.
J. Freeman: Edge of truth, *Opera News*, 19 November 1966, p. 6.
J. de Freitas Branco, LJ, o autor de Jenufa, *Arte musical*, 1959, No. 8, p. 206.
Hans Gal (ed.): LJ, in *The Musicians World* (Great Composers in their Letters), Thames & Hudson (London) 1965, p. 431.
G. Gavazzeni: LJ, *La Rassegna musicale*, May–June 1938.
— Musicisti del nostro tempo, LJ, *La Rassegna musicale*, July–August 1938.
M. Glinski: LJ *Muzyka*, October 1928.
H. Goldschmidt: Janáček und Stravinsky, *Musik und Gesellschaft*, February 1959, p. 21.
Vladimír Helfert: LJ, O. Pazdírek (Brno) 1939.
— Zwei Gegenpole des Tschechischen Musik —Smetana und Janáček, *Der Aufstieg*, April 1934, p. 63.
— Documents relating to the life and works of LJ, *Tempo*, December 1933.

— O Janáčkovi, Prague, 1949.
Vladimír Helfert & Erich Steinhard: Die Musik in der tschechoslovakischen Republik, Orbis (Prague) 1938.
Karl Holl: LJ, *Frankfurter Zeitung*, 1928, No. 615.
Hans Hollander: LJ e le sue opere, *Rivista musicale italiana*, 1927, No. 11.
— LJ and his operas, *MQ*, January 1929, p. 29.
— Erinnerungen an LJ, *Blätter der Staatsoper* (Berlin), 1931.
— Janáček, *Mundo musical*, March–April 1929.
— LJ und das Slawentum, *Der Auftakt*, 1934, Nos. 7–8, p. 105.
— LJ, der Mensch und Künstler, *Der Aufstieg*, April 1934; *Anbruch*, April 1934, p. 66.
— A man of the people, *Radio Times*, 21 June 1935, p. 13.
— LJ, Slav genius, *M&L*, July 1941, p. 248.
— LJ, a centenary approach, *MT*, June 1954, p. 305.
— LJ, *SM*, May 1954, p. 169.
— The music of LJ, its origin in folklore, *MQ*, 1955.
— LJ und seine Orchesterwerke, *SM*, November 1956, p. 433.
— LJ in seiner Beziehung zu Smetana und Dvorák, *NZfM*, March 1958.
— LJ in seinen Opern, *NZfM*, August 1958.
— Janáček's development, *MT*, August 1958, p. 427.
— LJ und das Streichquartett, *ÖM*, March 1962.
— Der Natur Impressionismus in Janáčeks Musik, *SM*, 1962, No. 2 (March–April), p. 61.
— LJ, his life and work (transl. Paul Hamburger), Calder (London) 1963.
K. Honolka: LJ, ein Schallplattenporträt, *Musica Schallplatte*, 1960, No. 1, p. 11.
Otakar Jeremiáš: LJ, Melpa (Prague) 1937.
Julius Kapp: LJs Leben und Werk, *Blätter der Staatsoper* (Berlin), 1941–2, No. 5, p. 2.
Ernst Krause: Der Musiker Mährens, *Musica*, 1954, No. 6, p. 230.
Jan Kunc: LJ, *Hudební Revue*, 1911.
Ludwig (Ludvík) Kundera: Janáčeks Stil, *Der Auftakt*, 1927, No. 11, p. 279.
— LJ a Klub přátel uměni, Olomouc, 1948.
— Janáčkova varhanická škola, Olomouc, 1948.

Janáček, Leoš

Ludwig (Ludvík) Kundera: LJ, *Canon*, July 1958, p. 366.
— So komponierte LJ, *Musik in der Schule*, 1962, Nos. 7–8, p. 372.
Jan Löwenbach: LJ, *Chesterian*, No. 54, April–May 1926.
A. McCredie: Janáček and opera, *Canon*, January 1959, p. 194.
Colin Mason: Janáček a victim of history, *The Listener*, 1953.
Wilfrid Mellers: A great Czech composer, *The Listener*, 20 April 1939, p. 861.
— A note on Janáček, *Chesterian*, No. 153, January 1948.
— Janáček, *New Statesman*, 21 February 1964, p. 307.
— The world of Janáček, *New Statesman*, 11 September 1964, p. 367.
Pierre Meylan: L'originalité de Janáček, *Revue musicale de Suisse Romande*, 1967, No. 5 (December), p. 5.
Jan Mikota: Janáček v Anglii, *Listy hudební matice*, 1926; LJ in England, *Anbruch*, September 1926, p. 330.
Daniel Müller: LJ, Editions Rieder (Paris) 1928.
Rosa Newmarch: LJ and Moravian music drama, *Slavonic Review*, December 1922, p. 362.
— LJ, *Chesterian*, No. 74, November 1928, p. 22.
— LJ, *Slavonic Review*, January 1929, p. 416.
— New works in Czechoslovakia—Janáček and Novák, *Chesterian*, No. 96, July 1931.
— The music of Czechoslovakia, O.U.P. (London) 1942.
Jeremy Noble: Janáček's humanity, *M&M*, April 1964, p. 24.
Fritz Oeser: Dvořák, Smetana, Janáček, *Musica*, 1957, Nos. 9–10, p. 497.
Willem Pijper: LJ, *De Muziek*, 1928, Nos. 11–12.
Peter J. Pirie: The chamber music of LJ, *MO*, April 1962, p. 401.
Jaroslav Procházka: The Lachian roots of LJ, Frýdek-Místel (Prague) 1948.
Jan Racek: LJ, Poznámky k tvurčimu profilu, Olomouc, 1937.
— Slovanské prvky v tvorbě Leoše Janáčka, Brno, 1952.
— Janáček—dramatík, *Slovenská Hudba*, 1958,

January p. 6, February p. 49, March p. 91, April p. 142.
— LJs und Béla Bartóks Bedeutung in der Weltmusik, *Studia musicologica*, 1964, Nos. 1–4, p. 501.
Jan Racek (ed.): LJ—Obraz života a díla, Brno, 1948.
Jan Racek & Artuš Rektorys (ed.): Correspondence of LJ with Maria Calma and Dr. František Veselý, Prague, 1951.
— Correspondence of LJ and Max Brod, Prague, 1953.
Malcolm Rayment: The composer who never grew old, *M&M*, June 1954, p. 15.
— The composer who had to fight for his operas, *M&M*, December 1956, p. 13.
Artuš Rektorys (ed.): Correspondence of LJ and Artuš Rektorys, Prague, 1934; second edition, 1949.
— Correspondence of LJ and Otakar Ostrčil, Prague, 1948.
— Correspondence of LJ and František S. Procházka, Prague, 1949.
— Correspondence of LJ and Gabriela Horvátová, Prague, 1950.
— Correspondence of LJ and Karel Kovařovic and the management of the National Theatre in Prague, Prague, 1950.
C. Rihtman: O tridesetoj godisnjici smrti LJ, *Zvuk*, 1959, Nos. 26–27, p. 249.
Adolfo Salazar: LJ, in *Sinfonía y ballet*, Editorial Mundo Latino (Madrid) 1929, p. 154.
C. Schoenbaum: LJ, *Dansk Musiktidsskrift*, April 1958, p. 43.
Erwin Schulhoff: LJ, *Anbruch*, May 1925, p. 237.
M. Schumach: A lesson learned from Janáček, *New York Times*, 2 February 1964, Section 2, p. 24.
Desmond Shawe-Taylor: Janáček in Prague and Berlin, *Opera*, September 1956, p. 542.
— The operas of LJ, *PRMA*, Vol. 85 (1960), p. 49.
Robert Smetana: Vyprávení o LJ, Olomouc, 1948.
Bohumír Stědron: LJ na mužském učitelském ústavu v Brně, *Tempo* (Prague), May 1934.
— LJ v dopisech a vzpomínkách, Prague, 1946; LJ, letters and reminiscences (transl. Geraldine Thomsen), Artia (Prague) 1955.

— Janáčkove oslavy v Brne, *Slovenska Hudba*, December 1959, p. 528.
— LJ und Ferenc Liszt, *Studia musicologica*, 1963, Nos. 1–4, p. 295.
Erwin Stein: LJ, *Pult und Taktstock*, September 1928.
Erich Steinhard: Janáček, *Der Auftakt*, 1928, No. 8, p. 191.
— LJ, *Leipziger Neueste Nachrichten*, 2 October 1928.
— Janáček, *The Dominant*, October–November 1928, p. 23.
H. H. Stuckenschmidt: LJ, in *Schöpfer der neuen Musik*, Suhrkamp Verlag (Frankfurt a. M.) 1958, p. 74.
Julien Tiersot: LJ, *Le Ménestrel*, 24 April 1931, p. 181.
Vladimír Úlehla: Živá písen, Fr. Borovy (Prague) 1949.
Adolf E. Vašek: Po stopách LJ, Brňenské knižní nakladatelství (Brno) 1930.
Adolf Veselý: LJ, Prague, 1924.
Jaroslav Vogel: LJ dramatík, Prague, 1948.
— LJ, his life and works (transl. Geraldine Thomsen-Muchová), Paul Hamlyn (London) 1962.
Boleslav Vomáčka: In memoriam LJ, *Tempo* (Prague), October 1928.
H. Weinstock: Minority report on Janáček, *Saturday Review*, 15 October 1960, p. 70.
— Janáček on Dostoievsky, *Saturday Review*, 27 May 1967, p. 63.

MISCELLANEOUS OR UNSIGNED
Erinnerungen an den Menschen LJ, *Blätter der Staatsoper* (Berlin), 1941–2, No. 5, p. 5.
— LJ, *The Times*, 9 July 1954, p. 2.

ZOLTÁN KODÁLY (1882–1967)

Kodály was born on 16 December 1882 at Kecskemét on the Great Hungarian Plain, where his father—a keen amateur musician—was employed as a booking-clerk by the State Railways; but most of the composer's childhood was spent in Galánta, to which his father was transferred as station-master in 1885, and Nagyszombat (now Trnava and part of Czechoslovakia), to which he moved seven years later. At Nagyszombat Kodály made his début as a composer with an overture for his school orchestra. In 1900 he went to Budapest to spend five years as a student at the Pázmány University (where he studied Modern Languages) and the Academy of Music (where his composition teacher was Hans Koessler). In 1905 he made his first folksong-collecting expedition and in the following year took his D.Phil. with a thesis on Hungarian folk music. It was at this time that Kodály met Béla Bartók, who was to be an intimate friend for nearly forty years and a close collaborator both in ethnomusicology and the promotion of new music in Hungary. After a six-month visit to Berlin and Paris, Kodály returned to Budapest in 1907 to become Professor of Musical Theory at the Academy. In 1910 he married Emma Gruber (*née* Sandor), his senior by nearly twenty years. During the First World War he continued with his teaching and fieldwork undisturbed, but in the following period of Hungarian political crisis (1918–20) he was appointed Deputy Director of the Academy on the establishment of the Republic and then reduced to the rank of professor again at the fall of the Communist government. His first great success as a composer came in 1923 with the *Psalmus Hungaricus*, and he soon became known as a visiting conductor of his own music in many parts of Europe, though it was not until 1946 that he visited the USA. The use of a boys' choir at the première of the *Psalmus* began to turn Kodály's attention to the problems of musical education, and a great deal of his time thereafter was devoted to the creation of a corpus of semi-didactic choral works for children. He stayed in Budapest during the Second World War and though he retired from teaching in 1942, came more and more to be seen as the Hungarian cultural figure *par excellence*. He became president of the Hungarian Arts Council in 1945 and in 1962, during the national celebrations of his eightieth birthday, was awarded the state's highest honour, the Order of the Hungarian People's Republic. His wife died in 1958 and in the following year he married Sarolta Péczeli, a music student nearly sixty years his junior; but he died himself in Budapest in March 1967.

Kodály, Zoltán

CATALOGUE OF WORKS

1. Ave Maria. For voice and organ. *c.* 1897.

2. Ave Maria. For voice and string orchestra. *c.* 1897.

3. Mass. For mixed chorus and orchestra. *c.* 1897. Fragments only.

4. Overture. For orchestra. 1897.

5. String Trio and String Quartet. *c.* 1899.

6. Ave Maria. For mixed chorus and organ. *c.* 1899.

7. Assumpta est. For baritone, mixed chorus and orchestra. 1902.

8. Evening (Este) (P. Gyulai). For soprano solo and mixed chorus (SSATBB) a cappella. 1904. Pub. 1931, Universal-Edition; Magyar Kórus; 1939, Hawkes (English version, Elisabeth M. Lockwood).

9. Adagio. For violin (or viola, or cello) and piano. 1905. Pub. 1910, Rózsavölgyi; Universal-Edition; Zeneműkiadó Vállalat.

10. Intermezzo. For string trio. 1905, Körül. Pub. 1957, in *Zoltán Kodály, 75. születésnapjára.*

11. Summer evening (Nyári este). For orchestra. 1906, rev. 1929–30. Ded. Arturo Toscanini. Dur. 20'.
fl, ob, ca, 2 cl, 2 bsn; 2 hn; strings.
fp: 3 April 1930, New York Philharmonic, cond. Arturo Toscanini.
fEp: 16 September 1930, Queen's Hall, Promenade Concert, BBC Symphony Orchestra, cond. Sir Henry Wood.
Pub. 1930, Universal-Edition; Hawkes.

12. Méditation sur un motif de Claude Debussy. For piano. 1907, Budapest.
fEbp: 8 March 1934, Katharine Goodson.
Pub. 1925, Universal-Edition.

13. Two folksongs from Zobor (Két Zoborvidéki Népdal). For SSSAAA soloists and SA chorus. 1908, Budapest.
1. *Woe is me* (Meghalok, Meghalok).
2. *The Leveret* (Piros Alma Mosolyog).
Pub. 1923, Universal-Edition; Universal-Edition (English versions by M. W. Pursey & M.-D. Calvocoressi).

14. Songs on Hungarian popular word (Énekszó) Op. 1. For voice and piano. 1907–9.
1. *Three the ways I must go*; 2. *Come to me, my little birdie*; 3. *The cage is open wide*; 4. *I neither toil nor spin*; 5. *My delightful brown-haired mistress*; 6. *Oh, how long it is since we met!*; 7. *He who loves a fair one*; 8. *I have always wondered*; 9. *Slender is a silk thread*; 10. *Ah, my beloved*; 11. *Let not your anger rise*; 12. *Now it's clear and now it's cloudy*; 13. *Never again shall I do what I have just done*; 14. *Do you think that I would sorrow*; 15. *Ah, but, you know*; 16. *I plucked the fairest flowers.*
fEbp (Nos. 4 & 5 only): 14 June 1926, Manchester station, Herbert Heyner.
fEbp (complete): 3 March 1939, Keith Falkner.
Pub. 1921, Rózsavölgyi.

15. String Quartet No. 1 Op. 2. 1908–9.
1. *Andante poco rubato—Allegro*; 2. *Lento assai, tranquillo*; 3. *Presto*; 4. *Allegro.*
Pub. 1910, Rózsavölgyi; Universal-Edition; Zeneműkiadó Vállalat.

16. Ten Pieces Op. 3. For piano. Dated: 17 March 1909, Budapest.
1. *Valsette* (rev. Frederick Delius); 2. *Lento*; 3. *Andante poco rubato*; 4. *Lento—Andante*; 5. *Allegretto scherzoso*; 6. *Furioso*; 7. *Moderato triste*; 8. *Allegro giocoso*; 9. *Allegretto grazioso*; 10. *Allegro commodo.*
Pub. 1910, Rózsavölgyi; 1945, Delkas (Los Angeles); Boosey & Hawkes.

16a. Valsette Op. 3. From Ten Pieces for piano. 1907, Budapest.
fEbp: 24 October 1927, Irene de Marik.
Pub. sep. 1921, Rózsavölgyi, and omitted from later editions of the Ten Pieces Op. 3 which then appeared as *Nine Pieces* Op. 4. Valsette arr. by Emil Telmányi for violin and piano pub. 1965, Boosey & Hawkes.

17. Cello Sonata. 1909.
Pub. 1957, in *Zoltán Kodály, 75. születésnapjára.*

18. Cello Sonata Op 4. 1909–10. Dated: February 1910, Budapest.
1. *Fantasia*; 2. *Allegro con spirito.*
fEp: 11 March 1914, Aeolian Hall, Livio Boni and Franz Liebich.

fEbp: 16 June 1928, George Roth and Endre Petri.
Pub. 1922, Universal-Edition.

19. Duo Op. 7. For violin and cello. 1914, Budapest.
1. *Allegro serioso, non troppo*; 2. *Adagio—Andante*; 3. *Maestoso e largamente, ma non troppo lento—Presto*.
fEp: 13 February 1924, London, concert of the Lener Quartet, Jeno Lener and Ìmro Hartman.
Pub. 1922, 1949, 1952, Universal-Edition.

20. Sonata for unaccompanied cello Op. 8. 1915, Budapest. Ded. Eugène de Kerpely.
1. *Allegro maestoso ma appassionato*; 2. *Adagio*; 3. *Allegro molto vivace*.
fEp: 5 February 1924, London Contemporary Music Centre concert, Beatrice Harrison.
fEp (public): 8 May 1924, Beatrice Harrison.
fEbp: 3 May 1928, Arts Theatre Club, Paul Hermann.
Pub. 1921, Universal-Edition.

21. Seven Songs Op. 6. 1912–16. For voice and piano.
1. *Solitude* (Einsamkeit) (Berzsenyi). 1912, Budapest.
2. *From a lover's letter* (Brieffragment an die Freundin) (Berzsenyi). 1916, Budapest.
3. *Life's noontide* (Am Zenith des Lebens) (Berzsenyi). 1913, Budapest.
4. *Spring* (Der Frühling) (Berzsenyi). 1913, Budapest.
fEbp: 14 June 1926, Manchester station, Herbert Heyner.
5. *Sadly rustle the leaves* (Braust der traurige Wald) (Kölcsey). 1915, Budapest.
6. *Weeping* (Tränenlos) (Kölcsey). 1913, Budapest.
7. *Farewell carnival!* (Faschings Abschied) (Csokonai). 1916, Budapest.
fEbp: 14 June 1926, Manchester station, Herbert Heyner.
Pub. 1923, Universal-Edition; 1939, Boosey & Hawkes: English version, Elisabeth Lockwood; German version, B. Szabolcsi.

22. Two Songs Op. 5. For low male voice and orchestra. 1913–16.

1. *Hervad marlige tünk* (Ady Andreas). 1913, Budapest.
3 fl, 2 ob, ca, 2 cl, 3 bsn; 4 hn; timp; hp, strings.
2. *Varni, ha ezfelt* (Ady Andreas). 1913–16, Budapest.
3 fl, pic, 2 ob, ca, 2 cl, bcl, 3 bsn, cbsn; 4 hn, 2 tpt, 3 tmb, bs tuba; timp, tamtam, tgle; hp, strings.
Pub. 1923, Universal-Edition. German version, Stephan Szabolcsi (No. 1), Josef Vészi (No. 2).

23. Four Songs. For voice and piano. 1907–1917.
1. *Haja, haja* (Dorfszene) (János Arany). 1907.
2. *Nausikaa*. 1907.
3. *Mezei dal* (Lied auf der Wiese). 1907.
4. *Fáj a szivem* (Schwer und trostlos) (Zsigmond Móricz). From 'Pacsirtaszó' (orig. scored for string quintet, cym and cl). 1917. See No. 25.
Pub. 1925, Universal-Edition. German version, B. Szabolcsi.

24. Two Drinking Songs. For male chorus. 1913–17.
1. *Bordal* (Trinklied) (Ferenc Kölcsey). 1913, Budapest.
2. *Mulató Gajd* (Zechergesang) (17th century, Anon.). 1917, Budapest.
Pub. 1923, Universal-Edition; 1952, Universal-Edition with English words by Matyas Seiber and Leo Black.

25. Pacsirtaszó. Music for a Schauspiel by Zsigmond Móricz. 1917. ? Unpub. See No. 23.

26. Sept Pièces Op. 11. For piano. 1910–18.
1. *Lento*. 13 November 1917.
2. *Rubato, parlando* (Chanson populaire Székely). November 1918.
3. *Allegretto malincolio* (Il pleut dans la ville). May 1910.
4. *Rubato* (Epitaphe). December 1918.
5. *Tranquillo*. 17 March 1918.
6. *Poco rubato* (Chanson populaire Székely). November 1917.
7. *Rubato*. 17 March 1917, Budapest.
fEbp (Nos. 1, 3 & 4): 7 August 1937, Eileen Ralph.

Pub. 1921, Universal-Edition; Zenemü-kiadó Vállalat.

26a. Seven Pieces for orchestra. Orch. György Ránki.

fp: 22 June 1963, Budapest, Radio Orchestra.

27. String Quartet No. 2 Op. 10. 1916(?)–1918. Dated: March 1918, Budapest. Ded. Hungarian Quartet (Waldbauer, Temesváry, Kornstein, Kerpely).

1. *Allegro*; 2. *Andante—Allegro giocoso*.

fEp: *c.* November 1922, Hungarian Quartet.

fEbp: 5 December 1927, Hungarian Quartet.

Pub. 1921, Universal-Edition.

28. Serenade Op. 12. For two violins and viola. 1919–20. Dated: March 1920, Budapest.

1. *Allegramente*; 2. *Lento, ma non troppo*; 3. *Vivo*.

fEp: 11 November 1922, members of the Lener Quartet.

fEbp: 5 October 1926, Grotrian Hall, Emeric Waldbauer, Jack Kessler and Jean de Temesváry.

Pub. 1921, Universal-Edition.

BIBLIOGRAPHY:

Béla Bartók: Kodály's Trio, *Musical Courier*, 1920.

29. Five Songs Op. 9. For voice and piano. 1916–23.

1. *Adám, hol vagy?* (Adam, wo bist du?) (Ady Endre). 1918, Budapest.

2. *Sappho, szerelmes éneke* (Sapphos Liebesgesang) (Ady Endre). 1916, Budapest.

3. *Éjjel* (Nachts) (Béla Balazs). 1918, Budapest.

4. *Kicsi virágom* (Blume, du holde) (Béla Balazs). 23 November 1923, Budapest.

5. *Azerdö* (Der Wald) (Béla Balazs). 1916, Budapest.

Pub. 1924, Universal-Edition; 1939, Boosey & Hawkes.

30. Psalmus Hungaricus Op. 13. For tenor, mixed chorus, children's voices and orchestra. 1923. Text: Mihály Kecskeméti Vég.

3 fl, 2 ob, 2 cl, 2 bsn; 4 hn, 3 tpt, 3 tmb; timp, cym; hp, organ, strings.

fp: 19 November 1923, Budapest Festival in celebration of the fiftieth anniversary of the union of Buda and Pest.

?fEp: 30 November 1927, Cambridge, Cambridge University Musical Society concert, Frank Mullings, London Symphony Orchestra conducted by Zoltán Kodály; performed in an English translation by E. J. Dent.

fEbp: 4 December 1927, Parry Jones, Wireless Chorus and Symphony Orchestra, cond. Stanford Robinson.

fAp: 19 December 1927, New York Philharmonic and Pro Musica, cond. Willem Mengelberg.

Pub. 1924, Universal-Edition; Zenemü-kiadó Vállalat.

BIBLIOGRAPHY:

József Ujfalussy: ZK et la naissance du Psalmus Hungaricus, *Studia musicologica*, 1962, Nos. 1–4, p. 357.

— A Psalmus Hungaricus, in *ZK 75. Születésnapjára*, Akadémiai Kiado (Budapest) 1957, p. 21.

31. Ballet Music (Ballettmusik). For orchestra. ?1925. Dur. 5'.

2 fl, pic, 2 ob, 2 cl, sax, bsn, cbsn; 4 hn, 3 tpt, 3 cornet, 3 tmb, tuba; timp, GC, cym, tamb pic, xyl, cimbalom, tgle, cast, celesta; strings.

fEp: 24 August 1937, Queen's Hall, Promenade Concert, BBC Symphony Orchestra, cond. Sir Henry Wood.

Pub. 1936, Universal-Edition.

32. The straw guy (Villö). Hungarian folksong for SSAA chorus a cappella. 1925.

fEp: 30 July 1935, BBC Chorus, cond. Trevor Harvey.

Pub. 1925, O.U.P.: English version, M.-D. Calvocoressi; German version, Emma Kodály.

33. See the gipsies (Túrót Eszik a Cigány). Hungarian folksong for SSAA chorus a cappella. 1925.

fEp: 30 July 1935, BBC Chorus, cond. Trevor Harvey.

Pub. 1925, O.U.P. (as 'See the gipsy'): English version, M.-D. Calvocoressi; German version, Emma Kodály; 1960, O.U.P.:

English words, Jacqueline Froom. Also pub. for SATB.

34. St. Gregory's Day (Gergekyjárás). Traditional Hungarian song for SSA chorus a cappella. 1926. Pub. 1929, 1933, O.U.P.: English version, Elisabeth M. Lockwood.

35. Háry János Op. 15. Opera. 1926. Libretto: Béla Paulini and Zsolt Harsányi, after a poem by János Garay.
fp: 16 October 1926, Budapest.
Pub. 1929, 1931, Universal-Edition. German version, R. S. Hoffmann.

BIBLIOGRAPHY:
Béla Abody: A Háry János felújítása, *Muzsika*, February 1963, p. 3.
Franz Blasl: ZKs Háry János, *Musikerziehung*, May 1968.
W. Kemp: Háry János auf der Bühne, *Anbruch*, November–December 1931, p. 209.
Fernando Rékai: La musique du Háry János de Kodály, *Crescendo*, November 1926.
István Volly: Ki volt Háry János?, *Muzsika*, November 1960, p. 46.

FILM:
Háry Janos. A Mafilm-Hungarofilm Production, 1965, directed by Miklós Szinetár. Hungarian State Opera Choir, Hungarian Radio and TV Children's Choir, cond. Jánas Ferencsiki with György Melis (Háry János), Mária Mátyás (Örzse), Judit Sándor (Marie-Louise), Jósef Réti (Ebelastin), Éva Gombos (The Empress), György Radnai (Marci).
fGBp: 1966, Edinburgh Festival.
Distributed in Britain by Eagle Films, 1969.

35a. Háry János: Suite. For orchestra. 1927.
1. *Prelude: The fairy tale begins* (Kezdödik a mese).
2. *Viennese musical clock* (Bécsi harangjátéz).
3. *Song* (Dal).
4. *The battle and defeat of Napoleon* (Napoleon csatája).
5. *Intermezzo* (Közjáték).
6. *Entrance of the Emperor and his court* (A császári udvar bevonulása).
3 fl, 3 pic, 2 ob, 2 cl, alto sax, 2 bsn; 4 hn, 3 tpt, 3 cornets, 3 tmb, bs tuba; timp, GC, cym, 4 campanelli, tamb basque, carillon,

tamtam, tamb pic, tgle; xyl, celesta, piano, cimbalom, strings.
fp: 15 December 1927, New York, New York Philharmonic, cond. Willem Mengelberg.
fEp: 23 August 1928, Queen's Hall, Promenade Concert, Wood Symphony Orchestra, cond. Sir Henry Wood.
Pub. 1927, Universal-Edition; Zenemükiadó Vállalat.

35b. Háry János: Intermezzo. Transcribed by Joseph Szigeti for violin and piano. Pub. 1951, Hawkes.

36. Dances of Marosszék (Marosszéki táncok). For piano. 1927. Dur. 12'.
fEp: 24 November 1930, BBC broadcast, Béla Bartók.
f London p: 13 January 1970, Elizabeth Hall, Tamas Vasary.
Pub. 1930, Universal-Edition; Zenemükiadó Vállalat.

36a. Dances of Marosszék. Version for orchestra. 1930.
2 fl, pic, 2 ob, 2 cl, 2 bsn; 4 hn, 2 tpt; timp, cym, GC, tamb pic; strings.
fp: 28 November 1930, Dresden, cond. Fritz Busch.
fAp: 11 December 1930, New York Philharmonic, cond. Arturo Toscanini.
fEp: 29 March 1931, BBC broadcast, BBC Orchestra, cond. Sir Henry Wood.
fEp (concert): 2 November 1933, Manchester, Halle Orchestra, cond. Robert Heger.
Pub. 1930, Universal-Edition; 1939, Hawkes; Zenemükiadó Vállalat.

37. King Ladislaus' Men (Magyars and Germans) (Lengyel László). For female voices (SSCC) a cappella. 1927. Based on Hungarian traditional fragments. Pub. 1929, O.U.P.: English version, Clement F. Rogers and Elisabeth M. Lockwood; 1961, O.U.P.: English version adapted.

38. Theatre Overture. For orchestra. 1927. Dur. 12'.
3 fl, pic, 2 ob, 2 cl, 2 bsn; 4 hn, 3 tpt, 3 tmb, bs tuba; timp, GC, cym, tamb pic, tgle; piano, strings.
fEp: 5 December 1932, Queen's Hall,

Kodály, Zoltán

Courtauld-Sargent concert, cond. (Sir) Malcolm Sargent.

Pub. 1932, Universal-Edition.

39. The Voice of Jesus (Jelenti Mágát Jézus). For female voices (SMzC) a cappella. 1927. A Zobor-side folksong. Pub. 1929, O.U.P.: English version, Clement F. Rogers and Elisabeth M. Lockwood; German version, B. Szabolcsi. Version for male voices (TBarB) pub. 1944, Magyar Kórus.

40. Gipsy lament (Cigánysirtaó). Traditional Hungarian song for female voices (SSA) a cappella. 1928. Pub. 1931, O.U.P.: English version, Elisabeth M. Lockwood; 1961, O.U.P.: English version, Jacqueline Froom.

41. God's blacksmith (Isten Kovácsa). A children's counting out song for female voices (SSA). 1928. Pub. 1931, O.U.P.: English version, Elisabeth M. Lockwood.

42. The deaf boatman (A Súket Sógor). For female voices (SSA) a cappella. 1928. Hungarian popular text. Pub. 1929, O.U.P.: English version, Clement F. Rogers.

43. Five Tantum Ergo. For female voices with (Nos. 1, 4, 5) organ acc. ?1928.

1. *Maestoso*; 2. *Andante*; 3. *Con moto*; 4. *Sostenuto*; 5. *Moderato*.

Pub. 1928, copyright Zoltán Kodály; 1941 (revised edition), Universal-Edition.

44. Whitsuntide (Pünkösdölö). For female voices (SMzC) a cappella. 1929. Based on traditional Hungarian melodies.

fEp (broadcast): 12 January 1936, BBC Chorus, cond. Zoltán Kodály.

Pub. 1929, O.U.P.: English version, Clement F. Rogers and Elisabeth M. Lockwood.

45. A Christmas Carol (Új Esztendöt Köszöntö). Traditional Hungarian song for female voices (SMzA) a cappella. 1929. Pub. 1929, 1962, O.U.P.: English version, Clement F. Rogers.

46. Dancing song (Táncnóta). Traditional Hungarian song for female voices (SMzA) a cappella. Pub. 1929, O.U.P.: English version, Elisabeth M. Lockwood.

47. Three Songs (Három ének) Op. 14. For voice and piano. 1924–9. Ded. Dr. Székelyhidy Ferencnek.

1. *Exile* (Siralmas nékem) (Balassa).

2. *Heart of fire* (Imhol nyvita én kebelem) (Anon., 17th century).

3. *Stay, sweet bird* (Várji, meg madaram) (Anon., 17th century).

Pub. 1929, 1930 (English version), Universal-Edition; 1939, Boosey & Hawkes. English version, A. H. Fox Strangways; German version, B. Szabolcsi (Nos. 1 & 2), Emma Kodály (No. 3).

47a. Three Songs. Version with orchestra. ?1937.

2 fl, 2 ob, 2 cl, 2 bsn; 2 hn; timp, pcssn; strings.

fEp (omitting No. 2): 12 September 1937, John McKenna and the BBC Orchestra, cond. Zoltán Kodály.

Pub. 1937, Universal-Edition.

48. The swallow's wooing (Gólyanóta). Hungarian children's song for female voices (SSA). 1929. Pub. 1929, O.U.P.: English version, Clement F. Rogers; 1961, O.U.P.: English version adapted.

49. A birthday greeting (Nagyszalontai) (Köszöntö). For male chorus a cappella. 1931. Ded. 'For March 17'. Dur. 1' 10".

?fEp (broadcast): 6 March 1937, BBC Singers, cond. Leslie Woodgate.

Pub. 1933, Universal-Edition; 1935, Universal-Edition: English version, M. W. Pursey. ?Arr. for mixed chorus.

50. Mátra Pictures (Mátrai Képek). A Set of Hungarian folksongs for mixed (SATB) chorus a cappella. 1931. Ded. The 'Székesfövárosi Énekkar' and its conductor V. Karvaly. Dur. 12'.

fEbp: 25 June 1933, Wireless Singers, cond. Cyril Dalmaine.

Pub. 1933, Universal-Edition: English version, Clement F. Rogers.

51. Pange lingua. For mixed voices and organ. ?1931.

fEp (broadcast): 12 January 1936, BBC Chorus, cond. Zoltán Kodály, with John Wills (organ).

Pub. 1931, Universal-Edition; 1939, Boosey & Hawkes.

52. The Spinning Room (Székely Fonó). Lyrical Scenes, with folksongs from Transylvania. 1924–32. Libretto: Zoltán Kodály.

53. Hungarian folk music (Magyar népzene). Collection of 57 ballads and folksongs for voice and piano. 1924–32. Variously published.

54. Epiphany (Vizkereszt). For female voices (SSA) a cappella. 1933. Pub. 1937, Universal-Edition; 1952, Universal-Edition: English version, Elisabeth M. Lockwood.

55. The Aged (Öregek) (Sándor Weöres). For mixed voices (SATB) a cappella. 1933. Pub. 1934, Magyar Kórus; 1935, Universal-Edition; 1939, Hawkes: English version, Elisabeth M. Lockwood.

56. Four Italian Madrigals (Négy Olasz Madrigal). For female voices. 1932–3. Pub. 1949, Editio Musica.

57. Dances from Galanta. For orchestra. 1933. Ded. Budapest Philharmonic Society on its eightieth birthday. Dur. 15'.

2 fl, 2 ob, 2 cl, 2 bsn; 4 hn, 2 tpt; timp, tamb pic, tgle, campanelle; strings.

fEp: 22 September 1934, Queen's Hall, Promenade Concert, BBC Symphony Orchestra, cond. Sir Henry Wood.

fAp: 11 December 1936, Philadelphia Orchestra, cond. Eugene Ormandy.

Pub. 1934, Universal-Edition; 1939, Hawkes; Zenemükiadó Vállalat. Piano version by Kenessey Jenö pub. 1935, Universal-Edition.

58. Jesus and the traders (Jézus és a kufárok). For mixed voices (SATB) a cappella. 1934. Ded. A. H. Tierie. Dur. 6' 30".

fEp: August 1935, BBC broadcast, BBC Chorus, cond. Trevor Harvey.

Pub. 1934, Magyar Kórus; 1936, Universal-Edition: English version, Edward Dent.

59. Too late (Akik Mindig Elkésnek) (E. Ady). For mixed voices (SATB) a cappella. 1934. Dur. 2' 20".

fEp: August 1935, BBC broadcast, BBC Chorus, cond. Trevor Harvey.

Pub. 1934, Magyar Kórus; 1935, Universal-Edition; 1939, Hawkes: English version, Elisabeth M. Lockwood.

60. Transylvanian lament (Székely Keserves) (Traditional Hungarian). For mixed voices (SATB) a cappella. 1934. Dur. 3' 30". Pub. 1934, Magyar Kórus; 1937, Universal-Edition: English version, Elisabeth M. Lockwood.

61. The Leveret (Nyúlacska) (Traditional Hungarian). For female voices (SS) a cappella. ?1934. Pub. 1937, Universal-Edition: English version, Elisabeth M. Lockwood.

62. Ave Maria. For female voices a cappella. ?1934. Pub. 1935, Universal-Edition.

63. The bachelor (Kit kéne élvenni). Folksong from Székely for male voices. 1934. Pub. 1935, Magyar-Kórus; 1935, Universal-Edition; 1951, Winthrop Rogers/Boosey: English version, Nancy Bush after a translation by Mátyás Seiber; 1952, Boosey & Hawkes: German version, Fritz Schröder.

64. The peacocks (Felszállott a páva) (E. Ady). For male voices (TBarB) a cappella. 1934. Pub. 1951, Winthrop Rogers/Boosey: English version, Nancy Bush after a translation by Mátyás Seiber; 1952, Boosey & Hawkes; German version, Fritz Schröder.

65. Songs from Karád (Karádi nóták). For male voices a cappella. 1934.

fEbp: 7 December 1952, BBC Men's Chorus, cond. Mátyás Seiber.

Pub. 1951, Winthrop Rogers/Boosey: English version, Nancy Bush after a translation by Mátyás Seiber; 1952, Boosey & Hawkes: German version, Fritz Schröder.

66. The Angel and the shepherds (Angyalok és pásztorok). For female voices (SA) a cappella. 1935.

fEp (broadcast): 12 January 1936, BBC Chorus, cond. Zoltán Kodály.

Pub. 1937, 1952, Universal-Edition: English version, Elisabeth M. Lockwood.

67. The ruins (Huszt) (Ferenc Kölcsey). For male voices (TBarB) a cappella. 1936. Dur. 3'.

fEp: 29 December 1936, BBC broadcast, Budapest University Chorus, cond. V. Vaszy.

Pub. 1938, Universal-Edition: English version, Elisabeth M. Lockwood; 1944, Magyar Kórus.

68. Ode to Franz Liszt (Liszt Ferenchez) (Mihály Vörösmarty). For mixed voices (SATB) a cappella. 1936. Dur. 7'. Pub. 1937, Universal-Edition: English version, Elisabeth M. Lockwood.

69. Shepherds' Christmas dance (Karácsonyi pásztortánc). For female voices (SA) and flute or recorder or wind ensemble. ?1936. Dur. 2'. Pub. 1938, Universal-Edition.

70. Budavári Te Deum. For soloists, mixed chorus and orchestra. 10 July 1936. Dur. 21'.

2 fl, 2 ob, 2 cl, 2 bsn; 4 hn, 3 tpt, 3 tmb, tuba; timp; organ (ad lib), strings.

fp: 11 September 1936, Budapest Cathedral.

fEp: 13 November 1936, BBC broadcast, BBC Chorus and Orchestra, cond. Sir Adrian Boult.

fEp (concert): 9 September 1937, Gloucester Cathedral, Three Choirs Festival, Isobel Baillie, Mary Jarred, Heddle Nash, Keith Falkner, Festival Choir and London Symphony Orchestra, cond. Zoltán Kodály.

Pub. 1937, Universal-Edition; 1939, Hawkes.

71. Annie Miller (Molnár Anna). Transylvanian folk ballad for mixed voices (SATB) a cappella. 1936.

fEbp: 29 July 1937, BBC Singers, cond. Trevor Harvey.

Pub. 1937, Magyar Kórus; 1937, Universal-Edition; 1939, Winthrop Rogers/Hawkes; 1942 (revised edition), Hawkes: English version, Elisabeth M. Lockwood.

72. To the Magyars (Dániel Berzsenyi). Four-part canon for mixed voices. ?1936. Pub. 1936, Magyar Kórus.

73. Hymn to King Stephen (Enek Szent István királyhoz). For mixed voices (SATB) a cappella. 1938. Pub. 1939, Magyar Kórus; 1939, Hawkes: English version specially written for the Fleet Street Choir by Nancy Bush. Version for male voices (TBarB) pub. 1944, Magyar Kórus.

74. Evening song (Esti dal). For mixed voices a cappella. 1938. Pub. ?1938, Editio Musica. Version for male voices (TBarB) pub. 1944, Magyar Kórus.

75. Variations on a Hungarian folksong (The Peacock) (Felszállott a páva). For orchestra. 1938–9. Composed for the fiftieth anniversary of the Concertgebouw Orchestra. Dur. 24½'.

3 fl, pic, 2 ob, ca, 2 cl, 2 bsn; 4 hn, 3 tpt, 3 tmb; timp, tgle, cinelli, campanello; hp, strings.

fp: 23 November 1939, Amsterdam, Concertgebouw Orchestra, cond. Willem Mengelberg.

fEp: 27 February 1946, BBC broadcast, BBC Symphony Orchestra, cond. Ernest Ansermet.

fEp (concert): 23 July 1956, Royal Albert Hall, Promenade Concert, BBC Symphony Orchestra, cond. Sir Malcolm Sargent.

Pub. 1941, Zoltán Kodály; 1947, Boosey & Hawkes.

76. Concerto for orchestra. 1939. Composed for the Golden Jubilee season of the Chicago Symphony Orchestra. Dur. 19'.

3 fl, pic, 2 ob, 2 cl, 2 bsn; 4 hn, 3 tpt, 3 tmb, tuba; timp, tgle; hp, strings.

fp: 6 February 1941, Chicago Symphony Orchestra, cond. Frederick Stock.

fEp: 5 October 1946, BBC broadcast, BBC Symphony Orchestra, cond. Zoltán Kodály.

Pub. 1942, Zoltán Kodály; 1958, Boosey & Hawkes.

77. Norwegian girls (Norvég leányok) (Sándor Weöres). For mixed voices (SATB) a cappella. 1940. Pub. 1951, Winthrop Rogers/Boosey: English version, Nancy Bush after a translation by Mátyás Seiber; 1952, Boosey & Hawkes: German version, Fritz Schröder.

78. Bicinia Hungarica. 180 progressive two-part songs in four volumes. 1937–41. Vols. 1–4 pub. 1957; 1962 (English edition), Boosey; Vol. 4 pub. 1958, Zenemükiadó Vállalet; 1962 (English edition), Boosey. Incorporated into *The Choral Method* (Vols. 4–7).

79. 15 Two-part exercises. 1941. Pub. 1941, Zoltán Kodály; Magyar Kórus; 1952, Boosey & Hawkes (except Hungary). Incorporated into *The Choral Method*.

80. Let us sing correctly. 107 two-part exercises (without words). 1941. Pub. 1941,

Zoltán Kodály; Magyar Kórus; 1952, Boosey & Hawkes; Zenemükiadö Vállalat.

81. The forgotten song of Bálint Balassi (Balassi Bálint Elfelejtett Eneke) (Erzsi Gazdag). For mixed voices a cappella. 1942. Pub. 1942, Magyar Kórus.

82. Missa Brevis. For mixed chorus and organ. 1942. Ded. 'Coniugi et consorti carissimae in anniversario XXXV'.

    1. *Introitus*; 2. *Kyrie*; 3. *Gloria*; 4. *Credo*; 5. *Sanctus*; 6. *Benedictus*; 7. *Agnus Dei*; 8. *Ite Missa Est.*

fEp (broadcast): 3 October 1946, BBC Chorus and George Thalben-Ball, cond. Zoltán Kodály.

fEp (concert): 21 April 1948, St. Martin-in-the-Fields, Westminster Music Society concert, Arnold Foster Choir, cond. Arnold Foster.

Pub. 1947, Boosey & Hawkes.

82a. Missa Brevis. Version for orchestra with (ad lib) organ. 1944.

3 fl, pic, 2 fl, 2 ob, 2 cl, 2 bsn; 4 hn, 3 tpt, 3 tmb, tuba; timp; organ, strings.

fEp: 9 September 1948, cond. Zoltán Kodály.

Pub. 1950, Boosey & Hawkes.

BIBLIOGRAPHY:

Mátyás Seiber: Kodály's Missa Brevis, *Tempo*, No. 4, summer 1947.

83. 333 elementary exercises in sight singing (Olvasógyakorlat). 1943. Pub. 1957, Magyar Kórus; Zenemükiadó Vállalat; 1963, Boosey & Hawkes (ed. Percy M. Young). Incorporated into *The Choral Method.*

84. Songs for schools. Vols I & II. 1943. Pub. Library of the Nation's Educators.

85. To the Transylvanians (A székelyekhez) (Sandor Petöfi). For mixed voices (SATB) a cappella. ?1943. Pub. 1943, Magyar Kórus; 1958, Boosey: English version, Thomas Rajna.

86. Veni, veni, Emmanuel (O come, O come, Emmanuel). From an eighteenth-century French missal, arr. for mixed voices (SAB) a cappella. ?1943. English words adapted by J. M. Neale (1818–66).

fEbp: 5 November 1949, Dorian Singers, cond. Mátyás Seiber.

Pub. 1963, Boosey & Hawkes.

87. Battle song (Csatadal) (Sandor Petöfi). For mixed voices (SATB–SATB) a cappella. 1943. Pub. 1959, Boosey & Hawkes: English version, Thomas Rajna; German version, Ernst Roth.

88. Psalm CXXI (121-ik Szoltár). For mixed voices (SATB) a cappella. 1943. Pub. 1959, Boosey & Hawkes: German version, Ernst Roth.

89. Communion (Elsö áldozás). Anthem for mixed voices (SATB) a cappella. 1943. Pub. 1963, Boosey & Hawkes: English version, Percy M. Young.

90. Cohors generosa. Old Hungarian student song of welcome for mixed voices (SAB) a cappella. 1943. Pub. 1944, Magyar Kórus; 1958, Boosey.

91. Song book for primary schools. With Jenö Adám. 1943. Pub. 1948, Hungarian Ministry of Education.

92. Mother listen (Kádár Kata). Folk Ballads for alto and chamber orchestra. 1943 (?1950). ?Pub. ?Universal-Edition.

93. The son of an enslaved country (Rab hazának fia). For male voices. 1944. Pub. 1947, Magyar Kórus.

94. Still by a miracle our country stands (Isten csodája) (Sándor Petöfi). For mixed voices a cappella. 1944. Pub. 1947, Magyar Kórus.

95. Sol-Mi. Eight volumes of educational works, with Jenö Adám. 1944–5. Pub. 1945, Magyar Kórus.

96. At the Martyrs' Grave. ?For orchestra. 1945. ?Unpub.

97. Twenty-four little canons on the black notes (24 kis kánon a fekete billentyűkön). For piano. June 1945, Budapest. Pub. 1946, Rózsavölgyi; 1957, Boosey & Hawkes. Incorporated into *The Choral Method.*

98. Children's dances (Gyermektáncok). Twelve dances for piano. May 1945, Budapest.

Kodály, Zoltán

1. *Allegretto*; 2. *Allegretto cantabile*; 3. *Vivace*; 4. *Moderato cantabile*; 5. *Allegro moderato, poco rubato*; 6. *Vivace*; 7. *Vivace, quasi marcia*; 8. *Friss*; 9. *Allegro marcato*; 10. *Allegro leggiero*; 11. *Vivace*; 12. *Allegro comodo*.
fEp: 14 December 1947, BBC broadcast, Ilona Kabos.
Pub. 1947, Hawkes.

99. Dirge (Sirató enek) (Pál Badrogh). For mixed voices. 1947. Pub. 1947, Magyar Kórus.

100. Czinka Panna. Singspiel by Béla Balázs. 1948. ?Unpub.

100a. Minuetto serio. For orchestra. From 'Czinka Panna'.
2 fl, 2 ob, 2 cl, 2 bsn; 4 hn, 2 tpt; timp; strings.
Pub. 1953, Zenemükiadó Vállalat.

101. Pentatonic music, Vols. I–IV. 1945–8. Pub. Zoltán Kodály; Magyar Kórus; Zenemükiadó Vállalat.

102. Cease your bitter weeping (Semmit ne bánkodjá) (Andrew Horváth de Szkhárosi). For mixed voices a cappella. ?Date. (Transcribed for chorus after the contemporary tune) and composed for the 100th anniversary of the Protestant teachers' college at Nagykörösi. Pub. 1951, Winthrop Rogers/Boosey: English version, Nancy Bush after a translation by Mátyás Seiber; 1952, Boosey & Hawkes: German version, Fritz Schröder. Also arr. Mátyás Seiber for female voices.

103. Soldier's song (Katonadal). For male voices, trumpet and drum. ?Date.
fEbp: 7 December 1952, BBC Men's Chorus, Jack Mackintosh (tpt), Ernest Gillegin (side dm), cond. Mátyás Seiber.
Pub. 1951, Winthrop Rogers/Boosey: English version, Nancy Bush after a translation by Mátyás Seiber; 1952, Boosey & Hawkes: German version, Fritz Schröder.

104. Kálló folk dances (Kállai kettös). For mixed chorus and orchestra. 1950.
1. *Slow dance*. Dur. $5\frac{1}{2}'$ (or 4′ with cut).
2. *Allegro*. Dur. $1\frac{1}{4}'$.
3. *Presto*. Dur $1\frac{1}{2}'$.
E-flat cl, 2 cl, 2 cimbalom, strings.
fp: 4 April 1951.

Pub. 1952, Zenemükiadó Vállalat; 1954, Hawkes: English words, Nancy Bush.

BIBLIOGRAPHY:
John S. Weissmann: Notes to Kodály's recent settings of Hungarian dances, *Tempo*, No. 32, summer 1954, p. 29.

105. Eight Little Duets. For soprano and tenor with piano, after the Bicinia Hungarica. 1953.
1. *Thus starts the Kalevala* (Igy kezdödik a Kalevala).
2. *Do not for gold and silver* (Arany ezüstért).
3. *From the woods a small bird* (Egy kicsi madárka).
4. *My little daughter* (Kis kece lányom).
5. *Maiden beauty* (Leány szépség).
6. *Tulip, tulip, fully blown* (Hej! tulipán, tulipán).
7. *Maker of the stars above us* (Csillagoknak terëmtöje).
8. *Counting song* (Kiolvasó).
Pub. 1954, Zenemükiadó Vállalat; 1957, Boosey; 1958, Boosey: English version, Thomas Rajna.

106. Wish for peace—The year 1801 (Békességohajtás) (Benedek Virág). For mixed voices. 1953. Pub. 1953, Zenemükiadó Vállalat.

107. Epigrams (Epigrammák). Nine vocalises for voice and piano (or for an instrument and piano). March 1954. Pub. 1954, Zenemükiadó Vállalat; 1963, Boosey & Hawkes (ed. Percy M. Young). Incorporated into *The Choral Method*.

108. 55 Two-Part Exercises. March 1954. Pub. 1964–5, Boosey & Hawkes (ed. Percy M. Young). Incorporated into *The Choral Method*.

109. 44 Two-Part Exercises. 1954. Pub. 1964–5, Boosey & Hawkes (ed. Percy M. Young). Incorporated into *The Choral Method*.

110. Tricinia. Twenty-nine progressive 3-part songs (SSA or TBB). 1954. Pub. 1964, Boosey & Hawkes (ed. Percy M. Young). Incorporated into *The Choral Method*.

111. 33 Two-Part Exercises. 1954. Pub.

1964, Boosey & Hawkes (ed. Percy M. Young). Incorporated into *The Choral Method*.

112. Hymn of Zrinyi (Zrinyi Szózata). For baritone soloist and mixed chorus a cappella. 1954. Ded. 'to the faithful companion of my life at her sickbed on our 45th anniversary'.

fp: ?1954, Imré Palló and the Hungarian Radio Choir, cond. Zoltán Vásárhelyi.

fEbp: 5 March 1958, Marian Zigmunt and the BBC Chorus, cond. Mátyás Seiber.

f London p: 13 January 1970, Elizabeth Hall, BBC Chorus, cond. Cecilia Vajda.

Pub. 1955, Zenemükiadó Vállalat; 1956, Hawkes; 1958, Hawkes: English version, Thomas Rajna; 1962, Hawkes: German version, Ernst Roth.

113. Psalm CXIV. For mixed voices and organ. ?Date. Pub. 1958, Zenemükiadó Vállalat; 1959, Boosey & Hawkes: German version, Ernst Roth.

114. Mountain nights (Hegyi Éjszakák). For female voices. 1923–56.

fEp: 28 August 1958, BBC broadcast, Zoltán Kodály Girls' Choir of Debrecen, cond. Georgy Gulyasi.

Pub. 1961–3, Boosey & Hawkes. Also known as 'Nights in the Mountains' or 'Evening in the Mountains'.

115. Song of faith (A Magyarokhoz) (Berzsenyi). Canon in 4 parts for SSATTB chorus a cappella. ?Date. Pub. 1959, Zenemükiadó Vállalat; 1964, Boosey & Hawkes: English version, Percy M. Young.

116. I will go look for death (John Masefield). For mixed voices (SATB) a cappella. 1959.

fEbp: 14 March 1962, Collegium Musicum Oxoniense, cond. László Heltay.

Pub. 1959, Boosey & Hawkes.

117. Homo perpende fragilis (In memoriam Mátyás Seiber). For mixed voices (SATB) a cappella. ?1960. Pub. 1960, Boosey.

118. Five songs of the Mountain-Tscheremis. For voice and piano. ?Date. Pub. 1961, Editio Musica.

119. Symphony. 1961. Commissioned by members of the Swiss Festival Orchestra. Ded. 'in memoriam Arturo Toscanini'. Dur. 30'.

1. *Allegro*; 2. *Andante moderato*; 3. *Vivo*.

3 fl, pic, 2 ob, 2 cl, 2 bsn; 4 hn, 3 tpt, 3 tmb, tuba; timp, tgle, cym; strings.

fp: 16 August 1961, Lucerne, cond. Ferenc Fricsay.

fEp: 7 December 1961, Royal Festival Hall, London Philharmonic Orchestra, cond. Ferenc Fricsay.

Pub. 1962, Boosey & Hawkes.

BIBLIOGRAPHY:
John S. Weissmann: Kodály première at the Lucerne Festival, *Musical Events*, October 1961, p. 14.
— Kodály's Symphony, a morphological study, *Tempo*, winter 1961–2, p. 19.

120. Media vita in morte sumus. For mixed voices. ?Date. Pub. 1962, Boosey & Hawkes.

121. Sik Sándor's Te Deum. For mixed voices. ?Date. Pub. 1962, Editio Musica.

122. Five Songs of Béla Bartók Op. 15. Orch. Kodály. 1961. Pub. 1962, Universal-Edition. For details see No. 61a in Bartók catalogue.

123. Fifty nursery songs with a range of five notes. 1962. Pub. 1963, Boosey & Hawkes; 1964, Boosey & Hawkes: English version, Percy M. Young. Incorporated into *The Choral Method*.

124. 66 Two-Part Exercises. 1963. Pub. 1964, Boosey & Hawkes (ed. Percy M. Young). Incorporated into *The Choral Method*.

125. An Ode for Music. Composed for Cork Choral Festival, 1963. Pub. 1963, Boosey & Hawkes.

126. Tell me where is fancy bred (Shakespeare). For female voices (SSA) a cappella. ?1964. Pub. 1964, Blond, in *Classical Songs for Children* (ed. Countess of Harewood and R. Duncan); 1965, Boosey & Hawkes.

127. An Ode (O'Shaughnessy). Composed for the quartercentenary of Merton College, Oxford, 1964. Unpub.

Kodály, Zoltán

128. Organoedia ad missam lectam. For organ ?1965. Pub. 1966, Boosey & Hawkes (ed. Martin Hall).

129. Sonatina. For cello and piano. ?1965. Pub. 1966, Boosey & Hawkes.

130. 22 Two-Part exercises. 1965. Pub. 1966, Boosey & Hawkes (ed. Percy M. Young). Incorporated into *The Choral Method*.

131. Laudes Organi. Fantasia on a twelfth-century Sequence for mixed chorus (SATB) and organ. 24 February 1966. Commissioned by the Atlanta Chapter for the 1966 National Convention of the American Guild of Organists, Atlanta, Georgia.
  fEp: 1966, London Student Chorale, cond. Roy Wales.
  Pub. 1966–7, Boosey & Hawkes.

132. Ladybird. For female voices (SSA) a cappella. ?1966. Based on a children's folksong. Pub. 1967, Boosey & Hawkes: English version, Geoffry Russell-Smith.

133. Wainamoinen makes music (From: The Kalevala). For female voices (SSAA) and harp or piano. ?1966. Pub. 1967, Boosey & Hawkes.

134. 77 Two-Part Exercises. ?Date. Pub. 1967, Boosey & Hawkes (ed. Percy M. Young).

BACH TRANSCRIPTIONS BY KODÁLY
Three Chorale Preludes. Arr. for cello and piano. ?1924.
  1. *Ach, was ist doch unser Leben*. Ded. Karl Straube.
  2. *Vater Unser im Himmelreich*.
  3. *Christus, der uns selig macht*.
  fEbp (complete): 15 June 1938, Douglas Cameron.
  Pub. 1924, 1951, Universal-Edition.

Fantasia cromatica. Arr. for viola solo. Pub. 1951, Boosey & Hawkes (ed. William Primrose).

Prelude and Fugue in E flat minor (From Book I). Arr. cello and piano. Pub. 1967, Boosey & Hawkes.

Prelude and Fugue in B minor (From Book I). Arr. string quartet.

'Lute' Prelude in C minor (Schm. 999). Arr. for violin and piano.

WRITINGS BY KODÁLY
The stanzaic structure of Hungarian folksong (A magyar népdal strófaszerkezete) 1906.
A plan for the new universal collection of folksongs (Az új egyetemes népdalgyüjtemény tervezete), in collaboration with Béla Bartók, *Ethnographia*, Vol. XXIV (1913), p. 313.
The pentatonic scale in Hungarian folk music (Ötfokú hangsor a magyar népzenében), *Zenei Szemle*, Vol. I (1917).
The Hungarians of Transylvania: folksongs (Erdélyi magyarság, Népdalok), in collaboration with Béla Bartók, 1921. Pub. 1923, Népies Irodalmi Társaság.
Bartóks Kinderstücke, *Anbruch*, 1921.
Béla Bartók, *RM*, 1921.
Lettera di Budapest, in various numbers of *Il Pianoforte*, 1922–3.
Les sonates de Béla Bartók, *RM*, 1923.
The Collection of Nagyszalonta (Nagyszalontai gyütjés), 1934. Pub. Magyar Népköltési Gyüjtemény (ed. Zsigmond Szendrei).
Children's choruses, 1929. Pub. *Zenei Szemle*, Vol. XIII.
Hungarian folk music (Magyar népzene), 1931. Pub. *Zenei Lexikon* (ed. Bence Szabolcsi & Aladár Tóth).
Ethnography and musical history (Néprajz és zenetörténet), 1933. Pub. *Ethnographia*, Vol. XLIV.
The structural peculiarities of Mari folk music (Sajátságos dallamszerkezet a cseremisz népzenében), 1934. Pub. in Memorial volume for the seventieth birthday of József Balassa, Budapest, 1934.
The folk music of Hungary (A magyar népzene), 1937. Pub. Royal Hungarian University Press, Budapest, 1937; 2nd edition (1943) with further additions; 3rd edition (1951) with further editions, completed by Lajos Vargyas, pub. Zeneműkiadó Vállalat: Ger. transl. 1956, Corvina (Budapest); Eng. transl. Ronald Tempest and Cynthia Jolly, Barrie & Rockliff (London) 1960.
Hungarian musical characteristics (Magyarság

a zenében) 1939. What is Hungarian? (Mi a magyar?) ed. Gyula Szekfü, Budapest, 1939.

Folk music and art music (Népzene és müzene), 1941; *Tempo*, winter 1962–3, p. 26.

Music in the kindergarten (Zene az óvodában), 1941. Pub. *Magyar Zenei Szemle*, Vol. I, No. 2.

Hungarian musical education (Magyar zenei nevelés), 1945.

The folksong collection of János Arany (Arany János népdalgyüjteménye), in collaboration with Ágost Gyulai, 1952. Pub. 1953, Hungarian Academy of Sciences, Budapest.

Who is a good musician? (Ki a jó zenész?), 1953. Pub. 1954, Zenemükiadó Vállalat.

Die ungarische Volksmusik, in *Musik der Zeit* (Ungarische Komponisten), Boosey & Hawkes (Bonn) 1954, p. 5.

The tasks of musicology in Hungary, *Studia musicologica*, 1961, Nos. 1–2, p. 5.

Musikunterricht und Erziehung, *ÖM*, November 1966, p. 587.

Folksong in Hungarian music education, *International Music Educator*, No. 15, March 1967, p. 486 (text also in French and German); repr. in *Musica* (Oxford), 1967, No. 1, p. 14.

Souvenirs (ed. D. Dille), *Studia musicologica*, 1967, Nos. 3–4, p. 255.

GENERAL BIBLIOGRAPHY

Béla Bartók: The greatest Hungarian musician, *Tempo*, winter 1962–3, p. 26; repr. from *Nyugat*, 1921.

S. Baud-Bovy: Hommage à ZK, *International Music Educator*, No. 7, April 1963, p. 225.

F. Bonis: ZKs Werke, *Studia musicologica*, 1962, Nos. 1–4, p. 11.

János Breuer: Kodály és a színpad, *Muzsika*, December 1962, p. 8.

Sir Ernest Bullock: Kodály's visit to College, *RCM Magazine*, 1960, No. 3, p. 66.

M.-D. Calvocoressi: ZK, *MT*, 1913.

— ZK, *MMR*, April 1922; repr. in *ZK* (Percy M. Young), Benn (London) 1964, p. 203.

— Choral music of Kodály, *The Listener*, 1936, p. 365.

Frank Choisy: Les chansons populaires

hongroises recueillies par Bartók et Kodály, *Revue des études hongroises et finno-oogriennes*, 1925, Vol. II, No. 2.

A. Darazs: The Kodály method for choral training, *American Choral Review*, 1966, No. 3, p. 8; *Council for Research in Music Education Bulletin*, No. 8, fall 1966, p. 59.

Suzanne Damrquez: Un musicien hongrois, ZK, *La Vie musicale*, No. 7, June 1951, p. 6.

A. E. F. Dickinson: Kodály's choral music, *Tempo*, No. 15, June 1946.

László Eösze: ZK, octogenarian, *New Hungarian Quarterly*, 1962, No. 6; ZK osemdesiatrocny, *Slovenska Hudba*, December 1962, p. 299.

— ZK, basnik hudby, *Hudebni Rozhledy*, 1962, No. 22, p. 956.

— Die Welt des Tondichters, *Studia musicologica*, 1962, Nos. 1–4, p. 95.

— ZK gyermekkarai, in *ZK 75. születésnapjára*, p. 105.

— ZK élete és művészete; transl. István Farkas and Gyula Gutyás as ZK, his life and work, Collet's (London)/Corvina (Budapest) 1962.

Imre Fabián: Kodály-hanglemezek, *Muzsika*, January 1963, p. 3.

Alan Fluck: Kodály, *Crescendo*, No. 75, March 1956, p. 123.

Andor Földes: Kodály, *Tempo*, No. 46.

Géza Frid: ZK zeventig jaar, *Mens en melodie*, December 1952, p. 376.

Willi Friese: Der Weggenosse Bartóks—ZK 70. Jahre, *NZfM*, 1952, p. 694.

R. G. Frost: Orff and Kodály, new teaching methods, *Music Journal*, February 1962, p. 34.

István Gábor: Kodály's music pedagogy, *New Hungarian Quarterly*, 1962, No. 5.

J. Gallois: ZK, le renovateur de la musique hongroise, *Musica* (Chaix), No. 105, December 1962, p. 4.

V. Gergely: ZK meets high fidelity, *High Fidelity*, December 1955, p. 58.

Scott Goddard: Hungarian master, *Radio Times*, 10 September 1937, p. 17.

Cecil Gray: ZK, in *A Survey of Contemporary Music*, London, 1924, p. 249.

— ZK, *MT*, May 1922, p. 312.

Edward Greenfield: Kodály on records, *Tempo*, winter 1962–3.

Kodály, Zoltán

E. Haraszti: ZK et la musique hongroise, *RM,* 1947.

Julian Herbage & Cynthia Jolly: Kodály, Hungary's music master, *M&M,* May 1967, p. 20.

Frank Howes: Kodály in English, *Tempo,* winter 1962–3, p. 17.

Pál Járdányi: Kodály and the folk song, *New Hungarian Quarterly,* 1962, No. 8.

Cynthia Jolly: The art songs of Kodály, *Tempo,* winter 1962–3, p. 2.

— Kodály, a personal view, *Tempo,* winter 1967–8, p. 16.

O. Karolyi: Kodály and musical literacy, *Making Music,* No. 59, autumn 1965, p. 8.

Harald Kaufmann: Letztes Gespräch mit ZK, *ÖM,* April 1967, p. 212.

A. Kendell: ZK, *Canon,* 1965, No. 2, p. 9.

György Kerényi: ZK e la musica sacra ungherese, *Magyar Kórus,* December 1932.

Dezsö Keresztúry: Kodály the writer, *New Hungarian Quarterly,* 1962, No. 8.

Iván Kertész: Unnepi Kodály-hangversenyek, *Muzsika,* February 1963, p. 1.

L. Kirwan: Kodály, *Making Music,* No. 23, autumn 1953, p. 8.

L. Kiss: ZK, *Zvuk,* No. 79 (1967), p. 37.

János Kovács: ZK szimfónikus müvei, in *ZK 75. születésnapjára,* p. 43.

Tábor Kozma: ZK, achievement and promise, *New Hungarian Quarterly,* 1962, No. 8.

Gerhard Krause: ZK, der Fünfzigjährige, *Signale,* 1932, No. 50, p. 995.

E. Kraus: ZK's legacy to music education, *International Music Educator,* No. 16, September 1967, p. 513.

Giulia Maróti: Kodály-hangverseny a rádioban, *Muzsika,* January 1963, p. 3.

Colin Mason: Hungary's history in Kodály's music, *The Listener,* 28 January 1960, p. 193.

— Kodály and chamber music, *Studia musicologica,* 1962, Nos. 1–4, p. 251.

W. H. Mellers: Kodály and the Christian epic, *M&L,* April 1941; in *Studies in Contemporary Music,* Dobson (London) 1947, p. 136.

Antal Molnár: Az ifú Kodály a zeneszerzés válaszútján, in *ZK 75. születésnapjára,* p. 9.

— Kodály und der Realismus, *Studia musicologica,* 1962, Nos. 1–4, p. 255.

— ZK, *Muzsika,* December 1962, p. 3.

Dorothy Moulton-Mayer: ZK, *Crescendo,* No. 48, November 1952, p. 13; No. 66, February 1955, p. 138.

Guido Pannain: ZK, *Il Pianoforte,* May 1926.

— ZK, in *Modern Composers,* London 1932.

Paul A. Pisk: Bartók und Kodály, *Berliner Börsen-Zeitung,* 9 June 1926.

Benjamin Rajezky: ZK in memoriam, *Musikforschung,* October–December 1967, p. 361.

Malcolm Rayment: Kodály at eighty, *M&M,* December 1963, p. 14.

— Kodály, folklorist, composer, educationalist, *Records & Recording,* August 1965, p. 14.

Willi Reich: Zum Tode von ZK, *SM,* 1967, No. 2 (March–April), p. 105.

Rudolf Réti: Gruss an Kodály, *Anbruch,* December 1932, p. 189.

M. H. Richards: Kodály's singing schools, *American Choral Review,* 1962, No. 4, p. 8.

— The legacy from Kodály, *Music Educators Journal,* 1963, No. 6, p. 27.

— The Kodály system in the elementary schools, *Council for Research in Music Education Bulletin,* No. 8, fall 1966, p. 44.

György Sandor: ZK was my teacher, *Etude,* April 1951, p. 12.

Robert Schollum: ZK und der ungarische musikalische Volksschule-zug, *Musikerziehung,* June 1962 (No. 4).

Mátyás Seiber & I. Szelengi: Kodály, *Crescendo,* November 1926.

Benedikt Szabolcsi: Die Instrumentalmusik ZKs, *Anbruch,* November 1922, p. 270.

— Die Lieder ZKs, *Anbruch,* August–September 1927, p. 283.

— Die Chöre ZKs, *Anbruch,* November–December 1928.

Bence Szabolcsi & D. Bartha (ed.): *ZK 75. születésnapjára,* 1957.

Bence Szabolcsi: Kodály and universal education, *Studia musicologica,* 1962, Nos. 1–4, p. 7.

— ZK's youth, *New Hungarian Quarterly,* 1962, No. 8.

Bence Szabolcsi (ed.): ZK, octogenario sacrum, Akademiai Kiado (Budapest) 1967.

Bence Szabolcsi & Imré Fábián: ZK zum 80. Geburtstag, *ÖM,* December 1962.

Etienne Szelényi: Kodály et le nouveau style du piano, *Crescendo,* November 1926.

András Szöllösy: Kodály's melody, *Tempo*, winter 1962–3, p. 12.
— Kodály müvészete, Budapest, 1943.
— ZK, povodom osamdesetagodisnjice rodenja, *Zvuk*, No. 57 (1963), p. 213.
Sándor Torday: ZK als paedagoog, *Mens en melodie*, September 1948, p. 272.
Aladar Tóth, ZK, *RM*, September–October 1929, p. 197.
— ZK zu seinem 50. Geburtstag, Vienna, 1932.
— ZK, *Anbruch*, December 1932, p. 191.
— The poetic world of ZK in the light of his choral works, *Music Journal*, May 1963, p. 53.
E. Szönyi: ZK's pedagogic activities, *International Music Educator*, No. 13, March 1966, p. 418 (text also in French and German).
Lajos Vargyas: Kodály's role in folk music, *New Hungarian Quarterly*, 1962, No. 8.
P. Varnai: 80-lecie Zoltana Kodály, *Ruch Muzyczny*, 1963, No. 5, p. 16.
P. Vidal: ZK, musicien aimé, *Musica* (Chaix), No. 145, April 1966, p. 26.
John Warrack: ZK, *Crescendo*, No. 136, October 1964, p. 33.
Imre Waldbauer: Kodály, in *Cobbett (I)*, 1929, p. 56.
John S. Weissmann: The contemporary movement in Hungary, *Music Today*, 1949.
— Kodály's later orchestral music, *Tempo*, No. 17, autumn 1950, p. 16; No. 18, winter 1950–1, p. 17.
— Kodálys späte Orchesterwerke, *Musik der Zeit*, Vol. 9 (Ungarische Komponisten), Boosey & Hawkes (Bonn) 1954, p. 16.
— Kodály Concerto-ja és Páva-variációi, in *ZK 75. születésnapjára*, p. 27.
— Kodály's songs, *The Listener*, 20 March 1958, p. 517.
Geoffrey Winters: The Kodály concept of music education, *Tempo*, No. 92, spring 1970, p. 15.
Percy M. Young: ZK, a Hungarian musician, Ernest Benn (London) 1964.
— ZK and the choral tradition, *American Choral Review*, 1965, No. 1, p. 1.

MISCELLANEOUS OR UNSIGNED
ZK, *Bollettino bibliografico musicale*, January 1933.

ZK, *Musikrevy*, 1963, p. 14.
ZK, Angliában, *Muzsika*, August 1960, p. 6.
Salute to Kodály, *Musica* (Oxford), 1967, No. 1, p. 44.
ZK, *Musica* (Oxford), 1967, No. 3, p. 31.

GUSTAV MAHLER (1860–1911)

The second of a succession of twelve children, Gustav Mahler was born on 7 July 1860 in the Bohemian village of Kalište, where his Jewish parents kept a liquor shop; but he moved with the family to Jihlava (=Iglau) in Moravia later the same year and lived there throughout his boyhood. In 1875 he was accepted as a student at the Vienna Conservatoire by Julius Epstein, who took a fatherly interest in him thereafter, as did Anton Bruckner. He spent three years at the Conservatoire, forming an intimate friendship with Hugo Wolf which, however, soured before Wolf's mental breakdown (1897). From 1880 to 1891 Mahler supported himself by taking increasingly important conducting posts at increasingly prestigious opera-houses (Bad Hall, Laibach, Olmütz, Cassel, Prague, Leipzig, Budapest); and from 1891 to 1897 he was principal conductor at the Hamburg Opera. His summer vacations in the Hamburg years, often spent at Steinbach-am-Attersee in the Salzkammergut, were devoted to composing. In October 1897, after a strategic conversion to Roman Catholicism which rendered him eligible for the post, Mahler became artistic director 'for life' of the Vienna Opera. During the next ten years his time was mainly divided between running the Vienna company with unprecedented perfectionism for nine months out of every twelve and in the remaining three composing his own music while staying in southern Austria, principally at Maiernigg on the Wörthersee in Carinthia. He was also principal conductor of the Vienna Philharmonic Orchestra from 1899 to 1901 and frequently toured Europe to conduct other orchestras. In 1902 he married Alma Schindler (1879–1964): they had two daughters, the elder of whom died in 1907. In the same year Mahler was manœuvred out of his position at the Vienna Opera and it was also discovered that he had a diseased heart. He made his first visit to the USA in 1908 to conduct the Metropolitan Opera for a season, and returned in 1909 to become conductor of the newly formed New York Philharmonic Orchestra. In all Mahler made four visits to America, but in February 1911, during the last, he suffered a serious breakdown in New York. He was taken back to Vienna mortally ill and died there from auto-intoxication of the blood in May of the same year.

CATALOGUE OF WORKS

1. Violin Sonata. 1876. Lost.
?fp: 12 September 1876, Jihlava.

2. Piano Quartet in A minor. First movement only. 1876.
?fp: 10 July 1876, ?Vienna Conservatoire.

BIBLIOGRAPHY:
Dika Newlin: GM's Piano Quartet in A minor (1876), *Chord and Discord*, 1963, No. 10, p. 180.

3. Piano Quartet. Fragment only. 1876.

4. 'Conservatoire' Symphony. ?1877. Lost.

5. Piano Quintet. ?Scherzo only. ?1875–?1878. Lost.
fp: 5 July 1878, Vienna Conservatoire.

6. Suite. For piano. 1875–?78.

7. Song Fragments. 1876–?79. Incl. Im wunderschönen Monat Mai (Heine).

8. Herzog Ernst von Schwaben. Opera. 1877–?78. Libretto: Josef Steiner (?after Uhland).

9. Piano Quartet. ?1879. Lost.

10. Quartet movement. For ? piano (?string) quartet. ?1879.

11. Das Klagende Lied. Original version. For soloists, chorus and orchestra. ?1878–November 1880.
1. *Waldmärchen*; 2. *Der Spielmann*; 3. *Hochzeitsstück*.
fp (No. 1): 28 November 1934, Radio Brno, cond. Alfred Rosé.
fp (complete): 8 April 1935, Vienna Radio, cond. Alfred Rosé.
fEp: 21 April 1970, Royal Festival Hall,

Elisabeth Söderström, Grace Hoffman, Ernst Häfliger, London Symphony Orchestra and Chorus, cond. Pierre Boulez.
Unpub. For final version of this work see No. 25.

BIBLIOGRAPHY:
Hans Holländer: Mahler-Uraufführung in Brünn, *Anbruch*, December 1934, p. 201.
— Ein unbekannter Teil von GMs Klagendem Lied, *Der Auftakt*, 1934, Nos. 11–12, p. 200.
Donald Mitchell: Mahler's Waldmärchen, *MT*, April 1970, p. 375.

12. Die Argonauten. Opera. 1880. Libretto: Gustav Mahler. Unpub.

13. Drei Lieder (Gustav Mahler). For tenor and piano. 1880.
1. *Im Lenz*. Dated: 19 February 1880.
2. *Winterlied*. Dated: 27 February 1880.
3. *Maitanz im Grünen*. Dated: 5 March 1880.
fp: 30 September 1934, Radio Brno, Zdenek Knittl, acc. Alfred Rosé.
Unpub.

14. Rübezahl. Opera. ?1879–83. Libretto: Gustav Mahler. Unfinished.

15. Nordische Symphonie (or Suite). ?1882–3. Lost.

16. Symphony in A minor. Three movements. 1882–3. Lost.

17. [Lieder und Gesänge aus der Jugendzeit]. For voice and piano. c. 1880–3.
1. *Frühlingsmorgen* (R. Leander).
2. *Erinnerung* (R. Leander).
3. *Hans und Grethe* (Trad.).
4. *Serenade aus 'Don Juan'* (Lenau, after Tirso de Molina).
5. *Phantasie aus 'Don Juan'* (Lenau, after Tirso de Molina).
Songs with words from 'Des Knaben Wunderhorn': c. 1888.
6. *Um schlimme Kinder artig zu machen*.
7. *Ich ging mit Lust durch einen grünen Wald*.
8. *Aus! Aus!*
9. *Starke Einbildungskraft*.
10. *Zu Strassburg auf der Schanz*.
11. *Ablösung im Sommer*.
12. *Scheiden und Meiden*.
13. *Nicht Wiedersehen!*

14. *Selbstgefühl.*
fp (No. 3): April 1886, Prague, Fräulein Frank.
Nos. 1–5 pub. as Vol. 1, 1885, Schott; Universal-Edition; Nos. 6–9 pub. as Vol. 2 & Nos. 10–14 pub. as Vol. 3, 1892, Schott; Universal-Edition.

18. **Begleitungsmusik zu lebenden Bildern nach Scheffels 'Der Trompeter von Säckingen'.** 1884. Lost.
fp: 23 June 1884, Cassel, cond. Mahler.

19. **Lieder eines fahrenden Gesellen.** For low voice and piano or voice and orchestra. December 1883–January 1885. Words: Gustav Mahler.
  1. *Wenn mein Schatz*; 2. *Ging heut' Morgen*; 3. *Ich hat ein glühend Messer*; 4. *Die zwei blauen Augen.*
  3 fl, pic, 2 ob, ca, 3 cl, bcl, 2 bsn; 4 hn, 3 tpt, 3 tmb; timp, GC, cym, tgle, glock; hp, strings.
  fp (version with orchestra): 16 March 1896, Berlin, Anton Sistermans and Berlin Philharmonic Orchestra, cond. Gustav Mahler.
  ?fEp: 3 November 1927, Queen's Hall, Royal Philharmonic Society concert, Maria Olczewska, cond. Sir Henry Wood. (NB: fEp originally announced for Promenade Concert, 17 October 1914.)
  Pub. 1897, Weinberger.

BIBLIOGRAPHY:
Rolf Urs Ringger: Zu GMs Lieder eines fahrenden Gesellen, *SM*, October 1959, p. 348.
— Mahlers Lieder eines fahrenden Gesellen, *Musica*, 1960, No. 6, p. 362.

20. **Symphony No. 1 in D major.** 1884–8.
  1. *Langsam, Schleppend*; 2. *Kräftig bewegt*; 3. *Feierlich und gemessen*; 4. *Stürmisch bewegt.*
  4 fl, 2 pic, 4 ob, ca, 3 cl, E-flat cl, bcl, 3 bsn, cbsn; 7 hn, 4 tpt, 3 tmb, tuba, Verstärkung hn; 2 timp, GC, cym, tgle, tamb, Turkish cym; hp, strings.
  fp: 20 November 1889, Budapest, cond. Gustav Mahler.
  fEp: 21 October 1903, Queen's Hall, Promenade Concert, Queen's Hall Orchestra, cond. (Sir) Henry Wood.
  fAp: 16 December 1909, New York, cond. Gustav Mahler.

Pub. 1898, Weinberger; *c.* 1905, Universal-Edition. Arr. by Bruno Walter for piano four hands, 1906, Universal-Edition.

BIBLIOGRAPHY:
Egon von Komorzynski: GMs erste Symphonie in D-dur, *NMZ*, 1905, Nos. 16–17.

20a. **Symphonic Movement: 'Blumine'.** Original second movement of preceding, probable source No. 18, discarded 1894. Dur. 8'.
  2 fl, 2 ob, 2 cl, 2 bsn; 4 hn, tpt; timp; hp, strings.
  Pub. 1967–8, Theodore Presser.

21. **Die drei Pintos.** Opera by Weber, completed by Gustav Mahler. 1887.
  fp: 20 January 1888, Leipzig, Municipal Theatre, cond. Gustav Mahler.
  Pub. Kahnt.

BIBLIOGRAPHY:
Winton Dean: The Three Pintos, *MT*, June 1962, p. 409.
Michael Marcus: The Three Pintos première, *M&M*, June 1962, p. 34.
John Warrack: Mahler and Weber, *MT*, February 1967, p. 120.
— Carl Maria von Weber, Hamish Hamilton (London) 1968.

22. **Lieder aus 'Des Knaben Wunderhorn'.** For voice and orchestra. 1892–96.
  1. *Der Schildwache Nachtlied.*
  2 fl, pic, 2 ob, ca, 2 cl, 2 bsn; 4 hn, 2 tpt; tgle, side dm, cym, GC, timp; hp, strings.
  2. *Verlorene Müh'.*
  2 fl, 2 ob, 2 cl, 2 bsn; 2 hn; tgle; strings.
  3. *Trost im Unglück.*
  2 fl, pic, 2 ob, 2 cl, 2 bsn; 4 hn, 2 tpt; tgle, side dm, timp; strings.
  4. *Wer hat dies Liedlein erdacht?*
  2 fl, 2 ob, 2 cl, 2 bsn; 2 hn; tgle; strings.
  5. *Das irdische Leben.*
  2 fl, 2 ob, ca, 2 cl, 2 bsn; 3 hn, tpt; cym; strings.
  6. *Des Antonius von Padua Fischpredigt.*
  2 fl, 2 ob, 2 cl, 3 bsn; 4 hn; tgle, Ruthe, cym, tamtam; GC, timp; strings.
  7. *Rheinlegendchen.*
  fl, ob, cl, bsn; hn; strings.
  8. *Lied des Verfolgten im Thurme.*

Mahler, Gustav

2 fl, 2 ob, 2 cl, 2 bsn; 4 hn, 2 tpt; timp; strings.

9. *Wo die schönen Trompeten blasen.*
2 fl, 2 ob, 2 cl; 4 hn, 2 tpt; strings.

10. *Lob des hohen Verstands.*
2 fl, 2 ob, 2 cl, E-flat cl, 2 bsn; 4 hn, tpt, tmb, tuba; timp, tgle; strings.

11. *Es sungen drei Engel.*
From Symphony No. 3.

12. *Urlicht.*
From Symphony No. 2.
Pub. 1899 (vocal score), Weinberger.

BIBLIOGRAPHY:
Robin Gregory: Mahler und Des Knaben Wunderhorn, *MMR*, 1953, pp. 227, 265.

23. **Symphony No. 2 in C minor** ('Resurrection'). For soloists, chorus and orchestra. 1887–94.
1. *Allegro maestoso*; 2. *Andante con moto*; 3. *In sehr ruhig fliessender Bewegung*; 4. *'Urlicht'*; 5. *Im Tempo des Scherzo's.*

4 fl, 4 pic, 4 ob, ca, 3 cl, bcl, 2 E-flat cl, 4 bsn, cbsn; 10 hn, 10 tpt, 4 tmb, bs tuba; timp, GC, cym, tamtam, tgle, side dm, glock, 3 bells, Ruthe; organ, 2 hp, strings.

fp (three instrumental movements only): 4 March 1895, Berlin, Berlin Philharmonic Orchestra, cond. Gustav Mahler.

fp (complete): 13 December 1895, Berlin, cond. Gustav Mahler.

f Vienna p: 9 April 1899, cond. Gustav Mahler.

f Ap: 8 December 1908, New York, cond. Gustav Mahler.

f Paris p: 17 April 1910, Concerts Colonne.

fEp: 16 April 1931, Queen's Hall, Courtauld-Sargent concert, Luise Helletsgruber and Enid Szanto, cond. Bruno Walter.

2Ep: 1 October 1949, Royal Albert Hall, Henry Wood Concerts Society, Dora van Doorn, Kathleen Ferrier, BBC Choral Society and BBC Symphony Orchestra, cond. Bruno Walter.

Pub. 1897, Hofmeister; 1898, Eberle; c. 1906 (?1910), Universal-Edition; 1939, Boosey & Hawkes. Arr. for piano four hands by Bruno Walter, 1899, Weinberger.

BIBLIOGRAPHY:
Alfredo Casella: GM et sa Deuxième Symphonie, *Revue S.I.M.*, 1910, p. 238.
Leonard Duck: 'Resurrection' Symphony, *Halle*, May 1958, p. 5.
G.R.H.: Mahler's Resurrection Symphony, *Gramophone*, December 1925, p. 335.
B. Stavenhagen: GM et sa deuxième, *Les Cahiers de la musique*, January 1938.

23a. **Symphony No. 2: Andante pastorale.**
Reduction for smaller orchestra by Erwin Stein. Dur. 8½′.
2 fl, pic, 2 ob, 2 cl, E-flat cl (ad lib), 2 bsn; 4 hn, 3(2) tpt, 3 tmb; timp; hp, strings.
Pub. 1942, Hawkes.

24. **Symphony No. 3 in D minor.** For alto voice, women's chorus, boys' chorus and orchestra. 1893–6.
1. *Kräftig entschieden*; 2. *Tempo di Menuetto*; 3. *Comodo (Scherzando)*; 4. *Sehr langsam—Misterioso*; 5. *Lustig im Tempo und keck im Ausdruck*; 6. *Lngsam—Ruhevoll—Empfunden.*

4 fl, 4 pic, ob, ca, 3 cl, 2 E-flat cl, bcl, 4 bsn, cbsn; 8 hn, 4 tpt, 4 tmb, bs tuba, Flügelhorn; 4 timp, 2 glock, tamb, tamtam, tgle, cym, GC, side dm, Ruthe, 5–6 bells; 2 hp, strings.

fp (2nd, 3rd & 6th movements): 1897, Berlin, cond. Felix Weingartner.

f complete p: 9 June 1902, Krefeld, Allgemeine Deutsche Musikverein, cond. Gustav Mahler.

f Ap: 8 February 1922, New York, cond. Willem Mengelberg.

?fEp: 29 November 1947, BBC broadcast, Kathleen Ferrier, Chesham Ladies Choir, boys from the London Choir School, BBC Symphony Orchestra, cond. Sir Adrian Boult.

fEp (concert): 28 February 1961, St. Pancras Town Hall, Jean Evans, Wimbledon Girls' Choir, William Ellis School Boys' Choir, Polyphonia Symphony Orchestra, cond. Bryan Fairfax.

Pub. 1898, Weinberger; 1906, Universal-Edition.

BIBLIOGRAPHY:
E. Chapman: Mahler's Third Symphony, *Musical Events*, January 1962, p. 26.
Bryan Fairfax: Mahler's Third for the first

time in England, *M&M*, February 1961, p. 9.

Georges Humbert: Autour de la IIIe symphonie de GM, *La Vie musicale* (Lausanne), 1909–10, No. 9.

Hans F. Redlich: Mahler's Third Symphony, *Chesterian*, No. 205, winter 1961.

Bruno Walter: GMs III. Symphonie (Zur Aufführung am 25. Oktober), *Der Merker*, 10 October 1909, p. 9.

Paul Zschorlich: GMs dritte Symphonie, *Leipziger Tageblatt*, 1904, p. 608.

Anon.: Derde Symphonie von GM, *Allgem. Handelsblad* (Amsterdam), 23 October 1903.

24a. What the flowers told me. From Symphony No. 3, arr. for reduced orchestra by Benjamin Britten. Pub. 1950, Boosey & Hawkes.

25. Das Klagende Lied. For soprano, alto, tenor, mixed chorus and orchestra. Final version: 1896–8.

3 fl, pic, 3 ob, ca, 3 cl, bcl, 2 bsn, cbsn; 4 hn, 4 tpt, 3 tmb, bs tuba; timp, tgle, cym, GC; 2 hp, strings.

fp: 17 February 1901, Vienna, Edith Walker, Elise Elizza, Anna von Mildenburg, Fritz Schrödter, cond. Gustav Mahler.

fEp: 13 May 1956, Royal Festival Hall, Joan Sutherland, Norma Proctor, Peter Pears, Goldsmiths Choral Union and London Symphony Orchestra, cond. Walter Goehr.

Pub. 1902, Weinberger; incl. vocal score by J. V. von Wöss.

BIBLIOGRAPHY:

Helene Nolthenius: GMs Klagende Lied, *Mens en melodie*, October 1952, p. 311.

26. Symphony No. 4 in G major. For orchestra, with soprano solo. 1899–1901. Words: from Des Knaben Wunderhorn. Dur. 54'.

1. *Bedächtig*; 2. *In gemächlicher Bewegung*; 3. *Ruhevoll*; 4. *Sehr behaglich*.

4 fl, 2 pic, 3 ob, ca, 3 cl, 2 E-flat cl, bcl, 3 bsn, cbsn; 4 hn, 3 tpt; timp, GC, tgle, small bells, glock, cym, tamtam; hp, strings.

fp: 25 November 1901, Munich, Kaim Saal, cond. Gustav Mahler.

fAp: 6 November 1904, New York, cond. Walter Damrosch.

fEp: 25 October 1905, Queen's Hall, Promenade Concert, Mrs. Henry J. Wood, Queen's Hall Orchestra, cond. Sir Henry Wood.

2Ep: 3 December 1907, Queen's Hall, Blanche Marchesi and New Symphony Orchestra, cond. (Sir) Thomas Beecham.

fFp: 18 January 1914, Paris, Salle Gaveau, Mme Faliero Dalcroze and Orchestre Lamoureux, cond. Camille Chevillard.

fEbp: 12 December 1926, Miriam Licette and Newcastle Station Orchestra, cond. Edward Clark.

Pub. 1901, Doblinger; 1906, Universal-Edition; revised edition, 1963, Universal-Edition/Internationale Gustav Mahler-Gesellschaft.

BIBLIOGRAPHY:

Raymond Bouyer: A propos d'une symphonie de feu GM, *Le Ménestrel*, 7 February 1914, p. 43.

Neville Cardus: A song symphony, *Halle*, February 1951, p. 4.

M. Chanan: Attitudes to death, *M&M*, February 1968, p. 39.

Max Kalbeck: GM, Vierter Symphonie, *Neues Wiener Tagblatt*, 16 January 1902.

Vincent d'Indy: La Quatrième Symphonie de Mahler, *La Revue S.I.M.*, 1 February 1914.

Arthur Seidl: GMs Vierter Symphonie, *Die Gesellschaft*, December 1901.

Erwin Stein: Eine unbekannte Ausgabe letzter Hand von Mahlers 4. Sinfonie, *Pult und Taktstock*, March–April 1929.

Anon.: Mahler Gusztáv—IV. szimfónia, *A Zene*, 1 February 1931, p. 140.

Anon.: Bruno Walter and Mahler's Fourth Symphony, *Philharmonic Post*, January 1947, p. 6.

27. Symphony No. 5 in C sharp minor. 1901–2. Dur. 65'.

1. *Trauermarsch*; 2. *Stürmisch bewegt, mit grösster Vehemenz*; 3. *Scherzo*; 4. *Adagietto* (for harp and strings); 5. *Rondo-Finale*.

4 fl, 2 pic, 3 ob, ca, 3 cl, bcl, 3 bsn, cbsn; 6 hn, 4 tpt, 3 tmb, bs tuba; 4 timp, cym, GC, side dm, tgle, glock, tamtam, wood clapper; hp, strings.

fp: 18 October 1904, Cologne, Gurzenich concert, cond. Gustav Mahler.

Mahler, Gustav

fAp: 24 March 1905, Cincinnati, cond. Frank van der Stucken.

fEp (Adagietto only): 31 August 1909, Queen's Hall, Promenade Concert, Queen's Hall Orchestra, cond. Sir Henry Wood.

fEp (complete): 21 October 1945, Stoll Theatre, London Philharmonic Orchestra, cond. Heinz Unger.

Pub. 1904, 1910, Peters; 1964, Peters/Internationale Gustav Mahler-Gesellschaft.

BIBLIOGRAPHY:

A. Eccerius: Die Uraufführung von GMs 5. Symphonie, *Neue Musikalische Presse* (Vienna), 1904, No. 20.

Philip H. Goepp: Mahler's Fifth Symphony, in *Great Works of Music*, 3rd series, Garden City Publishing Co. (USA) 1913, p. 244.

P. Grant: Mahler's Fifth Symphony, *Chord and Discord*, 1963, No. 10, p. 125.

E. O. Nodnagel: Mahlers Symphonie No. 5, *AMZ*, 1905.

— GMs fünfte Symphonie in Cis-moll—Technische Analyse, *Die Musik*, Vol. IV (1904–5), November (2) p. 243, December (1) p. 314.

28. Sieben Lieder aus [letzter zeit] (Seven Last Songs). For voice and orchestra or piano. *Five Rückert Songs*. 1901–3.

1. *Ich atmet' einen linden Duft.*
fl, ob, cl, 2 bsn; 4 hn; celesta, hp, violins, violas.

2. *Liebst du um Schönheit.*
2 ob, ca, 2 cl, 2 bsn; 4 hn; hp, strings.
Pub. 1907.

3. *Blicke mir nicht in die Lieder.*
fl, ob, cl, bsn; hn; hp, strings.

4. *Ich bin der Welt abhanden gekommen.*
ob, ca, 2 cl, 2 bsn; 2 hn; hp, strings.

5. *Um Mitternacht.*
2 fl, ob d'amore, 2 cl, 2 bsn, cbsn; 4 hn, 2 tpt, 3 tmb, bs tuba; timp; hp, piano.
Two Songs from 'Des Knaben Wunderhorn'. 1899.

6. *Revelge.* 1899.
2 fl, 2 ob, 2 cl, 2 bsn, cbsn; 4 hn, 3 tpt; timp, tgle, tamb mil, susp cym, GC, cym, tamtam; strings.

7. *Der Tamboursg'sell.* 1901.
2 ob, 2 cl, bcl, 2 bsn, cbsn; 4 hn, tuba; GC, side dm, tamtam, timp; cellos and basses.

Pub. 1905, Kahnt; English words by John Bernhoff.

29. Kindertotenlieder (Rückert). For voice and orchestra. 1901–4.
1. *Nun will die Sonn' so hell aufgeh'n*; 2. *Nun seh' ich wohl, warum so dunkle Flammen*; 3. *Wenn dein Mütterlein*; 4. *Oft denk' ich, sie sind nur ausgegangen!*; 5. *In diesem Wetter!*
2 fl, pic, 2 ob, ca, 2 cl, bcl, 2 bsn, cbsn; 4 hn; timp, glock, tamtam, bells; hp, strings.

fp: 29 January 1905, Vienna, Friedrich Weidemann, cond. Gustav Mahler.

fAp: 26 January 1910, New York, Ludwig Wüllner, cond. Gustav Mahler.

fEp: 28 May 1913, Bechstein Hall, Lula Mysz-Gmeiner, acc. Richard Epstein (piano).

?fEp (with orchestra): 27 May 1924, Queen's Hall, Elena Gerhardt and the London Symphony Orchestra, cond. Fritz Reiner. (NB: fEp originally announced for Promenade Concert, 14 October 1914.)

fEbp: 14 September 1925, Herbert Heyner and Newcastle Station Symphony Orchestra, cond. Edward Clark.

Pub. 1905, Kahnt.

BIBLIOGRAPHY:
P. Grant: Mahler's Kindertotenlieder, *Chord and Discord*, 1960, No. 9, p. 62.

30. Euryanthe. Opera by Weber: edition with revised text by Gustav Mahler. ?1902.
fp: 19 January 1903, Vienna.

31. Symphony No. 6 in A minor. 1903–5. Dur. 80′.
1. *Allegro energico, ma non troppo*; 2. *Scherzo (Wuchtig)*; 3. *Andante*; 4. *Finale (Allegro moderato)*.
4 fl, 2 pic, 4 ob, ca, cl in D, cl in E-flat, 3 cl in A, bcl, 4 bsn, cbsn; 8 hn, 6 tpt, 3 tmb, bs tmb, bs tuba; timp, glock, cowbells, bells, Rute, Hammer, cym, side dm, xyl; 2 hp, celesta, tgle, strings.

fp: 27 May 1906, Essen, Allgemeines Musikverein, cond. Gustav Mahler.

f Vienna p: 4 January 1907, Konzertverein, cond. Gustav Mahler.

fAp: 11 December 1947, New York, cond. Dimitri Mitropoulos.

?fEp: 16 October 1956, BBC broadcast, BBC Symphony Orchestra, cond. Norman Del Mar.

300

Pub. 1906, Kahnt; *c.* 1910, Universal-Edition; revised score, 1963, Kahnt/Internationale Gustav Mahler-Gesellschaft.

BIBLIOGRAPHY:
Hugo Daffner: Sechste Symphonie von GM—Erstaufführung unter Leitung des Komponisten am 8. November 1906, *NZfM* (Musikalisches Wochenblatt), 1906, No. 47 (22 November), p. 860.
Michael Kennedy: Mahler and his Sixth Symphony, *Halle*, No. 121, 1964–5, p. 9.
Ernst Otto Nodnagel: GMs A-moll Symphonie No. 6, *NZfM* (Musikalisches Wochenblatt), 1906, Nos. 21–22 (23 May), p. 465.
T.H.: Erstaufführung der 6. Symphonie von Mahler, *NZfM* (Musikalisches Wochenblatt), 1907, No. 3 (17 January), p. 56.
Klaus Pringsheim: Zur Uraufführung von Mahlers sechster Symphonie, *Anbruch*, September 1920, p. 496.
— Erinnerungen an die Uraufführungen von GMs sechster Sinfonie, *Neues Wiener Journal*, 15 September 1923.
Erwin Ratz: Zum Formproblem bei GM—Eine Analyse des Finales der VI. Sinfonie, *Die Musikforschung*, 1956 (Vol. 9, No. 2).
Eduard Reuss: Die sechste Symphonie von GM und ihre erste Aufführung, *Neue Musikalische Presse* (Vienna), 1906, No. 14.
Anon.: Mahler's Sixth Symphony in Vienna, *MS*, 19 January 1907, p. 41.

32. Symphony No. 7 in E minor. 1904–6. Dur. 80'.

1. *Langsam—Allegro*; 2. *Nachtmusik I*; 3. *Scherzo*; 4. *Nachtmusik II*; 5. *Rondo-Finale*.

4 fl, pic, 3 ob, ca, 3 cl, E-flat cl, bcl, 3 bsn, cbsn; tenor hn, 4 hn, 3 tpt, 3 tmb, tuba; timp, GC, tgle, cym, tamb, tamtam, bells, cowbells; 2 hp, guitar, mandoline, strings.

fp: 19 September 1908, Prague, Jubilee Exhibition hall, cond. Gustav Mahler.

f Amsterdam p: 3 October 1909, Concertgebouw Orchestra, cond. Gustav Mahler.

f Vienna p: 3 November 1909, Konzertverein, cond. Ferdinand Löwe.

fEp: 18 January 1913, Queen's Hall, Queen's Hall Orchestra (augmented to 110 players), cond. Sir Henry Wood.

fAp: 15 April 1921, Chicago, cond. Frederick Stock.

Pub. 1909, Bote & Bock; *c.* 1912, Universal-Edition; revised score, 1960, Bote & Bock/Internationale Gustav Mahler-Gesellschaft.

BIBLIOGRAPHY:
Theodor Helm: Mahlers VII. Symphonie, *NZfM*, 18 November 1909, p. 486.
Donald Mitchell: Mahler's enigmatic Seventh Symphony, *The Listener*, 11 April 1963, p. 649.
Ernest Newman: Mahler's Seventh Symphony, in *Testament of Music*, Putnam (London) 1962, p. 166.
William Ritter: La VIIe Symphonie de GM, *Revue S.I.M.*, 15 November 1908, p. 1154.
August Spanuth: GMs siebente Symphonie, *Signale*, No. 39, (23 September) 1908, p. 1189.
Richard Specht: Thematische Novitäten-Analysen, 1: Mahlers Siebente Symphonie, *Der Merker* (Suppl. No. 2), 25 October 1909.
B.: GMs Siebente, *Der Kunstwart*, December (2) 1909, p. 427.

33. Oberon. Opera by Weber; edition with rev. text by Gustav Mahler. *c.* 1906. Pub. 1919, Universal-Edition.

34. Symphony No. 8 in E flat major ('Symphony of a Thousand'). For soloists (SSSAATBarB), double chorus, boys' chorus and orchestra. 1906–7. Ded. to the composer's wife Alma Maria.

1. *Hymnus: Veni, creator spiritus*; 2. *Schlussszene aus 'Faust'*.

4 fl, pic, 4 ob, ca, E-flat cl, 3 cl, bcl, 4 bsn, cbsn; 8 hn, 4 tpt, 4 tmb, bs tuba; 3 timp, GC, cym, tamtam, tgle, bells (low), glock; celesta, piano, harmonium, organ, 2 hp, mandoline, strings; *also* 4 tpt, 3 tmb.

fp: 12 September 1910, Munich, Neue Musik Festhalle, Munich Exhibition concert, Gertrud Förstel, Marta Winternitz-Dorda, Irma Koboth, Otillie Meyzger, Tilly Koenen, Felix Senius, Nicola Geisse-Winkel, Richard Mayr, Leipzig Riedelverein, Vienna Singverein, Munich Central School Children's Chorus, cond. Gustav Mahler.

f Leipzig p: 1 March 1912, Alberthalle, cond. Georg Göhler.

Mahler, Gustav

f Vienna p: 14 March 1912, cond. Bruno Walter.

fAp: 2 March 1916, Philadelphia, cond. Leopold Stokowski.

fEp: 15 April 1930, Queen's Hall, Elsie Suddaby, May Blyth, Irene Mordern, Muriel Brunskill, Clara Serena, Walter Widdop, Harold Williams, Robert Easton, BBC National Chorus, chorus of boys from Southwark Cathedral, Holy Trinity (Sloane Square), St. Stephen's (Walbrook) and Alexandra Orphanage, BBC Symphony Orchestra, cond. Sir Henry Wood.

Pub. 1910 (vocal score), 1911 (full score), Universal-Edition; vocal score by J. V. von Wöss.

BIBLIOGRAPHY:

Robert Angles: Symphony of a Thousand, *Records & Recording*, December 1964, p. 28.

Friedrich Brandes: Mahlers achte Symphonie, *Der Kunstwart*, October (1) 1910, p. 51.

Havergal Brian: GM's Eighth Symphony, *MO*, March 1930, p. 525.

H. W. Draber: GMs achte Symphonie, eine Inhaltsangabe, *Signale*, 1910, No. 35 (31 August), p. 1339.

Paul Ehlers: GMs achte Symphonie, *AMZ*, 1910, No. 38.

Robert Holtzmann: GM und seine achte Symphonie, *AMZ*, 1910, No. 39.

— Mahlers achte Symphonie und die Kritik— Zugleich ein Beitrag zur Rassenfrage, *NMZ*, 1911, No. 8.

Cecil Gray & K. Sorabji: Mahler's Eighth Symphony, *MMR*, 1930, p. 169.

Georges Humbert: La VIIIme symphonie de GM, *La Vie musicale*, Vol. IV, Nos. 3 & 6.

Edgar Istel: The production of GM's 8th Symphony under the composer's direction at Munich, *MMR*, 1910, p. 218.

Heinrich Jalowetz: Mahler über die achte Symphonie, *Anbruch*, May 1923.

J. Alfred Johnstone: Mahler's Eighth Symphony, *MS*, 17 May 1930, p. 159.

Georg Klaren: Religiöses zu Mahlers VIII. Symphonie, *Anbruch*, November 1921, p. 312.

R. Piper: GM über die achte Symphonie, *Der Anbruch*, May 1923, p. 135.

William Ritter: La VIIIme Symphonie de GM, *Revue S.I.M.*, 1910, p. 571.

V. Ludwig Schittler: GMs achte Symphonie, *NZfM*, 29 September 1910, p. 273.

August Spanuth: GMs achte Symphonie, *Signale*, 1910, No. 38 (21 September), p. 1431.

— Mahlers 'Achte' in Leipzig, *Signale*, 1912, No. 10 (6 March), p. 317.

Richard Specht: Mahlers 'Achte' in München, *Der Merker*, 25 September 1910, p. 972.

— GMs VIII. Symphonie, thematische Analyse, 1912.

Paul Stefan: Zur Uraufführung der VIII. Symphonie GM in München, *NMZ*, 1910, No. 24.

P. de Stoecklin: (Symphony No. 8), *Le Courrier musical*, 1 October 1910.

A. Thomas-San Galli: Die Mahlersche 'Achte', *Rheinische Musik- und Theaterzeitung*, Vol. IX, Nos. 38–39.

Gerard Werke: De achtste symphonie van GM, *Mens en melodie*, June 1954, p. 164.

Anon.: Uraufführung von Mahlers achter Symphonie, *Signale*, 1910, No. 37 (14 September), p. 1398.

Anon.: In the Albert Hall—the world's largest symphony, *M&M*, March 1959, p. 19.

35. Das Lied von der Erde. Symphony for tenor and alto (or baritone) soloists and orchestra. 1907-9. Words: from Hans Bethge's 'Die chinesische Flöte'. Dur. 60'.

1. *Das Trinklied vom Jammer der Erde* (tenor); 2. *Der Einsame im Herbst* (alto); 3. *Von der Jugend* (tenor); 4. *Von der Schönheit* (alto); 5. *Der Trunkene im Frühling* (tenor); 6. *Der Abschied* (alto).

3 fl, pic, 3 ob, ca, E-flat cl, 3 cl, bcl, 3 bsn, cbsn; 4 hn, 3 tpt, 3 tmb; timp, celesta, mandoline, glock, tgle, cym, tamtam, tamb, GC; 2 hp, strings.

fp: 20 November 1911, Munich, two-day festival in memory of Mahler, cond. Bruno Walter.

fEp: 31 January 1914, Queen's Hall, Doris Woodall, Gervase Elwes, Queen's Hall Orchestra, cond. Sir Henry Wood.

fAp: 14 December 1916, Philadelphia, cond. Leopold Stokowski.

Pub. 1912 (score), 1912 (vocal score by J. von Wöss), Universal-Edition; revised score,

1962, Universal-Edition/Internationale Gustav Mahler-Gesellschaft.

BIBLIOGRAPHY:

Gerald Abraham: A great swan song, *Radio Times*, 31 January 1936, p. 12.

Gerth. Baruch: An unknown part of Mahler's Lied von der Erde, *MMR*, 1936, p. 62.

Eric Blom: GM, Das Lied von der Erde (notes for gramophone records), Columbia (London) 1937.

Neville Cardus: Mahler and Das Lied von der Erde, *Hallé*, April 1952, p. 4.

Mosco Carner: Form and technique in Mahler's Lied von der Erde, *MMR*, 1939, p. 48.

Hans Fischer: GMs Lied von der Erde und die Münchener Kritik, *NMZ*, 1916, No. 14, p. 207.

Edgar Istel: GM's Das Lied von der Erde, *MMR*, 1912, p. 10.

Ferdinand Keyfel: GM-Gedächtnisfeier, München, 19. u. 20. Nov.—Uraufführung Das Lied von der Erde, *Signale*, 1911, No. 48 (29 November), p. 1685.

H. Kralik: Das Lied von der Erde, 1933.

Rudolf Mengelberg: Eine Einführung in das Lied von der Erde, *Die Musikwelt*, 15 October 1922.

E. W. Mulder: Das Lied von der Erde, een critisch-analytische studie, 1951.

Henry Raynor: Walter, Klemperer and The Song of the Earth, *Chesterian*, No. 189, winter 1957, No. 190, spring 1957.

Eduard Reeser: Mahler's tekst—en vormbehandeling in Das Lied von der Erde, *Caecilia en De Muziek*, June 1936, p. 322.

Evelyn Reuter: Mahler et Le Chant de la Terre, *RM* (L'Oeuvre du XXᵉ Siècle), 1952, p. 99.

William Ritter: Le Chant de la Terre à Munich, *Revue S.I.M.*, January 1912, p. 66.

Richard Specht: Das Lied von der Erde, *Der Merker*, December (1) 1911, p. 1169.

— Mahlers Das Lied von der Erde, *Der Kunstwart*, December (2) 1911, p. 440.

Hans Tischler: Mahler's Das Lied von der Erde, *MR*, 1949, p. 111.

W. J. Turner: Das Lied von der Erde, *New Statesman*, 8 February 1930, p. 570.

J. von Wöss: Das Lied von der Erde, thematische Analyse, 1912.

36. Le Nozze di Figaro. Opera by Mozart, ed. Gustav Mahler. Pub. 1908, Peters.

37. Suite after Bach. For orchestra.
1. *Ouvertüre.*
fl, strings, hpschd.
2. *Rondeau & Badinerie.*
fl, strings, hpschd.
3. *Air.*
strings.
4. *Gavottes 1 & 2.*
3 tpt, 2 timp, 2 ob, strings, hpschd.
Pub. 1910, Schirmer.

38. Symphony No. 9 in D major. Autumn 1909–10. Dur. 75′.
1. *Andante comodo*; 2. *In tempo eines gemächlichen Ländlers*; 3. *Rondo-Burleske (Allegro assai)*; 4. *Adagio.*
4 fl, pic, 3 ob, ca, E-flat cl, 3 cl, bcl, 4 bsn, cbsn; 4 hn, 3 tpt, 3 tmb, bs tuba; timp, glock, cym, GC, side dm, tgle, tamb, 3 bells (low); 2 hp, strings.
fp: 26 June 1912, Vienna Festiva, Viennal Philharmonic Orchestra, cond. Bruno Walter.
fEp: 27 February 1930, Manchester, Halle Orchestra, cond. Sir Hamilton Harty: broadcast.
fAp: 16 October 1931, Boston, cond. Serge Koussevitzky.
f London p: 7 February 1934, BBC concert, Queen's Hall, BBC Symphony Orchestra, cond. Sir Adrian Boult.
Pub. 1912, 1940, 1952, Universal-Edition.

BIBLIOGRAPHY:

Richard Batka: GMs 'Neunte', *Der Kunstwart*, August (1) 1912, p. 193.

Henry Boys: Mahler and his Ninth Symphony, notes for HMV recording, 1938.

Jack Diether: The expressive content of Mahler's Ninth, an interpretation, *Chord and Discord*, 1963, No. 10, p. 69.

Eduard Reeser: 'Wie ein schwerer kondukt', *Caecilia en De Muziek*, 1936, p. 278.

Erwin Ratz: Zum Formproblem bei GM— Eine Analyse des ersten Satzes IX. Sinfonie, *Die Musikforschung*, 1955 (Vol. VIII), No. 2.

William Ritter: Le 'Neuvième' de Mahler, *Revue S.I.M.*, September–October 1912, p. 41.

Mahler, Gustav

Rolf Urs Ringger: Mahlers Neunte Symphonie und das Dramatische, *Musica*, March–April 1966, p. 58.
H. C. Schonberg: The mystic 'Ninth', *New York Times*, 7 January 1962, Section 2, p. 13.
August Spanuth: GMs posthume Symphonie, *Signale*, 1912, No. 27 (3 July), p. 915.
Richard Specht: Mahler's 'Neunte' (Uraufführung durch die Wiener Philharmoniker unter Bruno Walter im 3. Konzert der Wiener Musikfestwoche), *Der Merker*, July (2) 1912, p. 552.
Erwin Stein: Die Tempogestaltung in Mahlers neunter Sinfonie, *Pult und Taktstock*, October–November 1924.

39. Symphony No. 10. Sketched: 1909–10. Unfinished.
(a) Performing edition of Adagio and Purgatorio prepared by ?Ernst Krenek, ?Alban Berg, ?Franz Schalk.
3 fl, 3 ob, 3 cl, 3 bsn; 4 hn, 4 tpt, 3 tmb, tuba; 2 timp, cym, gong; hp, strings.
fp: 14 October 1924, Vienna, cond. Franz Schalk.
fEp (Adagio only): 20 November 1948, BBC broadcast, BBC Symphony Orchestra, cond. Hermann Scherchen.
fAp: 6 December 1949, Erie, cond. Fritz Mahler.
Pub. 1924 (facsimile), Paul Zsolnay (Vienna); 1966, Verlag Ricke (Munich), with additional sketches; 1951, Associated Music Publishers (New York), ed. Otto Jokl; 1964, Universal-Edition, ed. Erwin Ratz.
(b) Performing edition by Deryck Cooke.
fp (near complete): 19 December 1960, BBC broadcast, Philharmonia Orchestra, cond. Otto Goldschmidt.
fp (complete): 13 August 1964, Royal Albert Hall, Promenade Concert, London Symphony Orchestra, cond. Berthold Goldschmidt.

BIBLIOGRAPHY:
L. M. G. Arntzenius: Mahlers zehnte Sinfonie —ein Gespräch mit Willem Mengelberg, *De Telegraaf* (Amsterdam), 26 November 1924.
Elsa Bienenfeld: Mahlers zehnte Sinfonie, *Neues Wiener Journal*, 14 October 1924.

Deryck Cooke: Mahler's unfinished symphony, *The Listener*, 15 December 1960, p. 1121; repr. in *Essays on Music*, Cassell (London) 1967, p. 146.
— Mahler's Tenth Symphony: artistic morality and musical reality, *MT*, June 1961, p. 351.
— The facts concerning Mahler's Tenth Symphony, *Chord and Discord*, 1963, No. 10, p. 3.
— Bringing Mahler to life, *M&M*, August 1964, p. 15.
— Mahler's Tenth Symphony: sonority, texture and substance, *The Composer*, July 1965, p. 2.
M. du Pré Cooper: Mahler's sketches for a Tenth Symphony, *MT*, December 1932, p. 1083.
Rudolf Stephan Hoffmann: Mahlers Zehnte Symphonie, *NMZ*, 1925, No. 5, p. 114.
Karl Holl: Mahlers zehnte Sinfonie, *Frankfurter Zeitung*, No. 812, 30 October 1924.
Julius Korngold: Mahlers zehnte Sinfonie, *Neue Freie Presse*, 15 October 1924.
Heinz Kreutz: GMs zehnte Symphonie wird erklingen, *NZfM*, January 1964.
Alma Maria Mahler: Mahlers unvollendete Symphonie, *Anbruch*, December 1923, p. 281.
William Malloch: Deryck Cooke's Mahler Tenth, an interim report, *MR*, November 1962, p. 292.
Alfred Mathis: Mahler's Unfinished Symphony, *The Listener*, 11 November 1948, p. 740.
Claude Meylan: La Dixième Symphonie reconstituée de GM, *SM*, November–December 1964, p. 357.
Massimo Mila: Mahler's 10th Symphony, in *Musique contemporaine*, 1951.
Donald Mitchell: Some notes on Mahler's Tenth Symphony, *MT*, December 1955, p. 656.
Erwin Ratz: GMs X. Symphonie, *ÖM*, July 1964; *NZfM*, July–August 1964.
Charles Reid: Mahler's 'Tenth', *MR*, November 1965, p. 318.
E. Scherber: Mahlers 10. Symphonie und Schoenbergs Glückliche Hand, *Signale*, 12 November 1924.
Richard Specht: Mahlers letzte Sinfonie,

Vossische Zeitung (Berlin), No. 52, 31 January 1924.
— GM, nachgelassene zehnte Symphonie, Paul Zsolnay Verlag (Berlin), 1924.
Egon Wellesz: Mahlers Zehnte Sinfonie, *ÖM*, April 1961.
Anon.: Realising Mahler's uncompleted tenth symphony, *The Times*, 8 August 1963, p. 12.

GENERAL BIBLIOGRAPHY

Adolf Aber: Das Mahler-Fest in Amsterdam, *NZfM*, June (2) 1920, p. 174.
— Ein unbekannter Brief GMs, *Leipziger Neueste Nachrichten*, 29 January 1926.
Gerald Abraham: The symphonies of Mahler, *MS*, 1925, 13 June, p. 196, 27 June, p. 212.
— Mahler in heaven, *Radio Times*, 21 April 1933, p. 134.
— An outline of Mahler, *M&L*, October 1932; in *Slavonic and Romantic Music*, Faber (London) 1968, p. 323.
Guido Adler: GM, 1916.
— Zur Mahler-Fest in Amsterdam, *Anbruch*, April 1920, p. 255.
— Personality of Mahler, in *Great Composers through the Eyes of their Contemporaries*, Dutton (New York) 1951, p. 442.
Herbert Antcliffe: Mahler and modern Dutch music, *MMR*, 1954, p. 234.
E.F.B.: Four unknown Mahler symphonies found in Dresden, *Musical America*, 10 April 1938.
G. C. Bagster: GM, *MS*, 27 May 1911, p. 322.
Hermann Bahr: Mahler als Direktor, *Anbruch*, April 1920, p. 275.
Anna Bahr-Mildenburg, Marie Gutheil-Schoders, Selma Kurz & Leo Slezak: Die Mahler-Zeit der Wiener Oper—Erinnerungen, *Moderne Welt* (Vienna), Vol. III, No. 7.
R. W. Baker: Bruckner and Mahler, *The Gramophone*, December 1949.
— GM, *The Gramophone*, January 1950, p. 141.
Philip T. Barford: Mahler today, *MR*, August 1957, p. 177.
— Mahler, a thematic archetype, *MR*, November 1960, p. 297.
— Mahler Symphonies and Songs, BBC Publications (London) 1970 (BBC Music Guides).
Richard Batka: Das Jüdische bei GM, *Der Kunstwart*, July (2) 1910, p. 97.

— GM, *Der Kunstwart*, June (1) 1911, p. 313.
— Zwei Briefe von GM, *Die Musik*, January 1923.
Natalie Bauer-Lechner: Mahler-Aussprüche, *Anbruch*, April 1920, p. 306.
— Erinnerungen an GM, 1923.
Hermann Behn: GM, *Die Musikwelt*, 1928, No. 5.
Paul Bekker: GM, *Norddeutsche Allgemeine-Zeitung*, 1905, No. 2.
— GM, *Berliner Börsen-Courier*, 19 May 1911.
— GMs Sinfonien, 1921.
Elsa Bienenfeld: GM in Wien, *Der Tag* (Berlin), 30 May 1911.
— Mahler der Dirigent, *Moderne Welt* (Vienna), Vol. III (1922), No. 7.
— GM und Wilhelm Gericke, *Neues Wiener Journal*, 11 April 1926.
A. Bing: Zu Mahler Retuschen an Schumanns Symphonien, *Pult und Taktstock*, May–June 1928 and September 1928.
C. M. Blessinger: Mendelssohn, Meyerbeer, Mahler, Drei Kapitel Judentum in der Musik, 1939.
Ernest Bloch: Mahler, Strauss, Bruckner, *Die Musik*, June 1923, p. 664.
F. Bonis: GM und Ferenc Erkel: Beiträge zu ihren Beziehungen zueinander im Spiegel vier unbekannter Briefe von Mahler, *Studia musicologica*, 1961, p. 475.
John Boulton: GM, *Hallé*, No. 116, 1959–60.
Gerard Bourke: Mahler in Holland, *MO*, September 1960, p. 807.
Amedée Boutarel: Mahler, *Le Ménestrel*, 23 April 1910.
Richard Braungart: GM und die Programm-Musik, *Musikalische Rundschau* (Munich), 1905, No. 6; *Rheinisch-Westfälische Zeitung* (Essen), 1905, No. 97.
Havergal Brian: GM, *MO*, May 1946, p. 229.
S. Brichta: Ein Mahler-Denkmal in Wien, *Signale*, 1929, No. 3, p. 72.
— GM, *Signale*, 2 July 1930 (No. 27), p. 842.
— Mahler und Hugo Wolf, *Signale*, 1932, No. 21, p. 485.
Benjamin Britten: On behalf of GM, *Tempo* (American edition), October 1941.
Max Brod: GMs jüdische Melodien, *Anbruch*, May (2) 1920, p. 378.
— GM, 1961.

v

Emmanuel Buenzod: Solitude de Mahler, *Feuilles musicales*, October 1959.

Karel Burian: Zu GM, *Smetana*, 2 June 1911.

E. Byk: Mahlers Ekstase, *Der Auftakt*, February 1924.

Neville Cardus: GM, *Music*, winter 1947–8, p. 3.

— Elgar and Mahler, more than nationalists, *Radio Times*, 1 May 1931, p. 259.

Mosco Carner: GM's visit to London, *MT*, May 1936, p. 408.

— Mahler in his letters, *MMR*, 1936, p. 123.

— Mahler's re-scoring of the Schumann symphonies, *MR*, May 1941.

— Mahler's symphonic 'worlds', *The Listener*, 21 May 1964, p. 849.

Alfredo Casella: Mahler, *Revue S.I.M.*, 15 April 1910.

— Alfredo Casella's Festrede beim Mahlerfest in Amsterdam, *Anbruch*, June 1920, p. 415.

A.-E. Cherbuliez: GM, *Schweiz. Instrumentalmusik* (Lucerne), 1936, p. 221.

E. Combe: Les symphonies de Mahler, *RM*, June 1922, p. 42.

Deryck Cooke: the greatness of Mahler, *Music*, June 1953, p. 11, July 1953, p. 8.

— GM 1860–1961, BBC (London) 1960.

— The word and the deed ... the musical expression of Mahler's beliefs, *The Listener*, 2 July 1964, p. 22.

Ernst Decsey: Stunden mit Mahler, *Die Musik*, Vol. X (1910–11), No. 18 p. 352, No. 21 p. 143.

Norman Demuth & Herbert Antcliffe: GM (Stereoscopic Views No. 4), *The Dominant*, March–April 1927, p. 24.

M. Deutsch: Tchaikovsky–Mahler, *Mercure de France*, August–September 1955.

Jack Diether: Mahler and atonality, *MR*, May 1956, p. 130.

— Mahler—a musical existentialist, *New York Times*, 13 March 1960, Section 2, p. 12.

— Mahler's place in musical history, *Chord and Discord*, 1963, No. 10, p. 165.

— Mahler graduates, *The Gramophone*, August 1967, p. 97.

— Notes on some Mahler Juvenilia, *Chord and Discord*, 1969, Vol. 3, No. 1.

Friedhelm Döhl: GM, eine notwendige Revision, *NZfM*, August 1960.

Kurt Dorfmüller: GM-Dokumente in München, *Fontes Artis Musicae* (Cassel), January–April 1966.

David Drew: The price of popularity, *New Statesman*, 9 April 1965, p. 586.

Leonard Duck: Mahler again, *Hallé*, October 1954, p. 3.

L. Dunton Green: The problem of GM, *Chesterian*, No. 43, December 1924.

Ugo Duse: GM, 1962.

Alfred Einstein: GM, *Berliner Tageblatt*, 4 July 1930.

Gabriel Engel: GM, song-symphonist, Bruckner Society of America (New York) 1932.

Hermann Fähnrich: Musik und Musiker in Alma Mahler-Werfels 'And the Bridge is Love', *NZfM*, November 1959.

— GM, *Musica*, 1960, No. 6, p. 359; transl. F. Harling-Comyns, *MO*, October 1960, p. 17.

Erwin Felber: GM, der Mensch in seinem Werke, *Die Musik*, November 1931, p. 90.

Rudolf Felber: GM, *MT*, May 1923, p. 311.

Gerold Fierz: GM, eine Diskographie seiner Sinfonien, *SM*, May–June 1960, p. 185.

Ian F. Finlay: GM in England, *Chesterian*, No. 199, summer 1959.

Hugo R. Fleischmann: GM nelle sue lettere, *Musica d'oggi*, March 1925, p. 80.

— GM, twenty years after his death, *Chesterian*, No. 100, January–February 1932.

Paul Le Flem: GM, *Musica* (Chaix), No. 86, May 1961, p. 40.

Josef B. Foerster: Aus Mahlers Werkstatt—Erinnerungen, *Der Merker*, 10 September 1910, p. 921.

— Erinnerungen an GM, *Anbruch*, April 1920, p. 291.

— Mein Erlebnis GM, *Anbruch*, April (2) 1921, p. 147.

L. Frankenstein: GM, *NZfM*, 1 June 1911, p. 357.

Oskar Fried: Erinnerungen an Mahler, *Anbruch*, November 1919, p. 16.

Ernst Friedeggs: GM und Wien, *Nord und Süd* (Berlin), June 1911.

Martin Friedland: Das 'Erfinderische' und GM, *AMZ*, 18 May 1923.

R. Friedman: Souvenirs sur Mahler, *RM*, 1 November 1924, p. 95.

L. Fürnberg: GMs Heimkehr, *Musik und Gesellschaft*, May 1961, p. 264.

Adelheid Füsseli: Blick in Mahlers Seele, *Melos*, June 1950, p. 172.

Karl Heinz Füssl: Zur Literatur über GM, *ÖM*, July 1964.

E.E.G.: 'Mahler-Kult', *Anbruch*, November 1922, p. 257.

Hans Gal: GM, in *The Musicians World* (*Great Composers in their Letters*), Thames & Hudson (London) 1965, p. 375.

Oskar Geller: Wie GM nach Wien kam, *Neues Wiener Journal*, 24 May 1931.

Ugo Giardini: Mahler in New York, in *Great Composers through the Eyes of their Contemporaries*, Dutton (New York) 1951, p. 446.

Scott Goddard: GM, *Sackbut*, December 1921, p. 7.

— (transl.) A letter from GM, *British Musician*, February 1927, p. 236.

— GM, *MMR*, 1929, p. 355.

Georg Göhler: GM, *Der Kunstwart*, July (2) 1910, p. 69.

— GMs Lieder, *Der Kunstwart*, October (2) 1910, p. 146; *Die Musik*, Vol. X (1910–11), No. 18, p. 357.

Berthold Goldschmidt: GM, *Crescendo*, No. 122, October 1962, p. 30.

Franz Grasberger: GM und Richard Strauss, *ÖM*, 1966, Nos. 5–6 (May–June), p. 280.

Cecil Gray: (GM), *Nation*, 1 February 1930, p. 606.

Parks Grant: Bruckner and Mahler, the fundamental dissimilarity of their styles, *MR*, February 1971, p. 36.

Robin Gregory: Mahler's Rückert settings, *MMR*, 1954, p. 92.

Siegfried Günther: Teste und Textbehandlung in GMs Lyrik, *NZfM*, August (2) 1920, p. 268.

— Form und Wesen des Mahlerschen Liedes— Orchester- und Kammerlied, *NZfM*, January (1) 1921, p. 2.

Marie Gutheil-Schoder: Mahler bei der Arbeit, *Der Merker*, March (1) 1912, p. 165.

— Zwei Porträts, 2: GM, *Anbruch*, May 1937, p. 125.

Hans Gutman: Der Banale Mahler, *Anbruch*, March 1930, p. 102.

Emil Gutmann: GM als Organisator, *Die Musik*, Vol. X (1910–11), No. 18, p. 364.

A. Hamilton-Rowan: GM, *MMR*, 1914, p. 91.

F. Heinlein: GM, *Revista musicale Chilena*, No. 72 (1960), p. 8.

G. Hempel: GM in Leipzig, *Musik und Gesellschaft*, November 1967, p. 784.

Robert Hernried: Ungedruckte Briefe von GM, *Anbruch*, May 1936, p. 65.

Robert Hirschfeld: Mahler und Richard Strauss in Wien, *Österreichische Rundschau*, 1904, No. 9.

R. S. Hoffmann: Repräsentative Wiener Mahler-Aufführungen, *Anbruch*, April 1920, p. 310.

Artur Holde: 'And the Bridge is Love'—Die Lebenserinnerungen Alma Mahler-Werfels, *NZfM*, February 1959.

Karl Holl: GM in seinen Briefen, *NMZ*, 15 April 1925 (No. 14), p. 331.

Hans Holländer: Unbekannte Jugendbriefe GMs, *Die Musik*, August 1928, p. 807.

— Unbekannte Briefe aus GMs Jugend, *Neues Wiener Journal*, 16 September 1928.

— GM's jeugd., *De Muziek*, December 1928.

— Zwei deutsche Aufsätze des Gymnasiasten GM, *Der Auftakt*, 1929, No. 1, p. 5.

— GM, *MQ*, October 1931, p. 449.

— GM, ein tragisches Künstlerschicksal, *Der Auftakt*, 1936, Nos. 5–6, p. 82.

— GM, *Rivista musicale italiana*, December 1936.

— GM vollendet eine Oper von Carl Maria von Weber (Vier unbekannte Briefe Mahlers), *NZfM*, December 1955, p. 130.

B. Holmqvist: En man vid en gräns, *Röster i Radio*, 1951, No. 12, p. 4.

Richard Holt: GM, *The Gramophone*, March 1931, p. 510.

— The Mahler question again, *Philharmonic Post*, March–April 1948, p. 4.

Gervase Hughes: Mahler, in *The Handbook of Great Composers*, Arthur Barker (London) 1965, p. 205.

Llifon Hughes-Jones: Recognition after neglect, *M&M*, July 1960, p. 9.

Robert H. Hull, GM, *Contemporary Review*, September 1930, p. 348.

Edgar Istel: La personnalité et la vie de GM, *La Vie musicale*, Vol. IV, No. 3.

— GM, *MMR*, 1911, p. 138.

Edgar Istel: Erinnerungen an GM, *NMZ*, 1917, No. 6, p. 88.

— Mahlers Symphonien, erläutert mit Notenbeispielen, 1920.

Wilhelm Jelinek: GMs Persönlichkeit und Verhältnis zur Kunst, *NZfM*, 1910, 25 August p. 209, 1 September p. 223.

Ernst Jokl: GM in Amerika, *Anbruch*, April 1920, p. 289.

Alexander Jemnitz: GM als kgl. ung. Hofoperndirektor, *Der Auftakt*, 1936, Nos. 1–2 p. 7, Nos. 3–4 p. 63, Nos. 11–12 p. 183.

Albert Kareders: Zehn Jahr Direktion Mahler, *Wiener Fremdenblatt*, 30 May 1907.

Ludwig Karpath: GM und die Wiener Hofoper, *Bühne und Welt* (Berlin), 1904, No. 17.

— GM, *Strassburger Post*, No. 105, 1905.

— Mahler-Weingartner, der gehende und der kommende Herr, *Signale*, No. 56 (2 October), 1907, p. 998.

— Persönliches von GM, mit einem Brief Mahlers, *Der Merker*, April (1) 1913, p. 251.

— GM und der Kammersängertitel, *Neues Wiener Journal*, 14 October 1923.

— Begegnung mit dem Genius, 1934.

Hugo Kauder: Vom Geiste der Mahlerschen Musik, *Anbruch*, April 1920, p. 262.

— Mahlers Instrumentation, *Anbruch*, April 1920, p. 277.

Dieter Kerner: GMs Ende, *NZfM*, May 1961.

H. F. Kernkampf: GM, *Elsevier's Maandschrift* (Amsterdam), 1936, p. 312.

Otto Klemperer: Meine Erinnerungen an GM, 1920. Erinnerungen an GM, Atlantis Verlag (Zürich) 1960. Minor Recollections (transl. J. Maxwell Brownjohn), Dennis Dobson (London) 1964.

E. Klusen: Die Liedertexte GMs, *Sudetendeutsche Zs. f. Volkskunde*, Vol. VI, Nos. 5–6, p. 178.

— GM und das Volkslied seiner Heimat, *Journal of the International Folk Music Council*, 1963, p. 29.

E. von Komorzynski: GMs neue Lieder, *NMZ*, 1905, No. 10.

R. Konta: The life of GM, *Sackbut*, April 1930 p. 241.

Julius Korngold: GM, *Neue Freie Presse*, 4 June 1907 and 19 May 1911.

Heinrich Kralik: GMs Persönlichkeit, *ÖM*, May 1967, p. 271.

E. F. Kravitt: The trend towards the folklike, nationalism and their expression by Mahler and his contemporaries in the Lied, *Chord and Discord*, 1963, No. 10, p. 165.

Sven Kruckenberg: GM, *Musik och ljudteknik*, 1961, No. 3, p. 17.

Walther Krug: Mahler, in *Die neue Musik*, Eugen Rentsch (Erlenbach) 1919, p. 41.

Samuel Langford: The Mahler Festival at Amsterdam, *MT*, July 1920, p. 448.

Allan Lincoln Langley: Justice for GM, *MQ*, April 1926, p. 153.

Per Lindfors: GM, *Röster i Radio*, 1943, No. 40, p. 10.

Dolf Lindner: Zur Ausstellung 'GM und Seine Zeit', *ÖM*, June 1960.

K. List: Mahler, father of modern music, *Commentary*, July 1950, p. 42.

Anthony Lister: Comment on some criticisms of Mahler's symphonies, *MO*, March 1956.

Richard Litterscheid: Mahler, Mendelssohn und wir, *Die Musik*, March 1936, p. 413.

Edward Lockspeiser: Mahler in France, *MMR*, 1960, p. 52.

Friedrich Löhr: Zwei Jugendbriefe—von Mahler und über ihn, *Anbruch*, April 1920, p. 301.

Paul Lorenz: GM, ein Unvergessener, *ÖM*, October 1957.

Egon Lustgarten: Mahlers lyrisches Schaffen, *Anbruch*, April 1920, p. 255.

J. C. Lusztig: GM, *Rheinische Musik- und Theaterzeitung*, 1911, No. 20.

Joseph Machlis: GM, in *Introduction to Contemporary Music*, W. W. Norton (USA) 1961, Dent (London), p. 74.

Alma Maria Mahler: GM, Erinnerungen und Briefe, 1940; transl. GM, Memories and Letters, 1946; revised and enlarged edition (ed. Donald Mitchell), Viking Press (New York) 1969; John Murray (London) 1968.

— The end, in *Great Composers through the Eyes of their Contemporaries*, Dutton (New York) 1951, p. 448.

Gustav Mahler: Erneuerung, *Anbruch*, May 1924.

I. Maione: GM, *Il Baretti* (Naples), 1961, No. 8.

H. J. de Marez Oijens: GM in Holland, *Die Musikwelt*, 15 October 1922.

Jean Matter: De la réminiscence dans les

symphonies de Mahler, *SM*, October 1958, p. 377.
— La signification de l'humour dans la musique de Mahler, *Schweizerische Musik-pädagogische Blätter (Feuillets suisses de pédagogie musicale)*, January 1959.
— Le 'Knaben Wunderhorn' dans l'œuvre de Mahler, *Feuilles musicales*, October 1959.
— Mahler le démoniaque, 1959.
— Strauss et Mahler, *SM*, November–December 1964, p. 364.
Camille Mauclair: Hugo Wolf, Anton Bruckner, GM, in *Histoire de la musique européenne*, Librairie Fischbacher (Paris) 1914, p. 189.
Wilfrid Mellers: Mahler as key figure, *Scrutiny*, March 1941, p. 343; in *Studies in Contemporary Music*, Dennis Dobson (London) 1947, p. 109.
— Last romantics, *New Statesman*, 21 August 1964, p. 256.
— After Mahler, *New Statesman*, 29 January 1965, p. 172.
C. Rudolf Mengelberg: GM und Willem Mengelberg, *NMZ*, 1920, No. 15, p. 234.
— Mahlers Weg, *Anbruch*, May 1923, p. 134.
Willem Mengelberg: Mahler's music: comment on an article in the Daily Mail, *MMR*, 1930, p. 358.
E. H. Meyer: GM, *Musik und Gesellschaft*, May 1961, p. 257.
Donald Mitchell: GM, The Early Years, Rockliff (London) 1958.
— Mahler's early symphonies, *The Listener*, 26 February 1959, p. 393.
— Mahler and the English, *The Listener*, 10 March 1960, p. 473.
— Mahler on the gramophone, *M&L*, April 1960.
— GM—prospect and retrospect, *PRMA*, 1960–1, p. 83; *Chord and Discord*, 1963, No. 10, p. 138.
— Early and mature Mahler, *The Listener*, 25 October 1962, p. 695.
Erwin Mittag: GM als Dirigent, *ÖM*, June 1960.
Antal Molnár: GM, *Muzsika*, August 1960, p. 12.
Erich H. Mueller v. Asow: Ein ungedruckter Brief Mahlers, *ÖM*, February 1957.
A. Neisser: GM, mit Mahlers Bildnis, 1918.

Otto Neitzel: GM und das Amsterdamer Concertgebouw, *Anbruch*, April 1920, p. 256.
Zdeněk Nejedlý: GM mrtev, *Smetana*, 2 June 1911.
— GM, 1958.
Dika Newlin: Bruckner, Mahler, Schoenberg, 1947.
Paul Nettl: GM als Musikhistoriker, *Musica*, 1958, No. 10, p. 592.
— The controversial GM, *Music Journal*, June–July 1960, p. 32.
Jan Nevote: GM und die russische Musik, *Prager Presse*, No. 314, 15 November 1923.
E. O. Nodnagel: GM, *Der Kunstwart*, 1905, No. 9.
Z. Novacek: K. Mahlerovej storocnici, *Slovenska Hudba*, August 1960, p. 402.
A. Nyman: Livsproblem—GMs Musik, in *Musikalisk intelligens* (Stockholm), 1928, p. 59.
Werner Oehlmann: GM, *Musica*, 1955, No. 5, p. 199.
R. S. Olsen: Bruckner and Mahler, *MO*, December 1962, p. 143.
F. E. Pamer: GMs Lieder, *Studien zur Musikwissenschaft*, 1929, Band 16, 17.
D. C. Parker: Bruckner and Mahler, *MS*, 19 June 1920, p. 211.
Gösta Percy: GM, det universellas tondiktare, *Musikrevy*, 1960, p. 145.
Moses Pergament: Problemet GM, *Svenska Dagbladet*, 28 October 1936.
Emil Petschnig: Götze Mahler, *AMZ*, 20 January 1922.
C. Pichois & H. Trefz: GM s'est-il inspiré de Beaudelaire?, *Revue de littérature comparée*, October–December 1957.
Peter J. Pirie: Crippled splendour—Elgar and Mahler, *MT*, February 1956, p. 70.
B. Pleijel: Mahler paa LP-skivor, *Musikrevy*, 1960, No. 5, p. 155.
Bohdan Pociej: GM, *Ruch Muzyczny*, 1960, No. 24, p. 2.
L. Ponnelle: A Munich GM, 1913.
J. B. de Portugal: Notes para o processo de Mahler, *Arte musical*, 1960, No. 9, p. 236.
Robert W. F. Potter: A plea for the recording of the songs of GM, *The Gramophone*, June 1936, p. 8.

Mahler, Gustav

Klaus Pringsheim: GM, *Canadian Musical Journal*, autumn 1960, p. 17.
Max Puttmann: GM, *Blätter für Haus- und Kirchenmusik*, 1905, No. 5.
Erwin Ratz: GM, *NZfM*, December 1955, p. 127.
— Persönlichkeit und Werk, *ÖM*, June 1960.
— GM, *Musikrevy*, 1961, No. 8, p. 254.
— Musical form in GM, *MR*, February 1968, p. 34.
Henry Raynor: GM, without prejudice, *MMR*, 1953, p. 4.
— Mahler as a song writer, *MT*, July 1956, p. 352.
Hans F. Redlich: Die Welt der V., VI. und VII. Sinfonie Mahlers, *Anbruch*, April 1920, p. 265.
— GM, eine Erkenntnis, 1919.
— Mahlers Wirkung in Zeit und Raum, *Anbruch*, March 1930, p. 96.
— Bruckner & Mahler, 1955, 1963.
— La 'Trilogia della morte' di Mahler, *La Rassegna musicale*, September 1958, p. 177.
— The creative achievement of GM, *MT*, July 1960, p. 418.
Eduard Reeser: Onuitgegeven brieven van Mahler an Diepenbrock, *Caeceilia en De Muziek*, May 1934.
— GM, *Caecilia en De Muziek*, May 1936, p. 274.
Willi Reich: Kleines Mahler-Brevier, *Der Auftakt*, 1935, Nos. 9–10, p. 145.
— GM, *Musica Viva*, July 1936.
— GM zum Gedenken, *SMZ*, 1936, p. 303.
Josef Reitler: GM, *Rheinische Musik- und Theaterzeitung*, 1911, No. 17.
E. N. v. Reznicek: Erinnerungen an GM, *Anbruch*, April 1920, p. 298.
William Ritter: Deux symphonies de Mahler, *Feuilles musicales*, October 1959.
— Souvenirs de GM, *SM*, January–February 1961, p. 29.
Alfred Roller: Mahler und die Inszenierung, *Anbruch*, April 1920, p. 272; *Moderne Welt*, 1922, No. 7.
— Die Bildnisse von GM, 1922.
— Worte zu Bildnissen GMs, *Anbruch*, February 1922, p. 34.
Alfred Rosé: Aus GMs Sturm- und Drangperiode, *Hamburger Fremdenblatt*, 5 October

1928; From GM's storm and stress period, *Canadian Musical Journal*, winter 1957, p. 21.
K. H. Ruppel: Skizze zu einem Essay über GM, *Deutsche Kunstschau*, 15 March 1924.
H. Rutters: GM, 1919.
Edward Sackville West: GM, *Music Survey*, No. 2, winter 1948.
Adolfo Salazar: Bruckner y Mahler, in *Sinfonía y ballet*, Editorial Mundo Latino (Madrid) 1929, p. 120.
Ingrid Samson: GM, der Komponist, *Musik im Unterricht*, July–August 1960.
— Ein unveröffentlichter Brief GMs, *NZfM*, August 1960.
A. Schaefer: GMs Instrumentation, Bonn, 1933.
Hans Joachim Schaefer: GMs Wirken in Kassel, *Musica*, 1960, No. 6, p. 350.
Bernard Scharlitt: GM und das Wiener Hofoperntheater, *NZfM* (Musikalische Wochenblatt), 1907, No. 18 (2 May), p. 413.
— GM als Direktor des Wiener Hofoperntheaters, *Vereinigte Musikalische Wochenschriften* (Leipzig), 1907, No. 18.
— Gespräch mit Mahler, *Anbruch*, April 1920, p. 309.
A. Schering: GM als Liederkomponist, *NZfM*, 1905, Nos. 35–36 (30 August), p. 672, No. 37 (6 September), p. 691, No. 40 (27 September), p. 753.
Armin Schibler: L'élément mélodique dans les symphonies de Mahler, *Feuilles musicales*, October 1959.
— Zum Werk GMs, 1955.
L. Schiedermair: GM als Symphoniker, *Die Musik*, December (2) 1901, p. 506.
— GM, eine biographisch-kritische Würdigung, 1901.
— Tonsetzer der Gegenwart, VIII: GM, *NZfM*, 1905, No. 20 (10 May), p. 421.
Leopold Schmidt: GM, *Berliner Tageblatt*, 18 May 1911.
— Richard Specht über GM, *Der Kunstwart*, May (1) 1914, p. 148.
Hans Schnoor: Um Mahlers symphonisches Werk, *Die Musik*, April 1923, p. 481.
— Aus GMs Leipziger Zeit, *Leipziger Tageblatt*, 21 and 28 October 1923; *SM*, November 1924.
Arnold Schoenberg: GM, *Der Merker*, March (1) 1912, p. 182.

— Style and Idea, Faber (London) 1972.

K. Schubert: Vom Wesen der Sinfonik GMs, *Musik und Gesellschaft*, July 1960, p. 386.

G. Schünemann: Bekkers Mahler, *Zeitschrift für Musikwissenschaft*, Vol. IV, No. 2.

Gustav Schwarz: Der Entdecker GMs, *Neues Wiener Journal*, 1905, Nos. 6–8.

Paul Schwers: (GM), *AMZ*, 1911, Nos. 21–22.

Artur Seidl: Zu GMs Gedächtnis, *Der Merker*, March (1) 1912, p. 192.

— Pfitzner, Bruckner, Mahler, *Der Auftakt*, January 1924.

A. F. Seligmann: Silhouetten aus der Mahler-Zeit, *Moderne Welt*, 1922, No. 7.

Robert Simpson: Mahler and the BBC, *Music Survey*, No. 3, May 1948.

Iwan I. Sollertinsky: GM, 1932.

Robert Sondheimer: GM und Carl Loewe, *Die Musik*, February 1930, p. 356.

Kaikhosru Sorabji: Mahler and English audiences, *MM&F*, April 1932, p. 85.

August Spanuth: GM, *Signale*, 1911, No. 21 (24 May), p. 783.

— New York und GM, *Signale*, 1911, No. 24 (14 June), p. 879.

Richard Specht: GM, 1905, 1913, 1925.

— GM, *Die Musik*, May (1) 1908, p. 149.

— Mahler als Dirigent, *Der Kunstwart*, July (2) 1910, p. 94.

— Mahlers Weg, *Der Merker*, 10 September 1910, p. 913.

— GM, *Die Musik*, Vol. X (1910–11), No. 18, p. 335.

— Mahler, *Der Merker*, March (1) 1912, p. 161.

— GM als Operndirektor, *Die Musik*, December (2) 1913, p. 323.

— Mahler-Silhouette, *Der Merker*, 1 January 1919, p. 12.

— Mahlers Feinde, *Anbruch*, April 1920, p. 278.

— GMs Gegenwart, *Moderne Welt*, 1922, No. 7.

Theodore Spiering: Zwei Jahre mit GM in New York, *Vossische Zeitung*, 21 May 1911.

Eric Paul Stecel: Anton Bruckner, GM et l'école symphonique autrichienne, *Cahiers du Sud*, 1936, p. 138.

Paul Stefan: GMs Erbe, 1908.

— GM, ein Bild seiner Persönlichkeit, Munich, 1910.

— GM, 1912.

— GMs Kindheit, erste Jugend und Lehrjahre, *Die Musik*, Vol. X (1910–11), No. 18, p. 342.

— Richard Wagner und Mahler, *Der Merker*, March (1) 1912, p. 189.

— GM, a study of his personality and work, 1913.

— Mahlers Freunde, *Anbruch*, April 1920, p. 287.

— Der Mahler-Fest in Amsterdam, *NMZ*, 1920, No. 18, p. 288.

— GM, *Il Pianoforte*, Vol. II, No. 4.

— Mahler für Jedermann, *Anbruch*, September–October 1922, p. 227.

— Österreichische Musik seit Mahler, *Anbruch*, May 1923, p. 131.

— GM in der Literatur, *Moderne Welt*, 1922, No. 7.

— Mahler und das Theater, *Anbruch*, March 1930, p. 99.

— The man behind the symphony, *Radio Times*, 11 April 1930, p. 77.

— GM et la jeune generation, *RM*, March 1931, p. 195.

— GMs Kasseler Tage, *Vossische Zeitung*, 2 June 1928.

— Bruckner und Mahler, Amerika und Russland, *Anbruch*, October 1932, p. 183.

— Wiener Opernspiel in grossen Epochen, III: Mahler-Zeit, *Anbruch*, September 1936, p. 167 (repr. from *Die Wiener Oper*, Vienna, 1932).

Gerhard Stehmann: GMs Proben, *Moderne Welt*, 1922, No. 7.

Erwin Stein: Mahlers Instrumentationsretuschen, *Pult und Taktstock*, November–December 1927; *Anbruch*, February 1928, p. 42.

— Mahlers Sachlichkeit, *Anbruch*, March 1930, p. 99.

— Mahler today, *Tempo*, No. 6, February 1944.

— Mahler and the Vienna Opera, *Opera*, 1953, January, p. 4, March, p. 145, April, p. 200, May, p. 281.

Julius Steinberg: Aus Mahlers Prager Kapellmeisterzeit, *Fremdenblatt*, 25 May 1911.

Max Steinitzer: Erinnerungen an GM, *Anbruch*, April 1920, p. 296.

Helmut Storjohann: GMs Verhältnis zu Volksmusik, *Musica*, 1960, No. 6, p. 357.

Josef Stransky: Begegnungen mit GM, *Signale*, 1911, No. 29 (19 July), p. 1027.

Gustav A. Svoboda: O poslednich Mahlerových konzertech v Americe, *Smetana*, 2 June 1911.

H. Taubman: Appraising Mahler, *New York Times*, 28 February 1960, Section 2, p. 9.

Stainton Taylor: 'An Archangel slightly damaged'—GM and the Symphony, *Musical Mirror*, June 1930, p. 153.

Roland Tenschert: Der Faustische Zug in GMs Wesen und Werk, *Die Musik*, June 1927, p. 651.

Hans Tessmer: GMs Romantik, *NMZ*, 1919, No. 10, p. 116.

Heinz Tiessen: Die Briefe GMs, *Die Zeit*, 22 February 1925.

Hans Tischler: Mahler's impact on the crisis of tonality, *MR*, 1951, p. 113.

— Musical form in GM's works, *American Musicological Society Journal*, fall 1949, p. 199.

Harold Truscott: Some aspects of Mahler's tonality, *MMR*, 1957, p. 203.

— GM, in *The Symphony*, Vol. 2, Penguin Books (London) 1967, p. 29.

Hermann Ullrich: GM und Wien im Wandel der Zeiten, *ÖM*, June 1960.

Bruno Walter: Mahlers Weg, ein Erinnerungsblatt, *Der Merker*, March (1) 1912, p. 166.

— GM, Erinnerung-Betrachtung, Reichner (Vienna) 1936.

— Bruckner and Mahler, *Hallé*, October–November 1947, p. 1; *Chord and Discord*, November 1940, reprinted 1960, No. 9, p. 41.

— GM, Kegal Paul (London) 1937. GM (with a biographical essay by Ernst Křenek), Greystone Press (New York) 1941; new edition (transl. Lotte Walter Lindt) Hamish Hamilton (London) 1958.

— The young Kapellmeister, in *Great Composers through the Eyes of their Contemporaries*, Dutton (New York) 1951, p. 437.

— A propos GM, *ÖM*, June 1960.

Carmen Weingartner-Studer: GM und Felix Weingartner, *ÖM*, June 1960.

Adolph Weissmann: GM, *Sackbut*, October 1923, p. 76.

Egon Wellesz: Epilog zum Mahlerfest in Amsterdam, *Anbruch*, June 1920, p. 419.

— Mahlers Instrumentation, *Anbruch*, March 1930, p. 106; Mahler's orchestration, *MMR*, 1930, p. 321.

— GM, *Anbruch*, June–July 1935, p. 189.

— GM und die Wiener Oper, *Die neue Rundschau*, 1960, No. 2.

— Reminiscences of Mahler, *The Score*, No. 28, January 1961, p. 52.

Th. J. Wentholt: GM and Bruno Walter, *Gramophone Record Review*, July 1960, p. 513.

Erik Werba: Ein 'Mahler'-Brief, *ÖM*, June 1960.

Th. Wiesengrund-Adorno: Mahler Heute, *Anbruch*, March 1930, p. 86.

— Mahler: Eine musikalische Physiognomik, Suhrkamp (Frankfurt) 1960.

Friedrich Wildgangs: GM, *ÖM*, June 1946, p. 206.

— GM und Anton von Webern, *ÖM*, June 1960.

Franz Willnauer: Das Triviale und das Grotesk im Werke GMs, *NZfM*, August 1960.

H. C. Worbs: GM, *Canon*, December 1962–January 1963, p. 14.

MISCELLANEOUS OR UNSIGNED

GM, ein Selbstporträt in Briefen, *Der Merker*, March (1) 1912, p. 172.

Aus einem Tagebuch über Mahler, *Der Merker*, March (1) 1912, p. 184.

4 Briefe Mahlers an Bruno Walter, *Neue Freie Presse*, 31 December 1922.

Nachlassbriefe GMs (an Bruno Walter gerichtet), *Berliner Börsen-Courier*, 24 December 1922.

Ein Brief GMs an Ernst von Schuch, *Anbruch*, April 1922, p. 101.

GM, Briefe (ed. Alma Maria Mahler), Paul Zsolnay (Vienna), 1924.

Mahler's letters, *Sackbut*, 1923, January, p. 170, February, p. 204.

2 Briefe Mahlers an R. Batke, *Die Musik*, January 1923.

Ein Brief Mahlers an Bruckner, *Anbruch*, May 1923, p. 137.

Briefe von GM an Max Marschalk, *Vossische Zeitung*, 20 April 1924.

Erneuerung—Ein Brief GMs an Bruno
Walter, *Anbruch*, May 1924, p. 171.
Mahler: a study in nationality, *The Times*,
12 February 1927, p. 10.
Symphonies: Elgar and Mahler, *The Times*,
1 February 1930, p. 10.
Briefe an Theodor Reichmann, 1932.
Mahler e Hugo Wolf, *Musica d'oggi*, August–
September 1932, p. 349.
Een onbekende brief van GM, *De Muziek*,
August–September 1933.
Weber und Mahler—Mahlers Opernbearbei-
tungen, *Anbruch*, November 1936, p. 221.
GM und Hans von Bülow, *Die Musik*,
February 1930, p. 400.
GMs Instrumentation, *Anbruch*, 1936, Nos.
9–10, p. 285.
Kleines Mahler-Triptychon (Letters), *SM*,
January–February 1964, p. 21.

BOHUSLAV MARTINŮ (1890–1959)

Bohuslav Martinů's father, a shoemaker by
trade, was Keeper of the Church Tower of
St. James the Great in the small country town
of Polička on the borders of Bohemia and
Moravia; and it was in the tower that the
composer was born, 8 December 1890, and
lived—until he was eleven. Learning the violin
from the age of seven and beginning to compose three or four years later, Martinů had
enough local prestige by the time he was
fifteen for the Polička town council to
sponsor his further training as a violinist at
the Prague Conservatoire. He studied there
from 1906 until his expulsion 'for incorrigible
negligence' in 1910. During these years he
became a close friend of Stanislav Novák,
later the leader of the Czech Philharmonic
Orchestra, and from 1913 onwards played
irregularly himself among the second violins
of the Philharmonic. Avoiding service in the
Austrian army during the First World War,
Martinů eked out a living by giving piano and
violin lessons in Polička. In 1920 he became a
full-time member of the Czech Philharmonic,
directed at that time by Václav Talich, but
after a further brief spell at the Prague
Conservatoire (during which he studied with
Josef Suk) Martinů left for France in 1923 to
devote himself wholly to composition. At

first a private pupil of Albert Roussel's, he
lived in Paris for seventeen years, making
annual visits to Czechoslovakia and in 1931
marrying Charlotte Quennehen, a dress-
maker from Picardy. Martinů escaped from
Paris in June 1940 as the German army
reached the city, spent several months in
Aix-en-Provence and sailed for the United
States from Lisbon in March 1941. He was
Professor of Composition at the Berkshire
Music Center (Tanglewood, Mass.) in 1942,
and from 1943 to 1953 lived in New York
City, teaching at various institutions, including
Princeton University (1948–51). At the end of
the Second World War, while still in New
York, Martinů accepted a chair of composition
at the Prague Conservatoire; but in 1946,
during his second visit to Tanglewood, he
fell ten feet from a balcony and sustained
serious head and neck injuries which led to a
long convalescence in the United States. In
fact, Martinů never returned to Czechoslovakia, although from 1953 until his death
his homes were mainly European: principally
Nice, Rome (where he was Composer in
Residence at the American Academy from
1956 to 1957) and Schönenberg near Basle.
He died of stomach cancer at a sanatorium in
Liestal (Switzerland) in August 1959.

CATALOGUE OF WORKS

1. Three Horsemen. For string quartet.
1902, Polička. Unpub.

2. Village Wake. Suite for string orchestra
and flute. 1907, Polička. Unpub.

3. Dumka. For piano. 1909, Polička. Unpub.

4. Elegy. For violin and piano. Easter 1909,
Polička. Ded. S. Novák. Unpub.

5. Waltzes. For piano. 1910, Prague.
   1. *Andante* (A minor). 14 January 1910.
   2. *Valse mignonne.*
   3. *Tempo di valse* (G major). 1 February
1910.
   4. *Tempo di valse* (A minor). 3 February
1910.
   5. *Tempo di valse* (E-flat major). 4 February
1910.
Unpub.

Martinů, Bohuslav

6. Ballad. For piano. 10 October 1910, Prague. Unpub.

7. Sousedská. For piano. 14 October 1910, Prague. Unpub.

8. Idylla. For piano. 1910, Polička. Unpub.

9. Marche funèbre. For piano. 1910, Prague. Unpub.

10. Angel of Death. Study for piano. 1910, Polička. Unpub.

11. Angel of Death. Symphonic Poem for orchestra. 1910. Unpub.

12. Goldilocks. A Fairy Tale for piano. October–November 1910, Prague.
   1. Fairy tale; *2. Pastoral*; *3. Dumka*; *4. Barcarole*; *5. Waltz.*
Unpub.

13. Toilers of the Sea. Symphonic Poem for orchestra, after Victor Hugo. 1910, Polička. Sketch only.

14. The Death of Tintagile. Music to the puppet drama by Maurice Maeterlinck. For orchestra. 1910, Prague.

15. Symphony. 1910, Prague. First movement only.

16. Andante. For orchestra. 1910, Polička. Sketch only.

17. Violin Concerto. 1910, Polička.
   1. Moderato; *2. Largo*; *3. Allegretto.*
Unpub.

18. Romance. For violin and piano. 1910, Smiřice. Ded. Josef Vogner. Unpub.

19. The drowned maiden (Utonulá) (J. V. Sládek). For voice and piano. 1910, Prague. Unpub.

20. Before you know (Než se nadĕješ) (Jan Červenka). For voice and piano. 20 March 1910, Prague. Unpub.

21. In Nature (V přírodĕ) (V. Hálek). For voice and piano. 20 March 1910, Prague. Unpub.

22. Pastel (Bohdan Kaminský). For voice and piano. 20 March 1910, Prague. Unpub.

23. When we are old (Až budeme staří)

(A. Klášterský). For voice and piano. 1910, Prague.

24. The sleeper (Spící) (E. A. Poe). For voice and piano. 21 July 1910, Polička. Unpub.

25. Nokturno (A. Klášterský). For voice and piano. 1910, Prague. Unpub.

26. At night (Vnoci) (R. Mayer). For voice and piano. 19 July 1910, Prague. Two versions. Ded. (first version) Olga Valousková, (second version) J. Nováková-Tomášková. Unpub.

27. Maiden's dreams (Dívčí sny) (Ricarda Hugh). For voice and piano. Unpub.

28. Two Songs. For voice and piano. 5–6 August 1910.
   1. Why have you laughed at me? (Proč zoubky Tvé tak smály se) (V. Houdek).
   2. Where have I been? (Kde jsem to byla) (Růžena Jesenská).
Unpub.

29. Kiss, my sweetheart, kiss (Líbej, milá, líbej) (P. Manin). For voice and piano. 17 October 1910. Unpub.

30. Zpĕv a hudba. Song for voice and piano. 1910. Unpub.

31. Two Little Songs (in folk tone) (Xaver). for voice and piano. 1910. Ded. Olga Valoušková. Unpub.

32. A winter's night (Zimní noc) (A. Heyduk). For voice and piano. 1910, Prague. Unpub.

33. Picture of a mood (Náladová kresba) (V. Klen). 25 December 1910, Polička. Unpub.

34. Jašek's song (Jaškova zpĕvanka) (Tetmajer). For voice and piano. 1911, Prague. Unpub.

35. Two Songs (J. V. Sládek). For voice and piano. 26 May 1911. Ded. Olga Valoušková.
   1. A maiden's song; *2. When the day comes.*
Unpub.

36. Song (Mužík). For voice and piano. 1911, Prague. Unpub.

37. Tears (J. V. Sládek). For voice and piano. 24 December 1911, Polička. Unpub.

38. First love (První láska) (A. E. Mužík). For voice and piano. 1911. Unpub.

39. Berceuse. For violin and piano. 1911, Polička. Unpub.

40. Adagio. For violin and piano. 1911, Polička. Unpub.

41. Piano Quintet. 6 June–1 August 1911, Polička. Unpub.

42. Chanson triste. For piano. October 1911, Polička. Unpub.

43. Nocturnos. For string quartet. 1912, Polička.
 1. *Largo*; 2. *Presto.*
fp: 15 August 1912, Polička, Youth Band concert, S. Novák, B. Martinů, J. Vintr and J. Hruška.
Unpub.

44. Andante. For string quartet. 1912, Polička. Unpub.

45. Fantasy. For violin and piano. 1912, Polička.
fp: 15 July 1912, Polička.
Unpub.

46. Ballad on Miss Vilma's Umbrella. For piano. 1912, Polička. Unpub.

47. From Andersen's Fairy Tales. For piano. 1–7 January 1912, Polička.
 1. *Ballad*; 2. *Barcarole*; 3. *Novelette*; 4. *Polonaise*; 5. *Valse mignone*; 6. *Intermezzo*; 7. *Legend.*
Unpub.

48. Ballad (Chopin's Last Chords). For piano. 1912, Prague.
fp: 14 August 1912, Polička, Bohuslav Martinů.
Unpub.

49. Nocturne. For piano. 1912, Prague. Ded. Božena Pacovská. Unpub.

50. Song without words. For piano. 1912, Prague. Ded. Božena Pacovská. Pub. *Zlatá Praha* (Vol. XVI, No. 8) Musical Supplement.

51. Offertory. For soprano and organ. 1912, Polička. Unpub.

52. Ave Maria. For soprano and organ. 1912, Polička. Unpub.

53. Dance: Ei cimbore. For male choir, 2 violins, 2 violas and drum. Words: Folk text. Sketch only: undated.

54. The end of all (Konec všemu) (A. E. Mužík). For voice and piano. 14 January 1912, Prague. Unpub.

55. Dead love (Mrtvá láska) (A. E. Mužik). For voice and piano. 20 January 1912, Prague. Ded. Olga Valoušková. Unpub.

56. Early in the morning I weed the grain (Ráno raníčko, pleju oblíčko). For voice and piano. 10 March 1912, Prague. Unpub.

57. Lucie (Musset). For voice and piano. 13 March 1912, Prague. Unpub.

58. From childhood (Liliencron). For voice and piano. 16 March 1912, Prague. Unpub.

59. Hoar-frost fallen in the field (Padlo jíní na pole) (Heine). For voice and piano. 18 March 1912, Prague.

60. Marry me, mother, as long as I'm young (Vdejte mne, matičko, dokud jsem mladá). For voice and piano. 20 March 1912, Prague. Unpub.

61. You write to me (Ty píšeš mi) (A. Heyduk). For voice and piano. March 1912, Prague. Unpub.

62. The rose (Růže). For voice and piano. 1912, Prague. Unpub.

63. All this is what only remains (To všechno už jen zbylo) (J. V. Sládek). For voice and piano. 1912. Unpub.

64. I see you every night, my dear (Noc každou Tebe drahá zřím) (Heine). For voice and piano. 1912. Unpub.

65. Where was I? (Kde jsem to byla) (R. Jesenská). For voice and piano. 5 August 1912, Želiv. Unpub.

66. Speak on! (Mluv ke mně dál) (K. Tetmajer). For voice and piano. 22 August 1912. Unpub.

67. The jilted maiden (Opuštěná milá) (L. Grossmanová-Brodská). For voice and piano. 23 August 1912. Unpub.

68. Once upon a time (Kdysi) (L. Grossmanová-Brodská). For voice and piano. 9 September 1912. Unpub.

69. Dead eyes (O mrtvých očích) (V. Martínek). For voice and piano. 17 September 1912, Polička. Ded. Líba Zítková. Unpub.

70. The fiery man (Ohnivý muž) (Vrat. Hlavsa). For voice and piano. 1912. Unpub.

71. Song of the First of November (Vrat. Hlavsa). For voice and piano. 1912. Unpub.

72. Three maidens on a bright night (Tři panny za světlé noci) (Vrat. Hlavsa). For voice and piano. 1912. Unpub.

73. Nipponari. Seven songs for female voice and instrumental ensemble. 1912, Prague. Ded. Theo Drill Oridge.
 1. *Blue hour* (Nukada).
 fl, ca, v, 4 va, 4 c.
 2. *Old age* (Kinfsuna).
 va, hp. *Off stage:* ca, 5 va.
 3. *Reminiscence* (Kibino).
 fl, v, hp.
 4. *Life's dream* (Onomo Komadi).
 3 fl, 4 va.
 5. *Tracks in the snow* (Sidruka Gozen).
 pf, celesta, hp, 4 v, 4 va.
 6. *A backward glance* (Onomo Komadi).
 3 fl, hp, 4 v, 4 c.
 7. *At the sacred lake* (Kotsuna Ozi).
 3 fl, celesta, hp, tgle, tamtam.
 Unpub.

74. Old Song (Villiers de l'Isle Adam). For voice and piano. 1912. Unpub.

75. The gnat's wedding (Folksong words). For voice and piano. 1912. Unpub.

76. Let there be light, o God (Svítaj Bože). For voice and piano. 1912. Unpub.

77. In the garden at the castle (V zahradě na hradě) (In folk tone). For voice and piano. 1912. Unpub.

78. The swan (J. z Wojkovic). For voice and piano. 1912. Unpub.

79. I love old parks (Mám staré parky rád) (J. Borecký). For voice and piano. 1912. Unpub.

80. Song of Hanička (Písnička o Haničce) (Kalhus). For voice and piano. 1912. Unpub.

81. Enough of happiness (Štěstí to dost) (Liliencron). For voice and piano. 11 December 1912, Prague. Unpub.

82. Mother mine, I have a laddie (Matičko má, hocha mám). Song to the words of an old Spanish text, for voice and piano. 1913.

83. Le sapin de Noël. Song to a French text, for voice and piano. 1913, Prague. Unpub.

84. Le petit oiseau. Song to a French text, for voice and piano. 1913, Prague. Unpub.

85. Le soir. Song to a French text, for voice and piano. ?1913, Prague. Unpub.

86. Praeludium (based on the theme of the Marseillaise). For piano. 1913, Prague. Unpub.

87. Prelude No. 2 in F minor. For piano. 1913, Prague. Unpub.

88. Le soir. Lyrical melodrama, based on a poem by Albert Samain, with harp accompaniment. 1913, Prague. Unpub.

89. La libellule. Lyrical melodrama, based on a poem by Henri d'Orange, for violin, harp and piano. 1913, Prague. Unpub.

90. Danseuses de Java. Lyrical melodrama, based on a poem by Arthur Symonds, for viola, harp and piano. 1913, Prague. Unpub.

91. Night. 'Meloplastic scenic work' in one act. 1913–14. Libretto: F. Kohout. Unpub.

92. Dance with a veil. 'Meloplastic ballet'. 1912–14, Prague. Ded. Olga V. Gzovská. Unpub.

93. Four Little Songs (Goethe). For voice and piano. 1914–15.
 1. *Glückliche Fahrt* (Šťastná jízda); 2. *Elfenliedchen* (Písnička skřítků); 3. *Liebesglück* (Štěstí lásky).
 Unpub. No. 4 lost.

94. Nocturno No. 1. For orchestra. 1915, Polička. Unpub.

95. Nocturno (Les roses dans la nuit). Symphonic Dance No. 2 for orchestra. 1915, Polička. Lost.

96. Ballada (Villa by the sea). Symphonic

Dance No. 4 for orchestra. 1915, Polička. Unpub.

97. (Untitled work.) For large orchestra. 1915, Polička. Unpub.

98. Three Lyrical Pieces. For piano. November 1915, Prague. Ded. G. Čechová.
1. *Moderato—Allegro ma non troppo*; 2. *Moderato—Poco andante*; 3. *Scherzando*. Unpub.

99. Ruyana. For piano. February 1916, Borová. Ded. G. Čechová. Unpub.

100. Polkas. For piano. 1916, Polička.
1. *Allegretto (ma non troppo)*; 2. *Allegro vivo*; 3. *Allegro (D major)*; 4. *Temp à la polka, ma non troppo*; 5. *Moderato assai (E major)*. Unpub.

101. The Shadow. Ballet in one act. 1916, Polička. Unpub.

102. String Quartet. 1917, Polička. Unfinished.
1. *Allegro vivo*; 2. *Lento*; 3. *Allegro con brio*. Unpub.

103. Burlesque. For piano. 1917, Polička.
fp: 17 February 1917, Polička, Bohuslav Martinů. Unpub.

104. Snow. For piano. 1917, Polička.
1. *Snowflakes*; 2. *Evening*; 3. *Sledging—A recollection*.
fp: 17 March 1917, Polička, Bohuslav Martinů. Unpub.

105. Valse capriccio. For piano. 1917, Polička. Ded. Zdena Maxová. Unpub.

106. Mood (Nálada). For piano. 1917, Polička. Unpub.

107. Furiant. For piano. 1917, Polička. Unpub.

108. Evening (G. Moore). For voice and piano. 26 March 1917, Polička. Ded. Mrs. G. Čechová. Unpub.

109. Six Simple Songs. For voice and piano. 1917, Polička.
1. *The days are growing shorter* (Dny se tak krátí).

2. *An angel told me* (Řekl mi anděl).
3. *Oh, no one knows* (Ach, nikdo neví).
4. *Our hillside* (Ta naše stráň).
5. *In the distance thunder rumbles* (V dali hrom burácí).
6. *Good health, my love* (Bud, milý, zdráv). Unpub.

110. A shepherd's Sunday song (Uhland). For voice and piano. 1917, Polička.
fp: 3 August 1918, Polička, Zdeněk Otava. Unpub.

111. Puppets. Small pieces for piano. 1912–1914, Polička.
1. *Pierrot's tryst*; 2. *Valse sentimentale*; 3. *Columbine*; 4. *Puppets' ball*.
Pub. 1922, Chadim; 1957, 1959, State Publishing House.

111a. Puppets I. Small pieces for piano. 1914–?24, Polička.
1. *Columbine dances (Waltz)*; 2. *New puppets (Shimmy)*; 3. *The shy doll (Chanson)*; 4. *Fairytale*; 5. *Dance of the puppets (Waltz)*.
Pub. 1926, 1948, Urbánek; 1956, 1959, State Publishing House.

111b. Puppets II. Small pieces for piano. 1914–18, Polička.
1. *Puppet show (Waltz)*; 2. *Harlequin (Scherzo)*; 3. *Columbine remembers (Intermezzo)*; 4. *The sick puppet (Chanson triste)*; 5. *Columbine sings (Chanson à la Grieg)*.
Pub. 1925, 1948, Urbánek; 1956, 1959, State Publishing House.

112. Summer Suite. Six Lyrical Pieces for piano. New Year 1918, Polička.
1. *Moderato (Waltz)*; 2. *Tempo di minuetto*; 3. *Moderato*; 4. *Scherzando*; 5. *Allegretto*; 6. *Tempo di valse*. Unpub.

113. Lullabies. Children's songs for voice and piano. 1916–18, Polička. Texts of Nos. 4–8 from 'Des Knaben Wunderhorn'.
1. *To my child* (Mému dítěti) (G. Falke).
2. *The spinning top's lullaby* (Vlčkova ukolébavka) (Liliencron).
3. *Sleep, my little one* (Hajej, můj malý) (W. Raabe).
4. *Thanks to God the Creator* (Dík Bohu Stvořiteli).

317

Martinů, Bohuslav

5. *My little angel* (Andělíčku můj).
6. *Sleep, infant, sleep* (Spi, dítě, spi).
7. *Little red bootees* (Červené botičky).
8. *Fourteen little angels* (Čtrnáct andělíčků).
fp: 8 December 1920, Prague, Mozarteum, concert of contemporary songs.
Unpub.

114. Three Songs. 1917–18.
1. *Sweet death* (Nejkrásnější smrt) (Hafiz).
2. *A long pilgrimage* (Dlouhé putování).
3. *Restored to health* (Uzdraven).
fp: 8 December 1920, Prague, Mozarteum, concert of contemporary songs.
Unpub.

115. Three Songs for 'Cervená Sedma'. For voice and piano. ?1918.
1. *Summer Ballad* (Jiří Herold).
2. *Bar* (J. Dreman & J. Herold).
3. *Miners' song* (Fr. Gellner).
?Unpub.

116. String Quartet No. 1. 1918, Polička.
1. *Moderato*; 2. *Andante—Moderato*; 3. *Allegro non troppo*.
fp: 10 October 1927, Prague, Ševčík Quartet.
Unpub.

117. Czech Rhapsody. For baritone, chorus, large orchestra and organ. May–June 1918, Polička. Ded. Alois Jirásek.
fp: 12 January 1919, Prague, Czech Philharmonic, cond. L. V. Čelanský.
Unpub.

118. Magic Nights. Three songs to Chinese texts for soprano and orchestra. November–December 1918, Polička.
1. *Abroad* (Li-Tai-Po).
3 fl, 2 ob, ca, celesta, hp.
2. *Peach blossom* (Chan-Jo-Su).
4 fl, ob, hp, celesta, strings.
3. *The mysterious flute* (Li-Tai-Po).
4 fl, ob, cl, bsn; 2 hn, 2 tpt; cym, tgle, carillon; celesta, hp, strings.
fp (Nos. 1 & 2): 2 April 1924, Prague, Pavla Vachková and the Czech Philharmonic Orchestra.
Unpub.

119. Violin Sonata in C major. 30 January–1 March 1919. Ded. S. Novák and K. Šolc.
Unpub.

120. Choruses to Lithuanian folk texts. For male chorus. 2–3 March 1919, Polička.
1. *On the moon*; 2. *The woman dancer*.
fp: 1919, South Bohemian Vocal Society.
Unpub.

121. Small Dance Suite. For orchestra. 1919, Polička.
1. *Tempo di Valse*; 2. *Song*; 3. *Scherzo*; 4. *Allegro alla Polka*.
Unpub.

122. Cat's foxtrot. For piano. 1919, Polička. Written for the Polička Municipal Band and scored by J. Vintr. Unpub.

123. Grove of Satyrs. Cycle of three works for orchestra. 1920. Only No. 2 ('A Dream of the Past') extant. Unpub.

124. Spring in the Garden. Four children's pieces for piano. 1920, Prague. Pub. 1948, Zdeněk Vlk; 1961, State Publishing House (revised by Vilém Kurz).

125. Slovak Songs. Settings of 30 Slovak folksongs for voice and piano. 1920, Prague.
fp: 8 September 1920, Polička, K. Samohrdová, acc. Bohuslav Martinů.
Unpub.

126. Butterflies and Birds of Paradise. For piano. Christmas 1920, Polička. Ded. Ela Švabinská.
1. *Butterflies and flowers*; 2. *Butterflies and Birds of Paradise*; 3. *Birds of Paradise over the sea*.
Unpub.

127. Evenings on the shore. Three small pieces for piano. 1921, Luhačovice.
1. *Sailing boat returns to harbour in the evening*; 2. *Song on the shore*; 3. *The beating of the surf on the shore*.
Unpub.

128. Istar. Ballet in three acts and five scenes. 1918–22, Polička, Prague. Libretto by the composer, adapted from a Babylonian poem.
fp: 11 September 1924, Prague, National Theatre, cond. V. Maixner; choreography, R. Remislavsky; design, B. Feuerstein.
Unpub. *Suites Nos. 1 & 2* arr. František Bartoš (dur. 20' each) pub. 1961, Panton.

129. Vanishing Midnight. For orchestra. 1922, Prague.

1. *Satyrs in a grove of cypresses*; 2. *Blue hour*; 3. *Shadows*.
fp (No. 2): 18 February 1923, Prague, Czech Philharmonic Orchestra, cond. Václav Talich.
Unpub.

130. Improvisation to spring. For piano. 1922, Prague. Pub. in *Dalibor*, Vol. XXXIX, Nos. 6–7, Music Supplement.

131. Three Songs. For voice and piano. 1922, Prague.
   1. *On snow-swept paths* (Po cestách zavátých) (Karel Toman).
   2. *Thou, who dwellest in Heaven* (Ty jenž sídlíš v nebesích).
   3. *My brother has finished ploughing* (Můj bratr dooral) (Karel Toman).
   fp: 2 May (?1923), Paris, Société Nationale de Musique, Jane Bathori.
Unpub.

132. Folk Dances and Customs in Slovácko. Music for the film. 1922, Unpub.

133. Who is the most powerful in the world? Ballet Comedy in one act. 1922, Prague. Libretto by the composer, from an English fairy tale. Dur. 60'.
   fp: 31 January 1925, Brno, National Theatre, cond. Břetislav Bakala: choreography, J. Hladík.
Unpub. *Suite* (dur. 36'), 1922, Prague, unpub.

134. The Revolt. Ballet Sketch in one act. 1922–3, Prague.
   fp: 11 February 1928, Brno, National Theatre, cond. Fr. Neumann; producer, Ota Zítek; choreography, Ivo Váňa-Psota.
Unpub.

135. String Trio No. 1. 1923, Paris.
   fp: 1924, Paris.
   fCp: February 1925, members of Ondříček Quartet.
Unpub.

136. Fables. For piano. 1924, Paris. Ded. P. J. Osuský.
   1. *The humorous rabbit*; 2. *On the arm*; 3. *Monkeys*; 4. *The chicken*; 5. *The grumpy bear*.
   Pub. 1947, Urbánek; 1961, State Publishing House.

137. Quartet. For clarinet, horn, cello and drum. April 1924, Paris.
   1. *Allegro moderato*; 2. *Poco andante*; 3. *Allegretto ma non troppo*.
Unpub.

138. Half Time. Rondo for orchestra. Summer 1924, Polička. Dur. 9–10'.
   2 fl, pic, 2 ob, 2 cl, 2 bsn; 4 hn, 2 pistoni, 2 tpt, 3 tmb, tuba; timp, GC, cym, tamb pic, tgle; piano, strings.
   fp: 7 December 1924, Prague, Czech Philharmonic Orchestra, cond. Václav Talich.
   Pub. 1963, Panton.

139. Nonet. For violin, viola, cello, flute, clarinet, oboe, horn, bassoon and piano. 1924–5, Paris. Unpub.

140. Instructive duo for nervous players. For piano duet. 1925, Paris. Pub. 1925, Lidové noviny.

141. Film en miniature. For piano. 1925, Paris. Ded. Fína Taussigová.
   1. *Tango*; 2. *Scherzo*; 3. *Lullaby*; 4. *Waltz*; 5. *Chanson*; 6. *Carillon*.
   Pub. 1929, 1947, Hudební Matice.

142. Children's Songs. 1925, Paris. Ded. (Vol. 1) to the Osuský children, (Vol. 2) to the children of Fernand Couget. Unpub.

143. String Quartet No. 2. 1925, Paris, Prague. Ded. Novák-Frank Quartet.
   1. *Moderato—Allegro vivace*; 2. *Andante*; 3. *Allegro*.
   fp: November 1925, Berlin, Novák-Frank Quartet.
   fCp: 9 December 1925, Prague, Novák-Frank Quartet.
   ?fEp (broadcast): 3 April 1929, 2LO broadcast from Arts Theatre Club, Amar-Hindemith Quartet (Licco Amar, Walter Gaspar, Paul Hindemith and Maurits Franck).
   Pub. 1927, Universal-Edition.

144. Chinese Songs. For voice and piano. 1925, Prague. Ded. Fina Taussigová. Unpub.

145. Piano Concerto No. 1. 1925, Polička. Ded. Jan Heřman.
   1. *Allegro*; 2. *Andante*; 3. *Rondo*.
   fp: 21 November 1926, Prague, Jan Heřman and the Czech Philharmonic Orchestra, cond. Robert Manzer.

Martinů, Bohuslav

fFp: 11 February 1928, Paris, Concerts Colonne, Lucette Descaves and l'Orchestre Colonne, cond. Gabriel Pierné.
Unpub.

146. La Bagarre (Tumult). For orchestra. May 1926, Paris. Dur. 9–10′.
2 fl, pic, 2 ob, ca, E-flat cl, 2 cl, 2 bsn; 4 hn, 3 tpt, 3 tmb, tuba; timp, pcssn; strings.
fp: 11 November 1927, Boston, Boston Symphony Orchestra, cond. Serge Koussevitzky.
fEp: 26 November 1935, Queen's Hall, Prague Philharmonic Orchestra, cond. Václav Talich.
Pub. 1930, Leduc.

147. Divertimento (Concertino). For piano left hand and chamber orchestra. 1926, Paris. Ded. Otakar Hollmann. Title changed to Concertino in 1928. Dur. 19′ 45″.
1. *Allegro moderato* (4′ 36″); 2. *Andante* (7′ 06″); 3. *Allegro con brio* (8′ 03″).
fl, 2 ob, cl, 2 bsn; hn; strings.
fp: 26 February 1947, Prague, Otakar Hollmann and FOK Orchestra.
Pub. 1957, Czech Musical Fund Archives.

148. Violin Sonata in D minor. 1926, Paris.
1. *Allegro moderato*; 2. *Andante moderato*; 3. *Allegro*.
f London p: 20 June 1970, Wigmore Hall, Anthony Saltmarsh and Peter Croser.
Pub. 1966, Panton.

149. Habanera. For piano. 1926. Ded. Lydia Wisiakova. Unpub.

150. Three Czech Dances (Trois danses tchèques). For piano. 1926.
1. *Obkročák.* Ded. Jan Heřman.
2. *Dupák.* Ded. Denyse Molié.
3. *Polka.* Ded. Jane Mortier.
Pub. Eschig/Schott.

151. The butterfly that stamped. Ballet in one act. 1926, Paris. Libretto by the composer, after Rudyard Kipling. Unpub.

152. The Soldier and the Dancer: Overture. August 1926, Polička. Unpub.

152a. The Soldier and the Dancer. Comic Opera in three acts. July 1926–June 1927. Libretto: J. L. Budín, after Plautus.

fp: 5 May 1928, Brno, National Theatre, cond. Fr. Neumann; producer, Ota Zítek; choreography, Ivo Váňa-Psota.
Unpub.

153. Dance Music. For piano. 1927, Paris. Pub. 20 February 1927, Lidové noviny.

154. Duo. For violin and cello, Paris, 1927. Ded. S. Novák and M. Frank.
1. *Praeludium*; 2. *Rondo*.
fp: 17 March 1927, Stanislav Novák and Maurits Frank.
Pub. Sirène musicale; Eschig.

155. Trois esquisses de danses modernes. For piano. April 1927, Paris. Ded. Mme Vladimír Vaněk. Unpub.

156. La Revue de cuisine (The Kitchen Revue). Ballet. 1927, Paris. Libretto: Jarmila Kröschlová.
fp: 1927, Prague, cond. Stanislav Novák; with Jarmila Kröschlová.
Pub. 1932, Leduc.

156a. La Revue de cuisine: Suite. 1927, Paris. Ded. Mrs. Božena Nebeská.
1. *Prologue*; 2. *Tango*; 3. *Charleston*; 4. *Finale*.
cl, bsn; tpt; piano, v, c.
fp: 31 January 1930, Paris, Ecole Normale de Musique, Concerts Cortot.
fEbp: 2 December 1949, Leighton Lucas Orchestra, cond. Leighton Lucas.
Pub. 1930, Leduc.

157. Impromptu. For violin and piano. 1927, Paris. Dur. 6′.
1. *Poco allegro*; 2. *Andante moderato*; 3. *Allegretto moderato*.
Pub. 1933, Hedební Matice.

158. On tourne. Ballet in one act for a cartoon and puppet film. Summer 1927, Polička. Unpub.

159. Le Raid merveilleux. 'Ballet méchanique' for the Théâtre Bériza, Paris. 1927, Paris. Scored for two clarinets, trumpet and strings. Unpub.

160. String Quintet. 27 September–5 October 1927, Polička. Ded. Mrs. Elizabeth Sprague Coolidge.
1. *Allegro con brio*; 2. *Largo*; 3. *Allegretto*.

fp: 1928, Pittsfield (Mass.), Coolidge Festival.
fEbp: 21 June 1931, Roth Quartet with Bernard Shore (va).
Pub. 1930, Sirène musicale; Eschig.

161. Christmas (Le Noël). For piano. Christmas 1927, Paris. Ded. Anna Špačková.
 1. *Sledging*; 2. *A child's lullaby*; 3. *Christmas Carol*.
Pub. 1931, Urbánek.

162. Le Jazz. Movement for symphony orchestra (with three saxophones and banjo) and voice. January 1928, Paris. Dur. 5'. Unpub.

163. Les Larmes du couteau. Opera in one act. February–March 1928, Paris. Libretto: Georges Ribemont-Dessaignes. Dur. 20'. Unpub.
 2 v, c, bsn, sax, 2 tpt, 2 tmb, banjo, tamtam.

164. Quatre mouvements. For piano. Easter 1928. Ded. Miloš Šafránek.
 1. *Poco moderato—Allegretto*; 2. *Allegro—Poco largamento*; 3. *Adagio*; 4. *Allegro—Meno recitativo cantabile*.
Unpub.

165. Jazz-Suite. For orchestra. June 1928, Paris.
 1. *Prélude*; 2. *Musique d'entr'acte (Tempo di Blues)*; 3. *Musique d'entr'acte (Boston)*; 4. *Finale*.
fp: 1928, Baden-Baden Festival.
Unpub.

166. La Rhapsodie. For orchestra. 1928, Paris.
 fp: 14 December 1928, Boston, Boston Symphony Orchestra cond. Serge Koussevitzky.
Pub. 1930, Leduc.

167. Le Départ. For orchestra. 1929, Paris. Unpub.

168. Sextet. For piano and wind. 28 January–4 February 1929, Paris. Dur. 17'.
 1. *Prelude*; 2. *Adagio*; 3. *Scherzo*; 4. *Blues*; 5. *Finale*.
 piano, fl, ob, cl, 2 bsn.
Pub. 1960, Czech Musical Fund Archives; 1966, Panton.

168a. Divertimento No. 1. For flute and piano. Arr. of *Scherzo* from Sextet.

168b. Divertimento No. 2. ?For flute and piano. Arr. of *Blues* from Sextet.

169. String Quartet No. 3. 1929, Paris. Ded. Roth Quartet.
 1. *Allegro*; 2. *Andante*; 3. *Allegro vivo*.
fp: 1930, USA, Roth Quartet.
fFp: 20 April 1932, Paris, Société Musicale Indépendante, Roth Quartet.
Pub. 1931, Leduc.

170. Five Short Pieces (Cinq pièces brèves). For violin and piano. 1929, Paris. Ded. Miloš Šafránek.
 1. *Allegro moderato*; 2. *Andante*; 3. *Allegretto moderato*; 4. *Allegro vivo—Presto*; 5. *Allegro*.
fEbp: 7 December 1951, Suzanne Rozsa and Paul Hamburger.
Pub. 1930, 1953, Leduc.

171. Blues. For piano. 1929, Paris. Ded. Lydia Wisiakova. Unpub.

172. Borová (Seven Czech Dances). For piano. 1929, Paris. Ded. Anna Špačková.
 1. *Moderato*; 2. *Allegro moderato*; 3. *Allegro moderato*; 4. *Moderato*; 5. *Moderato*; 6. *Moderato*; 7. *Moderato*.
fEbp (three only): 24 August 1949, Leonard Cassini.
Pub. 1931, 1947, Leduc.

172a. Borová. Version for orchestra. 1931. Pub. 1931, Leduc, as *Czech Dances*.

173. La Danse. For piano. July 1929, Polička. Ded. Conrad Beck. Pub. 1929, Sirène musicale; Eschig (in 'Treize Danses').

174. Préludes (en forme de . . .). For piano. 1929. Ded. Charlotte Quennehen.
 1. *Blues*; 2. *Scherzo*; 3. *Andante*; 4. *Danse*; 5. *Capriccio*; 6. *Largo*; 7. *Etude*; 8. *Fox-Trot*.
Pub. 1930, Leduc.

175. Trois Souhaits (ou, Les Vicissitudes de la vie). Opera-film in three acts. January–May 1929, Paris. Libretto: Georges Ribemont-Dessaignes. Unpub.

175a. Les Vicissitudes de la vie. Film music for the opera. May 1929, Paris, Dur. 13'.

W

Martinů, Bohuslav

1. *Overture*; 2. *La chasse*; 3. *Banquet*; 4. *On board*; 5. *Shipwrecked*; 6. *Adolph and the Negress*; 7. *Indolende and Adolph*.
Unpub.

176. La Semaine de bonté. Opera in three acts. 1929, Paris. Libretto: Georges Ribemont-Dessaignes & Bohuslav Martinů, from an idea by Ilya Ehrenburg. Unfinished. Unpub.

177. Six Characters in Search of an Author. Improvisation at the piano: music for the play by Pirandello. 1929, Polička.
fp: 29 August 1929, Polička, opening of the J. K. Tyl Theatre.
Unpub.

178. Fantasie. For two pianos. September, Polička, Paris. Unpub.

179. Violin Sonata No. 1. November 1929, Paris.
1. *Allegro*; 2. *Andante*; 3. *Allegretto—Allegro con brio*.
Pub. 1930, 1952, Leduc.

180. A trois mains (avec un doigt). For piano. January 1930, Paris. Ded. M. & Mme Michel Dillart et le petit Jean Pierre. Pub. 1936, Sirène musicale; Eschig.

181. Quintet for wind. 1930, Paris. Unpub.

182. Rondes. A cycle of six pieces for seven instruments. 1930, Paris. Ded. Jan Kunc. Dur. 16'.
ob, cl, bsn; tpt; 2 v, piano.
fp: 18 March 1932, Paris, Concerts Cortot.
Pub. 1950, Orbis.

183. Checkmating the King (Echec au roi). Jazz Ballet in one act ('Ballet in black, white and red'). 16 January–17 February 1930, Paris. Libretto: André Coeuroy. Unpub.

184. Praeludium (in the form of a Scherzo). For orchestra. 1930, Paris. Arr. of a piano piece. Pub. 1930, Leduc.

185. Sonatine. For two violins and piano. 1930, Paris.
1. *Allegro*; 2. *Andante*; 3. *Allegretto*; 4. *Poco allegro*.
Pub. 1931, Leduc.

186. Ariette. For violin (or cello) and piano. 1930, Paris. Pub. 1931, Leduc.

186a. Vocalise-Etude. Version of preceding for voice and piano. 1930. Pub. 1930, Leduc.

187. Three Songs (Guillaume Apollinaire). 1930. Ded. Mrs. A. Pečírková.
1. *La blanche neige*; 2. *L'adieu*; 3. *Saltimbanques*.
fp: 9 January 1931, Prague, Anna Pečírková.
Unpub.

188. Cinq pièces brèves. For violin, cello and piano. 20–30 May 1930, Paris.
1. *Allegro moderato*; 2. *Adagio*; 3. *Allegro*; 4. *Allegro moderato*; 5. *Allegro*.
fp: 14 November 1930, Paris, Trio Filomusi.
fFp: 18 January 1933, Paris, Le Triton concert, Trio Hongrois.
Pub. 1931, Schott.

189. Concerto for cello and chamber orchestra. 1930, Paris. Ded. Gaspar Cassado. Dur. 22'.
1. *Allegro moderato*; 2. *Andante moderato*; 3. *Allegro con brio*.
fp: 13 December 1931, Berlin, Gaspar Cassado.
Pub. 1932, Schott.

189a. Cello Concerto. 1939. Transcription of preceding with full orchestra; rescored, 1955. Ded. Pierre Fournier. Dur. 27'.
2 fl, 2 ob, 2 cl, 2 bsn; 4 hn, 2 tpt, 3 tmb; timp, pcssn; strings.
fp: 1939, Paris, Pierre Fournier and the Société Philharmonique de Paris, cond. Charles Münch.
fbp: 27 February 1939, Pierre Fournier and BBC Orchestra, cond. Julian Clifford.
fp (1955 version): 6 March 1956, Helsinki, Miloš Sádlo and the Radio Orchestra, cond. Paavo Berglund.
Pub. 1931, Schott; new revised edition, 1956 (reduction by Helmut Degen).

190. Serenade for chamber orchestra. November 1930, Paris. Ded. Albert Roussel. Dur. 12'.
1. *Allegro*; 2. *Andantino moderato*; 3. *Allegretto*; 4. *Allegro*.
fp: 16 April 1931, Paris, Walter Straram Concerts.
Pub. 1931, Schott.

191. String Quartet with orchestra. 1931,
Paris. Ded. Pro Arte Quartet. Dur. 17'.
  1. *Allegro vivo*; 2. *Adagio*; 3. *Finale: Tempo
moderato*.
  2 fl, 2 ob, 2 cl, 2 bsn; 2 hn, 2 tpt, 2 tmb;
timp, side dm, GC, mil dm, cym, tgle;
strings.
  fp: 1931, Brussels, Pro Arte Quartet.
  fEp: 10 October 1932, Queen's Hall,
Courtauld-Sargent concert, Pro Arte Quartet
and the London Philharmonic Orchestra,
cond. (Sir) Malcolm Sargent.
  fAp: 23 December 1932, Boston, Richard
Burgin, Robert Gundersen, Jean Lefranc and
Jean Bedetti, Boston Symphony Orchestra,
cond. Serge Koussevitzky.
  f Prague p: 14 March 1934, Prague Quartet
and the Czech Philharmonic Orchestra, cond.
Václav Talich.
  f New York p: 9 April 1936, Pro Arte
Quartet and the New York Philharmonic
Symphony, cond. Hans Lange.
  Pub. 1932, Schott.

192. Etudes rythmiques. For violin and
piano. 1931, Paris. Pub. 1932, Schott.

193. Violin Sonata No. 2. 1931, Paris. Ded.
Hortense de Sampigny-Bailly.
  1. *Allegro moderato*; 2. *Larghetto*; 3. *Poco
allegretto*.
  fp: 22 January 1933, Paris, Hortense de
Sampigny-Bailly.
  Pub. 1932, Deiss; Salabert.

194. Etudes faciles. Nine Duets for two
violins in the first position. 1931, Paris.
  1. *Moderato*; 2. *Andante*; 3. *Moderato*;
4. *Andante*; 5. *Poco allegretto*; 6. *Allegro
moderato*; 7. *Andante*; 8. *Poco andante*;
9. *Moderato*.
  Pub. 1932, Leduc.

195. Pastorales. Six Pieces for cello and
piano. 1931, Paris.
  1. *Andante*; 2. *Allegretto moderato*; 3. *Adagio*;
4. *Moderato*; 5. *Largo*; 6. *Allegretto*.
  Pub. 1931, 1955, Leduc.

196. Nocturnes (Quatre Etudes). For cello
and piano. 1931, Paris. Ded. Karel Koštál.
  1. *Andantino moderato*; 2. *Lento*; 3. *Moderato*;
4. *Allegretto moderato*.

  fEbp: 5 August 1952, David Ffrangcon-
Thomas and Ernest Lush.
  Pub. 1931, 1950, Leduc.

197. Suite miniature. Seven Easy Pieces for
cello. 1931, Paris.
  1. *Moderato*; 2. *Poco andante*; 3. *Poco
moderato*; 4. *Andante*; 5. *Poco allegro*; 6. *Allegretto*; 7. *Moderato*.
  Pub. 1932, 1953, Leduc.

198. Arabesques (Etudes rythmiques). For
violin or cello and piano. 1931, Paris.
  1. *Poco allegro*; 2. *Moderato*; 3. *Andante
moderato*; 4. *Allegro*; 5. *Adagio*; 6. *Allegretto*;
7. *Allegretto moderato*.
  Pub. 1932, Deiss; Salabert.

**199. Festive Overture for the Sokol
Festival.** For orchestra. October 1931, Paris.
  fp: 3 July 1932, Czech Philharmonic
Orchestra, cond. F. Stupka.
  Unpub.

200. Sketches I and II. For piano. 1931, Paris.
Unpub.

200a. Four Pieces (?Jeux, Cahier I). For
piano. 1931, Paris.
  1. *Poco allegro*; 2. *Poco allegretto*; 3. *Allegretto*;
4. *Allegro*.
  Unpub.

200b. Jeux, Cahier II. Six Easy Pieces for
piano. 1931, Paris.
  1. *Poco allegretto*; 2. *Poco allegro*; 3. *Poco
andante*; 4. *Allegro*; 5. *Andante*; 6. *Allegro*.
  Unpub.

201. Little Songs for children. For voice
and piano. 1931, Polička.
  1. *Daddy's song*; 2. *Sonička's song*;
3. *Rozánka's song*.
  Unpub.

202. Špalíček (The Chap Book). Ballet in
three acts, with soloists, chorus and orchestra.
1931, Paris; rev. 1940.
  fp: 19 September 1933, Prague, National
Theatre, cond. J. Charvát; décors, J. M.
Gottlieb; choreography, Joe Jenčík.
  fp (revised version): 2 April 1949, Prague,
National Theatre, cond. V. Kašlík; design, J.
Svoboda; choreography, N. Jirskíková.
  Pub. 1947, Melantrich: piano score by

Martinů, Bohuslav

Karel Šolc. *Suites Nos. 1 & 2* (arr. Miloš Říhá) pub. 1959–60, Czech Musical Fund Archive; 1961, Panton.

202a. Two Dances from 'Špalíček'. For piano.
1. *Waltz*; 2. *Polka*.
Pub. 1950, Orbis.

203. String Sextet. 20–27 May 1932, Paris. Coolidge Prize, 1932. Ded. Elizabeth Sprague Coolidge.
1. *Lento—Allegro poco moderato*; 2. *Andantino—Allegro scherzando*; 3. *Allegretto poco moderato*.
fp: 24 April 1933, Washington, Library of Congress, Festival of Chamber Music, Kroll Sextet (William Kroll, Nicolas Berezovsky, Leon Barzin, O. Saltisow, Milton Prinz and Ossip Giskin).
fEbp: 22 November 1937, Menges String Sextet.
Pub. 1947, Associated Music Publishers.

203a. String Sextet. Version for orchestra.
fp: October 1959, Basle Chamber Orchestra, cond. Paul Sacher.

204. Sonata for two violins and piano. 1932, Paris. Composed for the Sonata Players, London.
1. *Allegro poco moderato*; 2. *Andante*; 3. *Allegretto—Vivo-Allegro*.
fp: February 1934, London, Sonata Players.
Pub. 1933, Deiss.

205. Four Children's Songs and Rhymes. For voice and piano. 1 June 1932, Paris. Ded. Anička Šafránková. Unpub.

206. Serenades. For chamber ensembles. 1932.
1. *First Serenade.* For six instruments. Dur. 7′.
   1. *Allegro moderato*; 2. *Larghetto*; 3. *Allegro*. cl, hn, 3 v, va.
2. *Second Serenade.* For three instruments. Dur. 7′.
   1. *Allegro*; 2. *Poco andante*; 3. *Allegro con brio*.
   2 v, va.
3. *Third Serenade.* For seven instruments. Theme with four variations. Dur. 7′.
   ob, cl, 4 v, c.

Pub. Melantrich. NB: For *Fourth Serenade* see No. 212 (Divertimento).

207. Esquisses de danse. Five Pieces for piano. 1932, Paris.
1. *Allegro moderato*; 2. *Poco andantino—Allegretto*; 3. *Allegro vivo*; 4. *Tempo di valse—Allegro*; 5. *Allegro*.
?fp: 25 November 1940, New York, Town Hall, Germaine Leroux.
fEbp (three only): 20 October 1949, Alfred Kitchin.
Pub. 1933, Schott.

207a. Pièce pour piano. 1932, Paris. Pub. Sirène musicale, in *Album des auteurs modernes*.

208. Sinfonia Concertante. For two orchestras. 1932, Paris. Dur. 16′.
1. *Allegro non troppo*; 2. *Vivace*; 3. *Andante*; 4. *Allegretto*.
Orch. 1: 3 ob, bsn; 2 hn; strings. Orch. 2: 2 fl, pic, 2 cl, bsn; 2 hn, 2 tpt, 3 tmb, tuba; timp, tamb pic, tamb, cym, tgle; strings.
Pub. 1953, Schott.

209. Les Ritournelles. For piano. 1932, Paris.
1. *Andante*; 2. *Andante moderato—Allegro moderato*; 3. *Intermezzo No. 1 (Andantino)*; 4. *Andante—Poco allegro*; 5. *Intermezzo No. 2 (Andante)*; 6. *Allegro vivo*.
?fp: 14 December 1941, New York, Town Hall, Rudolf Firkušný.
Pub. 1933, Schott.

210. Partita (Suite No. 1). For string orchestra. December 1932 (?1931), Paris. Dur. 11′.
1. *Poco allegro*; 2. *Moderato*; 3. *Andante moderato*; 4. *Poco allegretto*.
fp: 13 December 1932, Prague, Czech Philharmonic Orchestra, cond. Václav Talich.
fEp: 7 January 1947, Wigmore Hall, Riddick String Orchestra.
Pub. Schott.

211. Two Ballads to folksong texts. For contralto and piano. Christmas 1932, Paris. Ded. Olga Borová-Valoušková.
1. *Wandering musicians* (Putovali hudci).
2. *The orphan* (Sirotek).
fp: 29 April 1933, Prague, Olga Borová-Valoušková.

211a. Two Songs to Negro folk-poetry texts. Unknown date. Ded. Julie Nessy-Bächerová.
1. *Lullaby*; 2. *Desire*.
Unpub.

211b. Violin Concerto. 1932, Paris. Unfinished. Ded. Samuel Dushkin. Lost.

212. Divertimento (Serenade No. 4). For violin, viola, oboe, piano and string orchestra. 1932, Paris. Ded. Société d'études mozartiennes, Paris. Dur. 8'.
1. *Allegro*; 2. *Andante moderato*; 3. *Allegretto*.
fEp (broadcast): 10 May 1959, Chagrin Ensemble, cond. Francis Chagrin.
Pub. 1949, Melantrich.

213. Piano Quintet. March 1933, Paris.
1. *Poco allegro*; 2. *Andante* (*poco moderato*); 3. *Allegretto*; 4. *Allegro moderato*.
fp: 1933, Paris.
fAp: 7 March 1937, New York, American League of Composers, Irene Jacobi and the Pro Arte Quartet.
Pub. 1933, Sirène musicale; Eschig.

214. The Miracle of Our Lady (Hry o Marii). Opera in four parts. 1933–4, Paris.
1. *The Wise and the Foolish Virgins* (medieval text); 2. *Mariken de Nimègue* (Flemish miracle play; libretto, Henri Ghéon); 3. *The Nativity* (Moravian folk ballad texts); 4. *Sister Pascaline* (libretto, J. Zeyer and Bohuslav Martinů).
fp: 1934, Brno, National Theatre, cond. Antonín Balatka; producer, Branko Gavela (?R. Walter); décors, R. Muzika; choreography, Gabzdyl.
Unpub.

214a. Easter (K. J. Erben). For voice and piano. April 1933, Paris. Pub. 16 April 1933, Lidové noviny.

215. Concertino. For piano trio and orchestra. 20–30 August 1933, Paris. Ded. Trio Hongrois. Dur. 15'.
1. *Allegro* (*con brio*); 2. *Moderato*; 3. *Adagio*; 4. *Allegro*.
fp: 16 October 1936, Basle, Tibor Harsanyi and other soloists, Basle Chamber Orchestra, cond. Paul Sacher.
fFp: 1936, Paris, Le Triton concert, with Tibor Harsanyi.

fEp: 5 August 1948, Royal Albert Hall, Promenade Concert, Liza Fuchsova and other soloists, London Symphony Orchestra, cond. Stanford Robinson.
Pub. 1949, Melantrich.

216. Inventions. For orchestra. January 1934, Paris. Dur. $11\frac{1}{2}$–12'.
1. *Allegro moderato*; 2. *Andante moderato*; 3. *Poco allegro*.
2 fl, 2 ob, 2 cl, 2 bsn; 4 hn, 2 tpt, 2 tmb; timp, tamburo senza corda, 2 tamb pic, GC, cym, tgle, wood block, xyl; piano, strings.
fp: 1934, Venice Festival, cond. O. Piccardi.
Pub. 1949, Melantrich.

217. Piano Concerto No. 2. 1934, Paris; rescored, January 1944, New York. Composed for and ded. Germaine Leroux. Dur. 22–24'.
1. *Allegro moderato*; 2. *Poco andante*; 3. *Allegro con brio*.
2 fl, pic, 2 ob, 2 cl, 2 bsn; 4 hn, 2 tpt, 3 tmb; timp, tgle, tamb pic, GC, cym; strings.
fp: 1935, Prague, Rudolf Firkusný and the Czech Philharmonic Orchestra, cond. Václav Talich.
fFp: January 1937, Paris, Germaine Leroux and the Paris Conservatoire Orchestra, cond. Philippe Gaubert.
fGBp: 25 December 1937, Glasgow, Germaine Leroux and the Scottish Orchestra, cond. George Szell.
fEp: 15 November 1938, Queen's Hall, Rudolf Firkusný and the Czech Philharmonic Orchestra, cond. Rafael Kubelik.
fAp: 24 January 1940, New York, Germaine Leroux and the New York Philharmonic Symphony, cond. Herman Adler.
?fp (rev. version): 13 April 1945, Philadelphia, Rudolf Firkusný and the Philadelphia Orchestra, cond. Eugene Ormandy.
f New York p (rev. version): 22 October 1945, Czech Festival, Rudolf Firkusný and the New York Philharmonic Symphony, cond. Artur Rodzinsky.
fEp (rev. version): 29 July 1953, Royal Albert Hall, Promenade Concert, Rudolf Firkusný and the BBC Symphony Orchestra, cond. Sir Malcolm Sargent.
Pub. 1960, Czech Musical Fund Archive

Martinů, Bohuslav

(full score), Panton (reduction by Karel Šolc).

218. String Trio No. 2. 1934, Paris. Composed for and ded. Trio Pasquier. Dur. 14'.
1. *Allegro*; 2. *Poco moderato—Vivo—Poco andante—Allegro*.
fp: 15 February 1935, Paris, Le Triton concert, Trio Pasquier.
Pub. 1951, Heugel.

219. Four Marian Songs (Czech folksong texts). For SATB chorus. Autumn 1934, Paris. Ded. Karel Šejna.
1. *The Annunciation*; 2. *The Dream*; 3. *Virgin Mary's Breakfast*; 4. *The Picture of the Virgin Mary*.
fp: 12 April 1935, Vinohrady (Prague), Hlahol Choral Society, cond. Karel Šejna.
Unpub.

219a. Old Czech Nursery Rhymes. Six Choruses for female voices. July 1934, Paris. Ded. The Prague Teachers' Vocal Society. Dur. 11'.
fp: 1934, Prague, Prague Teachers' Vocal Society, cond. Metod Vymetal.
Unpub.

220. The Voice of the Forest (Hlas lesa). Radio opera in one act. April–May 1935, Paris. Libretto: Vítězslav Nezval. Dur. 30'.
fp: 6 October 1937, Czech Radio, cond. Otakar Jeremiáš.
Unpub.

220a. Le Jugement de Paris. Ballet in one act. 1935, Paris. Libretto: Boris Kochno. Commissioned by Ballets Russes de Monte Carlo.
Unpub.

221. Concerto for harpsichord and chamber orchestra. 1935, Paris. Ded. Marcelle de Lacour. Dur. 15'.
1. *Poco allegro*; 2. *Adagio*; 3. *Allegretto*.
fl, bsn; piano, strings.
fp: March 1936, Paris, house of Comtesse de Belagne, with Marcelle de Lacour as soloist.
fp (public): 2 June 1938, Paris, Le Triton concert, Marcelle de Lacour, cond. Vítězslava Kaprálová.
fEbp: 29 June 1958, Stanislav Heller and

the Kalmar Chamber Orchestra, cond. Maurice Miles.
Pub. 1958, Universal-Edition.

222. Two Pieces. For harpsichord. June 1935, Paris. Ded. Marcelle de Lacour.
1. *Lento*; 2. *Allegro con brio*.
Pub. 1962, Universal-Edition.

222a. A Piece for little Eva. For piano. 1935.
Pub. 1935, in *Eva* No. 9.

223. Unfaithful Marijka (Marijka nevěrnice). Music for a film directed by Vladislav Vančura from a novel by Ivan Olbracht. 1935.

224. The Suburban Theatre (Divadlo za bránou). Opera buffa in three acts. 1935–6, Paris. Libretto by the composer.
fp: 20 September 1936, Brno, National Theatre, cond. A. Balatka; producer, R. Walter; décors, F. Muzika; choreography, Ivo Váňa-Psota.
Unpub. *Commedia dell'arte* (Suite from 'The Suburban Theatre') arr. Miloš Říha, pub. 1960, Czech Musical Fund Archives; 1961, Panton.

225. City of Water of Life: Mariánské Lázně (Město živé vody: Mariánské Lázně). Music for a film. 1935, Prague.

225a. The Slipper (Střevíček). Music for a film. March 1935, Prague.
Unpub.

226. Comedy on a bridge. Comedy in one act, after the play by V. K. Klicpera. December 1935, Paris. Dur. 35'.
fl, pic, ob, cl, bsn; 2 hn, tpt, tmb; timp, GC, cym, tamb mil; piano, strings.
fp: 18 March 1937, Czech Radio, cond. Otakar Jeremiáš.
fEbp: 12 October 1951, BBC broadcast, London Philharmonic Orchestra, cond. John Pritchard; with Ian Wallace, Catherine Lawson, John Cameron, Marion Studholme, Frank Sale.
Pub. 1952, Boosey & Hawkes. German version, Ernst Roth; English version, Walter Schmolka.

226a. Little Suite. From the opera 'Comedy on a bridge'. 1952, New York City. Dur. 6'.

fl, pic, ob, cl, bsn; 2 hn, tpt, tmb; side dm, cym, GC, timp; piano, strings.
Pub. 1952, Boosey & Hawkes.

227. Oedipe. Incidental music (André Gide). 1936, Paris.
fp: 7 February 1936, Czech Radio; producer, Jindřich Honzl.
Unpub.

228. Dumka. For piano. 1936, Paris. Ded. J. Roudnická.
Pub. Hudební Matice (in 'Piano 1937').

228a. Dumka. For piano. 1936, Paris. Ded. Z. Kubíková.
Pub. 1936, in *Eva.*

228b. Dumka. For piano. 1936, Paris. Pub. 1937, Hudební Matice.

229. Concerto for flute, violin and chamber orchestra. 1936, Paris. Ded. Marcel Moyse. Dur. 20'.
1. *Allegro moderato*; 2. *Adagio*; 3. *Poco allegretto.*
fl, 2 ob, 2 cl, 2 bsn; 2 hn, tpt; pf, strings.
fp: ?1936, BBC broadcast, with Marcel Moyse and Blanche Honegger.
fp (concert): 26 December 1937, Geneva, with Marcel Moyse and Blanche Honegger.
fFp: 27 December 1937, Paris, Marcel Moyse, Blanche Honegger and the Paris Conservatoire Orchestra, cond. Philippe Gaubert.
Pub. 1961, Bärenreiter.

229a. Sonata for flute, violin and piano. 1936, Paris. Ded. Mme. Marcel Moyse. Pub. 1959, Baer; Novello.

230. Juliette, or The Key to Dreams. Lyric Opera in three acts. 17 May 1936–24 January 1937, Paris. Libretto: Bohuslav Martinů from the play by Georges Neveux.
fp: 16 March 1938, Prague, National Theatre, cond. Václav Talich; producer, Jindřich Honzl; decor, František Muzika; choreography, Joe Jenčík.
Pub. Melantrich.

BIBLIOGRAPHY:
H. H. Stuckenschmidt: Prague hears première of Martinů's Juliette, *Musical America,* 10 May 1938.

230a. Juliette: Three Fragments. For soprano, alto, tenor, baritone, bass and orchestra. 1938, Paris.
1. *Souvenirs*; 2. *Forest scene*; 3. *Finale.*
?Unpub.

231. Alexandre bis. Opera buffa in one act. 1937, Paris. Libretto: André Wormser. Unpub.

232. Quatre Madrigaux. For oboe, clarinet and bassoon. 1937, Nice. Ded. Trio d'Anches, Paris.
1. *Allegro moderato*; 2. *Lento*; 3. *Poco allegretto*; 4. *Poco allegro.*
Pub. 1951, Eschig.

233. A love carol (Koleda milostná). For voice and piano. 1937, Paris. Ded. Marie Raabová. Pub. 1937, in *Eva,* No. 3.

234. Duo Concertante. For two violins and orchestra. 1937, Nice. Ded. The Brothers Dezarsens.
fp: 1938, Radio Lausanne, Dezarsens Brothers.
Unpub.

235. Suite Concertante. For violin and orchestra. 1937, Paris; rev. 1945, New York. Ded. Samuel Dushkin.
1. *Toccata (Allegro un poco moderato)*; 2. *Aria (Andantino)*; 3. *Scherzo (Allegretto scherzando)*; 4. *Rondo (Poco allegro).*
fp: 1943, New York, Town Hall, Samuel Dushkin (with piano acc.).
fp (with orchestra): December 1945, St. Louis, Samuel Dushkin and the St. Louis Symphony, cond. Louis Golschmann.
fEp: 15 August 1956, Royal Albert Hall, Promenade Concert, Alan Loveday and the London Symphony Orchestra, cond. Basil Cameron.
fEp (broadcast): 9 January 1957, BBC broadcast, Alan Loveday and the BBC Northern Orchestra, cond. John Hopkins.
Pub. 1955, Schott: reduction violin part (ed. Samuel Dushkin); Associated Music Publishers.

236. Sonatina. For violin and piano. 1937, Paris. Dur. 15'.
1. *Moderato*; 2. *Andante*; 3. *Poco allegretto.*

Martinů, Bohuslav

?fEbp: 31 March 1946, Marie Wilson and Liza Fuchsová.
Pub. 1937, Melantrich.

237. Intermezzo. Four Pieces for violin and piano. 1937, Paris. Dur. 11′.
1. *Moderato*; 2. *Poco allegro*; 3. *Lento*; 4. *Poco allegro.*
Pub. 1937, Melantrich.

238. String Quartet No. 4. May 1937, Paris. Ded. Mme. Helene Pucová.
1. *Allegro poco moderato*; 2. *Allegro scherzando*; 3. *Adagio*; 4. *Allegro.*
fp: 13 June 1938, privately, Lejeune Quarter (Brussels).
fp (public): 15 October 1960, Donaueschingen, Novák Quartet.
Pub. 1963, State Publishing House.

239. Trio. For flute, violin and bassoon. 1937, Paris. Unpub.

240. Crotchets and Quavers. Instructive Pieces for piano. May 1937, Paris. Unpub.

241. Le train hauté. For piano. 1937, Paris. Ded. Marguerite Long. Pub. 1938, Eschig (in 'Parc d'attractions Expo 1937'),

242. A Garland (Folk texts). For soloists, chorus and orchestra. 1937, Paris. Dur. 41′.
fl, 2 ob, 2 cl; 2 hn, 2 tpt, tmb; pcssn; hmnm, 2 pianos, strings.
fp: May 1938, Prague, with Radio Symphony Orchestra, cond. Otakar Jeremiáš.
Pub. 1956, Czech Musical Fund Archives.

243. Concerto grosso. For small orchestra. 1938, Paris. Ded. Charles Münch. Dur. 14′.
1. *Allegro non troppo*; 2. *Lento*; 3. *Allegretto.*
fl, 3 ob, 3 cl, 2 hn; 2 pianos, strings.
fp: 14 November 1941, Boston, Boston Symphony Orchestra, cond. Serge Koussevitzky.
f New York p: 10 January 1942, Boston Symphony Orchestra, cond. Serge Koussevitzky.
fFp: 25 October 1945, Paris, Orchestre National, cond. Manuel Rosenthal.
fGBp: 24 August 1948, Edinburgh Festival, Concertgebouw Orchestra, cond. Charles Münch.
fEp: 18 November 1953, Royal Phil-

harmonic Society concert, Royal Philharmonic Orchestra, cond. Paul Sacher.
Pub. 1948, Universal-Edition.

244. String Quartet No. 5. May 1938, Paris. Composed for and ded. Pro Arte Quartet. Dur. 21′.
1. *Allegro non troppo*; 2. *Adagio*; 3. *Allegro vivo*; 4. *Lento—Allegro.*
fp: 25 May 1958, Prague, Novák Quartet.
Pub. 1959, State Publishing House; Baer.

245. Fenêtre sur le jardin. Four Pieces for piano. 1938, Vieux Moulin. Ded. Helena Pucová.
1. *Poco andante*; 2. *Allegro moderato*; 3. *Moderato*; 4. *Allegretto.*
Pub. 1957, Leduc.

246. Tre Ricercari. For chamber orchestra. 1938, Paris. Dur. 12′.
1. *Allegro poco;* 2. *Largo;* 3. *Allegro.*
fl, 2 ob, 2 bsn; 2 tpt; 2 pianos, 4v, 3c.
fp; 1938, Venice Festival.
fFp: 8 May 1939, Paris, Le Triton concert, Société Philharmonique, cond. Charles Münch.
fEp: 1 February 1941, London, Savoy Theatre, Sidney Beer Orchestra.
fAp: 22 May 1941, New York, ISCM Festival concert, WOR Sinfonietta, cond. Alfred Wallenstein.
Pub. 1939, Universal-Edition.

247. Double Concerto. For two string orchestras, piano and timpani. 1938, Paris, Pratteln. Ded. Paul Sacher. Dur. 20′.
1. *Poco allegro*; 2. *Largo*; 3. *Allegro.*
fp: 9 February 1940, Basle, Basle Chamber Orchestra, cond. Paul Sacher.
fFp: 23 February 1946, Paris, Société des Concerts, cond. Paul Sacher.
fGBp: 1949, Edinburgh Festival, Philharmonia Orchestra, cond. Rafael Kubelik, with Rudolf Serkin (piano).
f London p: 28 March 1950, Royal Albert Hall, Philharmonia Orchestra, cond. Rafael Kubelik.
Pub. 1946, Boosey & Hawkes.

248. Piano Concertino. June 1938, Paris. Ded. Juliette Aranyi. Dur. 21′.
1. *Allegro moderato*; 2. *Lento*; 3. *Allegro.*

2 fl, 2 ob, 2 cl, 2 bsn; 4 hn, 2 tpt, 2 tmb; timp, GC, cym, tamb pic; strings.

fp: 5 August 1948, London, Royal Albert Hall, Liza Fuchsová.

Pub. 1956, Cxech Musical Fund Archives; 1967, Panton.

249. Field Mass. For male chorus, baritone soloist and orchestra. 1939, Paris.

2 pic, 2 cl; 3 tpt, 2 tmb; timp, GC, cym, 2 tamb pic, tamb mil, crotales, tgle, campanelle, campana; piano, hmnm.

fp: 1946, Prague, Czech Philharmonic Orchestra, cond. Rafael Kubelik.

fEp: 28 May 1958, BBC broadcast, Frederick Harvey, BBC Men's Chorus, London Symphony Orchestra, cond. Stanford Robinson.

Pub. 1947, Melantrich.

250. Cello Sonata No. 1. 1939, Paris. Ded. Pierre Fournier. Dur. 19′.

1. *Poco allegro* (Dur. 7′ 20″); 2. *Lento* (Dur. 5′); 3. *Allegro con brio* (Dur. 6′ 40″).

fp: May 1940, Paris, Pierre Fournier and Rudolf Firkusný.

Pub. 1949, Heugel.

252. Madrigals. Eight Choruses for different combinations of voices. July 1939, Paris.

fp: 22 September 1965, London, Prague Madrigal Singers.

Unpub.

252. Fairy-tales. For piano. November 1939, Paris. Ded. Vítezslava Kaprálová on her twenty-fourth birthday. Unpub.

253. Military March. For orchestra. 1940, Paris. Ded. Czech Army in France. Unpub.

254. Bergerettes. For violin, cello and piano. 1940, Paris.

1. *Poco allegro*; 2. *Allegro con brio*; 3. *Andantino—Moderato*; 4. *Allegro*; 5. *Moderato*.

Pub. 1963, Southern Music.

255. Promenades. For flute, violin and harpsichord. 1940, Paris. Dur. 7½′.

1. *Poco allegro*; 2. *Adagio*; 3. *Scherzando*; 4. *Poco allegro*.

Pub. 1960, Baer; Novello.

256. Sonata da camera. For cello and chamber orchestra. 1940, Aix-en-Provence. Ded. Henri Honegger.

1. *Allegro*; 2. *Andante poco moderato*; 3. *Allegro.*

fp 1940, Basle, Henri Honegger and the Basle Chamber Orchestra, cond. Paul Sacher.

fEbp: 24 July 1952, Henri Honegger and l'Orchestre de la Suisse Romande, cond. Ernest Ansermet.

?Pub.

257. Fantasia and Toccata. For piano. September 1940, Aix-en-Provence. Ded. Rudolf Firkusný. Dur. 17′. Pub. Associated Music Publishers.

258. Sinfonietta giocosa. For piano and chamber orchestra. October–November 1940 Aix-en-Provence; rev. 1941, Pleasantville, New York. Dur. 32′ (according to the score).

1. *Poco allegro*; 2. *Allegretto moderato*; 3. *Allegro*; 4. *Andantino—Allegro.*

2(1) fl, 2 ob, 2 bsn; hn; strings (3/4-3-2-3-2).

fp: 16 March 1942, New York, Germaine Leroux and the National Orchestral Association, cond. Leon Barzin.

fEp: 19 March 1950, BBC broadcast, Liza Fuchsová and the London Chamber Orchestra, cond. Anthony Bernard.

Pub. 1951 (reduction by Karel Šolc), 1953 (full score), Boosey & Hawkes.

259. Mazurka (Hommage à Paderewski). For piano. 1941, New York City. Pub. 1942, appendix in I. J. Paderewski; 1967, Boosey & Hawkes.

260. Concerto da camera. For violin and string orchestra with piano and timpani. July–August 1941, Edgartown (Mass.). Ded. Paul Sacher and the Basle Chamber Orchestra. Dur. 20′.

1. *Moderato, poco allegro*; 2. *Adagio*; 3. *Poco allegro (Cadenza).*

fp: 23 January 1942, Basle, Gertrude Flügel and the Basle Chamber Orchestra, cond. Paul Sacher.

fEp: 4 July 1956, BBC broadcast, Louis Kaufman (violin), Charles Spinks (piano), Leighton Lucas Orchestra, cond. Leighton Lucas.

Pub. 1955, Universal Edition.

261. Cello Sonata No. 2. November–December 1941, Jamaica (L.I.). Ded. Frank Rybka. Dur. 18'.

1. *Allegro*; 2. *Largo*; 3. *Allegro*.

fp: 27 March 1942, New York, Lucien Laporte and Elly Bontempo.

fEbp: 24 July 1950, William Pleeth and Margaret Good.

Pub. 1944, Associated Music Publishers.

262. Piano Quartet No. 1. April 1942, Jamaica (L.I.). Dur. 25'.

1. *Poco allegro*; 2. *Adagio*; 3. *Allegretto poco moderato*.

fp: August 1942, Lenox (Mass.), Berkshire Music Center.

f New York p: 2 March 1943, Chamber Music Guild Quartet.

fEp: 19 April 1944, London, members of BBC Orchestra.

Pub. 1942, Associated Music Publishers.

263. Symphony No. 1. 1942, Jamaica (L.I.), Middlebury (Vt.), Lenox (Mass.) and Manomet (Mass.). Commissioned by the Koussevitzky Music Foundation. Ded. to the memory of Natalie Koussevitsky. Dur. 35'.

1. *Moderato*; 2. *Allegro*; 3. *Largo*; 4. *Allegro non troppo*.

fp: 13 November 1942, Boston, Boston Symphony Orchestra, cond. Serge Koussevitzky.

f New York p: 21 November 1942, Boston Symphony Orchestra, cond. Serge Koussevitzky.

f European p: 28 February 1945, Geneva, l'Orchestre de la Suisse Romande, cond. Ernest Ansermet.

fEp: 16 October 1945, Birmingham, City of Birmingham Orchestra, cond. (Sir) John Barbirolli.

fFp: November 1945, Paris, Conservatokre Orchestra, cond. Charles Münch.

f London p: 22 January 1946, London Philharmonic Orchestra, cond. Ernest Ansermet.

fEp (broadcast): 3 April 1955, Royal Philharmonic Orchestra, cond. Rafael Kubelik, in a series of concerts featuring Martinů's symphonies.

Pub. 1947, Boosey & Hawkes.

264. Madrigal Sonata. For flute, violin and piano. 9–10 October 1942, New York. 'Salute to the League of Composers in celebration of the League's twentieth anniversary.'

1. *Poco allegro*; 2. *Moderato*; 3. *Allegro*.

fp: 9 December 1942, New York, Town Hall, Ruth Freeman, Roman Totenberg and Elly Bontempo.

fEbp: 8 September 1946, Geoffrey Gilbert, Marie Wilson and Liza Fuchsová.

Pub. Associated Music Publishers.

265. Variations on a theme of Rossini. For cello and piano. October 1942, New York. Ded. Gregor Piatigorsky.

fp: May 1943, Frick Museum, Gregor Piatigorsky.

fEbp: 10 February 1950, William Pleeth and Margaret Good.

Pub. 1949, Boosey & Hawkes.

266. New Špaliček. Eight songs on Czech folk poetry for voice and piano. 1943, Jamaica (L.I.). Ded. Jan Masaryk. Pub. 1948, Melantrich.

267. Songs on one page (Písničky na jednu stránku). Seven songs to Moravian folk texts for voice and piano. 1943, New York. Ded. Olga Hurban. Pub. 1948, Melantrich.

268. Violin Concerto No. 2. 26 April 1943. New York. Composed for and ded. Mischa Elman. Dur. 27'.

1. *Andante—Poco allegro*; 2. *Andante noderato*; 3. *Poco allegro*.

2 fl, 2 ob, 2 cl, 2 bsn; 4 hn, 3 tpt, 3 tmb, tuba; timp, tamb pic, GC, cym, tgle; strings.

fp: 31 December 1943, Boston, Mischa Elman and the Boston Symphony Orchestra, cond. Serge Koussevitzky.

f New York p: 6 January 1944, Mischa Elman and the Boston Symphony Orchestra, cond. Serge Koussevitzky.

fEbp: 18 April 1951, Henry Holst and the BBC Northern Orchestra, cond. Charles Groves.

Pub. 1949, Melantrich.

269. Concerto for two pianos and orchestra. 1943, New York. Ded. Pierre Luboschutz and Genia Nemenoff.

1. *Allegro non troppo*; 2. *Adagio*; 3. *Allegro*.

fp: 5 November 1943, Philadelphia, Pierre

Luboschutz and Genia Nemenoff, Philadelphia Orchestra, cond. Eugene Ormandy.

f New York p: 9 November 1943, Pierre Luboschutz and Genia Nemenoff, Philadelphia Orchestra, cond. Eugene Ormandy.

fEp: 7 June 1951, Royal Festive Hall, Ethel Bartlett and Rae Robertson, Liverpool Philharmonic Orchestra, cond. Hugo Rignold.

Pub. 1946, Associated Music Publishers.

270. Symphony No. 2. 29 June–24 July 1943, Darien (Conn.). Ded. 'My Countrymen in Cleveland'. Dur. 24′.

1. *Allegro moderato*; 2. *Andante moderato*; 3. *Poco allegro*; 4. *Allegro*.

2 fl, pic, 3 ob, 2 cl, 3 bsn; 4 hn, 3 tpt, 3 tmb, tuba; timp, tgle, cym, GC, tamtam, side dm; hp, piano, strings.

fp: 26 October 1943, Cleveland (Ohio), Cleveland Orchestra, cond. Erich Leinsdorf.

f New York p: 30 December 1943, New York Philharmonic Symphony, cond. Arthur Rodzinski.

fFp: 19 October 1945, Paris, l'Orchestre National, cond. Manuel Rosenthal.

fEp: 9 December 1945, BBC Symphony Orchestra, cond. Sir Adrian Boult.

Pub. 1947, 1966, Boosey & Hawkes.

271. Memorial to Lidice. For orchestra. August 1943, Darien (Conn.). Dur. 8′.

3 fl, 2 ob, ca, 3 cl, 2 bsn; 4 hn, 2 tpt, 3 tmb, tuba; timp, GC, cym, tamtam; hp, piano, strings.

fp: 28 October 1943, New York, concert in commemoration of the twenty-fifth anniversary of the Czechoslovak Republic, New York Philharmonic Symphony, cond. Artur Rodzinski.

fEp: 6 January 1945, BBC broadcast, BBC Symphony Orchestra, cond. Clarence Raybould.

f Prague p: 14 March 1946, Czech Philharmonic Orchestra, cond. Rafael Kubelik.

Pub. 1946, Melantrich.

272. Madrigal Stanzas. Five Pieces for violin and piano. November 1943, New York. Ded. Albert Einstein. Pub. 1944, Associated Music Publishers.

273. Piano Quintet No. 2. April 1944, New York. Ded. Fanny P. Mason.

1. *Poco allegro*; 2. *Moderato*; 3. *Poco allegro*; 4. *Largo—Allegro non troppo—Largo—Vivace*.

fp (private): 31 December 1944, Boston, home of Mrs. Mason, Paul Degrau and members of the Boston Symphony Orchestra.

fp (public): 4 March 1945, New York, Elly Bontempo and the Guilet Quarter.

Pub. 1945, Associated Music Publishers.

274. Symphony No. 3. 2 May–14 June 1944, Ridgefield (Conn.). Ded. Serge Koussevitzky and the Boston Symphony Orchestra. Dur. 30′.

1. *Allegro*; 2. *Largo*; 3. *Allegro—Andante poco moderato*.

2 fl, pic, 2 ob, ca, 3 cl, 2 bsn; 4 hn, 3 tpt, 3 tmb, tuba; timp, tgle, cym, GC, tamtam, side dm; hp, piano, strings.

fp: 12 October 1945, Boston, Boston Symphony Orchestra, cond. Serge Koussevitzky.

fEbp: 23 May 1951, BBC Symphony Orchestra, cond. Rafael Kubelik.

Pub. 1949, 1967, Boosey & Hawkes.

275. Trio in F. For flute, cello and piano. 20–31 July 1944, Ridgefield (Conn.). Dur. 20′.

1. *Poco allegretto*; 2. *Andante*; 3. *Allegretto scherzando*.

fp: 28 February 1945, New York, Town Hall, René Le Roy, Janos Scholz and Sidney Foster.

fEp: 23 July 1947, BBC broadcast, Geoffrey Gilbert, James Whitehead and Liza Fuchsová.

Pub. 1945, Associated Music Publishers.

276. Songs on two pages. Seven songs to folk texts for voice and piano. October 1944, New York. Pub. 1948, Melantrich.

277. Violin Sonata No. 3. December 1944. New York.

1. *Poco allegro*; 2. *Adagio*; 3. *Scherzo*; 4. *Lento—Poco allegro*.

fp: 17 December 1945, New York, Angel Reyes.

fEbp: 25 September 1952, Yfrah Neaman and Howard Ferguson.

Pub. 1950, Associated Music Publishers.

278. Cello Concerto. 20 December 1944– 26 February 1945, New York.

Martinů, Bohuslav

1. *Moderato*; 2. *Andante poco moderato*;
3. *Allegro*.
Pub.

279. Symphony No. 4. 10 April–14 June
1945, New York, South Orleans, Cape Cod
(Mass.). Ded. Helen and Bill Ziegler. Dur. 30'.
1. *Poco moderato—Allegro*; 2. *Allegro vivo*;
3. *Largo*; 4. *Allegro*.
fp: 30 November 1945, Philadelphia, Philadelphia Orchestra, cond. Eugene Ormandy.
f New York p: 10 December 1945, Philadelphia Orchestra, cond. Eugene Ormandy.
fEp: 16 November 1946, BBC broadcast,
People's Palace, BBC Symphony Orchestra,
cond. Rafael Kubelik.
Pub. 1950, Boosey & Hawkes.

280. Flute Sonata. 25 June–3 July 1945,
South Orleans. Ded. Georges Laurent.
1. *Allegro moderato*; 2. *Adagio*; 3. *Allegro*.
fEbp: 7 March 1957, Harold Clarke and
Hubert Dawkes.
Pub. 1951, Associated Music Publishers.

281. Czech Rhapsody. ?For violin and
piano. July 1945, South Orleans. Ded. Fritz
Kreisler. Pub. 1961, Eschig.

282. Etudes and Polkas. For piano. Sixteen
pieces in three books. Summer 1945, South
Orleans, Cape Cod (Mass.).
Book I:
1. *Etude in D.* 31 July 1945, South Orleans.
2. *Polka in D.* Ded. Milunka Svobodová.
3. *Etude in A.*
4. *Polka in A.* 28 August 1945, South
Orleans.
5. *Pastorale.* 28 July 1945, South Orleans.
Ded. Mrs. Nora Stanley-Smith.
6. *Etude.* 27 July 1945, South Orleans.
Book II:
7. *Etude in C.*
8. *Polka in F.* Ded. Jean Weir-Jablonka.
9. *Dance-Etude.* 2 August 1945, South
Orleans.
10. *Polka in E.* Ded. Antonin Svoboda.
11. *Etude in F.*
Book III:
12. *Etude in A.*
13. *Polka in A.*
14. *Etude in F.*
15. *Polka in A.* Ded. Winifred Johnstone.

16. *Etude in F.*
fEp: 13 November 1946, Wigmore Hall,
Boosey & Hawkes concert, Dorothea Braus.
Pub. 1946, Boosey & Hawkes.

283. Fantasia. For theremin, with oboe,
string quartet and piano. November 1945,
New York. Ded. Lucie Bigelow Rosen.
fp: 3 November 1945, New York, Lucie
Bigelow Rosen, Robert Boom and the
Koutzen Quartet.
Unpub.

284. Symphony No. 5. 1946, New York.
Ded. Czech Philharmonic Orchestra. Dur. 27'.
1. *Adagio—Allegro*; 2. *Larghetto*; 3. *Lento—
Allegro*.
2 fl, pic, 3 ob, 3 cl, 3 bsn; 4 hn, 3 tpt, 2 tmb,
bs tmb, tuba; timp, GC, cym, side dm, tgle,
tamtam; piano, strings.
fp: 28 May 1947, Prague, Czech Philharmonic Orchestra, cond. Rafael Kubelik.
fEbp: 23 October 1947, BBC Symphony
Orchestra, cond. Ernest Ansermet.
Pub. 1950, Boosey & Hawkes.

285. Toccata e due canzone. For small
orchestra. 1946, New York. Ded. Paul Sacher
and the Basle Chamber Orchestra. Dur. 18'.
1. *Toccata (Allegro moderato)*; 2. *Canzone
No. 1 (Andante moderato)*; 3. *Canzone No. 2
(Allegro)*.
pic, 2 ob, cl, bsn; tpt; timp, cym, side dm,
tgle; piano, strings.
fp: 24 January 1947, Basle, Basle Chamber
Orchestra, cond. Paul Sacher.
fEbp: 15 February 1949, Philharmonia
Orchestra, cond. Paul Sacher.
Pub. 1952, Hawkes.

286. String Quartet No. 6. 25 December
1946, New York. Ded. Roe Barstow.
1. *Allegro moderato*; 2. *Andante*; 3. *Allegro*.
fp: 1 May 1947, Cambridge (Mass.), at
Symposium of Music Criticism, Harvard
University.
fEp: 4 October 1955, Wigmore Hall, Indig
Quartet.
fEbp: 5 May 1958, London Quartet.
Pub. 1950, Orbis.

287. Three Madrigals (Duo No. 1). For
violin and viola. 1947, New York City. Ded.
Lillian and Joseph Fuchs. Dur. 10'.

1. *Poco allegro*; 2. *Poco andante*; 3. *Allegro.*
fp: 1948, New York, Lillian and Joseph Fuchs.
fbp: 1 May 1950, Alan Loveday and Max Gilbert.
Pub. 1949, Boosey & Hawkes.

288. String Quartet No. 7 (Concerto da camera). June–July 1947, New York City, Dur. 23′.
1. *Poco allegro*; 2. *Andante*; 3. *Allegro vivo.*
fp: February 1949, New York, Kroll Quartet.
Pub. 1958, Southern.

289. Quartet. For oboe, violin, cello and piano. 15 September–21 October 1947, New York City. Ded. Leopold Mannes. Dur. 12′.
fp: October 1947, New York.
Pub. 1961, Eschig.

290. Piano Concerto No. 3. 10 March 1948, New York. Ded. Rudolf Firkusný, Dur. 25′.
1. *Allegro*; 2. *Andante poco moderato*; 3. *Moderato—Allegro.*
2 fl, 2 ob, 2 cl, 2 bsn; 4 hn, 3 tpt, 3 tmb, tuba; timp, tgle, tamb pic, tamtam, cym, GC; strings.
fp: 20 November 1949, Dallas, with Rudolf Firkusný as soloist.
fEbp: 16 April 1952, Rudolf Firkusný and the BBC Symphony Orchestra, cond. Sir Malcolm Sargent.
Pub. 1960 (full score) Czech Musical Fund Archives, (reduction) Panton.

291. Sinfonia concertante. For oboe, bassoon, violin, cello and small orchestra. March 1949, New York. Ded. Maja Sacher. Dur. 19′.
1. *Allegro (non troppo)*; 2. *Andante moderato*; 3. *Poco allegro.*
2 cl, 2 hn; piano, strings.
fp: 8 December 1950, Basle, Alexandre Gold (ob), Henri Bouchet (bsn), Petru Manoliu (v), Louis Fest (c), Basle Chamber Orchestra, cond. Paul Sacher.
fbp: 19 December 1950, BBC broadcast, Leon Goossens, Cecil James, Campoli, John Shinebourne and the Boyd Neel Orchestra, cond. Paul Sacher.
Pub. 1951, Boosey & Hawkes.

292. The fifth day of the fifth moon. For piano. 20 May 1948, New York. Ded. Hsien-Ming Lee Tcherepnine. Pub. 1951, Heugel.

293. Les bouquinistes du Quai Malaquais. For piano. 24 May 1948, New York. Ded. to the composer's wife Charlotte. Pub. 1954, Heugel.

294. Five Czech Madrigals. For SATB chorus. Czech folksong texts. June 1948, New York. Pub. 1953, Boosey & Hawkes.

295. The Strangler. Ballet for three dancers, with verses by Robert Fitzgerald. 1948, New York City. Libretto: Eric Hawkins. Composed for Martha Graham.
fp: 15 August 1958, New London (Conn.), American Dance Festival.
Unpub.

296. Three Czech Dances. For two pianos. 1949, New York. Ded. Ethel Bartlett and Rae Robertson.
1. *Allegro*; 2. *Andante*; 3. *Allegro (non troppo).*
fEbp: 25 January 1953, Ethel Bartlett and Rae Robertson.
Pub. 1951, Eschig.

297. Mazurka-Nocturne. For oboe, two violins and cello. August 1949, New York.
fp: 3 October 1949, Paris, UNESCO concert celebrating the centenary of Chopin's birth.
Unpub.

298. Barcarolle. For piano. December 1949, New York. Unpub.

299. Piano Trio No. 2 in D minor. February 1950, New York. Composed for the festive opening of the Haydn Library. Ded. MIT, Cambridge.
1. *Allegro moderato*; 2. *Andante*; 3. *Allegro.*
fp: 14 May 1950, Cambridge (Mass.), MIT.
fEbp: March 1956, London Czech Trio (Lisa Marketta, Suzanne Rozsa, Karel Horitz).
Pub. 1961, Eschig.

300. Sinfonietta La Jolla. For Chamber orchestra and piano. 21 March 1950, New York. Commissioned by and ded. The Musical Arts Society of La Jolla, California. Dur. 18–18½′.
1. *Poco allegro*; 2. *Largo—Andante moderato*; 3. *Allegro.*

Martinů, Bohuslav

fl, pic, 2 ob, 2 cl, 2 bsn; 2 hn, tpt; timp, pcssn; piano, strings.
fp: 1951, Los Angeles.
fEp: 12 February 1951. BBC broadcast, London Symphony Orchestra, cond. Nikolai Sokoloff.
Pub. 1953, Boosey & Hawkes.

301. Duo No. 2. For violin and viola. 1 April 1950, New York City. Ded. Lillian and Joseph Fuchs.
fp: 5 January, 1951, New York, Lillian and Joseph Fuchs.
Pub. 1951, Boosey & Hawkes.

302. New Czech songs. For six SSC choruses with one or two violins or clarinet and oboe ad lib. Folk texts. 1950, New York.
Pub. 1951, Boosey & Hawkes.

303. Intermezzo. For large orchestra. 1950, New York. Ded. St. Louis Orchestra. Dur. 10′.
fl, pic, 2 ob, 2 cl, 2 bsn; 4 hn, 2 tpt, 3 tmb; timp, cym, tgle, GC, tamtam, tamb; piano, strings.
fp: 29 December 1950, New York, St. Louis Orchestra, cond. Robert Whitney.
Pub. 1965, Southern.

304. Concerto for two violins and orchestra. 1 May–10 June 1950, New York. Ded. G. and H. Beal. Dur. 16′.
fp: 8 January 1951, Dallas.
f New York p: November 1951, Scherman Chamber Orchestra.
Pub. 1951, Boosey & Hawkes.

305. Piano Trio No. 3 in C major. 21 April–15 May 1951, New York. Ded. Leopold Mannes.
fp: 25 February 1952, New York, Mannes Trio.
Pub. 1961, Eschig.

306. Serenade. For violin, viola, cello and two clarinets. 8 October–5 November 1951, New York. Ded. Rosalie Leventritt.
1. *Moderato poco allegro*; 2. *Andante*; 3. *Poco allegro*; 4. *Adagio—Allegro—Molto adagio—Vivace*.
fp: 4 January 1952, New York.
Pub. 1962, Eschig.

307. Stowe Pastorals. For flute-à-bec (2

soprano, 2 tenor, bass), two violins, clarinet in C and cello. 5–25 November 1951, New York. Ded. The Trapp Family.
fp: 1952, Basle Radio.
Pub. 1960, Baer; Novello.

308. Improvisation. For piano. 1951, New York, Paris. Pub. Pierre Noel (in *Les Contemporains*, Part 3).

309. What Men Live By. Pastoral Opera in one act. 1951-2, New York. Libretto after Tolstoy.
fp: May 1953, New York.
Pub. 1953, Boosey & Hawkes.

310. Three-Part Sacred Songs. For three female choruses with violin. Czech folk texts. 1952, New York City. Pub. 1953, Boosey & Hawkes.

311. Cello Sonata No. 3. September 1952, Vieux Moulin. Ded. to the memory of Hans Kindler. Dur. 22′.
1. *Poco andante—Moderato*; 2. *Andante— Moderato—Allegro*; 3. *Allegro, ma non presto*.
fp: 1952, Washington D.C.
fEp: 20 June 1962, BBC broadcast, Milos Sadlo and Ernest Lush.
Pub. 1957, State Publishing House (revised by F. Smetana); Boosey & Hawkes.

312. The Marriage. Comic Opera in two acts for television. 5 October–30 November 1952, New York, Libretto: Bohuslav Martinů, after Gogol.
fp: 7 February 1953, New York Television.
Pub. 1953, Boosey & Hawkes.

BIBLIOGRAPHY:
J. Lyons: Martinů opera composed for television given first performance: Marriage, *Musical America*, February 1953, p. 247.

313. Fantaisies symphoniques (Symphony No. 6). 23 April 1953, Paris, New York. Ded. Charles Münch on the occasion of the seventy-fifth anniversary of the founding of the Boston Symphony Orchestra. Dur. 25–27′.
1. *Lento—Allegro*; 2. *Poco allegro*; 3. *Lento— Allegro*.
3 fl, pic, 3 ob, 3 cl, 3 bsn; 4 hn, 3 tpt, 3 tmb, tuba; timp, cym, GC, tamb pic, tamb basque, tgle, tamtam; strings.

fp: 12 January 1955, Boston, Boston Symphony Orchestra, cond. Charles Münch.
fEp: 11 June 1955, BBC broadcast, BBC Symphony Orchestra, cond. Vilem Tausky.
fCp: 8 February 1956, Prague, Czech Philharmonic Orchestra, cond. Karel Ancerl.
Pub. 1957, Boosey & Hawkes.

314. Rhapsody-Concerto. For viola and orchestra. 15 March–18 April 1952, New York.
fp: 19 February 1953, Cleveland, Jasha Weissi and the Cleveland Orchestra, cond. George Szell.
Unpub.

315. Three Partsongs. For three male choruses, two sopranos and contraltos. Czech folk texts. 1953, New York. Pub. 1953, Boosey & Hawkes.

316. La Plainte contre inconnu. Opera in three acts. 1953, Nice. Libretto: Bohuslav Martinů, from the play by Georges Neveux. Unfinished.

317. Concerto for violin and piano and orchestra. 1953, New York. Ded. Benno and Sylvia Rabinoff. Unpub.

318. Hymn to St. James. For soprano, contralto, bass, speaker, mixed chorus, organ and orchestra. 1954, Nice. Words: P. Jaroslav Daněk. Dur. 10.′
fp: 31 July 1955, Policka, St. James's, cond. Jaroslav Maděra.
Unpub.

319. Mirandolina. Comic Opera in three acts. 1954, Nice. Libretto: Bohuslav Martinů, after Goldoni.
fp: 17 May 1959, Prague, National Theatre, cond. Václav Kašlík; producer, Luděk Mandaus; design, Fr. Tröster; choreography, A. Landa.
Pub. 1959, Baer: vocal score by the composer.

320. Primrose. Five Duets to Moravian folk texts for soprano, contralto, violin and piano. 1–5 August 1954, Nice.
fp: December 1954 and February 1955, Brno, 'Opus', cond. Zdeněk Zouhar.
Pub. 1960, Panton.

321. The Hill of Three Lights. Small Oratorio for soloists, chorus and organ. 20–25 November 1954, Nice. Ded. The Haag Singers.
fp: 3 October 1955, Bern, Den Haag Singers.
Unpub.

322. Piano Sonata No. 1. December 1954, Nice. Ded. Rudolf Serkin.
1. *Poco allegro—Vivo*; 2. *Moderato (poco andante)*; 3. *Adagio—Poco allegro—Allegro*.
fp: 4 December 1957, New York, Rudolf Serkin.
Pub. 1958, Eschig.

323. The Epic of Gilgamesh. For soprano, tenor, baritone and bass soloists, speaker, mixed chorus and orchestra. 1954–5, Nice. Ded. Maja Sacher. Dur. 60′.
1. *Gilgamesh*; 2. *The death of Enkidu*; 3. *Invocation*.
2 fl, 2 cl; 3 tpt, 2 tmb; timp, pcssn (3 players); hp, piano, strings.
fp: 24 January 1958, Basle, Ursula Buckel, Hans Jonelli, Pierre Mollet and Derrik Olsen, Hans Haeser (speaker), Basle Chamber Chorus and Chamber Orchestra and Orchestral Society, cond. Paul Sacher.
fEp: 18 April 1959, BBC broadcast, April Cantelo, William Herbert, John Cameron and Trevor Anthony, BBC Chorus and BBC Symphony Orchestra, cond. Sir Malcolm Sargent.
Pub. 1957, Universal-Edition. English version, R. Campbell Thompson; German version, A. H. Eichmann.

324. Oboe Concerto. April–12 May 1955, Nice. Ded. Jiří Tancibudek (Australia). Dur. 17′.
1. *Moderato*; 2. *Poco andante*; 3. *Poco allegro*.
2 fl, 2 cl, bsn; 2 hn, tpt; piano, strings.
fp: 1956, Melbourne, Jiří Tancibudek.
fEp: 29 June 1958, BBC broadcast, Jiří Tancibudek and the Kalmar Chamber Orchestra, cond. Maurice Miles.
fEp (concert): 24 August 1959, Evelyn Rothwell and the Halle Orchestra, cond. Sir John Barbirolli.
Pub. 1961, Eschig.

325. The Opening of the Wells. For

female chorus, sopranos, contraltos and baritone soloists, speaker and instrumental ensemble of two violins, viola and piano. July 1955, Nice. Text from a poem by Miloslav Bureš. Ded. The 'Opus' Vocal Society in Brno. Dur. 21'.

fp: 7 January 1956, Polička, 'Opus' Society, cond. Zdenek Zouhar.

Pub. 1956, State Publishing House.

326. Les Fresques de Piero della Francesca. For orchestra. 1955, Nice. Ded. Rafael Kubelik. Dur. 21'.

1. *Andante poco moderato*; 2. *Adagio*; 3 *Poco allegro—Allegro molto*.

pic, 3 fl, 3 ob, ca, 3 cl, 3 bsn; 4 hn, 3 tpt, 3 tmb, tuba; timp, xyl, tgle, tamb pic, tamb, cym, GC, tamtam; hp, strings.

fp: 28 August 1956, Salzburg, Vienna Philharmonic Orchestra, cond. Rafael Kubelik.

fEp: 10 April 1957, Royal Festival Hall, Royal Philharmonic Orchestra, cond. Rafael Kubelik.

Pub. 1956, Universal-Edition.

326a. Viola Sonata. November 1955, New York. Ded. Lillian Fuchs.

1. *Poco andante—Moderato*; 2. *Allegro non troppo*.

fp: 12 March 1956, New York, Lillian Fuchs.

?Unpub.

327. Incantations. For piano and orchestra. 12 December 1955–5 February 1956. Dur. 20'.

fp: 4 December 1956, New York, Rudolf Firkusný, cond. Leopold Stokowski.

f European p: 30 August 1957, Edinburgh Festival, Rudolf Firkusný and the Philharmonia Orchestra, cond. Rafael Kubelik.

f London p: 5 September 1957, Royal Albert Hall, Promenade Concert, Rudolf Firkusný and the BBC Symphony Orchestra, cond. Sir Malcolm Sargent.

?Unpub.

328. Sonatina. For clarinet and piano. 1956, New York.

fEbp: 26 September 1958, Reginald Kell and Josephine Lee.

Pub. 1957, Leduc.

329. Sonatina. For trumpet and piano. 1956, New York. Pub. 1956, Leduc.

330. Brigands' Songs I. (Zbojnické I). Five Songs to folk texts for male chorus. January 1957, Rome. Ded. 'The Prague Teachers' Vocal Society'.

fp: 1957, Prague, Prague Teachers' Vocal Society cond. Miroslav Venhoda.

Pub. 1959, State Publishing House. English version, John Clapham.

330a. Brigands' Songs II (Zbojnické II). Details as preceding.

331. Legend from the Smoke of Potato Fires. For soloists, chorus and instrumental ensemble. 1957, Rome. Text: Miloslav Bureš. Ded. Mrs. Frances Ježková.

flute-à-bec, cl, hn, concertina, piano.

fp: 28 May 1957, Prague, Spring Festival, Czech Choral Society, cond. J. Kühn.

Pub. 1960, State Publishing House. English version, Iris Urwin.

332. Dandelion Romance. For tenor and soprano soloists and mixed chorus a cappella. 1957, Rome. Text: Miloslav Bureš. Ded. Jan and Markéta Kühn. Dur. 12'.

fp: 26 October 1958, Prague, Czech Choral Society, cond. Markéta Kühnová.

Pub. 1960, State Publishing House.

333. Reminiscences. For piano. 1957, Rome. Composed in memory of Václav Kaprál and Vítězslava Krprálová. Unpub.

334. The Rock. Symphonic Preludium for orchestra. 1957, Rome. Ded. The Cleveland Orchestra.

fp: 1958, Cleveland, Cleveland Orchestra, cond. George Szell.

Pub. 1959, Universal-Edition.

335. Duo. For violin and cello. 1957, Schönenberg. Ded. Mrs. Trauti Mohr. Dur. 10'. Pub. 1961, Eschig.

336. Divertimento. For two flute-à-bec. 1957, Schönenberg. Pub. 1958, Universal-Edition.

337. Fantasia concertante (Piano Concerto in B flat). For piano and orchestra. 1957, Schönenberg, Pratteln. Ded. Margrit Weber. Dur. 20'.

1. *Poco allegro risoluto*; 2. *Poco andante*; 3. *Poco allegro*.

2 fl, pic, 2 ob, 2 cl, 2 bsn; 4 hn, 2 tpt, 3 tmb; timp, GC, cym, xyl, tgle, tamb pic, tamb mil, wood block; strings.
fp: 1958, Berlin, Margrit Weber.
fEp: 13 June 1959, BBC broadcast, Margrit Weber and the BBC Symphony Orchestra, cond. Rudolf Schwarz.
Pub. 1959, Universal-Edition.

338. Parables. For orchestra. 1957-8. Ded. Charles Münch. Dur. 25-27'.
1. *Parable of a Sculpture.* 1 July 1957, Rome.
2. *Parable of a Garden.* 27 July 1957, Rome.
3. *Parable of a Labyrinth.* 9 February 1958, Schönenberg.
3 fl, pic, 3 ob, 3 cl, 3 bsn, dbsn; 4 hn, 3 tpt, 3 tmb, tuba; timp, xyl, tgle, tamb basco, tamb pic, 2 tamb mil, ten dm, GC, cym; strings.
fp: 13 February 1959, Boston, Boston Symphony Orchestra, cond. Charles Münch; relayed in Britain by the BBC.
Pub. 1959, Baer; 1961, Bärenreiter (without movement titles).

339. Estampes. For orchestra. 1958, Schönenberg. Ded. Robert Whitney and the Louisville Orchestra. Dur. 20'.
1. *Andante*; 2. *Adagio—Allegro molto*; 3. *Poco allegro.*
2 fl, pic, 2 ob, ca, 2 cl, 2 bsn; 4 hn, 2 tpt, 3 tmb; timp, cym, tgle, tenor dm, side dm, GC, xyl, tamb; hp, piano, strings.
Pub. 1958, 1962, Southern.

340. Ariadne. Lyric Opera in one act. 1958, Schönenberg. Libretto: Bohuslav Martinů, from the play 'Le Voyage de Thésée' by Georges Neveux. Dur. 45'.
fp: February 1961, Gelsenkirchen, cond. Ljubomir Romansky.
Pub. 1959, Baer; Novello. Reduction by the composer.

341. Harpsichord Sonata. 1958, Schönenberg. Ded. Antoinette Vischer. Dur. 5'.
1. *Poco allegro*; 2. *Poco moderato cantabile*; 3. *Allegretto.*
Pub. 1960, Eschig/Universal-Edition.

342. Greek Passion. Musical Drama in four acts. 1955-8, Nice, New York, Pratteln, Rome, Pratteln. Libretto: Bohuslav Martinů, from the novel by Nikos Kazantzakis.

fp: 12 June 1961, Zürich, cond. Paul Sacher.
Pub. 1958, Universal.

343. Piece for children. Duo for two cellos. 1959, Schönenberg. Pub. 1960, Baer.

344. Nonet. 19 January–1 March 1959, Schönenberg. Ded. Czech Nonet. Dur. 17'.
v, va, c, db; fl, cl, ob, bsn; hn.
fp: July 1959, Salzburg Festival.
fEp: 18 March 1966, Friends' House (London), Francis Chagrin Ensemble, cond. Francis Chagrin.
Pub. 1959, State Publishing House/Baer.

345. Les Fêtes nocturnes. For violin, viola, cello, clarinet, harp and piano. 14 February–4 March 1959, Schönenberg.
1. *Allegro moderato*; 2. *Andante moderato*; 3. *Poco allegro.*
fp: November 1959, Brunswick.
?Unpub.

346. Songs to Czech folksong texts. For four children's voices. January 1959, Schönenberg. Ded. Children and Youth Choral Society. Dur. 4'.
fp: 17 April 1960, Brno.
?Unpub.

347. Mikesh from the Mountains. For soloists, mixed chorus and instrumental ensemble (two violins, viola and piano). 2–13 February 1959, Schönenberg. Dur. 22'.
fp: 18 June 1959, Prague, Kühn Chamber Vocal Ensemble, cond. Pavel Kühn.
Pub. 1960, State Publishing House.

348. Variations about a Slovakian theme. For cello and piano. 14–20 March 1959, Schönenberg.
fp: October 1959, Prague, Saš Večtomov and V. Topinka.
Pub. 1960, Baer; Novello.

349. Impromptus. For harpsichord. 21 March 1959, Schönenberg. Ded. Antoinette Vischer. Dur. 4'. Pub. 1961, Eschig.

350. Partsong Book. Madrigals for SATB. March 1959, Schönenberg. Ded. Maruška Prazanová, Polička.
fp: 15 June 1959, Prague, New Madrigal Singers, cond. Miroslav Venhoda.
Pub. 1960. Baer.

Nielsen, Carl

351. The Bird Feast. For children's voices. Set to the text of a fifteenth-century Czech manuscript. March 1959, Schönenberg. Unpub.

352. Vigilie. For organ. 1959, Schönenberg. Ded. to and revised by B. Janácek. Pub. 1961, Eschig.

353. Prophecy of Isaiah. For male chorus, three soloists and instrumental ensemble (viola, trumpet, piano and timpani). 6 May 1959, Nice. Dur. 12'. Pub. 1962, Israeli Music Publications.

GENERAL BIBLIOGRAPHY

José Bruyr: BM, *Disques*, No. 114, January-February 1960, p. 24.
John Clapham: Martinů's instrumental style, *MR*, 1963, No. 2, p. 158.
O. Downes: Martinů at 60, *New York Times*, 7 January 1951.
V. Holzknecht: Za BM, *Hudební Rozhledy*, 1959 No. 17, p. 705.
B. Karasek: BM, compositeur tcheque, *Hudební Rozhledy*, 1960, No. 23, p. 969.
— Monografie o BM, *Hudební Rozhledy*, 1963, No. 17, p. 724.
Robert Layton: Martinů and the Czech tradition, in *The Symphony*, Vol. 2, Pelican Books (London) 1967, p. 218.
Miloslav Nedbal: BM, Panton (Prague) 1965.
M. Pinchard: Hommage à BM, *Musica*, (Chaix), No. 76, July 1960, p. 12.
Miloš Safránek: BM, with list of chief works, *MQ*, July 1943, p. 329.
— BH und das musikalische Theater, *Musica*, September 1959, p. 550.
— Nova dila a nove tisky skladeb BM, *Hudební Rozhledy*, 1959, No. 12, p. 504.
— BM, *Slovenska Hudba*, December 1960, p. 595.
— BM, the man and his music, New York, 1944; Dobson (London) 1946.
V. Sefl: Trikrat BM, *Hudební Rozhledy*, 1962, No. 9, p. 381.
D. Skrovan: BM, *Zvuk* No. 33–34 (1960) p. 129.
K. H. Wörner: BH, ein Blick auf sein Opernschaffen, *Musica*, March 1961, p. 117.
Zdenek Zouhar: BM, Krajské Nakladatelství (Brno) 1957
— Za BM, *Slovenska Hudba*, October 1959, p. 460.

CARL NIELSEN (1865–1931)

The seventh of twelve children brought up in great poverty, Carl Nielsen was born in the Danish village of Nørre-Lyndelse (near Odense on the island of Fyn) on 9 June 1865. His surname was formed in the once-standard Danish manner from the Christian name of his father, Niels Jørgensen, a journeyman painter who added to his income by organizing groups of musicians to play at local festivities. By the time Nielsen was ten he was playing the fiddle in one of these groups and in 1880, after spells as cowherd and grocer's assistant, he joined the military band in Odense to serve as a bugler for three years. In 1884 he entered the Royal Conservatoire at Copenhagen, studying with Niels Gade among others, but left in 1887 and made his début as a composer the following year with a performance of his Opus 1 in the Copenhagen Tivoli Gardens. He lived in Copenhagen for the rest of his life, though with frequent retreats to the country around Kolding in Jutland to compose. In 1889 Nielsen joined the Copenhagen Royal Orchestra as a second violinist, a post he held for sixteen years. In 1890–1 he visited Germany, Italy and France, and while in Paris (1891) met and married the Danish sculptress Anne Marie Brodersen. He made his conducting début in 1893, and in 1908, three years after leaving the violin section of the Royal Orchestra, he became co-conductor of the Royal Theatre with Frederick Rung. Soon after Rung's death he resigned (1914) to concentrate on composing. In 1915 he became conductor of the Copenhagen Musical Society, a position which allowed him the necessary time for his creative work and which he held for twelve years. By the second decade of the century Nielsen was beginning to achieve a firm reputation in his native land, and the enthusiastic celebrations in Copenhagen of his sixtieth birthday (1925) established that he had become the Danish musician *par excellence*. However, from 1922 onwards he was afflicted with angina pectoris, suffered a serious heart-attack in 1926 and died of a further attack in October 1931.

CATALOGUE OF WORKS

1. Polka in A major. For violin. *c.* 1874.

2. Skoma Gerens Brudevals. For piano. *c.* 1878.

3. Wind Quartet. For cornet, trumpet, alto trombone and tenor trombone. Date unknown.

4. Violin Sonata in G major. 1881–2. Unpub.

5. Quartet movement. For string quartet. ?*c.* 1882.

6. String Quartet ('No. 1') in D minor. 1882–3. Unpub.

7. Duet in A major. For two violins. 1882–3. Unpub.

8. Two Characteristic Pieces (Caraktér-stykker). For piano. *c.* 1882–3.

9. Vuggevise (Carl Nielsen). For voice and piano. *c.* 1883.

10. Fantasy. For clarinet and piano. 1883–7. Unpub.

11. Piano Trio in G major. 1882–3. Unpub.

12. String Quartet in F major. 1887.
fp: 21 January 1888, Carl Nielsen, Fr. Schnedler-Petersen, Ju. Borup and A. Bloch. Unpub.

13. Det bødes der for (J P. Jacobsen). For male chorus. 4 December 1887.

14. Laengsel (R. Burns). For male chorus. 1887.

15. Angst (E. Aarestrup). For voice and piano. 1887.

16. Til mit Hjertes Dronning (Shelley). For voice and piano. 1887.

17. Vejviseren synger (J. S. Welhaven). For voice and piano. 1887.

18. Serenade (I. Callanau). For voice and piano. 1887.

19. Tag Jer i Agt for Anna (R. Burns). For voice and piano. 1887.

20. Min Sjael er mørk (G. Byron). For voice and piano. 1887.

21. Byd mig at leve (R. Herrick). For 4-part male chorus. 1887.

22. Før drømte jeg fast (J. P. Jacobsen). For 4-part male chorus. 1887.

23. String Quartet No. 1 in G minor Op. 13. 1888. Ded. Johan S. Svendsen. Dur. 25'.
1. Allegro energico; *2. Andante amoroso*; *3. Scherzo: Allegro molto*; *4. Finale: Allegro (inquieto).*
fp: 3 February 1898, Anton Svendsen, Holger Møller. F. Marke and Ernst Høeberg. Pub. 1900, Hansen.

24. String Quintet in G major. 1888. Ded. Thorvald Nielsen, Erling Bloch, Hans Kassow and Louis Jensen. Dur. 30'.
1. Allegro pastorale; *2. Adagio*; *3. Allegretto scherzando*; *4. Finale: Allegro molto.*
fp: 28 April 1889, Copenhagen, Ludwig Holm, Carl Nielsen, Osv. Poulsen. F. O. Hansen and Kr. Sandby. Pub. 1937, Dania.

25. Little Suite Op. 1. For string orchestra. 1888. Ded. Orla Rosenhoff. Dur. 15–16'.
1. Prelude (Andante con moto); *2. Intermezzo (Allegro moderato)*; *3. Finale (Andante con moto).*
fp: 8 September 1888, Copenhagen, Tivoli Orchestra, cond. Balduin Dahl.
fEbp: 14 September 1952, Harvey Phillips String Orchestra, cond. Harvey Phillips. Pub. 1889. Hansen. Arr. for piano by Herman D. Koppel, 1949.

26. Symphonic Rhapsody. For orchestra. 1889.
2 fl, 2 ob, 2 cl, 2 bsn; 4 hn, 2 tpt, 3 tmb; timp; strings.
fp: 24 February 1893, Folkekoncerterne, cond. Victor Bendix. Unpub.

27. Fantasy Pieces (Fantasistykker) Op. 2. For oboe and piano. 1889. Ded. Olivo Krause. Dur. 6'.

Nielsen, Carl

1. *Romance*; 2. *Humoreske*.
fp: 16 March 1891, Olivo Krause and Victor Bendix.
Pub. 1890, Hansen.

27a. Romance. Op. 2 No. 1. Orch. Hans Sitt. Dur. 3′.
2 cl, 2 bsn; 2 hn; strings.
Pub. 1892, Hansen. Also arr. violin and piano by Emil Telmányi.

28. En Aften paa Giske. Historical Skuespil in one act. 1889. Text: A. Munch.
fp: 15 January 1890, Dagmarteatret.
Unpub.

29. Prelude (Forspil). For orchestra. ?1889.
fl, ob, 2 cl; 2 hn, 2 tpt, tmb; timp; strings.
Unpub.

30. Slutningskor. For SATB chorus and orchestra. ?1889. Unpub.

31. Five Piano Pieces Op. 3. 1890. Ded. Mrs. Orpheline Olsen (*née* Wexschall-Schram). Dur. 7′.
1. *Folketune*; 2. *Humoreske*; 3. *Arabeske*; 4. *Mignon*; 5. *Alfedans*.
fEbp: 6 September 1957, Esther Vagning.
Pub. 1891. Hansen.

32. String Quartet No. 2 in F minor Op. 5 (orig. Op. 6.). 1890. Ded. Anton Svendsen. Dur. 30′.
1. *Allegro non troppo ma energico*; 2. *Un poco Adagio*; 3. *Allegretto scherzando*; 4. *Finale: Allegro appassionato*.
fp (private): 18 December 1890, Berlin, home of Joseph Joachim.
fp (public): 8 April 1892, Copenhagen, Anton Svendsen, Holgar Møller, Chr. Petersen, Frits Bendix.
Pub. 1891, Hansen.

33. Five Poems by J. P. Jacobsen (Fem Digte af J. P. Jacobsen) Op. 4. For voice and piano. 1891. Ded. Anne Marie Carl Nielsen.
1. *Sundown (Solnedgang)*; 2. *In the garden of the harem (I Seraillets Have)*; 3. *To Asali (Til Asali)*; 4. *Irmelin Rose*; 5. *The day has gone (Har Dagen saenket)*.
fp: 28 April 1892, Copenhagen, Marie Nielsen, acc. G. Bruhn.
Pub. 1892, Hansen. Nos. 2, 4 & 5 also pub. 1895 in German version by Wilhelm Henzen.

33a. In the garden of the harem (I Seraillets Have) Op. 4 No. 2. Version by the composer for male chorus.

34. Songs and Verses by J. P. Jacobsen (Viser og Vers af J. P. Jacobsen) Op. 6. For voice and piano. 1891. Ded. Dr. Rudolph Bergh.
1. *Genre picture (Genrebillede)*; 2. *The seraphs (Seraferne)*; 3. *Silk shoes on a golden last (Silkesko over gylden Laest)*; 4. *That must be paid for (Det bødes der for)*; 5. *Song from 'Mogens' (Vise af 'Mogens')*; 6. *Had I, oh, had I (Havde jeg, o havde jeg)*.
fp: 28 April 1892, Copenhagen, Marie Nielsen, acc. G. Bruhn.
Pub. 1893, Hansen. Nos, 1, 3 & 4 also pub. 1895 in German version by Wilhelm Henzen.

35. Aldrig hans Ord kan jeg glemme. For voice and piano. 1891. Unpub.

36. I Drømmes Land (J. P. Jacobsen). ?For voice and piano. 1891. Unpub.

37. Symphony No. 1 in G minor Op. 7. 1892. Ded. Anne Marie Carl Nielsen. Dur. 34′.
1. *Allegro orgoglioso*; 2. *Andante*; 3. *Allegro comodo—Andante sostenuto*; 4. *Finale: Allegro con fuoco*.
3 fl, 2 ob, 2 cl, 2 bsn; 4 hn, 2 tpt, 3 tmb; timp; strings.
fp: 14 March 1894, Copenhagen, Royal Orchestra, cond. Johan Svendsen.
fEbp: 2 October 1947, BBC Symphony Orchestra, cond. Mogens Wöldike.
Pub. 1894, Hansen. Reduction by Henrik Knudsen, 1901.

38. Snefrid. Incidental music for a melodrama by Holger Drachmann. 1893, rev. 1899. Dated: 9 February 1899. Unpub.

38a. Snefrid: Prelude. For piano. Ded. Anna Kjaer. Pub. 1895, in *Ungt Blod*.

39. Six Songs (Seks Sange) Op. 10 (Ludvig Holstein). For voice and piano. 1894.
1. *You fine white apple blossom (Du fine, hvide Aebleblomst)*; 2. *Memory Lake (Erindringens Sø)*; 3. *Filled with flowers (Fyldt med Blomster)*; 4. *I walk in the sun (I Solen gaar jeg)*; 5. *The gold and white heavenlight (Det*

gyldenhvide Himmellys); 6. *Lazy fjord (Den dovne Fjord).*
fp: 3 February 1898, Margrethe Boye and Ida Møller.
Pub. 1895 (?1897), Hansen; German version, E. von Enzberg.

40. Symphonic Suite Op. 8. For piano. I August 1894. Ded. Victor Bendix. Dur. *c.* 15'.
1. *Intonation (Maestoso)*; 2. *Quasi allegretto*; 3. *Andante*; 4. *Finale (Allegro).*
fp: 4 May 1895, Copenhagen, Louis Glass.
fEp: 1 October 1959, BBC broadcast, Liza Fuchsová
Pub. 1895, Hansen.

41. Violin Sonata No. 1 in A major Op. 9. 23 August 1895. Ded. Henri Marteau. Dur. 22'.
1. *Allegro glorioso*; 2. *Andante*; 3. *Allegro piacevole e giovanile.*
fp: 15 January 1896, Copenhagen, Anton Svendsen and Johanne Stockmarr.
fEbp: 1 August 1946, Emil Telmányi.
Pub. 1896, Hansen. Revised edition, Emil Telmányi.

42. Hymnus amoris Op. 12. For soprano, tenor, baritone and bass soloists, children's chorus, mixed chorus, male chorus and orchestra. 27 December 1896. Text: Axel Olrik (Danish), J. L. Heiberg (Latin). Ded. Orla Rosenhoff. Dur. 25'.
3 fl, 2 ob, ca, 2 cl, 2 bsn; 4 hn, 3 tpt, 3 tmb, tuba; timp, tgle, campanelli; strings.
fp: 27 April 1897, Copenhagen, Musikforeningen, cond. Carl Nielsen.
fEbp: 11 February 1954, Carl Nielsen Festival (Copenhagen) performance with Danish State Radio Chorus and Orchestra.
?fEp: 14 June 1959, City of Birmingham Choir and Symphony Orchestra, cond. Meredith Davies.
Pub. 1897–98, Hansen.

43. Humoresque-Bagatelles Op. 11. For piano. 1894–7. Dated: 12 May 1897.
1. *How do you do? (Goddag! Goddag!)*; 2. *The spinning top (Snurretoppen)*; 3. *A little slow waltz (En lille langsom Vals)*; 4. *The jumping jack (Spraellemanden)*; 5. *Doll's march (Dukkemarsche)*; 6. *The musical box (Spillevaerket).*

fp: 3 February 1898, Copenhagen, Johanne Stockmarr.
fEbp: 18 February 1934, Johanne Stockmarr.
Pub. 1897, Hansen. Also version orch. Kjell Roikjer.

44. String Quartet No. 3 in E flat Op. 14. 1898. Ded. Edvard Grieg. Dur. 35'.
1. *Allegro con brio*; 2. *Andante sostenuto*; 3. *Allegretto pastorale*; 4. *Finale: Allegro coraggioso.*
fp: 4 October 1901, Copenhagen, Georg Høeberg, Louis Witzansky, Anton Bloch and Ernst Høeberg.
fEbp: 21 January 1952, Aeolian Quartet.
Pub. 1900, Hansen.

45. Festive Prelude to the New Century (Festpraeludium—ved Aarhundredskiftet). For piano. 1899. Ded. I. F. Willumsen.
fp: 4 March 1901, Copenhagen, Dagmar Borup.
fEp: 9 December 1965, St. Marylebone Parish Church, Christopher Dearnley.
Pub. 1901, Hansen. Also arr. for organ.

46. Edderkoppens Sang (Adam Oehlenschlaeger: 'Aladdin'). For SSA chorus. 4 December 1899. Pub. 1907, Hansen.

47. Cantata for the Lorens Frølich Festival 1900. Text: Axel Olrik.
fp: 30 November 1900, Peter Jerndorff (reciter) and Carl Nielsen (piano).
Unpub.

48. Gudhjaelp (Gustav Wied & Jens Petersen). For voice and piano. 1901. Unpub.

49. Saul and David. Opera in four acts. 1898–1901. Dated: 20 April 1901. Libretto: Einar Christiansen.
3 fl, 2 ob, 2 cl, 2 bsn; 4 hn, 3 tpt, 3 tmb, tuba; timp: hp, strings.
fp: 28 November 1902, Copenhagen, Royal Theatre, cond. Carl Nielsen.
fEbp: 10 May 1959, BBC Scottish Choral Society and Orchestra, cond. Berthold Goldschmidt; with Stanislav Pieczora, William Herbert, John Mitchinson, Joyce Barker, David Ward, Roger Stalman, Jean Watson, Pamela Petts.
Pub. 1904, Hansen. Also excerpts arr. for piano by Nicolaj Hansen, pub. 1912.

Nielsen, Carl

49a. Saul and David; Prelude, Act 2. 1900. Dur. 5½'.
3 fl, 2 ob, 2 cl, 2 bsn; 4 hn, 3 tpt, 3 tmb, tuba; timp; strings.
fp: 6 October 1901, Copenhagen, Royal Orchestra, cond. Johan Svendsen.
Pub. 1938, Hansen.

50. Come, thou white sun (Kom blankeste Sol) (Laurits Thura). For SSA and piano. 10 May 1901, Kolding. Pub. 1909, Hansen.

51. Cantata for the Students' Association (Kantate til Studentersamfundet). For soloists, piano and instruments. 1901. Text: Holger Drachmann.
fp: 1 June 1901, Emilie Ulrich and Helge Nissen (reciters), Emanuel Larsen (piano), cond. Carl Nielsen.
Unpub.

52. Symphony No. 2 ('The Four Temperaments'—'De Fire Temperamenter') Op. 16. 1901–2. Dated: 22 November 1902. Ded. Ferruccio Busoni. Dur. 30'.
1. *Allegro collerico*; 2. *Allegro comodo e flemmatico*; 3. *Andante malincolico*; 4. *Allegro sanguineo.*
3 fl, 2 ob, 2 cl, 2 bsn; 4 hn, 3 tpt, 3 tmb, tuba; timp; strings.
fp: 1 December 1902, Copenhagen, Dansk Koncertforening, cond. Carl Nielsen.
fGp: 5 November 1903, Berlin, Beethoven-Saal, cond. Ferruccio Busoni.
fEbp: 1 October 1951, Danish State Radio Symphony Orchestra, cond. Launy Grondahl.
fEp (concert): 12 February 1957, Chelsea Town Hall, Morley College Orchestra, cond. Lawrence Leonard. (NB: fEp orig. announced for 13 September 1921, Promenade Concert, but cancelled.)
Pub. 1903, Hansen. Reduction by Henrik Knudsen for piano four hands, 1917.

53. Helios Op. 17. Overture for orchestra. 23 April 1903. Ded. Julius Röntgen. Dur. 12'.
3 fl, 2 ob, 2 cl, 2 bsn; 4 hn, 3 tpt, 3 tmb, tuba; timp; strings.
fp: 8 October 1903, Copenhagen, Royal Orchestra, cond. Johan Svendsen.
fEbp: 24 September 1948, BBC Symphony Orchestra, cond. Clarence Raybould.

Pub. 1905, Hansen. Reduction by Henrik Knudsen for piano four hands, 1905.

54. Sleep (Søvnen) Op. 18. For chorus and orchestra. 10 November 1904. Text: Johannes Jørgensen. Dur. 20'.
3 fl, 2 ob, ca, 2 cl, 2 bsn; 4 hn, 3 tpt, 3 tmb, tuba; timp, campanelli; strings.
fp: 21 March 1905, Copenhagen, Musikforeningen, cond. Carl Nielsen.
fEp: 17 February 1958, St. James's Church (Piccadilly), Kensington Symphony Orchestra and Choir, cond. Leslie Head.
fEbp: 16 November 1958, Royal Philharmonic Orchestra, cond. Stanley Pope.
Pub. 1905 (piano score), 1907 (full score), Hansen. German version, C. Rocholl.

55. The dream of a merry Christmas (Drømmen om 'Glad Jul'). Fantasia for piano. 3 December 1905. Pub. 1905.

56. Thou Danish man (Du danske Mand) (Holger Drachmann). For voice and piano. 1906.
fp: 27 June 1906, Copenhagen, Tivoli, Henry Seemann.
Pub. 1906, Hansen.

57. Morten Børup's May Song (Morten Børups Majvise). For SSA. 1906.

58. String Quartet No. 4 in F major Op. 44 (orig. *Piacevolezza* Op. 19). 2 July 1906. Ded. Gunna Breuning, Gerhard Rafn, Ella Faber and Paulus Bache (Copenhagen String Quartet). Dur. 26'.
1. *Allegro non tanto e comodo*; 2. *Adagio con sentimento religioso*; 3. *Allegretto moderato ed innocente*; 4. *Allegro non tanto, ma molto scherzoso.*
fp: 30 November 1907, Copenhagen, Ludvig Holm, Johs. Schiørring, Kr. Sandby and Ernst Høeberg.
fEbp: 19 May 1953, Sebastian Quartet.
Pub. 1923, Peters.

59. Sir Oluf, he rides (Hr. Oluf, han rider). Incidental music for a drama by Holger Drachmann. 15 September 1906.
fp: 9 October 1906, Copenhagen, Royal Theatre, cond. Carl Nielsen.
Unpub.

59a. Four Songs. For voice and piano. From preceding.

1. *Hellidens Sang*; 2. *Olufs Sang*; 3. *Dansevise*; 4. *Elverdans*.

Pub. 1906, Hansen.

60. Jeg synes om din lette Gang (Carl Nielsen). For voice and piano. 11 July 1906. Unpub.

61. Maskarade. Opera in three acts. 1904–6. Dated: 3 November 1906. Libretto: Vilhelm Andersen, after Ludvig Holberg.

3 fl, 2 ob, 2 cl, bcl, 2 bsn; 4 hn, 3 tpt, 3 tmb, tuba; timp, GC; strings.

fp: 11 November 1906, Copenhagen, Royal Theatre, cond. Carl Nielsen.

Pub. 1906, Hansen. Also excerpts arr. piano by Axel Grandjean.

61a. Maskarade: Overture. 1906. Dur. 4′.

3 fl, 2 ob, 2 cl, 2 bsn; 4 hn, 3 tpt, 3 tmb, tuba; timp, GC; strings.

Pub. 1929, Samfundet; Hansen.

61b. Maskarade: Prelude, Act II. 1905. Dur. 4′.

3 fl, 2 ob, 2 cl, 2 bsn; 4 hn; strings.

fp: 11 November 1905, Copenhagen, Musikforeningen, cond. Carl Nielsen.

Pub. 1955, Hansen.

61c. Maskarade: Cock Dance (Hanedans). 1905. Dur. 4½′.

3 fl, 2 ob, 2 cl, 2 bsn; 4 hn, 3 tpt, 3 tmb, tuba; timp, tgle; strings.

fp: 11 November 1905, Copenhagen, Musikforeningen, cond. Carl Nielsen.

fEbp: 14 June 1933, BBC Orchestra, cond. J. L. Mowinckel.

Pub. 1914, Hansen. Also arr. for piano by Ludvig Schutte, pub. 1907.

61d. Maskarade: Selections. Arr. from the original score by Kjell Roikjer. Dur. 16′.

2 fl, 2 ob, cl; piano, tamb, strings.

Pub. Hansen.

62. Song of the Siskin (Sidskensang) (Emil Aarestrup). For SAT chorus a cappella. 5 December 1906.

fp: 7 April 1907, Caeciliaforeningen, cond. Fr. Rung.

Unpub.

63. Come, God's Angel (Kom Guds Engel) (Emil Aarestrup). For ATB chorus a cappella. 1906.

fp: 30 November 1907, Caecilienforeningen cond. Fr. Rung.

fEbp: 11 August 1952, Church Male Voice Choir of Copenhagen, cond. Arne Bertelsen. Unpub.

64. Strophic Songs (Strofiske Sange) Op. 21. For voice and piano. 1905–7. Ded. Dodil Neergaard.

Book I:

1. *Must the flowers fade?* (Skal Blomsterne da visne?) (Helge Rode).

2. *The Hawk* (Høgen) (Jeppe Aakjaer).

3. *The stonebreaker* (Jens Vejmand) (Jeppe Aakjaer).

Book II:

4. *Lower thy head* (Saenk kun dit Hoved) (Johannes Jørgensen).

5. *The first lark* (Den første Laerke) (Jeppe Aakjaer).

6. *Homeless* (Husvild) (Johs. V. Jensen).

7. *Good-night* (Godnat) (Johs. V. Jensen).

fp: 30 November 1907, Johanne Krarup-Hansen, acc. Henrik Knudsen.

Pub. 1907, Hansen.

65. Tove. Songs for the play by Ludvig Holstein. 1906–8. Ded. Vilhelm Herold.

1. *We sons of the plains* (Vi sletternes Sønner); 2. *Bird-catcher's song* (Fuglefaengervise); 3. *Tove's song* (Toves Sang); 3. *Hunter's song* (Jaegersang).

fp: 20 March 1908. Dagmarteatret.

Pub. 1908, Hansen.

66. Willemoes. Songs for the play by L. C. Nielsen, composed with Emilius Bangert. 1907–8. Dated: 30 January 1908. Ded. Helge Nissen.

1. *Fatherland* (Faedreland); 2. *Yes, take us, our mother* (Ja tag os, vor Moder); 3. *Følger hvo som følge kan*; 4. *Vibeke's song* (Vibekes Sang); 5. *Havet's song: The ocean round Denmark* (Havets Sang: Havet omkring Danmark).

fp: 7 February 1908, Folkteatret.

Pub. 1908, Hansen.

67. The Parents (Foraeldre). Music for a play by Otto Benzon. 1908.

fp: 9 February 1908.
Unpub.

68. The Dream of Gunnar (Saga-Drøm)
Op. 39. For orchestra. 1 April 1908. Ded.
Bror Beckman. Dur. 9–10'.

3 fl, 2 ob, 2 cl, 2 bsn; 4 hn, 3 tpt, 3 tmb,
tuba; timp, cym, glock; strings.

fp: 6 April 1908, Copenhagen, Musikforeningen, cond. Carl Nielsen.

fEbp: 23 November 1953, London Symphony Orchestra, cond. Walter Goehr.

Pub. 1920, Hansen.

69. Cantata for the anniversary of Copen-
hagen University (Kantate ved Universi-
tetets Aarsfest) Op. 24. For soprano, tenor,
bass, male chorus and orchestra. 1908.
Text: Niels Møller. Dur. 21'.

fp: 29 October 1908, Copenhagen University, Student Singers, cond. Salomon Levysohn.

Pub. 1908, Hansen: vocal score.

70. Evening Mood (Aftenstemning) (C.
Hauch). For male chorus a cappella. 1908.

fp: 19 October 1908, Herrekoret Bel Canto.

fEbp: 11 August 1952, Church Male Voice
Choir of Copenhagen, cond. Aine Bertelsen.

71. Cantata in celebration of the year 1659.
1909. Text: L. C. Nielsen.

fp: 11 February 1909, Copenhagen, Studentersangforeningen.

Unpub.

72. Son of the Wolf (Ulvens Søn). Songs
for the play by Jeppe Aakjaer. 1908.

1. *Gamle Anders Røgters Sang*; 2. *Kommer
I snart, I Husmaend!*

fp: 14 November 1909, Aarhus Teater.

Pub. 1909, Hansen.

73. In memoriam P. S. Krøyer (Kantate
til Mindefesten for Krøyer). Cantata for
reciter, soloists, chorus and piano. 1909.
Text: L. C. Nielsen.

fp: 4 December 1909.
Unpub.

74. Cantata for the National Exhibition
at Aarhus (Kantate ved Landsudstillingen i
Aarhus). Composed with Emilius Bangert.
1909. Text: L. C. Nielsen.

fp: 18 May 1909, Aarhus, cond. Carl
Nielsen.
Unpub.

75. Hagbart and Signe. Music for the play
by Adam Oehlenschlaeger. 1910. Ded.
Marie and Hother Ploug.

fp: 4 June 1910, Ulvedalene Friluftsteatret,
cond. Carl Nielsen.
Unpub.

75a. Halloges Sang. For voice and piano.
From preceding. Pub. 1910, Hansen.

76. At the bier of a young artist (Ved en
ung Kunstners Baare). Andante lamentoso
for string orchestra. 1910. Composed for the
funeral of the painter Oluf Hartmann,
January 1910. Pub. 1942, Skandinavisk og
Borups (Skandinavisk Musikforlag.)

77. Paaske-Liljen. For male chorus a cap-
pella. 1910. Pub. 1910, Hansen.

78. Symphony No. 3 (Sinfonia espansiva)
Op. 27. 1910–11. Dated: 30 April 1911. Dur.
35'.

1. *Allegro espansivo*; 2. *Andante pastorale*;
3. *Allegretto un poco*; 4. *Finale: Allegro*.

3 fl, pic, 3 ob, ca, 3 cl, 3 bsn, cbsn; 3 hn,
3 tpt, 3 tmb, tuba; timp; strings; soprano and
baritone voices.

fp: 28 February 1912, Copenhagen, Royal
Orchestra, cond. Carl Nielsen.

fEbp: 20 May 1937, Sylvia Schierbeck,
Holger Bruus-Gaard and the Danish State
Broadcasting Symphony Orchestra, cond.
Erik Tuxen.

f London p: 7 May 1962, St. Pancras Town
Hall, Polyphonia Symphony Orchestra, cond.
Bryan Fairfax.

Pub. 1913, Kahnt.

79. Violin Concerto Op. 33. 13 December
1911. Dur. 34–35'.

1. *Praeludium (Largo—Allegro cavalleresco)*;
2. *Poco adagio—Rondo: Allegretto scherzando*.

2 fl, 2 ob, 2 cl, 2 bsn; 4 hn, 2 tpt, 3 tmb;
timp; strings.

fp: 28 February 1912, Copenhagen, Peder
Møller and the Royal Orchestra, cond. Carl
Nielsen.

fEp: 22 June 1923, Queen's Hall, Emil

Telmányi and the London Symphony Orchestra, cond. Carl Nielsen.

fEbp: 25 October 1946, Henry Holst and the BBC Northern Orchestra, cond. Charles Groves.

Pub. 1919, Hansen.

80. Song for the Children's Relief Day (Bornehjaelpsdagens Sang). (Johannes Jørgensen). 1911. Pub. 1916, Hansen.

81. Nearer, my God, to Thee (Naermere, Gud, til Dig). Paraphrase for wind orchestra. 1912.

fp: 22 August 1915, cond. Carl Nielsen. Unpub.

82. Violin Sonata No. 2 Op. 35. 13 August 1912. Dur. 20'.

1. *Allegro con tiepidezza*; 2. *Molto adagio*; 3. *Allegro piacevole*.

fp: 7 April 1913, Copenhagen, Axel Gade and Henrik Knudsen.

fEbp: 17 October 1947, Henry Holst and Frank Merrick.

Pub. 1919, Hansen.

83. Sankt Hansaftenspil. Music for a Midsummer Eve's play by Adam Oehlenschlaeger. 1913. Unpub.

84. Johs. Jørgensens Ungdomssang. For piano with words. June 1913.

85. Ak, Julesne fra Bethlehem. For soprano and male chorus. 1914. Text: Johs. Jørgensen.

fp: 18 December 1914, Emilie Ulrich and Studentersangforeningen. Unpub.

86. Fredlys din Jord (Anders W. Holm). For male chorus a cappella. 1914.

fp: 1914, Studenterforeningen. Pub. 1914 (privately lithographed).

86a. Fredlys din Jord. Version for voice and piano. Pub. 1914, Hansen.

87. Serenata invano. For clarinet, bassoon, horn, cello and double bass. May 1914. Dur. 11'.

fp: 13 April 1915, Copenhagen. fEbp: 6 February 1952, Wigmore Ensemble (Jack Brymer, Gwydion Brooke, Dennis Brain, William Pleeth and Eugene Cruft).

Pub. 1942, Skandinavisk og Borups.

88. A Score of Danish songs (En Snes danske Viser.). With Thomas Laub. Book One: 22 December 1914. Includes twelve songs by Nielsen.

fp: 13 April 1915, Emilie Ulrich, Carl Madsen and Anders Brems, acc. S. Levysohn. Pub. 1915, Hansen.

89. Faedreland. Music for a play by Einar Christiansen. 1915.

fp: 5 February 1916, Copenhagen, Royal Theatre. Unpub.

90. Barnets Sang (Johannes Dam). For piano with words. 1915. Pub. 1915, Hansen.

91. Hil dig, vor Fane (N. F. S. Grundtvig). For male chorus. 1915.

fp: 1915, Studentersangforeningen. Unpub.

92. In memoriam Franz Neruda. Prologue for reciter and orchestra. 1915. Text: Jul. Clausen.

fp: 11 October 1915. Unpub.

93. Carl Nielsen's Melody Book for Johan Borup's Song Book. 1915. Includes some songs by Nielsen published for the first time. Pub. 1916, Hansen.

94. Symphony No. 4 (The Inextinguishable —Det Uudslukkelige) Op. 29. 1915–16. Dated: 14 January 1916. Dur. 37'.

1. *Allegro*; 2. *Poco allegretto*; 3. *Poco adagio quasi andante*; 4. *Allegro*.

2 fl, pic, 3 ob, 3 cl, 3 bsn; 4 hn, 3 tpt, 3 tmb, tuba; timp; strings.

fp: 1 February 1916, Copenhagen, Musikforeningen, cond. Carl Nielsen.

fEp: 22 June 1923, Queen's Hall, London Symphony Orchestra, cond. Carl Nielsen.

fEbp: 16 May 1951, BBC Scottish Orchestra, cond. Ian Whyte.

Pub. 1916, Hansen.

95. Tre Kompositioner for Langeleg. *c.* 1916.

1. *Naar Solen skinner*; 2. *Det tunge Budskab*; 3. *Som Fisken i Vandet*.

345

96. A Score of Danish Songs (En Snes danske Viser). For voice and piano. With Thomas Laub. Book Two: 1916. Includes eleven songs by Nielsen of which three had previously been published in melody form (in No. 93).

fp: 13 April 1917, Emilie Ulrich, Carl Madsen and Anders Brems, acc. S. Levysohn. Pub. 1917, Hansen.

97. Chaconne Op. 32. For piano. 1916. Dur. 9–10'.

fp; 13 April 1917, Copenhagen, Alexander Stoffregen.

fEp: 21 April 1923, Aeolian Hall, Victor Schiøler.

fEbp: 26 October 1951, France Ellegaard. Pub. 1917, Hansen.

98. Prologue to the Shakespeare Memorial Celebrations. 1916. Danish text: Helge Rode.

fp: 24 June 1916, Elsinore, Kronborg Castle, Anders Brems.

98a. Ariel's Song. From preceding. Pub. 1916, Hansen.

99. Theme with variations (Thema med Variationer) Op. 40. For piano. 1916. Dur. 15' 30"–16'.

fp: 29 November 1917, Copenhagen, Alexander Stoffregen.

fEbp: 4 April 1953, France Ellegaard. Pub. 1920, Hansen.

100. Study after Nature (Studie efter Naturen) (Hans Christian Anderson). For voice and piano. 1916. Pub. 1916, Hansen.

101. Hymns and Sacred songs (Salmer og aandelige Sange). For piano with words. 1912–16. Forty-nine songs, the majority to words by N. F. S. Grundtvig or H. A. Brorson. Pub. 1919, Hansen. Four additional songs unpub.

102. Blomstervise ('Danmarks Sommer gik sin Gang') (Ludvig Holstein). For voice and piano. 1917. Unpub.

103. Hymne. For chorus, 1917. Privately printed.

104. Cantata for the centenary of the Merchants' Committee (Kantate til Gros-serersocietet). 1917. Text: Valdemar Rørdam.

fp: 23 April 1917, Emilie Ulrich, Nelge Nissen, Peter Jerndorff and Anders Brems, Musikforeningens Kor, cond. Carl Nielsen. Unpub.

104a. Hymne til Danmark (Danmark i tusind Aar) (Valdemar Rørdam). For voice and piano. From preceding. Pub. 1917. Hansen. Also version for unison chorus.

104b. Købmands-Vise (Valdemar Rørdam). For voice and piano. From No. 104. Pub. 1917, Hansen.

105. Pan and Syrinx Op. 49. Pastorale for orchestra. 6 February 1917. Ded. Anne Marie and Emil Telmányi. Dur 8–9'.

2 fl, 2 ob, 2 cl, 2 bsn; 4 hn, 2 tpt; timp, tamb pic, tgle, tamb, crotales, cinelli; strings.

fp: 11 February 1918, Copenhagen, Royal Orchestra, cond. Carl Nielsen.

fEp: 22 June 1923, Queen's Hall, London Symphony Orchestra, cond. Carl Nielsen.

fEbp: 14 June 1933, BBC Orchestra, cond. J. L. Mowinckel.

Pub. 1925, Hansen.

106. The Lie (Løgnen). Song for a play by J. Sigurjonsson. 1918. Unpub.

107. Aladdin Op. 34. Music for a play by Adam Oehlenschlaeger. 1918–19.

fp: 15 February 1919, Copenhagen, Royal Theatre.

fp (concert): 12 November 1925, Dansk Koncertforening, cond. Carl Nielsen.

107a. Seven Pieces from 'Aladdin' Op. 34. For orchestra. Dur. 25'.

1. *Oriental festival march*; 2. *Aladdin's dream and Dance of the morning mists*; 3. *Hindu dance*; 4. *Chinese dance*; 5. *The market-place at Ispahan*; 6. *Prisoners' dance*; 7. *Negro dance*.

2 fl, 2 ob, 2 cl, 2 bsn; 4 hn, 2 tpt, 3 tmb, tuba; timp, xyl, tamb, tamb roulante, cym, tgle; celesta, strings.

fEp: 4 July 1959, Northern Polytechnic, Modern Symphony Orchestra, cond. Arthur Dennington.

Pub. Skandinavisk Musikforlag. Also Nos. 1, 2, 3, 4, & 7 for small orchestra, pub. 1926.

107b. Three Songs from 'Aladdin' Op. 34. For voice and piano. 1918.

1. *Cither, lad min Bøn dig røre*; 2. *Visselulle nu, Narnlil*; 3. *Alt oprejst Maanen staar.*
Pub. 1919, Hansen.

108. Christianshavn (O. Bauditz). For piano with words. 1916–18. Pub. *c.* 1918, Nodetrykkeriet Presto (Copenhagen).

109. Suite (Den Luciferiske) Op. 45. For piano. August 1919 (?rev. 1920). Ded. Artur Schnabel. Dur. 21'.
1. *Allegretto un pochettino*; 2. *Poco moderato;* 3. *Molto adagio e patetico*; 4. *Allegretto innocente*; 5. *Allegretto vivo*; 6. *Allegro non troppo ma vigoroso.*
fp: 14 March 1921, Copenhagen, Johanne Stockmarr.
fEbp: 4 March 1954, Arne Skjold Rasmussen
Pub. 1923, Peters.

110. To aandelige Sange. For piano with words. 1917–19.
1. *Den store Mester kommer* (B. S. Ingemann).
2. *Udrundne er de gamle Dage* (N. F. S. Grundtvig).
Pub. July 1919 in *Nordens Musik*; Choral arr. of No. 2 pub. 1921, Hansen.

111. Gry (H. Lorenzen). For piano with words. 1919–20. Pub. 1920. Hansen.

112. Moderen (The Mother) Op. 41. Music for the play by Helge Rode. 1920.
fp: 30 January 1921, Copenhagen, Royal Theatre, cond. Ebbe Hamerik.
Pub. 1921, Hansen: piano score.

112a. Moderen: Prelude to the Seventh Picture. Dur. 2½'.
2 fl, 2 ob, 2 cl, 2 bsn; 4 hn, 3 tmb; timp; strings.
Pub. 1955. Hansen. Also arr. for small orchestra by Walther Schrøder.

112b. Moderen: Suite. Arr. Emil Reesen.
1. *Marsch*; 2. *Prinsesse Tove*; 3. *Menuet*; 4. *Faedrelandssang.*
fl, ob, 2 cl, bsn; 2 hn, 2 tpt, tmb; timp; piano, strings.
Pub. 1942, Hansen.

112c. Faith and hope are playing (Tro og håb spiller). Duet for flute and viola, from 'Moderen'. Dur. 2'. Pub. 1952, Hansen. Also for flute solo.

112d. The fog is lifting (Taagen leeter). For flute and piano or harp, from 'Moderen'. Dur. 3½'. Pub. 1952, Hansen.

113. Twenty popular melodies (Tyve folkelige Melodier). For voice and piano or piano with words. 1917–21. Twenty songs of which thirteen are for piano with words. Pub. 1921, Hansen.

114. Springtime on Fyn (Fynsk Foraar) Op. 42. Lyric Humoresque for soprano, tenor. bass-baritone, mixed chorus and orchestra, 1921. Text: Aage Berntsen. Dur. 18–19'.
2 fl, 2 ob, 2 cl, 2 bsn; 4 hn, 2 tpt; timp; tgle; strings.
fp: 8 July 1922, Odense, Dagny Møller, Poul Widemann, Albert Høeberg, Dansk Korforening, cond. Georg Høeberg.
Pub. 1921 (piano score), 1945 (score), Hansen.

115. Symphony No. 5 Op. 50. 1921–22. Dated: 15 January 1922. Ded. Vera and Carl Johan Michaelsen. Dur. 39–40'.
1. *Tempo giusto—Adagio*; 2. *Allegro—Presto—Andante poco tranquillo—Allegro.*
3 fl, 2 ob, 2 cl, 2 bsn, cbsn; 4 hn, 2 tpt, 3 tmb, tuba; timp, cym, tgle, tamb, side dm; celesta, strings.
fp: 24 January 1922, Copenhagen, Musikforeningen, cond. Carl Nielsen.
fEbp: 17 October 1948, London Philharmonic Orchestra, cond. Erik Tuxen.
fGBp: 1950, Edinburgh Festival, Danish State Radio Orchestra, cond. Erik Tuxen.
Pub. 1926, Borups and Dania; 1950, Skandinavisk og Borups.

116. Cosmus. Music for a play by Einar Christiansen. 1921–2.
fp: 25 February 1922, Copenhagen, Royal Theatre.
Unpub.

117. Sof sött. For voice and piano. 1 March 1922. Ded. Veninde Sonja Helleberg. Unpub.

118. Quintet Op. 43. For flute, oboe/cor anglais, clarinet, horn and bassoon. April 1922. Ded. Paul Hagemann, S. Felumb, Aage Oxenvad, Knud Lassen and Hans Sørensen. Dur. 25'.

Nielsen, Carl

1. *Allegro ben moderato*; 2. *Menuet*; 3. *Praeludium* (*Adagio*)—*Tema con variazioni*.

f public p: 9 October 1922, Copenhagen, Copenhagen Wind Quintet (Paul Hagemann, Sv. Chr. Felumb, Aage, Oxenvad, Hans Sørensen and Knud Lassen).

fEbp: 12 June 1952, Copenhagen Wind Quintet.

Pub. 1923, 1928, Hansen.

119. Four folk melodies (Fire folkelige Melodier), For piano with words. August 1922.

1. *Laer mig, nattens stjerne* (Chr. Richardt).
2. *Sangen har lysning* (Bj. Björnson).
3. *Hvad synger du om* (C. Hostrup).
4. *Nu skal det åbenbares* (N. F. S. Grundtvig).

Pub. 1925, Hansen.

120. Homage to Holberg (Hyldest til Holberg). For soloists, chorus and orchestra. 1922. Text: Hans Hartvig Seedorff Pederson.

fp: 26 September 1922.

Unpub.

121. Song Book for the People's High Schools (Folkehøjskolens Melodibog). With Laub, Ring and Aagaard. 1922. Includes 33 songs by Nielsen, for piano with words, with a further five added to later editions. Pub. 1922, Hansen; and later editions.

122. Prelude and Theme with Variations Op. 48. For violin solo. 24 June 1923. Ded. Emil Telmányi. Dur. 15′–17′ 30″.

fp: 28 June 1923, London, Aeolian Hall, Emil Telmányi.

Pub. 1925, Peters.

123. Dansk Arbejde (Valdemar Rørdam). For piano with words. 1923. Pub. Hansen.

124. Christmas song: The Heavens darken, vast and silent (Julesang: Himlen mørkner) (Mogens Falck). For piano with words. 1923. Pub. 1923, Hansen.

125. Christmas song (Julesang: Kom Jul til Jord) (Ohs. Wiberg). For piano with words. 1923. Pub. 1923, Hansen.

126. Hjemlige Jul (Emil Bønnelycke). For piano with words. 1923. Pub. 23 December 1923, in *Magasinet*; 1926, Peder Friis.

126a. Hjemlige Jul. Version for voice and orchestra.

2 fl, 2 ob, 2 cl, 2 bsn; 4 hn, 2 tpt; timp; strings.

Unpub.

127. Ballad of the bear (Balladem om Bjornen) Op. 47. (Aage Bernsten, after C. J. L. Almquist). For voice and piano. 15 November 1923. Ded. Anders Brems.

fp: 13 January 1924, Copenhagen, Anders Brems, acc. Chr. Christiansen.

Pub. 1924, Hansen.

128. Danish National Anthem (Der er et yndigt Land) (Oehlenschlaeger). For SATTB chorus. 1924.

fp: 1 June 1924, Dansk Korforenings concert, cond. Georg Høeberg.

Pub. 1924, Hansen. Also version for SATB chorus, male chorus, voice and piano.

129. Danmark: Song Book (Sangbogen Danmark). With Hakon Anderson. 1924. Contains 44 melodies by Nielsen with a further eighteen incorporated in the revised edition. Pub. 1924, 1926–7 (revised edition), Hansen.

130. Det vi ved at siden Slangens Gift (C. Hostrup). For voice and piano. 1923–4. Unpub.

131. Hymne til Livet (Sophus Michaelis). For SSAA chorus. 1923–4.

fp: 12 March 1925, Damekoret Echo, cond. Poul Schierbeck.

Unpub.

132. Ten Little Danish Songs (Ti danske Smaasange). For voice and piano. 1923–4. Pub. 1926, Borups. Arr. for male chorus by Hakon Anderson pub. *c.* 1927.

133. Four Jutish songs (Fire Jydske Sange) (Anton Berntsen). For voice and piano. 1924–5. Pub. 1941, Skandinavisk og Borups.

134. Symphony No. 6 (Sinfonia semplice). 1924–5. Dated: 5 December 1925. Ded. Royal Orchestra, Copenhagen. Dur. 32–33′.

1. *Tempo giusto*; 2. *Humoreske* (*Allegretto*); 3. *Proposta seria* (*Adagio*); 4. *Thema med Variationer*.

2 fl, 2 ob, 2 cl, 2 bsn; 4 hn, 2 tpt, 3 tmb,

tuba; timp, glock, tgle, cym, side dm; strings.
fp: 11 December 1925, Copenhagen, Royal Orchestra, cond. Carl Nielsen.
fEp: 29 March 1954, Royal Festival Hall, Royal Philharmonic Orchestra, cond. Anthony Bernard.
Pub. Samfundet (revised edition, 1957).

BIBLIOGRAPHY:
Hugh Ottaway: Nielsen's Sixth Symphony, *MT*, July 1954, p. 363.

135. Ebbe Skammelsen. Music for a play by H. Bergstedt. 1925.
fp: 25 June 1925, Ulvedalene, Friluftsteatret.
Unpub.

136. Foraarsang (Marinus Børup). For chorus. 1926.
fp: 30 May 1926, Aarhus, Katedralskoles Børupfest.
Privately printed.

137. Flute Concerto. 1 October 1926. Florence. Dur. 18–21'.
1. *Allegro moderato*; 2. *Allegretto*.
2 ob, 2 cl, 2 bsn; 2 hn, bs tmb; timp; strings.
fp: 21 October 1926, Paris, Carl Nielsen concert, Salle Gaveau, Holger Gilbert Jesperson, cond. Emil Telmányi.
fp (new version, with revised last movement): 9 November 1926, Oslo.
fEp: 19 August 1953, BBC broadcast, Geoffrey Gilbert and the London Chamber Orchestra, cond. Anthony Bernard.
fEp (concert): 22 February 1954, Royal Festival Hall, Geoffrey Gilbert and the Royal Philharmonic Orchestra, cond. Anthony Bernard.
Pub. 1952, Samfundet.

138. New melodies for Johan Borup's Danish Song Book (Nye melodier til Borups Sangbog). 1926. Pub. Borup.

139. Det är höst (Alma Rogberg). For voice and piano. 1926. Unpub.

140. Dansk Vejr (Ove Rode). For piano with words. 1927. Pub. 1927, Borups.

141. An Imaginary Trip to the Faroe Islands (En Fantasirejse til Faerøerne). Rhapsodic Overture for orchestra. 6 November 1927. Dur. 10'.
3 fl, 2 ob, 2 cl, 2 bsn; 4 hn, 2 tpt, 3 tmb; timp, side dm, GC, cym, tgle; strings.
fp: 27 November 1927, Copenhagen, Royal Orchestra, cond. Carl Nielsen.
Pub. 1942, Skandinavisk og Borups.

142. Vocalise-Etude. For soprano and piano. 1927. Pub. 1928, Leduc.

143. Tillaeg til Folkehøjskolens Melodibog. 1927. Contains eighteen songs by Nielsen for piano with words.

144. Den traenger ud til hvert et sted (C. Hostrup). For piano with words. Pub. April 1928, in *Tidsskrift for dansk Folkeoplysning*.

145. Guldfloden (B. S. Ingemann). For piano with words. 1927. Pub. 1928, in *Ubberup Højskoles Aarsskrift*.

146. Preludio e Presto Op. 52. For violin solo. 1927–8. Dated: 28 March 1928. Ded. Fini Henriques. Dur. 12'.
fp: 14 April 1928, Copenhagen, Emil Telmányi.
Pub. 1930, Carl Nielsen; Samfundet.

147. Clarinet Concerto Op. 57. 15 August 1928. Ded. Aage Oxenvad. Dur. 24–27'.
2 bsn; 2 hn; side dm; strings.
f public p: 11 October 1928, Copenhagen, Aage Oxenvad and the Royal Orchestra, cond. Emil Telmányi. (NB: A private performance had been given on 14 September at Humlebaek by the same players.)
fEp (public): 5 February 1952, Wigmore Hall, Frederick Thurston and the Haydn Orchestra, cond. Harry Newstone.
Pub. 1931, Samfundet.

148. Bohemian-Danish Folksong (Bøhmisk dansk Folketone). Paraphrase for string orchestra. 24 October 1928. Dur. 8'.
fp: 1 November 1928, Copenhagen, State Radio Orchestra, cond. Jaroslav Krupka.
Pub. 1942, Skandinavisk og Borups.

149. Three Piano Pieces (Tre Klaverstykker) Op. 59. 1928.
1. *Impromptu: Allegro fluente*. 15 January 1928.

Nielsen, Carl

2. *Molto adagio.* 1 March 1928.
3. *Allegro non troppo.* 6 November 1928.
fp: 14 April 1929, Copenhagen, Chr. Christiansen.
fEbp: 2 May 1954, Arne Skjold Rasmussen.
Pub. 1937, Dania.

150. Canto serioso. For piano and horn. 1928 Pub. 1944, Skandinavisk Musikforlag. Also arr. by the composer for piano and cello.

151. Velkommen, Laerkelil (Chr. Richardt) For piano with words. 1928. Unpub.

152. Island. For recitation and orchestra. 29 October 1929. Text: Otto Lagoni. Scored by Emil Reesen. Unpub.

153. 29 Short Preludes Op. 51. For organ or harmonium. January–February 1929.
fp: 23 January 1930, Skovshoved Church, Poul Schierbeck.
Pub. 1930, Skandinavisk og Borups.

154. To efterladte Praeludier. For organ or harmonium. 1929. Pub. 1947, Skandinavisk Musikforlag.

155. To Skolesange (Viggo Stuckenberg). For SATB chorus. 1929. Unpub.

156. Three Motets (Tre Motetter) Op. 55. For mixed chorus a cappella. 1929. Ded. The Palestrina Choir and Mogens Wöldike. Dur. c. 15'.
1. *Afflictus sum.* For ATTB. 15 June 1929.
2. *Dominus regit me.* For SATB. 25 May 1929.
3. *Benedictus Dominus.* For SSATB. 28 June 1929.
fp: April 1930, Copenhagen, Palestrina Choir, cond. Mogens Wöldike.
fEbp (Nos. 2 & 3): 31 October 1951, BBC Singers, cond. Mogens Wöldike.
Pub. 1931, Skandinavisk og Borups.

157. Cantata for the centenary of the Polytechnic High School (Kantate til Polyteknisk Laereanstalt). For recitation, chorus and orchestra. 5 August 1929. Text: Hans Hartvig Petersen.
fp: 30 August 1929, Studentersangforeningen and Livgardens Orchestra, cond. Johan Hye-Knudsen.
Pub. choral score privately lithographed.

158. Hymn to Art (Hymne til Kunsten) (Sophus Michaelis). For soprano, tenor, chorus and wind orchestra. 1929. Dur. 10'.
fp: 12 October 1929, cond. Carl Nielsen.
Unpub.

159. Hjemstavn (Frederik Poulsen). For voice and piano. 1929. Pub. 1940, Hansen.

160. Der gaar et stille Tog (Harald Balslev & Uffe Hansen). For voice and piano. 1929. Pub. 1953, in *Ubberup Højskoles Aarsskrift.*

161. Til min Fødeø (S. P. Raben-Korch). For male chorus. 1929. Pub. 1934, Vilh. A. Langs (Odense). Also version for voice and piano arr. Kai Senstius.

162. Land of the future (Fremtidens Land) (Bj. Björnson). For piano with words. 28 November 1929. Pub. 1929, in *Ubberup Højskoles Aarsskrift.*

163. Denmark, now the clear night sleeps (Danmark, nu blunder den lyse Nat) (Thøger Larsen). For piano with words. 20 December 1929. Pub. 1930.

164. Vi Jyder. Song from Bartrumsen's play 'Fra Rold til Rebild', for voice and piano. 1929. Pub. 1929, A. Kaaber (Aarhus).

165. Piano music for young and old (Klavermusik for Smaa og Store) Op. 53. Twenty-four five-finger pieces in two books. January–February 1930. Foreword dated: July 1930.
fEp: 1 October 1959, BBC broadcast, Liza Fuchsová.
Pub. 1930, Skandinavisk og Borups.

166. Ligbraendings-Kantate. For 5-part mixed chorus with acc. 1930. Text: Sophus Michaelis.
fp: 30 March 1930, Danish Radio.
?Unpub.

167. Amor and the Poet (Amor og Digteren). Music for the Hans Christian Andersen Festival in Odense. 22 May 1930. Text: Sophus Michaelis.
fp: 12 July 1930, Odense Theater, cond. Carl Nielsen.
Unpub.

167a. Italian shepherd's air: In un boschetto (Italiensk Hyrdearie) Op. 54 (Guido

Cavalcanti). For soprano and piano or harpsichord. From preceding.

fp: 12 July 1930, Odense Theater, Mary Alice Therp.

Pub. 1930, Skandinavisk og Borups.

167b. Vi elsker dig (Sophus Michaelis). For voice and piano. From 'Amor og Digteren'. Pub. 1930, Skandinavisk og Borups.

168. Gensyn (Fr. Paludan-Müller). For piano with words. 1930. Pub. 1930, in *Højskolebladet* No. 14.

169. Kanons. Six canons, for 2-part or 4-part chorus, in a collection of 60 Danish canons. 1930.

170. Cantata for the 50th anniversary of the Young Merchants' Education Association (Kantate, Foreningen til unge Handelsmaends Uddannelse). For recitation, solo, chorus, and orchestra. 1930. Text: Hans Hartvig Seedorff Petersen.

fp: 3 November 1930, with Thorkild Roose, Hoger Byrding, Palestrina Choir (Palestrinakoret), cond. Mogens Wöldike.

Unpub.

171. Sjølunds Sangere (Karl Elnegaard). For SATTB chorus a cappella. 1930. Privately lithographed. Arr. by Kristian Ribers for SATB, pub. 1932.

172. Commotio Op. 58. For organ. 27 February 1931. Dur. 30'.

fp: 14 August 1931, Aarhus Domkirke, Emilius Bangert.

fEbp: 30 December 1954, Svend Aage Spange, organ of St. Mark's, North Audley Street.

Pub. 1932, Kistner & Siegel/Skandinavisk og Borups.

BIBLIOGRAPHY:

A. Gibbs: CN's Commotio, *MT*, March 1963, p. 208.

173. Cantata for the 50th anniversary of the Danish Cremation Union. March 1931. Text: Sophus Michaelis. Unpub.

174. Easter Eve Play (Paaskeaftens). Music for a play by N. F. S. Grundtvig. 1931.

fp: 4 April 1931, Copenhagen, Royal Theatre.

Unpub.

175. Allegretto. For two recorders. Composed for C. M. Savery's School. 1931 Pub. 1931, Skandinavisk og Borup.

176. Kvadet om Nordens Harpe (Aage Berntsen). For male chorus. 1931. Privately lithographed.

177. Piano Piece in C major (Klaverstykke). 1931. Pub. 1 January 1932. in *Dansk Musiktidsskrift*.

178. What lightens over the field (Det, som lysner over Vangen) (Frederik Poulsen). For piano with words. 23 August 1931. ?Pub.

WRITINGS BY CARL NIELSEN

Levende Musik, Martins Forlag (Copenhagen) 1925; Eng. transl. Reginald Spink as 'Living Music', 1953.

Min fynske Barndom, Martins Forlag (Copenhagen) 1927; Eng. transl. Reginald Spink as 'My Childhood', 1953.

CNs Breve, Gyldensalske Boghandel Nordisk Forlag (Copenhagen) 1954.

Breve fra CN til Emil B. Sachs, Skandinavisk Grammophon Aktieselskab, 1953.

I anledning af, *Dansk Musiktidsskrift*, 1953, No. 4, p. 73.

GENERAL BIBLIOGRAPHY

Jürgen Balzer: The dramatic music, in *CN, Centenary Essays*, p. 75.

William Behrend: CN, *RM*, 1 July 1927, p. 75.

— CN, *RM*, February 1932, p. 133.

— Zum Tode von CN, *NZfM*, November 1930, p. 989.

J. Bentzon: CN und der Modernismus, *Melos*, December 1927.

Gerard Bourke: Denmark's CN, *MO*, December 1962, p. 147.

Graham Carritt: CN, Danish composer, *MMR*, 1947, p. 211.

Fritz Crome: CNs 60. Geburtstag, *Signale*, 1925, No. 32, p. 1255.

— CN, *Signale*, 1931, No. 42 (7 October), p. 981.

Ludvig Dolleris: CN, en Musikografi, Fyns Boghandels Forlag/Viggo Madsen (Odense) 1949.

Leonard Duck: The case for CN, *MO*, May 1951, p. 401.

Nielsen, Carl

René Elvin: Who is this CN?, *M&M*, March 1953, p. 7.
Johannes Fabricius: CN, en billedbiografi (A pictorial Biography), Berlingske Forlag, n.d.; text in Danish and English.
Dan Fog: CN Kompositioner, Nyt Nordisk Forlag/Arnold Busck (Copenhagen) 1965.
Peter Garvie: CN, *Canadian Music Journal*, winter 1961, No. 2, p. 20.
Dudley Glass: Symphonist from the soil, *Halle*, January 1957, p. 2.
— CN's centenary, *MO*, June 1965, p. 529.
Poul Hamburger: Orchestral works and chamber music, in *CN Centenary Essays*, p. 19.
Knud Jeppesen: CN, *MR*, 1946, p. 170.
B. Johnnson: Et nyt 'Credo', *Dansk Musiktidsskrift*, 1953, No. 1, p. 4.
Robert Layton: CN and the stage, *The Listener*, 7 May 1959, p. 818.
— Nielsen and the string quartet, *The Listener*, 11 August 1960, p. 238.
H. Lenz: CN—'et stridens aeble', *Dansk Musikkultur*, October 1954, p. 86.
Sven Lunn: CN skildret af Henrik Knudsen, *Nordisk Musikkultur*, October 1957, p. 75.
J. Maegaard: Den sene CN, *Dansk Musiktidsskrift*, 1953, No. 4, p. 74.
S. Martinotti: Sibelius e Nielsen nel sinfonismo nordico, Chigiana, 1965.
Torben Meyer: CN, Kunstneren og Mennesket, Nyt Nordisk Verlag/Arnold Buseck (Copenhagen) 1947 (2 vols.).
— CN, *Musical America*, 1 November 1952, p. 8.
Thorvald Nielsen: Some personal reminiscences, in *CN Centenary Essays*, p. 7.
A. Nyman: CN, in *Musikalisk intelligens*, 1928, p. 202.
Hugh Ottaway: Impressions of CN, *Hallé*, February 1952, p. 6.
— Nielsen and Sibelius, *The Listener*, 25 February 1965, p. 313.
— CN, *M&M*, June 1965, p. 24.
— Some thoughts on CN, *MO*, January 1954, p. 211.
Anthony Payne: Nielsen's artistic scope, *The Listener*, 27 May 1965, p. 805.
Frede Schandorf Petersen: CN, the Danish composer, Press Department of the Ministry for Foreign Affairs (Copenhagen), n.d.

Andrew Porter: A CN festival, *MT*, November, 1953, p. 527.
— The CN Festival in Copenhagen, *London Musical Events*, November 1953, p. 527.
Charles Rose: CN, *Counterpoint* (Leeds), April 1958, p. 3.
Herbert Rosenberg: The concertos, in *CN Centenary Essays*. p. 47.
Nils Schiørring: The songs, in *CN Centenary Essays*, p. 117.
— CN, *Canon*, March–April 1960, p. 183.
E. Shawe: CN, *Canon*, August 1956, p. 17.
Desmond Shawe-Taylor: A CN festival, *New Statesman*, 12 September 1953, p. 285.
— Tribute to Nielsen: *New York Times*, 27 September 1953, Section 2, p. 7.
Arne Skjold-Rasmussen: The piano works, in *CN Centenary Essays*, p. 57.
Rudolf Simonsen: Dänischen Tonmeister CN, *Rheinische Musik-und Theater Zeitung*, 28 October 1922.
Robert Simpson: CNs Symfonier: en englaenders indtryk, *Dansk Musiktidsskrift*, 1952, No. 3, p. 90.
— CN Symphonist, Dent (London) 1952.
Søren Sørensen: The choral works, in *CN Centenary Essays*, p. 103.
Svend Erik Tarp: CN, a Danish view, *MT*, March 1949, p. 75.
Hans Tørsleff: CN, *AMZ*, November 1922.
Harold Truscott: The piano music of CN, *Chesterian*, No. 202, spring 1960, p. 103.
Fritz Tutenberg: CN zum 20. Todestage, *NZfM*, 1951, p. 526.
Finn Viderø: The organ works, in *CN Centenary Essays*, p. 69.
Nils L. Wallin: CN åt danskarna, *Prisma*, No. 2, p. 82.
John C. G. Waterhouse: Nielsen reconsidered, *MT*, 1965, June, p. 425, July, p. 515, August, p. 593.
Fleming Weis: CN and his art, *Chesterian*, No. 165, January 1951, p. 53.
J. H. Yoell: The big fist from the North, CN, *Hi Fi Music at Home*, February 1959, p. 20.

MISCELLANEOUS
Musikken og dens Maend, 4: CN, G. E. C. Gads Forlag, 1956.
CN, Centenary Essays, Nyt Nordisk Forlag/ Arnold Busck, 1965.

FRANCIS POULENC (1899–1963)

Born in Paris on 7 January 1899 Poulenc was descended from a line of Parisian craftsmen on his mother's side and from a deeply religious Aveyron family on his father's. Though he took piano lessons from Ricardo Viñes, as a composer he was very largely self-taught up to the time of his early success in 1917 with the *Rapsodie Nègre*. Soon after this he was conscripted into the French Army for three years. In his 'teens he was much influenced by the precocious talent of his exact contemporary Georges Auric and by the example of Erik Satie. The critic Henri Collet grouped together Auric and Poulenc, plus Milhaud, Honegger, Durey and Tailleferre, as *Les Six*; and in 1921 all collaborated (Durey excepted) to provide music for Jean Cocteau's scandal-provoking *Mariés de la Tour Eiffel*. But Poulenc soon returned to musical apprenticeship and between 1921 and 1924 took composition lessons from Charles Koechlin. He became well known as a pianist, especially as an accompanist, and from 1935 onwards partnered his friend the baritone Pierre Bernac in many recitals. In 1936 a spiritual crisis reawakened his dormant Catholicism. Poulenc stayed in occupied France between 1939 and 1945, having served again in the French army at the start of the war. He remained a bachelor and lived the greater part of his life in Paris, though with frequent visits to his country house at Noizay in the Touraine. He travelled further afield occasionally, notably with Milhaud to Italy and Vienna (where they met Schoenberg, Berg and Webern) in the early twenties, and with Bernac to the United States in the late forties. He died suddenly in Paris in January 1963.

CATALOGUE OF WORKS

1. Préludes. For piano. 1916. Unpub.

2. Rapsodie nègre. For piano, 2 violins, viola, cello, flute, clarinet and voice. Spring 1917, Paris; rev. 1933. Poem: 'Makoko Kangourou'. Ded. Erik Satie.
    1. *Prélude*; 2. *Ronde*; 3. *Honoloulou*; 4. *Pastorale*; 5. *Final*.
    fp: 11 December 1917, Paris, Théâtre du Vieux-Colombier, Jane Bathori concert, with Francis Poulenc (piano).

3. Trois Pastorales. For piano. 1918. Unpub. No. 1 rev. 1928 as No. 1 of Trois Pièces (see No. 30).

4. Toréador (Jean Cocteau). 'Chanson hispano-italienne' for voice and piano. 1918, rev. 1932. Ded. Pierre Bertin. Pub. 1933, Deiss.

5. Sonata for piano duet. June 1918, Boulogne-sur-Seine. Ded. Mlle. Simone Tilliard.
    1. *Prélude*; 2. *Rustique*; 3. *Final*.
    fEbp: 24 July 1933, Vitya Vronsky and Victor Babin.
    Pub. 1919, Chester.

6. Sonata for two clarinets. Spring 1918, Boulogne-sur-Seine; rev. 1945. Ded. Edouard Souberbielle.
    1. *Presto*; 2. *Andante*; 3. *Vif*.
    Pub. 1919, Chester: also reduction for piano solo by the composer.

7. Trois mouvements perpétuels. For piano. December 1918, Paris. Ded. Valentine Gross.
    1. *Balancé—Modéré*; 2. *Modéré;* 3. *Alerte*.
    fp: 1919, Paris, Lyre et Palette concert, Ricardo Viñes.
    fEbp: 10 October 1925, Manchester studio, Marcelle Meyer.
    Pub. 1919, Chester.

7a. Trois mouvements perpétuels. Version for orchestra.
    ?fp: 7 April 1927, Paris, Concerts Straram, cond. Walter Straram.
    fEbp: 26 October 1928, London Chamber Orchestra, cond. Anthony Bernard.

8. Le Bestiaire, ou Cortège d'Orphée (Guillaume Apollinaire). For voice and piano. 8 May 1919, Pont-sur-Seine. Ded. Louis Durey.
    1. *Le dromadaire*; 2. *La chèvre du Thibet*; 3. *La sauterelle*; 4. *Le dauphin*; 5. *L'écrevisse*; 6. *La carpe*.
    Pub. 1920, Eschig.

8a. Le Bestiaire. Version for voice, flute, clarinet, bassoon and string quartet. ?1919.
    fEbp: 4 February 1929, Arts Theatre Club, Claire Croiza.

8b. Le Bestiaire. Version for voice and orchestra.

Poulenc, Francis

fp: 17 March 1922, Paris, Salle du Conservatoire, Concerts Marthe Martine, cond. Roger Désormière.

9. Valse. For piano. July 1919, Pont-sur-Seine. Ded. Micheline Soulé. Pub. 1920, Demets (in 'Album des Six'); Eschig.

10. Cocardes (Jean Cocteau). For voice and piano. 1919. Ded. Georges Auric.
1. *Miel de Narbonne*; 2. *Bonne d'enfant*; 3. *Enfant de troupe*.
fp: 21 February 1920, Paris, Théâtre des Champs-Elysées, Koubitzky.
fEp: 20 April 1921, Aeolian Hall, Edward Clark concert, Gladys Moger.
fEbp: 14 July 1926, Newcastle station, Ellinora Hoggarth.
Pub. 1920, Editions de la Sirène.

10a. Cocardes. Version for voice, violin, cornet à piston, trombone, bass drum and triangle. 1919.

11. Suite in C. For piano. March 1920, Paris. Ded. Ricardo Viñes.
1. *Presto*; 2. *Andante*; 3. *Vif*.
fp: April 1920, Paris, Société Nationale de Musique, Ricardo Viñes.
Pub. 1920, Chester.

12. Impromptus (First Book). For piano. September 1920, Paris. Ded. Marcelle Meyer.
1. *Vite—Con fuoco*; 2. *Lent*; 3. *Allegro vivace*; 4. *Violent*; 5. *Andante*; 6. *Brusque*.
Pub. 1922, Chester.

13. Le Gendarme incompris. Incidental music (Jean Cocteau and Raymond Radiguet). 1921.
fp: May 1921, Paris, Théâtre des Mathurins. Unpub.

13a. Le Gendarme incompris: Suite. For orchestra.
1. *Overture*; 2. *Madrigal*; 3. *Finale*.
fEp: 11 July 1921, Prince's Theatre, ballet season.

14. Les Mariés de la Tour Eiffel. Ballet. Farce in one act by Jean Cocteau. Music by Georges Auric, Arthur Honegger, Darius Milhaud, Francis Poulenc and Germaine Tailleferre. 1921.
Poulenc's contributions: 1. *La Baigneuse de Trouville*; 2. *Discours du général*.

fp: 18 June 1921, Paris, Théâtre des Champs-Elysées, Ballets suédois; choreography, Jean Borlin.

BIBLIOGRAPHY:
Henri Béraud: Théâtre des Champs-Elysees—Les Mariés de la Tour Eiffel, *Mercure de France*, 15 July 1921, p. 449.

15. Promenades. Twelve pieces for piano. Summer 1921, Touraine. Ded. Artur Rubinstein.
1. *A pied*; 2. *En auto*; 3. *A cheval*; 4. *En bateau*; 5. *En avion*; 6. *En autobus*; 7. *En voiture*; 8. *En chemin de fer*; 9. *A bicyclette*; 10. *En diligence*.
fEp: 4 July 1923, Wigmore Hall, Artur Rubinstein.
Pub. 1923, Chester.

16. Esquisse d'une fanfare (Ouverture pour le Ve acte de 'Roméo et Juliette'). Summer 1921. Pub. 15 October 1921, in *Fanfare*, No. 2.

17. Chanson à boire (Anon., 17th century). For male choir (TTBB) a cappella. September 1922, Touraine. Ded. Harvard Glee Club.
fEbp: 23 April 1932, Wireless Chorus, cond. Stanford Robinson.
Pub. 1923, Rouart Lerolle.

18. Sonata for clarinet and bassoon. September 1922, Touraine. Ded. Audrey Parr.
1. *Allegro*; 2. *Romance*; 3. *Final (Très animé)*.
fEbp: 23 January 1931, Reginald Kell and Gilbert Vinter.
Pub. 1924, Chester. Also reduction for piano solo by the composer, 1925.

19. Sonata for horn, trumpet and trombone. August-October 1922, Houlgate-Touraine; revised, 1945. Ded. Mlle Raymonde Linossier.
1. *Allegro moderato*; 2. *Andante*; 3. *Rondeau (Animé)*.
?fEbp: 10 November 1952, Dennis Brain, William Overton and John Ashby.
Pub. 1924, Chester. Also reduction for piano solo by the composer, 1925.

20. Les Biches. Ballet in one act with chorus. 1923, Touraine. Words: Anon., 17th century.
1. *Overture*; 2. *Rondeau*; 3. *Chanson dansée*;

4. *Adagietto*; 5. *Jeu*; 6. *Rag-Mazurka*; 7. *Andantino*; 8. *Petite chanson dansée*; 9. *Final*.

fp: 6 January 1924, Théâtre de Monte-Carlo, cond. Edouard Flament; with Fouquet (tenor), Cérésol (baritone), Mme. Romanitza; scenery and costumes, Marie Laurençin; choreography, Nijinska; principal dancers, Vera Nemtchinova, Lydia Sokolova, Nijinska, Mme. Lubov Tchernicheva, Léon Woizikovsky, Anatole Vilzak.

fParis p: 26 May 1924, Théâtre des Champs-Elysées, cond. André Messager.

Pub. 1924, Heugel; reduction by Francis Poulenc, French and German text by J. Benoist-Méchin.

BIBLIOGRAPHY:

Jean Cocteau: Les Biches ... Notes de Monte-Carlo, *Nouvelle revue française*, 1924, No. 126, p. 275.

André Coeuroy: Jeune musique française, *Revue universelle*, 1 August 1924, p. 380.

Nigel Fortune: Les Biches, in *Decca Book of Ballet*, Muller (London) 1958, p. 233.

Darius Milhaud: FP et Les Biches, in *Etudes*, Claude Aveline (Paris) 1927, p. 61.

Boris de Schloezer: Théâtre S. de Diaghilew. I. Les Biches, II. Les Fâcheux, *Nouvelle revue française*, 1924, No. 133, p. 508.

20a. Les Biches: Suite. Suite for orchestra. Re-orchestrated. May 1939–January 1940, Noizay. Ded. Misia Sert. Dur. 15′ 30″.

I. *Rondeau* (Dur. 2′ 50″); 2. *Adagietto* (Dur. 3′ 10″); 3. *Rag-Mazurka* (Dur. 4′); 4. *Andantino* (Dur. 2′ 30″); 5. *Final* (Dur. 3′).

2 fl, pic, 2 ob, ca, 2 cl, bcl, 2 bsn, cbsn; 4 hn, 3 tpt, 3 tmb, tuba; timp, glock, tamb, small tamb, tamb mil, tamb de basque, cym, tgle, GC; hp, celesta, strings.

Pub. 1948, Heugel.

21. La Colombe. Gounod, recitatives by Francis Poulenc. 1923. Unpub.

22. Poèmes de Ronsard. For voice and piano. 1924–5.

1. *Attributs*. December 1924, Amboise. Ded. Mme. Charles Peignot.

2. *Le tombeau*. December 1924, Amboise. Ded. Marya Freund.

3. *Ballet*. December 1924. Amboise. Ded. Vera Janacopoulos.

4. *Je n'ai plus que les os*. January 1925, Amboise. Ded. Mme. Croiza.

5. *A son page*. January 1925, Amboise. Ded. Jane Bathori.

fp: 10 March 1925, Paris, Salle des Agriculteurs, Marcelle Meyer concert, Mme Charles (Suzanne) Peignot and Francis Poulenc.

fEbp (Nos. 1 & 3): 28 December 1931, Tatiana Makushina.

fEbp (No. 2): 12 March 1937, Marya Freund.

Pub. 1925, Heugel.

22a. Poèmes de Ronsard. Version with orchestra.

fp: 16 December 1934, Paris, Salle Gaveau, Suzanne Peignot and l'Orchestre Lamoureux, cond. Jean Morel.

23. Napoli. Suite for piano. 1922–25. Dated: September 1925, Nazelles. Ded. in memory of Juliette Meerovich.

1. *Barcarolle*; 2. *Nocturne*; 3. *Caprice italien*.

fp (excluding No. 3): 17 March 1924, Paris, Marcelle Meyer.

fEbp (No. 3 only): 12 March 1926, Manchester station, Marcelle Meyer.

fEbp (complete): 8 October 1926, Lucy Pierce.

Pub. 1926, Rouart Lerolle.

24. Chansons Gaillardes (Anon., 17th century). For voice and piano. 1925, Nazelles–1926, Clavary. Ded. Mme. Fernand Allard.

1. *La maîtresse volage*; 2. *Chanson à boire*; 3. *Madrigal*; 4. *Invocation aux Parques*; 5. *Couplets bachiques*; 6. *L'offrande*; 7. *La belle jeunesse*; 8. *Sérénade*.

fp: 2 May 1926, Paris, Salle des Agriculteurs, Pierre Bernac.

fEbp: 5 July 1933, Gilbert Moryn.

Pub. 1926, Heugel.

25. Trio for piano, oboe and bassoon. February–April 1926, Cannes. Ded. Manuel de Falla.

1. *Presto*; 2. *Andante*; 3. *Rondo* (*Très vif*).

fp: 2 May 1926, Paris, Salle des Agriculteurs, Auric-Poulenc concert. (NB: The second performance was given the following day at a *Revue Musicale* concert).

fEp: 8 December 1926, London Contemporary Music Centre concert. F. Ticciati, Léon Goossens and A. R. Newton.

fEbp: 5 July 1933, Francis Poulenc, Léon Goossens and Fred Wood.

Pub. 1926, Hansen.

BIBLIOGRAPHY:

André Schaeffner: Trio pour piano, hautbois et basson de FP, *RM*, May 1926, p. 295.

26. Pastourelle. For the one-act ballet 'L'Eventail de Jeanne'. 1927.

fp: 16 June 1927, Paris, private performance given by René and Jeanne Dubost, cond. Roger Désormière; choreography, Yvonne Franck and Alice Bourgat; costumes, Marie Laurençin; décor and lighting, Pierre Legrain and René Moulaërt; with Alice Bourgat.

f public p: 4 March 1929, Paris, Opéra, cond. J. E. Szyfer; choreography, Yvonne Franck and Alice Bourgat; with Tamara Toumanova, Mlle. Storms, Marcelle Bourgat, Odette Joyeux.

Pub. 1928, Heugel.

BIBLIOGRAPHY:

Maurice Brillant: L'Eventail de Jeanne, *RM*, 1 October 1927, p. 251.

26a. Pastourelle. Version for piano solo.
Pub. Chester.

27. Vocalise. For voice and piano. February 1927. Paris. Ded. to the memory of Evelyne Brélia.

?fp: 3 March 1928, Paris, Théâtre du Vieux-Colombier, Jane Bathori.

Pub. 1929, Leduc.

28. Airs chantés (Jean Moréas). For voice and piano. 1927–8.

1. *Air romantique*; 2. *Air champêtre*; 3. *Air grave*; 4. *Air vif.*

fp (incomplete): 3 March 1928, Paris, Théâtre du Vieux-Colombier, Jane Bathori.

fp (complete): 10 June 1928, Paris, Salle Chopin, Auric-Poulenc concert, Suzanne Peignot.

fEp (complete): 23 June 1929, BBC broadcast, Ninon Vallin.

Pub. Rouart Lerolle.

29. Deux Novelettes. For piano. 1927–8.

1. *C major.* October 1927, Nazelles. Ded. Aunt Liénard.

2. *B flat minor.* 1928, Amboise.

fp: 10 June 1928, Paris, Salle Chopin, Auric-Poulenc concert, Francis Poulenc.

fEbp: 20 December 1930, Henri Gil-Marchex.

Pub. 1930, Chester.

30. Trois Pièces. For piano. 1928. Ded. Ricardo Viñes.

1. *Pastorale.* 1918–28.
2. *Toccata.* 1928.
3. *Hymne.* 1928.

fp: 1928, Paris, Auric-Poulenc concert.

fEbp: (Nos. 2 & 3): 29 April 1936, Jehanne Chembard.

Pub. 1931, Heugel.

31. Concert Champêtre. For harpsichord and orchestra. April 1927–October 1928. Ded Wanda Landowska.

1. *Allegro molto*; 2. *Andante* (*Mouvement de Sicilienne*); 3. *Finale* (*Presto*).

2 fl, pic, 2 ob, ca, 2 cl, 2 bsn; 4 hn, 2 tpt, tmb, tuba; timp, xyl, tarolle & tambour (without timbre), tambour (with timbre), tamb de basque, tgle, GC, cym; strings (8–8–4–4–4).

f public p: 3 May 1929, Paris, Salle Pleyel, Wanda Landowska and l'Orchestre Symphonique de Paris, cond. Pierre Monteux.

fEp: 21 January 1931, Queen's Hall, Wanda Landowska and the BBC Symphony Orchestra, cond. Ernest Ansermet.

Pub. 1929 (reduction by composer), 1931 (min. score), Rouart Lerolle.

BIBLIOGRAPHY:

O. Corbiot: Le Concert Champêtre de FP, *L'Education musicale*, No. 133, December 1966.

André Schaeffner: Le Concert Champêtre pour clavecin et orchestre de FP, *RM*, May–June 1929, p. 75.

31a. Concert Champêtre. Version for piano and orchestra.

?fp: 10 March 1934, Paris, Salle Pleyel, Concerts Siohan, Mme. Durand-Texte, cond. R. Siohan.

fEp: 25 February 1939, Queen's Hall, Francis Poulenc and the London Philharmonic Orchestra, cond. Sir Thomas Beecham.

32. Hommage à Albert Roussel. For piano. 1929. Pub. Leduc.

33. Nocturne in C major. For piano. 1929. Ded. Suzette.
fEbp: 10 July 1936, Francis Poulenc.
Pub. 1932, Heugel.

34. Aubade. Choreographic Concerto for piano and 18 instruments. May–June 1929, Fontainebleau. Ded. Vicomte and Vicomtesse de Noailles. Dur. 21′.
1. *Toccata*; 2. *Récitatif: Les compagnes de Diane*; 3. *Rondeau*; *Diane et compagnes*; 4. *Entrée de Diane*; 5. *Sortie de Diane*; 6. *Presto: Toilette de Diane*; 7. *Récitatif: Introduction à la Variation de Diane*; 8. *Andante: Variation de Diane*; 9. *Allegro féroce: Désespoir de Diane*; 10. *Conclusion: Adieux et départ de Diane.*
2 fl, 2 ob, ca, 2 cl, 2 bsn; 2 hn, tpt; timp, strings (0–0–2–2–2).
fp (private): 18 June 1929, Paris, home of Vicomte and Vicomtesse de Noailles, with Francis Poulenc (piano); choreography, Nijinska; décor, Jean-Michel Franck.
fEp: 17 December 1929, Park Lane Hotel, New English Music Society concert, Francis Poulenc and the London Chamber Orchestra, cond. Anthony Bernard.
fFp (public): 21 January 1930, Paris, Théâtre des Champs-Elysées, with Vera Nemtchinova; choreography, Georges Balanchine.
fEbp: 5 September 1931, Queen's Hall, Promenade Concert, Francis Poulenc and BBC Symphony Orchestra, cond. Sir Henry Wood.
Pub. 1931, Rouart Lerolle; incl. min. score, reductions by the composer for piano solo or two pianos.

BIBLIOGRAPHY:
Terpander: Poulenc's Aubade, *The Gramophone* 1935, July p. 58, August p. 100.

35. Epitaphe. (Malherbe). For voice and piano. July 1930, Noizay. Ded. Raymonde Linossier. Pub. 1930, Rouart Lerolle.

36. Trois Poèmes de Louise Lalanne (Guillaume Apollinaire). For voice and piano. February 1931, Noizay. Ded. Comtesse Jean de Polignac.
1. *Le présent*; 2. *Chanson*; 3. *Hier.*

?fp: early 1932, Paris, Salle du Conservatoire, Concerts de la Sérénade, Roger Bourdin.
Pub. 1931, Rouart Lerolle. English version, Edward Agate; German version, Walther Klein.

37. Quatre Poèmes (Guillaume Apollinaire). For baritone or mezzo-soprano and piano. March 1931, Noizay.
1. *L'anguille*. Ded. Marie Laurençin.
2. *Carte postale*. Ded. Mme. Cole Porter.
3. *Avant le cinéma*. Ded. Mme. Picasso.
4. *1904*. Ded. Mme. Jean-Arthur Fontaine.
fEbp: 5 July 1933, Gilbert Moryn.
Pub. 1931, Rouart Lerolle.

38. Cinq Poèmes (Max Jacob). For voice and piano. July 1931, Nogent-sur-Marne– December 1931, Noizay.
1. *Chanson*. Ded. Marie Blanche.
2. *Cimetière*. Ded. Madeleine Vhita.
3. *La petite servante*. Ded. Suzanne Ch. Peignot.
4. *Berceuse*. Ded. Suzanne Balguerie.
5. *Souric et Mouric*. Ded. Eva Curie.
fp (Nos. 4 & 5): 24 May 1932, Paris, Salle du Conservatoire, Suzanne Peignot, acc. Francis Poulenc.
Pub. 1932, Rouart Lerolle.

39. Le Bal masqué. Cantata for baritone or mezzo-soprano, oboe, clarinet, bassoon, violin, cello, percussion and piano. February 1932, Noizay–10 April 1932, Cannes. Poem: Max Jacob. Ded. Vicomte and Vicomtesse de Noailles. Dur. 18′.
1. *Préambule et Air de Bravoure*; 2. *Intermède*; 3. *Malvina*; 4. *Bagatelle*; 5. *La dame aveugle*; 6. *Finale.*
fp: 20 April 1932, Hyères, home of Vicomte de Noailles, Gilbert Moryn (baritone), Francis Poulenc (piano.), cond. Roger Désormière.
fEbp: 1 June 1948, Pierre Bernac and Chamber Orchestra, cond. Leighton Lucas.
Pub. 1932, Rouart Lerolle.

39a. Caprice (d'après le Final du Bal masqué) For piano. May 1932, Paris.
fEbp: 5 June 1936, Stanislav de Niedzielski.
Pub. Rouart Lerolle.

39b. Capriccio (d'après Le Bal masqué). For two pianos. September 1952, Noizay. Ded. Sam. Barber. Pub. 1953, Rouart Lerolle.

40. Concerto in D minor for two pianos and orchestra. 1932. Ded. Princesse Edmond de Polignac.

1. *Allegro ma non troppo*; 2. *Larghetto*; 3. *Finale: Allegro molto.*

2 fl, pic, 2 ob, ca, 2 cl, 2 bsn; 2 hn, 2 tpt, 2 tmb, tuba; petit tamb, tamb mil, tamb, tamb de basque, GC, cast, tgle; strings.

fp: 5 September 1932, Venice, ISCM Festival, Francis Poulenc and Jacques Février, Orchestra of La Scala Milan, cond. Desiré Defauw.

fEp: 29 January 1933, Queen's Hall, Sunday Concert, Francis Poulenc and Jacques Février, London Philharmonic Orchestra, cond. Sir Thomas Beecham.

Pub. 1934, Rouart Lerolle.

41. Valse-improvisation sur le nom de Bach. For piano. 1932.

fEbp: 6 February 1946, Frank Laffitte.

Pub. 1932, La Revue musicale.

42. Six Improvisations. For piano. December 1932, Noizay.

1. *B minor. Presto ritmico.* Ded. Mme. Long de Marliave.

2. *A flat major. Assez animé.* Ded. Louis Duffey.

3. *B minor. Presto très sec.* Ded. Brigitte Manceaux.

4. *A flat major.* Presto con fuoco. Ded. Claude Popelin.

5. *A minor. Modéré mais sans lenteur.* Ded. Georges Auric.

6. *B flat major. A toute vitesse.* Ded. Jacques Février.

Pub. 1933, Rouart Lerolle.

43. Villageoises. Children's pieces for piano. February 1933, Montmartre.

1. *Valse Tyrolienne*; 2. *Staccato*; 3. *Rustique*; 4. *Polka*; 5. *Petite Ronde*; 6. *Coda.*

Pub. 1933, Rouart Lerolle.

44. Intermezzo. Incidental music (Jean Giraudoux). 1933.

fp: March 1933, Paris, Comédie des Champs-Elysées; with Valentine Tessier, Louis Jouvet, Pierre Renoir, Roman Bouquet and Robert Le Vigan.

45. Feuillets d'album. For piano. 1933.

1. *Ariette.* Ded. Yvonne Martin.

2. *Rêve.* Ded. Mme. A. Bassan.

3. *Gigue.* Ded. Marcelle Meyer.

Pub. 1933, Rouart Lerolle.

46. Improvisation No. 7 in C major. For piano. November 1933, Noizay. Ded. Comtesse A. J. de Noailles.

fEbp: 6 February 1946, Frank Laffitte.

Pub. 1934, Rouart Lerolle.

47. Bal de jeunes filles (Nocturne in A major). For piano. 24 December 1933, Paris. Ded. Janine Salles.

fEbp: 10 July 1936, Francis Poulenc.

Pub. 1934, Heugel.

48. Improvisation No. 9 in D major. For piano. January 1934, Noizay. Ded. Thérèse Dorny. Pub. 1934, Rouart Lerolle.

49. Nocturne No. 3 in F major. For piano. ?1934. Ded. Paul Collaer. Pub. 1934, Heugel.

50. Nocturne No. 4 in C minor. For piano. March 1934, Rome. Ded. Julien Green.

fEbp: 10 July 1936, Francis Poulenc.

Pub. 1934, Heugel.

51. Huit Chansons Polonaises. For voice and piano. 1934.

1. *La couronne* (Wianek). January 1934, Noizay. Ded. Ida Godebska.

2. *Le départ* (Odjazd). January 1934, Noizay. Ded. Misia Sert.

3. *Les gars polonais* (Polska mlodziez). January 1934, Paris. Ded. Mme. la Comtesse Elisabeth Potocka.

4. *Le dernier mazour* (Ostatni mazur). 30 April 1934, Paris. Ded. Marya Freund.

5. *L'adieu* (Pozegnanig). January 1934, Paris. Ded. Mme. Kochanska.

6. *Le drapeau blanc* (Biala choragiewka). February 1934, Noizay. Ded. Mme. Artur Rubinstein.

7. *La vistule* (Wisla). January 1934, Noizay. Ded. Wanda Landowska.

8. *Le lac* (Jezioro). 29 April 1934, Paris. Ded. Maria Modrakowska. Pub. 1934. Rouart Lerolle.

52. Nocturne No. 5 in D minor. For piano. ?1934. Ded. Jean Michel Frank. Pub. 1934. Heugel.

53. Improvisation No. 8 in A minor. For piano. May 1934, Noizay. Ded. Nora & Georges Auric. Pub. 1934, Rouart Lerolle.

54. Nocturne No. 6 in G major. For piano. May 1934, Noizay. Ded. Waldemar Streuger. Pub. 1934, Heugel.

55. Presto. For piano. July 1934, Le Tremblay. Ded. Vladimir Horowitz.
fEp: 26 October 1935, BBC Broadcast, Adolph Hallis.
Pub. Deiss.

56. Intermezzi. For piano. August 1934, Kerbastic.
1. *C major.* Ded. Dr. Raymond Mallet.
2. *D flat major.* Ded. Comtesse Jean de Polignac.
fEbp: 5 June 1936, Stanislas de Niedzielski.
Pub. 1934, Rouart Lerolle.

57. Improvisation No. 10 (Eloge des gammes) in F major. For piano. September 1934, Paris. Ded. Jacques Lerolle.
fEbp: 10 July 1936, Francis Poulenc.
Pub. 1934, Rouart Lerolle.

58. Badinage. For piano. December 1934, Noizay. Ded. Christiane.
fEp: 26 October 1935, BBC broadcast, Adolph Hallis.
Pub. Deiss.

59. Humoresque. For piano. ?1934. Ded. Walter Gieseking.
fEbp: 10 October 1937, Gwendoline Parke.
Pub. Rouart Lerolle.

60. Quatre chansons pour enfants. For voice and piano. 1934.
1. *Nous voulons une petite soeur* (Jean Nohain). 1934. Noizay. Ded. Marie-Blanche. Pub. 1935, Enoch.
2. *Le tragique histoire du petit René* (Jaboune). 1934, Besançon. Ded. Mme. H. Ledoux. Pub. 1935, Enoch.
3. *Le petit garçon trop bien portant* (Jaboune). Rondo for voice and piano. 1934, Vichy. Ded. Mario Beaugnies de St. Marceaux. Pub. 1937, Enoch.

4. *Monsieur Sans Souci* (Il fait tout lui-même) (Jaboune). 1934, Paris, Ded. Jean de Polignac. Pub. 1937, Enoch.

61. Villanelle. For pipe and piano. 1934. Ded. Mrs. Louise Dyre. Pub. 1934, Editions de l'Oiseau Lyre.

62. La Belle au bois dormant. Music for a film. 1935.

63. Nocturne No. 7 in E flat major. For piano. August 1935. Ded. Fred Timar. Pub. 1936, Heugel.

64. La Reine Margot. Incidental music (Edouard Bourdet). 1935. Composed in collaboration with Georges Auric.
fp: 1935, Paris, with Yvonne Printemps as Marguerite de Navarre.

65. A sa guitare (Ronsard). For voice and harp or piano. September 1935, Noizay. Ded. Yvonne Printemps.
fEbp: 5 October 1938, Maggie Teyte.
Pub. Durand.

66. Suite française (d'après Claude Gervaise). For 9 wind instruments. percussion and harpsichord. October 1935, Noizay.
1. *Bransle de Bourgogne*; 2. *Pavane*; 3. *Petite marche militaire*; 4. *Complainte*; 5. *Bransle de Champagne*; 6. *Sicilienne*; 7. *Carillon.*
2 ob, 2 bsn; 2 tpt, 3 tmb; tambour, cym, GC; hpschd.
Pub. 1948, Durand.

66a. Suite française. Version for piano, October 1935, Noizay. Ded. Edouard Bourdet.
fEbp: 10 February 1947, Francis Poulenc.
Pub. 1935, Durand.

67. Sept Chansons. For mixed chorus a cappella. April 1936, Noizay. (No. 1 dated March 1936, Noizay). Ded. André and Suzanne Latarget, and to the Chanteurs de Lyon.
1. *La Reine de Saba* (Jean Legrand); 2. *A peine défigurée* (Paul Eluard); 3. *Pour une nuit nouvelle* (Eluard); 4. *Tous les droits* (Eluard); 5. *Belle et ressemblante* (Eluard); 6. *Marie* (Apollinaire); 7. *Luire* (Eluard).
fp (No. 5 only): 15 November 1936, BBC broadcast, Ensemble, cond. Nadia Boulanger.

359

fp: 21 May 1937, Chanteurs de Lyon.
Pub. 1936, Durand.

68. Litanies à la Vierge Noire (Notre-Dame de Rocamadour). For women's or children's voices and organ. 22–29 August 1936, Uzerche.

fp: 17 November 1936, BBC broadcast, Ensemble, cond. Nadia Boulanger.
Pub. 1937, Durand.

69. Petites Voix (Songs for Children) (Madeleine Ley). Five easy choruses for 3-part children's choir a cappella. September 1936, Noizay.

1. *La petite fille sage* (The good little girl). Ded. Martine Paul Rouart.
2. *Le chien perdu* (The lost dog). Ded. Claude Lerolle.
3. *En rentrant de l'école* (When coming home from school). Ded. Emmanuel Hepp.
4. *Le petit garçon malade* (The little sick boy). Ded. Daniel Milhaud.
5. *Le hérisson* (The hedgehog). Ded. Jean Destouches.

Pub. 1936, Rouart Lerolle.

70. Les Soirées de Nazelles. For piano. Sketched, 1930. Dated: 1 October 1936, Noizay. Ded. to the composer's aunt Liénard.

1. *Préambule*; 2. *Variations*: (i) *Le comble de la distinction* (ii) *Le coeur sur la main* (iii) *La désinvolture et la discrétion* (iv) *La suite dans les idées* (v) *Le charme enjôleur* (vi) *Le contentement de soi* (vii) *Le goût du malheur* (viii) *L'alerte vieillesse*; 3. *Cadence*; 4. *Final*.

fp: 1 December 1936, BBC broadcast, Francis Poulenc.
fFp: 19 January 1937, Paris, Salle Gaveau, La Sérénade concert, Francis Poulenc.
Pub. 1937, Durand.

71. Tel jour, telle nuit (Paul Eluard). For voice and piano. 1936–7.

1. *Bonne journée*. January 1937, Lyon. Ded. Pablo Picasso.
2. *Une ruine coquille vide*. December 1936, Noizay. Ded. Freddy.
3. *Le front comme un drapeau perdu*. 27 January 1937, Monte Carlo. Ded. Nush.
4. *Une roulotte couverte en tuiles*. December 1936, Noizay. Ded. Valentine Hugo.

5. *A toutes brides*. January 1937, Paris. Ded Marie Blanche.
6. *Une herbe pauvre*. December 1936, Noizay. Ded. Marie Blanche.
7. *Je n'ai envie que de t'aimer*. December 1936, Noizay. Ded. Denise Bourdet.
8. *Figure de force brûlante et farouche*. January 1937, Paris. Ded. Pierre Bernac.
9. *Nous avons fait la nuit*. January 1937, Lyon. Ded. Yvonne Gouverné.

fp: 3 February 1937, Paris, Salle Gaveau, Pierre Bernac and Francis Poulenc.
fEbp: 23 February 1939, Pierre Bernac and Francis Poulenc.
Pub. 1937, Durand.

72. Bourrée au Pavillon d'Auvergne. For piano. 7 May 1937, Noizay. Ded. Marguerite Long. Pub. 1937, Deiss (in 'A l'Exposition'); Salabert.

73. Deux Marches et un Intermède. For chamber orchestra. June 1937. Composed for an entertainment at the Paris Exhibition (other contributions by Georges Auric). Ded. Antoinette d'Harcourt. Dur. 6'.

fl, ob, cl, bsn; tpt; strings.
1. *Marche 1889*. Dur. 1' 35".
2. *Intermède champêtre*. Dur. 2'.
3. *Marche 1937*. Dur. 1' 50".

fEbp: 25 June 1938, Boyd Neel Orchestra, cond. Boyd Neel.
Pub. 1938, Rouart Lerolle.

74. Mass in G major. For 4-part mixed choir a cappella. August 1937, Anost. Ded. to the memory of the composer's father.

1. *Kyrie* (Dur. 2' 30"); 2. *Gloria* (Dur. 2' 40"); 3. *Sanctus* (Dur. 1' 55"); 4. *Benedictus* (Dur. 3' 20"); 5. *Agnus Dei* (Dur. 4').

fp: May 1938, Paris, Dominican Chapel, Faubourg St. Honoré, Lyons Choir.
Pub. 1937, Rouart Lerolle.

75. Sécheresses (Edward James). Cantata for mixed chorus and orchestra. September–December 1937, Noizay. Ded. Yvonne de Casa Fuerte.

1. *Les sauterelles*; 2. *Le village abandonné*; 3. *Le faux avenir*; 4. *Le squelette de la mer*.

2 fl, pic, 2 ob, ca, 2 cl, 2 bsn; 4 hn, 2 tpt, 3 tmb, tuba; timp, tambour, tamb de basque, cym, tamtam; celesta, hp. strings.

fp: 1938, Paris, Concerts Colonne, cond. Paul Paray.

Pub. 1938 (voice parts), 1952 (score), Durand.

76. Trois Poèmes (Louise de Vilmorin). For voice and piano. December 1937. Ded. Marie Blanche de Polignac.

    1. *Le garçon de Liège*; 2. *Au-delà*; 3. *Aux officiers de la garde blanche.*

fp: 28 November 1938, Paris, Salle Gaveau, *La Sérénade* concert, with Francis Poulenc (piano).

fEbp: 12 November 1946, Geneviève Touraine, acc. Jean Michel Damase.

Pub. 1938, Durand.

77. Le Portrait (Colette). For voice and piano. March 1938, Paris. Ded. Hélène Jourdan-Morhange.

fp: 16 February 1939, Paris, Salle Gaveau, Pierre Bernac and Francis Poulenc.

fEbp: 27 June 1952, Pierre Bernac and Francis Poulenc.

Pub. 1939, Deiss.

78. Organ Concerto in G minor. For organ, string orchestra and timpani. April 1938, Noizay–August 1938, Anost. Ded. Princesse Edmond de Polignac.

fp: 21 June 1939, Paris, Salle Gaveau, *La Sérénade* concert, Maurice Duruflé and l'Orchestre Symphonique de Paris, cond. Roger Désormière.

?fEbp: 6 September 1950, Jeanne Demessieux and the BBC Northern Orchestra, cond. Joseph Post.

Pub. 1939, Deiss.

BIBLIOGRAPHY:
Norbert Dufourcq: Concerto en sol mineur pour orgue, orchestre à cordes et timbales par FP, *RM*, August–November 1939, p. 107.

79. Deux Poèmes de Guillaume Apollinaire. For voice and piano. 1938.

    1. *Dans le jardin d'Anna*. August 1938, Anost. Ded. Reine Bénard.

    2. *Allons plus vite*. May 1938, Noizay. Ded. Georges Auric.

fp: 16 February 1939, Paris, Salle Gaveau, Pierre Bernac and Francis Poulenc.

Pub. 1939, Rouart Lerolle.

80. La Grenouillère (Guillaume Apollinaire). For voice and piano. October 1938, Noizay. Ded. Marie-Blanche.

fp: 16 February 1939, Paris, Salle Gaveau, Pierre Bernac and Francis Poulenc.

Pub. 1939, Rouart Lerolle.

81. Priez pour Paix (Charles d'Orléans). For voice and piano. 28 October 1938, Noizay. Pub. 1939, Rouart Lerolle.

82. Nocturne No. 8 (pour servir de Coda au Cycle). For piano. December 1938, Noizay. Pub. 1939, Heugel.

83. Quatre Motets pour un temps de pénitence (Four Penitential Motets). For 4-part mixed choir a cappella. 1938–9.

    1. *Timor et Tremor*. January 1939, Noizay. Ded. M. L'Abbé Maillet. Pub. 1946, Rouart Lerolle.

    2. *Vinea mea electa*. December 1938, Noizay. Ded. Yvonne Gouverné. Pub. 1939, Rouart Lerolle.

    3. *Tenebrae factae sunt*. July 1938, Noizay. Ded. Nadia Boulanger. Dur. 3′ 35″. Pub. 1938, Rouart Lerolle.

    4. *Tristis est anima mea*. November 1938, Paris. Ded. Bournauck.

fEbp: 15 April 1953, Ensemble Chorale de Marcel Couraud.

Pub. 1946, Rouart Lerolle.

84. Miroirs brûlants (Paul Eluard). For voice and piano. 1938–9.

    1. *Tu vois le feu du soir*. August 1938, Anost. Ded. Pierre Bernac.

    2. *Je nommerai ton front*. 7 January 1939, Noizay. Ded. Marie-Laure.

fp: 16 February 1939, Paris, Salle Gaveau, Pierre Bernac and Francis Poulenc.

Pub. 1939, Salabert.

85. Ce doux petit visage (Paul Eluard). For voice and piano. April 1939, Noizay. Ded. to the memory of Raymonde Linossier. Pub 1941, Rouart Lerolle.

86. Fiançailles pour rire (Louise de Vilmorin). For voice and piano. September–October 1939, Noizay.

    1. *La Dame d'André*. Ded. Marie-Blanche.

    2. *Dans l'herbe*. Ded. Freddy.

    3. *Il vole*. Ded. Suzanne Peignot.

4. *Mon cadavre est doux comme un gant.* Ded. Ninon Vallin.

5. *Violon.* Ded. Denise Bourdet.

6. *Fleurs.* Ded. Solange d'Ayen.

Pub. 1940, Rouart Lerolle.

87. Bleuet (Guillaume Apollinaire). For voice and piano. October 1939, Noizay. Ded. André Bonnélie.

fEbp: 27 June 1952, Pierre Bernac and Francis Poulenc.

Pub. 1940, Durand.

88. Sextuor. For piano, flute, oboe, clarinet, bassoon and horn. 1932–9. Ded. Georges Salles. Dur. 20′.

1. *Allegro vivace* (Dur. 7′ 30″); 2. *Divertissement* (Dur. 5′ 30″); 3. *Finale: Prestissimo* (Dur. 7′).

fEp: 5 July 1933, BBC broadcast, Francis Poulenc, Robert Murchie, Léon Goossens, Haydn Draper, Fred Wood and Edmund Chapman.

fp (definitive version): 9 December 1940, Paris, Salle Chopin, Association Musicale Contemporaine concert, Quintette à vent de Paris.

fEp (definitive version): 3 December 1946, London Wind Quintet.

Pub. 1945, Hansen.

89. Deux Préludes posthumes et une Gnossienne. Erik Satie, orch. Francis Poulenc. 1939.

1. *Fête donnée par des Chevaliers Normands en l'Honneur d'une jeune Demoiselle.*

2 fl, 2 ob, 2 bsn, 2 hn; tpt, 2 tmb; strings.

2. *Ier Prélude du Nazaréen.*

ob, ca, 2 cl, 2 bsn; 2 hn, 2 tpt, 2 tmb; hp, strings.

3. *3ème Gnossienne.*

fl, ob, cl, 2 bsn; 2 hn; strings.

fEbp (No. 3): 11 September 1947, Leighton Lucas Orchestra, cond. Leighton Lucas.

fEbp (complete): 6 January 1952, Leighton Lucas Orchestra, cond. Leighton Lucas.

Pub. 1949, Rouart Lerolle.

90. Banalités (Guillaume Apollinaire). For voice and piano. October–November 1940.

1. *Chanson d'Orkenise.* November 1940, Paris. Ded. Claude Rostand.

2. *Hôtel.* October 1940, Noizay. Ded. Marthe Bosredon.

3. *Fagnes de Wallonie.* November 1940, Paris. Ded. Mme Henri Fredericq.

4. *Voyage à Paris.* October 1940, Noizay. Ded. Paul Eluard.

5. *Sanglots.* November 1940, Paris. Ded. Suzanne.

fp: 14 December 1940, Paris, Salle Gaveau, Pierre Bernac and Francis Poulenc.

Pub. 1941, Eschig.

91. Léocadia. Incidental music (Jean Anouilh) 1940.

91a. Les Chemins de l'Amour (Jean Anouilh). 'Valse chantée' from *Léocadia.* October 1940, Paris. Ded. Yvonne Printemps.

fEbp: 9 August 1952, Fanély Revoil, acc. Stanford Robinson.

Pub. Eschig.

92. Mélancolie. For piano. June 1940, Talence–August 1940, Brive. Ded. Raymond Destouches.

fp: 23 May 1941, Paris, Salle Gaveau, Marcelle Meyer. (NB: orig. announced for 9 May.)

Pub. Eschig.

93. Exultate Deo. For 4-part mixed choir a cappella. May 1941, Noizay. Ded. Georges Salles. Dur. 2′ 35″. Pub. 1941, Rouart Lerolle.

94. Salve Regina. For 4-part mixed choir a cappella. May 1941, Noizay. Ded. Hélène. Dur. 3′ 45″. Pub. 1941, Rouart Lerolle.

95. Improvisation No. 11 in G minor. For piano. June 1941, Paris. Ded. Claude Delvincourt. Pub. 1945, Rouart Lerolle.

96. Les Animaux modèles. Ballet in one act by Francis Poulenc after the Fables of La Fontaine. August 1940, Brive–September 1941, Noizay.

1. *Le Petit Jour*; 2. *L'Ours et les deux Compagnons*; 3. *La Cigale et la Fourmi*; 4. *Le Lion amoureux*; 5. *L'Homme entre deux âges et ses deux Maîtresses*; 6. *La Mort et le Bûcheron*; 8. *Le Repas de midi.*

fp: 8 August 1942, Paris, Opéra, cond. Roger Désormière; scenery and costumes, Maurice Brianchon, after Le Nain; choreography, Serge Lifar; with Mlle. Lorcia,

Solange Schwarz, Yvette Chauviré, Serge Peretti, Serge Lifar, Efimov.
Pub. 1942, Eschig (piano score.).

BIBLIOGRAPHY:
F. Reyna: Les Animaux Modèles, Opéra, *L'Information musicale*, 28 August 1942, p. 3.

96a. Les Animaux modèles: Ballet Suite. 1942.
fp: 7 March 1943, Paris, Salle du Conservatoire, Paris Conservatoire Orchestra, cond. Roger Désormière.

97. La Fille du jardinier. Incidental music (Exbrayat). 1941.

98. Improvisation No. 12 (Hommage à Schubert) in E flat major. November 1941, Paris. Ded. Edwige Feuillère. Pub. 1945, Rouart Lerolle.

99. La Duchesse de Langeais. Music for the film. 1942. Production, Films Orange; director, Jacques de Baroncelli; with Edwige Feuillère.

100. Chansons villageoises (Maurice Fombeure). For voice and piano. 1942.
1. *Chansons du clair tamis.* October 1942, Noizay. Ded. Louis Beydts.
2. *Les gars qui vont à la fête.* October–December 1942, Noizay-Paris. Ded. Jean de Polignac.
3. *C'est le joli printemps.* December 1942, Paris. Ded. Roger Bourdin.
4. *Le mendiant.* December 1942, Paris. Ded. André Schaeffer.
5. *Chanson de la fille frivole.* October 1942, Noizay. Ded. André Lecoeur.
6. *Le retour du sergent.* October 1942, Noizay. Ded. André Dubois.
fp: 28 June 1943, Paris, Salle Gaveau, *La Pléiade* concert.
Pub. 1943, Eschig.

100a. Chansons villageoises. Version for voice and chamber orchestra.
fl, pic, ob, ca, 2 cl, 2 bsn; 2 hn, tpt; hp, tgle, tamb, crécelle, whip, cym, glock, xyl, celesta; string quartet.
Pub. 1943, Eschig.

101. Intermezzo in A flat major. For piano. March 1943, Paris. Ded. Mme. Manty Rostand. Pub. 1947, Eschig.

102. Violin Sonata. Summer 1942–Easter 1943, Noizay; rev. 1949. Ded. to the memory of Federico Garcia Lorca.
1. *Allegro con fuoco*; 2. *Intermezzo: Très lent et calme*; 3. *Presto tragico*.
fp: 21 June 1943, Paris, La Pléiade concert, Ginette Neveu and Francis Poulenc.
fEbp: 10 March 1950, Campoli and Eric Gritton.
Pub. 1944, Eschig: violin part ed. Ginette Neveu.

103. Métamorphoses (Louise de Vilmorin). For voice and piano. 1943.
1. *Reine des mouettes.* Ded. Marie-Blanche.
2. *C'est ainsi que tu es.* August 1943, Beaulieu sur Dordogne. Ded. Marthe Bosredon.
3. *Paganini.* October 1943, Noizay. Ded. Jeanne Ritcher.
fEbp: 31 October 1943, Adrienne Cole, acc. Josephine Lee.
Pub. 1944, Rouart Lerolle.

104. Deux Poèmes (Louis Aragon). For voice and piano. 1943.
1. 'C'. September 1943, Noizay. Ded. Papoun.
2. *Fêtes galantes.* October 1943, Noizay. Ded. Jean de Polignac.
Pub. 1944, Rouart Lerolle.

105. Figure humaine (Paul Eluard). Cantata for double 6-part mixed choir a cappella. Summer 1943. Ded. Pablo Picasso.
fp: January 1945, BBC Choir, cond. Leslie Woodgate.
Pub. 1945, Rouart Lerolle. English version, Rollo H. Myers.

106. Le Voyageur sans bagages. Incidental music (Jean Anouilh). 1944.

106a. Le Voyageur sans bagages. Music for the film. 1944. Production, Eclair-Journal; director, Jean Anouilh; with Pierre Fresnay.

107. La Nuit de la Saint-Jean. Incidental music (James Barrie). 1944.

108. Les Mamelles de Tirésias. Comic Opera in two acts and a prologue. May–October 1944, Noizay. Libretto: Guillaume Apollinaire. Ded. Darius Milhaud.

fp: 3 June 1947, Paris, Opéra-Comique, cond. Albert Wolff; with Denise Duval (Thérèse and La Cartomancienne), Jane Atty (La Marchande de journaux), Irène Gromova (La Dame élégante), Yvonne Girard-Ducy (La grosse dame), Paul Payen (Le Mari), Emile Rousseau (Le Gendarme), Robert Jeantet (Le Directeur), Marcel Enot (Presto), Alban Derroja (Lacouf), Serge Rallier (Le Journaliste), Jacques Hivert (Le Fils), Gabriel Jullia (Le Monsieur barbu); producer, Max de Rieux; décor and costumes, Erté.

Pub. 1947, Heugel: vocal score.

BIBLIOGRAPHY:

Bernhard Gavoty: Les Mamelles de Tirésias, *Melos*, August–September 1947, p. 299.

R. Gelatt: Fare from France—recording of Les Mamelles de Tirésias, *Saturday Review*, 29 March 1954, p. 50.

Edward Lockspeiser: Tirésias at Aldeburgh, *Chesterian*, No. 196, autumn 1958.

M. Rivette: Father is a bachelor, *Opera* (San Francisco), March 1950, p. 18.

109. Un soir de neige. Short chamber cantata for six mixed voices or a cappella chorus. 24–26 December 1944. Poems: Paul Eluard. Ded. Marie-Blanche. Pub. 1945, Rouart Lerolle.

110. Montparnasse (Guillaume Apollinaire). For voice and piano. September 1941, Noizay-January 1945, Paris. Ded. Pierre Souvtchinsky. Pub. 1945, Eschig.

111. Hyde Park (Guillaume Apollinaire). For voice and piano. January 1945, Paris. Ded. to the memory of Audrey Norman Colville. Pub. 1945, Eschig.

112. Le Soldat et la Sorcière. Incidental music (Armand Salacrou). 1945.

113. L'Histoire de Babar (Babar the Elephant). For piano and reciter. Story: Jean de Brunhoff. 1940–5. Ded. 'For my little cousins Sophie, Sylvie, Benoit, Florence & Delphine Périer, Yvan, Alain, Marie-Christine & Margueritte-Marie Villotte, and my little friends Marthe Bosredon & André Lecoeur'. Dur. 22'.

fEbp: 5 September 1951, Pierre Bernac and Francis Poulenc.

Pub. 1949, Chester.

113a. L'Histoire de Babar. Version orch. Jean Francaix. 1962. Dur. 22'.

2 fl, pic, 2 ob, ca, 2 cl, bcl, 2 bsn, cbsn; 2 hn, 2 tpt, cornet, ten tmb, tuba; timp, tgle, caisse claire, GC, tambour, whip, 2 cym, tamtam, tamb, klaxon à manivelle, whistle; hp, strings.

Pub. 1963, Chester.

114. Chansons françaises. For mixed chorus a cappella. 1945-6. Ded. Henri Screpel.

1. *Margoton va t'a l'iau.* For SATB. August 1945, Larche.

2. *La belle se siet au pied de la tour.* For SATBarB. September 1945, Noizay.

3. *Pilons l'orge.* For SATBarB. August 1945, Larche.

4. *Clic, clac, dansez sabots.* For TBB. September 1945, Noizay.

5. *C'est la petit'fill' du prince.* For SATBarB. April 1946, Noizay.

6. *La belle si nous étions.* For TBB. April 1946, Noizay.

7. *Ah! mon beau laboureur.* For SATB. April 1945, Larche.

8. *Les tisserands.* For SATBarB. April 1946, Noizay.

fEbp: 24 April 1953, BBC Singers, cond. Leslie Woodgate.

Pub. 1948, Rouart Lerolle.

115. Deux Mélodies sur des poèmes de Guillaume Apollinaire. For voice and piano. 1946.

1. *Le pont.* July 1946, Le Tremblay. Ded. to the memory of Raymond Radiguet.

2. *Un poème.* 27 July 1946, Le Tremblay. Ded. Luigi Dallapiccola.

fEbp (No. 1): 27 June 1952, Pierre Bernac and Francis Poulenc.

Pub. 1947, Eschig.

116. Paul et Virginie (Raymond Radiguet). For voice and piano. August 1946, Noizay. Pub. 1947, Eschig.

117. Le Disparu (Robert Desnos). For voice and piano. Summer 1947, Le Tremblay. Ded. Henri Sauguet. Pub. 1947, Rouart Lerolle.

118. Main dominée par le cœur (Paul Eluard). For voice and piano. Summer 1947,

Noizay. Ded. Marie-Blanche. Pub. 1947, Rouart Lerolle.

119. Trois Chansons de F. Garcia Lorca. For voice and piano. 1947.

1. *L'enfant muet.* Summer 1947, Noizay. Ded. Geneviève Touraine.

2. *Adelina à la promenade.* September 1947, Noizay. Ded. Mme. Auguste Lambiotte.

3. *Chansons de l'oranger sec.* September 1947, Noizay. Ded. Gérard Souzay.

Pub. 1947, Heugel.

120. . . . Mais mourir (Paul Eluard). For voice and piano. October 1947, Noizay. Ded. 'to the memory of Nush'.

fEbp: 27 June 1952, Pierre Bernac and Francis Poulenc.

Pub. 1948, Heugel.

121. Amphytrion. Incidental music (Molière) 1947.

fp: 5 December 1947, Paris, Compagnie Madeleine Renaud-Jean-Louis Barrault; décor and costumes, Christian Bérard; director, Jean-Louis Barrault.

122. Sinfonietta. For orchestra. 1947, Noizay. Ded. Georges Auric. Dur. 24'.

1. *Allegro con fuoco*; 2. *Molto vivace*; 3. *Andante cantabile*; 4. *Finale: Prestissimo et très gai.*

2 fl, 2 ob, 2 cl, 2 bsn; 2 tpt, 2 tmb; timp; hp, strings.

fp: 24 October 1948, BBC broadcast, Philharmonia Orchestra, cond. Roger Désormière.

fEp (concert): 20 February 1950, Chelsea Town Hall, Chelsea Symphony Orchestra, cond. Norman Del Mar.

Pub. 1951, Chester.

123. Calligrammes (Guillaume Apollinaire). For voice and piano. July 1948. Dur. 9' 20".

1. *L'espionne.* May 1948, Noizay. Ded. Simone Tilliard. Dur. 1' 32".

2. *Mutation.* July 1948, Le Tremblay. Ded. Pierre Lelong. Dur. 40".

3. *Vers le Sud.* July 1948, Le Tremblay. Ded. Jacqueline Apollinaire. Dur. 1' 40".

4. *Il pleut.* August 1948, Noizay. Ded. to the memory of Emmanuel Fay. Dur. 1'.

5. *La grâce exilée.* July 1948, Le Tremblay. Ded. to the composer's sister Jeanne. Dur. 28".

6. *Aussi bien que les cigales.* August 1948, Noizay. Ded. Jacques Soulé. Dur. 1' 40".

7. *Voyage.* July 1948, Le Tremblay. Ded. to the memory of Raymonde Linossier.

fEp: 14 February 1949, BBC broadcast, Pierre Bernac and Francis Poulenc.

Pub. 1948, Heugel.

124. Quatres petites prières de Saint François d'Assise. For male chorus a cappella. Summer 1948, Noizay. Ded. 'Aux Frères mineurs de Champfleury et spécialement à Frère Jérôme en souvenir de son grand-père: mon oncle, Camille Poulenc.'

1. *Modéré, mais sans lenteur*; 2. *Majestueux et éclatant*; 3. *Très expressif et fervent*; 4. *Bien calme.*

Pub. 1949, Rouart Lerolle.

125. Cello Sonata. April–October 1948, Noizay. Ded. Marthe Bosredon and Pierre Fournier. Dur. 21' 25".

1. *Allegro: tempo di Marcia* (Dur. 5' 25"); 2. *Cavatine: Très calme* (Dur. 6' 30"); 3. *Ballabile: Très animé et gai* (Dur. 3' 20"); *Finale: Largo—Presto* (Dur. 6' 10").

fp: 18 May 1949, Paris, Pierre Fournier and Marthe Bosredon.

fEp: 15 June 1949, BBC broadcast, Pierre Fournier and Francis Poulenc.

Pub. 1949, Heugel.

126. Mazurka (Louise de Vilmorin). For voice and piano. July 1949, Le Tremblay. Pub. 1949, Heugel (in *Mouvements du Coeur*).

127. Piano Concerto. May–October 1949, Noizay. Ded. Denise Duval and Raymond Destouches.

1. *Allegretto*; 2. *Andante con moto*; 3. *Rondeau à la française.*

?fp: January 1950, Boston, Francis Poulenc and the Boston Symphony Orchestra, cond. Charles Münch.

fEp: 8 November 1950, Royal Albert Hall, Francis Poulenc and the BBC Symphony Orchestra, cond. Basil Cameron.

Pub. 1950, Salabert: reduction.

128. La Fraîcheur et le feu (Paul Eluard). For voice and piano. April 1950, Noizay–July 1950, Brive. Ded. Igor Stravinsky.

1. *Rayon des yeux . . .*; 2. *Le matin les branches attisent*; 3. *Tout disparut . . .*; 4. *Dans*

les ténèbres du jardin; 5. *Unis la fraîcheur et le feu* ...; 6. *Homme au sourir tendre* ...; 7. *La grande rivière qui va* ...
fbp: 16 November 1950, BBC broadcast, Pierre Bernac and Francis Poulenc.
Pub. 1951, Eschig.

129. Stabat Mater. For soprano, mixed choir (SCTBarB) and orchestra. Ded. to the memory of Christian Bérard. Summer 1950, Noizay.
2 fl, pic, 2 ob, ca, 2 cl, bcl, 3 bsn; 4 hn, 3 tpt, 3 tmb, tuba; timp; 2 hp, strings.
fp: 13 June 1951, Strasbourg Festival, Geneviève Moizan, les Choeurs de Saint-Guillaume and l'Orchestre Municipal de Strasbourg, cond. Fritz Münch.
fEp: 8 September 1955, Hereford, Three Choirs Festival, Jennifer Vyvyan, Festival Choir and London Symphony Orchestra, cond. Meredith Davies.
Pub. 1951, Rouart Lerolle: vocal score.

130. L'Embarquement pour Cythère. Valse-Musette for two pianos. July 1951, Paris. Ded. Henri Lavorelle. Pub. 1952, Eschig.

131. Thème varié. For piano. February–September 1951. Noizay. Ded. Geneviève Sienkewicz. Pub. 1952, Eschig.

132. Le Voyage en Amérique. Incidental music for the film. 1951. Production, Le Monde en Images; director, Henri Lavorel; with Pierre Fresnay and Yvonne Printemps.
fp: 14 August 1951, Cannes, Cinéma aux Etoiles. Distributed in Britain by Films de France, 1952.

133. Quatre Motets pour le temps de Noël (Four Christmas Motets). For mixed choir a cappella. 1951-2.
1. *O magnum mysterium.* April 1942, Noizay. Ded. Félix de Nobel.
2. *Quem vidistis pastores dicite.* December 1951, Marseille. Ded. Simone Gerard.
3. *Videntes stellam.* November 1951, Aix-en-Provence. Ded. Madeleine Bataille.
4. *Hodie Christus natus est.* 18 May 1952, Paris. Ded. Marcel Couraud.
Pub. 1952, Rouart Lerolle.

134. Ave Verum Corpus. Motet for three female voices (SMzA). 1952, Noizay. Ded. La Chorale féminine de Pittsburgh. Pub. 1952, Rouart Lerolle.

135. Matelote Provençale. For orchestra. Contribution to 'La Guirlande de Campra'. June 1952, Noizay. Ded. Roger Bigonnet.
fl, pic, 2 ob, 2 cl, 2 bsn; 2 hn, 2 tpt; timp; strings.
fp: 31 July 1952, Aix-en-Provence Festival, Paris Conservatoire Orchestra, cond. Hans Rosebaud.
Pub. 1954, Salabert.

136. Sonata for two pianos. Autumn 1952, Marseille–Spring 1953, Noizay. Commissioned by and ded. Arthur Gold and Robert Fizdale.
1. *Prologue* (*Extrêmement lent et calme*); 2. *Allegro molto* (*Très rythmé*); 3. *Andante lyrico* (*Lentement*); 4. *Epilogue* (*Allegro giocoso*).
fEbp: 2 November 1953, Arthur Gold and Robert Fizdale.
Pub. 1954, Eschig.

137. Bucolique. For orchestra. 1954. Contribution to 'Variations sur le nom de Marguerite Long.' Pub. Salabert.

138. Parisiana (Max Jacob). For voice and piano. April 1954, Noizay.
1. *Joueur du bugle.* Ded. to the memory of Pierre Colle.
2. *Vous n'écrivez plus?* Ded. Paul Chadourne.
Pub. 1954, Salabert.

139. Rosemonde (Guillaume Apollinaire). For voice and piano. May 1954, Noizay. Ded. Comtesse Pastré. Pub. 1955, Eschig.

140. Le Travail du peintre (Paul Eluard). For voice and piano. August 1956, Le Tremblay. Ded. Alice Esty.
1. *Pablo Picasso*; 2. *Marc Chagall*; 3. *Georges Braque*; 4. *Juan Gris*; 5. *Paul Klee*; 6. *Joan Miró*; 7. *Jacques Villon.*
fEbp: 1 January 1958, Pierre Bernac and Francis Poulenc.
Pub. 1957, Eschig.

141. Deux mélodies 1956. For voice and piano. September 1956.
1. *La souris* (Guillaume Apollinaire). Ded. Marya Freund.

2. *Nuage* (Mme. Laurence de Beylié). Ded.
Rose Plaut-Dercourt.
Pub. 1957, Eschig.

142. Dialogues des Carmélites. Opera in
three acts, August 1953–September 1955;
vocal score dated August 1955, Tourettes-
sur-Loup; orchestrated, June 1956. Text:
Georges Bernanos. Ded. 'to the memory of
the composer's mother, to Claude Debussy,
and to Claudio Monteverdi, Giuseppe Verdi
and Modeste Moussorgski'. Dur. 2½ hrs.

2 fl, pic, ob, ca, 2 cl, bcl, 3 bsn, cbsn; 4 hn,
3 tpt, 3 tmb, tuba; timp, pcssn; piano, 2 hp,
strings.

fp: 26 January 1957, Milan, La Scala, cond.
Nino Sanzogno; with Virginia Zeani (Blanche
de la Force), Gianna Pederzini (La Prieure),
Leila Genger (La nouvelle Prieure), Gigliola
Frazzoni (Mère Marie), Eugenia Ratti (Soeur
Constance), Vittoria Palombini (Mère Jeanne),
Fiorenza Cossoto (Soeur Mathilde), Scipio
Colombo (Le Marquis de la Force), Nicola
Filacuridi (Le Chevalier de la Force); producer,
Margherite Wallmann; décor and costumes,
Georges Wakhévitch.

fFp: 21 June 1957, Paris, Opéra, cond.
Pierre Dervaux; with Denise Duval (Blanche
de la Force), Denise Scharley (La Prieure),
Régine Crespin (La nouvelle Prieure), Rita
Gorr (Mère Marie), Liliane Berton (Soeur
Constance), Mme Fourrier (Mère Jeanne),
Mme. Desmoutiers (Soeur Mathilde), Xavier
Depraz (Le Marquis de la Force), Jean
Giraudeau (Le Chevalier de la Force); pro-
ducer, Maurice Jaquemont; décor and cos-
tumes, Suzanne Lalique.
Pub. 1957, Ricordi.

BIBLIOGRAPHY:
Felix Aprahamian: Dialogue des Carmélites,
Chesterian, No. 190. spring 1957.
A. Beguin: Georges Bernanos e i Dialogues
des Carmélites, *Ricordiana*, 1957, No. 1.
A. Beguin and Henri Hell: Le Dialogue des
Carmélites de Georges Bernanos et FP,
L'Opéra de Paris, 1956.
M. Derrick: The Carmelites at Covent
Garden, *Canon*, March–April 1958, p. 282.
Aloys Fornerod: Dialogue des Carmélites,
Schweizerische Musikpädagogische Blätter,
October 1958.

— Les Dialogues des Carmélites de FP,
Feuilles musicales, October 1958.
Eugenio Gara: Poulenc è andato a raggiun-
gere le sue Carmelitane, *Musica d'oggi*,
January–February 1963.
Edward Lockspeiser: Poulenc and The
Carmelites, *Opera*, January 1958, p. 9.
Francis Poulenc: Comment J'ai composé le
Dialogue des Carmélites, *L'Opéra de Paris*,
1957.
H. H. Stuckenschmidt: FP, Dialogue des
Carmélites, Maïlander Scala 1957, in *Oper
in dieser Zeit*, Friedrich Verlag (Hannover)
1964, p. 82.
H. Taubman: Opera of the spirit, *New York
Times*, 29 September 1957, Section 2, p. 9.
C. Thoresby: Carmelite dialogues, *New York
Times*, 10 February 1957, Section 2, p. 9.
E. de Weerth: The Carmelites fire La Scala,
Opera News, 11 March 1957, p. 10.
Anon: A new Poulenc opera comes to Covent
Garden, *M&M*, December 1957, p. 10.

143. Dernier Poème (Robert Desnos). For
voice and piano. December 1956, Hotel
Majestic, Cannes. Ded. Youri Desnos. Pub.
1957, Eschig.

144. Flute Sonata. ?December 1956. Ded.
to the memory of Elizabeth Sprague Coolidge.
fp: 18 June 1957, Strasbourg Festival, Jean-
Pierre Rampal and Francis Poulenc.
fEp: 17 February 1958, BBC broadcast,
Gareth Morris and Francis Poulenc.
Pub. Chester.

145. Elégie. For horn and piano. 1957. Ded.
to the memory of Dennis Brain. Dur. 8'.
fp: 17 February 1958, BBC broadcast, Neill
Sanders and Francis Poulenc.
Pub. 1958, Chester.

146. Improvisation No. 13 in A minor.
For piano. March 1958, Hotel Majestic,
Cannes. *Allegretto commodo*. Ded. Mme.
Auguste Lambiotte. Pub. Salabert.

147. Improvisation No. 14 in D flat major.
For piano. March 1958, Hotel Majestic,
Cannes. Ded. Henri Hell. Pub. 1958, Salabert.

148. La Voix Humaine. Lyric Tragedy in
one act. February–June 1958, Cannes, Saint

Poulenc, Francis

Raphaël, Noizay. Text: Jean Cocteau. Ded. Daisy and Hervé Dugardin. Dur. 40'.

2 fl, pic, ob, ca, 2 cl, bcl, 2 bsn; 2 hn, 2 tpt, tmb, tuba; timp, cym, tamb de basque, xyl; hp, strings.

fp: 6 February 1959, Paris, Opéra-Comique, cond. Georges Prêtre; with Denise Duval; producer and designer, Jean Cocteau.

f Ebp: 4 December 1959, Denise Duval and Orchestre de la Radio Lyrique, cond. Georges Prêtre.

BIBLIOGRAPHY:
Edward Lockspeiser: An introduction to Poulenc's La Voix Humaine, *Opera*, August 1960, p. 527.
Anon: Mme. Duval on the phone—La Voix Humaine, *Newsweek*, 7 March 1960, p. 65.
Anon: Vox Humana, *Röster i Radio*, 1962, No. 5, p. 36.

149. Une Chanson de porcelaine (Paul Eluard). For voice and piano. 1958. Pub. Eschig.

150. Laudes de Saint Antoine de Padoue. For male chorus a cappella.
  1. *O Jésu.* July 1957, Brive.
  2. *O Proles.* January 1958, Brive.
  3. *Laus Regi.* March 1959, Cannes.
  4. *Si Quaeris.* March 1959, Cannes.
  Pub. 1959, Salabert.

151. Improvisation No. 15 in C minor (Hommage à Edith Piaf). For piano. Summer 1959, Bagnols-en-Forêt. Pub. 1960, Salabert.

152. Elégie. For two pianos. Summer 1959, Bagnols-en-Forêt. Ded. to the memory of Marie-Blanche. Pub. 1960, Eschig.

153. Gloria. For soprano, mixed chorus and orchestra. May–December 1959. Commissioned by the Koussevitzky Music Foundation and ded. to the memory of Serge and Nathalie Koussevitzky. Dur. 28'.
  1. *Gloria*; 2. *Laudamus te*; 3. *Domine Deus*; 4. *Domine fili unigenite*; 5. *Dominus Deus*; *Agnes Dei*; 6. *Qui sedes ad dexteram Patris.*
  fp: 20 January 1961, Adela Addison, Chorus Pro Musica and the Boston Symphony Orchestra, cond. Charles Münch.
  f European p: 14 February 1961, Paris, Rosanna Cartteri, les Choeurs et l'Orchestre National de la R.T.F., cond. Georges Prêtre. Pub. 1960, Salabert.

BIBLIOGRAPHY:
Robert Taylor: Le Gloria de FP, *Feuilles musicales*, May–June 1961, op. 75.

154. La Courte Paille (Maurice Carème). For voice and piano. July–August 1960. Ded. Denise Duval and Richard Schilling.
  1. *Le sommeil*; 2. *Quelle aventure?*; 3. *La Reine de coeur*; 4. *Ba, Be, Bi, Bo, Bu*; 5. *Les Anges musiciens*; 6. *Le carafon*; 7. *Lune d'Avril.*
  Pub. 1960, Eschig.

155. La Dame de Monte Carlo. Monologue for soprano and orchestra (Jean Cocteau). April 1961, Monte Carlo. Ded. Denise Duval. Dur. 6' 30".

2 fl, 2 ob, 2 cl, 2 bsn; 2 hn, 2 tpt; timp, tgle, cast, cym, tamb de basque, tamtam; vib, hp, strings.

fEp: 15 January 1962, BBC broadcast, Elisabeth Robinson and BBC Northern Orchestra, cond. Stanford Robinson.
  Pub. 1961, Ricordi (Paris).

156. Sept Répons des Ténèbres. For soprano solo (child's voice), mixed choir (of boys' and men's voices) and orchestra. April–October 1961. Commissioned by the New York Philharmonic in celebration of its opening season in the Lincoln Center for the Performing Arts. Dur. 25'.

Jeudi Saint. 1. *Una hora non potuistis vigilare mecum*; 2. *Judas, mercator pessimus.* Vendredi Saint. 3. *Jesum tradidit*; 4. *Caligaverunt oculi mei*; 5. *Tenebrae factae sunt.* Samedi Saint. 6. *Sepulto Domino*; 7. *Ecce quomodo moritur justus.*
  Pub. 1962, Salabert.

157. Nos souvenirs qui chantent (d'après un thème de Francis Poulenc). Words by Robert Tatry, music by Francis Poulenc and Paul Bonneau. Pub. 1962, Heugel.

158. Renaud et Armide. Incidental music (Jean Cocteau). 1962.

159. Clarinet Sonata. 1962. Dur. 13'.
  1. *Allegro tristamente*; 2. *Romanza: Très calme*; 3. *Allegro con fuoco* (*Très animé*).
  Pub. 1963, Chester.

160. Oboe Sonata. 1962.
Pub. Chester.

161. Fancy (Shakespeare). For voice and piano. ?1962. Ded. Miles and Floria. Commissioned for 'Classical Songs for Children' (ed. The Countess of Harewood and Ronald Duncan). Pub. 1964, Anthony Blond.

WRITINGS BY POULENC
A propos de Mavra, *Les Feuilles libres*, June–July 1932.
Igor Stravinsky, *L'Information musicale*, 3 January 1941, op. 195.
Le coeur de Maurice Ravel, *Nouvelle revue française*, No. 323, February 1941, p. 237.
Centenaire de Chabrier, *Nouvelle revue française*, No. 329, December 1941, p. 110.
Oeuvres récentes de Darius Milhaud, *Contrepoints*, No. 1, January 1946, p. 59.
Tributes to Christian Bérard (contribution), *Ballet*, April 1949, p. 30.
Opera Forum (contribution), in *Music Today*, Dobson (London) 1949, p. 137.
Entretiens avec Claude Rostand, Julliard (Paris) 1954.
Lorsque je suis mélancolique, *Mercure de France*, 1 January 1956.
Inventur der modernen französischen Musik, *Melos*, February 1956, p. 35.
Comment j'ai composé le Dialogue des Carmélites, *L'Opéra de Paris*, 1957.
Emmanuel Chabrier, La Palatine (Paris) 1961.
Opera in the cinema era, *Opera*, January 1961, p. 11.
Journal de mes mélodies. Grasset, 1964.
Extrait du 'Journal de mes mélodies', *Feuilles musicales*, May–June 1961, p. 64.
A propos d'une lettre d'Arthur Honegger, *SM*, May–June 1962, p. 160.
Moi et mes amis (ed. Stéphane Audel), La Palatine (Paris) 1963.
Correspondance, 1915–1963 (ed. Hélène de Wendel, preface by Darius Milhaud), Editions du Seuil (Paris) 1967.

GENERAL BIBLIOGRAPHY
M.A. : FP, *Muzsika*, April 1963, p. 21.
J. A. Abbing: Op bezoek bij FP, *Mens en melodie*, November 1949, p. 332.
R. Allorto: Intervista con FP, *Ricordiana*, January 1957.

Felix Aprahamian: The operas of FP, *Ricordiana*, July 1960, p. 1.
— Poulenc, Cocteau and Monte Carlo, *Ricordiana*, January 1963, p. 7.
Stéphane Audel: Dernier souvenir de FP, *Revue musicale de Suisse Romande*, December 1965.
K. de Bergen: FP, ses maîtres et ses amis, *Beaux Arts* (Brussels), 1 November 1935.
Pierre Bernac: Notes sur l'interprétation des mélodies de FP, *Feuilles musicales*, May–June 1961, p. 68.
José Bruyr: FP, in *L'Ecran des musiciens*, Les Cahiers de France (Paris) 1930, p. 40.
W. A. Chislett: Neglected Composers, 7: FP, *The Gramophone*, November 1928, p. 236.
A. Cohn: Art of FP, *American Record Guide*, March, 1964, p. 622.
Paul Collaer: Les compositeurs issus du groupe des 'Six', in *La Musique moderne*, Elsevier (Paris) 1955, p. 163.
David Cox: Poulenc and Surrealism, *The Listener*, 11 July 1963, p. 69.
Laurence Davies: FP, Jongleur de Notre Dame, in *The Gallic Muse*, Dent (London) 1967, p. 157.
David Drew: The simplicity of Poulenc, *The Listener*, 16 January 1958, p. 137.
Louis Durey: FP, *Chesterian*, No. 25, September 1922, p.1.
André Espian de la Maestre: FP, *ÖM*, January 1959.
Nigel Fortune: FP, in *Decca Book of Ballet*, Muller (London) 1958, p. 232.
J. E. Fritschel: The study and performance of three extended choral works, *Dissertation Abstracts*, August 1961, p. 593.
Paul-André Gaillard: Moments profanes et religieux dans l'oeuvre de FP, *SM*, March–April 1965, p. 79.
R. Gelatt: Vote for FP, *Saturday Review of Literature*, 28 January 1950, p. 57.
— Stuff of legend, *Reporter*, 7 September 1967, p. 45.
André George: FP, *Chesterian*, No. 45, March–April 1925.
J. Gruen: FP, *Musical America*, April 1960, p. 6.
Jean-Michel Hayoz: In memorian—FP et son temps, *SM*, November–December 1963, p. 352.

Poulenc, Francis

Henri Hell: La musique religieuse de FP, *RM* (L'Oeuvre du XXe Siècle), 1952, p. 53.
— FP, musicien français, Plon (Paris) 1958.
— FP et le théâtre lyrique, *Feuilles musicales*, May–June 1961, op. 65.
— Hommage à FP, *Musica* (Chaix), No. 109, April 1963, p. 36.
Leigh Henry: FP, *MO*, April 1920, p. 542.
M. Houdin: La jeunesse nogentaise de FP, *Bulletin de la Société historique et archéologique de Nogent-sur-Marne*, 1964, No. 4.
A. Hughes: Les Six, a generation later, *Musical America*, 15 February 1954, p. 12.
— FP, *Musical America*, February 1963, p. 20.
Robert H. Hull: A master of Gallic wit, *Radio Times*, 30 June 1933, p. 810.
Hélène Jourdan-Morhange: Poulenc et ses poètes, *Feuilles musicales*, May–June 1961, p. 76.
I. Kolodin: Duval, Poulenc, *Saturday Review*, 26 March 1960, p. 36.
Paul Landormy: FP, in *La Musique française après Debussy*, Gallimard (Paris) 1943, p. 158.
George Linstead: The charm of Poulenc, *Chesterian*, No. 139, May–June 1938, p. 134.
Edward Lockspeiser: FP and modern French poets, *MMR*, 1940, p. 29.
— The wit and the heart: a study of FP, *High Fidelity*, July 1958, p. 35.
— Poulenc and his music, *Ricordiana*, April 1963, p. 7.
Joseph Machlis: FP, in *Introduction to Contemporary Music*, Norton (U.S.A.), Dent (London) 1961, p. 232.
Pierre Meylan: FP à Lausanne, *Feuilles musicales*, May–June 1961, p. 78.
Massimo Mila: Poulenc, *Espero* (Geneva), November 1942.
Jan Mul: Gesprekken met FP, *Mens en melodie*, June 1955, p. 205.
— De Componist FP, *Mens en melodie*, September 1955, p. 291.
Rollo H. Myers: FP, *MMR*, May 1931, p. 129.
F. de Nobel: Memories of FP, *Sonorum Speculum*, No. 15, June 1963, p. 39.
A. Payne: Tribute to Poulenc, *M&M*, June 1963, p. 44.
Gustave Pitteluga: FP and the praise of paradox in art, *Chesterian*, No. 124, November–December 1935, p. 37.

Henry Prunières: FP, *De Muziek*, January 1928.
— FP, *Sackbut*, February 1928, p. 190.
— FP, *Cahiers d'Art*, 1928, No. 3, p. 125.
Charles Ribeyre: Milhaud et Poulenc, *L'Orient musical*, 15 December 1924.
Knudage Riisager: Auric et Poulenc à Copenhague, *RM*, 1 December 1926, p. 171.
Ned Rorem: Poulenc, a memoir, *Tempo*, spring 1963, p. 28.
Claude Rostand: La musique religieuse—FP et ses trois styles, *Feuilles musicales*, May–June 1961, p. 71.
— Visages de Poulenc, *Revue musicale de Suisse Romande*, 30 April 1963, p. 9.
Jean Roy: FP, in *Musique française*, Nouvelles Editions Debresse (Paris) 1962, p. 237.
— FP, l'homme et son oeuvre, Editions Seghers (Paris) 1964.
Edmund Rubbra: Goossens and Poulenc, *MMR*, November 1931, p. 330.
R. Sabin: Poulenc, the essence is simplicity, *Musical America*, 15 November 1949, p. 27.
A. Salzman: The many paradoxes of Monsieur Poulenc, *New York Times*, 28 February 1960, Section 2, p. 9.
J.-P. Sarrautte: Os sessenta anos de FP, *Gazeta musical e de todas as artes*, July–August 1959, p. 325.
Adolfo Salazar: Poulenc, in *La música actual en Europa y sus problemas*, J. M. Yagües (Madrid) 1935, p. 462.
André Schaeffner: FP, musicien français, *Contrepoints*, No. 1, January 1946, p. 50.
M. Schubart: FP, *Opera* (San Francisco), April 1950, p. 22.
C. B. Selfridge: French Song since Ravel, *National Association of Singing Teachers Bulletin* (New York), September 1955, p. 17.
B. K. Spanjaard: Het Liedwerk van FP, *Mens en melodie*, January 1947, p. 17.
A. S. J. Tessimond: Words to music by Poulenc, *The Dominant*, March–April 1927, p. 32.
Irving Vein: FP, *Chesterian*, No. 179, July 1954.
Max Vredenburg: Twee vijftig-jarigen: Georges Auric en FP, *Mens en melodie*, February 1949, p. 43.
H. E. Wortham: Auric and Poulenc, *British*

Musician, 1927, February p. 205, April p. 288, May p. 17.
— Auric and Poulenc, *Apollo*, August 1926, p. 67.

MISCELLANEOUS OR UNSIGNED

Hommage à FP, *Feuilles musicales*, May–June 1961, p. 63.
Entretien avec FP, *Le Guide du Concert*, April–May 1929.
FP on his ballets, *Ballet*, September 1946, p. 57.
Poulenc's maturity, *The Times*, 27 January 1961, p. 43.

SERGE PROKOFIEV (1891–1953)

Serge Sergeyevich Prokofiev was a Ukrainian, born on 23 April 1891 in the village of Sontsovka (Ekaterinoslav Government), where his father was manager of a large estate. He was a precocious child and had written two 'operas' before taking lessons from the composer Reinhold Glière at Sontsovka in the summers of his eleventh and twelfth years. In 1904 he went to the St. Petersburg Conservatoire and studied there for ten years, concentrating in the first five on composition (under Lyadov and Rimsky-Korsakov) and in the second on orchestral conducting and the piano. At this time he formed lasting friendships with the composer Nikolai Miaskovsky and the critic Boris Asafyev. Prokofiev made his début as a composer-pianist in December 1908 at one of the 'Evenings of Modern Music' in St. Petersburg, and soon began to make a career as a pianist and (less often) conductor, mainly of his own works. As his father had died and left him 'head of a family' Prokofiev was not called up to serve in the First World War; and in 1917 his attitude to the Russian Revolution was ambiguous. With the permission of the People's Commissar for Education he left Russia in 1918 and, travelling via Japan, visited the United States, where he spent most of the next four years. It was in America that he met his first wife, the Spanish singer Lina Llubera. In 1922 he settled in Europe, living first in the Bavarian village of Ettal, then from 1923 in Paris. Important émigré figures in Prokofiev's life at this time were Kussevitsky (who did much to promote his music by conducting it and publishing it in his Edition Russe de Musique) and Diaghilev (with whose Russian Ballet he collaborated closely until the impresario's death in 1929). Prokofiev continued his concert tours of America and western Europe, but did not break with the Soviet Union. He made three tours of Russia between 1927 and 1932, and from 1933 onwards—though often visiting the West until the outbreak of the Second World War—lived mainly in the USSR. In the mid-1930s he taught composition in Moscow but thereafter concentrated almost exclusively on composing. In 1941 he divorced his first wife and married Mira Mendelson, and when Russia entered the Second World War was evacuated successively to the Causasus, Kazakhstan and the Urals, returning to Moscow in 1943. From 1946 onwards he lived in Zvenigorod, a village forty miles from Moscow, but his health deteriorated (the result of brain concussion after a fall in 1945) and he died in March 1953 from cerebral haemorrhage. Though an important Soviet musical figure, Prokofiev was sometimes officially accused of the vices of Modernism and Formalism, notably in the Communist Party Central Committee's resolution of 10 February 1948. Only after his death—he died the same day as Stalin—was his work fully 'reinstated' by the Party during de-Stalinization in 1958.

CATALOGUE OF WORKS

1. Piano Sonata No. 1 in F minor Op. 1. 1907, rev. 1909.
   fp: 6 March 1910, Moscow, Serge Prokofiev. Pub. 1911, Jurgenson.

2. Four Etudes Op. 2. For piano. 1909.
   1. *D minor* (*Allegro*); 2. *E minor*; 3. *C minor* (*Andante semplice*); 4. *C minor* (*Presto energico*).
   fp (Nos. 1, 2, 4): 6 March 1910, Moscow, Serge Prokofiev.
   Pub. 1912, Jurgenson.

3. Four Pieces Op. 3. For piano. 1907–8, rev. 1911.
   1. *Story* (*Erzählung*); 2. *Badinage* (*Scherz*); 3. *March*; 4. *Phantom* (*Trugbild*).
   fp (No. 1): 31 December 1908, St. Petersburg, Serge Prokofiev.

Prokofiev, Serge

fp (complete): 10 April 1911, St. Petersburg, Serge Prokofiev.

Pub. 1911, Jurgenson; 1925, Benjamin (Leipzig), rev. M. Frey.

4. Four Pieces Op. 4. For piano. 1908, rev. 1910–12.

1. *Reminiscence*; 2. *Elan*; 3. *Despair* (*Désespoir*); 4. *Suggestion diabolique*.

fp: 31 December 1908, St. Petersburg, Serge Prokofiev.

Pub. 1913, Jurgenson.

5. Sinfonietta in A major Op. 5. For orchestra. 1909, rev. 1914.

fp: 6 November 1915, Petrograd, Maryinsky Theatre, Siloti concert, cond. Serge Prokofiev.

Unpub. See also No. 50.

6. Dreams Op. 6. Symphonic Poem for orchestra. 1910.

fp: 5 December 1910, St. Petersburg, students' concert, cond. Serge Prokofiev.

f Moscow p: 14 July 1911, cond. K. D. Saradzhev.

Unpub.

7. Two poems (K. Balmont) Op. 7. For women's voices and orchestra. 1909–10.

1. *The white swan*; 2. *The wave*.

fp (No. 1): 1910, St. Petersburg, Conservatoire pupils' concert, cond. Serge Prokofiev.

Unpub. Lost. No. 1 reconstructed by the composer from surviving voice parts.

8. Autumnal Sketch Op. 8. For orchestra. 1910, rev. 1938.

fp: 1 August 1911, Moscow, cond. A.K. Medtner.

Unpub. Arr. for two pianos eight hands by N. Y. Myaskovsky.

9. Two Songs (Deux Poèmes) Op. 9. For voice and piano. 1910–11.

1. *Other planets are yonder* (Il est d'autres planètes) (K. Balmont). 1910.

2. *Unmoored is the vessel* (La Barque démarre). 1911.

fp (No. 1): 28 March 1914, St. Petersburg, A. G. Zherebtsova-Andreyeva, acc. Dulov.

Pub. 1917, Gutheil; Breitkopf & Härtel; Chester. French version, Louis Laloy; German version, Vera Miller; English version, R. Burness.

10. Piano Concerto No. 1 in D flat major Op. 10. In one movement. 1910–11. Ded. Nicholas Tcherepnin. Dur. 16–17'.

2 fl, pic, 2 ob, 2 cl, 2 bsn, cbsn; 4 hn, 2 tpt, 3 tmb, tuba; timp, campanelli; strings.

fp: 7 August 1912, Moscow, People's House, Serge Prokofiev, cond. K. D. Saradzhev.

f St. Petersburg p: 1912, Serge Prokofiev, cond. A. P. Aslanov.

fEp: 24 August 1920, Queen's Hall, Promenade Concert, Ellen M. Jensen and the Queen's Hall Orchestra, cond. Sir Henry Wood. Note also: 10 March 1923, Queen's Hall, Serge Prokofiev and the New Queen's Hall Orchestra, cond. Sir Henry Wood.

Pub. 1913, Jurgenson; Forberg (min. score); 1948, Leeds Music (reduction for two pianos, with annotations by György Sandor).

BIBLIOGRAPHY:

M. Montagu-Nathan: Prokofiev's First Piano Concerto, *MT*, January 1917, p. 12.

11. Toccata in C major Op. 11. For piano. 1912.

fp: 10 December 1916, Petrograd, Serge Prokofiev.

fEbp: 5 December 1927, Serge Prokofiev.

Pub. 1913, Jurgenson.

12. Ten Pieces Op. 12. For piano. 1906–13.

1. *Marche*. 1908–13.

2. *Gavotte*. 1908–10.

3. *Rigaudon*. 1913.

4. *Mazurka*. 1909.

5. *Caprice*. 1913.

6. *Légende*.

7. *Prélude*.

8. *Allemande*. 1913.

9. *Scherzo humoristique*.

10. *Scherzo*. 1912.

fp (three only): 5 February 1914, Moscow, Serge Prokofiev.

fEbp (complete): 27 December 1928, Arthur Benjamin.

Pub. 1914, Jurgenson.

12a. Scherzo Op. 12b. For four bassoons. Transcription of *Scherzo humoristique* Op. 12 No. 9.

Pub. 1915, Jurgenson.

13. Maddalena Op. 13. Opera in one act. 1911, rev. 1913. Libretto: M. Lieven. Unpub.

BIBLIOGRAPHY:
Christina Thoresby: Early Prokofiev opera found in Paris, *Musical America*, 15 January 1954, p. 25.
Rita McAllister: Prokofiev's early opera Maddalena, *PRMA*, 1969–70, p. 137.

14. Piano Sonata No. 2 in D minor Op. 14. 1912.
1. *Allegro ma non troppo*; 2. *Scherzo: Allegro marcato*; 3. *Andante*; 4. *Vivace*.
fp: 5 February 1914, Moscow, Serge Prokofiev.
Pub. 1913, Jurgenson.

15. Ballade Op. 15. For cello and piano. 1912.
fp: 5 February 1914, Moscow, E. Y. Belousov and Serge Prokofiev.
?fEp: 15 December 1927, Aeolian Hall, Paul Grummer and Tcherepnin.
Pub. 1915, Jurgenson; 1923, Gutheil/ Breitkopf & Härtel, ed. F. H. Schneider.

16. Piano Concerto No. 2 in G minor Op. 16. 1913.
1. *Andantino*; 2. *Scherzo: Vivace*; 3. *Intermezzo: Allegro molto*; 4. *Finale: Allegro tempestuoso*.
fp: 5 September 1913, Pavlovsk, Serge Prokofiev, cond. A. P. Aslanov.
fIp: 7 March 1915, Rome, Augusteo, Serge Prokofiev, cond. Bernardino Molinari.

16a. Piano Concerto No. 2 in G minor Op. 16. Revised version. 1923.
fp: 8 May 1924, Paris, Koussevitzky concert, Serge Prokofiev, cond. Serge Koussevitzky.
fEp: 9 December 1927, Serge Prokofiev and Wireless Orchestra, cond. Ernest Ansermet.
fEp (concert): 26 August 1955, Royal Albert Hall, Promenade Concert, Kyla Greenbaum and the London Symphony Orchestra, cond. Basil Cameron.
Pub. 1925, Gutheil (reduction for two pianos by the composer); Breitkopf & Härtel.

17. Sarcasms Op. 17. Five Pieces for piano. 1912–14.

1. *Tempestuoso*. 1912.
2. *Allegro rubato*. 1913.
3. *Allegro precipitato*. 1913.
4. *Smanioso*. 1914.
5. *Precipitosissimo*. 1914.
fp: 10 December 1916, Petrograd, Serge Prokofiev.
Pub. 1916, Jurgenson.

18. The Ugly Duckling (Le vilain petit canard) Op. 18. For voice and piano. 1914. Based on Andersen's fairy tale.
fp: 30 January 1915, Petrograd, A. G. Zherebtsova-Andreyeva, acc. Serge Prokofiev.
Pub. 1917, Gutheil; 1922, Breitkopf & Härtel: French version, Vera Janacopulos; German version, Kurt Hanow; English version, Robert Burness.

19. Violin Concerto No. 1 in D major Op. 19. 1916–17. Dur. 23'.
1. *Andantino*; 2. *Scherzo: Vivacissimo*; 3. *Moderato—Allegro moderato*.
2 fl, pic, 2 ob, 2 cl, 2 bsn; 4 hn, 2 tpt, tuba; timp, tamb, tamb mil; hp, strings.
fp: 18 October 1923, Paris, Marcel Darrieux, cond. Serge Koussevitzky.
fEp: 3 February 1932, Josef Szigeti and the BBC Symphony Orchestra, cond. Nikolai Malko.
Pub. 1921, Gutheil; 1924 (full score), Gutheil; 1947, Boosey & Hawkes.

20. Scythian Suite (Ala and Lolly) Op. 20. For orchestra. 1914–15.
1. *L'adoration de Vélèss et de Ala*; 2. *Le dieu ennemi et la danse des esprits noirs*; 3. *La nuit*; 4. *Le départ glorieux de Lolly et le cortège du Soleil*.
3 fl, pic, 3 ob, ca, E flat cl, 3 cl, bcl, 3 bsn, cbsn; tpt pic, 4(5) tpt, 8 hn, 3 tmb, bs tmb, tuba; timp, GC, 2 cym, tgle, tamb, tamb mil, tamtam, celesta, campanelli, xyl; piano, 2 hp, strings.
fp: 29 January 1916, Petrograd, Maryinsky Theatre, Siloti concert, cond. Serge Prokofiev.
fEp: 1 November 1920, London, London Symphony Orchestra, cond. Albert Coates.
f Paris p: 29 April 1921, cond. Serge Koussevitzky.
Pub. 1923, Gutheil: ed. F. H. Schneider.

373

Prokofiev, Serge

BIBLIOGRAPHY:
A. Getteman: La Suite Scythe de Prokofiev, *Arts et lettres d'aujourd'hui*, 1923, No. 2.

21. Chout (The Buffoon) Op. 21. Ballet in six scenes. 1915, rev. 1920. Scenario: Serge Prokofiev, from a story by A. Afanasyev.

Tableau 1: *1. La chambre du Bouffon; 2. Premier entr'acte.* Tableau 2: *3. Chez les sept bouffons; 4. Deuxième entr'acte.* Tableau 3: *5. Dans la cour du Bouffon; 6. Troisième entr'acte.* Tableau 4: *7. La chambre de réception des bouffons; 8. Quatrième entr'acte.* Tableau 5: *9. La chambre à coucher du marchand; 10. Cinquième entr'acte.* Tableau 6: *11. Le jardin du marchand.*

fp: 17 May 1921, Paris, Diaghilev's Ballets Russes, cond. Serge Prokofiev.

fEp: 9 June 1921, London, Prince's Theatre, Serge Diaghilev's Ballets Russes.

Pub. 1922, Gutheil/Breitkopf & Härtel.

BIBLIOGRAPHY:
M.-D. Calvocoressi: A jester with a magic whip, *Radio Times*, 16 October 1936, p. 14.
Edwin Evans: Chout, *MN&H*, 18 June 1921, p. 784.
Ralph Hill: Chout, *Gramophone Record*, December 1934, p. 4.
Jean Marnold: Chout, ballet de M. SP, *Mercure de France*, No. 583, 1 October 1922, p. 234.

21a. Chout: Symphonic Suite Op. 21b. 1920.

1. Le Bouffon et sa Bouffonne; 2. Danse des bouffonnes; 3. Les bouffons tuent leurs bouffonnes (Fugue); 4. Le Bouffon travesti en jeune femme; 5. Troisième entr'acte; 6. Danse des filles des bouffons; 7. L'arrivée du marchand, la danse des révérences et le choix de la fiancée; 8. Dans la chambre à coucher du marchand; 9. La jeune femme est devenue chèvre; 10. Cinquième entr'acte et l'enterrement de la chèvre; 11. La querelle du Bouffon avec le marchand; 12. Danse finale.

2 fl, pic, 2 ob, ca, 3 cl, 3 bsn; 3 tpt, 4 hn, 3 tmb, tuba; timp, tgle, tamb mil, cym, GC, campanelli, xyl; 2 hp, piano, strings.

fp: 15 January 1924, Brussels, F. Ruhlmann.

fEbp: 19 October 1934, BBC Orchestra, cond. Serge Prokofiev.

Pub. 1924, Gutheil/Breitkopf & Härtel: incl. reduction by the composer for piano solo.

22. Visions fugitives (Fugitive visions) Op. 22. For piano. 1915–17.

1. Lentamente; 2. Andante; 3. Allegretto; 4. Animato; 5. Molto giocoso; 6. Con eleganza; 7. (Arpa) Pittoresco; 8. Comodo; 9. Allegretto tranquillo; 10. ——; 11. Con vivacità; 12. Assai moderato; 13. Allegretto; 14. Feroce; 15. Inquieto; 16. Dolente; 17. Poetico; 18. Con una dolce lentezza; 19. Presto agitatissimo e molto accentuato; 20. Lento irrealmente.

fp: 15 April 1918, Petrograd, Serge Prokofiev.

Pub. 1917, Gutheil; 1922, Breitkopf & Härtel.

23. Five Songs (Cinq Poésies) Op. 23. For voice and piano. 1915.

1. The garret dweller (Sous le toit) (Valentine Goryansky).

2. The grey petticoat (De gris vêtu) (Zinaida Gippius).

3. Oh, trust in me (Suiv-moi sans crainte) (Boris Verin).

4. In garden bed (Dans mon jardin) (C. Balmont).

5. The wizard (Le sorcier) (Agnivtzeff).

fp (No. 5): 10 December 1916, Petrograd, I. Alchevsky, acc. Serge Prokofiev.

Pub. 1917, Gutheil; 1926, Breitkopf & Härtel: French version, Louis Laloy; German version, Vera Miller; English version, R. Burness.

24. The Gambler Op. 24. Opera in four acts, six scenes. 1915–16, rev. 1927–28. Libretto: Serge Prokofiev, from a story by Dostoievsky.

fp: 29 April 1929, Brussels, Théâtre de la Monnaie, cond. Corneil de Thoran.

Pub. 1930, Edition russe de musique: vocal score (by the composer) only; French version, P. Spaak; German version, Gustav von Festenberg.

BIBLIOGRAPHY:
Andrew Porter: Prokofiev's early operas— The Gambler, The Love of Three Oranges, *MT*, August 1962, p. 528.

25. Symphony No. 1 in D major Op. 25

('Classical'). For orchestra. Ded. Boris Asafyev.

1. *Allegro*; 2. *Larghetto*; 3. *Gavotta: Non troppo allegro*; 4. *Finale: Molto vivace.*

2 fl, 2 ob, 2 cl, 2 bsn; 2 tpt, 2 hn; timp; strings.

fp: 21 April 1918, Petrograd, cond. Serge Prokofiev.

fEp: 11 June 1921, London, Prince's Theatre Orchestra, cond. Serge Prokofiev.

Pub. 1925, Russian Music Publishers; also piano reduction by the composer, pub. 1931.

26. Piano Concerto No. 3 in C major

Op. 26. 1917–21. Dated: 28 September 1921.

1. *Andante—Allegro*; 2. *Theme and Variations*; 3. *Allegro, ma non troppo.*

fp: 16 December 1921, Chicago, Serge Prokofiev and the Chicago Symphony Orchestra, cond. Frederick Stock.

f New York p: 26 December 1921, Serge Prokofiev, cond. Albert Coates.

fEp: 24 April 1922, Queen's Hall, Serge Prokofiev and the London Symphony Orchestra, cond. Albert Coates.

fFp: 27 October 1922, Serge Prokofiev, cond. Serge Koussevitzky.

fRp: 22 March 1925, Moscow, S. Y. Feinberg, cond. K. S. Sarajev.

Pub. 1923, Gutheil; Breitkopf & Härtel; also reduction for two pianos by the composer.

BIBLIOGRAPHY:

Alan Frank: Piano Concerto No. 3 in C major, in *The Concerto*, Pelican Books (London) 1952, p. 382.

27. Five Songs (Cinq Poésies) (Anna Akhmatova) Op. 27. For voice and piano. 1916.

1. *Sunlight streaming in the chamber* (Dans la chambre la poussière d'or); 2. *There is nothing comparable with love* (La sincère tendresse); 3. *Thoughts of sunlight* (Souvenir du soleil); 4. *Greeting!* (Bonjour!); 5. *The grey-eyed king* (Le roi aux yeux gris).

fp: 18 February 1917, Moscow, Z. A. Artemyeva, acc. Serge Prokofiev.

Pub. 1917, Gutheil; 1925, Breitkopf & Härtel: French version, Louis Laloy; English version, R. Burness; German version, Vera Miller.

28. Piano Sonata No. 3 in A minor Op. 28.

In one movement. 1907, rev. 1917.

fp: 15 April 1918, Petrograd, Serge Prokofiev.

fEbp: 5 December 1927, Serge Prokofiev.

Pub. 1918, Gutheil; 1925, Benjamin (Leipzig), rev. M. Frey.

29. Piano Sonata No. 4 in C minor

(D'après des vieux cahiers') Op. 29. 1908, rev. 1917.

1. *Allegro molto sostenuto*; 2. *Andante assai*; 3. *Allegro con brio, ma non leggiere.*

fp: 17 April 1918, Petrograd, Serge Prokofiev.

Pub. 1918, Gutheil; 1921, Breitkopf & Härtel.

29a. Andante Op. 29b. From Op. 29, transcribed for orchestra. 1934.

2 fl, 2 ob, ca, 2 cl, bcl, 2 bsn, cbsn; 2 tpt, 4 hn, 3 tmb, tuba; timp, cym, GC; strings.

fp: 13 February 1958, Leningrad Philharmonic Orchestra, cond. G. Rozhdestvensky.

Pub. 1965, State Music Publishers.

30. Seven, They Are Seven (Sept, ils sont Sept) Op. 30. Akkadian Incantation for tenor, chorus and orchestra. 1917–18. Dated: 26 January 1918, Kislovdsk (Caucusus). Revised: 1933. Poem: K. Balmont.

3 fl, 2 pic, 3 ob, ca, 2 cl, bcl, 3 bsn, cbsn; pic tpt, 4 tpt, 8 hn, 3 ten tmb, bs tmb, tuba, cbs tuba; timp, 2 GC, cym, tamb mil, tamb, tamtam, campanelli, xyl; celesta, 2 hp, strings.

fp: 29 May 1924, Paris, cond. Serge Koussevitzky.

Pub. 1922 (full score), Moscow; 1933, Edition Russe de Musique: French version, Louis Laloy; English version, A. Flotat.

31. Tales of the old grandmother (Contes de la vieille grand'mère) Op. 31. For piano. 1918.

1. *Moderato*; 2. *Andantino*; 3. *Andante assai*; 4. *Sostenuto.*

fp: 7 January 1919, New York, Serge Prokofiev.

fEbp (Nos. 2 & 3): 5 December 1927, Serge Prokofiev.

Pub. 1922, Gutheil/Breitkopf & Härtel.

Prokofiev, Serge

32. Organ Prelude and Fugue by Buxtehude. Arr. by Serge Prokofiev for piano. 1918. Pub. 1923, Gutheil.

33. Four Pieces Op. 32. For piano. 1918.
1. *Danza*; 2. *Menuetto*; 3. *Gavotta*; 4. *Valse*.
fp: 30 March 1919, New York, ?Serge Prokofiev.
fEbp: 5 December 1927, Serge Prokofiev.
Pub. 1922, Gutheil; Breitkopf & Härtel.

34. Schubert Waltzes. Selected and combined into a Suite by Serge Prokofiev for piano. 1918. Pub. 1923, Gutheil.

35. The Love for Three Oranges Op. 33. Opera in four acts, ten scenes and a prologue. 1919. Libretto: Serge Prokofiev, from the play by Carlo Gozzi.
fp: 30 December 1921, Chicago, cond. Serge Prokofiev.
fRp: 18 February 1926, Leningrad Theatre of Opera and Ballet, cond. V. A. Dranishnikov; producer, S. E. Radlov; design, V. Dmitriev.
fEbp: 4 July 1935, BBC Chorus and Orchestra, cond. Albert Coates; with Oda Slobodskaya, Ina Souez, Constance Willis, Arthur Fear, Heddle Nash, Walter Widdop.
Pub. 1922, Gutheil (piano score only); Breitkopf & Härtel; 1947, Hawkes: German version, Jürgen Beythien; French version, Vera Janacopulos and Serge Prokofiev.

BIBLIOGRAPHY:
R. Caamaño: Prokofiev e la sua opera L'amore delle tre melarancie, *Polifonia* (Buenos Aires) 1952.
M.-D. Calvocoressi: Farce and fairy tale, *Radio Times*, 28 June 1935, p. 13.
Ernest Chapman: Prokofiev fantasy at Sadlers Wells, *Musical Events*, June 1963, p. 8.
Raymond Charpentier: Une grande première à Monte-Carlo—L'Amour des 3 Oranges de SP, *La Vie musicale*, June 1952.
Donald Mitchell: Prokofiev's Three Oranges, *Tempo*, No. 41, autumn 1956.
Andrew Porter: Prokofiev's early operas—The Gambler, The Love of Three Oranges, *MT*, August 1962, p. 528.
Malcolm Rayment: Chicago oranges, *M&M*, April 1963, p. 12.

Boris de Schloezer: L'amour des trois oranges, *Revue Pleyel*, 15 December 1925.
Henry W. Simon: The Love of the Three Oranges, in *Festival of Opera*, W. H. Allen (London) 1957, p. 236.
Eugen Szenkar: Die Liebe zu den drei Orangen, die deutsche Erstaufführung, Köln, 1925, *Musik der Zeit*, No. 5 (1953), p. 54.
Emile Vuillermoz: L'Amour des trois oranges, *Revue hommes et mondes*, May 1952, p. 141.
Karl Westermayer: Die Liebe zu den drei Orangen, *Signale*, 1926, No. 41, p. 1472.

35a. The Love for Three Oranges: Symphonic Suite Op. 33b. 1919, rev. 1924.
1. *Les Ridicules*; 2. *Le Magicien Tchélio et Fata Morgana jouent aux cartes (Scène infernale)*; 3. *Marche*; 4. *Scherzo*; 5. *Le prince et la princesse*; 6. *La fuite*.
2 fl, pic, 2 ob, ca, 2 cl, bcl, 3 bsn, cbsn; 3 tpt, 4 hn, 3 tmb, tuba; timp, GC, tamb mil, cym, xyl, campanelle, tamtam, tamb, tgle; 2 hp, strings.
fp (revised version): 29 November 1925, Paris, cond. Serge Kussevitsky.
Pub. 1922, Gutheil; 1926, Edition Russe de Musique (full score, ed. Albert Spalding).

35b. March and Scherzo Op. 33b. From 'The Love for Three Oranges', extracted from Symphonic Suite Op. 33b. Dur. 2′ + 3′.
fEp: 1 June 1922, Queen's Hall, London Symphony Orchestra, cond. Serge Kussevitsky.
fEbp: 23 May 1926, Newcastle Station Symphony Orchestra, cond. Edward Clark.
Pub. ?1922, ?Gutheil; 1926, Edition Russe de Musique; Hawkes (min. score).

35c. March and Scherzo Op. 33c. From 'The Love for Three Oranges', transcribed for piano solo by Serge Prokofiev. Pub. 1922, Gutheil; Breitkopf & Härtel.

36. Overture on Hebrew Themes Op. 34. For clarinet, piano and string quartet. 1919.
fp: 26 January 1920, New York, Zimro Ensemble with Serge Prokofiev (piano).
fEbp: 26 March 1925, Frederick Thurston, Stanford Robinson and the Snow Quartet (Jessie Snow, Kenneth Skeaping, Ernest Tomlinson and Edward J. Robinson).

Pub. 1922, Gutheil; Breitkopf & Härtel (ed. F. H. Schneider).

36a. Overture on Hebrew Themes Op. 34b. Version for orchestra. 1934.
2 fl, 2 ob, 2 cl, 2 bsn; 2 tpt, 2 hn; GC; piano, strings.
fp: ?1935, Prague, cond. Nikolai Malko.
Pub. 1935, Gutheil; Edition Russe de Musique.

37. Five Songs Without Words Op. 35. For voice and piano. 1920.
1. *Andante*; 2. *Lento, ma non troppo*; 3. *Animato, ma non allegro*; 4. *Andantino, un poco scherzando*; 5. *Andante non troppo*.
fp: 27 March 1921, New York, Nina Koshetz, acc. Serge Prokofiev.
Pub. 1922, Gutheil; Breitkopf & Härtel.

37a. Five Melodies Op. 35b. Version of Op. 35 for violin and piano. 1925.
1. *Andante*; 2. *Lento, ma non troppo*; 3. *Animato, ma non allegro*; 4. *Allegretto leggero e scherzando*; 5. *Andante non troppo*.
Pub. 1925, Russian Music Publishers.

38. Five Songs (K. Balmont) Op. 36. For voice and piano. Ded. Lina Llubera.
1. *An incantation for fire and water* (Une incantation du feu et de l'eau); 2. *The voice of birds* (La Voix des oiseaux); 3. *The butterfly* (Le Papillon); 4. *Think of me!* (*A Malayan incantation*) (Pense à moi!—Une incantation malaise); 5. *The pillars* (Les granits).
fEp (?fp) (Nos. 2–4): 5 December 1927, Lina Llubera, acc. ?Serge Prokofiev.
fp (complete): 14 June 1928, Paris, Lina Llubera, acc. Serge Prokofiev.
Pub. 1921 (?1923), Gutheil; 1923, Breitkopf & Härtel: French version, Lina Llubera and Serge Prokofiev; German version, Vera Miller; English version, Olga Mojaysky.

39. The Flaming Angel Op. 37. Opera in five acts. 1919–27. Libretto: Serge Prokofiev, from a story by V. Bryusov.
fp (excerpts only): 14 June 1928, Paris, cond. Serge Kussevitsky.
fp (complete, concert form): 25 November 1954, Paris, cond. S. Bruck.
fp (stage): 29 September 1955, Venice, Teatro Fenice, cond. Nino Sanzogno; with Dorothy Dow, Gabriella Carturan, Mafalda Masini, Rolando Panerei, Enrico Campi, Gino del Signore, Mario Carlin, Mario Borriello, Antonio Annaloro.
fEp: 27 July 1965, Sadlers Wells, New Opera Company, cond. Leon Lovett; with Marie Collier (Renata), John Shaw (Rupprecht), Elizabeth Bainbridge (Fortune-Teller), John Fryatt (Mephistopheles), John Noble (Innkeeper); producer, Peter Coe.
Pub. 1927; Gutheil: piano score only.

BIBLIOGRAPHY:
Ernest Chapman: Prokofiev's Angel of Fire, *Musical Events*, September 1965.
Martin Cooper: Prokofiev's Flaming Angel, *The Listener*, 10 April 1958, p. 637.
Piero Dallamano: L'angelo di fuoco di SP, *La Rassegna musicale*, 1962, p. 169.
Bernard Jacobson: Fiery Angel, *R&R*, March 1964, p. 14.
Alan Jefferson: The Angel of Fire, *M&M*, August 1965, p. 32.
David Lloyd-Jones: Prokofiev and The Angel of Fire, *The Listener*, 29 July 1965, p. 178.
R.-Aloys Mooser: L'ange de feu, in *Aspects de la musique contemporaine*, Editions Labor et Fidès (Geneva) 1957, p. 148.
Jeremy Noble: Unbalanced angel, *New Statesman*, 6 August 1965, p. 196.
Charles Reid: Frenzy at the Wells, *Spectator*, 6 August 1965, p. 178.
Leonid Sabaneev: The Angel of Fire, Prokofiev's new opera, *MT*, October 1928, p. 891.
Hans Swarenski: The Flaming Angel, *Tempo*, No. 39, spring 1956.
Christina Thoresby: The Flaming Angel given belated Paris première, *Musical America*, January 1955, p. 7.
— Prokofiev's opera heard after twenty-seven years, *Strad*, February 1955, p. 364.
— Prokofiev première in Venice, *New York Times*, 9 October 1955, Section 2, p. 11.
Anon.: First London production of The Angel of Fire, the opera that everyone refused, *Music Magazine*, August 1965, p. 7.

40. Piano Sonata No. 5 in C major Op. 38. 1923.
1. *Allegro tranquillo*; 2. *Andantino*; 3. *Un poco Allegretto*.
fp: 9 March 1924, Paris, Serge Prokofiev.

fRp: 6 March 1927, Moscow, Serge Prokofiev.

Pub. 1925, Gutheil; Breitkopf & Härtel.

41. Quintet in G minor Op. 39. For oboe, clarinet, violin, viola and double-bass. 1924. Incorporating material from an unpublished ballet, 'Trapeze'.

1. *Theme and Variations*; 2. *Andante energico*; 3. *Allegro sostenuto, ma con brio*; 4. *Adagio pesante*; 5. *Allegro precipitato, ma non troppo presto*; 6. *Andantino*.

fp: 6 March 1927, Moscow, N. V. Nazarov (ob), I. N. Mayorov (cl), O. M. Tsiganov (v), V. V. Borisovsky (va), I. F. Gertovich (db).

fEp: 5 March 1928, Contemporary Chamber Concert.

fEbp: 31 May 1938, Horace Green, Wilfrid Kealey, Antonio Brosa, Leonard Rubens, Victor Watson.

Pub. 1927, Gutheil; Boosey & Hawkes.

42. Symphony No. 2 in D minor Op. 40. 1924. In two movements. Ded. Serge Kussevitsky.

1. *Allegro ben articolato*; 2. *Tema & Variations*.

2 fl, pic, 2 ob, alto ob, 2 cl, bcl, 2 bsn, cbsn; 3 tpt, 4 hn, 3 tmb, tuba; timp, GC, tamb, cast, cym, tgle, tamb mil; piano, strings.

fp: 6 June 1925, Paris, Koussevitzky concert, cond. Serge Kussevitsky.

Pub. 1924, Editions Russe de Musique; also arr. for two pianos eight hands by P. A. Lamm.

BIBLIOGRAPHY:

Jack Diether: At last, Prokofiev's Second Symphony, *American Record Guide*, July 1964, p. 1016.

Jean Marnold: Concerts Koussevitzky—Deuxième Symphonie de M. SP, *Mercure de France*, No. 654, 15 September 1925, p. 806.

43. Le Pas d'acier Op. 41. Ballet in two scenes. 1925. Scenario: G. Yakulov and Serge Prokofiev.

1. *Entrée des personnages*; 2. *Train des paysans-ravitailleurs*; 3. *Les commissaires*; 4. *Les petits camelots*; 5. *L'orateur*; 6. *Matelot à bracelets et ouvrière*; 7. *Changement de décors*; 8. *Le matelot devient un ouvrier*; 9. *L'usine*; 10. *Les marteaux*; 11. *Finale*.

fp: 7 June 1927, Paris, Diaghilev's Ballets

russes, cond. Roger Desormière; choreography, L. Massine.

fEp: 9 July 1927, Prince's Theatre, Diaghilev's Ballets russes.

Pub. 1928, Editions Russe de Musique: reduction by Serge Prokofiev.

BIBLIOGRAPHY:

M. Kernochan: Pas d'acier, *Outlook*, 13 May 1931, p. 60.

43a. Le Pas d'acier: Symphonic Suite Op. 41b. 1926.

1. *Introduction of cast*; 2. *Commissars, orators and citizens*; 3. *Sailor and working woman*; 4. *Factory*.

fp: 27 May 1928, Moscow, cond. V. Savich.

?fEp: 5 March 1933, BBC broadcast, BBC Orchestra, cond. Albert Coates.

Pub. 1927, Editions Russe de Musique: score and piano reduction by Serge Prokofiev.

44. Overture in B flat Op. 42. For instrumental ensemble. First version. 1926.

fp: 7 February 1927.

Unpub.

44a. Overture in B flat Op. 42b. For orchestra. Second version. 1928. Dur. 8'.

fl, ob, 2 cl, 2 bsn; 2 tpt, tmb; timp, tamb mil, GC, cym; celesta, 2 hp, 2 pianos; cello, 2 double-basses.

fp: 22 December 1930, Paris, cond. Serge Prokofiev.

fEp: 22 February 1960, Chelsea Town Hall, Polyphonia Orchestra, cond. Bryan Fairfax.

Pub. 1930, 1948, Editions Russe de Musique.

45. Divertimento (Divertissement) Op. 43. For orchestra. 1925–9.

1. *Moderato, molto ritmato*; 2. *Larghetto*; 3. *Allegro energico*; 4. *Allegro non troppo e pesante*.

2 fl, 2 ob, 2 cl, 2 bsn; 2 tpt, 4 hn, 3 tmb, tuba; timp, GC, tamb mil, cym, tamb; strings.

fp: 22 December 1929, Paris.

Pub. 1930, Editions Russe de Musique: incl. reduction by Serge Prokofiev for piano.

45a. Divertimento (Divertissement) Op. 43b. Transcription for piano. 1938. Pub. 1940, State Music Publishers.

46. Symphony No. 3 in C minor Op. 44. 1928. Ded. Nicolas Miaskovsky. Dur. 33'.

1. *Moderato*; 2. *Andante*; 3. *Allegro agitato*; 4. *Andante mosso*.

2 fl, pic, 2 ob, ca, 2 cl, bcl, 2 bsn, cbsn; 3 tpt, 4 hn, 3 tmb, tuba; timp, GC, tamb, cym, cast, campana, tamb mil, tamtam; 2 hp, strings.

fp: 17 May 1929, Paris, l'Orchestre Symphonique de Paris, cond. Pierre Monteux.

fEp: 19 October 1934, BBC broadcast, invitation concert in Broadcasting House, BBC Orchestra, cond. Serge Prokofiev.

fGBp (concert): 4 September 1962, Edinburgh Festival, Usher Hall, Philharmonia Orchestra, cond. Gennadi Rozhdestvensky.

f London p (concert): 16 September 1962, Royal Festival Hall, London Symphony Orchestra, cond. Gennadi Rozhdestvensky.

Pub. 1931, Editions Russe de Musique. Arrangements: by N. Y. Miaskovsky for piano four hands; by P. A. Lamm for two pianos eight hands.

BIBLIOGRAPHY:

Israel Yampolsky: Prokofiev's Third Symphony, *Musical Events*, September 1962, p. 22.

47. Things in Themselves (Choses en soi) Op. 45. For piano. 1928.

1. *Allegro moderato*; 2. *Moderato scherzando*.

fp: 6 January 1930, New York, Serge Prokofiev.

Pub. 1930, Editions Russe de Musique.

48. The Prodigal Son (L'Enfant prodigue) Op. 46. Ballet in three scenes. 1928. Scenario: B. Kokhno.

1. *The departure* (Le départ); 2. *Meeting with friends* (Rencontre avec des Camarades); 3. *The beautiful woman* (L'Enjôleuse); 4. *Men's dance* (Les danseurs); 5. *The prodigal son and the beautiful woman* (L'Enfant prodigue et l'Enjôleuse); 6. *The drinking scene* (L'ivresse); 7. *The robbery* (Pillage); 8. *The awakening and repentance* (Réveil et Remords); 9. *Division of Spoils: Intermezzo* (Partage du Butin: Intermède); 10. *The return* (Le Retour).

fp: 21 May 1929, Paris, cond. Serge Prokofiev.

fEp: 1 July 1929, Covent Garden, Diaghilev's Russian Ballet, cond. Roger Desormière; choreography, Georges Balanchine; décor, Georges Rouault; with Serge Lifar, Fedorov, Woizikovsky, Dolin, Doubrovska.

Pub. 1929, Editions Russe de Musique: reduction by Serge Prokofiev.

48a. The Prodigal Son: Symphonic Suite Op. 46b. 1929.

1. *Adagio—Allegretto—Presto—Andantino espressivo—Presto*; 2. *Allegro fastoso*; 3. *Presto* (for three clarinets); 4. *Andante assai*; 5. *Andante pomposo—Allegro espressivo*.

fp: 7 March 1931, Paris, cond. Serge Prokofiev.

Pub. 1930, Editions Russe de Musique: incl. piano reduction by Serge Prokofiev.

49. Symphony No. 4 in C major Op. 47. First version. 1930.

fp: 14 November 1930, Boston, Boston Symphony Orchestra, cond. Serge Koussevitzky.

Unpub. See also Op. 112 (No. 120).

50. Sinfonietta in A major Op. 48. For orchestra. Third version. 1929. Ded. Nicolas Tcherepnine.

1. *Allegro giocoso*; 2. *Andante*; 3. *Intermezzo* (*Vivace*); 4. *Scherzo* (*Allegro risoluto*); 5. *Allegro giocoso*.

2 fl, 2 ob, 2 cl, 2 bsn; tpt, 4 hn; strings.

fp: 18 November 1930, Moscow, cond. K. S. Sarajev.

?fEbp: 2 February 1943, BBC Scottish Orchestra, cond. Ian Whyte.

Pub. 1931, Editions Russe de Musique: incl. reduction for piano by Serge Prokofiev.

51. Portraits Op. 49. Symphonic Suite from the opera 'The Gambler', for orchestra. 1930–1.

1. *Alexis*; 2. *La Grand'Mère*; 3. *Le Général*; 4. *Pauline*; 5. *Dénouement*.

2 fl, pic, 2 ob, ca, 2 cl, bcl, 2 bsn, cbsn; 3 tpt, 4 hn, 3 tmb, tuba; timp, GC, tamb, tamb mil, tgle, cym; 2 hp, piano, strings.

fp: 12 March 1932, Paris, cond. Serge Prokofiev (?F. Ruhlmann).

fEp: 26 January 1934, BBC concert, BBC Orchestra, cond. Nikolai Malko.

Pub. 1932, Editions Russe de Musique.

52. String Quartet No. 1 in B minor Op. 50. 1930.

Prokofiev, Serge

1. *Allegro*; 2. *Andante molto*; 3. *Andante*.
fp: 25 April 1931, Washington, Brosa Quartet.
fRp: 9 October 1931, Moscow, Roth Quartet.
fEp: 21 December 1931, BBC broadcast, Brosa Quartet.
Pub. 1931, Editions Russe de Musique.

52a. Andante Op. 50b. Arr. for string orchestra. 1930. Unperf. Unpub.

53. On the Dnieper (Sur le Borysthène) Op. 51. Ballet ('Poème choréographique') in two scenes. 1930. Scenario: Serge Lifar and Serge Prokofiev. Ded. to the memory of Serge Diaghilev.
Prélude. Tableau 1: *1. Rencontre*; *2. Scène*; *3. Pas de deux*; *4. Variation du premier danseur et finale.* Tableau 2: *5. Fiançailles*; *6. Danse du fiancé*; *7. Danse de la fiancée*; *8. Danse des jeunes gens*; *9. La Bagarre*; *10. Scène*; *11. Epilogue.*
fp: 16 December 1932, Paris Opéra, cond. Philippe Gaubert; choreography, Serge Lifar; décor and costumes, N. Gontcharova and M. Larionov.
Pub. 1932, Edition Russe de Musique: piano reduction by Serge Prokofiev.

53a. On the Dnieper (Sur le Borysthène): Symphonic Suite Op. 51b. 1933.
1. Prelude; *2. Variation of first dancer*; *3. The betrothal*; *4. The quarrel*; *5. Tableau*; *6. Epilogue.*
fp: 1934, Paris, cond. Serge Prokofiev.
Pub. Editions Russe de Musique: piano reduction by Serge Prokofiev.

54. Six Pièces Op. 52. Concert transcriptions for piano. 1930–1. From Op. 46, 48, 35, 50.
1. *Intermezzo.* (Comp. 1928.) Ded. Alexander Borovsky.
2. *Rondo.* (Comp. 1928.) Ded. Arthur Rubinstein.
3. *Etude.* (Comp. 1928.) Ded. Vladimir Horowitz.
4. *Scherzino.* (Comp. 1920.) Ded. Nicolas Orloff.
5. *Andante.* (Comp. 1930.)
6. *Scherzo.* (Comp. 1909.) Ded. Vladimir Horowitz.

fp: 27 May 1932, Moscow, Serge Prokofiev.
Pub. 1931, Editions Russe de Musique.

55. Piano Concerto No. 4 in B flat major for left hand Op. 53. 1931, Paris. Comp. for and ded. Paul Wittgenstein.
1. *Vivace*; 2. *Andante*; 3. *Moderato—Allegro molto*; 4. *Vivace*.
fp: 5 September 1956, West Berlin, S. Rapp.
fRp: 17 November 1959, Leningrad, A. Vedernikov, cond. G. Rozhdestvensky.
f London p: 25 September 1961, Royal Festival Hall, Malcolm Binns and the Royal Philharmonic Orchestra, cond. Kenneth V. Jones.
Pub. 1963, Moscow (State Music Publishers); piano score, ed. A. Vedernikov.

56. Two Sonatinas (Deux Sonatines) Op. 54. For piano. 1931–2.
No. 1 in E minor:
1. *Allegro molto*; 2. *Adagietto*; 3. *Allegretto*.
No. 2 in G major:
1. *Allegro sostenuto*; 2. *Andante amabile*; 3. *Allegro, ma non troppo*.
fp: 17 April 1932, BBC broadcast, Serge Prokofiev.
fRp: 27 November 1932, Moscow, Serge Prokofiev.
Pub. 1932, Editions Russe de Musique.

57. Piano Concerto No. 5 in G major Op. 55. 1932.
1. *Allegro con brio*; 2. *Moderato ben accentuato*; 3. *Toccata: Allegro con fuoco*; 4. *Larghetto*; 5. *Vivo*.
2 fl, pic, 2 ob, 2 cl, 2 bsn; 2 tpt, 2 hn, 2 tmb, tuba; timp, GC, tamb mil; strings.
fp: 31 October 1932, Berlin, Serge Prokofiev and the Berlin Philharmonic Orchestra, cond. Wilhelm Furtwängler.
fRp: 25 November 1932, Moscow, Serge Prokofiev, cond. N. S. Golovanov.
fEp: 31 January 1934, Serge Prokofiev and the BBC Symphony Orchestra, cond. Bruno Walter.
Pub. 1933, Editions Russe de Musique: incl. reduction by Serge Prokofiev for two pianos.

58. Sonata for two violins in C major Op. 56. 1932.

1. Andante cantabile; *2. Allegro*; *3. Comodo* (*quasi Allegretto*); *4. Allegro con brio*.

fp: 27 November 1932, Moscow, D. Tsiganov and V. Shirinsky.

fEp: *c.* March 1933, St. John's Institute, Music Society concert, Alfredo Poltronieri and Robert Soetens.

Pub. 1933, Editions Russe de Musique; 1947, Moscow (State Music Publishers).

59. Symphonic Song Op. 57. For orchestra. 1933.

fp: 14 April 1934, Moscow, cond. A. V. Gauk.

Unpub.

60. Cello Concerto in E minor Op. 58. 1933–8.

1. Andante; *2. Allegro giusto*; *3. Theme, Interlude & Variations*.

fp: 26 November 1938, Moscow, L. V. Berezovsky, cond. M. S. Melik-Pashayev.

fEbp: 24 March 1954, John Shinebourne and the BBC Scottish Orchestra, cond. Ian Whyte.

Pub. 1951, Anglo-Soviet Music: reduction.

BIBLIOGRAPHY:

Felix Aprahamian: Prokoviev's Cello Concerto Op. 58, *London Musical Events*, April 1957, p. 27.

61. Three Pieces (Trois Pièces) Op. 59. For piano. 1933–4.

1. Promenade. 1934.

2. Paysage. 1933.

3. Sonatine pastorale. 1934.

fp: 1935, Moscow, Serge Prokofiev.

Pub. 1935, Editions Russe de Musique.

62. Egyptian Nights. Incidental music for a play by A. Tayeerov, after Pushkin, Shakespeare and Shaw. 1933.

2 fl, pic, 2 ob, ca, 2 cl, alto sax, ten sax, bsn; corno da caccia, pic cornet, cornet, tpt, 2 hn, tmb; timp, tgle, tamb, tamb mil, cym, GC, tamtam, campanelli; hp, piano, strings; tenor and bass soloists and chorus.

fp: 1933, Moscow, Kamerny Theatre.

Pub. 1963, Moscow: score and piano score.

62a. Egyptian Nights: Symphonic Suite Op. 61. ?1934.

1. Night in Egypt; *2. Caesar, the Sphinx and Cleopatra*; *3. Alarm*; *4. Dances*; *5. Antony*; *6. Eclipse of Cleopatra*; *7. Roma militaria*.

fp: 22 December 1938, Moscow.

fEp: 16 March 1940, Queen's Hall, Courtauld-Sargent concert, London Philharmonic Orchestra, cond. (Sir) Malcolm Sargent.

Pub. 1934, Gutheil.

63. Lieutenant Kije. Music for the film produced by Belgoskino (Leningrad). 1933. Scored for small symphony orchestra.

63a. Lieutenant Kije Op. 60. Suite for orchestra, based on the film music. 1934.

1. Naissance de Kijé; *2. Romance*; *3. Noces de Kijé*; *4. Troika*; *5. Enterrement de Kijé*.

2 fl, pic, 2 ob, 2 cl, ten sax, 2 bsn; cornet à piston, 2 tpt, 4 hn, 3 tmb, tuba; GC, tgle, tamb mil, cym, tamb, sonagli; hp, celesta, piano, strings.

fp: 1934, Moscow.

fFp: 20 February 1937, Paris, l'Orchestre Lamoureux, cond. Serge Prokofiev.

f London p: 9 June 1942, Cambridge Theatre, as a ballet.

fEp (concert): 7 June 1944, Royal Albert Hall, Russian Music Festival, London Symphony Orchestra, cond. Anatole Fistoulari.

Pub. 1935, Gutheil; Breitkopf & Härtel.

BIBLIOGRAPHY:

Florent Schmitt: In den Tagen 'Lieutenant Kije', *Musik der Zeit*, No. 5 (1953), p. 33.

63b. Two Songs Op. 60b. 1934. From the film 'Lieutenant Kije'.

1. The little gray dove is cooing; *2. Troika*.

Pub. Editions Russe de Musique.

64. Thoughts (Pensées) Op. 62. For piano. 1933–4.

1. Adagio penseroso; *2. Lento*; *3. Andante*.

fp: 13 November 1936, Moscow, Serge Prokofiev.

Pub. 1936, Editions Russe de Musique.

65. Violin Concerto No. 2 in G minor Op. 63. Dated: 16 August 1935, Baku.

1. Allegro moderato; *2. Andante assai*; *3. Allegro, ben marcato*.

2 fl, 2 ob, 2 cl, 2 bsn; 2 tpt, 2 hn; GC, tamb mil, tgle, cym, cast; strings.

fp: 1 December 1935, Madrid, Robert

Soëtens and the Madrid Symphony Orchestra, cond. Enrique Arbós.

fEbp: 20 December 1936, Robert Soëtens and the BBC Orchestra, cond. Sir Henry Wood.

fEp (concert): 26 January 1938, Queen's Hall, Robert Soëtens and BBC Symphony Orchestra, cond. Serge Prokofiev.

Pub. 1937, Gutheil; Edition Russe de Musique; reduction by the composer, 1938, 1960, State Music Publishers; 1947, Leeds Music (ed. Louis Persinger).

66. Romeo and Juliet Op. 64. Ballet in four acts, ten scenes. 1935–6. Scenario: S. Radlov, A. Piotrovsky, L. Lavrovsky and Serge Prokofiev.

fp: December 1938, Brno.

fRp: 11 January 1940, Leningrad, Kirov Opera and Ballet Theatre, cond. I. Sherman; with Galina Ulanova (Juliet), K. Sergeyev (Romeo), A. Lopukhov (Mercutio), R. Gerbek (Tybalt), E. Biber (Nurse), L. Shavrov (Paris).

Pub. 1944, Muzfond; 1946, State Music Publishers (piano arr. only).

BIBLIOGRAPHY:

Gedeon Dienes: Romeo és Julia, *Muzsika*, July 1962, p. 6.

R.-Aloys Mooser: Romeo et Juliette, in *Aspects de la musique contemporaine*, Editions Labor et Fidès (Geneva) 1957, p. 250.

Iris Morley: Romeo and Juliet in Moscow, *Ballet*, August 1947, p. 19.

66a. Romeo and Juliet: Symphonic Suite No. 1 Op. 64b.

1. *Folk dance*; 2. *A scene* (*The street awakens*); 3. *Madrigal*; 4. *Minuet* (*The arrival of the guests*); 5. *Masks* (*Romeo and Mercutio masked*); 6. *Romeo and Juliet* (*The balcony scene*); 7. *The death of Tybalt*.

2 fl, pic, 2 ob, ca, 2 cl, bcl, ten sax, 2 bsn, cbsn; 4 hn, cornet, 2 tpt, 3 tmb, tuba; timp, snare dm, tgle, cym, GC, tamb, xyl, bells; hp, piano, strings.

fp: 27 November 1936, Moscow, Bolshoi Theatre, cond. George Sebastian.

fAp: 21 January 1937, Chicago Symphony Orchestra, cond. Serge Prokofiev.

f London p: 15 January 1954, Philharmonia Orchestra, cond. Sir Eugene Goossens.

Pub. 1938, State Music Publishers; 1946, Leeds Music (New York).

66b. Romeo and Juliet: Symphonic Suite No. 2 Op. 64c.

1. *The Montagues and the Capulets*; 2. *Juliet— the little girl*; 3. *Friar Laurence*; 4. *Dance*; 5. *Romeo and Juliet before parting*; 6. *Dance of the Maids from the Antilles*; 7. *Romeo and Juliet's grave*.

2 fl, pic, 2 ob, ca, 2 cl, bcl, ten sax, 2 bsn, cbsn; 4 hn, cornet, 2 tpt, 3 tmb, tuba; timp, snare dm, bells, tamb, cym, GC, maracas; hp, piano, celesta, strings.

fp: 15 April 1937, Leningrad, cond. Serge Prokofiev.

fEp: 26 January 1938, BBC Symphony Orchestra, cond. Sir Adrian Boult.

fAp: 25 March 1938, Boston Symphony Orchestra, cond. Serge Prokofiev.

Pub. 1938, State Music Publishers; 1946, Leeds Music (New York).

67. Music for children (Musiques d'enfants) Op. 65. Twelve easy pieces for children. 1935.

1. *Matin* (*Morning*); 2. *Promenade* (*Walk*); 3. *Historiette* (*Fairy tale*); 4. *Tarantelle*; 5. *Repentirs* (*Repentance*); 6. *Valse*; 7. *Cortège de sauterelles* (*Grasshoppers' parade*); 8. *La pluie et l'arc-en-ciel* (*Rain and rainbow*); 9. *Atrappe qui peut* (*Touch and run*); 10. *Marche*; 11. *Soir* (*Evening*); 12. *Sur les prés la lune se promène* (*The moon goes over the meadows*).

fp: 11 April 1936, Moscow, Serge Prokofiev.

Pub. 1936, Editions Russe de Musique; Peters (Leipzig).

67a. A Summer Day Op. 65b. Children's suite for small orchestra. 1941. Transcriptions of numbers from Op. 65.

1. *Morning*; 2. *Tag*; 3. *Waltz*; 4. *Repentance* (*Remorse*); 5. *March*; 6. *Evening*; 7. *The moon sails o'er the meadows*.

2 fl, 2 ob, 2 cl, 2 bsn; 2 tpt, 2 hn; timp, tgle, cym, GC, tamb, tamb mil, cast; strings.

fp: 1946, Moscow broadcast, cond. A. Stasevich.

Pub. 1947, State Music Publishers; 1948, Hawkes.

68. Six mass songs Op. 66. For voice and piano. 1935.

1. *Partisan Zheleznyak* (M. Golodny).

2. *Anyutka* (Anniutka) (Anon.).
3. *My country is growing* (A. Afinogenov).
4. *Through snow and fog* (A. Afinogenov).
5. *Beyond the hills* (Anon.).
6. *Song of Voroshilov* (Tatyana Siborskaya).
Pub. 1935, State Music Publishers (Nos. 1, 2); 1939, Iskusstvo Publishers (Nos. 3–6).

69. Peter and the Wolf Op. 67. Symphonic Tale for narrator and orchestra. 1936. Text: Serge Prokofiev. Dur. 35'.

fl, ob, cl, bsn; tpt, 3 hn; timp, tamb, tgle, cym, tamb mil, cast, GC; strings.

fp: 2 May 1936, Moscow Conservatory children's concert, Moscow Philharmonic Orchestra, cond. Serge Prokofiev, with T. Bobrova (speaker).

fAp (fp outside Russia): 25 March 1938, Boston Symphony Orchestra, cond. Leopold Stokowski.

f London p: January 1941, Savoy Theatre, Sidney Beer Symphony Orchestra, cond. Sidney Beer.

Pub. 1937 (reduction by Serge Prokofiev), 1940 (score), State Music Publishers. Min. score: 1942, Hawkes.

BIBLIOGRAPHY:
N. Saz: Wie Peter und der Wolf entstand, *Musik in Schule*, 1962, No. 9, p. 424.
E. Schicken: Peter und der Wolf—über die Arbeit mit Tonband und Lichtbildern, *Musik in Schule*, 1962, No. 10, p. 445.

70. Three children's songs Op. 68. For voice and piano. 1936–9.
1. *The chatterbox* (A. Barto).
2. *Lollipop song* (Sweet melody) (N. Sakonskaya).
3. *The little pigs* (L. Kvito, Russian version by S. Mikhalkova).
Pub. 1937 (Nos. 1, 2), 1946 (No. 3), State Music Publishers; 1948, Anglo-Soviet Music Press, with English texts by W. H. Easterbrook.

71. Four Marches Op. 69. For brass band. 1935–7.
1. *March for the Spartakiade*; 2. *Lyrical March*; 3. *Marching Song*; 4. *Cavalry March* (*with Chorus 'Over the Bridge'*).
Pub. (No. 1 only): 1937, State Music Publishers.

72. The Queen of Spades Op. 70. Music (24 numbers) for the film. 1936.
2 fl, 2 ob, ca, 2 cl, bcl, 2 bsn, alto sax, bar sax; 4 hn, 2 tpt, 3 tmb, tuba; timp, tamb, tamburo, cym, GC; cembalo, hp, piano, strings.
Pub. 1962, Moscow.

73. Boris Godunov Op. 70b. Incidental music (24 numbers) for the drama by Pushkin. 1936. Unpub.

74. Eugene Onegin Op. 71. Incidental music (45 numbers) for the play by Pushkin. 1936.
fp: Moscow, Kamerny Theatre.
Unpub.

75. Russian Overture Op. 72. For orchestra. 1936.
3 fl, pic, 3 ob, ca, 3 cl, bcl, 3 bsn, cbsn; 8 hn, 4 tpt, 3 tmb, tuba; timp, GC, cym, tamb, tamb mil, campanelli, cast, xyl, tamtam; 2 hp, piano, strings.
fp: 29 October 1936, Moscow, cond. Eugen Szenkar.
fEp: 29 June 1948, BBC broadcast, BBC Theatre Orchestra, cond. Walter Goehr.
Pub. 1936, Gutheil; 1946, State Music Publishers; Anglo-Soviet Music Press.

76. Three Romances (Pushkin) Op. 73. For voice and piano. ?1937.
1. *Pine trees*; 2. *Pink flush of dawn* (*Roseate dawn*); 3. *In your chamber.*
fp: 20 April 1937, Moscow broadcast.
Pub. 1937, State Music Publishers, in *A. S. Pushkin in Romances and Songs by Soviet Composers.*

77. Cantata for the Twentieth Anniversary of the October Revolution Op. 74. For symphony orchestra, brass band, orchestra of accordions, percussion and two choirs. 1936–7. Text: From writings and speeches of Marx, Lenin and Stalin.
1. *Introduction*; 2. *Philosophers*; 3. *Interlude*; 4. *We march together*; 5. *Interlude*; 6. *Revolution*; 7. *Victory*; 8. *Stalin's vow*; 9. *Symphony*; 10. *Constitution.*
Unpub.

78. Romeo and Juliet Op. 75. Ten pieces for piano. 1937.
1. *Folk dance*; 2. *Scene*; 3. *Minuet*; 4. *Juliet—*

the little girl; 5. *Masks*; 6. *The Montagues and the Capulets*; 7. *Friar Laurence*; 8. *Mercutio*; 9. *Dance of the maids from the Antilles*; 10. *Romeo and Juliet before parting.*

fp: 1937, Moscow, Serge Prokofiev.

Pub. 1938, Iskusstvo Publishers; 1956, Leeds Music (ed. Michael Fredericks).

79. Songs of our days Op. 76. For mezzo-soprano and baritone soloists, chorus and orchestra. 1937.

1. *March.*
2. *Cavalry song: Over the bridge* (A. Prishelets).
3. *Good health to you* (From the Byelorussian).
4. *Golden Ukraine* (Taken down as sung by U. Barabash on 'Krasny Prakhr' collective farm).
5. *Brother for brother* (V. Lebedev-Kumach).
6. *Girls* (A. Prishelets).
7. *Twenty-year-old* (S. Marshak).
8. *Lullaby* (V. Lebedev-Kumach).
9. *From East to West* (From the folksong).

2 fl, 2 ob, 2 cl, 2 bsn; 3 tpt, 4 hn, 3 tmb, tuba; tgle, legno, tamb, tamburo, cym, GC; hp, strings.

fp: 5 January 1938, Moscow, cond. A. V. Gauk.

Pub. 1939 (piano reduction by Serge Prokofiev), 1962 (full score), State Music Publishers.

80. Hamlet Op. 77. Incidental music for the play by Shakespeare. 1937–8.

1. *Ghost of Hamlet's father*; 2. *March of Claudius*; 3. *Ophelia's first song*; 4. *Ophelia's second song*; 5. *Ophelia's third song*; 6. *Ophelia's fourth song*; 7. *Fanfares 1 & 2*; 8. *Pantomime*; 9. *Song of the gravediggers*; 10. *Final march of Fortinbras.*

fp: 15 May 1938, Leningrad; producer, S. Radtov.

Unpub.

80a. Gavotte Op. 77b. For piano. 1938. Transcription of No. 4 from Op. 77.

fp: 30 (?22) November 1939, Moscow broadcast, H. Neuhaus.

Pub. 1939, Gutheil; 1940, State Music Publishers.

81. Alexander Nevsky. Music for the

Mosfilm production directed by Sergei M. Eisenstein. For mezzo-soprano, chorus and orchestra. 1938.

1. *Devastated Russia*; 2. *Dawn*; 3. *Pskov (I)*; 4. *Pskov (II)*; 5. *Pskov (III)*; 6. *Pskov (IV)*; 7. *The town square*; 8. *Mobilisation*; 9. *Ironwedge*; 10. *Russian horns*; 11. *A horn sinks*; 12. *Horns played in front of the square*; 13. *Fifes*; 14. *The square*; 15. *The duel*; 16. *After the duel*; 17. *Horns playing pursuit*; 18. *Cavalry charge*; 19. *Pursuit*; 20. *Entry into Pskov*; 21. *Finale.*

fEp: 8 December 1941, BBC broadcast version by Louis MacNeice of the film with Robert Donat as Nevsky; BBC Chorus and Theatre Chorus and BBC Symphony Orchestra, cond. Sir Adrian Boult.

Unpub.

81a. Alexander Nevsky Op. 78. Cantata for mezzo-soprano, chorus and orchestra. 1938–9. Words: V. Lugovskoi and Serge Prokofiev.

1. *Russia under the Mongolian yoke*; 2. *Song about Alexander Nevsky*; 3. *The crusaders in Pskov*; 4. *Arise, ye Russian people* (*Arise, men of Russia*); 5. *The battle on the ice*; 6. *Field of the dead*; 7. *Alexander's entry into Pskov.*

2 fl, pic, 2 ob, ca, 2 cl, bcl, sax, 2 bsn, cbsn; 4 hn, 3 tpt, 3 tmb, tuba; timp, tamb mil, tamb, maracas, legno, tgle, GC, xyl, tamtam, campana, campanelli; hp, strings.

fp: 17 May 1939, Moscow, V. D. Gagarina (mezzo-soprano), Moscow Philharmonic Chorus and Orchestra, cond. Serge Prokofiev.

Pub. 1941, State Music Publishers: incl. reduction by L. Atovmyan.

81b. Three Songs from Alexander Nevsky Op. 78b. For voice and piano.

1. *Arise men of Russia*; 2. *Hark, ye bright falcons*; 3. *On the Neva river* (for male chorus or duet).

Pub. 1939, State Music Publishers.

82. Seven Mass Songs Op. 79. For voice and piano. 1939.

1. *Song of the homeland* (A. Prokofiev).
2. *The Stakhanov girl* (A. Blagov).
3. *Over the Arctic Ocean* (M. Svetlov).
4. *Send-off* (Transl. from the Byelorussian).
5. *Forward!* (M. Mendelson).
6. *A Cossack came through the village* (P. Panchenko).

7. *Down the road* (Anon., from text published in *Pravda*, 9 November 1937).
Pub. 1940, State Music Publishers.

83. Violin Sonata No. 1 in F minor Op. 80. 1938–46.
1. *Andante assai*; 2. *Allegro brusco*; 3. *Andante*; 4. *Allegrissimo—Andante assai*.
fEp: 25 August 1946, BBC broadcast, Joseph Szigeti and Gerald Moore.
fRp: 23 October 1946, Moscow, David Oistrakh and Lev Oborin.
Pub. 1947, Muzfond; 1951, State Music Publishers.

84. Semyon Kotko Op. 81. Opera in five acts, seven scenes. 1939. Libretto: V. Katayev and Serge Prokofiev, from a story by V. Katayev.
fp: 23 June 1940, Moscow, Stanislavsky Opera Theatre, cond. M. N. Zhukov; producer, S. G. Birman; sets, A. G. Tyshler.
Pub. 1960, Moscow (vocal score).

BIBLIOGRAPHY:
H. Weinstock: Propaganda opera by Prokofiev, *Saturday Review*, 26 May 1962, p. 44.

84a. Semyon Kotko: Symphonic Suite Op. 81b. 1941.
1. *Introduction*; 2. *Semyon and his mother*; 3. *The betrothal*; 4. *The southern night*; 5. *Execution*; 6. *The village is burning* (*Village in flames*); 7. *Funeral*; 8. *Ours have come* (*Red Army arrives*).
2 fl, pic, 2 ob, ca, 2 cl, bcl, 2 bsn, cbsn; 4 hn, 3 tpt, 3 tmb, tuba; timp, GC, cym, tamb basque, tamb mil, campana, tamtam, sonagli, tgle, tamb di legno; hp, strings.
fp: 23 June 1940, Moscow.
Pub. 1947, State Music Publishers.

85. Piano Sonata No. 6 in A major Op. 82. 1939–40.
1. *Allegro moderato*; 2. *Allegretto*; 3. *Tempo di valzer lentissimo*; 4. *Vivace*.
fp: 8 April 1940, Moscow broadcast.
Pub. 1941, State Music Publishers; Anglo-Soviet Music Press; 1946, Leeds Music (ed. György Sandor).

BIBLIOGRAPHY:
Frank Merrick: SP's Sixth Piano Sonata, *MT*, January 1944, p. 9.

86. Piano Sonata No. 7 in B flat major Op. 83. 1939–42.
1. *Allegro inquieto*; 2. *Andante caloroso*; 3. *Precipitato*.
fp: 18 January 1943, Moscow, Sviatoslav Richter.
fEp: 20 November 1946, BBC broadcast, Nikita Magaloff.
Pub. 1943, State Music Publishers; Anglo-Soviet Music Press.

BIBLIOGRAPHY:
Frank Merrick: Prokofiev's Seventh and Eighth Piano Sonatas, *MT*, August 1948, p. 234.

87. Piano Sonata No. 8 in B flat major Op. 84. 1939–44.
1. *Andante dolce—Allegro moderato*; 2. *Andante sognando*; 3. *Vivace—Allegro ben marcato*.
fp: 30 December 1944, Moscow, Emil Gilels.
Pub. 1946, State Music Publishers; 1946, Anglo-Soviet Music Press.

BIBLIOGRAPHY:
Malcolm H. Brown: Prokofiev's Eighth Piano Sonata, *Tempo*, autumn 1964, p. 9.
Frank Merrick: Prokofiev's Seventh and Eighth Piano Sonatas, *MT*, August 1948, p. 234.

88. Zdravitsa (Hail to Stalin) (A Toast to Stalin) Op. 85. Cantata for chorus and orchestra on folk texts. 1939. Dur. 12½'.
2 fl, pic, 2 ob, ca, 2 cl, bcl, 2 bsn, cbsn; 3 tpt, 4 hn, 3 tmb, tuba; timp, legno, tamb mil, tamb, tgle, cym, GC, tamtam, xyl, campanelli; hp, piano, strings.
fp: 21 December 1939, Moscow, cond. N. S. Golovanov.
fEp: 21 December 1944, BBC broadcast, BBC Chorus and Orchestra, cond. Sir Adrian Boult. (NB: fEp originally announced for Promenade Concert, 11 August 1944.)
Pub. 1941, State Music Publishers: incl. reduction by L. Atovmyan.

89. The Duenna (orig. Betrothal in a Nunnery) Op. 86. Lyric-comic opera in four acts, nine scenes. 1940. Libretto: Serge Prokofiev, based on the play by Sheridan; verses by Mira Mendelson.

Prokofiev, Serge

2 fl, pic, 2 ob, ca, 2 cl, bcl, 2 bsn, cbsn; 4 hn, 3 tpt, 3 tmb, tuba; timp, pcssn; strings.
fp: 3 November 1946, Leningrad.
Pub. 1944, Muzfond (vocal score); 1948, 1954, Leeds Music (with English libretto by Jean Karsavina).

89a. Summer Night. Suite from the opera 'The Duenna'.
1. *Introduction*; 2. *Serenade*; 3. *Minuet*; 4. *Dreams*; 5. *Dance*.
2 fl, pic, 2 ob, ca, 2 cl, bcl, 2 bsn, cbsn; 4 hn, 3 tpt, 3 tmb, tuba; timp, tgle, legno, tamb, tamburo, maracas, cym, GC, campanelli; hp, strings.
Pub. 1965, State Music Publishers.

89b. Dance of the Masks. From 'The Duenna'.
2 fl, pic, 2 ob, ca, 2 cl, bcl, 2 bsn, cbsn; 4 hn, 3 tpt, 3 tmb, tuba; timp, legno, tamb, tamburo, cym, GC; hp, strings.
Pub. 1965, State Music Publishers.

90. Cinderella Op. 87. Ballet in three acts. 1940–4. Scenario: N. D. Volkov.
fp: 21 November 1945, Moscow, Bolshoi Theatre, cond. Y. Fayer; with Galina Ulanova (Cinderella), M. Gabovich (Prince).
fEp: 23 December 1948, Royal Opera House, Covent Garden, with Moira Shearer (Cinderella).
Pub. 1945, Muzfond (piano score); 1954, State Music Publishers (piano arr.).

BIBLIOGRAPHY:
Philip Hope-Wallace: Prokofiev's music for Cinderella, *Ballet*, February 1949, p. 34.
Edward Lockspeiser: Prokofiev ballet Cinderella presented in London, *Musical America*, 15 April 1949, p. 5.

91. Symphonic March in B flat major Op. 88. For orchestra. 1941. Unpub.

92. Seven mass songs Op. 89 No. 1. For voice and piano. 1941–2.
1. *Song* (V. Mayakovsky).
2. *Song of the brave* (A. Surkov).
3. *The tankman's vow*.
4. *Son of Kabarda*.
5. *The soldier's sweetheart*.
6. *Fritz*.
7. *Love of a soldier* (M. Mendelson).

fp (Nos. 3, 4): November 1941, Nalchik, A. Dolivo and Serge Prokofiev.
Pub. 1942, Muzfond (Nos. 3–6).

93. March in A flat major Op. 89 No. 2. For band. ?1941. Unpub.

94. The Year 1941 Op. 90. Symphonic Suite for orchestra. 1941.
1. *Night*; 2. *In battle*; 3. *For the brotherhood of nations*.
fp: 21 January 1943, Sverdlovsk, cond. N. S. Rabinovich.
Unpub.

95. War and Peace Op. 91. Opera in five acts, thirteen scenes, with a choral prologue (first version); in eleven scenes (second version). 1941–52. Libretto: Serge Prokofiev and M. Mendelson-Prokofieva.
fp (first version; first eight scenes only): 12 June 1946, Leningrad.
fp (second version): 31 March 1955, Leningrad.
Pub. 1943, Muzfond.

BIBLIOGRAPHY:
K. O. Hoover: Prokofiev's War and Peace, *Theatre Arts*, October 1950, p. 44.
J. Machlis: Prokofiev's War and Peace, *New York Times*, 6 January 1957, Section 2, p. 9.
Serge Prokofiev: Prokofiev's opera War and Peace, *MT*, February 1945, p. 51, reprinted from *Soviet War News*.
V. Seroff: Tolstoy's war, Prokofiev's peace, *Saturday Review*, 28 November 1959, p. 48.
M. Stempel: Prokofievs sista opera Krig och fred, *Musikrevy*, 1953, p. 116.
Emilia Zanetti: Prokofiev's Oper Krieg und Frieden (transl. Willi Reich), *Melos*, July–August 1953, p. 232.
Anon.: Prokofiev's War and Peace, *The Listener*, 22 February 1962, p. 357.

95a. Four Choruses from War and Peace. For SATB (No. 2, TTBB) and piano.
1. *So they came* (*First chorus of Kutuzov*); 2. *Brothers, we must go!* (*Second chorus of Kutuzov*); 3. *On this sombre night* (*Chorus of Muscovites*); 4. *The time is near* (*Chorus of the partisans*).
Pub. 1946, Russian-American Music Publishers (New York); English text, Elaine de Sincay; ed. Hugh Ross.

96. String Quartet No. 2 in F major
(Kabardinian Quartet) Op. 92. 1942, Nalchik.
  1. *Allegro sostenuto*; 2. *Adagio*; 3. *Allegro*.
fp: 7 April (?5 September) 1942, Moscow,
Beethoven Quartet.
  Pub. 1944, State Music Publishers; 1948,
International Music (New York).

97. Ballad of an unknown boy Op. 93.
Cantata for soprano, tenor, chorus and
orchestra. 1942–3. Text: P. Antokolsky.
  fp: 21 February 1944, Moscow, N.
Shpiller, F. Fedotov, Leningrad State Choir,
Republican Russian Choir and orchestra,
cond. A. V. Gauk.
  Unpub.

98. Flute Sonata in D major Op. 94. For
flute and piano. 1942–3.
  1. *Moderato*; 2. *Scherzo*; *Presto*; 3. *Andante*;
4. *Allegro con brio*.
  fp: 7 December 1943, Moscow, N. Khar-
kovsky and Sviatoslav Richter.
  Pub. 1953, Leeds Music; flute part ed.
Carleton Sprague Smith.

98a. Violin Sonata in D major Op. 94b.
Transcription of preceding. 1943–4.
  fp: 17 June 1944, Moscow, David Oistrakh
and Lev Oborin.
  Pub. 1946, State Music Publishers; 1956,
Leeds Music, violin part ed. Joseph Szigeti.

99. Three Pieces from Cinderella Op. 95.
For piano. 1942.
  1. *Intermezzo*; 2. *Gavotte*; 3. *Valse lente*.
  Pub. 1943, State Music Publishers; 1945,
Leeds Music (ed. Harry Cumpson); Anglo-
Soviet Music Press.

100. Lermontov. Music for the film. 1941–2.
A United Stalingrad and All-Union Children's
Film Studios production, directed by A.
Gendelstan, with A. Konsovsky as Lermontov.
Unpub.

101. Three Pieces Op. 96. For piano. 1941–
1942. Transcriptions from 'War and Peace'
and the film 'Lermontov'.
  1. *Waltz* (*from War and Peace*); 2. *Contra-
dance* (*from Lermontov*); 3. *Mephisto Waltz*
(*from Lermontov*).
  Pub. 1943, State Music Publishers; 1947,
Leeds Music.

102. Partisans in the Ukrainian Steppes.
Music for the Kiev Film Studio production,
directed by I. Savchenko. 1942. Unpub.

103. Kotovsky. Music for the Central
United Film Studio production directed by
A. Faintsimmer. 1942. Unpub.

104. Tonya. Music for the film. 1942.
Unpub.

105. Ten Pieces from Cinderella Op. 97.
For piano. 1943.
  1. *Fairy spring*; 2. *Fairy summer*; 3. *Fairy
autumn*; 4. *Fairy winter*; 5. *Grasshoppers and
dragonflies*; 6. *Orientalia*; 7. *Passepied*;
8. *Capriccio*; 9. *Bourrée*; 10. *Adagio*.
  Pub. 1944, State Music Publishers.

105a. Adagio from Cinderella Op. 97b.
For cello and piano. 1943–4.
  fp: 19 April 1944, Moscow broadcast, A. P.
Stogorsky.
  Pub. 1945, Muzfond; 1951, Leeds Music.

**106. Sketches for National Anthem of the
Soviet Union and National Anthem of the
R.S.F.S.R.** Op. 98. 1943. Unpub.

107. March in B flat major Op. 99. For
band. 1943–4.
  fp: 30 April 1944, Moscow broadcast, cond.
I. V. Petrov.
  Pub. 1946, State Music Publishers.

108. Symphony No. 5 in B flat major
Op. 100. 1944.
  1. *Andante*; 2. *Allegro marcato*; 3. *Adagio*;
4. *Allegro giocoso*.
  2 fl, pic, 2 ob, ca, pic cl, 2 cl, bcl, 2 bsn,
cbsn; 3 tpt, 4 hn, 3 tmb, tuba; timp, tgle, cym,
tamb, tamb mil, legno, GC, tamtam; hp,
piano, strings.
  fp: 13 January 1945, Moscow, cond. Serge
Prokofiev.
  fAp: 14 November 1945, Boston Symphony Orchestra, cond. Serge Koussevitzky.
  fEp: 21 August 1946, Royal Albert Hall,
Promenade Concert, London Symphony
Orchestra, cond. Basil Cameron.
  Pub. 1946, State Music Publishers; Anglo-
Soviet Music Publishers. Arrangements incl.
for piano solo by A. Vedernikov, for two
pianos eight hands by P. A. Lamm, concert

transcription of Scherzo for piano solo by Vedernikov.

BIBLIOGRAPHY:
William W. Austin: Prokofiev's Fifth Symphony, *MR*, August 1956, p. 205.
O. Corbiot: La cinquième symphonie Op. 100 de SP, *L'Education musicale*, No. 144, January 1968.
R.-Aloys Mooser: 5me Symphonie, in *Aspects de la musique contemporaine*, Editions Labor et Fidès (Geneva) 1957, p. 90.

109. Romeo and Juliet: Suite No. 3 Op. 101. 1944.

1. *Romeo at the fountain*; 2. *Morning dance*; 3. *Juliet*; 4. *Nurse*; 5. *Morning serenade (Aubade)*; 6. *Juliet's death*.

2 fl, pic, 2 ob, ca, 2 cl, bcl, 2 bsn, cbsn; 4 hn, 3 tpt, 3 tmb, tuba; timp, GC, legno, tamb mil, tgle, tamb, campanelli; celesta, piano, hp, strings.

fp: 8 March 1946, Moscow, cond. V. Degtyarenko.

Pub. 1947, Muzfond; 1949, State Music Publishers.

110. Six Pieces from Cinderella Op. 102. For piano. 1944.

1. *Waltz of Cinderella and the Prince*; 2. *Cinderella's variations*; 3. *The quarrel*; 4. *Waltz: Cinderella departs for the ball*; 5. *Dance with shawls*; 6. *Amoroso*.

Pub. 1944, Muzfond.

111. Piano Sonata No. 9 in C major Op. 103. 1945–7. Ded. Sviatoslav Richter.

1. *Allegretto*; 2. *Allegro strepitoso*; 3. *Andante tranquillo*; 4. *Allegro con brio, ma non troppo presto*.

fp: 21 April 1951, Moscow, Union of Soviet Composers concerts in celebration of Prokofiev's sixtieth birthday, Sviatoslav Richter.

fEp: 16 February 1957, BBC broadcast, Ross Pratt.

Pub. 1955, State Music Publishers, Anglo-Soviet Music Press, Leeds Music (ed. Menahem Pressler).

BIBLIOGRAPHY:
Frank Merrick: Prokofiev's Ninth Piano Sonata, *MT*, December 1956, p. 649.

112. Russian folksongs Op. 104. Twelve songs in two volumes for voice and piano. 1944.

1. *Guelder rose*; 2. *Green glade*; 3. *Guelder rose on the hill*; 4. *White snow*; 5. *Brown eyes*; 6. *Katerina*; 7. *Dream*; 8. *Beyond the woods*; 9. *Dunyushka*; 10. *My beloved is gone*; 11. *Sashenka*; 12. *The monk*.

fp: 25 March 1945, Moscow.

Pub. 1945, Muzfond.

113. Ode to the end of the War Op. 105.

For eight harps, four pianos, brass, percussion and double-basses. 1945.

fp: 12 November 1945, Moscow, cond. S. A. Samosud.

fEp: 7 July 1946, London, ISCM Festival.

Unpub.

114. Russian folksongs Op. 106. For tenor and bass and piano acc. 1945.

1. *Moscow road*; 2. *Every man must marry*.

Pub. 1946, Muzfond. Folk texts taken down by Y. Hippius.

115. Cinderella: Suite No. 1 Op. 107. 1946. Dur. 32'.

1. *Introduction*; 2. *Pas de chat (Dance with shawls)*; 3. *Quarrel*; 4. *Fairy godmother and Fairy winter*; 5. *Mazurka*; 6. *Cinderella goes to the ball*; 7. *Cinderella's waltz*; 8. *Midnight*.

2 fl, pic, 2 ob, ca, 2 cl, bcl, 2 bsn, cbsn; 4 hn, 3 tpt, 3 tmb, tuba; timp, tgle, cast, tamb, tamb mil, tamtam, cym, GC, campane, campanelli, xyl; piano, hp, strings.

fp: 12 November 1946, Moscow, cond. A. Stasevich.

fEp: 14 March 1948, BBC broadcast, BBC Theatre Orchestra, cond. Walter Goehr.

fEp (concert): 18 November 1949, Royal Albert Hall, Liverpool Philharmonic Orchestra, cond. Hugo Rignold.

Pub. 1949, Anglo-Soviet Music.

116. Cinderella: Suite No. 2 Op. 108. 1946.

1. *Cinderella's dreams*; 2. *Dancing lesson and gavotte*; 3. *Spring fairy and Summer fairy*; 4. *Bourrée*; 5. *Cinderella arrives at the ball*; 6. *Grand waltz*; 7. *Galop*.

Unpub.

117. Cinderella: Suite No. 3 Op. 109. 1946.

1. *Pavane*; 2. *Cinderella and the Prince*

(*Adagio*); 3. *Three oranges*; 4. *Southern hands* (*The Temptation*); 5. *Orientalia*; 6. *The Prince finds Cinderella*; 7. *Valse lente*; 8. *Amoroso*.

fp: 3 September 1947, Moscow broadcast, cond. A. Stasevich.

Pub. 1954, State Music Publishers.

118. Waltzes Op. 110. Suite for orchestra. 1946. From 'War and Peace', 'Cinderella' and 'Lermontov'.

1. *Since we met*; 2. *Cinderella in the palace*; 3. *Mephisto Waltz*; 4. *End of tale*; 5. *New Year's waltz*; 6. *Happiness*.

fp: 13 May 1947, cond. M. O. Steiman.

Pub. 1947, Muzfond.

119. Symphony No. 6 in E flat minor Op. 111. 1945–6.

1. *Allegro moderato*; 2. *Largo*; 3. *Vivace*.

2 fl, pic, 2 ob, ca, pic cl, 2 cl, bcl, 2 bsn, cbsn; 3 tpt, 4 hn, 3 tmb, tuba; timp, tgle, tamb, tamb mil, tamtam, legno, cym, GC; celesta, piano, hp, strings.

fp: 11 October 1947, Leningrad, cond. Y. A. Mravinsky.

f European p: 23 February 1950, London, Royal Albert Hall, London Philharmonic Orchestra, cond. Eduard van Beinum.

Pub. 1949, Anglo-Soviet Music Press; Leeds Music.

120. Symphony No. 4 in C major Op. 112. Second version. 1947.

1. *Andante—Allegro eroico*; 2. *Andante tranquillo*; 3. *Moderato, quasi allegretto*; 4. *Allegro risoluto*.

2 fl, pic, 2 ob, ca, pic cl, 2 cl, bcl, 2 bsn, cbsn; 3 tpt, 4 hn, 3 tmb, tuba; timp, tgle, wd bk, tamb, tamburo, cym, GC; strings.

fEp: 11 March 1950, BBC broadcast, BBC Symphony Orchestra, cond. Sir Adrian Boult.

Pub. 1962 (full score), Moscow.

121. Festive Poem ('Thirty Years') Op. 113. For orchestra. 1947.

fp: 3 October 1947, Moscow, cond. K. Ivanov.

Pub. 1947, Muzfond.

122. Prosper, our mighty land Op. 114. Cantata for chorus and orchestra. 1947. Text: A. Mashistov. Composed for the thirtieth anniversary of the October Revolution.

Originally called *Flourish, mighty land* and written to a text by Eugene Dolmatovsky.

2 fl, pic, 2 ob, ca, 2 cl, bcl, 2 bsn, cbsn; 3 tpt, 4 hn, 3 tmb, tuba; timp, tgle, tamb, cast, tamburo, cym, GC; hp, piano, strings.

fp: 12 November 1947, Moscow, Russian Federal S.S.R. Choir and State Symphony Orchestra, cond. N. P. Anosov.

Pub. 1947, Muzfond (piano score only); 1962, State Music Publishers (full score, revised edition with new text).

123. Sonata in D major Op. 115. For unacc. violins in unison. 1947.

fEbp: 10 July 1959, Ruggiero Ricci.

Pub. 1947, Muzfond; 1952, State Music Publishers; 1953, Leeds Music (for violin solo, ed. Louis Persinger).

124. Ivan the Terrible Op. 116. Music for films produced by Mosfilm and directed by Sergei M. Eisenstein. Part I ('Ivan the Terrible') 1942–4, Part II ('The Boyars' Plot') 1945. Scored for mezzo-soprano and orchestra. Music cond. A. L. Stasevich.

1. *Overture*; 2. *Ocean*; 3. *Shuisky and huntsmen*; 4. *Enter Ivan*; 5. *March of the young Ivan*; 6. *Swan*; 7. *Song of praise*; 8. *Rebellion*; 9. *God's fool*; 10. *Mystery play*; 11. *Tartars*; 12. *Enter Tartars*; 13. *Ivan's tent*; 14. *Attack*; 15. *Gunners*; 16. *Guns move on Kazan*; 17. *Capture of Kazan*; 18. *Malyuta's envy*; 19. *Ivan implores the Boyars*; 20. *The poisoning*; 21. *Anastasya's illness*; 22. *Ivan at the bier*; 23. *Song of the beaver*; 24. *'Come back'*; 25. *Long life*; 26. *Dance of the Oprichniks*; 27. *Oprichniks' song*; 28. *Oprichniks and Vladimir*; 29. *Oprichniks' vow*.

Unpub.

124a. Ivan the Terrible. Oratorio for narrator, soloists and orchestra. Completed by A. L. Stasevich, 1961. Text: Sergei M. Eisenstein. Texts of songs: V. Lugovskoy.

1. *Overture*; 2. *March of the young Ivan*; 3. *Ocean–Sea*; 4. *I'll be the Tsar!*; 5. *God is glorified!*; 6. *Long live our Tsar!*; 6a. *Ocean–Sea*; 7. *Simpleton*; 8. *The white swan*; 8a. *Glorification*; 9. *On the bones of foes*; 10. *The Tartars*; 11. *Cannoneers*; 12. *To Kazan!*; 13. *Ivan pleads with the Boyars*; 13a. *The Tartar plains*; 14. *Efrosiniya and Anastasia*; 15. *Song of the Beaver* (*The Lullaby of Efro-*

Prokofiev, Serge

siniya); 16. *Ivan at the coffin of Anastasia*; 17. *The choir of the Tsar's men*; 17a. *The oath of the Tsar's men*; 18. *Song of Fyodor Basmanov and the Tsar's men*; 19. *Dance of the Tsar's men*; 20. *Finale.*
Pub. 1962, Moscow, with English text and lyrics by Herbert Marshall.

125. The Story of a Real Man Op. 117. Opera in four acts. 1947–8. Libretto: M. Mendelson-Prokofieva and Serge Prokofiev, from a novel by Boris Polevoi.
fp: 3 December 1948, Leningrad.
Pub. 1962, Soviet Composers (Moscow): vocal score.

BIBLIOGRAPHY:
P. Eckstein: In der CSSR—Auf dem Wege zur Gegenwartsoper, *Musik und Gesellschaft*, August 1961, p. 488.
J. Jiranek: Cin hodny opery Narodniho divadla, *Hudební Rozhledy*, 1961, No. 10, p. 431.
J. Keldys: Posledni opera Sergeje Prokofieva, *Hudební Rozhledy*, 1960, No. 4, p. 148 (transl. by V. Solin from *Sovetskaya Muzyka*).
M. Ladmanova: Nad pribehom jednej epery, *Slovenska Hudba*, May 1961, p. 225.
N. Notowicz: Prokofievs Oper Der Wahre Mensch, *Musik und Gesellschaft*, January 1961, p. 18.
G. Polyanovsky: Prokofiev's last opera, *Opera*, April 1961, p. 261.
K. Schönewolf: Prokofievs Oper Der Wahre Mensch erstmals in deutsches Bearbeitung, *Musik und Gesellschaft*, July 1961, p. 431.
A. A. Zolotov: Prokofiev première, *Opera News*, 11 March 1961, p. 32.

126. The Stone Flower Op. 118. Ballet in four acts. 1948–50. Scenario: L. Lavrovsky and M. Mendelson-Prokofieva, from a story by P. Bazhov.
fp: 12 February 1954, Moscow, Bolshoi Theatre, cond. Y. Fayer; with Galina Ulanova (Katerina), V. Preobrazhensky (Danila), N. Chorokhova (Mistress of Copper Mountain).
Pub. 1956, State Music Publishers: piano score, arr. A. Vedernikov.

127. Cello Sonata in C major Op. 119. 1949.

1. *Andante grave*; 2. *Moderato*; 3. *Allegro ma non troppo.*
fp: 1 March 1950, Moscow, Mstislav Rostropovich and Sviatoslav Richter.
fAp: 25 February 1951, New York, Town Hall, Raya Garbousova.
fEbp: 13 April 1960, Janos Starker and Ernest Lush.
Pub. 1951, State Music Publishers; 1953, Leeds Music (ed. Raya Garbousova).

128. Two Pushkin Waltzes Op. 120. For orchestra. 1949.
fp: 1952, Moscow broadcast, cond. S. A. Samosud.
Unpub.

129. Soldiers' Marching Song (V. Lugovskoi) Op. 121. 1950. Unpub.

130. Winter Bonfire Op. 122. Suite for narrator, boys' chorus and orchestra. 1949. Text: S. Marshak.
1. *Departure*; 2. *Snow under the windows*; 3. *Waltz on the ice*; 4. *Bonfire*; 5. *Pioneer rally*; 6. *Winter evening*; 7. *On the march*; 8. *Return.*
2 fl, pic, ob, 2 cl, bsn; 2 tpt, 4 hn, tmb, tuba; timp, tamb mil, GC, tgle, cym, campanelli; celesta, piano, hp, strings.
fp: 19 December 1950, Moscow, Lyuda Pirogova and Natasha Zashchipina (reciters), boys' chorus of Moscow Choir School, cond. S. A. Samosud.
Pub. 1951, State Music Publishers.

131. Summer Night Op. 123. Suite for orchestra from the opera 'The Duenna'. 1950.
1. *Introduction*; 2. *Serenade*; 3. *Minuet*; 4. *Dreams*; 5. *Dance.*
2 fl, pic, 2 ob, ca, 2 cl, bcl, 2 bsn, cbsn; 4 hn, 3 tpt, 3 tmb, tuba; timp, tgle, legno, tamb, tamburo, maracas, cym, GC, campanelli; hp, strings.
Pub. 1965, State Music Publishers.

132. On Guard for Peace Op. 124. Oratorio for narrator, mezzo-soprano, mixed chorus, boys' chorus and orchestra. 1950. Text: S. Marshak.
fp: 19 December 1950, Moscow.
Pub. 1952, State Music Publishers: vocal score.

133. Sinfonia Concertante in E minor
Op. 125. For cello and orchestra. 1950–2.

fp: 18 February 1952, Moscow, in original form (as Cello Concerto No. 2), Mstislav Rostropovich, cond. Sviatoslav Richter.

fEp: 14 August 1955, BBC broadcast of a Danish recording by Mstislav Rostropovich and the Symphony Orchestra of Statsradio-fonien, cond. Thomas Jensen.

Unpub.

134. Wedding Suite Op. 126. Suite for orchestra from 'The Stone Flower'. 1951. Dur. 17'.

1. *Amorous dance*; 2. *Dance of the fiancée's girl friends*; 3. *Maidens' dance*; 4. *Ceremonial dance*; 5. *Wedding dance*.

2 fl, pic, 2 ob, ca, pic cl, 2 cl, bcl, 2 bsn, cbsn; 4 hn, 3 tpt, 3 tmb, tuba; timp, GC, cym, tgle, campanelli, tamb, tamb mil, legno; hp, piano, strings.

fp: 12 December 1951, Moscow, cond. S. A. Samosud.

Pub. 1960, Anglo-Soviet Music Press; Leeds Music.

135. Gipsy Fantasy Op. 127. For orchestra, from 'The Stone Flower'. 1951.

fp: 18 November 1951, Moscow, cond. S. A. Samosud.

Unpub.

136. Ural Rhapsody Op. 128. For orchestra, from 'The Stone Flower'. 1951. Unperf. Unpub.

137. The Mistress of the Copper Mountain Op. 129. Suite for orchestra, from 'The Stone Flower'. Projected but unrealized.

138. The Volga Meets the Don Op. 130. Festive Poem for orchestra. 1951.

fp: 22 February 1952, Moscow broadcast, cond. S. A. Samosud.

Pub. 1956, State Music Publishers: piano score arr. A. Vedernikov.

139. Symphony No. 7 in C sharp minor Op. 131. 1951–2. Dur. 32'.

1. *Moderato*; 2. *Allegretto*; 3. *Andante espressivo*; 4. *Vivace*.

2 fl, pic, 2 ob, ca, 2 cl, bcl, 2 bsn; 4 hn, 3 tpt, 3 tmb, tuba; timp, GC, tgle, tamb, tamb mil, cym, campanelli, xyl, legno; hp, piano, strings.

fp: 11 October 1952, Moscow, cond. S. A. Samosud.

fAp: 10 April 1953, Philadelphia, Philadelphia Orchestra, cond. Eugene Ormandy.

f New York p: 21 April 1953, Philadelphia Orchestra, cond. Eugene Ormandy.

fEp: 23 October 1954, Leeds Festival, Town Hall, Yorkshire Symphony Orchestra, cond. Nikolai Malko; broadcast by the BBC.

Pub. 1953 (arr. by A. Vedernikov for piano four hands), 1954 (score), State Music Publishers; Le Chant du Monde (Paris); Leeds Music (New York).

BIBLIOGRAPHY:

O. Downes: Prokofiev Seventh, *New York Times*, 26 April 1953, Section 2, p. 7.
I. Kolodin: First performance of Seventh Symphony, *Saturday Review*, 9 May 1953, p. 31.
Edward Lockspeiser: Prokofiev's Seventh Symphony, *Tempo*, No. 37, autumn 1955.
Hugh Ottaway: Prokofiev's Seventh Symphony, *MT*, February 1955, p. 74.
Andrew Porter: Prokofiev's Seventh Symphony, *London Musical Events*, June 1956, p. 25.

140. Cello Concertino in G minor Op. 132. For cello and orchestra. 1952. Unfinished. Completed by M. Rostropovich, scored by D. Kabalevsky.

1. *Andante mosso*; 2. *Andante*; 3. *Allegretto*.

2 fl, 2 ob, ca, 2 cl, 2 bsn; 2 tpt, 4 hn, 3 tmb, tuba; timp, tamb, tamburo, cym, GC; strings.

fp: 29 December 1956, Moscow Conservatoire (Smaller Hall), Mstislav Rostropovich and A. Dedyukhin (piano).

fp (with orchestra): 18 March 1960, Moscow Conservatoire (Great Hall), Mstislav Rostropovich, cond. Stasevich.

f London p: 25 July 1965, Royal Festival Hall, Mstislav Rostropovich and the London Symphony Orchestra, cond. Gennadi Rozhdestvensky.

Pub. 1960, State Music Publishers.

141. Concerto for two pianos and string orchestra Op. 133. 1952. Unfinished. Unpub.

Prokofiev, Serge

142. Cello Sonata in C sharp minor Op. 134. For unacc. cello. Unfinished. Unpub.

143. Piano Sonata No. 5 in C major Op. 135. Second version. 1952–3.
fp: 2 February 1954, Alma-Ata, A. Vedernikov.
Pub. 1955, State Music Publishers.

144. Symphony No. 2 in D minor Op. 136. Second version. Projected but unrealized.

145. Piano Sonata No. 10 Op. 137. Sketch only.

146. Piano Sonata No. 11 Op. 138. Projected but unrealized.

GENERAL BIBLIOGRAPHY

Gerald Abraham: Prokofiev as a Soviet composer, *MR*, 1943, No. 4, p. 241; Prokofiev als 'Sowjet' Komponist, *Musik der Zeit*, No. 5 (1953), p. 35.
B. Asafiev: SP, *Slovenska Hudba*, May 1958, p. 205.
Michel Astroff: Bei der Arbeit belauscht, *Musik der Zeit*, No. 5 (1953), p. 31.
K. Baekkelund: Prokofieff og Sjostakovitsj som pianister, *Norsk Musikerblad*, December 1961, p. 2.
George Brieger: Zum Tode SPs, *NZfM*, 1953, p. 213.
David Brown: Prokofiev and the opera, *The Listener*, 23 August 1962.
M. H. Brown: Prokofiev in America, *Listen*, December 1963, p. 2.
José Bruyr: Prokofiev, tel que je l'ai connu, *Musica* (Chaix), No. 108, March 1963, p. 4.
Humphrey Burton: Prokofiev, *Crescendo*, No. 115, October 1961, p. 29.
Geoffrey Bush: People who live in glass houses, *Composer*, No. 37, autumn 1970, p. 25.
M.-D. Calvocoressi: SP, *Anbruch*, 1922, Nos. 11–12, p. 172.
Jan Carlstedt: SP, *Nutida musik*, Vol. 5 (1961–2), No. 3, p. 25.
M. Cazden: Humour in the music of Stravinsky and Prokofiev, *Science and Society*, winter 1954, p. 52.
Abram Chasins: Prokofiev's nine piano sonatas, *Saturday Review*, 25 May 1957, p. 46.

André Coeuroy: Musiciens d'ailleurs, *Revue universelle*, 15 May 1922, p. 536.
Martin Cooper: SP, *London Musical Events*, May 1953, p. 22.
— Prokofiev—playboy or prodigal?, *The Listener*, 16 February 1961, p. 301.
— SP, in *Ideas and Music*, Barrie & Rockliff (London) 1965, p. 135.
A. della Corte: Opere e pensieri di Prokofiev e Kaciaturian, *La Scala*, March 1961.
O. Downes: A great composer, *New York Times*, 15 March 1953, Section 2, p. 7.
David Drew: Prokofiev's demon, *New Statesman*, 2 September 1966, p. 328.
P. Faltin: K niektorym tektonickym principom v klavirnych sonatach Sergeja Prokofieva, *Slovenska Hudba*, November 1960, p. 533.
Erwin Felber: SP, *Die Musik*, November 1932, p. 104.
P.-O. Ferroud: The ballets of SP, *Chesterian*, No. 114, March–April 1934, p. 89.
Raymond Forrer: SP, *L'Orient musical*, May 1929.
A. Fiewralski: Prokofiew i Meyerhold, *Ruch Muzyczny* 1963, No. 1, p. 18.
Andrew A. Fraser: SP, *Chesterian*, No. 78, April–May 1929.
J. Germain: Deux œuvres de jeunesse de Prokofiev, *Disques*, 1950, No. 22, p. 515.
Noël Goodwin: SP, *MO*, June 1953, p. 537.
Roy Harris: Roy Harris salutes SP, *Musical America*, May 1961, p. 12.
Leigh Henry: SP, *MO*, 1924, May p. 806, July p. 999.
Josef Hermann: SP, *Musica*, 1953, No. 6, p. 250.
Rotislav Hofmann: Autour de Prokofiev, *Revue musicale de France*, 1946, No. 5.
— SP, *Le Journal musical français*, 9 April 1953.
— SP, Editions Seghers (Paris) 1964.
Vincent d'Indy: Trois musiciens célèbres, *Le Courrier musical*, 15 March 1922.
I. Jirko: Prokofjevovy klavirni sonaty souborne, *Hudební Rozhledy*, 1961, No. 9, p. 393.
— 5x Prokofjev; hrst poznamek k prokofjevovske interpretaci, *Hudební Rozhledy*, 1962, Nos. 23–24, p. 1011.
— Drama zivota, *Hudební Rozhledy*, 1963, No. 14, p. 568.

E. Jenö Juhász: Prokofiev—Szkitákszvit, *Muzsika*, March 1963, p. 28.

János Kárpáti: SP, *Muzsika*, May 1961, p. 12.

Ernst Krause: Blick nach Osten—Shostakowitsch und Prokofiev, *Musica*, 1947, No. 2, p. 105.

Stanley D. Krebs: SP, in *Soviet Composers and the Development of Soviet Music*, George Allen & Unwin (London), 1970.

Gerald Larner: Prokofiev for piano, *R&R*, February 1965, p. 66.

Robert Layton: SP, in *The Symphony*, Penguin Books (London) 1967, p. 166.

— Prokofiev and the Sonata, *The Listener*, January 1967.

David Lloyd-Jones: Prokofiev and the opera, *Opera*, August 1962, p. 513.

Edward Lockspeiser: Prokofiev, Russia's Peter Pan of music, *M&M*, May 1953, p. 12.

— SP, *Crescendo*, No. 131, December 1963, p. 70.

Watson Lyle: The music of Prokofiev, *MM&F*, October 1932, p. 20.

Joseph Machlis: SP, in *Introduction to Contemporary Music*, Norton (USA) 1961, Dent (London), p. 273.

Carlo Marinelli: Romanticismo di Prokofiev, *Rassegna musicale*, June 1959, p. 143.

A. Martin: SP—la musique rencontre le cinéma, *Cahiers du Cinéma*, No. 23, May 1953, p. 24.

Frank Merrick: SP, *MN&H*, 31 March 1923, p. 306.

— Prokofiev's piano sonatas 1–5, *MT*, January 1945, p. 9.

— Prokofiev's piano sonatas, *PRMA*, 1948–9, p. 13.

— Prokofievs Werke für Klavier allein, *Musik der Zeit*, No. 5 (1953), p. 50.

A. Medvedev: Filmova providka u Prokofjevovi, *Hudební Rozhledy*, 1961, No. 20, p. 863.

Alain Messiaen: Mort et transfiguration de SP, *RM* (Les Carnets Critiques), 1953, p. 12.

M. Montagu-Nathan: SP, *MT*, May 1953, p. 209.

Serge Moreux: Mit den Augen des Freundes gesehen, *Musik der Zeit*, No. 5 (1953), p. 25.

Iris Morley: Cinderella und Romeo und Julia—Am Bolshoi-Theater und in Covent Garden, *Musik der Zeit*, No. 5 (1953), p. 56.

N. Nabokov: SP, *Atlantic Monthly*, July 1942, p. 62.

Antonio Odriozola: SP (discography), *Musica* (Madrid), 1953, p. 238.

D. Hugh Ottaway: SP and Benjamin Britten, *MO*, July 1950, p. 576.

R. Parmenter: Prokofiev's unknown legacy, *New York Times*, 24 May 1953, Section 2, p. 7.

L. Poljakova: Prokofjevova symfonicka tvorba (transl. V. Solin), *Hudební Rozhledy*, No. 20 (1959), p. 846.

G. Pugliese: Unknown world of Prokofiev's opera (with discography), *High Fidelity*, June 1966, p. 44.

Malcolm Rayment: Prokofiev as symphonist, *The Listener*, 18 February 1965, p. 277.

Charles Reid: SP, in *Decca Book of Ballet*, Muller (London) 1958, p. 234.

K. Riisager: Prokofiev, *Dansk Musiktidsskrift*, 1927, No. 1.

Luigi Rossi: Il balletti, paradigma di Prokofiev, *Musica d'oggi*, July–August (No. 4), 1963, p. 165.

L. Sabanyev: Russia's strong man, *Modern Music*, February 1929.

R. Sabin: Classicist but decadent, *Musical America*, 15 December 1951, p. 5.

M. Sabinina: Opera, kterou Prokofjev nenapsal, *Hudební Rozhledy*, 1962, No. 20, p. 854 (transl. from *Sovetskaya Muzyka*).

Semyon Scheifstein: SP, Moscow 1965; SP, Dokumente, Briefe, Erinnerungen (transl. E. Loesch), *VEB*, Deutscher Verlag für Musik (Leipzig) 1966.

Boris de Schloezer: Prokofiev, *RM*, July 1921, p. 50.

— Igor Stravinsky and SP, *Melos*, 1925, No. 10.

— SP, *Revue Pleyel*, March 1926.

— SP, *Nouvelle nouvelle revue française*, 1953, No. 4, p. 730.

Irving Schwerké: SP, his career and work, *Musical Courier*, 11 August 1934; in *Views and Interviews* (Paris), 1936, p. 49.

Gerald Seaman: The many sidedness of Prokofiev, *The Listener*, 9 April 1959, p. 647.

Desmond Shawe-Taylor: A Russian composer, *New Statesman*, 14 March 1953, p. 294.

M. Skorik: Prokofjev a Schönberg, *Hudební Rozhledy*, 1962, No. 11, p. 459 (transl. from *Sovetskaya Muzyka*).

Nicolas Slonimsky: Ugly duckling of Russian music, *Christian Science Monitor Magazine*, 27 January 1945, p. 7.

Denis Stevens: Prokofiev in Prague, *New York Times*, 23 June 1963, Section 2, p. 11.

Alan Stockdale: Prokofiev, *The Gramophone*, August 1939, p. 101.

H. H. Stuckenschmidt: SP, in *Schöpfer der neuen Musik*, Suhrkamp Verlag (Frankfurt a.M.) 1958, p. 258.

Hans Swarowski: Prokofievs Orchesterwerke, *Musik der Zeit*, No. 5 (1953), p. 41.

— Unknown works with a new aspect, *Tempo*, No. 30, winter 1953–4.

Joseph Szigeti: The Prokofiev I knew, *M&M*, June 1963, p. 10.

B. Ulanov: The death of Prokofiev, *Metronome*, May 1953, p. 34.

J. d'Urbano: Presentazione di SP, *Buenos Aires Musical*, 1 June 1953.

I. Vajda: SP a my, *Slovenska Hudba*, 1963, No. 3, p. 76.

J. Valek: O zakladech symfonismu Sergeje Prokofieva, *Hudební Rozhledy*, No. 20 (1959), p. 833.

A. Werth: Real Prokofiev—now it can be told, *Nation*, 4 April 1953, p. 285.

Robert Zanetti: Prokofiev und Diaghilev, *Melos*, December 1965, p. 443.

T. A. Zielinski: O muzyce bez kompleksow, *Ruch Muzyczny*, 1 February 1960, p. 3.

— Prokofiewowskie nieporozumenia, *Ruch Muzyczny*, 1 June 1960, p. 11.

MISCELLANEOUS OR UNSIGNED

Prokofiev's new line, *Time*, 1 February 1937, p. 38.

Prokofiev eats crow, *Musical America*, March 1949, p. 11.

Was Prokofiev a great composer?, *The Times*, 7 June 1963, p. 15.

GIACOMO PUCCINI (1858–1924)

Giacomo Puccini represents the last of four generations of Italian church-composers who lived in (Lucca) Tuscany, and when he was born there on 22 December 1858 it was widely assumed that like his father he would one day be director of music at the church of San Martino. He played the organ from the age of fourteen but did not begin to compose until he was seventeen. His ambition to become primarily an opera composer dates from a visit to Pisa in 1876 to see Verdi's *Aida*. He entered the Milan Conservatoire in 1880 with some help from a scholarship awarded by Queen Margherita, and studied there for three years, one of his composition teachers being Amilcare Ponchielli. In 1884 he had his first success with the première of *Le Villi* in Milan and this led to an almost exclusive attachment to the publishing house of Ricordi, whose director Giulio Ricordi had a profound influence on Puccini's subsequent career. 1884 also saw his elopement with Elvira Gemignani (*née* Bonturi), whom he married in 1904 after her husband's death, by which time her son by Puccini was eighteen years old. (The greater part of their married life was marked by varying degrees of estrangement.) In 1891 Puccini moved to Torre del Lago near Lucca and, except for winters in Milan, lived there until 1922. After the success of *Manon Lescaut* (1893) he began to amass a fortune from his operas and was able to indulge his enthusiasm for fast cars, motor boats and duck-shooting on the lake at Torre. In his maturity he did not teach or conduct, but did travel extensively to supervise the production of his operas, crossing the Atlantic first in 1905 *en route* for Buenos Aires and first visiting New York two years later. It was on a visit to London in 1905 that he met Sybil Seligman (wife of a London banker) who became a lifelong and intimate friend. In 1922 he moved to Viareggio and in 1924 the Italian Fascist government made him Senator of the Realm; but in the same year Puccini, a life-long chain-smoker, became badly afflicted with cancer of the throat. He travelled to Brussels in November for an operation at the Institut de la Couronne. The operation itself was a success but it put too great a strain on his heart and he died a few days later, leaving unfinished the final act of his last opera, *Turandot*.

CATALOGUE OF WORKS

1. Preludio sinfonico. For orchestra. 1876.

2. I Figli d'Italia bella. Cantata. 1877.

3. Motet and Credo. 1878. Composed for the annual Feast of San Paolino.
fp: 12 July 1878, Lucca, pupils of the Pacini Conservatoire.

3a. Mass. 1880. Incorporating preceding.
fp: 12 July 1880, Lucca.
Pub. 1951, as *Messa di Gloria*.

BIBLIOGRAPHY:
W. Elkin: Puccini's Messa di Gloria, *MT*, August 1957, p. 440.

4. Salve Regina. For soprano and harmonium. Before 1880.

5. Melancolia (Ghislanzoni). For voice and strings. 1881. Unpub.

6. Allor ch'io sarò morto (Ghislanzoni). ?For voice and piano. 1881.

7. Noi legger (Ghislanzoni). ?For voice and piano. 1882.

8. Spirto gentil (Ghislanzoni). ?For voice and piano. 1882.

9. Romanza (C. Romano). ?For voice and piano. 1883.

10. Storiella d'amore (G. Puccini). For voice and piano. 1883. Pub. 1883 (4 October), Sonzogno (in *La Musica Populare*).

11. Adagietto. For orchestra. 1883.

12. Piano Trio. ?Date. Fragment only.

13. Scherzo. For string quartet. 1880–3.

14. String Quartet in D. 1880–3.

15. Fugues. For string quartet. 1882–3.

16. Capriccio sinfonico. For orchestra. 1883. Ded. Carlo Poniatowski.
fp: 14 July 1883, Milan, Conservatoire, students' orchestra, cond. Franco Faccio.
Pub. 1884, Francesco Lucca (Milan): reduction by Giuseppe Frugatta for piano four hands.

BIBLIOGRAPHY:
Mosco Carner: Puccini's symphonic venture: the Capriccio sinfonico, *MO*, June 1938, p. 781.

17. Le Villi. Opera in one act. 1884. Libretto: Fontana. Ded. Arrigo Boito and Marco Sala.
fp: 31 May 1884, Milan, Teatro dal Verme, cond. Achille Panizza; with Caporetti (Anna), Antonio d'Andrade (Roberto).

17a. Le Villi. Revised version in two acts. 28 October 1884.
fp: 26 December 1884, Turin, Teatro Regio.
f Milan p: 24 January 1885, La Scala, cond. Franco Faccio; with Romilda Pantaleoni, Anton and Menotti.
fEp: 24 December 1897, Manchester, Carl Rosa Company, cond. Edgardo Levi; with Mrs. Arthur Rousby (Anna), Henry Beaumont (Roberto), Frank Lund (Wulf); given in the English version by Percy Pinkerton as 'The Witch-Dancers'.
f New York p: 17 December 1908, Metropolitan Opera House; with Alda (Anna), Bonci (Roberto), Amato (Wulf).
fGBbp: 10 February 1927, Glasgow Station Choir and Orchestra, cond. Herbert A. Carruthers; with Alice Moxon (Anna), Herbert Thorpe (Roberto), Arthur Cranmer (Wulf).
Pub. 1885 (vocal score), Ricordi: reduction by Carlo Chiusuri. English version by Percy Pinkerton, 1897.

BIBLIOGRAPHY:
R. Mariani: Prodromi pucciniani: Le Villi e Edgar, *Musica d'oggi*, April 1958, p. 218.
Anon.: Puccini as disciple of Wagner: Le Villi, *The Times*, 22 April 1955, p. 17.

18. Edgar. Opera in four acts. Summer 1884–autumn 1888. Libretto: Fontana, from Musset's 'La Coupe et les Lèvres'. Ded. J. Burgmein (pseud. Giulio Ricordi).
fp: 21 April 1889, Milan, La Scala, cond. Franco Faccio; with Romilda Pantaleoni Tigrana), Aurelia Cattaneo (Fidelia), De Negri (Edgar).
Pub. 1890, Ricordi: vocal score by Carlo Carignani.

18a. Edgar. Revised version in three acts. Summer 1889.

Puccini, Giacomo

fp: 28 February 1892, Ferrara, Teatro Communale.

fp outside Italy: 19 March 1892, Madrid, cond. Luigi Mancinelli; with Luisa Tetrazzini (Fidelia), Pasqua (Tigrana), Francesco Tamagno (Edgar).

Pub. 1892, Ricordi.

BIBLIOGRAPHY:

R. Mariani: Prodromi pucciniani: Le Villi e Edgar, *Musica d'oggi*, April 1958, p. 218.

Graham Stephens: The history of Edgar, *Ricordiana*, April 1967, p. 8.

19. Solfeggi. For voice and piano. 1888.

20. Sole e amore (G. Puccini). Mattinata for voice and piano. 1888. Pub. 1888, Paganini appendix (Genoa).

21. E l'uccellino (R. Fuccini). For voice and piano. 1898. Ded. Memmo Lippi. Pub. 1899, Ricordi; 1919, Ricordi (London): English version by Lute Drummond as 'A Little Birdie'; German version by Louise Perrot, 1915.

22. Tre Minuetti. For string quartet. 1890.
   1. Ded. S. A. R. Vittoria Augusta di Borbone, Principessa di Capua.
   2. Augusteo Michelangeli.
   3. Carlo Carignani.
Pub. c. 1892, Pigna (Milan).

22a. Deux Menuets. Republished version of preceding, omitting No. 2. Pub. 1898, Heugel: also arr. by Alberto d'Erasmo for piano, and by Guglielmo Andreoli for piano four hands; 1902, Ricordi.

23. Crisantemi. For string quartet. 1890 (?1889). Ded. to the memory of Amadeo di Savoia, Duc d'Aosta. Pub. 1890, Ricordi.

24. Manon Lescaut. Lyric Drama in four acts. 1890–October 1892. Libretto: Ruggiero Leoncavallo, Marco Praga, Domenico Oliva, Luigi Illica and Giacosa, from the novel by the Abbé Prévost.

3 fl, pic, 2 ob, ca, 2 cl, clarone, 2 bsn; 4 hn, 3 tpt, 3 tmb, bs tuba; timp, GC, cym, tgle, carillon; hp, strings.

fp: 1 February 1893, Turin, Teatro Regio, cond. Alessandro Pomé; with Cesira Ferrani (Manon), Cremonini (Des Grieux), Moro (Lescaut), Polonini (Geronte).

fEp: 14 May 1894, Covent Garden, cond. Al Seppilli; with Olghina (Manon), Beduschi (Des Grieux), Pini-Corsi (Lescaut), Arimondi (Geronte).

fEbp: 14 May 1928, Wireless Chorus and Symphony Orchestra, cond. Percy Pitt; with Miriam Licette (Manon), Parry Jones (Des Grieux), Percy Heming (Lescaut).

Pub. 1893, Ricordi: vocal score by Carlo Carignani. English version by Mowbray Marras, 1905; French version by Maurice Vicaire.

BIBLIOGRAPHY:

Robert Boas: The heroine Puccini did not love, *Opera*, June 1956, p. 335.

Mosco Carner: The two Manons, *MMR*, October 1937; *The Listener*, 17 March 1966, p. 412.

G. Gavazzeni: Ritratto della Manon Lescaut, *Musica d'oggi*, July 1958, p. 417.

J. Gheusi: Les avatars de Manon sur la scène lyrique, *Musica* (Chaix), No. 95, February 1962, p. 43.

C. S. Hiss: Abbé Prevost's Manon Lescaut as novel, libretto and opera, *Dissertation Abstracts*, February 1968, p. 3210A.

Anon.: La Manon Lescaut di Puccini alla Monnaie de Bruxelles, *Ars et Labor*, May 1911, p. 369.

— Gli esecutori della Manon Lescaut, *Ars et Labor*, May 1909, p. 359.

Various contributors: Manon Lescaut, *Opera News*, 13 November 1950, 26 March 1956, 12 January 1959, 10 December 1960.

25. La Bohème. Opera in four acts. 1892–5. Dated: 10 December 1895. Libretto: Giacosa and Illica, from the novel by Henri Murger.

2 fl, pic, 2 ob, ca, 2 cl, bcl, 2 bsn; 4 hn, 3 tpt, tmb, bs tmb; timp, tgle, GC, cym; hp, carillon, strings.

fp: 1 February 1896, Turin, Teatro Regio, cond. Arturo Toscanini; with Ferrani (Mimi), Pasini (Musetta), Gorga (Rodolfo), Wilmant (Marcello), Pini-Corsi (Schaunard), Mazzara (Colline).

fEp: 22 April 1897, Manchester, cond. Claude Jacquinet; with Alice Esty (Mimi), Bessie Macdonald (Musetta), Robert Cuningham (Rudolfo), William Paul (Marcello),

Charles Tilbury (Schaunard), Arthur Winckworth (Colline).

fFp: 13 June 1898, Paris, Opéra-Comique, with Mlle Giraudon (Mimi), Mlle Tiphaine (Musetta), Maréchal (Rodolfo), Bouvet (Marcello), Fugère (Schaunard), Isnardon (Colline); décors, Jusseaume.

fEbp: 19 August 1927, Wireless Chorus and Symphony Orchestra, cond. Percy Pitt; with Sylvia Nelis (Mimi), Doris Lemon (Musetta), Heddle Nash (Rodolfo), Percy Heming (Marcello), Frederick Collier (Schaunard).

Pub. 1896, Ricordi: vocal score by Carlo Carignani. English version by William Grist and Percy Pinkerton, 1897; German version by Ludwig Hartmann, 1897; French version by Paul Ferrier, 1898.

BIBLIOGRAPHY:

R. Bianchi: La Bohème, Rome, 1923.
A. Billeci: La Bohème di GP, studio critico, Palermo, 1931.
José Bruyr: Les véritables personnages de Bohème, Musica (Chaix), No. 76, July 1960, p. 2.
Max Chop: Die Bohème, Leipzig, n.d.
G. Confalonieri: Il significato di Bohème, Musica d'oggi, June 1958, p. 351.
O. Downes: Bohème debate: pros and cons of English versions qualities, New York Times, 18 January 1953, Section 2, p. 7.
P. Dragadze: Found—the missing act of La Bohème, Opera News, February 1959, p. 27.
E. Valenti Ferro: Carmen y la Bohème con mas pena que gloria, Buenos Aires Musical, No. 292 (1963), p. 1.
Arnaldo Fraccaroli: Bohème—Die Entstehung des Werkes, Blätter der Staatsoper (Berlin), October (No. 3) 1927, p. 6.
Arthur Jacobs & Stanley Sadie: La Bohème (Bohemian Life), in The Opera Guide, Hamish Hamilton (London) 1964, p. 273.
I. Kolodin: Beecham on Bohème (interview), Saturday Review, 25 August 1956, p. 36.
E. Markham Lee: Puccini's La Bohème, Alexander Moring (London), Nights at the Opera series, 1909.
Basil Maine: Latin Quarter love—set to melody, Radio Times, 24 January 1930, p. 197.
W. Maisch: Puccinis musikalische Formgebung, untersucht an der Oper La Boheme, Neustadt a. d. Aisch, 1934.
Ernest Newman: La Bohème, in More Opera Nights, Putnam (London) 1954, p. 38.
Arturo Rossato: La 'prima' di Bohème, Musica d'oggi, June 1923, p. 180.
Henry W. Simon: La Bohème, in Festival of Opera, W. H. Allen (London) 1957, p. 61.
Adolf Weissmann: Bohème—Kritische Betrachtungen, Blätter der Staatsoper (Berlin), October (No. 3) 1927, p. 15.
Various contributors: La Bohème, Opera News, 20 March 1950, 12 March 1951, 10 March 1952, 22 December 1952, 16 February 1953, 14 December 1953, 21 March 1955, 25 March 1957, 10 February 1958, 11 March 1961, 20 January 1962.
La Bohème, Norsk Musikerblad, October 1960, p. 9.
La Bohème: complete text of new English translation by H. Dietz, Theatre Arts, December 1953, p. 34.

26. Scossa elettrica. March for orchestra. 1896.

27. Inno a Diana. For chorus and piano. 1897. Text: F. Salvatore. (?Carlo Abeniacar.) Pub. 1899, G. Venturini (Florence). Later incorporated into 'Inno a Roma'. (See No. 39.)

28. Cantata a Giove. 1897.

29. Avanti, Urania! For chorus and piano. 1899 (?1896). Text: Renato Fuccini. Ded. Marchese Anna Ginori-Lisci. Pub. 1899, Genesio Venturini.

30. La Tosca. Melodrama in three acts. 1896–1900. Libretto: Giuseppe Giacosa and Luigi Illica, from the play by Victorien Sardou.

3 fl, pic, 2 ob, ca, 2 cl, bcl, 2 bsn, cbsn; 4 hn, 3 tpt, 3 tmb, bs tmb; timp, tgle, cannon, GC, cym, carillon, celesta, campane, hp, organ, strings.

fp: 14 January 1900, Rome, Teatro Costanzi, cond. Mugnone; with Hariclea Darclée (Tosca), De Marchi (Cavaradossi), Eugenio Giraldoni (Scarpia), Galli (Angelotti), Borelli (Sacristan); producer, Tito Ricordi.

fEp: 12 July 1900, Covent Garden, cond. Luigi Mancinelli; with Milka Ternina

(Tosca), Fernando De Lucia (Cavaradossi), Antonio Scotti (Scarpia), Eugène Dufriche (Angelotti), Charles Gilibert (Sacristan).

fAp: 4 February 1901, New York, Metropolitan Opera House; with Milka Ternina, Cremonini, Antonio Scotti, Eugène Dufriche, Charles Gilibert.

ffp: 13 October 1903, Paris, Opéra-Comique, with Claire Friché (Tosca), Beyle (Cavaradossi), Dufranne (Scarpia), Huberdau (Angelotti), Delvoye (Sacristan).

fEbp: 31 August 1927, Wireless Chorus and Symphony Orchestra, cond. Percy Pitt; with Rachel Morton (Tosca), Tudor Davies (Cavaradossi), Harold Williams (Scarpia), Arthur Fear (Angelotti).

Pub. 1899, Ricordi: vocal score by Carlo Carignani. German version by Max Kalbeck, 1900; French version by Paul Ferrier, 1900; English version by W. Beatty-Kingston, 1905.

BIBLIOGRAPHY:

Dennis Arundell: Tosca re-studied, *Opera*, April 1960, p. 262.

G. Breuer: Tosca, Jeritza and me, *High Fidelity*, December 1957, p. 56.

Max Chop: Tosca, Leipzig, 1924.

André Coeuroy: La Tosca de Puccini, étude historique et critique, Paris, 1923.

O. Downes: Elements of opera: fusion of music and play revealed in Tosca, *New York Times*, 21 September 1952, Section 2, p. 7.

A. Golea: La Tosca change de scène, *Musica* (Chaix), August 1960, p. 2.

Edward Greenfield: Tosca, *Opera*, January 1964, p. 6.

Arthur Jacobs & Stanley Sadie: Tosca, in *The Opera Guide*, Hamish Hamilton (London) 1964, p. 279.

Denis Mahon: A note on the staging of Tosca, *Opera*, March 1951, p. 162.

M. Mailhe: Les grandes roles et leurs interprètes: La Tosca, *Musica* (Chaix), No. 116, November 1963, p. 36.

Ernest Newman: Tosca, in *More Opera Nights*, Putnam (London) 1954, p. 187.

Harold D. Rosenthal: Tosca's golden jubilee, *Opera*, April 1950, p. 32.

K. G. Schuller: Verismo opera and the verists, *Dissertation Abstracts*, 1961, p. 596.

Henry W. Simon: Tosca, in *Festival of Opera*, W. H. Allen (London) 1957, p. 481.

L. Torchi: La Tosca, *Rivista musicale*, 1900.

G. Vigolo: Fascino e mistero di Tosca, *Musica d'oggi*, January 1958, p. 14.

Various contributors: Tosca, *Opera News*, 16 January 1950, 8 December 1952, 2 January 1956, 18 March 1957, 10 March 1958, 6 April 1959, 19 March 1960, 7 April 1962, 13 January 1968.

31. Madama Butterfly. Opera in three acts. 1900–3. Dated: 27 December 1903. Libretto: Giuseppe Giacosa and Luigi Illica, from a dramatized version by David Belasco of a story by John L. Long.

3 fl, pic, 2 ob, ca, 2 cl, clarone, 2 bsn; 4 hn, 3 tpt, 3 tmb, bs tmb; timp, tamburo, tgle, cym, tamtam, GC, campanelli a tastiera, campanelli giapponesi, campane, tamtam giapponesi (ad lib); strings. *On stage:* campanella, tubular bells, viola d'amore, bird whistle, tamtams (low & high).

fp: 17 February 1904, Milan, La Scala, cond. Cleofonte Campanini; with Rosina Storchio (Cio-Cio-San), Giovanni Zenatello (Pinkerton), Giuseppe De Luca (Sharpless); producer, Tito Ricordi; scenic design, Jusseaume.

31a. Madama Butterfly. Revised version.

fp: 28 May 1904, Brescia, Teatro Grande; with Salomea Krusciniski (Cio-Cio-San), Giovanni Zenatello (Pinkerton), Bellati (Sharpless).

fEp: 10 July 1905, Covent Garden, cond. Cleofonte Campanini; with Emmy Destinn (Cio-Cio-San), Enrico Caruso (Pinkerton), Antonio Scotti (Sharpless).

fAp: October 1906, Washington, D.C., Savage Opera Company.

fEbp: 16 September 1927, Wireless Chorus and Symphony Orchestra, cond. Percy Pitt; with Miriam Licette (Cio-Cio-San), Parry Jones (Pinkerton), Dennis Noble (Sharpless).

ffp: 28 December 1906, Paris, Opéra-Comique, with Marguerite Carré (Cio-Cio-San), Clément (Pinkerton), Périer (Sharpless).

Pub. 1904, Ricordi: vocal score, Carlo Carignani. English version by R. H. Elkin, 1906; French version by Paul Ferrier, 1906; German version by Alfred Brüggemann, 1907.

BIBLIOGRAPHY:
J. Brownlee: The history of Madame Butterfly, *Music Journal*, April 1962, p. 32.
Mosco Carner: The first version of Madam Butterfly, *MO*, April 1941, p. 294.
Max Chop: Madame Butterfly, Leipzig, n.d.
G. Confalonieri: Una Madama Butterfly italo-giapponese, *Musica d'oggi*, April 1958, p. 250.
Arnaldo Fraccaroli: Madame Butterfly, *Blätter der Staatsoper* (Berlin), February 1931, p. 9.
A. Golea: La millième de Madame Butterfly à l'Opéra-Comique, *Musica* (Chaix), No. 73, April 1960, p. 31.
H. Hugh Harvey: Fifty years of Butterfly, 2: The London première, *Opera*, March 1954.
— Fifty years of Madame Butterfly, *The Gramophone*, August 1955, p. 89.
Arthur Jacobs & Stanley Sadie: Madama Butterfly, in *The Opera Guide*, Hamish Hamilton (London) 1964, p. 285.
Herman Klein: The Gramophone and the Singer—Madam Butterfly, *The Gramophone*, May 1925, p. 464.
I. Kolodin: Authentic Butterfly: performance by Fujiwara opera company of Tokyo, *Saturday Review*, 25 October 1952, p. 32.
D. Miyasawa: La vera Cio-cio-san, *Musica d'oggi*, January 1959, p. 2.
Ernest Newman: Madam Butterfly, in *More Opera Nights*, Putnam (London) 1954, p. 484.
Arthur Notcutt: Madam Butterfly and its interpreters, *MO*, May 1950, p. 458.
Tito Ricordi: Henry W. Savage e Madam Butterfly negli Stati Uniti, *Ars et Labor*, February 1907, p. 110.
Antonio Salvucci: Fifty years of Butterfly, 1: The Milan première, *Opera*, March 1954.
H. Schmidt-Garre: Madame Butterfly und der Terminkalender, *NZfM*, February 1961, p. 66.
Henry W. Simon: Madama Butterfly, in *Festival of Opera*, W. H. Allen (London) 1957, p. 250.
A. Toni: Divagazioni su Madama Butterfly, *Musica d'oggi*, March 1958, p. 155.
Various contributors: Madama Butterfly, *Opera News*, 13 February 1950, 28 January 1952, 10 December 1956, 22 December 1958, 16 April 1960, 3 February 1962.
Anon.: Dopo la prima rappresentazione di Madama Butterfly al Royal Covent Garden di Londra (10 Luglio 1905), *Ars et Labor*, August 1905, p. 502.

32. Requiem. For soprano, tenor, bass and harmonium or organ. 1905.

33. Foglio d'album. For piano. 1907. Pub. 1942, Edward B. Marks (New York).

34. Piccolo Tango. For piano. 1907. Pub. 1942, Edward B. Marks (New York).

35. La Fanciulla del West. Opera in three acts. Dated: 6 August 1910. Libretto: Guelfo Civinini and Carlo Zangarini, from a drama by David Belasco. Ded. Queen Alexandria.

3 fl, pic, 3 ob, ca, 3 cl, clarone, 3 bsn, cbsn; 4 hn, 3 tpt, 3 tmb, bs tmb; timp, glock, celesta, GC, cym, tamburo, tgle, fonica (on stage); 2 hp, strings.

fp: 10 December 1910, New York, Metropolitan Opera House, cond. Arturo Toscanini; with Emmy Destinn (Minnie), Enrico Caruso (Johnson), Pasquale Amato (Sheriff); producer, Tito Ricordi.

f European p: 29 May 1911, London, Covent Garden, cond. Cleofonte Campanini; with Emmy Destinn (Minnie), Amadeo Bassi (Johnson), Dinh Gilly (Sheriff).

fIp: 12 June 1911, Rome, Teatro Costanzi, cond. Arturo Toscanini.

f Paris p: 16 May 1912, Opéra, cond. Tullio Serafin; with Carmen Mélis (Minnie), Enrico Caruso (Johnson), Titta Ruffo (Sheriff).

fEbp: 11 June 1928, Wireless Chorus and Symphony Orchestra, cond. Percy Pitt; with Stiles Allen (Minnie), Walter Widdop (Johnson), Roy Henderson (Sheriff).

Pub. 1910, Ricordi: vocal score, Carlo Carignani. English version by R. H. Elkin, 1910; French version by Maurice Vaucaire, 1911; German version by Alfred Brügemann, 1912.

BIBLIOGRAPHY:
F. G. Barker: Wells farrago, *M&M*, January 1963, p. 18.
David Drew: Horse opera: The Girl of the Golden West, *New Statesman*, 21 December 1962, p. 910.

A. Fraccaroli: Puccini et la Fanciulla del West, *Corriere della sera*, 15 October 1910.

A. Gasco: La musica della Fanciulla del West, *Tribuna*, 10 December 1910.

— La Fanciulla del West al Teatro Costanzi, *Tribuna*, 14 June 1911.

G. Gavazzeni: Nella Fanciulla del West protagonista e l'orchestra?, *Musica d'oggi*, November 1959, p. 545.

Arthur Jacobs & Stanley Sadie: La Fanciulla del West, in *The Opera Guide*, Hamish Hamilton (London) 1964, p. 290.

Ernest Newman: The first English performance of The Girl of the Golden West, in *Testament of Music*, Putnam (London) 1962, p. 97.

Marino Rinaldo: La Fanciulla del West, Instituto d'alta cultura (Milan) 1940.

Harold Rosenthal: The Girl of the Golden West, *Ricordiana*, October 1962, p. 1.

— Opera on the gramophone, 11: Puccini's Wild West, *Opera*, December 1962, p. 781.

Stanley Sadie: Puccini's Western, *Musical Events*, January 1963, p. 6.

Henry W. Simon: The Girl of the Golden West, in *Festival of Opera*, W. H. Allen (London) 1957, p. 198.

John S. Weissmann: Puccini's gangster opera, *Musical Events*, December 1962, p. 22.

C. Zangarini: Puccini et la Fanciulla del West, *Propaganda musicale*, 1930, Nos. 1–5.

Various contributors: La Fanciulla del West, *Opera News*, 6 January 1962.

Anon.: The Girl of the Golden West, *The Times*, 23 December 1910, p. 10.

Anon.: Puccini's new opera—production at Covent Garden: La Fanciulla del West, *The Times*, 30 May 1911, p. 10.

36. La Rondine. Operetta. 1917. Libretto: Giuseppe Adami, from a German libretto by Alfred Maria Willner and Heinz Reichert.

fp: 27 March 1917, Monte Carlo; cond. Gino Marinuzzi; with Gilda della Rizzi (Magda), Ines Farraris (Lisette), Tito Schipa (Ruggero).

fEbp: 24 June 1929, Wireless Chorus and Symphony Orchestra, cond. Percy Pitt; with Ina Souez (Magda), Olive Groves (Lisette), Tudor Davies (Ruggero).

Pub. 1917, Sonzogno: vocal score by Carlo

Carignani; 1917, Sonzogno (German version); 1920, Eibenschütz & Berté.

BIBLIOGRAPHY:

Giuseppe Adami: Ricordi pucciniana: il volo d'una Rondine, *Nuova antologia*, 1 December 1934, p. 435.

E. Bonner: La Rondine, *Outlook*, 4 April 1928, p. 547.

Mosco Carner: A Puccini operetta—La Rondine, in *Of Man and Music*.

I. Kolodin: Puccini as Lehar: recording of La Rondine, *Saturday Review*, 14 May 1955, p. 33.

C. Sartori: Rondine, a l'evasione dalla guerra, *Musica d'oggi*, October 1958, p. 484.

37. Il Trittico. 1915–18.

fp: 14 December 1918, New York, Metropolitan Opera House: for details see under individual operas.

fEp: 18 June 1920, Covent Garden: for details see under individual operas.

Pub. (complete), 1918, Ricordi: vocal score by Carlo Carignani.

BIBLIOGRAPHY:

Arnaldo Fraccaroli: Entstehung und erste Aufführung des Triptychon, *Blätter der Staatsoper* (Berlin), March (No. 21) 1928, p. 6.

Arthur Jacobs & Stanley Sadie: Il Trittico, in *The Opera Guide*, Hamish Hamilton (London) 1964, p. 294.

W. Kelch: Triptychon—Farben einer Palette, *Musik und Szene*, 1962–3, No. 6, p. 5.

Arthur Neisser: Puccini über sein Triptychon, *Blätter der Staatsoper* (Berlin), March (No. 21) 1928, p. 13.

Luigi Ricci: The three panels of Puccini, *Ricordiana*, January 1957, p. 1.

Harold Rosenthal: Puccini's Trittico, *London Musical Events*, February 1957, p. 19.

Edmund Tracey: Opera on the gramophone, 15: Puccini's Trittico, *Opera*, April 1965, p. 247.

R. Turro: El Triptico tres argumentos buscan y hallan un compositor, *Buenos Aires Musical*, No. 295 (1963), p. 1.

Adolf Weissmann: Das Triptychon, *Blätter der Staatsoper* (Berlin), March (No. 21) 1928, p. 6.

37a. Il Tabarro. Dated: 25 November 1916.

Libretto: Giuseppe Adami, from Didier Gold's 'La Houppelande'.

2 fl, pic, 2 ob, ca, 2 cl, clarone, 2 bsn; 4 hn, 3 tpt, 3 tmb, bs tmb; timp, tgle, tamburo, GC, cym, glock, cornetta, tromba d'automobile, siren, low bell; 2 hp, celesta, strings.

fp: 14 December 1918, New York, Metropolitan Opera House, cond. Roberto Moranzoni; with Claudia Muzio (Giorgetta), Giulio Crimi (Luigi), Luigi Montesanto (Michele).

f European p: 11 January 1919, Rome, Teatro Costanzi, cond. Gino Marinuzzi; with Labia (Giorgetta), Di Giovanni, i.e. Edward Johnson (Luigi), Galeffi (Michele).

fEp: 18 June 1920, Covent Garden, cond. Gaetano Bavagnoli; with Ida Quaiatti (Giorgetta), Thomas Burke (Luigi), Dinh Gilly (Michele).

Pub. 1918, Ricordi. German version by Alfred Brüggemann, c. 1920; French version by Didier Gold, 1921; English version by Joseph Machlis, 1956.

BIBLIOGRAPHY:
Mosco Carner: A grim drama of jealousy, *Radio Times*, 26 November 1937, p. 9.
Edward Greenfield: A lost Puccini aria, *Opera*, September 1957, p. 552.
R. Mariani: Fermenti e anticipazioni del Tabarro, *Musica d'oggi*, February 1959, p. 56.
Henry W. Simon: Il Tabarro, in *Festival of Opera*, W. H. Allen (London) 1957, p. 461.

37b. Suor Angelica. Dated: 14 September 1917. Libretto: Giovacchino Forzano.

2 fl, pic, 2 ob, ca, 2 cl, clarone, 2 bsn; 4 hn, 3 tpt, 3 tmb, bs tmb; timp, tgle, GC, cym, glock, cornetta; celesta, strings. *On stage:* pic, 2 pianos, organ, 3 tpt, campanella di bronzo, campane, piatti-tavolette.

fp: 14 December 1918, New York, Metropolitan Opera House, cond. Roberto Moranzoni; with Geraldine Farrar (Angelica), Flora Perini (Zia Principessa).

f European p: 11 January 1919, Rome, Teatro Costanzi, cond. Gino Marinuzzi; with Dalla Rizza (Angelica).

fEp: 18 June 1920, Covent Garden, cond. Gaetano Bavagnoli; with Dalla Rizza (Angelica), Jacqueline Royer (Princess).

Pub. 1918, Ricordi. German version by Alfred Brüggemann, c. 1920; French version by Paul Ferrier, 1921; English version by Herbert Withers, 1930.

BIBLIOGRAPHY:
Riccardo Allorto: Suor Angelica nella unita del Trittico, *Musica d'oggi*, May 1959, p. 198.
— The place of Suor Angelica, *Ricordiana*, October 1959, p. 4.
Henry W. Simon: Suor Angelica, in *Festival of Opera*, W. H. Allen (London) 1957, p. 459.

37c. Gianni Schicchi. Dated: 20 April 1918. Libretto: Giovacchino Forzano, based on an episode in Dante's Inferno.

2 fl, pic, 2 ob, ca, 2 cl, clarone, 2 bsn; 4 hn, 3 tpt, 3 tmb, bs tmb; timp, tgle, tamburo, GC, cym, low bell; hp, celesta, strings.

fp: 14 December 1918, New York, Metropolitan Opera House, cond. Roberto Moranzoni; with Giuseppe De Luca (Schicchi), Florence Easton (Lauretta), Giulio Crimi (Rinuccio).

f European p: 11 January 1919, Rome, Teatro Costanzi, cond. Gino Marinuzzi; with Galeffi (Schicchi), Dalla Rizza (Lauretta), Di Giovanni, i.e. Edward Johnson (Rinuccio).

fEp: 18 June 1920, Covent Garden, cond. Gaetano Bavagnoli; with Ernesto Badini (Schicchi), Dalla Rizza (Lauretta), Thomas Burke (Rinuccio).

Pub. 1918, Ricordi. German version by Alfred Brüggemann, c. 1920; French version by Paul Ferrier, 1921; English version by Percy Pitt, 1930; English version by Anne and Herbert Grossman, 1959.

BIBLIOGRAPHY:
M. Morini: Momento del Gianni Schicchi, *Musica d'oggi*, March 1959, p. 98.
Ernest Newman: Gianni Schicchi, in *Opera Nights*, Putnam (London) 1943, p. 39.
G. Setaccioli: Il contenuto musicale del Gianni Schicchi, Rome, 1920.
Henry W. Simon: Gianni Schicchi, in *Festival of Opera*, W. H. Allen (London) 1957, p. 192.
Various contributors: Gianni Schicchi, *Opera News*, 14 January 1952, 3 February 1958.
Anon.: Gianni Schicchi, *Blätter der Staatsoper* (Berlin), April 1923, p. 3.

38. Morire (G. Adami). For voice and piano. 1917. *c.* 1917 in an album (pub. Per la Croce Rossa Italiana).

39. Inno a Roma. For chorus and orchestra. 1919. Text: Fausto Salvatori. Ded. Princess Jolanda of Savoy.

fp: June 1920, Rome Stadium.

Pub. 1923, Sonzogno (Milan): reduction; 1942, Bahar-Edition Baltic (Berlin) in a German version by Ralph Maria Siegel and new orchestration by Josef Rixner.

40. Turandot. Opera in three acts. Libretto: Giuseppe Adami and Renato Simoni, from the play by Gozzi. Unfinished. Completed by Franco Alfano.

fp: 25 April 1926, Milan, La Scala, cond. Arturo Toscanini; with Rosa Raisa (Turandot), Maria Zamboni (Liu), Michele Fleta (Calaf).

fEp: 7 June 1927, Covent Garden, cond. Vincenzo Bellezza; with Bianca Scacciati (Turandot), Lotte Schoene (Liu), Aroldo Lindi (Calaf); producer, Charles Moor.

fFp: 2 April 1928, Paris, Opéra, cond. Philippe Gaubert; with Maurise Beaujon (Turandot), Georges Thill (Calaf), Marcelle Denya (Liu); décors and costumes, Dresa.

Pub. 1926, Ricordi: vocal score by G. Zuccoli. German version by Alfred Brügemann, 1926; French version by Paul Spaak, 1927; English version by R. H. Elkin, 1929.

BIBLIOGRAPHY:

Giuseppe Adami: Nascita di Turandot, *Nuova antologia*, 16 April 1935, p. 581.
— La principessa crudele, *Nuova antologia*, 1 June 1935, p. 420.
F. G. Barker: Chu Chin Turandot, *M&M*, April 1963, p. 40.
Adolphe Boschot: La dernière œuvre de Puccini, *Revue politique et littéraire* (Revue bleue), 1928, p. 314.
David Drew: Turandot, *New Statesman*, 13 January 1967, p. 57.
A. M. Gordon-Brown: Turandot records, *The Gramophone*, October 1929, p. 223.
Richard Holt: Turandot, *The Gramophone*, December 1938, p. 276.
Arthur Jacobs & Stanley Sadie: Turandot, in *The Opera Guide*, Hamish Hamilton (London) 1964, p. 304.
Alfred Kalisch: A Puccini pageant, *Sackbut*, June 1926, p. 301.
A. Kalmus: Critique and analysis, *MO*, November 1926, p. 142.
John W. Klein: Puccini's greatest work, *MO*, July 1948, p. 397.
I. Kolodin: Uncomplete Turandot, *Saturday Review of Literature*, 22 April 1950, p. 26.
Constant Lambert: The symphonic brilliance of Turandot, *Radio Times*, 1 June 1934, p. 673.
M. Lessona: Turandot di GP, *Rivista musicale italiana*, June 1926.
R. Marini: La Turandot di GP, Casa Editrice Monslavato (Florence) 1942.
Ernest Newman: Turandot, in *Opera Nights*, Putnam (London) 1943.
S. Procida: Turandot nel teatro di Puccini, *Nuovo antologia*, 16 May 1926, p. 180.
V. W. Russell-Forbes: Turandot, *The Gramophone*, September 1927, p. 145.
William Saunders: Turandot, *Sackbut*, July 1930, p. 336.
Henry W. Simon: Turandot, in *Festival of Opera*, W. H. Allen (London) 1957, p. 512.
Various contributors: Turandot, *Opera News*, 4 March 1961, 24 February 1962.
Anon.: Il trionfo successo di Turandot, *Musica d'oggi*, May 1926.

GENERAL BIBLIOGRAPHY

Giuseppe Adami: Puccini, S. A. Fratelli Treves (Milan) 1935.
— Il romanzo della vita di GP, Milan/Rome 1944 (3rd edition).
— GP, epistolario, Milan, 1928; Letters of GP (transl. Ena Makin), Harrap (London) 1931.
— Le opere che Puccini non scrisse, *La Lettura*, 1921.
— Ricordi pucciniana, *Nuova antologia*, 16 July 1932 p. 161, 16 January 1934 p. 232, 1 December 1934, p. 435.
H. H. Arnold: Puccini, victim and victor, *Opera News*, 28 January 1952, p. 12.
W. S. Ashbrook: Puccini as portraitist, *Opera News*, 8 December 1952, p. 26.
— Puccini and the soprano, *Opera News*, 12 January 1959, p. 8.
Giorgio Barini: Zoofonia Pucciniana, *Musica*

d'oggi, 1922, Nos. 8–9 (August–September), p. 227.

Clive Barnes: Present day taste and Puccini, *Ricordiana*, October 1965, p. 1.

Marcel Bitsch: Verdi et Puccini, *Revue internationale de musique*, No. 12, spring 1952, p. 48.

A. Bonaccorsi: Il caso Puccini, *Rivista nazionale di musica*, 2–16 May 1924.

— Le musiche sacre dei Puccini, *Bollettino Storico Lucchese*, Vol. VI, 1934.

— GP e i suoi antenati musicali, Edizione Curci (Milan) 1950.

— Puccini nella critica d'oggi, *Musica d'oggi*, 1962, No. 2, p. 70.

A. Bonaventura: GP, l'uomo-l'artista, Livorno, 1924.

F. Brusa: GP, *Rivista musicale italiana*, March 1925.

Thomas Burke: Case of Puccini, *London Mercury*, September 1934, p. 439.

Mosco Carner: The exotic element in Puccini, *MQ*, January 1936, p. 45; in *Of Men and Music*, 1945 (3rd edition).

— Puccini's early operas, *M&L*, July 1938, p. 295; in *Of Men and Music*, 1945 (3rd edition).

— In defence of Puccini, in *Of Men and Music*, 1945 (3rd edition).

— Puccini's first step into opera, *The Listener*, 3 April 1958, p. 597.

— Puccini, a critical biography, London, 1958.

— Three projected Puccini operas, *Opera*, January 1959, p. 7.

— What Verdi and Puccini really wrote, *Opera*, October 1961, p. 641.

— Ill-starred Puccini, *M&M*, April 1967, p. 22.

Alfredo Casella: GP, *Blätter der Staatsoper* (Berlin), June (No. 27) 1928, p. 1.

G. M. Ciampelli: Una curiosa lettera di GP donata al Museo Teatrale, *La Scala e il Museo Teatrale*, January–March 1928.

Ernest Closson: Puccini, *La Revue belge*, 15 December 1924, p. 559.

A Coppotelli: Per la musica d'Italia: Puccini nella critica del Torrefranca, Orvieto, 1919.

Géza Csáth: Über Puccini, eine Studie (transl. from the Hungarian by H. Horvath), Budapest, 1912.

— Über Puccini, *Blätter der Staatsoper* (Berlin), March (No. 21) 1928, p. 1.

Winton Dean: GP, in *The Heritage of Music*, Vol. 3, O.U.P. (London) 1951, p. 153.

Dante Del Fiorentino: Immortal Bohemian, an intimate memoir of GP, Gollancz (London) 1952.

— Puccinian reminiscences, *Music Journal*, November–December 1958, p. 32.

John N. Donald: Puccini's forgotten operas, *MO*, November–December 1950, p. 69.

Wakeling Dry: GP, John Lane/The Bodley Head (London) 1906.

G. A. D'Ecclesiis: The aria techniques of GP: a study in musico-dramatic style, *Dissertation Abstracts*, August 1961, p. 592.

B. dal Fabbro: Le partiture di Verdi e di Puccini, *Musica d'oggi*, July–August 1961, p. 168; repr. from *Illustrazione Italiana*.

Karl Gustav Fellerer: GP, Potsdam, 1937.

F. Fontana: Puccini visto dal suo primo librettista, *Musica d'oggi*, 1933.

Arnaldo Fraccaroli: La vita di GP, Ricordi (Milan) 1925.

— GP si confida e racconta, Milan, 1957.

Piero Gadda Conti: Vita e melodie di GP, Milan, 1955.

Eugenio Gara: Carteggi Pucciniani, Ricordi (Milan) 1958.

— Prospetto cronologico della vita e delle opere di GP, *L'Approdo musicale*, April–June 1959, p. 81.

Carlo Gatti: Puccini, in un gruppo di lettere inedite a un amico, Emilio Bestetti Edizione d'Arte (Milan) 1944.

G. M. Gatti: Rileggendo le opere di GP, *Il Pianoforte*, August 1927, p. 257.

— Works of GP (transl. T. Baker), *MQ*, January 1928, p. 16.

— Puccini dieci anni dopo la morte, *Pan*, 1934, No. 3, p. 407.

G. Gavazzeni: Problemi di tradizione dinamico-fraseologica e critica testuale in Verdi e in Puccini, *La Rassegna musicale*, 1959, March p. 27, June p. 106.

Cecil Gray: A note on Puccini, *Opera*, April 1950, p. 29.

— Three modern Italian composers, *Sackbut*, October 1920, p. 284.

Edward Greenfield: Puccini, Keeper of the Seal, Arrow Books (London) 1958.

Puccini, Giacomo

Eva M. Grew: Childhood of Puccini, *British Musician*, September 1935, p. 206.
Vittorio Gui: GP, *Il Pianoforte*, June–July 1922, p. 172.
— Puccini, *MO*, 1939, May p. 691, June p. 782.
F. P. Harvey: GP, *Canon*, November–December 1959, p. 137.
K. Homolka: Das Fluidum der Liebe: Frauengestalten in Puccinis Opern, *Musik und Szene*, 1962–3, No. 6, p. 1.
Gervase Hughes: Puccini, in *The Handbook of Great Composers*, Arthur Barker (London) 1965, p. 199.
Spike Hughes: Puccini and the public, *Ricordiana*, October 1958, p. 1.
H. E. Jacob: The essence of Puccini, *Opera News*, 12 March 1951, p. 6.
G. Jellinek: Puccini, master of monotone, *Opera News*, 14 December 1953, p. 4.
D. Johnson: The Puccini operas on records, *High Fidelity*, December 1959, p. 93.
Julius Kapp: GP, biographische Skizze, *Blätter der Staatsoper* (Berlin), October (No. 3) 1927, p. 1.
John W. Klein: The last phase, *MO*, 1937, October p. 16, November p. 118.
— A centenial assessment, *MT*, December 1958 p. 654.
— 'A masterly piece of trash', *MO*, March 1947, p. 183.
— Puccini's enigmatic activity, *M&L*, July 1965, p. 195.
G. G. Knosp: Puccini, Brussels, 1937.
K. Kornicher: GP, *Musikleben*, March 1955, p. 114.
Constant Lambert: In defence of Puccini, *Radio Times*, 10 June 1938, p. 13.
A. Lancellotti: Recuerdos de Puccini, *La Revista de musica*, August 1928.
G. M. Lane: Casa Puccini, *Opera News*, 11 March 1961, p. 21.
P. H. Lang: Melody—is it dated?, *Saturday Review of Literature*, 11 January 1947, p. 28.
Heinrich Lindlar: Puccini, auf dem Wege zum Musical?, *Musik und Szene*, 1962–3, No. 6, p. 7.
D. A. Mackinnon: Early Puccini, *Opera News*, 6 January 1958, p. 28.
L. Marchetti: Puccini nelle imagini, Milan, 1949.

G. R. Marek: Genius with a hat on, *Good Housekeeping*, November 1949, p. 4.
— Bohème, Butterfly and other tear jerkers, *Good Housekeeping*, February 1951, p. 124.
— Puccini, a biography, New York, 1951; Cassell (London) 1952.
R. Mariani: L'ultimo Puccini, *La Rassegna musicale*, 1936.
— GP, Turin, 1939.
Samuel J. Marino: GP, a check-list of works by and about the composer, *New York Public Library Bulletin*, February 1955.
Guido Marotti: GP intimo (with F. Pagni), Florence, 1926.
— GP, Florence, 1949.
— Aus 'GP intimo', *Blätter der Staatsoper* (Berlin), February 1931, p. 5.
Carlo Marsili: L'antica famiglia Puccini a Celle, *Ars et Labor*, October 1909, p. 738.
G. Martinelli: My association with the composers of the verismo school, *Recorded Sound*, No. 8, p. 232.
J. Marx: GP, *ÖM*, December 1959, p. 511.
C. and M. J. Matz: First ladies of the Puccini premières, *Opera News*, 1962, 6 January p. 14, 3 February p. 25.
M. J. Matz: Puccini in America, *American Heritage*, April 1959, p. 52.
C. H. Meltzer: Puccini as I knew him, *Outlook*, 10 December 1924, p. 585.
G. Monaldi: GP e la sua opera, Rome, 1924.
A. Neisser: GP, sein Leben und sein Werk, Leipzig, 1928.
Ernest Newman: The last Puccini, in *More Essays from the World of Music*, Calder (London) 1958, p. 94.
— A note on Puccini, in *Testament of Music*, Putnam (London) 1962, p. 211.
— Puccini, in *–do–*, p. 286.
P. Panichelli: Il 'Pretino' di GP racconta, Pisa, 1949 (3rd edition).
G. Petrocchi: L'opera di GP nel giudizio della critica, *Rivista musicale*, 1941.
H. F. Peyser: Puccini in perspective, *Musician*, January 1925, p. 11.
Ildebrando Pizzetti: GP, in *Musicisti contemporanei*, Milan, 1914.
— GP as we see him today (transl. F. Haring-Comyns), *MO*, May 1959, p. 529.
V. Raeli: GP, *Rivista nazionale di musica*, 5 December 1924.

Henry Raynor: Puccini in 1958, *MO*, June 1958, p. 575.

Charles Reid: Puccini, craftsman or genius?, in *Opera No. 3*, Calder (London) 1956, p. 64.

— 'Frau Majolica' and friends, *Spectator*, 16 April 1965, p. 505.

L. Ricci: Puccini interprete di se stesso, Ricordi (Milan) 1954.

G. Roncaglia: GP, *Il Pianoforte*, 1925, No. 1, p. 15.

O. Roux: Memorie giovanili autobiografiche, Florence, n.d.

F. Salerno: Le donne pucciniane, Palermo, 1928.

P. Sanborn: Puccini and Fauré, *Nation*, 24 December 1924, p. 714.

P. Santi: Senso comune e vocalità nel melodramma pucciniano, *La Rassegna musicale*, June 1958, p. 109.

Claudio Sartori: Puccini, Nuova Accademia Editrice (Milan) 1958.

Vincent Seligman: Puccini among friends, Macmillan (London) 1938.

M. de Schauensee: Puccini and Paris, *Opera News*, 10 December 1960, p. 17.

R. A. Simon: Operatic genius, *Saturday Review of Literature*, 11 June 1938, p. 6.

Richard Specht: GP, das Leben, der Mensch, das Werk, Max Hesses Verlag (Berlin) 1931; GP, the Man, his Life, His Work (transl. C. A. Phillips), Dent (London) 1933.

K. B. Stephens: Home of Puccini, *Mentor*, October 1926, p. 33.

Frank Thiess: Puccini, Versuch einer Psychologie seiner Musik, Paul Zsolnay Verlag (Berlin/Vienna/Leipzig) 1947.

E. Thomas: GP, *NZfM*, December 1958, p. 698.

Fausto Torrefranca: GP e l'opera internazionale, Fratelli Bocca (Turin) 1913.

Claude Trevor: What Puccini is doing, *MT*, September 1916, p. 418.

— Puccini and his operas, *MS*, 1921, 24 September, p. 111, 8 October, p. 127, 22 October, p. 148.

Denis Vaughan: Puccini's orchestration, *PRMA*, No. 87, 1960–1, p. 1.

— Variations on a theme (discrepancies between original manuscripts and printed scores), *Music Magazine*, October 1961, p. 9.

— I manoscritti di Verdi e di Puccini: una interpellanza al Senato della Republica, *Musica d'oggi*, March–April 1961, p. 65.

— 'Tradition' in Verdi and Puccini, *Opera*, May 1961, p. 301.

— The horse's mouth, *Opera News*, 7 April 1962, p. 8.

Adolf Weissmann: GP, Drei Masken Verlag (Munich) 1922.

Ralph W. Wood: A comi-tragedian, *MO*, November 1944, p. 37.

M. Zafred: L'orchestra nelle opere di Puccini, *Musica d'oggi*, April 1959, p. 146.

B. Zirato: The last days of Puccini, *Opera News*, 4 March 1961, p. 26.

MISCELLANEOUS OR UNSIGNED

Il maestro Puccini sul suo 'Ricochet', *Ars et Labor*, May 1909, p. 362.

Il maestro Puccini in viaggio per Nuova-York, *Ars et Labor*, December 1910, p. 954.

Il 'Cio-Cio-San', il magnifico canotto automobile del Maestro Puccini, *Ars et Labor*, January 1912, p. 40.

GP, commemorative supplement, *Musica d'oggi*, March 1925.

Puccini im deutschen Opernspielplan, *Blätter der Staatsoper* (Berlin), February 1931, p. 1.

Puccini revealed through his letters, *Musician*, October 1931, p. 13.

Gli anni giovanili di GP, *L'Approdo musicale*, April–June 1959, p. 28.

SERGEI RACHMANINOV (1873–1943)

Sergei Vassilievich Rachmaninov was born into a Russian aristocratic family on 2 April 1873 on the estate of Oneg in the Novgorod Government. By 1882 his father, a former captain in the Imperial Guard, had squandered all five of the estates which constituted Rachmaninov's mother's dowry, and in that year the parents separated. Rachmaninov went to live with his mother in St. Petersburg and studied at the Conservatoire there from 1883 to 1885. He then moved to Moscow and, apart from concert tours and a spell in Dresden (1906–9), his life for the next thirty-two years was divided between Moscow and the estate of Ivanovka near Tambov. Rachmaninov was a student at the Moscow Conservatoire from 1885 to 1892, spending his first five years there under the strictest pedagogic supervision in the house of a Conservatoire piano teacher, Nikolai Sverev. He studied composition with Taneyev and Arensky, becoming a protégé of Tchaikovsky and close friend of Scriabin. In January 1892 he made his début as a composer-pianist in Moscow and in September of the same year gave the première of the C Sharp Minor Prelude, which almost immediately made him world-famous. This was the start of a career which combined composition, teaching music in various Moscow girls' schools and appearing as conductor and pianist, largely of his own works, notably in England in 1899 and the USA ten years later. He also conducted opera, in 1897–8 for the Mamontov company (where he met and started a lifelong friendship with Fyodor Chaliapin) and in 1904–6 for the Bolshoi. In 1902 he married his cousin Natalia Satin and from 1909 to 1912, as Vice-President of the Imperial Russian Musical Society, worked to improve standards in the music schools of the smaller Russian cities. The greater part of his *œuvre* was written by the time of the Russian Revolution in 1917. In December that year he used the opportunity of a Scandinavian concert-tour to escape from Russia. He never returned, starting a new career in the West as a touring piano virtuoso. In 1921 he settled in New York City, which was to be his base for the next twenty years. From 1922 until 1939 he divided each year into two seasons of concert touring, one in the USA and the other in Europe. The summers of 1929–31 were spent at Clairefontaine near Paris and those thereafter at Rachmaninov's villa on Lake Lucerne. From 1931 his music was boycotted in the Soviet Union, though this attitude changed during the Second World War. In 1942 Rachmaninov moved to Beverly Hills in California, becoming an American citizen in February 1943 and dying of cancer the following month.

CATALOGUE OF WORKS

1. Scherzo. For orchestra. Dated: 5–12 February 1887.
2 fl, 2 ob, 2 cl, 2 bsn; hn, tpt; timp; strings.
fp: 2 November 1945, Moscow, cond. N. Anosov.

Pub. 1947, Muzgiz; ed. Paul Lamm.

2. Three Nocturnes. For piano. 1887–8.
1. Dated: 14–21 November 1887.
2. Dated: 22–25 November 1887.
3. Dated: 3 December 1887–12 January 1888.
Pub. 1949, Muzgiz.

3. Four Pieces. For piano. 1887.
1. *Romance* (F sharp minor).
2. *Prélude* (E flat minor).
3. *Melody* (E major).
4. *Gavotte* (D major).
Pub. 1948, Muzgiz.

4. Piano piece. *c.* 1887. Composed for harmony examination. Presumably lost but re-written from memory by the composer for publication in facsimile in *Rachmaninov's Recollections* (1934).

5. Esmeralda. Opera based on Victor Hugo's Notre Dame de Paris. Fragments only. Dated: 17 October 1888.

6. Piano Concerto. Sketches only. Dated: November 1889.

7. String Quartet No. 1. Two movements only. ?1889.
2. *Romance*; 3. *Scherzo*.
fp: October 1945, Moscow, Beethoven Quartet.
Pub. 1947, Muzgiz.

8. Deus Meus. Motet for 6-part mixed chorus. Spring 1890.
fp: February 1891, Moscow Conservatory, chorus, cond. Sergei Rachmaninov.
Unpub.

9. At the gate of the Holy Abode (Mikhail Lermontov). For voice and piano. Dated: 29 April 1890. Ded. Mikhail Slonov. Pub. 1947, Muzgiz.

10. I'll tell you nothing (Afanasy Fet). For voice and piano. Dated: 1 May 1890. Pub. 1947, Muzgiz.

11. Romance. For cello and piano. Dated: August 1890, Ivanovka. Ded. Vera Skalon. Pub. 1948, Muzgiz.

12. Manfred. For orchestra. *c.* 1890. ?Unfinished. Lost.

13. Russian Rhapsody. For two pianos. Dated: 12–14 January 1891.

fp: 17 November 1891, students' concert, Sergei Rachmaninov and Joseph Lhévinne. Pub. 1948, Muzgiz.

14. C'était en avril (E. Pailleron). For voice and piano. Dated: 1 April 1891. Pub. 1947, Muzgiz.

15. Dusk has fallen (Alexei Tolstoy). For voice and piano. Dated: 22 April 1891. Pub. 1947, Muzgiz.

16. Piano Concerto No. 1 in F sharp minor Op. 1. 1890–1. Dated: 6 July 1891, Ivanovka. Ded. Alexander Siloti. Revised edition dated: 10 November 1917.

1. *Vivace*; 2. *Andante*; 3. *Allegro vivace*.

2 fl, 2 ob, 2 cl, 2 bsn; 4 hn, 2 tpt, 3 tmb; timp, tgle, cym; strings.

fp (first movement only): 17 March 1892, students' concert, Sergei Rachmaninov, cond. Wassili Safonov.

fEp: 4 October 1900, Queen's Hall, Promenade Concert, Evelyn Suart and the Queen's Hall Orchestra, cond. (Sir) Henry Wood.

Pub. Gutheil, incl. reduction for two pianos by the composer; new revised edition, 1920, State Music Editions; 1947, Boosey & Hawkes.

17. Prelude in F major. For piano. Dated: 20 July 1891, Ivanovka. Pub. 1948, Muzgiz.

18. Valse and Romance. For piano six hands. 1890–1. Ded. Natalia, Ludmila and Vera Skalon.

1. *Valse*. Dated: 15 August 1890.
2. *Romance*. Dated: 20 September 1891.

Pub. 1948, Muzgiz.

19. Symphony in D minor. First movement only. Dated: 28 September 1891. Pub. 1947, Muzgiz (ed. P. Lamm).

20. Prince Rotislav. Poem for orchestra, from a ballad by Alexei Tolstoy. Dated: 9–15 December 1891. Ded. Anton Arensky.

2 fl, pic, 2 ob, ca, 2 cl, 2 bsn; 4 hn, 2 tpt, 2 pistoni, 3 tmb, tuba; timp, cym GC, tamtam; hp, strings.

fp: 2 November 1945, Moscow, cond. N. Anosov.

Pub. 1947, Muzgiz.

21. Again you leapt, my heart (Grekov). For voice and piano. ?1891. Pub. 1947, Muzgiz.

22. You recall that evening? (Alexei Tolstoy). For voice and piano. ?1891. Pub. 1947, Muzgiz.

23. Boris Godunov. Two fragments, based on the play by Pushkin. ?1891.

1. *Arioso by Boris* (three variants).
2. *Pimen's Monologue* (two variants).

Pub. 1947, Muzgiz (selected variants, ed. P. Lamm).

24. Masquerade (Mikhail Lermontov). Fragment in two variants for bass voice and piano. ?1891. Pub. 1947, Muzgiz (second variant, ed. P. Lamm).

25. Mazeppa (Pushkin). Fragment for vocal quartet. ?1891. Unpub.

26. String Quintet. ?1891. ?Lost.

27. Grianem-ukhnem. Russian boatmen's song arr. for voice and piano. ?1891. Ded. Adolf Yaroshevsky. Pub. 1944, Muzgiz.

28. Romance. For piano and violin. ?1891. Pub. 1951, Leeds Music (ed. Louis Persinger).

29. Piece. For cello and piano. ?1891. Pub. 1947, Composers Press (ed. Modeste Altschuler).

30. Trio élégiaque in G minor. For piano, violin and cello. Dated: 18–21 January 1892.

fp: 30 January 1892, Moscow, Sergei Rachmaninov, David Krein and Anatoli Brandukov.

Pub. 1947, Muzgiz (revised by Dobrokhotov).

31. Two Pieces Op. 2. For cello and piano. 1892. Ded. Anatoli Brandukov.

1. *Prelude in F major*; 2. *Oriental dance*.

fp: 30 January 1892, Moscow, Anatoli Brandukov and Sergei Rachmaninov.

31a. The Sleeping Beauty. Ballet score and Suite by Tchaikovsky, arr. by Rachmaninov for piano duet. Pub. 1892, Jurgenson.

32. Aleko. Opera in one act. Dated: 13 April

1892. Libretto: Vladimir Nemirovich-Danchenko, from Pushkin's 'Gipsies'.

fp: 27 April 1893, Moscow, Bolshoi Theatre, cond. Ippolit Altani.

Pub. 1892 (vocal score by the composer), Gutheil; 1953 (full score), Muzgiz.

33. Five Pieces Op. 3. For piano. Autumn 1892. Ded. Anton Arensky.

    1. *Elegy* (E flat minor).

    2. *Prelude* (C sharp minor).

    3. *Melody* (E major). Revised, 26 February 1940.

    4. *Polichinelle* (F sharp minor).

    5. *Serenade* (B flat minor). Revised, ?1940.

fp (No. 2): 26 September 1892, Moscow, Sergei Rachmaninov.

fp (complete): December 1892, Kharkov, ?Sergei Rachmaninov.

?fEp (No. 2): November 1893, St. James's Hall, Alexander Siloti.

?fEp (No. 5): 2 May 1904, Bechstein Hall, Evelyn Suart.

Pub. 1893, Gutheil (as 'Morceaux de Fantasie').

BIBLIOGRAPHY:

G. Maier: Rachmaninov's Prelude in C sharp minor, *Etude*, August 1945, p. 432.

Sergei Rachmaninov: My Prelude in C sharp minor, *Delineator*, February 1910.

Anon.: Why Rachmaninov's Prelude is preferred to twenty-three others, *Musician*, December 1926, p. 18.

34. Six Songs Op. 4. For voice and piano. 1890–3.

    1. *Oh, no! I beg you, don't forsake me* (Dmitri Merezhkovsky). Dated: 26 February 1892. Ded. Anna Lodyzhenskaya.

    2. *Morning* (M. Yanov). 1891. Ded. Yuri Sakhnovsky.

    3. *In the silence of the secret night* (Afanasy Fet). Dated: 17 October 1890. Ded. Vera Skalon.

    4. *Sing not, beauty, in my presence* (Alexander Pushkin). Summer 1893. Ded. Natalia Satina.

    5. *O thou, my field* (The harvest of sorrow) (Alexei Tolstoy). Summer 1893. Ded. Ye. Lysikova.

    6. *How long, my friend?* (Arseni Golenishchev-Kutuzov). Ded. Countess Olga Golenishcheva-Kutuzova.

Pub. Gutheil. Nos. 3 & 4 revised by the composer for voice, violin and piano (violin obbligato by Fritz Kreisler), pub. 1922, Fischer.

35. Fantasia (Suite No. 1) Op. 5. For two pianos. Summer 1893, Lebedin.

    1. *Barcarole*; 2. *O night, O love*; 3. *Tears*; 4. *Holy night*.

fp: 30 November 1893, Moscow, Sergei Rachmaninov and Paul Pabst.

Pub. Gutheil; 1960, Moscow.

36. O Mother of God, perpetually praying. For mixed 3-part choir. Summer 1893, Lebedin.

fp: 12 December 1893, Moscow, Synodical Choir.

Unpub.

37. Two Pieces Op. 6. For violin and piano. Summer 1893, Lebedin. Ded. Julius Conus.

    1. *Romance in D minor*; 2. *Hungarian dance*.

Pub. Gutheil.

38. The Crag (The Rock) Op. 7.* Fantasia for orchestra. Summer 1893, Lebedin. Ded. Nikolai Rimsky-Korsakov.

fp: 20 March 1894, Moscow, cond. Vasili Safonov.

?fEp: 19 April 1899, Philharmonic Society of London, cond. Sergei Rachmaninov.†

f New York p: 28 January 1904, Russian Symphony Orchestra, cond. Modeste Altschuler.

Pub. Jurgenson: incl. reduction for piano four hands by the composer.

39. Six Songs Op. 8. For voice and piano. Autumn 1893, Lebedin.

    1. *The water lily* (Heine). Ded. Adolf Yaroshevsky.

    2. *Child, thou art as beautiful as a flower* (Taras Shevchenko). Ded. Leonid Yakovlev.

---

* For the sake of consistency I follow Bertensson and Leyda in listing *The Crag* as the preferable title, but in Britain it is usually known as *The Rock* and has also been performed as *The Cliff*.

† Rachmaninov was making his English début on this occasion which was the 'official' and generally accepted British première of the work; but there is a possibility, unconfirmed, that it had been given the previous year in a performance conducted by Sacheverell Coke.

3. *Meditation* (Taras Shevchenko). Ded. Maria Olferyeva.

4. *My love has brought me sorrow* (The soldier's wife) (Heine). Ded. Mikhail Slonov.

5. *A dream* (Heine). Ded. Natalia Skalon.

6. *A prayer* (Goethe). Ded. Maria Deisha-Sionitzkaya.

Pub. 1894, Gutheil; Russian words, Alexei Pleshcheyev.

40. Trio élégiaque in D minor Op. 9. For piano, violin and cello. Dated: 25 October–15 December 1893. Ded. 'In memory of a great artist' (i.e. Tchaikovsky).

1. *Moderato*; 2. *Quasi variazione*; 3. *Allegro risoluto.*

fp: 31 January 1894, Moscow, Sergei Rachmaninov, Julius Conus and Anatoli Brandukov.

fEp: 22 February 1898, Queen's (Small) Hall, Walenn Chamber Concert, Herbert Parsons (piano), Gerald Walenn and Herbert Walenn.

fEbp: 12 October 1924, Birmingham station, Nigel Dallaway, Frank Cantell, Arthur Kennedy.

Pub. 1894, Gutheil; revised edition, 1907, Gutheil; final revised edition 1950, Muzgiz (ed. Goldenweiser).

Bibliography:

Alex Cohen: Modern chamber music, 1: A Russian Elegy, *Music Student*, June 1912, p. 367.

41. Romance in G major. For piano duet. ?1893. Pub. 1950, Muzgiz.

42. Song of the disillusioned (Dmitri Rathaus). For voice and piano. ?1893. Pub. 1947, Muzgiz.

43. The flower had faded (Dmitri Rathaus). For voice and piano. ?1893. Pub. 1947, Muzgiz.

44. Seven Pieces Op. 10. For piano. Dated: December 1893–January 1894. Ded. Paul Pabst.

1. *Nocturne* (A minor).
2. *Valse* (A major).
3. *Barcarole* (G minor).
4. *Melody* (E minor).

5. *Humoresque* (G major). Rev. 3 March 1940. Pub. Charles Foley.
6. *Romance* (F minor).
7. *Mazurka* (D flat major).

fp: 31 January 1894, ?Sergei Rachmaninov. Pub. 1894, Gutheil (as 'Morceaux de Salon').

45. Six Duets Op. 11. For piano duet. April 1894.

1. *Barcarole* (G minor).
2. *Scherzo* (D major).
3. *Russian song* (B minor).
4. *Valse* (A major).
5. *Romance* (C minor).
6. *Slava!* (Glory!) (C major).

Pub. Gutheil.

46. Capriccio bohémien (Capriccio on gipsy themes) Op. 12. For orchestra. Summer 1894. Ded. Pyotr Lodyzhensky (Lodijensky).

fp: 22 November 1895.

f New York p: 20 December 1906, Russian Symphony Orchestra, cond. Modeste Altschuler.

fEbp: 11 December 1935, BBC Orchestra, cond. Warwick Braithwaite.

Pub. Gutheil: incl. reduction for piano four hands by the composer.

47. Two episodes à la Liszt. Summer 1894. Unfinished. Unpub.

47a. Chorus of Spirits from 'Don Juan'. For mixed chorus a cappella. Relating to preceding project. Unpub.

48. Symphony No. 1 in D minor Op. 13. January–August 1895. Ded. A. L. (Anna Lodyzhenskaya).

1. *Grave—Allegro ma non troppo*; 2. *Allegro animato*; 3. *Larghetto*; 4. *Allegro con fuoco.*

3 fl, pic, 2 ob, 2 cl, 2 bsn; 4 hn, 3 tpt, 3 tmb, tuba; timp, tgle, tamb mil, tamb, cym, GC, tamtam; strings.

fp: 15 March 1897, St. Petersburg, con. Alexander Glazunov.

fEp: 2 January 1964, Royal Festival Hall, Polyphonia Symphony Orchestra, cond. Bryan Fairfax.

Original score lost: reconstruction by B. Shalman pub. 1947, Muzgiz. Original arr. (1896) for piano four hands by the composer pub. 1950, Muzgiz.

49. Six Choruses Op. 15. For women's or children's voices and piano. 1895.

1. *Slavsya!* (Be praised!) (Nikolai Nekrasov).
2. *The night* (Vladimir Ladyzhensky).
3. *The pine tree* (Mikhail Lermontov).
4. *The waves slumbered* (Dreaming waves) (Konstantin Romanov).
5. *Bondage* (Captivity) (N. Tziganov).
6. *The angel* (Mikhail Lermontov).
Pub. 1895–6, Jurgenson.

50. Twelve Songs Op. 14. For voice and piano. September 1896.

1. *I wait for thee* (M. Davidova). Ded. Ludmila Skalon.
2. *The isle* (Shelley, transl. Konstantin Balmont). Ded. Sophia Satina.
3. *For long love has brought little consolation* (How few the joys) (Afanasy Fet). Ded. Zoya Pribitkova.
4. *I came to her* (Alexei Koltzov). Ded. Yuri Sakhnovsky.
5. *These summer nights* (Midsummer nights) (Dmitri Rathaus). Ded. Maria Gutheil.
6. *How everyone loves thee!* (Alexei Tolstoy). Ded. A. Ivanovsky.
7. *Believe me not, friend!* (Alexei Tolstoy). Ded. Anna Klokacheva.
8. *Oh, do not grieve!* (Alexei Apukhtin). Ded. Nadezhda Alexandrova.
9. *She is lovely as the noon* (Nikolai Minsky). Ded. Yelizaveta Lavrovskaya.
10. *In my soul* (Love's flame) (Nikolai Minsky). Ded. Yelizaveta Lavrovskaya.
11. *Floods of spring* (Spring waters) (Fyodor Tiutchev). Ded. Anna Ornatzkaya.
12. *'Tis time!* (Semyon Nadson).
Pub. 1896, Gutheil.

51. Six Moments Musicaux Op. 16. For piano. October–December 1896. Ded. Alexander Zatayevich.

1. *Andantino* (B flat minor).
2. *Allegretto* (E flat minor).
3. *Andante cantabile* (B minor).
4. *Presto* (E minor).
5. *Adagio sostento* (D flat major).
6. *Maestoso* (C major).
Pub. Jurgenson.

52. String Quartet No. 2. First two movements only. 1896.

1. *Allegro moderato*; 2. *Andante molto sostenuto.*
fp: October 1945, Moscow, Beethoven Quartet.
Pub. 1948, Muzgiz.

53. Improvisations. For piano. 1896. In-included in *Four Improvisations* (comp. with Arensky, Glazunov and Taneyev). Pub. 1925–6 in *Sergei Taneyev* (Moscow), ed. K. Kuznetzov.

54. Symphony. Discarded sketches only. Dated: 5 April 1897. Unpub.

55. Glazunov's Symphony No. 6 Op. 58. Transcribed for piano duet by Sergei Rachmaninov. Pub. 1897, Belaiev.

56. Fantasy Pieces. For piano.

1. *Morceau de Fantaisie in G minor.* Dated: 11 January 1899.
2. *Untitled piece in D minor.* Undated.
Pub. 1950, Muzgiz.

57. Fughetta in F major. For piano. Dated: 4 February 1899, Moscow. Pub. 1950, Muzgiz.

58. Two Russian and Ukrainian songs. Arr. for chorus. 1899.

1. *At the gate.* Lost.
2. *Shoes.* Pub. Muzgiz.

59. Were you hiccuping (P. Viazemsky, adapted by Sergei Rachmaninov). A song-jest. Dated: 17 May 1899. Pub. 1947, Muzgiz (ed. P. Lamm).

60. Pantelei, the healer (Alexei Tolstoy). For mixed chorus a cappella. June–July 1900.
fp: ?1901, Moscow, Synodical Choir.
Pub. ?Gutheil.

61. Suite No. 2 Op. 17. For two pianos. December 1900–April 1901. Ded. Alexander Goldenweiser.

1. *Introduction*; 2. *Valse*; 3. *Romance*; 4. *Tarantelle.*
fp: 24 November 1901, Moscow, Sergei Rachmaninov and Alexander Siloti.
fEbp (omitting No. 4): 22 June 1926, Isabel Gray and Claud Pollard.
Pub. 1901, Gutheil.

62. Piano Concerto No. 2 in C minor Op. 18. Dated: Autumn 1900–21 April 1901. Ded. Nikolai Dahl.

1. *Moderato*; 2. *Adagio sostenuto*; 3. *Allegro scherzando*.

2 fl, 2 ob, 2 cl, 2 bsn; 4 hn, 2 tpt, 3 tmb, tuba; timp, GC, cym; strings.

fp (last two movements): 2 December 1900, Moscow, Nobility Hall, Sergei Rachmaninov, cond. Alexander Siloti.

fp (complete): 27 October 1901, Moscow, Philharmonic Society concert, Sergei Rachmaninov, cond. Alexander Siloti.

fEp: 29 May 1902, Queen's Hall, Philharmonic Society of London, Sapellnikov.

fEbp: 29 October 1923, Cecil Dixon and London Wireless Orchestra, cond. L. Stanton Jefferies.

Pub. 1901, Gutheil: incl. reduction for two pianos by the composer. Min. score: Boosey & Hawkes.

BIBLIOGRAPHY:

H. G. Sear: A concerto, *MS*, 15 February 1919, p. 57.

63. Cello Sonata in G minor Op. 19. Summer 1901. Ded. Anatoli Brandukov.

1. *Lento—Allegro moderato*; 2. *Allegro scherzando*; 3. *Andante*; 4. *Allegro mosso*.

fp: 2 December 1901, Moscow, Anatoli Brandukov and Sergei Rachmaninov.

fEp: 18 January 1904, St. James's Hall, Monday Popular Concert, Percy Such and Lucy Polgreen.

fEbp: 27 August 1924, Beatrice Eveline and Maurice Cole.

Pub. 1902, Gutheil.

BIBLIOGRAPHY:

Felix Salmond: Sonata of Rachmaninov for piano and violoncello (Op. 19), *Strad*, 1915, August p. 100, September p. 155.

64. Spring Op. 20. Cantata for baritone, mixed chorus and orchestra. January–February 1902. Ded. Nikita Morozov (N. S. Marasoff). Text: Nikolai Nekrasov.

fp: 11 March 1902, Moscow.

Pub. 1903, Gutheil: incl. vocal score by the composer; German text, Vladimir Czumikow.

65. Twelve Songs Op. 21. For voice and piano. April 1902, Ivanovka.

1. *Fate* (Alexei Apukhtin). Dated: 18 February 1900. Ded. Fyodor Chaliapin.

2. *By the new grave* (Semyon Nadson).

3. *Twilight* (M. Guyot, transl. Korneli Tkhorzhevsky). Ded. Nadezhda Zabela-Vrubel.

4. *They answered* (The answer) (Victor Hugo, transl. Lev Mey). Ded. Yelena Kreutzer.

5. *Lilacs* (Ekaterina Beketova).

6. *Fragment from Musset* (Loneliness) (Transl. Apukhtin). Ded. Princess Alexandra Lieven.

7. *How nice it is here* (How fair this spot) (Glafira Galina).

8. *On the death of a linnet* (Vasili Zhukovsky). Ded. Olga Trubnikova.

9. *Melody* (Semyon Nadson). Ded. Natalia Lanting.

10. *Before the ikon* (Arseni Golenishchev-Kutuzov). Ded. Maria Ivanova.

11. *No prophet I!* (Alexander Kruglov).

12. *How painful for me* (Sorrow in springtime) (Glafira Galina).

Pub. 1902, Gutheil.

65a. Lilacs Op. 21 No. 5. Transcribed by the composer for piano solo. 1913. Pub. 1919, Gutheil.

66. Variations on a theme by Chopin Op. 22. For piano. August 1902–February 1903. Ded. Theodore Leschetizky.

fp: 10 February 1903, Moscow, Sergei Rachmaninov.

fEp: 26 June 1911, Bechstein Hall, Max Pauer.

Pub. 1904, Gutheil.

67. Ten Preludes Op. 23. For piano. 1903. Ded. Alexander Siloti.

1. *Largo* (F sharp minor).
2. *Maestoso* (B flat major).
3. *Tempo di menuetto* (D minor).
4. *Andante cantabile* (D major).
5. *Alla marcia* (G minor). 1901.
6. *Andante* (E flat major).
7. *Allegro* (C minor).
8. *Allegro vivace* (A flat major).
9. *Presto* (E flat minor).
10. *Largo* (G flat major).

fp: 10 February 1903, Moscow, ?Sergei Rachmaninov.

fEbp: 22–27 February 1926, 2LO broadcast, Stephen Wearing.
Pub. 1904, Gutheil.

68. Night (Dmitri Rathaus). For voice and
piano. Pub. 1904, Jurgenson (in *Works by
Contemporary Russian Composers*, Vol. 2).

69. The Miserly Knight Op. 24. Opera in
three scenes from a play by Pushkin. August
1903–28 February 1904; scored, 1905. Dated:
19 May 1905 (Scene 1), 30 May 1905 (Scene 2),
7 June 1905 (Scene 3).
fp: 11 January 1906, Moscow, Bolshoi
Theatre, cond. Sergei Rachmaninov.
Pub. 1905, Gutheil: incl. vocal score by the
composer.

70. Francesca da Rimini Op. 25. Opera in
two scenes with prologue and epilogue.
Summer 1904; orchestrated, 1905. Dated:
22 July 1905. Libretto: Modeste Tchaikovsky,
from an episode in Dante's Inferno.
fp: 11 January 1906, Moscow, Bolshoi
Theatre, cond. Sergei Rachmaninov.
Pub. 1905, Gutheil: incl. vocal score by the
composer; German text, Lina Esbeer.

71. Fifteen Songs Op. 26. For voice and
piano. 1906. Ded. Maria and Arkadi Kerzin.
1. *There are many sounds* (The heart's secret)
(Alexei Tolstoy). 14 August 1906.
2. *He took all from me* (All once I gladly
owned) (Fyodor Tiutchev). Dated: 15 August
1906.
3. *Let us rest* (Anton Chekhov). Dated:
14 August 1906.
4. *Two partings, a dialogue* (Alexei Koltzov).
For baritone and soprano. Dated: 22 August
1906.
5. *Let us leave, my dear* (Beloved, let us fly)
(Arseni Golenishchev-Kutuzov). Dated: 22
August 1906.
6. *Christ is risen* (Dmitri Merzehkovsky).
Dated: 23 August 1906.
7. *To the children* (A. Khomyakov). Dated:
9 September 1906.
8. *I implore pity!* (Dmitri Merezhkovsky).
Dated: 25 August 1906.
9. *Again I am alone* (Let me rest here alone)
(Taras Shevchenko, transl. Ivan Bunin).
Dated: 4 September 1906.

10. *Before my window* (Glafira Galina).
Dated: 17 September 1906.
11. *The fountain* (Fyodor Tiutchev). Dated:
6 September 1906.
12. *The night is mournful* (Ivan Bunin).
Dated: 3 September 1906.
13. *When yesterday we met* (Yakov
Polonsky). Dated: 3 September 1906.
14. *The ring* (Alexei Koltzov). Dated:
10 September 1906.
15. *All things pass* (Dmitri Rathaus).
Dated: 5 September 1906.
fp (complete): 12 February 1907, Moscow,
Kerzin Concerts.
Pub. 1907, Gutheil. No. 12 arr. by Sergei
Rachmaninov for cello and piano.

72. Symphony No. 2 in E minor Op. 27.
October 1906–April 1907. Ded. Serge.
Taneyev.
1. *Largo—Allegro moderato*; 2. *Allegro molto*;
3. *Adagio*; 4. *Allegro vivace*.
3 fl, 2 ob, ca, 2 cl, bcl, 2 bsn; 4 hn, 3 tpt,
3 tmb, tuba; timp, cym, GC; strings.
fp: 26 January 1908, St. Petersburg, cond.
Sergei Rachmaninov.
fEp: 19 May 1910, Queen's Hall, Philharmonic Society of London, cond. Arthur
Nikisch.
fEbp: 4 March 1925, Bristol, Colston Hall,
Bristol Symphony Orchestra, cond. (Sir)
Eugene Goossens.
Pub. 1908, Gutheil. Reduction by Vladimir
Wilshaw for piano duet pub. 1910, Gutheil.

BIBLIOGRAPHY:
David Rubin: Transformations of the 'Dies
Irae' in Rachmaninov's Second Symphony,
MR, May 1962, p. 132.

73. Polka italienne. For piano duet. 1906, or
later. Ded. Sergei Siloti. Pub. 1938, Charles
Foley.

74. Piano Sonata No. 1 in D minor Op. 28.
Dated: 14 May 1907, Dresden.
1. *Allegro moderato*; 2. *Lento*; 3. *Allegro molto*.
fp: 17 October 1908, Moscow, Konstantin
Igumnov.
fEbp: 12 February 1937, Charles Lynch.
Pub. 1908, Gutheil.

75. Monna Vanna. Unfinished opera. Piano
score of Act I dated: 15 April 1907, Dresden.

Fragments only of Act II. Libretto: Mikhail Slonov, based on the play by Maurice Maeterlinck.

76. Letter to K. S. Stanislavsky. For voice and piano. October 1908, Dresden.
fp: 14 October 1908, Moscow Art Theatre, Fyodor Chaliapin.
Pub. Gutheil.

77. The Isle of the Dead Op. 29. Symphonic Poem for orchestra, after a painting by Böcklin. Dated: 17 April 1909. Ded. Nikolai Struve.
3 fl, pic, 2 ob, ca, 2 cl, bcl, 2 bsn, cbsn; 6 hn, 3 tpt, 3 tmb, tuba; timp, GC, cym; hp, strings.
fp: 18 April (O.S.)/1 May 1909, Moscow, Philharmonic Society, cond. Sergei Rachmaninov.
fEp: 23 February 1910, Royal College of Music concert, cond. Sir Charles Stanford.
fEp (professional): 25 August 1915, Queen's Hall, Promenade Concert, Queen's Hall Orchestra, cond. Sir Henry Wood.
Pub. 1909, Gutheil. Reduction by Otto Taubmann for piano duet pub. 1910, Gutheil.

BIBLIOGRAPHY:
Robert H. Hull: Mysterious music, *Radio Times*, 17 January 1936, p. 12.

78. Piano Concerto No. 3 in D minor Op. 30. Summer 1909, Ivanovka. Ded. Josef Hofmann.
1. *Allegro ma non tanto*; 2. *Intermezzo* (*Adagio*); 3. *Finale* (*Alla breve*).
2 fl, 2 ob, 2 cl, 2 bsn; 4 hn, 2 tpt, 3 tmb, tuba; timp, GC, cym, tamb mil; strings.
fp: 28 November 1909, New York, Sergei Rachmaninov, cond. Walter Damrosch.
fEp: 24 October 1911, Liverpool, Liverpool Philharmonic Society concert, Sergei Rachmaninov, cond. Simon Speelman.
f London p: 7 November 1911, Queen's Hall, Philharmonic Society, Sergei Rachmaninov, cond. Willem Mengelberg.
Pub. 1910, Gutheil: incl. reduction for two pianos by the composer. Min. score: Boosey & Hawkes.

79. Liturgy of Saint John Chrysostom Op. 31. For mixed choir. Dated: 30 July 1910, Ivanovka.

fp: 25 November 1910, Moscow, Synodical Choir, cond. Nikolai Danilin.
Pub. Gutheil.

80. Preludes Op. 32. For piano. 1910.
1. *Allegro vivace* (C major). Dated: 30 August.
2. *Allegretto* (B flat minor). Dated: 2 September.
3. *Allegro vivace* (E major). Dated: 3 September.
4. *Allegro con brio* (E minor). Dated: 28 August.
5. *Moderato* (G major). Dated: 23 August.
6. *Allegro appassionato* (F minor). Dated: 25 August.
7. *Moderato* (F major). Dated: 24 August.
8. *Vivo* (A minor). Dated: 24 August.
9. *Allegro moderato* (A major). Dated: 26 August.
10. *Lento* (B minor). Dated: 6 September.
11. *Allegretto* (B major). Dated: 23 August.
12. *Allegro* (G sharp minor). Dated: 23 August.
13. *Grave* (D flat major). Dated: 10 September.
fEbp: 22–27 February 1926, 2LO broadcast, Stephen Wearing.
Pub. 1911, Gutheil.

81. Polka de W.R. (Polka V.R.). For piano. Based on a theme by Vasili Rachmaninov. Dated: 11 March 1911. Ded. Leopold Godowsky. Pub. 1911, Editions Russe de Musique.

82. Etudes-Tableaux Op. 33. For piano. August 1911.
1. *Allegro non troppo* (F minor). Dated: 11 August.
2. *Allegro* (C major). Dated: 16 August.
3. *Non Allegro—Presto* (E flat minor). Dated: 23 August.
4. *Allegro con fuoco* (E flat major). Dated: 17 August.
5. *Moderato* (G minor). Dated: 15 August.
6. *Grave* (C sharp minor). Dated: 13 August.
Pub. 1914, Gutheil.

82a. Etudes-Tableaux. For piano. August–September 1911. Composed for Op. 33 but omitted before publication.

413

1. *Grave* (C minor). Orig. No. 3. Dated: 18 August. Pub. 1948, Muzgiz.

2. *Allegro* (A minor). Orig. No. 4. Dated: 8 September. Unpub. in this form.

3. *Moderato* (D minor). Orig. No. 5. Dated: 11 September. Pub. 1948, Muzgiz.

83. Fourteen Songs Op. 34. For voice and piano. June 1912.

1. *The muse* (Alexander Pushkin). Dated: 6 June. Ded. 'Re' (i.e. Marietta Shaginyan).

2. *In the soul of each of us* (The soul's concealment) (Apollon Korinfsky). Dated: 5 June. Ded. Fyodor Chaliapin.

3. *The storm* (Pushkin). Dated: 7 June. Ded. Sobinov.

4. *The migrant wind* (Konstantin Balmont). Dated: 9 June. Ded. Leonid Sobinov.

5. *Arion* (Pushkin). Dated: 8 June. Ded. Leonid Sobinov.

6. *The raising of Lazarus* (A. Khomyakov). Dated: 4 June. Ded. Fyodor Chaliapin.

7. *It cannot be* (So dread a fate I'll never believe) (Apollon Maikov). Dated: 7 March 1910, rev. 13 June 1912. Ded. to the memory of Vera Komissarzhevskaya.

8. *Music* (Yakov Polonsky). Dated: 12 June. Ded. P. Ch.

9. *You knew him well* (The poet) (Fyodor Tiutchev). Dated: 12 June. Ded. Fyodor Chaliapin.

10. *I remember that day* (The morn of life) (Fyodor Tiutchev). Dated: 10 June. Ded. Leonid Sobinov.

11. *With holy banner firmly held* (Afanasy Fet). Dated: 11 June. Ded. Fyodor Chaliapin.

12. *What happiness* (What wealth of rapture) (Afanasy Fet). Dated: 19 June. Ded. Leonid Sobonov.

13. *Dissonance* (Discord) (Yakov Polonsky). Dated: 17 June. Ded. Felia Litvin.

14. *Vocalise.* Dated: April 1912, rev. 21 September 1915. Ded. Antonina Nezhdanova. Also arr. by the composer for orchestra, or violin and piano, or cello and piano. Pub. 1913, Gutheil.

84. The Bells Op. 35. Poem for orchestra, chorus and soloists. January–April 1913, Rome; orchestration completed, 27 July 1913, Ivanovka; rev. 1936. Text: Edgar Allan Poe, transl. Konstantin Balmont. Ded. Willem Mengelberg and the Concertgebouw Orchestra of Amsterdam.

1. *Allegro, ma non tanto*; 2. *Lento*; 3. *Presto*; 4. *Lento lugubre.*

fp: 30 November 1913, St. Petersburg, cond. Sergei Rachmaninov.

f Moscow p: 8 February 1914, Moscow, Philharmonic Society concert, cond. Sergei Rachmaninov.

fEp: 15 March 1921, Liverpool, Liverpool Philharmonic Society, Doris Vane, Arthur Jordan, Norman Williams, Philharmonic Choir, cond. Sir Henry Wood.

Revised version:

fp: 21 October 1936, Sheffield Festival, Isobel Baillie, Parry Jones, Harold Williams, Philharmonic Choir, London Philharmonic Orchestra, cond. Sir Henry Wood.

f London p: 10 February 1937, Queen's Hall, Isobel Baillie, Parry Jones, Roy Henderson, Philharmonic Choir, BBC Orchestra, cond. Sir Henry Wood.

Pub. Gutheil: incl. vocal score by Alexander Goldenweiser; English version, Fanny S. Copeland.

BIBLIOGRAPHY:

L. S. Ashton: Bells, *Etude*, March 1952, p. 54.

Robert Hull: Rachmaninov's The Bells, *MMR*, October 1936, p. 171.

Anon.: Poe à la russe—recording of The Bells, *Musical America*, September 1953, p. 13.

85. Piano Sonata No. 2 in B flat minor Op. 36. Dated: 13 September 1913, Ivanovka; rev. summer 1931. Ded. Matvei Pressman.

1. *Allegro agitato*; 2. *Non allegro*; 3. *Allegro molto.*

?fEp: 30 January 1914, Bradford, Sergei Rachmaninov.

fEbp: 21 June 1938, Cyril Smith.

Pub. 1914, Gutheil; revised version, 1931, Tair.

86. From the Gospel of St. John. For voice and piano. Autumn 1914. Pub. 1915, Jurgenson, in *Klich* (Appeal).

87. Night Vigil (Vesper Service) Op. 37. For mixed choir. January–February 1915. Ded. to the memory of Stepan Smolensky.

fp: 10 March 1915, Moscow, Synodical Choir, cond. Nikolai Danilin.
Pub. Editions Russe de Musique; English edition, 1920, as *Songs of the Church*.

88. The Scythians. Ballet. 1915. Unfinished. Lost.

88. Six Songs Op. 38. For soprano and piano. 1916. Ded. Nina Koshetz.
  1. *In my garden at night* (Isaakian, transl. Alexander Blok). Dated: 12 September.
  2. *To her* (Andrei Belyi). Dated: 12 September.
  3. *Daisies* (Igor Severyanin).
  4. *The rat-catcher* (Valeri Briusov). Dated: 12 September.
  5. *The dream* (Fyodor Sologub). Dated: 2 November.
  6. *A-oo* (Konstantin Balmont). Dated: 14 September.
  fp: 24 October 1916, Mme Koshetz and Sergei Rachmaninov.
  Pub. 1916, Editions Russe de Musique. No. 3 transcribed by the composer for piano, pub. 1924, Tair.

89. Two Songs. For voice and piano. 1916. Sketches only.
  1. *Prayer* (Konstantin Romanov); 2. *All wish to sing* (Glory to God) (Fyodor Sologub). Unpub.

90. Etudes-Tableaux Op. 39. For piano. Autumn 1916–February 1917.
  1. *Allegro agitato* (C minor). Dated: 5 October 1916.
  2. *Lento assai* (A minor). 1917.
  3. *Allegro molto* (F sharp minor). Dated: 14 October 1916.
  4. *Allegro assai* (B minor). Dated: 24 September 1916.
  5. *Appassionato* (E flat minor). Dated: 17 February 1917.
  6. *Allegro* (A minor). Dated: 8 September 1911, rev. 27 September 1916.
  7. *Lento lugubre* (C minor). 1917.
  8. *Allegro moderato* (D minor). 1917.
  9. *Allegro moderato—Tempo di marcia* (D major). Dated: 2 February 1917.
  fp (incomplete): 29 November 1916, Petrograd, ?Sergei Rachmaninov.
  fEp (Nos. 3 & 9): 1 December 1917, Aeolian Hall, Mark Hambourg. (NB: Four were performed by Rachmaninov at his Queen's Hall recital on 20 May 1922.)
  Pub. 1920, Editions Russe de Musique.

91. Oriental Sketch. For piano. Dated: 14 November 1917, Moscow.
  fp: 12 November 1931, New York, Juilliard School.
  Pub. 1938, Charles Foley.

92. (Untitled piece.) For piano. Dated: 14 November 1917. Unpub.

93. Fragments. For piano. Dated: 15 November 1917, Moscow. Pub. October 1919, in *The Etude*.

94. The Star Spangled Banner. Transcription for piano. ?1918.
  fp: 15 December 1918, Boston, Sergei Rachmaninov.

95. Cadenza for Liszt's Hungarian Rhapsody No. 2. ?1919.
  fp: 10 January 1919, Boston, Sergei Rachmaninov.

96. Luchinushka (The splinter). Russian song arr. (for John McCormack) for tenor and piano. Dated: 3 July 1920, Goshen. Unpub.

97. Apple tree, O apple tree. Russian song harmonisation for a collection by Alfred J. Swan. 1920. Pub. 1921, Enoch, in *Songs from many lands*.

98. Along the street. Russian song arrangement. 1920. Sketch only.

99. Liebesleid. Kreisler, arr. by Rachmaninov for piano solo. ?1921.
  fp: 20 November 1921, Chicago, Sergei Rachmaninov.
  Pub. 1923, Charles Foley.

100. Minuetto from L'Arlésienne Suite No. 1. Bizct, arr. by Rachmaninov for piano solo. ?1903.
  fp: 19 January 1922, Tulsa (Oklahoma), Sergei Rachmaninov.
  Pub. 1923, Charles Foley.

101. Gopak from Fair at Sorochintzi. Mussorgsky, arr. by Rachmaninov for piano solo. Dated: 1 January 1924.
  fp: ?13 November 1923, Scranton (Penn.),

Sergei Rachmaninov (?before committed to paper).
Pub. 1924, Charles Foley.

101a. Gopak from Fair at Sorochintzi. Mussorgsky, arr. by Rachmaninov for violin nd piano. Pub. 1926, Charles Foley.

102. Liebesfreud. Kreisler, arr. by Rachmaninov for piano solo. ?1925.
fp: 29 October 1925, Stamford (Conn.), Sergei Rachmaninov.
Pub. 1926, Charles Foley.

103. Quickly, quickly, from my cheeks. Russian song arrangement for voice and piano. 1925. Unpub.

104. Wohin? (The brooklet). Song by Schubert, from 'Die Schöne Müllerin', arr. by Rachmaninov for piano solo. ?1925.
fp: 29 October 1925, Stamford (Conn.), Sergei Rachmaninov.
Pub. 1926, Charles Foley.

105. Piano Concerto No. 4 in G minor Op. 40. January–25 August 1926, New York, Dresden; rev. 1941. Ded. Nicolas Medtner.
1. *Allegro vivace*; 2. *Largo*; 3. *Allegro vivace*.
2 fl, pic, 2 ob, ca, 2 cl, 2 bsn; 4 hn, 2 tpt, 3 tmb, tuba; timp, tgle, tamb, tamb mil, cym, GC; strings.
fp: 18 March 1927, Philadelphia, Sergei Rachmaninov and the Philadelphia Orchestra, cond. Leopold Stokowski.
Pub. 1928, Tair: incl. reduction by the composer. Revised version pub. 1944 (score), 1946 (reduction by Sergei Rachmaninov and Robert Russell Bennett), Charles Foley.

106. Russian Songs (Chansons russes) Op. 41. For chorus and orchestra. 1926. Ded. Leopold Stokowski.
1. *Over the little river* (See! a wooden bridge).
2. *Oh, Vanka, you bold fellow* (Oh, my Johnny!). Dated: 16 November 1926.
3. *Quickly, quickly, from my cheeks.*
2 fl, pic, 2 ob, ca, 2 cl, bcl, 2 bsn, cbsn; 4 hn, 2 tpt, alto tpt, 3 tmb, tuba; timp, tgle, cym, campanelli, verghe, tamb mil; hp, piano, strings.
fp: 18 March 1927, Philadelphia, chorus and

Philadelphia Orchestra, cond. Leopold Stokowski.
fEp: 11 March 1930, Liverpool, Philharmonic Hall, chorus and Liverpool Philharmonic Orchestra, cond. Sir Henry Wood; broadcast by the BBC.
Pub. 1928, Tair: incl. vocal score by the composer; English version, Kurt Schindler; French version, M.-D. Calvocoressi; German version, H. Müller.

107. Variations on a theme of Corelli Op. 42. For piano. Dated: 19 June 1931. Ded. Fritz Kreisler.
fp: 12 October 1931, Montreal, Sergei Rachmaninov.
fbp: 27 November 1937, BBC broadcast, Maurice Reeve.
Pub. Tair.

108. Flight of the bumble bee. Rimsky-Korsakov, arr. by Rachmaninov for piano solo. Pub. 1931, Charles Foley.

109. Songs. Settings of verses by the composer's granddaughter. 1933. Lost.

110. Scherzo from A Midsummer Night's Dream. Mendelssohn, arr. by Rachmaninov for piano solo. Dated: 6 March 1933.
fp: 23 January 1933, San Antonio (Texas), Sergei Rachmaninov (?before committed to paper).
Pub. 1933, Tair/Charles Foley.

111. Prelude, Gavotte and Gigue from Violin Partita in E major. Bach, arr. by Rachmaninov for piano solo. Dated: 9 September 1933.
fp (Prelude only): 20 February 1933, Portland (Oregon), Sergei Rachmaninov.
fp (complete): 9 November 1933, Harrisburg (Penn.), Sergei Rachmaninov.
Pub. (Prelude only) 1933, Tair/Charles Foley; (complete) 1941, Charles Foley.

112. Rhapsody on a theme of Paganini Op. 43. For piano and orchestra. Dated: 3 July–18 August 1934. Senar.
2 fl, pic, 2 ob, ca, 2 cl, 2 bsn; 4 hn, 2 tpt, 3 tmb, tuba; timp, tamburo, tgle, cym, GC, campanelli; hp, strings.
fp: 7 November 1934, Baltimore, Sergei

Rachmaninov and the Philadelphia Orchestra, cond. Leopold Stokowski.

f New York p: 27 December 1934, Sergei Rachmaninov and the New York Philharmonic-Symphony, cond. Bruno Walter.

fEp: 7 March 1935, Manchester, Sergei Rachmaninov and the Halle Orchestra, cond. Nikolai Malko.

f London p: 21 March 1935, Queen's Hall, Royal Philharmonic Society concert, Sergei Rachmaninov and the London Philharmonic Orchestra, cond. Sir Thomas Beecham.

Pub. 1934, Charles Foley: incl. reduction by the composer for two pianos.

113. Symphony No. 3 in A minor Op. 44. 1935–6.

1. *Lento—Allegro moderato.* Dated: 18 June–22 August 1935.

2. *Adagio ma non troppo.* Dated: 26 August–18 September 1935, Senar.

3. *Allegro.* Dated: 6–30 June 1936, Senar.

2 fl, pic, 2 ob, ca, 2 cl, bcl, 2 bsn, cbsn; 4 hn, 2 tpt, alto tpt, 3 tmb, tuba; timp, xyl, tgle, tamburo, GC, cym; 2 hp, strings.

fp: 6 November 1936, Philadelphia, Philadelphia Orchestra, cond. Leopold Stokowski.

f European p: 18 November 1937, London, Queen's Hall, Royal Philharmonic Society concert, London Philharmonic Orchestra, cond. Sir Thomas Beecham.

Pub. 1937, Charles Foley.

BIBLIOGRAPHY:

Robin Hull: Rachmaniov's Third Symphony, *MMR*, November 1937, p. 201.

114. Symphonic Dances Op. 45. For orchestra. 1940. Ded. Eugene Ormandy and the Philadelphia Orchestra.

1. *Non allegro.* Dated: 22 September–8 October.

2. *Andante con moto* (Tempo di valse). Dated: 27 September.

3. *Lento assai—Allegro vivace.* Dated: 29 October, New York.

2 fl, pic, 2 ob, ca, 2 cl, bcl, alto sax, 2 bsn, cbsn; 4 hn, 3 tpt, 3 tmb, tuba; timp, tgle, tamb, tamburo, campanelli, xyl, tamtam, campane, cym, GC; hp, piano, strings.

fp: 3 January 1941, Philadelphia, Philadelphia Orchestra, cond. Eugene Ormandy.

fEp: 27 January 1954, BBC broadcast, BBC Symphony Orchestra, cond. Sir Malcolm Sargent.

fEp (concert): 14 August 1954, Royal Albert Hall, Promenade Concert, BBC Symphony Orchestra, cond. Sir Malcolm Sargent.

Pub. 1941, Charles Foley.

114a. Symphonic Dances Op. 45. Arr. by the composer for two pianos. Dated: 10 August 1940, Long Island. Pub. 1941, Charles Foley.

115. Lullaby. Tchaikovsky (Op. 16 No. 1) arr. by Rachmaninov for piano solo. Dated: 12 August 1941.

fp: 14 October 1941, Syracuse (New York), Sergei Rachmaninov.

Pub. 1941, Charles Foley.

GENERAL BIBLIOGRAPHY

John Amis: The unfamiliar Rachmaninov, *Records & Recording*, January 1963, p. 19.

W. R. Anderson: Rachmaninov and his pianoforte concertos, Hinrichsen Edition (London), No. 7, n.d.

Victor Belaiev: SR (transl. S. W. Pring), *MQ*, July 1927, p. 359.

Sergei Bertensson: Rachmaninov as I knew him, *Etude*, March 1948, p. 138.

Sergei Bertensson & Jay Leyda: SR, New York University (1956), Allen & Unwin (London) 1965.

Erik Brewerton: Rachmaninov's songs, *M&L*, January 1934, p. 32, April 1934, p. 109.

A. Chasins: Rachmaninov legacy, *Saturday Review*, 29 October 1955, p. 37, 26 November 1955, p. 46.

J. Chernukhin: With the enemy at the gates, Moscow holds Rachmaninov exhibition, *Musician*, September 1942, p. 136.

W. A. Chislett: Rachmaninov's piano concertos, *The Gramophone*, August 1934, p. 84.

— SR, *Halle*, No. 117, 1960–1, p. 13.

Israel Citkowitz: Orpheus with his lute, *Tempo*, No. 22, winter 1951–2, p. 8.

John Culshaw: SR, Dennis Dobson (London) 1949.

— SR, the man and his music, O.U.P. (London) 1951.

— The popularity of Rachmaninov's piano concertos, *Halle*, April 1951, p. 19.

Rachmaninov, Sergei

— Rachmaninov, the legacy, *The Listener*, 3 March 1966, p. 328.

R. Ericson: Rachmaninov, a discography, *High Fidelity*, May 1955, p. 76.

Edwin Evans: Rachmaninov (obituary notice), *MR*, August 1943.

A. Favia-Artsay: Rachmaninov, *Hobbies*, October 1959, p. 28.

Clintom Gray-Fisk: Rachmaninov's seventieth birthday, *MO*, April 1943, p. 221.

William Flanagan: SR, a twentieth-century composer, *Tempo*, No. 22, winter 1951–2, p. 4.

Jonathan Frank: Rachmaninov and Medtner, a comparison, *MO*, March 1958, p. 387.

Anton Gronowicz: SR, Dutton (New York) 1946.

A. M. Henderson: Rachmaninov at home, *MO*, April 1938, p. 593.

— Personal memories of Rachmaninov, *MO*, May 1943, p. 257.

— Rachmaninov at home, *M&M*, November 1956, p. 15.

— Rachmaninov as I knew him, *Etude*, April 1954, p. 9.

W. J. Henderson: Master of piano and orchestra, *Mentor*, March 1926, p. 38.

Ralph Hill: Rachmaninov, *Gramophone Record*, September 1934, p. 4.

J. Holcman: Hidden treasures of Rachmaninov, *Saturday Review*, 30 August 1958, p. 31.

Richard Holt: The genius of Rachmaninov, *The Gramophone*, January 1928, p. 352.

Frank Howes: Rachmaninov, *MMR*, 1943, p. 81.

Robin Hull: The problem of Rachmaninov, *MO*, April 1942, p. 229.

W. C. De Jong: Rachmaninova persoonlijkheid, *Mens en melodie*, March 1953, p. 69.

R. Kammerer: Golden age of pianists preserved on old records, *Musical America*, February 1957, p. 172.

— Golden art of SR, *American Record Guide*, October 1966, p. 156.

I. Korzuchin: SR, *Music*, February 1920, p. 15.

Maria Kurenko: The songs, an appreciation, *Tempo*, No. 22, winter 1951–2, p. 25.

Constant Lambert: Enjoying Rachmaninov, *Radio Times*, 16 September 1938, p. 14.

F. Lliurat: Les interpretacions de SR, *Revista musical Catalan*.

Watson Lyle: Rachmaninov, a personal sketch, *MN&H*, 17 June 1922, p. 740.

— Rachmaninov and music today, *Apollo*, August 1928, p. 81.

— Rachmaninov, a biography, William Reeves (London) 1938.

Basil Maine: Conversation with Rachmaninov, *MO*, October 1936, p. 14.

Benno Moiseiwitsch: Rachmaninov remembered, *Music Magazine*, May 1962, p. 14.

— Reminiscences of Rachmaninov, *Music Journal*, January 1963, p. 67.

Nicholas Nadejine: Rachmaninov, *The Gramophone*, March 1935, p. 383.

M. Montagu Nathan: The story of Russian music, 15: SR, *Music Student*, March 1918, p. 280.

John F. Porte, Gramophone celebrities, XII: SR, *The Gramophone*, August 1925, p. 128.

R. Quilti: Rachmaninov, the last romantic composer, *Hi Fi Music at Home*, October 1959, p. 26.

Sergei Rachmaninov: National and radical impressions in the music of today and yesterday, *Etude*, October 1917.

— Beware of the indifferent piano teacher, warns Rachmaninov (interview with H. Brower), *Musician*, February 1925, p. 11.

— Some critical moments in my career, *MT*, June 1930; Fr. transl., *Candide*, 4 September 1930.

— The artist and the gramophone, *The Gramophone*, April 1931, p. 525.

— Interpretation depends on talent and personality (ed. F. Leonard), *Etude*, April 1932, p. 239.

— Regrets of a musician, *Musical Mirror*, November 1929, p. 285.

— Composer as interpreter, *MMR*, 1934, p. 201.

— Rachmaninov's recollections, see under Oskar von Riesemann.

P. H. Reed: Rachmaninov left priceless recordings, *Etude*, June 1943, p. 369.

Joseph Reither: Chronicle of exile, *Tempo*, No. 22, winter 1951–2, p. 29.

Oskar von Riesemann: Rachmaninov's recollections (transl. Dolly Rutherford), Allen & Unwin (London) 1934.

Edward Sackville-West: Rachmaninov, *British Institute of Recorded Sound Bulletin*, No. 4, spring 1957, p. 13.

Victor Seroff: Rachmaninov, Cassell (London) 1951.

— Notes on a translation—curious biography of Rachmaninov recently published in Paris, *Saturday Review*, 31 July 1954, p. 37.

William Seymer: Våra dagars stora pianister, 3—SR, *Förena des pianoblad*, Vol. 4 (1939), No. 2, p. 4.

Robert Simpson: SR, in *The Symphony*, Vol. 2, Penguin Books (London) 1967, p. 128.

R. Slenczynska: Rachmaninov's Preludes, *Clavier*, 1963, No. 6, p. 27.

S. Smolian: Da capo, *American Record Guide*, October 1966, p. 154.

A J. & Katherine Swan: Rachmaninov, personal reminiscences, *MQ*, 1944, January p. 1, April p. 174.

Eric H. Thiman: A note on Rachmaninov's Preludes, *MO*, September 1926, p. 1199.

Ellen von Tideböhl: SR, *MMR*, 1906, p. 148.

Rosalyn Tureck: Virtuoso—SR by Sergei Bertensson, *New Statesman*, 25 February 1966, p. 268.

M. Varro: Rachmaninov e Strawinsky, *Musica d'oggi*, January 1937.

Joseph Yasser: Progressive tendencies in Rachmaninov's music, *Musicology*, Vol. 2 (1948), No. 1; *Tempo*, No. 22, winter 1951–1952, p. 11.

MISCELLANEOUS OR UNSIGNED

Some Russian songs: Moussorgsky and Rachmaninov, *The Times*, 14 October 1911, p. 8.

SR, *MO*, December 1930, p. 213.

Last pictures taken of Rachmaninov before death, *Life*, 12 April 1943, p. 4.

Composer of the month, *Etude*, April 1953, p. 32.

Rachmaninov's reputation after the critical twenty years, *The Times*, 29 March 1963, p. 15.

MAURICE RAVEL (1875–1937)

Ravel was born on 7 March 1875 at Ciboure near St.-Jean-de-Luz in the French-Basque *département* of Basses Pyrénées. His mother was probably Basque and his father—a mechanical engineer who almost invented the motorcar—was Swiss. When he was three months old the Ravels moved to Paris (first Montmartre, later Levallois); and apart from frequent retreats to St.-Jean-de-Luz, the composer was to live in or near Paris for the rest of his life. Between 1889 and 1904 he studied at the Conservatoire (where his composition teacher from 1897 was Gabriel Fauré) and began fruitful friendships with the pianist Ricardo Viñes and the composer Erik Satie. In the two decades following, his closest companions (apart from his adored mother) were the self-styled 'Apaches', a group which in addition to Viñes and himself included the critic M.-D. Calvocoressi, the composer Florent Schmitt and the poet Léon-Paul Fargue. Between 1901 and 1905 Ravel was four times candidate for the Prix de Rome and the fact that he was never awarded the Grand Prix made him the centre of much controversy, as did the debate over his musical debt to Debussy, especially at the time of the noisy première of the *Histoires Naturelles* in 1907. In the years just before the First World War he was associated with Diaghilev's Ballets Russes, and during the War itself served as a hospital orderly and truck driver. Ravel's mother died in 1917, and from this time onward his health slowly deteriorated. However, he was able to make a tour of the United States in 1927–8 as pianist and conductor of his own work, rôles he rarely undertook in public. From 1921 until his death, Ravel—who remained a bachelor—lived at Montfort l'Amaury about fifteen miles outside Paris; but from 1933 he was increasingly afflicted by apraxia, probably the result of a car accident. Musical and some other sorts of activity became impossible, and although he was able to enjoy a holiday trip to Morocco and Spain in 1934 with the sculptor Léon Leyritz, his condition became so bad that a major operation on the brain had to be performed in December 1937. Ravel died a few days later.

CATALOGUE OF WORKS

1. **Sérénade grotesque.** For piano. 1863. Unpub.

Ravel, Maurice

2. Ballade de la reine morte d'aimer (Roland de Marès). For voice and piano. 1894. Unpub.

3. Le Rouet. For voice and piano. 1894. Unpub.

4. Menuet antique. For piano. 1895. Ded. Ricardo Viñes. Dur. 6′ 50″.

fp: 13 April 1901, Paris, Société Nationale de Musique concert, Ricardo Viñes.

fEbp: 26 March 1924, Newcastle station, Maurice Cole.

Pub. 1895 (?1898), Enoch; repr. 1923.

4a. Menuet antique. Version for orchestra. 1929.

2 fl, pic, 2 ob, ca, 2 cl, bcl, 2 bsn, cbsn; 4 hn, 3 tpt, 3 tmb, tuba; 2 timp; hp, strings.

fp: 11 January 1930, Paris, Concerts Lamoureux, cond. Maurice Ravel.

Pub. 1930, Enoch.

5. Un Grand sommeil noir (Verlaine). For voice and piano. 1895. Dur. 3′ 30″. Pub. Fondation Maurice Ravel (Durand).

6. Les Sites auriculaires. For two pianos. 1895–6.

1. *Habanera.* 1895. Dur. 4′ 15″.
2. *Entre cloches.* 1896.

fp: 5 March 1898, Paris, Société Nationale de Musique concert, Marthe Druon and Ricardo Viñes.

Unpub. No. 1 incorporated in 'Rapsodie espagnole' (see No. 29); No. 2 lost.

7. Sainte (Mallarmé). For voice and piano. 1896. Ded. Mme Edmond Bonniot (*née* Mallarmé). Dur. 2′ 50″.

fEbp: 26 January 1927, Helen Henschel.

Pub. 1907, Durand; Eng. words by Nita Cox.

8. Deux épigrammes (Clément Marot). For voice and piano. 1898. Ded. Hardy Thé.

1. *D'Anne qui me jecta de la neige.* Dur. 3′.
2. *D'Anne jouant de l'espinette.* Dur. 5′ 45″.

fp: 27 January 1900, Société Nationale de Musique concert, Hardy Thé and Maurice Ravel.

Pub. 1898, Demets; 1923, Schott; Eng. words by P. Pinkerton.

9. Schéhérazade. Overture ('Ouverture de féerie') for orchestra. 1898.

fp: 27 May 1899, Paris, Société Nationale de Musique concert, cond. Maurice Ravel. Unpub.

BIBLIOGRAPHY:
Pierre de Breville: Schéhérazade, *Mercure de France,* July 1899.

10. Pavane pour une infante défunte. For piano. 1899. Ded. Princess Edmond de Polignac. Dur. 5′ 45″.

fp: 5 April 1902, Paris, Société Nationale de Musique concert, Ricardo Viñes.

?fEp: 7 November 1908, Bechstein Hall, Evelyn Suart.

Pub. Demets; Eschig; arr. violin and piano by L. Fleury, 1923, Schott; arr. two pianos by Mario Castelnuovo-Tedesco, 1950, Leeds Music Corp. (New York).

BIBLIOGRAPHY:
Cuthbert Whitemore: How to interpret Ravel's Pavane, *Music Teacher,* March 1925.

10a. Pavane pour une infante déunte. Version for orchestra. 1910.

2 fl, ob, 2 cl, 2 bsn; 2 hn; hp, strings.

fp: 25 December 1910, Paris, cond. Alfredo Casella.

f London p: 16 August 1911, Queen's Hall, Promenade Concert, Queen's Hall Orchestra, cond. (Sir) Henry Wood.

fEbp: 25 November 1923, cond. A. Corbett-Smith.

Pub. 1910, Demets; Eschig.

11. Si morne (Verhaeren). For voice and piano. 1899. Unpub.

12. Myrrha. Cantata. Text: Fernand Beissier. 1901. Composed for the Prix de Rome. Unpub.

13. Jeux d'eau. For piano. 1901. Ded. 'Mon cher Maître Gabriel Fauré'.

fp: 5 April 1902, Paris, Société Nationale de Musique concert, Ricardo Viñes.

fEp: 2 May 1904, Bechstein Hall, Evelyn Suart.

fEbp: 18 October 1924, Birmingham station, Irene Scharrer.

Pub. 1906, Demets; 1923, Eschig/Schott.

14. Alcyone. Cantata. Text: A. and F. Adenis. 1902. Composed for the Prix de Rome. Unpub.

15. String Quartet in F. 1902–3. Ded. 'A mon cher maître Gabriel Fauré'. Dur. 30′ 20″.

1. *Allegro moderato*; 2. *Assez vif*; 3. *Très lent*; 4. *Vif et agité*.

fp: 5 March 1904, Paris, Société Nationale de Musique concert, Heymann Quartet.

fEp: 6 December 1907, Leighton House (Kensington), concert of French music, Parisian Quartet.

fEbp: 26 March 1925, Snow Quartet (Jessie Snow, Kenneth Skeaping, Ernest Tomlinson, Edward J. Robinson).

Pub. 1904, Astruc; 1910, Durand; arr. for piano solo and for two pianos by Lucien Garban; arr. for piano duet by Maurice Delage.

BIBLIOGRAPHY:

M.-D. Calvocoressi: Le Quatuor de M. Ravel, *RM*, 15 April 1904.

Alex. Cohen: Ravel's String Quartet in F, *Chamber Music* (Music Student supplement), No. 4, December 1913, p. 28.

André Mangeot: The Ravel String Quartet, *The Gramophone*, September 1927, p. 138.

Jean Marnold: Le Quatuor de Maurice Ravel, *Mercure de France*, April 1904.

— Le Quatuor de Maurice Ravel, in *Musique d'autrefois et d'aujourd'hui*, Dorbon-Aîné (Paris) 1912, p. 150.

Pierre Lalo: Le Quatuor de M. Ravel, *Le Temps*, 19 April 1904.

16. Alysse. Cantata. 1903. Composed for the Prix de Rome.

17. Manteau de fleurs (Paul Gravollet). For voice and piano. 1903. Dur. 3′ 20″. Pub. 1903, 1920, Hamelle. Also version for voice and orchestra.

18. Schéhérazade (Tristan Klingsor). Song cycle for voice and orchestra. 1903. Dur. 17′.

1. *Asie*. Ded. Mlle Jane Hatto. Dur. 10′ 20″.
2. *La Flûte enchantée*. Ded. Mme René de Saint-Marceaux. Dur. 3′.
3. *L'Indifférent*. Ded. Mme Sigismond Bardac. Dur. 3′ 40″.

2 fl, pic, 2 ob, ca, 2 cl, 2 bsn; 4 hn, 2 tpt, 3 tmb, tuba; timp, tgle, tamb, side dm, GC, cym, gong, glock; celesta, 2 hp, strings.

fp: 17 May 1904, Paris, Nouveau-Théâtre, Société Nationale de Musique concert, Jane Hatto as soloist, cond. Alfred Cortot.

tEp: 26 April 1909, Bechstein Hall, Société des Concerts Français concert, Jane Bathori.

fEbp: 24 July 1927, Susanne Bertin and Wireless Symphony Orchestra, cond. Edward Clark.

Pub. 1904, Astruc; 1910, Durand (1914, full score); Eng. version by H. Klein.

BIBLIOGRAPHY:

René Chalupt: Schéhérazade, *La Phalange*, February 1913.

Jean Marnold: Schéhérazade, *Mercure de France*, July 1904.

19. Le Noël des jouets (Maurice Ravel). For voice and piano. 1905. Ded. Mme Jean Cruppi. Dur. 3′ 10″.

fp: 24 March 1906, Jane Bathori.

Pub. 1905, Bellon Ponscarme; Mathot; Salabert.

19a. Le Noël des jouets. Version for voice and orchestra.

2 fl, pic, 2 ob, ca, 2 cl, bcl, 2 bsn, cbsn; 4 hn, 2 tpt, 3 tmb, tuba; timp, tgle, cliquet, tambour, tamb de basque, cast, glock, xyl, GC, tamtam; 2 hp, celesta, strings.

fp: 26 April 1906, Paris, Société Nationale de Musique concert, Jane Bathori.

20. Margot la Rouge. Opera by Frederick Delius; vocal score prepared by Maurice Ravel, *c.* 1905.

21. Sonatine. For piano. 1905. Ded. Ida and Cipa Godebski. Dur. 14′ 20″.

1. *Modéré, doux et expressif*; 2. *Mouvement de Menuet*; 3. *Animé*.

fp: 10 March 1906, Lyon, Paule de Lestang.

fEp: 26 April 1909, Bechstein Hall, Société des Concerts Français, Mary Vadot.

fGBbp: 19 May 1924, Cardiff station, Desirée McEwen.

Pub. 1905, Durand.

22. Miroirs. For piano. 1905. Dur. 28′ 10″.

1. *Noctuelles*. Ded. Léon-Paul Fargue. Dur. 6′.
2. *Oiseaux tristes*. Ded. Ricardo Viñes. Dur. 2′ 30″.

Ravel, Maurice

3. *Une Barque sur l'océan.* Ded. Paul Sordes. Dur. 10'.

4. *Alborada del gracioso.* Ded. M.-D. Calvocoressi. Dur. 5' 30".

5. *La Vallée des cloches.* Ded. Maurice Delage. Dur. 4' 10".

fp: 6 January 1906, Paris, Société Nationale de Musique concert, Ricardo Viñes.

fEp (No. 4): 2 December 1909, Queen's Hall, Ernest Schelling.

fGBbp (No. 4): 25 September 1924, Glasgow station, Angus Morrison.

fEbp (No. 2): 12 March 1926, Newcastle station, Marcelle Meyer.

Pub. 1906, Demets; 1924, Eschig/Schott. Arr. for piano four hands by J. Jemain.

BIBLIOGRAPHY:

Gaston Carraud: Barque sur l'océan, *La Liberté,* 5 February 1907.

Pierre Lalo: Les Miroirs, la Suite pour piano, *Le Temps,* 30 January 1906.

Jean Marnold: Miroirs, *Mercure musical,* 1 February 1906; *Mercure de France,* 1 March 1906.

22a. Alborada del gracioso. Version for orchestra. Dur. 5' 30".

2 fl, pic, 2 ob, ca, 2 cl, 2 bsn, cbsn; 4 hn, 2 tpt, 3 tmb, tuba; 3 timp, crotales, tgle, tamb de basque, cast, tamb mil, cym, GC, xyl; hp, strings.

fp: 17 May 1919, Paris, Concerts Pasdeloup.

fEp (concert): 9 November 1921, Queen's Hall, Goossens Orchestra, cond. Eugene Goossens (but previously heard as an interlude at the Russian Ballet).

Pub. 1923, Demets; Eschig.

22b. Une Barque sur l'océan. Version for orchestra. ?1906.

3 fl, 3 ob, 3 cl, 2 bsn; 4 hn, 2 tpt, 2 tmb, tuba; timp, GC, cym, tgle, glock, celesta, tamtam; hp, strings.

fp: 3 February 1907, Paris, Concerts Colonne, cond. Gabriel Pierné.

fEp: 31 March 1951, BBC broadcast, BBC Symphony Orchestra, cond. Sir Adrian Boult.

Second version fp: 30 October 1926, Paris, Théâtre-Mogador, Orchestre Pasdeloup, cond. Albert Wolff.

Pub. Demets; Eschig; second version unpub.

23. Introduction and Allegro. For harp, string quartet, flute and clarinet. 1906. Ded. Albert Blondel. Dur. 13'.

fp: 22 February 1907, Paris, Cercle Musical concert, with Micheline Kahn (hp).

fEp: 4 September 1907, Queen's Hall, Promenade Concert, with Alfred Kastner (hp).

fEbp: 3 April 1925, Sidonie Goossens and members of Newcastle Station Symphony Orchestra, cond. Edward Clark.

Pub. 1906, Durand. Arr. for two pianos by Maurice Ravel; for piano duet by Léon Roques; for piano solo by Lucien Garban.

24. Les Grands vents venus d'outre-mer (Henri de Régnier). For voice and piano. 1906. Ded. Jacques Durand. Dur. 2' 40".

fp: 8 June 1907, Le Havre, 'Cercle d'art moderne' concert, Hélène M. Luquiens, acc. Maurice Ravel.

f Paris p: 12 December 1907, Engel-Bathori recital, Jane Bathori.

Pub. 1907, Durand; Eng. words by Nita Cox.

25. Cinq mélodies populaires grecques (M.-D. Calvocoressi). For voice and piano (or orchestra). 1904–6. Dur. 6' 35".

1. *Le Réveil de la mariée.* Dur. 1' 45". Orch. Maurice Ravel.

2. *Là-bas vers l'église.* Dur. 55". Orch. Manuel Rosenthal.

3. *Quel galant!* Dur. 55". Orch. Manuel Rosenthal.

4. *Chanson des cueilleuses de lentisques.* Dur. 2'. Orch. Manuel Rosenthal.

5. *Tout gai!* Dur. 1'. Orch. Maurice Ravel.

2 fl, 2 ob, 2 cl, 2 bsn; 2 hn, tpt; 2 timp, tamb mil, tamb de basque, cym, tgle, xyl, vibraphone, celesta; hp, strings.

fEp: 26 April 1909, Bechstein Hall, Société des Concerts Français, Jane Bathori and Emile Engel, acc. Mary Vadot.

fEbp: 9 February 1925, Newcastle station, Elsie Treweek.

Pub. 1906, Durand.

BIBLIOGRAPHY:

Marguerite Babaian: MR et les chansons

popularies Grecques, *RM*, December 1938, p. 302.

26. Histoires naturelles (Jules Renard). For voice and piano. 1906.
   1. *Le Paon*. Ded. Mme Jane Bathori. Dur. 4' 40".
   2. *Le Grillon*. Ded. Mlle Madeleine Picard. Dur. 2' 50".
   3. *Le Cygne*. Ded. Mme Alfred Edwards (*née* Godebska). Dur. 2' 35".
   4. *Le Martin-Pêcheur*. Ded. Emile Engel. Dur. 2' 45".
   5. *La Pintade*. Ded. Roger-Ducasse. Dur. 2' 40".
   fp: 19 March (?12 January) 1907, Paris (Salle Erard), Société Nationale de Musique concert, Jane Bathori, acc. Maurice Ravel.
   fEp (Nos. 1, 4, 5 only): 26 April 1909, Bechstein Hall, Société des Concerts Français, Jane Bathori and Emile Engel, acc. Mary Vadot.
   fEbp: 20 October 1930, Claire Croiza.
   Pub. 1907, Durand.

26a. Histoires naturelles. Version orch. Manuel Rosenthal.
   2 fl, ob, 2 cl, bsn; 2 hn, tpt; cym, GC, bells, tamtam, tgle, crécelle, caisse claire, vibraphone, celesta; hp, strings.

BIBLIOGRAPHY:
M.-D. Calvocoressi: Les Histoires Naturelles de Maurice Ravel et l'imitation debussyste, *Grande Revue*, 10 May 1907.
— Histoires naturelles, *Mercure musicale*, 1907, p. 155.
Gaston Carraud: Les Histoires naturelles de M. Ravel, *La Liberté*, 15 January 1907.
Ami Châtelain: Jules Renard et les Histoires naturelles, *SM*, March–April 1963, p. 82.
Scott Goddard: Histoires naturelles, *MN&H*, 30 July 1921.
Ingrid Hermann: Ravels Histoires naturelles, *Musik im Unterricht* (Vienna), March 1965.
Louis Laloy: Les deux cotes, in *La musique retrouvée*, Librairie Plon (Paris) 1928, p. 161.
Terpander: Ravel's Histoires naturelles, *The Gramophone*, April 1935, p. 428.
D. Le Touzé: Les Histoires naturelles de MR, *L'Education musicale*, No. 138, 1 May 1967.

27. Sur l'herbe (Verlaine). For voice and piano. 1907. Dur. 2' 10".
   fp: 12 December 1907, Paris, Engel-Bathori recital, Jane Bathori.
   Pub. 1907, Durand; Eng. words by Nita Cox.

28. Vocalise en forme d'Habanera. For voice and piano. 1907. Dur. 3' 10". Pub. 1907, Leduc.

28a. Pièce en forme d'Habanera. Version of preceding for violin and piano. Also transcr. by Doney for flute (or oboe, or violin) and piano, pub. 1924 Leduc; arr. for wind quintet by Clarke S. Kessler, 1933.

29. Rapsodie espagnole. For orchestra. 1907. Ded. 'A mon cher maître Charles de Bériot'. Dur. 18' 35".
   1. *Prélude à la nuit*. Dur. 4' 30".
   2. *Malaguena*. Dur. 2' 20".
   3. *Habañera*. Dur. 4' 15".
   4. *Feria*. Dur. 7' 30".
   2 fl, 2 pic, 2 ob, ca, 2 cl, bcl, 3 bsn, sarrusophone (or cbsn); 3 tpt, 3 tmb, tuba; 4 timp, side dm, cym, tgle, tamb de basque, cast, GC, gong, xyl; celesta, 2 hp, strings.
   fp: 15 March 1908, Paris, Concerts Colonne, cond. Edouard Colonne.
   fEp: 21 October 1909, Queen's Hall, Promenade Concert, Queen's Hall Orchestra, cond. (Sir) Henry Wood.
   f New York p: 21 November 1909, New York Symphony Society, cond. Walter Damrosch.
   fGBbp: 9 May 1926, Glasgow Station Orchestra, cond. Herbert A. Carruthers.
   Pub. 1908, Durand; incl. min. score. Arr. for piano solo, piano duet, two pianos. No. 3 arr. by Fritz Kreisler for violin and piano, 1928, Schott.

BIBLIOGRAPHY:
Gaston Carraud: La Rapsodie espagnole, *La Liberté*, 17 March 1908.
Pierre Lalo: La Rapsodie espagnole de M. Ravel, *Le Temps*, 17 and 24 March 1908.
Louis Laloy: La Rapsodie espagnole, *Grande Revue*, 25 March 1908.
Jean Marnold: La Rapsodie espagnole, *Mercure de France*, 16 April 1908.

30. L'Heure espagnole. Opera ('comédie

musicale') in one act. Libretto: Franc Nohain. 1907. Ded. Jeanne Cruppi.

2 fl, pic, 2 ob, ca, 2 cl, 2 bsn, sarrusophone; 4 hn, 2 tpt, 3 tmb, tuba; timp, pcssn; celesta, 2 hp, strings.

fp: 19 May 1911, Paris, Opéra-Comique, with Geneviève Vix, Jean Périer, Coulomb, Delvoye and Cazeneuve, cond. François Ruhlmann.

fEp: 24 July 1919, Covent Garden, with Pauline Donalda (Concepción), André Gilly (Gonzalve), Octave Dua (Torquemada), Alfred Maguenat (Ramiro), Edouard Cotreuil (Don Iñigo Gómez), cond. Percy Pitt. (The 'Air de Concepcion' had already been heard separately in the concert hall: 7 May 1918, Aeolian Hall, Zonia Rosowski, acc. Mme Poldowski.)

fEbp: 29 December 1947, l'Orchestre National, cond. Ernest Bour; with Geori Boué (Concepción), Louis Arnoult (Gonzalve). Jean Planel (Torquemada), Roger Bourdin (Ramiro), Charles Paul (Don Iñigo Gómez).

Pub. 1908 (vocal score, arr. Maurice Ravel), 1911 (full score), Durand.

BIBLIOGRAPHY:

Camille Bellaigue: L'Heure espagnole, Revue des deux mondes, 1 July 1911.
Adolphe Boschot: L'Heure espagnole, Echo de Paris, 20 May 1911.
Maurice Brillant: Sur 'L'Heure espagnole' et la qualité comique de MR, Le Correspondant, 25 December 1921.
Gaston Carraud: L'Heure espagnole, La Liberté, 21 May 1911.
René Chalupt: L'Heure espagnole, La Phalange, June 1911.
Jean Chantavoine: L'Heure espangole, Revue hebdomadaire, 24 June 1911.
R. Gelatt: Hour with Ansermet—recording of L'Heure espagnole, Saturday Review, 29 August 1953, p. 59.
— Opéra-Comique recording of L'Heure espagnole, Saturday Review, 28 November 1953, p. 95.
Henri Ghéon: L'Heure espagnole, Nouvelle Revue française, 1 July 1911.
Scott Goddard: Some notes on Maurice Ravel's L'Heure espagnole, Sackbut, 1925, May p. 282, June p. 340.

Arthur Hoérée: Ravel's 'Spanische Stunde', Blätter der Staatsoper (Berlin), October (No. 4) 1929, p. 5.
G. Jean-Aubry: A propos d'une comédie musicale: L'Heure espagnole de MR, in La Musique française d'aujourd'hui, Perrin (Paris) 1916, p. 116.
Pierre Lalo: L'Heure espagnole, Le Temps, 28 May 1911.
— L'Heure espagnole à l'Opéra, in De Rameau à Ravel (Portraits et Souvenirs), Editions Albin Michel (Paris) 1947, p. 377.
Pierre de Lapommeraye: Opéra—L'Heure espagnole, Le Ménestrel, 16 December 1921, p. 498.
Jean Marnold: Opéra National—l'Heure espagnole de MM. MR et Franc-Nohain, Mercure de France, No. 567, 1 February 1922, p. 763.
Ernest Newman: L'Heure espagnole, in Opera Nights, Putnam (London) 1943, p. 582.
Phonos: First impressions of the Ravel opera, MMR, 1919, p. 198.
Arthur Pougin: L'Heure espagnole, Le Ménestrel, 27 May 1911, p. 163.
R. Sabin: Intimate and witty, L'Heure espagnole, Musical America, February 1953, p. 182.
Henry W. Simon: L'Heure espagnole, in Festival of Opera, W. H. Allen (London) 1957, p. 205.
C. Smith: L'Heure espagnole, Musical America, 15 December 1950, p. 7.
Emile Vuillermoz: L'Heure espagnole, Revue S.I.M., 15 June 1911.
Various: L'Heure espagnole—Revue de la Presse Quotidienne (reviews by Pierre Laloy, Reynaldo Hahn, Louis de Fourcaud and Adolphe Boschot), Revue S.I.M., June 1911, p. 74.

31. Ma Mère l'Oye. Children's pieces for piano four hands. 1908. Ded. Mimie and Jean Godebski.

1. *Pavane de la Belle au bois dormant*; 2. *Petit Poucet*; 3. *Laideronette, Impératrice des Pagodes*; 4. *Les Entretiens de la Belle et la Bête*; 5. *Le Jardin féerique*.

fp: 20 April 1910, Paris, Société de Musique Indépendante concert, Jeanne Leleu and Geneviève Durony.

fEp: 30 June 1922, London, reception given for Ravel by Mme Alvar, Maurice Ravel and (Sir) Eugene Goossens; also: 26 April 1924, Aeolian Hall, Maurice Ravel and Henri Gil-Marchex.

Pub. 1910, Durand.

31a. Ma Mère l'Oye. Version for orchestra. 1911. Ded. Jacques Rouché. Dur. 28′ 30″.

Prélude; 1. *Danse du rouet*; 2. *Pavane*; 3. *La Belle et la Bête*; 4. *Petit Poucet*; 5. *Laideronette*; 6. *Le Jardin féerique*.

2 fl, pic, 2 ob, ca, 2 cl, 2 bsn, cbsn; 2 hn; timp, tgle, cym, side dm, GC, xyl, glock; celesta, hp, strings.

fp: 21 (?28) January 1912, Paris, Théâtre des Arts, as a ballet (scenario, Maurice Ravel) with Ariane Hugon, cond. Gabriel Grovlez.

fEp: 4 May 1912, Queen's Hall, Casals concert, Queen's Hall Orchestra, cond. (Sir) Henry Wood.

fAp: 8 November 1912, New York, Aeolian Hall, New York Symphony Orchestra.

fEp (complete): 28 January 1951, BBC broadcast, Leighton Lucas Orchestra, cond. Leighton Lucas.

Pub. 1912, Durand; piano reduction by J. Charlot.

BIBLIOGRAPHY:

R. Bernier: Ma Mère l'Oye de Ravel, *Syrinx*, June–July 1938.

René Chalupt: Ma Mère l'Oye, *La Phalange*, May 1911.

Henry-Jacques: Ma Mère l'Oye de MR, *Disques*, December 1951.

Henri Malherbe: La Renaissance du ballet français—Ma Mère l'Oye, *Musica*, March 1913.

Louis Vuillemin: Ma Mère l'Oye, *Comoedia*, 7 March 1913.

Emile Vuillermoz: Les Théâtres—Ma Mère l'Oye, *Revue Musicale S.I.M.*, February 1912, p. 55.

L. R. Wyckoff: Ma Mère l'Oye by Ravel, *Musician*, November 1934, p. 15.

Anon.: Ravel's Mother Goose, *Etude*, August 1949, p. 462.

32. Gaspard de la nuit. Poems for piano after Aloysius Bertrand. 1908. Dur. 26′.

1. *Ondine*. Ded. Harold Bauer. Dur. 7′.
2. *Le Gibet*. Ded. Jean Marnold. Dur. 7′.
3. *Scarbo*. Ded. Rudolph Ganz. Dur. 12′.

fp: 9 January 1909, Paris, Société Nationale de Musique concert, Ricardo Viñes.

fEp (No. 2): 8 December 1910, Bechstein Hall, Evlyn Howard-Jones.

fEp (complete): 4 February 1914, Aeolian Hall, Leonard Borwick; note also: 23 March 1914, Aeolian Hall, F. B. Ellis concert, Ricardo Viñes.

fEbp (No. 1): 22 October 1924, Newcastle station, Edgar Bainton.

Pub. 1909, Durand.

BIBLIOGRAPHY:

Gaston Carraud: Gaspard de la nuit, *La Liberté*, 12 January 1909.

I. Freundlich: MR's Gaspard de la nuit, *Etude*, December 1956, p. 16.

Louis Laloy: Gaspard de la nuit, *Grande Revue*, 25 January 1909.

Friederike Lichtenthäler: Bertrand und Ravel, *ÖM*, June 1967, p. 325.

W.P. (?Wouter Paap): Gaspard de la nuit van MR, *Mens en melodie*, February 1953, p. 51.

L. Perracchio: Gaspard de la nuit di Ravel, *Il Pianoforte*, January 1921.

32a. Le Gibet. Orch. Sir Eugene Goossens.

fEp: 11 August 1961, Royal Albert Hall, Promenade Concert, BBC Symphony Orchestra, cond. Sir Eugene Goossens.

?Unpub.

33. Nocturnes. Debussy, transcribed for two pianos by Maurice Ravel. 1909.

34. Menuet sur le nom d'Haydn. For piano. 1909.

fp: March 1911, Paris, Société Nationale de Musique concert.

fEbp: 27 September 1926, Birmingham station, Gordon Bryan.

Pub. 1909, La Revue musicale; 1910, Durand.

35. Tripatos. Greek Dance (Danse chantée) for voice and piano. 1909. Ded. Marguerite Babaian. Dur. 1′ 30″.

Pub. December 1938, La Revue musicale.

36. Prélude à l'après-midi d'un faune.

Ravel, Maurice

Debussy, transcribed for two pianos by Maurice Ravel. Pub. 1910, Fromont.

37. Valses nobles et sentimentales. For piano. 1911. Ded. Louis Aubert. Dur. 14′ 25″.
fp: 9 May 1911, Paris, Société Musicale Indépendante concert, Louis Aubert.
fEp: 11 February 1914, Aeolian Hall, Leonard Borwick.
fEbp: 6 December 1934, Kathleen Long.
Pub. 1911, Durand. Arr. for piano four hands by Lucien Garban.

37a. Valses nobles et sentimentales. Version for orchestra. 1912. Dur. 14′ 25″.
2 fl, 2 ob, ca, 2 cl, 2 bsn; 4 hn, 2 tpt, 3 tmb, tuba; timp, GC, side dm, cym, tgle, dm, tamb de basque, glock; celesta, 2 hp, strings.
fp: 22 April 1912, Paris, Théâtre du Châtelet, as a ballet entitled 'Adélaïde, ou le langage des fleurs' (scenario, Maurice Ravel), Trouhanova season, cond. Maurice Ravel.
fEp: 25 September 1913, Queen's Hall, Promenade Concert, Queen's Hall Orchestra, cond. Sir Henry Wood.
fEbp: 25 November 1923, cond. A. Corbett-Smith.
Pub. 1912, Durand.

BIBLIOGRAPHY:
Camille Bellaigue: Adélaïde, *Mercure de France*, 16 July 1917, p. 340.
René Chalupt: Adélaïde, *La Phalange*, June 1912.
Pierre Lalo: Adélaïde à l'Opéra, *Le Temps*, 17 May 1917.
Francis de Miomandre: Adélaïde, *Le Théâtre*, September 1912.
Jean Poueigh: Adélaïde (à l'Opéra), *La Rampe*, 12 April 1917; *Le Carnet de la Semaine*, 15 April 1917.
Roland-Manuel: Adélaïde, *Revue indépendante*, 7 May 1912.

38. Daphnis et Chloë. Ballet (Michel Fokine, after Longus): Choreographic Symphony in three movements. 1909–11. Ded. Serge de Diaghilev.
2 fl, pic, fl in G, 2 ob, ca, cl in E flat, 2 cl, bcl, 3 bsn, dbsn; 4 hn, 4 tpt, 3 tmb, tuba; timp, side dm, cast, crotales, cym, wind machine, GC, dm, tamb, gong, tgle, glock,

xyl; celesta, 2 hp, strings; mixed chorus (offstage).
Suite No. 1: 1. Nocturne; 2. Interlude; 3. Danse guerrière.
Suite No. 2: 1. Lever du jour; 2. Pantomime; 3. Danse générale.
fp (Suite No. 1): 2 April 1911, Paris, Théâtre du Châtelet, Concerts Colonne, cond. Gabriel Pierné.
fp (ballet): 8 June 1912, Paris, Théâtre du Châtelet, Diaghilev's Ballets Russes, cond. Pierre Monteaux; with Tamara Karsavina, Nijinsky and Bolm; choreography, Fokine; décors, Léon Bakst.
fEp (ballet): 9 June 1914, Drury Lane, Diaghilev's Ballets Russes, cond. Pierre Monteaux; with Fokine (Daphnis), Tamara Karsavina (Chloë).
fEp (concert): 13 December 1913, Royal Philharmonic Society concert, cond. Sir Thomas Beecham.
fEbp (Suite No. 2): 31 March 1927, Royal Albert Hall, National Orchestra, cond. Ernest Ansermet.
fEp (concert, complete with chorus): 5 January 1928, Royal Philharmonic Society concert, with chorus of students from the Royal Academy of Music, cond. Ernest Ansermet.
Pub. 1913, Durand (Suite No. 1, 1912). Arr. for piano solo, piano four hands, two pianos.

BIBLIOGRAPHY:
Eric Blom: Daphnis and Chloë ballet, *Music Teacher*, October 1930, p. 589.
R. Brussel: Daphnis et Chloë, *Le Figaro*, 9 June 1912.
Gaston Carraud: Daphnis, *La Liberté*, 11 June 1912.
René Chalupt: Daphnis et Chloë, *La Phalange*, July 1912.
Jean Chantavoine: Daphnis et Chloë, *Excelsior*, 9 June 1912.
Henri de Curzon: Daphnis et Chloë, *Guide musical*, 23 and 30 June 1912.
Henry Gauthier-Villars: Daphnis et Chloë, *Comoedia illustré*, 15 June 1912.
Scott Goddard: Ravel's ballet Daphnis et Chloë, *M&L*, July 1926.
Basil Hogarth: Masterpieces of the Ballet,

3: Ravel's Daphnis and Chloe, *The Gramophone*, November 1935, p. 225.

Tamara Karsavina, Elsa Brunelleschi, Tony Mayer & Alexander Bland: Four opinions on Daphnis and Chloe, *Ballet*, June 1951, p. 4.

Pierre Lalo: Daphnis et Chloë, *Le Temps*, 11 June 1912.

Jean Marnold: Daphnis et Chloë, *Mercure de France*, 16 August 1917, p. 696.

Roland-Manuel: Daphnis et Chloë, *Revue indépendante*, 18 June 1912.

W. Rooke-Ley: Daphnis and Chloe, Arcadian lovers, *Radio Times*, 17 October 1930, p. 169.

Julie Sazonova: La reprise de Daphnis et Chloë, *Nouvelle revue française*, 1934, No. 247, p. 740.

Emile Vuillermoz: Daphnis et Chloë, *Revue S.I.M.*, 15 June 1912.

Anon.: Return of the Russian Ballet: Ravel's Daphnis et Chloé, *The Times*, 10 June 1914, p. 11.

Daphnis et Chloe: Protest from MR, *The Times*, 9 June 1914, p. 9; Diaghilev's reply, 10 June, p. 11; M. Ravel's rejoinder, 17 June, p. 9.

39. Khovantschina. Opera by Mussorgsky, completed and orchestrated by Maurice Ravel and Igor Stravinsky. Lost.

40. Trois Poèmes de Stéphane Mallarmé. For voice and chamber ensemble. August 1913, St. Jean-de-Luz. Dur. 11' 20".

1. *Soupir*. Ded. Igor Stravinsky. Dur. 3' 50".
2. *Placet futile*. Ded. Florent Schmitt. Dur. 4' 30".
3. *Surgie de la croupe et du bond*. Ded. Erik Satie. Dur. 3'.

2 fl, 2 cl, bcl, string quartet and piano.

fp: 14 January 1914, Paris, Société Musicale Indépendante concert, Jane Bathori.

fEp: 17 March 1915, Aeolian Hall, Classical Concert Society, Jane Bathori, cond. (Sir) Thomas Beecham.

Pub. 1914, Durand; also reduction for voice and piano.

BIBLIOGRAPHY:

Helga Böhmer: Alchimie der Töne (Die Mallarmé-Vertonungen von Debussy und

Ravel, *Musica*, 1968, No. 2 (March–April).

D. K. Sorabji: Trois Poèmes de Stéphane Mallarmé, *MS*, 13 March 1915, p. 196.

41. Prélude. For piano. 1913. Ded. Mlle Jeanne Leleu. Composed for a sight-reading test at the Paris Conservatoire. Dur. 1' 20". Pub. 1913, Durand.

42. A la manière de . . . For piano. 1913.
1. *Borodin*. Dur. 2'.
2. *Chabrier*. Dur. 2' 40".

fp: 10 December 1913, Paris, Société Musicale Indépendante, Alfredo Casella.

fEp: 11 June 1915, Aeolian Hall, Société des Concerts Français, Alfredo Casella.

Pub. 1914, Mathot; 1948, Salabert.

BIBLIOGRAPHY:

Anon.: Recent music in Paris: Ravel as parodist, *The Times*, 24 December 1913, p. 9.

43. Le Prélude du fils des étoiles. Erik Satie, orchestrated by Maurice Ravel. 1913. Unpub.

44. Deux mélodies hébraïques. For voice and piano. May 1914. Ded. Mme Alvina-Alvi.
1. *Kaddisch* (Dur. 4' 30").
2. *L'Enigme éternelle* (Dur. 1' 5").

fp: 3 June 1914, Paris, Mme Alvina-Alvi and Maurice Ravel.

fEp: 24 March 1917, Aeolian Hall, Marguerite Nielka, acc. Anthony Bernard.

fEbp (No. 1): 27 August 1933, Charles Panzéra.

Pub. 1915, Durand; also arr. for violin and piano; No. 1 arr. for piano by A. Ziloti.

44a. Deux mélodies hébraïques. Version for voice and orchestra.

2 fl, 2 ob, 2 cl, 2 bsn; 2 hn; tamtam; hp, strings.

fp: 17 April 1920, Paris, Concerts Pasdeloup, Madeleine Grey.

Pub. 1920, Durand.

45. Piano Trio. 1914. Ded. André Gédalge. Dur. 23' 25".

1. *Modéré* (Dur. 8' 10"); 2. *Pantoum: assez vif* (Dur. 4' 15"); 3. *Passacaille: très large* (Dur. 6'); 4. *Final: animé* (Dur. 5').

Ravel, Maurice

fp: 28 January 1915, Paris, Alfredo Casellà, Georges Enesco, Feuillard.

fEp: 11 June 1915, Aeolian Hall, Société des Concerts Français, concert in aid of L'Oeuvre Fraternelle des Artistes, Alfredo Casella, Yvonne Astruc, M. J. Charron.

fEbp: 26 April 1925, Newcastle station, Edgar L. Bainton, Alfred M. Wall, Carl Fuchs.

Pub. 1915, Durand; also arr. for piano four hands by Lucien Garban.

46. Carnaval. Schumann, orchestrated by Maurice Ravel. 1914. Unpub.

47. Trois chansons (Maurice Ravel). For 4-part a cappella chorus. 1915. Dur. 5′ 25″.
   1. *Nicolette.* Ded. Tristan Klingsor. Dur. 1′ 40″.
   2. *Trois beaux oiseaux du paradis.* Ded. Paul Painlevé. Dur. 2′ 10″.
   3. *Ronde.* Ded. Mme Paul Clemenceau. Dur. 1′ 35″.

fEbp: 22 April 1932, Wireless Chorus, cond. Stanford Robinson.

Pub. 1916, Durand; Eng. version by Mme Swayne Saint René Taillandier.

47a. Trois chansons. Version for voice and piano. 1916.

fEp: 29 October 1919, Wigmore Hall, Classical Concerts Society, Olga Haley, acc. Emile Bosquet.

fEbp (No. 1): 15 December 1927, Anne Thursfield.

BIBLIOGRAPHY:
Arthur Hoérée: Maurice Ravel—Trois Chansons transcrites pour cordes par Malcolme Holmes (Concert Jane Evrard), *RM*, April 1935, p. 288.

48. Le Tombeau de Couperin. For piano. 1917. Dur. 23′ 10″.
   1. *Prélude.* Ded. to the memory of Lt. Jacques Charlot. Dur. 2′ 50″.
   2. *Fugue.* Ded. to the memory of Lt. Jean Cruppi. Dur. 3′ 15″.
   3. *Forlane.* Ded. to the memory of Lt. Gabriel Deluc. Dur. 4′ 40″.
   4. *Rigaudon.* Ded. to the memory of Pierre and Pascal Gaudin. Dur. 3′ 15″.
   5. *Menuet.* Ded. to the memory of Jean Dreyfus. Dur. 5′ 30″.

6. *Toccata.* Ded. to the memory of Capt. Joseph de Marliave. Dur. 3′ 40″.

fp: 11 April 1919, Paris, Société Musicale Indépendante concert, Marguerite Long.

fEp: 29 October 1919, Wigmore Hall, Classical Concert Society concert, Emile Bosquet.

fEbp (No. 6): 9 September 1924, Birmingham station, Angus Morrison.

fGBbp (Nos. 4 & 5): 25 September 1924, Glasgow station, Angus Morrison.

Pub. 1918, Durand.

48a. Le Tombeau de Couperin. Version for orchestra. ?1919. Dur. 16′ 15″.
   1. *Prélude*; 2. *Forlane*; 3. *Menuet*; 4. *Rigaudon.*
   2 fl, 2 ob, ca, 2 cl, 2 bsn; 2 hn; tpt; hp, strings.

fp: 28 February 1920, Paris, Concerts Pasdeloup, cond. Rhené-Baton.

fp (ballet): 8 November 1920, Paris, Théâtre des Champs-Elysées, Ballets suédois de Rolf de Maré, cond. D.-E. Inghelbrecht; with Jean Borlin and Mlle Hasselquist; choreography, Jean Borlin.

fAp: 20 November 1920, Boston Symphony Orchestra, cond. Pierre Monteux.

fEp (ballet): ?early 1921, Princes' Theatre, London.

fEp (concert): 22 March 1921, Queen's Hall, New Queen's Hall Orchestra, cond. Sir Henry Wood.

fEbp: 25 April 1927, Wireless Symphony Orchestra, cond. Percy Pitt.

Pub. 1919, Durand. Arr. for piano duet and for two pianos.

BIBLIOGRAPHY:
R. Bernier: Le Tombeau de Couperin de Ravel, *Syrinx*, May 1938.
Pierre Lalo: Le Tombeau de Couperin, *Le Temps*, 16 November 1922.
M. Perrin: Le Tombeau de Couperin, *Le Monde musical*, 31 July 1933.

49. Chants populaires. For voice and piano. 1910–17.
   1. *Chanson espagnole* (Dur. 2′ 45″); 2. *Chanson française* (Dur. 2′ 40″); 3. *Chanson italienne* (Dur. 1′ 25″); 4. *Chanson hebraïque* (Dur. 6′ 25″); 5. *Chanson écossaise*; 6. *Chanson flamande*; 7. *Chanson russe.*

Nos. 1–4 pub. 1910, Jurgenson (Moscow); 1925, Durand. Nos. 5–7 unpub.

49a. Chanson hebraïque. Version for voice and orchestra. Orch. Maurice Delage. Pub. 1957, Durand.

50. Menuet pompeux. Chabrier, orchestrated by Maurice Ravel. 1918.

2 fl, pic, 2 ob, 2 cl, 2 bsn; 4 hn, 2 tpt, 3 tmb, tuba; timp, tgle, tamb de basque, tamb mil, cym, GC; hp, strings.

fp: March 1936, Concerts Pasdeloup, cond. Albert Wolff.

51. Frontispiece. For two pianos. 1918 (?1919). Pub. 1919, Feuillets d'Art No. 2. Dur. 1' 30".

52. La Valse. Choreographic poem for orchestra. 1919–20. Ded. Misia Sert. Dur. 17'.

2 fl, pic, 2 ob, ca, 2 cl, bcl, 2 bsn, dbsn; 4 hn, 3 tpt, 2 tmb, tuba; 3 timp, tgle, tamb, dm, side dm, cym, cast, gong, glock, crotales; 2 hp, strings.

fp: 12 December 1920, Paris, Théâtre du Châtelet, Concerts Lamoureux, cond. Camille Chevillard.

fEp: 3 May 1921, Queen's Hall, New Queen's Hall Orchestra, cond. Sir Henry Wood.

fEbp: 9 December 1927, Wireless Symphony Orchestra, cond. Ernest Ansermet.

fp (ballet): 20 November 1928, Paris Opéra, Ida Rubinstein recital, cond. Walter Straram.

Pub. 1921, Durand. Arr. for piano solo by Maurice Ravel; for piano duet by Lucien Garban; for two pianos by Maurice Ravel (pub. 1920).

BIBLIOGRAPHY:

T. Lindenlaub: La Valse, *Le Temps*, 28 December 1920.

Jean Poueigh: La Valse, *Comoedia*, 13 December 1920.

Roland-Manuel: La Valse, *L'Eclair*, December 1926.

53. Le Tombeau de Claude Debussy. Duo for violin and cello. ?1920.

fp: 24 January 1921, Paris, Salle des Agriculteurs, Société Musicale Indépendante concert.

Pub. 1920 (December), La Revue Musicale.

54. Sarabande. Debussy, orchestrated by Maurice Ravel. 1920. Dur. 4' 30".

2 fl, ob, ca, 2 cl, 2 bsn; 2 hn, tpt; cym, tamtam; hp, strings.

fp: 18 March 1923, Paris, Salle Gaveau, Orchestre Lamoureux, cond. Paul Paray.

Pub. 1923, Jean Joubert.

55. Sonata for violin and cello. 1920–2. Ded. to the memory of Claude Debussy. Dur. 19' 10".

1. *Allegro* (Dur. 5'); 2. *Très vif* (Dur. 3' 20"); 3. *Lent* (Dur. 5' 20"); 4. *Vif* (Dur. 5' 30").

fp: 1922, Paris, Hélène Jourdan-Morhange and Maurice Maréchal.

fEp: 30 June 1922, reception given for Maurice Ravel by Mme Alvar, Jelly d'Aranyi and Hans Kindler.

fEp (public): 28 April 1923, Wigmore Hall, Margaret Harrison and Beatrice Harrison.

fEbp: 30 May 1928, Margaret Harrison and Beatrice Harrison.

Pub. 1922, Durand.

BIBLIOGRAPHY:

Florent Schmitt: Une Sonate de M. MR, *La Revue de France*, 1 November 1922.

56. Berceuse sur le nom de Gabriel Fauré. For violin and piano. 1922. Ded. Claude Roland-Manuel. Dur. 2' 30".

fEbp: 17 April 1925, Cyril Dalmaine.

Pub. October 1922, La Revue Musicale; Durand. Arr. for piano solo, piano duet, cello and piano, flute and piano.

57. Tableaux d'une Exposition. Mussorgsky, orchestrated by Maurice Ravel. 1922, Lyons-la-Forêt.

2 fl, pic, 3 ob, ca, 2 cl, bcl, 2 bsn, cbsn; 4 hn, 3 tpt, 3 tmb, tuba; alto sax; timp, tgle, tamburo, cym, tamtam, campanelle, GC, xyl; celesta, piano, hp, strings.

fp: 19 October 1922, Paris Opéra, cond. Serge Koussevitzky.

fEp: 5 February 1923, Queen's Hall, London Symphony Orchestra, cond. Serge Koussevitzky.

Pub. Editions russe de musique/Boosey & Hawkes.

58. Danse. Debussy, orchestrated by Maurice Ravel. 1923. Dur. 5' 10".

Ravel, Maurice

2 fl, 2 ob, 2 cl, 2 bsn; 4 hn, 2 tpt; timp, tgle, tamb de basque, tambour, GC, crotales; strings.

fp: 18 March 1923, Paris, Salle Gaveau, Orchestre Lamoureux, cond. Paul Paray.

Pub. 1923, Jean Joubert.

59. Ronsard à son âme. For voice and piano. 1924. Ded. Marcelle Gérar. Dur. 1′ 50″.

fEp (?fp): 26 April 1924, Aeolian Hall, Marcelle Gérar.

fFp: 10 May 1924, Paris, Théâtre du Vieux Colombier, *Revue Musicale* concert ('Hommage à Ronsard').

Pub. May 1924, Revue Musicale; Durand.

59a. Ronsard à son âme. Version with orchestral accompaniment.

2 fl, 2 ob, 2 cl, bsn; vibraphone, tamtam; piano, strings.

Pub. Durand.

BIBLIOGRAPHY:

Maurice Bex: Le Tombeau de Ronsard, *Revue hebdomadaire*, 7 June 1924, p. 108.

60. Tzigane. Concert rhapsody for violin and piano. April–May 1924, Montfort-l'Amaury. Ded. Jelly d'Aranyi.

fp: 26 April 1924, London, Jelly d'Aranyi and Henri Gil-Marchex.

Pub. 1924, Durand.

BIBLIOGRAPHY:

L. Dunton Green: Une œuvre nouvelle de Ravel—Tzigane, *RM*, May 1924, p. 263.

Henry Prunières: Tzigane de MR à la S.M.I., *RM*, 1 November 1924, p. 59.

60a. Tzigane. Version for violin and orchestra. 1924.

2 fl, pic, 2 ob, 2 cl, 2 bsn; 2 hn, tpt; tgle, glock, cym; celesta, hp, strings.

?fp: 7 December 1924, Paris, Société Musicale Indépendante concert, with Samuel Dushkin (violin).★

★ Usually quoted as the first performance, thereby discounting a suggestion that the première was given with Jelly d'Aranyi as soloist on 30 November 1924. It is certain that Jelly d'Aranyi had played the version with piano in Paris, but details of any performance of the orchestral version before Dushkin's are strangely difficult to trace: unless given in private, the occasion would surely have been publicised and widely noticed.

fEp: 13 January 1925, Chelsea Town Hall, Chelsea Music Club concert, Bernard Reillie (violin), cond. Eugene Goossens.

Pub. 1924, Durand.

BIBLIOGRAPHY:

Arthur Hoérée: Tzigane, Rapsodie de concert (violon et orchestre) écrite par Maurice Ravel pour Jelly d'Aranyi, *RM*, 1 January 1925, p. 173.

61. L'Enfant et les sortilèges. Lyrical Fantasy in two parts. 1920–5. Text: Colette.

2 fl, pic, 2 ob, E flat cl, 2 cl, bcl, 2 bsn, dbsn; 4 hn, 3 tpt, 3 tmb, tuba; 2 timp, small timp, tgle, tambour, cym, GC, tamtam, whip, rattle, cheese-grater, wood block, wind machine, crotales, side flute (flûte à coulisse), xyl; celesta, piano (or luthéal), hp, strings.

fp: 21 March 1925, Théâtre de Monte-Carlo, cond. Victor de Sabata; with Mlle Gauley (L'Enfant), Mme Orsoni (La Maman), Mme Narsay (La Bergère).

f Paris p: 1 February 1926, Opéra-Comique, cond. Albert Wolff; with Mme Gauley, Germaine Féraldy, Roger Bourdin.

fEbp: 20 December 1947, l'Orchestre National, cond. Ernest Bour; with Nadine Sautereau, Marthe Angelici, Odette Turba-Rabier, Mado Robin, Hélène Bouvier, Lucienne Jourfier, Solange Michel, Denise Scharley, Claudine Verneuil, Charles Cambon, Hughes Cuenod, Yvon le Marc Hadour, Maurice Prigent.

fEp (concert): 13 June 1951, Royal Festival Hall, London Philharmonic Choir and Orchestra, cond. Victor de Sabata.

f London p: 17 March 1965, Sadler's Wells, cond. John Matheson; with Janet Coster (The child), Elizabeth Robinson (The chair, The bat, A shepherd), Shirley Chapman (The mother, The Chinese cup, The dragonfly), Louise Lebrun (The fire, The princess, The nightingale), Maureen Morelle (The cat, The squirrel, A shepherd), Jean Manning (The little owl), Denis Dowling (The armchair, The tree), John Hauxvell (Grandfather clock, The tomcat), John Fryatt (The teapot, A little old man, The frog); producer, John Cox; scenery and costumes, John Truscott; English transl. Viola Tunnard.

Pub. 1925, Durand; incl. vocal score.

'Sauve-toil' pub. I April 1925, La Revue musicale.

BIBLIOGRAPHY:

Georges Auric: L'Enfant et les sortilèges, *Nouvelles littéraires*, April 1925.

Adolphe Boschot: L'Enfant et les sortilèges, *Revue politique et littéraire*, 1926, p. 156.

Maurice Brillant: L'Enfant et les sortilèges, *Le Correspondant*, February 1926.

André Coeuroy: A l'Opéra-Comique: Laparra et Ravel, *Revue universelle*, 15 February 1926, p. 508.

— L'Enfant et les sortilèges, *Paris-Midi*, 2 February 1926; transl. Claire Stransky, *Anbruch*, May 1926, p. 235.

R. Dezarneaux: L'Enfant et les sortilèges, *La Liberté*, 3 February 1926.

André George: L'Enfant et les sortilèges, *Nouvelles littéraires*, February 1926.

Scott Goddard: French composers, with a note on MR's latest work, *MT*, June 1925, p. 503.

Rudolf Hartmann: MR, 'Das Zauberwort', *Signale*, 1927, No. 22, p. 802.

Arthur Hoérée: Opéra-Comique, L'Enfant et les sortilèges, *Beaux Arts*, 15 March 1926, p. 126.

Arthur Honegger: L'Enfant et les sortilèges, *Musique et théâtre*, 15 April 1925.

Louis Laloy: L'Enfant et les sortilèges, *Revue des deux mondes*, 1 August 1939, p. 701.

Henri Malherbe: L'Enfant et les sortilèges, *Le Temps*, 3 February 1926.

André Mangeot: L'Enfant et les sortilèges de Colette et MR à Montecarlo, *Le Monde musical*, March 1925.

Jean Marnold: Opéra-Comique, L'Enfant et les sortilèges, *Mercure de France*, No. 666, 15 March 1926, p. 701.

André Messager: L'Enfant et les sortilèges, *Le Figaro*, February 1926.

C. L. Osborne: 'L'Enfant' in its stereo debut, *High Fidelity*, August 1961, p. 50.

Henry Prunières: L'Enfant et les sortilèges à l'Opéra de Monte Carlo, *RM*, 1 April 1925, p. 105.

— MR's L'Enfant et les sortilèges, *Sackbut*, 1925, May p. 282, June p. 340.

— L'Enfant et les sortilèges de MR à l'Opéra-Comique, *RM*, 1 March 1926, p. 258.

Roland-Manuel: L'Enfant et les sortilèges, *Le Ménestrel*, 5 February 1926, p. 60.

Henry W. Simon: L'Enfant et les sortilèges, in *Festival of Opera*, W. H. Allen (London) 1957, p. 130.

C. Tenroc: L'Enfant et les sortilèges, *Le Courrier musical*, 15 April 1925.

62. Chansons madécasses (Evariste Parny). For voice, flute, cello and piano. 1925–7. Commissioned by Elizabeth Sprague Coolidge. Dur. 10′ 25″.

1. *Nahandova* (Dur. 3′ 20″); 2. *Aoua!* (Dur. 3′ 45″); 3. *Il est doux . . .* (Dur. 3′ 20″).

fp: 13 June 1926, Paris, Salle Erard, Jane Bathori.

fEbp: 10 April 1928, Claire Croiza.

fEp (concert): 19 October 1928, Aeolian Hall, Gordon Bryan chamber concert, Odette de Foras with Joseph Slater (fl), May Mukle and Maurice Ravel (p).

Pub. 1926, Durand.

BIBLIOGRAPHY:

Arthur Hoérée: Chanson madécasse, par MR, *RM*, 1 October 1925, p. 243.

— Festival MR à la S.M.I., *Beaux Arts*, 1 November 1926, p. 284.

Henry Prunières: Trois chansons madécasses de MR (Soirée de Mrs. Coolidge), *RM*, 1 July 1926, p. 60.

Roland-Manuel: Chansons madécasses, *Revue Pleyel*, February 1927.

63. Rêves (Léon-Paul Fargue). For voice and piano. 1927. Dur. 1′ 15″.

fp: 19 March 1927, Paris, Théâtre du Vieux-Colombier, Jane Bathori.

Pub. 1927, Durand.

64. Violin Sonata. 1923–7. Ded. Hélène Jourdan-Morhange. Dur. 17′ 50″.

1. *Allegretto* (Dur. 7′ 35″); 2. *Blues: moderato* (Dur. 5′ 30″); 3. *Perpetuum mobile: Allegro* (Dur. 4′).

fp: 30 May 1927, Paris, Salle Erard, Georges Enesco and Maurice Ravel.

fEp: *c.* November 1927, Music Club concert, Jelly d'Aranyi and Myra Hess.

fEbp: 29 April 1930, Licco Amar and Philipp Jarnach.

Pub. 1927, Durand.

BIBLIOGRAPHY:
Maurice Boucher: La Sonate de MR pour piano et violon, *RM*, 1 July 1927, p. 53.

65. Fanfare. For the one-act ballet 'L'Eventail de Jeanne'. 1927. Dur. 1'.

pic, cl, bsn; hn, tpt; tambour, GC, tamtam, glock; strings.

fp: 16 June 1927, Paris, private concert given by René and Jeanne Dubost, cond. Roger Désormière; choreography, Yvonne Franck and Alice Bourgat; costumes, Marie Laurençin; décor and lighting, Pierre Legrain and René Moulaërt; with Alice Bourgat.

fp (public): 4 March 1929, Paris Opéra, cond. J.-E. Szyfer; choreography, Yvonne Franck and Alice Bourgat; with Tamara Toumanova, Mlle Storms, Marcelle Bourgat, M. le Joyeux.

Pub. 1928, Heugel.

66. Boléro. For orchestra. 1928. Ded. Ida Rubinstein.

2 fl, pic, 2 ob, ob d'amore, ca, cl in E flat, 2 cl, bcl, 2 bsn, cbsn; 4 hn, small tpt, 3 tpt, 3 tmb, tuba, 3 sax; 3 timp, 2 tambours, cym, tamtam; celesta, hp, strings.

fp: 22 November 1928, Paris Opéra, Ida Rubinstein season, cond. Walter Straram.

fAp: 14 November 1929, New York (Carnegie Hall), New York Philharmonic-Symphony Orchestra, cond. Arturo Toscanini.

f Paris p (concert): 11 January 1930, Salle Gaveau, Orchestre Lamoureux, cond. Albert Wolff.

fEp: 7 March 1930, BBC concert, cond. Frank Bridge (in place of Sir Thomas Beecham).

Pub. 1929, Durand. Arr. for piano solo and for piano duet; arr. for two pianos by Maurice Ravel, 1930.

BIBLIOGRAPHY:
B. M. Cadman: Rhythm that made a man?—MR's Bolero, *Etude*, June 1940, p. 377.
Piero Coppola: Boléro de Ravel, in *Dix-sept ans de musique à Paris*, Librairie F. Rouge (Lausanne) 1944, p. 103.
Léon-Paul Fargue: Ravel and the Bolero are one, *Arts and Decoration*, July 1937, p. 30.
Serge Lifar: Boléro et Istar, *L'Information musicale*, 24 December 1941, p. 503.

Anon.: Bolero, a musical earthquake, *Literary Digest*, 7 December 1929, p. 19; Ravel defends his Bolero, *Literary Digest*, 15 August 1931, p. 17.

67. Piano Concerto for left hand. 1931. Ded. Paul Wittgenstein. Dur. 17' 45".

2 fl, pic, 2 ob, ca, cl in E flat, 2 cl, bcl, 2 bsn, cbsn; 4 hn, 3 tpt, 3 tmb, tuba; timp, tgle, tamburo, cym, GC, wd bk, tamtam; hp, strings.

fp: 27 November 1931, Vienna, with Paul Wittgenstein as soloist.

fEp: 16 August 1932, Queen's Hall, Promenade Concert, Paul Wittgenstein and the BBC Symphony Orchestra, cond. Sir Henry Wood.

f Paris p: 17 January 1933, Salle Pleyel, Festival Ravel, Paul Wittgenstein and l'Orchestre Symphonique de Paris, cond. Maurice Ravel.

Pub. 1931, Durand.

BIBLIOGRAPHY:
Arthur Hoérée: MR, son temps, particularités, Le Concerto pour la main gauche, *Beaux Arts* (Brussels), 28 January 1938.
Hélène Jourdan-Morhange: Pour l'anniversaire de Ravel—Le concerto pour la main gauche, *Feuilles musicales*, December 1957.
Edward Lockspeiser: Piano Concerto in D major for left hand, in *The Concerto* (ed. Ralph Hill), Pelican Books 1952, p. 312.
Henry Prunières: Ravel—Concerto pour la main gauche, *RM*, 1 February 1933, p. 127.
L. Rognoni: Concerto pour la main gauche di Ravel, *Rivista Musicale Italiana*, 1937.
Anon.: Left-hand music, *Living Age*, November 1931, p. 271.

68. Piano Concerto in G major. 1931. Ded. Marguerite Long. Dur. 20' 45".

1. *Allegramente*; 2. *Adagio assai*; 3. *Presto*.

fl, pic, ob, ca, cl in E flat, cl, 2 bsn; 2 hn, tpt, tmb; 2 timp, tgle, tamburo, cym, GC, tamtam, wd bk, whip; hp, strings.

fp: 14 January 1932, Paris, Marguerite Long and l'Orchestre Lamoureux, cond. Maurice Ravel.

fEp: 25 February 1932, Royal Philharmonic Society concert, Marguerite Long, cond. Maurice Ravel.

Pub. 1932, Durand; reduction by Lucien Garban.

BIBLIOGRAPHY:
Edward Lockspeiser: Piano Concerto in G major, in *The Concerto* (ed. Ralph Hill), Pelican Books 1952, p. 309.
A Mendel: Golden-haired standard, new Ravel piano concerto, *Nation*, 28 December 1932, p. 652.
R.-A. Mooser: Le concerto pour piano de MR, *Dissonances*, March 1933.
Henry Prunières: MR—Concerto pour piano et orchestre, *RM*, 1 February 1932, p. 123.

69. Don Quichotte à Dulcinée (Paul Morand). For voice and piano. 1932. Dur. 5′ 50″.
   1. *Chanson romanesque.* Ded. Robert Zoucinou. Dur. 2′.
   2. *Chanson épique.* Ded. Martial Singher. Dur. 2′ 10″.
   3. *Chanson à boire.* Ded. Roger Bourdin. Dur. 1′ 40″.
   Pub. 1934, Durand; Eng. words by Edward Lockton.

69a. Don Quichotte à Dulcinée. Version for voice and orchestra.
   2 fl, 2 ob, ca, 2 cl, 2 bsn; 2 hn, tpt; cast, vib; hp, strings.
   fp: 1 December 1934, Paris, Théâtre du Châtelet, Martial Singher and l'Orchestre Colonne, cond. Paul Paray.
   Pub. 1934, Durand.

BIBLIOGRAPHY:
Fred. Goldbeck: 3 Mélodies de Ravel—Don Quichotte à Dulcinée, *RM*, January 1935, p. 42.
Arthur Hoérée: Don Quichotte à Dulcinée de Ravel, *Le Monde musical*, December 1935.

GENERAL BIBLIOGRAPHY
Jules van Ackere: MR, Editions Elsevier (Brussels) 1957; foreword by Roland-Manuel.
— Ravel, de orkestrater, *Revue Belge de musicologie*, 1951, No. 1, p. 23.
— MR, in *MGG*, Vol. 11 (1963), p. 58.
Kurt Ackeret: Studen zum Klavierwerke von MR, Zurich, 1941.

István Albert: MR, *Muzsika*, January 1963, p. 32.
Edmond Appia: MR et l'esprit romand, *Suisse Romande*, 1938, No. 5.
Felix Aprahamian: The unfamiliar Ravel, *Records & Recording*, February 1963, p. 17.
Felix Aprahamian & Freda Pitt: MR, in *Decca Book of Ballet*, Muller (London) 1958, p. 245.
Tony Aubin: Hommage à MR, *Revue Musicale de France*, No. 2, 1946.
Louis Aubert: Souvenir, *RM*, December 1938, p. 298.
Georges Auric: MR, *Nouvelles littéraires*, 29 December 1937.
— MR, *Marianne*, 5 January 1938.
J. Balzer: MR, *Dansk Musiktidsskrift*, January 1938.
Henry Barraud: Das Wahre gesicht von MR, *Cahiers franco-allemands*, 1938, Nos. 3–4.
Jane Bathori: Souvenir, *RM*, December 1938, p. 371.
— Les musiciens que j'ai connu, *Recorded Sound*, winter 1961–2, p. 144.
Sten Beite: Franska smaken, *Orfeus* (Stockholm), 1926, p. 238.
Arnold Bennett & G. Jean-Aubry: MR, his music and his home, *British Musician*, February 1938, p. 32.
J. R. Bennett: Ravel and his tribute to eighteenth-century French music, *Halle*, January 1954, p. 4.
Robert Bernard: MR, *RM*, January 1938, p. 1.
— MR, *Le Journal de Genève*, 8 February 1938.
— La gloire de Ravel, *RM*, December 1938, p. 199.
Georges Bernard: MR, *Etudes*, 20 January 1938.
R. Bernier: Considérations sur l'art de MR, *Syrinx*, January 1938.
— A propos de MR, *Syrinx*, February 1938.
— Le Tombeau de Couperin, Ma Mère l'Oye, de Ravel, *Syrinx*, June–July 1938.
Albert Bertelin: MR, *La Petite Maîtrise*, January–February 1938.
René Berthelot: Affinités de Ravel et Valéry, *Revue Musicale de France*, No. 2, 1946.
Henri Bidon: Les fantômes de Ravel, *RM*, December 1938, p. 236.
Arthur Bliss & Hubert J. Foss: MR (Stereoscopic Views, No. 1), *The Dominant*, April 1928, p. 22.

Jean-Richard Bloch: MR ou les Monstres domptés, *RM*, January–February 1939, p. 8.

André Boll: La présentation décorative de l'œuvre de Ravel, *RM*, December 1938, p. 252.

Pierre Boulez: Trajectoires: Ravel, Stravinsky, Schoenberg, *Contrepoints*, 6ᵉ cahier, 1949.

Havergal Brian: MR, *MO*, November 1939, p. 63.

Sten Broman: MR, *Sydsvenska Dagbladet*, 7 March 1935.

Donald Brook: Ravel, in *Five Great Composers*, Rockliff 1946, p. 185.

J. G. Brennan: MR, *Catholic World*, May 1938, p. 198.

Robert Brussel: La mort de MR, *Le Figaro*, 29 December 1937.

José Bruyr: MR ou Le Lyrisme et les Sortilèges, Librairie Plon (Paris) 1950.

— Mes rencontres avec MR, *Le Guide du Concert*, 1938, 7, 14, 21, 28 January and 4, 11 February.

— MR, *Revue internationale de musique*, March–April 1938, p. 89.

— Ravel, tel que je l'ai connu, *Musica* (Chaix), No. 99, June 1962, p. 4.

Richard Brycesn: MR, *Gramophone Record*, April 1935, p. 2.

Edward Burlingame Hill: Une opinion américaine sur MR, *Le Mercure musical*, 15 November 1906.

— News from Ravel, *Boston Journal*, c. December 1921.

— MR, *MQ*, January 1927, p. 130.

M.-D. Calvocoressi: MR, *Bulletin de la S.I.M.*, April 1909.

— MR, *MT*, December 1913, p. 785.

— MR, in *Musicians Gallery*, Faber & Faber (London) 1933, chapters IV, VI, VII; Vaughan Williams and Ravel, chapter XXX, p. 283.

— MR, *MT*, January 1938, p. 22.

— MR, *MMR*, 1938, p. 33.

— When Ravel composed to order, *M&L*, January 1941.

— Ravel's letters to Calvocoressi, *MQ*, January 1941, p. 1.

Antonio Capri: MR, *Bollettino mensile di vita e cultura musicale*, December 1937.

— MR, in *Musica e musicisti d'Europa*, Ulrico Hoepli (Milan) 1939, p. 196.

Alfredo Casella: L'harmonie, *RM*, April 1925, p. 28; Ravel's harmony, *MT*, February 1926, p. 124.

— MR, *Musica d'oggi*, March 1938.

René Chalupt: Ravel au miroir de ses lettres, Laffont (Paris) 1956.

— MR et les prétextes littéraires de sa musique, *RM*, April 1925, p. 75.

— La féerie et MR, *RM*, December 1958, p. 320.

René Chambrillac: Survie de Ravel, *La Page musicale*, 7 January 1938.

Gilbert Chase: Death takes Ravel, leading French composer, *Musical America*, 10 January 1938.

Ami Châtelain: La famille de MR et ses origines, *SM*, 1945.

— MR et les 'Juifs', *Revue musicale de la Suisse Romande*, 10 September 1965, p. 5.

Jean Cocteau: À MR, *RM*, January 1930, p. 16.

— Ravel et nous, *RM*, December 1938, p. 396.

André Coeuroy: MR, *Musical Digest*, 29 November 1921.

— MR, in *La Musique française moderne*, Librairie Delagrave (Paris) 1922, p. 31.

— MR, *MN&H*, 21 April 1923, p. 386 (repr. from *Quinze Musiciens Français*).

— La dernière œuvre de MR, *Muzika* (Warsaw), 1925, No. 3.

— Images de Ravel au miroir de ses lettres, *RM*, April 1925, p. 75.

— Autour de Ravel, *Beaux Arts* (Brussels), 7 January 1938.

L. Colacicchi: MR, *Il Musicista*, January–February 1938.

A. Comhaire: Ravel et quelques poètes, *Syrinx*, February 1938.

Martin Cooper: MR, *The Gramophone*, February 1938, p. 374.

Piero Coppola: MR, in *Dix-sept ans de musique à Paris*, Librairie F. Rouge (Lausanne) 1944, pp. 31 and 212.

Covielle: M. Ravel et le Prix de Rome, *Le Matin*, 22 May 1905.

H. de Curzon: MR, *Journal des Débats*, 30 December 1937.

— MR, *La Métropole* (Anvers), 9 January 1938.

Charles C. Cushing: MR, *Modern Music*, March–April 1938.

Laurence Davies: MR, music's Dr. Coppelius,

in *The Gallic Muse*, J. M. Dent (London) 1967, p. 121.

Norman Demuth: Ravel, Dent: Master Musicians series (London) 1947.

— MR, in *Musical Trends in the 20th Century*, Rockliff (London) 1952, p. 70.

P. Donostia: Hommage à Maurice Ravel, *Gure Herria* (Ustaritz), October–December 1937.

Leonard Duck: Debussy and Ravel, *Halle*, No. 118, 1961–2, p. 26.

Norbert Dufourcq: MR, in *La Musique française*, Librairie Larousse (Paris) 1949, p. 311.

René Dumesnil: MR, in *Portraits de musiciens français*, Librairie Plon (Paris) 1938, p. 225.

— MR, *Mercure de France*, 1 February 1938.

— MR, poète, *RM*, December 1958, p. 316.

Maurice Dumesnil: MR, the man, the musician, the critic, *Etude*, September–October 1934, pp. 513, 583.

— MR, 1875–1937, *Etude*, April 1938, p. 215.

— Three Ravels, *Etude*, February 1946, p. 65.

— Teacher's roundtable: characteristics of Ravel's piano music, *Etude*, November 1952, p. 23.

Louis Durey: MR, *Chesterian*, No. 14, April 1921.

Edwin Evans: Great song writers, VII: MR, *MM&F*, July 1931, p. 207.

David Ewan: MR, *Musical Record* (Philadelphia), December 1933.

Manuel de Falla: Notes sur Ravel, *RM*, March 1939, p. 81; Manuel de Falla et MR, *Le Monde musical*, June–July 1939.

Léon-Paul Fargue: MR, Editions Domat: Collection 'Au voilier' 1949.

— MR, *Plaisir de France*, August 1936.

Georges Favre: MR, *Bulletin Mensuel de l'Union Française des Oeuvres Laïques d'Education Artistique* (Paris), April 1950.

Jacques Février: MR, *L'Art musical*, 28 January 1938.

— Exigences de Ravel, *Revue Internationale de Musique*, April 1939, p. 892.

Gerold Fierz: Eine Gesamtaufnahme der Orchesterwerke von MR, *SM*, September–October 1963, p. 306.

R. Franquinet: In memoriam MR, A. A. M. Stols (Maastricht) 1937.

Hans Gal (ed.): MR, in *The Musicians World* (Great Composers in their Letters), Thames & Hudson (London), p. 412.

Henry Gauthier-Villars: Pierre Lalo contra Ravel, Louis Laloy pro Ravel, *Mercure de France*, 1 April 1907.

R. Gelatt: Ravel, early and late, *Saturday Review*, 28 May 1949, p. 47.

André George: Féerie et mystère de MR, *Les Nouvelles littéraires*, 1 January 1938.

— A la gloire de Ravel, *Les Nouvelles littéraires*, 26 November 1938.

Jaap Geraedts: Ravel, J. H. Gottmer (Haarlem) 1957.

Walter Gieseking: Wie spielt man Ravels Klaviermusik, *Melos*, December 1947, p. 412.

Henri Gil-Marchex: La technique de piano, *RM*, April 1925, p. 38; Ravel's pianoforte technique, *MT*, December 1926, p. 1087.

— Les concertos de Ravel, *RM*, December 1938, p. 275.

Teocrito di Giorgio: La matematica di Ravel, *Tribuna d'Italia*, 30 January 1938.

Scott Goddard: Baudelaire, Ravel, Debussy, *MN&H*, 4 June 1921, p. 717.

— Some notes on the piano works of Maurice Ravel, *Sackbut*, October 1921, p. 8.

— The published songs of MR, *Sackbut*, June 1922, p. 6.

— MR, *M&L*, October 1925.

— Ravel's orchestral music, *MM&F*, December 1932, p. 75.

— MR, *Music*, autumn 1947, p. 24.

Frederick Goldbeck: Sur Ravel et ses concertos, *RM*, January 1933, p. 193.

Madeleine Goss: Bolero (The life of MR), Holt (New York) 1940.

Cecil Gray: MR, in *A Survey of Contemporary Music*, O.U.P. 1927, p. 114.

Madeleine Grey: Souvenir d'une interprète, *RM*, December 1938, p. 367.

— Working with Ravel (transl. C. G. Burke), *Saturday Review*, 26 July 1952, p. 37.

F. V. Grunfeld: Unravelling Ravel: the great leap sideways, *Reporter*, 6 May 1965, p. 35.

Léon Guichard: Prestiges de Ravel, *Le Point*, September 1938.

Pierre Guillet: MR, *Göteborgs Handels- och Sjöfartstidning*, 12 April 1935.

Paul Guinard: Ravel à Madrid, *RM*, May 1924, p. 261.

Ravel, Maurice

R. Hammond: MR, *Modern Music*, February 1928.

Leigh Henry: MR, *MO*, May p. 689, June p. 774.

— MR in London, *MS*, 15 July 1922, p. 23.

Arthur Hoérée: MR, *Beaux Arts*, 21 January 1938.

— La mélodie et l'œuvre lyrique, *RM*, April 1925, p. 46.

Basil Hogarth: MR, *The Gramophone*, May 1931, p. 569.

— L'œuvre vocale, *RM*, December 1938, p. 294.

Karl Holl: Zum Tode von MR, *Neues Musikblatt*, January 1938.

Arthur Honegger: Ravel et Debussysme, *RM*, December 1938, p. 258.

Valentine Hugo: Trois souvenirs de Ravel, *RM* (La Littérature française et la musique), 1952, p. 137.

Maurice Imbert: MR, *L'Art musical*, 7 January 1938.

E. Jade: MR, *Franco-American Society Bulletin*, December 1923.

Vladimir Jankélévitch: Ravel et les sortilèges, *Europe* (Paris), 15 January 1938.

— MR, Editions du Seuil (Paris) 1956; transl. Margaret Crosland, Grove Press (New York), John Calder (London) 1959.

— La sérénade interrompue, *RM*, December 1958, p. 337.

G. Jean-Aubry: Profils perdus, M. Ravel, *Le Censeur*, 20 July 1907.

— MR, in *La Musique française d'aujourd'hui*, Perrin (Paris) 1916, p. 182.

— Modern French composers, 1: MR, *MMR*, 1918, pp. 31, 57.

— MR, *Arts Gazette*, 1 July 1922.

— MR, *Chesterian*, No. 137, January–February 1938.

Joel: Mozart et Ravel, *L'Information musicale*, 3 March 1944, p. 215.

William W. Johnson: Profile—MR, *Crescendo*, No. 20, February 1949, p. 14.

Hélène Jourdan-Morhange: Le monde entier écoute Ravel, *La République*, 19 January 1938.

— Mon ami Ravel, *RM*, December 1938, p. 384.

— Ravel et nous, Editions 'Le Milieu du Monde' (Geneva) 1945.

Hélène Jourdan-Morhange & Vlado Perlemuter: Ravel d'après Ravel, Editions du Cervin (Lausanne) 1957.

P. Kaldor: MR, *Commune*, February 1938.

Tristan Klingsor: Ravel et l'art de son temps, *RM*, April 1925, p. 9.

— MR et les vers libre, *RM*, December 1958, p. 313.

Tristan Klingsor & André Mangeot: MR, sa vie et ses œuvres, *Le Monde musical*, 31 January 1938.

D. Kostic: Jedna zelena kravata, jedan drapsko i nestro o Ravelu, *Zvuk*, No. 37 (1960), p. 368.

J. Koral: Ravel, *Wiadomosci Muzyczne*, 1925, No. 1.

J. Kresanek: MR, *Slovenska Hudba*, January 1958, p. 12.

P.-F. Lacome: Ravel et l'Espagne, *L'Information musicale*, 1 October 1943, p. 13.

J. de Lacratelle: Memories of MR, *Canon*, October 1956, p. 88.

R. Lagas: Bij een uitspraak van Ravel, *Mens en melodie*, January 1955, p. 13.

Pierre Lalo: M. Ravel, *Le Temps*, 13 June 1899.

— Le concours du prix de Rome en 1905: Le cas de M. Ravel, *Le Temps*, 11 July 1905.

— Quelques ouvrages nouveaux de M. Ravel et le Debussysme. L'art Debussyste et l'art de M. Debussy, *Le Temps*, 19 March 1907.

— Encore le Debussysme. Une lettre de M. Ravel, *Le Temps*, 9 April 1907.

— MR, in *De Rameau à Ravel: Portraits et Souvenirs*, Editions Albin Michel (Paris) 1947, p. 196.

Louis Laloy: MR, *Mercure musical et bulletin mensuel français de la S.I.M.*, 1907, p. 279.

— Au Conservatoire, *Mercure musical*, 1 June 1905.

— MR, *Mercure musical*, February and March 1905.

— Les Partis musicaux en France, *Grande Revue*, 25 December 1907.

Paul Landormy: MR, in *La Musique française après Debussy*, Gallimard (Paris) 1943, p. 105.

— La musique française de piano, 1. MR, *Le Ménestrel*, 27 May 1932, p. 225.

— MR, *Le Ménestrel*, 7 and 14 January 1938, p. 1.

— MR (transl. W. Wagner), *MQ*, October 1939, p. 430.

W. L. Landowsky: MR, sa vie, son œuvre, Editions Ouvrières (Paris) 1950.

Daniel Lesur: Ravel und die Opernbühne, *Melos*, December 1947, p. 405.

Serge Lifar: MR et le ballet, *RM*, December 1938, p. 266.

Heinrich Lindlar: Ravels Tanzpoetik, *Musica*, 1960, No. 8, p. 483.

E. Lliurat: MR, *Revista Musica Catalana*, July 1924.

Edward Lockspeiser: Roussel and Ravel, *M&L*, July 1938, p. 245.

Marguerite Long: MR, *La Page musicale*, 7 January 1938.

— Souvenir de MR, *RM*, December 1938, p. 365.

C. Loubet: Pour le 25ᵉ anniversaire de sa mort: Ravel et Montfort, *Pays d'Yvelines, de Hurepoix et de Beauce*, 1962, No. 6.

Pierre Lucas: Quelques souvenirs sur MR, *L'Age nouveau*, March 1938.

Watson Lyle: MR, a personal impression, *MN&H*, 27 October 1923, p. 360.

Armand Machabey: MR, Editions Richard-Masse (Paris) 1947.

— Ravels Orchesterwerke, *Melos*, December 1947, p. 408.

Joseph Machlis: MR, in *Introduction to Contemporary Music*, Norton (USA) 1961, Dent (London), p. 133.

G. E. Magnat: Ravel ou les sortilèges de l'intelligence, in *Portraits de quelques musiciens*, Foetisch-Frères (Lausanne) 1948, p. 99.

Charles Malherbe: MR, *Revue S.I.M.*, August–September 1910.

A. Mantelli: MR, *La Rassegna musicale*, February 1938, p. 63.

— Razionalismo e sensibilità di MR, *L'Approdo musicale*, April–June 1958.

Gabriel Marcel: La musique français en deuil, *La Vie intellectuelle*, 25 February 1938.

Georgette Marnold: Quelques lettres de MR, *RM*, December 1938, p. 260.

Jean Marnold: Scandale du prix de Rome, *Mercure musical*, 15 June and 1 July 1905.

— L'affaire Ravel, *Revue musicale de Lyon*, 1 May 1907.

— Oeuvres de M. Ravel, *Mercure de France*, 16 January 1908.

Frank Martin: MR, *SM*, 15 March 1938.

Paul-Marie Masson: MR, *La Dépêche* (Toulouse), 29 December 1938.

Camille Mauclair: La musique de piano de MR, *Le Courrier musical*, 1906.

— Sensations récentes, 1. MR, *Le Courrier musical*, 1906, No. 13.

John Maycock: The music of Ravel, *Halle*, September 1952, p. 18.

Wilfrid Mellers: Debussy and Ravel, in *Man and his Music*, Barrie & Rockliff (London) 1962, p. 935.

Pierre Meylan: Igor Stravinsky et MR ont collaboré à Clarens en 1913, *Revue musicale de Suisse Romande*, 1 March 1965, p. 5.

Darius Milhaud: MR, *Le Soir*, 29 December 1937.

— MR, *L'Art musical populaire*, December 1937–January 1938.

— Reminiscences of Debussy and Ravel, *The Listener*, 29 May 1958, p. 896; repr. in *Essays on Music* (ed. Felix Aprahamian), Cassell (London) 1967, p. 78.

André Mirambel: L'inspiration grecque dans l'œuvre de Ravel, *Néoellinika Grammata* (Athens), 12 February 1938; *RM*, December 1958, p. 304.

M. Montabré: Entretien avec MR, *L'Intransigeant*, 28 January 1923.

R.-A. Mooser: MR, *Dissonances*, January 1938.

R. O. Morris: MR, *M&L*, July 1921.

Rollo (H.) Myers: Ravel, life and works, Gerald Duckworth (London) 1960.

— Ravel on the stage, *M&M*, April 1965, p. 14.

Gérard Neuhaus: MR, *Schweizer. Musikpädag. Blätter*, 1937, Nos. 27–28.

Gösta Nystroem: MR, *Göteborgs Handels- och Sjöfartstidning*, 27 January 1938.

Antonio Odriozola: MR (discography), *Musica* (Madrid), 1953, Nos. 3–4, p. 215.

Frank Onnen: MR, Amsterdam; Engl. transl. Continental Book Co., Stockholm.

Selim Palmgren: MR, *Hufsudstadsbladet*, 29 December 1937.

Guido Pannain: MR, *La Rassegna musicale*, January 1928, p. 22.

— In morte di MR, *Rivista musicale Italiana*, 1938, No. 1.

Domenico de Paoli: MR, *Bollettino bibliografico musicale*, May 1929.

Claude Peracchio: MR, *Revue des artistes*, February 1938.

Moses Pergament: MR, *Svensk Dagbladet*, 29 December 1937.

Constantin Photiadès: MR, *Revue de Paris*, 1 March 1938.

Bohdan Pilarski: Une conférence de MR à Houston, *Revue de musicologie*, December 1964, p. 208.

— Ravel w Polsce, *Ruch Muzyczny*, 1963, No. 11, p. 12.

Ildebrando Pizzetti: MR, in *Musicisti contemporanei*, Fratelli Treves (Milan) 1914, p. 171.

Jean Poueigh: A propos du dixième anniversaire de la morte de MR, *Revue hommes et mondes*, No. 18, January 1947, p. 161.

Francis Poulenc: Le cœur de MR, *Nouvelle revue française*, February 1941.

Henry Prunières: Stravinsky and Ravel, *Modern Music*, January 1929.

Muñoz de Quedo: Debussy el antiguo y Ravel el moderno, *Mercurio Musical* (Buenos Aires), 1936, No. 61, p. 8.

K. Regamey: MR, *Muzyka Polska*, January 1938.

Jan Reisser: MR, *Rytmus*, January 1938.

K. Riisager: MR à Copenhague, *RM*, 1 March 1926, p. 277.

— MR, *Dansk Musiktidsskrift*, January 1938.

E. Robinson: Naïve Ravel, *American Mercury*, May 1932, p. 115.

Lionel Rogg: MR, *Musikalische Rundschau der Schweiz*, May 1955.

Paul Rosenfeld: MR, *New Republic*, 11 December 1929, p. 68.

Roland-Manuel: MR, *L'Echo musical*, February 1913.

— MR et son œuvre, Durand (Paris) 1914; 2nd edn. 1926.

— MR, *RM*, April 1921, p. 1.

— New work by Ravel, *MN&H*, 29 April 1922, p. 535.

— MR, *Lyrica*, April 1923.

— Ravel and the new French school, *League of Composers' Review*, January 1925.

— MR ou l'esthétique de l'imposture, *RM*, April 1925, p. 16.

— Notes sur le style de MR, *Revue Pleyel*, No. 47, August 1927; *Musique*, No. 1, 15 October 1927.

— MR et son œuvre dramatique, Librairie de France (Paris) 1928.

— MR et la jeune école française, *Nouvelles littéraires*, June 1937.

— A la gloire de Ravel, *Nouvelle Revue Critique* (Paris), 1938, revised edn. Gallimard (Paris) 1948; Eng. transl. Cynthia Jolly, Dobson (London) 1947.

— Réflexions sur Ravel, *La Grande Revue*, April 1938.

— Le génie de MR, *Les Temps présents*, 7 January 1938.

— MR à travers sa correspondance, *RM*, January–February 1939, p. 1.

— Ravel, in *Les Musiciens célèbres*, Editions d'Art Lucien Mazenod (Geneva) 1948, p. 282.

— Lettres de MR et documents inédits, *Revue de musicologie*, July 1956, p. 49.

Kajsa Rootzén: MR, in *Fransk musik* (Stockholm), 1957, p. 60.

Daniel Ruyneman: In memoriam MR, *Maandblad voor Hedrendaagsche Muziek*, February 1938.

Leonid Sabaneev: MR, *MO*, August 1938, p. 943.

Adolfo Salazar: Ravel, in *La música actual en Europa y sus problemas*, J. M. Yagües (Madrid) 1935, p. 451.

Gustave Samazeuilh: Quelques souvenirs sur MR, *Le Temps*, 29 December 1937; *La Petite Gironde* (Bordeaux), 22 January 1938.

— MR en pays basque, *RM*, December 1938, p. 392; *Monde illustré*, 31 January 1948.

— Le souvenir de Gabriel Pierné—Albert Roussel, MR, in *Musiciens de mon temps*, Editions Marcel Daubin (Paris) 1947, p. 198.

Charlotte Sanford: Ravel's first trip to New York, *Musical Courier*, May 1955, p. 8.

Henri Sauguet: Mes rencontres avec MR, *RM*, January–February 1939, p. 11.

Boris de Schloezer: MR, *Nouvelle revue française*, 1938, No. 293, p. 298.

— Chronique musicale, *Nouvelle revue française*, 1939, No. 306, p. 499.

E. R. Schmitz: What Debussy and Ravel told me about their piano music, *Proceedings of Music Teachers National Association* (Pittsburgh), 1949.

Herbert Schmolzi: Hartmann, Mussorgsky, Ravel, *NZfM*, October 1963.

Paul Segalla: Ravel's songs, *MMR*, 1955, p. 264.

Victor Seroff: MR, Hold (New York) 1953.

Frank Shera: Debussy and Ravel, O.U.P. 1925.

B. van den Sigtenhorst Meijer: MR, *De Wereld der Muziek*, February 1938.

Ernst Silz: Debussy und Ravel als Wegbereiter der Neuen Musik, *Musikerziehung*, September 1965.

Speculum: Ravel, *La Rassegna musicale*, January 1938, p. 23.

Paul Stefan: Ravel und Casella, *Der Merker*, 1 October 1920, p. 467.

— Ravel in Wien, *Anbruch*, April 1929, p. 168.

J. Stehmann: Ravel, *Le Rouge et le Noir*, 5 January 1938.

Heinrich Strobel: Bildnis des Menschen MR, *Melos*, December 1947, p. 414.

H. H. Stuckenschmidt: MR, in *Schöpfer der neuen Musik*, Suhrkamp Verlag (Frankfurt a.M.) 1958, p. 52.

— MR, Variationen über Person und Werk, Suhrkamp Verlag (Frankfurt a.M.) 1966.

J. Suarès: Pour Ravel, *RM*, April 1925, p. 3.

— Ravel, *Blätter der Staatsoper* (Berlin), October (No. 4) 1929, p. 1.

— Ravel, esquisse, *RM*, December 1938, p. 240.

H. S. Sulzberger: MR, *Neue Zürcher Zeitung*, 17 November 1926.

J. H. Swanson: Ravel is fun, *Repertoire*, October 1951, p. 23.

Karel Szymanowski: Hommage à Ravel, *Muzika* (Warsaw), 1925, No. 3.

Magda Tagliaferro: Debussy et Ravel, *Le Monde musical*, July 1936.

Willy Tappolet: MR, Leben und Werk, O. Walter (Olten) 1950.

— MR 'der Baske', *SM*, November 1955, p. 421.

Léon Vallas: Le nouveau style pianistique, *Revue musicale de Lyon*, 6 January 1907.

— Encore l'affaire Ravel et le Debussysme, *Revue musicale de Lyon*, 14 April 1907.

Ralph Vaughan Williams: MR's music, *Living Age*, 28 May 1921, p. 553.

Ricardo Viñes: Fragments, *RM*, December 1938, p. 360.

Max Vredenburg: Ravel, de Bask, *Mens en melodie*, February 1948, p. 51.

Emile Vuillermoz: En l'an 2000, *Revue S.I.M.*, August–September 1910.

— Portrait de MR, *Cahiers d'aujourd'hui*, 1922, No. 10, p. 196.

— Le style orchestrale, *RM*, April 1925, p. 22.

— MR est mort, *Excelsior*, 29 December 1937.

— Une grande figure de la musique française, *L'Illustration*, 8 January 1938.

— Défendons Ravel, *Candide*, 13 January 1938.

— MR, *RM*, December 1938, p. 245.

Ernest Walker: A study of Ravel, *MMR*, 1939, p. 110.

Egon Wellesz: Ravel, *Der Auftakt*, May 1922.

— MR, *Anbruch*, October (2) 1920 (No. 16), p. 544.

Theodor Wiesengrund-Adorno: Ravel, *Anbruch*, April–May 1930, p. 151.

Rudolf Wittelbach: MR, *SM*, January–February 1963, p. 13.

Ralph W. Wood: Ravel and the orchestra, *MO*, November 1946, p. 41.

K. H. Wörner: MR, das Heitere und das Magische, *Musik und Szene*, 1962–3, No. 14, p. 1.

E. Zanetti: La critica di Ravel, *Musica d'oggi*, October 1958.

Berta Zuckerkandl-Szeps: Bei MR, *Neues Wiener Journal*, 18 October 1925.

SYMPOSIA

Maurice Ravel, par quelques-uns de ses familiers, Editions du Tambourinaire (Paris) 1939. Contributions by Colette, Maurice Delage, Léon-Paul Fargue, Hélène Jourdan-Morhange, Tristan Klingsor, Roland-Manuel, Dominique Sordet, Emile Vuillermoz, Jacques de Zogheb.

Maurice Ravel, Les Publications techniques et artistiques (Paris) 1945. Contributions by Tony Aubin, Léon-Paul Fargue, Arthur Hoérée, Hélène Jourdan-Morhange, Georges Pioch.

MISCELLANEOUS OR UNSIGNED

Some French scores—Ravel, Roger-Ducasse, Roussel, *The Times*, 4 January 1913, p. 10.

Ravel, *Nouvelle revue musicale* (Lyon), October 1924.

The art of MR, *The Times*, 20 December 1913, p. 11.

Raveliana, *RM*, April 1925, p. 80.

Ravel et la critique contemporaine, *RM*, April 1925, p. 89.

MR e l'ora presente, *Musica d'oggi*, July 1925, p. 217.

Debussy en Ravel, *Muziekbode*, October and November 1927.

Intervista con MR, *Musica d'oggi*, August–September 1931, p. 360.

MR, *British Musician*, October 1930, p. 271.

Le style pianistique de Debussy et de Ravel, *Dissonances*, April 1932.

Entretien avec Ravel, *RM*, March 1931, p. 193.

MR, *Les Echos de l'Ecole César Franck*, February–March 1938.

Correspondances, *RM*, January–February 1939, p. 13.

MR: Catalogue de l'œuvre, A. Durand (Paris) 1954.

MR, *Disques*, No. 70, February–March 1955, p. 242.

Festival Ravel à l'Opéra, *L'Opéra de Paris*, XV, 1958.

ALBERT ROUSSEL (1869–1937)

Roussel's environment as a young man was not especially musical and he was well advanced on a naval career before deciding to devote himself to composition. He was born at Tourcoing near Lille in France on 5 April 1869, was brought up by his grandfather and uncle after being orphaned at the age of seven, and started to train as a naval officer in 1887, having little formal instruction in music. Between 1889 and 1894 he spent much time at sea, notably in the Far East, becoming a lieutenant in 1893. It was a fellow officer, Adolphe Calvet, who encouraged him to seek informed comment on his early compositions. The comment being favourable, Roussel left the navy in June 1894, studied under the organist Eugène Gigout and in 1898 entered the recently founded Schola Cantorum in Paris. After being a pupil of Vincent d'Indy's at the Schola, he was appointed Professor of Counterpoint there (1902–14), his most remarkable pupils at this time being Erik Satie and Edgar Varèse. He married Blanche Preisach in 1908 and the following year toured India and South-East Asia with her, intensify-

ing an interest in oriental civilization which had a considerable influence on his music. Apart from service in the Red Cross and French Artillery during the First World War, Roussel's later life was externally uneventful and devoted almost exclusively to composition. From 1921 until the year of his death he lived on the coast at Varengeville near Dieppe and only rarely travelled abroad, most notably to the USA in 1930 to hear the Boston Symphony Orchestra give the first performance of the symphony (No. 3 in G minor) which it had commissioned from him. His sixtieth birthday the previous year was celebrated in Paris with a series of concerts of his work. Roussel overtaxed his strength organizing the festival of the International Society for Contemporary Music in Paris in 1937, and he died in the August of that year while taking a rest-cure for *angina pectoris* at Royan (Charente-Maritime).

CATALOGUE OF WORKS

1. Fantaisie. For violin and piano. 1892. Destroyed.

2. Andante (Ave Maria). For violin, viola, cello and organ. 1892. Destroyed.

3. Marche nuptiale. For orchestra. 1893.

4. Deux Madrigaux à quatre voix. 1897.
  1. *Chanson du XVe siècle*; 2. *Words: Le Soucy*.
  fp: 3 May 1898, Paris, Salle Pleyel, Société des Compositeurs, Mlles Elinora and C. O'Rorke, Lubet and De Clynsen, cond. Albert Roussel.
  Unpub. ?Destroyed.

5. Des heures passent Op. 1. Suite for piano. 1898. Dur. 14′.
  1. *Graves, légères*. Ded. Mme Ricour de Bourgies.
  2. *Joyeuses*. Ded Mme E. Henry-Baudot.
  3. *Tragiques*. Ded. Mlle Léontine Wattel.
  4. *Champêtres*. Ded. Mlle J. Taravent.
  Pub. Hamelle.

6. Quintet. For strings and horn. c. 1901.
  fp: 2 February 1901, Paris, Société Nationale de Musique concert, Parent, Lammers, Denayer, Baretti and Reine.
  ?Destroyed.

7. Violin Sonata. *c.* 1902.

fp: 5 May 1902, Paris, Société Nationale de Musique concert, Saïller and Blanche Selva. ?Destroyed.

8. Les Rêves (Armand Silvestre). For voice and piano. Unknown date.

9. Pendant l'attente (Catulle Mendès). For voice and piano. Unknown date.

10. Tristesse au jardin (L. Tailhade). For voice and piano. Unknown date.

11. Music for a film. Unidentified. Unknown date.

12. Piano Trio Op. 2. For piano, violin and cello. May–October 1902, rev. 1927. Dur. 30′.

1. *Modéré sans lenteur—Très animé*; 2. *Lent*; 3. *Finale: Très lent—Vif et gaiment.*

fp (private): 14 April 1904, Paris, home of Mme Taravent.

fp (public): 4 February 1905, Paris, Salle Pleyel, Société Nationale de Musique concert, Marthe Dron (piano), A. Parent (violin) and L. Fournier (cello).

fEp: 24 March 1909, London, Société des Concerts Français, Antoinette Velnard, Baillon and Maurech.

Pub. Rouart Lerolle; new edition, 1927.

13. Quatre poèmes Op. 3 (Henri de Régnier). For voice and piano. September–October 1903.

1. *Le départ.* Ded. Mme Jeanne Raunay. Dur. 2′ 15″.

2. *Vœu.* Ded. Mary Garden. Dur. 3′.

3. *Le jardin mouillé.* Ded. Maurice Bagès. Dur. 2′ 30″.

4. *Madrigal lyrique.* Ded. Mme Albert Groz. Dur. 4′ 45″.

fp: 21 April 1906, Paris, Salle Pleyel, Société Nationale de Musique concert, Jane Bathori, acc. Alfred Cortot.

?fEp (No. 3 only): 5 January 1909, Folkestone, Hotel Metropole, Incorporated Society of Musicians Conference concert, Mme Willaume-Lambert.

Pub. 1921, Rouart Lerolle; Eng. version, Rosa Newmarch.

14. Résurrection Op. 4. Symphonic Prelude for orchestra, after the novel by Tolstoy. Dated: 17 August 1903. Ded. Edouard Brunel.

2 fl, pic, 2 ob, ca, 2 cl, bcl, 2 bsn; 4 hn, 3 tpt, 3 tmb, tuba; timp; hp, strings.

fp: 17 May 1904, Paris, Nouveau-Théâtre, Société Nationale de Musique concert, cond. Alfred Cortot.

Pub. Rouart Lerolle; reduction for piano.

15. Conte à la poupée. For piano. 1904. Dur. 3′. Pub. in Album de la Schola Cantorum.

16. Vendanges. Symphonic Sketch for orchestra. *c.* 1905.

fp: 18 April 1905, Paris, Nouveau-Théâtre, Concerts Cortot, cond. Alfred Cortot. Destroyed.

17. Rustiques Op. 5. Suite for piano. 1904–6, Cormeilles, Paris. Ded. Mme Sérieyx Taravent. Dur. 13′.

1. *Danse au bord de l'eau.* 1904.

2. *Promenade sentimentale en forêt.* 1904.

3. *Retour de fête.* 1906.

fp: 17 February 1906, Paris, Salle Pleyel, Société Nationale de Musique, Blanche Selva.

Pub. Durand.

18. Divertissement Op. 6. For flute, oboe, clarinet, bassoon, horn and piano. 1906. Ded. Société moderne des instruments à vent. Dur. 7′.

fp: 10 April 1906, Paris, Salle des Agriculteurs, E. Wagner (piano) and Société moderne des instruments à vent.

?fEp: 14 May 1924, Aeolian Hall, Eugene Goossens concert, Kathleen Long and the London Wind Quartet.

fEbp: 28 February 1926, Newcastle Station Wind Quintet, with Olive Tomlinson (piano).

Pub. Rouart Lerolle.

19. Le Poème de la forêt Op. 7. For orchestra. 1904–6. Ded. Alfred Cortot. Dur. 35′.

1. *Forêt d'hiver.* Dated: 14 June 1906.

2. *Renouveau.* Dated: 15 July 1905.

3. *Soir d'été.* Dated: 20 October 1904, Cormeilles.

4. *Faunes et Dryades.* Dated: 27 September 1906.

3 fl, pic, 2 ob, ca, 2 cl, 2 bsn; 4 hn, 2 tpt,

441

3 tmb, tuba; timp, cym, tamb de basque, tgle; 2 hp, strings.

fp (No. 3): 15 December 1904, Paris, Concerts Cortot, cond. Alfred Cortot.

fp (No. 4): 10 November 1907, Paris, Concerts Lamoureux, cond. Camille Chevillard.

fp (complete): 22 March 1908, Brussels, Théâtre de la Monnaie, Concerts Populaires, cond. Sylvain Dupuis.

fFp (complete): 7 February 1909, Paris, Concerts Lamoureux, cond. Vincent d'Indy.

fEbp: 4 October 1935, BBC Midland Orchestra, cond. Leslie Heward.

Pub. 1910, Rouart Lerolle; incl. min. score, and reduction by Albert Roussel for piano four hands.

20. Quatre poèmes Op. 8 (Henri de Régnier). For voice and piano. February–July 1907.

1. *Adieux.* Ded. Paul Poujaud. Dur. 4′ 30″.
2. *Nuit d'automne.* Ded. Emile Engel. Dur. 3′.
3. *Invocation.* Ded. Jane Bathori. Dur. 3′ 15″.
4. *Odelette.* Ded. Mme Octave Maus. Dur. 4′ 30″.

fp: 11 January 1908, Paris, Salle Erard, Société Nationale de Musique concert, Jane Bathori, acc. Albert Roussel.

Pub. 1921, Rouart Lerolle; Eng. version by Rosa Newmarch.

20a. Adieux Op. 20 No. 1. Version with orchestra. 1907. Dur. 4′ 30″.

2 fl, 2 ob, ca, 2 cl, 2 bsn; 2 hn, 2 tpt, 3 tmb, tuba; timp; hp, strings.

Pub. Rouart Lerolle.

21. La Menace Op. 9 (Henri de Régnier). For voice and orchestra or piano. Comp. 1907, orch. 1908. Dated: 2 November 1908. Ded. Mme Gustave Samazeuilh. Dur. 6′.

2 fl, 2 ob, ca, 2 cl, 2 bsn; 4 hn, 2 tpt, 3 tmb; timp, tgle; celesta, hp, strings.

fp: 11 March 1911, Paris, Concerts Hasselmans, Emile Engel, cond. Louis Hasselmans.

Pub. 1910, Rouart Lerolle; incl. reduction by Albert Roussel; Eng. version by Rosa Newmarch ('The Threat').

22. Flammes Op. 10 (G. Jean-Aubry). For voice and piano. Dated: 15 February 1908. Ded. Mlle Madeleine Aubry. Dur. 5′.

fp: 14 February 1909, Le Havre, Cercle d'art moderne, S. Berchut.

Pub. Rouart Lerolle; Eng. version by Rosa Newmarch.

23. Violin Sonata No. 1 in D minor Op. 11. September 1907–July 1908, rev. 1931. Ded. Vincent d'Indy. Dur. 32′.

1. *Lent—Très animé*; 2. *Assez animé*; 3. *Très animé.*

fp: 9 October 1908, Paris, Salon d'Automne, Armand Parent and Marthe Dron.

Pub. 1909, Rouart Lerolle; new edition revised by the composer, 1931.

BIBLIOGRAPHY:

M. Montagu-Nathan: Some modern French sonatas for piano and violin, II: AR, *Chamber Music (Music Student Supplement)*, No. 7, March 1914, p. 67.

24. Deux poèmes chinois Op. 12 (H. P. Roché, after Giles). For voice and piano. 1907–1908.

1. *Ode à un jeune gentilhomme.* Dated: 9 March 1907. Ded. Mme Alfred Cortot. Dur. 1′ 30″.
2. *Amoureux séparés* (Fu-Mi). Dated: 28 February 1908. Ded. Mlle Pironnay. Dur. 2′.

fp (No. 1): 28 June 1907, Le Havre, Cercle d'art moderne.

f Paris p (No. 1): 11 January 1908, Salle Erard, Société Nationale de Musique concert, Jane Bathori, acc. Albert Roussel.

fp (No. 2): 14 February 1909, Le Havre.

Pub. 1921, Rouart Lerolle.

25. Le Marchand de sable qui passe Op. 13. Incidental music to a 'conte lyrique' in one act by G. Jean-Aubry. Dated: 23 October 1908. Ded. Mlle Suzanne Berchut (Mme Suzanne Balguérie). Dur. 19′.

1. *Prélude*; 2. *Scène II*; 3. *Interlude et Scène IV*; 4. *Scène finale.*

fl, cl; hn; hp, strings.

fp: 16 December 1908, Le Havre, cond. Albert Roussel.

?fEp: May 1914, London, Société des Concerts Français, cond. Albert Roussel.

Pub. 1910, Demets; incl. piano reduction.

25a. Le Marchand de sable qui passe: Suite Op. 13. Dur. 15′.

fl, cl; hn; hp, strings.

fp: 18 November 1919, Amsterdam, Concertgebouw Orchestra.
?fEp: 15 December 1919, Birmingham, Midland Institute, cond. (Sir) Granville Bantock.
Pub. Demets; Eschig.

26. Suite in F sharp minor Op. 14. For piano. July 1909–April 1910, Arromanches, Paris. Ded. Blanche Selva. Dur. 20′.
  1. *Prélude*. Dated: July 1909.
  2. *Sicilienne*. Dated: 1 September 1909.
  3. *Bourrée*. Dated: August 1909.
  4. *Ronde*. Dated: April 1910.
fp: 28 January 1911, Paris, Salle Pleyel, Société Nationale de Musique concert, Blanche Selva.
fEbp: 14 December 1933, Frank Mannheimer.
Pub. 1910, Rouart Lerolle.

27. Evocations Op. 15. Symphonic Poem for baritone, tenor, contralto, mixed chorus and orchestra (M.-D. Calvocoressi). 1910–11. Dur. 42′.
  1. *Les Dieux dans l'ombre des cavernes*. Ded. Gustave Samazeuilh. Dur. 16′.
  2. *La Ville rose*. Ded. Carlos de Castera. Dur. 10′.
  3. *Aux bords du fleuve sacré*. Ded. Octave Maus. Dur. 16′.
3 fl, pic, 2 ob, ca, 2 cl, bcl, 2 bsn, cbsn; 4 hn, 3 tpt, 3 tmb, tuba; 3 timp, tgle, tamtam, caisse roulante, GC, cym, tambour, jeu de timbres; celesta, 2 hp, strings.
fp: 18 May 1912, Paris, Salle Gaveau, Société Nationale de Musique concert, Carbelly, Mallet and Mlle Ticier, cond. Rhené-Bâton.
fEp (No. 1): 24 March 1917, Queen's Hall, Queen's Hall Orchestra, cond. Sir Henry Wood. (NB: fGBp of No. 2 originally announced for 26 January 1914, Edinburgh, McEwen Hall, Scottish Orchestra, cond. Rhené-Bâton: cancelled.)
?fEp (complete): 8 October 1960, BBC broadcast, London Philharmonic Choir and BBC Symphony Orchestra, cond. Rudolf Schwarz.
Pub. 1912, Durand: incl. min. score, reduction by Albert Roussel for two pianos, reduction by L. Roques for piano four hands.

BIBLIOGRAPHY:
M.-D. Calvocoressi: Les Evocations, *Comoedia-illustré*, June 1912.
Alfredo Casella: Les Evocations, *Le Monde musical*, April 1913.
G. Jean-Aubry: Les Evocations d'AR, in *La Musique française d'aujourd'hui*, Perrin (Paris) 1916, p. 133.
Florent Schmitt: The Evocations of M. AR, *MS*, 19 April 1913, p. 334; reprinted from *La France*, 2 April 1913.

28. Sonatine Op. 16. For piano. Dated: 3 September 1912, Port-Goulphar. Ded. Marthe Dron. Dur. 10′.
  1. *Modéré—Vif et très léger*; 2. *Très lent—Modéré*.
fp: 18 January 1913, Paris, Salle Erard, Marthe Dron.
fEp: 23 October 1925, Lucie Caffaret.
fEbp: 29 April 1938, Frank Mannheimer.
Pub. 1912, Durand.

29. Le Festin de l'Araignée Op. 17. Ballet-pantomime in one act. 1912. Scenario: Count Gilbert de Voisins. Ded. Jacques Rouché. Dur. 38′.
2 fl, pic, 2 ob, ca, 2 cl, 2 bsn; 2 hn, 2 tpt; timp, GC, cym, tgle, tamb de basque, tambour, tamtam; celesta, hp, strings.
fp: 3 April 1913, Paris, Théâtre des Arts, cond. Gabriel Grovlez; with Sahari Djeli (L'Araignée); décors, Maxime Dethomas; choreography, Léo Staats.
Pub. Durand; incl. reduction by Albert Roussel for piano solo.

BIBLIOGRAPHY:
José Bruyr: AR et le Festin de l'Araignée, *Radio Magazine*, 5 September 1937.
Raymond Charpentier: Le Festin de l'Araignée, *Comoedia*, 7 December 1922.
Henri de Curzon: Le Festin de l'Araignée, *Le Théâtre*, September 1913.
Robert Dézarneaux: Le Festin de l'Araignée, *La Liberté*, 8 December 1922.
Louis Laloy: Le Festin de l'Araignée, *Revue des deux mondes*, 1 August 1939, p. 704.
M. Montagu-Nathan: AR's Spider's Web, *MO*, August 1914, p. 886.

29a. Le Festin de l'Araignée: Fragments

symphoniques. October–December 1912, Bois-le-Roy, Paris. Dur. 17′.

2 fl, pic, 2 ob, ca, 2 cl, 2 bsn; 2 hn, 2 tpt; 2 timp, GC, cym, tambour, tgle; celesta, hp, strings.

fEp: 23 October 1920, Queen's Hall, New Queen's Hall Orchestra, cond. Sir Henry Wood.

fEbp: 21 August 1933, BBC Orchestra, cond. Edward Clark.

Pub. 1913, Durand; incl. reduction by Léon Roques for piano four hands.

30. Petit canon perpétuel. For piano. 1913. Ded. Mme la Comtesse de Chaumont-Quitry.

fEbp: 27 May 1934, Esther Fischer.
Pub. Durand.

31. Padmâvatî Op. 18. Opera-ballet in two acts. 1914–18. Full score dated: 2 July 1918. Poem: Louis Laloy. Ded. Mme Albert Roussel. Dur. 95′.

4 fl, 2 pic, 3 ob, ca, E flat cl, 2 cl, bcl, 3 bsn, cbsn; 4 hn, 4 tpt, 3 tmb, tuba; 3 timp, tgle, tambour, tamb de basque, cym, GC, tamtam; celesta, 2 hp, strings.

fp: 1 June 1923, Paris, Opéra, cond. Philippe Gaubert; with Mlle Lapeyrette (Padmâvatî), Mlle Laval (Nakamti), Franz (Ratan-Sen), Rouard (Alaouddin), Fabert (Le Brahmane); producer, Pierre Chéreau; décors, Valdo-Barbey; choreography, Léo Staats.

fEp (excerpts only): 9 November 1937, BBC broadcast, BBC Orchestra, cond. Nadia Boulanger; with Nathalie Kédroff (Padmâvatî), Irène Kédroff (Nakamti), Hugues Cuenod (Le Brahmane).

Pub. 1919 (vocal score), 1924 (full score), Durand.

BIBLIOGRAPHY:

Georges Auric: Padmâvatî, *Les Nouvelles littéraires*, 9 June 1923.

Paul Bertrand: Padmâvatî, *Le Ménestrel*, 8 June 1923, p. 256.

Maurice Bex: Padmâvatî, *Revue hebdomadaire*, 4 August 1923, p. 110.

Adolphe Boschot: Padmâvatî, *Revue politique et littéraire* (*Revue bleue*), 1923, p. 462.

André Coeuroy: Padmâvatî, opéra-ballet, *Revue universelle*, 1 August 1923, p. 370.

Martin Cooper: Padmâvatî, *The Listener*, 5 July 1962, p. 37.

Xavier de Courville: La mise en scène de Padmâvatî, *RM*, July 1923.

Paul Dukas: Padmâvatî, *Le Quotidien*, 7 June 1923.

— Padmâvatî, *Le Monde musical*, June 1923.

René Dumesnil: Le Padmâvatî d'AR, *SM*, 1947.

Arthur Hoérée: Hommage à Louis Laloy et à AR, *L'Information musicale*, 31 March 1944, p. 247.

Jean Marnold: Padmâvatî, opéra-ballet, poème de M. Louis Laloy, musique de M. AR, *Mercure de France*, No. 609, 1 November 1923, p. 776.

Jean Poueigh: Opéra, réprise de Padmâvatî, *Revue hommes et mondes*, No. 7, February 1947, p. 393.

Gustave Samazeuilh: Opéra, Padmâvatî, *Beaux Arts*, 15 June 1923, p. 172.

C. Tenroc: Padmâvatî, *Le Courrier musical*, 15 June 1923.

Valdo-Barbey: Naissance de Padmâvatî, *RM*, November 1937, p. 344.

31a. Padmâvatî: Suite No. 1. Dur. 17′. Pub. Durand.

31b. Padmâvatî: Suite No. 2. Dur. 14′.

fp: 24 January 1926, Paris, Théâtre du Châtelet, Orchestre Colonne, cond. Gabriel Pierné.

Pub. Durand.

32. Deux mélodies Op. 19. For voice and piano. 1918.

1. *Light* (G. Jean-Aubry). Ded. Mme Gaston Frager. Dur. 4′.

2. *A Farewell* (E. Oliphant). Ded. Edwin Evans. Dur. 3′ 30″.

fp: 27 December 1919, Paris, Salle des Agriculteurs, Société Nationale de Musique concert, Lucy Vuillemin and Louis Vuillemin.

fEbp: 14 December 1933, Anne Thursfield.
Pub. 1919, Durand.

33. Deux mélodies Op. 20 (René Chalupt). For voice and orchestra or piano. 1919.

1. *Le Bachelier de Salamanque*. Ded. Jacques Durand. Dur. 1′ 30″.

2. *Sarabande*. Ded. Lucy Vuillemin. Dur. 2′ 30″.

2 fl, 2 ob, 2 cl, 2 bsn; 2 hn, 2 tpt; tgle, cym, GC; celesta, hp, strings.

fp (with orchestra): 9 December 1928, Paris, Claire Croiza and l'Orchestre Symphonique de Paris, cond. Louis Fourestier.

fEbp (No. 1): 6 July 1927, Sara Fischer.

fEbp (complete): 31 October 1932, Claire Croiza.

Pub. 1919, Durand.

34. Impromptu Op. 21. For harp. March 1919. Ded. Lily Laskine. Dur. 5′.

fp (private): 6 April 1919, Paris, home of Mlle Goupil, Lily Laskine.

fp (public): 14 December 1919, Paris, Salle Gaveau, Société Musicale Indépendante concert, Lily Laskine.

?fEp: 28 January 1925, Wigmore Hall, Maria Korchinska.

fEbp: 20 August 1934, Maria Korchinska.

Pub. 1919, Durand.

35. Doute. For piano. 1919. Ded. Claude Duboscq. Dur. 4′.

fp: 15 May 1920, Paris, Société Nationale de Musique concert, Mme Grovlez.

Pub. 15 December 1919, in *Feuillets d'Art*, No. 4; 1948, Durand.

36. Pour une fête de printemps Op. 22. Symphonic Poem for orchestra, January–February 1920. Ded. Eugène Gigout. Dur. 12′.

2 fl, pic, 2 ob, ca, 2 cl, 3 bsn; 4 hn, 2 tpt, 3 tmb, tuba; timp, tgle, tamb de basque, cym, GC; hp, strings.

fp: 29 October 1921, Paris, Théâtre du Châtelet, Orchestre Colonne, cond. Gabriel Pierné.

fEp: 3 October 1922, Queen's Hall, Promenade Concert, New Queen's Hall Orchestra, cond. Sir Henry Wood.

fGBbp: 13 January 1925, Glasgow, St. Andrew's Hall, Scottish Orchestra, cond. Vaclav Talich.

Pub. 1921, Durand; incl. min. score, reduction by Albert Roussel for two pianos four hands, reduction by L. Garban for piano four hands.

BIBLIOGRAPHY:

P. Giriat: Pour une fête de printemps, *Gazette artistique*, 1 March 1924.

Darius Milhaud: Pour une fête de printemps, *Le Courrier musical*, November 1921.

37. Symphony No. 2 in B flat Op. 23. 1919–20 (?orch. 1921). Ded. Rhené-Bâton. Dur. 40′.

1. *Lent—Assez animé*. Dated: July–September 1919.

2. *Modéré*. Dated: April 1920.

3. *Très lent—Modérément animé*. Dated: June–August 1920.

3 fl, pic, 2 ob, ca, 2 cl, bcl, 3 bsn, cbsn; 4 hn, 4 tpt, 3 tmb, tuba; timp, tgle, tamb de basque, cym, GC; celesta, 2 hp, strings.

fp: 4 March 1922, Paris, Théâtre des Champs-Elysées, Orchestre Pasdeloup, cond. Rhené-Bâton.

?fEp: 6 October 1937, Leeds Festival, London Philharmonic Orchestra, cond. Sir Thomas Beecham.

Pub. Durand; incl. min. score, reduction by Albert Roussel for two pianos four hands, reduction by L. Garban for piano four hands.

BIBLIOGRAPHY:

Roland-Manuel: Roussel's new symphony, *MN&H*, 22 April 1922, p. 501.

38. L'Accueil des Muses. For piano. September 1920. Ded. to the memory of Claude Debussy. Dur. 4′.

fp: 24 January 1921, Paris, Salle des Agriculteurs, Société Musicale Indépendant concert in memory of Debussy, Ernest Lévy.

Pub. December 1920, Revue musicale; Durand.

39. Fanfare pour un sacre païen. For brass and drums. October 1921.

fp: 25 April 1929, Paris Opéra, Orchestre Lamoureux, cond. Albert Wolff.

Pub. December 1921, in *Fanfare* (London), for 4 tpt, 3 drums; Durand, for 4 hn, 4 tpt, 3 tmb, 3 timp.

40. La Naissance de la Lyre Op. 24. Music for a 'conte lyrique' in one act and three tableaux, after Sophocles. Text: Théodore Reinach. Dated: (piano score) 15 September 1923, Ste. Marguerite-sur-mer; (full score) 28 March 1924. Ded. Serge Koussevitzky. Dur. 75′.

2 fl, 2 pic, 2 ob, ca, 2 cl, bcl, 3 bsn; 4 hn, 4 tpt, 3 tmb, tuba; timp, cym, GC, tgle, tamb

de basque, tambour, tamtam; celesta, 2 hp, strings.

fp: 1 July 1925, Paris, Opéra, cond. Philippe Gaubert; with (singers) Mlle Denya, Mlle Delvair, (dancer) Mlle de Craponne; producer, Pierre Chéreau; décors, Legueult, Brianchon; choreography, Mme Nijinska.

Pub. 1924, Durand; incl. vocal score by Albert Roussel.

BIBLIOGRAPHY:

Jean Chantavoine: La Naissance de la lyre, *Le Ménestrel*, 10 July 1925, p. 303.

A. Dayrolles: La Naissance de la lyre, *Revue politique et littéraire*, 12 July 1925, p. 38.

Arthur Hoérée: Académie Nationale de Musique—La Naissance de la lyre, *Beaux Arts*, 15 July 1925, p. 234.

A. Jullien: La Naissance de la lyre, *Journal des Débats*, 24 July 1925, p. 150.

Gabriel Marcel: La Naissance de la lyre, *L'Europe nouvelle*, 11 July 1925.

Emile Vuillermoz: La Naissance de la lyre à l'Opéra, *RM*, August 1925, p. 139.

40a. La Naissance de la Lyre: Symphonic Fragments. Dur. 22′.

1. *Prélude*; 2. *Queste des Satyres*; 3. *Lutte des nymphes et des satyres*; 4. *La grotte d'Hermès*; 5. *Danse des nymphes*; 6. *Danse des satyres*.

Orchestration as for No. 40.

fp: 13 November 1927, Paris, Salle Gaveau, Orchestre Lamoureux, cond. Paul Paray.

Pub. 1927, Durand.

41. Madrigal aux Muses Op. 25 (Gentil Bernard). For three female voices (SSC) a cappella. Dated: 16–20 October 1923. Ded. Poul Schierbeck.

fp: 6 February 1924, Paris, Salle Pleyel, Société Musicale Indépendante concert, Groupe Nivard.

Pub. 1923, Durand.

42. Deux Poèmes de Ronsard Op. 26. For voice and flute. Dated: April 1924.

1. *Rossignol, mon mignon*. Ded. Ninon Vallin. Dur. 3′ 30″. Pub. May 1924, Revue musicale.

2. *Ciel, aer et vens*. Ded. Claire Croiza. Dur. 2′ 30″.

fp (No. 1): 15 May 1924, Théâtre du Vieux-Colombier, Revue Musicale 'Hommage à Ronsard' concert, Ninon Vallin.

fp (No. 2): 28 May 1924, Paris, Claire Croiza.

fEp (Nos. 1 & 2): 5 July 1928, Arts Theatre Club, Sara Fischer and Robert Murchie.

Pub. 1924, Durand.

BIBLIOGRAPHY:

Maurice Bex: Le Tombeau de Ronsard, *Revue hebdomadaire*, 7 June 1924, p. 108.

43. Joueurs de flûte Op. 27. For flute and piano. August–September 1924, Vasterival.

1. *Pan*. Ded. Marcel Moyse.
2. *Tityre*. Ded. Gaston Blanquart.
3. *Krishna*. Ded. Louis Fleury.
4. *Mr. de la Péjaudie*. Ded. Philippe Gaubert.

fp: 17 January 1925, Paris, Théâtre du Vieux-Colombier, Revue Musicale concert, Louis Fleury and Janine Weill.

fEbp (No. 2): 19 August 1934, Joseph Slater and Angus Morrison.

fEbp (No. 1): 25 October 1937, Arthur Gleghorn.

Pub. 1925, Durand.

44. Violin Sonata No. 2 in A major Op. 28. January–September 1924. Ded. J. Guy Ropartz. Dur. 17′.

1. *Allegro con moto*; 2. *Andante*; 3. *Presto*.

fp: 15 October 1925, Paris, Salle Gaveau, Société Musicale Indépendante concert, Asselin and Lucie Caffaret.

fEp: April 1927, Westminster, Joseph Szigeti and Max Pirani.

fEbp: 13 July 1931, Alphonse Onnou and Stefan Askenase.

Pub. Durand.

45. Ségovia Op. 29. For guitar. Dated: April 1925. Ded. Andrès Segovia. Dur. 3′.

fp: 25 April 1925, Madrid, ? Segovia.

f Paris p: 13 May 1925, Segovia.

Pub. 1925, Durand; incl. version by Albert Roussel for piano solo.

46. Sérénade Op. 30. For flute, violin, viola, cello and harp. July–September 1925. Dated: 7 September 1925, Vasterival, Ste. Marguerite-sur-mer.

1. *Allegro*; 2. *Andante*; 3. *Presto*.

fp: 15 October 1925, Paris, Salle Gaveau, Société Musicale Indépendante concert, Quintette Instrumentale de Paris (René Le Roy, Pierre Jamet, René Bas, Pierre Grout, R. Boulmé).

?fEp: 30 November 1930, Quintette Instrumentale de Paris.

Pub. 1926, Durand; incl. reduction by L. Garban for piano four hands.

47. Duo. For bassoon and cello or double-bass. 1925. Ded. Serge Koussevitzky (on the occasion of his nomination as Chevalier de la Légion d'Honneur). Dur. 5′.

fp: 23 December 1940, Paris, Salle Chopin, F. Oubradous and G. Marchésini.

Pub. 1943, Durand.

48. Odes Anacréontiques Op. 31 & Op. 32 (Transl. Leconte de Lisle). For voice and piano. April–September 1926.

Op. 31:

1. *Ode XVI: Sur lui-même.* Ded. Tony Jourdan. Dur. 1′ 15″.

2. *Ode XIX: Qu'il faut boire.* Ded. Charles Sautelet. Dur. 1′.

3. *Ode XX: Sur une jeune fille.* Ded. René Dommange. Dur. 1′ 45″.

Op. 32:

1. *Ode XXVI: Sur lui-même.* Ded. Henry Fabert. Dur. 1′ 15″.

2. *Ode XXXIV: Sur une jeune fille.* Ded. Edmond Warnery. Dur. 1′ 15″.

3. *Ode XLIV: Sur un songe.* Ded. Henry Le Boeuf. Dur. 1′ 15″.

fp (Odes XX & XLIV): 17 May 1926, Concerts Bathori.

fp (complete): 30 May 1927, Concerts Durand, Edmond Warnery.

Pub. 1927, Durand.

48a. Odes Anacréontiques Op. 31 & Op. 32. Version with orchestra.

1. *Ode XVI* (Op. 31 No. 1).

2. *Ode XXVI* (Op. 32 No. 1).

3. *Ode XXXIV* (Op. 32 No. 2).

2 fl, 2 ob, 2 cl, 2 bsn; 2 hn, 2 tpt; timp, pcssn; hp, strings.

Pub. Durand.

49. Suite in F Op. 33. For orchestra. January–September 1926. Ded. Serge Koussevitsky. Dur. 16′.

1. *Prélude.* Dur. 4′.

2. *Sarabande.* Dur. 7′.

3. *Gigue.* Dur. 5′.

50. Le Bardit des Francs. For four-part male chorus a cappella. 1926. Ded. to the memory of Christian Preisach. Dur. 6′.

fp: 21 April 1928, Strasbourg, Chorale Strasbourgeoise, cond. E. G. Münch.

Pub. in Le Renouveau Choral (Colmar).

50a. Le Bardit des Francs. Version with brass and percussion. 1926.

2 tpt, 2 hn, 3 tmb, tuba; 2 timp, 2 cym, GC, tamtam.

Pub. 1934, Durand.

51. Concert Op. 34. For small orchestra. October 1926–February 1927. Ded. Walther Straram. Dur. 15′.

1. *Allegro*; 2. *Andante*; 3. *Presto.*

2 fl, pic, 2 ob, 2 cl, 2 bsn; 2 hn, 2 tpt; timp; strings.

fp: 5 May 1927, Paris, Concerts Straram, cond. Walther Straram.

fEbp (?fEp): 23 October 1932, BBC broadcast, BBC Orchestra, cond. Percy Pitt.

Pub. 1927, Durand.

BIBLIOGRAPHY:

Gustave Bret: Concert pour petit orchestre, *Intransigeant*, 10 May 1927.

52. Sarabande. For the ballet 'L'Eventail de Jeanne'. April 1927. Ded. Jeanne Dubost.

2 fl, 2 ob, 2 cl, 2 bsn; 2 hn, 2 tpt; cym, GC; strings.

fp: 16 June 1927, Paris, privately given by René and Jeanne Dubost, cond. Roger Désormière; choreography, Yvonne Franck and Alice Bourgat; costumes, Marie Laurencin; décors and lighting, Pierre Legrain and René Moulaërt; with Alice Bourgat.

fp (public): 4 March 1929, Paris, Opéra, cond. J.-E. Szyfer; choreography, Yvonne Franck and Alice Bourgat; with Tamara Toumanova, Mlle Storms, Marcelle Bourgat, M. le Joyeux.

fEbp: 11 July 1949, Leighton Lucas Orchestra, cond. Leighton Lucas.

Pub. 1928, Heugel.

52a. Sarabande. Version for piano duet.

Roussel, Albert

fEbp: 28 December 1933, Vitya Vronsky and Victor Babin.
Pub. Heugel.

53. Deux poèmes chinois Op. 35 (H. P. Roché, from the English translation by Herbert Gilles). For voice and piano. 1927.
1. *Des fleurs font une broderie* (Li-Ho, 9th cent.). Dated: 25 June 1927, Vasterival. Ded. Pierre Bernac. Dur. 1' 30".
2. *Réponse d'une épouse sage* (Chang-Chi, 8th–9th cent.). Ded. Marcelle Gérar. Dur. 3'.
fp (No. 1): 5 July 1928, Fontainebleau, Pierre Bernac.
fp (No. 2): 23 May 1927, Paris, Marcelle Gérar.
fEbp (No. 1): 22 February 1939, Pierre Bernac and Francis Poulenc.
fEbp (No. 2): 6 September 1949, Geneviève Touraine and Frederick Stone.
Pub. 1927, Durand.

53a. Réponse d'une épouse sage. Version with orchestra.
2 fl, 2 ob, 2 cl, 2 bsn; 2 hn, 2 tpt; timp, tgle; strings.
fp: 9 December 1928, Paris, Claire Croiza and l'Orchestre Symphonique de Paris, cond. Louis Fourestier.
Pub. Durand.

54. Piano Concerto in G Op. 36. July–October 1927. Ded. Lucie Caffaret. Dur. 16'.
1. *Allegro molto*; 2. *Adagio*; 3. *Allegro con spirito*.
2 fl, pic, ob, ca, 2 cl, 2 bsn; 2 hn, 2 tpt; 3 timp, cym, GC, caisse claire, tgle; strings.
fp: 7 June 1928, Paris, Concerts Koussevitsky, Alexandre Borovsky, cond. Serge Koussevitzky.
?fEp: 14 December 1937, BBC broadcast, Roussel memorial concert, Frank Mannheimer and the BBC Orchestra, cond. Sir Henry Wood.
Pub. 1928, Durand; incl. reduction for two pianos four hands.

55. Vocalise No. 1. For voice and piano. 1927. Dur. 1' 45".
fp: 20 December 1928, Mlle J. Darnay.
Pub. 1928, Lemoine.

56. Vocalise No. 2. For voice and piano.

1928. Ded. Mme Régine de Lormoy. Dur. 2' 30".
fp: 13 April 1929, Paris, Régine de Lormoy and Pierre Maire.
Pub. 1930, Leduc.

56a. Vocalise No. 2. Version orchestrated by Arthur Hoérée.
fl, cl, bsn; tpt, hn; celesta, tgle; hp, strings.
fp: 17 December 1930, Charleroi, Roussel Festival, Régine de Lormoy, cond. Fernand Quinet.
Pub. 1930, Leduc; also arr. by Arthur Hoérée as *Aria* for flute (or oboe, or clarinet, or violin, or viola, or cello) and piano or orchestra.

57. Psalm 80 Op. 37. For tenor, mixed chorus and orchestra. April–August 1928. Dated: 31 August 1928. Ded. Her Majesty Queen Elisabeth of the Belgians. Dur. 23'.
2 fl, pic, 2 ob, ca, 2 cl, bcl, 2 bsn, dbsn; 4 hn, 4 tpt, 3 tmb, tuba; timp, cym, GC, tgle, snare dm, tamtam; hp, strings.
fp: 25 April 1929, Paris, Théâtre National de l'Opéra, Jouatte (tenor), Chorale de la Schola de Nantes, Orchestre Lamoureux, cond. Albert Wolff.
fEp: 28 July 1931, ISCM Festival, Parry Jones, BBC Wireless Chorus and BBC Symphony Orchestra, cond. Sir Adrian Boult; sung in English.
Pub. 1929, Birchard (Boston, Mass.); incl. vocal score.

BIBLIOGRAPHY:
Maurice Brillant: Psaume LXXX, *Le Correspondant*, 25 June 1929.
Paul Collaer: Psaume LXXX, *Pult und Taktstock*, 1930, No. 7.
Pierre Leroi: Psaume LXXX, *Excelsior*, 30 November 1931.
Henry Prunières: Le Psaume LXXX, *RM*, April 1929, p. 45.
— AR and the Eightieth Psalm (transl. F. H. Martens), *MQ*, January 1930, p. 52.

58. O bon vin, où as-tu crû? 'Chanson du terroir' from Champagne, collected by Mme G. Dévignes, harmonised by Albert Roussel. October 1928. Ded. Régine de Lormoy.
fp: 13 April 1929, Régine de Lormoy and Albert Roussel.
Pub. 1935, Durand.

59. Jazz dans la nuit Op. 38 (René Dommange). For voice and piano. December 1928. Ded. Mme René Dommange. Dur. 3′ 30″.

fp: 18 April 1929, Paris, Salle Gaveau, Festival Roussel, Claire Croiza.

fEbp: 27 November 1937, Claire Croiza.

Pub. 1929, Durand; Eng. version by Rosa Newmarch.

59a. Jazz dans la nuit Op. 38. Version orchestrated by P. Vellones.

2 tpt, ten tmb, alto sax, ten sax, bar sax; banjo; timp, pcssn; piano; cbs.

60. Petite Suite Op. 39. For orchestra. January–June 1929.

1. *Aubade*. Dated: 31 January 1929, Paris. Ded. Mme Henry Le Boeuf.

2. *Pastorale*. Dated: June 1929, Vesterival. Ded. Mme Kristoffer Nirop.

3. *Mascarade*. Dated: 31 January 1929, Paris. Ded. Mme Jules Destrée.

2 fl, pic, 2 ob, 2 cl, 2 bsn; 2 hn, 2 tpt; timp, tgle, GC, cym, tamb de basque, tambour, cast; strings.

fp (Nos. 1 & 3): 11 April 1929, Paris, Théâtre des Champs-Elysées, Festival Roussel, cond. Walter Straram.

fp (complete): 6 February 1930, Paris, Concerts Straram, cond. Walter Straram.

fEbp: 28 April 1937, BBC Orchestra, cond. Constant Lambert.

Pub. 1929, Durand; incl. reduction by Albert Roussel for piano four hands.

61. Trio Op. 40. For flute, viola and cello. Dated: 22 September 1929, Vasterival. Ded. Mrs. Elizabeth Sprague Coolidge. Dur. 13′.

1. *Allegro grazioso*; 2. *Andante*; 3. *Allegro non troppo*.

?fp: 29 October 1929, Paris, Concerts Coolidge, Barrère (flute), Lionel Tertis (viola) and Hans Kindler (cello).

fEp: 27 November 1930, Armitage Hall (Great Portland Street), Quintette Instrumentale de Paris concert.

fEbp: 18 December 1930, Robert Murchie, Germain Prevost and Robert Maas.

Pub. 1930, Durand.

62. Prélude et Fughette Op. 41. For organ. July 1929. Ded. Nadia Boulanger. Dur. 4′ 30″.

fp: 18 May 1930, Paris, Mlle Pédelièvre.

fEbp: 17 October 1952, Arnold Richardson, All Souls', Langham Place.

Pub. 1930, Durand. Also transcribed by F. Goldbeck for string orchestra.

63. Symphony No. 3 in G minor Op. 42. August 1929–29 March 1930, Vasterival, Paris. Ded. Boston Symphony Orchestra and its conductor Serge Koussevitzky. Dur. 23′.

1. *Allegro vivo*; 2. *Adagio*; 3. *Vivace*; 4. *Allegro con spirito*.

3 fl, pic, 2 ob, ca, 2 cl, bcl, 2 bsn, cbsn; 4 hn, 4 tpt, 3 tmb, tuba; timp, tgle, cym, GC, tamb de basque, tamb, tamtam; celesta, 2 hp, strings.

fp: 24 October 1930, Boston, Boston Symphony Orchestra, cond. Serge Koussevitzky.

fFp: 28 November 1931, Paris, Salle Gaveau, Orchestre Lamoureux, cond. Albert Wolff.

fEp: 20 January 1933, BBC concert before an invited audience, BBC Orchestra, cond. Sir Adrian Boult. Note also: 22 April 1934, BBC broadcast, BBC Orchestra, cond. Ernest Ansermet.

Pub. 1931, Durand.

BIBLIOGRAPHY:

Henry Prunières: La Troisième Symphonie en sol mineur d'AR à l'Orchestre Symphonique de Boston, *RM*, January 1931, p. 77.

Charles Stuart: Roussel's Third Symphony, *Halle*, October 1950, p. 3.

Emile Vuillermoz: 3e Symphonie, *Excelsior*, 30 November 1931.

64. Bacchus et Ariane Op. 43. Ballet in two acts. June–December 1930. Scenario: Abel Hermant. Ded. Mme Hélène Tony-Jourdan. Dur. 39′.

2 fl, pic, 2 ob, ca, 2 cl, bcl, 2 bsn, cbsn; 4 hn, 4 tpt, 3 tmb, tuba; timp, GC, cym, tamtam; celesta, 2 hp, strings.

fp: 22 May 1931, Paris, Opéra, cond. Philippe Gaubert; décors, Georges de Chirico; choreography, Serge Lifar; with Serge Lifar, Mlle Spessitziva, Peretti, Rosita Cérès, Mlle Simoni.

Pub. 1931, Durand; incl. reduction by Albert Roussel for piano solo.

Roussel, Albert

BIBLIOGRAPHY:
André Coeuroy: Bacchus et Ariane, *Paris-Midi*, 25 May 1931.
Henri de Curzon: Bacchus et Ariane, *Journal des Débats*, 5 June 1931, p. 945.
Henriette Denizeau: Bacchus et Ariane, *Appogiature*, June 1931.
Louis Laloy: Bacchus et Ariane, *Revue des deux mondes*, 1 July 1931, p. 219.
André Levinson: Bacchus et Ariane, in *Visages de la Danse*, Grasset (Paris), p. 134.

64a. Bacchus et Ariane: Suite No. 1 Op. 43. Dur. 18'.
Orchestration as for No. 64.
fp: 2 April 1933, Paris, Salle Pleyel, Orchestre Symphonique de Paris, cond. Charles Münch.
?fEp: 10 June 1949, BBC broadcast, BBC Symphony Orchestra, cond. Sir Adrian Boult.

64b. Bacchus et Ariane: Suite No. 2 Op. 43. Dur. 21'.
Orchestration as for No. 64.
fp: 2 February 1934, Paris, Salle Pleyel, Orchestre Symphonique de Paris, cond. Pierre Monteux.
fEp: 5 November 1945, BBC broadcast, Paris Conservatoire Orchestra, cond. Charles Münch.

65. Deux Idylles Op. 44 (Transl. Leconte de Lisle). For voice and piano. 1931.
1. *Le Kérioklèpte* (Theocritus). Dated: 5 May 1931. Ded. Régine de Lormoy. Dur. 1' 30".
2. *Pan aimait Ekho* (Moskhos). Dated: 16 October 1931. Ded. Yvonne Brothier. Dur. 1' 30".
fp: 5 March 1932, Paris, Société Nationale de Musique concert, Régine de Lormoy, acc. Arthur Hoérée.
Pub. 1931, Durand.

66. A flower given to my daughter Op. 44 (James Joyce). For voice and piano. 1931. Dur. 1' 45".
fp: 16 March 1932, London, Dorothy Moulton.
Pub. 1932, in The Joyce Book, Sylvan Press (London); 1948, Durand; Fr. transl. by Rollo H. Myers.

67. String Quartet in D major Op. 45. December 1931–4 June 1932, Vasterival. Ded. Henry Le Boeuf.
1. *Allegro*; 2. *Adagio*; 3. *Allegro vivo*; 4. *Allegro moderato*.
fp: 9 December 1932, Brussels, Pro Arte Quartet.
f Paris p: 16 December 1932, Le Triton concert, Roth Quartet.
fEbp: 26 June 1933, Griller Quartet.
Pub. 1932, Durand.

68. Le Testament de la Tante Caroline. Opéra-bouffe in three acts. 1932–3. Libretto: Nino. Ded. Julia and Jan Reisser. Dur. 115'.
fl, ob, cl, bsn; hn, tpt, tmb; timp, pcssn; strings.
fp: 14 November 1936, Olmütz, cond. A. Heller: sung in Czech.
fFp: 11 March 1937, Paris, Opéra-Comique, cond. Roger Désormière; with Suzanne Dehelly, Fanely Revoil, Mlle Sibille; décors and costumes, Georges Pitoëff; sung in French.
Pub. Heugel.

BIBLIOGRAPHY:
Louis Aubert: Le Testament de Tante Caroline, *Le Journal*, 11 March 1937.
Reynaldo Hahn: Le Testament de Tante Caroline, *Le Figaro*, 24 March 1937.
Louis Laloy: La Tante Caroline, *Revue des deux mondes*, 15 April 1937, p. 940.
Constantin Photiadès: Le Testament de Tante Caroline, *Revue de Paris*, 1 April 1937.
Henry Prunières: Le Testament de Tante Caroline, opéra-bouffe de Nino, musique d'AR, à l'Opéra-Comique, *RM*, 15 April 1937, p. 194.

68a. Suite-Fantaisie. For small orchestra, arranged by Albert Roussel from 'Le Testament de Tante Caroline'. Dur. 12'.

69. Prelude and Fugue Op. 46. For piano. 1932–4. Ded. Henri Gil-Marchex. Dur. 5'.
1. *Prelude*. 1934.
2. *Fugue* (sur le nom de Bach). September 1932. Pub. December 1932 in Revue Musicale.
fp: 23 February 1935, Paris, Société Nationale de Musique concert, Henri Gil-Marchex.
Pub. 1934, Durand.

70. Deux poèmes chinois Op. 47 (H. P. Roché, after English translations by Herbert Gilles). For voice and piano. September 1932, Vasterival.

    1. *Favorite abandonnée*. Ded. Mme Bourdette-Vial. Dur. 1′ 30″.

    2. *Vois, de belles filles*. Ded. Vera Janacopulos. Dur. 1′ 30″.

fp: 4 May 1934, Paris, Le Triton concert, Mme Bourdette-Vial.

fEbp: 29 January 1953, Myra Verney, acc. Clifton Helliwell.

Pub. 1934, Durand.

71. A Glorious Day Op. 48. For military band. November–December 1932.

fp: July 1933, Paris, Garde Républicaine.

Pub. Durand; incl. conductor's condensed score by Albert Roussel. Arranged also for French and American bands.

72. Trois Pièces Op. 49. For piano. August–November 1933, Vasterival. Ded. Robert Casadesus. Dur. 7′.

    1. *Allegro con brio*; 2. *Allegro grazioso*; 3. *Allegro con spirito*.

fp: 14 April 1934, Paris, Société Nationale de Musique concert, Robert Casadesus.

fEbp: 19 October 1953, Frank Laffitte.

Pub. 1934, Durand.

73. Deux mélodies Op. 50 (René Chalupt). For voice and piano. 1933–4.

    1. *L'heure du retour*. January 1934. Ded. Lucy Vauthrin. Dur. 4′.

    2. *Cœur en péril*. December 1933. Ded. Marcelle Bunlet. Dur. 2′.

fp (No. 1): January 1935, Marcelle Bunlet.

fp (No. 2): December 1934, Marcelle Bunlet.

fEbp (No. 2): 8 September 1935, Anne Thursfield.

Pub. 1934, Durand.

74. Andante and Scherzo Op. 51. For flute and piano. January–April 1934. Ded. Georges Barrère. Dur. 5′.

fp: 17 December 1934, Convegno de Milan.

Pub. 1934, Durand.

75. Pipe in D major. For French flageolet and piano. 1934. Ded. Mrs. James Dyer. Dur. 1′ 15″. Pub. 1934, Editions de l'Oiseau-Lyre.

76. Sinfonietta Op. 52. For string orchestra. Dated: 12 June–6 August 1934. Ded. Jane Evrard. Dur. 8′.

    1. *Allegro molto*; 2. *Andante*; 3. *Allegro*.

fp: 19 November 1934, Paris, Salle Gaveau, Evrard ladies' orchestra, cond. Jane Evrard.

fEp: 8 December 1939, BBC broadcast, BBC Orchestra, cond. Anthony Bernard.

Pub. 1934, Durand.

BIBLIOGRAPHY:

Arthur Hoérée: AR, Sinfonietta, *RM*, January 1935, p. 44.

77. Symphony No. 4 in A major Op. 53. Dated: 10 August–31 December 1934. Ded. Albert Wolff.

    1. *Lento—Allegro con brio*; 2. *Lento molto*; 3. *Allegro scherzando*; 4. *Allegro molto*.

2 fl, pic, 2 ob, ca, 2 cl, bcl, 2 bsn, cbsn; 4 hn, 4 tpt, 3 tmb, tuba; timp, tamb, tgle, cym, GC; hp, strings.

fp: 19 October 1935, Paris, Opéra-Comique, Orchestre Pasdeloup, cond. Albert Wolff.

fEp: 9 February 1936, BBC broadcast, BBC Orchestra, cond. Sir Adrian Boult.

Pub. 1935, Durand.

BIBLIOGRAPHY:

Robert Bernard: La Quatrième Symphonie d'AR, *RM*, November 1935, p. 275.

Paul Dambly: 4ᵉ Symphonie, *Le petit journal*, 21 October 1935.

George Linstead: Roussel and the Fourth Symphony, *Halle*, March 1957, p. 4.

78. Aenéas Op. 54. Ballet with chorus in one act and two tableaux. March–April 1935. Text: Joseph Weterings. Ded. to the memory of Henry Le Boeuf. Dur. 37′.

    1. *Prélude*; 2. *Introduction*; 3. *Les Epreuves d'Aenéas*; 4. *Hymne Final*.

2 fl, pic, 2 ob, ca, 2 cl, bcl, 2 bsn, cbsn; 4 hn, 3 tpt, 3 tmb, tuba; timp, tgle, cym, GC, tamtam; piano, strings.

fp: 31 July 1935, Brussels, Palais des Beaux Arts, Chorale de la Société Philharmonique, cond. Hermann Scherchen; décors, Hélène Scherbatow; choreography, Léonide Katchourowsky; with Léonide Katchourowsky (Aenéas), Marie Tchernova (Didon).

f Paris p: 4 April 1938, Odéon, cond.

451

Roussel, Albert

Philippe Gaubert; choreography, Serge Lifar; décors and costumes, René Moulaërt.

fEp (concert): 19 November 1954, Royal Festival Hall, London Philharmonic Choir and Orchestra, cond. Jean Martinon.

fEp (broadcast): 3 December 1954, London Philharmonic Choir and BBC Symphony Orchestra, cond. Walter Goehr.

Pub. 1936, Durand; incl. vocal score by the composer.

BIBLIOGRAPHY:

André Coeuroy: Aenéas et hommage à Roussel, *Beaux Arts*, 15 April 1938.

André George: Aenéas de Roussel, *Les Nouvelles littéraires*, 7 May 1938.

Fr. Goldbeck: Le Ballet d'Aenéas: Quelques refléxions sur les rapports de la musique et de la choréographie, *RM*, April–May 1938, p. 282.

Guido Pannain: Aenéas, *Il Mattino* (Naples), 20 January 1937.

Henry Prunières: Le Ballet Aenéas d'AR à Bruxelles, *SM*, September–October 1935, p. 237.

Willi Reich: Aenéas, *Beaux Arts*, 9 August 1935.

79. Deux mélodies Op. 55 (Georges Ville). For voice and piano. 1935.

1. *Vieilles cartes, vieilles mains*. Dated: September 1935, Vasterival. Ded. Mme Blanc-Audra. Dur. 1′ 30″.

2. *Si quelquefois tu pleures...* Dated: October 1935, Vasterival. Ded. Madeleine Vhita. Dur. 1′ 30″.

fp: 24 January 1936, Paris, Mme Blanc-Audra.

Pub. 1936, Durand.

80. Prélude. Incidental music for 'Le Quatorze Juillet' by Romain Rolland. 1936.

4 fl, 2 pic, 4 ob, 8 cl, 4 bsn, 2 cbn, 2 alto sax, 2 ten sax, 2 bar sax; 6 hn, 6 tpt, 3 tmb, bs tmb, 2 tubas; timp, GC, cym, tgle, tamb, tamtam.

fp: 14 July 1936, Paris, Théâtre de l'Alhambra, cond. Roger Désormière.

Pub. Chant du Monde. Other contributions to the complete score were by Ibert, Auric, Milhaud, Koechlin, Honegger and Daniel Lazarus.

BIBLIOGRAPHY:

Léon Kochnitzky: Le Quatorze Juillet, action populaire de Romain Rolland, *RM*, July–August 1936, p. 42.

81. Rapsodie flamande Op. 56. For orchestra. April–3 July 1936, Vasterival. Ded. Erich Kleiber. Dur. 10′.

2 fl, pic, 2 ob, ca, 2 cl, bcl, 2 bsn, cbsn; 4 hn, 3 tpt, 3 tmb, tuba; 3 timp, tgle, tamb, tamb de basque, tamtam, caisse claire, cym, GC; hp, strings.

fp: 12 December 1936, Brussels, Société Philharmonique, cond. Erich Kleiber.

fFp: 21 January 1937, Paris, Orchestre Philharmonique de Paris, cond. Charles Münch.

fEp: 14 December 1937, BBC broadcast, Roussel memorial concert, BBC Orchestra, cond. Sir Henry Wood.

fEp (concert): 8 September 1938, Queen's Hall, Promenade Concert.

Pub. 1936, Durand.

BIBLIOGRAPHY:

Arthur Hoérée: Rapsodie flamande par AR, *RM*, February 1937, p. 129.

82. Concertino Op. 57. For cello and orchestra. August–September 1936. Ded. Marix Loevensohn. Dur. 12′.

1. *Allegro moderato*; 2. *Adagio*; 3. *Allegro molto*.

2 fl, 2 ob, 2 cl, 2 bsn; 2 hn, 2 tpt; timp; strings.

fp: 6 February 1937, Paris, Salle Pleyel, Concerts Poulet-Siohan, Pierre Fournier, cond. Robert Siohan.

fEp: 29 October 1937, Pierre Fournier and the BBC Orchestra, cond. Clarence Raybould.

fEp (concert): 5 April 1946, Wigmore Hall, Pierre Fournier and the Leighton Lucas Orchestra.

Pub. 1937, Durand; incl. reduction by the composer.

BIBLIOGRAPHY:

Henry Prunières: Roussel, Concertino pour violoncelle et orchestre, *RM*, February 1937, p. 125.

83. String Trio Op. 58. For violin, viola and cello. June–July 1937. Ded. Pasquier Trio. Dur. 15′.

1. *Allegro moderato*; 2. *Adagio*; 3. *Allegro con spirito*.

fFp: 4 April 1938, Paris, Ecole Normale, Le Triton concert, Pasquier Trio.

fbp: 22 October 1938, BBC broadcast, Pasquier Trio.

Pub. Durand.

BIBLIOGRAPHY:

Conrad Beck: Une création d'AR à Bale: Trio pour violon, alto et violoncelle, *RM*, February 1938, p. 153.

84. Elpénor Op. 59. Incidental music for a 'poème radiophonique' by Joseph Weterings. For flute and string quartet. ?1937. Ded. Juliette Weterings. Dur. 30'. Pub. 1947, Durand.

85. Andante (from an unfinished Trio). For oboe, clarinet and bassoon. July–August 1937.

fp (privately): 30 November 1937, Trio d'Anches de Paris.

Pub. November 1937, Revue Musicale.

GENERAL BIBLIOGRAPHY

Helene Abraham: AR, *L'Art musical populaire*, October–November 1937.

Annèlen: Une visite chez AR, *Algemeen Handelsblad*, 7 May 1928.

Georges Auric: Un de nos Maîtres, *Gringoire*, 19 April 1929.

J. Balzer: AR, *Dansk Musiktidsskrift*, October 1937.

Jane Bathori: Les musiciens que j'ai connus, *Recorded Sound*, winter 1961–2, p. 144.

Robert Bernard: A la mémoire d'AR, *RM*, November 1937, p. 289.

— Dans le souvenir d'AR, in *–do–*, p. 322.

— Les amis d'AR, *RM*, July–August 1938, p. 33.

— AR, *La Revue mensuelle*, September 1938.

— Le souvenir d'AR, *L'Information musicale*, 12 September 1941, p. 3.

— AR, sa vie, son œuvre, La Colombe (Paris) 1948.

Eric Blom: The chamber music of AR, *MO*, July 1921, p. 848.

Nadia Boulanger: L'œuvre théâtrale d'AR, *RM*, May–June 1929, p. 52.

Maurice Brillant: Portrait d'AR, *RM*, April 1929, p. 3.

— AR, *L'Aube*, 29 August 1937.

Robert Brussel: Hommage à un musicien français, *Le Figaro*, 21 May 1929.

— AR, *Le Figaro*, 24 August 1937.

José Bruyr: Un Maréchal de la musique française, *Midi* (Brussels), 16 April 1929.

M.-D. Calvocoressi: AR, in *Musicians Gallery*, Faber & Faber (London) 1933, chapter 5.

— AR, *MT*, October 1937, p. 868.

— AR, *Radio Times*, 10 December 1937, p. 19.

P. Capdevielle: Défense de Roussel, *L'Information musicale*, 13 December 1940, p. 102.

Gaston Carraud: AR, *Le Monde musical*, 15 and 30 January 1920.

René Chalupt: AR, *La Phalange*, 20 August 1910.

— AR, *Nouveautes musicales*, April 1914.

— Conseil aux Sirènes, *Le Courrier musical*, 1 March 1929.

— Hommage à AR, *RM*, April 1929, p. 1.

— Le reflet du monde éxterieur dans l'œuvre d'AR, *RM*, April 1929, p. 20.

— Quelques souvenirs sur AR, *RM*, November 1937, p. 324.

René Chauvet: Souvenirs, *RM*, November 1937, p. 332.

André Coeuroy: AR, in *La Musique française moderne*, Librairie Delagrave (Paris) 1922, p. 59.

— L'inspiration d'AR, *La Revue universelle*, 15 April 1922, p. 263.

— AR, *Anbruch*, April 1921, p. 130.

— AR, *La Chronique de Paris*, July 1944, p. 62.

L. Cortese: AR, *Rivista musicale italiana*, 1937, 6e fasc.

Alfred Cortot: AR, *Le Monde musical*, November 1937.

— L'œuvre pianistique d'AR, *RM*, November 1937, p. 293.

— L'interpretation des œuvres de Ravel et de Roussel, *Le Monde musical*, September 1938.

— AR, in *La Musique française de piano* (troisième série), Paris, 1944.

Henri de Curzon: AR, *Journal des Débats*, 21 September 1937.

— AR, *La Métropole* (Anvers), 10 October 1937.

Georges Dandelot: AR, *Le Monde musical*, August–September 1937.

Basil Deane: AR, Barrie & Rockliff (London) 1961.

André Delacour: AR, ou l'inquiétude créatrice, *L'Européen*, 20 May 1931.

Marcel Delannoy: Un souvenir, *RM*, November 1937, p. 339.

Claude Delvincourt: Le langage harmonique d'AR, *RM*, November 1937, p. 336.

Suzanne Demarquez: Les mélodies d'AR, *Musique*, 15 May 1929.

Norman Demuth: AR—a study, United Music Publishers (London) 1947.

— Roussel and the French tradition, *Music Survey*, No. 3, May 1948.

— Roussel and the French operatic tradition, *Chesterian*, No. 159, July 1949.

— AR, in *Musical Trends in the 20th Century*, Rockliff (London) 1952, p. 59.

Norbert Dufourcq: AR, in *La Musique française*, Librairie Larousse (Paris) 1949, p. 301.

Robert Dumaine: AR, *Le Guide du concert*, 1 and 8 October 1937.

René Dumesnil: AR, *Le Courrier musical*, 1 December 1930.

— AR, *Mercure de France*, 15 September 1937.

— Souvenirs, *RM*, November 1937, p. 336.

— AR, in *Portraits de musiciens français*, Librairie Plon (Paris) 1938, p. 212.

— AR, souvenirs d'amitié, *L'Opéra de Paris*, 1958.

Maurice Emmanuel: Les premières œuvres orchestrales, *RM*, November 1937, p. 309.

Edwin Evans: AR, *Chesterian*, No. 51, December 1925.

— AR, *Chesterian*, No. 138, March–April 1938.

Georges Favre: AR, *Bulletin mensuel de l'Union française des œuvres laïques d'education artistique*, July 1950.

P.-O. Ferroud: La musique de chambre d'AR, *RM*, April 1929, p. 52.

— Un musicien français—AR, *Latinité*, May 1929.

Paul Le Flem: L'œuvre symphonique d'AR, *RM*, April 1929, p. 35.

Alice Gabeaud: AR—six mélodies, *L'Education musicale*, No. 130, July 1966.

R. Gelatt: Chabrier, Roussel, and others, *Saturday Review*, 29 November 1952, p. 74.

André George: AR et la mélodie, *RM*, April 1929, p. 29.

— Témoignage, *RM*, November 1937, p. 334.

Henri Gil-Marchex: La musique de piano d'AR, *RM*, April 1929, p. 65.

Leigh Henry: AR, *MO*, 1923, September p. 1148, October p. 51.

Ralph Hill: AR, *Gramophone Record*, May 1935, p. 4.

Arthur Hoérée: Paying a call on AR, *Eolus*, January 1928.

— Une visite à AR, *Le Courrier musical*, 15 April 1929.

— L'homme, la vie, l'œuvre, *Le Courrier musical*, 1929 (?1 March).

— La technique, *RM*, April 1929, p. 84.

— Für AR, *SM*, 15 May and 1 June 1929.

— A propos du soixentenaire d'AR, *Cahiers de Belgique*, March 1930.

— Le classicisme d'AR, *Le Mois*, December 1932.

— AR et son temps, *Beaux Arts*, 29 June 1934.

— AR, *RM*, August–September 1937, p. 155.

— AR, Editions Rieder (Paris) 1938.

Arno Huth: AR, *Anbruch*, September 1937, p. 226.

G. Jean-Aubry: AR, *Bulletin de la S.I.M.*, 15 October 1908, p. 1083.

— AR, in *La Musique française d'aujourd'hui*, Perrin (Paris) 1916, p. 173.

— AR, *MO*, April 1919, p. 418.

— Une première rencontre, *RM*, April 1929, p. 16.

P. Kaldor: La musique française porte le deuil d'AR, *Commune*, October 1937.

Tristan Klingsor: Festival AR, *Le Monde musical*, November 1937.

Charles Koechlin: Sur AR, *RM*, November 1937, p. 335.

J. Kricka: Odpoledne u Alberta Roussela, *Tempo* (Prague), 1 December 1937.

Paul Landormy: AR (transl. M. M. Marble), *MQ*, October 1938, p. 512.

— AR, in *La Musique française après Debussy*, Gallimard (Paris) 1943, p. 78.

— Pour la mémoire d'AR, *RM*, November 1937, p. 328.

Albert Laurent: Un entretien avec A,R *Guide du concert*, 12 and 19 October 1928.

Edward Lockspeiser: Roussel and Ravel, *M&L*, July 1938, p. 245.

Armand Machabey: AR, *Disques*, September 1937.

Joseph Machlis: AR, in *Introduction to Con-*

temporary *Music*, W. W. Norton (USA) 1961, Dent (London), p. 241.

Henry Malherbe: AR, *Le Temps*, 8 May 1929.

— AR, *MMR*, 1929, p. 200.

John Manduell: AR, in *The Symphony*, Vol. 2, Penguin Books (London) 1967, p. 104.

André Mangeot: AR, *Le Monde musical*, August–September 1937.

Gabriel Marcel: Hommage à AR, *RM*, November 1937, p. 330.

— La musique française en deuil, *La Vie intellectuelle*, 25 February 1938.

Ernest Marion: In memoriam AR, *Les Cahiers du Sud*, November 1937.

Colin Mason: Roussel's chamber music, *The Listener*, 5 February 1959, p. 264.

Pierre Meylan: Lettres inédites d'AR à Auguste Sérieyx, *Feuilles musicales*, February 1959.

— AR et le Suisse, d'après une correspondance inédite, *Schweizerische Musikpädagogische Blätter*, October 1959, No. 4.

Wilfrid Mellers: AR et 'La Musique Française', in *Studies in Contemporary Music*, Dobson (London) 1947, p. 73.

Darius Milhaud: Adieu à AR, *RM*, November 1937, p. 339.

Donald Mitchell: AR, in *Decca Book of Ballet*, Muller (London) 1958, p. 269.

Rollo H. Myers: AR, a forgotten French composer?, *The Listener*, 23 January 1964.

Guido Pannain: Compositori del nostro tempo—AR, *La Rassegna musicale*, 6 June 1929, p. 302.

Henri Petit: AR, *L'Art musical*, 1 October 1937.

R. Petit: Roussel ave vale, *Modern Music*, November–December 1937.

Marc Pincherle: Les cours d'interprétation de M. Vincent d'Indy et AR, *Le Monde musical*, June 1925.

— AR, Geneva, 1957.

Gaston Poulet: Hommage, *RM*, November 1937, p. 343.

V. Reisser: AR als Lehrer, *Der Auftakt*, 1937, Nos. 7–8.

Rhené-Bâton: In memoriam, *RM*, November 1937, p. 340.

Helene Rieder: AR, *Suisse Romande*, November 1937.

Roland-Manuel: AR, *RM*, November 1922, p. 11.

— AR, *Musique*, 15 May (No. 8) 1929.

— AR, *Der Auftakt*, 1937, Nos. 3–4, p. 38.

Kajsa Rootzén: AR, in *Fransk musik*, 1957, p. 69.

Jean Roy: AR, in *Musique française*, Debresse (Paris) 1962, p. 79.

Edmund Rubbra: AR, *MMR*, 1932, p. 217.

Gustave Samazeuilh: AR, *L'Amour d'art*, June 1920.

— Le théâtre d'AR, *Le Courrier musical*, 15 April 1929.

— Mort de M. AR, *Le Temps*, 25 August 1937.

— Le souvenir de Gabriel Pierné, Albert Roussel, Maurice Ravel, in *Musiciens de mon temps*, Editions Marcel Daubin (Paris) 1947, p. 198.

Boris de Schloezer: AR, *Nouvelle revue française*, 1937, No. 289, p. 681.

Louis Schneider: AR, *La Revista de musica*, August 1928.

Marius Schneider: AR, *Anbruch*, April–May 1930, p. 158.

Octave Séré: AR, in *Musiciens français d'aujourd'hui*.

Louis de Serres: AR, *Les Echos de l'Ecole César Franck*, October–November 1937.

R. Turro: Retrato de Roussel, el musico joven, *Buenos Aires Musical*, No. 287 (1963), p. 2.

A. Van der Linden: AR et Octave Maus, *Revue belge de musicologie*, 1950, No. 4, p. 198.

Louis Vuillemin: AR et son œuvre, Durand (Paris) 1924.

J. Weterings: AR, *Cahiers de Belgique*, March 1930.

— Un musicien indépendant, *Beaux Arts*, 2 March 1934.

— A Vasterival avec AR, *Beaux Arts*, 4 December 1936.

— AR, *La Sirène*, September 1937.

G. M. Witkowski: Souvenirs, *RM*, November 1937, p. 342.

H. Woollett: La musique française moderne, *Le Monde musical*, March 1922.

MISCELLANEOUS OR UNSIGNED
AR, *The Times*, 9 November 1945, p. 8.

Acquired tastes—Roussel and Berg, *The Times*, 15 December 1950, p. 8.

AR et la Schola (Une lettre de Paul Poujaud à AR), *Revue internationale de musique*, No. 11, autumn 1951, p. 522.

ERIK SATIE (1866–1925)

Eric Satie—he changed the spelling to 'Erik' in 1888—was born on 17 May 1866 in in Normandy at Honfleur, where his father was a ship-broker. His parents moved to Paris when he was four, leaving him in the charge of grandparents and much under the influence of an eccentric Uncle Adrien. His mother, a Scotswoman, died in 1872 and in 1878 Satie went to live in Paris with his father. He was to live exclusively in Paris for the rest of his life, apart from army service in Arras (1886–7) and a tour of Belgium in the early 1920s. He studied ineffectively at the Paris Conservatoire from 1879 to 1886, served a year in the French Army and then earned a living until the turn of the century as a Montmartre café pianist at the 'Chat-Noir', the 'Auberge du Clou' and the 'Café de la Nouvelle Athènes'. He was also much involved between 1890 and 1895 in Rosicrucianism (as interpreted by Joséphin Péladan) and related mysteries, including his own 'Eglise Métropolitaine d'Art de Jésus Conducteur'. In 1898 he went to live permanently in the Paris suburb of Arcueil-Cachan, where he joined the Radical Socialists and took some part in municipal affairs (children's outings, concerts, the local militia). In 1905, in his fortieth year, he embarked on a three-year course in counterpoint and analysis under Roussel and d'Indy at the Schola Cantorum. Public performances by Debussy and Ravel in 1911 of some of Satie's early works brought about a turning point in his career. Nevertheless, though he always had many friends in the artistic *avant garde*, notably Debussy and Cocteau (whom he met in 1891 and 1915 respectively), he remained an isolated, poor and celibate eccentric. It was Cocteau who arranged that Satie should collaborate with himself, Massine and Picasso on the Diaghilev ballet *Parade*, the stormy première of which in 1917 turned the composer into a father-figure of the New Music in Paris, especially of those musicians (Milhaud and Poulenc among them) who later came to be known as *Les Six*. Other young composers, calling themselves the Arcueil School, gathered around Satie in 1923, while his close association with the Surrealists and the Dadaists was brought to fruition in a further controversial ballet première, that of *Relâche* in November 1924. Soon afterwards it was discovered that Satie (for long a heavy drinker) was suffering from cirrhosis of the liver. This led to pleurisy and his death in July 1925.

CATALOGUE OF WORKS

1. Elégie (J. P. Contamine de Latour). For voice and piano. 1886. Ded. Mlle Céleste Le Prédour. Pub. ?1889, Alfred Satie; 1968, Salabert, as *Trois Mélodies de 1886*, No. 2.

2. Les Anges (J. P. Contamine de Latour). For voice and piano. 1886. Ded. Charles Levadé. Pub. ?1889, Alfred Satie, as *Trois Mélodies* No. 1; 1968, Salabert, as *Trois Mélodies de 1886*, No. 1.

3. Les Fleurs (J. P. Contamine de Latour). For voice and piano. 1886. Ded. Mlle la Comtesse Gérald de Marguenat. Pub. ?1889, Alfred Satie, as *Trois Mélodies* No. 2; 1968, Salabert, as *Trois Autres Mélodies* No. 3.

4. Sylvie (J. P. Contamine de Latour). For voice and piano. 1886. Ded. Mlle Olga Satie. Pub. ?1889, Alfred Satie, as *Trois Mélodies* No. 3; 1968, Salabert, as *Trois Mélodies de 1886* No. 3.

5. Chanson (J. P. Contamine de Latour). For voice and piano. 1887. Ded. Mlle Valentine de Bret. Pub. ?1889, Alfred Satie; 1968, Salabert, as *Trois Autres Mélodies* No. 1.

6. Valse Ballet. For piano. 1885.

7. Fantaisie Valse. For piano. 1885.

8. Ogives. For piano. 1886.

9. Trois Sarabandes. For piano. September 1887. No. 2 ded. Maurice Ravel.
  Pub. Rouart Lerolle.

9a. Trois Sarabandes. Orch. Robert Caby.

2 fl, 2 ob, 2 cl, 2 bsn, sarrusophone; 2 hn, 2 tpt, tmb, tuba; hp, strings.
Pub. Salabert.

10. Trois Gymnopédies. For piano. 1888.
1. *Lent et douloureux.* Ded. Mlle Jeanne de Bret.
2. *Lent et triste.* Ded. Conrad Satie.
3. *Lent et grave.* Ded. Charles Levadé.
Pub. Rouart Lerolle.

10a. Gymnopédies. Nos. 1 & 3 orch. Claude Debussy.
No. 1: 2 fl, ob, 4 hn, strings.
No. 2: 2 fl, ob, 4 hn, cym, 2 hp, strings.
fp: 20 February 1897, Paris, Salle Erard, Société Nationale de Musique concert.
fbp: 10 February 1925, Glasgow station, Scottish Orchestra.
Pub. E. Baudoux.

10b. Gymnopédie No. 2. Orch. Herbert Murrill.
fbp: 31 December 1949, Leighton Lucas Orchestra, cond. Leighton Lucas.

10c. Gymnopédie No. 2. Orch. Roland-Manuel. Pub. Salabert.

11. Trois Gnossiennes. For piano. 1890. Nos. 1 & 3 marked: *Lent.* No. 1 ded. Roland-Manuel. Pub. 1913, Rouart Lerolle.

11a. Gnossienne No. 4. For piano. 1891. Pub. 1968, Salabert. Also version orch. R. Caby.

11b. Gnossienne No. 5. For piano. 8 July 1889. Pub. 1968, Salabert. Also version orch. R. Caby.

11c. Gnossienne No. 6. For piano. 1897. Pub. 1968, Salabert. Also version orch. R. Caby.

11d. Gnossiennes Nos. 1–3. Orch. Lanchberry. Pub. Salabert.

11e. Gnossienne No. 3. Orch. Francis Poulenc. 1939.
fl, ob, cl, 2 bsn; 2 hn; strings.
fEp: 11 September 1947, BBC broadcast, Leighton Lucas Orchestra, cond. Leighton Lucas.
Pub. 1949, Rouart Lerolle.

12. Première pensée Rose + Croix. For Piano. 20 January 1891. Dur. 1′ 16″. Pub. 1968, Salabert.

13. Le Fils des Etoiles. Incidental music (Jules Bois) for flutes and harps. 1891.

13a. Trois Préludes (from 'Le Fils des Etoiles'). For piano. 1891.
1. *Act I: La Vocation.*
2. *Act II: L'Initiation.*
3. *Act III: L'Incantation.*
Pub. Rouart Lerolle.

13b. Le Fils des Etoiles: Prelude, Act I. Reorch. Maurice Ravel. 1913.

13c. Le Fils des Etoiles. Version orch. Roland-Manuel. Pub. Salabert.

14. Hymne au drapeau (pour le Prince de Byzance du Sâr Péladan). For voice and piano. 1891. Pub. 1968, Salabert as *Hymne pour le* 'Salut drapeau'. Also version orch. R. Caby.

15. Uspud. 'Ballet chrétien' in three acts by J. P. Contamine de Latour. 1892. Privately printed. Version orch. R. Caby pub. Salabert.

16. Petite ouverture à danser. For piano. Before 1900. Pub. 1968, Salabert. Also version orch. R. Caby.

17. Poudre d'or. Valse for piano. *c.* 1900. Ded. Mlle Stéphanie Nantas. Pub. ?1901, Rouart Lerolle. Version for café orchestra pub. Salabert.

18. Tendrement (Vincent Hyspa). 'Valse chantée'. *c.* 1900. Pub. ?1902, E. Baudoux/ Bellon Ponscarme. Version with café orchestra acc. pub. Salabert.

19. La Diva de 'L'Empire' (Dominique Bonnaud & Numa Blès). 'Marche chantée' from the revue 'Dévidons la Bobine'. 'Répertoire Paulette Darty.' *c.* 1900. Pub. 1904, Bellon Ponscarme. Version with orchestra pub. Salabert.

19a. La Diva. 'Intermezzo Américain' arr, for piano by Hans Ourdine. Pub. 1919. Rouart Lerolle; also arr. for café orchestra.

20. Je te veux (Henry Pacory). 'Valse chantée.' 'Répertoire Paulette Darty.' *c.* 1900. Pub. ?1905, Bellon Ponscarme.

20a. Je te veux. Version for voice and orchestra.

fl, ob, 2 cl, bsn; 2 tpt, tmb; hp, strings.
Pub. Salabert. Also version for voice and café orchestra.

20b. Valse (Je te veux). For piano. Ded. Paulette Darty. Pub. 1904, Bellon Ponscarme.

20c. Je te veux. Version for small orchestra (?arr. Constant Lambert).
fEp: 14 June 1949, BBC broadcast, section of the London Symphony Orchestra, cond. Constant Lambert.

21. Sonneries de la Rose + Croix. For piano. 1892.
  1. *Air de l'Ordre.*
  2. *Air du Grand Maître.* Ded. Joséphin Péladan.
  3. *Air du Grand Prieur.* Ded. Le Comte Antoine de la Rochefoucauld.
Pub. Rouart Lerolle.

22. Danses gothiques. For piano. Dated: 23 March 1893, 6 rue Cortot.
  1. *A l'occasion d'une grande peine*; 2. *Dans lesquelles les Pères de la Très Véritable et Très Sainte Eglise sont invoqués*; 3. *En faveur d'un malheureux*; 4. *A propos de Saint Bernard et de Sainte Lucie*; 5. *Pour les pauvres trépassés*; 6. *Où il est question du pardon des injures reçues*; 7. *Par pitié pour les ivrognes, honteux, débauchés, imparfaits, désagréables, et faussaires en tous genres*; 8. *En le haut honneur du venéré Saint Michel, le gracieux Archange*; 9. *Après avoir obtenu la remise de ses fautes.*
Pub. 1929, Rouart Lerolle.

23. Quatre Préludes. For piano. 1893.
  1. *Fête donnée par des Chevaliers Normands en l'honneur d'une jeune demoiselle*; 2. *Prélude d'Eginhard*; 3. *1ère Prélude du Nazaréen*; 4. *2me Prélude du Nazaréen.*
Pub. 1929, Rouart Lerolle.

23a. Deux Préludes. Orch. Francis Poulenc. 1939.
No. 1: 2 fl, 2 ob, 2 bsn; 2 hn, tpt, tmb, strings.
No. 3: ob, ca, 2 cl, 2 bsn; 2 hn, 2 tpt, 2 tmb; hp, strings.
Pub. 1949, Rouart Lerolle.

24. Prélude de la Porte Héroïque du Ciel. For piano. 1894. Ded. Erik Satie ('Je me dédie cette œuvre').

fEbp: 5 October 1953, Angus Morrison.
Pub. 1912, Rouart Lerolle.

24a. Prélude de la Porte Héroïque du Ciel. Orch. Roland-Manuel. 1912.
fEp: 14 June 1949, BBC broadcast, section of the London Symphony Orchestra, cond. Constant Lambert.

25. Messe des Pauvres. For organ or piano. 1895.
  1. *Kyrie eleison*; 2. *Dixit domine*; 3. *Prière des Orgues*; 4. *Commune qui mundi nefas*; 5. *Chant Ecclésiastique*; 6. *Prière pour les voyageurs et les marins en danger de mort, à la très bonne et très auguste Vierge Marie, mère de Jésus*; 7. *Prière pour le salut de mon âme.*
fEbp: 16 December 1951, Paris, Institut des Jeunes Aveugles, Marie-Louise Girod.
Pub. 1929, Rouart Lerolle.

25a. Messe des Pauvres. Version orch. David Diamond. Dur. 8'.
2 fl, 2 ob, 2 cl, 2 bsn; 2 hn, 2 tpt; timp, tgle; hp, strings; small chorus (ad lib).
fEbp: 17 October 1960, Leighton Lucas Orchestra, cond. Leighton Lucas.
Pub. Salabert.

BIBLIOGRAPHY:
Bryan Hesford: The performance and problems of ES's 'Messe des Pauvres', *MO*, June 1966, p. 533.

26. Pièces froides. For piano. 1897.
  1. *Airs à faire fuir.* Ded. Ricardo Viñes.
  2. *Danses de travers.* Ded. Mme J. Ecorcheville.
fEbp: 9 June 1949, Robert Collet.
Pub. 1912, Rouart Lerolle.

26a. Nouvelles pièces froides. For piano. After 1897 but before 1910.
  1. *Sur un mur*; 2. *Sur un arbre*; 3. *Sur un pont.*
Pub. 1968, Salabert.

27. Geneviève de Brabant. Miniature opera for marionettes. 1899.
  1. *Prélude*; 2. *Chorus, Act I*; 3. *Entrée des soldats*; 4. *Entr'acte, Act II*; 5. *Air de Geneviève*; 6. *Sonnerie de cor*; 7. *Entrée des soldats*; 8. *Entr'acte, Act III*; 9. *Air de Golo*; 10. *Entrée des soldats.*
Pub. 1930, Universal-Edition: vocal score.

27a. Geneviève de Brabant. Scored by Roger Désormière.
fl, ob, 2 cl, bsn; 2 hn, cornet à piston, tmb; cym, GC, tarolle, tamb; strings.
Pub. 1930, Universal-Edition.

28. Jack-in-the-Box. Pantomime. 1900. Unperf.

28a. Jack-in-the-Box. Orch. Darius Milhaud. 1926.
1. *Prélude.* Dur. 2½′.
2. *Entr'acte.* Dur. 2′.
3. *Final.* Dur. 2′.
2 fl, pic, 2 ob, 2 cl, 2 bsn; 2 hn, 2 tpt, 2 tmb; timp, tarolle, GC, 2 cym; strings.
fEbp (No. 1): 3 April 1934, BBC Orchestra, cond. H. Foster Clark.
Pub. 1929, Universal-Edition.

29. Rêverie du pauvre. For piano. 1900· Dur. 4′ 05″. Pub. 1968, Salabert.

30. The Dreaming Fish (Le Poisson rêveur). Esquisse for piano. March 1901, Arceuil. Dur. 5′ 15″. Pub. 1968, Salabert. Also version for piano and orchestra by R. Caby.

31. Trois Morceaux en forme de poire. For piano four hands. Dated: September 1903.
1. *Manière de commencement* (*Gnossienne from Fils des Etoiles, 1891*)—*Prolongation du même*; 2. *Lentement*; 3. *Enlevé*; 4. *Brutal*; 5. *En plus*; 6. *Redite.*
fEbp: 9 June 1949, Geraldine and Mary Peppin.
Pub. 1911, Rouart Lerolle.

31a. Trois Morceaux en forme de poire. Version orch. Roger Désormière.
2 fl, 2 ob, ca, 2 cl, 2 bsn; 3 hn, 2 tpt, 2 tmb, tuba; pcssn; celesta, hp, strings.
Pub. Salabert.

32. Chanson médiévale. For voice and piano. 1906. Pub. 1968, Salabert, as *Trois Autres Mélodies* No. 2.

33. Douze petits chorals. For piano. *c.* 1906. Pub. 1968, Salabert.

34. Prélude en tapisserie. For piano. Dated: 12 October 1906, Arceuil.
fEbp: 30 June 1950, Robert Collet.
Pub. 1929, Rouart Lerolle.

35. Passacaille. For piano. Dated: July 1906, Arceuil-Cachan. Pub. 1929, Rouart Lerolle. Version orch. David Diamond, pub. Salabert.

36. Aperçus désagréables. For piano four hands. Dated: September 1908–October 1912.
1. *Pastorale*; 2. *Choral*; 3. *Fugue.*
Pub. 1913, Demets.

37. Deux rêveries nocturnes. For piano. 1910–11. Dur. 3′ 50″.
1. *Pas vite*; 2. *Très modérément.*
Pub. 1968, Salabert.

38. (Carnet de croquis et d'esquisses.) For piano. After 1895 but before 1913. Pub. 1968, Salabert.

39. En habit de cheval. For orchestra. 1911.
1. *Chorale*; 2. *Fugue litanique*; 3. *Autre choral*; 4. *Fugue de papier.*
2 fl, 2 ob, 2 cl, 2 bsn; 2 hn, 2 tpt, 3 tmb, tuba, cbs tuba; strings.
fEp: 11 September 1947, BBC broadcast, Leighton Lucas Orchestra, cond. Leighton Lucas.
Pub. Salabert.

39a. En habit de cheval. Version for piano four hands. Dated: June–August 1911.
fEbp: 22 November 1953, Denis Matthews and Howard Ferguson.
Pub. 1911, Rouart Lerolle.

40. Véritables préludes flasques (pour un chien). For piano. 1912.
1. *Sévère réprimande.* Dated: 12 August 1912.
2. *Seul à la maison.* Dated: 17 August 1912.
3. *On joue.* Dated: 23 August 1912.
Pub. 1912, Demets; Eschig.

41. Descriptions automatiques. For piano. 1913.
1. *Sur un vaisseau.* Dated: 21 April 1913. Ded. Mme Fernand Dreyfus.
2. *Sur une lanterne.* Dated: 22 April 1913. Ded. Mme Joseph Ravel.
3. *Sur un casque.* Dated: 26 April 1913. Ded. Mme Paulette Darty.
Pub. 1913, Demets; Eschig.

42. Embryons desséchés. For piano. 1913.
1. *d'Holothurie.* Dated: 30 June 1913. Ded. Mlle Suzanne Roux.

2. *d'Edriophthalma.* Dated: 1 July 1913. Ded. Edouard Dreyfus.

3. *de Podophthalma.* Dated: 4 July 1913. Ded. Mme Jane Mortier.

Pub. 1913, Demets; Eschig.

43. Croquis et agaceries d'un gros bonhomme en bois. For piano. 1913.

1. *Tyrolienne turque.* Dated: 28 July 1913. Ded. Mlle Elvira Viñes Soto.

2. *Danse maigre.* Dated: 2 June 1913. Ded. Hernando Viñes Soto.

3. *Españaña.* Dated: 25 August 1913. Ded. Mlle Claude Emma Debussy.

Pub. 1913, Demets; Eschig.

44. Chapitres tournés en tous sens. For piano. 1913.

1. *Celle qui parle trop.* Dated: 23 August 1913. Ded. Robert Manuel.

2. *Le porteur de grosses pierres.* Dated: 25 August 1913. Ded. Fernand Dreyfus.

3. *Regrets des Enfermés.* Dated: 5 September 1913. Ded. Mme Claude Debussy.

fp: 14 January 1914, Paris, Société Musicale Indépendante concert, Ricardo Viñes.

Pub. 1913, Demets; Eschig.

45. Vieux séquins et vieilles cuirasses. For piano. 1913.

1. *Chez le marchand d'or.* Dated: 9 September 1913. Ded. Ricardo Viñes.

2. *Danse cuirassée.* Dated: 17 September 1913. Ded. M.-D. Calvocoressi.

3. *La défaite des Cimbres.* Dated: 14 September 1913. Ded. Emile Vuillermoz.

Pub. 1913, Demets; Eschig.

46. Enfantines. For piano. 1913.

1. *Menus propos enfantins.* Dated: 10 October 1913. Ded. Mlle Valentine Gross.

1. Chant guerrier du roi des haricots.

2. Ce que dit la petite princesse des Tulipes.

3. Valse du Chocolat aux amandes.

2. *Enfantillages pittoresques.* Dated: 22 October 1913. Ded. Mme Léon Verneuil.

1. Petite prélude à la journée.

2. Berceuse.

3. Marche du grand escalier.

3. *Peccadilles importunes.* Dated: 26 October 1913. Ded. Mme Marguerite Long.

1. Etre jaloux de son camarade qui a une grosse tête.

2. Lui manger sa tartine.

3. Profiter de ce qu'il a des cors aux pieds pour lui prendre son cerceau.

Pub. 1914, Demets; Eschig.

47. Le Piège de Méduse. Lyric Comedy with music. 1913. Pub. 1921, Galerie Leiris.

47a. Le Piège de Méduse. Seven pieces for piano.

1. *Quadrille*; 2. *Valse*; 3. *Pas vite* 4. *Mazurka*; 5. *Un peu vif*; 6. *Polka*; 7. *Quadrille.*

Pub. 1954, Salabert. Version for eight instruments pub. 1968, Salabert.

48. Les Pantins dansent. For piano. Dated: 16 November 1913. Pub. 1929, Rouart Lerolle.

48a. Les Pantins dansent. Version for orchestra by the composer. Dur. 2' 30".

fl, cl, ob, bsn; hn, tpt; strings.

Pub. 1967, Salabert.

49. (Musiques intimes et secrètes.) For piano. 1906–13.

1. *Nostalgie*; 2. *Froide songerie*; 3. *Fâcheux exemple.*

Pub. 1968, Salabert.

50. (Six Pièces de la periode 1906–13.) For piano.

1. *Désespoir agréable.* January 1908. Dur. 1'.

2. *Effronterie.* n.d. Dur. 2' 53".

3. *Poésie.* ?1913.

4. *Prélude canin.* c. 1910. Dur. 40–45".

5. *Profondeur.* n.d. Dur. 1' 52".

6. *Songe-creux.* n.d. Dur. 1' 35".

Pub. 1968, Salabert.

51. Choses vues à droite et à gauche (sans lunettes). For piano and violin. 1914. Ded. Marcel Chailley.

1. *Choral hypocrite.* Dated: 17 January 1914.

2. *Fugue à tâtons.* Dated: 21 January 1914.

3. *Fantaisie musculaire.* Dated: 30 January 1914.

Pub. 1916, Rouart Lerolle.

52. Trois Poèmes d'Amour (Erik Satie). For voice and piano. 1914. Ded. Henri Fabert.

1. *Ne suis que grain de sable*; 2. *Suis chauve de naissance*; 3. *Ta parure et secrète.*

fEbp: 30 June 1950, Donald Munro, acc. Clifton Helliwell.

Pub. 1916, Rouart Lerolle.

53. Cinq Grimaces. Composed for an unrealized production by Jean Cocteau of 'A Midsummer Night's Dream'. 1914.

1. *Modéré*; 2. *Peu vite*; 3. *Modéré*; 4. *Temps de Marche*; 5. *Modéré*.

3 fl, pic, 2 ob, ca, 2 cl, 2 bsn, cbsn; 2 hn, 3 tpt, 3 tmb, tuba; timp, cym, GC, tambour; strings.

fEp: 1926, London, His Majesty's Theatre, Diaghilev's Ballets Russes.

Pub. 1929, Universal-Edition.

54. Sports et divertissements. For piano. 1914.

1. *Choral inappétissant.* Dated: 15 May 1914.
2. *Balançoire.* Dated: 31 March 1914.
3. *La Chasse.* Dated: 7 April 1914.
4. *Comédie italienne.* Dated: 29 April 1914.
5. *La Mariée.* Dated: 16 May 1914.
6. *Colin-Maillard.* Dated: 27 April 1914.
7. *La Pêche.* Dated: 14 March 1914.
8. *Yachting.* Dated: 22 March 1914.
9. *Bain de mer.* Dated: 11 April 1914.
10. *Le Carnaval.* Dated: 3 April 1914.
11. *Le Golf.* Dated: 20 May 1914.
12. *La Pieuvre.* Dated: 17 March 1914.
13. *Les Courses.* Dated: 26 March 1914.
14. *Les Quatre Coins.* Dated: 24 April 1914.
15. *Pique-Nique.* Dated: 19 April 1914.
16. *Water-Chute.* Dated: 14 April 1914.
17. *Le Tango.* Dated: 5 May 1914.
18. *Traîneau.* Dated: 2 May 1914.
19. *Flirt.* Dated: 28 March 1914.
20. *Feu d'artifice.* Dated: 6 April 1914.
21. *Le Tennis.* Dated: 21 April 1914.

fEbp: 5 October 1953, Angus Morrison.

Pub. Publications Lucien Vogel; drawings by Charles Martin.

55. Heures séculaires et instantanées. For piano. 1914.

1. *Obstacles venimeux.* Dated: 25 June 1914.
2. *Crépuscule matinal* (de midi). Dated: 3 July 1914.
3. *Affolements granitiques.*

Pub. 1916, Demets.

56. Trois Valses du précieux degoûté. For piano. 1914.

1. *Sa taille.* Dated: 21 July 1914. Ded. Roland-Manuel.
2. *Son binocle.* Dated: 22 July 1914. Ded. Mlle Linette Chalupt.
3. *Ses jambes.* Dated: 23 July 1914. Ded. René Chalupt.

fEbp: 9 June 1949, Robert Collet.

Pub. 1916, Rouart Lerolle.

56a. Trois Valses du précieux degoûté. Orch. Greenbaum.

fEbp: 18 August 1937, BBC Orchestra, cond. Constant Lambert.

57. Avant-dernières pensées. For piano. 1915.

1. *Idylle.* Dated: 23 August 1915. Ded. Debussy.
2. *Aubade.* Dated: 3 October 1915. Ded. Paul Dukas.
3. *Méditation.* Dated: 6 October 1915. Ded. Albert Roussel.

Pub. 1916, Rouart Lerolle.

58. Trois mélodies. For voice and piano. 1916.

1. *Daphénéo* (M. God). Dated: 14 April 1916. Ded. Emile Engel.
2. *La Statue de bronze* (Léon-Paul Fargue). Dated: 26 May 1916. Ded. Jane Bathori.
3. *Le chapelier* (René Chalupt). Dated: 14 April 1916. Ded. Igor Stravinsky.

fEbp: 26 August 1952, Hugues Cuenod, acc Margaret Kitchin.

Pub. 1917, Rouart Lerolle. Version orch. R. Caby, Salabert (hire).

59. Parade. 'Ballet réaliste.' 1917. Theme, Jean Cocteau. Ded. Mme Edwards (*née* M. Godebska).

1. *Choral—Prélude du rideau rouge—Prestidigitateur chinois*; 2. *Petite fille américaine*; 3. *Acrobates*; 4. *Final—Suite au 'Prélude du rideau rouge'.*

2 fl, pic, 2 ob, ca, E-flat cl, 2 cl, 2 bsn; 2 hn, 2 piston, 2 tpt, 3 tmb, tuba; timp, tamb, tamb basque, sirène aigue, tarolle, roue de loterie, typewriter, flaques sonores, tamtam, cym, GC, bouteillophone, xyl, tgle, organ pedal; hp, strings.

fp: 18 May 1917, Paris, Théâtre du Châtelet, Diaghilev, cond. Ernest Ansermet; with Léonide Massine, Mlle Chabelska,

Woizikovsky, Statkevitsch, Lopokova; choreography, Léonide Massine; curtain, décors and costumes, Pablo Picasso.

fEp (concert): 11 September 1947, BBC broadcast, Leighton Lucas Orchestra, cond. Leighton Lucas.

Pub. 1917, Rouart Lerolle; Salabert.

BIBLIOGRAPHY:

Georges Auric: Préface à Parade, 1917.
— Parade et Socrate, *Littérature*, March 1919.
— Les Ballets russes: Parade, *Nouvelle revue française*, February (No. 89) 1921, p. 224.
Jean Cocteau: Parade, in *Cock and Harlequin* (transl. Rollo H. Myers), The Egoist Press 1921, p. 24.
— The collaboration of Parade, in –do–, p. 53.
William Lieberman: Parade and the New Spirit, *Dance Index*, November–December 1946.
Wilfrid Mellers: Parade, in *Decca Book of Ballet*, Muller (London) 1958, p. 278.
Darius Milhaud: A propos de Parade au concert, in *Etudes*, Claude Aveline 1927, p. 41.

59a. Parade. Ballet Suite for piano four hands. 1917.

1. *Prélude du Rideau Rouge*; 2. *Prestidigitateur Chinois*; 3. *Petite fille Américaine*; 4. *Ragtime du Paquebot*; 5. *Acrobates*; 6. *Suite au Prélude du Rideau Rouge*.

Pub. 1917, Rouart Lerolle. 'Rag-Time Parade' arr. for piano by Hans Ourdine pub. 1919, Rouart Lerolle.

60. Sonatine bureaucratique. For piano. July 1917. Ded. Juliette Meerovitch.

fEbp: 21 May 1925, Manchester station, Marcelle Meyer.

Pub. 1917, S. Chapelier.

61. Cinq Nocturnes. For piano. 1919.
No. 1. Dated: August 1919. Ded. Mme Marcelle Meyer.
No. 2. Dated: September 1919. Ded. André Salomon.
No. 3. Dated: October 1919. Ded. Mme Jean Hugo.
No. 4. Dated: October 1919. Ded. Mme la Comtesse Etienne de Beaumont.
No. 5. Dated: November 1919. Ded. Mme Georges Cocteau.

Pub. 1919 (Nos. 1–3) Rouart Lerolle, 1920 (Nos. 4 & 5) Demets; Eschig.

62. Socrate. Symphonic Drama in three parts for four voices and orchestra. 1919. Text: Plato, transl. Victor Cousin. Ded. Mme la Princesse Edmond de Polignac and to the memory of Prince Edmond de Polignac.

1. *Portrait de Socrate*; 2. *Les Bords de l'Ilissus*; 3. *Mort de Socrate*.

fEp: 17 June 1949, BBC broadcast, Megan Foster, Sophie Wyss and a section of the London Symphony Orchestra, cond. Constant Lambert.

Pub. 1919, Editions de la Sirène: vocal score.

BIBLIOGRAPHY:

David Cox: Peculiar homage to Socrates, *The Listener*, 21 December 1961, p. 1089.
Guido M. Gatti: Sokrates von ES, *Anbruch*, February (2) 1921, p. 75.
Albert Jeanneret: Le Socrate d'ES, *L'Esprit nouveau*, No. 9, July 1921.
Jean Marnold: M. Cocteau et la musique— Socrate de M. ES, *Mercure de France*, 1920, No. 524 (15 April) p. 495, No. 525 (1 May) p. 782.
Henry Prunières: ES, a propos de Socrate, *Nouvelle revue française*, No. 79, 1920, p. 605.

63. Trois petites pièces montées. For orchestra. 1919.

1. *De l'enfance de Pantagruel (Rêverie)*; 2. *Marche de Cocagne (Démarche)*; 3. *Jeux de Gargantua (Coin de Polka)*.

fEbp: 18 December 1925, Newcastle Station Symphony Orchestra, cond. Edward Clark.

BIBLIOGRAPHY:

Terpander: ES's Trois petites pièces montées, *The Gramophone*, January 1935, p. 321.

63a. Trois petites pièces montées. Version for piano four hands. 1920. Ded. Mme Julien Henriquet. Pub. 1920, Editions de la Sirène.

64. La belle excentrique. For music-hall orchestra. 1920.

1. *Grande Ritournelle*; 2. *Marche 'Franco-Lunaire'*; 3. *Valse du 'mystérieux baiser dans l'œil'*; 4. *Cancan 'Grand-Mondain'*.

fEp: 1926, London, His Majesty's Theatre, Diaghilev's Ballets Russes.

fEbp: 14 June 1949, BBC broadcast, section

of the London Symphony Orchestra, cond. Constant Lambert.

Pub. 1922: Editions de la Sirène: reduction for piano four hands.

65. Premier Menuet. For piano. Dated: June 1920. Ded. Claude Dubosq.

fp: 24 January 1921, Paris, Salle des Agriculteurs, Société Musicale Indépendante concert in memory of Debussy, Ernst Lévy.

Pub. 1922, Editions de la Sirène.

66. Quatre petites mélodies. For voice and piano. 1920.
1. *Elégie* (Lamartine).
2. *Danseuse* (Jean Cocteau).
3. *Adieu* (Raymond Radiguet).
Pub. Eschig.

67. Ludions. For voice and piano. 1923. Poems: Léon-Paul Fargue.
1. *Air du Rat*; 2. *Spleen*; 3. *La Grenouille américaine*; 4. *Air du Poète*; 5. *Chanson du Chat*.
fEbp: 30 June 1950, Donald Munro, acc. Clifton Helliwell.
Pub. 1926, Rouart Lerolle.

68. Mercure. Ballet ('Poses Plastiques'). 1924. Ded. Mme la Comtesse Etienne de Beaumont.
1. *Marche-Ouverture. Premier Tableau:* 2. *La Nuit*; 3. *Danse de tendresse*; 4. *Signes du zodiaque*; 5. *Entrée de Mercure. Deuxième Tableau:* 6. *Danse des Grâces*; 7. *Bain des Grâces*; 8. *Fuite de Mercure*; 9. *Colère de Cerbère. Troisième Tableau:* 10 *Polka des Lettres*; 11. *Nouvelle Danse*; 12. *Le Chaos*; 13. *Rapt de Proserpine*.
fEbp: 13 July 1932, BBC Orchestra, cond. Constant Lambert.
Pub. 1930, Universal-Edition.

69. Relâche. 'Ballet instantanéiste' in two acts and cinematographic entr'acte by René Clair. 1924. Dur. 25′.
fl, ob, cl, bsn; 2 hn, 2 tpt, tmb; timp; strings.
fp: 29 November 1924, Paris, Théâtre des Champs-Elysées, Ballets suédois; scenario and décors, Francis Picabia.
fEbp ('Suite'): 18 August 1937, BBC Orchestra, cond. Constant Lambert.
Pub. 1926, Rouart Lerolle: piano score.

BIBLIOGRAPHY:

Jean Marnold: Ballets suédois—Relâche, ballet instantanéiste en deux actes et un entr'acte cinématographique de René Clair et la queue du chien de M. Francis Picabia, musique de M. ES, *Mercure de France*, No. 637, 1 January 1925, p. 219.

69a. Cinéma. 'Entr'acte symphonique' from 'Relâche' arr. for piano four hands by Darius Milhaud. Dur. 18′.

Pub. 1926, Rouart Lerolle.

WRITINGS BY ERIK SATIE

Les Six, *Feuilles libres*, February 1922.
L'Origine d'instruction, *Feuilles libres*, June–July 1922.
Igor Stravinsky, *Feuilles libres*, October–November 1922.
Conférence, *Anbruch*, January 1923.
Les Périmés, *Feuilles libres*, No. 31, 1923.
Chronique musicale, *L'Approdo musicale*, 1965, Nos. 19–20.
Mémoires d'un amnésique, *L'Approdo musicale*, 1965, Nos. 19–20.

GENERAL BIBLIOGRAPHY

Georges Auric: La leçon d'ES, *RM*, August 1925, p. 98.
— Découverte de Satie, *RM*, June 1952, p. 17.
William Austin: Satie before and after Cocteau, *MQ*, April 1962, p. 216.
Pierre Bertin: ES, *Les Annales*, February 1951.
— Comment j'ai connu ES, *RM*, June 1952, p. 73.
Robert Caby: (ES), *Le Monde*, 1 December 1928.
— (ES), *Montparnasse*, January 1929.
J. Cage & A. Skulsky: Satie controversy, *Musical America*, 15 December 1950, p. 12.
J. Cage: Letters to the editor—More Satie, *Musical America*, 1 April 1951, p. 26.
M.-D. Calvocoressi: (ES), *Musica*, April 1911.
— ES, *MMR*, 1925, p. 6.
— Milhaud on Satie, *The Dominant*, February 1929, p. 23.
— Concerning ES, *MM&F*, April 1933, p. 208.
— ES, in *Musicians Gallery*, Faber & Faber (London) 1933, p. 124.
René Chalupt: Quelques souvenirs sur ES, *RM*, June 1952, p. 39.

Antonio Capri: ES, in *Musica e musicisti d'Europa*, Ulrico Hoepli (Milan) 1939, p. 209.

Rydhyar D. Chennevière: ES and the music of irony, *MQ*, October 1919.

Jean Cocteau: ES, *Action*, No. 2, March 1920.
— Satie versus Satie, in *Cock and Harlequin* (transl. Rollo H. Myers), The Egoist Press 1921, p. 18.
— ES, *Fanfare*, No. 1, 15 October 1921.
— Fragments d'une conférence sur ES (1920), *RM*, March 1924, p. 217.
— L'exemple d'ES, *RM*, August 1925, p. 97.
— (ES), *Comoedia*, 17 May 1926.
— Deux de mes collaborateurs, *Anbruch*, April–May 1930, p. 146.
— Satie, *RM*, June 1952, p. 17.
— ES, Editions Dynamo (Liège) 1957.

André Coeuroy: The cure by literature, *League of Composers Review*, April 1925.
— Fauré–Caplet–Satie, *Anbruch*, 1925, No. 7, p. 430.
— Erik Leslie Satie, *Larousse mensuel*, No. 225 (1925), p. 962.
— ES, in *La Musique française moderne*, Librairie Delagrave (Paris) 1922, p. 153.

Paul Collaer: (ES), *Action*, 1921.
— (ES), *Arts et lettres d'aujourd'hui*, July 1924.
— (ES), *Sélection*, January 1925.
— ES et les Six, in *La Musique moderne*, Elsevier (Paris) 1955, p. 141.

Henri Collet: Un livre de Rimsky et un livre de Cocteau—les cinq Russes, les six Français et ES, *Comoedia*, 16 and 23 January 1920.

Alfred Cortot: Le cas ES, *RM*, April–May 1938, p. 248.
— La musique française de piano, Vol. III, 1924.

David Cox: ES, inspired eccentric, *The Listener*, 13 October 1960, p. 657.

Werner Danckert: Der Klassizismus ESs und seine geistesgeschichtliche Stellung, *Zeitschrift für Musikwissenschaft*, 1929, No. 2, p. 105.

Yves Dautun: (ES), *Ceux qui viennent*, September 1925.

Laurence Davies: ES, the nightingale and the tramcar, in *The Gallic Muse*, Dent (London) 1967, p. 91.

Norman Demuth: ES, in *Musical Trends in the 20th Century*, Rockliff (London) 1952, p. 22.

F. Deshayes: ES, *Musik* (Copenhagen), Vol. 4, No. 1.

Peter Dickinson: ES, *MR*, May 1967, p. 139.

René Dumesnil: ES, les Six et la Génération de la Guerre, in *La Musique contemporaine en France*, Librairie Armand Colin (Paris) 1930, Vol. 2, Chapter X, p. 5.
— ES, in *Portraits de musiciens français*, Librairie Plon (Paris) 1938, p. 103.

Louis Durey: ES, *The Arts*, December 1930.

J. Ecorcheville: ES, *Revue S.I.M.*, 15 March 1911, p. 29.

Gabriel Fournier: ES et son époque, *RM*, June 1952, p. 129.

Stanislas Fumet: Eironeia, *RM*, June 1952, p. 19.

André George: (ES), *Les Nouvelles littéraires*, December 1923.

Léon Guichard: Prélude à l'œuvre d'ES, *Le Point*, April 1938.
— ES et la musique grégorienne, *RM*, November 1936, p. 334.

Everett Helm: ES zum 100. Geburtstag, *ÖM*, 1966, Nos. 5–6 (May–June), p. 239.
— The man with a mask, *High Fidelity*, December 1963, p. 54.

Leigh Henry: ES, *MO*, March 1920, p. 459.
— ES, a tribute, *MS*, 25 July 1925, p. 23.

Julius Hijman: Satie's dood en wederrdood, *Caecilia en de Muziek*, August–September 1935.

Martin Howe: ES and his ballets, *Ballet*, August–September 1948 p. 25, October 1948 p. 25.

Valentine Hugo: Le Socrate que j'ai connu—Lettres inédites, *RM*, June 1952, p. 139.

Maurice Imbert: (ES), *Le Courrier musical*, July 1925.

Z. Jachimecki: ES, *Muzyka*, March and May 1927.

Dom Clément Jacob: ES et le chant grégorien, *RM*, June 1952, p. 85.

Maxime Jacob: L'exemple d'ES, *Vigile*, 1930, 2e cahier, p. 123.

G. Jean-Aubry: ES, in *La Musique française d'aujourd'hui*, Perrin (Paris) 1916, p. 198.

Albert Jeanneret: ES, *L'Esprit nouveau*, No. 2, 1920.

M. Kisling: Souvenir de Satie, *RM*, June 1952, p. 107.

Charles Koechlin: ES, *RM*, March 1924, p. 193.
— ES, in *Von neuer Musik*, 1925, p. 154.
— (ES), *Journal des Débats*, 16 May 1926.
Marcel Laloe: ES, *Les Réverbères*, April 1938.
Louis Laloy: Ce que je pense d'ES, *Le Courrier musical*, 15 May 1925.
Constant Lambert: ES and his 'musique d'ameublement' in *Music Ho!*, Faber & Faber (London) 1934; Penguin Books (London) 1948; ES et la musique abstraite, *RM*, June 1952, p. 101 (repr. from *Music Ho!*).
Paul Landormy: ES, in *La Musique française après Debussy*, Gallimard (Paris) 1943, p. 54.
Michel Leiris: L'humour d'ES, *Nouvelle revue française*, No. 292, 1938, p. 163.
Fernand Léger: Satie inconnu, *RM*, June 1952, p. 137.
André Mangeot: ES, *Le Monde musical*, 31 January 1933.
Joseph Machlis: ES, in *Introduction to Contemporary Music*, W. W. Norton (USA), Dent (London) 1961, p. 209.
Louis de Marval: A propos d'ES, *SM*, 1967, No. 6 (November–December), p. 340.
Robert Le Masle: ES évoqué et interpreté à Londes, *Contrepoints*, No. 1, January 1946, p. 119.
Pierre de Massot: Quelques propos et souvenirs sur ES, *RM*, June 1952, p. 125.
W. H. Mellers: ES and the 'problem' of contemporary music, *M&L*, July 1942; in *Studies in Contemporary Music*, Dennis Dobson (London) 1947, p. 16.
— ES et la musique 'fonctionnelle', *RM*, June 1952, p. 33.
— ES, in *Decca Book of Ballet*, Muller (London) 1958, p. 276.
E. L. T. Messens: Le souvenir d'ES, *RM*, June 1952, p. 147.
Darius Milhaud: Chronique musicale, *Intentions*, December 1923.
— La mort d'ES, in *Études*, Claude Aveline 1927, p. 89.
— ES et l'art de la fugue, *Musique*, January 1930.
— Les derniers jours d'ES, *Le Figaro littéraire*, 23 April 1949.
— Werdegang von ES, *Anbruch*, April–May 1930, p. 144.

— Note sur ES, in *Oeuvres nouvelles*, Maison Française (New York) 1946.
Rollo (H.) Myers: ES, Dennis Dobson (London) 1948.
— Poet or buffoon?, *Radio Times*, 13 August 1937, p. 11.
— L'importance de Satie dans la musique contemporaine, *RM*, June 1952, p. 77.
— The strange case of ES, *MT*, July 1945, p. 201.
— ES, *M&M*, May 1966, p. 16.
Ronald Pearsall: Satie forty years after, *MO*, March 1965, p. 335.
Francis Picabia: ES, *Paris-Journal*, 27 June 1924.
Francis Poulenc: La musique de piano d'ES, *RM*, June 1952, p. 23.
Fred W. Prieberg: ES, *Musica*, 1955, No. 8, p. 366.
Henry Prunières: ES, *Il Pianoforte*, August–September 1925.
Rosette Renshaw: ES, *La Nouvelle Revue Canadienne*, April–May 1951.
Charles Ribeyre: ES, *L'Orient musical*, 1 August 1925.
W. Wright Roberts: The problem of Satie, *M&L*, October 1923.
Roland-Manuel: (ES), *L'Echo musical*, April 1913.
— ES, 11-page brochure, publisher not stated, 1916.
— Excuses à Satie, *Revue Pleyel*, March 1926.
— Satie tel que je l'ai vu, *RM*, June 1952, p. 9.
Kajsa Rootzén: En musikalisk galghumorist, *Svensk dagbladet*, 18 June 1940.
Claude Rostand: Picasso et la musique, *SM*, November–December 1961, p. 374.
Albert Roussel: A propos d'un récent festival, *Le Gaulois*, 12 June 1926.
Jean Roy: Satie poète, *RM*, June 1952, p. 55.
— ES, in *Musique française*, Debresse (Paris) 1962, p. 15.
K. H. Ruppel: Monsieur le Pauvre, *Melos*, July–August 1966, p. 205.
Adolfo Salazar: ES, in *Música y músicos de hoy*, Editorial Mundo Latino (Madrid) 1928, p. 338.
Gustave Samazeuilh: ES, in *Musiciens de mon temps*, Editions Marcel Daubin (Paris) 1947, p. 297.

William G. Sasser: Le développement du style d'ES, *RM*, June 1952, p. 111.

Conrad Satie: (ES), *Le Cœur*, June 1895.

Henri Sauguet: Souvenirs et réflexions autour d'ES, *RM*, June 1952, p. 95.

William Saunders: ES, *Musical News*, 1 September 1917, p. 131.

— ES's forms and harmonies, *Musical News*, 8 September 1917, p. 147.

Boris de Schloezer: ES, *Nouvelle revue française*, 1925, No. 143, p. 251.

— Le cas Satie, *RM*, August 1924.

Florent Schmitt: ES, *Montjoie*, 14 March 1913.

Roger Shattuck: Satie et la musique de placard, *RM*, June 1952, p. 47.

— ES, composer to the School of Paris, *Art News Annual*, 1957.

— ES, in *The Banquet Years*, Faber & Faber (London) 1959.

A. Skulsky: ES, *Musical America*, July 1950.

Pierre Soccanne: (ES), *Le Guide du concert*, 7 January 1927.

Paul Souday: (ES), *Paris-Midi*, 22 May 1927, 16 June 1924, 5 December 1924.

H. H. Stuckenschmidt: ES, *Vossische Zeitung*, 11 December 1926.

— ES, *Anbruch*, 11 February 1929, p. 60.

— ES, *Der Auftakt*, 1934, Nos. 1–2, p. 6.

— ES, in *Schöpfer der neuen Musik*, Suhrkamp Verlag (Frankfurt a. M.) 1958, p. 42.

Pierre-Daniel Templier: ES, Editions Rieder, 1932.

Vincenzo Terenzio: ES, un bilancio, *Musica d'oggi*, July–August 1963.

Virgil Thomson: La place de Satie dans la musique du XXᵉ siècle, *RM*, June 1952, p. 13.

— (ES), in *The Musical Scene*, New York 1951.

— (ES), in *Music Left and Right*, New York 1951.

Yvonne Tiénot & O. d'Estrade-Guerra: Debussy et ES, *Feuilles musicales*, June–July 1962, p. 86.

J. van der Veen: ES, *Mens en melodie*, December 1953, p. 389.

Carl van Vaechten: (ES), in *Interpreters and Interpretations*, New York 1917.

— (ES), in *Excavations*, New York 1929.

Egon Wellesz: ES, *Tempo* (Prague), October–November 1929.

J. Weterings: ES, *Beaux Arts*, 1 January 1937.

MISCELLANEOUS OR UNSIGNED

ES, nota biografica, *Bollettino bibliografico musicale*, August–September 1928, p. 1.

Précision sur le cas ES, *Dissonances*, June 1931.

ES, *Le Monde musical*, July 1925.

ES, the velvet gentleman, *RM*, March 1924, p. 208.

Trois lettres d'ES à Claude Debussy, *Revue de musicologie*, 1962, No. 125, p. 71.

ARNOLD SCHOENBERG (1874–1951)

Schoenberg spent all but five of the first fifty years of his life in Vienna, where he was born on 13 September 1874. Though he took violin lessons as a boy, he was self-taught in composition, except for a few months' instruction in counterpoint from Alexander von Zemlinsky, whose sister Mathilde he was to marry in 1901. After working in a bank from 1891 to 1895, Schoenberg devoted himself wholly to music, supporting himself around the turn of the century by scoring and conducting music for operetta and cabaret. He soon became a noted teacher of composition, his outstanding pupils in the first decade of this century being Alban Berg and Anton Webern. (Later pupils were to include Roberto Gerhard, Nikos Skalkottas and John Cage.) The completion of his *Treatise on Harmony* in 1911 showed his gifts as a theorist, and at about the same time he was making his mark as a painter connected with the *Blauer Reiter* group. Although forty years old in 1914, he was twice conscripted into the Austrian army (December 1915 and July 1917), and on final demobilisation in October 1917 devoted himself to teaching in Vienna, to running the Society for Private Musical Performances (1918–22) and to formulating his 'method of composition with twelve notes'. His wife died in 1923 and the following year he married Gertrud Kolisch, sister of the leader of the Kolisch Quartet. He left Vienna in 1926 to take over Busoni's master class in composition at the Prussian Academy of Arts in Berlin. With the rise of Hitler, Schoenberg was dismissed his post (1933), left Berlin, formally resumed his lapsed Jewish faith in Paris and set out for the United States. His health could not stand the climate of New

York and Boston, where he had taken teaching posts, and he settled in Los Angeles, where he was later appointed to a professorship at the University of California (1936–44). Schoenberg assumed United States nationality in 1940, survived a near-fatal illness in 1946 and died in Los Angeles in July 1951.

CATALOGUE OF WORKS

1. String Quartet in D major. 1897.
1. *Allegro molto*; 2. *Intermezzo (Andantino grazioso)*; 3. *Andante con moto*; 4. *Allegro*.
fp: 1897, Vienna, Fitzner Quartet.
fEbp: 5 July 1961, Aeolian Quartet.
Pub. 1966, Faber Music; foreword by O. W. Neighbour; introductory article in *Faber Music News*, autumn 1966, p. 21.

2. Zwei Lieder Op. 1. For voice and piano. 1897 (?1898). Words: Karl Freiherr von Levetzow. Ded. Alexander von Zemlinsky.
1. *Dank*; 2. *Abschied*.
Pub. 1903, Birnbach (Berlin).

3. Vier Lieder Op. 2. For voice and piano. 1899. Ded. Alexander von Zemlinzky.
1. *Erwartung* (Richard Dehmel). 9 August 1899.
2. *Schenk mir deinen goldenen Kamm* (Richard Dehmel).
3. *Erhebung* (Richard Dehmel). 16 November 1899.
4. *Waldsonne* (Johannes Schlaf).
fEbp (No. 4): 4 March 1930, Ruzena Herlinger.
fEbp (Nos. 1–3): 15 November 1931, Enid Cruickshank.
Pub. 1903, Birnbach (Berlin)/Universal-Edition (Vienna).

4. Sechs Lieder Op. 3. For voice and piano. 1899–1903. Ded. Carl Redlich.
1. *Wie Georg von Frundsberg von sich selber sang* (From 'Das Knaben Wunderhorn'). 18 March 1903, Berlin.
2. *Die Aufgeregten* (Gottfried Keller). 9 November 1903.
3. *Warnung* (Richard Dehmel). 7 May 1899.
4. *Hochzeitslied* (Jens Peter Jacobsen).
5. *Geübtes Herz* (Gottfried Keller).
6. *Freihold* (Hermann Lingg). 20 November 1900.

Pub. 1904, Birnbach (Berlin)/Universal-Edition (Vienna).

5. Verklärte Nacht Op. 4. String sextet, based on a poem by Richard Dehmel (from 'Weib und Welt'). 1 December 1899.
fp: 1903, Vienna, augmented Rosé Quartet.
fEp: 15 January 1914, Grafton Galleries, Music Club concert, London String Quartet (leader, Albert Sammons) with James Lockyer (second viola) and Cedric Sharpe (second cello).
fEbp: 17 December 1928, Samuel Kutcher, George Whitaker, Raymond Jeremy, James Lockyer, Cedric Sharpe, Edward Robinson.
Pub. Birnbach (Berlin).

BIBLIOGRAPHY:
Neville Cardus: Verklärte Nacht, *Halle*, January 1949, p. 9.
Jascha Horenstein: Verklärte Nacht, *Pult und Taktstock*, March–April 1927.
Alfred Kalisch: The Schönberg Sextet, some notes, *Chamber Music* (Music Student Supplement), No. 10, September 1914, p. 7.
János Kárpáti: Schönberg: Verklärte Nacht, *Muzsika* (Budapest), August 1963, p. 33.
F. G. Youens: Schönbergs Verklärte Nacht, *The Gramophone*, July 1939, p. 82.

5a. Verklärte Nacht. Version by Arnold Schönberg for string orchestra. 1917, rev. 1943.
fEbp: 14 December 1924, Newcastle Station String Orchestra, cond. Edward Clark.
fEp (concert): 3 February 1927, Royal Albert Hall, National Orchestra, cond. Hermann Scherchen.
Pub. Universal-Edition; revised version pub. 1943, Associated Music Publishers (New York).

6. Gurrelieder. For soloists, mixed chorus and orchestra (Jens Peter Jacobsen). 1900–11.
4 pic, 8 fl, 5 ob, 2 ca, 7 cl, 2 cl in E flat, 2 bcl, 3 bsn, 2 cbsn; 10 hn, 6 tpt, bs tpt, alto tmb, 4 tmb, bs tmb, cbs tmb, 4 Wagner tuba, cbs tuba; 6 timp, GC, cym, tgle, glock, side dm, ten dm, xyl, rattle, iron chains, tamtam; 4 hp, celesta, strings.
fp: 23 February 1913, Vienna, Musikverein

Hall, Philharmonic Chorus and Wiener Ton-künstlerorchester, cond. Franz Schreker; with Martha Winternitz-Dorda (Tove), Marya Freund (Forest Dove), Hans Nachod (Waldemar), Boruttau (Klaus the Fool), Nosalewicz (The Peasant) and Gregory (Speaker).

fEp: 27 January 1928, Queen's Hall, 2LO broadcast, National Chorus and National Orchestra, cond. Arnold Schönberg; with Stiles Allen (Tove), Gladys Palmer (Wood Dove), Parry Jones (Waldemar), John Perry (Klaus the Fool), Frank Phillips (The Peasant) and Arthur Wynne (Speaker).

Pub. 1912, Universal-Edition; also vocal score by Alban Berg. German text by Robert Franz Arnold.

BIBLIOGRAPHY:

Alberto Basso: I Gurre-Lieder di Schoenberg, *La Rassegna musicale*, September 1957, p. 219.

Richard Batka: Schönbergs Gurrelieder, *Der Kunstwart*, March (2) 1913, p. 435.

Paul Bekker: Die Gurrelieder in Duisberg, *Anbruch*, September–October 1922, p. 248.

Arthur Bliss: Gurrelieder and its composer, *Musical News*, January 1928, p. 12.

Mosco Carner: An early Schoenberg master-piece, *The Listener*, 17 August 1961, p. 257.

Jack Diether: At last in stereo, Schönberg's Gurre-lieder, *American Record Guide*, November 1965, p. 208.

— Schoenberg's Gurrelieder on LP, *Chord and Discord*, No. 7 (1954), p. 62.

R. Ericson: New life for Gurre-lieder, *Saturday Review*, 30 October 1965, p. 85.

R. Eyer: End of an era: recording of Gurre-lieder, *Musical America*, March 1954, p. 18.

Theodor Helm: ASs Gurrelieder—Urauffüh-rung in Wien am 27. Februar, *NZfM*, 1913, No. 11 (13 March), p. 154.

Heinrich Jalowetz: Die Gurrelieder, *Anbruch*, May 1923, p. 138; *Pult und Taktstock*, March–April 1927.

I. Kolodin: Lieder of Gurre, recordings, *Saturday Review*, 30 January 1954, p. 50.

R. Lawrence: Schönberg's Gurrelieder, an event for a generation, *High Fidelity*, October 1954, p. 79.

H. Nachod: The very first performance of Schoenberg's Gurrelieder, *Music Survey*, summer 1950, p. 38.

Ernest Newman: AS's Gurre-Lieder, *MT*, January 1914, p. 11.

D. E. Pike: The Gurrelieder of AS, *Chesterian*, No. 24, June 1922.

Paul A. Pisk: Schönbergs Gurrelieder, *Deutsche Kunstschau*, 1924, No. 21.

Percy Scholes: 140 players and some 'big iron chains', *Radio Times*, 13 January 1928, p. 49.

Richard Specht: Zur Uraufführung der Gurrelieder, *Der Merker*, February (1) 1913, p. 89.

— ASs Gurrelieder, *Der Merker*, March (1) 1913, p. 161.

Erwin Stein: The Gurrelieder, in *Orpheus in New Guises*, Rockliff (London) 1953, p. 55.

W. J. Turner: Schönberg's Gurrelieder, *New Statesman*, 4 February 1928, p. 530.

John S. Weissmann: Introducing Schoenberg, *Musical Events*, May 1961, p. 16.

6a. Lied der Waldtaube (from 'Gurre-lieder'). For voice and chamber orchestra. 1922.

fl, pic, ob, ca, cl in E flat, 2 cl, bcl, bsn, cbsn; 2 hn; hmnm, piano; string quintet.

fEbp: 8 May 1931, Enid Cruickshank and the BBC Orchestra, cond. Anton Webern.

Pub. 1923, Universal-Edition.

7. Pelleas und Melisande Op. 5. Symphonic poem for orchestra, from the drama by Maurice Maeterlinck. 1902–3. Dated: 28 February 1903, Berlin.

3 fl, 2 pic, 3 ob, ca, cl in E flat, 3 cl, bcl, 3 bsn, cbsn; 8 hn, 4 tpt, alto tmb, 4 tmb, cbs tuba; 2 timp, tgle, cym, GC, ten dm, tam-tam, glock; 2 hp, strings.

fp: 26 January 1905, Vienna, Verein der Schaffenden concert, Wiener Konzertvereins-orchester, cond. Arnold Schönberg.

fRp: 21 December 1912, St. Petersburg, Siloti concert, cond. Arnold Schönberg.

fEp: 10 December 1930, Queen's Hall, BBC Symphony Orchestra, cond. Hermann Scherchen.

Pub. 1911, Universal-Edition; also arr. for piano four hands by Heinrich Jalowetz.

BIBLIOGRAPHY:

Alban Berg: AS, Pelleas und Melisande:

Kurze thematische Analyse, Universal-Edition, n.d.

Edwin Evans: Giant symphonic poem, *Radio Times*, 17 January 1936, p. 13.

Erwin Felber: Pelleas und Melisande, *Pult und Taktstock*, March–April 1927.

Philipp Jarnach: Schönbergs Pelleas bei Kleiber, *Anbruch*, March 1927, p. 135.

Carl von Perinella: Berichte—ASs Pelleas und Melisande in Berlin, *Der Merker*, 10 November 1910, p. 129.

Paul Stefan: Schönbergs symphonische Dichtung Pelleas und Melisande, *NMZ*, 1923, No. 7, p. 105.

8. Acht Lieder Op. 6. For voice and piano. 1903–5.

1. *Traumleben* (Julius Hart). 18 December 1903.
2. *Alles* (Richard Dehmel). 6 September 1905, Traunstein.
3. *Mädchenlied* (Paul Remer).
4. *Verlassen* (Hermann Conradi). 19 December 1903.
5. *Ghasel* (Gottfried Keller). 23 January 1904.
6. *Am Wegrand* (John Henry Mackay).
7. *Lockung* (Kurt Aram).
8. *Der Wanderer* (Friedrich Nietzsche). 15 October 1905.

fEbp (No. 8): 15 November 1931, Ruzena Herlinger.

Pub. 1907, Birnbach (Berlin)/Universal-Edition (Vienna).

9. Sechs Orchesterlieder Op. 8. For voice and orchestra. 1904.

1. *Natur* (Heinrich Hart). 7 March 1904.
2 fl, 2 ob, ca, cl, bcl, 2 bsn; 4 hn, 2 tpt, 3 tmb, bs tuba; hp, strings.
2. *Das Wappenschild* (from 'Des Knaben Wunderhorn'). 25 May 1904, Vienna.
2 fl, pic, 3 ob, 3 cl, 3 bsn, cbsn; 4 hn, 3 tpt, 3 tmb; 3 timp, GC, tgle, cym; strings.
3. *Sehnsucht* (from 'Des Knaben Wunderhorn'). 7 April 1904, Vienna.
2 fl, ob, ca, cl, bcl, 2 bsn; 4 hn; strings.
4. *Nie ward' ich, Herrin, müd . . .* (Petrarch). 3 July 1904, Mödling.
3 fl, 2 ob, ca, 2 cl, bcl, 2 bsn, cbsn; 4 hn, 3 tpt, 3 tmb, bs tuba; 3 timp; strings.

5. *Voll jener Süsse* (Petrarch). November 1904, Vienna.
Instrumentation as for No. 4.
6. *Wenn Vöglein klagen* (Petrarch).
3 fl, pic, 2 ob, ca, 2 cl, bcl, 2 bsn, cbsn; 4 hn, 2 tpt, 3 tmb, bs tuba; strings.

Pub. 1911 (voice and piano), 1913 (voice and orchestra), Universal-Edition.

10. String Quartet No. 1 in D minor Op. 7. 26 September 1905.

fp: 5 February 1907, Vienna, Rosé Quartet.
fEp: 1 November 1913, Bechstein Hall, Flonzaley Quartet.
fEbp: 3 October 1927, Vienna Quartet.
Pub. 1907, Birnbach (Berlin)/Universal-Edition. Arr. for piano four hands by Felix Greissle.

BIBLIOGRAPHY:

A. Basso: A proposito dei primi Quartetti di Schoenberg, *Musica d'oggi*, June 1960, p. 250.

11. Kammersymphonie Op. 9. For fifteen solo instruments. 25 July 1906, Rottach-Egern.

fl, ob, ca, 2 cl, bcl, bsn, cbsn; 2 hn; strings.
fp: 1907, Vienna, Hofoper wind ensemble and the Rosé Quartet.
fEp: 6 May 1921, Aeolian Hall, ensemble, cond. Edward Clark.
Pub. 1912, Universal-Edition; also piano reduction by Eduard Steuermann; arr. for piano four hands by Felix Greissle.

BIBLIOGRAPHY:

Alban Berg: AS Kammersymphonie Op. 9—Thematische Analyse, Universal-Edition, n.d.

Theodor Helm: Konzert der Bläserkammermusik-Vereinigung der k.k. Hofoper (Die neue Kammersymphonie von AS), *Musikalisches Wochenblatt* (*NZfM*), 1907, No. 8 (21 February), p. 203.

Hans Keller: Schoenberg, the problem of performance, *MR*, May 1957, p. 150.

Ernst Kunwald: Die Kammersinfonie, *Pult und Taktstock*, March–April 1927.

11a. Kammersymphonie Op. 9. Version for orchestra by the composer. Pub. 1922, Universal-Edition. Arr. for piano four hands by Arnold Schönberg, unpub.

Schoenberg, Arnold

11b. First Chamber Symphony Op. 9b. New version for orchestra by the composer. 18 April 1935, Hollywood.

2 fl, pic, cl in E flat, cl, bcl, 3 ob, ca, 2 bsn, cbsn; 4 hn, 2 tpt, 3 tmb; strings.

Pub. 1936, Schirmer.

11c. Kammersymphonie Op. 9. Arr. by Anton Webern for flute (or violin), clarinet (or viola), violin, cello and piano. 1922.

fEp: 7 April 1930, BBC broadcast, cond. Anton Webern.

12. Zwei Balladen Op. 12. For voice and piano. 1907.

1. *Der verlorene Haufen* (Viktor Klemperer). 15 March–April 1907.

2. *Jane Grey* (Heinrich Ammann). 28 April 1907.

fEbp (No. 2): 29 November 1930, Emmy Heim.

Pub. 1920, Universal-Edition.

13. Friede auf Erden Op. 13. For mixed chorus a cappella. Words: C. F. Mayer. 9 March 1907.

fEbp: 7 January 1931, Wireless Chorus, cond. Stanford Robinson.

Pub. 1931, Tischer & Jagenberg; 1955, Schott. Eng. words by A. Fagge.

BIBLIOGRAPHY:

Siegfried Günther: Das trochäische Prinzip in ASs Op. 13, *Zeitschrift für Musikwissenschaft*, 1907–8.

1923, No. 3, p. 158.

14. String Quartet No. 2 in F sharp minor Op. 10. For string quartet and soprano voice. Words: Stefan George. 1907–8. Dated: 11 July 1908.

1. *Mässig (moderato)*; 2. *Sehr rasch*; 3. *Litanei*; 4. *Entrückung*.

fp: December 1908, Vienna, Rosé Quartet with Marie Gutheil-Schoder.

fEp: 10 June 1914, Bechstein Hall, London String Quartet (leader, Arthur Catterall) with Carrie Tubb.*

---

* Three movements only were performed. It is possible that the first complete performance in London was that given on 20 February 1924 at a chamber concert given in Aeolian Hall by Eugene Goossens, the interpreters being the Hungarian Quartet with Dorothy Moulton.

fFp: 30 March 1922, Paris, Salle Gaveau, Concerts Jean Wiéner, Pro Arte Quartet with Marya Freund.

fEbp: 15 October 1928, Arts Theatre Club, Vienna Quartet with Margot Hinnenberg-Lefebre.

Pub. 1910, Universal-Edition; reduction for voice and piano of last two movements by Alban Berg; arr. for piano four hands by Felix Greissle.

BIBLIOGRAPHY:

A. Basso: A proposito dei primi Quartetti di Schoenberg, *Musica d'oggi*, October 1960, p. 369.

14a. String Quartet No. 2 in F sharp minor Op. 10. Version for string orchestra by the composer. Pub. 1929.

15. Zwei Lieder Op. 14. For voice and piano. 1907-8.

1. *Ich darf nicht dankend* (Stefan George: 'Waller im Schnee').

2. *In diesen Wintertagen* (Georg Henckel). 2 February 1908.

Pub. 1920, Universal-Edition.

16. Zwei Lieder. For voice and piano.

1. *Gedenken*.

2. *Am Strande* (Rainer Maria Rilke). 8 February 1909.

Pub. 1966, Schott/Universal-Edition, in Arnold Schoenberg Sämtliche Werke (Reihe A, Band 1).

17. Das Buch der hängenden Gärten Op. 15. Fifteen songs for soprano and piano (Stefan George). 1908-9.

fp: 14 January 1910, Vienna, Martha Winternitz-Dorda.

fEbp: 1 November 1929, Margot Hinnenberg-Lefebre, acc. Eduard Steuermann.

Pub. 1914, Universal-Edition.

BIBLIOGRAPHY:

Karl Heinrich Ehrenforth: Ausdruck und Form (Schönbergs Durchbruch zur Atonalität in den George-Lieder Op. 15), H. Bouvier (Bonn) 1963.

Humphrey Searle: George-Lieder Op. 15, *Music Survey*, June 1952, p. 491.

18. Drei Klavierstücke Op. 11. 1909, rev. 1924.

1. *Mässige*. 19 February 1909. Dur. 4'.
2. *Mässige*. 22 February 1909. Dur. 6'.
3. *Bewegte*. 7 August 1909. Dur. 2½'.
fp: 14 January 1910, Vienna, Verein für Kunst und Kultur, Etta Werndorff.
fEp: 22 January 1912, Steinway Hall, Richard Bühlig.
fEbp: 7 May 1928, Eduard Steuermann.
Pub. 1910, Universal-Edition. Concert version of No. 2 by Ferruccio Busoni pub. 1910, Universal-Edition.

BIBLIOGRAPHY:
Frederick Corder: An epoch-making composer, *MT*, December 1911, p. 781.
A. Koperberg: Van Wermeskerken: Bij een Pianostuk van Schönberg, *Mens en melodie*, December 1952, p. 382.
Leonhard Welker: ASs Op. 11, *Die Musik*, October (2) 1912, p. 109.

19. Fünf Orchesterstücke Op. 16. For large orchestra. 1909, rev. 1922. 1. Dated: 9 June 1909; 2. Dated: 15 June 1909; 3. Dated: 1 July 1909, Steinakirchen; 4. Dated: 18 July 1909; 5. 11 August 1909, Steinakirchen.
3 fl, 2 pic, 3 ob, ca, 4 cl, bcl, cbcl, 3 bsn, cbsn; 6 hn, 3 tpt, 4 tmb, bs tuba; timp, xyl, cym, tgle, tamtam, GC; celesta, hp, strings.
fp: 3 September 1912, Queen's Hall, Promenade Concert, Queen's Hall Orchestra, cond. Sir Henry Wood. Note also: 17 January 1914, Queen's Hall, Queen's Hall Orchestra, cond. Arnold Schönberg.
fFp: 22 April 1922, Paris, Théâtre des Champs-Elysées, Orchestre Pasdeloup, cond. André Caplet.
Pub. 1912, Peters-Edition. Arr. for chamber orchestra (fl, pic, ob, cl, bsn, hn, hmnm, piano, strings) by Felix Greissle, pub. 1925, Peters-Edition. Reduction to normal orchestral size by the composer, September 1949, pub. 1952, Peters.

BIBLIOGRAPHY:
Max Deutsch: Les cinq pièces pour orchestre d'AS, *SM*, December 1948.
Ernest Newman: Schoenberg's Five Orchestral Pieces, in *Testament of Music* (ed. Herbert Van Thal), Putnam (London) 1962, p. 111.
Paul Rosenfeld: Five orchestral pieces, *Dial*, January 1922, p. 111.
H. H. Stuckenschmidt: Drömvisioner ur det

undermedvetna—Om ASs fem orkesterstycken Op. 16, *Nutida musik*, Vol. 3 (1959–60), No. 2, p. 14.
John Warrack: Seven Works That Shook the World, 7: Schoenberg's Five Orchestral Pieces, *Crescendo*, No. 127, March 1963, p. 142.
Theodor Wiesengrund-Adorno: Orchesterstücke Op. 16, *Pult und Taktstock*, March–April 1927.

19a. Fünf Orchesterstücke. Arr. for two pianos by Anton Webern.
fEbp: 16 November 1961, Cornelius Cardew and John Tilbury.

20. Erwartung Op. 17. Monodrama for voice and orchestra. Poem: Marie Pappenheim. 27 Aug.–12 Sept. 1909, Vienna.
3 fl, 2 pic, 4 ob, ca, 4 cl, bcl, 3 bsn, cbsn; 4 hn, 3 tpt, 4 tmb, bs tuba; timp, cym, GC, side dm, tamtam, rattle, tgle, glock, xyl; celesta, hp, strings.
fp: 6 June 1924, Prague, Neues Deutsches Theater, Marie Gutheil-Schoder, cond. Alexander von Zemlinsky.
fEp: 9 January 1931, BBC broadcast, Margot Hinnenberg-Lefebre and BBC Orchestra, cond. Arnold Schönberg.
Pub. 1916 (full score), Universal-Edition; vocal score by Eduard Steuermann.

BIBLIOGRAPHY:
Paul Bekker: Erwartung, *Anbruch*, 1924, Nos. 8–9.
A. Berger: Spotlight on the moderns: Erwartung, *Saturday Review*, 28 June 1952, p. 46.
Robert Craft: Schoenberg's Erwartung, *Counterpoint*, September 1952, p. 13.
Hans Keller: What happens in Erwartung?, *The Listener*, 13 August 1964, p. 250.
I. Kolodin: Erwartung by Pilarczyk, *Saturday Review*, 23 February 1963, p. 55.
Jeremy Noble: Schoenberg's Erwartung at Sadler's Wells, *Musical Events*, April 1960, p. 10.
Hans F. Redlich: Schönbergs Erwartung in Wiesbaden, *Anbruch*, February 1928, p. 60.
Paul Stefan: Erwartung, *Anbruch*, May 1924, p. 200.
H. H. Stuckenschmidt: Erwartung und Die

Schoenberg, Arnold

glückliche Hand—Schönberg-Abend in der Krolloper, *Anbruch*, June 1930, p. 221.
— ASs Erwartung, *Scheinwerfer*, 1931, No. 9.
Egon Wellesz: ASs Erwartung, *Der Auftakt*, June 1924.
Alexander Zemlinsky: Einige Wörte über das Stadium von Schönbergs Erwartung, *Pult und Taktstock*, March–April 1927.

20a. Der Nöck. Carl Löwe, orch. Arnold Schönberg. ?1910.

20b. Three Little Pieces. For chamber orchestra. Untitled and unfinished. 1910.
fEbp: 22 December 1960, Wigmore Ensemble, cond. George Malcolm.

21. Sechs kleine Klavierstücke Op. 19. 1911.
1. *Leicht, zart*; 2. *Langsam*; 3. *Sehr langsame*; 4. *Rasch, aber leicht*; 5. *Etwas rasch*; 6. *Sehr langsam*.
fp: 14 January 1910, Vienna, Verein für Kunst und Kultur, Etta Werndorff.
fEp: 14 February 1914, Newcastle, Geographic Institute, meeting of the Northern Section of the Incorporated Society of Musicians, lecture on Schönberg given by Edgar L. Bainton.
?f Paris p: 10 May 1921, Léo-Pol Morin.
fEbp (5 pieces): 7 May 1928, Eduard Steuermann.
fEbp (complete): 6 April 1936, Edmund Rubbra.
Pub. 1913, Universal-Edition.

BIBLIOGRAPHY:
Carl-Olof Anderberg: Kommentar till ett pianostycke, *Musikrevy*, 1960, No. 7, p. 253, No. 8, p. 297.
Gunnar Hallhagen: ASs Sex små pianostycken Opus 19, *Nutida musik*, Vol. 6 (1962–3), No. 2, p. 29.
Hugo Leichtentritt: ASs Op. 19, *Die Musik*, March 1933, p. 405.

22. Herzgewächse Op. 20. For high soprano, celesta, harmonium and harp. Text: Maurice Maeterlinck. 9 December 1911.
fEp: 1 December 1960, BBC invitation concert, Dorothy Dorow (soprano), Susan Bradshaw (celesta), Charles Spinks (hmnm), Renata Scheffel-Stein (hp), cond. Henry Washington.

Pub. 1914, in Der blaue Reiter (Munich); 1920, Universal-Edition; also piano score by Felix Greissle, 1925.

23. Pierrot Lunaire Op. 21. 21 Melodramas for speaking voice and chamber ensemble. Words: Albert Giraud, Ger. transl. Otto Erich Hartleben. 1912. Ded. Albertine Zehme.
Part 1:
1. *Mondestrunken.* 17–29 April 1912.
2. *Colombine.* 20 April 1912.
3. *Der Dandy.* 1–2 April 1912.
4. *Eine blasse Wäscherin.* 18 April 1912.
5. *Valse de Chopin.* 7 May 1912.
6. *Madonna.* 9 May 1912.
7. *Der kranke Mond.* 18 April 1912.
Part 2:
8. *Die Nacht.* 9–21 May 1912.
9. *Gebet an Pierrot.* 12 March 1912.
10. *Raub.* 9 May 1912.
11. *Rote Messe.* 22–24 April 1912.
12. *Galgenlied.* 12 May 1912.
13. *Enthauptung.* 23 May 1912.
14. *Die Kreuze.* 27 April–9 July 1912.
Part 3:
15. *Heimweh.* 5–22 May 1912.
16. *Gemeinheit.* 26 April–6 June 1912.
17. *Parodie.* 4 May 1912.
18. *Der Mondfleck.* 28 May 1912.
19. *Serenade.* 25 April 1912.
20. *Heimfahrt.* 9 May 1912.
21. *O alter Duft.* 30 May 1912.
piano, fl/pic, cl/bcl, v/va, c.
fp: 16 October 1912, Berlin, Albertine Zehmer (speaker), Eduard Steuermann (p), H. W. de Vries (fl/pic), K. Essberger (cl/bcl), Jakob Maliniak (v/va), Hans Kindler (c), cond. Arnold Schoenberg.
fFp: 16 January 1922, Paris, Salle Gaveau, Concerts Wiéner, Marya Freund (speaker), Jean Wiéner (p), Louis Fleury, H. Delacroix, Roelens, Feuillard, cond. Darius Milhaud.
fEp: 19 November 1923, Kensington Town Hall, Kensington Music Club concert, Marya Freund (speaker), Jean Wiéner (p), Louis Fleury, H. Delacroix, H. Denayer, P. Mas, cond. Darius Milhaud.
Pub. 1914, Universal-Edition.

BIBLIOGRAPHY:
Richard Batka: ASs Pierrot Lunaire, *Der Kunstwart.* December (1) 1912, p. 353.

Marion Bauer: The text of Pierrot Lunaire, *MN&H*, 3 November 1923, p. 385.

Paul Bekker: ASs Pierrot Lunaire in Frankfurt, *Frankfurter Zeitung*, 11 December 1921; *Anbruch*, January 1922, p. 15.

Maurice Bex: Pierrot Lunaire, *Revue hebdomadaire*, 11 February 1922, p. 239.

L. Castle: Schoenberg and his Pierrot Lunaire, *MS*, 17 May 1924, p. 161.

J. Diether: Not one but three new versions of Pierrot Lunaire, *American Record Guide*, April 1963, p. 68.

Q. Eaton: New friends of music revive Schoenberg's Pierrot Lunaire, *Musical America*, March 1949, p. 13.

Louis Fleury: About Pierrot Lunaire, *M&L*, April 1929.

Guido M. Gatti: Schönberg Pierrot Lunaire in Italien, *Anbruch*, April 1924, p. 164.

Robert Godet: Après une audition de Pierrot Lunaire, *RM*, May 1923, p. 19.

Cecil Gray: Schoenberg's Pierrot Lunaire, *Radio Times*, 17 November 1933, p. 481.

Charles Koechlin: Pierrot Lunaire, mélodramme d'AS, *Le Monde musical*, February 1922.

— Evolution et tradition; à propos du Pierrot Lunaire de M. Schönberg, *Le Ménestrel*, 17 March 1922, p. 117.

Jan Maegaard: Schoenbergs George-Lieder og 1961), No. 5, p. 2.

A. Mendel: Pierrot Lunaire, *Nation*, 10 May 1933, p. 538.

Darius Milhaud: Paris und unser Pierrot Lunaire, *Anbruch*, February 1922, p. 44.

Rollo H. Myers: Schönberg's Pierrot Lunaire, *Chesterian*, No. 22, April 1922.

G. A. Pfister: Pierrot Lunaire, *MN&H*, 6 October 1923, p. 280.

Hugo Rasch: ASs Lieder des Pierrot Lunaire, *AMZ*, 25 October 1912, p. 1078.

— Der wiedererstandene Pierrot Lunaire, *AMZ*, 1922, No. 41, p. 748.

Paul Reisenfeld: Ästhetische Ammerkungen zu ASs Pierrot Lunaire, *AMZ*, December 1912.

Florent Schmitt: Pierrot Lunaire, *Revue de France*, 1 May 1922.

Erwin Stein: Il Pierrot Lunaire di Schönberg, *Il Pianoforte*, April 1924.

— Die Behandlung der Sprechstimme in

Pierrot Lunaire, *Pult und Taktstock*, March–April 1927; Engl. transl. as 'The treatment of the speaking voice in Pierrot Lunaire' in *Orpheus in New Guises*, Rockliff (London) 1953, p. 86.

— The moonstruck Pierrot comes to London, *Radio Times*, 4 April 1930, p. 9.

Roland Tenschert: Eine Passacaglia von AS, *Die Musik*, May 1925, p. 590.

— Der 'Musikingenieur' Schönberg—Niederländerkünste im Pierrot Lunaire, *Der Auftakt*, 1926, No. 1, p. 13.

Emile Vuillermoz: Pierrot Lunaire, *Excelsior*, 1 May 1922.

Ralph Wood: An interim note on Pierrot Lunaire, *MMR*, 1945, p. 57.

Anon.: Pierrot Lunaire, *Röster i Radio*, 1957, No. 7, p. 12.

— Pierrot Lunaire, *Disques*, No. 77, January–February 1956, p. 97.

24. Die glückliche Hand Op. 18. Drama with music. Text: Arnold Schönberg. 9 September 1910–18 November 1913.

3 fl, 2 pic, 3 ob, ca, cl in D, 3 cl, bcl, 3 bsn, cbsn; 4 hn, 3 tpt, 4 tmb, bs tuba; hp, celesta, glock, xyl, timp, cym, GC, side dm, tamtam, bells (high & low), tgle, Metallrohr, tamb, hammer; strings.

fp: 14 October 1924, Vienna Volksoper, cond. Fritz Stiedry; with Alfred Jerger (The Man), Hedy Pfundtmayr (The Woman), Josef Hustinger (The Gentleman).

fEbp: 11 December 1957, Eberhard Wächter and section of chorus of Oesterreichischen Rundfunk, Vienna Symphony Orchestra, cond. Michael Gielen.

fEp (public): 17 October 1962, Royal Festival Hall, Derrick Olsen and section of the BBC Chorus, BBC Symphony Orchestra, cond. Michael Gielen.

Pub. 1916 (full score), Universal-Edition; also reduction for two pianos by Eduard Steuermann.

BIBLIOGRAPHY:

Rudolph Stephan Hoffmann: Die glückliche Hand—Drama mit Musik von AS, *NMZ*, 1925, No. 4.

H. Hutchinson: Die glückliche Hand, *Nation*, 21 May 1930, p. 605.

R.-Aloys Mooser: Die glückliche Hand, in

Aspects de la musique contemporaine, Editions Labor et Fidès (Geneva) 1957, p. 275.

Alfred Rosenzweig: Schönberg's Die glückliche Hand, *Sackbut*, October 1925, p. 83.

E. Scherber: Mahlers 10. Symphonie und Schönbergs Glückliche Hand, *Signale*, 12 November 1924.

Humphrey Searle: Schoenberg's Die glückliche Hand, *Musical Events*, October 1962, p. 8.

H. H. Stuckenschmidt: Schönbergs Glückliche Hand in Breslau, *Der Auftakt*, 1928, No. 4, p. 97.

G. Vernon: Modernism in extremis—presentation by the Philadelphia symphony orchestra of Die glückliche Hand, *Commonweal*, 14 May 1930, p. 53.

Karl H. Wörner: Die glückliche Hand, *SM*, September–October 1964, p. 274.

Die glückliche Hand—Drama mit Musik von AS (Text of the opera), *Der Merker*, June (1) 1911, p. 718.

25. Vier Lieder Op. 22. For voice and orchestra. 1913–16.

1. *Seraphita* (Ernest Dowson, Ger. transl. Stefan George). 6 October 1913.

24 v, 12 c, 9 db; 6 cl; tpt, 3 tmb, bs tuba; timp, cym, xyl, tamtam.

2. *Alle, welche dich suchen* (Rainer Maria Rilke: 'Das Stundenbuch'). 3 December 1914.

4 fl, ca, 3 cl, 2 bcl, cbsn; hp; 3 c, db.

3. *Mach mich zum Wächter deiner Weiten* (Rainer Maria Rilke: 'Das Stundenbuch'). 3 December 1914–1 January 1915.

3 fl, 2 pic, 3 ob, ca, 3 bcl, cbs cl; 4 v, 5 c, db.

4. *Vorgefühl* (Rainer Maria Rilke: 'Das Buch der Bilder'). 28 July 1916.

3 fl, pic, 3 ob, ca, 3 cl, bcl, 3 bsn, cbsn; 4 hn, tpt, bs tuba; strings.

fp: 21 February 1932, Frankfurt a.M., Hertha Reinecke (soprano) and the Radio Orchestra, cond. Hans Rosbaud.

fEp: 9 February 1952, BBC broadcast, Mary Jarred and the BBC Symphony Orchestra, cond. Clarence Raybould.

fEp (concert): 19 October 1960, Royal Festival Hall, cond. Bruno Maderna.

Pub. 1917, Universal-Edition.

BIBLIOGRAPHY:

Arnold Schönberg: Analysis of the Four

Orchestral Songs Op. 22, *PNM*, spring–summer 1965, p. 1.

Peter Stadlen: Schoenberg problems, *Musical Events*, October 1960, p. vi.

26. Die Jakobsleiter. Oratorio (unfinished) for soloists, chorus and orchestra. 1917–22. Scoring completed by Winfried Zillig.

fp (opening portion): 12 January 1958, Hamburg, Orchestra and Chorus of the North German Radio, cond. Hans Rosbaud.

fp (completed version): 1961, Vienna.

fEp: December 1965, Royal Festival Hall, BBC concert, Ilse Hollweg, Günther Reich, Joseph Ward, Robert Tear, John Shirley-Quirk, Otakar Kraus, Zurich Speaking Chorus, BBC Chorus, London Symphony Orchestra, cond. Erich Schmid.

BIBLIOGRAPHY:

Walter Klein: AS—Die Jakobsleiter, *NMZ*, 1920, No. 8, p. 123.

Hansjörg Pauli: Zu ASs Jakobsleiter, *SM*, November–December 1962, p. 351.

Anthony Payne: First performances: Schoenberg's Jacob's Ladder, *Tempo*, No. 75, winter 1965–6, p. 21.

Berthold Wiertel: Schönberg's Die Jakobsleiter, in *Schoenberg*, Schirmer (New York) 1937, p. 165.

Karl H. Wörner: Schoenbergs Oratorium Die Jakobsleiter, *SM*, September–October 1965, p. 250 and November–December 1965, p. 333.

Winfried Zillig: Notes on Die Jakobsleiter, *The Score*, No. 25, June 1959, p. 7.

27. Fünf Klavierstücke Op. 23. 1920–3.

1. *Sehr langsam*; 2. *Sehr rasch*; 3. *Langsam*; 4. *Schwungvoll*; 5. *Walzer*.

fEp: 7 January 1929, Arts Theatre Club, BBC concert of modern chamber music, Eduard Steuermann.

Pub. 1928, Wilhelm Hansen.

28. Serenade Op. 24. For chamber ensemble and baritone voice. Words (4th movement): Petrarch: Sonnet No. 217. 1920–3. Dated: 27 April 1923.

1. *Marsch*; 2. *Menuett*; 3. *Variationen*; 4. *Sonett von Petrarca*; 5. *Tanzscene*; 6. *Lied (ohne Worte)*; 7. *Finale*.

cl, bcl; mandoline, guitar; v, va, c.

fp (privately): 2 May 1924, Vienna, home of Dr. Norbert Schwarzmann.

fp (public): 20 July 1924, Donaueschingen, cond. Arnold Schönberg.

Pub. 1924, Wilhelm Hansen; also reduction for piano four hands by Felix Greissle; arr. for p, v and c by Felix Greissle; reduction of 4th movement for low voice and piano by Felix Greissle.

BIBLIOGRAPHY:

Paul A. Pisk: ASs Serenade, *Anbruch*, May 1924, p. 201.

Erwin Stein: ASs Serenade, *Anbruch*, August–September 1925, p. 421.

29. Suite Op. 25. For piano. 1921.
  1. *Präludium*; 2. *Gavotte*; 3. *Musette*; 4. *Intermezzo*; 5. *Menuett*; 6. *Gigue*.

fEp: 7 January 1929, Arts Theatre Club, BBC concert of modern chamber music, Eduard Steuermann.

Pub. 1925, Universal-Edition.

30. Chorale-Preludes (J. S. Bach). Arr. for orchestra by Arnold Schönberg.
  1. *Komm, Gott, Schöpfer, Heiliger Geist*.

2 fl, 2 pic, 2 ob, 2 ca, 2 E-flat cl, 2 cl, 2 bcl, 2 bsn, 2 cbsn; 4 hn, 4 tpt, 4 tumb, tuba; 4 timp, tgle, glock; 2 hp, strings.
  2. *Schmücke Dich, o liebe Seele*.

2 fl, 2 pic, 2 ob, 2 ca, 2 E-flat cl, 2 cl, 2 bcl, 2 bsn, 2 cbsn; 4 hn, 4 tpt, 4 tmb, tuba; timp, tgle, cym, glock; celesta, hp, strings.

fp: 7 December 1922, New York, New York Philharmonic Orchestra, cond. Josef Stransky.

fEp: 20 September 1928, Queen's Hall, Promenade Concert, cond. Sir Henry Wood.

Pub. 1925, Universal-Edition.

BIBLIOGRAPHY:

H. F. Redlich: Zu Schönbergs Instrumentierung zweier Bachscher Choralvorspiele, *Pult und Taktstock*, March–April 1927.

31. Wind Quintet Op. 26. For flute (piccolo), oboe, clarinet, horn and bassoon. 1923–4. Ded. Bubi Arnold.
  1. *Schwungvoll*; 2. *Anmutig und Leiter: scherzando*; 3. *Etwas langsam*; 4. *Rondo*.

fp: 13 September 1924, Vienna, wind group from the Vienna Philharmonic Orchestra, cond. Felix Greissle.

f Paris p: 3 May 1926, Revue Musicale concert, Fleury (fl), Lamorlette (ob), Cahuzac (cl), Entraigue (hn) and Dhérin (bsn), cond. Vladimir Golschmann.

fEbp: 9 March 1952, Dennis Brain Wind Quintet.

Pub. 1925, Universal-Edition. Arr. as Sonata for violin (or flute) and piano, or for clarinet and piano, by Felix Greissle. Also reduction for piano four hands.

BIBLIOGRAPHY:

Robert Craft: Performance notes for Schoenberg's Quintet, *Woodwind Magazine*, June 1952, p. 6.

Felix Greissle: Die formalen Grundlagen des Bläserquintetts von AS, *Anbruch*, February 1925, p. 63.

R.-Aloys Mooser: Bläserquintett Op. 26, in *Aspects de la musique contemporaine*, Editions Labor et Fidès (Geneva) 1957, p. 226.

Th. Wiesengrund-Adorno: Schönbergs Bläserquintett, *Pult und Taktstock*, May–June 1928 and September 1928.

32. Suite (Septet) Op. 29. For piano, piccolo clarinet (or flute), clarinet, bass clarinet (or bassoon), violin, viola and cello. 1924–6. Ded. 'Meiner lieben Frau'.
  1. *Ouverture*; 2. *Tanzschritte*; 3. *Thema mit Variationen*; 4. *Gigue*.

fp: 15 December 1927, Paris, cond. Arnold Schoenberg.

?fEp: 24 November 1933, BBC concert in Broadcasting House, Frederick Thurston (cl), Ralph Clark (cl), Walter Lear (bcl), Rudolf Kolisch (v), Eugen Lehner (va), Benar Heifetz (cl), Eduard Steuermann (piano).

Pub. 1927, Universal-Edition.

BIBLIOGRAPHY:

Lamar Crowson: Playing Schoenberg's Opus 29, *RCM Magazine*, 1962, No. 3, p. 54.

Hans Schnoor: Schönberg Op. 29 bei Paul Aron, *Anbruch*, January 1929, p. 46.

Erwin Stein: Zu Schönbergs neuer Suite Op. 29, *Anbruch*, August–September 1927, p. 280.

33. Kaiserwalzer (Johann Strauss). Arr. for chamber ensemble (flute, clarinet, string quartet and piano) by Arnold Schönberg. 1925. Pub. *c.* 1960.

34. Vier Stücke Op. 27. Nos. 1–3 for unacc. SATB; No. 4 with acc. of mandoline, clarinet, violin and cello. 1925.

   1. *Unentrinnbar* (Arnold Schönberg). 30 September 1925.

   2. *Du sollst nicht, du musst* (Arnold Schönberg). 17 October 1925.

   3. *Mond und Menschen* (from Hans Bethge's 'The Chinese Flute'). 16 October 1925.

   4. *Der Wunsch des Liebhabers* (from Hans Bethge's 'The Chinese Flute'). 10 November 1925.

   fEp: 2 February 1961, BBC broadcast, London New Music Singers cond. Graham Treacher, with Hugo D'Alton (mandoline), Gervase de Peyer (cl), Emanuel Hurwitz (v) and Terence Weil (c).

   Pub. 1926, Universal-Edition.

35. Drei Satiren Op. 28 (Arnold Schönberg). For unacc. SATB. 1925.

   1. *Am Scheideweg.* 12 November 1925.

   2. *Vielseitigkeit.* 31 December 1925.

   3. *Der neue Klassizismus.* Short cantata for SATB chorus with viola, cello and piano. 13 November–30 December 1925.

Appendix. 1925–6.

   1. *Ein Spruch und zwei Variationen über ihn*; 2. *Canon für Streichquartett*; 3. *Legitimation als Canon.*

   Pub. 1926, Universal-Edition.

BIBLIOGRAPHY:

Erwin Stein: Neue Choere von Schönberg, *Anbruch*, December 1926, p. 421.

Th. Wiesengrund-Adorno: Choruses Op. 27 & 28, *Anbruch*, November–December 1928.

36. Variations for orchestra Op. 31. 1926–1928. 20 September 1928, Roquebrune. Dur. 16′ 12″.

   4 fl, 2 pic, 4 ob, ca, E-flat cl, 4 cl, bcl, 4 bsn, cbsn; 4 hn, 3 tpt, 4 tmb, bs tuba; timp, cym, GC, side dm, tamtam, tgle, tamb, glock, xyl, flexatone; celesta, mandoline, hp; strings.

   fp: 2 December 1928, Berlin, Berlin Philharmonic Orchestra, cond. Wilhelm Furtwängler.

   fEp: 13 November 1931, BBC broadcast, BBC Studio Symphony Orchestra, cond. Sir Adrian Boult. (Note also: 8 February 1933, BBC Symphony Orchestra, cond. Arnold Schoenberg.)

   fEp (concert): 22 September 1958, Liverpool, Philharmonic Hall, Musica Viva concert, Royal Liverpool Philharmonic Orchestra, cond. John Pritchard.

   Pub. 1929, Universal-Edition.

BIBLIOGRAPHY:

Hans Ulrich Engelmann: Schoenbergs Variationen für Orchester, *Melos*, December 1966, p. 396.

R.-Aloys Mooser: Variationen für Orchester Op. 31, in *Aspects de la musique contemporaine*, Editions Labor et Fidès (Geneva) 1957, p. 130.

Peter S. Odegard: Schoenberg's Variations: an addendum, *MR*, May 1966, p. 102.

Arnold Schönberg: The Orchestral Variations Op. 31 (A radio talk, Frankfurt Radio, 1931), *The Score*, No. 27, July 1960, p. 27.

Erwin Stein: Zur Uraufführung der Variationen für Orchester von Schönberg, *Anbruch*, January 1929, p. 45.

Wgd. (i.e. Theodor Wiesengrund-Adorno): Variationen für Orchester Op. 31 von AS, *Anbruch*, January 1930, p. 35.

37. String Quartet No. 3 Op. 30. 8 March 1927. Ded. Elizabeth Sprague Coolidge.

   1. *Moderato*; 2. *Adagio*; 3. *Intermezzo* (*Allegro moderato*); 4. *Rondo* (*Molto moderato*).

   fp: 19 September 1927, Vienna, Coolidge invitation concert, Kolisch Quartet.

   fEp: 13 February 1928, BBC chamber concert, Vienna Quartet.

   Pub. 1927, Universal-Edition.

BIBLIOGRAPHY:

R.-Aloys Mooser: 3ᵐᵉ Quatuor, in *Aspects de la musique contemporaine*, Editions Labor et Fidès (Geneva) 1957, p. 191.

Erwin Stein: Schönberg's Third String Quartet, *The Dominant*, March 1928, p. 14.

38. Prelude and Fugue in E flat major. J. S. Bach, arr. for orchestra. 1928.

   2 fl, 2 pic, 2 ob, 2 ca, 2 E-flat cl, 2 cl, 2 bcl, 2 bsn, 2 cbsn; 4 hn, 4 tpt, 4 tmb, tuba; timp, tgle, cym, glock, xyl, GC; celesta, hp, strings.

   fp: 10 November 1929, Vienna, cond. Anton Webern.

   fEp: 9 January 1931, BBC broadcast, BBC Orchestra, cond. Arnold Schoenberg.

fEp (concert): 16 November 1964, Royal Academy of Music (Duke's Hall), Kensington Symphony Orchestra, cond. Michael Head.
Pub. 1929, Universal-Edition.

39. Klavierstücke Op. 33a. 1928.
fEbp: 23 December 1932, Else C. Kraus.
Pub. 1929, Universal-Edition.

40. Drei Volksliedsätze. Three German folksongs (15th and 16th centuries) for mixed chorus a cappella. 1928.
1. *Schein uns, du liebe Sonne*; 2. *Es gingen zwei Gespielen gut*; 3. *Herz liebchen Lieb, durch scheiden.*
fp: November 1929, Vienna, Singverein, cond. Anton Webern.
fEbp (No. 2): 25 June 1933, Wireless Singers, cond. Cyril Dalmaine.
Pub. 1930, Peters-Edition in *Volksliederbuch für die Jugend.*

41. Von Heute auf Morgen Op. 32. Opera in one act. Libretto: Max Blonda (i.e. Gertrud Schoenberg). 1928-9.
2 fl, pic, 2 ob, ca, E-flat cl, 2 cl, bcl, sop sax, alto sax, bs sax, bsn, cbsn; 2 hn, 2 tpt, 3 tmb, bs tuba; timp, cym, GC, side dm, tamtam, tgle, tamb, glock, xyl, flexaton; hp, piano, celesta, mandoline, guitar; strings.
fp: 1 February 1930, Frankfurt a.M., Municipal Theatre, cond. William Steinberg; with Else Gentner-Fischer (Wife), Elisabeth Friedrich (Girl Friend), Benno Zieglier (Husband), Anton M. Topitz (Singer).
fEbp: 21 September 1958, 1958 Holland Festival recording, cond. Hans Rosbaud; with Erika Schmidt (Wife), Magda Laszlo (Girl Friend), Derrick Olsen (Husband), Herbert Schachtschneider (Singer).
fEp: 13 November 1963, Royal Festival Hall, BBC Symphony Orchestra, cond. Antal Dorati; with Heather Harper, Erika Schmidt, Herbert Schachtschneider and Derrik Olsen.
Pub. 1929-30 (piano score) Edition Benno Balan; 1951 (piano score) Ars Viva Verlag Hermann Scherchen; 1961 (score) Schott.

BIBLIOGRAPHY:
Alois Hába: AS—Von heute auf morgen, Opern-première in Frankfurt a.M., *Der Auftakt*, 1930, No. 2, p. 54.

Hans Keller: Schoenberg's comic opera, *The Score*, No. 23, July 1958, p. 27.
Paul A. Pisk: Schönberg's twelve-tone opera, *Modern Music*, April–May 1930.
Willi Reich: Schönberg-Premiere nach 22 Jahren, *Melos*, January 1953, p. 27.
— Schoenberg-Première, *Musikleben*, February 1953, p. 63.
George Schott: Schönbergs Von heute auf morgen, *Signale*, 1930, No. 7, p. 179.
Theodor Wiesengrund-Adorno: AS: Von heute auf morgen—Uraufführung in Frankfurt am Main, *Anbruch*, February 1930, p. 72; *Die Musik*, March 1930, p. 445.

42. Deutsche Volkslieder. German folksongs arr. for voice and piano. Pub. 1930, Peters-Edition in *Volksliederbuch für die Jugend*; 1961, Peters.

43. Begleitungsmusik zu einer Lichtspielszene (Accompaniment to a Film Scene) Op. 34. For orchestra. 15 October 1929–14 February 1930, Berlin.
1. *Drohende Gefahr*; 2. *Angst*; 3. *Katastrophe.*
fl, pic, ob, 2 cl, bsn; 2 hn, 2 tpt, tmb; timp, cym, GC, side dm, tamtam, tgle, tamb, glock, xyl; piano, strings.
fp: 1930, Berlin, Orchestra of the Kroll Opera, cond. Otto Klemperer.
fEp: 8 May 1931, BBC broadcast, BBC Orchestra, cond. Anton Webern.
Pub. 1930, Heinrichshofens Verlag (Magdeburg).

BIBLIOGRAPHY:
A. Berger: Schoenberg for sound-track; recording of Begleitmusik, *Saturday Review*, 28 April 1956, p. 56.
R.-Aloys Mooser: Begleitungsmusik zu einer Lichtspielszene, in *Aspects de la musique contemporaine*, Editions Labor et Fidès (Geneva) 1957, p. 101.
H. Swarsenki: Au sujet de la Musique pour un Film Imaginaire de Schoenberg, *Musique et Radio*, September 1962, p. 295.

44. Sechs Stücke Op. 35. For male chorus (TTBB). Words: Arnold Schönberg, transl. D. Millar Craig and Adolph Weiss. 1929-30.
1. *Hemmung* (Restraint). 19 February 1930.
2. *Das Gesetz* (The law). 5-9 March 1930, Berlin-Charlottenburg.

3. *Ausdrucksweise* (Means of expression).
4. *Glück* (Happiness).
5. *Landsknechte* (Yeomen). 5–8 March 1930, Berlin–Charlottenburg.
6. *Verbundenheit* (Obligation). 16–19 April 1929.
Pub. 1930, Bote & Bock.

BIBLIOGRAPHY:
Josef Polnauer: Schönbergs 'Verbundenheit', in *Arnold Schönberg zum 60. Geburtstag*, Universal-Edition, p. 44.
Willi Reich: Schönberg's new Männerchor, *Modern Music*, January–February 1932; Schönbergs neue Männerchöre, *Der Auftakt*, May–June 1932, p. 124.

45. Piano Piece Op. 33b. 10 October 1931, Barcelona.
f Ebp: 23 December 1932, Else C. Kraus.
Pub. New Music Society of California.

46. Moses und Aron. Opera in three acts (final act unfinished). 1930–2.

3 fl, 3 pic, 3 ob, ca, E-flat cl, 2 cl, bcl, 2 bsn, cbsn; 4 hn, 3 tpt, 3 tmb, tuba; timp, side dm, GC, large tenor dm, tamb, cym, tamtam, gong, tgle, glock, xyl, flexatone, high & low bells, high bell without specific pitch, rattle; hp, piano, celesta, 2 mandolines; strings. For stage music in Act II: tmbs, ca, hn, 2 mando-lines, 2 guitars, 2 tpt, pic, fl, cl, timp, GC (muffled), tamb, gongs, cym, xyl, piano.

fp (Der Tanz um das goldene Kalb): 2 July 1951, Darmstadt, Orchestra and Chorus of the Landestheater, cond. Hermann Scherchen.

fEp: 10 March 1952, BBC broadcast, BBC Chorus and London Philharmonic Orchestra, cond. Hermann Scherchen; with Elizabeth Cooper, Tatiana Magic, Joan Gray, Marjorie Thomas, Frank Sale, Lloyd Strauss-Smith and Dennis Noble.

fp (complete opera, concert form): 12 March 1954, Hamburg, Nordwestdeutscher Rundfunk Chorus and Orchestra, cond. Hans Rosbaud; with Hans Herbert Fiedler, Helmut Krebs, Ilona Steingruber, Horst Gunter, Helmut Kistschmar, Hermann Rieth; the performance was relayed by the BBC and a recording broadcast on 26 February 1955.

fp (stage): 6 June 1957, Zürich, Stadttheater, cond. Hans Rosbaud; with Ilse Wallenstein, Ilse Friedrich, Mary Davenport, H. H. Fiedler, Helmut Melchert, Charles Gillig; producer, Karl Heinz Krahl.
Pub. 1957, Schott. Reduction by Winfried Zillig. English transl. Allen Forte.

BIBLIOGRAPHY:
Herbert Fleischer: Il testamento artistico di AS: La danza intorno al vitello d'oro, *Il Diapason*, 1951, Nos. 5–6.
Ernest Chapman: Moses and Aron at Covent Garden, *Musical Events*, August 1965, p. 12.
Robert Henderson: Moses und Aron, *M&M*, July 1965, p. 18.
Heinz Joachim: Die Stimme aus dem Dornbusch: ASs Moses und Aron, *NZfM*, May 1957.
János Kárpáti: Schoenberg: Mózes és Áron, *Muzsika*, 1962, October p. 20, November p. 6.
Hans Keller: Moses und Aron, *The Score*, No. 20, June 1957, p. 69; No. 21, October 1957, p. 30.
— After 25 years, an 'unfinished' opera makes a bow on the stage, *M&M*, August 1957, p. 11.
— Moses, Freud and Schoenberg, *MMR*, 1958, pp. 12, 63.
— Schoenberg and the first sacred opera, *The Listener*, 12 November 1959, p. 848.
B. Kortsen: Schoenbergs opera Moses og Aron, *Dansk Musiktidsskrift*, 1963, No. 6, p. 222.
J. Maegaard: Moses og Aron, *Nordisk Musik-kultur*, October 1957, p. 85.
Colin Mason: Schoenberg's late success: Moses und Aron, *Manchester Guardian*, 15 June 1957, p. 4.
P. Moor: Schoenberg's Moses and Aron in Hamburg, *New York Times*, 4 April 1954, Section 2, p. 7.
Oliver Neighbour: Moses und Aron, *MT*, 1965, p. 422.
Willi Reich: Ein Briefwechsel über Moses und Aron, *SM*, 1957, p. 259.
— ASs Oper Moses und Aron, *SM*, July 1957, p. 296.
— Moses und Aron, *SM*, April 1954, p. 143.
Charles Reid: Operatic tradition in Schönberg's Moses und Aron, *The Listener*, 24 June 1965, p.953

Geoffrey Skelton: Schönberg's Moses und Aron, *MT*, June 1954, p. 304.

Erwin Stein: Moses und Aron, *Opera*, August 1957, p. 485.

George Steiner: Schönberg's Moses und Aron, *Encounter*, July 1965, p. 40.

H. H. Stuckenschmidt: A Schönberg first performance at Darmstadt (transl. William Mann), *Foyer*, No. 1, autumn 1951, p. 26.

— Moses und Aron di Schönberg, *La Rassegna musicale*, 1962, p. 210.

— AS Moses und Aron, Nordwestdeutscher Rundfunk Hamburg, in *Oper in dieser Zeit*, Friedrich Verlag (Hannover) 1964, p. 10.

— AS Moses und Aron, Städtische Oper Berlin 1959, in *–do–*, p. 12.

John J. Weissmann: Moses and Aron at Covent Garden, *Musical Events*, June 1965, p. 6.

Jacques Wildberger: Moses och Aron, *Nutida musik*, Vol. 2 (1958–9), No. 2, p. 12.

Karl H. Wörner: Schoenberg-Urauff. im NWDR, Hamburg, *Musikleben*, April 1954, p. 136.

— Schoenberg's Moses and Aron, *London Musical Events*, May 1954, p. 23.

Peter Yates: Moses and Aron by Schoenberg, *Art and Architecture*, 1958, September p. 4, October p. 6.

Anon.: Moses und Aron, Uraufführung in NWDR Hamburg, *Melos*, April 1954, p. 115.

— Bible on the stage, *Music Magazine*, June 1965, p. 7.

— Opera on records: Moses und Aron, *Opera News*, 8 April 1961, p. 25.

47. Cello Concerto. After the Concerto for Clavicembalo composed in 1746 by Georg Matthias Monn (1717–1750). 1932–3. Ded. Pablo Casals.

　1. *Allego moderato*; 2. *Andante, alla marcia*; 3. *Tempo di Minuetto*.

　2 fl, 2 pic, 2 cl, 2 bsn; 2 hn, 2 tpt, 2 tmb; timp, glock, xyl, tgle, cym, GC, snare dm, tamb; celesta, hp, strings.

　fEp (?fp): 5 February 1933, BBC broadcast, Antonio Sala and the BBC Orchestra, cond. Edward Clark.

　fEp (concert): 7 December 1935, Queen's Hall, Royal Philharmonic Society concert,

Emanuel Feuermann and the London Philharmonic Orchestra.

　Pub. 1935, Schirmer; reduction by the composer, 1936.

48. Three Songs Op. 48 (Jakob Haringer). For voice and piano. 1933.

　1. *Sommermäd*. 14–16 January 1933, Berlin.

　2. *Tot*. 17 February 1933, Berlin.

　3. *Mädchenlied*. 23 February 1933, Berlin.

　Pub. 1952, Bomart (New York).

49. Concerto for string quartet and orchestra. After the Concerto grosso Op. 6 No. 7 of Handel. 20 May–16 August 1933.

　2 fl, 2 ob, 2 cl, 2 bsn; 2 hn, 2 tpt; pcssn; hp, strings.

　fp: 26 September 1934, Prague, Kolisch Quartet and Radio Orchestra, cond. Karl B. Jirak.

　fEbp: 7 March 1937, Kolisch Quartet and the BBC Orchestra, cond. Sir Adrian Boult.

　Pub. c. 1935, Schirmer.

50. Suite for string orchestra. 1934.

　1. *Ouverture*; 2. *Adagio*; 3. *Menuet*; 4. *Gavotte*; 5. *Gigue*.

　fp: 18 May 1935, Los Angeles, Los Angeles Philharmonic Orchestra, cond. Otto Klemperer.

　fEp: 1 February 1936, BBC broadcast, Boyd Neel String Orchestra, cond. Boyd Neel.

　Pub. 1935, Schirmer.

51. Violin Concerto Op. 36. 1934–6. Ded. Anton von Webern. Dur. 30′.

　1. *Poco allegro*. 2 September 1934.

　2. *Andante grazioso*. 27 August 1936.

　3. *Finale: Allegro*. 23 September 1936.

　3 fl, pic, 3 ob, E-flat cl, cl, bcl, 4 bsn; 4 hn, 3 tpt, 3 tmb, tuba; timp, xyl, glock, general pcssn; strings.

　fp: 6 December 1940, Philadelphia, Louis Krasner and the Philadelphia Orchestra, cond. Leopold Stokowski.

　fEbp: 20 March 1952, Antonio Brosa and the BBC Symphony Orchestra, cond. Rudolf Schwarz.

　fGBp (public): 29 April 1960, Glasgow, St. Andrew's Hall, Musica Viva concert, Wolfgang Marschner and the Scottish National

Orchestra, cond. Alexander Gibson; broadcast.

f London p: 3 October 1960, Wolfgang Marschner and the London Symphony Orchestra, cond. Alexander Gibson.

Pub. 1939, Schirmer; also reduction by Felix Greissle.

BIBLIOGRAPHY:

André Mangeot: AS's concerto for violin and orchestra, *Strad*, 1940, March p. 420, April p. 450.

Josef Rufer: ASs violinkonsert Opus 36, *Nutida musik*, Vol. 6 (1962–3), No. 7, p. 15.

H. Schnippering: Bemerkungen zu Schönberg's Violinkonzert—Wie ein Musikfreund Schönberg hört, *Melos*, June 1950, p. 167.

Unsigned: AS's Violin Concerto, *MO*, February 1940, p. 205.

52. String Quartet No. 4 Op. 37. 1936. Ded. Elizabeth Sprague Coolidge and the Kolisch Quartet.

1. *Allegro molto, energico.* 27 April–12 June 1936.

2. *Comodo.* 24 May–10 June 1936.

3. *Largo.* 10 June–18 June 1936.

4. *Allegro.* 18 June–26 July 1936.

fp: 9 January 1937, Los Angeles, Kolisch Quartet.

f European p: 12 March 1937, BBC broadcast, Kolisch Quartet.

f Paris p: 17 February 1939, Société Nationale concert, Kolisch Quartet.

Pub. 1939, Schirmer.

53. Piano Quartet Op. 25 (Brahms). Orchestrated by Arnold Schönberg. 2 May–19 September 1937.

fp: 7 May 1938, Los Angeles, Los Angeles Philharmonic Orchestra, cond. Otto Klemperer.

fEbp: 10 April 1961, BBC Scottish Orchestra, cond. Norman Del Mar.

fEp (concert): 21 August 1962, Royal Albert Hall, Promenade Concert, Philharmonia Orchestra, cond. Sir Adrian Boult.

Pub. *c.* 1938, Schirmer.

BIBLIOGRAPHY:

Gordon Jacob, Schönberg and Brahms's Op. 25, *M&L*, July 1951.

54. Kol Nidre Op. 39. For rabbi, chorus and orchestra. 1 August–8 September 1938.

2 fl, pic, ob, E-flat cl, cl, bcl, bsn; 2 tpt, 2 hn, 2 tmb, tuba; timp, cym, gong, bell, GC, flexatone, xyl; strings.

fp: 4 October 1938, Los Angeles, cond. Arnold Schönberg.

Pub. 1953, Boelke Bomart (Hillsdale, New York).

55. Second Chamber Symphony Op. 38a. Begun: 1906. Completed: October 1939. Dur. 24'.

1. *Adagio.* 15 August 1939, Brentwood Park.

2. *Con fuoco—Molto adagio.* 21 October 1939, Brentwood Park.

2 fl, pic, 2 ob, ca, 2 cl, 2 bsn; 2 hn, 2 tpt; string quintet.

fp: 15 December 1940, New York, orchestra of the New Friends of Music, cond. Fritz Stiedry.

fEp: 15 November 1948, BBC broadcast, Philharmonia Orchestra, cond. Hermann Scherchen.

Pub. Schirmer; 1952, study score.

55a. Second Chamber Symphony Op. 38b. Version by the composer for two pianos. First movement dated: 25 December 1941; second movement dated: 12 January 1942, Brentwood Park. Unpub.

56. Variations on a recitative Op. 40. For organ. 25 August–12 October 1941.

fp: March 1944, concert of the U.S. Section of the ISCM, Carl Weinrich.

fEbp: 17 March 1952, Ralph Downes.

Pub. 1947, H. W. Gray (New York), ed. Carl Weinrich; arr. for two pianos by Celius Dougherty, 1955.

BIBLIOGRAPHY:

M. Mason: An organist plays Mr. Schoenberg, *Organ Institute Quarterly*, spring 1956, p. 19.

57. Ode to Napoleon Buonaparte Op. 41. For string quartet, piano and reciter. Text: Byron. 12 June 1942, Brentwood Park.

fEbp: 18 July 1951, Aeolian Quartet, Leonard Cassini and George Baker.

Pub. 1944, Schirmer.

57a. Ode to Napoleon Buonaparte Op.

41b. Transcription by the composer for string orchestra, piano and reciter.

fp: 23 November 1944, New York, Mack Harrell (reciter), Eduard Steuermann (piano) and the New York Philharmonic, cond. Artur Rodzinski.

fEp: 28 May 1945, Cambridge Theatre (London), Cuthbert Kelly (reciter), Else Cross (piano), strings of the London Philharmonic Orchestra, cond. Karl Rankl.

58. Piano Concerto Op. 42. 30 December 1942. Ded. Henry Clay Shriver. Dur. 28'.

2 fl, pic, 2 ob, 2 cl, 2 bsn; 4 hn, 2 tpt, 3 tmb, tuba; timp, bells, gong, cym, xyl, GC, side dm; strings.

fp: 6 February 1944, New York, NBC broadcast, Eduard Steuermann and the NBC Symphony Orchestra, cond. Leopold Stokowski.

fEp: 7 September 1945, Royal Albert Hall, Promenade Concert, Kyla Greenbaum and the BBC Symphony Orchestra, cond. Basil Cameron.

Pub. 1944, Schirmer; also reduction for two pianos by Eduard Steuermann.

BIBLIOGRAPHY:

Yvonne Lefébure: A propos du Concerto pour piano de Schoenberg, *Contrepoints*, No. 1, January 1946, p. 68.
René Leibowitz: Schönbergs Klavierkonzert, *Melos*, February 1949, p. 44.
R.-A. Mooser: Concerto pour piano Op. 42, in *Aspects de la musique contemporaine*, Editions Labor et Fidès (Geneva) 1957, p. 256.

59. Birthday Canons. For three voices. 1943. Ded. Carl Engel. Pub. 1943, Schirmer, in *A Birthday Offering*; also pub. 1963, Bärenreiter, in *Thirty Canons* (ed. Josef Rufer).

60. Theme and Variations Op. 43a. For band. 24 August 1943. Dur. 11'.

2 fl, 2 pic, 2 ob, 2 bsn, E-flat cl, 3 cl, alto E-flat cl, bcl; 2 alto sax, ten sax, bar sax; 2 cornets, 2 tpt, 2 Flugelhorns, 4 hn in F, 4 hn in E flat, 3 tmb, baritone, euphonium, basses and tubas; double bass; timp, cym, GC, side dm, glock, tamb, tgle, xyl, gong.

Pub. 1944, Schirmer.

60a. Theme and Variations Op. 43b. Version for orchestra. 1943.

fp: 20 October 1944, Boston, Boston Symphony Orchestra, cond. Serge Koussevitzky.

fEp: 5 July 1947, BBC broadcast, London Philharmonic Orchestra, cond. Walter Goehr.

Pub. 1944, 1949, Schirmer.

BIBLIOGRAPHY:

W. C. M. Kloppenburg: Het Thema van Schönbergs Variationen for orchester, *Mens en melodie*, December 1957.
Peter S. Odegard: Schönberg's Variations: an addendum, *MR*, May 1966, p. 102.

61. Prelude Op. 44 ('Genesis' Prelude). For mixed chorus (SATB) and orchestra. 30 September 1945. Commissioned by Nathaniel Shilkret.

2 fl, pic, 3 ob, E-flat cl, 2 cl, bcl, 2 bsn, cbsn; 4 hn, 3 tpt, 3 tmb, tuba; xyl, glock, GC, cym, tgle, side dm, tamtam, timp; hp, celesta, strings.

fp: 18 November 1945, Los Angeles, Werner Janssen Symphony Orchestra, cond. Werner Janssen.

fEp: 29 November 1961, Royal Festival Hall, BBC Symphony Orchestra, cond. Bruno Maderna.

Pub. 1962, Edition Shilkret (Malverne, Long Island, N.Y.).

62. String Trio Op. 45. 20 August–23 September 1946. Commissioned by the Department of Music, Harvard University.

fp: March 1947, Harvard University.

fbp: 14 January 1950, BBC broadcast, London String Trio (Maria Lidka, Watson Forbes and Vivian Joseph).

Pub. 1950, Boelke Bomart (Hillsdale, New York).

BIBLIOGRAPHY:

William Hymanson: Schoenberg's String Trio (1946), *MR*, 1950, p. 184.
O. W. Neighbour: Dodecaphony in Schoenberg's String Trio, *Music Survey*, June 1952, p. 489.

63. A Survivor from Warsaw Op. 46. For narrator, men's chorus and orchestra. 11–23 August 1947. Composed for the Koussevitzky Music Foundation and ded. to the memory of

Nathalie Kousseveitzky. Text: Arnold Schön-berg; Fr. version by René Leibowitz, Ger. version by Margaret Peter.

2 fl, pic, 2 ob, 2 cl, 2 bsn; 4 hn, 3 tpt, 3 tmb, tuba; xyl, bells, chimes, mil dm, GC, timp, cym, tgle, tamb, tamtam, cast; hp, strings.

fp: 4 November 1948, Albuquerque (New Mexico), Albuquerque Civil Symphony Orchestra, cond. Kurt Frederick.

fEbp: 9 January 1951, Antonio Kurbinsky, Venetian Theatre Choir and Symphony Orchestra of Radio Italiana, cond. Hermann Scherchen.

fEp: 19 June 1951, George Baker, London Philharmonic Choir and Orchestra, cond. Clarence Raybould; broadcast.

Pub. 1949, Boelke-Bomart (Hillsdale, New York).

BIBLIOGRAPHY:

Henry Cowell: Current Chronicle—Survivor from Warsaw, *MQ*, July 1950, p. 450.

P. Hamburger: AS's Survivor from Warsaw, *Music Survey*, winter 1950, p. 183.

René Leibowitz: AS's Survivor from Warsaw or the possibility of 'committed' art, *Horizon*, August 1949, p. 122.

P. Righini: Il sopravvissuto di Varsavia d'AS, *Rivista musicale italiana*, October–December 1951, p. 393.

64. Three Folksongs Op. 49. For mixed chorus (SATB) a cappella. 1948.

1. *Es gingen zwei Gespielen gut.* 24 June 1948.
2. *Der Mai tritt ein mit Freuden.* 26 June 1948.
3. *Mein Herz in steten Treuen.*

Pub. 1949, Edward B. Marks (New York); English words by Harold Heiberg.

65. Phantasy Op. 47. For violin with piano acc. 3–22 March 1949. Ded. in memory of Adolph Koldofsky.

fp: 13 September 1949, Los Angeles, Adolph Koldofsky and Leonard Stein.

fEbp: 18 July 1951, Tibor Varga and Kyla Greenbaum.

Pub. 1952, C. F. Peters (New York).

66. Dreimal tausend Jahre (God's Return) Op. 50a. For mixed chorus (SATB) a cappella. Poem: Dagobert D. Runes. 20 April 1949.

fp: 29 October 1949, Fylkingen (Sweden), Lilla Chamber Chorus, cond. Eric Ericson.

fEbp: 2 March 1961, London New Music Singers, cond. Graham Treacher.

Pub. Prisma, 1949, No. 4 (as Op. 49b); 1955, Schott.

BIBLIOGRAPHY:

D. M. Epstein: Late Schönberg work is released—Dreimal tausend Jahre, *Musical America*, 1 December 1956, p. 24.

67. De Profundis (Psalm 130) Op. 50b. For mixed chorus (SSATBB) a cappella. 20 June–2 July 1950.

fp: 29 January 1954, Cologne, Chorus of the West German Radio, cond. Bernhard Zimmermann.

fEp (broadcast): 11 February 1960, London New Music Singers, cond. Graham Treacher.

Pub. 1953, Israeli Music Publishers.

68. Moderne Psalmen Op. 50c. For mixed chorus, speaker and orchestra. 1950. Text: Arnold Schönberg.

fp: 29 May 1956, Cologne, Chorus and Orchestra of the West German Radio, cond. Nino Sanzogno.

Pub. 1956, Schott.

BIBLIOGRAPHY:

Hans Keller: Schoenberg, the last work, *MR*, August 1957, p. 221.

H. H. Stuckenschmidt: Moderne Psalmen von AS, *ÖM*, February 1957.

Roman Vlad: Moderne Psalmen von AS, *Melos*, September 1957.

Karl H. Wörner: 'Und trotzdem bete ich'. Schönbergs Moderne Psalmen, *NZfM*, March 1957.

69. 30 Canons. 1905–49. Collected post-humously, ed. Josef Rufer. Pub. 1963, Bärenreiter.

SCHOENBERG'S MAJOR WRITINGS.

Harmonielehre, Vienna, 1911; Eng. transl. by D. Adams (abridged), Theory of Harmony, New York, 1947.

Models for Beginners in Composition, New York, 1942.

Style and Idea, New York, 1950. New and enlarged edition, ed. Leonard Stein, Faber, (London), 1972.

Structural Functions of Harmony, New York, 1954, ed. Humphrey Searle; Der formbildenden Tendenzen der Harmonie, Schott (Mainz) 1957; Structural Functions of Harmony, 2nd edition rev. Leonard Stein, Benn (London) 1969.

Ausgewählte Briefe, ed. Erwin Stein, Mainz, 1958; Letters, ed. Erwin Stein, transl. Eithne Wilkins & Ernst Kaiser, Faber (London) 1964.

Preliminary Exercises in Counterpoint, ed. Leonard Stein, Faber (London), St. Martin's Press (New York) 1963.

Fundamentals of Musical Composition, ed. Gerald Strang & Leonard Stein, Faber (London) 1967.

For a comprehensive list of Schoenberg's writings see:

Josef Rufer: The Works of Arnold Schoenberg, Faber (London) 1962.

GENERAL BIBLIOGRAPHY

Oskar Adler: Von der ewigen Jugend des Genies, in AS zum 60. Geburtstag, Universal-Edition, p. 31.

Ernest Ansermet: Music—expression or representation?, Musical America, February 1949, p. 6.

Merle Armitage: Transition, in Schoenberg, Schirmer (New York) 1937, p. 1.

David Josef Bach: AS und Wien, Der Merker, 1 June 1921, p. 254; Anbruch, 1921, No. 12, p. 216.

— A note on AS, MQ, October 1935 and January 1936.

— Du sollst nicht, du musst, in AS zum 60. Geburtstag, Universal-Edition, p. 62.

Edgar L. Bainton: AS, a critical study, MO, December 1913, p. 187.

Béla Bartók: ASs Musik in Ungarn, Anbruch, December (2), p. 647.

Paul Bekker: Schönberg-Abend in Frankfurt, Anbruch, March 1920, p. 195.

— Schönberg, Melos, 1921, No. 7, p. 123.

M. Bendiner: Modernism in general, Schönberg in particular, Musician, May 1935, p. 9.

N. V. Bentzon: Omkring AS, Dansk Musiktidsskrift, February 1956, p. 9.

— Hommage à Schoenberg, Dansk Musiktidsskrift, 1950, No. 9, p. 176.

Alban Berg: Der Lehrer (contribution), in AS, R. Piper (Munich) 1912, p. 89.

— Warum ist Schönbergs Musik so schwer verständlich?, Anbruch, August–September 1924; Why is Schönberg's music so hard to understand?, MR, August 1952, p. 187.

S. Bergel: Schönbergs sång om Warszawa, Musikrevy, 1951, p. 170.

A. Berger: Spotlight on the moderns, Saturday Review, 24 November 1951, p. 80, and 28 November 1953, p. 72.

— Later Schönberg, two new lp's, Saturday Review, 25 July 1953, p. 52.

— Chamber music by Schönberg and others, Saturday Review, 27 February 1954, p. 71.

— Berg, Schönberg and Krasner, Saturday Review, 24 April 1954, p. 56.

Otto Besch: AS, der Mann der Zukunft?, AMZ, 1912, No. 12.

Klaus Bessel: Revolutionär wird dogmatisch: AS als Anreger der modernen Musik, Berufsmusiker (Aachen), 1949, No. 10, p. 168.

Joachim Birke: Richard Dehmel und AS, ein Briefwechsel, Die Musikforschung, 1958, No. 3, p. 279.

— Nachträge zum Briefwechsel zwischen Dehmel und Schönberg, Die Musikforschung, January–March 1964.

Leo Black: The songs of AS, The Listener, 20 January 1966, p. 112.

F. Blanks: AS, Canon, March–April 1958, p. 273.

Werner Bollert: Zwischen Schönberg und Klebe, Musica, 1951, No. 3, p. 109.

Benjamin Boretz & Edward Cone (ed.): Perspectives on Schoenberg and Stravinsky, Princeton University Press (Princeton, N.J.) 1968.

Pierre Boulez: Trajectoires: Ravel, Stravinsky, Schönberg, Contrepoints, 6e cahier, 1949.

— Schönberg is dead, The Score, No. 6, May, 1952.

Havergal Brian: AS, MO, 1921, February p. 420, March p. 511.

Maurice Brillant: Les œuvres et les hommes [Honegger & Schönberg], Le Correspondant, 25 May 1922.

Alfred Brasch: Der letzte Romantiker, Rheinischer Merkur (Koblenz), 1949, No. 26, p. 6.

R. Breuer: Schönberg in his letters, Saturday Review, 30 January 1960, p. 35.

Schoenberg, Arnold

Hermann Broch: Irrationale Erkenntnis in der Musik, in *AS zum 60. Geburtstag*, Universal-Edition, p. 49.

A. J. Broekema: A stylistic analysis and comparison of the solo vocal works of AS, Alban Berg and Anton Webern, *Dissertation Abstracts*, November 1962, p. 1730.

Sten Broman: Schönberg och de atonala, *Sydsvenska Dagbladet*, 27 January 1932.

D. J. Buch: Schönberg und Wien, *Anbruch*, August 1921.

Richard Bühlig: Schönberg and the classical tradition, in *Schoenberg*, Schirmer (New York) 1937, p. 109.

K. Burke: Schönberg, *National*, 29 November 1933, p. 633.

G. Cablid: Den 'degenererade' Schönberg, *Musikvärlden*, 1949, p. 230.

John Cage: East in the West, *Modern Music*, 1946, No. 2, p. 111.

M.-D. Calvocoressi: AS and others, *Music Student*, March 1914, p. 133.

— The classicism of AS, *MT*, April 1914, p. 234.

— A visit to Schönberg in Berlin, in *Musicians Gallery*, Faber & Faber (London) 1933, chapter XXV.

Laura Remick Capp: The secret of modernist music—an interview with the foremost of modern impressionist composers, AS, *The Etude*, 1934, No. 10, p. 573.

P. Carpenter: The piano music of AS, *Piano Quarterly*, No. 41, fall 1962, p. 26.

Alfredo Casella: AS e la nuova musica italiana, *Musica d'oggi*, October 1924, p. 300; AS und die italienische Musik, *Der Auftakt*, September 1925, p. 255.

— Schönberg in Italy, *League of Composers' Review*, Vol. 1, No. 3, November 1924.

L. Castle: Schönberg's 'Treatise on Harmony', *MS*, 14 and 18 June 1924, pp. 193, 208.

G. Cervin: AS i praktiken, *Musikrevy*, 1954 p. 274, 1955 p. 170.

Carlos Chavez: Antecedents and consequences, *Eolus*, January 1927.

L. Chevaillier: Les idées de Schönberg, *Le Monde musical*, 31 January 1928.

Israel Citkowitz: Stravinsky and Schönberg: a note on syntax and sensibility, *Juilliard Review*. No. 3, fall 1954, p. 17.

Philip Greeley Clapp: Schönberg, futurist in music, *Musical News*, 1913, p. 297.

Edward Clark, Robert Donington & Paul Hamburger: After Schönberg's 75th birthday, *Music Survey*, Vol. III, No. 3, p. 180.

André Coeuroy: Schönberg in Paris (transl. Claire Stransky), *Anbruch*, January 1928, p. 21.

— Concerning AS, *Chesterian*, No. 69, March 1928.

— AS, in *Panorama de la musique contemporaine*, Simon Kra (Paris) 1928.

— Musiciens d'ailleurs, *Revue universelle*, 15 May 1922, p. 536.

A. Cohn: Music of AS, *American Record Guide*, November 1963 p. 192, January 1964 p. 394, September 1965 p. 12.

Paul Collaer: Le cas Schönberg, *La Revue internationale de musique* (Brussels), July-September 1938, p. 432.

— AS, Anton Webern, Alban Berg, in *La Musique moderne*, Elsevier (Paris) 1955, p. 35.

A. Collins: Bartók, Schönberg and some songs, *M&L*, April 1929.

Herbert Connor: Schönberg, *Signale*, 1926, No. 21, p. 879.

J. D. Cook: Composer tells how, *Saturday Review*, 26 June 1954, p. 41.

John Culshaw: Atonal preliminaries—Shoenberg, in *A Century of Music*, Dobson (London) 1952, p. 68.

George Coulter: An open letter to Schönberg and Company, *Musical Mirror*, May 1928, p. 117.

Henry Cowell: Current Chronicle, *MQ*, January 1949, p. 106.

Robert Craft: In memoriam, *Saturday Review of Literature*, 25 August 1951, p. 41.

D. Crew: Schoenberg, a humble petition and advice to English critics, *Music Survey*, February, p. 438.

Carl Dahlhaus: Ansermets Polemik gegen Schönberg, *NZfM*, 5 May 1966, p. 179.

— Schönberg und Bach, *NZfM*, March 1967, p. 109.

— Die Schönberg-Gesamtausgabe beginnt, *Melos*, April 1967, p. 116.

Luigi Dallapiccola: Der 13. September, *Stimmen* (Berlin), No. 16, 1949.

Louis Danz: Schönberg the inevitable, in

Schoenberg, Schirmer (New York) 1937, p. 207.

Winton Dean: Schönberg's ideas, *M&L*, October 1950, p. 295.

Ernst Decsey: Zur Schönberg-Kritik, *Signale*, 1914, No. 5 (4 February), p. 173.

Norman Demuth: AS, in *Musical Trends in the 20th Century*, Rockliff (London) 1952, p. 209.

E. J. Dent: (AS), *Nation*, 14 May 1921, p. 261.
— Music of AS, *Living Age*, 9 July 1921, p. 112.

Max Deutsch: AS, *La Vie musicale*, No. 9, September 1951, p. 3.

O. Downes: AS, *New York Times*, 22 July 1951, Section 2, p. 5.

Leonard Duck: Schönberg and Webern, *Halle*, No. 117, 1960–1, p. 17.

Antoine Duhamel: AS, la critique, et le monde musical contemporain, *RM* (L'Oeuvre du XXe Siècle), 1952, p. 77.

Herbert Eimert: (AS), *Die Musikleben* (Mainz), September 1951.
— AS, der Fünfundsiebzigjährige, *Melos*, September 1949, p. 226.

Hans Eisler: AS, der musikalische Reaktionär, *Anbruch*, 1924, p. 312.
— Schönbergova dvanasttonava technika, *Slovenska Hudba*, October 1958, p. 416.
— AS, Sinn und Form, in *Eine Auswahl von Reden* (Leipzig), 1961, p. 112.

Carl Engel: Schönberg and 'sentiment', in *Schoenberg*, Schirmer (New York) 1937, p. 157.

Richard Engländer: Kring AS, *Musikrevy*, 1950, p. 225.

E. Erdmann: Von Schönberg und seinen Liedern, *Melos*, 1920, No. 9, p. 207.

Edwin Evans: Schoenberg, dreamer and mathematician, *Radio Times*, 13 November 1931, p. 509.

Hermann Erpf: Für AS, *NMZ*, 1921, No. 3, p. 37.
— AS, *Neue Badische Landeszeitung* (Mannheim), No. 461, 11 September 1924.
— AS, *NMZ*, 1 October 1924.
— AS—Zu seinem 50. Geburtstag am 13. September 1924, *NMZ*, 1925, No. 1, p. 18.

R. Evett: What is atonality?, *New Republic*, 8 September 1952, p. 22.

David Ewen: AS, *MMR*, 1934, p. 147.

A. Felber: AS, *La Nuova Italia musicale*, September 1931.

Erwin Felber: Schönberg, *Deutsche Kunstschau*, No. 21, 1924.
— AS, *Die Musik*, May 1931, p. 566.
— AS und die Oper, *Anbruch*, January–February 1937, p. 67.

A. Helmut Fiechtner: Ein jüdischer Komponist der Moderne, *Gemeindeblatt* (Düsseldorf), 1949, No. 13, p. 9.
— Theodor Berger und Schönberg, *Melos*, 1952, No. 2, p. 55.
— Zwischen Schönberg und Berger, *Musica*, 1952, No. 3, p. 121.

H. T. Finck: Musical Messiah—or Satan?, *Nation*, 25 November 1915, p. 635.

Herbert Fleischer: Il problema Schönberg, *La Rassegna musicale*, 1935, No. 2, p. 111.

Hugo Fleischer: Für und wider AS, *Die Merker*, December (2) 1912, p. 919.

H. Fleischmann: Schönberg e le sue opere orchestrali, *Musica d'oggi*, December 1927.

Hugo Robert Fleischmann: AS, *ZfM*, 1920, No. 18, September (2), p. 307.

Hubert Foss: Schönberg, *MT*, September 1951, p. 401.

A. Franckenstein: Schönberg from Pelléas to Genesis, *High Fidelity*, December 1963, p. 68.

Peter Racine Fricker: Two song cycles, *The Listener*, 24 January 1963, p. 185.

Ruth Friedburg: The solo keyboard works of AS, *MR*, February 1962, p. 39.

Philip Friedheim: Tonality and structure in the early works of Schönberg, New York University, 1963.

Martin Friedland: Noch einmal der Fall Schönberg, *AMZ*, 1924, No. 45, p. 811.

Walther Friedlander: Musik der Einsamkeit— Werke von Schönberg, *Hier und Heute* (Frankfurt a.M.), 1951, No. 9, p. 22.

Viktor Fuchs: AS als Soldat im ersten Weltkrieg, *Melos*, June 1966, p. 178.

F.G.: Schönberg, ou le musicien saisi par la sonate, *RM*, September–October 1934, p. 211.

M.L.G.: The coming of Schönberg, *MS*, 24 January 1914, p. 79.

Rudolf Gail: Der Expressionismus ASs, *Ostsee-Zeitung* (Stettin), 13 January 1925.

Hans Gal (ed.): AS, in *The Musicians World*

Schoenberg, Arnold

(Great Composers in their Letters), Thames & Hudson (London) 1965, p. 439.

Guido M. Gatti: Schönberg, Casella ed un nuovo stile musicale italiano, *L'Esame*, April 1924.

Herbert Gerigk: Eine Lanze für Schönberg! Anmerkungen zu einem Geburtstagsaufsatz, *Die Musik*, November 1934, p. 87.

Matteo Glinsky: Il mesaggio di AS, *L'Osservatore Romano*, 1951, No. 168.

— Intorno all'enigma schönberghiano, *L'Osservatore Romano*, 1951, No. 170.

Franz Glück: Briefe von AS an Adolf Loos, *ÖM*, January 1961.

Alexander Goehr: Schönberg's late tonal works, *The Listener*, 16 January 1964, p. 132.

— Schönberg, *M&M*, July 1965, p. 16.

Alfred Goetze: AS, *Berliner Börsen-Zeitung*, No. 429, 12 September 1924.

Fred. Goldbeck: The strange case of Schönberg, *The Score*, No. 6, May 1952.

Noël Goodwin: Man and Superman?, *M&M*, January 1965, p. 16.

M. Groczycka: Teatra Arnolda Schönberga, *Ruch Muzyczny*, 1962.

Glenn Gould: The dodecaphonist's dilemma, *Canadian Music Journal*, 1956, No. 1, p. 20.

— AS, a perspective, University of Cincinnati, *Occasional Papers*, No. 3, 1964.

Peter Gradenwitz: Schönbergs religiöse Werke, *Melos*, November 1959; The religious works of AS, *MR*, February 1960, p. 19.

— Gustav Mahler and AS, in *Leo Baeck Institute Yearbook*, V, 1960, p. 262.

Max Graf: AS's Basso Continuo, *Signale*, 1913, No. 14 (2 April), p. 505.

— Der neueste Schönberg, *Anbruch*, December 1927, p. 432.

— Recollections of Schönberg's early career, *Musical America*, August 1951, p. 14.

Cecil Gray: AS, a critical study, *M&L*, January 1922, p. 73.

— AS, in *A Survey of Contemporary Music*, O.U.P. 1927, p. 162.

Paris von Gütersloh: Schönberg der Maler, in *AS*, R. Piper (Munich) 1912, p. 65.

Alois Hába: Schönberg und die weiteren Möglichkeiten der Musikentwicklung, in *AS zum 60. Geburtstag*, Universal-Edition, p. 15.

A. Hallenberg: AS och den nya musiken, *Kyrkosångsförbundet*, 1951, p. 85.

Bengt Hambraeus: Den siste Schönberg, *Musikrevy*, 1958, p. 92.

Tibor Harsanyi: Schönberg in Paris, *Literatura*, April 1928.

W. Hart: Kulturband—Diskussion um AS und die klingende Ergänzung, *Berliner Musikbericht*, 1947, No. 2, p. 11.

Katherine Hayward: An interview with AS, *Southwestern Musician*, September 1949, p. 4.

H. W. Heinsheimer: Schönberg's Odyssey, *Opera News*, 13 March 1965, p. 6.

Robert L. Henderson: Schönberg and 'Expressionism', *MR*, May 1958, p. 283.

— Portrait of Debussy, 3: Debussy and Schoenberg, *MT*, March 1967, p. 222.

Leigh Henry: AS, *MO*, 1921, February p. 420, March p. 511.

Philip Heseltine: AS, *MS*, 21 September 1912, p. 176.

Alfred Heuss: Über AS, *ZfM*, March 1924, p. 110.

— AS, Preussischer Kompositionslehrer, *ZfM*, October 1925, p. 583.

Peter Heyworth: The unfamiliar Schönberg, *Records & Recording*, April 1963, p. 27.

— Listening to Schönberg, *High Fidelity*, August 1963, p. 51.

Richard S. Hill: Schönberg's tone rows and the tonal system of the future, *MQ*, January 1936, p. 14.

Margot Hinnenberg-Lefèvre: Begegnung mit Schönberg, *Stimmen* (Berlin), No. 16, 1949.

Walther Hirschberg: Schönberg-Abend in der Krolloper, *Signale*, 1930, No. 25 (18 June), p. 808.

André Hodeir: AS, in *Since Debussy* (transl. Noel Burch), Secker & Warburg (London) 1961, p. 39.

Arthur Hoérée: Schönberg à Paris, *Beaux Arts*, 1 January 1928; *Musique*, 15 February 1928.

H. Holewa: AS, *Utsikt*, 1946, No. 6, p. 25.

Karl Holl: Schönberg, *Der Auftakt*, 1924, No. 8.

— AS fünfzigjährig, *Frankfurter-Zeitung*, No. 687, 13 September 1924.

G. W. Hopkins: Schoenberg and the 'logic' of atonality, *Tempo*, No. 94, autumn 1970, p. 15.

Karl Horwitz: Der Lehrer (contribution), in *AS*, R. Piper (Munich) 1912, p. 89.

A. E. Hull: Schönberg explained, *MMR*, 1914, pp. 59, 87, 116, 145, 176.

— Light on Schönberg, *MMR*, 1925, p. 163.

— Schönberg and his poets, *MO*, July 1925, p. 1020.

Reginald Hunt: Schönberg and the atonal idiom, *MO*, October 1950, p. 13.

Dyneley Hussey: Schönberg and his times, *Britain Today*, No. 192, April 1952.

Vincent d'Indy: Trois musiciens modernes, *Le Courrier musical*, 15 March 1922.

Heinrich Jalowetz: Die Harmonielehre, in *AS*, R. Piper (Munich) 1912, p. 49.

— Der Lehrer (contribution), in same, p. 82.

— Schönbergs Werk in der Zeit, in *AS zum 60. Geburtstag*, Universal-Edition, p. 4.

— On the spontaneity of Schönberg's music, *MQ*, October 1944, p. 385.

Gunnar Jeanson: AS, *Göteborgs Handels- cho Sjöfartstidning*, 13 October 1934.

Hildegard Jone: AS zum 60. Geburtstag, in *AS zum 60. Geburtstag*, Universal-Edition, p. 2.

Arthur Kahne: AS, *Berliner Tageblatt*, 23 December 1926.

W. Kandinsky: Die Bilder, in *AS*, R. Piper (Munich) 1912, p. 59.

Michael Kassler: The decision of AS's twelve-note-class system and related systems, Princeton University (Princeton, New Jersey) 1961.

— AS: a perspective, by Glenn Gould, *PNM*, fall–winter 1966, p. 161.

Adele T. Katz: Schönberg, in *A Challenge to Musical Tradition* (A new concept of tonality), Putnam 1945 (USA), 1947 (GB), p. 350.

Hans Keller: Schönberg-Anekdoten, *Stimmen* (Berlin), No. 16, 1949.

— AS, *MR*, February 1952, p. 83.

— The BBC's victory over Schönberg (with a footnote by Donald Mitchell), *MR*, May 1952, p. 130.

— Unpublished Schoenberg letters, *Music Survey*, June 1952, p. 449.

— Schönberg and the string quartet, *The Listener*, 21 April 1960, p. 731.

— Schoenberg—first performances, *Musical Events*, November 1961, p. 11.

— Schönberg; too great to be called great?, *The Listener*, 3 October 1963.

— Schönberg as music, *The Listener*, 7 January 1965, p. 34.

— Schönberg again or Schönberg anew, *Halle*, No. 122, 1965–6, p. 17.

— Schoenberg's four concertos, *The Listener*, 16 February 1967, p. 240.

Dieter Kerner: Schönberg als Patient, *Melos*, November 1959.

— AS, *Medizinischer Monatsspiegel*, May 1959.

Frd. Keyfel: Der Fall Schönberg, *Signale*, 1911, No. 10 (8 March), p. 383.

Walter Klefisch: Die Liquidierung der Atonalität—Ein Referat über die Wandlung ASs, *Neue Musikzeitschrift* (Munich), 1949, No. 3, p. 76.

Rudolf Klein: AS in Selbstzeugnissen, *ÖM*, February 1961.

Walter Klein: ASs Harmonielehre, *Der Merker*, March (2) 1912, p. 209.

— Das theosophische Element in Schönbergs Weltanschauung, *Anbruch*, 1924, Nos. 8–9.

Otto Klemperer: My recollections of Schönberg, in *Schoenberg*, Schirmer (New York) 1937, p. 183.

— AS, teacher, composer and transcriber, *Canon*, September 1949, p. 102.

Paul von Klenau: Tonal, A-tonal, *Anbruch*, 1924, Nos. 8–9.

Charles Koechlin: Schönberg in Paris, *Pult und Taktstock*, February 1928.

Josef Koffler: Drei Begegnungen, in *AS zum 60. Geburtstag*, Universal-Edition, p. 36.

Rudolf Kolisch: Schönberg als nachschaffender Künstler, *Anbruch*, 1924, Nos. 7–8, p. 306.

B. Kortsen: Forholdet Thomas Mann—AS, *Dansk Musiktidsskrift*, October 1959, p. 175.

Ernst Křenek: AS, in *Schoenberg*, Schirmer (New York) 1937, p. 79.

— AS 75 år, *Prisma* (Stockholm), 1949, No. 4, p. 40.

Paul Königer: Der Lehrer (contribution), in *AS*, R. Piper (Munich) 1912, p. 87.

Walther Krug: Schönberg, in *Die neue Musik*, Eugen Rentsch (Erlenbach) 1919, p. 57.

Paul Landormy: Schönberg, Bartók und die französische Musik, *Anbruch*, 1922, Nos. 9–10, p. 142.

Schoenberg, Arnold

Paul Landormy; AS, in *La Musique française*, Gallimard (Paris) 1943, p. 61.

Juliane Lange: Schönbergs Methode mit 12 Tönen zu komponieren, *Wirtschafts-Zeitung* (Stuttgart) 1949, No. 73, p. 15.

Warren M. Langlie: AS as a teacher, University of California, 1960.

Yvonne Lefébure: La révolution Schoenbergienne, *Formes et Couleurs*, 1948, No. 2.

Hugo Leichtentritt: AS's Harmonielehre, *Signale*, 1912, No. 22 (29 May), p. 731.

— Schönberg and tonality, *Modern Music*, April (?June) 1928.

René Leibowitz: Les œuvres dramatiques d'AS ou la conscience du drame futur dans la musique contemporaine, *Polyphonie*, premier cahier 1947–8.

— The traditional significance of the music of AS, *Horizon*, January 1947, p. 55.

— Besuch bei AS, *SM*, 1948, Nos. 8–9 (September), 324.

— La rhétorique d'AS, *Cahiers du Sud* (Paris), 1949, No. 297, p. 291.

— Stufen zur Vollendung, *Stimmen* (Berlin), No. 16, 1949.

— (AS), *The Canon*, September 1949.

Amadeo Solé Leris: AS, *Musica* (Madrid), No. 7, January–March 1954, p. 29.

Monica Lichtenfeld: Schönberg und Hauer, *Melos*, April 1965, p. 118.

Karl Linke (Lincke): Gedanken zu Schönberg, *Der Merker*, June (1) 1911, p. 710.

— Der Lehrer (contribution), in *AS*, R. Piper (Munich) 1912, p. 75.

K. List: Schönberg disc-course, *Saturday Review*, 1957, 30 November, p. 62, 14 December, p. 33.

Edward Lockspeiser: Schönberg, Nietzsche and Delius, *The Listener*, 9 March 1961, p. 463.

F. Lliurat: En torn de Schönberg, *Revista Musical Catalana*, May 1932; En torna a Schönberg, *Musicografia* (Monovar), May 1934.

W. Loewenfels (ed.): Eisler on Schönberg, *Saturday Review*, 31 August 1963, p. 33.

Max Loewengard: ASs Harmonielehre, *Der Merker*, September (1) 1913, p. 653.

Rudolf Lück: Die Generalbass-Aussetzungen ASs, in *Deutsches Jahrbuch der Musikwissenschaft*, 1964, p. 26.

Joseph Machlis: AS, in *Introduction to Contemporary Music*, Norton (USA), Dent (London) 1961, p. 344.

Charles Maclean: Schönberg, a short sketch of his life, *MT*, May 1914, p. 302.

Armand Machabey: Notes sur la musique allemande contemporaine: Schönberg, *Le Ménestrel*, 1930, 21 February p. 81, 30 May p. 245, 6 June p. 257.

Jan Maegaard: A study of the chronology of Op. 23–26 by AS, in *Dansk aarbog for musikforskning*, 1962, p. 93.

— Schönbergs George-Lieder og Pierrot Lunaire, *Nutida musik*, Vol. 4 (1960–1), No. 5, p. 2.

Luigi Magnani: Schönberg e la sua scuola, *La Rassegna musicale*, 1945, p. 29.

— Schönberg e il simbolismo, *Il Diapason* (Milan), July–August 1952.

Basil Maine: Schönberg and Stravinsky, *Apollo*, September 1926, p. 99.

Michael Mann: Problems of interpretation: Mozart–Schnabel–Schönberg, *Musicology* (Brooklyn, New York), 1949, p. 138.

William Mann: The anatomy of Schoenberg, *M&M*, May 1963, p. 17.

Gertrud Marbach: Schlemmers Begegnungen mit Schönberg, Scherchen und Hindemith, *NZfM*, December 1962.

Frank Martin: Schönberg and ourselves, *The Score*, No. 6, May 1952, p. 15.

Hans Joachim Marx: Don der Gegenwärtigkeit historischer Musik—Zu ASs Bach Instrumentation, *NZfM*, February 1961.

Colin Mason: Schoenberg and the orchestra, *The Listener*, 23 November 1961, p. 889.

Renzo Massarini: AS in Italy, *Sackbut*, July 1924, p. 364.

Alois Melichar: Schönberg und die Folgen, Eduard Wancura Verlag (Vienna) 1960.

Wilfrid Mellers: Wagner, Schönberg and Freud, *The Listener*, 4 August 1960, p. 201.

— Schönberg and Hindemith, in *Man and his Music*, Barrie & Rockliff (London) 1962, p. 982.

C. Rudolf Mengelberg: AS und die deutsche Musik, *Anbruch*, 1921, No. 6 (March), p. 108.

— Schönberg in Amsterdam, *Anbruch*, April 1921, p. 129.

Darius Milhaud: (Untitled contribution), in *AS zum 60. Geburtstag*, Universal-Edition, p. 30.
— To AS on his seventieth birthday: personal recollections, *MQ*, October 1944, p. 379.
— Begegnungen mit Schönberg, *Melos*, April 1955, p. 100.
— Erinnerungen an AS, *ÖM*, December 1955.
Donald Mitchell: Schoenberg the traditionalist, *Chesterian*, No. 159, July 1949.
— Bartók, Stravinsky and Schönberg, *Chesterian*, No. 175, July 1953.
H. K. Moderwell: AS's music, *New Republic*, 25 December 1915, p. 189.
P. Moor: Two titans: Schönberg and Ives, *Theatre Arts*, February 1950, p. 49.
Alfred Morgenroth: AS, ein Führer zur neuen Musik, *Halbmonatsschrift für Schulmusikpflege* (Dortmund), October 1924.
Arno Nadel: AS, Wesenhafte Richtlinien in der neueren Musik, *Die Musik*, 1912, No. 18 (June), p. 353.
Oliver (O.W.) Neighbour: In defence of Schönberg, *M&L*, January 1952.
— Schönberg: a talk given to Composers' Concourse, *The Score*, No. 16, June 1956, p. 19.
Robert U. Nelson: Schönberg's variation seminar, *MQ*, April 1964, p. 141.
Robert Neumann: Der Lehrer (contribution), in *AS*, R. Piper (Munich) 1912, p. 81.
Dika Newlin: Schoenberg in America, *Music Survey*, No. 5, 1949.
— The Schoenberg–Nachod collection, a preliminary report, *MQ*, 1968, No. 1, p. 31.
Ernest Newman: The Schönberg case, in *More Essays from the World of Music* (ed. Felix Aprahamian), Calder (London) 1958, p. 106.
— The case of AS, in *Testament of Music* (ed. Herbert Van Thal), Putnam (London) 1962, p. 163.
Hans Oesch: Hauer und Schönberg, *ÖM*, March 1960.
Ates Orga: Schönberg's 'free' atonality, *The Listener*, 19 May 1966, p. 736.
Eberhard Otto: Bahnbreches der Neuen Musik: AS, *ZfM*, 1951, p. 421.
Wouter Paap: AS, *Mens en melodie*, August 1951, p. 253.
Enzo Pachi & Luigi Rognoni: Schönberg . . .

e Strawinsky, *Aut-Aut* (Milan) 1952, No. 7.
Guido Pannain: AS, *La Rassegna musicale*, November 1928, p. 591.
— AS, *Der Auftakt*, January 1930, p. 17 (transl. Viktor Joss).
— AS, *MMR*, 1932, p. 121.
— AS, in *Musicisti dei tempi nuovi*, Turin, 1932, p. 55.
— Schönberg a la 'filosofia della musica nuova', *La Rassegna musicale*, July 1953, p. 193.
D. C. Parker: Schönberg hangs by a thread, *MS*, 15 May 1915, p. 372.
Hansjörg Pauli: ASs Briefe, *SM*, February 1959, p. 60.
Juan Carlos Paz: AS, o, el fin de la era tonal, Buenos Aires, 1958.
L. S. Peppercorn: Revolutionary music, *Radio Times*, 15 March 1935, p. 14.
George Perle: Schönberg's late style, *MR*, November 1952, p. 274.
— Serial composition and atonality: an introduction to the music of Schoenberg, Berg and Webern, Berkeley, 1962.
— Babbitt, Lewin and Schönberg: a critique, *PNM*, spring 1963, p. 120.
G. Perlman: AS, prophet or iconoclast?, *Instrumentalist*, November 1962, p. 42.
H. A. Peter: Kompromisslöshetens geni, *Skolmusik*, 1954, No. 6, p. 7; *Kyrkosångsförbundet*, 1957, p. 21.
Emil Petschnig: AS the Psychopath, *AMZ*, 1924, Nos. 48, 49, pp. 875, 895.
Hermann Pfrogner: Das Inhalt-Form-Problem im Schaffen ASs, *ÖM*, 1947, No. 10, p. 266.
M. Phillippot: L'école de Vienne, *Musical Information Récord*, No. 11, winter 1953–4, p. 9.
A. D. Pierce: Herr Schönberg, *American Mercury*, October 1931, p. 243.
D. E. Pike: AS as song writer, *Chesterian*, No. 68, January–February 1928.
Marc Pincherle: Aspects de Schönberg, *Journal musical français*, 25 September 1951; *SM*, April 1953, p. 158.
Paul A. Pisk: Schönberg's twelve-tone opera, in *Schoenberg*, Schirmer (New York) 1937, p. 187.
— (AS), *The Canon* (Sydney), September 1949.

Schoenberg, Arnold

Gertrud Pliquett: Schönbergs Theorie der Dissonanz, *Musikblätter*, 1948, No. 4, p. 20.

Rudolf Ploderer: Divination, in *AS zum 60. Geburtstag*, Universal-Edition, p. 60.

Fred K. Prieberg: Die junge Schönberg und seine Kritiker, *Melos*, September 1964, p. 264.

Klaus Pringsheim: Zwischen Helmholtz und Schönberg, *SM*, October 1956, p. 385.

C.J.P.: AS im Lichte seiner Zeit, *Anbruch*, 1924, No. 10, p. 432.

Karl Rankl: AS, *The Score*, No. 6, May 1952, p. 83.

Hugo Rasch: Nach der AS-Matinee, *AMZ*, 1912, No. 6.

Hans F, Redlich: Schönbergs Tonalität, *Pult und Taktstock*, March–April 1927.

— AS, *MR*, 1951, p. 304.

— Schönberg's religious testament, *Opera*, June 1965, p. 401.

Hans Reich: Schönberg als Zeitgenosse, *Der Auftakt*, 1934, No. 9 (September), p. 138.

Willi Reich: Musikerporträts im Rundfunk—Schönberg, *Anbruch*, May 1931, p. 100.

— AS e la suoa scuola viennese, *Pan*, 1934, No. 4, p. 566.

— AS et son école viennoise, *Les Cahiers de la musique*, 1 December 1936.

— Bitte der Jüngeren, in *AS zum 60. Geburtstag*, Universal-Edition, p. 40.

— Ein neues Buch von AS, *Melos*, December 1950, p. 351.

— Freiwillige für Schönberg, *Melos*, September 1951, p. 246.

— AS, *SM*, 1951, No. 9 (September), p. 354.

— AS, *Musiker* (Zürich), 1951, No. 4, p. 224.

— AS, *Neue Schweizer Rundschau*, Vol. 19 (1951–2), p. 224.

— Schönbergs musikpädagogisches Vermächtnis, *Melos*, December 1958.

— Ein unbekannter Brief von AS an Alban Berg, *ÖM*, January 1959.

— Zwei verschollene Porträts von AS und Alban Berg, *SM*, July–August 1963, p. 186.

— Vom Wiener 'Schönberg-Verein'. Mit unbekannten Briefen von Alban Berg, *SM*, November–December 1965, p. 340.

Schönberg: oder Der Konservative Revolutionär, Vienna, 1968; transl. by Leo Black, Schoenberg: a critical biography, Longmans, London, 1971.

Rudolf Réti: Formale Erläuterungen zu ASs Klavierstucken, *Der Merker*, June (1) 1911, p. 715.

A. Rich: Schönberg revealed by Gould, *Saturday Review*, 24 September 1966, p. 78.

José Rodriguez: Conversation with a legend, in *Schoenberg*, Schirmer (New York), 1937, p. 135.

Wolfgang Rogge: Das Klavierwerke ASs, Gustav Bosse Verlag (Regensburg) 1964.

Luigi Rognoni: Posizione di Schönberg, *L'Ambrosiano* (Milan), 1937, No. 177.

— AS, *La Rassegna musicale*, 1948, p. 291.

— Ritratto del Maestro della dodecafonia: AS, *La Fiera Letteraria* (Rome), No. 42, 1951.

— Espressionismo e dodecafonia, Giulio Einaudi, 1954.

— Gli scritti e i dipinti di AS, *L'Approdo musicale* (Turin), 1960, No. 12.

— La contradiction de Schoenberg, *L'Arc* (Aix-en-Provence), No. 27, 1965.

Paul Rosenfeld: Concerning Schönberg's music, *New Republic*, 22 January 1916, p. 309.

H. Rosenwald: Schoenberg between 1911 and 1950, *Musical News* (Chicago), June 1950, p. 6.

Walter H. Rubsamen: Schönberg in America, *MQ*, October 1951, p. 469; AS in Amerika, *Melos*, 1953, May, p. 132, June, p. 168.

Josef Rufer: AS, *Deutsche Allgemeine Zeitung*, 24 June 1927.

— The salient point in Schönberg's works, *Pro Musica*, June 1928.

— Über neue Musik im allgemeinen und Schönberg im besonderen, *Doppelpunkt* (Berlin), 1947, No. 3.

— Schöpferische Synthese, *Stimmen* (Berlin), No. 16, 1949.

— Rede auf AS, *Melos*, December 1957.

— A talk on AS, *The Score*, No. 22, February 1958, p. 7.

— ASs Nachlass, *ÖM*, March 1958.

— Das Werk ASs, Bärenreiter-Verlag (Kassel) 1959; transl. Dika Newlin as The Works of AS, New York, 1963, Faber & Faber (London) 1962.

— Schönberg—gestern, heute und morgen, *SM*, July–August 1965, p. 190.

— Spielgelungen des Eros, *ÖM*, May–June 1965.

K. H. Ruppel: Schönberg—ein Ereignis, *Melos*, April 1953, p. 118.

John Russell: Schönberg, the end of a myth, *20th Century*, December 1960, p. 432.

R. Saathen: AS, *ÖM*, 1951, Nos. 8–9.

St. Freund: Schönberg, *Le Monde musical*, 30 November 1927.

César Saerchinger: The truth about Schönberg, in *Schoenberg*, Schirmer (New York) 1937, p. 89.

Adolfo Salazar: Scriabin y Schönberg, in *Sinfonía y ballet*, Editorial Mundo Latino (Madrid) 1929, p. 147.

— AS post-mortem, *Nuestra Musica* (Mexico), August 1951.

Lazare Saminsky: Schönberg and Bartók, pathbreakers, *League of Composers' Review*, February 1924.

P. Sanborn: Another Schönberg Dithyramb, *MQ*, April 1925.

André Schaeffner: AS à Paris, *RM*, February 1928, p. 63.

— Variations Schönberg, *Contrepoints*, 1950, p. 110.

Ferdinand Scherber: AS als Dirigent, *Signale*, 1915, No. 19 (12 May), p. 289.

Hermann Scherchen: AS, *Melos*, 1920, p. 9.

Boris de Schloezer: The way of understanding, in *Schoenberg*, Schirmer (New York) 1937, p. 41.

E. Schmid: Studie über Schönbergs Streichquartette, *SM*, 1934, 15 January, 15 February, 15 March.

Ernst Schoen: AS, *Cahiers d'art*, 1927, No. 1, p. 36.

Boris Schwarz: AS in Soviet Russia, *PNM*, fall–winter 1965, p. 86.

Paul Schwers: Ein Nachwort zur Berliner Schönberg-Affaire, *AMZ*, 1922, No. 43, p. 784.

— Der 50jährige AS, *AMZ*, 12 September 1924 (No. 37), p. 629.

— Schönbergs Berufnung nach Berlin, *AMZ*, 1925, No. 39, p. 775.

Humphrey Searle: Schönberg and the future, *Hinrichsen Music Book*, Vol. VII, 1952, p. 134.

— AS, *World Review*, April 1952, p. 36.

— Two concertos by AS, *Gramophone Record Review*, June 1958, p. 657.

Roger Sessions: Music in crisis, in *Schoenberg*, Schirmer (New York) 1937, p. 9.

— Schönberg in the United States, *Tempo*, No. 9, December 1944; Schönberg in den USA, *Stimmen* (Berlin), No. 16, 1949.

— Some notes on Schönberg and the 'Method of Composing with Twelve Tones', *The Score*, No. 6, May 1952.

Maud G. Sewall: Hucbald, Schönberg and others on parallel octaves and fifths, *MQ*, April 1926, p. 248.

A. Skulsky: AS, *Musical America*, September 1951, p. 5.

Nicholas Slonimsky: A Schönberg chronology, in *Schoenberg*, Schirmer (New York) 1937, p. 215.

— Modern immortals, *Saturday Review of Literature*, 30 September 1950, p. 54.

— Musical oddities, *Etude*, April 1955, p. 5.

Carlo Somigli: Il modus operandi di AS, *Revista musicale italiana*, 1913, p. 583.

Richard Specht: AS, eine Vorbemerkung, *Der Merker*, June (1) 1911, p. 697.

— AS, *Nation*, 14 October 1925, p. 444.

Claudio Spies: Schönberg by Pittsburgh and Steinberg, *PNM*, spring–summer 1966, p. 172.

Paul Stefan: Schönberg-Abend, *Der Merker*, 25 October 1910, p. 79.

— Aus ASs Wedegang. Erinnerungen, *Der Merker*, June (1) 1911, p. 734.

— Schönberg's operas, *League of Composers' Review*, January 1925; *MQ*, January 1925; *Modern Music*, December 1929–January 1930; in *Schoenberg*, Schirmer (New York) 1937, p. 195.

— AS, Zeitkunst-Verlag (Vienna) 1924.

— Zur Schönberg-Feier, *Anbruch*, 1935, No. 7 (September), p. 135.

Eduard Steuermann: The piano music of Schönberg, in *Schoenberg*, Schirmer (New York) 1937, p. 125.

Erwin Stein: ASs neuer Stil, *Der Merker*, 1 January 1921, p. 3.

— Zur neuen Auflage von Schönbergs Harmonielehre, *Anbruch*, December (Nos. 19–20) 1922, p. 291.

— Über den Vortrag von Schönbergs Musik, *Pult und Taktstock*, September 1924.

— Einige Bemerkungen zu Schönbergs

Zwölftonreihen, *Anbruch*, June–July 1926, p. 251.

Erwin Stein: Schönberg and the Germanic line, *Modern Music*, June 1926.

— Der Lehrer (contribution), in *AS*, R. Piper (Munich) 1912, p. 82.

— Neue Formprinzipien, *Anbruch*, 1924, Nos. 8–9.

— Beethoven und Schönberg, *Anbruch*, March 1927.

— Idées d'AS, *RM*, November 1928, p. 1.

— Schönberg's new structural form, *Modern Music*, July 1930.

— AS, *RM*, March 1931, p. 201.

— Schönbergs Klang, in *AS zum 60. Geburtstag*, Universal-Edition, p. 25; Schönberg's sound, in *Schoenberg*, Schirmer (New York) 1937, p. 119.

— Leitfaden zur Harmonielehre, Vienna, 1951.

— Berg and Schönberg, *Tempo*, No. 44, summer 1957.

— AS: Ausgewählte Briefe, B. Schott's Söhne (Mainz) 1958; transl. Eithne Wilkins & Ernst Kaiser, Faber & Faber (London) 1964.

Rudolf Steiner: Der unbekannte Schönberg: aus unveröffentlichten Briefen an Hans Nachod, *SM*, September–October 1964, p. 284.

Rudolf Steiner & Ena Steiner: AS, an unknown correspondence, *Saturday Review*, 27 March 1965.

Erich Steinhard: Die Kunst ASs, *NMZ*, 1912, No. 18.

Eduard Steuermann: Zukunftsmusik, in *AS zum 60. Geburtstag*, Universal-Edition, p. 28.

— The piano music of Schoenberg, in *Schoenberg*, Schirmer (New York) 1937, p. 125.

R. Stevenson: The significance of Schoenberg, *Southwestern Musician*, September 1951, p. 13.

F. Stiedry: Schönberg-Proben, *Stimmen* (Berlin), No. 16, 1949.

Igor Stravinsky: Schönberg speaks his mind. *The Observer*, 18 October 1964.

— Schoenberg and I, *Show*, February 1963, p. 30.

— Schönberg's letters, *High Fidelity*, May 1965, p. 136.

Heinrich Strobel: Abschied von Schönberg, *Melos*, August 1951, p. 209.

— Der Bannerträger Schönbergs, *Melos*, 1952, No. 1, p. 13.

H. H. Stuckenschmidt: AS, *Das Kunstblatt*, February 1925.

— Das Problem Schönberg, *Melos*, April 1947 (No. 6), p. 161.

— Schönbergs Theorie der Dissonanz, *Musikblätter* (Berlin), 1948, No. 4, p. 20.

— Der Eigentliche. Die Dissonanzen zwischen AS und Thomas Mann, *Der Monat* (Munich), Vol. 1 (1948–9), No. 6, p. 76.

— Aesthetische Grundlagen, *Stimmen* (Berlin), No. 16, 1949.

— AS, Atlantis Verlag (Zürich/Freiburg) 1951; transl. Edith Temple Roberts and Humphrey Searle, John Calder (London) 1959.

— Schönbergs religiöse Werk, *SM*, 1957, p. 256.

— Stil und Ästhetik Schönbergs, *SM*, March 1958, p. 97; in *Schöpfer der neuen Musik*, Suhrkamp Verlag 1957, p. 162.

— Schönberg honoured at Hamburg anniversary, *Musical America*, March 1958, p. 6.

— Kandinsky und Schönberg, *Melos*, July–August 1964, p. 209.

— Luft von anderem Planeten, *Melos*, April 1965, p. 109.

H. A. Stuckey: Herr Schönberg and Mr. Masefield: a similarity and a contrast, *MS*, 5 September 1914, p. 176.

L. O. Symkins: AS's new world of dodecaphonic music, *Etude*, September 1950, p. 12.

Noel Heath Taylor: The Schönberg concept, *M&L*, April 1939, p. 183.

Roland Tenschert: Schönbergs neue Notenschrift, *Der Auftakt*, 1925, No. 9, p. 264.

— Der Musikingénieur, *Anbruch*, January 1926.

Virgil Thomson: How dead is Schönberg, *The New York Review of Books*, 22 April 1965, p. 6.

Alf Thoor: Genstörtig man med lissplan, *Musiklevet*, 1960, p. 8.

Michael Tippett: Schönberg's letters, *The Composer*, No. 15, spring 1965, p. 2.

Ernst Toch: AS, *Neue Badische Landeszeitung* (Mannheim), No. 226, 5 May 1925.

Roy Travis: Direct motion in Schönberg and

Webern, *PNM*, spring–summer 1966, p. 85.

T. Temple Tuttle: Schönberg's compositions for piano solo, *MR*, November 1957, p. 300.

R. Cort Van Den Linden: AS, *M&L*, October 1926 and January 1927.

Roman Vlad: L'ultimo Schönberg, *La Rassegna musicale*, 1948, p. 106.

Emile Vuillermoz: AS, *Deutsche Allgemeine Zeitung*, 18 August 1926.

J. Vyslouzil: Dva vyznamne schönbergovske dokumenty, *Hudební Rozhledy*, 1962, No. 18, p. 771.

Mayo Wadler: An American's impression of Schönberg, *The Musical Leader*, 1925,

Alan Walker: Schönberg's classical background, *MR*, November 1958, p. 283.

— Back to Schönberg, *MR*, May 1960, p. 140.

C. Henry Warren: Schönberg and his English critics, *Sackbut*, January 1932, p. 93.

Glenn E. Watkins: Schönberg and the organ, *PNM*, fall–winter 1965, p. 119.

Anton Webern: Über AS, *Rheinische Musik- und Theater-Zeitung*, 1912, pp. 99, 118.

— Schönbergs Musik, in *AS*, R. Piper (Munich) 1912, p. 22.

— Der Lehrer (contribution), in same, p. 85.

— Aus Schönbergs Schriften, in *AS zum 60. Geburtstag*, Universal-Edition, p. 11.

— Bekännelse till AS, *Nutida musik*, Vol. 6 (1962–3), No. 7, p. 18.

Adolph Weiss: The Lyceum of Schönberg, *Modern Music*, March–April 1932.

— The twelve-tone series, in *Schoenberg*, Schirmer (New York) 1937, p. 75.

Adolf Weissmann: Der 50jahrige AS, *Allgemeine Zeitung*, No. 336, 26 August 1924.

Egon Wellesz: AS, *Les Cahiers d'aujourd'hui*, série I (1912–14), p. 520.

— Les dernières œuvres d'AS, *Les Cahiers d'aujourd'hui*, nouvelle série (1920–1), No. 6, p. 286.

— Der Lehrer AS, *Melos*, 1921, No. 1, p. 12, No. 2, p. 36, No. 3, p. 57.

— Schönberg's treatise on harmony, *Sackbut*, December 1922, p. 133.

— Arnold Schönbergs Buhnenwerke, *Anbruch*, 1920, No. 18, p. 604.

— AS et son œuvre, *RM*, May 1923, p. 1.

— AS, *RM*, 1926, April, p. 12, July, p. 11, August, p. 126, November, p. 38.

— Der Lehrer (contribution), in *AS*, R. Piper (Munich) 1912, p. 81.

— AS, *Zeitschrift in der Internationalen Musik-gesellschaft*, 1911, No. 12.

— Schönberg et la jeune école viennoise, *Bulletin S.I.M.*, March 1912, p. 21.

— Schönberg and beyond, *MQ*, January 1916, p. 76.

— AS, E. P. Tal (Leipzig) 1921; rev. version transl. W. H. Kerridge, J. M. Dent (London) 1925.

— (Untitled article), in *AS zum 60. Geburtstag*, Universal-Edition, p. 23.

— AS, Counterpoint Publications (Oxford) 1945.

— The origins of Schönberg's twelve-tone system, Washington D.C., 1958.

— Schönberg und die Anfänge der Wiener Schule, *ÖM*, May 1960, p. 237.

— AS i poceci dodekafonije, *Zvuk*, 1960, Nos. 33–34, 1960, p. 113.

— Schönberg and the twelve-note system, *The Listener*, 10 August 1961, p. 199.

— Recollections of Schönberg, *The Composer*, No. 17, October 1965, p. 8.

M. A. Prick van Wely: AS en het expressionisme, *Symphonia* (Hilversum), Vol. XIX (1936), p. 5.

Franz Werfel: A tribute, in *Schoenberg*, Schirmer (New York) 1937, p. 205.

Fritz Werle: Zwei Kunstlerhoroskope, *Anbruch*, April 1927, p. 166.

Kurt Westphal: ASs Weg zur Zwolftöne-Musik, *Die Musik*, April (No. 7) 1929, p. 491.

Theodor Wiesengrund-Adorno: Der dialektische Komponist, in *AS zum 60. Geburtstag*, Universal-Edition, p. 18.

— Philosophie der neuen Musik, Tübingen 1949; new edition, Frankfurt 1938; Fr. transl. by Hildenbrand and Lindenberg as 'Philosophie de la nouvelle musique', Paris, 1962.

— Schoenbergs Klavierwerke, *Musica Schallplatte*, 1961, No. 4, p. 73.

— AS, in *Die grossen Deutschen*, Vol. IV, 1957, p. 508.

Hans E. Wind: Die Endkrise der bürgerlichen Musik und die Rolle ASs, Krystall-Verlag (Vienna) 1935.

Kurt v. Wolfurt: AS und der musikalische

Sibelius, Jean

Expressionismus, *Berliner Börsen-Zeitung*, 9 February 1927.
Ralph W. Wood: Concerning 'Sprechgesang', *Tempo*, No. 2 (17) December 1946.
Karl H. Wörner: AS, *Musica*, 1949, No. 9, p. 310.
— AS and the theater, *MQ*, October 1962, p. 444.
— Der unbekannte Schönberg, *Melos*, December 1952, p. 343.
J. Yasser: A letter from AS, *American Musicological Society Journal*, spring 1953, p. 53.
P. Yates: Leverkühn and the magician, *Saturday Review of Literature*, 26 February 1949, p. 47.
— Five decades of Schönberg, *Saturday Review of Literature*, 27 August 1949, p. 43.
— Apostle of atonality, *New York Times Magazine Section*, 11 September 1949, p. 19.
— Los Angeles moderns, *Saturday Review*, 29 September 1956, p. 44.
— Demi-wasteland, *High Fidelity*, January 1962, p. 38.
Alexander Zemlinzky: Jugenderinnerungen, in *AS zum 60. Geburtstag*, Universal-Edition, p. 33.
W. Zillig: Begegnung mit Schönberg, *Stimmen* (Berlin), No. 16, 1949.

<small>MISCELLANEOUS OR UNSIGNED</small>
AS, stages of musical growth, *The Times*, 17 January 1914, p. 11.
Leigh Henry on AS, *MS*, 20 June 1914, p. 579.
Herr Schoenberg and the Queen's Hall Orchestra, *The Times*, 23 January 1914, p. 8.
Blüten aus der Schönberg-Literatur, *AMZ*, 1924, No. 50, p. 919.
Nuovi trovati formali di AS, *Musica d'oggi*, May 1925, p. 152.
Une conversation avec AS, *RM*, November 1928; *Revue internationale de musique*, No. 7, January 1940, p. 96.
ASs Meisterklasse, *Signale*, 19 June 1929.
AS, *Musica d'oggi*, July 1931, p. 312.
Interviewing Schönberg, *Living Age*, 15 March 1928, p. 552.
Die ersten 'Schönberg-Platten', *Der Auftakt*, 1931, No. 3, p. 95.
Repercussions from a recent broadcast, *Music Teacher*, March 1933, p. 129.

Modernist to teach classes in America, *News Week*, 11 November 1933, p. 29.
Schönberg as a humorist, *Literary Digest*, 16 December 1933, p. 24.
Aus Schönbergs Schriften, *Anbruch*, September 1934, p. 138.
Letters from Webern and Schönberg to Roberto Gerhard, *The Score*, No. 24, November 1958, p. 36.
Twelve-tone puzzle, *Newsweek*, 4 December 1944, p. 90.
Doctor Faustus Schönberg?, *Saturday Review of Literature*, 1 January 1949, p. 22.
Destiny unknown, *Time*, 30 June 1961, p. 53.
Hollywood series to honour Schönberg, *Musical America*, October 1952, p. 32.
Aspects of Schönberg: recordings, *Musical America*, 15 November 1953, p. 17.
AS, *Musical Information Record*, No. 13, summer–autumn 1954, p. 24.
Schönberg quartets: recordings, *Musical America*, 1 February 1954, p. 15.
Schönberg legacy listed in Berlin, *Musical America*, 15 November 1957, p. 9.
El legado de Schoenberg, *Revista Musical Chilena*, January–February 1958, p. 80.
Aus Briefen ASs, *NZfM*, December 1958.
Schönberg revisited, *Time*, 30 June 1961, p. 53.
Schönberg for people who like Tristan, *The Times*, 1 November 1963, p. 16.
Das Werk ASs, *SM*, 1968, No. 2 (March–April), p. 121.

JEAN SIBELIUS (1865–1957)
Johan Sibelius—he changed the 'Johan' to 'Jean' in his early twenties—was born on 8 December 1865 into a middle-class family of mixed Finnish and Swedish blood at Hämeenlinna in southern Finland, where his father was a garrison doctor. The composer's mother-tongue was Swedish, but by adolescence he was almost equally fluent in Finnish. He wrote music from the age of ten, but did not decide to make a career of composition until much later: when he entered the Tsar Alexander University in Helsinki in 1885 it

was to study law, and though he did take courses at the Music Institute both at the same time and subsequently (studying there from 1885 to 1889 and giving up the law after one year), his prime ambition was to be a violin virtuoso. While at the Music Institute he was the protégé and composition-pupil of the Director, Martin Wegelius, and also began lifelong friendships with Ferruccio Busoni (then teaching piano in Helsinki) and several members of the Järnefelt family, who introduced him to their influential nationalistic circle of artists and administrators. In 1889 Sibelius left Finland for two years to study composition under Albert Becker in Berlin and under Robert Fuchs and Carl Goldmark in Vienna. Soon after his return to Helsinki he began to teach violin and music theory at the Music Academy. He married Aino Järnefelt in 1892 and in the same year had his first major success with the première of *Kullervo*. In 1897, as compensation for his not being appointed to a vacant musical post at the Tsar Alexander University, the state awarded Sibelius an annual stipend, which was turned into a life pension in 1907 and further enlarged in 1912 and 1925. By 1900 this had enabled him to retire from teaching altogether and concentrate on composition. In 1904 Sibelius moved from Helsinki to the nearby village of Järvenpää, which was to be his permanent home. However, he travelled widely during the next twenty years, largely to conduct his own music, notably making five trips to England and one (in 1914) to the United States. By the outbreak of the First World War he had become the Finnish cultural figure *par excellence* and there were national celebrations on his fiftieth and sixtieth birthdays. However, after writing *Tapiola* in 1926 he virtually retired from composition and from the world; and although he lived for a further thirty years—enjoying a great reputation at this time in Britain and the USA—he published nothing of consequence and rarely left Järvenpää. When he died there of a cerebral haemorrhage in September 1957, tenacious rumours of the survival in manuscript of an 'Eighth Symphony' supposedly written in the 1930s were proved groundless.

CATALOGUE OF WORKS

1. Water drops. For violin and cello, pizzicato. 1876. Unpub.

2. Piano Trio in A minor. 1881–2. Fragments only. Unpub.

3. Piano Quartet in E minor. 1881–2. Unpub.

4. Violin Sonata in D minor. 1881–2. Unpub.

5. Andantino. For cello and piano. ?1884.

6. String Quartet in E flat major. 1885. Unpub.

7. String Trio in G minor. ?1885. Unpub.

8. Violin Sonata in F major. 1889. Unpub.

9. Piano Trio ('Korpo Trio'). 1887. Unpub.

10. Longing (Trånaden). For piano. 1887. To accompany the recitation of verses by Stagnelius. Unpub.

11. Quartet in G minor. For piano, harmonium, violin and cello. Unpub.

12. Au crépuscule. For piano. 1887. Unpub.

13. Andante cantabile. For violin and piano. 1887. Unpub.

14. Andantino. For piano. 1888. ?Unpub.

15. Scherzo. For piano. ?1888. Unpub.

16. The watersprite (Näcken). Two songs for the fairy-tale drama by G. Wennerberg. 1888. Unpub.

17. Piano Trio in C major ('Loviisa Trio'). 1888. Unpub.

18. Serenade (Runeberg). For voice and piano. 1888. Pub. 1888, in *Det sjungande Finland*, No. 45.

19. Nights of jealousy (Svartsjukans nätter). For violin, cello and piano. 1888. To accompany the recitation of verses by Runeberg. Unpub.

20. Theme and Variations in C sharp minor. For string quartet. 1888. Unpub.

21. Two Pieces Op. 1. For violin and piano. 1888, rev. 1912.

1. *Romance*; 2. *Epilogue*.

Pub. 1890 (No. 1), Nornan; 1891 (No. 2, as *Perpetuum mobile*), Nuori Suomi; (Nos. 1 & 2), Universal-Edition.

22. String Quartet in B flat major Op. 4. 1889–90. Unpub.

22a. Presto. From preceding, arr. for string orchestra. Unpub.

23. Piano Quintet in G minor. 1889. Unpub.

24. String Quartet in A minor. 1889. Unpub.

25. Suite in A major. For string trio. 1889. Unpub.

26. Allegretto. For piano. 1889. Unpub.

27. Florestan. Suite for piano. Dated: 22 April 1889. With descriptive text by the composer.

1. *Moderato*; 2. *Molto moderato*; 3. *Andante*; 4. *Tempo primo*.
Unpub.

28. Andantino. For clarinet, 2 cornets, 2 horns, baritone and tuba. 1890–1. Unpub.

29. Menuetto. For clarinet, 2 cornets, 2 horns, baritone and tuba. 1890–1. Unpub.

30. Overture in E major. For orchestra. 1890–1.

2 fl, 2 ob, 2 cl, 2 bsn; 4 hn, 2 tpt, 2 tmb, tuba; timp, pcssn; strings.
Unpub.

31. Ballet Scene. For orchestra. 1891.

2 fl, 2 ob, 2 cl, 2 bsn; 4 hn, 2 tpt, 2 tmb, tuba; pcssn; strings.
Unpub.

32. Piano Quartet in C major. 1891. For piano, two violins and cello. 1891. Unpub.

33. Seven Songs of Runeberg Op. 13. For voice and piano. 1891–2.

1. 'Neath the fir trees (Under strandens granar). 1892.
2. A kiss's hope (Kyssens hopp). 1892.
3. The heart's morning (Hjärtats morgon). 1891.

4. *Spring is flying* (Våren flyktar hastigt). 1891.
5. *The dream* (Drömmen). 1891.
6. *To Frigga* (Till Frigga). 1892.
7. *The young hunter* (Jägargossen). 1891.

Pub. 1904/1906/1908, Breitkopf & Härtel: English words, (Nos. 1–3) Rosa Newmarch, (Nos. 4–6) William Wallace; French words (Nos. 1–3) Amédée Boutarel, (Nos. 4–6) J. d'Offoël.

33a. Spring is flying (Våren flyktar hastigt) Op. 13 No. 4. Version with orchestra. 1914.

2 fl; 4 hn; pcssn; strings.
Unpub.

34. Kullervo Op. 7. Symphonic Poem for soprano and baritone soloists, male chorus and orchestra. 1892.

1. *Introduction*; 2. *The youth of Kullervo*; 3. *Kullervo and his sister*; 4. *Kullervo leaves for the war*; 5. *Kullervo's death*.

2 fl, 2 ob, 2 cl, 2 bsn; 4 hn, 3 tpt, 3 tmb, tuba; timp, pcssn; strings.

fp: 29 April 1892.

fEp: 19 November 1970, Bournemouth, Raili Kostia, Usko Viitanen, Helsinki University Choir, Bournemouth Symphony Orchestra, cond. Paavo Berglund.

Pub. Breitkopf & Härtel.

BIBLIOGRAPHY:

Robert Layton: Sibelius's Kullervo Symphony, *The Listener*, 16 September 1965, p. 433.
Jean Matter: Kullervo, ou Comment naît un grand musicien, *SM*, 1967, No. 6 (November–December), p. 343.
H.R.: First and last Sibelius, *MR*, February 1971, p. 71.
E. Tanzberger: Kullervo, *Sibelius-Miteillungen*, No. 3, March 1960, p. 9.

35. En Saga Op. 9. Tone Poem for orchestra. 1892.

fp: 16 February 1893, Helsinki, cond. Jean Sibelius.
Unpub.

35a. En Saga Op. 9. Tone poem for orchestra. Revised version. 1901.

2 fl, 2 ob, 2 cl, 2 bsn; 4 hn, 3 tpt, 3 tmb; GC, cym, tgle; strings.

fEp: 24 March 1906, Liverpool, Orchestral Society concert, cond. Jean Sibelius (?Granville Bantock).

f London p: 4 October 1906, Queen's Hall, Promenade Concert, Queen's Hall Orchestra, cond. (Sir) Henry Wood.

fEbp: 9 August 1925, Wireless Orchestra, cond. (Sir) Eugene Goossens.

Pub. 1903, Breitkopf & Härtel. Arr. for piano solo by F. H. Schneider, pub. 1908, Breitkopf & Härtel.

BIBLIOGRAPHY:
Leslie Head: 'Lost' Sibelius music for the first time here, *M&M*, March 1959, p. 13.

36. Rondo. For viola and piano. 1893. Unpub.

37. Arioso (Runeberg) Op. 3. For voice and piano. 1893, rev. 1913. Pub. R. E. Westerlund Oy (Helsinki); also version with string orchestra.

38. Six Impromptus Op. 5. For piano. 1893.
   1. *Moderato* (G minor).
   2. *Lento—Vivace* (G minor).
   3. *Moderato—alla marcia* (A minor).
   4. *Andantino* (E minor).
   5. *Vivace* (B minor).
   6. *Commodo* (E major).
Pub. Breitkopf & Härtel. Nos. 5 & 6 arr. for string orchestra.

39. Karelia. Incidental music. 1893.
   1. *Overture*; 2. *Più lento*; 3. *Moderato assai*; 4. *March in the old style*; 5. *Tempo di menuetto*; 6. *Moderato, ma non tanto*; 7. *Alla marcia* ('*Based on an old motif*'); 8. *Vivace*; 9. *Moderato—Allegro molto—Vivace molto—Maestoso e largamente* (The Finnish national anthem 'Vårt Land' by Pacius).
   2 fl, 2 ob, 2 cl, 2 bsn; 4 hn, 3 tpt, 3 tmb, tuba; timp, pcssn; strings.
fp: 13 November 1893, entertainment promoted by the Student Corporation of Viipuri.
Unpub.

39a. Karelia Overture Op. 10. For orchestra. 1893. No. 1 of preceding.
   2 fl, pic, 2 ob, 2 cl, 2 bsn; 4 hn, 3 tpt, 3 tmb, tuba; timp, GC, tamb, tgle; strings.

fEp: 25 October 1907, Queen's Hall, Promenade Concert, Queen's Hall Orchestra, cond. (Sir) Henry Wood.

fEbp: 24 April 1927, Birmingham Station Orchestra.

Pub. 1906, Breitkopf & Härtel. Arr. for piano solo by Otto Taubmann pub. 1907, Breitkopf & Härtel.

39b. Karelia Suite Op. 11. For orchestra. 1893.
   1. *Intermezzo*; 2. *Ballade*; 3. *Alla marcia*.
   2 fl, pic, 2 ob, ca, 2 cl, 2 bsn; 4 hn, 3 tpt, 3 tmb, tuba; timp, tgle, GC, cym; strings.
fEp: 23 October 1906, Queen's Hall, Promenade Concert, Queen's Hall Orchestra, cond. (Sir) Henry Wood.
Pub. 1906, Breitkopf & Härtel. Nos. 1 & 2 arr. for piano (1897), pub. Axel Lindgren (Helsinki). Complete arr. for piano, 1907, Breitkopf & Härtel.

40. Piano Sonata in F major Op. 12. 1893.
   1. *Allegro molto*; 2. *Andantino*; 3. *Vivacissimo*.
   f London p (No. 2 only): 17 April 1907, Evelyn Suart.
Pub. 1906, Breitkopf & Härtel.

41. Rakastava (The Lover) Op. 14. For male chorus a cappella. 1893. Words: from Kanteletar, Book I.
   1. *Where is my beloved?* (Missä armahani?).
   2. *My beloved's path* (Armahan kulku).
   3. *Good evening, my little bird* (Hyvää iltaa, lintuseni).
   fp: 28 April 1894, Helsinki, University Chorus.
Pub. Ylioppilaskunnan Laulajat (Helsinki).

41a. Rakastava Op. 14. Version for male chorus and string orchestra. 1894. Unpub.

41b. Rakastava Op. 14. Version for mixed chorus a cappella. 1898. Pub. Sävelisto, Vol. 3.

41c. Rakastava Op. 14. Rewritten version for string orchestra, triangle and timpani. 1911.
   1. *The lover*; 2. *The path of the beloved*; 3. *Good night—farewell!*
   fEbp: 28 June 1928, Wireless String Orchestra, cond. Stanford Robinson.
Pub. 1913, Breitkopf & Härtel. Arr. for piano solo by Leo Funtek, 1913.

42. Cantata for the University Ceremonies of 1894. For mixed chorus and orchestra. 1894. Text: Kasimir Leino.

2 fl, 2 ob, 2 cl, 2 bsn; 2 hn, 2 tpt, 2 tmb, tuba; timp, pcssn; strings.

fp: 31 May 1894, Helsinki.

Unpub.

43. Menuetto. For orchestra. 1894.

fl, ob, 2 cl, 2 bsn; 4 hn, 3 tpt, 3 tmb, tuba; pcssn; strings.

Unpub.

44. A Song for Lemminkäinen (Laulu Lemminkäiselle) (Veijola) Op. 31 No. 1. For chorus and orchestra. ?1894.

2 fl, 2 ob, 2 cl, 2 bsn; 4 hn, 2 tpt, 3 tmb, tuba; timp; strings.

Unpub.

45. The Wood Nymph (Skogsrået) Op. 15. For piano, two horns and strings. 1894. To accompany the recitation of verses by Rydberg. Unpub.

45a. The Wood Nymph (Skogsrået) Op. 15. Tone Poem for orchestra. 1895. Revised version of preceding.

2 fl, 2 ob, 2 cl, 2 bsn; 4 hn, 3 tpt, 3 tmb; timp, pcssn; strings.

fp: 1895, Helsinki, cond. Jean Sibelius.

Pub. Breitkopf & Härtel.

46. Spring Song (Vårsång) Op. 16. Tone Poem for orchestra. 1894.

2 fl, 2 pic, 2 ob, 2 cl, 2 bsn; 4 hn, 3 tpt, 3 tmb, tuba; timp, bells; strings.

fp: 21 June 1894, Vaasa, Festival of the Society for National Education.

?fEp: 31 October 1905, Birmingham, cond. Johan Hock.

Pub. 1902–3, Breitkopf & Härtel (orig. as *La Tristesse du printemps*). Arr. for piano solo by Otto Taubman, 1907.

47. Finnish Runos. Seventeen fragments transcribed by Sibelius. 1895.

48. Serenade (Stagnelius). For baritone and orchestra. 1895.

2 ob, 2 cl, 2 bsn; 4 hn; strings.

fp: 1895, Helsinki, cond. Jean Sibelius.

Unpub.

49. Morning mist (Aamusumussa) (Erkko). For three children's voices a cappella. 1896.

Pub. Kustannusosakeyhtiö Otava (Helsinki). Also version for male chorus. Version for mixed chorus pub. Sävelisto Vol. 4.

50. Cantata for the Coronation of Nicolas II. For soloists, mixed chorus and orchestra. 1896. Text: Cajander.

fp: November 1896, Helsinki.

51. The Maid in the Tower (Jungfrun i tornet). Opera in one act. 1896. Libretto: Hertzberg. Composed for a lottery soirée for the benefit of Kajanus's Orchestra and Orchestra School.

fl, ob, 2 cl, bsn; 2 hn, tpt, tmb; pcssn; strings.

Unpub.

52. Workers' March (Työkansan marssi) (J. H. Erkko). For mixed chorus a cappella. 1893–6. Pub. 1896, Työväen kalenteri, Vol. 4 (Viipuri).

53. Natus in curas Op. 21 (Gustafsoon). For male chorus (TTBB) a cappella. 1896. Composed for the unveiling of a monument to Professor Pippingskjöld. Pub. 1906, Breitkopf & Härtel, as Op. 21 No. 2.

54. Lemminkäinen Suite (Four Legends) Op. 22. For orchestra. 1893–5.

1. *Lemminkäinen and the Maidens of the Island* (pub. as Lemminkäinen and the Maidens of Saari). 1895, rev. 1897, 1939.

2 fl, 2 ob, 2 cl, 2 bsn; 4 hn, 3 tpt, 3 tmb; timp, pcssn; strings.

2. *Lemminkäinen in Tuonela.* 1895, rev. 1897, 1939.

2 fl, 2 ob, 2 cl, 2 bsn; 4 hn, 3 tpt, 3 tmb; pcssn; strings.

3. *The Swan of Tuonela.* 1893, rev. 1897, 1900.

ob, ca, cl, 2 bsn; 4 hn, 3 tmb; timp, pcssn; hp, strings.

4. *Lemminkäinen's homeward journey.* 1895, rev. 1897, 1900.

2 fl, pic, 2 ob, 2 cl, 2 bsn; 4 hn, 3 tpt, 3 tmb, tuba; timp, tgle, tamb, cym, GC, campanelli; strings.

fp: 13 April 1896, Helsinki, cond. Jean Sibelius.

fp (1897 revision): November 1897, Helsinki, cond. Jean Sibelius.

fAp (Nos. 3 & 4): 1901, Chicago Symphony Orchestra, cond. Frederick Stock.

f London p (No. 3): 31 August 1905, Queen's Hall, Promenade Concert, Queen's Hall Orchestra, cond. (Sir) Henry Wood.

fEbp (No. 4): 26 January 1925, BBC broadcast, Newcastle Station Orchestra, cond. Edward Clark.

fp outside Finland (Nos. 1 & 2): 24 February 1937, Bournemouth Festival, Bournemouth Municipal Orchestra, cond. Sir Henry Wood (in place of Georg Schneevoigt).

fEbp (No. 1): 5 January 1938, BBC Orchestra, cond. Georg Schneevoigt.

fp (complete, 1939 revision): 11 November 1950, BBC broadcast, BBC Symphony Orchestra, cond. Basil Cameron.

Pub. Breitkopf & Härtel. Nos. 3 & 4 arr. for piano solo by Otto Taubman, 1907.

BIBLIOGRAPHY:
Robert L. Jacobs: Sibelius's Lemminkäinen and the Maidens of Saari, *MR*, May 1963, p. 147.
Harold E. Johnson: Jean Sibeliuksen 'Lemminkäis-sarja', *Helsingin Sanomat*, 19 May 1957.
Egon von Komorzynski: Tuonelas svan af JS utförd i Wien, *Finsk Musikrevy*, April 1905.
Anon.: Four Legends for orchestra—first performance of complete cycle, *Strad*, November 1950, p. 254.

55. Cantata for the University Ceremonies of 1897 Op. 23. For soloists, mixed chorus and orchestra. 1897. Text: Koskimics. Unpub.

55a. Songs for mixed chorus (Lauluja sekaköörille). Excerpts from preceding.
1. *We the youth of Finland* (Me nuoriso Suomen).
2. *The wind rocks* (Tuuli tuudittele).
3. *Oh hope, hope, you dreamer* (Oi toivo, toivo, sä lietomieli).
4. *Many on the sea of life* (Montapa elon merellä).
5. *The fading thoughts of the earth* (Sammuva sainio maan).
6a. *Let thanks ring unto the Lord* (Soi kiitokseksi Luojan). For women's chorus.
Pub. Fazerin Musiikkikaupa Oy (Helsinki).

6b. *Blow, blow gentler* (Tuule, tuule leppeämmin).
7. *Love, your realm is limitless* (Lempi, sun valtas ääretön on).
8. *As the swift current* (Kuin virta vuolas).
9. *Oh precious Finland, incomparable mother* (Oi kallis Suomi, äiti verraton).
Pub. 1899, Frazer & Westerlund.

56. The Rapids-Shooter's Brides (Koskenlaskijan morsiamet) (The Ferryman's Brides) Op. 33. For baritone or mezzo-soprano and orchestra. 1897. Text: A. Oksanen. Ded. Maikki Järnefelt.
2 fl, 2 ob, 2 cl, 2 bsn; 4 hn, 2 tpt, 3 tmb; timp, pcssn; strings.
fp: November 1897, Helsinki, cond. Jean Sibelius.
fEp: 10 September 1936, Queen's Hall, Promenade Concert, Muriel Brunskill and the BBC Symphony Orchestra, cond. Sir Henry Wood.
Pub. Breitkopf & Härtel.

BIBLIOGRAPHY:
Scott Goddard: An early ballad, *Radio Times*, 4 September 1936, p. 14.

57. Tiera. Tone poem for brass and percussion. 1898.
3 cornets, alto tenor, baritone, tuba; cym, GC.
Pub. Kustannusosakeyhtiö Otava (Helsinki).

58. Seven Songs Op. 17. For voice and piano. 1891–8.
1. *And I questioned then no further* (Sen har jag ej frågat mera) (Runeberg). 1894.
2. *Slumber* (Sov in!) (K. A. Tavaststjerna). 1894.
3. *Enticement* (Fågellek) (K. A. Tavaststjerna). 1891.
4. *Astray* (Vilse) (K. A. Tavaststjerna). 1894.
5. *The dragonfly* (En slända) (Oscar Levertin). ?1894.
6. *To evening* (Illalle) (A. V. Forsman-Koskimies). 1898.
7. *Driftwood* (Lastu lainehilla) (Ilmari Calamnius). 1898.
Pub. 1904–8, Breitkopf & Härtel: German version, Alfred J. Boruttau; English version, William Wallace or Rosa Newmarch;

Sibelius, Jean

French version, J. d'Offoël or Amédée Boutarel or May de Rudder.

58a. And I questioned them no further (Sen har jag ej frågat mera) Op. 17 No. 1. Version with orchestra. 1903.
2 fl, 2 ob, 2 cl, 2 bsn; 4 hn; timp, pcssn; strings.
Unpub.

58b. Slumber (Sov in!) Op. 17 No. 2. Version with orchestra.
2 fl, 2 cl, 2 bsn; hn; timp; strings.
Unpub.

58c. Enticement (Fågellek) Op. 17 No. 3. Version with orchestra.
fl, ob; hn; pcssn; hp, strings.
Unpub.

59. King Kristian II Op. 27. Incidental music for a play by Adolf Paul. 1898.
1. *Elegie*; 2. *Musette*; 3. *Menuetto*; 4. *Fool's song of the spider*; 5. *Nocturne*; 6. *Serenade*; 7. *Ballade*.
2 fl, 2 ob, 2 cl, 2 bsn; 4 hn, 2 tpt, 3 tmb; timp, tgle, tamb, GC, cym; hp, strings; solo voice.
fp: 28 February 1898, Helsinki, Swedish Theatre, cond. Jean Sibelius.
Pub. 1899, Breitkopf & Härtel.

59a. King Kristian II Op. 27. Suite for orchestra. 1898.
1. *Elegie*; 2. *Musette*; 3. *Menuetto*; 4. *Nocturne*; 5. *Serenade*; 6. *Ballade*.
fAp: 1900, Cincinnati, cond. Frank Van der Stucken.
fEp: 26 October 1901, Queen's Hall, Promenade Concert, Queen's Hall Orchestra, cond. (Sir) Henry Wood.
Pub. Breitkopf & Härtel. Nos. 1–4 also arr. for piano solo.

60. Sandels Op. 28. Improvisation for male chorus and orchestra. 1898, rev. 1915. Text: Runeberg.
2 fl, 2 ob, 2 cl, 2 bsn; 4 hn, 2 tpt, 3 tmb; timp, pcssn; strings.
fp: March 1900, Helsinki, Muntra Musikanter.
Unpub.

61. The Breaking of the ice on the Uleå River (Islossningen i Uleå älv) Op. 30.

Improvisation for male chorus, recitation and orchestra. 1898. Text: Zachris Topelius.
2 fl, 2 ob, 2 cl, 2 bsn; 4 hn, 3 tpt, 3 tmb, tuba; timp, pcssn; strings.
fp: October 1899, Helsinki, cond. Jean Sibelius.
Unpub.

62. Carminalia. Latin songs for students arr. for SAB a cappella or soprano and alto with piano and harmonium. 1899. From melodies and texts collected by Elise Stenbäck.
1. *Ecce novum guadium*; 2. *Angelus emittitur*; 3. *In studio laboris*.
Pub. K. F. Wasenius (Helsinki).

63. Lullaby (Kehtolaulu). For violin and kantele. 1899. Pub. December 1935, Musiikkitieto.

64. 'Press Celebrations' Music. 1899.
fp: November 1899, Helsinki.
Unpub.

64a. Scènes historiques I Op. 25. Suite for orchestra. 1899, rev. 1911. From the 'Press Celebrations' Music (tableaux 1, 2 & 3).
1. *All'Overtura*.
2 fl, 2 ob, 2 cl, 2 bsn; 4 hn, 3 tpt, 3 tmb; timp; strings.
2. *Scena*.
2 fl, pic, 2 ob, 2 cl, 2 bsn; 4 hn, 3 tpt, 3 tmb; timp, tgle, GC, cym, tamburo; strings.
3. *Festivo*.
2 fl, 2 ob, 2 cl, 2 bsn; 4 hn, 3 tpt, 3 tmb; timp, tgle, cast, tamburo, GC, cym; strings.
Pub. 1912, Breitkopf & Härtel.

64b. Finlandia Op. 26. For orchestra. 1899, rev. 1900. From the 'Press Celebrations' Music (Tableau 6).
2 fl, 2 ob, 2 cl, 2 bsn; 4 hn, 3 tpt, 3 tmb, tuba; timp, GC, cym, tgle; strings.
fp: 2 July 1900, Helsinki, cond. Robert Kajanus.
fEp: 18 March 1905, Liverpool, Liverpool Orchestral Society, cond. (Sir) Granville Bantock.
f London p: 13 October 1906, Queen's Hall, Promenade Concert, Queen's Hall Orchestra, cond. (Sir) Henry Wood.
Pub. 1905, Breitkopf & Härtel: incl. arr. for piano solo.

BIBLIOGRAPHY:
Harold E. Johnson: Finlandia ja 'Sanomaleh-distön päivän' musiikki, *Helsingin Sanomat*, 5 October 1958.

65. Sailing (Segelfahrt) (Öhqvist). For voice and piano. 1899. Pub. 1899, in *Brohige blad*.

66. Row, row duck (Souda, souda sinisorsa) (Koskimies). For voice and piano. 1899. Pub. 1899, Fazerin Musiikkikaupa Oy (Helsinki).

67. Song of the Athenians (Atenarnes sång) Op. 31 No. 3. For boys' and men's voices with wind and percussion. 1899. Text: Rydberg.
3 cornets, alto, euphonium, ten hn, tuba; tgle, cym, GC.
fp: 26 April 1899, Helsinki, cond. Jean Sibelius.
Pub. 1904–6, Breitkopf & Härtel: English version, William Wallace; German version, Alfred J. Boruttau; Finnish version, Yrjö Weijola. Also version with piano acc. Also version (unpub.) with orchestra.

68. Six Songs Op. 36. For voice and piano. 1899.
1. *Black roses* (Svarta rosor) (E. Josephson).
2. *But my bird is long in homing* (Men min fågel märks dock icke) (Runeberg).
3. *Tennis at Trianon* (Bollspelet vid Trianon) (G. Fröding).
4. *Sigh, sedges, sigh* (Säv, säv, susa) (G. Fröding).
5. *March snow* (Marssnön) (J. J. Wecksell). Pub. 1912.
6. *The diamond on the March snow* (Demanten på marssnön) (J. J. Wecksell).
Pub. 1904, Breitkopf & Härtel: English version, William Wallace; French version, J. d'Offoël.

68a. Tennis at Trianon (Bollspelet vid Trianon) Op. 36 No. 3. Version with orchestra.
2 fl, cl, bsn; pcssn; hp, strings.
Unpub.

68b. The diamond on the March snow (Demanten på marssnön) Op. 36 No. 6.
2 fl, 2 cl; hp, strings.
Unpub.

69. Symphony No. 1 in E minor Op. 39. 1899.

1. *Andante ma non troppo—Allegro energico*; 2. *Andante (ma non troppo lento)*; 3. *Scherzo (Allegro)*; 4. *Finale—quasi una fantasia (Andante —Allegro molto)*.
2 fl, 2 ob, 2 cl, 2 bsn; 4 hn, 3 tpt, 3 tmb, tuba; timp, GC, cym; hp, strings.
fp: 26 April 1899, Helsinki, cond. Jean Sibelius.
fEp: 13 October 1903, Queen's Hall, Promenade Concert, Queen's Hall Orchestra, cond. (Sir) Henry Wood.
fEbp: 25 May 1927, Wireless Symphony Orchestra, cond. Georg Schneevoigt.
Pub. 1902, Breitkopf & Härtel.

BIBLIOGRAPHY:
Gerald Abraham: Sibelius's symphonic methods—No. 1 in E minor, *MO*, October 1937, p. 19.
Jack Diether: Two views of the Sibelius First, *American Record Guide*, August 1964, p. 1126.
Julian Herbage: Symphony No. 1 in E minor, in *The Symphony*, Pelican Books (London) 1949, p. 329.
Karl Thiessen: Sinfonie Nr. 1 (E-moll) von JS, *Signale*, 1903, Nos. 12–13 (11 February), p. 190.
Anon.: The First Symphony, *British Musician*, March 1931, p. 55.

70. Snöfrid Op. 29. Improvisation for mixed chorus, recitation and orchestra. ?1900. Text: Rydberg.
2 fl, ob, 2 cl, bsn; 2 hn, 3 tpt, tmb; timp, pcssn; strings.
Pub. Hansen (vocal score), F. Tilgmann (choral parts).

71. Björneborgarnes March. Arr. for orchestra. 1900.
2 fl, 2 ob, 2 cl, 2 bsn; 4 hn, 3 tpt, 3 tmb; pcssn; strings.
Unpub.

72. Fantasia. For cello and piano. 1900. ?Unpub.

73. Hymn to Thais (Borgström). For voice and piano. 1900. Unpub.

74. The Cavalier (Kavaljeren). For piano. 1900. Pub. December 1900, in *Fyren*.

75. Cortège. For orchestra. ?1901. Existence uncertain.

76. Malinconia Op. 20. For cello and piano. 1901. Pub. 1911, Breitkopf & Härtel.

77. Symphony No. 2 in D major Op. 43. 1901–2. Ded. Axel Carpelan.

1. *Allegretto—Poco allegro*; 2. *Tempo andante ma rubato—Allegro—Andante sostenuto*; 3. *Vivacissimo*; 4. *Allegro moderato*.

2 fl, 2 ob, 2 cl, 2 bsn; 4 hn, 3 tpt, 3 tmb; timp; strings.

fp: 3 March 1902, Helsinki, cond. Jean Sibelius.

fEp: 2 March 1905, Manchester, Halle Orchestra, cond. Hans Richter.

fEbp: 8 December 1927, Bournemouth, Winter Gardens, Bournemouth Municipal Orchestra, cond. Sir Dan Godfrey.

Pub. Breitkopf & Härtel.

BIBLIOGRAPHY:

Gerald Abraham: Sibelius's symphonic methods—No. 2 in D, *MO*, December 1937, p. 211.

Scott Goddard: Sibelius's Second Symphony, *M&L*, April 1931, p. 156.

Julian Herbage: Symphony No. 2 in D major, in *The Symphony*, Pelican Books (London) 1949, p. 331.

R.-Aloys Mooser: 2me Symphonie en ré majeur Op. 43, in *Aspects de la musique contemporaine*, Editions Labor et Fidès (Geneva) 1957, p. 195.

78. Nostalgia (Kotikaipaus) (Von Konow). For three women's voices a cappella. 1902. Pub. December 1935, in *Suomen Musiikkilehti*.

79. To Thérèse Hahl (Till Thérèse Hahl) (Wasastjerna). For mixed chorus a cappella. 1902. Pub. Sävelisto, Vol. 3.

80. Overture in A minor. For orchestra. 1902.

2 fl, 2 ob, 2 cl, 2 bsn; 4 hn, 4 tpt, 2 tmb, tuba; timp; strings.

fp: 3 March 1902, Helsinki, cond. Jean Sibelius.

Unpub.

81. Impromptu Op. 19. For women's chorus and orchestra. 1902, rev. 1910. Text: V. Rydberg.

2 fl, 2 ob, 2 cl, 2 bsn; 4 hn; timp, pcssn; hp, strings.

fp: 3 March 1902, Helsinki, cond. Jean Sibelius.

Pub. 1910, Breitkopf & Härtel: incl. vocal score; English version, Rosa Newmarch; German version, A. J. Boruttau.

82. The Origin of Fire (Tulen synty) Op. 32. For baritone, male chorus and orchestra. 1902, rev. 1910. Text: from the Kalevala.

2 fl, 2 ob, 2 cl, 2 bsn; 4 hn, 2 tpt, 3 tmb, tuba; timp, pcssn; strings.

fp: 9 April 1902, Helsinki, inauguration of new Finnish National Theatre, Ojenperä (baritone), Philharmonic Society, cond. Jean Sibelius.

fEp: 5 October 1937, Leeds Festival, Festival Chorus and London Philharmonic Orchestra, cond. Sir Thomas Beecham.

Pub. 1911, Breitkopf & Härtel: vocal score; English version, Rosa Newmarch (as *Ukko the Firemaker*); German version, Alfred J. Boruttau.

83. Finnish folksongs. Arr. for piano. 1903.

1. *My beloved (Minun kultani)*; 2. *I love you with all my heart (Sydämestäni rakastan)*; 3. *Evening comes (Ilta tulee)*; 4. *That beautiful girl (Tuopa tyttö, kaunis tyttö)*; 5. *The brother's murderer (Velisurmaaja)*; 6. *Wedding memory (Häämuistelma)*.

Pub. Breitkopf & Härtel.

84. Romance in C major Op. 42. For string orchestra. 1903. Ded. José Eibenschütz.

fp: March 1904, Turku, cond. Jean Sibelius.

fEp: 12 February 1910, Queen's Hall, Queen's Hall Orchestra, cond. (Sir) Henry Wood.

Pub. 1909, Breitkopf & Härtel.

BIBLIOGRAPHY:

Harold Rawlinson: Romance (in C major) Op. 42 (Some famous works for string orchestra, No. 5), *Strad*, August 1946, p. 102.

85. Kuolema (Death) Op. 44. Incidental music to a drama by Arvid Järnefelt. 1903. Six 'scenes' for string orchestra, bass drum and church bell.

fp: 2 December 1903, Helsinki, Finnish

Theatre, cond. Jean Sibelius.
Unpub. See also No. 118.

85a. Valse triste Op. 44. For orchestra. 1904.
From 'Kuolema', revised version.
fl, cl; 2 hn; timp; strings.
fp: 25 April 1904, Helsinki, cond. Jean
Sibelius.
Pub. 1904, Breitkopf & Härtel; also arr. for
piano solo.

BIBLIOGRAPHY:
Jussi Jalas: Valse triste och musiken till
'Kuolema', *Musik-Världen*, May 1948,
p. 138.

85b. Scene with cranes Op. 44. For
orchestra. 1906. Revised version of Nos. 3 & 4
from 'Kuolema'. Unpub.

86. Violin Concerto Op. 47. 1903, rev.
1905. Ded. Franz von Vecsey.
   1. *Allegro moderato*; 2. *Adagio di molto*;
3. *Allegro ma non tanto*.
   2 fl, 2 ob, 2 cl, 2 bsn; 4 hn, 2 tpt, 3 tmb;
timp; strings.
   fp (original version): 8 February 1904,
Helsinki, Viktor Nováček, cond. Jean Sibelius.
   fp (revised version): 19 October 1905,
Berlin, Karl Halir, cond. Richard Strauss.
   fAp: 30 November 1906, New York,
Carnegie Hall, Maud Powell and the New
York Philharmonic.
   fEp: 1 October 1907, Queen's Hall,
Promenade Concert, Henri Verbrugghen and
the Queen's Hall Orchestra, cond. (Sir)
Henry Wood.

BIBLIOGRAPHY:
Eric Blom: Sibelius, Concerto in D minor for
   violin and orchestra, *Music Teacher*, September 1933, p. 467.
Neville Cardus: Before listening, please
   remove labels, *Radio Times*, 12 September
   1930, p. 535.
Julian Herbage: Violin Concerto in D minor,
   in *The Concerto*, Pelican Books (London)
   1952, p. 278.
Walter Legge: Sibelius and his Violin Concerto, *Halle*, December 1946–January 1947,
   p. 5.
Donald F. Tovey: Violin Concerto, in *EMA*,
   Vol. 3, O.U.P. (London) 1936, p. 211.

87. Nine Partsongs Op. 18. For male
chorus (TTBB) a cappella. 1893–1904.
   1. *To the Fatherland* (Isänmaalle) (Cajander).
1900. Pub. Kustannusosakeyhtiö Otava (Helsinki). Also known as *Yks' voima* (One power).
Also version for mixed chorus a cappella.
   2. *My brothers abroad* (Veljeni vierailla
mailla) (Aho). 1904. Pub. Laulu-Miehet
(Helsinki).
   3. *Fire on the island* (Saarella palaa) (From:
Kanteletar). 1895. Pub. Breitkopf & Härtel.
Also known as *Työnsä kumpasellaki* (Each has
his job). Also version for mixed chorus
a cappella (1898) pub. Sävelisto, Vol. 4.
   4. *Busy as a thrush* (Min rastas raataa)
(From: Kanteletar). 1898. Also version for
mixed chorus a cappella (1898) pub. Sävelisto,
Vol. 4.
   5. *The woodman's song* (Metsämiehen laulu)
(Kivi). 1898. Pub. Breitkopf & Härtel.
   6. *The song of my heart* (Sydämeni laulu)
(Kivi). 1898. Pub. Breitkopf & Härtel. Also
version for mixed chorus a cappella (1907)
pub. Sävelisto, Vol. 8.
   7. *The broken voice* (Sortnut ääni) (From:
Kanteletar). 1898. Pub. 1907, Breitkopf &
Härtel (with English version by Rosa Newmarch as *The song now stilled*). Also version
for mixed chorus a cappella (1898) pub.
Sävelisto Vol. 3.
   8. *Hail, moon!* (Terve kuu) (From: Kalevala). 1901. Pub. 1907, Breitkopf & Härtel
(English version, Rosa Newmarch).
   9. *The boat journey* (Venematka) (From:
Kalevala). fp: April 1893, University Chorus.
Pub. 1907, Breitkopf & Härtel (with English
version by Rosa Newmarch as *Sailing sea-
wards*). Also version for mixed chorus a cappella pub. Kustannusosakeyhtiö Otava
(Helsinki).
   fEbp (Nos. 3, 6, 9): 11 February 1938,
Helsinki University Chorus.

88. Ten Pieces Op. 24. For piano. 1894–1903.
   1. *Impromptu.* 1894.
   2. *Romance in A major.* 1894.
   3. *Caprice.* 1895.
   4. *Romance in D minor.* 1895.
   5. *Waltz in E major.* 1895.
   6. *Idyll.* 1898.
   7. *Andantino.* 1898.
   8. *Nocturne.* 1900.

9. *Romance in D flat major.* 1903.
10. *Barcarola.* 1903.
Pub. 1904, Breitkopf & Härtel.

89. Har du mod? Op. 31 No. 2. For male chorus and orchestra. 1904. Text: Wecksell.
2 fl, 2 ob, 2 cl, 2 bsn; 4 hn, 2 tpt, 3 tmb, tuba; timp, pcssn; strings.
Pub. (piano score) Axel Lindgren, (choral parts) R. E. Westerlund Oy.

90. Five Songs Op. 38. For voice and piano. 1903–4.
1. *Autumn evening* (Höstkväll) (C. V. Rydberg). 1903.
2. *On a balcony by the sea* (På verandan vid havet) (C. V. Rydberg). 1902.
3. *In the night* (I natten) (C. V. Rydberg). 1903.
4. *The harper and his son* (Harpolekaren och hans son) (C. V. Rydberg). 1904.
5. *I wish I dwelt in India land* (Jag ville jag vore i Indialand) (Gustaf Fröding). 1904.
Pub. 1904–8, Breitkopf & Härtel: English version, Rosa Newmarch; German version, Alfred J. Boruttau; French version, Amédée Boutarel.

90a. Autumn evening (Höstkväll) Op. 38 No. 1. Version with orchestra.
2 ob, 2 cl, bcl, 3 bsn; 4 hn, 3 tmb, tamburo; hp, strings.
Pub. 1907, Breitkopf & Härtel.

90b. On a balcony by the sea (På verandan vid havet) Op. 38 No. 2. Version with orchestra.
2 ob, 2 cl, 2 bsn; 4 hn, pcssn; hp, strings.
Unpub.

90c. In the night (I natten) Op. 38 No. 3. Version with orchestra.
cl, 2 bsn; 4 hn; timp, pcssn; strings.
Unpub.

91. Cassazione Op. 6. For orchestra. 1904.
No. 1.
2 fl, 2 ob, 2 cl, 2 bsn; 4 hn, 2 tpt, 3 tmb, tuba; timp; strings.
No. 2.
2 fl, 2 cl; 2 hn, tpt, tmb; timp; strings.
Unpub.

92. Kyllikki Op. 41. Three Lyric Pieces for piano. 1904.

1. *Largamente—Allegro*; 2. *Andantino*; 3. *Commodo.*
fEbp: 20 April 1936, Ernest Lush.
Pub. Breitkopf & Härtel.

93. Dance Intermezzo Op. 45 No. 2. For piano. 1904. Pub. Breitkopf & Härtel.

93a. Dance Intermezzo Op. 45 No. 2. Version for orchestra. 1907.
2 fl, ob, 2 cl, bsn; 4 hn, 2 tpt; timp, pcssn; hp, strings.
Alternative orchestration: fl, 2 cl; 2 hn, tpt; timp, pcssn; strings. ?Unpub.
fEp: 31 August 1907, Queen's Hall, Promenade Concert, Queen's Hall Orchestra, cond. (Sir) Henry Wood.
Pub. Breitkopf & Härtel.

94. Not with lamentations (Ej med klagan) (Runeberg). For mixed chorus a cappella. 1905. Pub. Sävelisto, Vol. 8. Also known as *To the memory of Albert Edelfelt* (Till minnet av Albert Edelfelt).

95. Pelléas et Mélisande Op. 46. Incidental music for the play by Maurice Maeterlinck. 1905.
fp: 17 March 1905, Helsinki, Swedish Theatre, cond. Jean Sibelius.
fEbp: 2 December 1926, Newcastle Station Repertory Company, Station Symphony Orchestra, cond. Edward Clark; producer, Eric Barber; English transl. Laurence Alma Tadema.

95a. Pelléas et Mélisande: Suite Op. 46.
1. *At the castle gate* (Prelude, Act I Scene 1).
2. *Mélisande* (Prelude, Act I Scene 2).
3. *At the seashore* (Melodrama, Act I Scene 4).
4. *A spring in the park* (Prelude, Act II Scene 1).
5. *The three blind sisters* (Mélisande's song, Act III Scene 2).
6. *Pastorale* (Melodrama, Act III Scene 4).
7. *Mélisande at the spinning wheel* (Prelude, Act III Scene 1).
8. *Entr'acte* (Prelude, Act IV Scene 1).
9. *Mélisande's death* (Prelude, Act V Scene 2).
fl, ob, 2 cl, 2 bsn; 2 hn; timp, pcssn; strings.
f London p: 3 April 1906, Aeolian Hall concert given by the pianist Kathleen Chabot,

Queen's Hall Orchestra, cond. (Sir) Henry Wood.
Pub. 1905, Robert Lienau. Unpub.: Prelude, Act IV Scene 2 & Mélisande's song (No. 5, original version).

BIBLIOGRAPHY:
Erik Furuhjelm: Sibelius's musik till Pelléas . och Mélisande, *Finsk Musikrevy*, April 1905.
G. Sievers: Sibelius und die Komponisten seiner Zeit: Vergleich der Pelleas et Mélisande Vertonungen, *Sibelius-Miteilungen*, No. 4, April 1961, p. 10.

96. Extinct (Erloschen) (Busse-Palmo). For voice and piano. 1906. Pub. Suomen Musiikkilehti.

97. The Countess's portrait (Grefvinnans konterfej). For string orchestra. 1906. To accompany the recitation of verses by Z. Topelius. Also known as *Portraits* (Porträtterna). Unpub.

98. The liberated Queen (Vapautettu kuningatar) Op. 48. Cantata for mixed chorus and orchestra. 1906. Text: Paavo Cajander.
2 fl, 2 ob, 2 cl, 2 bsn; 4 hn, 2 tpt, 3 tmb; timp, pcssn; strings.
fp: 12 May 1906, Helsinki.
Pub. 1907, Jurgenson (Moscow); Robert Lienau (Berlin) to a German text as *Die gefangene Königin* (The captive Queen)—German version, Th. Rehbaum; English version, Rosa Newmarch. Also known as *There sings the Queen* (Siell'laulavi kuningstar) and *Snellman's Fest Cantata*.

99. Pohjola's Daughter Op. 49. Symphonic Fantasia for orchestra. 1906. Ded. Robert Kajanus.
3 fl, 2 ob, ca, 2 cl, bcl, 3 bsn; 4 hn, 2 cornets, 2 tpt, 3 tmb, tuba; timp; hp, strings.
fp: 29 December 1906, St. Petersburg, Siloti concert, cond. Jean Sibelius.
f New York p: spring 1918, Carnegie Hall, Boston Symphony Orchestra, cond. Karl Muck.
fEp: 4 July 1932, Queen's Hall, Sibelius Society concert, London Symphony Orchestra, cond. Robert Kajanus.
Pub. Robert Lienau.

100. Six Songs Op. 50. For voice and piano. 1906.
1. *Spring song* (Lenzgesang) (A. Fitger).
2. *Longing* (Sehnsucht) (Rudolf Weiss).
3. *In the field a maiden sings* (Im Feld ein Mädchen singt) (Margarete Susman).
4. *Oh, wert thou here* (Aus banger Brust) (Richard Dehmel).
5. *The silent city* (Die stille Stadt) (Richard Dehmel).
6. *Song of the roses* (Rosenlied) (Anna Ritter).
fEbp: 31 December 1933, John Armstrong.
Pub. 1907, Robert Lienau: English version, Rosa Newmarch.

100a. Oh, wert thou here (Aus banger Brust) Op. 50 No. 4. Version with orchestra.
fl, cl, 2 bsn; 2 hn; hp, strings.
Unpub.

101. Belshazzar's Feast Op. 51. Incidental music, for small orchestra, for a play by Hjalmar Procopé. 1906.
1. *Alla marcia* (Act I).
2. *Nocturne* (Prelude, Act II).
3. *The Jewish girl's song* (Act II).
4. *Allegretto* (Act III).
5. *Dance of life* (Act III).
6. *Dance of death* (Act III).
7. *Tempo sostenuto* (Act IV).
8. *Allegro* (Act IV).
fl, 2 cl, 2 hn; pcssn; strings.
fp: 7 November 1906, Helsinki, Swedish Theatre, cond. Jean Sibelius.
Unpub.

101a. Belshazzar's Feast: Suite Op. 51.
1. *Oriental procession* (No. 1, orig. version).
2. *Solitude* (Accompaniment for No. 3, orig. version).
3. *Night music* (No. 2, orig. version).
4. *Khadra's dance* (Nos. 5 & 6, orig. version).
2 fl, ob, 2 cl; 2 hn; pcssn; strings.
fp: 25 September 1907, Helsinki, cond. Jean Sibelius.
fEbp: 29 October 1924, Bournemouth, Winter Gardens, Bournemouth Municipal Orchestra, cond. Sir Dan Godfrey.
Pub. 1907, Robert Lienau.

102. Pan and Echo Op. 53. Dance Intermezzo for orchestra. 1906.

3 fl, 3 ob, 3 cl, 3 bsn; 4 hn, 4 tpt, 3 tmb, tuba; timp; hp, strings.
fp: 1906, Vaasa, cond. Jean Sibelius.
f Helsinki p: April 1907, cond. Jean Sibelius.
Pub. Robert Lienau.

103. Symphony No. 3 in C major Op. 52.
For orchestra. 1907. Ded. Granville Bantock.
1. *Allegro moderato*; 2. *Andantino con moto quasi allegretto*; 3. *Moderato*.
2 fl, 2 ob, 2 cl, 2 bsn; 4 hn, 2 tpt, 3 tmb; timp; strings.
fp: 26 September 1907, Helsinki, cond. Jean Sibelius.
fEp: 27 February 1908, Queen's Hall, Philharmonic Society of London concert, cond. Jean Sibelius. (NB: fEp originally announced for a concert of the Liverpool Philharmonic Society on 2 May 1907, to have been conducted by the composer.)
?fAp: 2 March 1913, New York, New York Symphony Society, cond. Walter Damrosch.
Pub. Robert Lienau.

BIBLIOGRAPHY:
Gerald Abraham: Sibelius's symphonic methods—No. 3 in C, *MO*, February 1938, p. 403.
Julian Herbage: Symphony No. 3 in C major, in *The Symphony*, Pelican Books (London) 1949, p. 334.
F. O. Souper: A Sibelius symphony, *Strad*, January 1929, p. 532.
Donald F. Tovey: Symphony in C major No. 3 Op. 52, in *EMA*, Vol. 2, O.U.P. (London) 1935, p. 121.

104. Night ride and sunrise Op. 55. Tone Poem for orchestra. 1907.
3 fl, 2 ob, 3 cl, 3 bsn; 4 hn, 2 tpt, 3 tmb, tuba; timp, pcssn; strings.
fp: January 1909, St. Petersburg, Siloti concert, cond. Alexander Siloti.
f Finnish p: 3 April 1911, Helsinki, cond. Jean Sibelius.
fAp: spring 1918, New York, Carnegie Hall, Boston Symphony Orchestra, cond. Karl Muck.
fEp: February 1930, Hastings Festival, Hastings Municipal Orchestra, cond. Basil Cameron.

fEbp: 25 October 1931, BBC Studio Orchestra, cond. Basil Cameron.
Pub. Robert Lienau.

105. Two Songs Op. 35. For voice and piano. 1907–8.
1. *Jubal* (Josephson).
2. *Teodora* (Gripenberg).
Pub. Breitkopf & Härtel.

105a. Jubal Op. 35 No. 1. Version with orchestra.
2 fl, ob, 2 cl, 2 bsn; 2 hn; pcssn; strings.
Unpub.

106. Swanwhite Op. 54. Incidental music for a play by A. Strindberg. 1908. Original score of fourteen scenes.
fp: 8 April 1908, Helsinki, Swedish Theatre, cond. Jean Sibelius.
?fEp: 7 February 1949, BBC performance of the play with Sibelius's music, BBC Theatre Orchestra, cond. Walter Goehr.
Unpub.

106a. Swanwhite: Suite Op. 54.
1. *The peacock*; 2. *The harp*; 3. *The maiden with the roses*; 4. *Listen, the robin sings*; 5. *The prince alone*; 6. *Swanwhite and the prince*; 7. *Song of praise*.
2 fl, 2 ob, 2 cl, 2 bsn; 4 hn; timp, cast, tgle; hp, strings.
fEp: 29 September 1909, Queen's Hall, Promenade Concert, Queen's Hall Orchestra, cond. (Sir) Henry Wood.
Pub. 1909, Robert Lienau.

107. The Lizard (Ödlan) Op. 8. Incidental music (Mikael Lybeck). For solo violin and string quintet. 1909.
fp: 6 April 1910, Helsinki, Swedish Theatre, cond. Jean Sibelius.
Unpub.

108. String Quartet in D minor (Voces intimae) Op. 56. 1909.
1. *Andante—Allegro molto*; 2. *Vivace*; 3. *Adagio di molto*; 4. *Allegretto (ma pesante)*; 5. *Allegro*.
fEp: 4 March 1914, Leeds, Leeds Bohemian Quartet.
fEbp: 19 October 1931, Kutcher Quartet (Samuel Kutcher, Frederick Grinke, Raymond Jeremy, Douglas Cameron).
Pub. Robert Lienau.

109. Eight Songs Op. 57 (Ernst Josephson). For voice and piano. 1909.

1. *The fairy and the snail* (Älvan och snigeln); 2. *A flower stood by the path* (En blomma stod vid vägen); 3. *The millwheel* (Kvarnhjulet); 4. *May* (Maj); 5. *I am a tree* (Jag är ett träd); 6. *Duke Magnus* (Hertig Magnus); 7. *The flower of friendship* (Vänskapens blomma); 8. *The watersprite* (Näcken).

Pub. 1910, Robert Lienau: English version, Herbert Harper; German version, Th. Rehbaum.

110. Ten Pieces Op. 58. For piano. 1909.

1. *Rêverie*; 2. *Scherzino*; 3. *Air varié*; 4. *The shepherd*; 5. *The evening*; 6. *Dialogue*; 7. *Tempo di menuetto*; 8. *Fisher song*; 9. *Sérénade*; 10. *Summer song*.

Pub. Breitkopf & Härtel.

111. In Memoriam Op. 59. Funeral March for orchestra. 1909.

2 fl, 3 ob, 3 cl, 3 bsn; 4 hn, 3 tpt, 3 tmb, tuba; timp, pcssn; strings.

fp: 3 April 1911, Helsinki, cond. Jean Sibelius.

fEp: 27 October 1938, Queen's Hall, inauguration of the Sibelius Festival, Royal Philharmonic Society concert, London Philharmonic Orchestra, cond. Sir Thomas Beecham.

Pub. Breitkopf & Härtel.

112. Two Songs for Shakespeare's 'Twelfth Night' Op. 60. For voice and guitar or piano. 1909. Composed for a production at the Swedish Theatre, Helsinki.

1. *Come away, death* (Kom nu hit, död); 2. *When that I was and a little tiny boy* (Och när som jag ver en liten smådräng).

Pub. 1911, Breitkopf & Härtel. Version of No. 1 with harp and string orchestra, unpub.

113. Ballet Scene. For orchestra. 1909.

2 fl, 2 ob, 2 cl, 2 bsn; 4 hn, 2 tpt, 3 tmb; timp, pcssn; strings.

Unpub.

114. Folk School children's march (Kansakoululaisten marssi). For children's voices a cappella. 1910. Pub. 1910, in *Kansakouluan lauluja*. Also known as *To the memory of Uno Cygnaeus* (Uno Cygnaeuksen muistolle).

115. The Dryad Op. 45 No. 1. Tone Poem for orchestra. 1910.

2 fl, pic, 2 ob, 2 cl, bcl, 2 bsn; 4 hn, 3 tpt, 3 tmb, tuba; tamb, cast, tamburo, GC; strings.

Pub. 1910, Breitkopf & Härtel: incl. reduction for piano solo.

116. Eight Songs Op. 61. For voice and piano. 1910.

1. *Slowly as the evening sun* (Shall I forget thee) (Långsamt som kvällskyn) (K. A. Tavaststjerna).

2. *Lapping waters* (Vattenplask) (V. Rydberg).

3. *When I dream* (När jag drömmer) (K. A. Tavaststjerna).

4. *Romeo* (K. A. Tavaststjerna).

5. *Romance* (K. A. Tavaststjerna). Ded. Arthur Borgström.

6. *Dolce far niente* (K. A. Tavaststjerna).

7. *Idle wish* (Fåfäng önskan) (Runeberg).

8. *Spell of springtime* (Vårtagen) (Gripenberg).

Pub. 1911, Breitkopf & Härtel: English version, Rosa Newmarch; German version, Alfred J. Boruttau.

BIBLIOGRAPHY:

Scott Goddard: Great song writers, XII: Sibelius Opus Sixty-One, *MM&F*, March 1932, p. 67.

117. Luonnotar Op. 70. Tone Poem for soprano and orchestra. ?1910. Text: from The Kalevala. Ded. Aïno Ackté.

2 fl, 2 ob, 3 cl, 2 bsn; 4 hn, 2 tpt, 3 tmb; timp; 2 hp, strings.

fp: 10 September 1913, Gloucester, Shire Hall, Three Choirs Festival concert, with Aïno Ackté.

Pub. 1915, Breitkopf & Härtel: vocal score: German version, Alfred J. Boruttau.

118. Two Pieces Op. 62. 1911. Composed for revised version of 'Kuolema' at the Finnish National Theatre, 8 March 1911.

1. *Canzonetta*. For string orchestra.

2. *Valse romantique*. For orchestra.

2 fl, 2 cl; 2 hn; timp; strings.

fEp (Nos. 1 & 2): 2 December 1911, Queen's Hall, Queen's Hall Orchestra, cond. Sir Henry Wood.

Pub. Breitkopf & Härtel.

119. Symphony No. 4 in A minor Op. 63. 1911. Ded. Eero Järnefelt.

1. *Tempo molto moderato, quasi adagio*; 2. *Allegro molto vivace*; 3. *Il tempo largo*; 4. *Allegro*.

2 fl, 2 ob, 2 cl, 2 bsn; 4 hn, 2 tpt, 3 tmb; timp, glock; strings.

fp: 3 April 1911, Helsinki, cond. Jean Sibelius.

fEp: 1 October 1912, Birmingham Festival, cond. Jean Sibelius.

fAp: 1913, New York, cond. Walter Damrosch.

2Ep: December 1913, Bournemouth, Bournemouth Municipal Orchestra, cond. (Sir) Dan Godfrey.

f London p: 20 March 1920, Queen's Hall, New Queen's Hall Orchestra, cond. Sir Henry Wood.

Pub. 1912, Breitkopf & Härtel.

BIBLIOGRAPHY:

Gerald Abraham: Sibelius's symphonic methods—No. 4 in A minor, *MO*, April 1938, p. 598.

Eric Blom: Sibelius, Symphony No. 4 in A minor, *Music Teacher*, December 1933, p. 633.

Julian Herbage: Symphony No. 4 in A minor, in *The Symphony*, Pelican Books (London) 1949, p. 337.

Harold E. Johnson: Sibelius fjärde symfoni— en stråkkvartett?, *Nya Pressen*, 7 June 1958.

Ernest Newman: Sibelius No. 4, its English history, in *From the World of Music*, Calder (London) 1956, p. 127.

Edmund Rubbra: Sibelius's Fourth Symphony, *MT*, February 1934, p. 127.

120. Two Partsongs Op. 65. For mixed chorus a cappella. 1911–12.

1. *People from land and sea* (Män från slätten och havet) (Ernst W. Knape). 1911.

2. *Bell melody of Berghäll Church* (Klockmelodin i Berghälls kyrka) (Engström). 1912.

fp (No. 1): June 1912, Vaasa, Swedish music festival.

Pub. 1927 (No. 1), 1914 (No. 2), Breitkopf & Härtel: German version, Alfred J. Boruttau.

121. Cantata. For women's chorus a cappella. Text: W. von Konow. 1911. Pub. Affärstryckeriet (Turku).

122. Wedding March. For orchestra. 1911. Composed for Act III of 'Die Sprache der Vögel', a drama by A. Paul.

2 fl, ob, 3 cl, 2 tpt, 2 tmb; timp, pcssn; strings.

fp: March 1911, Vienna.

Unpub.

123. Dreams (Drömmarna) (Reuter). For mixed chorus a cappella. 1912. Pub. Svenska Folkskolans Vänner (Helsinki).

124. Song for the People of Uusimaa (Uusmaalaisten laulu) (Terhi). For mixed chorus a cappella. 1912. Commissioned by the South Finnish Student Corporation. Pub. Kustannusosakeyhtiö Otava. Also version for mixed chorus a cappella.

125. Scènes historiques II Op. 66. For orchestra. 1912.

1. *The Chase (Overture)*; 2. *Love song*; 3. *At the drawbridge*.

2 fl, pic, 2 ob, 2 cl, 2 bsn; 4 hn; timp, tgle, tamtam; hp, strings.

Pub. Breitkopf & Härtel.

126. Three Sonatinas Op. 67. For piano. 1912. Ded. Martha Tornell.

No. 1 in F sharp minor.

1. *Allegro*; 2. *Largo*; 3. *Allegro*.

No. 2 in E major.

1. *Allegro*; 2. *Andantino*; 3. *Allegro*.

No. 3 in B flat minor.

1. *Allegro moderato*; 2. *Andante—Allegretto*.

Pub. 1912, Breitkopf & Härtel.

BIBLIOGRAPHY:

Cedric Thorpe Davie: Sibelius's piano sonatinas, *Tempo*, No. 10, March 1945.

127. Two Rondinos Op. 68. For piano. 1912.

1. *G sharp minor*; 2. *C sharp minor*.

fEbp: 3 July 1935, Max Pirani.

Pub. Universal-Edition.

128. Two Serenades Op. 69. For violin and orchestra. 1912–13.

1. *D major*; 2. *G minor*.

2 fl, 2 ob, 2 cl, 2 bsn; 4 hn; timp, pcssn; strings.

Pub. 1913, Breitkopf & Härtel: reduction by Hermann Gärtner.

129. Scaramouche Op. 71. Music for a tragic pantomime by Poul Knudsen and Mikael Trepka Bloch. 1913. Ded. Svend Borberg.

2 fl, 2 ob, 2 cl, 2 bsn; 4 hn, tpt; timp, pcssn; hp, strings.

fp: 12 May 1922, Copenhagen, Royal Theatre.

Pub. 1919, Hansen: German version, Mathilde Mann; French version, Samuel Prahl; English version, Alexander W. I. Worster; also piano score by Otto Olsen.

BIBLIOGRAPHY:
Friederike von Krosigk: Scaramouche, *Signale*, 1927, No. 25, p. 964.

130. The Bard Op. 64. Tone Poem for orchestra. 1913, rev. 1914.

2 fl, 2 ob, 3 cl, 2 bsn; 4 hn, 2 tpt, 3 tmb; timp, pcssn; hp, strings.

fp: 1913, Helsinki, cond. Jean Sibelius.

fEp: 13 October 1935, BBC broadcast, BBC Orchestra, cond. Sir Adrian Boult.

fEp (concert): 27 October 1938, Queen's Hall, Royal Philharmonic Society concert inaugurating the Sibelius Festival, London Philharmonic Orchestra, cond. Sir Thomas Beecham.

Pub. Breitkopf & Härtel.

131. Five Christmas Songs Op. 1. With piano. 1895–1913. Nos. 1–4, Topelius; No. 5, Joukahainen.

1. *Now Christmas stands at the snowy gate* (Nu står jul vid snöig port); 2. *Now Christmas comes* (Nu så kommer julen); 3. *Outside it grows dark* (Det mörknar ute); 5. *Give me no splendour* (Giv mig ej glans); 5. *High are the snowdrifts* (On hanget korkeat).

Pub. R. E. Westerlund Oy.

132. Spagnuolo. For piano. 1913. Printed in facsimile by Karisto (Hämeenlinna).

133. Three Songs for American schools. 1913.

1. *Autumn song* (Dixon); 2. *The sun upon the lake is low* (Scott); 3. *A cavalry catch* (Macleod).

Pub. 1915, Silver Burdett (Boston) in Progressive Music Series.

134. Pensés lyriques Op. 40. For piano. 1912–14.

1. *Valsette*; 2. *Chant sans paroles*; 3. *Humoresque*; 4. *Menuetto*; 5. *Berceuse*; 6. *Pensée mélodique*; 7. *Rondoletto*; 8. *Scherzando*; 9. *Petite sérénade*; 10. *Polonaise*.

Pub. (Nos. 1–8) Breitkopf & Härtel, (Nos. 9–10) R. E. Westerlund Oy.

135 The Oceanides Op. 73. Tone poem for orchestra. 1914. Ded. Mr. and Mrs. Carl Stoeckel.

3 fl, 3 ob, 3 cl, 3 bsn; 4 hn, 3 tpt, 3 tmb; timp, pcssn; 2 hp, strings.

fp: 4 June 1914, Norfolk (Conn.), Litchfield County Choral Union Musical Festival, cond. Jean Sibelius.

?fEp: 1 May 1932, BBC broadcast, BBC Orchestra, cond. Leslie Heward.

Pub. Breitkopf & Härtel.

BIBLIOGRAPHY:
Ulrich Dibelius: Form und Impression, Die Okeaniden von Sibelius, *NZfM*, December 1956.

136. Four Lyric Pieces Op. 74. For piano. 1914.

1. *Eclogue*; 2. *Soft west wind*; 3. *At the dance*; 4. *In the old home*.

Pub. 1915, Breitkopf & Härtel.

137. Five Pieces Op. 75. For piano. 1914.

1. *When the mountain-ash is in flower*; 2. *The lonely fir*; 3. *The aspen*; 4. *The birch*; 5. *The fir*.

Pub. 1922, Hansen.

138. Thirteen Pieces Op. 76. For piano. *c.* 1914.

1. *Esquisse*; 2. *Etude*; 3. *Carillon*; 4. *Humoresque*; 5. *Consolation*; 6. *Romanzetta*; 7. *Affettuoso*; 8. *Pièce enfantine*; 9. *Arabesque*; 10. *Elegiaco*; 11. *Linnea*; 12. *Capricietto*; 13. *Harlequinade*.

Pub. Hansen.

139. Two Pieces Op. 77. For violin (or cello) and orchestra. 1914.

1. *Cantique* (Laetare anima mea). Ded. Ossian Fohström.

2 fl, 2 cl; 2 hn; timp hp, strings.

2. *Devotion* (Ab imo pectore).

2 fl, cl, 2 bsn; 4 hn, 3 tmb; strings.

Pub. 1922 (No. 1), 1923 (No. 2), Hansen.

140. Six Songs Op. 72. For voice and piano. 1907–15.

 1. *Farewell* (Vi ses igen) (Viktor Rydberg). 1914.

 2. *Orion's girdle* (Orions bälte) (Z. Topelius). 1914.

 3. *The kiss* (Kyssen) (Viktor Rydberg). 1915.

 4. *The echo nymph* (Kaiutar) (Larin Kyösti). 1915.

 5. *Der Wanderer und der Bach* (Martin Greif). 1915.

 6. *A hundred ways* (Hundra vägar) (J. C. Runeberg). 19 ∴7.

 Pub. 1916, Breitkopf & Härtel.

141. Four Pieces Op. 78. For violin (or cello) and piano. 1915–19.

 1. *Impromptu.* 1915.

 2. *Romance.* 1915.

 3. *Religioso.* 1919. Ded. Rev. Dr. Chr. Sibelius.

 4. *Rigaudon.* 1915.

 Pub. 1923, Hansen.

142. Six Pieces Op. 79. For violin and piano. 1915.

 1. *Souvenir*; 2. *Tempo di menuetto*; 3. *Danse caractéristique*; 4. *Sérénade*; 5. *Dance idyll*; 6. *Berceuse*.

 Pub. 1922, Hansen.

143. Sonatina in E major Op. 80. For violin and piano. 1915.

 1. *Lento—Allegro*; 2. *Andantino*; 3. *Lento—Allegretto—Vivace*.

 fEbp: 19 October 1931, Samuel Kutcher and Ernest Lush.

 Pub. 1921, Hansen.

144. Five Pieces Op. 81. For violin and piano. *c.* 1915.

 1. *Mazurka*; 2. *Rondino*; 3. *Waltz*; 4. *Aubade*; 5. *Menuetto*.

 Pub. 1916–17, R. E. Westerlund Oy & Breitkopf & Härtel.

145. Symphony No. 5 in E flat major Op. 82. 1915, rev. 1916 and 1919.

 1. *Molto moderato—Allegro moderato*; 2. *Andante mosso quasi allegretto*; 3. *Allegro molto*.

 2 fl, 2 ob, 2 cl, 2 bsn; 4 hn, 3 tpt, 3 tmb; timp; strings.

 fp (1915 version): 8 December 1915,

Helsinki, Sibelius's fiftieth birthday concert, Municipal Orchestra, cond. Robert Kajanus.

 fp (1916 version): 14 December 1916, Helsinki, cond. Jean Sibelius (?or previously in Turku).

 fp (1919 version): 24 November 1919, Helsinki.

 fEp: 12 February 1921, Queen's Hall, New Queen's Hall Orchestra, cond. Jean Sibelius.

 fEbp: 6 October 1927, Birmingham, Town Hall, City of Birmingham Orchestra, cond. Sir Adrian Boult.

 Pub. 1921, Hansen.

BIBLIOGRAPHY:

Gerald Abraham: Sibelius's symphonic methods—No. 5 in E flat, *MO*, June 1938, p. 785.

Eric Blom: Symphony No. 5 in E flat major, *Music Teacher*, July 1932, p. 341.

K. W. Gehrkens: What did Sibelius mean?— Spacing of the final chords in Fifth Symphony, *Etude*, April 1943, p. 243.

Julian Herbage: Symphony No. 5 in E flat major, in *The Symphony*, Pelican Books (London) 1949, p. 342.

Donald F. Tovey: Symphony in E flat major, No. 5 Op. 82, in *EMA*, Vol. 2, O.U.P. (London) 1935, p. 125.

146. Five Partsongs Op. 84. For male chorus a cappella. 1914–15.

 1. *Herr Lager* (Fröding). 1914.

 2. *On the mountain* (På berget) (Gripenberg). 1915.

 3. *A dream chord* (Ett drömackord) (Fröding). 1915.

 4. *Eternal Eros* (Evige Eros) (Gripenberg). 1915.

 5. *At sea* (Till havs) (Reuter). 1915.

 Pub. (Nos. 1–4) Muntra Musikanter (Helsinki), (No. 5) R. E. Westerlund Oy.

147. The thought (Tanken) (Runeberg). Duet for two sopranos and piano. 1915. Unpub.

148. Ten Pieces Op. 34. For piano. 1914–16.

 1. *Waltz*; 2. *Dance air*; 3. *Mazurka*; 4. *Humorous*; 5. *Drollery*; 6. *Rêverie*; 7. *Pastoral dance*; 8. *The harper*; 9. *Reconnaissance*; 10. *Souvenir*.

Pub. (Nos. 1–6) Breitkopf & Härtel, (Nos. 7–10) R. E. Westerlund Oy.

149. In the moonlight (Kuutamolla) (Suonio). For male chorus a cappella. 1916. Pub. Ylioppilaskunnan Laulajat (Helsinki).

150. Everyman (Jedermann) (Jokamies) Op. 83. Incidental music for a play by Hugo von Hofmannsthal. For mixed chorus, piano, organ and orchestra. 1916.
2 fl, ob, 2 cl, bsn; 2 hn, 2 tpt; timp, pcssn; strings.
fp: 5 November 1916, Helsinki, Finnish National Theatre.
Unpub.

151. Five Pieces Op. 85. For piano. 1916.
1. *Bellis*; 2. *Oeillet*; 3. *Iris*; 4. *Aquileja*; 5. *Campanula*.
Pub. Hansen.

152. Six Songs Op. 86. For voice and piano. 1916.
1. *The coming of spring* (Vårförnimmelser) (K. A. Tavaststjerna).
2. *Longing is my heritage* (Längtan heter min arfvedel) (E. A. Karlfeldt).
3. *Hidden union* (Dold förening) (C. Snoilsky).
4. *And is there a thought?* (Och finns det en tanke?) (K. A. Tavaststjerna).
5. *The singer's reward* (Sångarlön) (C. Snoilsky).
6. *Ye sisters, ye brothers* (I systrar, I bröder) (Mikael Lybeck).
Pub. 1923, Hansen.

153. Two Humoresques Op. 87. For violin and orchestra. 1917.
1. *D minor.*
2 fl, 2 ob, 2 cl, 2 bsn; 2 hn; timp; strings.
2. *D major.*
2 hn; timp; strings.
Pub. 1923, Hansen: reduction by Karl Ekman. See also No. 155.

154. Six Songs Op. 88. For voice and piano. 1917.
1. *The anemone* (Blåsippan) (Fr. M. Franzén).
2. *The two roses* (De bägge rosorna) (Fr. M. Franzén).

3. *The star-flower* (Hvitsippan) (Fr. M. Franzén).
4. *The primrose* (Sippan) (J. L. Runeberg).
5. *The thorn* (Törnet) (J. L. Runeberg).
6. *The flower's destiny* (Blommans öde) (Runeberg).
Pub. 1923, Hansen.

155–158. Four Humoresques (Nos. 3–6) Op. 89. For violin and orchestra. 1917. For violin and orchestra. 1917.
3. *G minor.* With string orchestra.
4. *G minor.* With string orchestra.
5. *E flat major.*
2 fl, 2 cl, 2 bsn; strings.
6. *G. minor.*
2 fl, 2 bsn; strings.
Pub. 1922–23, Hansen: reduction by Karl Ekman.

159. Six Songs Op. 90 (J. L. Runeberg). For voice and piano. 1917.
1. *The north* (Norden); 2. *Her message* (Hennes budskap); 3. *The morning* (Morgonen); 4. *The birdcatcher* (Fågelfängaren); 5. *Summer night* (Sommarnatten); 6. *Who has brought you here?* (Hvem styrde hit din väg?).
Pub. R. E. Westerlund Oy.

160. March of the Finnish (27th Royal Prussian) Jaeger Battalion Op. 91 No. 1. For male chorus a cappella. 1917. Text: Nurmio. Pub. in hectograph.

160a. March of the Finnish Jaeger Battalion Op. 91 No. 1. Version for male chorus and orchestra. ?1917.
2 fl, 2 ob, 3 cl, 2 bsn; 4 hn, 3 tpt, 3 tmb, timp, pcssn; strings.
fp (public): 19 January 1918, Helsinki, City Orchestra, cond. Robert Kajanus.
Pub. Breitkopf & Härtel. Also version for voice and piano pub. Breitkopf & Härtel.

161. Scount March Op. 91 No. 2. For mixed chorus a cappella. 1917. Text: Finne-Procopé.
Pub. Hansen.

161a. Scout March Op. 91 No. 2. Version for mixed chorus and orchestra. ?1917.
2 fl, 2 ob, 2 cl, 2 bsn; 4 hn, 3 tpt, 3 tmb, tuba; timp; strings.
Pub. 1922, Hansen. Also version for voice and piano pub. Hansen.

162. Fridolin's folly (Fridolins dårskap) (Karlfeldt). For male chorus a cappella. 1917. Pub. Abraham Hirsch (Stockholm).

163. Mandolinato. For piano. 1917. Pub. Hansen.

164. The roaring of a wave (Brusande rusar en våg) (Schybergson). For male chorus a cappella. 1918. Pub. R. E. Westerlund Oy.

165. Jonah's voyage (Jone havsfärd) (Karlfeldt). For male chorus a cappella. 1918. Pub. Werner Söderström (Helsinki), as *Joonaan meriretki.*

166. Narciss (Gripenberg). For voice and piano. ?1918. Pub. R. E. Westerlund Oy.

167. One hears the storm outside (Ute hörs stormen) (Schybergson). For male chorus a cappella. 1918. Pub. R. E. Westerlund Oy.

168. Our native land (Oma maa) Op. 92. Cantata for mixed chorus and orchestra. Text: Kallio (i.e. Kustaa Samuli Berg). 1918. Commissioned by the National Chorus for its tenth anniversary.
2 fl, 2 ob, 2 cl, 2 bsn; 4 hn, 2 tpt, 3 tmb; timp, pcssn; strings.
Pub. (choral parts only) R. E. Westerlund Oy.

169. Song of the earth (Jordens sång) Op. 93. Cantata for mixed chorus and orchestra. 1919. Text: Hemmer. Composed for the inauguration of the Swedish Åbo Academy, Turku.
2 fl, 2 ob, 2 cl, 2 bsn; 3 hn, 2 tpt, 2 tmb; timp; strings.
Pub. (choral parts only) R. E. Westerlund Oy.

170. Six Pieces Op. 94. For piano. 1919.
1. *Dance*; 2. *Novelette*; 3. *Sonnet*; 4. *Berger et bergerette*; 5. *Mélodie*; 6. *Gavotte.*
Pub. 1922, Hansen; R. E. Westerlund Oy (Finland only).

171. Academic March (Promotiomarssi). For orchestra. 1919. 2 fl, 2 ob, 2 cl, 2 bsn; 4 hn, 2 tpt; timp, pcssn; hp, strings.
Unpub.

172. Small girls (Små flickorna) (Procopé). For voice and piano. 1920. Pub. 1920, in *Lucifer.*

173. Honour March of the Singing Brothers of Viipuri (Viipurin Laulu-Veikkojen kunniamarssi) (Eerola). For male chorus a cappella. 1920. Two versions. Pub. (first version) in *Viipurin Laulu-Veikot,* (second version) J. Wikstedtin Kivipaino (Helsinki).

174. Hymn of the earth (Maan virsi) Op. 95. Cantata for mixed chorus and orchestra. 1920. Text: E. Leino.
2 fl, 2 ob, 2 cl, 2 bsn; 4 hn, 2 tpt, 3 tmb; timp; strings.
fp: June 1920, Helsinki, trade fair concert, cond. Jean Sibelius.
Pub. R. E. Westerlund Oy.

175. Valse lyrique Op. 96 No. 1. For orchestra. 1920.
2 fl, 2 ob, 2 cl, 2 bsn; 4 hn, 2 tpt, 3 tmb; timp, pcssn; strings.
Pub. Hansen. Arr. for piano solo pub. 1920, Hawkes.

176. Autrefois (Scène pastorale) Op. 96 No. 2. For two voices (ad lib) and orchestra. 1919.
2 fl, 2 cl, 2 bsn; 2 hn; timp; strings.
Pub. Hansen. Also arr. for piano solo.

177. Valse chevaleresque Op. 96 No. 3. For orchestra. 1920.
2 fl, 2 ob, 2 cl, 2 bsn; 4 hn, 2 tpt, 3 tmb; timp, pcssn; strings.
Pub. Hansen. Also arr. for piano solo.

178. Six Bagatelles Op. 97. For piano. 1920.
1. *Humoresque I*; 2. *Song*; 3. *Little waltz*; 4. *Humorous march*; 5. *Impromptu*; 6. *Humoresque II.*
Pub. 1921, Breitkopf & Härtel.

179. Suite mignonne Op. 98 No. 1. For flute and strings. 1921.
1. *Petite scène*; 2. *Polka*; 3. *Epilogue.*
Pub. Chappell. Also arr. for piano solo.

180. Suite champêtre Op. 98 No. 2. For string orchestra. 1921.
1. *Pièce caractéristique*; 2. *Mélodie élégiaque*; 3. *Danse.*
Pub. ?1922, Hansen. Also arr. for piano solo pub. 1922, Hansen.

181. Andante festivo. For string quartet.

1922. Pub. 28 December 1922, in *Kertomus Säynatsalon tehtaitten 25-vuotisjuhlasta*.

181a. Andante festivo. Version for string orchestra and (ad lib) timpani. Pub. R. E. Westerlund Oy.

182. Resemblance (Likhet) (Runeberg). For male chorus a cappella. 1922. Pub. Musices Amantes (Turku).

183. Eight Pieces Op. 99. For piano. 1922.
  1. *Pièce humoristique*; 2. *Esquisse*; 3. *Souvenir*; 4. *Impromptu*; 5. *Couplet*; 6. *Animoso*; 7. *Moment de valse*; 8. *Petite marche*.
  Pub. Fazerin Musiikkikaupa Oy.

184. Suite caractéristique Op. 100. For harp and string orchestra. 1922.
  1. *Vivo*; 2. *Lento*; 3. *Commodo*.
  Unpub. Version for piano solo pub. 1924, Hansen.

185. Five Romantic Pieces Op. 101. For piano. 1923.
  1. *Romance*; 2. *Chant du soir*; 3. *Scène lyrique*; 4. *Humoresque*; 5. *Scène romantique*.
  Pub. 1925, Hansen; Carl Fischer (New York).

186. Novelette Op. 102. For violin and piano. 1923. Pub. 1923, Hansen.

187. Five Pieces Op. 103. For piano. 1924.
  1. *The village church*; 2. *The fiddler*; 3. *The oarsman*; 4. *The storm*; 5. *In mournful mood*.
  Pub. 1925, Hansen; Carl Fischer (New York).

188. Symphony No. 6 in D minor Op. 104. 1923. Ded. Wilhelm Stenhammar.
  1. *Allegro molto moderato*; 2. *Allegro moderato*; 3. *Poco vivace*; 4. *Allegro molto*.
  2 fl, 2 ob, 2 cl, bcl, 2 bsn; 4 hn, 3 tpt, 3 tmb; timp; hp, strings.
  fp: 19 February 1923, Helsinki, Helsinki City Orchestra, cond. Jean Sibelius.
  fEp: 10 September 1925, Gloucester, Three Choirs Festival concert, cond. Jean Sibelius.
  f London p: 20 November 1926, New Queen's Hall Orchestra, cond. Sir Henry Wood.
  Pub. Abraham Hirsch (Stockholm).

BIBLIOGRAPHY:
Gerald Abraham: Sibelius's symphonic methods—No. 6 in D minor, *MO*, August 1938, p. 945.
Eric Blom: Sibelius, Symphony No. 6 in D minor, *Music Teacher*, September 1931, p. 467.
J. H. Elliot: The Sixth Symphony of Sibelius, *M&L*, July 1936, p. 234.
Julian Herbage: Symphony No. 6 in D minor, in *The Symphony*, Pelican Books (London) 1949, p. 345.

189. Symphony No. 7 in C major Op. 105. 1924.
  2 fl, 2 ob, 2 cl, 2 bsn; 4 hn, 3 tpt, 3 tmb; timp; strings.
  fp (as *Fantasia sinfonica*): 24 March 1924, Stockholm, cond. Jean Sibelius.
  f Ap: 3 April 1926, Philadelphia, Philadelphia Orchestra, cond. Leopold Stokowski.
  f Finnish p: April 1927, Helsinki.
  fEp: 8 December 1927, Queen's Hall, Royal Philharmonic Society concert, cond. Sir Henry Wood.
  Pub. 1925, Hansen.

BIBLIOGRAPHY:
Gerald Abraham: Sibelius's symphonic methods—No. 7 in C major, *MO*, October 1938, p. 21.
Edward Crankshaw: Sibelius's Seventh, *Bookman*, November 1933, p. 110.
Vittorio Gui: Note sulla Settima di Sibelius, *La Rassegna musicale*, January 1956, p. 33.
Julian Herbage: Symphony No. 7 in C major, in *The Symphony*, Pelican Books (London) 1949, p. 349.
Harold E. Johnson: Sibeliuksen seitsemäs sinfonia ja 'Fantasia sinfonica', *Helsingin Sanomat*, 22 September 1957.

190. Five Danses Champêtres Op. 106. For violin and piano. 1925. Pub. Hansen.

191. Hymn Op. 107. For chorus and organ. 1925. Unpub.

192. Two Partsongs Op. 108 (Larin Kyösti). For male chorus a cappella. 1925.
  1. *Humoreski*; 2. *Wanderers on the long way* (Ne pitkän matkan kulkijat).
  Pub. Laulu-Miehet.

193. The Tempest Op. 109. Incidental music for the play by Shakespeare. 1925. Original

Sibelius, Jean

score in 34 parts for soloists, mixed chorus, harmonium and orchestra.

fp: 16 March 1926, Copenhagen, Royal Theatre.

193a. The Tempest Op. 109. Concert version for orchestra.
Prelude.
2 fl, pic, 2 ob, 3 cl, 2 bsn; 4 hn, 3 tpt, 3 tmb, tuba; timp, pcssn; strings.
fEp: February 1930, Hastings Festival, Hastings Municipal Orchestra, cond. Basil Cameron.
Suite No. 1.
1. *The oak tree*; 2. *Humoresque*; 3. *Caliban's song*; 4. *The harvesters*; 5. *Canon*; 6. *Scena*; 7. *Intrada-Berceuse*; 8. *Entr'acte—Ariel's song*; 9. *The storm.*
2 fl, pic, 2 ob, 3 cl, 2 bsn; 4 hn, 3 tpt, 3 tmb, tuba; timp, pcssn; hp, strings.
fEp: 4 October 1934, Leeds Festival.
f London p: 18 October 1934, Queen's Hall, Royal Philharmonic Society concert, cond. Sir Thomas Beecham.
Suite No. 2.
1. *Chorus of the winds*; 2. *Intermezzo*; 3. *Dance of the nymphs*; 4. *Prospero*; 5. *Song I*; 6. *Song II*; 7. *Miranda*; 8. *The Naiads*; 9. *Dance episode.*
2 fl, 2 ob, 2 cl, 2 bsn; 4 hn; timp; hp, strings.
Pub. Hansen. Also some Suite numbers arr. for piano.

194. The lonely ski trail (Ett ensamt skidspår). For piano. 1925. To accompany the recitation of verses by B. Gripenberg. Pub. Nordiska Musikförlaget (Stockholm). Also version for harp and string orchestra (1948), unpub.

195. Introductory Antiphons (Johdantovuorolauluja). For mixed chorus. 1925.
1. *Palm Sunday* (Palmusunnuntaina); 2. *All Saints Day* (Pyhäinpäivänä); 3. *General Prayers* (Rukouspäivänä).
Pub. Werner Söderström (Helsinki).

196. The way to school (Koulutie) (Koskenniemi). For children's voices a cappella. 1925. Pub. Werner Söderström (Helsinki).

197. Morceau romantique sur un motif de

M. Jacob de Julin. For piano. 1925. Pub. Delanchy-Dupre (Asnières).

197a. Pièce romantique. Version for orchestra of preceding. 1925. Composed for General Mannerheim's Children's Fund.
fp: 9 March 1925, Helsinki, gala concert, Helsinki City Orchestra, cond. Jean Sibelius. Unpub.

198. Väinö's song (Väinön virsi) Op. 110. For mixed chorus and orchestra. 1926. Text: from The Kalevala.
2 fl, 2 ob, 2 cl, 2 bsn; 4 hn, 3 tpt, 3 tmb; timp, pcssn; strings.
fp: 28 June 1926, Sortavala Festival, cond. Robert Kajanus.
Pub. 1945, R. E. Westerlund Oy.

199. Tapiola Op. 112. Tone Poem for orchestra. 1926. Ded. Walter Damrosch. Commissioned by the New York Symphony Society.
3 fl, pic, 2 ob, ca, 2 cl, bcl, 2 bsn, cbsn; 4 hn, 3 tpt, 3 tmb; timp; strings.
fp: 26 December 1926, New York, New York Symphony Orchestra, cond. Walter Damrosch.
f Finnish p: April 1927, Helsinki.
fEp: 1 September 1928, Queen's Hall, Promenade Concert, Wood Symphony Orchestra, cond. Sir Henry Wood: broadcast by the BBC.
Pub. 1926, Breitkopf & Härtel.

200. You are mighty, O Lord (Suur' olet, Herra). Hymn for mixed chorus a cappella. 1927. Text: Korpela. Pub. Suomen Laulajain ja Soittájain Liitto (Helsinki). Also version for male chorus pub. Laulu-Miehet (Helsinki).

201. Masonic Ritual Music Op. 113. For male voices, piano and organ. 1927– .
1. *Introduction.* 1927.
2. *Thoughts be our comfort* (Schiller).
3. *Introduction and Hymn* (Confucius).
4. *Marcia* (Goethe).
5. *Light* (Simelius).
6. *Salem* (Rydberg).
7. *Whosoever hath a love* (Rydberg).
8. *Ode to fraternity* (Sario). 1946.
9. *Hymn* (Sario).
10. *Marche funèbre.* 1927.
11. *Ode* (Korpela).

514

12. *Finlandia Hymn* (Sola). 1938.
Pub. 1935 (first edition), 1950 (second, enlarged edition) Grand Lodge of Free and Accepted Masons of the State of New York.

BIBLIOGRAPHY:
E. Tanzberger: Rituelle Freimaurer-Musik Op. 113 von JS, *Sibelius-Mitteilungen*, No. 7, October 1963, p. 1.

202. Five Esquisses Op. 114. For piano. 1929.
1. *Landscape*; 2. *Winter scene*; 3. *Forest lake*; 4. *Song in the forest*; 5. *Spring vision.*
Unpub.

203. Four Pieces Op. 115. For violin and piano. 1929.
1. *On the heath*; 2. *Ballade*; 3. *Humoresque*; 4. *The Bells.*
Pub. 1930, Breitkopf & Härtel.

204. Three Pieces Op. 116. For violin and piano. 1929.
1. *Scène de danse*; 2. *Danse caractéristique*; 3. *Rondeau romantique.*
Pub. 1930, Breitkopf & Härtel.

205. Two Pieces Op. 111. For organ. 1925–1931.
1. *Intrada.* 1925.
2. *Mournful music* (Surusoitto). 1931.
Pub. R. E. Westerlund Oy.

206. Karelia's fate (Karjalan osa) (Nurminen). March for male chorus and piano. 1930. Pub. Musiikkikeskus (Helsinki).

207. The Guard of the bridge (Sittavahti) (Sola). For male chorus a cappella. ?Date. Pub. 1938, in *Helsingin työväen mieskuoro.*

208. Two Italian songs. For mixed chorus. ?Date. Unpub.

209. Symphony No. 8. Destroyed.

BIBLIOGRAPHY:
Basil Cameron: Sibelius's Eighth Symphony, *Composer*, No. 13, spring 1964, p. 5.
Arnold Whittall: Sibelius's Eighth Symphony, *MR*, August 1964, p. 239.

GENERAL BIBLIOGRAPHY
Fannie Aavatsmark: A visit to Sibelius, *Musical America*, 10 December 1935.

G.E.H.A.: The art of JS, *Musical Mirror*, October 1921, p. 8.
Gerald Abraham: The symphonies, in *Sibelius: a symposium* (ed. Gerald Abraham), Lindsay Drummond (London) 1947.
— Sibelius, *Radio Times*, 22 September 1933, p. 659.
W. R. Anderson: Some songs by Sibelius, *MT*, September 1932, p. 799.
Otto Andersson: Finlandssvenska musikfester under 50 år, Förlaget Bro (Åbo) 1947.
— JS i Amerika, Förlaget Bro (Åbo) 1955.
— JS och Svenska Teatern, Förlaget Bro (Åbo) 1956.
— När JS erhöll statsstipendium, *Hufvudstadsbladet*, 3 January 1957.
— Sibelius-Nummer I–II, *Tidning för Musik*, Nos. 14–16, December 1915.
— Sibelius och Kajanus som konkurrenter, *Hufvudstadsbladet*, 8 December 1956.
H. Orsmond Anderston: Old Vainämöinen, *MO*, July 1919, p. 619.
Elliott Arnold: Finlandia—The story of Sibelius, Henry Holt (New York) 1941.
Henry Askeli: A sketch of Sibelius the man, *MQ*, January 1940, p. 1.
Frank Baker: Couple the tubas—notes upon Sibelius, *Chesterian*, No. 119, January–February 1935, p. 64.
Sir Granville Bantock: JS, *MMR*, December 1935, p. 217.
Sir John Barbirolli (& others): JS, *Hallé*, November 1957, p. 15.
Sir Thomas Beecham: Sibelius the craftsman, *Living Age*, February 1939, p. 576.
Ralph H. Bellairs: Debussy and Sibelius, *MO*, July 1908, p. 748.
Rodney Bennett: Song writers of today, 3—Sibelius, *Music Teacher*, August 1926, p. 461.
H. Berman: Indomitable Finn, *Etude*, December 1955, p. 26.
Eric Blom: The piano music, in *Sibelius, a symposium*, Lindsay Drummond (London) 1947.
Kim Borg: JS und die Finnen: Gesamtverzeichnis der Werke von JS, *ÖM*, October 1957.
Elsa von Born: Den underbara resan, Finlands Röda Kors, Julhälsning, 1935, p. 5.

Gerard Bourke: The Sibelius festival, *MO*, August 1954, p. 636.

— Sibelius festival at Helsinki, *MO*, August 1955, p. 661.

L. V. Brant: Sibelius today, *Etude*, December 1948, p. 725.

José Bruyr: Le premier Finlandais, *Le Ménestrel*, 26 January/2 February 1940, p. 17.

Gordon Bryan: The piano music of Sibelius, *M&M*, December 1955, p. 9.

— Sibelius, the soul of geniality, *Radio Times*, 22 November 1946, p. 5.

— Sibelius at Ainola, *RCM Magazine*, 1957, No. 1, p. 5.

Frederick Bye: JS, an essentially *national* composer, *Musical Mirror*, October 1930, p. 276.

Neville Cardus: Sibelius, in *Ten Composers*, Jonathan Cape (London) 1945.

— Finland's true laureate, *Radio Times*, 6 December 1929, p. 704.

— Sibelius, national composer of Finland, *Radio Times*, 23 October 1931, p. 259.

David Cherniavsky: The use of germ motives by Sibelius, *M&L*, January 1942, p. 1.

— The special characteristic of Sibelius's style, in *Sibelius, a symposium*, Lindsay Drummond (London) 1947.

— Two unpublished tone-poems by Sibelius, *MT*, August 1949, p. 272.

— Sibelius and Finland, *MT*, January 1950, p. 15.

— Sibelius's tempo corrections, *M&L*, January 1950, p. 53.

— Besuch bei JS, *Musica*, 1955, No. 12, p. 598.

— Finland and Sibelius, *Canon*, November 1956, p. 137.

C. Clemens: Glimpse of JS, with some letters, *Hobbies*, April 1953, p. 128.

Anthony Collins: Sibelius, the man and his music, *London Musical Events*, November 1955, p. 22.

Edward Crankshaw: JS, *Bookman*, July 1934, p. 197.

A. Walter Cranmer: A clouded view of the master, Sibelius, *Musical America*, July 1932.

Fritz Crome: Hos Finlands stote Mester—En Samtale med Sibelius, *Musik* (Copenhagen), August (No. 8) 1919.

— Ein Gesprach mit Sibelius, *Signale*, 1919, No. 39 (24 September), p. 595 (repr. from *Musik*, Copenhagen).

— JS in Kopenhagen, *Signale*, 1924, No. 46, p. 1746.

John Culshaw: Sibelius and the symphonic revival, in *A Century of Music*, Dennis Dobson (London) 1952, p. 107.

— Sibelius and the future of symphonic music, in –do–, p. 159.

Norman Demuth: JS, in *Musical Trends in the 20th Century*, Rockliff (London) 1952, p. 253.

Astra Desmond: The songs, in *Sibelius, a symposium*, Lindsay Drummond (London) 1947.

N. DeVore: Sphinx speaks through Finland's Sibelius, *Musician*, December 1941, p. 185.

Olin Downes: Symphonic prophet, *New York Times Magazine*, 8 December 1940, p. 6.

— Sibelius today and tomorrow, *Saturday Review*, 10 December 1955, p. 30.

— Sibelius the symphonist, Philharmonic Society of New York, 1956.

Leonard Duck: Sibelius, man and mystic, *Halle*, October 1953, p. 2; February 1955, p. 1.

(Sir) George Dyson: Sibelius, *MT*, November 1936, p. 987.

Friedrich Ege: JS, *SM*, December 1955, p. 473.

Karl Ekman: JS, en Konstnärs Liv och Personlighet, Helsinki, 1935; Eng. transl. as JS, his life and personality, Alan Wilmer (London) 1936.

— JS och hans verk, Holger Schildts Förlag (Helsinki) 1956.

E. Elisofon: Sibelius revisited, *Time*, 23 October 1944, p. 60.

J. H. Elliott: Sibelius, *MMR*, February 1931, p. 33.

— JS, a modern enigma, *Chesterian*, No. 92, January–February 1931, p. 93.

Edwin Evans: A chat with Sibelius, *MN&H*, 26 February 1921, p. 268.

Frank Feldman: JS, *M&M*, November 1957, p. 12.

Karl Flodin: JS, fosterlandets tonsättare, *Finsk Musikrevy*, December 1905.

— Finska musiker, Söderström (Helsingfors) 1900.

— JS nya Kompositioner, *Euterpe* (Helsingfors), 1904, No. 7.

— JS, in *Finnische Rundschau*, 1901, No. 4.
— Musikliv och reseminnen, Söderström (Helsingfors) 1931.
K. Flor: JS, *Nordisk Musikkultur*, December 1955, p. 110.
Benjamin Frankel: Sibelius and his critics, *The Listener*, 29 June 1961, p. 1130.
Nils-Erik Fougstedt: Sibelius's Tonsättningar till Rydberg-Texter, *Musik-Världen* (Stockholm), December (No. 10) 1945.
Sigurd Frosterus: Sibelius-koordinater, *Nya Argus* (Helsinki), 1932, pp. 79, 94.
Erik Furuhjelm: JS, hans tondiktning och drag ur hans liv, Holger Schildts Förlag (Borgå) 1916.
E. Gamber: Mein Besuch in Ainola, *Sibelius-Mitteilungen*, No. 3, March 1960, p. 16.
G. Gavazzeni: JS, *La Rassegna musicale*, 1939, p. 256.
P. E. Gerschefski: The thematic, temporal, and dynamic processes in the symphonies of JS, *Dissertation Abstracts*, April 1963, p. 3920.
Lionel Gilman: And what of Sibelius?, *The Gramophone*, September 1931, p. 124.
— Sibelius, *Catholic World*, February 1939, p. 610.
Dudley Glass: Salute to Sibelius, *MO*, December 1965, p. 149.
Scott Goddard: The chamber music *and* The choral music, in *Sibelius, a symposium*, Lindsay Drummond (London) 1947.
— JS, *Halle*, September 1949, p. 3.
Joan Goodacre: JS, *The Gramophone*, December 1938, p. 273.
N. R. Graves: Visit to the home of Sibelius, *Etude*, March 1937, p. 149.
— Master of Järvenpää, *Etude*, June 1952, p. 9.
Cecil Gray: JS, in *A Survey of Contemporary Music*, O.U.P. (London) 1927, p. 184.
— Sibelius, or music and the future, *Nation and Athenaeum*, 24 December 1927, p. 483.
— Sibelius, the symphonies, O.U.P. (London) 1935.
— Sibelius's tone poems, *Radio Times*, 11 October 1935, p. 12.
— The enduring art of Sibelius, *Radio Times*, 20 August 1937, p. 11.
— Sibelius at 80, *London Philharmonic Post*, November 1945, p. 4.
Robin Gregory: Sibelius and the Kalevala, *MMR*, March–April 1951, p. 59.

Axel Hambraeus: JS, in *Mästare i tonernas värld*, 1933.
Ilmari Hannikainen: Sibelius and the development of Finnish music, Hinrichsen Edition (London) 1948.
Michael G. Heenan: The symphonic poems of Sibelius, *The Gramophone*, 1950, July, p. 22, August, p. 39.
Veikko Helasvuo: Sibelius and the music of Finland, Otava (Helsinki) 1957.
— JS, *Halle*, November 1955, p. 10.
T. Heinitz: Sibelius without society, *Saturday Review*, 31 December 1955, p. 40.
Julian Herbage: JS, in *The Symphony*, Pelican Books (London) 1949, p. 326.
— JS, *The Gramophone*, December 1955, p. 256.
Ralph Hill: a new book on Sibelius, *MM&F*, February 1932, p. 38.
— Sibelius talks, *Radio Times*, 4 September 1936, p. 14.
— Sibelius the man, in *Sibelius, a symposium*, Lindsay Drummond (London) 1947.
William G. Hill: Some aspects of form in the symphonies of Sibelius, *MR*, August 1949, p. 165.
Richard Holt: JS, *The Gramophone*, November 1931, p. 211.
A. E. Hull: JS, *MMR*, December 1927, p. 357.
Dyneley Hussey: Sibelius, *Weekend Review*, 24 October 1931, p. 515.
M. Jalas: Sibelius und seine Kinder, *Sibelius-Mitteilungen*, No. 5, December 1961, p. 10.
Harold E. Johnson: JS, the recorded music, R. E. Westerlund Oy (Helsinki) 1957.
— Jean Sibeliuksen alkusoitto, *Helsingin Sanomat*, 28 February 1958.
— Jean Sibeliuksen 'Työkansan marssi', *Helsingin Sanomat*, 5 July 1958.
— Sibelius ja ohjelmamusiikki, *Helsingin Sanomat*, 8 June 1958.
— Sibelius, Faber (London) 1959.
S. Jordan: Smaa glimt av JS, *Dansk Musiktidsskrift*, 1962, No. 2, p. 43.
A. Kalisch: JS, *British Music Bulletin*, March 1921, p. 63.
Michael Kennedy: Sibelius and Vaughan Williams, *Hallé*, No. 117, 1960–1, p. 10.
I. Kolodin: Sibelius and Sargent in Helsinki, *Saturday Review*, 7 July 1956, p. 20.

Walter von Konow: Janne, *Veckans Krönika*, 4 December 1915, p. 429.

Muistoja Jean Sibeliuksen poikavuosilta, Aulos (Helsinki) 1925.

nstant Lambert: The symphonies of Sibelius, *The Dominant*, May–June 1927, p. 14.

— Sibelius and the integrations of form, in *Music Ho*, Faber (London) 1934.

— Sibelius and the music of the future, in *–do–*.

Robert Layton: Sibelius, the early years, *PRMA*, 1964–5, p. 73.

— Sibelius (Master Musicians), Dent (London) 1965, 1971.

— Sibelius and his world, Thames & Hudson (London) 1970.

Walter Legge: Conversations with Sibelius, *MT*, March 1935, p. 218.

— Sibelius's position today, *MMR*, December 1935, p. 224.

René Leibowitz: Sibelius, le plus mauvais compositeur du monde, Editions Dynamo (Liège) 1955.

Santeri Levas: Nuori Sibelius, Werner Söderström (Helsinki) 1957.

— JS och hans hem, Helsinki, 1925.

K. E. Limbert: JS, *Parents Review*, April 1939, p. 244.

— Sibelius—music for the summer term, *Parents Review*, March 1947, p. 69.

Robert Lorenz: Afterthoughts on the Sibelius Festival, *MT*, January 1939, p. 13.

— The Nordic element—Bax and Sibelius, *MO*, February 1957, p. 277.

George Lowe: Two modern song-writers, Sibelius and Delius, *MS*, 9 July 1910, p. 25.

William Luke: Sibelius, the contemporary Master, *Apollo*, July 1953, p. 24.

F. L. Lunghi: Ricordo di Sibelius, *Santa Cecilia*, December 1957.

Watson Lyle: The 'nationalism' of Sibelius, *MQ*, October 1927, p. 617.

Joseph Machlis: JS, in *Introduction to Contemporary Music*, Norton (USA) 1961, Dent (London), p. 93.

Charles Maclean: Sibelius in England, *Zeitschrift der Internationalen Musikgesellschaft*, Vol. IX (1907–8), p. 271.

Leevi Madetoja: JS oppetajana, Aulos, 1925.

William Mann: Sibelius, *Crescendo*, No. 56, November 1953, p. 54.

S. Martinotti: Sibelius e Nielsen nel sinfonismo nordico, Chigiana, 1955.

Einari Marvia: Jean Sibeliuksen musikaalinen sukuperintö, *Uusi Musiikkilehti*, 1955, No. 9, p. 49.

Jean Matter: Sibelius et Debussy, *SM*, March–April 1965, p. 82.

— Quelques aspects de l'être symphonique de Sibelius, *SM*, 1966, No. 1 (January), p. 31.

Wilfrid Mellers: Sibelius at ninety—a revaluation, *The Listener*, 1 December 1955, p. 969; repr. in *Essays on Music*, Cassell (London) 1967, p. 236.

— Delius, Sibelius and nature, in *Man and his Music*, Barrie & Rockliff (London) 1962, p. 923.

O. A. Merritt-Hawkes: Suomi, called Finland —the country of Sibelius, *National Review*, July 1937, p. 78.

Alfred H. Meyer: Sibelius, symphonist, *MQ*, January 1936, p. 68.

Georges Migot: JS, *RM*, March 1922, p. 256.

P. C. Moreton: JS, a salute for his 87th birthday, *Music*, December 1952, p. 21.

Béla C. Nagy: Sibelius, *Muzsika*, December 1965, p. 28.

O. C. Zur Nedden: JS, Wollen, Werden, Wirken, *Sibelius-Mitteilungen*, No. 1, March 1958, p. 5.

Boyd Neel: A visit to Sibelius, *Crescendo*, No. 36, March 1951, p. 207.

Ernest Newman: Two symphonies, in *More Essays from the World of Music*, John Calder (London) 1958, p. 113.

— Sibelius, most personal of great composers, in *–do–*, p. 116.

— Sibelius on composition, in *–do–*, p. 121.

— The independence of Sibelius, obituary notice, in *–do–*, p. 127.

— Mozart and Sibelius's 'Form' as seen in historical perspective, in *–do–*, p. 222.

Rosa Newmarch: JS, a Finnish composer, Breitkopf & Härtel (Leipzig) 1906.

— JS, a short history of a long friendship, C. C. Birchard (Boston) 1939, Goodwin & Tabb (London) 1944.

— Sibelius, *Chesterian*, No. 14, April 1921, p. 417.

Walter Niemann: JS, *Signale*, 1904, Nos. 12–13 (10 February), p. 185.
— JS und die finnische Musik, *Die Musik*, November (2) 1913, p. 195.
— JS, Breithopf & Härtel (Leipzig) 1917.
A. Nyman: JS, in *Musikalisk intelligens*, 1928, p. 107.
Hugh Ottaway: Nielsen and Sibelius, *The Listener* 1965, p. 313.
Martti Pajanne: Muusikkojen muistelmia mestarista orkesterinjohtajana, *Uusi Musiikkilehti*, 1955, No. 9, p. 15.
A. Balogh Pál: Sibelius, *A Zene*, 1 December 1940, p. 59.
D. C. Parker, Sibelius, *MS*, 1932, p. 81.
Simon Parmet: Sibelius Symfoniker, Söderström (Helsinki) 1955; transl. Kingsley A. Hart as *The Symphonies of Sibelius*, Cassell (London) 1959.
Anthony Payne: The scope of Sibelius, *M&M*, December 1965, p. 20.
O. Pesonen: An immortal composer, *London Musical Events*, November 1957, p. 40.
— Sibelius, *London Musical Events*, October 1955, p. 20.
Walter Petzet: Besuch bei Sibelius, *Signale*, 1927, No. 36, p. 1231.
E. Peyser: JS, tonal patriot, *Scholastic*, 7 December 1935, p. 6.
Peter J. Pirie: The Nordic element—Bax and Sibelius, *MO*, February 1957, p. 277.
R. Pollak: JS, *Magazine of Art*, January 1938, p. 8.
Laurence Powell: JS, *Disques*, November–December 1930.
L. Price: Portrait of Sibelius at Järvenpää, *Yale Review*, December 1934, p. 356.
— Sibelius at seventy-five, *Atlantic Monthly*, January 1941, p. 71.
Heinrich Pudor: Biographisches, JS, *Musikalisches Wochenblatt*, 11 October 1900, p. 554.
Bernard Rands: Sibelius and his critics, *MR*, May 1958, p. 105.
Malcolm Rayment: Sibelius, a centenary guide to his symphonies on record, *R&R*, December 1965, p. 29.
Henry Raynor: Sibelius, an attempted postscript, *Chesterian*, No. 199, summer 1959.
L. Redmond: Face of greatness, *Coronet*, April 1952, p. 68.

P. E. Reed: Seventy-fifth birthday, *Etude*, February 1941, p. 86.
Nils-Eric Ringbom: Helsingfors orkesterföretag 1882–1932, Frenckellska Tryckeri (Helsinki) 1932.
— Litteraturen om JS, *Svenska Tidskrift för Musikforskning* (Stockholm), 1942.
— JS, Bonniers (Stockholm), 1948; Nyt Nordisk Forlag (Copenhagen) 1950; JS, a master and his work, University of Oklahoma Press 1954.
Edward Robinson: JS, *American Mercury*, February 1932, p. 245.
Eino Roiha: Die Symphonien von JS, K. J. Gummerus (Jyväskylä) 1941.
I Ronke: The Sibelius I knew, *International Musician*, September 1961, p. 18.
Paul Rosenfeld: Sibelius, in *Musical Portraits*, Kegan Paul (London) 1922.
— Beethoven of the North, *New Republic*, 21 April 1941, p. 526.
Alec Rowley: The pianoforte works of JS, *Musical Mirror*, May 1929, p. 121.
Adolfo Salazar: JS, un sinfonista de otros climas, in *La música actual en Europa y sus problemes*, J. M. Yagües (Madrid) 1935, p. 434.
E. M. Salzer: Letzter Besuch bei JS, *Sibelius-Mitteilungen*, No. 1, March 1958, p. 8.
M. Salzer: Begegnung mit JS, *Musikleben*, March 1955, p. 113.
E. Salzman: Seven of Sibelius, *Saturday Review*, 29 October 1966, p. 68.
Börje Sandberg: Sibelius, Helsinki, 1940.
H. J. Schäfer: JS zum Gedenken, *Sibelius-Mitteilungen*, No. 1, March 1958, p. 2.
— JS, Auszüge aus seinem Vortrag, *Sibelius-Mitteilungen*, No. 2, March 1959, p. 4.
E. Silfverhjelm: Ved JS gravsted, *Norsk Musikerblad*, December 1961, p. 9.
Robert Simpson: Sibelius and musical movement, *The Listener*, 2 January 1964, p. 38.
Oili Sinimi: JS, *Neues Wiener Journal*, 6 November 1931.
P. Sjöblom: Master as seen by his wife—interview with A. Sibelius, *Etude*, October 1938, p. 641.
C. Smith: Sibelius, close-up of a genius, *American Mercury*, February 1941, p. 144.
Lauri Solanterä: JS—manuscripts, R. E. Westerlund Oy (Helsinki) 1945.

Sibelius, Jean

Lauri Solanterä: The works of JS, R. E. Westerlund Oy (Helsinki) 1955.

F. O. Souper: The symphonies of Sibelius, *MM&F*, March 1932, p. 65.

Carl Stoeckel: Some recollections of the visit of JS to America in 1914, Yale University Library (MS).

Ernst Tanzberger: Sibelius in den Vereinigten Staaten, *Sibelius-Mitteilungen*, No. 5, December 1961, p. 1.

— JS und Béla Bartók, *–do–*, p. 4.

— Die symphonischen Dichtungen von JS, Würzburg, 1943.

— JS als Sinfoniker, *NZfM*, December 1955, p. 134.

— JS, Wiesbaden, 1962.

Erik Tawaststjerna: The pianoforte compositions of Sibelius, Kustannusosakeyhtiö (Helsinki) 1957.

— Sibelius, Otava (Helsinki), Vols. I–III; Bonniers (Stockholm) 1967 (I).

V. Terenzio: Le sinfonie di Sibelius, *Musica d'oggi*, May 1959, p. 204.

Bengt de Törne: Sibelius, a close-up, Faber (London) 1937.

— Sibelius as a teacher, *Criterion*, January 1937, p. 220.

Baroness von Troil: Sibelius's jubilee in Finland, *MMR*, 1935, p. 230.

W. R. Trotter: Sibelius and the tide of taste (incl. discography), *High Fidelity*, December 1965, p. 48.

Harold Truscott: The greatness of Sibelius, *The Listener*, 15 August 1963, p. 253.

— A Sibelian fallacy, *Chesterian*, No. 192, autumn 1957.

— Sibelius, in The Penguin Symphony (ed. Robert Simpson), Penguin Books (London) 1966.

W. J. Turner: The pure cold water of Sibelius's music, *Radio Times*, 1 July 1932, p. 3.

A. O. Väisänen: Sibelius ja kansanmusiiki, *Kalevalan vuosikirja*, 1936, No. 16.

— Sibelius om sina Kalevala-kompositioner, *Musikern*, 1 December 1925, p. 663.

Kees Van Hoek: Musical lighthouse by a sea of change, *Christian Science Monitor Magazine*, 19 August 1950, p. 14.

— JS, *Contemporary Review*, December 1953, p. 348.

Ralph Vaughan Williams: Sibelius, *RCM Magazine*, 1955, No. 3, p. 58.

Anni Voipio: Sibelius as his wife sees him, *New York Times*, 28 January 1940.

Ernest Walker: Some music of Sibelius, in *Essays on Music*, Cassell (London) 1967, p. 232.

John C. G. Waterhouse: Sibelius and the twentieth century, *MT*, December 1965, p. 939.

E. von Wendt: Hos JS på Ainola, *Bonniers veckotidn*, Vol. V (1928), No. 52, p. 38.

J. A. Westrup: JS, *MT*, November 1957, p. 601.

MISCELLANEOUS OR UNSIGNED

Mélodies de Sibelius, *Le Guide musical* (Brussels), 1906.

JS, *Musical Herald*, April 1919, p. 107.

Sibelius and the music of Finland, *British Musician*, 1930, November p. 302, December p. 341, and January 1931 p. 9.

Giovanni Sibelius, *Bollettino bibliografico musicale*, March 1932.

Sibelius at seventy, *Time*, 16 December 1935, p. 53.

Composer who works at night—day is too precious, *Newsweek*, 7 December 1935, p. 19.

JS, *MO*, November 1936, p. 121.

Seventieth birthday anniversary, *Etude*, April 1936, p. 200.

Finland's king, *Time*, 6 December 1937, p. 33.

The achievement of Sibelius, *The Times*, 8 December 1945, p. 6.

Gesprach mit Sibelius, *SM*, July 1953, p. 297.

JS, *Disques*, No. 66, July–August 1954, p. 456.

L'œuvre de JS, *Disques*, No. 62, January–February 1954, p. 76.

Features of Sibelius's style: music of the north, *The Times*, 9 December 1955, p. 3.

Musical wizard of the north, *M&M*, December 1955, p. 7.

Nature boy at ninety, *Time*, 12 December 1955, p. 73.

Giant from the north—Britain's Sibelius centenary performances, *Music Magazine*, December 1965, p. 4.

RICHARD STRAUSS (1864–1949)

Richard Strauss was born on 11 June 1864 in Munich, where his father was the principal horn player in the Court Orchestra. His precocious talent was developed skilfully though conservatively by his parents, and the young Strauss was able to hear his Symphony in D Minor at a public concert in 1881, the year before he entered Munich University. Leaving the University after a year to concentrate entirely on music, he soon came to the notice of Hans von Bülow, who in 1885 made him his assistant conductor at Meiningen; and for the next half-century Strauss was to be as celebrated a conductor as he was a composer. After brief appointments at Munich and Bayreuth, he became conductor of the Court Theatre at Weimar in 1889, staying until 1894. In that year he married the singer Pauline de Ahna (who had played the heroine in the première of his first opera, *Guntram*) and returned to Munich to spend four years as Court Conductor there. In 1898 he started a twenty-year term as conductor of the Berlin Court Opera, during the second half of which he was also the opera's musical director. It was in Paris in 1900 that Strauss first met the Austrian poet Hugo von Hofmannsthal, who was to be the author of six of his libretti and an influential friend for the next thirty years. 1905 saw the rapturous première in Dresden of *Salome*, and although all Strauss's music was the source of much controversy, he was now receiving a considerable income from it. One of the results was that in 1908 he was able to move into the villa he had built for himself at Garmisch-Partenkirchen in Bavaria, his home for most of the rest of his life. Strauss's final appointment was to the co-directorship of the Vienna State Opera in 1919, his partner being the conductor Franz Schalk; and his life after resigning from this in 1924 (over disagreements with Schalk) was made up of travelling, composing and free-lance conducting. He remained in Germany during the Nazi period and the Second World War. At first he worked with the Nazis, accepting the presidency of their Reichsmusikkammer in 1933; but he fell foul of the régime because his current librettist, Stefan Zweig, was Jewish,

and he was made to resign the presidency in 1935. He was tolerated by the Nazis thereafter because of his prestige, but was *persona non grata*. At the end of the War he left Garmisch and lived mainly in Switzerland, visiting London for a festival of his music in 1947; but he returned to Garmisch in May 1949 and died there the following September.

CATALOGUE OF WORKS

1. Schneider-Polka. For piano. 1871.

2. Weihnachtslied 'Op. 1'. For voice and piano. 1871. Ded. Uncle George and Aunt Johanna. Pub. in *Die Woche* and in *Die Musik* (1905, No. 8).

3. Einkehr 'Op. 1 No. 2' (Uhland). For voice and piano. Dated: 21 August 1871. Ded. Aunt Johanna (Pschorr). Pub. 1905, in *Die Musik* (No. 8).

4. Winterreise 'Op. 2' (Uhland). For voice and piano. 1871. Pub. 1964, Fürstner/Boosey & Hawkes.

5. Panzenberg-Polka 'Op. 6'. For piano. 1872.

6. Gavotte No. 1. For piano. 1872 (?1872–1873). Pub. in *Musikalisches Bilderbuch für Pianoforte*, Vol. I, No. 1.

7. Hochlands Treue 'Op. 3'. Overture for orchestra. 1872.

8. Two Sonatinas. For piano. 1873.

9. Der müde Wanderer 'Op. 7 No. 1' (Heinrich Hoffmann von Fallersleben). For voice and piano. 1873. Pub. 1964, Fürstner/ Boosey & Hawkes.

10. Husarenlied 'Op. 7 No. 2' (Heinrich Hoffmann von Fallersleben). For voice and piano. 1873. Pub. 1964, Fürstner/Boosey & Hawkes.

11. Sechs kleine Sonaten. For piano. 1874.

12. Der Fischer (Goethe). For voice and piano. 1877. Pub. 1964, Fürstner/Boosey & Hawkes.

13. Phantasie. For piano. 1874. Ded. 'Seinem lieben Papa'.

14. Fünf Klavierstücke. 1873.

15. Zwei Klavierstücke. 1875.

16. Concertante. For piano, two violins and cello. 1875. Ded. 'Seinem Vettern Pschorr'.

17. Festmarsch No. 1 in E flat Op. 1. For orchestra. 1876, Munich. Ded. to the composer's uncle, Georg Pschorr.
  2 fl, pic, 2 ob, 2 cl, 2 bsn; 4 hn, 4 tmb, tuba; timp; strings.
  fp: 26 March 1881, Munich, 'Wilde Gung'l', cond. Franz Strauss.
  fEp: 6 October 1898, Queen's Hall, Promenade Concert, Queen's Hall Orchestra, cond. (Sir) Henry Wood.
  fEbp: 13 August 1926, Newcastle Station Symphony Orchestra, cond. Edward Clark.
  Pub. 1881, Breitkopf & Härtel.

18. Arie der Almaide. 1878. Unfinished.

19. Kyrie, Sanctus & Agnus Dei Op. 12. 1877. Ded. 'Papa'.

20. Serenade 'Op. 13'. For orchestra. 1877. Ded. Meyer.
  2 fl, 2 ob, 2 cl, 2 bsn; 2 hn, 2 tpt, 2 tmb; timp; strings.
  fp: ?29 April 1920, Munich, 'Wilde Gung'l'.

21. Trio No. 1 in A 'Op. 15'. 1877. Ded. 'Onkel Anton' (von Knözinger).

22. Piano Sonata No. 1 in E 'Op. 10'. 1878. Ded. Ludwig Thuille.

23. Spielmann und Zither 'Op. 12 No. 1' (Theodor Körner). For voice and piano. 1878. Pub. 1964, Fürstner/Boosey & Hawkes.

24. Wiegenlied 'Op. 12 No. 2' (Heinrich Hoffmann von Fallersleben). For voice and piano. 1878. Pub. 1964. Fürstner/Boosey & Hawkes.

25. Abend- und Morgenrot (Heinrich Hoffmann von Fallersleben). For voice and piano. 1878. Pub. 1964, Fürstner/Boosey & Hawkes.

26. Im Walde (Emanuel von Geibel). For voice and piano. 1878. Pub. 1964, Fürstner/ Boosey & Hawkes.

27. Die Drossel 'Op. 14 No. 2' (Ludwig Uhland). For voice and piano. 1878. Pub. 1964, Fürstner/Boosey & Hawkes.

28. Lass ruhn die Toten 'Op. 14 No. 3' (Adalbert von Chamisso). For voice and piano. 1878. Pub. 1964, Fürstner/Boosey & Hawkes.

29. Lust und Qual 'Op. 14 No. 4' (Goethe). For voice and piano. 1878. Pub. 1964, Fürstner/Boosey & Hawkes.

30. Scherzo 'Op. 14'. For piano. 1878.

31. 12 Variations. For piano. 1878. Ded. Pauline Nagiller.

32. Der Spielmann und sein Kind 'Op. 15' No. 2. For voice and orchestra. 1878.

33. Alphorn 'Op. 15 No. 3' (Justinus Kerner). For voice, horn and piano. 1878 (?1876). Ded. 'Papa'. Pub. 1964, Fürstner/Boosey & Hawkes.

34. Introduction, Theme and Variations in E flat 'Op. 17'. For horn and piano. 1878. Ded. 'Papa'.

35. Nebel 'Op. 18 No. 1' (Nikolaus von Lenau). For voice and piano. 1878. Pub. 1964, Fürstner/Boosey & Hawkes.

36. Soldatenlied 'Op. 18 No. 2' (Heinrich Hoffmann von Fallersleben). For voice and piano. 1878. Pub. 1964, Fürstner/Boosey & Hawkes.

37. Das Röslein 'Op. 18 No. 3' (Heinrich Hoffmann von Fallersleben). For voice and piano. 1878. Pub. 1964, Fürstner/Boosey & Hawkes (as 'Ein Röslein zog ich mir im Garten').

38. Overture in E 'Op. 16'. 1879.

38a. Overture in A minor 'Op. 17 No. 2'. 1879. Ded. Meyer.

39. Gavotte No. 4. For orchestra. July 1879.
  2 fl, pic, 2 ob, 2 cl, 2 bsn; 2 hn, 2 tpt, tmb; timp; strings.
  fp: 29 May 1880, Munich, 'Wilde Gung'l', cond. Franz Strauss.
  Unpub.

40. Trio No. 2 in D 'Op. 20'. 1879. Ded. 'Onkel Georg Pschorr'.

41. Weihnachtsgefühl (Greif). For baritone and piano. 1879.

42. Für Musik (Geibel). For voice and piano. 1879. Ded. Sophie Diez.

43. Die Lilien glühn in Düften (Geibel). For voice and piano. 1879. Ded. C. Meysenheim.

44. Waldgesang 'Op. 25' (Geibel). For voice and piano. 1879. Ded. C. Meysenheim.

45. O schneller, mein Ross 'Op. 23 No. 5' (Geibel). For voice and piano. 1879. Ded. C. Meysenheim.

46. Introduction, Theme and Variations in G. For flute and piano. 1879.

47. Es rauscht das Laub/Frühlingsanfang 'Op. 26' (Geibel). For voice and piano. 1879.

48. Piano Sonata No. 2 in C minor 'Op. 22'. 1879. Ded. 'Onkel Karl Hörburger'.

49. Fünf kleine Klavierstücke 'Op. 24' 1879.

50. Romanze 'Op. 27'. For clarinet and orchestra. 1879.
fp: late 1879, Munich, Kgl. Ludwigsgymnasium.
Unpub.

51. Drei Lieder 'Op. 30 No. 1' (Uhland). For voice and piano. 1879.

52. In Vaters Garten 'Op. 30 No. 2' (Heine). For voice and piano. 1879.

53. Der Morgen 'Op. 30 No. 4' (Sallet). For voice and piano. 1880.

54. Die erwachte Rose 'Op. 30 No. 3' (Friedrich Sallet). For voice and piano. 1880. Pub. Peters, as *Drei Liebeslieder* No. 2 (ded. Lotte Speyer); 1958, Peters (New York).

55. Ständchen. For piano quartet. 1880.

56. Chorus from Sophocles' 'Elektra'. With small orchestra. 1880.
2 cl; 2 hn, 2 tpt; timp; strings.
fp: 1880, Munich, Ludwigsgymnasium.
Pub. ?1902.

57. String Quartet in A major Op. 2. 1879–80. Dated: 14 November 1880, Munich. Ded. Benno Walter Quartet. Dur. 26'.

fp: 14 March 1881, Munich, Museumsaal, Benno Walter Quartet.
fGBbp: 6 July 1925, Aberdeen station, 2BD Quartet.
Pub. Josef Aibl; Universal-Edition.

58. Symphony [No. 1] in D minor (orig. Op. 4). 1880.
2 fl, 2 ob, 2 cl, 2 bsn; 4 hn, 2 tpt, 3 tmb; timp; strings.
fp: 30 March 1881, Munich, Akademie, Hoforchester, cond. Hermann Levi.
Unpub.

59. Sechs Lieder 'Op. 21'. For unacc. chorus. 1880. Ded. 'Papa'.

60. Zwei Lieder. For unacc. chorus. 1880.

61. Scherzando. For piano. 1880.

62. Immer leise wird mein Schlummer (Lingg). For voice and piano. 1880.

63. Fugue on four themes. For piano. 1880. Ded. 'Papa'.

64. Mutter, O sing mich zur Ruh (Felicia Hemans). For voice and piano. 1880.

65. John Anderson, mein Lieb (Burns). For voice and piano. 1880.

66. Festchor. For chorus and piano. 1880.
fp: 1881, Munich, Festival in Ludwigsgymnasium.
Unpub.

67. Piano Sonata in B minor Op. 5. 1880–1. Ded. Joseph Giehrl.
1. *Allegro molto appassionato*; 2. *Adagio cantabile*; 3. *Scherzo (Presto)*; 4. *Allegretto vivo*.
Pub. 1883, Joseph Aibl; Universal-Edition.

68. Fünf Klavierstücke Op. 3. 1880–1.
1. *Andante*; 2. *Allegro vivace scherzando*; 3. *Largo*; 4. *Allegro molto*; 5. *Allegro marcatissimo*.
Pub. 1881, Joseph Aibl; Universal-Edition.

69. Serenade in E flat for thirteen wind instruments Op. 7. 1881–2. Ded. F. W. Meyer. Dur. 10'.
2 fl, 2 ob, 2 cl, 2 bsn, cbsn; 4 hn.
fp: 27 November 1882, Dresden, Tonkünstlerverein concert, wind group of the Court Orchestra, cond. Franz Wüllner.

fEp: 7 July 1893, Royal College of Music students' concert, cond. (Sir) Charles V. Stanford.

f British p (professional): 4 February 1899, Glasgow, Scottish Orchestra concert.

fAp: 12 February 1898, New York, New York Symphony Society, cond. Walter Damrosch.

f London p (professional): 6 November 1900, Queen's Hall, Promenade Concert, members of the Queen's Hall Orchestra, cond. (Sir) Henry Wood.

fEbp: 14 July 1927, wind instrumentalists of the Wireless Symphony Orchestra, cond. Edward Clark.

Pub. 1882, Joseph Aibl; Universal-Edition.

70. Geheiligte Stätte (Fischer). For voice and piano. 1881.

71. Violin Concerto in D minor Op. 8. 1881–2. Ded. Benno Walter. Dur. 29′.

1. *Allegro*; 2. *Lento ma non troppo*; 3. *Rondo* (*Prestissimo*).

2 fl, 2 ob, 2 cl, 2 bsn; 4 hn, 2 tpt; timp; strings.

fp: 5 December 1882, Vienna, Bösendorfer-saal, Benno Walter (violin) and Richard Strauss (piano).

fp (with orchestra): 17 February 1896, Leipzig, Alfred Krasselt and Liszt Verein, cond. Richard Strauss.

fEp: 7 April 1902, Bournemouth, Philip Cathie and the Bournemouth Municipal Orchestra, cond. (Sir) Dan Godfrey.

f London p: 18 February 1904, St. James's Hall, Achille Rivarde and the Queen's Hall Orchestra.

?fEbp: 2 October 1936, Campoli and the BBC Orchestra, cond. Julian Clifford.

Pub. 1883, Joseph Aibl; Universal-Edition: incl. reduction.

72. Waldgesang (Karl Stieler). For voice and piano. 1882.

73. Ballade ('Jung Friedel wallte am Rheines-strand') (Becker). For voice and piano. 1882.

74. Im Waldesweben ist es Ruh'. For voice and piano. 1882.

75. Rote Rosen (Karl Stieler). For voice and piano. 1883. Pub. Peters, as *Drei Liebeslieder*

No. 1 (ded. Lotte Speyer); 1958, Peters (New York).

76. Begegnung (Friedrich Gruppe). For voice and piano. ?1883 (?1878–9). Pub. Peters, as *Drei Liebeslieder* No. 3 (ded. Lotte Speyer); 1958, Peters (New York).

77. Cello Sonata in F major Op. 6. 1882–3. Ded. Hans Wihan. Dur. 24′.

1. *Allegro con brio*; 2. *Andante ma non troppo*; 3. *Finale: Allegro vivo.*

fp: 8 December 1883, Nuremberg, Hotel Goldner Adler, Hans Wihan and Hildegard von Königsthal.

fEp: 5 March 1898, St. James's Hall, Monday Popular Concert, Hugo Becker and Fanny Davies.

fEbp: 10 April 1924, Beatrice Eveline and Dorothy Howell.

Pub. 1883, Aibl; Universal-Edition.

78. Stimmungsbilder Op. 9. For piano. 1882–4. Dated: 5 February 1884.

1. *Auf stillen Waldespfad*; 2. *An einsamer Quelle*; 3. *Intermezzo*; 4. *Träumerei*; 5. *Heide-bild.*

fEp (Nos. 1, 3, 4): 13 February 1903, Bechstein Hall, Georg Liebling.

79. Overture in C minor (orig. Op. 10). For orchestra. 1883. Ded. Hermann Levi.

fp: 26 November 1883, Munich, Akademie Hoforchester, cond. Hermann Levi.

Unpub.

80. Acht Lieder (Gedichte) aus 'Letzte Blätter' Op. 10 (Hermann von Gilm. For voice and piano. 1882–3. Ded. Heinrich Vogel.

1. *Zueignung*; 2. *Nichts*; 3. *Die Nacht*; 4. *Die Georgine*; 5. *Geduld*; 6. *Die Verschwie-genen*; 7. *Die Zeitlose*; 8. *Allerseelen.*

Pub. ?1885, 1907, Joseph Aibl; Universal-Edition/Boosey & Hawkes: English version, John Bernhoff; French version. A. L. Hettich.

80a. Zueignung Op. 10 No. 1. Version with orchestra. Dated: 19 June 1940, Garmisch. Ded. Viorica Ursuleac.

2 fl, 2 ob, 2 cl, 3 bsn; 4 hn, 3 tpt; timp; 2 hp, strings.

fp: 4 July 1940, Rome, Viorica Ursuleac, cond. Clemens Krauss.

Pub. 1964, Fürstner/Boosey & Hawkes.

80b. Allerseelen Op. 10 No. 8. Arr. by Max Reger for piano solo. Pub. 1904, Joseph Aibl; Universal-Edition.

81. Horn Concerto No. 1 in E flat Op. 11. 1882–3, Munich. Ded. Oscar Franz. Dur. 17'.
1. *Allegro*; 2. *Andante*; 3. *Rondo: Allegro*.
2 fl, 2 ob, 2 cl, 2 bsn; 2 hn, 2 tpt; timp; strings.
fp (with orchestra): 4 March 1885, Meiningen, Gustav Leinbos and Hofkapelle, cond. Hans von Bülow.
fEp: February 1898, Bournemouth, Mr. Trevisone and Bournemouth Municipal Orchestra, cond. ?(Sir) Dan Godfrey.
Pub. 1884, Joseph Aibl; Universal-Edition.

82. Romanze (orig. Op. 13). For cello and orchestra. 1883.

83. Variations on a theme of Cesare Negri (1604). For string quartet. 1883. Ded. August Pschorr.

84. Symphony [No. 2] in F minor Op. 12. 1883–4. Dated: 25 February 1884, Berlin. Dur. 45'.
1. *Allegro ma non troppo, un poco maestoso*; 2. *Scherzo: Presto*; 3. *Andante cantabile*; 4. *Finale: Allegro assai, molto appassionato*.
2 fl, 2 ob, 2 cl, 2 bsn; 4 hn, 2 tpt, 3 tmb, bs tuba; timp; strings.
fp: 13 December 1884, New York, New York Philharmonic Society, cond. Theodore Thomas.
fGp: 13 January 1885, Cologne, Gürzenich concert, Städtisches Orchester, cond. Franz Wüllner.
fEp: 28 November 1896, Crystal Palace, cond. August Manns.
fbp: 1 April 1938, BBC Orchestra, cond. Clarence Raybould.
Pub. 1885, Joseph Aibl; Universal-Edition; 1933, Peters. Also arr. by Richard Strauss for piano duet.

BIBLIOGRAPHY:
Adam Carse: First Symphony in F minor Op. 12, *MO*, November 1920, p. 143.

85. Suite in B flat Op. 4. For thirteen wind instruments. 1883–4. Dated: 23 October 1884. Dur. *c.* 22–25'.
1. *Präludium: Allegretto*; 2. *Romanze: Andante*; 3. *Gavotte: Allegro*; 4. *Introduktion und Fuge: Andante cantabile—Allegro con brio*.
2 fl, 2 ob, 2 cl, 2 bsn, cbsn, 4 hn.
fp: 18 November 1884, Munich, wind group from the Meiningen Court Orchestra, cond. Richard Strauss.
fEp: 7 May 1900, Queen's (Small) Hall, George A. Clinton chamber concert, wind ensemble, cond. George A. Clinton.
Pub. 1911, Leuckart. Also arr. for piano duet.

86. Piano Quartet in C minor Op. 13. 1883–4, Munich. Ded. George II of Sachsen-Meiningen. Dur. 38'. First prize, Berlin Tonkünstlerverein competition, 1885.
1. *Allegro—Molto meno mosso*; 2. *Scherzo: Presto*; 3. *Andante*; 4. *Finale: Vivace*.
?fp: 8 December 1885, Weimar, Richard Strauss and the Halir Quartet. (?fp: 6/8 January 1886, Meiningen.)
fEp: 13 February 1897, London concert given by Else Mathis, Else Mathis (piano), L. Szczepanowski, Rene Ortmans and B. Albert.
fEbp: 5 March 1925, Philharmonic Piano Quartet (Charles Kelly, Paul Beard, Frank Venton, Johan C. Hock).
Pub. 1886, Joseph Aibl; Universal-Edition.

87. Aus den Hebräischen Melodien (Byron). ?For voice and piano. 1884.

88. Aus Mirza Schaffy (Bodenstedt). ?For voice and piano. 1884.

89. Festmarsch. For orchestra. 1884.

90. Wandrers Sturmlied Op. 14. For six-part chorus and orchestra. 1884, Munich. Text: Goethe. Ded. Franz Wüllner. Dur. 15'.
2 fl, 2 ob, 2 cl, 2 bsn, cbsn; 4 hn, 2 tpt, 3 tmb; timp; strings.
fp: 8 March 1887, Cologne, Gürzenich, chorus and Städtisches Orchester, cond. Richard Strauss.
fEp: 2 October 1902, Sheffield Festival, cond. (Sir) Henry Wood.
Pub. 1886, Joseph Aibl; Universal-Edition.

91. Improvisations and Fugue. On an

original theme, for piano. 1884. Ded. Hans von Bülow. Pub. (Fugue only) 1898, Bruckmann (Munich) in *Das Klavier und seine Meister*.

92. Cadenzas (to Mozart's Piano Concerto in C minor K.491). 1885.
fp: 18 October 1885, Meiningen, Richard Strauss and the Court Orchestra, cond. Hans von Bülow.
Unpub.

93. Schwäbische Erbschaft (Feodor Loewe). For four-part male chorus. 1885. Pub. 1950, Leuckart.

94. Burleske in D minor. For piano and orchestra. 1885–6. Ded. Eugen d'Albert. Dur. 17'.
2 fl, pic, 2 ob, 2 cl, 2 bsn; 4 hn, 2 tpt; timp; strings.
fp: 21 June 1890, Eisenach, Tonkünstlerfest, Eugen d'Albert (piano), cond. Richard Strauss.
fEp: 13 March 1903, Queen's Hall, Royal Academy of Music concert, Mary Burgess (piano), cond. Sir Alexander Mackenzie.
fEp (professional): June 1903, St. James's Hall, Strauss Festival, Wilhelm Backhaus and the Concertgebouw Orchestra, cond. Willem Mengelberg.
fEbp: 1 December 1927, Bournemouth, Winter Gardens, Ethel Cobban and the Bournemouth Municipal Orchestra, cond. Sir Dan Godfrey.
Pub. 1894, Steingräber (Leipzig).

95. Bardengesang (Kleist). For male chorus and orchestra. 1886.
fp: January 1886, Meiningen Court Theatre.
Unpub. See also No. 150.

96. Fünf Lieder Op. 15. For medium voice and piano. 1884–6 (?88). Words: Michelangelo (No. 1), A. F. von Schack (Nos. 2–5). Ded. Victoria Blank (Nos. 1, 3, 4), Johanna Pschorr (Nos. 2, 5).
1. *Madrigal*; 2. *Winternacht*; 3. *Lob des Leidens*; 4. *Dem Herzen ähnlich*; 5. *Heimkehr*.
Pub. Rahter; Universal-Edition. Note: No. 5 was orchestrated by L. Weniger.

97. Aus Italien Op. 16. Symphonic Fantasy for orchestra. 1886. Ded. Hans von Bülow. Dur. 47'.

1. *Auf der Campagna*; 2. *In Roms Ruinen*; 3. *Am Strande von Sorrent*; 4. *Neapolitanisches Volksleben*.
2 fl, pic, 2 ob, ca, 2 cl, 2 bsn, cbsn; 4 hn, 2 tpt, 3 tmb; timp, cym, tgle, tamb, side dm; hp, strings.
fp: 2 March 1887, Munich, Musikalische Akademie, Court Orchestra, cond. Richard Strauss.
fEps: (Nos. 1, 3) 28 November 1889, St. James's Hall, London Symphony Concert, cond. (Sir) George Henschel; (Nos. 3, 4) 9 June 1903, Richard Strauss Festival, Concertgebouw Orchestra, cond. Willem Mengelberg; (Nos. 1, 2) 27 August 1903, Queen's Hall, Promenade Concert, cond. (Sir) Henry Wood.
f Vienna p: 19 November 1899, Vienna Philharmonic Orchestra, cond. Gustav Mahler.
fFp: 29 March 1903, Paris, Nouveau-Théâtre, l'Orchestre Lamoureux, cond. Richard Strauss.
?fGBp (complete): 8 December 1903, Glasgow, Scottish Orchestra, cond. Richard Strauss.
Pub. 1887, Aibl; Universal-Edition; 1933, Peters.

98. Sechs Lieder Op. 17 (A. F. von Schack). For voice and piano. ?1885–summer 1887.
1. *Seitdem dein Aug'*; 2. *Ständchen*; 3. *Das Geheimnis*; 4. *Von dunklem Schleier umsponnen* (*Aus den Liedern der Trauer*); 5. *Nur Muth!*; 6. *Barcarole*.
fp (No. 2): 28 October 1889, Weimar, Heinrich Zeller, acc. Richard Strauss.
Pub. 1897, Rahter; Universal-Edition.

98a. Ständchen Op. 17 No. 2. Version orch. Felix Mottl.

99. Mädchenblumen Op. 22 (Felix Dahn). Four Poems for voice and piano. 1888. Ded. Hans Giessen.
1. *Kornblumen*; 2. *Mohnblumen*; 3. *Efeu*; 4. *Wasserrose*.
Pub. Fürstner/Boosey & Hawkes.

100. Violin Sonata in E flat Op. 18. 1887–8. Ded. to the composer's cousin Robert Pschorr. Dur. 27'.
1. *Allegro ma non troppo*; 2. *Improvisation: Andante cantabile*; 3. *Finale: Andante—Allegro*.

fp: 3 October 1888, Elberfeld (?Munich), Robert Heckmann and Julius Buths (?Richard Strauss).

fEp: October 1897, Queen's (Small) Hall, Edith Robinson and Isidor Cohn.

fFp: 1897, Paris, Eugène Ysaÿe and Raoul Pugno.

Pub. 1888, Joseph Aibl; Universal-Edition.

101. Romeo and Juliet. Incidental music for the play by Shakespeare. 1887.

1. *Tanzlied—Moresca*; 2. *Trätterlied*; 3. *Vor dem Hochzeitsbette*; 4. *Trauermusik*.

fp: 23 October 1887, Munich, National Theatre.

Unpub.

BIBLIOGRAPHY:

Hermann Fries: Eine Bühnenmusik zu Shakespeares Romeo und Julia, *Richard Strauss Jahrbuch 1959–60*, p. 51.

102. Sechs Lieder aus Lotusblättern Op. 19 (A. F. von Schack). For voice and piano. 1887 (?1888) (?1885–8). Ded. Emilie Herzog.

1. *Wozu noch, Mädchen*; 2. *Breit über mein Haupt*; 3. *Schön sind, doch kalt die Himmelssterne*; 4. *Wie sollten wir*; 5. *Hoffen und wieder verzagen*; 6. *Mein Herz ist stumm*.

Pub. 1897, Joseph Aibl; Universal-Edition; Boosey & Hawkes.

103. Don Juan Op. 20. Tone Poem after Nikolaus Lenau for orchestra. 1887. Ded. Ludwig Thuille. Dur. 17′.

3 fl, pic, 2 ob, ca, 2 cl, 2 bsn, cbsn; 4 hn, 3 tpt, 3 tmb, tuba; timp, tgle, cym, glock; hp, strings.

fp: 11 November 1889, Weimar, Court Orchestra, cond. Richard Strauss.

fAp: 30 October 1891, Boston, Boston Symphony Orchestra, cond. Arthur Nikisch.

fFp: 25 November 1891, Paris, l'Orchestre Lamoureux, cond. Charles Lamoureux.

fEp: 24 May 1897, St. James's Hall, cond. Hans Richter.

fEbp: 7 October 1924, Birmingham, Town Hall, City of Birmingham Symphony Orchestra, cond. (Sir) Adrian Boult.

Pub. 1890, 1904, Joseph Aibl.

BIBLIOGRAPHY:

Eric Blom: RS, Don Juan, *Music Teacher*, September 1932, p. 425.

René Kopf: Le Don Juan de RS, *L'Education musicale*, No. 141, 1 October 1967.

Donald F. Tovey: Tone poem (after Nicolaus Lenau) Don Juan, in *EMA*, Vol. 4, O.U.P. (London) 1937, p. 154.

104. Schlichte Weisen Op. 21 (Felix Dahn). Five Poems for voice and piano. 1887–8. Ded. to the composer's sister Johanna.

1. *All' mein Gedanken*; 2. *Du meines Herzens Krönelein*; 3. *Ach Lieb, ich muss nun scheiden*; 4. *Ach weh mir unglückhaftem Mann*; 5. *Die Frauen sind oft fromm und still*.

Pub. Joseph Aibl; Universal-Edition; Boosey & Hawkes.

104a. All' mein Gedanken Op. 21 No. 1. Arr. for piano by Max Reger. Pub. 1904, Joseph Aibl; Universal-Edition.

105. Festmarsch in D major. For orchestra. 1888.

2 fl, 2 ob, 2 cl, 2 bsn; 3 hn, 2 tpt, tmb; timp, pcssn; strings.

106. Macbeth Op. 23. Tone Poem after Shakespeare for orchestra. First version, 1886–1888. Ded. Alexander Ritter. Dur. 18′. Unperf. Unpub. Arr. for piano duet.

106a. Macbeth Op. 23. Tone Poem after Shakespeare for orchestra. Second version, 1889–90. Ded. Alexander Ritter. Dur. 18′.

3 fl, pic, 2 ob, ca, 2 cl, bcl, 2 bsn, cbsn; 4 hn, 3 tpt, bs tpt, 3 tmb, tuba; timp, cym, tamtam, GC, side dm; strings.

fp: 13 October 1890, Weimar, Court Orchestra, cond. Richard Strauss.

fEp: 5 June 1903, St. James's Hall, Richard Strauss Festival, Concertgebouw Orchestra, cond. Willem Mengelberg.

f Vienna p: 11 March 1903, Konzertverein, cond. Ferdinand Löwe.

fAp: 17 March 1911, Boston, Boston Symphony Orchestra, cond. Max Fiedler.

fEbp: 18 October 1931, BBC Studio Orchestra, cond. Richard Strauss.

Pub. Joseph Aibl; Universal-Edition; 1933, Peters.

107. Tod und Verklärung Op. 24. Tone Poem for orchestra. 1888–9. Dated: 18 November 1889. Ded. Friedrich Rösch. Dur. 24′.

3 fl, 2 ob, ca, 2 cl, bcl, 2 bsn, cbsn; 4 hn, 3 tpt, 3 tmb, bs tuba; timp, tamtam; 2 hp, strings.

fp: 21 June 1890, Eisenach, Stadttheater, Tonkünstlerfest, cond. Richard Strauss.

f Vienna p: 15 January 1893, Vienna Philharmonic Orchestra, cond. Hans Richter.

fAp: 5 February 1897, Boston, Boston Symphony Orchestra, cond. Emil Pauer.

fFp: 28 February 1897, Paris, Théâtre du Châtelet, l'Orchestre Colonne, cond. Richard Strauss.

fEp: 7 December 1897, Queen's Hall, cond. Richard Strauss.

fGBbp: 6 July 1924, Cardiff Station Symphony Orchestra, cond. Warwick Braithwaite.

Pub. Joseph Aibl; Peters.

108. Scherzquartett ('Utan svafvel och fosfor'). For male voices. Dated: 7 December 1889.

fp: 14 December 1889, Weimar.

Pub. 1926, in *Neue Musik Zeitung* (No. 24).

109. Iphigénie en Tauride. Opera in three acts by Gluck, newly translated and arranged for the German stage by Richard Strauss. 1890.

2 fl, 2 ob, 2 cl, 2 bsn; 3 hn, 2 tpt, 3 tmb, tuba; timp, pcssn; strings.

?fp: 9 June 1900, Weimar, Court Theatre, cond. Rudolf Krzyzanowski.

Pub. Fürstner/Boosey & Hawkes.

110. Second Festmarsch in C. For orchestra. 1889. Composed for the twenty-fifth anniversary of the 'Wilde Gung'l'.

2 fl, 2 ob, 2 cl, 2 bsn; 3 hn, 2 tpt, 3 tmb, tuba; timp, pcssn; strings.

fp: 1 February 1889, Munich, 'Wilde Gung'l', cond. Franz Strauss.

Unpub.

111. Zwei Lieder Op. 26 (Nikolaus Lenau). For high voice and piano. 1891. Ded. Heinrich Zeller.

1. *Frühlingsgedränge*; 2. *O wärst du mein.*

Pub. Joseph Aibl; Universal-Edition; Boosey & Hawkes.

112. Festmusik. For orchestra. 1892. Composed to accompany tableaux vivants on the occasion of the golden wedding of the Grand Duke and Duchess of Weimar.

1. *Bernhard von Weimar in der Schlacht bei Lützen*; 2. *Vor Wilhelm von Oranien seine Schätze opfernd*; 3. *Begegnung und Friedensschluss zwischen Oranien und Spinola*; 4. *Versöhnung der Admirale.*

2 fl, pic, 2 cl, 2 bsn, cbsn; 4 hn, 3 tpt, 3 tmb, tuba; timp, pcssn; hp, strings.

fp: 8 October 1892, Weimar, Court Orchestra, cond. Richard Strauss.

Unpub.

112a. Kampf und Sieg. New version of No. 1 from preceding. Dated: 8 February 1930, Vienna.

2 fl, pic, 2 ob, 2 cl, 2 bsn; 4 hn, 3 tpt, 3 tmb, bs tuba; timp, GC, side dm, cym, tgle; strings.

fp: 3 February 1931, Vienna, Eighth Vienna Philharmonic Ball.

Pub. 1930, Heinrichshofen (Magdeburg).

113. Guntram Op. 25. Opera in three acts. 1888–93. Dated: 5 September 1893. Text: Richard Strauss. Ded. 'to my dear parents'. Dur. 195'.

3 fl, pic, 3 ob, ca, 3 cl, bcl, 3 bsn, cbsn; 4 hn, 3 tpt, bs tpt, 2 tmb, bs tmb, bs tuba; timp, tamb, tgle, cym, small cym, GC, ten dm; 2 hp, lute, strings (16-16-12-10-8). *Stage music:* 4 hn, 4 tenor hn, 4 tpt, 3 tmb, 4 side dm.

fp: 10 May 1894, Weimar, Court Theatre, cond. Richard Strauss; with Pauline de Ahna (Freihild), Heinrich Zeller (Guntram), Schwarz (Robert), Wiedey (Friedhold), Karl Buchta (Fool); producer, F. Wiedey.

Pub. 1895, Aibl New version, Boosey & Hawkes.

BIBLIOGRAPHY:

Richard Batka: Die Guntramlegende, *Der Kunstwart*, October 1901.

Joachim Moser: Zu RS' Guntram, *NZfM*, December 1940, p. 784.

Erwin Völsing: Guntram, Erstaufführung in der Berliner Staatsoper, *Die Musik*, July 1942, p. 325.

113a. Guntram. New version. 1934–9. Dur. 105'.

fp: 29 October 1940, Weimar, Deutsches Nationaltheater.

113b. Guntram: Prelude.

fEp: 2 October 1895, Queen's Hall,

Promenade Concert, Queen's Hall Orchestra, cond. (Sir) Henry Wood.

114. Zwei Stücke. For piano quartet. 1893. Ded. Georg Pschorr, Christmas 1893.

1. *Arabischer Tanz*; 2. *Liebesliedchen*.

Unpub.

115. Vier Lieder Op. 27. For high voice and piano. 1893–4. Ded. 'To my beloved Pauline on the 10th September 1894'.

1. *Ruhe, mine Seele* (Karl Henckell).

2. *Cäcilie* (Heinrich Hart).

3. *Heimliche Aufforderung* (John Henry Mackay).

4. *Morgan* (John Henry Mackay).

Pub. 1894, 1897, Aibl; Universal-Edition; Boosey & Hawkes. Nos. 2, 3, 4 arr. by Max Reger for piano solo.

115a. Ruhe, meine Seele Op. 27 No. 1. Version with orchestra. Dated: 9 June 1948, Montreux.

2 fl, pic, 2 ob, ca, 2 cl, bcl, 2 bsn; 4 hn, 2 tpt, 3 tmb, tuba; timp; celesta, hp, strings.

Pub. 1964, Boosey & Hawkes.

115b. Cäcilie Op. 27 No. 2. Version with orchestra. 1897.

2 fl, 2 ob, 2 cl, 2 bsn; 4 hn, 2 tpt, 3 tmb, tuba; timp; hp, strings.

f Ep: 3 June 1903, London, Strauss Festival, Pauline Strauss.

Pub. 1911, Universal-Edition.

115c. Heimliche Aufforderung Op. 27 No. 3. Version orch. Robert Heger.

115d. Morgen Op. 27 No. 4. Version with orchestra. Dated: 20 September 1897, Marquartstein.

3 hn; hp, solo violin, strings.

f Ep: 3 June 1903, London, Strauss Festival, Pauline Strauss.

Pub. 1911, Universal-Edition.

BIBLIOGRAPHY:

Elisabeth Schumann: Morgen (master lesson with score), *Etude*, February 1951, p. 26.

116. Till Eulenspiegels lustige Streiche Op. 28. 'After the old rogue's tune—in Rondeau form—set for full orchestra.' 1894–5. Dated: 6 May 1895, Munich. Ded. Arthur Seidl. Dur. 18'.

3 fl, pic, 3 ob, ca, cl in D, 2 cl, bcl, 3 bsn, cbsn; 4 hn, 4 hn in D (ad lib), 6 tpt, 3 tmb, bs tuba; timp, tgle, cym, GC, side dm, Ratsche; strings (16-16-12-12-8).

fp: 5 November 1895, Cologne, Gürzenich concert, Städtische Orchester, cond. Franz Wüllner.

f Vienna p: 5 January 1896, Vienna Philharmonic Orchestra, cond. Hans Richter.

fAp: 21 February 1896, Boston, Boston Symphony Orchestra, cond. Emil Paur.

fEp: 21 March 1896, Crystal Palace, cond. August Manns.

fFp: 27 November 1897, Paris, Théâtre du Châtelet, l'Orchestre Colonne, cond. Richard Strauss.

fEbp: 2 April 1924, Manchester, Free Trade Hall, 2ZY Orchestra, cond. Sir Dan Godfrey.

Pub. 1895, Joseph Aibl; Universal-Edition; 1933, Peters.

BIBLIOGRAPHY:

Annette Guyot: Le Till Eulenspiegel de RS, *L'Education musicale*, No. 138, 1 May 1967.

Alfred Lorenz: Der formale Schwung in RS' Till Eulenspiegel, *Die Musik*, June 1925, p. 658.

W. McNaught: Is Till Eulenspiegel a Rondo?, *MT*, 1937, p. 789.

Kurt Wilhelm: Die geplante Volksoper Till Eulenspiegel, *Richard Strauss Jahrbuch 1954*, p. 102.

117. Drei Lieder Op. 29 (O. J. Bierbaum). For high voice and piano. 1894–5. Ded. Eugen Gura.

1. *Traum durch die Dämmerung*.

2. *Schlagende Herzen*.

3. *Nachtgang*.

Pub. Aibl; Universal-Edition; Boosey & Hawkes. Nos. 1 & 3 arr. by Max Reger for piano solo pub. 1904, Aibl; Universal-Edition.

117a. Traum durch die Dämmerung Op. 29 No. 1. Version orch. Robert Heger.

2 fl, 3 cl, 2 bsn; 4 hn, tmb; hp, strings.

118. Also sprach Zarathustra Op. 30. Tone poem, freely after Friedrich Nietzsche, for orchestra. 1895–6. Dated: 24 August 1896, Munich.

3 fl, 2 pic, 3 ob, ca, E-flat cl, 2 cl, bcl, 3 bsn, cbsn; 6 hn, 4 tpt, 3 tmb, 2 bs tubas; timp, GC, cym, tgle, glock, deep bell in E flat; 2 hp, organ, strings (16-16-12-12-8).

fp: 27 November 1896, Frankfurt a.M., Museum Concert, Städtisches Orchester, cond. Richard Strauss.

f Berlin p: 30 November 1896, Berlin Philharmonic Orchestra, cond. Arthur Nikisch.

fEp: 6 March 1897, Crystal Palace, cond. August Manns.

f Vienna p: 24 March 1897, Vienna Philharmonic Orchestra, cond. Hans Richter.

fAp: 29 October 1897, Boston, Boston Symphony Orchestra, cond. Emil Paur.

f New York p: 16 December 1897, Metropolitan Opera, Boston Symphony Orchestra, cond. Emil Paur.

fFp: 22 January 1899, l'Orchestre Lamoureux, cond. Richard Strauss.

Pub. 1896, Joseph Aibl; Universal-Edition; Peters.

BIBLIOGRAPHY:

Edward A. Baughan: Also sprach Zarathustra, *MMR*, 1904, p. 41.

L.L.: Also sprach Zarathustra, an aperçu, *MS*, 31 March 1906, p. 197.

Karl Schmalz: RS' Also sprach Zarathustra und Ein Heldenleben, *Die Musik*, January (2) 1905, p. 102.

119. 'Drei' Lieder Op. 31. For voice and piano. 1895-6. Ded. (Nos. 1-3) composer's sister Johanna, (No. 4) Marie Ritter.

1. *Blauer Sommer* (Carl Busse).

2. *Wenn* (Carl Busse). Orig. pub. 1896, in *Jugend* (Munich).

3. *Weisser Jasmin* (Carl Busse).

4. *Stiller Gang* (Richard Dehmel). With viola solo. Dated: 1895. Later addition.

Pub. Fürstner/Boosey & Hawkes.

120. Wir beide wollen springen (Otto Julius Bierbaum). For voice and piano. Dated: 7 June 1896. Pub. 1896, in *Jugend* (No. 42, 17 October); May 1956, in *Mitteilungen der Internationalen Richard Strauss Gesellschaft* (No. 9).

121. Fünf Lieder Op. 32. For voice and piano. 1896. Ded. composer's wife.

1. *Ich trage meine Minne* (Karl Henckell).

2. *Sehnsucht* (Detlev von Liliencron).

3. *Liebeshymnus* (Karl Henckell).

4. *O süsser Mai* (Karl Henckell).

5. *Himmelsboten zu Liebchens Himmelbett* (from: Das Knaben Wunderhorn).

fp (Nos. 1-4): 9 November 1896, Munich.

Pub. Universal-Edition; Boosey & Hawkes. No. 1 arr. by Max Reger for piano solo pub. 1904, Joseph Aibl; Universal-Edition.

121a. Ich trage meine Minne Op. 32 No. 1. Version orch. Robert Heger.

121b. Liebeshymnus Op. 32 No. 3. Version with orchestra. Dated: 27 September 1897, Munich.

3 fl, 2 ob, 2 cl, 2 bsn; 4 hn, tpt; 4 violins, strings.

Pub. 1911, Universal-Edition.

122. Vier Gesänge Op. 33. For voice and orchestra. 1896-7.

1. *Verführung* (John Henry Mackay). Dated: 5 July 1896, Marquartstein.

2 fl, 2 ob, ca, 2 cl, bcl, 3 bsn, cbsn; 4 hn, 2 tpt, 3 tmb, tuba; timp; hp, strings.

2. *Gesang der Apollopriesterin* (Emanuel von Bodmann). Dated: 1 October 1896, Munich.

3 fl, 3 ob, 3 cl, 3 bsn, cbsn; 4 hn, 3 tpt, 4 tmb; timp, cym; solo violin, strings.

3. *Hymnus* (Anon., wrongly attributed to Schiller). Dated: 5 January 1897, Munich.

2 fl, 2 ob, 2 cl, bcl, 2 bsn; 4 hn, 2 tpt, 3 tmb; timp, tgle; hp, strings.

4. *Pilgers Morgenlied* (An Lila) (Goethe). Dated: 25 January 1897, Munich.

2 fl, pic, 2 ob, E-flat cl, 2 cl, 3 bsn; 4 hn, 2 tpt, 3 tmb, tuba; timp; strings.

fp (No. 2): 6 December 1896, Brussels, Théâtre de la Monnaie, Milka Ternina, cond. Richard Strauss.

fGp (No. 2): 18 February 1903, Frankfurt a.M., Elsa Schweitzer, cond. Richard Strauss.

fEp (No. 2): 1903, Ash Wednesday concert, Queen's Hall, Marie Brema.

fp (No. 3): 5 June 1903, Ffrangcon-Davies and the Concertgebouw Orchestra, cond. Richard Strauss.

fGp (No. 3): 8 March 1905, Dresden, Karl Scheidemantel and Königliche Hofkapelle, cond. Richard Strauss.

Pub. 1897, Bote & Bock; incl. reduction for voice and piano.

123. Zwei Gesänge Op. 34. For 16-part mixed chorus a cappella. 1897.

1. *Der Abend* (Schiller). Dated: 16 March 1897, Munich. Ded. Julius Buths.
2. *Hymne* (Rückert). Dated: 18 March–7 May 1897, Munich. Ded. Philipp Wolfrum.

fp (No. 1): 2 May 1898, Cologne, Konservatoriumschor, cond. Franz Wüllner.

fp (No. 2): 21 May 1898, Amsterdam, Klein-koor a Cappella, cond. Anton Averkamp.

Pub. 1897, Joseph Aibl; Universal-Edition.

BIBLIOGRAPHY:
Chr. A. Rappard: Twee Vocale-Oorkesterwerken van RS, *Weekblad for Muziek* (Amsterdam), 1906, Nos. 2–4.

124. Hymne ('Licht, du ewiglich eines'). For mixed chorus and orchestra. 1897. Composed for the opening of the Secession Art Exhibition in Munich.

fp: 1 June 1897, Munich, Court Orchestra and Chorus, cond. Richard Strauss.

Unpub.

125. Don Quixote Op. 35. Fantastic Variations on a theme of knightly character for full orchestra. Dated: 29 December 1897, Munich. Ded. Joseph Dupont. Dur. 35'.

1. *Introduzione*; 2. *Tema con 10 variazioni*; 3. *Finale*.

2 fl, pic, 2 ob, ca, E-flat cl, 2 cl, bcl, 3 bsn, cbsn; 6 hn, 3 tpt, 3 tmb, ten tuba, bs tuba; timp, tgle, bells, tamb, wind machine; hp, strings (16-16-12-10-8).

fp: 8 March 1898, Cologne, Gürzenich concert, Friedrich Grützmacher (cello) and Städtisches Orchester, cond. Franz Wüllner.

fFp: 11 March 1900, Paris, Lamoureux Concert, cond. Richard Strauss.

fEp: 4 June 1903, St. James's Hall, Strauss Festival, Concertgebouw Orchestra, cond. Richard Strauss.

fAp: 12 February 1904, Boston, Boston Symphony Orchestra, cond. Wilhelm Gericke.

f Vienna p: 17 December 1904, Konzertverein, cond. Ferdinand Löwe.

fEbp: 13 December 1927, Liverpool, Philharmonic Hall, Liverpool Philharmonic Orchestra, cond. Paul von Klenau.

Pub. 1898, Joseph Aibl; Universal-Edition;

1933, Peters. Reduction for piano four hands by Otto Singer pub. 1898, Joseph Aibl.

BIBLIOGRAPHY:
Eric Blom: RS, Don Quixote Op. 35, *Music Teacher*, February 1932, p. 71.
Roland Tenschert: Die Wandlungen einer Kadenz—Absonderlichkeiten der Harmonik im Don Quixote von RS, *Die Musik*, June 1934, p. 663.
Anon.: Don Quixote by RS, *British Musician*, February 1933, p. 30.

126. Enoch Arden Op. 38. Melodrama for piano. Dated: 26 February 1897. Poem: Tennyson, transl. Adolf Strodtmann. Ded. Emil von Possart.

fp: 24 March 1897, Munich, Emil von Possart (reciter) and Richard Strauss (piano).

f Vienna p: 13 January 1899, Tonkünstlerverein, Josef Lewinsky and Alexander von Zemlinsky.

fEp: 2 June 1902, Queen's Hall, Emil von Possart and Richard Strauss.

Pub. 1898, Robert Forberg. Arrangement: by Adalbert Baranski as a symphonic poem for orchestra, 1958.

BIBLIOGRAPHY:
Sydney Grew: Strauss's Enoch Arden, *MO*, May 1914, p. 624.
S. Magrini: Enoch Arden di RS, *Il Pianoforte*, December 1921.
Ernest Newman: Drama allied to music, *Radio Times*, 21 August 1936, p. 7.

127. Vier Lieder Op. 36. For voice and piano. 1898, Munich. Ded. (No. 1) Marie Riemerschmid (*née* Hörburger), (Nos. 2–4) Raoul Walter.

1. *Das Rosenband* (Klopstock).
2. *Für fünfzehn Pfennige* (from: Das Knaben Wunderhorn).
3. *Hat gesagt* (from: Das Knaben Wunderhorn).
4. *Anbetung* (Rückert).

Pub. Joseph Aibl; Universal-Edition; Boosey & Hawkes.

127a. Der Rosenband Op. 36 No. 1. Version with orchestra. Dated: 22 September 1897.

2 fl, pic, 2 ob, 2 cl, bcl, 2 bsn; 2 hn; strings.

fEp: 3 June 1903, London Strauss Festival, Pauline Strauss.

Pub. 1911, Universal-Edition.

128. Sechs Lieder Op. 37. For voice and piano. 1897–8. Ded. Pauline Strauss ('to my beloved wife on the 12th April').

1. *Glückes genug* (Detlev von Liliencron).
2. *Ich liebe dich* (Detlev von Liliencron).
3. *Meinem Kinde* (Gustav Falke).
4. *Mein Auge* (Richard Dehmel).
5. *Herr Lenz* (Emanuel von Bodmann).
6. *Hochzeitlich Lied* (Anton Lindner).

Pub. 1898, Joseph Aibl; Universal-Edition; Boosey & Hawkes. No. 1 arr. by Max Reger for piano solo pub. 1904, Joseph Aibl; Universal-Edition.

128a. Ich liebe dich Op. 37 No. 2. Version with orchestra. Dated: 30 August 1943, Garmisch.

2 fl, 2 ob, 2 cl, 2 bsn; 4 hn, 2 tpt, 3 tmb; timp; strings.

Pub. 1964, Boosey & Hawkes.

128b. Meinem Kinde Op. 37 No. 3. Version with orchestra. 1897.

2 fl, 2 bsn; hp, strings.

Pub. 1911, Universal-Edition.

128c. Mein Auge Op. 37 No. 4. Version with orchestra. Dated: 5 September 1933, Bad Wiessee.

2 fl, 2 ob, 2 cl, 2 bsn; 2 hn, tpt; hp, strings.

Pub. 1964, Boosey & Hawkes.

129. Fünf Lieder Op. 39. For voice and piano. 1897–8. Ded. Fritz Sieger.

1. *Leises Lied* (Richard Dehmel).
2. *Jung Hexenlied* (Bierbaum).
3. *Der Arbeitsmann* (Richard Dehmel).
4. *Befreit* (Richard Dehmel). Dated: 2 June 1898.
5. *Lied an meinen Sohn* (Richard Dehmel).

Pub. 1898, Forberg.

129a. Der Arbeitsmann Op. 39 No. 3. ?Version with orchestra.

129b. Befreit Op. 39 No. 4. Version with orchestra. Dated: 10 September 1933, Bad Wiessee.

2 fl, 2 ob, ca, 2 cl, bcl, 2 bsn, cbsn; 4 hn, 2 tpt, 3 tmb, tuba; timp; hp, harmonium, strings.

Pub. 1964, Boosey & Hawkes.

130. Ein Heldenleben Op. 40. Tone Poem for orchestra. 1897–8. Dated: 27 December 1898, Berlin, Charlottenburg. Ded. Willem Mengelberg and the Concertgebouw Orchestra, Amsterdam. Dur. 40'.

3 fl, pic, 4 ob, ca, E-flat cl, 2 cl, bcl, 3 bsn, cbsn; 8 hn, 5 tpt, 3 tmb, ten tuba, bs tuba; timp, GC, cym, snare dm, big dm; 2 hp, strings (16-16-12-12-8).

fp: 3 March 1899, Frankfurt a. M., Museum Concert, Städtisches Orchester, cond. Richard Strauss, with Alfred Hess as solo violinist.

fFp: 4 March 1900, Paris, l'Orchestre Lamoureux, cond. Richard Strauss.

f Vienna p: 23 January 1901, Kaim Orchestra of Munich, cond. Richard Strauss.

fAp: 6 December 1901, Boston, Boston Symphony Orchestra, cond. Wilhelm Gericke.

fEp: 6 December 1902, Queen's Hall, Saturday Concert, Queen's Hall Orchestra, cond. Richard Strauss.

fEbp: 25 March 1926, Manchester, Free Trade Hall, Halle Orchestra, cond. Sir Thomas Beecham.

Pub. 1899, Leuckart; 1927, Leuckart; 1931, Associated Music Publishers (min. score).

BIBLIOGRAPHY:

J.H.G.B.: Herr RS's tone poem Ein Heldenleben—a first impression only, *MS*, 13 December 1902, p. 364.

J. H. Elliot: Ein Heldenleben, *Halle*, February 1958, p. 1.

Robert Ralph: Strauss's Heldenleben, *Music Student*, 1912, November p. 75, December p. 115.

Karl Schmalz: RS' Also sprach Zarathustra und Ein Heldenleben, *Die Musik*, January (2) 1905, p. 102.

Ralph Vaughan Williams: Ein Heldenleben, *Vocalist*, January 1903, p. 295.

Anon.: Ein Heldenleben and its English critics, *MS*, 24 January 1903, p. 49.

131. Fünf Lieder Op. 41. For voice and piano. 1899. Ded. 'Frau Marie Rösch (*née* Ritter) in most cordial admiration'.

1. *Wiegenlied* (Richard Dehmel). Dated: 22 August 1899, Marquartstein.
2. *In der Campagna* (John Henry Mackay). Dated: 1899, Marquartstein.

3. *Am Ufer* (Richard Dehmel). Dated: 15 August 1899, Marquartstein.

4. *Bruder Liederlich* (Detler von Liliencron). Dated: 16 August 1899, Marquartstein.

5. *Leise Lieder* (Christian Morgenstern). Dated: 4 June 1899, Berlin, Charlottenburg.

Pub. 1899, Leuckart; Universal-Edition; Boosey & Hawkes.

131a. Wiegenlied Op. 41 No. 1. Version with orchestra.

2 fl, 2 ob, ca, 2 cl, 2 bsn; 2 hn; 2(1) hp, strings.

Pub. ?1916, Leuckart.

132. Zwei Männerchöre Op. 42. From Herder's 'Stimmen der Völker'. 1899.

1. *Liebe*; 2. *Altdeutsches Schlachtlied*.

fp: 8 December 1899, Vienna, Wiener Schubertbund, cond. Adolf Kirchl.

Pub. 1899, Leuckart.

133. Soldatenlied (August von Kopisch). For male chorus a cappella. ?1899. Pub. 1909, O. Bauer (Munich).

134. Drei Gesänge Op. 43. After classical German poets, for voice and piano. Ded. Ernestine Schumann-Heink.

1. *An Sie* (Klopstock).

2. *Muttertändelei* (G. A. Bürger). Dated: 15 August 1899.

3. *Die Ulme zu Hirsau* (Uhland). Dated: 4 September 1899.

Pub. 1899, Challier.

134a. Muttertändelei Op. 43 No. 2. Version with orchestra. Dated: 21 February 1900.

2 fl, 2 ob, ca, 2 cl, 2 bsn; 2 hn; tgle, cym; strings (without double-basses).

Pub. 1911, Challier.

135. Zwei grössere Gesänge Op. 44. For low voice and orchestra. 1899.

1. *Notturno* (Richard Dehmel). Dated: 4–16 September 1899, Charlottenburg. Ded. Anton van Rooy. Dur. 5'.

2 fl, pic, 2 ob, ca, 2 cl, bcl, 2 bsn, dbsn; 3 tmb; solo violin, strings (12-12-8-7-6).

2. *Nächtlicher Gang* (Rückert). Dated: 10 November 1899, Charlottenburg. Ded. Karl Scheidemantel. Dur. 7'.

4 fl, 2 pic, 2 ob, ca, E-flat cl, 2 cl, 2 bsn, dbsn; 6 hn, 4 tpt, 3 tmb, tuba; timp, GC, cym, tamtam, cast, Rute, Holzinstrument; hp, strings (12-12-8-8-6).

fp: 3 December 1900, Berlin, Wagnersverein concert, Baptist Hoffmann, cond. Richard Strauss.

Pub. 1899 (No. 1), 1900 (No. 2), Forberg.

136. Drei Männerchöre Op. 45. From Herder's 'Stimmen der Völker'. 1899. Ded. 'to my dear father'.

1. *Schlachtgesang*.

2. *Lied der Freundschaft* (Simon Dach).

3. *Der Brauttanz* (Simon Dach).

Pub. 1900, Fürstner/Boosey & Hawkes.

137. Das Schloss am Meere. Melodrama after Uhland with piano. 1899.

fp: 23 March 1899, Berlin, E. von Possart and Richard Strauss.

Pub. 1911, Fürstner/Boosey & Hawkes.

138. Fünf Gedichte Op. 46 (F. Rückert). For voice and piano. 1899–1900. Ded. 'to my dear parents-in-law'.

1. *Ein Obdach gegen Sturm und Regen.* Dated: 16 January 1900.

2. *Gestern war ich Atlas.* Dated: 16 January 1900.

3. *Die sieben Siegel.* Dated: 18 November 1899.

4. *Morgenrot.* Dated: 4 February 1900.

5. *Ich sehe wie in einen Spiegel.* Dated: 7 February 1900, Charlottenburg.

Pub. 1900, Fürstner/Boosey & Hawkes.

139. Fünf Lieder Op. 47 (Ludwig Uhland). For voice and piano. 1900. Ded. J. C. Pflüger.

1. *Auf ein Kind.* Dated: 5 May 1900.

2. *Des Dichters Abendgang.* Dated: 8 May 1900.

3. *Rückleben.* Dated: 23 May 1900.

4. *Einkehr.* Dated: 1900, Charlottenburg.

5. *Von den sieben Zechbrüdern.*

Pub. 1900, Fürstner/Boosey & Hawkes.

139a. Des Dichters Abendgang. Version with orchestra. Dated: 15 June 1918.

3 fl, 2 ob, ca, 2 cl, bcl, 2 bsn; 4 hn, 3 tpt, 3 tmb, tuba; timp; 2 hp, strings.

Pub. 1918, Fürstner/Boosey & Hawkes.

140. Fünf Lieder Op. 48. For voice and piano. 1900.

Strauss, Richard

1. *Freundliche Vision* (Bierbaum). Dated: 5 October 1900.
2. *Ich schwebe* (Henckell). Dated: 25 September 1900.
3. *Kling!* (Henckell). Dated: 30 September 1900.
4. *Winterweihe* (Henckell). Dated: 23 September 1900.
5. *Winterliebe* (Henckell). Dated: 2 October 1900, Charlottenburg.
   Pub. 1901, Fürstner/Boosey & Hawkes.

140a. Freundliche Vision Op. 48 No. 1. Version with orchestra. Dated: 1 July 1918, Garmisch.
   2 fl, 2 bsn; 4 hn, 2 tpt, 2 tmb; strings.
   Pub. 1918, Fürstner; 1943, Boosey & Hawkes.

140b. Winterweihe Op. 48 No. 4. Version with orchestra. Dated: 28 June 1918.
   ob, 2 cl, 2 bsn; 3 hn; strings (10-10-6-6-4).
   Pub. 1918, Fürstner; 1943, Boosey & Hawkes.

140c. Winterliebe Op. 48 No. 5. Version with orchestra. Dated: 29 June 1918, Garmisch.
   2 fl, pic, 2 ob, 2 cl, 2 bsn; 4 hn, 2 tpt, 3 tmb; timp, pcssn; strings.
   Pub. 1918, Fürstner; 1943, Boosey & Hawkes.

141. Acht Lieder Op. 49. For voice and piano. 1900–1.
1. *Waldseligkeit* (Richard Dehmel). Dated: 21 September 1901. Ded. composer's wife.
2. *In goldener Fülle* (Paul Renner). Dated: 13 September 1901. Ded. Ernst Kraus.
3. *Wiegenliedchen* (Richard Dehmel). Dated: 20 September 1901. Ded. Grete Kraus.
4. *Das Lied des Steinklopfers* (Henckell). Dated: 24 September 1901. Ded. Consul Simon.
5. *Sie wissen's nicht* (Oscar Panizza). Dated: 14 September 1901. Ded. Walter Ende.
6. *Junggesellenschwur* (from: Das Knaben Wunderhorn). Dated: 11 May 1900. Ded. Baron A. von Stengel.
7. *Wer lieben will* (from: Elsässische Volkslieder). Dated: 23 September 1901, Charlottenburg.

8. *Ach, was Kummer, Qual und Schmerzen* (from: Elsässische Volkslieder). Dated: 23 September 1901, Charlottenburg.
   fEp (No. 1): 12 May 1903, Bechstein Hall, Alex Disraeli, acc. H. Bird.
   Pub. 1902, Fürstner/Boosey & Hawkes.

141a. Waldseligkeit Op. 49 No. 1. Version with orchestra. Dated: 24 June 1918, Garmisch.
   2 fl, 2 cl, bcl, 2 bsn; 2 hn; harmonium, hp, strings (12-12-8-8-6).
   Pub. 1918, Fürstner; 1943, Boosey & Hawkes.

142. Feuersnot Op. 50. 'Singgedicht' in one act. 1900–1. Dated: 22 May 1901, Berlin, Charlottenburg. Text: Ernst von Wolzogen. Ded. Friedrich Rösch. Dur. 85'.
   3 fl, pic, 3 ob, 2 ca, cl in D, 2 cl, bcl, 3 bsn, cbsn; 4 hn, 3 tpt, 3 tmb, bs tuba; timp, tgle, tamb, cast, tamtam, side dm, GC, cym, glock; 2 hp, strings (12-12-8-8-6). *Stage music* (ad lib): glock (ad lib), harmonium, solo violin, solo cello, 2 small drums, 3 hp (ad lib).
   fp: 21 November 1901, Dresden, Court Opera, cond. Ernst von Schuch; with Annie Krull (Diemut) and Karl Scheidemantel (Kunrad); producer, Maximilian Moris.
   f Vienna p: 29 January 1902, Hofoper, cond. Gustav Mahler.
   fEp (Love Scene only): 1 February 1902, Queen's Hall, Saturday Concert, Queen's Hall Orchestra, cond. (Sir) Henry Wood.
   fEp (complete): 9 July 1910, His Majesty's Theatre, The Thomas Beecham Opera Comique season, cond. Sir Thomas Beecham; with Maud Fay (Diemut), Mark Oster (Kunrad), Robert Radford (Burgomaster), Lena Maitland (Elsbeth), Stella Phelps (Wigelis), Lilian Coomber (Margret); sung in English; producer, Louis Verande.
   Pub. 1901, Fürstner/Boosey & Hawkes: English version, William Wallace; French version, Jean Marnold; Italian version, Ottone Schanzer.

BIBLIOGRAPHY:
Ludwig Hartmann: Feuersnot, *Bühne und Welt*, December 1901.
A.K.: RS' Feuersnot in Berlin, *MT*, December 1902, p. 808.

Ernest Newman: Feuersnot, in *Testament of Music*, Putnam (London) 1962, p. 270.

Erich Urban: RS' Feuersnot, *Die Musik*, December (1) 1901, p. 417.

Paul Zschorlich: Gedanken über die Feuersnot, *Die Zeit*, 1902, No. 6.

143. Zwei Gesänge Op. 51. For bass and orchestra. 1902–6.

1. *Das Thal* (Uhland). Dated: 11 December 1902, Charlottenburg. Ded. Paul Knüpfer.

3 fl, 2 ob, 2 cl, 2 basset hn, bcl, 2 bsn, dbsn; 4 hn, 2 tpt; strings (12-12-8-8-6).

2. *Der Einsame* (Heine). Dated: 18 February 1906, Berlin.

strings.

fp (No. 1): 7 April 1903, Berlin, Paul Knüpfer, ?with piano acc. by Richard Strauss.

fp (No. 2): 5 March 1906, Leipzig, Paul Knüpfer, ?with piano acc. by Richard Strauss.

Pub. 1903 (No. 1), 1906 (No. 2), Fürstner; 1943, Boosey & Hawkes.

144. Taillefer Op. 52. Ballad of Uhland for mixed chorus, soloists and orchestra. 1902–3. Ded. Faculty of Philosophy, Heidelberg University. Dur. 16'.

4 fl, 2 pic, 4 ob, 2 ca, 2 cl in D, 2 cl in B flat, 2 cl in A, bcl, 4 bsn, cbsn; 8 hn, 6 tpt, 4 tmb, 2 bs tubas; timp, pcssn; glock, strings (24-24-16-14-12).

fp: 26 October 1903, Heidelberg, Festival of Music, cond. Richard Strauss.

fEp: 12 October 1905, Bristol Festival, with Amy Perry, John Coates and Andrew Black as soloists.

f London p: 3 March 1906, Queen's Hall, Perceval Allen, Henry Turnpenny and Montague Borwell, Leeds Choral Union and Queen's Hall Orchestra, cond. (Sir) Henry Wood.

Pub. 1903, Fürstner/Boosey & Hawkes; vocal score by Otto Singer; English version, P. England.

145. Kanon ('Hans Huber in Vitznau'). For four voices. 1903. Pub. (facsimile) in Edgar Refardt, *Hans Huber, Leben und Werk eines Schweizer Musikers*, Atlantis-Verlag (Zürich) 1944.

146. Sinfonia Domestica Op. 53. For orchestra. 1902–3. Ded. 'To my dear wife and our son'. Dur. 41–45'.

3 fl, pic, 2 ob, ob d'amore, ca, cl in D, 3 cl, 4 bsn, cbsn; 4 sax, 8 hn, 4 tpt, 3 tmb, bs tuba; timp, cym, GC, tgle, tamb, glock; 2 hp, strings (16-16-12-10-8).

fp: 21 March 1904, New York, Carnegie Hall, Strauss Festival, Wetzler Symphony Orchestra, cond. Richard Strauss.

fGp: 1 June 1904, Frankfurt a.M., Tonkünstlerfest, Städtisches Orchester, cond. Richard Strauss.

fEp: 25 February 1905, Queen's Hall, Saturday Concert, Queen's Hall Orchestra, cond. (Sir) Henry Wood.

2Ep: 1 April 1905, Queen's Hall, Queen's Hall Orchestra, cond. Richard Strauss.

fFp: 25 March 1906, Paris, l'Orchestre Colonne, cond. Richard Strauss.

Pub. 1904, Bote & Bock. Also reduced wind orchestration by G. E. Lessing.

BIBLIOGRAPHY:

J.H.G.B.: Symphonia Domestica—The performance, *MS*, 8 April 1905, p. 213.

Wilhelm Klatte: Die Symphonia domestica, *Die Musik*, January (2) 1905, p. 124.

L.L.: Symphonia Domestica—First impressions, *MS*, 8 April 1905, p. 212.

Walther Riezler: Symphonia domestica, *Freistatt*, 1904, No. 51.

Anon.: RS's Symphonia Domestica, a description, *MS*, 1905, 25 February p. 119, 4 March p. 133.

147. Zwei Lieder. From Calderón's 'Richter von Zalamea', for voice (mezzo-soprano/tenor) and guitars or harp. 1904. Composed for a production of the play at the Lessingtheatre, Berlin, but probably not performed.

1. *Liebesliedchen*. For tenor.

2. *Lied der Chispa*. For mezzo-soprano.

Pub. 1954, *Strauss Jahrbuch*.

148. Salome Op. 54. Drama in one act. 1903–5. Dated: 10 June 1905. Text: Oscar Wilde; Ger. transl. by Hedwig Lachmann. Ded. Edgar Speyer. Dur. 95–100'.

3 fl, pic, 2 ob, ca, heckelphone, E-flat cl, 4 cl, bcl, 3 bsn, cbsn; 6 hn, 4 tpt, 4 tmb, bs tuba; timp, pcssn, xyl, glock; 2 hp, celesta, strings.

Reduced orchestration: 3 fl, pic, 2 ob, ca, 2 cl,

bcl, 3 bsn; 4 hn, 3 tpt, 3 tmb, bs tuba; timp, pcssn; hp, celesta, strings.

Stage music: harmonium, organ.

fp: 9 December 1905, Dresden, Hofoper, cond. Ernst von Schuch; with Marie Wittich (Salome), Irene von Chavanne (Herodias), Karl Burrian (Herod), Carl Perron (Jokanaan), Rudolf Jäger (Narraboth).

fEp: 8 December 1910, Royal Opera House, Covent Garden, cond. Sir Thomas Beecham; with Aïno Ackté (Salome), Ottilie Metzger (Herodias), Ernst Kraus (Herod), Clarence Whitehill (Jokanaan), Maurice D'Oisly (Narraboth).

fEbp: 6 November 1934, BBC Orchestra, cond. Albert Coates; with Oda Slobodskaya (Salome), Constance Willis (Herodias), Francis Russell (Herod), Arthur Fear (Jokanaan), Trefor Jones (Narraboth).

Pub. Fürstner/Boosey & Hawkes. Vocal score by Otto Singer.

BIBLIOGRAPHY:

Richard Batka: RS, Salome, in *Aus den Opernwelt*, Georg D. W. Callwey (Munich) 1907, p. 193.

Robert Breuer: Salome in New York 1907, *SM*, March 1957, p. 97.

Raoul Brunel: La Salomé de RS au cinéma, *Le Ménestrel*, 21 March 1924, p. 129.

Paul Colberg: First performance of RS's opera Salome, *MS*, 16 December 1905, p. 384.

Hans Curjel: Salome, das Werk des Jugendstils, *Blätter der Staatsoper* (Berlin), 1929.

Victor Debay: La Salome de RS, *Le Courrier musical*, 1907, No. 10.

Alfred Einstein: Strauss's Salome, *Radio Times*, 2 November 1934, p. 365.

W. Frost: Salome at fifty, *Opera News*, 5 March 1956, p. 33.

F. A. Geissler: Salome von RS, *Die Musik*, January (1) 1906, p. 56.

Herbert Gerigk: Ammerkungen zu RS' Salome, *Die Musik*, March 1942, p. 202.

Lawrence Gilman: Strauss's Salome, its art and its morals, in *Aspects of Modern Opera*, New York, 1909.

The Earl of Harewood: Salome at Covent Garden, *Opera*, February 1950, p. 4.

Günter Hausswald: Salome als Höfoper, in *Richard Strauss Jahrbuch 1959–60*, p. 99.

Friedrich Hofmann: Eindrücke von Salome, *Baltische Blätter für Musik*, 1907.

A. Ingman: Salome in Dresden, *Finsk Musikrevy*, December 1905.

Arthur Jacobs & Stanley Sadie: Salome, in *The Opera Guide*, Hamish Hamilton (London) 1964, p. 325.

Victor Junk: Aus den Salome—Proben in der Wiener Volksoper, *NZfM*, February 1934, p. 137.

René Kerdyk: L'hypothèse d'une rédemption dans Salome, *Le Journal musical*, 1907, No. 10.

Wilhelm Kienzl: RS' Salome, *Das Blaubuch*, 1906, No. 27.

Frederick Kitchener: Strauss's Salome (uncensored) in the East, *MS*, 4 March 1911, p. 134.

M. Kufferath: Salome de RS, Fischbacher, 1907.

Rudolf Louis: Die erlöste Salome, *Süddeutsche Monatshefte*, 1907, No. 2.

William Mann: Opera on the gramophone, 3: Salome, *Opera*, July 1957, p. 420.

Paul Marsop: Italien und der 'Fall Salome', *Die Musik*, 1907, No. 9, p. 139.

Otto Neitzel: Salome von Oskar Wilde und RS, *NMZ*, 1907, Nos. 17–18.

Ernest Newman: Salome, in *More Opera Nights*, Putnam (London) 1954, p. 3.

— Salome, in *Testament of Music*, Putnam (London) 1962, p. 287.

Paul Pfitzner: Salome, *Musikalisches Wochenblatt*, 1905.

Alberta von Puttkamer: Die Salome von Wilde-Strauss als Kulturerscheinung, *Der Tag*, 12 October 1907.

Leopold Schmidt: Salome von RS—Zur Erstaufführung des Werkes im Berliner Kgl. Opernhaus, *Die Musik*, 1907, No. 7, p. 54.

Richard Specht: Salome, *Blätter der Staatsoper* (Berlin), 1929.

Roland Tenschert: RS' Opernfassung der deutschen Übersetzung von Oscar Wildes Salome, *Richard Strauss Jahrbuch 1959–60*, p. 99.

Kurt Westphal: Die psychologische Aufgabe des Orchesters im Musikdrama von Strauss —dargestellt an Salome, *Strauss*, Nos. 54–55, December 1967, p. 3.

Strauss's *Salome*, *MO*, January 1906, p. 261; repr. from *The Times*.

Salome et la presse, *Le Monde musical*, 1907, No. 10.

Salome in London—production at Covent Garden, *The Times*, 9 December 1910, p. 10.

Salome at Covent Garden, the second performance, *The Times*, 12 December 1910, p. 10.

Strauss and Salome, *The Times*, 10 December 1910, p. 12.

Salome and shock (first New York performance in 1907), *Center*, March 1954, p. 7.

Salome, *Musical Courier*, 10 March 1958.

Salome, issues of *Opera News*, 14 January 1952, 3 February 1958, 17 February 1962.

149. Sechs Lieder Op. 56. For voice and piano. 1903–6. Ded. (No. 1) Pauline Strauss, (Nos. 2–6) Strauss's mother.

1. *Gefunden* (Goethe). Dated: 8 August 1903.
2. *Blindenklage* (Henckell).
3. *Im Spätboot* (C. F. Meyer).
4. *Mit deinen blauen Augen* (Heine).
5. *Frühlingsfeier* (Heine).
6. *Die heiligen drei Könige* (Heine).

fEp (No. 1): 9 December 1903, St. James's Hall, Pauline Strauss, acc. Richard Strauss.

Pub. 1906, Bote & Bock.

149a. Frühlingsfeier Op. 56 No. 5. Version with orchestra. Dated: 3 September 1933, Bad Wiessee.

2 fl, pic, 2 ob, ca, 2 cl, bcl, 2 bsn, dbsn; 4 hn, 2 tpt, 3 tmb; timp, cym; hp, strings (14-12-8-8-6).

Pub. 1934, Bote & Bock.

149b. Die heiligen drei Könige Op. 56 No. 6. Version with orchestra. Dated: 7 October 1906, Berlin, Charlottenburg.

3 fl, 2 ob, ca, 2 bsn; 3 hn, 2 tpt, 3 tmb, tuba; timp, tgle, tamb, cym, GC; celesta, 2 hp, solo violin, viola & cello, strings (12-12-8-8-6).

Pub. 1906, Bote & Bock.

150. Bardengesang Op. 55 (Klopstock). For male chorus and orchestra. 1906. Ded. Gustav Wohgemuth. Dur. 12′.

4 fl, 2 ob, 4 cl, 3 bsn; 6 hn, 4 tpt, 3 tmb, tuba; timp, pcssn; 4 hp, strings.

fp: 6 February 1907, Dresden, Lehrergesangverein and Gewerbehauskapelle, cond. Friedrich Brandes.

Pub. 1906, Fürstner/Boosey & Hawkes: vocal score, Otto Singer.

151. Zwei Militärmarsche Op. 57. For orchestra. 1906.

1. *Militärmarsch* (E flat).

2 fl, pic, 2 ob, 3 cl, 2 bsn; 4 hn, 2 tpt, 3 tmb; timp, pcssn; strings.

2. *Kriegsmarsch* (C minor).

4 fl, 2 pic, 2 ob, 4 cl, 2 bsn; 6 hn, 4 tpt, 3 tmb, tuba; timp, pcssn; strings.

fp: 6 March 1907, Berlin, Court Concert, cond. Richard Strauss.

Pub. 1907, Peters.

152. Sechs Volksliedbearbeitungen (Folksong arrangements). For male chorus a cappella. 1905–6.

1. *Christlicher Maien*; 2. *Misslungene Liebesjagd*; 3. *Tummle*; 4. *Hüt' dich*; 5. *Wächterlied*; 6. *Kuckuck*.

Pub. 1906, Peters; 1952, Leuckart (three only).

153. Zwei Parademärsche. For the 'Königsjäger zu Pferde' Regiment and for cavalry. ?1905. Ded. Kaiser Wilhelm II.

fp: 6 March 1907, Berlin.

Pub. 1906–7, Fürstner/Boosey & Hawkes. No. 2 arr. by A. Peschke. No. 1 pub. for piano.

154. Königsmarsch. For orchestra. 1905–6. Ded. 'H.M. the Emperor and King Wilhelm II in deepest homage'.

8 tpt, 12 drums; 2 fl, 2 pic, 2 ob, 2 E-flat cl, 2 cl, 2 bsn, cbsn; 8 hn, 4 tpt, 4 tmb, bs tuba; timp, side dm, GC & cym; 2 hp, strings (12-12-8-8-6).

fp: 6 March 1907, Berlin.

Pub. 1906, Fürstner/Boosey & Hawkes.

155. De Brandeburgsche Mars. Presentation March arr. for orchestra. 1906.

fp: 6 March 1907, Berlin.

Pub. Fürstner/Boosey & Hawkes.

156. Der Graf von Rom. Wordless. For voice and piano. 1906. Pub. (facsimile) 1961, in programme of Berlin State Opera production of 'Der Rosenkavalier'.

157. Elektra Op. 58. Tragedy in one act. 1906–8. Dated: 22 September 1908, Garmisch. Text: Hugo von Hofmannsthal. Ded. Natalie and Willy Levin. Dur. 95–102'.

3 fl, pic, 3 ob, ca, heckelphone, E-flat cl, 4 cl, 2 basset hn, bcl, 3 bsn, cbsn; 8 hn (2 tubas in B flat, 2 tubas in F), 6 tpt, bs tpt, 3 tmb, cbs tmb, cbs tuba; timp, pcssn, glock; 2(4) hp, celesta (ad lib), strings.

Reduced orchestration: 3 fl, 2 ob, ca, 4 cl, 3 bcl, 3 bsn; 4 hn, 6 tpt, 3 tmb, bs tuba; timp, pcssn; 2 hp, strings.

fp: 25 January 1909, Dresden, Hofoper, cond. Ernst von Schuch; with Annie Krull (Elektra), Margarethe Siems (Chrysothemis), Ernestine Schumann-Heink (Klytemnestra), Carl Perron (Orestes), Johannes Sembach (Aegisthus); producer, Georg Toller.

fEp: 19 February 1910, Royal Opera House, Covent Garden, cond. Sir Thomas Beecham; with Edyth Walker (Elektra), Frances Rose (Chrysothemis), Anna von Bahr-Mildenburg (Klytemnestra), Friedrich Weidemann (Orestes), Maurice D'Oisly (Aegisthus).

fEbp: 9 May 1938, Covent Garden, cond. Sir Thomas Beecham; with Rose Pauly (Elektra), Kerstin Thorborg (Klytemnestra), Hilde Konetzni (Chrysothemis), Herbert Janssen (Orestes).

Pub. 1908, Fürstner/Boosey & Hawkes. Vocal score, Otto Singer. English version, Alfred Kalisch; French version, H. Gauthier-Villars.

BIBLIOGRAPHY:

Felix Adler: Richard Straussens Elektra, *Neue Revue*, 5 February 1909, p. 217.

Alfred Bonaccorsi: Elettra di Strauss, *La Rassegna musicale*, 1962, p. 127.

G. A. Borgese: Elektra, *La Stampa*, 24 October 1908; transl. & condensed by Richard Saville, *MS*, 16 January 1909, p. 37.

André Coeuroy: Elektra à l'Opéra, *Revue universelle*, 15 March 1932, p. 762.

Paul Corder: RS at Dresden, *MS*, 6 February 1909, p. 85.

O. Downes: Elektra in 1952, *New York Times*, 24 February 1952, Section 2, p. 7.

C.L.G.: Elektra, *MO*, April 1910, p. 488; repr. from *The Spectator*.

F. A. Geissler: Elektra von RS, *Faschingsheft Musik*, Vol. 8 (1909), No. 10, p. 243.

Noel Goodwin: Elektra, *MO*, May 1953, p. 467.

David Irvine: The enthusiasm for Elektra, *MS*, 2 April 1910, p. 211.

Alan Jefferson: Opera on the gramophone, 14: Elektra, *Opera*, May 1953, p. 266.

Alfred Kalisch: Impressions of Strauss's Elektra, *Bulletin S.I.M.*, April 1909.

Julius Kapp: Elektra, *Blätter der Staatsoper* (Berlin), May 1923, p. 3; November 1926, p. 1.

Walter Klein: Die Harmonisation in Elektra von RS, *Der Merker*, 1911, April (1) p. 540, April (2) p. 590.

Constant Lambert: Strauss's Elektra, in *Essays on Music*, Cassell (London) 1967, p. 240.

William Mann: An introduction to Strauss's Elektra, *Opera*, May 1953, p. 266.

— A note on Elektra, *MT*, June 1954, p. 322.

Jean Marnold: Elektra, in *Musique d'autrefois et d'aujourd'hui*, Dorbon-Aîné (Paris) 1912, p. 335.

Carl Mennicke: Über RS' Elektra, *Die Musik*, August 1935, p. 808.

G. Montagu: RS's Elektra, *London Musical Events*, May 1953, p. 27.

Ernest Newman: Elektra, *Radio Times*, 6 May 1938, p. 13.

Henry Prunières: Elektra de RS à l'Opéra, *RM*, March 1932, p. 212.

Alfred Roller: Anmerkungen zu den Dekorationsskizzen für Elektra, *Der Merker*, 10 December 1909, p. 187.

Camille La Senne: Elektra de RS au théâtre de Dresde, *Bulletin S.I.M.*, 15 February 1909, p. 204.

Henry W. Simon: Elektra, in *Festival of Opera*, W. H. Allen (London) 1957, p. 125.

Emerson Whithorne: An interview with Edyth Walker, Strauss's Elektra, *MS*, 16 April 1910, p. 242; repr. from *Musical America*.

MISCELLANEOUS OR UNSIGNED:

Strauss's Elektra in Vienna, *MS*, 3 April 1909, p. 212.

RS's Elektra, *MMR*, 1910, p. 27.

Elektra in New York, *The Times*, 3 February 1910, p. 8.

Royal Opera, Covent Garden: Elektra by RS, *The Times*, 21 February 1910, p. 12.

Aus dem Werdegang der Elektra: Briefe von RS und Hugo von Hofmannsthal, *Blätter der Staatsoper* (Berlin), November 1926, p. 6.

Elektra, issues of *Opera News*, 18 February 1952, 25 March 1961.

Presse-Stimmen über Elektra nach der Berliner Erstaufführung am 15. Februar 1909, *Blätter der Staatsoper* (Berlin), November 1926, p. 10.

158. Feierlicher Einzug der Ritter des Johanniterordens. For brass and drums. 1909.

   3 solo tpt, 12 tpt, 4 hn, 4 tmb, 2 tubas, timp. Pub. 1909, Schlesinger'sche Buch und Musikhandlung (Berlin). Arrangement: for organ, by Max Reger.

159. Der Rosenkavalier Op. 59. Comedy for music in three acts. 1909–10. Dated: 26 September 1910, Garmisch. Text: Hugo von Hofmannsthal. Ded. 'To my dear kinsfolk the Pschorr Family in Munich'. Dur. 132'.

   3 fl, pic, 3 ob, ca, 3 cl (incl. E-flat cl), bcl, basset hn, 3 bsn, cbsn; 4 hn, 3 tpt, 3 tmb, bs tuba; timp, pcssn; 2 hp, celesta, strings. *Stage music:* 2 fl, ob, cl in C, 2 cl, 2 bsn; 2 hn, tpt; side dm, piano, harmonium; string quintet (solo or substantially doubled).

   fp: 26 January 1911, Dresden, Hofoper, cond. Ernst von Schuch; with Margarethe Siems (Marschallin), Eva von den Osten (Octavian), Minnie Nast (Sophie), Carl Perron (Ochs), Karl Scheidemantel (Faninal), Fritz Soot (Tenor singer); design, Alfred Roller; producers, Max Reinhardt and Georg Toller.

   fEp: 29 January 1913, Covent Garden, cond. Sir Thomas Beecham; with Margarethe Siems (Marschallin), Eva von der Osten (Octavian), Claire Dux (Sophie), Paul Knüpfer (Ochs), Friedrich Brodersen (Faninal), Frederick Blamey (Tenor singer), Annie Gura-Hummel (Annina), Hans Bechstein (Valzacchi); producer, Hermann Gura.

   f New York p: 9 December 1913, Metropolitan Opera; with Frieda Hempel (Marschallin), Margaret Ober (Octavian), Otto Goritz (Ochs).

   Pub. 1910, Fürstner/Boosey & Hawkes. Vocal score, Carl Besl. English version, Alfred Kalisch; French version, Jean Chantavoine; Italian version, Ottone Schanzer.

BIBLIOGRAPHY:

E. A. Baughan: RS's Der Rosenkavalier, *Glasgow Herald*, 30 January 1913, *MS*, 8 February 1913, p. 120.

Maurice Bex: Le Chevalier à la Rose par RS, *Revue hebdomadaire*, 26 February 1927, p. 493.

Iwan Block: Kulturpsychologisches zum Rosenkavalier, *Berliner Tageblatt*, 6 February 1911.

Eric Blom: The Rose Cavalier of Strauss, O.U.P. (London) 1930.

Rutland Boughton: Der Rosenkavalier, *MO*, March 1913, p. 405.

Friedrich Brandes: Der Rosenkavalier (nach der Dresdner Uraufführung), *Der Kunstwart*, February (2) 1911, p. 273.

Gustav Brecker: Ein Brief über den 'Rosenkavalier', *Der Merker*, March (2) 1911, p. 496.

Paul Colberg: Der Rosenkavalier, *MS*, 11 February 1911, p. 84.

J. F. Cooke: Der Rosenkavalier, *Etude*, May 1924, p. 345.

H. W. Draber: Der Rosenkavalier, *Rheinische Musik- und Theaterzeitung*, 1911, No. 4.

Martin Friedland: Wie Strauss' Rosenkavalier entstand, *AMZ*, 1924, No. 14, p. 179.

F. A. Geissler: Der Rosenkavalier, *Die Musik*, 1911, No. 10, p. 225.

Hugo von Hofmannsthal: Ungeschriebenes Nachwort zum Rosenkavalier, *Der Merker*, March (2) 1911, p. 488.

Hans Holländer: Das Satyrmotiv in den Meistersingern und im Rosenkavalier, *NZfM*, May 1958.

Edgar Istel: RS's Der Rosenkavalier, *MMR*, 1911, p. 56.

Alan Jefferson: Opera on the gramophone, 12: Der Rosenkavalier, *Opera*, March 1963, p. 162.

Arthur Jacobs & Stanley Sadie: Der Rosenkavalier, in *The Opera Guide*, Hamish Hamilton (London) 1964, p. 329.

Strauss, Richard

A. Kalisch: Der Rosenkavalier, *MT*, March 1911, p. 165.

C.-G. Stellan Mörner: Rosenkavaljeren på Operan, *Studiekamraten*, 1959, p. 45.

Ernest Newman: Der Rosenkavalier, in *Opera Nights*, Putnam (London) 1943, p. 508.

— Der Rosenkavalier, the new Strauss opera at Covent Garden, 1913, in *Testament of Music*, Putnam (London) 1962, p. 107.

Fritz Oeser: Der Rosenkavalier, *Musica*, 1957, No. 1, p. 3.

Lazare Ponnelle: Le Chevalier de la Rose, *Bulletin S.I.M.*, March 1911, p. 73.

Michael Rose: Der Rosenkavalier: Extracts from the letters between Strauss and Hofmannsthal during the composition of the opera, *Opera*, June 1959, p. 356.

Gustav Röttger: Study of harmony in Rosenkavalier, Munich, 1931.

Willi Schuh: Die Entstehung des Rosenkavalier, *Trivium* (Zürich), 1951.

— Original version of Act II of Rosenkavalier, *Die neue Rundschen*, 1953.

Paul Schwers: Die Uraufführung des Rosenkavalier in der Dresdener Hofoper, *AMZ*, 1911, No. 5.

Henry W. Simon: Der Rosenkavalier, in *Festival of Opera*, W. H. Allen (London) 1957, p. 419.

Ethel Smyth: Der Rosenkavalier, *The Suffragette*, 21 February 1913.

Richard Specht: Vorlautiges vom Rosenkavalier, *Der Merker*, January (2) 1911, p. 331.

— Der Rosenkavalier in Dresden, *Der Merker*, February (1) 1911.

Paul Stefan: Rosenkavalier und Filmmusik, *Anbruch*, February 1926, p. 65.

Richard Strauss: Der Rosenkavalier, *AMZ*, 1910, No. 39.

Roland Tenschert: Die Meistersinger und Der Rosenkavalier, *NMZ*, 1926, No. 11, p. 228.

— Fünfzig Jahre Der Rosenkavalier, *ÖM*, January 1961.

Heinz Thiessen: Wo steht Strauss mit seinem Rosenkavalier?, *AMZ*, 1911, No. 14.

Claude Trevor: RS's Der Rosenkavalier, *MMR*, 1911, p. 6.

U. W. Weisstein: Studies in the libretto—

Otello, Der Rosenkavalier: Prologomena to a poetics of opera, *Dissertation Abstracts*, October 1954, p. 1738.

MISCELLANEOUS OR UNSIGNED:

Der Rosenkavalier, *The Times*, 21 January 1911, p. 13.

Der Rosenkavalier at Dresden, *The Times*, 27 January 1911, p. 10.

A side-issue of thought at Strauss's Der Rosenkavalier, *MMR*, 1914, p. 15.

Brief über den Rosenkavalier, *Anbruch*, November 1925, p. 479.

Der Rosenkavalier, issues of *Opera News*, 23 February 1953, 13 February 1956, 17 March 1958, 26 December 1959, 22 December 1962.

Straussov Gavalier s ruzou v Narodnom divadle, *Slovenska Hudba*, March 1958, p. 121.

159a. Der Rosenkavalier: (Second) Waltz Sequence from Act III. For orchestra. 1911.

fEp: 23 August 1911, Queen's Hall, Promenade Concert, Queen's Hall Orchestra, cond. Sir Henry Wood.

Pub. 1911, Fürstner/Boosey & Hawkes.

Arrangements: for piano by J. Doebber, 1911; concert transcription by Anne-Marie Ørbeck (dur. 8') pub. 1939, Fürstner.

159b. Der Rosenkavalier: First Waltz Sequence (from Acts I & II). For orchestra. 1944. Dur. 12–12½'.

3 fl, 3 ob, E-flat cl, 2 cl, corno di bassetto, 3 bsn; 4 hn, 3 tpt, 3 tmb, tuba; timp, tamb, tgle, cym, GC; 2 hp, strings.

fp: 4 August, London, London Philharmonic Orchestra, cond. Erich Leinsdorf.

Pub. 1947, Fürstner/Boosey & Hawkes.

159c. Der Rosenkavalier: Suite. For orchestra. 1945. Dur. 22'.

fp: 14 April 1946, Manchester, Halle Orchestra, cond. Sir John Barbirolli.

Pub. Boosey & Hawkes.

160. Ariadne auf Naxos Op. 60. Opera in one act, for performance after Molière's 'Le Bourgeois Gentilhomme' (incidental music). First version. Dated: 20 April 1912. Text: Hugo von Hofmannsthal. Ded. Max Reinhardt. Dur. 85'.

2 fl, 2 pic, 2 ob, 2 cl, 2 bsn; 2 hn, tpt, tmb;

timp, pcssn; 2 hp, celesta, piano, harmonium, strings.

fp: 25 October 1912, Stuttgart, Kleines Haus (Hoftheater), cond. Richard Strauss; with Maria Jeritza (Ariadne), Margarethe Siems (Zerbinetta), Hermann Jadlowker (Bacchus), Albin Swoboda (Harlequin).

fEp: 27 May 1913, His Majesty's Theatre, cond. Sir Thomas Beecham; with Eva Plaschke von der Osten (Ariadne), Hermine Bosetti (Zerbinetta), Otto Marak (Bacchus), Carl Armster (Harlequin); the play (in English) adapted by W. Somerset Maugham; producer, Max Beerbohm Tree; opera (in German) produced by Emil Gerhauser and T. C. Fairbairn.

Pub. 1912, Fürstner/Boosey & Hawkes.

BIBLIOGRAPHY:

Rutland Boughton: Ariadne in Naxos, MO, July 1913, p. 721.

Friedrich Brandes: Ariadne in Dresden, Der Kunstwart, December (2) 1912, p. 431.

Harrison Frewin: RS's opera Ariadne auf Naxos, MS, 7 June 1913, p. 496.

Hugo von Hofmannsthal: Ce que nous avons voulu en écrivant Ariane à Naxos et le Bourgeois Gentilhomme, Revue S.I.M., September–October 1912, p. 1.

Edgar Istel: Production of RS's Ariadne auf Naxos at Stuttgart, MMR, 1912, p. 315.

Oswald Kühn: Ariadne auf Naxos—Bericht über die Uraufführung, NMZ, No. 3, January 1913.

Jacques Mayer: Begging RS's pardon— Ariadne auf Naxos, MS, 22 March 1913, p. 236.

Leopold Schmidt: Ariadne auf Naxos, Der Kunstwart, November (2) 1912, p. 240.

Oscar Schröter: Ariadne auf Naxos, Oper in einem Aufzuge von Hugo von Hofmannsthal, Musik von RS—Uraufführung im Stuttgarter Hoftheater am 25. Oktober 1912, Die Musik, November (2) 1912, p. 226.

— Ariadne auf Naxos, AMZ, No. 43, October 1912.

Paul Schwers: Die Stuttgarter Uraufführung der Ariadne auf Naxos, AMZ, No. 44, November 1912.

Richard Specht: Gespräch über Ariadne auf Naxos, Der Merker, November (1) 1912, p. 793.

Hermann Starcke: Ariadne auf Naxos in der Dresdener Hofoper, AMZ, No. 47, November 1912.

Hans Winand: Zur Regie der Ariadne, NMZ, No. 3, January 1913.

Anon.: Strauss's new opera: Ariadne auf Naxos, The Times, 26 October 1912, p. 9.

— Strauss's new opera, The Times, 28 October 1912, p. 10.

160a. Ariadne auf Naxos Op. 60. Second version (with Prologue). 1915–16. Dated: 20 June 1916. Dur. 125′ (Prologue 40′).

fp: 4 October 1916, Vienna, Hofoper, cond. Franz Schalk; with Maria Jeritza (Ariadne), Selma Kurz (Zerbinetta), Lotte Lehmann (Composer), A. von Környey (Bacchus), Hans Duhan (Music Teacher and Harlequin).

fGp: 1 November 1916, Berlin, Hofoper, cond. Leo Blech.

fEp: 27 May 1924, Covent Garden, cond. Karl Alwin; with Elisabeth Schumann (Composer), Lotte Lehmann (Ariadne), Maria Ivogün (Zerbinetta), Karl Fischer-Niemann (Bacchus), Karl Renner (Music Teacher and Harlequin).

BIBLIOGRAPHY:

Anthony Besch: Ariadne auf Naxos, MT, January 1961, p. 18.

G. M. Ciampelli: Arianna a Nasso di RS al Teatro di Torino, Fiamma, November–December 1925.

Attilio Cimbro: L'Arianna a Nasso di RS, Il Pianoforte, December 1925.

René Dumesnil: Sur Ariane à Naxos de Strauss, Mercure de France, 15 October 1937.

Walter Eilert: ;Ariadne auf Naxos, Scheinwerfer, 1931, No. 15.

O. Erhardt: Fünfzig Jahre Ariadne auf Naxos, Strauss, No. 34, September 1962, p. 4; 50 anos de Ariadne en Naxos, Buenos Aires Musical, No. 283 (1962), p. 1.

Herbert Fleischer: Ariadne und die Musikbühne der Gegenwart, Blätter der Staatsoper (Berlin), May 1932, p. 14; Arianna a Nasso nel teatro d'oggi, La Scala, 15 March 1950.

Rudolph Stephan Hoffmann: Ariadne auf Naxos, NMZ, 1917, No. 3, p. 40.

Arthur Jacobs & Stanley Sadie: Ariadne auf

Naxos, in *The Opera Guide*, Hamish Hamilton (London) 1964, p. 336.

Julius Kapp: Entstehung und Wandlungen der Ariadne auf Naxos, *Blätter der Staatsoper* (Berlin), May 1932, p. 2.

Istvan Kertesz: Ariadne Naxos szigeten, *Muzsika*, January 1968, p. 4.

H. Krellmann: Verbundenheit im Nichtverstehen: zur Entstehung der Oper Ariadne auf Naxos, *Deutsche Oper*, No. 11, 1964–5, p. 7.

Else Mayer-Lisman: Introduction to Ariadne auf Naxos, *Opera*, August 1951, p. 21.

Ernest Newman: Ariadne auf Naxos, in *Testament of Music*, Putnam (London) 1962, p. 174.

Stanley Sadie: RS's Ariadne in Naxos, *London Musical Events*, February 1961, p. 12.

Willi Schuh: RS, Ariadne auf Naxos, in *Musik der Zeit*, Vol. 6 (Oper im XX. Jahrhundert), 1954, p. 18.

Max See: Ariadne I oder II?, *NZfM*, July–August 1961.

Henry W. Simon: Ariadne auf Naxos, in *Festival of Opera*, W. H. Allen (London) 1957, p. 44.

Egon Vietta: Die Entstehung der Ariadne im Briefwechsel von Hugo von Hofmannsthal und RS, *Das Musikleben*, July–August 1954, p. 269.

E. Werba: Neueinstudierte Ariadne auf Naxos, *ÖM*, December 1967, p. 754.

Hugo von Hofmannsthal über Ariadne auf Naxos, *Blätter der Staatsoper* (Berlin), October 1926, May 1932 p. 5.

Various contributors: Ariadne auf Naxos, *Opera News*, 16 February 1963.

160b. Le Bourgeois gentilhomme (Der Bürger als Edelmann) Op. 60. Comedy with dances by Molière; free stage adaptation in three acts by Hugo von Hofmannsthal. 1917. (The original incidental music augmented by pieces.)

1. *Overture, Act I*; 2. *Auftritt des Jourdain & Couplet des Jourdain*; 3. *Musikalisches Gespräch*; 4. *Menuett*; 5. *Szene des Fechtmeisters*; 6. *Auftritt und Tanz der Schneider*; 7. *Finale, Act I*; 8. *Prelude, Act II*; 9. *Auftritt des Cleonte*; 10. *Intermezzo, Act II*; 11. *Das Diner*; 12. *Courante (in Canonform)*; 13. *Finale, Act II*; 14. *Prelude (alla Siciliene), Act III*;

15. *Melodram*; 16. *Die türkische Zeremonie*; 17. *Finale, Act III.*

2 fl, pic, 2 ob, 2 cl, 2 bsn; 2 hn, tpt, tmb; timp, glock, side dm, tamb, tgle, GC, cym; piano, hp, strings.

fp: 9 April 1918, Berlin, Deutsches Theater; producer, Max Reinhardt.

Pub. 1918, Fürstner/Boosey & Hawkes. Vocal score, Otto Singer.

160c. Le Bourgeois gentilhomme: Suite Op. 60. For orchestra. 1918. Dur. 35'.

1. *Overture*; 2. *Minuet*; 3. *The fencing master*; 4. *Entry and dance of the tailors*; 5. *Lully's minuet*; 6. *Courante*; 7. *Entry of Cleonte*; 8. *Prelude, Act II*; 9. *Intermezzo*; 10. *The dinner.*

2 fl, pic, 2 ob, 2 cl, 2 bsn; 2 hn, tpt, tmb; timp, glock, side dm, tamb, tgle, GC, cym; hp, piano, strings.

fp: 31 January 1920, Vienna, Vienna Philharmonic Orchestra, cond. Richard Strauss.

fEp: 3 November 1921, Manchester, Halle Orchestra, cond. (Sir) Hamilton Harty.

f London p: 23 November 1922, Queen's Hall, Royal Philharmonic Society concert, cond. Albert Coates.

fEbp: 18 October 1925, Newcastle Station Symphony Orchestra, cond. Edward Clark.

Pub. 1923, Fürstner/Boosey & Hawkes.

161. Festliches Präludium Op. 61. For orchestra. 1913. Composed for the opening of the Konzerthaus, Vienna. Dur. 12'.

4 fl, pic, 4 ob, ca, 4 cl, bcl; 8 hn, 6 tpt, 12(6) distant tpt, 4 tmb, bs tuba; timp, pcssn; organ, strings (96).

fp: 19 October 1913, Vienna, Konzertverein Orchester, cond. Ferdinand Löwe.

fEp: 4 November 1913, Queen's Hall, Royal Philharmonic Society concert, cond. Willem Mengelberg.

f Berlin p: 1 December 1913, Berlin Philharmonic Orchestra, cond. Artur Nikisch.

fEbp: 9 November 1926, Royal Albert Hall, National Orchestra, cond. Richard Strauss.

Pub. 1913, Fürstner/Boosey & Hawkes.

162. Deutsche Motette Op. 62 (F. Rückert). For four soloists and 16-part mixed chorus

a cappella. 1913. Ded. Hugo Rüdel and the Hoftheatersingchor, Berlin.

fp: 2 December 1913, Berlin, Hoftheatersingchor (?Berlin Cathedral Choir), cond. Hugo Rüdel.

Pub. 1913, Fürstner/Boosey & Hawkes. English version, Alfred Kalisch.

163. Tüchtigen stellt das schnelle Glück (Hugo von Hofmannsthal). Cantata for male chorus a cappella. 1914. Ded. Nicolaus Count Seebach on his twentieth anniversary as Generalintendant of the Royal Saxon Court Theatre. Pub. 1935, Juncker & Dünnhaupt (Berlin).

164. Josephslegende Op. 63. Action in one act. 1912–14. Dated: 2 February 1914, Berlin. Scenario: Harry Count Kessler and Hugo von Hofmannsthal. Ded. Edouard Hermann. Dur. 60–65'.

4 fl, pic, 4 ob, heckelphone, 3 cl, bcl, 3 bsn, cbsn; 6 hn, 4 tpt, 4 tmb, tuba, bs tuba; timp, pcssn, xyl; 4 hp, celesta, piano, organ, strings.

fp: 14 May 1914, Paris, Opéra, Diaghilev's Ballet Russe, cond. Richard Strauss; with Maria Kusnetzova (Potpihar's Wife), Leonid Massine (Joseph); choreography, Michel Fokine; scenery, Sert; costumes, Léon Bakst.

fEp: 23 June 1914, Drury Lane, Beecham season, with Leonid Massine, Tamara Karsavina, Mme Fokina.

fGp: 4 February 1921, Berlin, State Opera, cond. Richard Strauss.

Pub. 1914, Fürstner/Boosey & Hawkes. Vocal score, Otto Singer.

BIBLIOGRAPHY:

M.-D. Calvocoressi: RS's Legend of Joseph, *MT*, May 1914, p. 300.

Alfred Heuss: Über die Josephs-Legende von RS—Erstaufführung am Neuen Theater zu Leipzig am 22. Januar, *NZfM*, March (1) 1922, p. 110.

R. S. Hoffmann: Straussens Josefslegende, Feuersnot—Zur Erstaufführung an der Wiener Staatsoper, *Anbruch*, April 1922, p. 110.

Count Harry Kessler: Joseph in opera: Venetian setting of the Bible story, *The Times*, 9 May 1914, p. 6.

William Mann: The Legend of Joseph, in *Decca Book of Ballet*, Muller (London) 1958, p. 295.

Gustav Renker: Der Fall Josephs-Legende, *Berliner Tagblatt*, 1923.

Leopold Schmidt: Die Josephslegende von RS, *Der Kunstwart*, June (2) 1914, p. 402.

— Zu Richard Straussens neuestem Bühnenwerke, *Der Kunstwart*, February (1) 1915, p. 106.

Felix Vogt: Die Uraufführung der Josephslegende von RS in Paris, *Die Musik*, June (1) 1914, p. 312.

Anon.: The new Strauss ballet: first rehearsal impressions, *The Times*, 13 May 1914, p. 7; La Légende de Joseph: brilliant production in Paris, *The Times*, 15 May 1914, p. 7; A medieval Joseph: Strauss's new ballet and its music—spectacular splendours, *The Times*, 24 June 1914, p. 11.

164a. Josephslegende: Symphonic Fragment. For orchestra. 1947. Dur. 20'.

2 fl, 2 ob, 2 cl, 2 bsn; 4 hn, 3 tpt, 3 tmb, tuba; timp, pcssn; 2 hp, strings.

fp: March 1949, Cincinnati, Cincinnati Symphony Orchestra, cond. Fritz Reiner.

fLondon p: 8 November 1953, Royal Festival Hall, London Symphony Orchestra, cond. Sir Eugene Goossens.

Pub. Fürstner/Boosey & Hawkes.

165. Eine Alpensinfonie Op. 64. For orchestra and organ. 1911–15. Dated: 8 February 1915. Ded. Nicolaus Seebach and the Royal Orchestra, Dresden. Dur. 50'.

4 fl, 2 pic, 2 ob, ca, heckelphone, E-flat cl, 2 cl, cl in C or bcl, 4 bsn, cbsn; 8(4) hn, 4 tpt, 4 tmb, 4 tubas, 2 bs tubas; timp, GC, side dm, tgle, tamtam, cowbells, glock, wind & thunder machine; 2 hp, celesta, organ (ad lib). *In addition:* 12 hn, 2 tpt, 2 tmb (offstage, if necessary to be taken from the orchestra).

fp: 28 October 1915, Berlin, Dresden Court Orchestra, cond. Richard Strauss.

fEp: 13 November 1923, Queen's Hall, cond. Aylmer Buesst.

fEbp: 9 November 1926, Royal Albert Hall, National Orchestra, cond. Richard Strauss.

Pub. 1915, Leuckart.

543

Strauss, Richard

BIBLIOGRAPHY:

Friedrich Brandes: Richard Straussens Alpensymphonie, *Deutsche Wille* (Der Kunstwart), December (1) 1915, p. 174.

F. Cattaneo: Eine Alpensymphonie di RS, *Rivista musicale italiana*, March 1924.

Jean Chantavoine: La Symphonie Alpestre de M. RS (première audition à Paris, Salle Gaveau), *Le Ménestrel*, 6 March 1925, p. 114.

Geoffrey Crankshaw: Grandiose peaks, *M&M*, January 1968, p. 43.

Lawrence Gilman: RS and his Alpine symphony, *North American Review*, December 1916, p. 920.

Arthur Hoérée: Symphonie Alpestre par RS, *Beaux Arts*, 1 April 1925, p. 108.

D. G. Mason: Strauss in the Alps, *New Republic*, 13 May 1916, p. 38.

Ernest Newman: Strauss's new Symphony, in *Testament of Music*, Putnam (London) 1962, p. 179.

Christopher Palmer: Strauss's Alpine Symphony, *MR*, May 1968, p. 106.

André Schaeffner: L'Alpensinfonie de RS, *RM*, 1 May 1925, p. 173.

166. Die Frau ohne Schatten Op. 65. Opera in three acts. 1914–18. Dated: February 1918, Garmisch. Text: Hugo von Hofmannsthal. Dur. 201′.

4 fl, 2 pic, 3 ob, ca, cl in E-flat, cl in D, 2 cl in C, basset hn, bcl, 4 bsn, cbsn; 8 hn (2 tubas in F, 2 tubas in B flat), 4 tpt, 4 tmb, bs tuba; timp, pcssn, glock, 4 Chinese gongs; 2 hp, 2 celestas, glass harmonica, strings. *Stage music:* 2 fl, ob, 2 cl in C, bsn; hn, 6 tpt, 6 tmb; 4 tamtams, organ.

fp: 10 October 1919, Vienna, State Opera, cond. Franz Schalk; with Maria Jeritza (Empress), Lotte Lehmann (Barak's Wife), Lucy Weidt (Nurse), Aagard Oestvig (Emperor), Richard Mayr (Barak), Josef von Manowarda (Messenger); producer, Hans Breuer; design, Alfred Roller.

Pub. ?1919, Fürstner/Boosey & Hawkes. Vocal, score, Otto Singer.

BIBLIOGRAPHY:

Günther Baum: Zur Entstehung von Strauss-Hofmannsthals Frau ohne Schatten, *NZfM*, November 1956.

Heinrich Blabecker: RS, Die Frau ohne Schatten, *NMZ*, 1920, No. 5, p. 76.

Eric Blom: Die Frau ohne Schatten, *MO*, May 1921, p. 692.

E. Valenti Ferro: La Mujer sin Sombra, triunfo de la musica, *Buenos Aires Musical*, No. 334 (1965), p. 1.

Erich Graf: Zur Thematik der Frau ohne Schatten, *ÖM*, May–June 1964.

Theodor Helm: Die Frau ohne Schatten—Uraufführung im Wiener Operntheater am 10. Oktober 1919, *NZfM*, 6 November 1919, p. 275.

Donald Mitchell: Die Frau ohne Schatten, *The Listener*, 17 April 1958, p. 673.

Walter Petzet: Die Frau ohne Schatten, *Signale*, 1927, No. 12, p. 410.

Heinz Röttger: Das Formproblem bei RS gezeigt an der Oper Die Frau ohne Schatten mit Einschluss von Guntram und Intermezzo, Munich, 1937.

Edward Sackville-West: Strauss, Hofmannsthal and Die Frau ohne Schatten, *Opera*, December 1953, p. 725.

Gustav Samazeuilh: La Femme sans ombre, *RM*, June 1938, p. 364.

Lynn Snook: The myth and the 'Shadow', *Opera*, June 1967, p. 470.

Roland Tenschert: Die Frau ohne Schatten, *ÖM*, May 1953.

Claude Trevor: Strauss's new opera, *MS*, 3 July 1920, p. 6.

Adolf Weissmann: Die Frau ohne Schatten, *Anbruch*, May 1920, p. 344.

Egon Wellesz: Die Frau ohne Schatten, *Anbruch*, November 1919, p. 10.

Various contributors: Die Frau ohne Schatten, *Opera News*, 17 December 1966.

166a. Die Frau ohne Schatten: Fantasy. For orchestra. 1946. Ded. Manfred von Mautner-Markhoff. Dur. 14–19′.

3 fl, 3 ob, 3 cl, 3 bsn; 4 hn, 3 tpt, 3 tmb, tuba; timp, pcssn; celesta, hp, strings.

fp: 26 June 1947, Vienna, Vienna Symphony Orchestra, cond. Karl Böhm.

fEp: 5 October 1947, Drury Lane Theatre, Royal Philharmonic Orchestra, cond. Norman Del Mar.

Pub. Fürstner/Boosey & Hawkes.

167. Krämerspiegel Op. 66 (Alfred Kerr).

For voice and piano. 1918. Ded. Dr. Friedrich Rösch.

1. *Es war einmal ein Bock*; 2. *Einst kam der Bock als Bote*; 3. *Es liebt einst ein Hase*; 4. *Drei Masken*; 5. *Hast du ein Tongedicht vollbracht*; 6. *O lieber Künstler*; 7. *Unser Feind*; 8. *Von Händlern wird die Kunst bedroht*; 9. *Es war mal eine Wanze*; 10 *Die Künstler sind Schöpfer*; 11. *Der Händler und die Macher*; 12. *O Schröpferschwarm.*

fp: 1 November 1926, Berlin, Sigrid Johannsen, acc. Michael Raucheisen.

Pub. 1921, Cassirer: limited edition; 1959, Boosey & Hawkes.

BIBLIOGRAPHY:
Strauss und Kerr über den Krämerspiegel, *Strauss*, No. 48, March 1966, p. 16.

168. Sechs Lieder Op. 67. For voice and piano. 1918.
I. *Lieder der Ophelia* (Shakespeare):

1. *Wie erkenn' ich mein Treulieb?*; 2. *Guten Morgen, 's ist Sankt Valentinstag*; 3. *Sie trugen ihn auf der Bahre bloss.*
II. *Aus den Büchern des Unmuts des Rendsch Nameh* (Goethe):

4. *Wer wird von der Welt verlangen*; 2. *Hab' ich euch denn je geraten*; 6. *Wanderers Gemütsruhe.*

fp (II only): 27 June 1919, Dresden, Mary Grasenick.

Pub. Bote & Bock.

169. Sechs Lieder Op. 68 (Clemens Brentano). For high voice and piano. Ded. Elisabeth Schumann.

1. *An die Nacht*; 2. *Ich wollt' ein Sträusslein binden*; 3. *Säusle, liebe Myrthe*; 4. *Als mir dein Lied erklang*; 5. *Amor*; 6. *Lied der Frauen.*

fp (Nos. 1–5): 30 May 1919, Berlin, Birgitt Engell, acc. Georg Schumann.

fp (No. 6): 29 September 1920, Dresden, Mary Gravenick, acc. Alfred Klietmann.

Pub. Fürstner/Boosey & Hawkes.

169a. Brentano Lieder Op. 68. Version with orchestra. 1940. No. 6 orch. 1933.

fp: 9 February 1941, Düsseldorf, Erna Schlüter.

fEbp: 9 February 1962, Barbara Holt and the BBC Scottish Orchestra, cond. Norman Del Mar.

170. Fünf kleine Lieder Op. 69. For voice and piano. 1918.

1. *Der Stern* (A. von Arnim).
2. *Der Pokal* (A. von Arnim).
3. *Einerlei* (A. von Arnim).
4. *Waldesfahrt* (Heine).
5. *Schlechtes Wetter* (Heine).
Pub. Fürstner/Boosey & Hawkes.

171. Sinnspruch ('Alle Menschen gross und klein') (Goethe). For voice and piano. 1919. Pub. 1920, Mosse (Almanac); 1959–60, in *Richard Strauss Jahrbuch.*

172. Drei Hymnen Op. 71 (Hölderlin). For high voice and orchestra. 1921. Ded. Minnie Untermayr.

1. *Hymne an die Liebe*. Dated: 6 April 1921, Vienna. Dur. 10'.
2. *Rückkehr in die Heimat*. Dated: 2 January 1921, Vienna. Dur. 10'.
3. *Die Liebe*. Dated: 20 January 1921, Vienna. Dur. 9'.

fp: 9 November 1921, Berlin, Barbara Kemp and the Berlin Philharmonic Orchestra, cond. Gustav Brecher.

fEp: 21 October 1931, BBC concert, Margarete Teschemacher and the BBC Symphony Orchestra, cond. Richard Strauss.

Pub. 1921, Fürstner/Boosey & Hawkes. Vocal score, Otto Singer.

173. Schlagobers Op. 70. Gay Viennese Ballet in two acts. 1921–2. Dated: 16 October 1922, Garmisch. Ded. Ludwig Karpath. Dur. 90'.

4 fl, pic, 3 ob, 3 cl, bcl, 3 bsn, cbsn; 4 hn, 3 tpt, 3 tmb, bs tuba; timp, pcssn; 2 hp, celesta, strings.

fp: 9 May 1924, Vienna, State Opera, cond. Richard Strauss.

fGp: 9 October 1924, Breslau, Stadttheater, cond. Richard Strauss.

Pub. 1923, Fürstner/Boosey & Hawkes; incl. piano reduction by Otto Singer.

173a. Schlagobers: Suite. 1932. Dur. 25'.

fEp: 15 December 1932, Manchester, Halle Orchestra, cond. Sir Hamilton Harty.

fEbp: 9 April 1933, BBC Orchestra, cond. Sir Adrian Boult.

Pub. Fürstner/Boosey & Hawkes.

Strauss, Richard

BIBLIOGRAPHY:

Ernst Decsey: Schlagobers, *Die Musik*, June 1924, p. 665.

P. Gorini: Panna montata (Schlagobers) di RS, *Il Pensiero musicale*, May–June 1924.

R. S. Hoffmann: Schlagobers von RS, *Anbruch*, May 1924, p. 203.

— Schlagobers von RS—Zur Uraufführung in Wien, *NMZ*, 1924, No. 5, p. 118.

O. Mancini: RS e la panna montata, *Rivista nazionale di musica*, 1 January 1933.

Ferdinand Scherber: Das neue Strauss-Ballett, *Signale*, 28 May 1924 (No. 22), p. 11.

174. Hans Adam war ein Erdenkloss (Goethe). For bass and piano. 1922. Ded. Michael Bohnen. Pub. 1951, Oertel; 1964, Boosey & Hawkes (as Op. 87 No. 1).

175. Tanzsuite. After keyboard pieces by François Couperin, assembled and arranged by Richard Strauss for small orchestra. 1922–3. Dur. 25–30′.

1. *Pavane*; 2. *Courante*; 3. *Carillon*; 4. *Sarabande*; 5. *Gavotte*; 6. *Tourbillon*; 7. *Allemande e Minuet*; 8. *March*.

2 fl, 2 ob, ca, 2 cl, 2 bsn; 2 hn, tpt, tmb, glock, tamb; hp, hpschd, celesta, strings (4-3-2-2-2).

fp (ballet): 17 February 1923, Vienna, Hofburg (Redoutensaal), Vienna State Opera, cond. Clemens Krauss.

fp (concert): 21 December 1923, Dresden, State Orchestra, cond. Fritz Busch.

fEp: 13 January 1926, 2LO broadcast, Wireless Symphony Orchestra, cond. Percy Pitt. (NB: Originally announced for a 5XX High Power Programme, Daventry, on 1 September 1925, but evidently not transmitted.)

Pub. 1923, Leuckart; ?Fürstner.

176. Intermezzo Op. 72. A Bourgeois Comedy with symphonic interludes in two acts. 1918–23. Dated: 21 August 1923, Buenos Aires. Ded. to the composer's son, Franz Strauss. Dur. 115′.

2 fl, pic, 2 ob, ca, 2 cl, bcl, 2 bsn; 3 hn, 2 tpt, 2 tmb; timp, pcssn; hp, piano, hmnm, strings.

fp: 4 November 1924, Dresden, Schauspielhaus, State Opera, cond. Fritz Busch; with Lotte Lehmann (Christine), Liesel von Schuch (Anna), Josef Correck (Storch), Theo Strack (Lummer); design, Adolf Mahnke.

Pub. 1924, Fürstner/Boosey & Hawkes. Vocal score, Otto Singer.

BIBLIOGRAPHY:

Prof. Besser: Intermezzo von RS, *Signale*, 1924, No. 52, p. 2031.

Max Chop: Erstaufführung von RS' Intermezzo an der Berliner Staatsoder, *Signale*, 1925, No. 14, p. 590.

Erich Graf: Die Bedeutung von RS' Intermezzo, *ÖM*, May 1963.

Julius Kapp: Einführung in das Werk, *Blätter der Staatsoper* (Berlin), March 1925, p. 7.

William Mann: Intermezzo, *M&M*, December 1964, p. 14.

Heinrich Platzbecker: Intermezzo von RS—Uraufführung in der Dresdner Staatsoper, *NMZ*, 1925, No. 5, p. 116.

Harold Rosenthal: New light on Intermezzo, *Opera*, September 1965, p. 626.

P. Schwers: Intermezzo von RS, *AMZ*, 14 November 1924.

Eugen Schmitz: Das Intermezzo von RS, *Die Musik*, December 1924, p. 199.

Otto Siegl: RS' Intermezzo, *Musikbote*, December 1924.

Paul Stefan: RS, Das Intermezzo, einer Demission, *Anbruch*, November–December 1924, p. 412.

Richard Strauss: RS über das Stilproblem seines Intermezzo, *Melos*, 17 October 1924.

— Vorwort zu Intermezzo, *Ausblick* (Blätter der Dresdener Staatstheater), November 1924; *Blätter der Staatsoper* (Berlin), October 1924 p. 16, March 1925 p. 1.

Wilh. Virneisel: RS' Intermezzo, *NZfM*, 1929, March, p. 131, April, p. 201.

Adolf Weissmann: L'Intermezzo di RS alla Staatsoper di Dresda, *Musica d'oggi*, January 1925, p. 6.

176a. Vier sinfonische Zwischenspiele aus Intermezzo. Dur. 25′.

1. *Reisefieber und Walzerszene*; 2. *Träumerei am Kamin*; 3. *Am Spieltisch*; 4. *Fröhlicher Beschluss*.

fEp: 24 May 1931, BBC broadcast, BBC Orchestra, cond. (Sir) Eugene Goossens.

fEp (concert): 1 September 1932, Queen's

Hall, Promenade Concert, BBC Symphony Orchestra, cond. Sir Henry Wood.

Pub. Fürstner/Boosey & Hawkes.

177. Hochzeitspräludium. For two harmoniums. 1924. Composed for the wedding of Franz and Alice Strauss.

fp: 15 January 1924, Vienna, Karl Alwin and Prof. Friedel.

fp (public): 4 May 1948, Vienna, Louis Dité and Adolf Broschek.

Pub. January 1924, in *Neue Freie Presse* (Vienna).

178. Wiener Philharmoniker-Fanfare. For brass and timpani. 1924. Ded Vienna Philharmonic Orchestra.

6 tpt, 8 hn, 6 tmb, 2 bs tuba; timp.

fp: 4 March 1924, first Vienna Philharmonic Ball.

Pub. 1961, Boosey & Hawkes.

179. Wiener Rathaus-Fanfare. For brass and timpani. 1924. Composed for the opening of Vienna Music Week.

6 tpt, 8 hn, 6 tmb, 4 bs tuba; timp.

fp: 14 September 1924, Vienna, Rathaus tower.

Pub. 1961, Boosey & Hawkes.

180. Die Ruinen von Athen. Beethoven, newly edited and revised by Hugo von Hofmannsthal and Richard Strauss. 1924.

fp: 20 September 1924, Vienna, State Opera, cond. Richard Strauss.

Pub. Fürstner/Boosey & Hawkes.

181. Parergon zur Sinfonia domestica Op. 73. For piano left hand and orchestra. 1924–5. Ded. Paul Wittgenstein. Dur. 25'.

2 fl, 2 ob, ca, 2 cl, bcl, 2 bsn, cbsn; 4 hn, 2 tpt, 3 tmb, bs tuba; timp; hp, strings.

fp: 6 (?16) October 1925, Dresden, Paul Wittgenstein and the Saxon State Orchestra, cond. Fritz Busch.

fEp: 25 August 1928, Queen's Hall, Promenade Concert, Paul Wittgenstein and the Wood Symphony Orchestra, cond. Sir Henry Wood.

'Exclusive property of Herr Paul Wittgenstein.' Private print, pub. 1950, Boosey & Hawkes.

BIBLIOGRAPHY:

Donald F. Tovey: Parergon to the Sinfonia Domestica for pianoforte with orchestra in E, in *EMA*, Vol. 3, O.U.P. (London) 1936, p. 200.

182. Durch allen Schall und Klang (Goethe). For voice and piano. 1925. Ded. Romain Rolland on his sixtieth birthday (29 January 1926). Pub. Rotapfel ('Liber Amicorum Romain Rolland'); 1959–60, in *Richard Strauss Jahrbuch*.

183. Aus dem westöstlichen Divan (Goethe). For voice and piano. Dated: 11 June 1925, Garmisch. Pub. 1949, in *Tempo*, No. 12 (same work as preceding).

BIBLIOGRAPHY:

Willi Schuh: A forgotten Goethe song, *Tempo*, No. 12, summer 1949, p. 20.

184. Military March in F. 1925. Composed for the film 'Der Rosenkavalier' (script, Hugo von Hofmannsthal; director, Robert Wiene; musical arrangement, Alwin and Singer).

fp: 10 January 1926, Dresden, State Opera, Saxon State Orchestra, cond. Richard Strauss.

fEbp: 12 April 1926, BBC broadcast, cond. Richard Strauss.

Pub. Fürstner/Boosey & Hawkes.

185. Panathenäenzug Op. 74. Symphonic Etudes in the form of a Passacaglia for piano left hand and orchestra. 1926–7. Dated: 14 February 1927, Vienna. Ded. Paul Wittgenstein. Dur. 20'.

3 fl, pic, 2 ob, ca, 2 cl, bcl, 2 bsn, cbsn; 4 hn, 3 tpt, 3 tmb, bs tuba; timp, pcssn; celesta, hp, strings.

fp: 11 March 1928, Vienna, Paul Wittgenstein and the Vienna Philharmonic Orchestra, cond. Franz Schalk.

fEp: 13 September 1954, BBC broadcast, Gordon Watson and the BBC Scottish Orchestra, cond. Ian Whyte.

'Exclusive property of Herr Paul Wittgenstein.' Private print, pub. 1950, 1953 (reduction), Boosey & Hawkes.

186. Die ägyptische Helena Op. 75. Opera in two acts. 1924–7. Dated: 8 October 1927, Garmisch. Dur. 130'.

4 fl, 2 pic, 2 ob, ca, cl in C, 2 cl, bcl, 3 bsn, cbsn; 6 hn, 6 tpt, 3 tmb, bs tuba; timp, pcssn; 2 hp, celesta, organ, strings. *Stage music:*

6 ob, 6 cl, 4 hn, 2 tpt, 4 tmb, pcssn, wind machine.

fp: 6 June 1928, Dresden, State Opera, cond. Fritz Busch; with Elisabeth Rethberg (Helena), Maria Rajdl (Aithra), Helene Jung (Sea-shell), Curt Taucher (Menelaus), Friedrich Plaschke (Altair), Guglielmo Fazzini (Da-ud); producer, Otto Erhardt; décor, Leonhard Fanto.

Revised version. 1932–3. Dur. 125'.

fp: 14 August 1933, Salzburg, Festspielhaus, cond. Clemens Krauss; producer, Lothar Wallerstein.

Pub. 1928, Fürstner/Boosey & Hawkes. Vocal score, Otto Singer.

BIBLIOGRAPHY:

E. Bonner: Much ado about Helena— première of Die ägyptische Helena, *Outlook*, 21 March 1928, p. 466.

— Egyptian Helen comes to Vienna, *Outlook*, 11 July 1928, p. 426.

Max Chop: RS, Die ägyptische Helena, *Signale*, 1928, No. 42, p. 1249.

Hermann Fähnrich: Dreimal Helena—Die Helena-Tragödie von Euripides, Goethe und RS, *NZfM*, January 1959.

Hugo von Hofmannsthal: Die ägyptische Helena, *Schallkiste*, June 1928.

— Writing of Egyptian Helen, *Dial*, August 1928, p. 147.

— Hugo von Hofmannsthal über die Dichtung, *Blätter der Staatsoper* (Berlin), October 1928, p. 4.

— The Egyptian Helen, *Journal of Aesthetics*, December 1956, p. 205.

Julius Kapp: Einführung in die Oper, *Blätter der Staatsoper* (Berlin), October 1928, p. 12.

Walter Petzet: Die ägyptische Helene, *Signale*, 1928, No. 24, p. 774.

Eugen Schmitz: Die ägyptische Helene— Uraufführung der neuen Oper von RS im Dresdner Opernhaus, *Die Musik*, July 1928, p. 741.

Erich Steinhard: RS, Ägyptische Helena, *Der Auftakt*, 1928, No. 7, p. 150.

Richard Strauss: RS über das Werk, *Blätter der Staatsoper* (Berlin), October 1928, p. 2.

187. Die Tageszeiten Op. 76 (Joseph von Eichendorff). Song cycle for male chorus and orchestra. 1927 (?1927–8). Ded. Vienna

Schubert-Bund and its conductor Viktor Keldorfer. Dur. 30'.

1. *Der Morgen*; 2. *Mittagsruh*; 3. *Der Abend*; 4. *Die Nacht*.

2 fl, 2 ob, ca, 2 cl, bcl, 2 bsn, cbsn; 4 hn, 2 tpt, 3 tmb; timp, pcssn; hp, organ, strings.

fp: 21 July 1928, Vienna, Schubert-Bund and Wiener Symphonie-Orchester, cond. Viktor Keldorfer.

fEp: 24 November 1928, Huddersfield, Home Valley Male Voice Choir and the Halle Orchestra, cond. Irving Silverwood; sung in an English translation by Rosa Newmarch.

Pub. 1928, Leuckart.

BIBLIOGRAPHY:

Viktor Keldorfer: Les heures du jour (Tageszeiten) de RS, *Feuilles musicales*, August–September 1959.

Ferdinand Scherber: RS, Die Tageszeiten, *Signale*, 1928, No. 31, p. 929.

188. Gesänge des Orients Op. 77 (Hans Bethge). For voice and piano. 1927 (?1928).

1. *Ihre Augen*; 2. *Schwung*; 3. *Liebesgeschenke*; 4. *Die Allmächtige*; 5. *Huldigung*.

fp: 5 June 1929, Vienna, Koloman von Pataky, acc. Richard Strauss.

Pub. 1929, Leuckart: English version, Rosa Newmarch; French version, J. Bevet.

189. Austria Op. 78 (Anton Wildgans). Austrian song for orchestra and male chorus. 1929. Ded. Wiener Männergesangverein.

3 fl, 2 ob, ca, 2 cl, bcl, 2 bsn, cbsn; 4 hn, 4 tpt, 3 tmb, tuba; timp, cym; 2 hp, strings.

fp: 10 (?20) January 1930, Vienna, Männergesangverein, cond. Richard Strauss (?F. Grossmann).

Pub. 1930, Bote & Bock. Vocal score, Otto Singer.

BIBLIOGRAPHY:

Ferdinand Scherber: RS, Österreichisches Lied, *Signale*, 29 January 1930, No. 5, p. 111.

190. Idomeneo. Mozart, newly arranged by Richard Strauss and Lothar Wallerstein. 1930.

fp: 16 April 1931, Vienna, State Opera, cond. Richard Strauss.

Pub. Heinrichshofen.

BIBLIOGRAPHY:

Walther Hirschberg: Mozart–Strauss Idomeneo—Erstaufführung in der Berliner Staatsoper, 1932, No. 47, p. 909.

191. Arabella Op. 79. Lyrical comedy in three acts. 1929–32. Dated: 12 October 1932, Garmisch. Text: Hugo von Hofmannsthal. Ded. Alfred Reucker and Fritz Busch. Dur. 155′.

3 fl, pic, 2 ob, ca, cl in C, 2 cl, bcl, 3 bsn, cbsn; 4 hn, 3 tpt, 3 tmb, bs tuba; timp, pcssn; hp, strings.

fp: 1 July 1933, Dresden, State Opera, cond. Clemens Krauss; with Viorica Ursuleac (Arabella), Margit Bokor (Zdenka), Camilla Kallab (Adelaide), Elice Illiard (Fiakermilli), Alfred Jerger (Mandryka), Friedrich Plaschke (Waldner), Martin Kremer (Matteo); producer, Josef Gielen; design, Leonhard Fanto.

fEp: 17 May 1934, Covent Garden, cond. Clemens Krauss; with Viorica Ursuleac (Arabella), Margit Bokor (Zdenka), Ruth Berglund (Adelaide), Elice Illiard (Fiakermilli), Alfred Jerger (Mandryka), Berthold Sterneck (Waldner), Martin Kremer (Matteo); producer, Otto Erhardt; design, Benno von Arent.

Pub. 1933, Fürstner/Boosey & Hawkes. Vocal score, Felix Wolfes.

BIBLIOGRAPHY:
Joseph Gregor: Arabella, ÖM, 1947, Nos. 7–8, p. 188.
Ralph Hill: RS's Arabella, *Gramophone Record*, November 1933, p. 7.
Alan Jefferson: An introduction to Arabella, *Opera*, January 1965, p. 9.
William Mann: Two of Strauss's later operas, *Opera*, September 1953, p. 523.
W. Petzet: Arabella, Oper von RS, *Signale*, 5–12 July 1933.
Hans F. Redlich: RS, Arabella (Première audition à l'Opéra de Dresden), *RM*, September–October 1933, p. 212.
Eugen Schmitz: Arabella, die neue Oper von RS, *Die Musik*, August 1933, p. 842.
Henry W. Simon: Arabella, in *Festival of Opera*, W. H. Allen (London) 1957, p. 40.
Paul Stefan: Arabella, *Anbruch*, November–December 1933, p. 143.
Roland Tenschert: Arabella, die letzte Gemeinschaftsarbeit von Hugo von Hofmannsthal und RS, ÖM, July–August 1958.

John S. Weissmann: Strauss's Arabella at Covent Garden, *Tempo*, No. 72, spring 1965, p. 18.
— Arabella di Strauss al Covent Garden, *Musica d'oggi*, 1965, No. 3, p. 80.
Anon.: Arabella—Strauss Richard bemutató az Operaházban, *A Zene*, 15 January 1935, p. 135.
Anon.: The last great singing opera, *Music Magazine*, January 1965, p. 10.
Various contributors: Arabella, issues of *Opera News*, 21 February 1955, 4 February 1957, 21 January 1961, 18 December 1965.

192. Das Bächlein (attrib. Goethe). For voice and piano. 1933. Pub. 1951, Universal-Edition; 1964, Boosey & Hawkes (as Op. 88 No. 1, together with the Weinheber Songs of 1942).

192a. Das Bächlein. Version with orchestra. 1935. Written for Viorica Ursuleac.

fp: 19 June 1942, Berlin, Viorica Ursuleac and the Berlin Philharmonic Orchestra, cond. Clemens Krauss.

Pub. Boosey & Hawkes.

193. Drei Lieder (Rückert). For voice and piano. 1929–35.
1. *Von künftigen Alter.* 1929.
2. *Und dann nicht mehr.* 1929.
3. *Im Sonnenschein.* 1935.

Pub. Universal-Edition (as Op. 87 Nos. 1, 3, 4).

194. Die schweigsame Frau Op. 80. Comic opera in three acts. 1932–5. Dated: 20 October 1934, Garmisch. Overture dated: 17 January 1935, Garmisch. Text: Stefan Zweig, freely adapted from Ben Jonson. Dur. 175′.

3 fl, 3 pic, 2 ob, ca, cl in D, 2 cl, bcl, 3 bsn, cbsn; 4 hn, 3 tpt, 3 tmb, bs tuba; timp, pcssn; 4 bells, hp, celesta, hpschd, organ, strings.

fp: 24 June 1935, Dresden, State Opera, cond. Karl Böhm; with Maria Cebotari (Aminta), Friedrich Plaschke (Morosus), Martin Kremer (Henry), Mathieu Ahlersmeyer (Barber).

fEp: 20 November 1961, Covent Garden, cond. Rudolf Kempe; with Barbara Holt (Aminta), David Ward (Morosus), Kenneth

549

Macdonald (Henry), Joseph Ward (Razor-blade); producer, Franz Josef Wild; design, Martin Battersby.

Pub. 1935, Fürstner/Boosey & Hawkes. Vocal score, Felix Wolfes.

BIBLIOGRAPHY:

E. Downes: A witty Strauss, *New York Times*, 5 October 1958, Section 2, p. 9.

Norman Feasey: The Silent Woman: an introduction, *Opera*, November 1961, p. 692.

Willi Reich: RS-Premiere in Dresden, *Anbruch*, June–July 1935, p. 194.

— RS, La Femme Silencieuse, première audition à Dresde, *RM*, September–October 1935, p. 232.

John S. Weissmann: RS at Covent Garden—English première of Die schweigsame Frau, *Musical Events*, January 1962, p. 6.

Anon.: Die schweigsame Frau (synopsis), *The Listener*, 29 October 1959, p. 752.

194a. Potpourri (Overture to 'Die schweigsame Frau'). 1935. Dur. 4'.

fEbp: 19 January 1936, BBC Orchestra, cond. Oswald Kabasta.

Pub. Fürstner.

195. Die Göttin im Putzzimmer (Rückert). For 8-part mixed chorus a cappella. 1935. Dur. 9'.

fp: 2 March 1952, Vienna, State Opera Chorus, cond. Clemens Krauss.

Pub. 1958, Boosey.

196. Zugemessne Rhythmen (Goethe). For voice and piano. 1935. Ded. Peter Raabe. Pub. 1954, in *Strauss Jahrbuch*.

197. Drei Männerchore (Rückert). A cappella. 1935.

1. *Vor den Türen*; 2. *Traumlicht*; 3. *Fröhlich im Maien*.

fp: 5 April 1936, Cologne, Kölner Männergesangverein, cond. Eugen Papst.

Pub. 1958, Leuckart.

198. Olympische Hymne (Robert Lubahn). For mixed chorus and orchestra. 1936 (?1934). Dur. 4'.

3 fl, 3 ob, 3 cl, 3 bsn; 4 hn, 6 tpt, 6 tmb, 2 tuba; timp, pcssn; strings; 4 offstage tpt.

fp: 1 August 1936, Berlin, Olympiade opening ceremony, cond. Richard Strauss.

Pub. 1936, Fürstner/Boosey & Hawkes. Incl. arr. for male chorus, or voice, and piano.

BIBLIOGRAPHY:

Wolfgang von Bartels: Olympiahymne von RS und Paul Winters Olympia-fanfaren, *NZfM*, September 1936, p. 1100.

199. Friedenstag Op. 81. Opera in one act. 1935–6. Dated: 16 June 1936. Text: Joseph Gregor. Ded. Viorica Ursuleac and Clemens Krauss. Dur. 80'.

3 fl, 2 ob, ca, cl in C, 2 cl, bcl, 3 bsn, cbsn; 6 hn, 4 tpt, 4 tmb, bs tuba; timp, pcssn; strings. *Stage music:* bells, organ.

fp: 24 July 1938, Munich, State Opera (National Theatre), cond. Clemens Krauss; with Viorica Ursuleac (Maria), Hans Hotter (Commandant), Ludwig Weber (Holsteiner), Georg Hann (Sergeant-Major), Julius Patzak (Private), Peter Anders (Piedmontese); producer, Rudolf Hartmann.

Pub. 1938, Fürstner/Boosey & Hawkes. Vocal score, Ernst Gernot Klussmann.

BIBLIOGRAPHY:

E. H. Müller von Asow: Zu RS' unveröffentlichtem Opus 81, *Musikerziehung*, June 1960, p. 235; *Musikhändel*, 1960, No. 3, p. 116.

Herbert Gerigk: Friedenstag, RS—Uraufführung im München, *Die Musik*, August 1938, p. 769.

Harald Kaufmann: Ästhetische Manipulationen im Friedenstag von RS, *NZfM*, July–August 1961.

O. von Pander: Der Friedenstag von RS, *SM*, June 1938.

Gustave Samazeuilh: Jour de Paix de RS, *Le Temps*, 13 August 1938.

— Daphne et Jour de Paix de Strauss à Dresde, *Le Temps*, 5 November 1938.

Speculum: Jour de Paix, *La Rassegna musicale*, May–June 1938.

200. Daphne Op. 82. Bucolic Tragedy in one act. 1936–7. Dated: 24 December 1937, Taormina. Text: Joseph Gregor. Ded. Karl Böhm. Dur. 100'.

3 fl, pic, 2 ob, ca, cl in C, 2 cl, basset hn, bcl, 3 bsn, cbsn; 4 hn, 3 tpt, 3 tmb, bs tuba; timp, pcssn; 2 hp, strings. *Stage music:* Alphorn, organ.

fp: 15 October 1938, Dresden, Saxon State Opera, cond. Karl Böhm; with Margarete Teschemacher (Daphne), Helene Jung (Gaea), Torsten Ralf (Apollo), Martin Kremer (Leukippos), Sven Nilsson (Peneios); design, Leonhard Fanto.

fEp (concert, excerpts only): 9 April 1951, Royal Albert Hall, Elisabeth Schwarzkopf and the Philharmonia Orchestra, cond. Paul Kletzki.

Pub. 1938, Ortel; Schott/Boosey & Hawkes. Vocal score, Ernst Gernot Klussmann.

BIBLIOGRAPHY:

Alfred Burgatz: Der Motivkranz des Straussischen Daphne, *Die Musik*, April 1939, p. 451.

André Coeuroy: Daphne de RS, *Beaux Arts*, 11 November 1938.

H. Gerigk: Daphne von RS, *Die Musik*, October 1938.

Gustave Samazeuilh: Daphne et Jour de Paix de Strauss à Dresde, *Le Temps*, 5 November 1938.

Malcolm Rayment: Maiden into tree, *R&R*, June 1965, p. 19.

Eugen Schmitz: RS' Daphne, Uraufführung in Dresden, *NZfM*, November 1938, p. 1225.

201. Durch Einsamkeiten (Anton Wildgans). For male chorus a cappella. 1938 (?1939). Composed for the seventy-fifth anniversary of the Vienna Schubert-Bund.

fp: 1 April 1939, Vienna, Wiener Schubert-Bund, cond. Otto Nurrer.

Unpub.

202. München. Occasional Waltz for orchestra. 1938–9. First version. Dur. 4½′. Unpub.

3 fl, pic, 2 ob, E-flat cl, 2 cl, 2 bsn, cbsn; 4 hn, 3 tpt, 3 tmb, tuba; timp, glock; hp, strings.

fp: 24 May 1939, Munich.

202a. München. Second version, 1945. Dur. 9–10′. Instrumentation as for No. 202. Dur. 10′.

fp: 31 March 1951, Vienna, Vienna Symphony Orchestra, cond. Fritz Lehmann.

fEp: 13 March 1955, Royal Festival Hall, Philharmonia Orchestra, cond. Norman Del Mar.

Pub. 1951, Fürstner.

203. Die Liebe der Danae Op. 83. 'Heitere Mythologie' in three acts. 1938–40. Dated: 28 June 1940, Garmisch. Text: Joseph Gregor, from a draft by Hugo von Hofmannsthal. Ded. Heinz Tietjen. Dur. 165′.

3 fl, pic, 2 ob, ca, 3 cl, basset hn, bcl, 3 bsn, cbsn; 6 hn, 4 tpt, 4 tmb, tuba; timp, pcssn; 2 hp, celesta, piano, strings.

fp: 16 August 1944, dress rehearsal for cancelled world première, Salzburg, Festspielhaus, cond. Clemens Krauss; with Viorica Ursuleac (Danae), Horst Taubmann (Midas), Hans Hotter (Jupiter); producer, Rudolf Hartmann; design, Emil Preetorius.

f public p: 14 August 1952, Salzburg Festspielhaus, cond. Clemens Krauss; with Annelies Kupper (Danae), Josef Gostić (Midas), Paul Schöffler (Jupiter); producer, Rudolf Hartmann; design, Emil Preetorius.

fEp: 16 September 1953, Covent Garden, Bavarian State Opera, cond. Rudolf Kempe; with Annelies Kupper (Danae), Howard Vandenburg (Midas), Ferdinand Frantz (Jupiter); producer, Rudolf Hartmann; scenery, Helmut Jürgens; costumes, Rosemary Jakameit.

Pub. 1944, Oertel.

BIBLIOGRAPHY:

Everett Helm: Die Liebe der Danae, *Musical America*, October 1952, p. 5.

Rudolf Hartmann: Erinnerungen an die Einstudierung von RS' Oper Die Liebe der Danae in Salzburg im Jahre 1944, *SM*, June 1952, p. 241.

Andrew Porter: Die Liebe der Danae, *London Musical Events*, October 1952, p. 32.

Willi Reich: Die letzte RS-Première, *Neue Schweizer Rundschau*, Vol. 20 (1952–3), p. 311.

Evelyn Reuter: L'Amour de Danaé de RS, *RM* (Les Carnets Critiques), 1952, p. 21.

K. H. Ruppel: Die Liebe der Danae, keine heitere Mythologie, *Melos*, September 1952, p. 255.

Roland Tenschert: Zu RS' Oper Die Liebe der Danae, *SM*, October 1952, p. 403.

Kurt Westphal: Die Liebe der Danae in Berlin *Musikleben*, December 1952, p. 369.

203a. Die Liebe der Danae: Symphonic

Fragment. For orchestra. Arr. posthumously by Clemens Krauss. Dur. $13\frac{1}{2}'$.

3 fl, pic, ca, 3 cl, corno di bassetto, bcl, 3 bsn, cbsn; 6 hn, 3 tpt, 3 tmb, tuba; timp, GC, cym, celesta, glock; 2 hp, strings.

fp: 14 November 1952, London, Royal Albert Hall, Vienna Philharmonic Orchestra, cond. Clemens Krauss.

Pub. 1954, Hawkes.

204. Japanische Festmusik Op. 84. For orchestra. 1940. Composed for the celebration of the 2,600th anniversary of the Japanese Empire. Dur. 15'.

3 fl, 2 ob, ca, 4 cl, bcl, 3 bsn, cbsn; 8 hn, 7 tpt, 8 tmb, 2 tubas; 2 hp, timp, pcssn; organ, strings.

fp: 11 December 1940, Tokyo, United Symphony Orchestra, cond. Helmut Fellmer.

f European p: January 1942, Vienna, Vienna Symphony Orchestra, cond. Rudolf Moralt.

fEp: 18 November 1961, BBC broadcast, BBC Symphony Orchestra, cond. Charles Groves.

Pub. 1941, Fürstner.

205. Verklungene Feste. 'Dance vision from two centuries' after two centuries. 1940. Couperin-Tanzsuite augmented by six further pieces.

fp: 5 April 1941, Munich, Bayerische Staatsoper, cond. Clemens Krauss.

?Pub. Oertel.

See also No. 207.

206. Capriccio Op. 85. Conversation Piece for music in one act by Clemens Krauss and Richard Strauss. 1940–1. Dated: 3 August 1941, Garmisch. Ded. Clemens Krauss. Dur. 130'.

3 fl, pic, 2 ob, ca, cl in C, 2 cl, basset hn, bcl, 3 bsn, cbsn; 4 hn, 2 tpt, 3 tmb; timp, pcssn; 2 hp, hpschd, strings. *Stage music:* string sextet (in the wings), violin, cello, hpschd (in costume).

fp: 28 October 1942, Munich, State Opera (National Theatre), cond. Clemens Krauss; with Viorica Ursuleac (Countess Madeleine), Hildegard Ranczak (Clairon), Horst Taubmann (Flamand), Hans Hotter (Olivier), Walter Höfermayer (Count), Georg Hann (La Roche), Irma Beilke and Franz Klarwein

(Italian duettists); producer, Rudolf Hartmann; design, Rochus Gliese.

fEp (concert excerpts): 9 April 1951, Royal Albert Hall, Elisabeth Schwarzkopf and the Philharmonia Orchestra, cond. Paul Kletzki.

fEp: 22 September 1953, Covent Garden, Bavarian State Opera, cond. Robert Heger; with Maud Cunitz (Countess Madeleine), Herta Töpper (Clairon), Richard Holm (Flamand), Albrecht Peter (Olivier), Karl Schmitt-Walter (Count), Benno Kusche (La Roche).

Pub. 1942, Oertel; 1964, Boosey & Hawkes.

BIBLIOGRAPHY:

Robert Breuer: Capriccio, Strauss's One Testament, *Musical America*, February 1954.

— Strauss, Krauss and Capriccio, *Saturday Review*, 26 October 1963, p. 60.

Henry W. Simon: Capriccio, in *Festival of Opera*, W. H. Allen (London) 1957, p. 73.

Richard Strauss: Preface to Capriccio, *Juilliard Review*, spring 1954.

Roland Tenschert: Das Sonett in RS' Oper Capriccio, *SM*, January 1958, p. 1; transl. H. C. R. Landon, *Tempo*, No. 47, spring 1958, p. 7.

John S. Weissmann: Capriccio at Glyndebourne, *Musical Events*, July 1963, p. 11.

206a. String Sextet. From 'Capriccio' Op. 85. ?1942. Dur. 10'.

fEp: 13 November 1946, Wigmore Hall, Boosey & Hawkes concert, Blech Quartet with Watson Forbes and John Shinebourne.

Pub. 1942, Oertel; Schott/Boosey & Hawkes.

206b. Suite for harpsichord. From 'Capriccio' Op. 85. Composed for Isolde Ahlgrimm. ?1944.

fp: 7 November 1946, Vienna, Isolde Ahlgrimm.

Unpub.

207. Divertimento Op. 86. For small orchestra, after keyboard pieces by François Couperin. 1941. The new pieces of 'Verklungene Feste' (No. 205) with two further numbers. Dur. 40'.

2 fl, 2 ob, ca, 2 cl, 2 bsn; 2 hn, tpt, tmb;

timp, pcssn; celesta, hpschd, hp, organ (hmnm), strings.

fp: 31 January 1943, Vienna, Vienna Philharmonic Orchestra, cond. Clemens Krauss.

Pub. 1942, Oertel.

208. Zwei Lieder (J. Weinheber). For voice and piano. 1942. Composed for Weinheber's fiftieth birthday.

1. *St. Michael*; 2. *Blick vom oberen Belvedere*.

fp: 9 March 1942, Vienna, Alfred Poell and Hilde Konetzni, acc. Karl Hermann.

Pub. 1964, Boosey & Hawkes (as Op. 88 Nos. 3 & 2, together with 'Das Bächlein').

209. Horn Concerto No. 2 in E flat. 1942. Dur. 25'.

1. *Allegro—Andante con moto*; 2. *Rondo: Allegro molto*.

2 fl, 2 ob, 2 cl, 2 bsn; 2 hn, 2 tpt; timp; strings.

fp: 11 August 1943, Salzburg, Gottfried von Freiberg and the Vienna Philharmonic Orchestra, cond. Karl Böhm.

fEp (concert): 31 May 1949, Chelsea Town Hall, Dennis Brain and the Chelsea Symphony Orchestra, cond. Norman Del Mar.

Pub. 1950, Boosey & Hawkes.

210. Xenion (Distichon) ('Nichts von Vergänglichen') (Goethe). For voice and piano. 1942. Ded. Gerhart Hauptmann on his eightieth birthday. Pub. 1959–60 in *Strauss Jahrbuch*.

211. Festmusik für den Trompetercorps der Stadt Wien. 1942–3.

fp: 9 April 1943, Vienna, Rathaus tower, cond. Richard Strauss.

Pub. Boosey & Hawkes.

212. Sonatina No. 1 in F. For 16 wind instruments. 'From the workshop of an invalid.' 1943. Composed for the ninetieth anniversary of the Dresden Tonkünstlerverein. Dur. 20–23'.

2 fl, 2 ob, cl in C, 2 cl, basset hn, bcl, 2 bsn, cbsn, 4 hn.

fp: 17 (?18) June 1944, Dresden, wind group from the Saxon State Orchestra, cond. Karl Elmendorff.

Pub. 1952, Boosey & Hawkes.

213. An den Baum Daphne (J. Gregor).

Epilogue to 'Daphne' for 9-part mixed chorus a cappella. 1943. Ded. Konzertvereinigung of the Vienna State Chorus on its twentieth anniversary. Dur. 15'.

fp: 5 January 1947, Vienna, State Opera Chorus and Boys' Choir of the Kanotei, cond. Felix Prohaska.

Pub. 1958, Boosey & Hawkes.

214. Metamorphosen. Study for 23 solo strings. 1944–5. Dated: 12 April 1945, Garmisch. Ded. Paul Sacher and the Collegium Musicum, Zürich. Dur. 26–30'.

10 violins, 5 violas, 5 cellos, 3 double basses.

fp: 25 January 1946, Zürich, Collegium Musicum, cond. Paul Sacher.

fEp: 12 December 1946, London, St. Bartholomew concert, Boyd Neel Orchestra.

Pub. 1946, Boosey & Hawkes.

BIBLIOGRAPHY:

Ernest Newmann: De Senectute, in *More Essays from the World of Music*, John Calder (London) 1958, p. 129.

K. Wilhelm: Die Metamorphosen von RS, *SM*, February 1951, p. 51.

215. Sonatina No. 2 in E flat (Symphony for wind instruments). 'Merry Workshop.' 1944–5. Ded. 'to the divine Mozart at the end of a life filled with gratitude'. Dur. 36–40'.

2 fl, 2 ob, cl in C, 2 cl, basset hn, bcl, 2 bsn, cbsn, 4 hn.

fp: 25 March 1946, Winterthur, Musikkollegium, Stadtorchester, cond. Hermann Scherchen.

fEp: 2 January 1953, Royal Festival Hall, London Baroque Ensemble, cond. Karl Haas.

fEbp: 28 January 1953, London Baroque Ensemble, cond. Karl Haas.

Pub. 1952, Boosey & Hawkes.

216. Oboe Concerto. 1945–6. Dur. 22–23'.

2 fl, ca, 2 cl, 2 bsn; 2 hn; strings.

fp: 26 February 1946, Zürich, Marcel Saillet and the Tonhalle Orchestra, cond. Volkmar Andreae.

fEp: 17 September 1946, Promenade Concert, Royal Albert Hall, Leon Goossens and the BBC Symphony Orchestra, cond. Sir Adrian Boult.

Pub. 1948, Boosey & Hawkes: incl. reduction by Arthur Willner.

217. Duet Concertino. For clarinet and bassoon with string orchestra and harp. 1947. Composed for Radio Lugano. Dur. 20'.

fp: 4 April 1948, Lugano (Radio Monte Ceneri), Armando Basile and Bruno Bergamaschi with the Orchestra della Radio Svizzera Italiana, cond. Otmar Nussio.

fEp: 4 May 1949, Manchester, Halle Orchestra, cond. Sir John Barbirolli.

f London p: 29 July 1949, Promenade Concert, Royal Albert Hall, Frederick Thurston and Archie Camden with the London Symphony Orchestra, cond. Sir Malcolm Sargent.

Pub. 1949, Hawkes.

218. Vier letzte Lieder. For high voice and orchestra. 1948. Dur. 22½'.

1. *Frühling* (Hermann Hesse). Dated: 18 July 1948, Pontresina. Ded. Willi Schuh and his wife. Dur. 4½'.

2 fl, 2 ob, ca, 2 cl, bcl, 3 bsn; 4 hn; hp, strings.

2. *September* (Hermann Hesse). Dated: 20 September 1948, Montreux. Ded. Mr. and Mrs. Seery. Dur. 4½'.

3 fl, 2 ob, ca, 2 cl, bcl, 2 bsn; 4 hn, 2 tpt; hp, strings.

3. *Beim Schlafengehen* (Hermann Hesse). Dated: 4 August 1948, Pontresina. Ded. Adolf Jöhr and his wife. Dur. 5½'.

2 fl, 2 pic, 2 ob, ca, 2 cl, bcl, 2 bsn; 4 hn, 2 tpt, 3 tmb, tuba; celesta, strings.

4. *Im Abendrot* (Eichendorff). 1946-8. Dated: 27 April 1948, Montreux. Ded. Ernst Roth. Dur. 8'.

2 fl, 2 ob, ca, 2 cl, bcl, 2 bsn, cbsn; 4 hn, 3 tpt, 2 tmb, bs tmb, tuba; timp; strings.

fp: 22 May 1950, London, Royal Albert Hall, Kirsten Flagstad and the Philharmonia Orchestra, cond. Wilhelm Furtwängler.

fGp: 25 September 1950, Frankfurt a.M., Museum, Christel Goltz and the Städtisches Orchester, cond. B. Vondenhoff.

Pub. 1950, Boosey.

BIBLIOGRAPHY:

Arthur Hutchings: Strauss's Four Last Songs, *MT*, December 1950, p. 465.

Willi Schuh: Die vier letzten Lieder von RS, *SM*, 1950.

WRITINGS BY RICHARD STRAUSS

Spielplan grosser Opernhäusen, *Blätter der Staatsoper* (Berlin), October 1925.

Persönliche Erinnerungen an Hans von Bülow, *Neueste Nachrichten*, 8 November 1925.

Schön gesungene Friedenshymne jedenfalls unschädlich, *Acht Uhr Abendblatt*, 26 June 1928.

Über Komponieren und Dirigieren, *Berliner Börsen-Courier*, 8 June 1929.

Cosi fan tutte, *Blätter der Staatsoper* (Berlin), 1932, No. 5.

Die Bedeutung des Wortes in der Oper, *Nürnberger Zeitung*, 14 August 1932.

Begrüssungsansprache anlässlich des ersten deutschen Komponistentages in Berlin, *NZfM*, March 1934.

The artistic testament of RS (transl. and with an introduction by Alfred Mann), *MQ*, January 1950, p. 1.

Views and recollections, *Symphony*, February 1952, p. 9.

Kythere, Ballettszenarium (1900), *Strauss Jahrbuch*, 1959-60, p. 59.

Anmerkungen zur Aufführung von Beethovens Symphonien, *NZfM*, June 1964.

Über mein Schaffen, *ÖM*, May–June 1964.

Zeitgemässe Glossen für Erziehung zur M, *Musik im Unterricht*, July–August 1964.

GENERAL BIBLIOGRAPHY

Adolf Aber: Stunden mit RS, *Die Musikwelt*, 15 September 1922; *Blätter der Staatsoper* (Berlin), May 1923, p. 5.

— RS, *Crescendo*, No. 35, February 1951, p. 179; No. 43, November 1951, p. 47.

— The waltz in the works of RS, *Crescendo*, No. 68, March 1955, p. 175.

— Strauss and Hofmannsthal, *MT*, May 1954, p. 242.

Gerald Abraham: RS, a case of self-misunderstanding, *MS*, 1931, April, p. 24, May, p. 148.

Theodor W. Adorno: RS, zum 60. Geburtstage, *NZfM*, 1924, No. 6, p. 289.

— Glosse zu RS, *Anbruch*, June 1929, p. 250.

— RS, *PNM*, fall–winter 1965 p. 14, spring–summer 1966 p. 113.

J. Amenabar: Un juicio sobre RS, *Revista musical Chilena*, August–November 1949, p. 11.

A. de Angelis: Interview, *Living Age*, 14 October 1922, p. 96.

Herbert Antcliffe: Elgar and Strauss, *MMR*, 1905, p. 84.

— Berlioz, Liszt and RS, *MMR*, 1906, p. 4.

William Armstrong: Interview with RS, in *Composers Through the Eyes of Their Contemporaries*, Dutton (New York) 1951, p. 419.

Thomas Armstrong: Strauss's tone poems, O.U.P. (London) 1931.

E. H. Mueller von Asow: RS, Thematisches Verzeichnis, Doblinger (Vienna) 1959, 2 vols.

Kurt Atterberg: RS, *Stockholmstidningen*, 11 June 1939.

E. A. B.: RS, *MS*, 7 June 1902, p. 356.

G. Bagier: RS der Sechzigjährige, *Der Auftakt*, July 1924, p. 180.

Hermann Bahr: RS, *Der Merker*, May (2) 1914, p. 379.

— RS, *Blätter der Staatsoper* (Berlin), 1921, No. 4, p. 19.

Sir John Barbirolli: RS, a tribute, *Halle*, November 1949, p. 21.

Clive Barnes: Strauss in collaboration, *M&M*, June 1964, p. 16.

Richard Batka: Der Monatsplauderer RS, *NMZ*, 1907, No. 17, p. 372.

— RS, Berlin/Charlottenburg 1908.

E. A. Baugham: RS and programme music, *Living Age*, 14 October 1905, p. 110.

— RS and an operatic problem, *Fortnightly Review*, April 1913, p. 717.

Gunther Baum: Briefe als Spiegel der Persönlichkeit, *Musica*, 1959, No. 3, p. 167.

(Sir) Arnold Bax: RS, in *Music Magazine*, Rockliff (London) 1953, p. 76.

Paul Bekker: RS, *Berliner Börsen-Courier*, 1905, No. 9.

— RS, *Westermanns Monatshefte*, 1907, No. 1.

— RS als Dirigent, *AMZ*, No. 43, October 1912.

— RS, *Kunstwart*, June 1924, p. 96.

— RS, *Anbruch*, June–July 1924, p. 219.

— Brief an RS, *Die Musik*, November 1932, p. 81.

Anton Berger: RS als geistige Macht, Schröder (Garmisch), ?1965.

Oscar Bie: Die Moderne Musik von RS, Berlin, 1916.

— RS' Lieder, *Blätter der Staatsoper* (Berlin), November 1926, p. 15.

Ernest Blake: RS, *MS*, 31 May 1902, p. 342.

Leo Blech: Zu RS' 60. Geburtstag, *Neue Freie Presse*, 8 June 1924.

— RS, *Die Theater- und Musikwoche*, 1919, No. 29, p. 7.

Ernest Bloch: Mahler, Strauss, Bruckner, *Die Musik*, June 1923, p. 664.

Sidney S. Bloch: The greatest conductor of his time, in *Great Composers Through the Eyes of Their Contemporaries*, Dutton (New York) 1951, p. 422.

Eric Blom: RS, *Chesterian*, No. 7, September–October 1926.

Karl Böhm: Begegnung mit RS (ed. F. E. Dostal), Doblinger (Vienna) 1964.

A. M. Bonisconti: L'ultimo Strauss, *La Rassegna musicale*, January 1950, p. 37.

Wilhelm Bopp: RS, *Neue Badische Landeszeitung*, 20 November 1927.

G. Bourke: The domesticity of Strauss, *Music Magazine*, April 1962, p. 18.

Willi Brandl: RS, Leben und Werk, Wiesbaden, 1950.

Gustav Brecher: RS, Leipzig, 1900.

Wilfried Brennecke: Die Metamorphosen-Werke von RS und Paul Hindemith, *SM*, 1963, May–June p. 129, July–August p. 199.

Robert Breuer: New light on Strauss, *New York Times*, 13 June 1954, Section 2, p. 9.

— My brother RS, an interview with Johanna von Rauchenberger, *Saturday Review*, 27 December 1958, p. 31.

— RS memories—as told by his sister: interview with Frau Rauchenberger-Strauss, *Opera Annual*, No. 6, 1959, p. 121.

— Strauss–Zweig correspondence reflects Nazi persecution, *Musical America*, February 1958, p. 236.

— Drei 'neue' Lieder von RS, *SM*, January 1959, p. 10.

— Strauss and Shakespeare, *Opera News*, 25 March 1961, p. 6.

— Das 'Kunstlerische Vermächtnis' von RS in zweiter Version (ed. Willi Schuh), *Strauss-Mitteilungen*, No. 32, March 1962, p. 1.

— Case of hard-earned bread—Strauss's tours of America, *High Fidelity*, June 1964, p. 42.

Strauss, Richard

Max Broesike-Schoen: Das Straussische Lied, *Die Musikwelt*, 1 June 1924.

Richard Bryceson: RS, *Gramophone Record*, March 1934, p. 8.

Paul Bülow: RS' Pilgerfahrt nach Bayreuth, *NZfM*, June 1934, p. 605.

Alfred Burgatz: RS und wir, *Die Musik*, June 1939, p. 577.

C. G. Burke: RS on microgroove, *High Fidelity*, April 1954, p. 59.

Antonio Capri: RS e i più recenti compositori della Germania, in *Musica e musicisti d'Europa*, Ulrico Hoepli (Milan) 1939, p. 364.

Neville Cardus: RS, in *Ten Composers*, London, 1945.

— RS, *Halle*, March 1949, p. 4.

Mosco Carner: The 'first-class second-rate composer', *Music Magazine*, June 1964, p. 4.

Jean Chantavoine: RS, *La Revue Rhénane*, No. 11, August 1922.

Heinrich Chevalley: RS und wir, *Die Musikwelt*, 1 June 1924.

Max Chop: RS, der Neuromantiker und 'Moderne', *Signale*, 1924, No. 24 p. 971, No. 25 p. 1003, No. 26 p. 1035, No. 27 p. 1073.

A. Cimbro: RS, i poemi sinfonici, Milan, 1926.

Anthony Clyne: The decline of RS, *Bookman*, May 1921, p. 111.

André Coeuroy: RS héros de roman et d'opéra, *Nouvelles littéraires*, 29 November 1924.

Deryck Cooke: Strauss, Stravinsky and Mozart, *The Listener*, 9 November 1961, p. 789.

J. F. Cooke: RS, *Etude*, November 1949, p. 7.

Martin Cooper: RS, *Chesterian*, No. 160, October 1949.

Hans Corrodi: Musiköpfe der Gegenwart, *Neue Schweizer Rundschau*, Vol. 2 (1934–5), p. 453.

W. I. Corver: Alfred Tennyson en RS, *Weekblad for Muziek*, 1906.

George Cowe: The songs of RS, *MO*, January 1909, p. 251.

John Culshaw: RS and the decline of romanticism, in *A Century of Music*, Dobson (London) 1952, p. 68.

Gerald Cumberland: Studies in musical psychology, No. 1: Dr. RS, *MO*, February 1911, p. 330.

M.D.: Les Lieder de RS, *Bulletin de la S.I.M.*, November 1911, p. 85.

A. Dami: Position de RS, *Le Courrier musical*, 1 June 1928.

Ernst Decsey: Strauss, der Süddeutsche, *Die Musikwelt*, 1 June 1924.

E. Desderi: RS, *Rivista musicale italiana*, October–December 1949.

Hans Herbert Dettelbach: RS und Italien, *Deutsche Allg. Zeitung*, 21 July 1925.

F. Deutsch: RS today, *Living Age*, May 1932, p. 238.

O. Downes: Strauss on opera: problems of management, *New York Times*, 15 August 1954, Section 2, p. 7.

Alfred Dressler: Der Stoff der neuen Oper von RS, *Signale*, 1931, No. 42 (7 October), p. 986.

Franz Dubitzky: RS' Kammermusik, *Die Musik*, June (1) 1914, p. 283.

Paul Ehlers: RS in München, *Der Merker*, 25 July 1910, p. 868.

— Proteus Strauss, *AMZ*, 1914, No. 24.

— RS, *Münchener Neueste Nachrichten*, No. 156, 11 June 1924.

Alfred Einstein: Konvention, *Der Auftakt*, July 1924.

— Strauss und Hofmannsthal, in *Von Schütz bei Hindemith*, Pan-Verlag (Zürich/Stuttgart) 1957, p. 129.

J. Elias: Strauss in search of an answer, *High Fidelity*, January 1959, p. 45.

Nancy van der Elst: Romain Rolland en RS, *Mens en melodie*, August 1954, p. 252.

Robert Engel: RS und Russland, *Die Musik*, June 1934, p. 658.

Otto Erhardt: The later operatic works of RS, *Tempo*, No. 12, summer 1949, p. 23.

— RS, Buenos Aires, 1950.

— RS, Leben, Wirken, Schaffen, Olten/Freiburg 1953.

— RS und die Dresdner Oper, Erinnerungen unseres Ehrenmitgliedes, *Strauss*, No. 49, June 1966, p. 1.

Neville d'Esterre: Richard the Second, *British Musician*, March 1938, p. 52.

David Ewen: Also sprach RS, *MQ*, April 1930, p. 207.

Hermann Fähnrich: Semiramis (Eine unge-schriebene Oper von RS), *Musical*, 1958, No. 4, p. 204.

— Europäische Begegnung, *Musical*, 1957, No. 2, p. 65.

— RS über das Verhältnis von Dichtung und Musik (Wort und Ton) in seinem Opern-schaffen, *Die Musikforschung*, January–March 1961, p. 22.

— RS und Prag, *NZfM*, June 1964.

J. Feschotte: RS et la communaute humaine, *Strauss*, No. 33, June 1962, p. 3.

Helmut A. Fiechtner: Wien und das Testa-ment von RS, *Musica*, 1956, No. 12, p. 817.

Gerold Fierz: Opera von RS auf Schallplatten, *SM*, March–April 1962, p. 108.

H. T. Finck: RS, the man and his works, Boston, 1917.

J. Franze: RS and Mozart, *Revista de Estudias Musicales*, August 1949.

V. Fuchs: Mountaineering with RS, *Opera News*, 26 December 1959, p. 12.

Hans Gal (ed.): RS, in *The Musicians World—Great Composers in their Letters*, Thames & Hudson (London) 1965, p. 384.

Hugh F. Garten: The Strauss–Hofmannsthal letters, *Opera*, May 1953, p. 274.

— Hofmannsthal as librettist, *Opera*, August 1951, p. 15.

R. Gelatt: Late operas of RS, *Reporter*, 3 October 1957, p. 37.

Elena Gerhardt: Strauss and his Lieder, *Tempo*, No. 12, summer 1949, p. 9.

R. Gerlach: Tonalität und tonale Konfigura-tion im Œuvre von RS, *Die Musikforschung*, 1966, No. 2, p. 195.

— Don Juan und Rosenkavalier: Studien zu Idee und Gestalt einer tonalen Evolutions im Werk RS, Haupt (Berlin) 1966.

H. L. Gideon: Music dramas of RS, *Forum*, April 1910, p. 381.

Lawrence Gilman: RS, Tchaikovsky and the idea of death, *Musical World*, 1903, No. 8.

— Achievement of Strauss, *Modern Music*, Vol. III, p. 25.

— Strauss and the Greeks, in *Nature in Music*, New York, 1914.

— Strauss and the music of death, *North American Review*, December 1920, p. 847.

— RS, *New Republic*, 9 November 1921, p. 321.

H. Glass: RS on microgroove (discography), *High Fidelity*, March 1962, p. 50.

Georg Göhler: RS, *Die Zukunft*, 1907, No. 42, p. 98.

— RS, der Bekenner und der Schriftsteller, *Neue Revue*, December (1) 1907, p. 193.

— Ein neues Werk über RS, *NZfM*, October (1) 1922, p. 421; 1931, No. 9, p. 713.

Fred. Goldbeck: RS et le petit monstre tutelaire, *RM*, April 1936, p. 287.

Antoine Goléa: RS in französischer Sicht, *NZfM*, 6 June 1966, p. 218.

Glenn Gould: Strauss and the electronic future, *Saturday Review*, 30 May 1964, p. 58.

— An argument for Strauss, *Records & Recording*, July 1964, p. 11.

Max Graf: The Strauss–Hofmannsthal letters, *Musical America*, February 1953, p. 17.

— Strauss and his librettist, *Opera News*, 23 February 1953, p. 4.

Georg Gräners: Zum Kapitel: RS, *Vossische Zeitung*, 14 September 1907.

Franz Grasberger: Gustav Mahler und RS, *ÖM*, May–June 1966, p. 280.

— RS-Bibliographie, Teil I (1882 bis 1944) (ed. O. Ortner), Prachner (Vienna) 1964.

— Der Strom der Töne trug mich fort—Die Welt um RS in Briefen (ed. F. Grasberger), Hans Schneider (Tutzing) 1967.

Cecil Gray: RS, in *A Survey of Contemporary Music*, O.U.P. (London) 1927, p. 33.

Josef Gregor: RS, der Meister der Oper, Munich, 1939.

— Briefwechsel, Salzburg, 1955.

— RS zum 10. Todestag, *ÖM*, September 1959.

Ernst Groell: Erinnerung an RS, *NZfM*, July–August 1962.

Vittorio Gui: Ricordi su RS, *L'Approdo musicale*, January–March 1959.

Fritz Gysi: RS, Potsdam, 1934.

Franz Hadamowsky: Die Wiener Ur- and Erstaufführung der Werke von RS, *ÖM*, May–June 1964.

— Regisseure und Bühnenbilder um RS in Saltzburg, *ÖM*, August 1964.

Paul Hamburger: Strauss the song writer, *M&M*, June 1964, p. 14.

Fred. Hamel: Analyse des Ruhmes—Zum Abschied von RS, *Musica*, 1949, No. 10, p. 345.

Rudolf Hartmann: Letzter Besuch bei RS, *SM*, 1950.
— Last visit to RS, in *Great Composers Through the Eyes of Their Contemporaries*, Dutton (New York) 1951, p. 429.
Siegmund von Hausegger: Strauss-Glosse, *Der Merker*, May (2) 1914, p. 386.
— RS und Alexander Ritter, *Münchener Neueste Nachrichten*, No. 156, 11 June 1924.
R. Heger: Musical problems in the operas of RS, *Canon*, December 1962–January 1963, p. 76.
Günter Hausswald: Antiker Mythos bei RS, *Musica*, 1958, No. 6, p. 323.
— RS, heute, *Musica*, 1964, No. 1, p. 6.
A. Henderson: Genius of Strauss, *Forum*, October 1911, p. 452.
W. J. Henderson: Genius of RS, *Mentor*, February 1929, p. 23.
Kurt Herbst: Das Verhältnis von Mozart und RS—eine zeitgenössische Komponistenfrage!, *Die Musik*, December 1935, p. 182.
H. Herzfeld: Strauss and Hofmannsthal, *Commonweal*, 21 June 1935, p. 203.
Alfred Heuss: Musikdramatische Parallelen bei RS und Monteverdi, *NZfM*, May 1929, p. 264.
Peter Heyworth: The unfamiliar Strauss, *Records & Recording*, September 1962, p. 37.
Ralph Hill: RS's tone poems, *Gramophone Record*, June 1934, p. 4.
— A note on RS, *Radio Times*, 24 August 1934, p. 487.
B. Himmler: Last glimpse of Strauss, *Opera News*, 26 December 1959, p. 4.
Robert Hirschfeld: Mahler und RS in Wien, *Österreichische Rundschau*, 1904, No. 9.
Rudolf Stephan Hoffmann: RS als Operndirektor in Wien, *NMZ*, No. 10, p. 236.
— Ein Brief an RS, *Anbruch*, February 1922, p. 61.
— Strauss als Wiener Operndirektor, *Thüringer Allg. Zeitung*, No. 158, 11 June 1924.
Basil Hogarth: The strange case of RS, *The Gramophone*, January 1935, p. 297.
Artur Holde: Unbekannte Briefe und Lieder von RS, *NZfM*, December 1958.
K. Hommel: Das RS-Bild im Buch der Gegenwart, *Strauss*, No. 37, June 1963, p. 7.
Frank Howes: Nimrod on Strauss, *MT*, June 1970, p. 590.

— He portrayed himself in music, *Radio Times*, 8 November 1929, p. 392.
W. Huder: Alfred Kerr und RS, eine Darstellung, *Strauss*, No. 48, March 1966, p. 18.
Gervase Hughes: Strauss, in *The Handbook of Great Composers*, Arthur Barker (London) 1965, p. 218.
James Huneker: RS, *Die Musik*, January (2) 1905, p. 79.
Hermann Inderan: RS, *Rheinische Musikblätter*, June 1924.
David Irvine: The survival value of RS, *MS*, 1910, 5 March p. 145, 12 March p. 160.
Ernst Isler: Zur RS' 60. Geburtstag, *Neue Zürche Zeitung*, No. 847, 7 June 1924.
Edgar Istel: The RS week at Munich, *MMR*, 1910, p. 171.
— RS zum 50. Geburtstage, *NZfM*, 1914, No. 24, p. 343.
S. Jahnke: RS und der Geist des XX. Jahrhunderts, *Strauss*, No. 52, March 1967, p. 2.
Alan Jefferson: The operas of RS in Britain 1910–1963, Putnam (London) 1963.
— Strauss on the couch, *M&M*, June 1964, p. 297.
Cyril Jenkins: RS, his significance, *Welsh Outlook*, September 1914, p. 397.
Heinz Joachim: Der Briefwechsel von RS und Stefan Zweig, *NZfM*, March 1958.
M. Joubert: Hugo von Hofmannsthal and his collaboration with RS, *Contemporary Review*, November 1929, p. 632.
A. Kalisch: RS on the stage, *Sackbut*, July 1924.
S. Kallenberg: RS, Leben und Werk, Leipzig, 1926.
D. Kämper (ed.): RS und Franz Wüllner im Briefwechsel, Arno (Cologne) 1963.
Julius Kapp: RS und die Berliner Oper, *Blätter der Staatsoper* (Berlin), June 1924.
Herbert von Karajan: Karajan über RS, *ÖM*, August 1964.
A. E. Keeton: RS as man and musician, *Contemporary Review*, June 1903, p. 845.
Viktor Keldorfer: Erlebnisse mit RS, *Neues Wiener Journal*, 31 March 1929.
Götz Klaus Kende: Clemens Krauss über seine Zusammenarbeit mit RS, *SM*, February 1957, p. 45.
— RS und Clemens Krauss, *Musica*, 1960, No. 1, p. 5.

— RS und Clemens Krauss bei den Salzburger Festspielen, *ÖM*, August 1964.

Franz Seraph Kerschensteiner: Familiengeschichte um RS und die Walter Parkstein, *NZfM*, June 1934, p. 596.

C. Kistler: Deutsche Komponisten der Gegenwart: RS, *NMZ*, 1898, No. 1, p. 6, No. 2, p. 21, No. 3, p. 3.

Wilhelm Klatte: Aus RS' Werkstatt, *Die Musik*, June 1924, p. 636.

Gaston Knosp: Notes sur RS, *Bulletin S.I.M.*, 1907, p. 393.

— Un manifeste de RS, *Bulletin S.I.M.*, 1907, p. 872.

Gustav Kobbe: RS the tone-poet, *MS*, 21 June 1902, p. 393; repr. from *North American Review*.

Horst Koegler: RS without successor?, *MO*, June 1953, p. 535.

Hans Költzsch: RS, *NZfM*, June 1935, p. 643.

Julius Kopsch: Der Siebzigjährige RS, *Die Musik*, June 1934, p. 641.

— Freiheit des Schaffens Idee und Tat bei RS, *Strauss*, No. 35, December 1962, p. 8.

— RS der grosser Kämpfer für das Recht des künstlerisch Schaffenden, *Strauss*, No. 44, March 1965, p. 10.

J. Korngold: RS, *Neue Freie Presse*, 3 May 1924.

Heinrich Kralik: RS und Wien, *Die Musik*, June 1934, p. 652.

— Genie in unserer Welt—Zum 100. Geburtstag von RS, *ÖM*, May–June 1964.

— RS, Weltbürger der Musik, Wollzeilen (Vienna) 1963.

Ernst Krause: Fülle des Lebens—Zum 85. Geburtstag von RS, *Musica*, 1949, No. 6, p. 202.

— RS, Gestalt und Werk, Leipzig, 1956.

— Ein Brief an Dora Wihan-Weis (1889), *Strauss Jahrbuch*, 1959–60, p. 55.

— Spielkasino und Warenhaus: zum Schicksal zweier Wagner- und Strauss-Gedenkstätten, *Musik und Gesellschaft*, May 1961, p. 273.

— Zwei vernachlässigte Strauss-Opern, *Musik und Gesellschaft*, July 1965, p. 450.

Willy Krienitz: RS in Münchner Konzertleben, in *RS und seine Vaterstadt*, Munich, 1934.

Walther Krug: Strauss, in *Die neue Musik*, Eugen Rentsch (Erlenbach) 1919, p. 37.

Karl-Joachim Krüger: Hugo von Hofmannsthal und RS, Berlin, 1935.

O. Kühn: Zum 50. Geburtstag von RS, *NMZ*, 1914, No. 19, p. 376.

Frederic S. Law: RS, *MS*, 29 December 1906, p. 405, 5 January 1907, p. 6.

H. Lawrence: RS, vintage years, *Audio Engineering*, November 1954, p. 10.

Lotte Lehmann: RS, *Die Theater- und Musikwoche*, 1919, No. 29, p. 10.

— Tribute, *Musical America*, September 1949, p. 14.

— Singing with RS (transl. Ernst Pawel), Hamish Hamilton (London), Macmillan (New York) 1964.

— Five operas and RS (transl. Ernst Pawel), Macmillan (New York) ? 1965.

Erich Leinsdorf: Genius of RS, *Atlantic*, August 1965, p. 79.

A. Leonardi: RS, *Corriere Musicale dei Piccoli*, June 1927.

H. Wilhelm Lichtenberg: Kurz-Geschichten über RS, *NZfM*, June 1934, p. 675.

Heinrich Lindlar: 'Ironische Verbundenheit', *Musica*, 1953, No. 12, p. 565.

R. Littlehale: Dr. Strauss's last appearance in America, *MS*, 4 June 1904, p. 353.

R. M. Longyear: Schiller, Moszkowski and Strauss: John of Arc's 'Death and Transfiguration', *MR*, 1967, p. 209.

Rudolf Louis: RS, *Blätter für Haus- und Kirchenmusik*, 1904, No. 6, p. 81.

Watson Lyle: The personality and art of Strauss, *Review of Reviews*, February 1922, p. 146.

Joseph Machlis: RS, in *Introduction to Contemporary Music*, Norton (USA) 1961, Dent (London), p. 84.

André Espiau de la Maestre: Debussys Deklamationstechnik in Pelléas et Mélisande im Lichte des Briefwechsels von RS und Romain Rolland, *ÖM*, January 1962.

O. Mancini: RS, Debussy ed il modernismo musicale, *Revista Nazionale di Musica*, April–May and August 1933.

Richard Mandl: Meine Begegnung mit RS, *Der Merker*, May (2) 1914, p. 391.

William Mann: Modern composers: RS, *Crescendo*, No. 58, February 1954, p. 95.

— A Strauss diary, *Opera*, November 1953, p. 648.

William Mann: RS, in *Decca Book of Ballet*, Muller (London) 1958, p. 294.

— Strauss, 20th century classicist, *Musical America*, July 1964, p. 14.

— RS, a critical study of the operas, Cassell (London) 1964; RS, Das Opernwerk (transl. Willi Reich), Beck (Munich).

A. Mantelli: Il tempo di Strauss, *L'Approdo musicale*, January–March 1959.

Norman Del Mar: RS, a critical commentary on his life and works, Barrie & Rockliff (London), Vol. 1, 1962; Vol. 2, 1968; Vol. 3, 1972.

Michael Marcus: RS, *Crescendo*, No. 133, February 1964, p. 111.

George R. Marek: RS, the life of a non-hero, Victor Gollancz (London) 1967.

Jean Marnold: RS, *Le Guide musical* (Brussels), 1900, Nos. 40–50.

— RS, in *Musique d'autrefois et d'aujourd'hui*, Dorbon-ainé (Paris) 1912, p. 107.

Max Marschalk: Revelations of his working methods, in *Great Composers Through the Eyes of Their Contemporaries*, Dutton (New York) 1951, p. 426.

Paul Marsop: RS und das Theater, *Die Musik*, June 1924, p. 630.

— Kleine Erinnerungsbilder, *Münchener Neueste Nachrichten*, No. 156, 11 June 1924.

Daniel Gregory Mason: Study of Strauss, *MQ*, April 1916, p. 171.

Jean Matter: Strauss et Mahler, *SM*, November–December 1964, p. 364.

Camille Mauclair: RS und die Musik seit Wagner, *NMZ*, 1903, Nos. 19–20.

W. Mauke: RS, *Bühne und Welt*, 1899, No. 17, p. 785.

— RS, *Das neue Jahrhundert*, 1899, No. 50.

Ludwig Karl Mayer: Das Werk des Dramatikers RS, *Thüringer Allg. Zeitung*, No. 158, 11 June 1924.

L. Mazzucchetti: RS e Stefan Zweig, *L'Approdo musicale*, January–March 1959.

Wilfrid Mellers: Two traditionalists: Faure and Strauss, in *Man and his Music*, Barrie & Rockliff (London) 1962, p. 923.

Jacques de Menasce: RS in retrospect, *Juilliard Review*, spring 1954.

André Messager: Die Musiker unserer Epoche: RS zum 60. Geburtstag, *Neue Freie Presse*, 8 June 1924.

F. N. Mennemeier: RS und seine Librettisten, *Musik und Szene*, 1962–3, No. 2, p. 8.

E. H. W. Meyerstein: RS, *MR*, 1949, p. 285.

P. Mies: RS in Wechselnder Sicht, *Musikhandel*, December 1964, p. 323.

Franz Mikorey: RS, *Münchener Zeitung*, 24 August 1932.

F. Milburn: Sentimental Strauss, *Opera News*, 13 February 1956, p. 9.

Sister Mirelda: RS centenarian—his money and his music, *Music Journal*, February 1965, p. 72.

Donald Mitchell: The case of RS, *Disc*, spring 1950, p. 10.

— Strauss as a conversationalist, *Opera*, November 1953, p. 658.

Edward S. Mitchell: The Strauss revivals, *Sackbut*, November 1920, p. 143.

Erwin Mittag: RS, musikhistoriskt och privat, *Musiklevet*, 1960, p. 54.

P. Mlakar: Susreti sa Richardom Straussom, *Zvuk*, No. 63 (1965), p. 257.

Hans Joachim Moser: RS, Leben und Werk, Cracow, 1944.

— Begegnungen mit RS, *Musikerziehung*, March 1960, p. 179.

E. H. Mueller: RS und Giuseppe Verdi, *ÖM*, August 1961.

Robert Müller-Hartmann: Max Steinitzer über RS, *AMZ*, 1911, No. 13.

Theodor Müngersdorf: RS als Vokalkomponist, *Die Stimme*, September 1924.

E. W. Murphy: Harmony and tonality in the large orchestral works of RS, *Dissertation Abstracts*, July 1965, p. 408.

R. C. Muschler: RS, *Revue Rhénane*, June 1925.

— RS, Hildesheim, 1924.

Rollo H. Myers: RS, *MT*, October 1949, p. 347.

— Retrospective RS, *Contrepoints*, No. 6, 1950, p. 25.

Rollo Myers (ed.): RS and Romain Rolland: correspondence, diary and essays, Calder & Boyars (London) 1968.

Otto Neitzel: Zur Würdigung von RS, *NMZ*, 1907, No. 19.

Ernest Newman: The recent RS festival in London, *Musical World*, 1903, No. 8.

— Strauss and the music of the future, *Fortnightly Review*, January 1903, p. 30.
— RS, Music of the Masters series (London) 1908.
— RS, in *More Essays from the World of Music, Calder* (London) 1958, pp. 132, 134.
— Mozart and Strauss, in *Testament of Music*, Putnam (London) 1962, p. 101.
— The Newman–Shaw controversy concerning RS, in *–do–*, p. 115.
— RS, in *–do–*, p. 264.
Gunther von Noé: Das Zitat bei RS, *NZfM*, June 1964.
Albert Noelte: RS zu seinem 60. Geburtstag, *Der Sammler*, No. 67, 11 June 1924.
Arthur Notcutt: RS, some recollections of the London premières, *MO*, December 1949, p. 135.
Gerhard Ohlhoff: RS' Berefung nach Weimar, *SM*, May–June 1964, p. 155.
Alfred Orel: RS als Begleiter seiner Lieder, *SM*, January 1952, p. 12.
— RS, *Wiener Zeitung*, 11 June 1924.
Helmuth Osthoff: Mozarts Einfluss auf RS, *SM*, November 1958, p. 409.
Alfons Ott: Festvortrag zur Eröffnung der Ausstellung 'RS und seine Zeit' in der neuen Deutschen Oper Berlin, *Strauss*, No. 44, March 1965, p. 4.
— Frauengestalten im Werk von RS, *Strauss*, No. 43, December 1964, p. 2.
— Couperin als Quelle für RS, Fontes Artis Musicae, January–April 1966.
Hugh Ottaway: Some thoughts on RS, *Halle*, March 1954, p. 1.
Selim Palmgren: RS, *Hufvudstadsbladet*, 11 June 1939.
W. Panofsky: RS, Partitur eines Lebens, Piper (Munich) 1965.
R. Paoli: Le lettere di RS, *L'Approdo musicale*, January–March 1959.
D. C. Parker: Criticisms of RS, *MS*, 21 August 1909, p. 116.
— RS, his place in modern music, *MS*, 21 June 1913, p. 88.
— Roses from the South (Italian influence upon Strauss), *Opera News*, 26 December 1959, p. 6.
Julius Patzak: RS als Mozart-Dirigent, *ÖM*, July–August 1956.

Bernhard Paumgartner: RS, *ÖM*, 1947, Nos. 11–12, p. 299.
— RS in der Schweiz, *ÖM*, August 1964.
Emil Petschnig: Wirtschaftliches von der jüngsten Wiener Strauss-Première, *NMZ*, 1920, No. 4, p. 52.
W. Petzet: RS, *Signale*, 30 May 1934.
— Die Richard Strausstage in Dresden, *Signale*, 12 November 1924.
H. F. Peyser: Strauss—delayed curtain on an era, *Musical America*, October 1949, p. 4.
Ferdinand Pfohl: RS und der Hamburgische Geist, *NZfM*, January 1935, p. 24.
Robert Pitrou: Hugo von Hofmannsthal, librettiste de RS, d'après leur correspondance, *RM*, May 1930, p. 417.
Alfred Planyarsky: Strauss vor dem Orchester, *ÖM*, August 1964.
John F. Porte: RS as conductor, *The Gramophone*, September 1931, p. 147.
Robert W. F. Potter: The songs of RS, *The Gramophone*, March 1936, p. 407.
C. M. Prerauer: More on RS, from his own hand (hitherto unknown letters), *Musical Courier*, August 1961, p. 12.
Helene Raff: Um RS herum, *NZfM*, June 1939, p. 590.
Johanna von Rauchenberger-Strauss: Jugenerinnerung, *Strauss Jahrbuch*, 1959–60, p. 7.
— My brother RS (ed. R. Breuer), *Saturday Revue*, December 1958, p. 31.
Herbert Raynor: RS, *MO*, December 1953, p. 145.
Hans F. Redlich: RS, *Der Aufstieg*, April 1934.
E. Reeser: RS und Alphons Diepenbrock, ein Briefwechsel, *Strauss*, No. 32, March 1962, p. 5.
Willi Reich: RS und Romain Rolland, *Melos*, March 1951, p. 70.
Hugo Reichenberger: Die Münchener RS-Woche, *Der Merker*, 25 July 1910, p. 870.
Charles Reid: Strauss and the heroic ideal, *M&M*, June 1964, p. 10.
Jon Reil: RS-Geschichtchen, *NZfM*, June 1934, p. 672.
Gustav Renker: Der Mensch und seinem Werken, *Die Musik*, June 1924, p. 624.
Paul Riesenfeld: Das RS-Fest in Breslau, *Signale*, 1924, No. 43, p. 1617.
— RS, eine Seelenanalyse, *Nord und Süd*, 1902, No. 305.

Strauss, Richard

Romain Rolland: RS, *La Revue de Paris*, 1899, No. 12 (15 June).

— RS, in *Musiciens d'aujourd'hui*, Paris, n.d.

— A propos de quelques articles sur RS, *Bulletin S.I.M.*, 1909, 15 June, p. 513, 15 July, p. 625.

— Meinem Freund RS, *Neue Freie Presse*, 8 June 1924.

— RS, Correspondance, Fragments de Journal, Paris, 1951.

Paul Rosenfeld: RS, *Dial*, February 1920, p. 137.

Harold Rosenthal: Munich commemorates Strauss, *Opera*, May 1964, p. 309.

A. Rosenzweig: Les adaptations de Lulli et de Couperin par RS, *RM*, April 1926.

Claude Rostand: RS, l'ambiance, les origines, la vie, l'œuvre, l'esthetique et le style, Paris, 1949.

— Position et evolution de RS, *Disques*, December 1952, p. 660.

Ernst Roth: The operas of RS, *Ballet*, October 1949, p. 33.

— RS in London 1947, *Strauss Jahrbuch*, 1954, p. 132.

Rubato: RS, *Vocalist*, July 1902, p. 122.

J. Rufer: RS (transl. V. Solin), *Hudební Rozhledy*, 1959, No. 16, p. 670.

K. Ruhrberg: Genie an der Wende der Zeit, *Deutsche Oper*, No. 8, 1964–5, p. 8.

Ernst Rychnovsky: Ein literarisches Denkmal für RS, *Die Musik*, June (1) 1914, p. 316.

C. Saerchinger: RS as I knew him, *Saturday Review of Literature*, 29 October 1949, p. 47.

Adolfo Salazar: RS, in *Música y músicos de hoy*, Editorial Mundo Latino (Madrid) 1928, p. 255.

Lionel Salter: RS, *The Gramophone*, October 1949, p. 75.

Gustave Samazeuilh: Un hommage à RS, *Le Ménestrel*, 5 November 1937, p. 289.

— RS, in *Musiciens de mon temps*, Marcel Daubin (Paris) 1947, p. 317.

— RS and France, *Tempo*, No. 12, summer 1949, p. 31.

— Persönliche Erinnerungen an RS, *Das Musikleben*, January 1952, p. 2.

— Zum Abschluss des Strauss-Jahres 1964; ein Brief aus Paris, *Strauss*, No. 44, March 1965, p. 1 (in French and German).

L. Saminsky: The downfall of Strauss, *League of Composers Review*, November 1924.

Pitts Sanborn: RS in Munich, *Modern Music*, November–December 1938.

Francesco Santoliquido: Il dopo Wagner: Claude Debussy e RS, Rome, 1909.

F. Sargeant: RS, *Life*, 19 September 1949, p. 127.

Richard Saville: The songs of RS, *MS*, 26 November 1904, p. 339, 28 January 1905, p. 53, 4 February 1905, p. 71; repr. from *The Musician* (Boston).

K. Schaezler: RS, *Commonweal*, 22 June 1934, p. 207.

Theo. Schäfer: RS, *Halbmonatsschrift für Schulmusikpflege*, 5 June 1924.

— Das Psychologische bei RS, *Dortmunder Zeitung*, 12–13 June 1924.

Franz Schalk: RS, *Die Theater- und Musikwoche*, 1919, No. 29, p. 1.

Hans F. Schaub: RS und wir, *Die Musikwelt*, 15 August 1922.

Ferdinand Scherber: Die Strauss-Affäre, *Signale*, 1924, No. 47 (19 November), p. 1783.

L. Schiedermair: RS in amerikanische Beleuchtung, *Freistatt*, 1902, No. 34.

Willi Schmid: The Munich element in RS, *MT*, January 1935, p. 20.

Leopold Schmidt: RS, *NZfM*, 1905, No. 40, p. 747.

— RS, Leipzig, 1906.

— RS als Dramatiker, *Die Musikwelt*, 1 June 1924.

— RS als Dirigent, *Blätter der Staatsoper* (Berlin), October 1926.

Eugen Schmitz: RS als Musikdramatiker, Munich, 1907.

Percy Scholes: Strauss, *Radio Times*, 16 October 1931, p. 177.

Walter Schrenk: Der Meister und sein Werk, *Deutsche Allg. Zeitung*, 11 June 1924.

— RS und die Gegenwart, *Blätter der Staatsoper* (Berlin), March 1925, p. 13.

— RS und die moderne Musik, Berlin, 1934.

Oscar Schröter: Besuch bei RS, *Stuttgarter Neues Tagblatt*, No. 554, 27 November 1925.

Margarete Schuch-Mankiewicz: Ernst von Schuch über RS, *Der Merker*, March (2) 1911.

Friedrich von Schuch: RS, Ernst von Schuch und Dresdens Oper, Leipzig, 1953.

Willi Schuh: RS, in *Les Musiciens célèbres*, Editions d'Art Lucien Mazenod (Geneva) 1948, p. 232.

— Hofmannsthal und die Oper, *Melos*, July–August 1949, p. 180.

— In memoriam RS, *SM*, October 1949, p. 361.

— In honour of RS, *Tempo*, No. 12, summer 1949, p. 5.

— Über Opern von RS, Zürich, 1947.

— RS—Zyklus des Zürcher Stadttheaters, *SM*, July 1953, p. 308.

— Zürcher RS-Zyklus, *SM*, July 1954, p. 284.

— Das Bühnenwerk von RS, in den letzten unter Mitwirkung des Komponisten geschaffenen Münchner Inszenierungen, Zürich, 1954.

— Betrachtungen und Erinnerungen, Atlantis-Verlag (Zürich) 1957; Eng. transl. L. J. Lawrence, Boosey & Hawkes (London) 1957.

— Das Szenarium und die musikalischen Skizzen zum Ballet 'Kythere', *Strauss-Jahrbuch*, 1959–60, p. 84.

— Verstreute Goethe-Vertonungen, in *–do–*, p. 147.

Willi Schuh & Ernst Roth: RS, complete catalogue, Boosey & Hawkes/Fürstner, 1964.

Max See: RS und die 'griechische Operette', *NZfM*, June 1964.

W. Seibert: RS, *Blätter der Staatsoper* (Berlin), 1924, No. 16.

Arthur Seidl: Steinitzers RS-Biographie, *Die Musik*, May 1912, p. 256.

— RS als Politiker, *AMZ*, 25 October 1912, p. 1058.

— Straussiana, Regensburg, 1913.

— Drei kleinere Kapitel zur Strauss-Biographie, *Der Merker*, May (2) 1914, p. 387.

Arthur Seidl & Willi Klatte: RS, ein Charakterskizze, 1896.

William Seymer: RS, *Nya Dagligt Allehanda*, 11 June 1939.

Desmond Shawe-Taylor: RS, *Halle*, November 1949, p. 23.

N. Slonimsky: Straussiana, *Etude*, February 1951, p. 4.

W. S. Smith: Bruckner vs Brahms, and Mahler vs Strauss: a study in contrasts, *Chord and Discord*, 1958, No. 8, p. 91.

M. L. Smyser: RS, *M&L*, January 1931, p. 46.

August Spanuth: RS, *AMZ*, 1904, No. 22, p. 386; No. 23, p. 405.

— Der fünfzigjährige RS, *Signale*, 1914, No. 23, p. 963.

Richard Specht: Strauss-Silhouette, *Der Merker*, March (2) 1911, p. 490.

— Strauss, *Der Merker*, May (2) 1914, p. 362.

— RS, Glossen zu seinem Wesen und zu seinem Werk, *Die Musik*, June (1) 1914, p. 259.

— Der Kampf und RS, *Der Merker*, 1 December 1919, p. 756.

— Dirigenten RS, *Anbruch*, March 1920, p. 185.

— RS und sein Werk, Leipzig, 1921.

— Strauss-Metamorphosen, *Die Musikwelt*, 1 June 1924.

— RS der Klassiker unserer Zeit, *Die Musik*, June 1924, p. 621.

— Zur Strauss-Diskussion, *Neue Freie Presse*, 15 November 1924.

P. Spencer: 20th century waltz king, *Opera News*, 13 February 1956, p. 12.

Paul Stefan: RS, 50. Geburtstag, *Hamburger Fremdenblatt*, 11 June 1914.

— RS verlässt die Wiener Oper, *Anbruch*, May 1931, p. 86.

D. Steinbeck: Strauss und die Stagnation der Oper, *Strauss*, Nos. 54–55, December 1957, p. 9.

Max Steinitzer: Der unbekannte Strauss, *Die Musik*, November 1911, p. 131.

— RS, Berlin/Leipzig, 1911 (various editions).

— RS' Leben bis zum Jahre 1885, *Die Musik*, November 1911, p. 131.

— Weggelassene Vorrede zu meinem 'RS', *AMZ*, No. 43, 25 October 1912.

— RS als Persönlichkeit, *NMZ*, No. 3, January 1913.

— Das Kapitel Weimar in RS' Leben, *Die Musik*, 1914, June (1) p. 297, June (2) p. 345.

— Zum 60. Geburtstag von RS, *Die Musikwelt*, 1 June 1924.

— Meister RS—Zur seinem 60. Geburtstag am 11. Juni, *Reclams Universum*, 1924, No. 34, p. 147.

— RS' Werke für Klavier, *Die Musik*, November 1931, p. 105.

Strauss, Richard

— Strauss-Programme, *Die Musik*, June 1934, p. 656.
— Die Reden vom Wiener RS-Bankett, *NZfM*, June 1934, p. 585.
W. Stephens: Visit to RS, *Musician*, January 1912, p. 12.
— Dr. RS, *Musical News*, 1912, No. 1089, p. 46.
R. Sternfeld: Strauss und Pfitzner, *AMZ*, 13 December 1924.
Denis Stevens: Strauss in Munich, *Opera News*, 2 May 1964, p. 28.
Teresa Stich-Randall: Singing Strauss, *Musical America*, July 1964, p. 16.
Otto Strasser: RS und die Wiener Philharmoniker, *ÖM*, August 1964.
Heinrich Strobel: Dank an RS, *Melos*, July–August 1949, p. 177.
Hans Swarowsky: Persönliches von RS, *ÖM*, April–May 1957.
Arthur Symons: Music of Strauss, *Living Age*, 10 January 1903, p. 113.
— RS, *Bulletin S.I.M.*, 1907, p. 117 (transl. Edouard & Louis Thomas).
— RS, *Le Mercure musical*, 1907, No. 11.
Reinhard Syz: RS und die Musik, *März*, 1907, No. 1.
Walter Szmolyan: Literatur über RS, *ÖM*, August 1964.
O. Taubmann: RS, *Sängerhalle*, 1900, Nos. 1–2.
Roland Tenschert: Das Verhältnis von Wort und Ton, *NZfM*, June 1934, p. 591.
— Die Tonsymbolik bei RS, *Die Musik*, June 1934, p. 646.
— Autobiographisches im Schaffen von RS, *NZfM*, June 1939, p. 582.
— Hosenrollen in den Bühnenwerken von RS, *NZfM*, June 1939, p. 586.
— 3 × 7 Variationen über das Thema RS, Vienna, 1944.
— Anekdoten von RS, Vienna, 1945.
— RS—eine Wahlverwandschaft, Vienna, 1949.
— Richard Wagner im Urteil von RS, *SM*, September 1954, p. 327.
— RS—Gedenken an der Rhein-Oper, *ÖM*, October 1959.
— Erinnerungen an RS, *ÖM*, May–June 1964.
— RS und die Salzburger Festspiele, *Strauss Jahrbuch*, 1954, p. 150; *ÖM*, August 1964.

— RS und Stefan Zweig, *ÖM*, February 1968.
Hans Tessmer: RS, *Deutsche Tonkünstler-Zeitung*, 1924, p. 405.
— RS, *Ausblick* (Blätter der Dresdener Staatstheater), November 1924.
— RS—Zu seinem 60. Geburtstage am 11. Juni, *NMZ*, 1924, No. 5, p. 104.
Emil Thilo: RS als Chorkomponist, *Die Musik*, June (1) 1914, p. 304.
Walter Thomas: RS und seine Zeitgenossen, Langen-Müller (Munich, Vienna) 1964.
Heinz Tiessen: Die reine Wirkung der Straussischen Programme-Symphonie, *NMZ*, 1913, No. 8.
— Erinnerungen an RS in seiner Berliner Jahren, *Strauss*, Nos. 54–55, December 1967, p. 24.
Willy Tiktin: Strauss Triumphator, *Das Blaubuch* (Berlin), 1907, No. 1.
Franz Trenner: RS und die 'Wilde Gung'l', *SM*, 1950, Nos. 8–9, p. 403.
— Richard's start in life, in *Great Composers Through the Eyes of Their Contemporaries*, Dutton (New York) 1951, p. 416.
— RS und Ernst von Wolzogen, *Strauss Jahrbuch*, 1954, p. 110.
— RS Dokumente seines Lebens und Schaffens, Munich, 1954.
Emil Tschirch: Mit RS auf Reisen, *Die Musik*, June 1924, p. 657.
— Reise mit Strauss nach England, *Deutsche Allg. Zeitung*, 11 June 1924.
A. Tubeuf: Pour le rayonnement de RS en France, *Strauss*, No. 36, March 1963, p. 4.
Hermann Ullrich: RS, *ÖM*, September 1958.
Erich Urban: RS in neuen Werken, *Vossische Zeitung*, 1 December 1901.
— RS in neuen Liedern, *Die Musik*, September (2) 1902, p. 2137.
— RS, in *Moderne Essays zur Kunst*, Berlin, 1902.
— Strauss contra Wagner, Berlin, 1902.
B. Vogel: Deutsche Komponisten der Gegenwart: RS, *NMZ*, 1891, No. 7, p. 78.
Fritz Vollbach: Die orchestrale Farbengebung bei RS, *Der Merker*, 1909, No. 6.
— RS als Meister der Farbe, *NMZ*, 1910, No. 8.
— RS, *AMZ*, 1914, No. 24, p. 919.
Jürgen Völckers: Die untrennbare Ver-

schmelzung: RS und Hugo von Hofmanns-thal, *NZfM*, 1954, p. 712.

— RS und sein 'musikalisches Testament': 'Prima la parole—dopo la musica', *NZfM*, July–August 1957.

Emile Vuillermoz: La Festwoche RS à Stuttgart, *Revue S.I.M.*, November 1912, p. 49.

Edmund Wachten: Das Formproblem in den sinfonischen Dichtungen von RS, Berlin, 1933.

— RS als nationale Erscheinung, *AMZ*, 19 January 1934.

— RS, sein Leben in Bildern, Leipzig, 1940.

Hermann W. Waltershausen: RS, Munich, 1921.

— RS, *Hellweg*, No. 32, 9 August 1922.

— Wie sieht unserer Zeit RS, *München-Augsburger Abendzeitung*, No. 159, 13 June 1924.

John S. Weissmann: RS, *Musical Events*, July 1964, p. 21.

— Strauss on the stage, *MR*, 1967, No. 4, p. 331.

Egon Wellesz: RS, *MR*, 1950, p. 23.

— Hofmannsthal and Strauss, *M&L*, 1952.

— L'epistolario Strauss–Hofmannsthal commentato da Egon Wellesz, *Rivista musicale italiana*, January–March 1953, p. 80.

Erik Werba: Der 'Mueller-Asow'—das Thematische Strauss-Verzeichnis, *ÖM*, August 1964.

Gerard Werker: RS, *Mens en melodie*, November 1949, p. 337.

Theo W. Werner: Des Meisters sinfonisches Schaffen, *Thüringer Allg. Zeitung*, No. 158, 11 June 1924.

Kurt Westphal: Das Musikdramatische Prinzip bei RS, *Die Musik*, September 1927, p. 859.

Rolf Wilhelm: Die Donau (Fragment einer sinfonischen Dichtung), *Strauss Jahrbuch*, 1954, p. 125.

A. C. Williams: The domestic genius, *Halle*, October 1958, p. 5.

Herbert Windt: RS und die Atonalität, *Die Musik*, June 1924, p. 642.

K. Wörner: RS und Mozart, *AMZ*, 6 October 1933.

Leo Wurmser: RS as an opera conductor, *M&L*, January 1964, p. 4.

— Strauss and some classical symphonies, *M&L*, July 1964, p. 233.

W. von Wymetal: Wiener Wünsche für RS, *AMZ*, 9–15 June 1924 (No. 26), p. 513.

Wilhelm Zentner: RS, *NZfM*, June 1939, p. 577.

Paul Zschorlich: RS in Leipzig, *Leipziger Tageblatt*, 1905, No. 108.

— RS und das Publikum, *Musikalische Rundschau*, 1906, No. 1.

— RS über den Fortschritt in der Musik, *Die Hilfe*, 1907, No. 25.

Hans Zurlinden: Ein Sonntag bei RS, *Neue Schweizer Rundschau*, Vol. 17 (1949–50), p. 367.

F. M. Zweig: Friderike Maria Zweig über RS, *Strauss*, Nos. 54–55, December 1967, p. 24.

MISCELLANEOUS OR UNSIGNED

RS, *MT*, January 1898, p. 25.

Concerning RS and programme music, *MS*, 12 July 1902, p. 22.

So much for Strauss, *MS*, 21 June 1902, p. 390.

Musical 'progress' and RS, *MS*, 5 July 1902, p. 9.

RS, Tchaikovsky and the idea of death, *MS*, 29 August 1903, p. 136.

James Huneker on RS, *MS*, 12 September 1903, p. 165 (condensed from *New York Sun*).

RS and his works, *MS*, 19 December 1903, p. 389.

RS, *MT*, January 1903, p. 9.

Strauss and tone-poems: a word to composers, *The Vocalist*, November 1903, p. 228.

From Guntram to Elektra, *The Times*, 23 July 1910, p. 10.

RS über Johannes Brahms und Hans von Bülow, *AMZ*, 1910, No. 2.

Ernest Hutchinson on RS, *MS*, 12 February 1910, p. 101.

Strauss in his summer home, *MS*, 23 July 1910, p. 61; reprinted from *Musical America*.

A new view of RS, *MS*, 11 March 1911, p. 153.

Unsere Strauss-Rundfrage, *AMZ*, 25 October 1912, p. 1058.

Un interview de RS, *Le Monde musical*, June 1919.

RS, eine Umfrage, *Anbruch*, May 1924, p. 205.

L'esthétique de RS formulée par lui-même, *Le Monde musical*, 31 January 1928.

RS, *Midland Musician*, March 1929, p. 64.

RS, *A Zene*, 15 November 1932, p. 57.

Le declin de RS, *Dissonances*, October 1933.

RS Spiegelung in Büchern, *Anbruch*, May 1934, p. 89.

Strauss v. Hitler, *Time*, 17 July 1944, p. 46.

The artistic testament of RS, *Opera*, June 1950, p. 20.

Anderman zieht den Vorhang auf, *Melos*, July–August 1949, p. 185.

Neue Briefe von RS, *Melos*, February 1954.

Claude Debussy über RS, *Musikleben*, June 1954, p. 229.

Der Kapellmeister-Souffleur: ein unveröffentlichter Brief von RS an Hans Pringsheim, *Musikleben*, March 1954, p. 91.

Wie RS arbeitete, *Musikleben*, July–August 1954, p. 269.

Ein Kinderbild von RS, *Musikleben*, October 1954, p. 349.

RS, *Disques*, No. 65, May–June 1954, p. 351.

RS und Anton Kippenberg: Briefwechsel, *Strauss Jahrbuch*, 1959–60, p. 114.

Erlebnis und Bekenntnis des jungen RS, *Strauss*, No. 30, September 1961, p. 1.

Ein bisher unveröffentlichter Brief des 19-jährigen RS, *Strauss*, No. 33, June 1962, p. 8.

Dichter und Musiker—Aus dem Briefwechsel Strauss–Hofmannsthal, *Musica*, 1952, No. 1, p. 1.

Briefe an Fritz Busch, *SM*, July–August 1964, p. 210.

Auf dem Briefwechsel RS/Clemens Krauss, *SM*, January 1966, p. 2.

Kerr schreibt an Strauss, *Strauss*, No. 47, December 1965, p. 8.

Wortlaut des auf S. 18/19 im Faksimile wiedergegebenen Strauss-Briefes in der originalen Schreibweise von Strauss, *Strauss*, No. 49, June 1966, p. 16.

Aus dem Tagebuch von RS, *Strauss*, No. 51, December 1966, p. 1.

RS et Romain Rolland, Albin Michel (Paris) 1961; transl. Rollo Myers, Calder & Boyars (London) 1968.

The correspondence between RS and Hugo von Hofmannsthal (transl. Hanns Hammelmann and Ewald Osers), Collins (London) 1961.

IGOR STRAVINSKY (1882–1971)

Igor Fedorovich Stravinsky was born on 17 June 1882 at Oranienbaum (now Lomosonov) near St. Petersburg, and St. Petersburg —where his father was a bass in the Imperial Opera—was his home until 1910, though the summers were often spent on relations' country estates, especially the Nossenko estate at Ustilug in Volhynia. Though as a boy he had private tuition in piano and composition, his parents forbade him to make a career of music and he ineffectually studied law at St. Petersburg University from 1901 to 1905. From 1903 to 1906 he was a private composition pupil of Rimsky-Korsakov and virtually became a member of Rimsky's family circle. In 1906 he married Catherine Nossenko, a first cousin whose close friend he had been since he was ten. In February 1909 he met the impresario Serge Diaghilev and agreed to help with musical arrangements for his Russian Ballet in Paris. This was the beginning of a collaboration which lasted until shortly before Diaghilev's death in 1929. Stravinsky travelled extensively with Ballet in Europe and wrote a series of works for it, including *L'Oiseau de Feu*, the Paris première of which in 1910 was his first great success, and *Le Sacre du Printemps*, also first performed in Paris but amid remarkable uproar (1913). From 1910 to 1914 Stravinsky divided the year between Ustilug and Clarens in Switzerland, where he met the conductor Ernest Ansermet, who was to be a great champion of his work. He was not called up by the Russian Army at the declaration of World War I because of poor health and stayed on in Switzerland, living from 1915 to 1920 at Morges. After the Russian Revolution Stravinsky elected to continue his career in the West and lived in France during the 1920s and 1930s, at Biarritz, Nice, Voreppe (near Grenoble) and finally from 1934—the year in which he became a French citizen—in Paris. He toured widely as conductor and pianist in performances of his own music, notably with the violinist Samuel Dushkin from 1931 to 1935 and in the mid-1930s with his own son, the pianist Soulima Stravinsky. In 1939 Stravinsky's wife died of tuberculosis (a disease which also afflicted the composer and his daughters) and he visited the USA for the fourth time, using the delivery of the Charles Eliot Norton lectures at Harvard University (*Poétique Musicale*, 1939–40) as the stepping stone to a new life away from the War. In 1940 he married Vera de Bosset (formerly wife of the painter Sergei Soudeikine and an intimate friend for nearly twenty years) and settled permanently in Los Angeles, becoming an American citizen in 1945. In 1947 he met the young American musician Robert Craft, who became his musical assistant, biographer and mentor in the music of Webern. In the late 1950s and early 1960s Stravinsky undertook concert tours on a world scale with Craft, revisiting Moscow and Leningrad in 1962 after half a century's absence. He survived a series of strokes (1956, 1967) but died of heart failure in New York on 6 April 1971.

CATALOGUE OF WORKS

1. Sonata in F sharp minor. For piano. 1903–4, Samara, St. Petersburg. Ded. Nicolas Richter.

1. *Allegro*; 2. *Andante*; 3. *Scherzo*; 4. *Finale*.
fp (private): 9 February 1905, Nicolas Richter.
Unpub.

2. The Mushrooms going to war. Song for bass and piano. 1904. Unpub.

3. Faune et Bergère (Faun and Shepherdess) (Op. 2). Song Suite for mezzo-soprano and orchestra. Words: A Pushkin. 1906, Imatra, St. Petersburg. Ded. to the composer's wife. Dur. 10'.

1. *La Bergère*; 2. *Le Faune*; 3. *Le Torrent*.
2 fl, pic, 2 ob, 2 cl, 2 bsn; 4 hn, 2 tpt, 3 tmb, tuba; timp, cym, GC; strings.
fp (private): 27 April 1907, St. Petersburg, Court Orchestra, cond. H. Wahrlich.
fp (public): 16 February 1908, St. Petersburg, Belaiev's season of Russian Symphony Concerts, cond. Felix Blumenfeld.
Pub. 1908, Belaiev. Also reduction for voice and piano by the composer. French

version, A. Komaroff; German version, Heinrich Möller.

4. Symphony in E flat (Op. 1). 1905–7, Ustilug. Ded. 'to my dear teacher N. A. Rimsky-Korsakov'. Dur. 30'.

1. *Allegro moderato*; 2. *Scherzo: Allegretto*; 3. *Largo*; 4. *Finale: Allegro molto*.
2 fl, pic, 2 ob, 3 cl, 2 bsn; 4 hn, 3 tpt, 3 tmb, tuba; timp, tgle, cym & GC; strings.
fp (private): 27 April 1907, St. Petersburg, Court Orchestra, cond. H. Wahrlich.
fp (public): 22 January 1908, St. Petersburg, Belaiev's season of Russian Symphony Concerts, cond. Felix Blumenfeld.
fp (in slightly revised version): 2 April 1914, Montreux, cond. Ernest Ansermet.
fEp: 16 April 1914, Torquay, Festival Concert, cond. Basil Hindenberg.
fFp: 16 November 1928, Paris, l'Orchestre Symphonique de Paris, cond. Igor Stravinsky.
Pub. 1914, Jurgenson; State Publishing House (Moscow).

5. Pastorale. Song without words for soprano and piano. 1907, Ustilug. Ded. Nadezhda Rimsky-Korsakov. Dur. 4'.

fp (private): 31 October 1907, at one of Rimsky-Korsakov's private gatherings, Igor Stravinsky and Maximilian Steinberg.
fp (public): winter 1908, St. Petersburg, at one of the Evenings of Contemporary Music.
Pub. 1910, Jurgenson.

5a. Pastorale. Version for soprano, oboe, cor anglais, clarinet and bassoon. December 1923, Biarritz. Pub. Schott.

5b. Pastorale. Lengthened version for violin and piano by Igor Stravinsky and Samuel Dushkin. 1933. Dur. 6'. Pub. 1934, Schott.

5c. Pastorale. Lengthened version for violin, oboe, cor anglais, clarinet and bassoon. 1933. Pub. 1934, Schott.

6. Mélodies (Serge Gorodetsky) (Op. 6). For mezzo-soprano and piano. Dur. 8'.

1. *La Novice* (*Chanson de printemps*)—The Cloister (Spring). December 1907, Ustilug. Ded. Elizabeth Theodorovna Petrenko.
2. *La Rosée sainte* (*Chant mystique des Vieux-Croyants Flagellants*)—A Song of the Dew

(Mystic Song of the Ancient Russian Flagellants). 1908, Ustilug.

fp: winter 1908, St. Petersburg, one of the
Evenings of Contemporary Music, Elizabeth
Petrenko and Igor Stravinsky.

fEp (No. 1): 31 March 1914, Steinway Hall,
Alys Bateman and Parlovitz.

fEp (No. 2): 29 May 1912, Steinway Hall,
Mme Aktzery and Yowanowitch.

fEbp (No. 2): 5 December 1927, Lina
Llubera.

Pub. ?1912, Jurgenson; 1968, Boosey &
Hawkes. French and English versions, M.-D.
Calvocoressi.

7. Scherzo fantastique (Op. 3). For large
orchestra. June 1907–March 1908, Ustilug.
Ded. Alexander Siloti. Dur. 16′.

3 fl, alto fl, pic, 2 ob, ca, 3 cl, bcl, 2 bsn,
cbsn; 4 hn, 2 tpt, alto tpt; cym, celesta;
2 (orig. 3) hp, strings.

fp: 6 February 1909, St. Petersburg, cond.
Alexander Siloti.

fEp: 26 August 1914, Queen's Hall,
Promenade Concert, Queen's Hall Orchestra,
cond. Sir Henry Wood.

fEbp: 13 May 1928, Wireless Symphony
Orchestra, cond. Igor Stravinsky.

Pub. Jurgenson; Schott.

7a. Les Abeilles. Ballet adaptation of
preceding.

fp: 10 January 1917, Paris, Opéra; choreography, Leo Staats.

BIBLIOGRAPHY:

Jean Marnold: Les Abeilles, ballet de M. IS,
Mercure de France, 1 March 1917.

8. Feu d'artifice (Fireworks) (Op. 4).
Fantasy for large orchestra. May–June 1908,
Ustilug. Ded. Nadia and Maximilian Stein-
berg. Dur. 4′.

3 fl, 2 ob, 3 cl, 2 bsn; 6 hn, 3 tpt, 3 tmb, tuba;
timp, tgle, cym, GC, celesta, campanelli; 2 hp,
strings.

fp: 6 February 1909. St. Petersburg, Siloti
concerts, cond. Alexander Siloti.

fEp: 14 February 1914, Queen's Hall,
Saturday Afternoon Concert, Queen's Hall
Orchestra, cond. Sir Henry Wood. (Repeated,
'by request', a fortnight later.)

fEbp: 4 March 1926, Manchester, Free

Trade Hall, Halle Orchestra, cond. Sir
Hamilton Harty.

Pub. 1910, Schott. Reduction for piano four
hands by Otto Singer pub. 1924, Schott.

BIBLIOGRAPHY:

O. Corbiot: La fantasie orchestrale Feu
d'artifice, *L'Education musicale*, No. 144,
January 1968.

9. Chant funèbre (Funeral Dirge) (Op. 5).
For wind instruments, in memory of Rimsky-
Korsakov. Summer 1908, Ustilug.

fp: autumn 1908, St. Petersburg, Belaiev's
season of Russian Symphony Concerts, cond.
Felix Blumenfeld.

Unpub. Lost.

10. Four Studies (Op. 7). For piano. June–
July 1908, Ustilug.

1. *Con moto* (C minor). Ded. E. Mitusov.

2. *Allegro brillante* (D major). Ded. Nicolas
Richter.

3. *Andantino* (E minor). Ded. Andrey
Rimsky-Korsakov.

4. *Vivo* (F sharp major). Ded. Vladimir
Rimsky-Korsakov.

fp: 1908, Igor Stravinsky.

Pub. 1910, Jurgenson; Benjamin (Hamburg).

11. Kobold. Grieg, orch. Igor Stravinsky
for the ballet 'Le Festin'. 1909.

fp: 19 May 1909, Paris, Théâtre du Châtelet,
Diaghilev's Russian Ballet.

Unpub.

**12. Nocturne in A flat and Valse Brillante
in E flat.** Chopin, orch. Igor Stravinsky for
the ballet 'Les Sylphides'. 1909.

fp: 2 June 1909, Paris, Théâtre du Châtelet,
Diaghilev's Russian Ballet.

Unpub.

13. Two Songs of the Flea. Orch. Igor
Stravinsky. 1910.

1. *Song of the Flea* (Beethoven, Op. 75
No. 3). For bass and orchestra.

2 fl, 2 ob, 2 cl, 2 bsn; 2 hn; strings.

2. *Song of the Flea* (Mussorgsky). For
baritone or bass and orchestra.

3 fl, 2 ob, 2 cl, 2 bsn; 4 hn, 2 tpt, 3 tmb,
tuba; timp, hp, strings.

Pub. W. Bessell & Co.; Boosey & Hawkes.

14. L'Oiseau de feu (The Firebird). Ballet ('conte dansé') in two scenes. November 1909–18 May 1910. Ded. Andrey Rimsky-Korsakov. Dur. 45'.

1. *Introduction*. Scene One: 2. *Kaschei's Enchanted Garden*; 3. *Appearance of the Firebird pursued by Ivan Tsarevich*; 4. *Dance of the Firebird*; 5. *Ivan Tsarevich Captures the Firebird*; 6. *Supplication of the Firebird*; 7. *Appearance of Thirteen Enchanted Princesses*; 8. *The Princesses' Game with the Golden Apples (Scherzo)*; 9. *Sudden Appearance of Ivan Tsarevich*; 10. *The Princesses' Khorovod (Round Dance)*; 11. *Daybreak*; 12. *Magic Carillon; Appearance of Kashchei's Guardian Monsters; Capture of Ivan Tsarevich*; 13. *Arrival of Kashchei the Immortal; His Dialogue with Ivan Tsarevich; Intercession of the Princesses*; 14. *Appearance of the Firebird*; 15. *Dance of Kashchei's Retinue under the Firebird's Spell*; 16. *Infernal Dance of all Kashchei's Subjects*; 17. *Lullaby (Firebird)*; 18. *Kashchei's Death*. Scene Two: 19. *Disappearance of the Palace and Dissolution of Kashchei's Enchantments; Animation of the Petrified Warriors; General Thanksgiving*.

3 fl, 2 pic, 3 ob, ca, 3 cl, pic cl, bcl, 3 bsn, 2 cbsn; 4 hn, 3 tpt, 3 tmb, tuba; timp, tgle, tamb de basque, cym, GC, tamtam, campanelli; xyl, celesta, pf, 3 hp; strings (16-16-14-8-6). On stage: 3 tpt, 2 ten tuba, 2 bs tuba.

fp: 25 June 1910, Paris, Opéra, Diaghilev's Russian Ballet, cond. Gabriel Pierné; with Tamara Karsavina (The Firebird), Fokina (Tsarevna), Fokine (Ivan Tsarevich), Boulgakov (Kaschei the Immortal); choreography, Michel Fokine; décor and costumes, Alexander Golowine; costumes for The Firebird and Tsarevna, Léon Bakst.

Pub. 1910, Jurgenson; Schott.

14a. L'Oiseau de feu (The Firebird). Suite. 1911. Dur. 21'.

1. *Introduction—Kashchei's Enchanted Garden—Dance of the Firebird*; 2. *Supplication of the Firebird*; 3. *The Princesses' Game with the Golden Apples*; 4. *The Princesses' Khorovod*; 5. *Infernal Dance of all Kashchei's Subjects*.

Orchestration as for complete ballet.

fEp: 4 September 1913, Queen's Hall, Promenade Concert, Queen's Hall Orchestra, cond. Sir Henry Wood.

Pub. 1912, Jurgenson. Also *Berceuse* pub. separately with reduced wind.

14b. L'Oiseau de feu (The Firebird). Suite, revised version. 1919, Morges. Dur. 26'.

1. *Introduction—The Firebird and its Dance—Variation of the Firebird*; 2. *The Princesses' Khorovod*; 3. *Infernal Dance of King Kashchei*; 4. *Lullaby*; 5. *Finale*.

2 fl, pic, 2 ob, ca, 2 cl, 2 bsn; 4 hn, 2 tpt, 3 tmb, tuba; timp, GC, cym, tamb, xyl, tgle; piano, hp, strings.

fEp: 8 April 1921, Queen's Hall, first of Edward Clark's series of concerts, cond. Edward Clark.

fEbp: 23 March 1924, Augmented Wireless Orchestra, cond. Percy Pitt.

Pub. Chester.

14c. L'Oiseau de feu (The Firebird). Suite, new version. 1945. Dur. 28'.

1. *Introduction—Prelude and Dance of the Friebird—Variations (Firebird)*; 2. *Pantomime I*; 3. *Pas de deux (Firebird and Ivan Tsarevich)*; 4. *Pantomime II*; 5. *Scherzo (Dance of the Princesses)*; 6. *Pantomime III*; 7. *Rondo (Khorovod)*; 8. *Infernal Dance*; 9. *Lullaby (Firebird)*; 10. *Final Hymn*.

Orchestration as for 14b, plus snare dm.

Pub. 1946-7, Leeds Music Corporation.

BIBLIOGRAPHY:

Arthur Dennington: The three orchestrations of Stravinsky's Firebird, *Chesterian*, No. 201, winter 1960.

14d. Prélude et Ronde des Princesses. For violin and piano. Transcribed by the composer. 1926. Ded. Paul Kochanski. Pub. Schott.

14e. Berceuse. For violin and piano. Transcribed by the composer. 1926. Ded. Paul Kochanski. Pub. Schott.

14f. Berceuse. For violin and piano. New version, transcribed by Igor Stravinsky and Samuel Dushkin. 1933. Pub. Schott.

14g. Scherzo. For violin and piano. New version, transcribed by Igor Stravinsky and Samuel Dushkin. 1933. Pub. Schott.

14h. Summer Moon. Song 'adapted from

the Firebird Suite'. Words: John Klenner. Pub. 1946, Leeds Music Corporation.

BIBLIOGRAPHY:

Frank Onnen: De Waarheid over Summermoon, *Mens en melodie*, March 1948, p. 85.

14i. Canon (on a Russian Popular Tune). For orchestra. 1965. (Theme from Finale of 'Firebird'). Dur. 0' 30".

3 fl, pic, 2 ob, ca, 2 cl, bcl, 2 bsn, cbsn; 4 hn, 3 tpt, 3 tmb, tuba; timp, GC, piano, hp; strings.

fp: 16 December 1965, Toronto, CBC, cond. Robert Craft.

Pub. 1966, Boosey & Hawkes.

15. Two Poems of Verlaine (Op. 9). For baritone and piano. July 1910, La Baule. Ded. to the composer's brother Gury Stravinsky.

1. *Un grand sommeil noir* (*Sagesse*); 2. *La lune blanche . . .* (*La Bonne Chanson*).

fEbp: 14 September 1924, Norman Allin.

Pub. 1911, Jurgenson; 1954, Boosey & Hawkes. Russian version, S. Mitusov; English version, M.-D. Calvocoressi; German version, M.-D. Calvocoressi.

15a. Two Songs (Paul Verlaine). Version of preceding for baritone and orchestra. 1951. Same dedication. Dur. 4'.

1. *La Bonne Chanson*; 2. *Sagesse*.

2 fl, 2 cl; 2 hn; strings.

Pub. 1953, Boosey & Hawkes.

16. Pétrouchka (Petrushka). Burlesque in four scenes. August 1910–May 1911, Lausanne–Clarens–Beaulieu–Rome. Dated: 13–26 May 1911, Rome. Ded. Alexandre Benois. Dur. 43'.

Scene 1: *The Shrove-tide Fair*; *Legerdemain scene*; *Russian Dance*. Scene 2: *In Petrushka's Cell*. Scene 3: *In the Blackamoor's Cell*; *Dance of the Ballerina*; *Valse*. Scene 4: *The Shrove-tide Fair* (evening); *Wet-Nurses'. Dance*; *Dance of the Coachmen*; *Masqueraders' Scene*.

4 fl, 2 pic, 4 ob, ca, 3 cl, bcl, 3 bsn, cbsn; 4 hn, 2 pistoni, 2 tpt, pic tpt, 3 tmb, tuba; timp, GC, cym, tamtam, tgle, tamb de basque, tamb mil, tamb de Provence (tambourin) campanelli, celesta (2 & 4 hands), pf, 2 hp, xyl; strings.

fp: 13 June 1911, Paris, Théâtre du Châtelet, Diaghilev's Russian Ballet, cond. Pierre Monteux; with Tamara Karsavina (The Ballerina), Nijinsky (Petrushka), Orlov (The Moor), Ceccheti (The Showman); choreography, Michel Fokine; décors and costumes, Alexandre Benois.

fEbp: 23 May 1926, Newcastle Station Orchestra, cond. Edward Clark.

Pub. 1912, Edition Russe de Musique; Boosey & Hawkes. Incl. reduction for piano four hands by the composer.

BIBLIOGRAPHY:

C. Barnes: Birth and death of Petrouchka, *Dance Magazine*, September 1957, p. 16.

Maurice Delage: A propos de Petrouchka, *Gazette artistique*, 1 January 1924.

G. Edgerton: Petroushka, IS's famous ballet, *Arts and Decoration*, February 1925, p. 17.

J. H. Elliot: Petrouchka in new apparel, *Halle*, September 1948, p. 8.

Edwin Evans: Stravinsky—The Firebird and Petrushka, O.U.P. (London) 1933.

Noël Goodwin: Petrushka and the ballet, *Crescendo*, No. 129, November 1963, p. 23.

Leigh Henry: Petroushka, his pedigree and some ponderings thereon, *MO*, June 1919, p. 555.

F.P.: IS, Petrusca, *NMZ*, 15 June 1925.

André Schaeffner: Petrushka, *Le Ménestrel*, 5 June 1931, p. 241; Petrouchka, *MMR*, 1932, p. 55.

H. M. Tomlinson: Petroushka, *Saturday Review of Literature*, 5 December 1925, p. 394.

16a. Pétrouchka (Petrushka). Revised '1947' version. Dated: October 1946, Hollywood. Dur. 42'.

First Part: 1. *The Shrove-Tide Fair*; 2. *Danse Russe*. Second Part: 3. *Petrouchka*. Third Part: 4. *The Blackamoor*; 5. *Valse*. Fourth Part: 6. *The Shrove-Tide Fair*; 7. *Wet-Nurses' Dance*; 8. *Peasant With Bear*; 9. *Gypsies and a Rake Vendor*; 10. *Dance of the Coachmen*; 11. *Masqueraders*; 12. *The Scuffle*; 13. *Death of Petrouchka*; 14. *Police and the Juggler*; 15. *Vociferation of Petrouchka's Double*.

3 fl, pic, 2 ob, ca, 3 cl, bcl, 2 bsn, dbsn; 4 hn, 3 tpt, 3 tmb, tuba; timp, tgle, cym, GC, tamb, side dm, tamtam, xyl, celesta; hp, pf, strings

Pub. 1947/8, Boosey & Hawkes.

BIBLIOGRAPHY:
Henry Boys: Note on the new Petrouchka, *Tempo*, No. 8, summer 1948, p. 15.
— Anmerkungen zum neuen Petruschka, *Musik der Zeit*, Vol. 1, Boosey & Hawkes (1952), p. 22.
Rudolph Stephan: Vom alten und von neuen Petrushka—Stravinsky 1910 und 1946, *NZfM*, June 1962.

16b. Trois Mouvements de Pétrouchka (Three Movements from Petrushka). Transcribed for piano solo by the composer. 1921, Anglet. Ded. Artur Rubinstein.

1. *Russian Dance*; 2. *In Petrushka's Cell*; 3. *The Shrove-tide Fair*.

Pub. 1922, Edition Russe de Musique. A version for two pianos by Victor Babin also exists. Also *Suite de cinq pièces tirée du ballet Petrouchka* transcribed for piano by Théodore Szántó (1922) pub. 1922, Edition Russe de Musique.

17. Deux Poésies de K. Balmont (Two Poems of Balmont). For high voice and piano. 1911, Ustilug. Dur. 2½'.

1. *Myosotis, d'amour fleurette* (Forget-me-nots) (The Flower). Ded. 'to my Mother'.

2. *Le Pigeon* (The Dove). Ded. 'to my sister-in-law Ludmila Beliankin'.

fEbp (No. 1): 17 June 1928, Valentina Aksarova.

Pub. 1912, Edition Russe de Musique; Boosey & Hawkes. French version, M.-D. Calvocoressi; German version, Berthold Feiwel; English version, Robert Burness; later English version, Robert Craft.

17a. Two Poems of Balmont. Version for high voice and chamber orchestra. 1954.

2 fl, 2 cl; pf; 2 v, va, c.

fEbp: 6 October 1955, Emelie Hooke, ensemble, cond. Hermann Scherchen.

Pub. Boosey & Hawkes.

18. Le Roi des Etoiles. For male chorus (TTBB) and orchestra. 1911–12, Ustilug. Text: K. Balmont. Ded. Claude Debussy. Dur. 6'.

3 fl, pic, 4 ob, ca, 3 cl, E-flat cl, 3 bsn, cbsn; 8 hn, 3 tpt, 3 tmb, tuba; timp, GC, tamtam, celesta; 2 hp, strings.

fp: 19 April 1939, Brussels, Institut Nationale de Radiodiffusion Belge, cond. Franz André.

fEp: 28 November 1957, BBC/ICA concert, male voices of the Elizabethan Singers and orchestra, cond. Manuel Rosenthal.

Pub. 1913, Jurgenson. Incl. vocal score by the composer. French version, M.-D. Calvocoressi.

BIBLIOGRAPHY:
Darius Milhaud: A propos d'une première audition d'IS, *RM*, May–June 1939, p. 309.

19. Le Sacre du Printemps (The Rite of Spring). Scenes of Pagan Russia in two parts. 1911–13, Ustilug-Clarens. Ded. Nicolas Roerich. Dur. 34'.

Part I: The Adoration of the Earth. *Introduction*; *Auguries of Spring* (Dances of the Young Girls); *Mock Abduction*; *Spring Khorovod* (Round Dance); *Games of the Rival Clans*; *Procession of the Wise Elder*; *Adoration of the Earth* (the Wise Elder); *Dance of the Earth.* Part II: The Sacrifice. *Introduction*; *Mystical Circles of the Young Girls*; *Glorification of the Chosen Victim*; *The Summoning of the Ancients*; *Ritual of the Ancients*; *Sacrificial Dance* (the Chosen Victim).

3 fl, alto fl, 2 pic, 4 ob, 2 ca, pic cl, 3 cl, 2 bcl, 4 bsn, 2 cbsn; 8 hn, pic tpt, 4 tpt, bs tpt, 3 tmb, 2 tuba; timp, pic timp, tgle, cym antique, GC, tamtam, guero rape, tamb de basque, cym; strings.

fp: 29 May 1913, Paris, Théâtre des Champs-Elysées, Diaghilev's Russian Ballet, cond. Pierre Monteux; with Marie Piltz (The Chosen Victim), Varontsov (The Wise Elder); choreography, Nijinsky.

fEp: 11 July 1913, Drury Lane, Diaghilev's Russian Ballet, cond. Pierre Monteux; with Marie Piltz.

Pub. 1913 (reduction for piano four hands by the composer), 1921 (full score), Edition Russe de Musique; Boosey & Hawkes. Sketches (1911–13) pub. 1969, Boosey & Hawkes. *Danse sacrale* revised (1943) version pub. 1945, Associated Music Publishers (New York).

BIBLIOGRAPHY:
Th. W. Adorno: On Stravinsky's Sacre, *Stimmen*, 1949, No. 17.

J. Balzer: Le Sacre du Printemps for any generation, *Musikrevy*, Vol. 4 (1949–50), p. 16.

Eric Blom: The Listener's Repertoire—Stravinsky's The Rite of Spring, *Music Teacher*, January 1931, p. 25.

Paul Collaer: Le Sacre du Printemps, *Arts et Lettres d'Aujourd'hui*, 1923, No. 17.

— Le Sacre du Printemps, *Les Beaux Arts* (Brussels), 30 November 1934.

J. H. Elliot: The Rite of Spring then and now, *Halle*, November 1957, p. 2.

Noël Goodwin: Genesis of the Rite, *M&M*, May 1970, p. 26.

Cecil Gray: Sacre reheard, *Nation*, 2 February 1929, p. 616.

A. Getteman: Le Sacre du Printemps, *Arts et Lettres d'Aujourd'hui*, 1923, No. 19.

Basil Hogarth: Le Sacre du printemps, *The Gramophone*, August 1936, p. 5.

Louis Laloy: Le Sacre du Printemps, *S.I.M.*, May 1914, p. 45.

Igor Markevitch: Une Messe Naturelle, *Musik der Zeit*, Vol. 1, Boosey & Hawkes (1952), p. 3.

Massimo Mila: Il Sacre du Printemps ha trentacinque anni, *La Rassegna musicale*, 1945, p. 185.

Lennert Reimers: Stravinskys Vårofer, *Musick*, 1963, No. 1, p. 4.

André Schaeffner: Storia e significato del Sacre du Printemps di Stravinsky, *La Rassegna musicale*, November 1929, p. 536.

Horst Scharschuch: Analyse zu ISs Sacre du Printemps, Gustav Bosse Verlag (Regensburg) 1960.

Sacheverell Sitwell: Stravinsky's Sacre du Printemps, *Radio Times*, 23 January 1931, p. 173.

Roger Smalley: The sketchbook of The Rite of Spring, *Tempo*, No. 91, winter 1969–70, p. 2.

Pierre Souvtchinsky: Das Wunder des Sacre du Printemps, in *IS*, Pressestelle Westdeutscher Rundfunk (Cologne) 1963, p. 15.

Igor Stravinsky: A propos Le Sacre du Printemps, *Saturday Review*, 26 December 1959, p. 29.

— Stravinsky on 50 years of the Rite of Spring, *Records & Recording*, April 1961, p. 18.

John Warrack: Seven works that shook the world, 6: Stravinsky's The Rite of Spring, *Crescendo*, No. 123, November 1962, p. 51.

Anon.: Le Sacre in 1913, *MN&H*, 11 June 1921, p. 749.

20. Trois Poésies de la Lyrique Japonaise (Three Japanese Lyrics). For voice and piano. 1912–13. Dur. 3½'.

1. *Akahito*. Dated: 6–19 October 1912, Ustilug. Ded. Maurice Delage.

2. *Mazatsumi*. Dated: 5–18 December 1912, Clarens. Ded. Florent Schmitt.

3. *Tsaraiuki*. Dated: 9–22 January 1913, Clarens. Ded. Maurice Ravel.

Pub. 1913, Edition Russe de Musique; Boosey & Hawkes. French version, Maurice Delage; English version, Robert Burness; German version, Ernst Roth; Russian version, A. Brandta.

20a. Trois Poésies de la Lyrique Japonaise (Three Japanese Lyrics). For voice and chamber orchestra. 1912–13. Dur. 3½'.

1. *Akahito*. Dated: 16–29 December 1912, Clarens. Ded. Maurice Delage.

2. *Mazatsumi*. Dated: 8–21 December 1912, Clarens. Ded. Florent Schmitt.

3. *Tsaraiuki*. Dated: 9–22 January 1913, Clarens. Ded. Maurice Ravel.

2 fl, pic, 2 cl, bcl, pf, 2 v, va, c.

?fp: 14 January 1914, Paris, Société Musicale Indépendante.

fEbp: 23 October 1925, Newcastle Station, Vivienne Chatterton, cond. Edward Clark.

Pub. as No. 20.

21. Khovanschina. Version of Mussorgsky's opera by Igor Stravinsky and Maurice Ravel. Commissioned by Serge Diaghilev. March–April 1913.

fp: 5 June 1913, Paris, Théâtre des Champs-Elysées.

fEp: 1 July 1913, Drury Lane.

Final Chorus (arr. & orch. Stravinsky) pub. (vocal score), 1914, Bessel.

22. Three Little Songs (Recollections of my Childhood). For voice and Piano. Comp. *c.* 1906, definitive version October–November 1913. Words: Russian popular texts. Dur. 1' 30".

1. *La Petite Pie* (The Magpie). Dated: 6–

19 October 1913, Clarens. Ded. to the composer's son Sviatoslav Soulima.

2. *Le Corbeau* (The Rook). Ded. to the composer's daughter Ludmila.

3. *Tchitcher-Iatcher* (The Jackdaw). Dated: October–November 1913, Clarens. Ded. to the composer's son Theodore.

Pub. 1914, Edition Russe de Musique; Boosey & Hawkes. French version, C.-F. Ramuz; English version, Robert Burness.

22a. Three Little Songs (Recollections of my Childhood). Lengthened version for voice and small orchestra. 1929–30, Nice. Dur. 3'.

1. *La Petite Pie* (The Magpie). 25–26 December 1929.

fl, 2 ob, 2 cl, 2 bsn; strings.

2. *Le Corbeau* (The Rook). 29 December 1929.

2 cl, 2 bsn; strings.

3. *Tchitcher-Iatcher* (The Jackdaw). 4 January 1930.

fl, 2 ob, 2 cl, 2 bsn; strings.

Pub. 1934, Edition Russe de Musique; Boosey & Hawkes.

23. Le Rossignol (The Nightingale). Musical fairy tale ('Conte lyrique') in three acts. 1908–1914, Ustilug–Clarens–Leysin. Text: S. Mitusov, from the story by Hans Andersen. ?Ded. S. Mitusov. Dur. 45'.

2 fl, pic, 2 ob, ca, 3 cl, bcl, 3 bsn, cbsn; 4 hn, 4 tpt, 3 tmb, tuba; timp, cym, tamb mil, tgle, antique cym, campanelle, tamb, tamtam; pf, celesta, 2 hp, guitar (ad lib), mandoline (ad lib); strings.

fp: 26 May 1914, Paris, Opéra, Diaghilev's Russian Ballet, cond. Pierre Monteux.

fEp: 18 June 1914, Drury Lane, cond. Pierre Monteux; with Mlle Dobrovlska (The Nightingale).

Pub. 1914 (vocal score by the composer), 1923 (full score), Edition Russe de Musique; 1947, Boosey & Hawkes. French version, M.-D. Calvocoressi; English version, Basil T. Timotheieff & Charles C. Hayne; German version, Liesbeth Wienhold. *Revised (1962) version*, A. Elukhen & B. Feiwel.

BIBLIOGRAPHY:

M.-D. Calvocoressi: IS's opera The Nightingale, *MT*, June 1914, p. 372.

23a. Chant du Rossignol (Song of the Nightingale). Symphonic Poem in three parts. Based on music from 'Le Rossignol'. 4 April 1917, Morges. Dur. 20'.

1. *The Fête in the Emperor of China's Palace*; 2. *The Two Nightingales*; 3. *Illness and Recovery of the Emperor of China*.

2 fl, pic, 2 ob, 2 cl, 2 bsn; 4 hn, 3 tpt, 3 tmb, tuba; timp, tgle, tamb de basque, tamburo, cym, GC, tamb, tamtam, tamb mil, caisse claire; celesta, pf, 2 hp; strings.

fp: 6 December 1919, Geneva, L'Orchestre de la Suisse Romande, cond. Ernest Ansermet.

fEp: July 1920, Royal Opera House, Covent Garden.

fEbp: 31 January 1930, Queen's Hall, BBC Symphony Orchestra, cond. Ernest Ansermet.

Pub. 1921, Edition Russe de Musique; Boosey & Hawkes. Reduction for piano solo by the composer pub. 1927.

BIBLIOGRAPHY:

Edward J. Dent: Le Chant du Rossignol, *Athenaeum*, 23 July 1920, p. 102.

Henry Prunières: IS's Chant du Rossignol, *Chesterian*, No. 9, September 1920.

23b. Songs of the Nightingale and Chinese March. For violin and piano, transcribed by Igor Stravinsky and Samuel Dushkin. 1932, Voreppe.

fEp: 13 March 1933, BBC broadcast, Samuel Dushkin and Igor Stravinsky.

Pub. Edition Russe de Musique; Boosey & Hawkes.

24. Three Pieces for string quartet. 1914, Salvan. Ded. Ernest Ansermet. Dur. 8'.

1. *crotchet* = 126; 2. *crotchet* = 76; 3. *minim* = 40.

fEp: 13 February 1919, Wigmore Hall, Philharmonic Quartet.

fEbp: 7 November 1927, Pro Arte Quartet.

Pub. 1922, Edition Russe de Musique; 1947, Boosey & Hawkes. Ed. F. H. Schneider.

For orchestral version, incorporated into *Four Studies for Orchestra*, see No. 60.

BIBLIOGRAPHY:

Terpander: Stravinsky's Three Pieces for string quartet, *The Gramophone*, May 1935, p. 469.

25. Pribaoutki. Song Games ('Chansons plaisantes') for voice and instrumental ensemble. 1914, Salvan. Words: Russian popular texts. Ded. to the composer's wife. Dur. 5'.

1. *L'Oncle Armand* (*Kornillo*); 2. *Le Four* (*Natashka*); 3. *Le Colonel* (*The Colonel*); 4. *Le Vieux et le Lièvre* (*The Old Man and the Hare*).

fl, ob, ca, cl, bsn; v, va, c, db.

fp: 22 February 1918, Aeolian Hall, Olga Haley and ensemble, cond. (Sir) Eugene Goossens.

Pub. 1917, Ad. Henn; Chester. French version, C.-F. Ramuz; German version, R. St. Hoffmann. Incl. reduction for voice and piano by the composer.

26. Valse des fleurs. For two pianos. 30 August 1914, Clarens.

perf: 1949, New York, concert organized by Robert Craft.

Unpub. Lost.

27. Three Easy Pieces. For piano four hands (easy left hand). 1914–15, Clarens. Dur. 3'.

1. *March*. Ded. Alfredo Casella.
2. *Waltz*. Ded. Erik Satie.
3. *Polka*. Ded. Serge Diaghilev.

fp: 8 November 1919, Lausanne, José Iturbi and Igor Stravinsky.

Pub. 1917, Ad. Henn; Chester.

For orchestral version see No. 31a and No. 31b.

27a. Polka. Transcribed for cimbalom solo by the composer. 1915. Unpub.; MS reproduced in *Feuilles musicales*, March–April 1962.

27b. March. For twelve instruments. 25 March 1915. Unpub.

28. Souvenir d'une marche boche. For piano. 1 September 1915, Morges. Pub. (in facsimile) in *The Book of the Homeless* (ed. Edith Wharton), Macmillan (London) 1916.

29. Berceuses du chat (Cat's cradle songs). Song cycle ('Suite des chants') for contralto and three clarinets. 1915–16, Clarens-Morges. Words: Russian popular texts. Ded. Natalie Gontcharova and Michel Larionov. Dur. 5'.

1. *Sur le poêle*; 2. *Intérieur*; 3. *Dodo . . .*; 4. *Ce qu'il a le chat*.

fEp: 20 July 1920, Wigmore Hall, Olga Haley.

Pub. 1917, Ad. Henn; Chester. Incl. reduction for voice and piano by the composer. French version, C.-F. Ramuz; German version, R. St. Hoffmann.

30. Renard (The Fox). A Burlesque in song and dance. Spring 1915, Château d'Oex— 1916, Morges. Vocal score dated: 1 August 1916, Morges. Text: Igor Stravinsky, from Russian popular tales. Ded. Princesse Edmond de Polignac. Dur. 20'.

fl, ob, ca, cl, E-flat cl, bsn; 2 hn, tpt; cimbalom, timp, cym & GC, 2 tamb de basque, caisse claire, tgle; solo string quintet; 2 solo tenors, 2 solo basses.

fp: 18 May 1922, Paris, Opéra, Diaghilev's Russian Ballet, cond. Ernest Ansermet; choreography, Nijinska; décor and costumes, Michel Larionov.

fEbp: 12 April 1935, Broadcasting House, invitation concert, cond. Ernest Ansermet; with Bradbridge White, Martin Boddey, Stanley Riley, Samuel Dyson.

f concert p: 17 October 1955, Geneva, Michel Sénéchal, Hugues Cuénod, Heinz Rehfuss, Xavier Dépraz, l'Orchestre de la Suisse Romande, with Istvan Arato, cond. Ernest Ansermet.

Pub. 1917, Ad. Henn; Chester. French version, C.-F. Ramuz; German version, Rupert Koller; English version, Rollo H. Myers. Vocal score by the composer.

BIBLIOGRAPHY:

Antonio de Bernardi: Renard di Stravinsky, *Il Convegno musicale* (Turin), No. 1, January–March 1964.

Else Kolliner: Bemerkungen zu Stravinskys Renard, *Anbruch*, May 1926, p. 214.

Pierre Meylan: Reflections sur Renard de Stravinsky-Ramuz, *Feuilles musicales*, November 1961, p. 154.

R.-Aloys Mooser: Renard, in *Aspects de la musique contemporaine*, Editions Labor et Fidès (Geneva) 1957, p. 187.

André Schaeffner: Renard et l'epoque russe de Stravinsky, *Cahiers de la Compagnie Madeleine Renaud/Jean-Louis Barrault*, 3e cahier 1954.

31. Five Easy Pieces. For piano four hands (easy right hand). 1916–17, Morges. Ded. 'à Madame Eugenia Errazuriz—hommage très respectueux'. Dur. 9'.
1. *Andante*; 2. *Española*; 3. *Balalaika*; 4. *Napolitana*; 5. *Galop*.
fp: 8 November 1919, Lausanne, José Iturbi and Igor Stravinsky.
Pub. 1917, Ad. Henn; Chester.

31a. Suite No. 1. For small orchestra. 1917–1925. Dated: 31 December 1925. Dur. 5'.
1. *Andante*; 2. *Napolitana*; 3. *Española*; 4. *Balalaika*.
2 fl, pic, ob, 2 cl, 2 bsn; hn, tpt, tmb, tuba; GC; strings.
fEbp: 1 February 1931, BBC Orchestra, cond. Igor Stravinsky; near-integral performance of Suites 1 & 2 as '8 pièces faciles pour petit orchestre'.
Pub. Chester.

31b. Suite No. 2. For small orchestra. 1921. Dur. 7'.
1. *March*; 2. *Waltz*; 3. *Polka*; 4. *Galop*.
2 fl, pic, ob, 2 cl, 2 bsn; hn, 2 tpt, tmb, tuba; caisse claire, cym, GC; piano, strings.
fEp: 16 June 1922, Queen's Hall, cond. (Sir) Eugene Goossens.
fEbp: 17 November 1924, Bournemouth, Winter Gardens, Bournemouth Municipal Orchestra, cond. Sir Dan Godfrey.
Pub. Chester.

32. Trois Histoires pour Enfants (Three Tales for Children). For voice and piano. 1915–17. Ded. 'Pour mon fils cadet'. Dur. 2'.
1. *Tilimbom*. 22 May 1917, Morges.
2. *Les canards, les cygnes, les oies*. 1917, Morges.
3. *L'ours* (Petite histoire avec une chanson). 30 December 1915, Morges.
fEp: late 1920, Steinway Hall, Miss Baddeley.
Pub. 1920, Chester. French version, C.-F. Ramuz. New edition of No. 1 pub. 1927, Chester (with English version by Rosa Newmarch).

32a. Tilimbom. Lengthened version for voice and orchestra. December 1923, Biarritz.
3 fl, 2 ob, 2 cl; 2 hn, tpt; timp; strings.
Pub. Schott.

See also No. 98.

33. Valse pour les enfants (Waltz for children). For piano. *c.* 1917, Morges. Pub. 21 May 1922, in *Le Figaro*.

34. Song of the Volga Boatmen. Russian folksong orch. Igor Stravinsky. 8 April 1917. Dur. 2' (4').
2 fl, 2 ob, 2 cl, 2 bsn, cbsn; 4 hn, 3 tpt, 3 tmb, tuba; timp, pcssn.
fp: 9 April 1917, Rome, Costanzi Theatre, cond. Ernest Ansermet.
fEbp: 23 May 1926, Newcastle Station Orchestra, cond. Edward Clark.
Pub. 1920, Chester.

35. Four Russian Peasant Songs ('Saucers'). For unacc. female voices. 1914–17. Words: after Afanasiev's collection of Russian popular texts. Dur. 3'.
1. *On Saints' Days in Chigisakh*. For 4-part chorus. 22 October 1916, Morges.
2. *Ovsen*. For 2-part chorus. 1917, Morges.
3. *The Pike*. For three solo voices and 4-part chorus. 1914, Salvan.
4. *Master Portly*. For solo voice and 4-part chorus. 1915.
fEbp: 23 December 1932, BBC Chorus, cond. Cyril Dalmaine.
Pub. *c.* 1930, Schott; 1932, Chester.

35a. Four Russian Peasant Songs. New version for equal voices with accompaniment of four horns. 1954. Dur. 3' 40".
fp: 11 October 1954, Los Angeles, Monday Evening Concerts, cond. Robert Craft.
Pub. 1958, Chester.

BIBLIOGRAPHY:
Pierre Meylan: Une nouvelle instrumentation de Stravinsky, Les Quatres Chants russes, *Schweizerische Musikpädagogische Blätter*, October 1957.
— Une intéressante transcription de Stravinsky, Les Quatre Chants, *Feuilles musicales*, March–April 1962, p. 39.

36. Canons for two horns. 1917. Unpub.

37. Study. For pianola. 1917, Morges–Les Diablerets. ?Ded. Mme Eugenia Errazuriz. Dur. 2' 15".
fp: 13 October 1921, London, Aeolian Hall.

fEbp: 11 May 1927, player-piano operated by Reginald Reynolds.

Pub. Aeolian Company: pianola roll T967B.

BIBLIOGRAPHY:

Anon.: Stravinsky and the 'Pleyela', *MS*, 10 September 1927, p. 94.

37a. Madrid. Transcription of preceding for two pianos by Soulima Stravinsky. Pub. 1951, Boosey & Hawkes.

For orchestral version see No. 60.

38. Berceuse. For voice and piano. 10 December 1917, Morges. Text: Russian words by Igor Stravinsky, French translation by C.-F. Ramuz. Ded. 'à ma fillette'. Dur. 0′45″. Pub. 1962, Faber & Faber (London) in *Expositions and Developments*.

39. Duet for two bassoons. 1918. Sketch only. Unpub.

40. Prologue from 'Boris Godunov'. Mussorgsky, arr. for piano by Igor Stravinsky for his children. 1918, Morges. Unpub.

41. L'Histoire du Soldat (The Soldier's Tale). 'To be read, played and danced.' In two parts. 1918, Morges. Text: C.-F. Ramuz. Ded. Werner Reinhart. Dur. 35′.

Part I: 1. *The Soldier's March*; 2. *Music to Scene* 1; 3. *Music to Scene* 2; 4. *Closing music to Scene* 3. Part II: 5. *Introduction*; 6. *The Royal March*; 7. *Little Concert*; 8. *Three Dances* (*Tango, Valse, Ragtime*); 9. *The Devil's Dance*; 10. *Little Chorale*; 11. *Great Chorale*; 12. *Triumphal March of the Devil*.

cl, bsn; cornet à pistons, tmb; 2 caisses claires, 2 tambours, GC, cym, tamb de basque, tgle.

fp: 28 September 1918, Lausanne, Théâtre Municipal, cond. Ernest Ansermet; with Elie Gagnebin (Narrator), Gabriel Rosset (The Soldier), Jean Villard-Gilles (The Devil, acted part), Georges Pitoëff (The Devil, danced part), Ludmila Pitoëff (The Princess, danced part); Allegra (cl), de Beir (bsn), Schöldlin (cornet à pistons), Miene (tmb), Jacobi (pcssn), Closset (v), Fricke (db).

Pub. 1924, Chester. Piano reduction by the composer. English version, Rosa Newmarch; German version, Hans Reinhart. Later English version, Michael Flanders and Kitty Black.

BIBLIOGRAPHY:

Ernest Ansermet: L'Histoire du Soldat, *Chesterian*, No. 10, October 1920.

Paul Collaer: L'Histoire du Soldat, *Arts et Lettres d'Aujourd'hui*, 1923, No. 17.

A. Mantelli: Intorno alla Storià del soldato, *La Rassegna musicale*, 1949, p. 220.

Otto Mayer: La Historia del Soldat, *Mirador*, 16 May 1935.

W. S. Meadmore: Stravinsky's The Soldier's Tale, *MS*, 30 July 1927, p. 38.

H. Pringsheim: Stravinskys Geschichte vom Soldaten auf der Berliner Volksbühne, *AMZ*, 25 January 1924.

C.-F. Ramuz: Historien av en soldat, *Dansk Musiktidsskrift*, 1952, Nos. 224–6.

Ferdinand Scherber: Technische Musik—Glossen zu Stravinskys Geschichte vom Soldaten, *Signale*, 1926, No. 15, p. 528.

H. Schnoor: Stravinsky, Geschichte vom Soldaten, *Der Auftakt*, November 1924.

Marc Semenoff: L'Histoire du Soldat, texte de Ramuz, musique de Stravinsky, *Revue musicale de France*, 1946, No. 5.

Sacheverell Sitwell: Stravinsky's L'Histoire du Soldat, *Radio Times*, 8 July 1927, p. 55.

Theodore Stravinsky: Sieg des Geistes über das Temperament, *Melos*, June 1952, p. 174.

41a. L'Histoire du Soldat: Suite.

1. *The Soldier's March*; 2. *The Soldier's Violin*; 3. *Royal March*; 4. *The Little Concert*; 5. *Three Dances: Tango, Waltz, Ragtime*; 6. *The Devil's Dance*; 7. *Chorale*; 8. *The Devil's Triumphal March*.

Instrumentation as No. 41.

fp: 20 July 1920, London, Wigmore Hall, cond. Ernest Ansermet.

Pub. 1922, Chester.

41b. L'Histoire du Soldat: Suite. Version for violin, clarinet and piano. Autumn 1919. Dur. 25′.

1. *The Soldier's March*; 2. *The Soldier's Violin*; 3. *The Little Concert*; 4. *Tango, Waltz, Ragtime*; 5. *The Devil's Dance*.

fp: 8 November 1919, Lausanne.

Pub. 1920, Chester.

42. Rag-time. For eleven instruments. 11

November 1918, Morges. Ded. Mme Eugenia Errazuriz. Dur. 4'.

fl, cl; hn, cornet à pistons, tmb; caisse claire à corde, caisse claire sans corde, GC, cym; cimbalom, 2 v, va, db.

fp: 27 April 1920, London, Aeolian Hall, Arthur Bliss Chamber Concert, ensemble, cond. (Sir) Arthur Bliss.

Pub. 1919, Editions de la Sirène; 1920, Chester. Transcription for piano solo by the composer.

BIBLIOGRAPHY:

Anon.: Stravinsky, *British Musician*, June 1935, p. 122.

43. La Marseillaise. Arr. for unaccompanied violin. 1 January 1919, Morges. Unpub.

44. Four Russian Songs. For voice and piano. December 1918–October 1919. Words: from Russian popular texts. Ded. Maja and Bela Strozzi-Pečić. Dur. 4' 45".

1. *Canard* (Ronde). 28 December 1918, Morges.

2. *Chanson pour compter*. 16 March 1919, Morges.

3. *Le Moineau est assis . . .* 23 October 1919, Morges.

4. *Chant dissident*. March 1919, Morges.

Pub. 1920, Chester. French version, C.-F. Ramuz.

45. Piano-Rag-Music. For piano solo. 28 June 1919, Morges. Ded. Artur Rubinstein. Dur. 3'.

fp: ?8 November 1919, Lausanne (?20 November 1919, Zürich, Tonhalle), José Iturbi.

Pub. 1920, Chester.

46. Three Pieces for clarinet solo. 1919, Morges. Ded. Werner Reinhart. Dur. 3' 45".

fp: 8 November 1919, Lausanne, Werner Reinhart.

fEp: 20 July 1920, Wigmore Hall, Haydn Draper.

Pub. 1920, Chester.

47. Pulcinella. Ballet with song, after Giambattista Pergolesi. 1919–20 April 1920, Morges. Dur. 35'.

1. *Overture*; 2. *Serenata* (tenor solo); 3. *Scherzino*; 4. *Allegro*; 5. *Andantino*; 6. *Alle-*

gro; 7. *Allegretto* (soprano solo); 8. *Allegro assai*; 9. *Allegro* (bass solo); 10. *Largo* (trio)—*Allegro* (duet, soprano and tenor)—*Presto* (tenor solo); 11. *Allegro alla breve*; 12. *Allegro moderato*; 13. *Andantino* (soprano solo); 14. *Allegro*; 15. *Gavotta con due variazioni*; 16. *Vivo*; 17. *Tempo di minué* (trio); 18. *Allegro assai*.

2 fl, 2 ob, 2 bsn; 2 hn, tpt, tmb; string quintet (concertino), strings (ripieno) (4+4-4-3-3).

fp: 15 May 1920, Paris, Opéra, Diaghilev's Russian Ballet, cond. Ernest Ansermet; with Léonide Massine (Pulcinella) and Tamara Karsavina (Pimpinella); singers, Zoia Rosowska, Aurelio Anglada, Gino de Vecchi; chor. Massine; décor and costumes, Pablo Picasso.

Pub. (vocal score by the composer) 1920, Chester; (full score), Edition Russe de Musique; Boosey & Hawkes. Revised (1965) edition pub. 1966, Boosey & Hawkes.

BIBLIOGRAPHY:

Edward J. Dent: Pulcinella, *Athenaeum*, 23 July 1920, p. 102.

A. Mantelli: Pulcinella di Stravinsky, *La Rassegna musicale*, 1946, p. 90.

Yvonne Rihouet: Aux ballets russes, Pulcinella, *Nouvelle revue française*, 1920, No. 83, p. 326.

Adolfo Salazar: Pulcinella and Maese Pedro, *Chesterian*, No. 44, January–February 1925.

Raoul de Roussy de Seles: IS's Pulcinella, *Chesterian*, No. 6, March 1920.

47a. Pulcinella: Suite. For small orchestra. c. 1922, rev. 1947. Dur. 22'.

1. *Sinfonia* (*Overture*); 2. *Serenata*; 3. *Scherzino—Allegro—Andantino*; 4. *Tarantella*; 5. *Toccata*; 6. *Gavotta con due variazioni*; 7. *Duetto* (*Vivo*, rev. ed.); 8. *Minuetto—Finale*.

Orchestration as No. 47.

fp: 22 December 1922, Boston Symphony Orchestra, cond. Pierre Monteux.

fEp: 4 October 1925, BBC broadcast, London Chamber Orchestra, cond. Anthony Bernard.

fEp (concert): 24 October 1925, Queen's Hall, New Queen's Hall Orchestra, cond. Sir Henry Wood.

Pub. 1924, Edition Russe de Musique;

Stravinsky, Igor

Boosey & Hawkes. Revised edition pub. 1949, Boosey & Hawkes.

BIBLIOGRAPHY:
R. Bernier: Introduction à la Suite de Pulcinella de Stravinsky, *Syrinx*, April 1938.

47b. Suite (after themes, fragments and pieces by Giambattista Pergolesi). For violin and piano. Summer 1925, Nice. Dated: 24 August 1925. Ded. Paul Kochanski.
    1. *Introduction*; 2. *Serenata*; 3. *Tarantella*; 4. *Gavotta con due variazioni*; 5. *Minuetto e Finale*.
    Pub. 1926, Edition Russe de Musique.

47c. Suite Italienne. Transcription for cello and piano by Igor Stravinsky and Gregor Piatigorsky. 1932.
    1. *Introductione*; 2. *Serenata*; 3. *Aria*; 4. *Tarantella*; 5. *Minuetto e Finale*.
    Pub. 1934, Edition Russe de Musique; Boosey & Hawkes.

47d. Suite Italienne. Transcription for violin and piano by Igor Stravinsky and Samuel Dushkin. *c.* 1933.
    1. *Introduzione*; 2. *Serenata*; 3. *Tarantella*; 4. *Gavotta con due variazioni*; 5. *Scherzino*; 6. *Minuetto e Finale*.
    fEp: 13 March 1933, BBC broadcast, Samuel Dushkin and Igor Stravinsky.
    Pub. 1934, Edition Russe de Musique.

48. Concertino. For string quartet. July–September 1920, Carantec, Garches. Ded. Flonzaley Quartet. Dur. 6′.
    fEp: 1924, details untraced.
    fEbp: 7 November 1927, Pro Arte Quartet.
    Pub. 1923, Wilhelm Hansen. Reduction for piano four hands by the composer. Also reduction for piano solo by Arthur Lourié (pub. 1925).

48a. Concertino. For twelve instruments. 1952. Dur. 6′.
    fl, ob, ca, cl, 2 bsn; 2 tpt, ten tmb, bs tmb; v, c.
    fp: 11 November 1952, Los Angeles Chamber Symphony Orchestra.
    fEp: 22 July 1957, BBC broadcast, London Symphony Orchestra, cond. Walter Goehr.
    Pub. 1953, Wilhelm Hansen.

49. Symphonies of wind instruments. Summer–20 November 1920, Carantec, Garches. Ded. to the memory of Claude Achille Debussy. Dur. 12′.
    3 fl, alto fl, 2 ob, ca, cl, alto cl, 3 bsn, dbsn; 4 hn, 3 tpt. 3 tmb, tuba.
    fp: 10 June 1921, Queen's Hall, concert of Russian music, London Symphony Orchestra, cond. Serge Koussevitzky.
    fEbp: 28 April 1928, Wireless Symphony Orchestra, cond. Ernest Ansermet.
    Pub. 1926 (piano reduction by Arthur Lourié), Edition Russe de Musique. (A fragment for piano solo pub. December 1920, *Revue musicale*.)

49a. Symphonies of wind instruments. Revised version, 1945–7.
    3 fl, 2 ob, ca, 3 cl, 3 bsn, cbsn; 4 hn, 3 tpt, 3 tmb, tuba.
    Pub. 1952, Boosey & Hawkes.

BIBLIOGRAPHY:
Paul Collaer: Symphonies d'instruments à vent d'IS, *Cahiers de Belgique*, April 1928.

50. Les Cinq Doigts (The Five Fingers). Eight very easy melodies on five notes. 18 February 1921, Garches. Dur. 8′.
    1. *Andantino*; 2. *Allegro*; 3. *Allegretto*; 4. *Larghetto*; 5. *Moderato*; 6. *Lento*; 7. *Vivo*; 8. *Pesante*.
    Pub. 1922, Chester.

50a. Eight Instrumental Miniatures. For fifteen players. 1962. Ded. Lawrence Morton. Dur. 8′ (?6′).
    1. *Andantino*; 2. *Vivace* (7); 3. *Lento* (6); 4. *Allegretto* (3); 5. *Moderato alla breve*; 6. *Tempo di Marcia* (2); 7. *Larghetto* (4); 8. *Tempo di Tango*.
    fp (first four pieces only): 26 March 1962, Los Angeles, Monday Evening Concerts, cond. Robert Craft.
    fp (complete): 29 April 1962, Toronto, Massey Hall, CBC Symphony Orchestra, cond. Igor Stravinsky.
    f London p: 19 January 1964, Royal Festival Hall, Park Lane Ensemble, cond. Norman Del Mar.
    Pub. 1963, Chester.

51. Mavra. Opera buffa in one act, for soprano, mezzo-soprano, contralto, tenor and orchestra. Libretto: Boris Kochno, after Pushkin. 1921–2, Anglet, Biarritz. Dated: 9 March 1922, Biarritz. *Overture* written a few weeks later. Ded. to the memory of Pushkin, Glinka and Tchaikovsky. Dur. 25′.

2 fl, pic, 2 ob, ca, 2 cl, E-flat cl, 2 bsn; 4 hn, 4 tpt, 3 tmb, tuba; strings (1+1–1–3–3).

fp: 3 June 1922, Paris, Opéra, Diaghilev's Russian Ballet, cond. Gregor Fitelberg; with Oda Slobodskaya (Parasha), Mme Sadovène (The Neighbour), Zoïa Rosovska (The Mother), Bélina Skoupevski (The Hussar); décor and costumes, Léopold Survage; producer, Nijinska.

fEp (Overture): 28 January 1931, BBC Symphony Orchestra, cond. Ernest Ansermet.

fEbp (complete): 27 April 1934, Oda Slobodskaya, Kate Winter, Betty Bannerman, Mary Jarred, Tudor Davies, Wireless Chorus, BBC Symphony Orchestra, cond. Ernest Ansermet.

fEp (stage): 16 November 1964, Royal Academy of Music, Duke's Hall, Pauline Tinsley, Oda Slobodskaya, Monica Sinclair, Kenneth Macdonald, Kensington Symphony Orchestra, cond. Michael Head.

Pub. 1925, Edition Russe de Musique; 1947, Boosey & Hawkes. Vocal score by the composer. English version, Robert Burness (1925), Robert Craft; French version, Jacques Larmanjat; German version, A. Elukhen.

BIBLIOGRAPHY:
Leslie Head: Stravinsky and his opera buffa, *M&M*, November 1964, p. 27.
Darius Milhaud: Stravinskys neue Bühnenwerke, *Anbruch*, November 1922, p. 260.
Francis Poulenc: A propos de Mavra, *Les Feuilles libres*, June–July 1922.
Roland-Manuel: Mavra, *Musical News*, 1 July 1922, p. 13.

51a. Mavra. Arrangement for jazz band by Jack Hylton (with the agreement of the composer). *c.* 1930.

fp: 28 January 1931, Jack Hylton's Band, rehearsal attended by the composer.

BIBLIOGRAPHY:
Anon.: Stravinsky and Jack Hylton's Band, *MMR*, 1931, p. 85.

51b. Chanson de Paracha (from 'Mavra').

Arranged and transcribed for soprano and orchestra by the composer. 1922–3.

2 ob, 2 cl, 2 bsn; 4 hn, tuba; 2 v, va, several cellos and basses.

Pub. ?1933, Edition Russe de Musique.

51c. Chanson Russe (Russian Maiden's Song). Arr. for violin and piano by Igor Stravinsky and Samuel Dushkin. April 1937, New York. Pub. 1938, Edition Russe de Musique; Boosey & Hawkes.

51d. Chanson Russe (Russian Maiden's Song). Arr. for cello and piano by Igor Stravinsky and Dimitri Markevitch. Pub. Edition Russe de Musique; 1951, Boosey & Hawkes.

52. Les Noces (The Wedding). Russian Choreographic Scenes. For 4-part chorus (SATB), soprano, mezzo-soprano, tenor and bass soloists and orchestra. Words: adapted by Igor Stravinsky from Russian popular texts. Composed: 1914, Clarens—4 April 1917, Morges. Orchestrated: 1921, Garches—6 April 1923, Monaco. Ded. Serge de Diaghilev. Dur. 35′.

Part I. Scene 1: *At the Bride's House* (*The Tresses*); Scene 2: *At the Bridegroom's House*; Scene 3: *The Bride's Departure*. Part II. Scene 4: *The Wedding Feast* (*The Red Table*).

4 pianos, xyl, timp, 2 crotales, bell, 2 side dms (with and without snare), tamb, GC, cym, tgle.

fp: 13 June 1923, Paris, Théâtre de la Gaieté, Diaghilev's Russian Ballet, cond. Ernest Ansermet; with Georges Auric, Edouard Flament, Hélène Léon and Marcelle Meyer (pianos); choreography, Nijinska; décor and costumes, Natalia Goncharova.

fEp: 14 June 1926, His Majesty's Theatre, cond. (Sir) Eugene Goossens; with Georges Auric, Francis Poulenc, Vittorio Rieti and Vladimir Dukelsky (pianos).

Pub. 1922 (vocal score), *c.* 1923 (full score), Chester. Vocal score by the composer. French version, C. F. Ramuz; English version, D. Millar Craig; German version, K. Gutheim and H. Kruger.

BIBLIOGRAPHY:
Victor Belaiev: IS's Les Noces, an outline, O.U.P. (London) 1928.

Stravinsky, Igor

Adolphe Boschot: Les Noces de Stravinsky, *Revue politique et littéraire* (Revue bleue), 1923, p. 462.

M. Castelnuovo-Tedesco: Leggendo Les Noces di Stravinsky, *Il Pianoforte*, January 1928.

André Coeuroy: Les Noces, *Larousse mensuel*, 1 November 1923.

— Les Noces, *Revue universelle*, 1 August 1923, p. 373.

Paul Dukas: Les Noces de Stravinsky, *Gaceta musical*, January 1928.

Nathalie Gontcharova: The creation of Les Noces, *Ballet*, September 1949, p. 23.

R. Hammond: Viewing Les Noces in 1929, *Modern Music*, March–April 1929.

E. J. Hermann: IS, Der Siebzigjährige, *Musica*, 1952, No. 6, p. 223.

Arthur Hoérée: Les Noces de Stravinsky, *Les Cahiers de Belgique*, May 1928.

— Les Noces de Stravinsky, *Les Beaux Arts* (Brussels), 4 April 1936.

G. Jeanneret: Les Noces, *L'Esprit nouveau*, 1923, No. 18.

Jan Ling: Reflexionen kring Les Noces, *Nutida musik*, Vol. 6 (1962–3), No. 4, p. 45.

R.-A. Mooser: Les Noces d'IS, *Dissonances*, January 1934.

Paul Moresi: A rustic wedding, *Gramophone Record*, October 1934, p. 10.

C.-F. Ramuz: Über Stravinskys Les Noces, *Musica*, 1950, No. 4.

Roland-Manuel: IS's Les Noces, *Chesterian*, No. 33, September 1923.

André Schaeffner: Gaité-Lyrique, Ballets russes—Noces d'IS, *Le Ménestrel*, 29 June 1923, p. 287.

Florent Schmitt: Les Arts et la Vie, *Revue de France*, 15 September 1923.

Emile Vuillermoz: Noces, IS, *RM*, 1 August 1923, p. 69.

Anon.: Our Russian Bulletin 1: Stravinsky's latest compositions, *Music Student*, October 1915, p. 26.

53. The Sleeping Beauty: Variation d'Aurore & Entr'acte symphonique. Tchaikovsky, orch. Stravinsky for Diaghilev's revival of the ballet at the Alhambra, London, 2 November 1921. Unpub.

54. Octuor (Octet). For wind instruments.

Late 1922, Biarritz–20 May 1923, Paris. Dur. 16'.

1. *Sinfonia*; 2. *Tema con variazioni*; 3. *Finale.* fl, cl, 2 bsn; 2 tpt, ten tmb, bs tmb.

fp: 18 October 1923, Paris, Opéra, Concerts Koussevitzky, cond. Igor Stravinsky.

fEp: 9 February 1926, Chenil Galleries, Music Society concert, members of London Chamber Orchestra, cond. Anthony Bernard.

fEbp: c. January 1928, BBC studio concert, cond. Ernest Ansermet.

Pub. 1924, Edition Russe de Musique; 1947, Boosey & Hawkes. Ed. Albert Spalding. Reduction for piano solo by Arthur Lourié pub. 1926. Revised (1952) version pub. Boosey & Hawkes.

55. Concerto for piano and wind instruments. Mid-1923–April 1924, Biarritz. Ded. Nathalie Koussevitzky. Dur. 20'.

1. *Largo—Allegro*; 2. *Larghissimo* (*Largo*, rev. ed.); 3. *Allegro*.

2 fl, pic, 2 ob, ca, 2 cl, 2 bsn, cbsn; 4 hn, 4 tpt, 3 tmb, tuba; timp; contrabasses.

fp: 22 May 1924, Paris, Opéra, Concerts Koussevitzky, Igor Stravinsky (piano), cond. Serge Koussevitzky.

fAp: 23 January 1925, Boston, Igor Stravinsky and Boston Symphony Orchestra, cond. Serge Koussevitzky.

fEp: 19 June 1927, BBC broadcast, Igor Stravinsky and Wireless Symphony Orchestra, cond. Edward Clark.

fEp (concert): 19 June 1929, Queen's Hall, Igor Stravinsky (piano), cond. (Sir) Eugene Goossens.

Pub. 1924 (reduction), 1936 (full score), Edition Russe de Musique. Reduction for two pianos by the composer. Revised (1950) edition pub. Boosey & Hawkes.

BIBLIOGRAPHY:

A. Baresel: Stravinskys Klavierkonzert, *NMZ*, 1925, No. 14, p. 339.

Boris de Schloezer: Concerto pour piano de Stravinsky, *RM*, 1 July 1924, p. 69.

Adolf Weissmann: Stravinsky spielt sein Klavierkonzert, *Anbruch*, 1924, No. 10, p. 407; *Il Pianoforte*, November–December 1924.

56. Sonata. For piano. 1924, Biarritz, Nice.

Ded. Mme la Princesse Edmond de Polignac.
1. *crotchet* = 112. 21 August 1924, Biarritz.
2. *Adagietto*. 6 October 1924, Nice.
3. *crotchet* = 112. 21 October 1924, Nice.
fp: July 1925, Donaueschingen.
fEp: 19 November 1925, Stefan Askenase.
fEbp: 16 March 1926, Marcelle Meyer.
Pub. 1925, Edition Russe de Musique;
Boosey & Hawkes. Ed. Albert Spalding.

BIBLIOGRAPHY:
Arthur Lourié: La Sonate de Stravinsky, *RM*,
August 1925, p. 100.

57. Serenade in A. For piano. April–
Autumn 1925, Nice. Ded. to the composer's
wife. Dur. 12′.
1. *Hymne*; 2. *Romanza*; 3. *Rondoletto*;
4. *Cadenza Finala*.
fEp: 3 April 1929, Arts Theatre Club,
Marcelle Meyer (broadcast).
Pub. 1926, Edition Russe de Musique;
Boosey & Hawkes. Ed. Albert Spalding.

BIBLIOGRAPHY:
Alfred Cortot: Serenade in A, *Musik der Zeit*,
Vol. 1, Boosey & Hawkes (1952), p. 30.
Terpander: Stravinsky's Serenade for piano-
forte, *The Gramophone*, May 1936, p. 504.

58. Pater Noster. For mixed (SATB) choir
a cappella. 1926. Dur. 1′ 10″. Pub. 1932.
Edition Russe de Musique; Boosey & Hawkes.

58a. Pater Noster. New version with Latin
text. March 1949. Pub. Boosey & Hawkes.

59. Oedipus Rex. Opera-oratorio in two
acts after Sophocles. Text: Jean Cocteau,
translated into Latin by J. Daniélou. Composed: 11 January 1926–14 March 1927, Nice.
Orchestration completed: 10 May 1927.
Dur. 52′.
3 fl, 2 ob, ca, 3 cl, 2 bsn, cbsn; 4 hn, 4 tpt,
3 tmb, tuba; timp; hp, pf, strings.
fp: 30 May 1927, Paris, Théâtre Sarah
Bernhardt, Diaghilev's Russian Ballet, cond.
Igor Stravinsky.
fEp: 12 May 1928, BBC broadcast, R. E.
Jeffrey (Speaker), Astra Desmond, Walter
Widdop, Roy Henderson, Frank Phillips,
Hardy Williamson, Wireless Chorus and
Symphony Orchestra, cond. Igor Stravinsky.
fEp (concert): 12 February 1936, Queen's

Hall, Philip Cunningham (narrator), Oda
Slobodskaya, Walter Widdop, Harold
Williams, Norman Walker, Tudor Davies,
Philharmonic Choir, BBC Symphony Orches-
tra, cond. Ernest Ansermet.
Pub. 1927, Edition Russe de Musique;
Boosey & Hawkes. Vocal score by the
composer. New (1948) version pub. 1949,
Boosey & Hawkes (English version, E. E.
Cummings).

BIBLIOGRAPHY:
E. Bonner: Oedipus Rex of Stravinsky,
Outlook, 28 March 1928, p. 504.
K. Burke: Oedipus Rex, *Dial*, 18 March 1928,
p. 445.
Jean Cocteau: La collaboration Oedipus Rex,
RM ('L'Œuvre du XXᵉ Siècle'), 1952, p. 51.
André Coeuroy: Oedipus Rex, *NMZ*, 1927,
No. 4.
Aaron Copland: Stravinsky's Oedipus Rex,
New Republic, 29 February 1928, p. 68.
Rudolf Ficker: Stimmen zum Oedipus Rex,
NMZ, 1928, No. 16, p. 513.
E. Lindegren: Stravinsky och Oedipus Rex,
Nutida musik, Vol. 1 (1957–8), No. 1, p. 2.
Heinrich Lindlar: IS, Oedipus Rex, *Musik der
Zeit*, Vol. 6 (Oper im XX. Jahrhundert),
Boosey & Hawkes (1954), p. 35.
Arthur Lourié: Oedipus Rex de Stravinsky,
RM, June 1927, p. 240.
Wilfrid Mellers: Stravinsky's Oedipus, *The
Listener*, 27 July 1961, p. 149.
— Stravinsky's Oedipus as 20th Century
Hero, *MQ*, July 1962, p. 300; in *Stravinsky:
a new appraisal of his work*, New York, 1963.
R.-A. Mooser: Oedipus Rex, in *Aspects de la
musique contemporaine*, Editions Labor et
Fidès (Geneva) 1957, p. 97.
Rollo H. Myers: A modern oratorio, *Radio
Times*, 7 February 1936, p. 12.
Leonid Sabaneef: Stravinsky's Oedipus,
Chesterian, No. 64, July–August 1927.
André Schaeffner: Oedipus Rex, *Le Ménestrel*,
10 June 1927, p. 257.
Boris de Schloezer: Oedipus Rex, *Nouvelle
revue française*, 1927, No. 167, p. 244.
Roger Sessions: On Oedipus Rex, *Modern
Music*, April 1928.
Heinrich Strobel: Stravinskys Neuklassizismu,
—Oedipus Rex in Berlin, *NMZ*, 1928s
No. 14, p. 433.

H. Straus: Oedipus Rex, *Nation*, 4 April 1928, p. 387.

Adolf Weissmann: Stravinskys Oratorien-Oper König Ödipus, *Auftakt*, 1927, No. 10, p. 257.

60. Four Studies. For orchestra. 1914–28. Transcriptions of *Three Pieces for string quartet* (orch. 1914–18, Morges) and *Study for pianola* (orch. 2 October 1928). Dur. 12'.

1. *Dance*; 2. *Eccentric*; 3. *Canticle*; 4. *Madrid*.
3 fl, pic, 3 ob, ca, E-flat cl, 2 cl, bcl, 2 bsn; 4 hn, 3 tpt, 2 tmb, tuba; timp; pf, hp, strings.
fp: 7 November 1930, Berlin.
fEp: 28 January 1931, Queen's Hall, BBC Symphony Orchestra, cond. Ernest Ansermet.
Pub. Edition Russe de Musique; Boosey & Hawkes.

BIBLIOGRAPHY:
Normal Del Mar: Confusion and error, *The Score*, October 1957.

61. Apollon musagète (Apollo musagetes). Ballet in two scenes for string orchestra. July 1927–January 1928, Nice. Dur. 30'.
Tableau I (Prologue): *Naissance d'Apollon*. Tableau II: *Variation d'Apollon—Pas d'Action—Variation de Calliope—Variation de Polymnie—Variation de Terpsichore—Variation d'Apollon—Pas de deux—Coda—Apothéose*.
fp: 27 April 1928, Washington, Library of Congress.
f European p: 12 June 1928, Paris, Théâtre Sarah-Bernhardt, Diaghilev's Russian Ballet, cond. Igor Stravinsky.
fEp: 25 June 1928, His Majesty's Theatre, Diaghilev's Russian Ballet, cond. Igor Stravinsky; with Serge Lifar, Mmes Nikitina, Tchernicheva, Doubrovska.
fEbp: 27 June 1929, BBC broadcast from Kingsway Hall, Wireless Symphony Orchestra, cond. Igor Stravinsky.
Pub. 1928, Edition Russe de Musique; Boosey & Hawkes. Piano reduction by the composer. Revised (1947) version pub. 1949, Boosey & Hawkes.

BIBLIOGRAPHY:
Hanns Gutman: Apollo Musagetes, Urauf-führung in Paris, *Auftakt*, 1928, No. 9, p. 224.

Arthur Lourié: A propos de l'Apollon de Stravinsky, *Musique*, 15 December 1927.
— Stravinsky's Apollo, *The Dominant*, August–September 1928, p. 20.
Hans F. Redlich: Stravinskys Apollon Musagète, *Anbruch*, January 1929, p. 41.
Charles Reid: Apollonian Stravinsky, *Records & Recording*, January 1965, p. 15.
André Schaeffner: Apollon musagète d'IS, *Le Ménestrel*, 22 June 1928, p. 279.
Boris de Schloezer: Apollon Musagète, *Tempo* (Prague), December 1928; *La Revista de musica*, December 1928.

62. Le Baiser de la Fée (The Fairy's Kiss). Ballet-Allegory in four scenes. April–October 1928, Talloires, Nice. Ded. to the memory of Tchaikovsky. Dur. 45'.
Tableau I: *Berceuse de la tempête*. Tableau II: *Une fête au village*. Tableau III: *Au moulin—Pas de deux—Adagio—Variation—Coda (Presto)—Scène*. Tableau IV (Epilogue): *Berceuse des demeures éternelles*.
3 fl, pic, 2 ob, ca, 3 cl, bcl, 2 bsn; 4 hn, 3 tpt, 3 tmb, tuba; timp, GC; hp, strings.
fp: 27 November 1928, Paris, Opéra, Ballets Ida Rubinstein, cond. Igor Stravinsky; choreography, Nijinska.
fEp (concert): 27 June 1929, BBC broadcast from Kingsway Hall, Wireless Symphony Orchestra, cond. Igor Stravinsky.
Pub. 1928, Edition Russe de Musique; Boosey & Hawkes. Revised (1950) version pub. 1954, Boosey & Hawkes.

BIBLIOGRAPHY:
Lawrence Morton: Stravinsky and Tchaikovsky: Le Baiser de la Fée, *MQ*, July 1962, p. 313; in *Stravinsky: a new appraisal of his work*, New York, 1963.
Charles Reid: Kiss of Ice, *Records & Recording*, October 1963, p. 15.
L. E. Reindl: IS, Kuss der Fee (Magdeburg Stadttheater), *Die Musik*, January 1933, p. 284.
Roland-Manuel: Le Baiser de la Fée, *Musique*, 15 December 1928.

62a. Ballad. Transcription for violin and piano by Igor Stravinsky and Jeanne Gautier. 1947. Pub. 1951, Boosey & Hawkes.

62b. Divertimento. From 'Le Baiser de la

Fée'. Symphonic Suite for orchestra. 1934. Dur. 20'.

1. *Sinfonia*; 2. *Danses suisses*; 3. *Scherzo*; 4. *Pas de deux* (*Adagio, Variation, Coda*).

2 fl, pic, 2 ob, ca, 2 cl, bcl, 2 bsn; 4 hn, 3 tpt, 3 tmb, tuba; timp; GC; hp, strings.

fEp: 8 June 1940, Northern Polytechnic, Modern Symphony Orchestra, cond. Arthur Dennington.

Pub. 1938, Edition Russe de Musique. Revised (1949) version pub. 1950, Boosey & Hawkes.

62c. Divertimento. Transcribed for violin and piano by Samuel Dushkin and Igor Stravinsky. 1932. Pub. Edition Russe de Musique; Boosey & Hawkes.

63. Capriccio. For piano and orchestra. December 1928–September 1929, Nice, Echarvines; orchestration completed 9 November 1929. Dur. 20'.

1. *Presto*; 2. *Andante rapsodico*; 3. *Allegro capriccioso ma tempo giusto*.

2 fl, pic, 2 ob, ca, 2 cl, bcl, 2 bsn; 4 hn, 2 tpt, 3 tmb, tuba; timp; strings (concertino & ripieni).

fp: 6 December 1929, Paris, Salle Pleyel, Igor Stravinsky and l'Orchestre Symphonique de Paris, cond. Ernest Ansermet.

fEp: 21 March 1931, Queen's Hall, Concert Club concert, Igor Stravinsky and London Symphony Orchestra, cond. (Sir) Malcolm Sargent.

Pub. 1930, Edition Russe de Musique; Boosey & Hawkes. Reduction for two pianos by the composer. Revised (1949) version pub. 1952, Boosey & Hawkes.

BIBLIOGRAPHY:
Arthur Lourié: Le Capriccio de Stravinsky, *RM*, April 1930, p. 353.

64. Symphonie des Psaumes (Symphony of Psalms). For mixed (SATB) chorus and orchestra. January–15 August 1930, Nice, Charavines. Ded. 'Cette symphonie composée à l'occasion du cinquantaire de son existence'. Dur. 23'.

5 fl, pic, 4 ob, ca, 3 bsn, cbsn; 4 hn, pic tpt, 4 tpt, 2 tmb, bs tmb, tuba; timp, GC; hp, 2 pianos, cellos and basses.

fp: 13 December 1930, Brussels, Palais des Beaux Arts, Chorus and Orchestra of Société Philharmonique de Bruxelles, cond. Ernest Ansermet.

fAp: 19 December 1930, Boston, Boston Symphony Orchestra, cond. Serge Koussevitzky.

fEp: 16 November 1931, Queen's Hall, Courtauld–Sargent concert, Bach Choir and London Symphony Orchestra, cond. Igor Stravinsky.

Pub. 1930 (vocal score), 1931 (full score), Edition Russe de Musique; Boosey & Hawkes. Vocal score by Sviatoslav (Soulima) Stravinsky. Revised (1948) edition pub. 1948, Boosey & Hawkes.

BIBLIOGRAPHY:
Ingemar von Heijne: Stravinskys Psalmsymfoni—Några impressioner, *Nutida musik*, Vol. 5 (1961–2), No. 5, p. 23.

F. Olivier: La Symphonie des Psaumes de Stravinsky, *Le Monde musical*, 31 March 1931.

Henry Prunières: Symphonie des Psaumes d'IS, *RM*, January 1931, p. 79.

Anon.: Stravinsky's Symphony of Psalms, *British Musician*, December 1931 p. 257, January 1932 p. 16.

65. Violin Concerto in D. Spring–summer 1931, Nice, Voreppe. Dur. 22'.

1. *Toccata*; 2. *Aria I*; 3. *Aria II*; 4. *Capriccio*.

2 fl, pic, 2 ob, ca, E-flat cl, 2 cl, 3 bsn, cbsn; 4 hn, 3 tpt, 3 tmb, tuba; timp; strings (8+8–6–4–4).

fp: 23 October 1931, Berlin broadcast, Samuel Dushkin and Berlin Radio Orchestra, cond. Igor Stravinsky.

fEp: 16 November 1931, Queen's Hall, Courtauld–Sargent concert, Samuel Dushkin and London Symphony Orchestra, cond. Igor Stravinsky.

Pub. 1931, Schott. Reduction for violin and piano by the composer.

BIBLIOGRAPHY:
Hanns Gutman: Stravinsky, alt und neu—Uraufführung seines Violinkonzertes, *Auftakt*, 1931, Nos. 11–12, p. 278.

66. Duo Concertant. For violin and piano. December 1931–15 July 1932, Voreppe. Dur. 16'.

Stravinsky, Igor

1. *Cantilène*; 2. *Eglogue I*; 3. *Eglogue II*; 4. *Gigue*; 5. *Dithyrambe*.

fp: 28 October 1932, Berlin, Funkhaus, Samuel Dushkin and Igor Stravinsky.

fEp: 13 March 1933, BBC broadcast, Samuel Dushkin and Igor Stravinsky.

Pub. 1933, Edition Russe de Musique; Boosey & Hawkes.

BIBLIOGRAPHY:

Terpander: A note on the Duo Concertant, *The Gramophone*, May 1934, p. 469.

67. Credo. For mixed (SATB) choir a cappella. 1932. Dur. 3'. Pub. 1933, Edition Russe de Musique; Boosey & Hawkes.

67a. Credo. New version with Latin text. 1949. Pub. Boosey & Hawkes.

67b. Credo. New version with Slavonic text. 1964.

68. Perséphone. Melodrama in three scenes for tenor, mixed (SATB) chorus, children's (SA) chorus and orchestra. Text: André Gide. May 1933–24 January 1934, Voreppe, Paris. Dur. 45'.

1. *Perséphone ravie*; 2. *Perséphone aux Enfers*; 3. *Perséphone renaissante*.

3 fl, 3 ob, 3 cl, 3 bsn; 4 hn, 3 tpt, 3 tmb, tuba; timp, xyl, GC, tamb; 2 hp, piano, strings.

fp: 30 April 1934, Paris, Opéra, Ballets Ida Rubinstein, cond. Igor Stravinsky; producer, Jacques Copeau; choreography, Kurt Joos; décors and costumes, Barsacq.

fEp: 28 November 1934, Queen's Hall, Ida Rubinstein (reciter), René Maison (tenor), BBC Chorus and BBC Symphony Orchestra, cond. Igor Stravinsky.

Pub. 1934, Edition Russe de Musique; Boosey & Hawkes. Reduction by Sviatoslav Stravinsky. Revised (1949) edition pub. 1950, Boosey & Hawkes.

BIBLIOGRAPHY:

Charles-Albert Cingria: Perséphone et la critique, *Nouvelle revue française*, 1934, No. 251, p. 297.

Frederick Jacobi: On hearing Stravinsky's Perséphone, *Modern Music*, March–April 1935.

Rollo H. Myers: Stravinsky and Persephone, *Radio Times*, 23 November 1934, p. 641.

Henry Prunières: Perséphone d'IS aux Ballets de Mme Ida Rubinstein, *RM*, May 1934, p. 380.

Paul Rosenfeld: Mystery of Perséphone, *New Republic*, 3 April 1935, p. 213.

Victor Seroff: Gide and Stravinsky—Perséphone, *Saturday Review*, 30 November 1957, p. 49.

H. H. Stuckenschmidt: IS, Perséphone, Grosse Oper Paris 1934, in *Oper in dieser Zeit*, Friedrich Verlag (Hannover) 1964, p. 53.

69. Ave Maria. For mixed (SATB) choir a cappella. 4 April 1934. Dur. 1'. Pub. 1934, Edition Russe de Musique; Boosey & Hawkes.

69a. Ave Maria. New version with Latin text. March 1949. Pub. Boosey & Hawkes.

70. Concerto for two pianos. 1931, Voreppe–1935, Paris. Dated: 9 November 1935. Dur. 20'.

1. *Con moto*; 2. *Notturno (Adagietto)*; 3. *Quattro variazioni*; 4. *Preludio e Fuga*.

fp: 21 November 1935, Paris, Salle Gaveau, Igor Stravinsky and Soulima Stravinsky.

f London p: 8 October 1936, Royal Academy of Music New Music Society, Dorothy Manley and Myers Foggin.

?fEbp: 27 February 1938, BBC broadcast, Ethel Bartlett and Rae Robertson.

Pub. 1936, Schott.

BIBLIOGRAPHY:

André Schaeffner: Stravinsky's new concerto, *Modern Music*, June 1936.

71. Jeu de Cartes (A Card Game). Ballet in three deals. 6 December 1936, Paris. Dur. 23'.

2 fl, pic, 2 ob, ca, 2 cl, 2 bsn; 4 hn, 2 tpt, 3 tmb, tuba; timp, GC; strings (12+10–8–6–6).

fp: 27 April 1937, New York, Metropolitan Opera House, American Ballet, cond. Igor Stravinsky; choreography, Balanchine.

fEp (concert): 18 October 1937, Queen's Hall, Courtauld–Sargent concert, London Philharmonic Orchestra, cond. Igor Stravinsky.

fEp (stage): 16 June 1947, Winter Garden Theatre, Ballets des Champs-Elysées, cond. André Girard.

Pub. 1937, Schott. Piano reduction by the composer.

BIBLIOGRAPHY:
Paul Le Flem: Jeu de Cartes d'IS, *Les Heures de Paris*, 14 December 1937.
Boris de Schloezer: Jeu de Cartes d'IS, *Nouvelle revue française*, 1938, No. 292, p. 149.

72. Preludium (Praeludium). For jazz band. December 1936, Paris–1937, New York. Unpub.

72a. Preludium (Praeludium). New arrangement, 1953.
fp: 18 October 1953, Los Angeles, Evenings-on-the-Roof concerts, cond. Robert Craft.
Pub. 1968 (full score), Boosey & Hawkes.

73. Petit Ramusianum harmonique. Words: Igor Stravinsky. For solo voice or voices in unison, unaccompanied. 11 October 1937, Paris. Pub. 1938, in *Hommage à C.-F. Ramuz*, V. Porchet (Lausanne); also facsimile in *Feuilles musicales*, March–April 1962.

74. Concerto in E flat ('Dumbarton Oaks'). For chamber orchestra. Spring 1937 – 29 March 1938, Paris. Score inscribed: 'Dumbarton Oaks, 8.v.38'. Dur. 12'.
1. *Tempo giusto*; 2. *Allegretto*; 3. *Con moto*.
fl, E-flat cl, bsn; 2 hn; strings (3-3-2-2).
fp: 8 May 1938, Washington D.C., cond. Nadia Boulanger.
fp (public): 4 June 1938, Paris, Concerts de la Sérénade, cond. Igor Stravinsky.
fEp: 4 November 1938, BBC invitation concert, BBC Orchestra, cond. Nadia Boulanger.
Pub. 1938, Schott. Reduction for two pianos by the composer.

BIBLIOGRAPHY:
Herbert Eimert: Stravinskys Dumbarton Oaks, *Melos*, July 1947, p. 247.
Boris de Schloezer: Concerto pour petit orchestre d'IS, *La Nouvelle Revue Française*, 1938, No. 298, p. 152.

75. Symphony in C. Autumn 1938, Paris–19 August 1940, Beverly Hills, Hollywood. Ded. 'This symphony, composed to the Glory of God, is dedicated to the Chicago Symphony Orchestra on the occasion of the Fiftieth Anniversary of its existence'. Dur. 28'.
1. *Moderato alla breve*; 2. *Larghetto concertante*; 3. *Allegretto*; 4. *Largo—Tempo giusto, alla breve*.
2 fl, pic, 2 ob, 2 cl, 2 bsn; 4 hn, 2 tpt, 3 tmb, tuba; timp; strings.
fp: 7 November 1940, Chicago, Chicago Symphony Orchestra, cond. Igor Stravinsky.
fEp: 17 November 1943, Bedford, Corn Exchange, BBC broadcast, BBC Orchestra, cond. Sir Adrian Boult.
Pub. 1948, Schott.

BIBLIOGRAPHY:
Sol Babitz: Stravinsky's Symphony in C, *MQ*, January 1941, p. 20.

76. Tango. For piano. 1940, Hollywood. Dur. 4' 30". Pub. 1941, Mercury Music Corp. (New York).

76a. Tango. Version for orchestra (orch. Felix Guenther).
3 fl, 2 ob, 2 cl, bcl, 2 bsn; 2 alto sax, tenor sax; 2 hn, 3 tpt, 3 tmb, tuba; pcssn; guitar, piano, strings.
fp: July 1941, Robin Hood Dell, cond. Benny Goodman.
Pub. 1941, Mercury Music Corp. (New York).

76b. Tango. Version for orchestra (orch. Igor Stravinsky). 1953.
4 cl, bcl, 4 tpt, 3 tmb; guitar; strings (3-1-1-1).
fp: 18 October 1953, Los Angeles, Evenings-on-the-Roof concerts, cond. Robert Craft.
Pub. 1954, Mercury Music Corp. (New York).

76c. Tango. Version for violin and piano by Samuel Dushkin. Unpub.

77. The Sleeping Beauty: Bluebird Pas-de-Deux. Tchaikovsky, arr. for small orchestra by Igor Stravinsky, for Ballet Theater, New York. 1941. Dur. 5' 15".
fl, ob, 2 cl, bsn; hn, 2 tpt, 2 tmb; timp; piano, strings.
Pub. 1953, Schott.

78. The Star Spangled Banner. Harmonised and orchestrated by Igor Stravinsky. 4 July 1941, Los Angeles.

3 fl, 3 ob, 2 cl, 2 bsn; 4 hn, 3 tpt, 3 tmb, tuba; timp; strings; mixed chorus (ad lib).

fp: 14 October 1941, Los Angeles, cond. James Sample.

Pub. Mercury Music Corporation.

79. Danses Concertantes. For chamber orchestra. 1941–13 January 1942, Hollywood. Dur. 20′.

1. *Marche—Introduction*; 2. *Pas d'Action*; 3. *Thème varié*; 4. *Pas de Deux*; 5. *Marche—Conclusion*.

fl, ob, cl, bsn; 2 hn, tpt, tmb; timp; strings (6-4-3-2).

fp: 8 February 1942, Los Angeles, Werner Janssen Orchestra, cond. Igor Stravinsky.

Pub. 1942, Associated Music Publishers (New York).

80. Circus Polka. For a young elephant. Composed for the Barnum and Bailey Circus. 1942. Version for wind band (scored by David Reksin).

fl, 2 solo cl, 2 cl, alto sax, bar sax, 2 solo cornets, 3 cornets, 2 baritone cornets, 2 hn, 4 tmb, 2 tubas; GC, side dm, cym, xyl.

fp: Spring 1942, New York, Barnum and Bailey Circus, Ballet of Elephants.

80a. Circus Polka. Symphonic version by the composer. 5 October 1942. Dur. 4′.

fl, pic, 2 ob, 2 cl, 2 bsn; 4 hn, 2 tpt, 3 tmb, tuba; timp, snare dm, GC, cym; strings.

fp: 13 January 1944, Cambridge (Mass.), Sanders Theatre, Boston Symphony Orchestra, cond. Igor Stravinsky.

fEp: 10 February 1952, London Symphony Orchestra, cond. George Weldon.

Pub. 1944, Associated Music Publishers (New York).

80b. Circus Polka. Version for piano by the composer. 5 February 1942, Hollywood. Dur. 4′.

fEbp: 12 May 1948, BBC broadcast, Colin Horsley.

Pub. 1942, Associated Music Publishers. Version for two pianos by Victor Babin pub. 1943.

81. Four Norwegian Moods. For orchestra. 18 August 1942, Hollywood. Dur. 8′ 30″.

1. *Intrada*; 2. *Song*; 3. *Wedding Dance*; 4. *Cortège*.

2 fl, pic, 2 ob, ca, 2 cl, 2 bsn; 4 hn, 2 tpt, 2 tmb, tuba; timp; strings.

fp: 13 January 1944, Cambridge (Mass.), Sanders Theatre, Boston Symphony Orchestra, cond. Igor Stravinsky.

fEp: 31 July 1944, Royal Albert Hall, Promenade Concert, BBC Symphony Orchestra, cond. Sir Henry Wood.

Pub. 1944, Associated Music Publishers (New York).

82. Ode. Elegiacal Chant in three parts. For orchestra. 25 June 1943, Hollywood. Ded. to the memory of Natalie Koussevitzky. Dur. 8′.

1. *Eulogy (Lento)*; 2. *Eclogue (Con moto)*; 3. *Epitaph (Lento)*.

3 fl, pic, 2 ob, 2 cl, 2 bsn; 4 hn, 2 tpt; timp; strings.

fp: 8 October 1943, Boston Symphony Orchestra, cond. Serge Koussevitzky.

fEp: 21 April 1949, BBC broadcast, Royal Philharmonic Orchestra, cond. Walter Goehr.

fEp (concert): 12 May 1950, Westminster (Central Hall), Morley College concert, Royal Philharmonic Orchestra, cond. Walter Goehr.

Pub. 1947, Schott.

83. Babel. Cantata for male chorus, narrator and orchestra. Words from the Book of Moses. 12 April 1944, Hollywood. Dur. 7′.

3 fl, pic, 2 ob, 2 cl, bcl, 2 bsn, cbsn; 4 hn, 3 tpt, 3 tmb; timp; hp, strings.

fp: 18 November 1945, Los Angeles, Wilshire Ebell Theater, cond. Werner Janssen. Part of the 'Genesis' cycle.

fEbp: 19 February 1953, BBC Chorus, Frank Phillips, BBC Symphony Orchestra, cond. Walter Goehr.

Pub. 1952 (vocal score), 1953, Schott. Vocal score by the composer. German version, L. Andersen.

84. Scherzo à la Russe. Original version for Paul Whiteman's Band. 1944, Hollywood.

fp: 1944, Blue Network Programme.

84a. Scherzo à la Russe. Symphonic version for orchestra. 1943–4, Hollywood. Dur. 4′.

2 fl, pic, 2 ob, 2 cl, 2 bsn; 4 hn, 3 tpt, 3 tmb, tuba; xyl, timp, tamb, tgle, cym, side dms

(with & without snares), GC; piano, hp; strings.

fp: March 1946, San Francisco, San Francisco Symphony Orchestra, cond. Igor Stravinsky.

fEp: 12 August 1946, Royal Albert Hall, Promenade Concert, London Symphony Orchestra, cond. Sir Adrian Boult.

Pub. 1945, Chappell (New York). Transcription for two pianos by the composer, pub. 1945, Associated Music Publishers.

BIBLIOGRAPHY:
R.-Aloys Mooser: Scherzo à la russe, in *Aspects de la musique contemporaine*, Editions Labor et Fidès (Geneva) 1957, p. 95.

85. Scènes de Ballet. For orchestra. 23 August 1944, Hollywood. Dur. 18'.

1. *Introduction*; 2. *Danses* (Corps de Ballet); 3. *Variation* (Ballerina); 4. *Pantomime*; 5. *Pas de deux*; 6. *Pantomime*; 7. *Variation* (Dancer); 8. *Variation* (Ballerina); 9. *Pantomime*; 10. *Danses* (Corps de Ballet); 11. *Apothéose*.

2 fl, pic, 2 ob, 2 cl, bsn; 2 hn, 3 tpt, 3 tmb, tuba; timp; piano, strings.

fp (stage): 1944, Philadelphia, Billy Rose's revue 'The Seven Lively Arts', cond. Maurice Abravnel.

fp (concert): winter 1945, New York, New York Philharmonic Orchestra, cond. Igor Stravinsky.

fEp (stage): 11 February 1948, Covent Garden, Sadler's Wells Ballet; with Margot Fonteyn and Michael Somes; choreography, Frederick Ashton; scenery and costumes, André Beaurepaire.

fEp (concert): 27 May 1954, Royal Philharmonic Society, Royal Philharmonic Orchestra, cond. Igor Stravinsky. (At this concert, Stravinsky was presented by Sir Arthur Bliss with the Gold Medal of the Royal Philharmonic Society.)

Pub. 1945, Chappell (New York).

BIBLIOGRAPHY:
J. Baly Gay: Las Excenas de Ballet de Stravinsky, *Nuestra Musica*, No. 8, October 1947.

86. Sonata for two pianos. 1943–4, Hollywood. Dur. 11'.

1. *Moderato*; 2. *Theme with variations*; 3. *Allegretto*.

fp: July 1944, Madison (Wisconsin), Nadia Boulanger and Richard Johnson.

Pub. 1945, Chappell (New York).

87. Elégie (Elegy). For unacc. viola (or violin). 1944. 'Composée à l'intention de Germain Prévost, pour être jouée à la mémoire de Alphonse Onnou fondateur du Quatuor Pro Arte.' Dur. 4' 30".

Pub. 1945, Chappell (New York).

88. Symphony in three movements. 1942–5. Ded. New York Philharmonic Symphony Society. Dur. 24'.

1. *crotchet = 160*; 2. *Andante*; 3. *Con moto*.

2 fl, pic, 2 ob, 2 cl, bcl, 2 bsn, cbsn; 4 hn, 3 tpt, 3 tmb, tuba; timp, GC; piano, hp, strings.

fp: 24 January 1946, New York, New York Philharmonic Symphony, cond. Igor Stravinsky.

fEp: 21 December 1946, BBC broadcast, London Philharmonic Orchestra, cond. Ernest Ansermet.

fEp (concert): 5 March 1948, Royal Albert Hall, Philharmonia Orchestra, cond. Otto Klemperer.

Pub. 1946, Associated Music Publishers (New York).

BIBLIOGRAPHY:
F.G.: Notes sur la Symphonie en trois mouvements de Stravinsky, *Contrepoints*, No. 5, December 1946, p. 109.
Michael Kennedy: Stravinsky and his 1945 Symphony, *Halle*, January 1959, p. 5.
Heinrich Strobel: Stravinskys Symphony in three movements, *Melos*, October 1948, p. 271; ISs Symfoni i tre satser, *Nutida musik*, Vol. 6 (1962–3), No. 7, p. 21.

89. Ebony Concerto. For clarinet and orchestra. 1 December 1945, Hollywood. Ded. Woody Herman. Dur. 11'.

1. *Allegro moderato*; 2. *Andante*; 3. *Moderato —Vivo*.

3 cl, 2 alto sax, 2 ten sax, bar sax, bcl; hn, 5 tpt, 3 tmb; pf, hp, guitar, double-bass; tom-tom, cym, drums.

fp: 25 March 1946, New York, Carnegie Hall, Woody Herman and his Band.

Pub. 1946, Charling Music Corporation; 1954, Edwin H. Morris & Co. (London).

90. Concerto in D. For string orchestra. 8 August 1946, Hollywood. Ded. 'Dédié à la Basler Kammerorchester et son chef Paul Sacher'. Dur. 12'.

　1. *Vivace*; 2. *Arioso* (*Andantino*); 3. *Rondo* (*Allegro*).

　fp: 27 January 1947, Basle, Basle Kammerorchester, cond. Paul Sacher.

　fEp: 5 January 1948, BBC broadcast, Boyd Neel Orchestra, cond. Paul Sacher.

　Pub. 1947, Boosey & Hawkes.

91. Little Canon (Petit canon pour la fête de Nadia Boulanger). For two tenors. Words: Jean de Meung. 1947, Hollywood. Unpub.

92. Orpheus (Orphée). Ballet in three scenes. 23 September 1947, Hollywood. Dur. 30'.

　First Scene: 1. *Orpheus weeps for Eurydice*; 2. *Air de Danse*; 3. *Dance of the Angel of Death*; 4. *Interlude*. Second Scene: 5. *Pas de Furies*; 6. *Air de Danse*; 7. *Interlude*; 6a. *Air de Danse* (*conclusion*); 8. *Pas d'Action*; 9. *Pas de Deux*; 10. *Interlude*; 11. *Pas d'Action*. Third Scene: 12. *Orpheus's Apotheosis*.

　2 fl, pic, 2 ob, ca, 2 cl, 2 bsn; 4 hn, 2 tpt, 2 tmb, bs tmb; timp; hp, strings.

　fp: 28 April 1948, New York, City Center, Ballet Society; with Nicholas Magallanes (Orpheus) and Maria Tallchief (Eurydice); choreography, Balanchine; scenery and costumes, Isamu Noguchi.

　f European p: September 1948, Venice, Teatro Fenice, Festival of Contemporary Music, cond. Igor Markevitch.

　fEp (concert): 16 February 1949, Royal Albert Hall, BBC Symphony Orchestra, cond. Ernest Ansermet.

　Pub. 1948, Boosey & Hawkes.

BIBLIOGRAPHY:
Ferdinando Ballo: Introduction to Stravinsky's Orpheus, *Tempo*, No. 10, winter 1948–9.
— Orpheus, *Musik der Zeit*, Vol. 1, Boosey & Hawkes (1952), p. 20.
Marius Monnikendam: Het jongste œuvre van Stravinsky—De Mis en Orpheus, *Mens en melodie*, June–July 1949, p. 190.

93. Mass. For mixed chorus and double wind quintet. 1944–8. Dated: 15 March 1948. Dur. 17'.

　1. *Kyrie*; 2. *Gloria*; 3. *Credo*; 4. *Sanctus*; 5. *Agnus Dei*.

　2 ob, ca, 2 bsn, 2 tpt, 3 tmb.

　fp: 27 October 1948, Milan, Teatro alla Scala, Chorus and Orchestra of La Scala, cond. Ernest Ansermet.

　fEp: 19 February 1949, Elsie Suddaby, Anne Wood, René Soames, Bruce Boyce, BBC chorus and double wind quintet from BBC Symphony Orchestra, cond. Ernest Ansermet.

　Pub. 1949, Boosey & Hawkes.

BIBLIOGRAPHY:
Ernest Ansermet: Stravinsky's newest work, *Tempo*, No. 10, winter 1948–9.
— La Messe de Stravinsky, *SM*, April 1949, p. 143.
Helmut Bader: Die Messe von Stravinsky, *Melos*, October 1950, p. 279.
Fritz Bouquet: Die Messe von Stravinsky— Deutsche Erstaufführung unter Rosbaud, *Melos*, May–June 1949, p. 160.
R. Goldman: Current comment—new Mass (1948), *MQ*, July 1949, p. 451.
— La Messa di Stravinsky, *Prospetti* (Florence), 1953, No. 3.
Massimo Mila: Das jüngste Werk Stravinskys, Die Messe, *Melos*, December 1948, p. 343.
Edmund Rubbra: Stravinsky's Mass, *Month*, April 1949, p. 250.
W. H. Rubsamen: First liturgical performance of Mass for mixed chorus and double woodwind quintet, *MQ*, October 1950, p. 581.
Willi Schuh: ISs Messe, *SM*, December 1948.

94. The Rake's Progress. Opera in three acts: fable by W. H. Auden and Chester Kallman. 1948–51. Dur. 150'.

　2 fl, 2 ob, 2 cl, 2 bsn; 2 hn, 2 tpt; cembalo (piano); timp; strings.

　fp: 11 September 1951, Venice, Teatro la Fenice, Chorus and Orchestra of La Scala (Milan), cond. Igor Stravinsky; with Rafaël Arié (Trulove), Elisabeth Schwarzkopf (Anne), Robert Rounseville (Tom Rakewell), Otakar Kraus (Nick Shadow), Nell Tangeman (Mother Goose), Jennie Tourel (Baba the Turk), Hugues Cuénod (Sellem), Emanuel Menkes (Keeper of the Madhouse). Broadcast by the BBC.

f Ep (concert excerpts): Royal Festival Hall, Elisabeth Schwarzkopf, Philharmonia Orchestra, cond. Harry Blech.

f Br p: 25 August 1953, Edinburgh Festival, Glyndebourne Opera.

Pub. 1951, Boosey & Hawkes.

BIBLIOGRAPHY:

Felix Aprahamian: Stravinsky's The Rake's Progress, *World Review*, November 1951, p. 17.

W. H. Auden: Reflexionen über die Oper, in *Musik der Zeit*, Vol. 1, Boosey & Hawkes (1952), p. 51.

Richard Capell: Stravinsky's opera, *MT*, November 1951, p. 498.

Deryck Cooke: 'The Rake' and the 18th century, *MT*, January 1962, p. 20.

A Della Corte: The Rake's Progress d'IS, *Rivista Musicale Italiana*, July–September 1951.

Robert Craft: The Rake's Progress, *The Score*, September 1954.

C.C.: The Rake's Progress, *MO*, February 1952, p. 271.

R. Eyer: Metropolitan Opera introduces Rake's Progress to America, *Musical America*, March 1953, p. 3.

— Rake on discs, *Musical America*, December 1953, p. 15.

Noël Goodwin: Stravinsky's road to Bedlam, *M&M*, May 1965, p. 18.

John W. Klein: The Rake's Progress, *The Listener*, 10 July 1958, p. 69.

— The Rake's Progress, *MO*, May 1962, p. 465.

Angela Lemkin: Impressions of The Rake's Progress, *London Symphony Observer*, March–April 1952, p. 125.

G. F. Malipiero: The Rake's Progress de Stravinsky, in *Musique Contemporaine*, 1951.

Colin Mason: Stravinsky's opera, *M&L*, January 1952.

Herbert Murrill: The Rake's Progress, *The Score*, May 1952.

Walter Panofsky: Die neue Oper von Stravinsky, The Rake's Progress, *Melos*, October 1951, p. 283.

Henry Raynor: Britten, Stravinsky and the future of opera, *MO*, October 1952 p. 19, November 1952 p. 83.

Claude Rostand: Rake's Progress in Frankreich, *Melos*, February 1953, p. 59.

Boris de Schloezer: Le Libertin, *Nouvelle revue française*, 1953, No. 9, p. 536.

Willi Schuh: ISs neue Opera The Rake's Progress, *SM*, October (No. 10) 1951, p. 400.

Gabriel Smit: Stravinsky's opera The Rake's Progress, *Mens en melodie*, October 1951, p. 298.

Igor Stravinsky: Come ho composto The Rake's Progress, *La Biennale* (Venice), October 1951.

Heinrich Strobel: The Rake's example, *Melos*, January 1952, p. 7.

Roman Vlad: The Rake's Progress di Stravinsky, ultima opera classica, *La Rassegna musicale*, 1962, p. 248.

Eric Walter White: Stravinsky's The Rake's Progress, *Tempo*, No. 20, summer 1951.

A. Williamson: Rake's Progress—Hogarth's paintings contrasted with Stravinsky's opera, *Musical America*, 1 January 1953, p. 6.

Various authors: The Rake's Progress, in *Musik der Zeit*, Vol. 1, Boosey & Hawkes (1952), p. 51.

94a. Lullaby. From 'The Rake's Progress'. Recomposed for two (soprano and alto) recorders. Pub. 1960, Boosey & Hawkes.

95. Cantata. For soprano, tenor, female chorus and instrumental ensemble. April 1951–August 1952. Words: Anon. (15/16th century lyrics). Ded. Los Angeles Chamber Symphony Society. Dur. 30'.

1. *A Lyke-Wake Dirge* (*Versus I*), *Prelude*. Chorus.

2. *Ricercar I* (*The maidens came*). Soprano.

3. *A Lyke-Wake Dirge* (*Versus II*), *1st Interlude*. Chorus.

4. *Ricercar II* (*Tomorrow shall be*) (*Sacred History*). Tenor.

5. *A Lyke-Wake Dirge* (*Versus III*), *2nd Interlude*. Chorus.

6. *Westron Wind*. Soprano and tenor.

7. *A Lyke-Wake Dirge* (*Versus IV*), *Postlude*. Chorus.

2 fl, 2 ob, ca, cello.

fp: 11 November 1952, Los Angeles Chamber Society, cond. Igor Stravinsky.

fEp: 17 November 1953, Royal Festival

Hall, Arda Mandikian, Peter Pears, English Opera Group Chorus and Ensemble, cond. Paul Sacher.

Pub. 1952, Boosey & Hawkes. Vocal score by the composer.

BIBLIOGRAPHY:

John Garbutt & Matthew Patterson: An approach to Stravinsky's Cantata and The Wedding, *M&L*, January 1957.

Heinrich Lindlar: IS's Cantata, *Tempo*, No. 27, spring 1953; *SM*, October 1953, p. 397.

Colin Mason: Serial procedures in the Ricercar II of Stravinsky's Cantata, *Tempo*, spring–summer 1962, p. 6.

96. Septet. For clarinet, horn, bassoon, piano, violin, viola and cello. July 1952–February 1953. Ded. Dumbarton Oaks Research Library and Collection. Dur. 11′.

1. *(Untitled)*; 2. *Passacaglia*; 3. *Gigue*.

fp: 23 January 1954, Dumbarton Oaks, Washington D.C., cond. Igor Stravinsky.

fEp: 23 May 1954, BBC broadcast, Virtuoso Chamber Ensemble, cond. Nadia Boulanger.

Pub. 1953, Boosey & Hawkes. Reduction for two pianos by the composer.

BIBLIOGRAPHY:

Hans Ludwig Schilling: Zur Instrumentation in ISs Spätwerk, aufgezoigt an seinem Septett 1953, *Archiv für Musikwissenschaft*, 1956, Nos. 3–4.

Erwin Stein: Stravinsky's Septet, *Tempo*, No. 31, spring 1954.

97. Three Songs from William Shakespeare. For mezzo-soprano, flute, clarinet and viola. Autumn 1953. Ded. 'Evenings on the Roof' (Los Angeles). Dur. 6′ 30″.

1. *Musick to heare*; 2. *Full fadom five*; 3. *When daisies pied*.

fp: 8 March 1954, Los Angeles, Evenings-on-the-Roof concerts, cond. Robert Craft.

fEbp: 29 March 1955, Nancy Evans, Gareth Morris, Stephen Waters, Watson Forbes.

Pub. 1954, Boosey & Hawkes. Reduction for voice and piano by the composer.

98. Four Songs for voice, flute, harp and guitar. Instrumented 1953–4. Phonetic Russian

text by the composer; English translation by Robert Craft and Rosa Newmarch.

1. *The Drake.* (No. 1 of *Four Russian Songs.*) 1953. Dur. 1′ 14″.

2. *A Russian Spiritual.* (No. 4 of *Four Russian Songs.*) 1954. Dur. 1′ 40″.

3. *Geese and Swans.* (No. 2 of *Three Tales for Children.*) 1954. Dur. 31″.

4. *Tilimbom.* (No. 1 of *Three Tales for Children.*) 1954. Dur. 58″.

fp: 21 February 1955, Los Angeles, Monday Evening Concerts, cond. Robert Craft.

Pub. 1955, Chester.

99. In Memoriam Dylan Thomas. Dirge-Canons and Song for tenor, string quartet and four trombones. February–March 1954. Dur. 6′.

1. *Dirge-Canons (Prelude)*; 2. *Song: Do not go gentle . . .* (Dylan Thomas); 3. *Dirge-Canons (Postlude)*.

fp: 20 September 1954, Los Angeles, Monday Evening Concert, cond. Robert Craft.

Pub. 1954, Boosey & Hawkes. Reduction for voice and piano by the composer.

BIBLIOGRAPHY:

Hans Keller: In Memoriam Dylan Thomas—Stravinsky's Schoenbergian technique, *Tempo*, No. 35, spring 1955.

100. Greeting Prelude. 'For the eightieth birthday of Pierre Monteux'. For orchestra. 1955. Dur. 45″.

2 fl, pic, 2 ob, 2 cl, 2 bsn, cbsn; 4 hn, 2 tpt, 3 tmb, tuba; timp, GC; piano, strings.

fp: 4 April 1955, Boston Symphony Orchestra, cond. Charles Munch.

Pub. 1956, Boosey & Hawkes.

101. Canticum Sacrum (ad honorem Sancti Marci nominis). For tenor and baritone soloists, chorus and orchestra. 1955. Dur. 17′.

Dedicatio; 1. *Euntes in mundum*; 2. *Surge, aquilo*; 3. *Ad Tres Virtutes Hortationes (Caritas—Spes—Fides)*; 4. *Brevis Motus Cantilenae*; 5. *Illi autem profecti*.

fl, 2 ob, ca, 2 bsn, cbsn; 3 tpt, bs tpt, 2 ten tmb, bs tmb, cbs tmb; hp, organ; violas and double-basses.

fp: 13 September 1956, Venice, St. Mark's Cathedral, cond. Igor Stravinsky.

fEp: 11 December 1956, ICA concert, St. Martin-in-the Fields, Duncan Robertson, Michel Roux, London Bach Society and St. Cecilia Orchestra, cond. Robert Craft; performed twice, and broadcast.

Pub. 1956, Boosey & Hawkes. Vocal score by the composer.

BIBLIOGRAPHY:

Heinrich Lindlar: Stravinskys Canticum Sacrum, *NZfM*, October 1956.

Klaus Freiherr von Loeffelholz: IS's Canticum Sacrum, *NZfM*, April 1968.

R.-Aloys Mooser: Canticum Sacrum, in *Aspects de la musique contemporaine*, Editions Labor et Fidès (Geneva) 1957, p. 231.

Luigi Pestalozza: IS, Canticum Sacrum, *Il Verri* (Milan), November 1956.

Albert von Reck: Gestalzusammenhänge im Canticum Sacrum von Stravinsky, *SM*, February 1958, p. 49.

Willi Schuh: Stravinskys Canticum Sacrum, *SM*, October 1956, p. 398.

Erwin Stein: IS's Canticum Sacrum, *Tempo*, No. 40, summer 1956.

Paul Steinitz: On rehearsing a choir for the Canticum Sacrum, *The Score*, March 1957, p. 56.

102. Choral-Variationen über das Weihnachtslied 'Vom Himmel hoch da komm' ich her'. J. S. Bach, arr. Igor Stravinsky for mixed chorus and orchestra. December 1955–February 1956, New York-Hollywood. Ded. Robert Craft. Dur. 15'.

2 fl, 2 ob, ca, 2 bsn, cbsn; 3 tpt, 3 tmb; hp, violas and double-basses.

fp: 27 May 1956, Ojai, California, cond. Robert Craft.

fEp: 11 December 1956, ICA concert, St. Martin-in-the-Fields, London Bach Society and St. Cecilia Orchestra, cond. Robert Craft; broadcast.

Pub. 1956, Boosey & Hawkes.

103. Agon. Ballet for twelve dancers. December 1953–27 April 1957. Ded. Lincoln Kirstein and George Balanchine. Dur. 20'.

1. *Pas de quatre—Double Pas de quatre—Triple Pas de quatre. Prelude.* 2. *First Pas de trois: Saraband Step—Gailliarde—Coda. Interlude.* 3. *Second Pas de trois: Bransle Simple—*

Bransle Gay—Bransle de Poitou. Interlude. 4. *Pas de deux—Four Duos—Four Trios.*

3 fl, pic, 2 ob, ca, 2 cl, bcl, 2 bsn, cbsn; 4 hn, 4 tpt, 2 ten tmb, bs tmb; hp, mandoline, piano; timp, 3 tomtoms or high timp, xyl, cast; strings.

fp (concert): 17 June 1957, Los Angeles, cond. Robert Craft.

fp (stage): 1 December 1957, New York, New York City Ballet.

fEp (concert): 21 May 1928, Collegium Musicum Londonii, cond. John Minchinton.

fEp (ballet): 20 August 1958, Covent Garden, cond. Hugo Rignold.

fEbp: 10 December 1958, Royal Festival Hall, BBC Symphony Orchestra, cond. Rudolf Schwarz.

Pub. 1957, Boosey & Hawkes. Reduction for two pianos by the composer.

BIBLIOGRAPHY:

Hans Keller: Stravinsky's performance of Agon, *Tempo*, No. 50, winter 1958–9.

Horst Koegler: Balanchine choreographiert Agon, *Melos*, July–August 1963.

Bernard Lewkovitch: Agon-musiken, *Nutida musik*, Vol. 3 (1959–60), No. 4, p. 4.

104. Threni (id est Lamentationes Jeremiae Prophetae). For six soloists (soprano, contralto, two tenors, bass and basso profondo), mixed chorus and orchestra. Summer 1957–21 March 1958. Ded. Norddeutscher Rundfunk. Dur. 35'.

1. *De Elegia Prima*; 2. *De Elegia Tertia* (1. *Querimonia*; 2. *Sensus Spei*; 3. *Solacium*); 3. *De Elegia Quinta*.

2 fl, 2 ob, ca, 2 cl, alto cl, bcl, sarrusophone; 4 hn, 3 tmb (alto, ten, bs), contralto bugle (Flugelhorn), tuba; timp, tamtam, piano, celesta, hp; strings.

fp: 23 September 1958, Venice, Sala della Scuola Grande di San Rocco, cond. Igor Stravinsky.

fFp: 14 November 1958, Paris, Salle Pleyel, Chorale des J.M.F., l'Orchestre des Concerts Lamoureux, cond. Robert Craft.

fEp: 2 June 1959, Royal Festival Hall, April Cantelo, Helen Watts, Wilfred Brown, Denis Dowling, David Galliver, Roger Stalman, London Philharmonic Choir and

Stravinsky, Igor

Orchestra, cond. William Steinberg; broadcast.

Pub. 1958, Boosey & Hawkes. Vocal score by Erwin Stein.

BIBLIOGRAPHY:

I. Kolodin: First American performance of Threni, *Saturday Review*, 17 January 1959, p. 83.

Hansjörg Pauli: On Stravinsky's Threni, *Tempo*, No. 49, autumn 1958.

— Zur seriellen Struktur von ISs Threni, *SM*, December 1958, p. 450.

Malcolm Rayment: Threni, a programme note, *Gramophone Record Review*, December 1960, p. 77.

Willi Schuh: Strukturanalyse eines Fragments aus Stravinskys Threni, *SM*, December 1958, p. 456.

105. Movements. For piano and orchestra. 1958–30 July 1959. Ded. Margrit Weber. Dur. 10′.

2 fl, 2 ob, 2 cl, bsn; 2 tpt, 3 tmb; hp, celesta, strings.

fp: 10 January 1960, New York, Town Hall, Stravinsky Festival, Margrit Weber, cond. Igor Stravinsky.

fEp: 22 March 1961, Royal Festival Hall, Aloys Kontarsky and the BBC Symphony Orchestra, cond. Hans Rosbaud.

Pub. 1960, Boosey & Hawkes. Reduction for two pianos by the composer.

BIBLIOGRAPHY:

Robert Breuer: IS, Movements for piano and orchestra, *SM*, March–April 1960, p. 113.

Willi Reich: Stravinskys 'Klavier-Konzert' für Margrit Weber, *ÖM*, April 1962.

106. Epitaphium. For flute, clarinet and harp. 'Für das Grabmal des Prinzen Max Egon zu Fürstenberg.' 1959. Dur. 1′ 16″.

fp: 17 October 1959, Donaueschingen Festival.

fEp: 12 November 1959, BBC broadcast, Virtuoso Ensemble, cond. Robert Craft.

Pub. 1959, Boosey & Hawkes.

107. Double Canon (Raoul Dufy in memoriam). For string quartet. 1959. Dur. 1′ 16″.

fp: 10 January 1960, New York, Town Hall, Stravinsky Festival.

fEbp: 10 April 1961, Melos Ensemble.

Pub. 1960, Hawkes.

108. Tres Sacrae Cantiones. Carlo Gesualdo di Venosa, reconstructed by Igor Stravinsky. 1957–9.

1. *Da pacem Domine*; 2. *Assumpta est Maria*; 3. *Illumina nos*.

fEbp: 2 May 1960, London Bach Group, cond. John Minchinton.

Pub. 1957 (No. 3), 1960 (complete), Boosey & Hawkes.

109. Momentum pro Gesualdo di Venosa ad CD annum. Three Madrigals recomposed for instruments by Igor Stravinsky. March 1960, Hollywood. Dur. 6′ 54″.

1. *Asciugate i begli occhi* (Madrigale XIV, Libro quinto). Dur. 2′ 24″.

2. *Ma tu, cagion di quella* (Madrigale XVIII, Libro quinto). Dur. 1′ 50″.

3. *Beltà poi che t'assenti* (Madrigale II, Libro sesto). Dur. 2′ 40″.

2 ob, 2 bsn; 4 hn, 2 tpt, 2 ten tmb; strings.

fp: 27 September 1960, Venice Biennale, Orchestra del Teatro la Fenice, cond. Igor Stravinsky.

fEp: 10 March 1961, BBC broadcast, BBC Symphony Orchestra, cond. Hans Rosbaud.

Pub. 1960, Boosey & Hawkes.

BIBLIOGRAPHY:

Robert Craft: A note on Gesualdo and Stravinsky, *Tempo*, No. 45, autumn 1957.

— Gesualdo–Stravinsky: Illumina nos (transl. Ernest Roth), *SM*, December 1957, p. 475.

Colin Mason: Stravinsky and Gesualdo, *Tempo*, Nos. 55–56, autumn–winter 1960.

Willi Schuh: ISs Momentum pro Gesualdo di Venosa, *SM*, November–December 1960, p. 368.

110. A Sermon, a Narrative and a Prayer. Cantata for alto and tenor soloists, speaker, chorus and orchestra. 1960–1. Hollywood. Dated: 31 January 1961. Ded. Paul Sacher. Dur. 16′.

1. *A Sermon* (from St. Paul).

2. *A Narrative* (The Stoning of St. Stephen —from the 'Acts').

3. *A Prayer* (from Thomas Dekker). 'In memoriam the Reverend James McLane.'

fl, alto fl, 2 ob, cl, bcl, 2 bsn; 4 hn, 3 tpt, 2 ten tmb, bs tmb, tuba; 3 tamtams, piano, hp; strings (8+7-6-5-4).

fp: 23 February 1962, Basle, Basle Chamber Orchestra, cond. Paul Sacher.

fEp: 31 May 1962, Royal Festival Hall, ISCM concert, BBC Symphony Orchestra, cond. Hans Rosbaud.

Pub. 1961, Boosey & Hawkes.

BIBLIOGRAPHY:

Colin Mason: Stravinsky's new work, *Tempo*, autumn 1961, p. 5.

Hans Oesch: Die Kantata des neuen Testaments von IS, *Melos*, April 1962, p. 124.

Constantin Regamey: L'œuvre la plus récente d'IS, A Sermon, a Narrative and a Prayer, *Feuilles musicales*, March–April 1962, p. 46; Stravinskys jüngster Werk, A Sermon, a Narrative and a Prayer, *SM*, May–June 1962, p. 134.

111. Anthem (The Dove descending breaks the air). For mixed (SATB) chorus a cappella. Words T. S. Eliot (from 'Four Quartets'). 2 January 1962, Hollywood. Ded. T. S. Eliott Dur. 2′ 10″.

fp: 19 February 1962, Los Angeles, Monday Evening Concerts, cond. Robert Craft.

fEp: 24 May 1962, BBC broadcast, BBC Chorus, cond. Peter Gellhorn.

Pub. Faber & Faber (in appendix to English edition of *Expositions and Developments*); Boosey & Hawkes.

112. The Flood. A Musical Play. Text chosen and arranged by Robert Craft, derived principally from the Book of Genesis and the York and Chester cycles of miracle plays (set down between 1430 and 1500). 1961–2. Dated: 14 March 1962. Dur. 24′.

1. *Prelude*; 2. *The Building of the Ark*; 3. *The Catalogue of the Animals*; 4. *The Comedy*; 5. *The Flood*; 6. *The Covenant of the Rainbow*.

3 fl, pic, alto fl, 2 ob, ca, 2 cl, bcl, cbcl, 2 bsn, cbsn; 4 hn, 3 tpt, 2 ten tmb, alto tmb, bs tmb, cbs tuba; timp, 3 tomtoms, xyl-marimba, cym, GC; celesta, piano, hp; strings.

fp: 14 June 1962, CBS Television Network.

fp (Stage): 30 April 1963, Hamburg, Staatsoper, cond. Robert Craft.

fEp: 2 October 1963, Royal Festival Hall, Norman Shelley (Noah), Betty Hardy (Noah's wife), BBC Chorus (Noah's sons), Godfrey Kenton (Narrator), John Noble and Roger Stalman (God), John Mitchinson (Lucifer, Satan), BBC Symphony Orchestra, cond. Antal Dorati.

Pub. 1962, 1963 (full score), Boosey & Hawkes.

BIBLIOGRAPHY:

Benjamin Boretz: Stravinsky, a Flood of Genius, *London Magazine*, January 1963.

Anthony Payne: Stravinsky's The Flood, *Tempo*, autumn 1964, p. 2.

Willi Schuh: IS, Die Sinflut, *SM*, May–June 1963, p. 159.

113. Abraham and Isaac. A Sacred Ballad for baritone and chamber orchestra. 1962–3 March 1963. Ded. to the people of the State of Israel. Dur. 12′.

2 fl, alto fl, ob, ca, cl, bcl, 2 bsn; hn, 2 tpt, ten tmb, bs tmb, tuba; strings.

fp: 21 August 1964, Jerusalem, Ephraim Biran, Israel Festival Orchestra, cond. Robert Craft.

Pub. 1965, Boosey & Hawkes.

BIBLIOGRAPHY:

Benjamin Boretz: Stravinsky's Abraham and Isaac, *Nation*, 11 January 1965, p. 39.

Willi Schuh: IS, Abraham and Isaac, A Sacred Ballad, *SM*, November–December 1964, p. 379.

Claudio Spies: Notes on Stravinsky's Abraham and Isaac, *PNM*, fall–winter 1966, p. 148.

Igor Stravinsky: Abraham and Isaac, *Musical Events*, August 1964, p. 8.

114. Canzonetta. Jean Sibelius, arr. Igor Stravinsky. 1963.

4 hn, 2 cl, hp, double-bass.

Pub. 1964, Breitkopf & Härtel.

115. Elegy for J.F.K. For mezzo-soprano. or baritone and three clarinets. Words: W. H. Auden. March 1964, Hollywood. Dur. 1′ 30″.

fp: 6 April 1964, Los Angeles, Monday Evening Concerts, cond. Robert Craft.

fEp: 13 October 1964, Manchester Institute

Stravinsky, Igor

of Contemporary Arts, John Shirley-Quirk
with Jack Brymer, Herbert New and Walter
Lear; broadcast.
Pub. 1964, Boosey & Hawkes.

116. Fanfare for a new theatre. For two
trumpets. Winter 1964, Hollywood. Ded. 'to
Lincoln and George' (Lincoln Kirstein and
George Balanchine).
fp: 19 April 1964, New York State Theater
in the Lincoln Center.
f London p: 3 October 1968, Wigmore
Hall, members of Philip Jones Brass Quintet.
Pub. 1968, Boosey & Hawkes.

117. Variations (Aldous Huxley in
Memoriam). For orchestra. 1963–4. Dated:
28 October 1964, Hollywood. Dur. 5′.
2 fl, alto fl, 2 ob, ca, 2 cl, bcl, 2 bsn; 4 hn,
3 tpt, 3 tmb; hp, piano, strings (12-10-8-6).
fp: 17 April 1965, Chicago, Chicago
Symphony, cond. Robert Craft.
f European p: 28 May 1965, Warsaw
Philharmonic, cond. Robert Craft.
Pub. 1965, Boosey & Hawkes.

BIBLIOGRAPHY:
Claudio Spies: Notes on Stravinsky's Variations, *PNM*, fall–winter 1965, p. 62.

118. Introitus (T. S. Eliot in memoriam).
For male chorus and chamber ensemble.
17 February 1965, Hollywood. Dur. 3′ 30″
(?4′).
hp, piano, 2 tamtams, 2 timp, va, double-
basses.
fp: 17 April 1965, Chicago Symphony,
cond. Robert Craf.
Pub. 1965, Boosey & Hawkes.

119. Requiem Canticles. For contralto,
bass, chorus and orchestra. 1965–6. Dated:
13 August 1966. Ded. to the memory of
Helen Buchanan Seeger. Dur. 15′.
1. *Prelude*; 2. *Exaudi*; 3. *Dies irae*; 4. *Tuba
Mirum*; 5. *Interlude*; 6. *Rex Tremendae*;
7. *Lacrimosa*; 8. *Libera me*; 9. *Postlude*.
3 fl, pic, alto fl, 2 bsn; 4 hn, 2 tpt, 3 tmb;
timp (2 players), xyl, vib, campane; hp, piano,
celesta; strings.
fp: 8 October 1966, Princeton University,
cond. Robert Craft.
Pub. 1967, Boosey & Hawkes.

BIBLIOGRAPHY:
B. Jacobson: Stravinsky's new Requiem
Canticles, *High Fidelity*, December 1966.
Anthony Payne: Requiem Canticles, *Tempo*,
No. 81, summer 1967, p. 10.
Eric Walter White: Stravinsky's Requiem
Canticles, *Tempo*, No. 79, winter 1966–7,
p. 14.

120. The Owl and the Pussy-Cat (Edward
Lear). For voice and piano. 1966. Ded. 'to
Vera'.
fp: 31 October 1966, Los Angeles, Monday
Evening Concerts, Peggy Bonini, acc. Ingolf
Dahl.
Pub. 1967, Boosey & Hawkes.

GENERAL BIBLIOGRAPHY
Jules van Ackere: IS, Standaard-Boekhandel
(Antwerp) 1954.
A. D. Allatt: Stravinsky and the dance, *Dance
Magazine*, May 1962, p. 39.
Ernest Ansermet: IS, the man and his work,
Musical Courier, 25 November 1915, p. 41.
— L'œuvre d'IS, *RM*, July 1921, p. 1.
— Einführung in das Schaffen ISs, *Anbruch*,
1922, Nos. 11–12, p. 169.
— Introduction à l'œuvre de Strawinsky,
Revue Pleyel, March 1925.
— Stravinsky's gift to the West, *Dance Index*,
1947, Nos. 10–12, p. 235.
— Music—expression of representation?,
Musical America, February 1949, p. 6.
— Ein Werk des Glaubens, *Musik der Zeit*,
Vol. 1 (1952), p. 33.
— Das Phänomen Strawinsky, *ÖM*, April
1962.
Ernest Ansermet & J.-Claude Piguet: (IS), in
Entretiens sur la musique (Neuchâtel), 1963,
p. 86.
Merle Armitage (ed.): IS, G. Schirmer (New
York) 1936.
— The age of Stravinsky, in *IS*, Duell, Sloan
& Pearce (New York) 1949, p. 169.
Boris Asagfieff: Über die Art der Einflusses
Strawinskys auf die zeitgenössische Musik,
Der Auftakt, 1929, No. 4, p. 106.
Georges Auric: Du 'Sacré' au 'Mavra', *Les
Nouvelles littéraires*, 6 January 1923.
— Hommage à IS, *RM*, May–June 1939,
p. 333.

Milton Babbitt: Remarks on recent Stravinsky, *PNM*, spring–summer 1964, p. 35.

Sol Babitz: Stravinsky's rhythmic innovations, *International Musician*, 1949, p. 22.

George Balachine: The dance element in Stravinsky's music, *Dance Index*, 1947, p. 250.

Stanley Bayfield: IS, *New Music Review*, 1925, p. 396.

Cyril W. Beaumont: Some memorable occasions, *Tempo*, No. 8, summer 1948, p. 9.

John Beckwith: A Stravinsky triptych, *Canadian Musical Journal*, summer 1962, p. 5.

W. Behrend: Omkring IS, *Musik* (Copenhagen), September 1924.

K. Benes: Revolutionäre Musik, *Der Auftakt*, November 1924.

Arthur Berger: Stravinsky and his firmament, *Saturday Review*, 27 November 1954, p. 58.

— A Stravinsky panorama, in *IS*, Duell, Sloan & Pearce (New York) 1949, p. 105.

— Stravinsky from the source, *Saturday Review*, 26 March 1955, p. 58.

— Stravinsky and the young American composers, *The Score*, June 1955, p. 38.

H. Berman: Colossus of modern music, *Etude*, May 1957, p. 11.

G. Bernard: Le formalisme en musique— Stravinski et Antheil, *La Revue nouvelle*, 15 November 1926.

Paul Bertrand: Les idées de M. IS sur le Disque et la Radio, *Le Ménestrel*, 1936, 31 January p. 33, 24 April p. 140, 8 May p. 155, 5 June p. 187, 3 July p. 220.

Arthur Bliss: A short note on Stravinsky's orchestration, *MS*, 30 July 1921, p. 43.

Marc Blitzstein: The phenomenon of Stravinsky, *MQ*, July 1935, p. 330.

J. M. Boonin: Stravinsky records Stravinsky, *Musical America*, June 1962, p. 12.

André Boll: La présentation décorative de l'œuvre d'IS, *RM*, June 1933, p. 13.

— L'œuvre de Théâtre de Strawinsky—sa présentation décorative, *RM*, May–June 1939, p. 347.

Benjamin Boretz: Stravinsky, a Flood of Genius—with selective list of recent recordings, *Nation*, 28 July 1962, p. 34; *London Magazine*, January 1963.

Benjamin Boretz and Edward T. Cone (ed.): Perspectives on Schoenberg and Stravinsky, Princeton University Press (Princeton, N.J.), 1968.

M. Boretzky: Die Wege der Musik und der Revolution, *Der Auftakt*, April 1929.

André Boucourechliev: Strawinsky et un multiple, in *Stravinsky*, Librairie Hachette (Paris) 1968, p. 149.

— Stravinsky, maintenant, *Preuves*, No. 140, October 1962, p. 70.

— Stravinsky à l'Opéra, *Preuves*, No. 172, June 1965, p. 64.

Pierre Boulez: Trajectoires—Ravel, Stravinsky, Schoenberg, *Contrepoints*, 6e cahier, 1949.

Pierre Boulez, Paul Sacher & Oscar Fritz Schuh: Persönlichkeit und Erscheinung, in *IS*, Pressestelle Westdeutscher Rundfunk (Cologne) 1963, p. 78.

Martin Boykan: 'Neoclassicism' and late Stravinsky, *PNM*, spring 1963, p. 155.

Henry Boys: Stravinsky, *MMR*, 1934, pp. 152, 195, 226.

— Stravinsky—critical categories needed for a study of his music, *The Score*, August 1949, p. 3.

— Organic continuity, in *IS*, Duell, Sloan & Pearce (New York) 1949. p. 93.

— Stravinsky—a propos his aesthetic, *The Score*, January 1950, p. 61.

— Stravinsky—the musical materials, *The Score*, 1951, p. 11.

— A note on Stravinsky's setting of English, *The Score*, June 1957, p. 14.

Andres Briner: Neues von Strawinsky über sich selbst, *Melos*, June 1962.

A. H. Browne: Aspects of Stravinsky's work, *M&L*, October 1930, p. 360.

G. Bucht: IS, ett porträtt, *Exposé*, 1957, p. 32.

M.-D. Calvocoressi: A Russian composer of today—IS, *MT*, August 1911, p. 511.

E. T. Canby: Stravinsky, *Saturday Review of Literature*, 21 September 1946, p. 39.

— Beethoven touch, *Saturday Review of Literature*, 21 June 1947, p. 47.

Carl D. Carls: Strawinsky, der eine und der andere, *Der Neue Weg* (Berlin), 1928, No. 13.

Andres Caro: Palabras a Stravinsky, *Compas* (Buenos Aires), 1936, No. 2.

Stravinsky, Igor

Elliott Carter: Stravinsky and the other moderns in 1940, *Modern Music*, March–April 1940.

Alfredo Casella: IS, Formiggini (Rome) 1926; new edition, La Scuola (Brescia) 1951.

Norman Cazden: Humor in the music of Stravinsky and Prokofiev, *Science and Society*, 1954, p. 52.

Gert Cervin: IS och tidens gång, *Nutida musik*, Vol. 6 (1962–3), No. 9, p. 19.

J. Chailley: L'axiome de Strawinsky, *Journal de psychologie normale et pathologique*, 1963, No. 4.

Theodore Chandler: Stravinsky's apologia, *Modern Music*, 1942, p. 17.

Gilbert Chase: Stravinsky, his autobiography, *British Musician*, August 1935, p. 171.

Julia Chatterton: Stravinsky the strategist, *MS*, 19 April 1930, p. 127.

R. D. Chennevière: Two trends of modern music in Stravinsky's works, *MQ*, April 1919, p. 169.

Max Chop: Strawinsky-Abend in der Staatsoper, *Signale*, 1925, No. 24, p. 1055.

A. Cimbro: Stravinski, *Il Pianoforte*, February 1922.

Charles-Albert Cingria: Les lauzangiers, *RM*, May–June 1939, p. 335.

Juan Eduardo Cirlot: IS, su tiempo, su significación, su obra, G. Gili (Barcelona) 1949.

Israel Citkowitz: Stravinsky and Schoenberg, *Juilliard Review*, No. 3, fall 1954, p. 17.

Jean Cocteau: Strawinsky dernière heure, *RM*, December 1923, p. 142.

— IS und das russische Ballett, *Melos*, October 1948, p. 268.

— Critics and the comic spirit, in *IS*, Duell, Sloan & Pearce (New York) 1949, p. 21.

— Meine Liebe zu Strawinsky und Picasso, *Musik der Zeit*, Vol. 1 (1952), p. 7.

— Über Strawinsky, in *IS*, Pressestelle Westdeutscher Rundfunk (Cologne) 1963, p. 46.

André Coeuroy: Strawinsky et nos poètes, *RM*, December 1923, p. 149.

— Picasso et Stravinski, in *La Revue hebdomadaire*, 2 April 1927, p. 95; *Modern Music*, February 1928, p. 3.

— La leçon de Stravinski, in *Panorama de la musique contemporaine*, Simon Kra (Paris) 1928.

Selma Jeanne Cohen: Ballet productions, 1910–1962, in *Stravinsky and the dance*, New York Public Library (New York) 1962, p. 38.

Paul Collaer: Strawinsky, Editions Equilibres (Brussels) 1930.

— IS, in *La Musique moderne*, 1955, p. 79.

Edward T. Cone: Stravinsky—the progress of a method, *PNM*, fall 1962, p. 18.

— The uses of convention—Stravinsky and his models, *MQ*, July 1962, p. 287.

Herbert Connor: Stravinsky, *Signale*, 1926, No. 19, p. 723.

J. D. Cook: Composer tells how, *Saturday Review*, 26 June 1954, p. 43.

Deryck Cooke: Strauss, Stravinsky and Mozart, *The Listener*, 9 November 1961, p. 789.

Aaron Copland: The personality of Stravinsky, in *IS*, Duell, Sloan & Pearce (New York) 1949, p. 121.

Edwin Corle (ed.): IS, Duell, Sloan & Pearce (New York) 1949.

F. J. Cornwell: Some Russian backgrounds in music, *Etude*, February 1932, p. 139.

Alfred Cortot: IS, le piano et les pianistes, *RM*, May–June 1939, p. 264.

Joseph Cottler: Stravinsky's testament, *Disques* (Philadelphia), October 1931.

Milein Cosman: Stravinsky at rehearsal (text by Hans Keller), Dennis Dobson (London) 1962.

Harry Cox: Zur geistlichen Musik ISs, *Katholische Kirchenmusik*, July 1962.

Robert Craft: Stravinsky's pieces, *Musical America*, February 1949, p. 16.

— Stravinsky's revisions, *Counterpoint*, 1953, p. 14.

— Reihenkompositionen—vom Septett zum Agon, *Musik der Zeit*, 1955, p. 43.

— A personal preface, *The Score*, June 1957, p. 7.

— Stravinsky at seventy-five is still the explorer, *New York Times Magazine*, 16 June 1957, p. 8.

— Stravinsky, *Look*, 26 December 1967, p. 50.

Robert Craft, Alessandro Piovesan & Roman Vlad: Le Musiche religiose d'IS, Lombroso (Venice) 1956.

Gordon Cross: Personal viewpoints, *Tempo*, No. 81, summer 1967, p. 24.

John Culshaw: Stravinsky and neo-classicism, in *A Century of Music*, Dennis Dobson (London) 1952, p. 68.

Hans Curjel: Strawinsky oder die künstlerische Atmosphäre von Paris, *Melos*, 1929, No. 4, p. 167.

— Strawinsky und die Bildende Kunst, in *IS*, Pressestelle Westdeutscher Rundfunk (Cologne) 1963, p. 56.

— Strawinsky und die Maler, *Melos*, June 1967, p. 203.

O. Daniel: Twelve-tone Stravinsky, *Saturday Review*, 17 October 1959, p. 84.

Colin Davis: Stravinsky and the conductor, *M&M*, June 1962, p. 26.

Norman Demuth: IS, in *Musical Trends in the 20th Century*, Rockliff (London) 1952, p. 277.

Roger Désormière: A propos de l'évolution de Strawinsky, *RM*, May–June 1939, p. 259.

G. Devaise: Stravinsky 37, *Gringoire*, 26 August 1938.

Ulrich Dibelius: Strawinskys musikalische Wirklichkeit, *Melos*, June 1967, p. 189.

Erich Doflein: Über Strawinsky, *Melos*, 1926, Nos. 4–5, p. 158.

O. Downes: Rites of Stravinsky—order in art, *New York Times Magazine*, 15 June 1952, p. 20.

David Drew: Stravinsky and his work, *Music*, June 1952, p. 9.

— Stravinsky's revisions, *The Score*, June 1957, p. 47.

Jacob Druckman: Stravinsky's orchestral style, *Juilliard Review*, spring 1957.

M. Druskin: Das Klavier in ISs Kunst, *Der Auftakt*, April 1929, p. 109.

— Stravinsky za sebe si i za svoeto vreme, *Bulgarska Muzika*, 1967, No. 2, p. 77.

Leonard Duck: Reflections upon Stravinsky, *Halle*, April 1956, p. 1.

Samuel Dushkin: Working with Stravinsky, in *IS*, Duell, Sloan & Perce (New York) 1949, p. 179.

Werner Egk: 'Dogmatische Bekenntnisse', *Musik der Zeit*, Vol. 1 (1952), p. 34.

A. Einstein: Das Barbarische in der neuen Musik, *Der Auftakt*, November 1924.

T. S. Eliot: London letter, *Dial*, October 1921, p. 452.

J. H. Elliot: Stravinsky and his forerunners, *Halle*, October 1956, p. 1.

A. Epstein: Stravinsky, *Modern Music*, April 1934.

Edwin Evans: The Stravinsky debate, *Music Student*, December 1920, p. 139.

— IS, Contrapuntal Titan, *Musical America*, 1921, No. 16, p. 9.

— Concerning Stravinsky, *MN&H*, 4 June 1921, p. 711.

— A chat with Stravinsky, *MN&H*, 12 November 1921, p. 474.

Peter Evans: Stravinsky's elegies, *The Listener*, 11 February 1965, p. 241.

— Stravinsky — information and illusion, *Tempo*, spring 1961, p. 2.

R. Evett: Quo vadis, Igor?, *New Republic*, 8 February 1954, p. 21.

David Ewen: The decline of Stravinsky, *MMR*, 1933, p. 179.

Imre Fábián: IS nyokvan éves, *Muzsika*, June 1962, p. 7.

— IS Magyarországon, *Muzsika*, July 1963, p. 1.

L. Fábián: Stravinski, *Zenei Szemble*, January 1927.

Mayorino Ferrariá: Stravinsky, magnifico camaleón lirico, *El Momento musical* (Buenos Aires), July 1937.

P.-O. Ferroud: The role of the abstract in IS's works, *Chesterian*, No. 85, March 1930, p. 141.

— Das aesthetische Problem bei Strawinsky, *Melos*, 1930, Nos. 8–9, p. 365.

Gerold Fierz: IS, Komponist und Dirigent, *SM*, March–April 1961, p. 45.

Herbert Fleischer: IS, Russischer Musik Verlag (Berlin) 1931.

— Rhythmische Veränderungen durch Strawinskij, *Die Musik*, June 1933, p. 654.

Maurice Fleuret: Debussy speaks of Stravinsky, Stravinsky speaks of Debussy (transl. F. Harling-Comyns), *MO*, January 1963, p. 211.

Marius Flothuis: Purcell, Stravinsky en de vooruitgang, *Mens en melodie*, March 1949, p. 82.

J. de Freitas Branco: Stravinsky em Lisboa, *Arte musical*, 1967, Nos. 25–26, p. 89.

Geza Frid: Het Problem Stravinsky, *Mens en melodie*, December 1948, p. 374.

F.G.: La théorique d'IS, *Contrepoints*, No. 3, March–April 1946, p. 12.

John Garbutt & Matthew Patterson: An approach to Stravinsky's Cantata and The Wedding, *M&L*, January 1957.

André George: Strawinsky, *Les Nouvelles littéraires*, 18 December 1937.

A. Getteman: L'esthétique d'IS, *Arts et Lettres d'aujourd'hui*, 20 January 1924.

Michel Georges-Michel: Sur Strawinsky, *RM*, December 1923, p. 146.

Roberto Gerhard: Twelve-note technique in Stravinsky, *The Score*, June 1957, p. 32.

Alberto Ginastera: Personal viewpoints, *Tempo*, No. 81, summer 1967, p. 4.

Igor Glebov: Kniga o Stravinskom, Triton (Leningrad) 1929.

— Prozess der Formbildung bei Strawinski, *Der Auftakt*, April 1929, p. 101.

Scott Goddard: Stravinsky's autobiography, *MMR*, 1935, p. 106.

Alexander Goehr: Personal viewpoints, *Tempo*, No. 81, summer 1967, p. 4.

Noël Goodwin: Stravinsky at the crossroads, *M&M*, July 1966, p. 16.

Eugene Goossens: Whole-hearted champion, in *IS*, Duell, Sloan & Pearce (New York) 1949, p. 99.

Bryan Gray: How he wants us to hear his music, *M&M*, June 1954, p. 19.

Cecil Gray: IS, in *A Survey of Contemporary Music*, O.U.P. (London) 1927, p. 127.

Will Grohmann: Künstler sehen Strawinsky, *Musik der Zeit*, Vol. 1 (1952), p. 12.

F. Grunfeld: Rebel at eighty, *Reporter*, 21 June 1966, p. 38.

B. H. Haggin: Stravinsky's guest appearance with the Ballet theater, *Nation*, 17 April 1943, p. 572.

David Hall: Brief note and discography, in *IS*, Duell, Sloan & Pearce (New York) 1949, p. 217.

Bengt Hambraeus: Variationer kring IS, *Musikrevy*, 1958, p. 219.

— Stravinsky åter i Stockholm, *Musikrevy*, 1961, p. 235.

Jacques Handschin: IS, Versuch einer Einführung, Zürich 1933.

Hamilton Harty: The Stravinsky dispute, *The Musician*, July 1921, p. 225.

Baird Hastings: Stravinsky and his choreo-graphers, *Chrysalis*, 1951, Nos. 11–12, p. 5.

Ingemar von Heijne: Musiken kring Stravin-sky, *Musikrevy*, 1963, p. 117.

Everett Helm: Stravinsky, a tribute, *Musical America*, June 1962, p. 5.

Gerald Hendrie: Stravinsky, *Halle*, No. 122, 1965–6, p. 19.

Leigh Henry: The humour of Stravinsky, *MT*, December 1919, p. 670.

— IS, *MT*, June 1919, p. 268.

— IS and the ballet, *Musical News*, 1919, 5 July p. 4, 19 July p. 22, 16 August p. 50.

— Les ballets de Stravinsky, *Action* (Paris), No. 1, February 1920, p. 83.

— IS and the objective dissection in contemporary music, *Chesterian*, No. 4, January 1920.

— IS, *MO*, February 1920, p. 371.

— The chamber music of Stravinsky, *MS*, 31 July 1920, p. 39.

— Stravinsky and the pragmatic criterion in contemporary music, *English Review*, 1921, p. 67.

— Stravinsky in the concert hall, *MS*, 18 June 1921, p. 212.

— Stravinsky and the enfranchisement of sound, *MS*, 30 July 1921, p. 41.

Friedrich Herzfeld: IS, Rembrandt-Verlag (Berlin) 1961.

Alfred Heuss: IS im Gewandhaus, *NZfM*, 1923, No. 18 (December), p. 19.

E. B. Hill: Russian nationalist composers, *Etude*, December 1941, p. 815.

Walther Hirschberg: Strawinsky-Abend der Städtischen Oper zu Berlin, *Signale*, 1927, Nos. 51–52, p. 1757.

— Strawinsky-Abend der Staatsoper, *Signale*, 1928, No. 10, p. 304.

Arthur Hoérée: 'A propos de Strawinsky' de B. de Schloezer, *RM*, December 1929, p. 153.

— Invention pure et matière musicale chez Strawinsky, *RM*, May–June 1939, p. 340.

André Hodeir: IS, in *Since Debussy* (transl. Noel Burch), Secker & Warburg (London) 1961, p. 21.

Basil Hogarth: IS, *The Gramophone*, June 1935, p. 5.

— The Firebird and Petroushka, *The Gramophone*, June 1936, p. 5.

Arthur Honegger: Strawinsky, homme de metier, *RM*, May–June 1939, p. 261.
— Franck et Strawinsky, *L'Information musicale*, 1941, 19 September p. 39, 26 September p. 63.
— 'Zar Igor', *Musik der Zeit*, Vol. 1 (1952), p. 10.
G. W. Hopkins: Stravinsky's chords, *Tempo*, No. 76, spring 1966, p. 6; No. 77, summer 1966, p. 2.
E. M. von Hornbostel: Musikalischer Exotismus, *Der Auftakt*, November 1924.
Reginald Hunt: Stravinsky and others, *MO*, May 1947, p. 253.
Aldous Huxley: Conversation with Stravinsky, *Vogue*, 15 February 1953, p. 94.
B. Jacobson: Stravinsky, his heritage and his legacy, *High Fidelity*, October 1966.
E. Jade: Stravinski, *France-American Music Society Bulletin*, March 1924.
Heinz Joachim: Der 'Wüstlung' als Beispiel (zum 70. Geburtstag von IS), *Das Musikleben*, June 1952.
— IS, *NZfM*, June 1957.
Donald C. Johns: An early serial idea of Stravinsky, *Music Review*, November 1962, p. 305; Eine frühe Reihenarbeit Stravinskys, *ÖM*, May–June 1964.
Alfred Kalisch: Stravinsky day by day, *MT*, January 1922, p. 27.
Alexis Kall: Stravinsky in the chair of poetry, *MQ*, July 1940, p. 283.
O. Karpfen: IS zum 50. Geburtstag, *Signale*, 1 June 1932.
Tamara Karsavina: A recollection of Stravinsky, *Tempo*, No. 8, summer 1948, p. 7.
— Träuenreiches Lernen, *Musik der Zeit*, Vol. 1 (1952), p. 14.
Hans Keller: Rhythm—Gershwin and Stravinsky, *The Score*, June 1957, p. 19.
— Schoenberg and Stravinsky: Schoenbergians and Stravinskyans, *Music Review*, 1954, p. 307.
— 'Conversations with IS', *Tempo*, No. 52, autumn 1959.
— Me about us and Stravinsky, *M&M*, June, 1962, p. 23.
— Stravinsky the downbeater, *The Listener*, 19 October 1967, p. 509.
Wilhelm Keller: Strawinskys Musik im

Spiegel seiner 'Poetik', *NZfM*, June 1952, p. 321.
K. Kirchberg: Stravinsky, der Klassiker, *Musikhandel*, 1967, No. 4, p. 163.
Helmut Kirchmeyer: IS, Zeitgeschichte im Persönlichkeitsbild, Gustav Bosse Verlag (Regensburg) 1958.
— Stravinsky im Lichte der zeitgenössischen Musikkritik, in *IS*, Pressestelle Westdeutscher Rundfunk (Cologne) 1963, p. 22.
L. Kirstein: Homage to Stravinsky, *Arts and Decoration*, May 1937, p. 14.
— IS, *Nation*, 15 June 1957, p. 530.
— Purity through the will, *Nation*, 8 October 1960, p. 233.
M. Kolisch: Stravinsky, Russian of the Russians, *Independant*, 16 May 1925, p. 559.
Endre Kollár: Stravinsky hangversenyén, *Muzsika*, November 1962, p. 2.
I. Kolodin: Stravinsky in the king's English, *Saturday Review*, 19 September 1953, p. 33.
— Stravinsky on Stravinsky, *Saturday Review*, 29 April 1961, p. 47.
— Six new discs, with a Stravinsky discography, *Saturday Review*, 12 May 1962, p. 58.
— Stravinsky in Santa Fe, *Saturday Review*, 18 August 1962, p. 29.
Ernst Krenek: ISs Memoiren, *Anbruch*, August 1935 p. 222, January 1936 p. 17.
Fr. A. Kypta: IS, Prague, 1957.
Louis Laloy: Stravinsky, in *La Musique retrouvée*, Librairie Plon (Paris) 1928, p. 213.
Paul Henry Lang: Stravinsky, the enigma, *Saturday Review of Literature*, 3 May 1947, p. 36.
— Fusillade from Stravinsky, *Saturday Review*, 27 June 1959, p. 50.
— (ed.): Stravinsky, a new appraisal of his work, Norton Library (New York) 1963.
Minna Lederman (ed.): Stravinsky in the theatre, Pelegrini & Cudahy (New York), Peter Owen (London) 1951.
Jacques Leduc: Les écrits de Stravinsky, *Cahiers musicaux*, 1958, No. 16, p. 37.
René Leibowitz: IS, *Les Temps modernes*, 1 April 1946, p. 1320.
— Schoenberg and Stravinsky, *Partisan Review*, 1948, p. 361.
Richard Anthony Leonard: Stravinsky, in

The Stream of Music, Hutchinson (London), third edn. 1967, p. 375.

François Lesure: Debussy e Stravinsky, *Musica d'oggi*, June 1959.

Andre Levinson: Strawinsky et la danse, *RM*, December 1923, p. 156; Stravinsky and the dance, *Theatre Arts Monthly*, November 1924, p. 741.

Anthony Lewis: Stravinsky, the music materials, *The Score*, January 1951.

Serge Lifar: IS, législateur du ballet, *RM*, May–June 1939, p. 321.

Heinrich Lindlar: ISs Sakraler Gesang, Gustav Bosse Verlag (Regensburg) 1957.

— Der schöpferische Universalist, *Musica*, 1957, No. 6, p. 311.

— Stravinsky, Kontakte zur Bildkunst, *Musica*, 1963, No. 3, p. 99.

— Die geistlichen Werke, in *IS*, Pressestelle Westdeutscher Rundfunk (Cologne) 1963, p. 49.

— Zum 85. Geburtstag von IS, *Musica*, 1967, No. 4, p. 186.

Edward Lockspeiser: Stravinsky in London, *20th Century*, January 1959, p. 57.

C. J. Luten: Stravinsky conducts, 1960, *American Record Guide*, June 1961, p. 772.

— Happy birthday, *American Record Guide*, June 1962, p. 772.

John McClure: IS at eighty, *The Gramophone*, June 1962, p. 1.

C. J. McNaspy: Interview with Stravinsky, *America*, 31 August 1963, p. 219.

Basil Maine: Stravinsky and pure music, *MT*, February 1922, p. 93.

— Schoenberg and Stravinsky, *Apollo*, September 1926, p. 99.

G. F. Malipiero: Stravinsky, Cavallino (Venice) 1945.

— IS a Venezia, *La Biennale* (Venice), April 1951.

— Elixiere im Exil . . ., *Musik der Zeit*, Vol. 1. (1952), p. 9.

William Mann: IS, *Crescendo*, No. 60, April 1954, p. 135; No. 118, February 1962, p. 108.

— IS at 80, *Crescendo*, No. 123, November 1962, p. 51.

A. Mantelli: IS e le sue opere più recente, *La Rassegna musicale*, 1941, p. 41.

— La posizione di Strawinsky nella musica moderna, *La Rassegna musicale*, 1944.

C. Marinelli: Discografia Strawinskiana, *La Rassegna musicale*, 1949, p. 230.

Colin Mason: Stravinsky's contribution to chamber music, *Tempo*, No. 43, spring 1957.

— Stravinsky's newest works, *Tempo*, Nos. 53–54, spring–summer 1960.

— Awaiting Stravinsky's ninth decade, *Guardian*, 16 June 1962, p. 8.

Otto Mayer: IS, *Revista Ford* (Barcelona), August 1935.

Wilfrid Mellers: Stravinsky and jazz, *Tempo*, No. 81, summer 1967, p. 29.

— Stravinsky and Bartók, in *Man and his Music*, Barrie & Rockliff (London) 1962, p. 1002.

C. H. Meltzer: Stravinsky the enigma, *Forum*, September 1921, p. 241.

Jacques de Menasce: Anniversary of IS, *Juilliard Review*, spring 1957.

Olivier Merlin: Musiques pour la danse du temps présent, in *Stravinsky*, Librairie Hachette (Paris) 1968, p. 113.

A. Mendel: Stravinsky, *Nation*, 11 March 1931, p. 279.

H. Mersmann, E. Preussner, H. Strobel & F. Warschauer: Stravinsky auf der Schallplatte, *Melos*, March 1930.

Hans Mersmann: Stravinsky, *Musik der Zeit*, Vol. 1 (1952), p. 65.

Pierre Meylan: Une amitié célèbre—C.-F. Ramuz, IS, Editions du Cervin (Lausanne) 1961.

— Au sujet d'IS et de René Morax, *SM*, May–June 1964, p. 170.

— C.-F. Ramuz et les musiciens, *Revue musicales de Suisse Romande*, 1967, No. 2, p. 6.

Peter Mieg: Zu Stravinskys Klavierwerk, *SM*, 1947.

Massimo Mila: Serietà di Strawinsky, *La Rassegna musicale*, 1949, p. 201.

— Europeismo di Strawinsky, *Nuova antologia*, 16 April 1933, p. 572.

Anthony Milner: Melody in Stravinsky's music, *MT*, July 1957, p. 370.

Aurel von Miloss: Stravinsky und das Ballett, in *IS*, Pressestelle Westdeutscher Rundfunk (Cologne) 1963, p. 31; *ÖM*, January 1965.

Donald Mitchell: Bartók, Stravinsky and Schoenberg, *Chesterian*, No. 175, July 1953.
— Stravinsky and neo-classicism, *Tempo*, spring–summer 1962, p. 9.
Edward Mitchell: The Stravinsky theories, *MT*, March 1922, p. 162.
Mario Mohr: Strawinsky-Fest in Frankfurt am Main, *Signale*, 1925, No. 50, p. 1915.
Marius Monnikendam: IS, J. H. Gottmer (Haarlem) 1958, 1966.
M. Montagu-Nathan: IS, 19 April 1913, p. 330.
Lawrence Morton: Incongruity and faith, in *IS*, Duell, Sloan & Pearce (New York) 1949, p. 193.
Herbert Murill: Stravinsky and Sorabji, a rejoinder, *MMR*, 1933, p. 36.
— Stravinsky today, *Chesterian*, No. 158, April 1949.
— Aspects of Stravinsky, *M&L*, April 1951.
Rollo H. Myers: Introduction to the music of Stravinsky, Dennis Dobson (London) 1950.
— Stravinsky at seventy-five, *MT*, June 1957, p. 313.
— Stravinsky on music, *Chesterian*, No. 201, winter 1960.
Nicolas Nabokov: IS, *Atlantic Monthly*, November 1949, p. 21.
— Christmas with Stravinsky, in *IS*, Duell, Sloan & Pearce (New York) 1949, p. 123.
— Stravinsky intime, *Dansk Musiktidsskrift*, 1952, Nos. 224–6.
— IS, Colloquium Verlag (Berlin) 1964.
Robert U. Nelson: Stravinsky's concept of variations, *MQ*, July 1962, p. 327.
Ernest Newman: Stravinsky on himself, *Sunday Times*, 12 May 1929.
P. Nielsen: Om Johann Sebastian Stravinsky, *Dansk Musiktidsskrift*, 1967, No. 5, p. 100.
Jeremy Noble: The self-exposed Stravinsky, *M&M*, June 1962, p. 20.
— Debussy and Stravinsky, *MT*, January 1967, p. 22.
— IS, *MT*, June 1971, p. 534.
Ove Nordwall: IS, ett porträtt med citat, P. A. Norstedt & Söners (Stockholm) 1967.
— Der späte Strawinsky, *Melos*, February 1967, p. 52.
John Ogdon: Stravinsky and the piano, *Tempo*, No. 81, summer 1967, p. 36.

Leon Oleggini: Connaissance de Stravinsky, Foetisch (Lausanne) 1952.
Frank Onnen: Stravinsky, Continental Book Company (Stockholm), Sidgwick & Jackson (London) 1948.
— Stravinsky en de vooruitgang, *Mens en melodie*, February 1949, p. 53.
— Stravinsky parmi nous, *RM* (L'Œuvre du XXe Siècle), 1952, p. 47.
Charles Oulmont: Besuch bei Strawinsky, *Melos*, February 1947, p. 107.
A.P.: Las idéas de IS, *El Momento musical* (Buenos Aires), February 1937.
Guido Pannain: IS, *La Rassegna musicale*, May 1928, p. 281.
— In margine ad alcune opere di Stravinsky, *La Rassegna musicale*, 1946, p. 36.
— La poetica di Stravinsky, *Gazzetta musicale di Napoli*, April 1956.
Domenico de Paoli: IS, *Bollettino bibliografico musicale*, December 1927, p. 1.
— L'Opera di Stravinsky, Milan 1931.
— (Stravinsky at home), *L'Ambrosiano* (Milan), 31 August 1933.
— IS, a L'Oiseau de Feu a Persefone, G. B. Paravia (Turin) 1934.
A. Parente: L'ultimo Stravinsky, *Gazzetta musicale di Napoli*, September 1956.
Ralf Parland: Den egensinnige Stravinsky, *Fönstret*, 1959, p. 21.
Ralph Parker: Stravinsky in Russia, *New Statesman*, 2 November 1962, p. 613.
P. Patera: IS, Revolutionär och eller reaktionär, *Svensk linje*, 1948, No. 4, p. 9.
— Den religiöse Stravinsky, *Vår lösen*, 1950, p. 181.
— Stravinsky som politiskt fenomen, *Ung höger*, 1952, No. 11, p. 7.
Juan Carlos Paz: Stravinsky, a distancia, *Compás* (Buenos Aires), August 1936.
Maurice Perrin: Stravinsky in a composition class, *The Score*, June 1957, p. 38.
Michel Philippot: L'illusoire expression, in *Stravinsky*, Librairie Hachette (Paris) 1968, p.221.
Armand Pierhal: De Stravinsky et de l'expression dans la musique, *La Nef*, April 1945, p. 152.
A. Pironti: Stravinsky a Venezia, *Il Punto* (Rome), 22 September 1956.

Stravinsky, Igor

Francis Poulenc: IS, *L'Information musicale*, 3 January 1941, p. 195.

Heinz Pringsheim: Aus Strawinskijs Falsch-münzerwerkstatt, *AMZ*, 1924, Nos. 51–52, p. 939.

Henry Prunières: Stravinsky and Ravel, winter 1928, *Modern Music*, January 1929.

Yvonne Rácz-Barblau: IS vu par le cymbaliste Aladár Rácz, *Feuilles musicales*, March–April 1962, p. 35.

C.-F. Ramuz: Souvenirs sur IS, Editions Mermod (Lausanne) 1929, 1946, 1952; Nouvelle Revue Française (Paris) 1929.

— Erinnerungen an Stravinsky, *Melos*, May 1954, p. 129.

Henry Raynor: Stravinsky, the teacher, *Chesterian*, Nos. 188 (autumn) and 189 (winter) 1956.

Herbert Read: Stravinsky and the muses, in *Stravinsky and the dance*, New York Public Library (New York) 1962, p. 8; *Tempo*, spring–summer 1962, p. 13.

Günther Rennert: Stravinsky's conception of opera (transl. Anne Ross), *Opera*, August 1956, p. 473.

Richard RePass: Stravinsky and the music drama, *MT*, February 1952, p. 66.

Knudåge Riisager: Stravinsky på teatret, *Dansk Musiktidsskrift*, 1952, Nos. 224–6.

N. Roerich: IS über seine Musik—Ein Ge-spräch mit Stravinsky, *Berliner Börsen-Courier*, No. 309, 5 July 1925.

Roland-Manuel: Stravinsky et la critique, *Revue Pleyel*, June 1924.

— Démarche de Stravinsky, *RM*, May–June 1939, p. 255.

Kajsa Rootzén: En musikalisk avantgardist, *Svenska Dagblatt*, 24 September 1935.

— En nutids musikers konståskådning, *Svensk Dagblatt*, 12 May 1936.

— Den kristne Stravinsky, *Credo*, 1961, p. 6.

P. Rosenfeld: IS, *Anbruch*, June 1921, p. 191.

— Stravinsky, *New Republic*, 14 April 1920, p. 207.

Claude Rostand: De crainte d'être trahi, in *Stravinsky*, Librairie Hachette (Paris) 1968, p. 189.

Ernst Roth: A great mind and a great spirit, *Tempo*, No. 81, summer 1967, p. 4.

— Gruss an IS, *SM*, 1967, No. 4, p. 190.

K. H. Ruppel: Stravinsky, der Meister des

Neoklassizismus, in *IS*, Pressestelle West-deutscher Rundfunk (Cologne) 1963, p. 38.

— Die Prinzessin Edmond de Polignac, *Melos*, June 1967, p. 198.

Hans Rutz: Stravinsky in Venice, *Music Review*, 1951, p. 329.

— Stravinsky und die Zukunft der Oper, *SM*, March 1952, p. 93.

Leonid Sabaneev: The Stravinsky legends, *MT*, September 1928, p. 785.

Gustav Samazeuilh: Les 'Chroniques' d'IS, in *Musiciens de mon temps*, Editions Marcel Daubin (Paris) 1947, p. 354.

Claude Samuel: Histoire d'une bataille, in *Stravinsky*, Librairie Hachette (Paris) 1968, p. 49.

P. Sanborn: Stravinsky, *Independent*, 12 April 1924, p. 212.

Erik Satie: Propos à propos IS, *Les Feuilles libres*, November 1922.

— A composer's conviction, in *IS*, Duell, Sloan & Pearce (New York) 1949, p. 25.

Henri Sauguet: Portrait d'IS, in *Stravinsky*, Librairie Hachette (Paris) 1968, p. 7.

André Schaeffner: Stravinsky, Editions Rieder (Paris) 1931.

— On Stravinsky, early and late, *Modern Music*, November–December 1934.

— Critique et thématique, *RM*, May–June 1939, p. 241.

Ferdinand Scherber: Ein Interview oder ISs Kritik an der Kritik, *Signale*, 27 March 1929, No. 13, p. 408.

Boris de Schloezer: IS, *RM*, December 1923, p. 97.

— Les Ballets russes: Trois créations—La Belle au bois dormant de Tchaikovsky, Renard et Mavra de Stravinsky, *Nouvelle revue française*, 1922, No. 106, p. 115.

— Stravinsky und Prokofiev, *Melos*, 1925, No. 10, p. 469.

— Stravinsky, *Dansk Musiktidsskrift*, 1927, No. 1.

— IS, Claude Aveline (Paris) 1929.

— Stravinsky, his technique, *The Dial*, January 1929.

— Sur Stravinsky, *RM*, February 1929, p. 1.

— IS, *Mundo musical* (Buenos Aires), July 1929.

— IS, *Revue de Genève*, January 1929, p. 38.

— The enigma of Stravinsky, *Modern Music*,

602

November–December 1932; L'enigma di Stravinsky, *La Rassegna musicale*, March–April 1934, p. 89.

— Le cas Stravinsky, *Nouvelle revue française*, 1938, No. 308 p. 891.

—Stravinsky, *Nouvelle reuve française;* 1939, No. 313, p. 630.

— An abridged analysis (transl. Ezra Pound), in *IS*, Duell, Sloan & Pearce (New York) 1949, p. 33.

Marcel Schneider: Stravinsky face à la société, in *Stravinsky*, Librairie Hachette 1968, p. 97.

Ernest Schoen: Über Stravinskys Einfluss, *Melos*, 1929, No. 4, p. 162.

Percy A. Scholes: Stravinsky in the nursery, *The Observer*, 4 June 1922.

— What does Stravinsky mean?, *Radio Times*, 3 May 1929, p. 224.

Karl Schönewolf: Gespräch mit Stravinsky, *Die Musik*, April 1929, p. 491.

Leo Schrade: Stravinsky, die Synthese einer Epoche, in *IS*, Pressestelle Westdeutscher Rundfunk (Cologne) 1963, p. 9.

Reinhold Schubert: Stravinsky und das musikalische Theater, in *IS*, Pressestelle Westdeutscher Rundfunk (Cologne) 1963, p. 65.

Willi Schuh: Stravinsky und die Tradition, *Melos*, November 1956, p. 308.

— Zur Harmonik ISs, *SM*, June 1952, p. 243.

Boris Schwarz: Stravinsky in Soviet Russian criticism, *MQ*, July 1962, p. 340.

E. Schulhoff: Paraphrase über Herrn Stravinsky, *Der Auftakt*, November 1924.

Daniel Scott-Maddocks: Stravinsky on disc, *Records & Recording*, June 1962, p. 15.

— A flood of Stravinsky, *Records & Recording*, September 1962, p. 25.

Max See: Stravinsky und die Oper, *Musik der Zeit*, Vol. 1 (1952), p. 45.

Roger Sessions: Thoughts on Stravinsky, *The Score*, June 1957, p. 32.

Robert Siohan: Stravinsky, Editions du Seuil (Paris) 1959, John Calder (London) 1966.

Sir Osbert Sitwell: English discernment, in *IS*, Duell, Sloan & Pearce (New York) 1949, p. 115.

A. Skulsky: IS, *Musical America*, February 1952, p. 27.

Nicolas Slonimsky: 'Centenari de Stravinsky, 1982', *Revista musical Catalana*, July 1931.

Roger Smalley: Personal viewpoints, *Tempo*, No. 81, summer 1967, p. 19.

Cecil Smith: Stravinsky and classicism, in *IS*, Duell, Sloan & Pearce (New York) 1949, p. 207.

Harvey Sollberger: Footnote to Stravinsky, *PNM*, fall–winter 1966, p. 148.

Federico Sopena: Strawinsky, vida, obra y estilo, Sociedad de Estudios y Publicaciones (Madrid) 1956.

André Souris: Debussy et Stravinsky, *Revue belge de musicologie*, 1962.

Pierre Souvtchinsky: Le Stravinsky d'Igor Glebov, *Musique*, March 1930.

— La notion du temps et la musique, *RM*, May–June 1939, p. 311.

— IS, *Contrepoints*, No. 2, February 1946, p. 19.

— Qui est Strawinsky?, *Cahiers musicaux*, 1958, No. 16, p. 7.

Pierre Souvtchinsky & John Warrack: Stravinsky as a Russian, *Tempo*, No. 81, summer 1967, p. 5.

Paul Stefan: Lärm bei Stravinsky, *Anbruch*, March 1925, p. 186.

— Stravinsky, Zeit und Raum, *Anbruch*, April–May 1932, p. 70.

— Stravinsky-Memoiren, Zweiter Teil, *Anbruch*, 1936, No. 1, p. 17.

Erich Steinhard: IS, *Die Musik*, May 1931, No. 8, p. 574.

H. Straus: On the giving of Stravinsky, *Nation*, 30 April 1924, p. 512.

Igor Stravinsky: Chroniques de ma vie, Editions Denoël et Steel, 1935/36; Eng. transl. Gollancz (London) 1936. Also other translations and editions.

— Pushkin: poetry and music. Pamphlet, printed 1940, USA.

— Poetique musicale, Harvard University Press, 1942, 1947 (English translation).

Themes and conclusions, Faber (London) 1972.

Articles include the following:

— Stravinsky et Tchaikovsky, *RM*, 1922, No. 9, p. 87.

— Art or routine—A justification of the

modern school, *Musical Mirror*, December 1928, p. 313.

— I, as I see myself, *The Gromophone*, August 1934, p. 85.

— Über die musikalische Komposition, *Melos*, October 1948, p. 257.

— Diaghilev I knew, *Atlantic Monthly*, November 1953, p. 33; Diaghilev, wie ich ihn kannte, *Melos*, December 1955, p. 1.

— St. Petersburg childhood, *New Yorker*, 24 September 1960, p. 146.

— Edgar Varèse, *Ricordiana*, April 1961, p. 4.

— Thoughts on contemporary music and recording, *Records & Recording*, September 1962, p. 21.

— Sacre de Diaghilev, *Vogue*, 15 April 1965, p. 124.

— Schoenberg's letters, *High Fidelity*, May 1965, p. 136.

Igor Stravinsky & Robert Craft: Conversations with IS, Doubleday (New York), Faber (London) 1959.

— Memories and Commentaries, Doubleday (New York), Faber (London) 1960.

— Expositions and Developments, Doubleday (New York), Faber (London) 1962.

— Dialogues and a Diary, Doubleday (New York) 1963.

Soulima Stravinsky: Stravinsky and Stravinsky, *Newsweek*, 2 August 1948, p. 72.

— What makes a composer great?, *Etude*, September 1949, p. 17.

Théodore Stravinsky: Le Message d'IS, Librairie F. Rouge (Lausanne) 1948; IS, Mensch und Künstler (transl. Heinrich Strobel), Schott (Mainz) 1952; The Message of IS (transl. Robert Craft & André Marion), Boosey & Hawkes (London) 1953.

— Causerie sur IS, *SM*, 1943.

— Le Message d'IS, *SM*, October 1949, No. 365.

— Stravinsky, la Russià e l'Occidente, *La Rassegna musicale*, 1949, p. 227.

— Stravinsky und die Musik, *Melos*, December 1949, p. 321.

V. Stravinsky: Stravinsky at home, *Musical America*, January 1963, p. 10.

Charles Stuart: Stravinsky, the Dialectics of Dislike, *Music Survey*, winter 1949, p. 142.

— Recent works examined, *Tempo*, No. 8, summer 1948, p. 20.

— Der 'neue' Stravinsky, *Musik der Zeit*, Vol. 1 (1952), p. 25.

Heinrich Strobel: Strawinskys Weg, *Melos*, 1929, No. 4, p. 158.

— Neue Funkmusiken—Stravinsky vor dem Mikrophon, *Melos*, 1930, No. 2, p. 90.

— Strawinsky privat, *Melos*, October 1931 (No. 10), p. 315.

— Schöpferischer Klassizismus Strawinsky, *Melos*, May–June 1947, p. 199.

— IS, *Melos*, 1947, October p. 328, November p. 377.

— Stravinsky, classic humanist (transl. Hans Rosenwald), Merlin Press (New York) 1955.

— IS, Atlantis Verlag (Zürich) 1956.

— Puccini und Strawinsky, *Melos*, 1931, No. 3, p. 104.

— Vom Apollon zur Psalmensinfonie, *Melos*, 1931, No. 7, p. 219.

H. H. Stuckenschmidt: Strawinsky oder die Vereinigung des Unvereinbaren, *Anbruch*, April–May 1932 (No. 4), p. 67.

— Assoziationen um einen Namen, *Musik der Zeit*, Vol. 1 (1952), p. 3.

— IS, in *Schöpfer der neuen Musik*, Suhrkamp Verlag (Frankfurt a.M.) 1958, p. 128.

— Stravinsky und sein Jahrhundert, Akademie der Künstle (Berlin) 1957.

— Strawinsky-Abend, Krolloper, Berlin 1928, in *Oper in dieser Zeit*, Friedrich Verlag (Hannover) 1964, p. 52.

W. Sutton: Stravinsky and synthetic melody, *MO*, November 1967, p. 91.

Joseph Szigeti: Stravinsky at work, *M&M*, June 1964, p. 23.

Herbert Tachezi: IS, *Musikerziehung*, December 1962.

Alexandre Tansman: IS, *Blok* (Warsaw), 1924, Nos. 3–4.

— IS, Amiot-Durant (Paris) 1948; transl. Therese & Charles Bleefield, Putnam (New York) 1949.

Willy Tappolet: Stravinsky am Genfersee, *Melos*, 1929, No. 4, p. 172.

John Taverner: Personal viewpoints, *Tempo*, No. 81, summer 1967, p. 25.

Ronald Taylor: Stravinsky and the problems of 20th century music, *Cambridge Journal*, March 1953, p. 363.

Stainton de B. Taylor: Stravinsky and the Plain Man, *MM&F*, August 1931, p. 229.

Terpander: Stravinsky, 1932, *The Gramophone*, February 1932, p. 373.

Juan Ma Thomas: Un musicien méditerranéen, *Musique*, 1928.

Ottavio Tiby: Stravinsky, *Il Pianoforte*, August 1924.

Otto Tomek (ed.): IS, Eine Sendereihe des Westdeutscher Rundfunks zum 80. Geburtstag, Westdeutscher Rundfunk (Cologne) 1963.

W. Tschuppik: Gespräch mit Strawinsky, *Der Auftakt*, 1924.

J. Urrutia-Blondel: Conversando con IS, *Revista Musical Chilena* (Santiago), September–October 1960.

M. Varro: Rachmaninov e Stravinsky, *Musica d'oggi*, January 1937.

M. Vermeulen: Rondom Stravinsky, *De Muziek*, October 1927.

G. Vigolo: Un despota del gusto musicale nel Novecenteo—Stravinsky, *La Rassegna musicale*, 1949, p. 206.

Emile Vuillermoz: IS, *S.I.M.*, May 1912, p. 15.

— Igor-le-Terrible, *Candide*, 16 June 1938.

Roman Vlad: Le musiche sacre di Stravinsky, *La Rassegna musicale*, 1948, p. 106.

— Esordi di Stravinsky, *La Rassegna musicale*, April 1956, p. 100.

— Stravinsky, dal neoclassicismo alla dodecafonia, *Il Punto* (Rome), 22 September 1956.

— Stravinsky, Giulio Einaudi (Rome) 1958; transl. Frederick & Ann, Fuller, O.U.P. (London) 1960.

— Die jüngste Schaffensperiode, in IS Pressestelle Westdeutscher Rundfunk (Cologne) 1963, p. 72.

Caroll D. Wade: A selected bibliography, *MQ*, July 1962, p. 372.

Stephen Walsh: Stravinsky's choral music, *Tempo*, No. 81, summer 1967, p. 41.

John Warrack: Stravinsky as a Russian, *Tempo*, No. 81, summer 1967, p. 7.

Franz Warschauer: Der Fall Strawinsky, *Die Weltbühne*, 1928, No. 13.

Adolf Weismann: Stravinsky, *Vossische Zeitung*, 21 February 1924.

— Stravinsky, *Anbruch*, June–July 1924, p. 228.

— IS, *Blätter der Staatsoper*, June 1925.

John S. Weissmann: Stravinsky in Venice, *Chesterian*, No. 169, January 1952.

Eric Walter White: Stravinsky's Sacrifice to Apollo, Hogarth Press (London) 1930.

— Stravinsky, a critical survey, John Lehmann (London) 1947; Philosophical Library (New York) 1948.

— Stravinsky, latter-day symphonist, *Horizon*, November 1947, p. 290.

— Stravinsky as a writer, *Tempo*, No. 8, summer 1948, p. 18.

— Stravinsky als Schriftsteller, *Musik der Zeit*, Vol. 1 (1952), p. 3.

— Stravinsky and Debussy, *Tempo*, spring–summer 1962, p. 2.

— Listening to Stravinsky's music in the twenties, *Tempo*, No. 81, summer 1967, p. 32.

— Stravinsky, the composer and his works, Faber (London) 1966.

Theodor Wiesengrund Adorno: Strawinsky-Fest, *Anbruch*, 1925, No. 10, p. 531.

R. Williams: Stravinsky, from enfant terrible to old master, *House Beautiful*, September 1954, p. 162.

— Man who made dissonance respectable, *House Beautiful*, June 1958, p. 76.

E. Wilson: Stravinsky and the modernists, *New Republic*, 1 April 1925, p. 156.

C. S. Wise: Impressions of IS, *MQ*, April 1916, p. 249.

Hellmuth Christian Wolff: Zur Chromatik des 17. Jahrhunderts—Ein Brief an IS, *NZfM*, June 1962.

W. Woronoff: Stravinsky et nous, *Syrinx*, January 1938.

Emilia Zanetti: Stravinsky hat gesagt (interview), *Musik der Zeit*, Vol. 1 (1952), p. 41.

MISCELLANEOUS OR UNSIGNED

Dionysian spirit which vitalizes the music of IS, *Current Opinion*, August 1914, p. 108.

Stravinsky's strange new sniffs and snorts, *Current Opinion*, October 1920, p. 491.

Scriabin and Stravinsky, *The Times*, 11 June 1921.

Lettre à Serge Diaghilev, *Comoedia*, 14 November 1921.

Stravinsky—Aufregung, *Der Auftakt*, November–December 1924.

Interview, *Prager Presse*, 13 November 1924.

Stravinsky, visitor, *Outlook*, 21 January 192 p. 92.

Stravinsky previsions a new music, *Current Opinion*, March 1925, p. 329.

Stravinsky talks, *Musical Mirror*, August 1926, p. 160.

'Warum meine Musik nicht geschätzt wird'— ein Interview mit IS, *Musik und Gesellschaft*, November 1930.

Stravinsky the extremist, *British Musician*, August 1934, p. 181.

Stravinsky contado por elé mesmo, *Revista Brasileira de Musica*, December 1935, p. 312.

IS raconté par lui-même, *Le Monde musical*, April 1935.

Le premier article sur IS, *L'information musicale*, 10 October 1941, p. 136.

ISs Werk, *Melos*, October 1948, p. 262.

The old master, *M&M*, May 1954, p. 9.

Music Mirror meets Stravinsky, *Music Mirror*, July 1954, p. 7.

Fantastic world of Stravinsky, *Life*, 25 November 1957, p. 94.

IS, 35 Antworten auf 35 Fragen, *Melos*, June 1957.

Answers to 34 questions: an interview with Stravinsky, *Encounter*, July 1957, p. 3.

IS, *Röster i Radio*, 1958, pp. 213, 214, 228.

10 år Stravinsky-verken 1948–58, *Nutida musik*, Vol. 1 (1957–8), No. 6, p. 17.

Nearly half a century of Stravinsky, *M&M*, December 1958, p. 9.

Stravinsky replies to Walt Disney, *Saturday Review*, 12 March 1960, p. 81.

Genius looks back, *Newsweek*, 22 August 1960, p. 88.

Stravinsky at eighty, *Newsweek*, 21 May 1962, p. 53.

Stravinsky in person, on records, in writing, *Life*, 8 June 1962, p. 17.

Stravinsky still a life force at eighty, *The Times*, 8 June 1962, p. 6.

IS, paroles et souvenirs, *Feuilles musicales*, March–April 1962, p. 31.

IS parle, *Feuilles musicales*, October 1962, p. 121.

Conversations with Stravinsky, *M&M*, June 1962, p. 16.

IS, *Röster i Radio*, 1962, No. 25, p. 26.

Stravinsky's scrapbook, *Musical America*, January 1963, p. 12.

IS, *Musikern*, 1963, No. 14, p. 7.

Stravinsky off the cuff, *M&M*, July 1963, p. 13.

IS, *Röster i Radio*, 1963, No. 24, p. 20; No. 50, p. 24.

Music and the statistical age (interview), *Commentary*, September 1966, p. 49.

EDGAR VARÈSE (1883–1965)

Edgar Varèse—he occasionally spelt his Christian name with a final 'd'—was born on 22 December 1883 in Paris, but spent most of his early childhood with grandparents in Villars, a village on the Saône near Tournus. From 1892 to 1903 he lived with his industrialist father (whom he loathed) in Turin. He was precocious enough to write a Jules Verne opera at the age of eleven, and while in Turin took secret composition lessons from the director of the Conservatoire, Giovanni Bolzoni; but his early education was mainly in mathematics and science, as his father was determined that he should become a physicist. However, instead of entering the Zürich Polytechnic as planned, Varèse returned to Paris to study music, first under d'Indy and Roussel at the Schola Cantorum in 1904 and then under Widor at the Conservatoire. In 1907 he married the actress Suzanne Bing and left Paris for Berlin, where he lived until the outbreak of the First World War. During these years Varèse conducted choral and orchestral groups (some of his own founding) in Paris, Berlin and Prague, and as a composer won the friendship and encouragement of Busoni and Debussy (both of whom he met in 1908). Varèse and his wife separated in 1913 and in 1915 he was mobilized into the French Army. However, he was soon discharged for medical reasons and left Europe for the USA, settling in 1916 in New York City, which was to be his home for most of the rest of his life. In 1917 he met Louise Norton (*née* McCutcheon) and married her in 1921, after both had obtained divorces. The manuscripts of many of his compositions (all unpublished) having been destroyed by fire in Berlin during the War, Varèse decided to disown all the work written before his arrival in the USA and launched on a second composing career. He did much to promote modern music in

America, becoming an American citizen in 1927 and helping to found the New Symphony Orchestra (1919), the International Composers' Guild (1921) and the Pan-American Association of Composers (1928). From 1928 to 1933 he lived in Paris and from 1936 to 1940 mainly in New Mexico and California. The late 1930s were a period of profound depression for him, caused partly by his disenchantment with conventional musical instruments and his lack of resources to develop new ones. As a result he produced no new music from 1936 to 1947, his musical activities during the Second World War being largely restricted to founding and conducting the Greater New York Chorus. However, the development of electronic music after the War stimulated him to compose again, and he was beginning to achieve a belated celebrity with the international *avant-garde* at the time of his death, following a thrombosis, in New York in November 1965.

CATALOGUE OF WORKS

1. Trois Pièces. For orchestra. ?1905. Lost.

2. La Chanson des jeunes hommes. For orchestra. 1905. Lost.

3. Le Prélude à la fin d'un jour. For orchestra. 1905. Lost.

4. Rhapsodie romane. For orchestra. 1906. Lost.

5. Bourgogne. For orchestra. 1907–8.
fp: 15 December 1910, Berlin, Blüthner Orchestra, cond. Josef Stransky.
Unpub. Destroyed.

6. Gargantua. For orchestra. 1909. Unfinished. Lost.

7. Mehr Licht. For orchestra. ?1911. Lost.

8. Les Cycles du Nord. For orchestra. ?1912. Lost.

9. Oedipus und die Sphynx. Opera. 1908–1914. Text: Hugo von Hofmannsthal. Unfinished. Lost.

10. Offrandes. For soprano and chamber orchestra. 1921.

1. *Chanson de hà-haut* (Vincent Huidobro). Ded. Louise.
2. *La croix du sud* (J. J. Tablada). Ded. Carlos Salzedo.
2 fl, pic, ob, cl, bsn; hn, 3 tpt, tmb; hp, strings; Ratsche, tamb mil, GC, cast, tamb basque, tgle, tamtam.
fp: 23 April 1922, New York, International Composers Guild concert, Nina Koshetz with ensemble, cond. Carlos Salzedo.
Pub. 1927, C. C. Birchard.

11. Amériques. For large orchestra. 1918–1922. Ded. 'to my unknown friends of the Spring of 1921'.
4 fl, 3 pic, fl grave, 4 ob, ca, heckelphone (or baritone ob), E-flat cl, 4 cl, bcl, cbscl, 4 bsn, 2 cbsn; 8 hn, 6 tpt, 4 tmb, bs tmb, tuba, cbs tuba (also 4 tpt, 2 tmb & bs tmb for fanfare); 2 timp, celesta, glock, xyl, 2 hps; sleighbells, cyclone whistle, steamboat whistle, siren (hand siren as used by New York Fire Department on fire engines), string dm, crow call, big rattle, tamb mil, GC, mammoth bs dm, 2 cym, crash cym, tgle, cast, tamb de basque, slap stick, Rute, tamtam; strings.
fp: 9 April 1926, Philadelphia, Philadelphia Orchestra, cond. Leopold Stokowski.
f New York p: 13 April 1926, Philadelphia Orchestra, cond. Leopold Stokowski.
f London p: 7 July 1969, Royal Festival Hall, English Bach Festival, Orchestre National de l'ORTF, cond. Marius Constant.
Pub. 1925, Curwen (full score).

12. Hyperprism. For small orchestra and percussion. 1923. Ded. José Juan and Nena Tablada.
fl, pic, E-flat cl; 3 hn, 2 tpt, ten tmb, bs tmb, snare dm, Indian dm, mammoth GC, tamb, crash cym (large), 2 cym, tamtam, tgle, anvil, slap stick, 2 Chinese blocks, lion roar (string dm), rattle, big rattle, sleighbells, siren.
fp: 4 March 1923, New York, International Composers Guild concert, cond. Edgar Varèse.
f European p: 30 July 1924, Wireless Symphony Orchestra, cond. (Sir) Eugene Goossens.
Pub. 1923, Ricordi (New York).

13. Octandre. For small orchestra. 1923. Ded. E. Robert Schmitz.

fl, pic, ob, cl, E-flat cl, bsn; hn, tpt, ten tmb; double bass.

fp: 13 January 1924, New York, International Composers Guild concert, cond. Robert Schmitz.

?fEp: 23 March 1934, BBC invitation concert of contemporary music, London Symphony Orchestra, cond. Edward Clark.

Pub. 1924, Curwen; 1956, Ricordi (New York).

BIBLIOGRAPHY:
Göran Fant: EVs Octandre, *Nutida musik*, Vol. 6 (1962–3), No. 7, p. 29.

14. Intégrales. For small orchestra and percussion. 1923. Ded. Mrs. Juliana Force.

2 pic, E-flat cl, cl, ob; hn, 2 tpt, 3 tmb; susp cym, side dm, ten dm, string dm, cast, cym, Chinese blocks, sleighbells, chains, tamb, gong, tamtam, tgle, crash cym, Rute, GC, slap stick.

fp: 1 March 1925, New York, International Composers Guild concert, cond. Leopold Stokowski.

Pub. 1925, Ricordi (New York); 1926, Curwen.

BIBLIOGRAPHY:
M. Andersen: Musik er lyd—en analyse med efterskrift, *Dansk Musiktidsskrift*, 1963, No. 4, p. 128.

15. Arcana. For large orchestra. 1925–7.

2 fl, 3 pic, 3 ob, ca, heckelphone, 4 cl, bcl, 3 bsn, 2 cbsn; 8 hn, 5 tpt, 2 ten tmb, bs tmb, cbs tmb, tuba, cbs tuba; timp, 6 pcssn; strings (16-16-14-12-10).

fp: 8 April 1927, Philadelphia, Philadelphia Orchestra, cond. Leopold Stokowski.

f New York p: 12 April 1927, Philadelphia Orchestra, cond. Leopold Stokowski.

Pub. 1952, Ricordi (New York).

BIBLIOGRAPHY:
Paul Rosenfeld: Musical chronicle—Arcana, *Dial*, June 1927, p. 537.

16. Ionisation. For percussion. Dated: 13 November 1931, Paris. Dur. 6½'.

crash cyms, GC; gong, 2 tamtams; 2 bongos, side dm, 2 GC laid flat; tamb mil, side dm; high siren, string dm; lown siren, slap stick, guiro; 3 Chinese blocks, claves

tgle; snare dm, maracas; tarole, snare dm, susp cym; cym, sleighbells, tubular chimes; guiro, cast, celesta; tamb, anvils, grand tamtam; slap stick, tgle, sleighbells, piano.

fp: 6 March 1933, New York, Pan-American Association of Composers, cond. Nicolas Slonimsky.

Paul Rosenfeld: Musical chronicle—Arcana, fEbp: 4 June 1951, 1950 Darmstadt Festival, cond. Hermann Scherchen.

?fEp: 25 February 1957, Royal Festival Hall, London Philharmonic Orchestra, cond. Hermann Scherchen.

Pub. 1934, Max Eschig; 1958, Ricordi.

BIBLIOGRAPHY:
A. Cohn: Percussion up to date, or new roles for palpitant rolls, *American Record Guide*, December 1957, p. 182.

17. Metal. For soprano and orchestra. ?1932. ?Unfinished. ?Lost.

18. Ecuatorial. For bass voice and orchestra. 1933–4. Text: from the sacred book of the Maya Quiché, the 'Popul Vuh' (Spanish transl. Father Jimines). Ded. L.V.

4 tpt, 4 tmb, piano, organ, 2 Ondes Martenot, timp, 2 snare dms, 2 ten dms, 3 GC, 3 tamtams, gong, cym, susp cym, 2 temple blocks, tamb.

fp: 15 April 1934, New York, Pan-American Association of Composers, Chase Baromeo (bass), cond. Nicolas Slonimsky.

fEp: 28 July 1966, Royal Albert Hall, Promenade Concert, BBC Symphony Orchestra, cond. Frederick Prausnitz.

Pub. 1961, Ricordi (New York). NB: original version was for chorus of bass voices instead of bass solo and Theremins instead of Ondes Martenot.

19. Density 21.5. For solo flute. January 1936.

fp: 16 February 1936, New York, Georges Barrère.

Pub. March 1957, *The Score*, No. 19, p. 15.

21. Déserts. For orchestra. 1953–4. Ded. Red Heller. Dur. 13' 20" (instr.) and 10' 08" (interp.) = 23' 28".

2 fl, pic, 2 cl, E-flat cl, bcl; 2 hn, 3 tpt, 3 tmb, bs tuba, cbs tuba; piano; *I.* 4 timp, vib, susp cym, side dm, claves; *II.* glock, snare dm, field dm, side dm, 2 timbales or

tomtoms, 2 susp cym, cencerro, tamb & Chinese blocks; *III.* 2 GC with attached cym, field dm, side dm, cencerro, guiro, claves, tamb, chimes (tubular bells); *IV.* vib, 3 gongs, 2 lathes, guiro, tamb; *V.* xyl, 3 Chinese blocks, 3 wooden dms (dragon heads), guiro, claves, 2 maracas; 2 magnetic tapes (ad lib).

fp: 2 December 1954, Paris, Orchestre National, cond. Hermann Scherchen.

?fEbp: 26 October 1961, cond. Robert Craft.

Pub. 1959, Ricordi/Franco Colombo (New York).

BIBLIOGRAPHY:

J. B. Felton: Camera concert, New York: Deserts, *Etude*, March 1956, p. 22.

Genêt: Letter from Paris: première of Deserts, *New Yorker*, 18 December 1954, p. 100.

Oliver Gilman: Deserts, *High Fidelity*, November 1955, p. 45.

W. Sargeant: Musical events: first New York performance of Deserts at Town Hall, *New Yorker*, 10 December 1955, p. 212.

Maria Scriabine: Le Désert, *Nouvelle nouvelle revue française*, No. 25 (1955), p. 162.

Y. Tinayre: Varèse composition causes furore in Paris, *Musical Courier*, 15 January 1955, p. 36.

22. Good Friday Procession in Verges. Electronic composition for the film 'Around and About Joan Miró'. 1955-6.

fp: 26–28 April 1957, New York, Metropolitan Museum of Art, Third International Art Film Festival.

23. Poème électronique. 1957-8. Composed for the Philips Pavilion at the Brussels World's Fair.

24. Nocturnal. For soprano and orchestra. Text: Anaïs Nin (from 'House of Incest'). Unfinished.

pic, fl/pic, ob, cl, E-flat cl, bsn, hn, 2 tpt, 3 tmb, strings, piano, pcssn (5 playcrs).

fp: 1 May 1961, New York, Composers' Showcase, Donna Precht (soprano), cond. Robert Craft.

WRITINGS BY VARÈSE

Jérôm' s'en va-t-en guerre, *Sackbut*, December 1923, p. 144.

Organised sound for the sound film, *Commonweal*, 13 December 1940, p. 204.

Answers, *Possibilities*, winter 1947-8, p. 96.

Musik auf neuen Wegen, *Stimmen*, 1949, No. 15, p. 401.

A communication, *MQ*, 1955, p. 574.

Les instruments de musique et la machine électronique, *L'Age nouveau*, No. 92, May 1955, p. 28.

Tout jeune homme j'habitais Berlin, in *Le Poème électronique Le Corbusier*, Editions de Minuit (Paris) 1958.

Le destin de la musique est de conquérir la liberté, *Liberté 59*, (Montreal), September–October 1959.

Erinnerungen und Gedanken, *Darmstädter Beiträge zur neuen Musik*, 1960, No. 3, p. 65.

The liberation of sound, *PNM*, fall–winter 1966, p. 11.

GENERAL BIBLIOGRAPHY

José-Antonio Alcarez: EV, *The Listener*, 10 February 1966, p. 218.

István Anhalt: Varèse, *Canadian Musical Journal* 1961, No. 2, p. 34.

Milton Babbitt: EV, a few observations of his music, *PNM*, spring–summer 1966, p. 14.

Olle Bonnier: Apropå Varèse, *Nutida musik*, Vol. II (1958–9), No. 1, p. 1.

B. Boretz: Varèse, *Nation*, 29 November 1965, p. 426.

André Boucourechliev: Vous entendez demain..., *Preuves*, No. 145, March 1963, p. 69.

— Tone Roads I, *Preuves*, No. 156, February 1964.

— EV, *Preuves*, No. 178, December 1965, p. 71.

P. Castaldi: Spunti e appunti: note su EV, *Musica d'oggi*, November–December 1961, p. 257.

Wen-Chung Chou: Varèse, a sketch of the man and his music, *MQ*, April 1966, p. 151

— Varèse, Current, *Musicology* (New York), winter 1965.

— 'Open rather than bounded', *PNM*, fall–winter 1966, p. 1.

— A Varèsce chronology, *–do–*, p. 7.

Carlos Chavez: Antecedents and consequences, *Eolus*, January 1927.

A. Cohn: Varèse, the stark individual,

American Record Guide, January 1962, p. 386.

Henry Cowell: The music of EV, *Modern Music*, February 1928, p. 9; in *American Composers* (New York), 1933, p. 43.

— Composing with tape, *Hi-Fi Music at Home*, January–February 1956, p. 58.

Robert Craft: EV talking, *Ricordiana*, January 1962, p. 2.

Luigi Dallapiccola, Elliott Carter (etc.): In memoriam EV, *PNM*, spring–summer 1966, p. 1.

Peter Dickinson, Varèse, sonic pioneer, *M&M*, December 1965, p. 28.

— EV, *Ricordiana*, April 1966, p. 1.

O. Downes: Rebel from way back, *New York Times*, 16 November 1958, Section 2, p. 11.

J. Edmunds: EV, engineer-composer, *Hi-Fi Music at Home*, March 1958, p. 28.

H. A. Fiechtner: Das Werk EV, *Musica*, 1962, No. 3, p. 155.

F. V. Grunfeld: The well-tempered ioniser, *High Fidelity*, September 1954, p. 39.

Everett Helm: Aussenseiter Varèse, *Melos*, December 1965, p. 433.

— Reconnaissance à EV, *Zvuk*, No. 67, 1966.

Robert Henderson: Varèse, *MT*, December 1965, p. 942.

Bengt Hambraeus: En kommentar till Varèse och hans musik, *Ord och bild*, Vol. 68 (1959), p. 145.

— Offrandes och Arcana samten liten Varèse-mosaik, *Nutida musik*, Vol. 6 (1962–3), No. 1, p. 15.

Pierre Hugli: EV, *SM*, 1966, No. 3 (May–June), p. 155.

J. H. Klarén: EV, pioneer of new music in America, Boston, 1928.

François Lesure: Debussy et EV, in *Debussy et l'évolution*, Paris, 1965, p. 333.

Ann McMillan: Samtal med EV, *Nutida musik*, Vol. 4 (1960–1), No. 4, p. 9.

Joseph Machlis: EV, in *Introduction to Contemporary Music*, Norton (USA), Dent (London) 1961, p. 624.

Wilfried Mellers: The retreat from the West—science and magic: Charles Griffes, Henry Cowell and EV, in *Music in a New Found Land*, Barrie & Rockliff (London) 1964, p. 145.

— EV, a great central figure, *Composer*, No. 18, January 1966, p. 10.

Heinz Klauss Metzger: Hommage à EV, *Darmstädter Beiträge zur neuen Musik*, No. 2 (1959), p. 54.

Henry Miller: Med EV i öknen Gobi, *Nutida musik*, Vol. 2 (1958–9), No. 1, p. 1.

M. Powell: Volley for Varèse, *Saturday Review*, 31 December 1960, p. 34.

Paul Rosenfeld: EV, *The Dial*, March 1924, p. 298.

— New American music, *Scribner's Magazine*, June 1931, p. 624.

— Varèse and Monteverde, *New Republic*, 26 April 1933, p. 310.

— Assault on the battery, *New Republic*, 24 January 1934, p. 309.

Jean Roy: EV, in *Musique française*, Nouvelles Editions Debresse (Paris) 1962, p. 123.

E. Salzman: Records: Varèse, *New York Times*, 30 October 1960, Section 2.

Gunther Schuller: Conversation with Varèse, *PNM*, spring–summer 1965, p. 32.

Igor Stravinsky: EV, *Ricordiana*, April 1962, p. 4.

H. H. Stuckenschmidt: EV, in *Schöpfer der neuen Musik*, Suhrkamp Verlag (Frankfurt a.M.) 1958, p. 64.

— 188 Sullivan Street: EV 75 Jahre alt, *Melos*, February 1961, p. 45.

Sigrid Sundequist: EV och Romain Rolland—Om en brevväxling, *Nutida musik*, Vol. 6 (1962–3), No. 1, p. 18.

Odile Vivier: Innovation instrumentale d'EV, *RM*, 1955, No. 226, p. 188.

Frederick Waldmann: EV, an appreciation, *Juilliard Review*, fall 1954, p. 3.

Arnold Whittall: Varèse and organic athematicism, *MR*, 1967, No. 4, p. 311.

Marc Wilkinson: An introduction to the music of EV, *The Score*, No. 19, March 1957, p. 5.

— EV, pioneer and prophet, *Melos*, March 1961.

T. A. Zielinski: Prekursor nowej muzyki, *Ruch Muzyczny*, 1961, No. 17, p. 4.

RALPH VAUGHAN WILLIAMS
(1872–1958)

Related on his mother's side to the Darwin

and Wedgwood families, Ralph Vaughan Williams was born at Down Ampney in Gloucestershire on 12 October 1872, the son of the Anglican vicar. He was taken to live at Leith Hill Place near Dorking in Surrey when his father died two years later. He spent his childhood and youth (and also the years 1928–53) in Dorking but lived the rest of his life mainly in London. He was educated at Charterhouse, the Royal College of Music and Trinity College, Cambridge, taking his Cambridge Doctorate of Music in 1901. His composition teachers included Parry and Stanford at the Royal College, Charles Wood at Cambridge, Max Bruch (Berlin, 1897) and Ravel (Paris, 1908); but equally important factors in his musical development were a deep friendship with Gustav Holst (whom he met in 1895), the collecting of English folksongs (from 1902) and the musical editorship of the *English Hymnal*, which was published in 1906. Vaughan Williams married Adeline Fisher in 1897, directed the first Leith Hill Festival in 1905 (and all subsequent Festivals for fifty years) and served during the First World War in the Royal Army Medical Corps and the Royal Garrison Artillery. After the War he became an important figure in London musical life, being appointed Professor of Composition at the Royal College of Music in 1919 (retiring in 1938) and conducting the Bach Choir from 1921 to 1928. He was awarded the Order of Merit in 1935. He made three visits to the United States (New England in 1922, Bryn Mawr College in 1932 and Cornell University in 1954) to conduct and teach. In 1951 Adeline Vaughan Williams died and two years later the composer married the poet Ursula Wood. He died in August 1958 at the age of eighty-five.

CATALOGUE OF WORKS

1. (Juvenilia and early unpublished works). 1878–95.

BIBLIOGRAPHY:

Michael Kennedy: *The works of RVW*. O.U.P. (London) 1964, pp. 395–9.

2. Rondel (Swinburne). For voice and piano. *c.* 1895–6.

fp: 28 May 1906, Bechstein Hall, Gregory Hast, acc. Henry Bird.

3. Echo's lament for Narcissus (Ben Jonson). Madrigal for double chorus. *c.* 1895–1896. Unpub.

4. Sonnet 71 (Shakespeare). For six voices (SSATBB) a cappella. Unpub.

5. Spring (Tennyson). Valse for voice and piano. 17 February 1896. Unpub.

6. Vine, vine and eglantine (Tennyson). Valse for soprano, alto, tenor and bass with piano acc. 12–16 March 1896. Unpub.

7. Winter (Tennyson). Valse for voice and piano. 16 March 1896. Unpub.

8. The willow song. Trad. English tune arr. for voice and piano. 19 February 1897. Unpub.

9. String Quartet in C minor. Winter 1898.

fp: 30 June 1904, Oxford and Cambridge Musical Club.

Unpub.

10. Serenade. For orchestra. 1898. Unpub.

1. *Prelude*; 2. *Scherzo*; 3. *Intermezzo and Trio*; 4. *Finale*.

2 fl, 2 ob, 2 cl, 2 bsn; 2 hn, 2 tpt; timp; strings.

fp: 4 April 1901, Bournemouth, Winter Gardens, Bournemouth Municipal Orchestra, cond. (Sir) Dan Godfrey.

f London p: 3 March 1908, Aeolian Hall, concert given by Dorothea Walenn, Aeolian Hall Orchestra, cond. Rosabel Watson.

11. Quintet in D major. For clarinet, horn, violin, cello and piano. 1898.

fp: 5 June 1900, Queen's (Small) Hall, George A. Clinton chamber concert, Llewella Davies (piano), Gordon Clinton (cl), Adolf Borsdorf (hn), Jessie Grimson (v) and B. P. Parker (c).

Unpub.

12. The garden of Proserpine (A. C. Swinburne). For soprano, chorus and orchestra. 1899. Unpub.

13. Three Elizabethan songs. For SATB chorus a cappella. *c.* 1890–1902.

Vaughan Williams, Ralph

1. *Sweet day* (George Herbert); 2. *The willow song* (Shakespeare); 3. *O mistress mine* (Shakespeare).

?fp: 5 November 1913, Shirehampton, Public Hall, Avonmouth and Shirehampton Choral Society, cond. R. Vaughan Williams.
Pub. 1913, Joseph Williams.

14. How can the tree but wither? (Thomas, Lord Vaux). For voice and piano.
?fp: 5 June 1907, Magpie Madrigal Society concert, Francis Harford.
Pub. 1934, O.U.P.

15. Claribel (Tennyson). For voice and piano. *c.* 1896–1902.
?fp: 2 December 1904, Bechstein Hall, Beatrice Spencer, acc. (Sir) Hamilton Harty.
Pub. 1906, Boosey.

16. Come away death (Shakespeare). For SSATB. *c.* 1896–1902. Pub. 1909, Stainer & Bell.

17. Rise early sun. Madrigal. *c.* 1896–1902. Lost.

18. Mass. For soloists, mixed double chorus and orchestra. 1897–9. Unpub.

19. Bucolic Suite. For orchestra. 1900.
fp: 10 March 1902, Bournemouth, Municipal Orchestra, cond. (Sir) Dan Godfrey.
Unpub.

20. Heroic Elegy and Triumphal Epilogue. For orchestra. 1900–2, rev. 1907.
fp: 5 March 1901, Royal College of Music, cond. Sir Charles Stanford.

21. Linden Lea (William Barnes). For voice and piano. 1901. Ded. Mrs. Edmund Fisher. Dur. $2\frac{1}{2}'$.
fp: 4 September 1902, Hooton Roberts Musical Union, J. Milner.
f London p: 2 December 1902, St. James's Hall, Frederick Keel, acc. C. A. Lidgey.
Pub. 1902, *The Vocalist*.

22. Fantasia. For piano and orchestra. 1896–1902, rev. 1904. Unpub.

23. Ring out your bells (Sir Philip Sidney). Madrigal for SSATB a cappella. 1902. Ded. Lionel Benson and the members of the Magpie Madrigal Society. Pub. Laudy; Bosworth.

24. Rest (Christina Rossetti). Madrigal for SSATB a cappella. 1902. Ded. Lionel Benson and the Magpie Madrigal Society.
fp: 14 May 1902, St. James's Hall, Magpie Madrigal Society, cond. Lionel Benson.
Pub. *c.* 1904–5, Laudy; 1909, Novello.

25. Blackmwore by the Stour (William Barnes). Dorset folk-song for voice and piano. *c.* 1901. Pub. May 1902, *The Vocalist*.

26. Entlaubet ist der Walde. Old German Volkslied for voice and piano. 1902. English text: Walter Ford. Ded. Walter Ford. Pub. 1937, O.U.P.

27. Whither must I wander? (Robert Louis Stevenson). For voice and piano. 1902.
fp: 27 November 1902, St. James's Hall, Campbell McInnes, acc. C. A. Lidgey.
Pub. June 1902, *The Vocalist*.

28. Boy Johnny (Christina Rossetti). For voice and piano. 1902. Ded. J. Campbell McInnes.
fp: 1902, Oxford.
f London p: 22 April 1903, St. James's Hall, Francis Harford, acc. Ernest Walker.
Pub. September 1902, *The Vocalist*.

29. If I were Queen (Christina Rossetti). For voice and piano. 1902.
fp: 16 April 1903, Exeter, A. Foxton Ferguson acc. Miss Wood.
Pub. November 1902, *The Vocalist*.

30. Tears, idle tears (Tennyson). For voice and piano. 1903. Ded. J. Francis Harford.
fp: 5 February 1903, St. James's Hall, Francis Harford, acc. Evlyn Howard-Jones.
Pub. June 1903, *The Vocalist*.

31. Silent noon (D. G. Rossetti). For voice and piano. 1903.
fp: 10 March 1903, St. James's Hall, Francis Harford, acc. Philip L. Agnew.
Pub. 1904, Willcocks.

32. Willow-Wood (D. G. Rossetti). Cantata. First version: 1903, for voice and piano. Revised version: 1908–9, for voice and orchestra with (ad lib) women's chorus.

2 fl, ob, ca, 2 cl, 2 bsn; 4 hn, 2 tpt, 3 tmb, bs tuba; timp; hp, strings.

fp: 25 September 1909, Liverpool, Music League Festival, Frederic Austin and Liverpool Welsh Choral Union, cond. Harry Evans.

Pub. 1909, Breitkopf & Härtel.

33. Sound sleep (Christina Rossetti). Trio for SSA and piano. 1903. Ded. Mrs. Massingberd.

fp: 27 April 1903, Spilsby, East Lincolnshire Musical Festival.

Pub. 1903, Novello.

33a. Sound sleep. Version with orchestra. 7 October 1903. Pub. Novello.

34. Adieu. German folksong for soprano and baritone with piano acc. 1903. English words: A. Foxton Ferguson. Pub. October 1903, *The Vocalist.*

35. Think of me. German folksong for soprano and baritone with piano acc. 1903. English words: A. Foxton Ferguson. Pub. October 1903, *The Vocalist.*

36. Cousin Michael. German folksong for soprano and baritone with piano acc. 1903. English words: A Foxton Ferguson. ?Unpub.

37. Orpheus with his lute (Shakespeare). For voice and piano. 1902. Ded. Lucy Broadwood.

fp: 2 December 1904, Beatrice Spencer, acc. (Sir) Hamilton Harty.

Pub. 1904, Prowse.

38. When I am dead, my dearest (Christina Rossetti). For voice and piano. 1903.

fp: 28 November 1905, Aeolian Hall, Alice Venning, acc. Samuel Liddle.

Pub. 1903, Prowse.

39. Réveillez-vous, Piccars (Adapt. by Paul England of fifteenth-century French battle song). For voice and piano. 1903, Pub. 1907, Boosey.

40. The winter's willow (William Barnes). In Dorset dialect, for voice and piano. Pub. November 1903, *The Vocalist.*

41. In the New Forest. Four Impressions for orchestra. 1902–3.

1. *Burley Heath*; 2. *The Solent.* Incomplete. Unpub.

42. Piano Quintet in C minor. For piano, violin, viola, cello and double bass. 27 October 1903, rev. 1904–5. Unpub.

f London p: 14 December 1905, Aeolian Hall, Broadwood concert, Richard Epstein (piano), Louis Zimmerman, Alfred Hobday, Paul Ludwig and Claude Hobday.

43. Jean Renaud. Fifteenth-century French song arr. for voice and piano. 1904. English adaptation: Paul England.

fp: 11 February 1904, St. James's Hall, Francis Harford, acc. May Christie.

Unpub.

44. L'Amour de Moy. Fifteenth-century French song arr. for voice and piano. 1904. English words: Paul England.

fp: as No. 43.

Pub. 1907, Boosey.

45. Symphonic Rhapsody. 1901–3. Destroyed.

fp: 7 March 1904, Bournemouth, Municipal Orchestra, cond. (Sir) Dan Godfrey.

46. In the Fen country. Symphonic Impression for orchestra. 10 April 1904, rev. February 1905, July 1907, April 1908, 1935. Dur. 14'.

3 fl, 2 ob, ca, 2 cl, bcl, 2 bsn; 4 hn, 2 tpt, 3 tmb, bs tuba; timp; solo violin, strings.

fp: 22 February 1909, Queen's Hall, Beecham Orchestra, cond. (Sir) Thomas Beecham.

Pub. 1969, O.U.P.

47. Ballade and Scherzo. For string quintet. 22 May 1904, rev. 1 October 1906. Unfinished.

48. Two Impressions. For orchestra. July 1904–7.

1. *Harnham Down*; 2. *Boldrewood.*

fp: 12 November 1907, Queen's Hall, New Symphony Orchestra, cond. Emil von Reznicek.

Unpub. No. 2 lost.

49. Andante sostenuto. For piano. 17 July 1904. Unpub.

50. Two Duets (Walt Whitman). For

soprano, baritone, piano and string quartet (ad lib) with violin obbligato. 1904.

1. *The last invocation*; 2. *The love-song of the bird*.

fp: 24 October 1904, Reading, Town Hall, A. Foxton Ferguson and Beatrice Spencer, with Miss Hedley (piano), Maurice Sons and Dorothy Blount (violins), Alfred Hobday (viola) and W. E. Whitehouse (cello).

Unpub.

51. The House of Life (D. G. Rossetti). Cycle of six sonnets for voice and piano. ?1903.

1. *Love-sight*; 2. *Silent noon*; 3. *Love's minstrels*; 4. *Heart's haven*; 5. *Death in love*; 6. *Love's last gift*.

fp: 2 December 1904, Bechstein Hall, Edith Clegg, acc. (Sir) Hamilton Harty.

Pub. 1904, Willcocks; 1933, Ashdown.

52. Songs of travel (Robert Louis Stevenson). For voice and piano. 1904. Dur. 23′.

1. *The vagabond*; 2. *Let beauty awake*; 3. *The roadside fire*; 4. *Youth and love*; 5. *In dreams*; 6. *The infinite shining heavens*; 7. *Whither must I wander?*; 8. *Bright is the ring of words*; 9. *I have trod the downward slope*.

fp (Nos. 1–8): 2 December 1904, Bechstein Hall, Walter Creighton, acc. (Sir) Hamilton Harty.

fp (complete): 21 May 1960, BBC broadcast, Hervey Alan, acc. Frederick Stone.

Pub. 1905 (Nos. 1, 8, 3), Boosey; 1907 (Nos. 2, 4, 5, 6), Boosey; 1960 (complete), Boosey & Hawkes.

52a. Songs of travel. Version for voice and orchestra. Orch. by the composer, 1905 (Nos. 1, 3 & 8 only), and Roy Douglas, 1960 (remainder).

2 fl, pic, 2 ob, 2 cl, 2 bsn; 4 hn, 2 tpt; timp, side dm, tgle; hp, strings.

53. Two French folksongs. Arr. for voice and piano. ?1904.

1. *Chanson de quête*; 2. *La Ballade de Jésus Christ*.

Pub. 1935, O.U.P.

54. French folksongs. Arr. for voice and piano. 1904.

1. *Quand le rossignol*; 2. *Que Dieu se montre seulement*.

Unpub.

55. Pezzo ostinato. For piano. 27 January 1905. Unpub.

56. Ye little birds (Thomas Heywood). For voice and piano. 1905.

fp: 3 February 1905, Aeolian Hall, H. Plunket Greene, acc. S. Liddle.

Unpub.

57. A cradle song (S. T. Coleridge). For voice and piano. Date uncertain (?1894). Pub. April 1905, *The Vocalist*.

58. Pan's Anniversary. A masque by Ben Jonson, music composed and arranged by R. Vaughan Williams, in association with Gustav Holst.

fp: 24 April 1905, Stratford-upon-Avon, Chorus and Orchestra of the Choral Union, cond. R. Vaughan Williams.

Unpub.

59. The splendour falls (Tennyson). For voice and piano. 1905. Pub. May 1905, *The Vocalist*.

60. Dreamland (Christina Rossetti). For voice and piano. 1905.

fp: 31 October 1905, Aeolian Hall, Gervase Elwes, acc. F. B. Kiddle.

Pub. 1906, Boosey.

61. Welcome Songs (Part I). Purcell, ed. R. Vaughan Williams for the Purcell Society (Works of Henry Purcell, Vol. XV). Pub. 1905, Novello.

62. Hymn tunes. Compositions and arrangements for The English Hymnal, pub. 1906, O.U.P.

63. Norfolk Rhapsody No. 1 in E minor. For orchestra. 1906. Dur. 10½′.

2 fl, 2 ob, ca, 2 cl, E-flat cl (ad lib), 2 bsn; 4 hn, 2 tpt, 3 tmb, tuba; timp, side dm; hp, strings.

fp: 23 August 1906, Queen's Hall, Queen's Hall Orchestra, cond. (Sir) Henry Wood.

fbp: 19 October 1924, Manchester, Free Trade Hall, Halle Orchestra, cond. (Sir) Hamilton Harty.

Pub. 1925, O.U.P.

64. Norfolk Rhapsody No. 2 in D minor. For orchestra. 1906.

2 fl, 2 ob, ca, 2 cl, 2 bsn; 4hn, 2 tpt, 3 tmb, bs tuba; timp, tgle; hp, strings.

fp: 27 September 1907, Cardiff Festival, London Symphony Orchestra, cond. R. Vaughan Williams.

f London p: 17 April 1912, Queen's Hall, Balfour Gardiner concert, New Symphony Orchestra, cond. Balfour Gardiner.

Unpub. Partly lost.

65. Norfolk Rhapsody No. 3 in G minor/ major. For orchestra. 1906.

Instrumentation and performance information as for No. 64.

Unpub. Lost.

66. Music for 'The Pilgrim's Progress'. For soprano, contralto, mixed chorus and strings.

fp: December 1906, Reigate Priory, cond. Ralph Vaughan Williams.

Unpub.

67. Toward the unknown region (Walt Whitman). Song for SATB chorus and orchestra. 1907. Ded. F.H.M. (Florence Maitland). Dur. 11½'.

3 fl, 2 ob, ca, 2 cl, bcl, 2 bsn; 4 hn, 3 tpt, 3 tmb, tuba; timp; 2 hp (or piano), strings. *Alternative:* 2 fl, ob, 2 cl, 2 bsn; 2 hn, 2 tpt; timp; hp (or piano), strings.

fp: 10 October 1907, Leeds Festival, Town Hall, Leeds Festival Chorus and Orchestra, cond. R. Vaughan Williams.

fbp: 17 January 1926, Wireless Chorus and Symphony Orchestra, cond. Percy Pitt.

Pub. 1907 (vocal score), Breitkopf & Härtel; 1924 (full score), Stainer & Bell.

68. Fain would I change that note (Anon.). Canzonet for four voices (SATB) a cappella. 1907. Pub. 1907, Novello.

69. Folksongs from the Eastern Counties. Collected and set with piano acc. by R. Vaughan Williams. Folksongs of England, Book II (ed. Cecil J. Sharp). Pub. 1908, Novello.

70. The jolly ploughboy. Sussex folksong arr. for TTBB a cappella. ?1908. Pub. 1908, Novello.

71. Buonaparty (Thomas Hardy). For voice and piano. 1908. Pub. 1909, Boosey.

72. The sky above the roof (Paul Verlaine, transl. Mabel Dearmer). For voice and piano. 1908. Pub. 1909, Boosey.

73. Three Nocturnes. For baritone, semichorus and orchestra. 1908. Words: Walt Whitman. Unpub.

74. Aethiopia saluting the colours (Whitman). Sketch only. *c.* 1908. Unpub.

75. The Future (Matthew Arnold). For soprano, chorus and orchestra. *c.* 1908. Unfinished. Unpub.

76. Is my team ploughing? (A. E. Housman). For voice and piano. *c.* 1908.

fp: 25 January 1909, Aeolian Hall, Gervase Elwes, acc. Frederick Kiddle.

Unpub. Eventually incorporated into *On Wenlock Edge* (see No. 78).

77. String Quartet in G minor. 1908, rev. 1921. Dur. 28'.

1. *Allegro moderato*; 2. *Minuet and Trio*; 3. *Romance* (*Andante sostenuto*); 4. *Finale* (*Rondo capriccioso*).

fp: 8 November 1909, Novello's Rooms, Society of British Composers meeting, Schwiller Quartet.

fp (public): 15 November 1909, Aeolian Hall, Schwiller Quartet.

fp (revised version): 6 March 1922, Central YMCA Drawing Room, Contemporary Music Centre/British Music Society concert.

fbp: 10 April 1924, Snow Quartet (Jessie Snow, Kenneth Skeaping, Ernest Tomlinson and Edward J. Robinson).

Pub. 1923, Goodwin; Curwen.

78. On Wenlock Edge (A. E. Housman). Song cycle for tenor with piano and (ad lib) string quartet. 1909. Dur. 24'.

1. *On Wenlock Edge*; 2. *From far, from eve and morning*; 3. *Is my team ploughing?*; 4. *Oh, when I was in love with you*; 5. *Bredon Hill* (*In summertime on Bredon*); 6. *Clun*.

fp: 15 November 1909, Aeolian Hall, Gervase Elwes, Frederick Kiddle and the Schwiller Quartet.

fbp: 17 February 1924, Seymour Dosser and the Clifton Quintet.

Pub. 1911, Novello.

78a. On Wenlock Edge. Version for tenor and orchestra. *c.* 1921–3.

2 fl, ob, ca, 2 cl, 2 bsn; 4 hn, 2 tpt, 3 tmb; timp, pcssn; celesta, hp, strings.

fp: 24 January 1924, Queen's Hall, Royal Philharmonic Society concert, John Booth, cond. Ralph Vaughan Williams.

79. The Wasps. Incidental music (Aristophanes, transl. H. J. Edwards) for tenor, baritone, male chorus and orchestra. 1909.

fp: 26 November 1909, Cambridge, New Theatre, cond. Charles Wood.

Pub. 1909, Cambridge.

79a. The Wasps: Aristophanic Suite. Dur. 25½'.

1. *Overture*; 2. *Entr'acte*; 3. *March-Past of the Kitchen Utensils*; 4. *Entr'acte*; 5. *Ballet and Final Tableau.*

2 fl, pic, 2(1) ob, 2 cl, 2(1) bsn; 4(2) hn, 2(1) tpt, 2(1) tmb; timp, tgle, cym, GC; hp, strings.

fp: 23 July 1912, Queen's Hall, Patron's Fund concert, New Symphony Orchestra, cond. R. Vaughan Williams.

fbp: 5 November 1924, Newcastle Augmented Station Orchestra, cond. Edward Clark.

Pub. 1914, Schott; 1933, Curwen. Arr. by Constant Lambert for piano duet pub. 1926, Curwen.

79b. The Wasps: Overture. Extracted from preceding.

2 fl, pic, 2 ob, 2 cl, 2 bsn; 2 hn, 2 tpt; timp, tgle, cym, GC; hp, strings.

80. A Sea Symphony. For soprano, baritone, mixed chorus and orchestra. 1909. Words: Walt Whitman. Ded. R.L.W. (Sir Ralph Wedgwood). Dur. 67'.

1. *A Song for All Seas, All Ships.* Dur. 19¼'.
2. *On the beach at night, alone.* Dur. 11½'.
3. *Scherzo* (The Waves). Dur. 7'.
4. *The Explorers.* Dur. 29¼'.

2 fl, 2(1) ob, ca, 3(2) cl, bcl (ad lib), 2 bsn, dbsn (ad lib); 4 hn, 3 tpt, 3 tmb, tuba; timp, pcssn; 2(1) hp, organ (ad lib); strings.

fp: 12 October 1910, Leeds Festival, Leeds Town Hall, Cicely Gleeson-White, Campbell McInnes, Festival Chorus and orchestra, cond.

R. Vaughan Williams, with Edward Bairstow (organ).

f London p: 4 February 1913, Queen's Hall, Agnes Nicholls, Campbell McInnes, Bach Choir and Queen's Hall Orchestra, cond. Hugh P. Allen, with Harold Darke (organ).

Pub. 1909, Breitkopf & Härtel (vocal score: revised edition, 1918, 1961); 1924 (full score), Stainer & Bell.

BIBLIOGRAPHY:

Gerald Abraham: VW and his symphonies, 1: The Sea Symphony, *MS*, 20 February 1926, p. 56.

Eric Blom: A Sea Symphony, *Music Teacher*, November 1930, p. 661.

Scott Goddard: VW's Sea Symphony, *The Listener*, 3 February 1955, p. 217.

Neville Cardus: Surge and sting of the sea in a symphony, *Radio Times*, 31 October 1930, p. 307.

81. Fantasia on English folk song. For orchestra. 1910.

fp: 1 September 1910, Queen's Hall, Promenade Concert, Queen's Hall Orchestra, cond. Sir Henry Wood.

Unpub. Lost.

82. Welcome Songs (Part 2). Purcell, ed. R. Vaughan Williams for the Purcell Society (Works of Henry Purcell, Vol. XVIII). Pub. 1910, Novello.

83. Fantasia on a theme by Thomas Tallis. For double string orchestra with solo quartet. 1910. Rev. 1913, 1919. Dur. 14½'.

fp: 6 September 1910, Gloucester Cathedral, Three Choirs Festival, London Symphony Orchestra, cond. R. Vaughan Williams.

f London p: 11 February 1913, Queen's Hall, Balfour Gardiner concert, New Symphony Orchestra, cond. R. Vaughan Williams.

fbp: 13 June 1926, Wireless String Orchestra, cond. Percy Pitt.

Pub. 1921, Goodwin & Tabb; Curwen; 1943, Boosey & Hawkes.

BIBLIOGRAPHY:

Eric Blom: VW, Fantasia on a theme by Tallis, *Music Teacher*, May 1931, p. 257.

Harold Rawlinson: Some famous works for

string orchestra, 24: Fantasia on a theme of Thomas Tallis, *Strad*, July 1951, p. 76.

84. Church songs. Collected by Rev. S. Baring-Gould, music arr. by Rev. H. Fleetwood Sheppard and R. Vaughan Williams. 1911. Pub. 1911, Society for the Promotion of Christian Knowledge.

85. Five Mystical Songs. For baritone, mixed chorus (ad lib) and orchestra. 1911. Words: George Herbert. Dur. 19'.

1. *Easter*; 2. *I got me flowers*; 3. *Love bade me welcome*; 4. *The call*; 5. *Antiphon*.

2 fl, 2 ob, 2 cl, 2 bsn; 4 hn, 2 tpt, 3 tmb, tuba; timp; hp, strings. *Or:* string quintet and piano.

fp: 14 September 1911, Worcester Cathedral, Three Choirs Festival, Campbell McInnes, Festival Chorus, London Symphony Orchestra, cond. R. Vaughan Williams.

f London p: 21 November 1911, Campbell McInnes, acc. (Sir) Hamilton Harty (piano).

fbp: 10 April 1924, Gilbert Bailey with the Snow Quartet and Maurice Cole (piano).

Pub. 1911, Stainer & Bell.

86. London Pageant. May Day Scene. 1911. Unpub.

87. The Bacchae. Incidental music. *c.* 1911–1914. Unpub.

88. Where is the home for me? (Gilbert Murray, after 'The Bacchae' of Euripides). For voice and piano. *c.* 1911–14. Pub. 1922, Ashdown.

89. Iphigenia in Tauris. Incidental music. *c.* 1911–14. Unpub.

90. Electra. Incidental music. *c.* 1911–14. Unpub.

91. Down among the dead men. Old English Air arr. for male voices (TTBB) a cappella. 1906. Pub. 1912, Joseph Williams.

92. The Spanish ladies. Arr. for voice and piano. 1912. Traditional words and tune. Pub. 1912, Boosey.

93. Alister McAlpine's lament (Robert Allan). Scottish Air arr. for mixed voices (SATB) a cappella. 1912. Pub. 1912, Curwen.

94. The winter is gone. English folksong arr. for male voices (TTBB) a cappella. 1912. Pub. 1912, Novello.

95. Phantasy Quintet. For string quintet. 1912. Ded. W. W. Cobbett and members of the London String Quartet. Dur. 16'.

1. *Prelude* (*Lento ma non troppo*); 2. *Scherzo* (*Prestissimo*); 3. *Alla sarabanda*; 4. *Burlesca* (*Allegro moderato*).

fp: 23 March 1914, Aeolian Hall, F. B. Ellis chamber concert, London String Quartet.

fbp: 3 May 1926, Chenil Galleries, Music Society Quartet (André Mangeot, Boris Pecker, Henry J. Berly, John Barbirolli) and Jean Pougnet.

Pub. 1921, Stainer & Bell.

96. Fantasia on Christmas Carols. For baritone, mixed chorus and orchestra. 1912. Ded. Cecil Sharp. Dur. 8'.

2 fl, 2 ob, 2 cl, 2 bsn; 4 hn, 3 tpt, 3 tmb, tuba; timp, bells (ad lib); organ, strings.

fp: 12 September 1912, Hereford Cathedral, Three Choirs Festival, Campbell McInnes, Festival Chorus, London Symphony Orchestra, cond. R. Vaughan Williams.

f London p: 4 March 1913, Queen's Hall, Balfour Gardiner concert, Campbell McInnes, London Choral Society, New Symphony Orchestra, cond. R. Vaughan Williams.

fbp: 21 December 1924, Bournemouth, Herbert Heyner, 6BM Choir and Wireless Orchestra, cond. Capt. W. A. Featherstone.

Pub. 1912, 1924 (full score), Stainer & Bell. Also versions with acc. for (a) string orchestra and organ or piano; (b) organ; (c) piano and cello.

97. Folksongs for schools. Arr. for unison voices and piano. Pub. 1912, Novello.

98. Folksongs from Sussex. Folk Songs of England, V. Ed. Cecil J. Sharp. Collected by W. Percy Merrick. With piano acc. by R. Vaughan Williams and Albert Robins. Pub. 1912, Novello.

99. Evening Hymn. Purcell, arr. for voice and string orchestra by R. Vaughan Williams. ?Date. Full score lost.

100. Ward the pirate. English folksong arr. for mixed chorus and small orchestra. ?1912. Unpub.

101. Tarry Trowsers. English folksong arr. for mixed chorus and small orchestra. ?1912. Unpub.

102. And all in the morning (On Christmas Day). Derbyshire carol arr. for mixed chorus and small orchestra. ?1912. Unpub.

103. The carter. English folksong for flute and piano. 1912. Unpub.

104. Minehead hobby-horse. English folk dance arr. for small orchestra. 1912. Unpub.

105. Phil the fluter's dancing. English folk dance arr. for flute and strings. 1912. Unpub.

106. Mannin Veen (Dear Mona). Manx traditional melody arr. for mixed chorus a cappella. ?1912. Pub. 1913, Curwen.

107. Love is a sickness (Samuel Daniel). Ballet for four voices (SATB) a cappella.

108. O praise the Lord of Heaven. Anthem for two full choirs and semi-chorus a cappella. 1913.
fp: 13 November 1913, St. Paul's Cathedral, London Church Choir Association, cond. (Sir) Walford Davies.
Pub. 1914, Stainer & Bell.

109. Five English folksongs. Freely arranged for mixed chorus a cappella. 1913.
fbp: 19 October 1925, Wireless Chorus, cond. Stanford Robinson.
Pub. 1913, Stainer & Bell.

110. A London Symphony. 1913. Ded. to the memory of George Butterworth. Dur. 44' (original version, c. 55–60').
1. _Lento—Allegro risoluto_; 2. _Lento_; 3. _Scherzo_ (_Nocturne_): _Allegro vivace_; 4. _Finale: Andante con moto—Maestoso alla marcia_ (_quasi lento_)—_Allegro. Epilogue: Andante sostenuto._
3 fl, 2 ob, ca, 2 cl, bcl, 2 bsn, dbsn; 4 hn, 2 tpt, 2 cornets, 3 tmb, tuba; timp, side dm, tgle, GC, cym, glock, jingles; hp, strings.
fp (original version): 27 March 1914, Queen's Hall, F. B. Ellis concert, Queen's Hall Orchestra, cond. Geoffrey Toye. MS lost.
fp (reconstructed version): 11 February 1915, Bournemouth, Winter Gardens, Bournemouth Municipal Orchestra, cond. (Sir) Dan Godfrey.

fp (revised version): 18 March 1918, Queen's Hall, New Queen's Hall Orchestra, cond. (Sir) Adrian Boult.
fp (second revision): 4 May 1920, Queen's Hall, British Music Society first annual congress concert, New Queen's Hall Orchestra, cond. Albert Coates.
fbp: 16 May 1924, Manchester, 2ZY Orchestra, cond. (Sir) Dan Godfrey.
fp (third revision): 22 February 1934, Queen's Hall, Royal Philharmonic Society concert, London Philharmonic Orchestra, cond. Sir Thomas Beecham.
Unpub. until second (1920) revision. Pub. 1920, c. 1936 (third revision), Stainer & Bell.

BIBLIOGRAPHY:
Gerald Abraham: VW and his symphonies, 2: The London Symphony, _MS_, 6 March 1926, p. 74.
W. R. Anderson: VW's London Symphony, _Halle_, October 1946, p. 17.
Eric Blom: RVW, a London Symphony, _Music Teacher_, August 1933, p. 383.
George Butterworth: VW's London Symphony, _RCM Magazine_, 1914, No. 2, p. 44; in _George Butterworth, a memoir_, 1918, p. 95.
H. C. Colles: The London Symphony, in _Essays and Lectures_, O.U.P. (London) 1945, p. 89.
Sydney Grew: VW's London Symphony, _Midland Musician_, January 1926, p. 33.
R. O. Morris: VW's London Symphony, _The Nation_, 15 May 1920, p. 199.
Charles O'Connell: A London Symphony, in _The Victor Book of Symphonies_, Simon & Schuster (New York) 1948, p. 531.
H. G. Sears: An introduction to VW's London Symphony, _Philharmonic Post_, September–October 1952, p. 66.
Bernard Shore: VW's London Symphony, in _Sixteen Symphonies_, Longmans, Green (London) 1949, p. 287.
Anon.: Composers in action: VW's new London Symphony, _The Times_, 28 March 1914, p. 6.
Anon.: The London Symphony—a matter of fact, _The Times_, 8 May 1920, p. 14.
Anon.: A London Symphony by RVW, _British Musician_, December 1926, p. 149.

111. The Death of Tintagiles. Incidental music (Maurice Maeterlinck). ?Date. Unpub.

112. The Blue Bird. Incidental music (Maurice Maeterlinck). ?Date.

113. The Merry Wives of Windsor. Incidental music (Shakespeare). 1913. Unpub.

114. King Richard II. Incidental music (Shakespeare). 1913. Unpub.

115. King Henry IV, Part 2. Incidental music (Shakespeare). 1913. Unpub.

116. King Richard III. Incidental music (Shakespeare). 1913. Unpub.

117. King Henry V. Incidental music (Shakespeare). 1913. Unpub.

118. The Devil's Disciple. Incidental music (G. B. Shaw). 1913. Unpub.

119. Four Hymns. For tenor and piano with viola obbligato (or string orchestra and viola obbligato). 1914. Ded. J.S.W. (Sir Steuart Wilson). Dur. 15′.
 1. *Lord! Come away* (Bishop Jeremy Taylor).
 2. *Who is this fair one?* (Isaac Watts).
 3. *Come love, come Lord* (Richard Crashaw).
 4. *Evening hymn* (transl. Robert Bridges, from the Greek).
 fp: 26 May 1920, Cardiff, Steuart Wilson, Alfred Hobday and the London Symphony Orchestra, cond. Julius Harrison.
 f London p: 19 October 1920, Aeolian Hall, Steuart Wilson, Alfred Hobday and chamber orchestra (leader, W. H. Reed), cond. R. Vaughan Williams.
 Pub. 1920, Boosey.

120. O God of earth and altar (G. K. Chesterton). Harmonisation of English traditional melody. 1919. Pub. Stainer & Bell in *Motherland Song Book I*.

120a. Motherland Song Book II. Ed. R. Vaughan Williams. 1919. Pub. Stainer & Bell.

120b. Motherland Song Book III. Includes arrs. of four sea shanties for unison and mixed voices by R. Vaughan Williams. 1919, Stainer & Bell; also pub. separately.

120c. Motherland Song Book IV. Arrs. of three sea shanties, as No. 120b.

121. Eight traditional English carols. Arr. for voice and piano or mixed choir a cappella. 1919. Pub. Stainer & Bell.

122. The turtle dove. Folksong arr. for male voices (TBB) and piano acc. ad lib. 1919. Pub. 1919, Curwen.

123. Three Preludes (founded on Welsh hymn tunes). For organ. 1920. Ded. Alan Gray. Dur. 8½′.
 1. *Bryn calfaria*; 2. *Rhosymedre*; 3. *Hyfrydol*.
 Pub. 1920, Stainer & Bell. Arr. for two pianos by Leslie Russell, 1939, Stainer & Bell. Nos. 2 & 3 orch. Arnold Foster pub. 1938 and 1951 respectively, Stainer & Bell.

124. O clap your hands. Motet for mixed chorus (SATB) and organ. 1920. Pub. 1920, Stainer & Bell.

124a. O clap your hands. Version with orch. acc.
 3 tpt, 3 tmb, tuba (ad lib); timp, cym (ad lib), organ.
 Pub. Stainer & Bell (hire).

125. Our love goes out to English skies (Harold Child). Patriotic Song for unison and mixed choir with acc., or for mixed or male chorus a cappella. 1920. Adapted from a march in 'The Indian Queen' by Henry Purcell. Pub. 1920, Stainer & Bell.

126. Twelve traditional carols from Herefordshire. Collected, edited and arr. for voice and piano, or to be sung unacc. (SATB), by Mrs. E. M. Leather and R. Vaughan Williams. Pub. 1920, Stainer & Bell.

127. The Lark Ascending. Romance for violin and orchestra. 1914–20. Ded. Marie Hall. Dur. 13′.
 2 fl, ob, 2 cl, 2 bsn; 2 hn; tgle; strings. *Chamber orchestra alternative:* fl, ob, cl, bsn; hn; tgle; strings.
 fp: 15 December 1920, Shirehampton, Public Hall, concert of the Avonmouth and Shirehampton Choral Society, Marie Hall with Geoffrey Mendham (piano).
 f London p: 14 June 1921, Queen's Hall, concert of the second congress of the British Music Society, Marie Hall and the British Symphony Orchestra, cond. (Sir) Adrian Boult.

fbp: 5 November 1924, Alfred M. Wall and Newcastle Station Augmented Orchestra, cond. Edward Clark.

Pub. 1925 (min. score), 1926 (full score) (reduction), O.U.P.

BIBLIOGRAPHY:

E. Spurgeon Knights: The Lark Ascending, a postscript, *Strad*, December 1941, p. 187.

128. Suite of six short pieces. For piano. *c.* 1920. Dur. 12′.

1. *Prelude*; 2. *Slow dance*; 3. *Quick dance*; 4. *Slow air*; 5. *Rondo*; 6. *Pezzo ostinato.*
Pub. 1921, Stainer & Bell.

128a. Charterhouse Suite. Version of preceding for string orchestra by James Brown in collaboration with the composer.

fbp: 8 April 1928, Wireless String Orchestra, cond. John Ansell.

Pub. 1923, Stainer & Bell.

129. Suite de ballet. For flute and piano. *c.* 1920. Dur. 7′.

1. *Improvisation*; 2. *Humoresque*; 3. *Gavotte*; 4. *Passepied.*
fp: 9 April 1962, BBC broadcast, Geoffrey Gilbert and Frederick Stone.

Pub. 1961, O.U.P.

130. Lord, Thou hast been our refuge. Motet for mixed chorus and semi-chorus (SATB) and orchestra (or organ). 1921. Dur. 7′.

2 fl, 2 ob, 2 cl, 2 bsn; 4 hn, 2 tpt, 3 tmb, tuba; timp; organ, strings.
Pub. 1921, Curwen.

131. The lass that loves a sailor. Words and music by Charles Dibdin, ed. and arr. for unison or SATB voices and piano. Pub. 1921, Stainer & Bell.

132. The mermaid. Old Song arr. for SATB voices a cappella or unison voices with piano. Pub. 1921, Stainer & Bell.

133. Heart of oak. Tune by William Boyce, arr. for unison voices and piano, or male voices (TTB) a cappella, or SATB voices and piano. Pub. 1921, Stainer & Bell.

134. The farmer's boy. Old English Air arr. for male voices (TTBB) a cappella. Pub. 1921, Stainer & Bell.

135. Loch Lomond. Scottish Air arr. for male voices (TTBB) a cappella. Pub. 1921, Stainer & Bell.

136. Old folks at home. Melody by Stephen Foster, arr. for male voices a cappella. Pub. 1921, Stainer & Bell.

137. Merciless Beauty. Three Rondels for high voice and string trio or piano. 1921. Words: doubtful authorship, attrib. Geoffrey Chaucer. Dur. 7′.

1. *Your eyën two*; 2. *So hath your beauty*; 3. *Since I from love.*
fp: 4 October 1921, Aeolian Hall, Steuart Wilson (tenor), Dorothy Longman and Kitty Farrer (violins), Valentine Orde (cello).

Pub. 1922, Curwen.

138. Fanfare. For double chorus of women's voices (SA), trumpets, cello, double bass and bells. Pub. 15 November 1921, in *Fanfare.*

139. A Pastoral Symphony. For orchestra with soprano (or tenor) voice. 1921. Dur. 35′.

1. *Molto moderato*; 2. *Lento moderato* (orig. *Andantino*); 3. *Moderato pesante*; 4. *Lento.*
3 fl, pic, 2 ob, ca, 3 cl, bcl, 2 bsn; 4 hn, 3 tpt, 3 tmb, bs tuba; timp, side dm, tgle, GC, cym, glock; hp, celesta, strings.

fp: 26 January 1922, Queen's Hall, Royal Philharmonic Society concert, Flora Mann (soprano), cond. (Sir) Adrian Boult.

fbp: 9 February 1924, relayed from Southwark Cathedral, London Symphony Orchestra.

Pub. 1924, Curwen.

BIBLIOGRAPHY:

Gerald Abraham: VW and his symphonies, 3: The Pastoral Symphony, *MS*, 1 May 1926, p. 142.

Eric Blom: VW, a Pastoral Symphony, *Music Teacher*, 12 December 1931, p. 666.

(Sir) Adrian Boult: Pastoral Symphony, *MN&H*, 1926, 9 January p. 27, 23 January p. 75.

H. C. Colles: A Pastoral Symphony, in *Essays and Lectures*, O.U.P. (London) 1945, p. 92.

Edwin Evans: A Pastoral Symphony, *MN&H*, 22 April 1922.

Eva Mary Grew: VW's Pastoral Symphony, *Midland Musician*, January 1926, p. 33.

Herbert Howells: VW's Pastoral Symphony, *M&L*, April 1922, p. 122.

— English Pastoral, *Radio Times*, 25 August 1933, p. 412.

D. Hugh Ottaway: VW and The Pastoral Symphony, *MT*, November 1949, p. 404.

— VW's Pastoral Symphony, *Halle*, December 1951, p. 4.

A. H. Fox Strangways: VW, the Pastoral Symphony, in *Music Observed*, Methuen (London) 1936, p. 131.

Donald F. Tovey: VW, Pastoral Symphony, in *EMA*, Vol. 2, O.U.P. (London) 1945, p. 92.

Anon.: Pastoral Symphony, *The Times*, 18 September 1926, p. 8.

Anon.: A Pastoral Symphony: Thought in sound, *The Times*, 28 January 1922, p. 8.

140. A farmer's son so sweet. Folksong arr. for male voices (TBarB) and piano (ad lib). 1921. Ded. The English Singers. Pub. 1923, Stainer & Bell.

141. Dirge for Fidele (Shakespeare). For two mezzo-sopranos and piano. Early composition, probably 1895. Pub. 1922, Ashdown.

142. O vos omnes (Is it nothing to you?). Motet for mixed voices (SSAATTBB) a cappella. 1922. Ded. Dr. R. R. Terry.

fp: 13 April 1922, Westminster Cathedral Choir, cond. R. R. Terry.

Pub. 1922, Curwen.

143. It was a lover and his lass (Shakespeare). Partsong for two voices and piano. Pub. 1922, Curwen.

144. Ca' the yowes (Robert Burns). Scottish folksong arr. for tenor and mixed chorus a cappella. Pub. 1922, Curwen.

145. Mass in G minor. For SATB soloists and double chorus a cappella (with ad lib organ part). c. 1920-1. Ded. Gustav Holst and his Whitsuntide Singers. Dur. 25'.

1. *Kyrie*; 2. *Gloria in excelsis*; 3. *Credo*; 4. *Sanctus—Osanna I—Benedictus—Osanna II*; 5. *Agnus Dei*.

fp: 6 December 1922, Birmingham, Town Hall, City of Birmingham Choir, cond. Joseph Lewis.

f liturgical p: 12 March 1923, Westminster

Cathedral, Choir of Westminster Cathedral, cond. R. R. Terry.

f London p (concert): 7 April 1923, Queen's Hall, Wolverhampton Music Society, cond. Joseph Lewis.

fbp: 26 June 1925, Aberystwyth Festival, University Hall, cond. R. Vaughan Williams.

Pub. 1922, Curwen.

145a. Communion Service in G minor. English version of preceding, adapted by Maurice Jacobson and revised by the composer.

1. *Responses to Commandments*; 2. *Kyrie*; 3. *Creed*; 4. *Sanctus*; 5. *Benedictus*; 6. *Agnus Dei*; 7. *Gloria in excelsis*.

Pub. 1923, 1951, Curwen.

146. The Shepherds of the Delectable Mountains. A Pastoral Episode founded upon 'The Pilgrim's Progress' by John Bunyan, in one act. For soloists, women's chorus (offstage) and small orchestra. 1922. Dur. 23'.

2 fl, ob, ca, strings. *Offstage*: 2 tpt, hp, 3 bells.

fp: 11 July 1922, Royal College of Music, cond. (Sir) Arthur Bliss, offstage orchestra cond. Gordon Jacob; with Archibald Winter, Leonard A. Willmore and Keith Falkner (Shepherds), Richard B. Kyle (Pilgrim), John K. Mckenna (Celestial Messenger); Dorcas M. Tomkins (Voice of a bird); producer, Humphrey Procter-Gregg.

fbp: 14 October 1935, BBC Midland Orchestra, cond. H. Foster Clark; with George Gibbs, Geoffrey Dams and Arthur Cranmer (Shepherds), Roy Henderson (Pilgrim), Harry Porter (Celestial Messenger), Jack Roberts (Voice of a bird).

Pub. 1925, O.U.P.

BIBLIOGRAPHY:

Scott Goddard: Pastoral episode, *Radio Times*, 11 October 1935, p. 12.

Hugh Ross: Medieval drama redivivus, *American Scholar*, winter 1936, p. 49.

147. High Germany. Folksong arr. for male voices and piano (ad lib). 1923. Pub. 1923, Novello.

148. Old King Cole. Ballet for orchestra and (ad lib) chorus. 1923. Dur. 22'.

3(2) fl, 2(1) ob, 2 cl, 2 bsn; 4(2) hn, 2 tpt,

2 ten tmb, bs tmb (ad lib if tuba is used), tuba; timp, glock (ad lib), tgle, side dm, GC, cym; celesta (ad lib), hp, strings.

fp: 5 June 1923, Cambridge, Nevile's Court, Trinity College, Festival of British music inaugurated by the University Musical Society, cond. Bernhard Ord.

fbp: 8 September 1924, Cardiff Station Orchestra, cond. ?Warwick Braithwaite.

Pub. 1924, 1925 (full score), Curwen. Piano reduction by Maurice Jacobson with violin obbligato (ad lib) by the composer, 1924.

149. English Folk Songs. Suite for military band. 1923. Dur. 11'.

1. *March: Seventeen come Sunday*; 2. *Intermezzo: My bonny boy*; 3. *March: Folk songs from Somerset*.

fp: 4 July 1923, Kneller Hall, Band of Royal Military School of Music, cond. Lieut. Hector E. Adkins.

Pub. 1924, Boosey & Hawkes. Arr. for piano solo by Michael Mullinar, 1949. Arr. for full orchestra by Gordon Jacob, 1942, Boosey & Hawkes. Arr. for brass band by Gordon Jacob, 1956, Boosey & Hawkes.

150. Sea Songs. Quick March for military and brass band. 1923. Dur. 4'.

?fp: April 1924, Wembley, British Empire Exhibition.

Pub. 1924, Boosey & Hawkes.

150a. Sea Songs. Version for orchestra by the composer. 1942.

2 fl, 2 ob, 2 cl, 2 bsn; 2 hn, 2 tpt, 2 tmb; timp, pcssn; strings. *Or:* 2 fl, cl; tpt, 2 tmb; timp, pcssn; strings.

Pub. 1943, Boosey & Hawkes.

151. Let us now praise famous men. Unison song with piano, organ or small orchestra (orch. version by Arnold Foster). 1923. Words from Ecclesiasticus. Pub. 1923, Curwen.

152. Two Pieces. For violin and piano. Composition date uncertain: possibly pre-1914.

1. *Romance*; 2. *Pastorale*.

Pub. 1923, Goodwin; Curwen.

153. Toccata marziale. For military band. 1924. Dur. 4'.

fp: 1924, Wembley, British Empire Exhibition, Band of Royal Military School of Music, cond. Lieut. H. E. Adkins.

Pub. 1924, Hawkes.

154. Hugh the Drover (or, Love in the Stocks). Romantic Ballad Opera in two acts. 1924. Words: Harold Child. Ded. Sir Hugh Allen. Dur. *c.* 120'.

2 fl, 2 ob, 2 cl, 2 bsn; 4 hn, 2 tpt, 3 tmb, tuba; timp, 4 pcssn; hp, strings; stage band.

fp: 4 July 1924, Royal College of Music (Parry Opera Theatre), cond. S. P. Waddington; with Trefor Jones (Hugh the Drover), H. Leyland White (John the Butcher), Keith Falkner (The Constable), William Wait (The Turnkey), Odette de Foras (Mary), Mona Benson (Aunt Jane); producer, Cairns James.

fbp & f public p: 14 July 1924, His Majesty's Theatre, British National Opera Company, cond. (Sir) Malcolm Sargent; with Tudor Davies (Hugh the Drover), Frederic Collier (John the Butcher), William Anderson (The Constable), Frederick Davies (The Turnkey), Mary Lewis (Mary), Constance Willis (Aunt Jane); producer, Cairns James.

Pub. 1924, Curwen.

BIBLIOGRAPHY:

R. Terence Casey: Hugh the Drover, *The Gramophone*, September 1950, p. 60.

J.D.: Hugh the Drover, *Opera*, No. 7, July 1924, p. 19.

A. H. Fox Strangways: Hugh the Drover, *London Mercury*, October 1924, p. 650.

Sir Steuart Wilson: Hugh the Drover, *Opera*, February 1950, p. 29.

155. Twenty-five vocal exercises. Founded on Bach's Mass in B minor. By Gertrude Sichel and R. Vaughan Williams. Pub. 1924, Stainer & Bell.

156. Mr. Isaacs Maggot. English traditional country dance tune arr. for clarinet, piano, triangle and strings. 1924. Unpub.

157. Two Poems by Seumas O'Sullivan. For voice and piano or unacc. voice. 1925.

1. *The twilight people*; 2. *A piper*.

fp: 27 March 1925, Aeolian Hall, Steuart Wilson, acc. Anthony Bernard.

Pub. 1925, O.U.P.

158. Three Songs from Shakespeare. For voice and piano. 1925.

1. *Take, o take, those lips away*; 2. *When icicles hang by the wall*; 3. *Orpheus with his lute.*

fp: 27 March 1925, Aeolian Hall, Steuart Wilson, acc. Anthony Bernard.

Pub. 1925, O.U.P.

159. Four Poems by Fredegond Shove. For voice and piano. 1925.

1. *Motion and stillness* (Comp. 1922); 2. *Four nights*; 3. *The new ghost*; 4. *The water mill.*

fp: 27 March 1925, Aeolian Hall, Steuart Wilson, acc. Anthony Bernard.

Pub. 1925, O.U.P.

160. Three Poems by Walt Whitman. For voice and piano. 1925.

1. *Nocturne*; 2. *A clear midnight*; 3. *Joy, shipmate, joy!*

Pub. 1925, O.U.P.

161. Flos Campi. Suite for viola, small wordless mixed chorus and small orchestra. Ded. Lionel Tertis. Dur. 20′.

fl, pic, ob, cl, bsn; hn, tpt; GC, cym, tgle, tabor; hp, celesta, strings.

fp: 10 October 1925, Queen's Hall, Lionel Tertis, choir from Royal College of Music, Queen's Hall Orchestra, cond. Sir Henry Wood.

Pub. 1928, O.U.P. Reduction by Gordon Jacob.

BIBLIOGRAPHY:

Eric Blom: King Solomon and VW, *The Listener*, 11 July 1940, p. 69.

Cecil Gray: VW and Holst, *The Nation*, 21 November 1925, p. 290.

162. Sancta Civitas (The Holy City). Oratorio for tenor, baritone, mixed chorus, semi-chorus, distant chorus and orchestra. 1923–5. Dur. 31′.

3 fl, 2 ob, ca, 2 cl, 2 bsn, dbsn; 4 hn, 3 tpt, 3 tmb, tuba; side dm, GC, cym; piano, hp, organ, strings.

fp: 7 May 1926, Oxford, Sheldonian Theatre, Arthur Cranmer, Trefor Jones, Oxford Bach Choir and Oxford Orchestral Society, cond. H. P. Allen.

f London p: 9 June 1926, Central Hall (Westminster), Roy Henderson, Steuart Wilson, The Bach Choir, The Temple Choristers, G. Thalben-Ball (organ), London Symphony Orchestra, cond. R. Vaughan Williams.

Pub. 1925, Curwen. Vocal score, Havergal Brian.

BIBLIOGRAPHY:

A. H. Fox Strangways: Sancta Civitas, *British Musician*, October 1927, p. 165.

163. Concerto in D minor (orig. Concerto Accademico). For violin and string orchestra. 1924–5. Ded. Jelly d'Aranyi. Dur. 14′.

1. *Allegro pesante*; 2. *Adagio—tranquillo*; 3. *Presto.*

fp: 6 November 1925, Aeolian Hall, Gerald Cooper concert, Jelly d'Aranyi and the London Chamber Orchestra, cond. Anthony Bernard.

fbp: 3 June 1928, William Primrose and National Orchestra of Wales, cond. Warwick Braithwaite.

Pub. 1927, O.U.P. Reduction by Constant Lambert.

BIBLIOGRAPHY:

Herbert Howells: VW's Concerto Accademico, *The Dominant*, March 1928, p. 24.

William Mann: VW, Concerto accademico, in *The Concerto*, Pelican Books (London) 1952, p. 422.

D. F. Tovey: VW, Concerto accademico, in *EMA*, Vol. 2, O.U.P. (London) 1935, p. 205.

164. Darest thou now, o soul (Walt Whitman). Unison song for voice and piano or strings. Pub. 1925, Curwen.

165. The Giant Fugue. J. S. Bach, arr. for strings by R. Vaughan Williams and Arnold Foster. 1925.

fbp: 18 April 1926, Newcastle Station String Orchestra, cond. Edward Clark.

Pub. 1925, Curwen.

166. Magnificat & Nunc Dimittis (The Village Service). For mixed chorus and organ. Pub. 1925, Curwen.

167. Songs of Praise. Music Editors, R. Vaughan Williams and Martin Shaw. Includes original tunes and arrangements by Vaughan Williams. Pub. 1925, O.U.P.

168. Six Studies in English folksong. For cello and piano. 1926. Ded. May Mukle. Dur. 10'.

1. *Adagio*; 2. *Andante sostenuto*; 3. *Larghetto*; 4. *Lento*; 5. *Andante tranquillo*; 6. *Allegro vivace*.

fp: 4 June 1926, Scala Theatre (London), English Folk Dance Society Festival, May Mukle and Anne Mukle.

Pub. 1927, Stainer & Bell.

169. Along the Field. Eight Housman songs for voice and violin. ?1926.

1. *We'll to the woods no more*; 2. *Along the field*; 3. *The half-moon westers low*; 4. *In the morning*; 5. *The sigh that heaves the grasses*; 6. *Goodbye*; 7. *Fancy's knell*; 8. *With rue my heart is laden*.

fp (seven only): 8 August 1926, BBC broadcast, Joan Elwes and Samuel Kutcher.

f concert p (seven only): 24 October 1927, Grotrian Hall, Joan Elwes and Marie Wilson.

fp (revised version): 26 May 1955, Wigmore Hall, Nancy Evans and Leonard Hirsch.

Pub. 1954, O.U.P.

170. On Christmas Night. A Masque with dancing, singing and miming, freely adapted from Dickens's 'A Christmas Carol' by Adolf Bolm and R. Vaughan Williams. Music by R. Vaughan Williams devised as a quodlibet of folk-tunes and country dances. Ded. Douglas Kennedy. Dur. 30'.

fl, pic, ob, cl, bsn; hn, tpt, ten tmb; timp, 2 pcssn; hp, celesta (ad lib), piano, strings.

fp: 26 December 1926, Chicago (Ill.), Eighth Street Theatre, Bolm Ballet. the Delamarter Orchestra, cond. Eric Delamarter.

f concert p (as *A Christmas Carol Suite*): 17 December 1929, Park Lane Hotel, New English Music Society concert, cond. Anthony Bernard.

fEp (as a ballet): 29 December 1935, Cecil Sharp House, cond. Imogen Holst; with Douglas Kennedy (The Watchman), Anna Walker (The Virgin Mary); producer, Frederick Wilkinson.

Pub. 1957, O.U.P. Vocal score, Roy Douglas.

171. Te Deum in G. For men's and boys' voices with organ or orchestra. 1928. Orch. Arnold Foster. Composed for the enthrone-ment of Dr. Cosmo Gordon Lang as Arch-bishop of Canterbury.

2 fl, 2 ob, 2 cl, 2 bsn; 4(2) hn, 2 tpt, 3 tmb, tuba (ad lib); timp, cym; piano, strings.

fp: 4 December 1928, Canterbury Cathe-dral, Choirs of Canterbury Cathedral and the Chapel Royal, Charlton Palmer (organ), cond. H. Walford Davies.

Pub. 1928, O.U.P.

172. The Oxford Book of Carols. Music editors, R. Vaughan Williams and Martin Shaw. Includes original tunes and arrange-ments by R. Vaughan Williams. Pub. 1928, O.U.P.

173. Sir John in Love. Opera in four acts, after Shakespeare. 1924–8. Ded. S. P. Wad-dington. Dur. *c*. 120'.

2 fl, 2 ob, ca, 2 cl, 2 bsn; 2 hn, 2 tpt, tmb; timp, pcssn, rattle, bells; hp, strings.

fp: 21 March 1929, Royal College of Music (Parry Opera Theatre), cond. (Sir) Malcolm Sargent; with Leyland White (Sir John Falstaff), Clifford White (Ford), May Moore (Mrs. Page), Olive Evers (Anne Page), Veronica Mansfield (Mrs. Ford), Hilda Rickard (Mrs. Quickly), A. Bamfield Cooper (Fenton), Douglas Tichener (Dr. Caius); producer, Cairns James; scenery, H. Procter-Gregg and Simpson Robinson.

Pub. 1930, O.U.P.

173a. Prologue, Episode and Interlude. From 'Sir John in Love'.

Instrumentation as for No. 173.

fp: 30 October 1933, Clifton (Victoria Rooms), cond. Robert Percival; with Dorothy Hill (The Queen), Percival Goodway (Fal-staff); producer, Robert Percival.

Pub. 1936, O.U.P. *Prologue* withdrawn.

173b. In Windsor Forest. Cantata for mixed chorus and orchestra, adapted from 'Sir John in Love'. Dur. 16'.

2 fl, 2 ob, 2 cl, 2 bsn; 2 hn, 2 tpt, tmb; timp, pcssn; hp (or piano), strings. *Or:* strings and piano.

1. *The conspiracy*; 2. *Drinking song*; 3. *Fal-staff and the fairies*; 4. *Wedding chorus*; 5. *Epilogue*.

fp: 9 November 1931, Windsor, Royal Albert Institute, Choir of H.M. Free Chapel of St. George and H.M. Private Chapel, Windsor Castle, Henry Ley (piano), cond. R. Vaughan Williams.

Pub. 1931, O.U.P.

174. Benedicite. For soprano, mixed chorus and orchestra. 1929. Ded. L.H.M.C. (Leith Hill Musical Competition) Towns Division. Dur. 15'.

2 fl, pic, 2 ob, 2 cl, 2 bsn; 4 hn, 2 tpt, 3 tmb; timp, pcssn; celesta (ad lib), piano, strings. *Or:* 2 fl, ob, 2 cl, bsn; 2 hn, tpt, tmb; piano, strings. *Or:* strings and piano.

fp: 2 May 1903, Dorking (Drill Hall), Leith Hill Musical Festival, Margaret Rees, Leith Hill Festival Chorus and Orchestra, cond. R. Vaughan Williams.

f London p: 21 February 1931, Southwark Cathedral, Joan Elwes, special choir, C. Thornton Lofthouse (piano), London Symphony Orchestra, cond. Edgar T. Cook.

fbp: 19 March 1931, Aeolian Hall, New English Choir and London Chamber Orchestra, cond. Anthony Bernard.

Pub. 1929, O.U.P.

175. The Hundredth Psalm. For mixed chorus and orchestra. 1929. Ded. L.H.M.C. (Leith Hill Musical Competition) Division II. Dur. 8'.

2 fl, 2(1) ob, 2 cl, 2 bsn, dbsn (ad lib); 4(2) hn, 2 tpt, tmb (ad lib), tuba; timp (ad lib), cym (ad lib); organ (ad lib), strings. *Or:* strings and organ or piano.

fp: 29 April 1930, Dorking (Drill Hall), Leith Hill Festival Chorus and Orchestra, cond. R. Vaughan Williams.

f London p: 24 May 1930, Morley College Chorus and Orchestra, cond. Arnold Foster.

Pub. 1929, Stainer & Bell.

176. Three Choral Hymns. For baritone (or tenor), mixed chorus and orchestra. 1929. Words: Miles Coverdale, Bishop of Exeter, transl. from the German. Ded. L.H.M.C. (Leith Hill Musical Competition) Division I. Dur. 11'.

1. *Easter hymn*; 2. *Christmas hymn*; 3. *Whitsunday hymn*.

fp: 30 April 1930, Dorking (Drill Hall), Ian Glennie, Leith Hill Festival Chorus and Orchestra, cond. R. Vaughan Williams.

f London p: 21 February 1931, Southwark

Cathedral, William Groves, special choir and London Symphony Orchestra, cond. Edgar T. Cook.

Pub. 1930, Curwen.

177. Three children's songs for a Spring festival. For unison voices and strings. 1929. Words: Frances M. Farrer. Ded. L.H.M.C. (Leith Hill Musical Competition) Children's Division.

1. *Spring*; 2. *The singers*; 3. *An invitation*.

fp: 1 May 1930, Dorking (Drill Hall), Leith Hill Festival Children's Choirs, cond. R. Vaughan Williams.

Pub. 1930, O.U.P.

178. Songs of Praise for boys and girls. Editors, Rev. Percy Dearmer, R. Vaughan Williams and Martin Shaw. Includes one original tune (No. 95, *Marathon*) especially written for the volume and various arrangements by Vaughan Williams. Pub. 1929, O.U.P.

179. Fantasia on Sussex folk tunes. For cello and orchestra. 1929. Ded. Pablo Casals.

2 fl, pic, ob, 2 cl, 2 bsn; 2 hn, tpt; timp; strings.

fp: 13 March 1930, Queen's Hall, Royal Philharmonic Society concert, Pablo Casals, cond. (Sir) John Barbirolli.

Unpub.

180. Hymn Tune Prelude on 'Song 13' by Orlando Gibbons. For piano. 1928. Ded. Harriet Cohen.

fp: 14 January 1930, Wigmore Hall, Harriet Cohen.

fbp: 18 April 1930, Harriet Cohen.

Pub. 1930, O.U.P.

181. Prelude and Fugue in C minor. For orchestra. 1921–30. Ded. Henry Ley. Dur. 10'.

1. *Prelude*. September 1921, rev. July 1923, March 1930.

2. *Fugue*. August 1921, rev. July 1923, March 1930.

3 fl, 2 ob, 2 cl, 2 bsn, dbsn; 4 hn, 3 tpt, 3 tmb, tuba; timp, 2 pcssn; organ, strings.

fp: 12 September 1930, Hereford Cathedral, Three Choirs Festival, London Symphony Orchestra, cond. R. Vaughan Williams.

Pub. O.U.P. (Hire).

182. Job. A Masque for dancing, founded on Blake's Illustrations of the Book of Job. 1930. Scenario: Geoffrey Keynes and Gwendolen Raverat. Ded. (Sir) Adrian Boult. Dur. 45'.

2(1) fl, bs fl, 2(1) ob, ca, 3(2) cl, bcl (ad lib), sax, 2 bsn, dbsn (ad lib); 4 hn, 3(2) tpt, 3 tmb, tuba; timp, side dm, tgle, cym, GC, xyl, glock, tamtam; 2(1) hp, organ (ad lib), strings.

Instrumentation for theatre orchestra (by Constant Lambert): 2 fl, pic, ob, 2 cl, sax; 2 hn, 2 tpt, tmb; timp, cym, GC, xyl, glock, tamtam; hp, strings.

fp: 23 October 1930, Norwich Festival, St. Andrew's Hall, Queen's Hall Orchestra, cond. R. Vaughan Williams.

fbp: 13 February 1931, BBC Symphony Orchestra, cond. R. Vaughan Williams.

f public p: 3 December 1931, Queen's Hall, Royal Philharmonic Society concert, Royal Philharmonic Society Orchestra, cond. Basil Cameron.

fp (stage version): 5 July 1931, Cambridge Theatre (London), cond. Constant Lambert; with John MacNair (Job), Anton Dolin (Satan), Stanley Judson (Elihu); scenery and costumes, Gwendolen Raverat; choreography, Ninette de Valois.

Pub. 1934 (full score), 1935 (min. score), O.U.P. Piano reduction, Vally Lasker, pub. 1931.

BIBLIOGRAPHY:
Eric Blom: Job, *Music Teacher*, February 1934, p. 93.
H. C. Colles: Job, in *Essays and Lectures*, O.U.P. (London) 1945, p. 101.
A. E. F. Dickinson: War in heaven, *The Listener*, 8 January 1948, p. 76.
Dyneley Hussey: VW and the masque of Job, *Dancing Times*, 1948, June, p. 461, July, p. 529.
Frank Howes: The music of Job, in *Job and the Rake's Progress,* Sadler's Wells Ballet Books No. 2, Bodley Head (London) 1949, p. 35.
Geoffrey Keynes: Job, in *–do–*, p. 24.
Michael Kennedy: VW's Job, *Halle*, April 1955, p. 2.
Herbert Murrill: William Blake and VW, *Radio Times*, 17 February 1933, p. 389.

183. Piano Concerto in C major. 1926–31. Ded. Harriet Cohen. Dur. 25'.

1. *Toccata (Allegro moderato)*; 2. *Romanza (Lento)*; 3. *Fuga chromatica, con finale alla tedesca.*

2 fl, pic, 2 ob, 2 cl, 2 bsn; 4 hn, 2 tpt, 3 tmb, tuba; timp, side dm, cym, GC, tamtam; organ pedal (ad lib), strings.

fp: 1 February 1933, Queen's Hall, Harriet Cohen and the BBC Symphony Orchestra, cond. Sir Adrian Boult.

Pub. 1936, O.U.P.

BIBLIOGRAPHY:
Frank Howes: VW's Pianoforte Concerto, *MT*, October 1933, p. 883.
William Mann: VW, piano concerto, in *The Concerto*, Pelican Books (London) 1952, p. 425.

183a. Concerto for two pianos and orchestra. Version of preceding by Joseph Cooper in collaboration with the composer.

fp: 22 November 1946, Royal Albert Hall, Cyril Smith and Phyllis Sellick, London Philharmonic and London Symphony Orchestras, cond. Sir Adrian Boult.

Unpub.

184. Magnificat. For contralto, women's choir, flute and orchestra. 1932. Ded. Astra Desmond. Dur. 12'.

2 fl, 2(1) ob, ca, 2 cl, 2 bsn; 4 hn, 2 tpt; timp; hp, celesta (ad lib), strings. *Or:* organ (or piano) with flute or violin obbligato.

fp: 8 September 1932, Worcester Cathedral, Three Choirs Festival, Astra Desmond, Festival Chorus and London Symphony Orchestra, cond. R. Vaughan Williams.

f London p: 1 May 1934, Queen's Hall, Blodwen Caerleon, Philharmonic Choir and London Symphony Orchestra, cond. C. Kennedy Scott.

Pub. 1932, O.U.P.

185. Choral and Choral Prelude. 'Ach, Bleib bei uns, Herr Jesu Christ.' J. S. Bach, freely arr. for piano. 1932. For 'A Bach Book for Harriet Cohen'. Pub. 1932, O.U.P.

186. The Running Set. For orchestra. 1933. Founded on traditional dance tunes. Dur. 5'.

fl, pic, 2(1) ob, 2 cl, 2 bsn; 2(1) hn, 2(1) tpt; side dm, tgle; piano (ad lib), strings.

fp: 6 January 1934, Royal Albert Hall, National Folk Dance Festival, orchestra cond. R. Vaughan Williams.

fp (concert): 27 September 1934, Queen's Hall, BBC Symphony Orchestra, cond. R. Vaughan Williams.

Pub. 1936 (arr. for two pianos by Vally Lasker and Helen Bidder), 1952 (full score), O.U.P.

187. Passacaglia on B.G.C. For organ. 1933. Unpub.

188. Henry the Fifth. Overture for brass band. 1933. Unpub.

189. The Golden Vanity. March for military band. 1933. Unpub.

190. Fantasia on 'Greensleeves'. Adapted from 'Sir John in Love', arr. for strings and harp (or piano) with one or two optional flutes by Ralph Greaves. Dur. 5'.

fp (concert): 27 September 1934, Queen's Hall, BBC Symphony Orchestra, cond. R. Vaughan Williams.

Pub. 1934, O.U.P.

191. An acre of land. English folksong for male voices (TTBB) with piano acc. ad lib. Pub. 1934, O.U.P.

192. John Dory. English folksong arr. for mixed voices (SATB) a cappella. Pub. 1934, O.U.P.

193. I'll never love thee more (James Graham). For mixed voices (SATB) a cappella. Pub. 1934, O.U.P.

194. The world it went well with me then. Old English Air from Chappell's 'Popular Music', arr. for male voices (TTBB) a cappella. Pub. 1934, O.U.P.

195. Tobacco's but an Indian weed. Old English Air from Chappell's 'Popular Music', arr. for male voices (TTBB) a cappella. Pub. 1934, O.U.P.

196. The ploughman. English folksong arr. for male voices (TTBB) with piano acc. ad lib. Pub. 1934, O.U.P.

197. The Pilgrim Pavement (Margaret Ridgeley Partridge). Hymn for soprano, mixed chorus and organ. Pub. 1934, O.U.P.

198. Six teaching pieces. For piano.

Book I: *Two 2-part Inventions*; Book II: *Valse Lente & Nocturne*; Book III: *Canon & 2-part Invention*.

Pub. 1934, O.U.P.

199. Music for 'The Pageant of Abinger'. 1934.

199a. O how amiable. Anthem for the dedication of a church or other festivals, for mixed chorus and organ. Originally composed for preceding. Ded. F.F. (Dame Frances Farrer). Pub. 1940, O.U.P.

200. Suite for viola and small orchestra. 1934. Ded. Lionel Tertis.

Group I: *Prelude*; *Carol*; *Christmas dance*. Group II: *Ballad*; *Moto perpetuo*. Group III: *Musette*; *Polka mélancolique*; *Galop*.

2 fl, pic, ob, 2 cl, 2 bsn; 2 hn, 2 tpt; timp, side dm, tgle; celesta, hp, strings.

fp: 12 November 1934, Queen's Hall, Lionel Tertis and the London Philharmonic Orchestra, cond. (Sir) Malcolm Sargent.

Pub. 1936 (reduction), 1963 (full score), O.U.P.

201. Folksongs from Newfoundland. Piano accompaniments for some numbers in the collection pub. 1934, O.U.P.

202. Symphony (No. 4) in F minor. 1931–1934. Ded. Arnold Bax. Dur. 33'.

1. *Allegro*; 2. *Andante moderato*; 3. *Scherzo (Allegro molto)*; 4. *Finale con Epilogo fugato (Allegro molto)*.

3(2) fl, pic, 3 ob, ca, 2 cl, bcl (ad lib), 2 bsn, dbsn (ad lib); 4 hn, 2 tpt, 3 tmb, tuba; timp, side dm, tgle, cym, GC; strings.

fp: 10 April 1935, Queen's Hall, BBC Symphony Orchestra, cond. Sir Adrian Boult.

Pub. 1935, O.U.P.

BIBLIOGRAPHY:

Frank Howes: A powerful symphony, *Radio Times*, 5 April 1935, p. 12.

N. Gerrard Long: VW's fourth symphony, a study in interpretation, *MMR*, June 1947, p. 116.

D. Hugh Ottaway: VW's Symphony in F minor, *Halle*, November 1950, p. 11.

— VW's F minor Symphony, *The Listener*, 8 August 1963, p. 217.

Vaughan Williams, Ralph

Ursula Vaughan Williams: Symphony No. 4 in F minor, *Crescendo*, No. 140, March 1965, p. 110.

203. Folk Songs Vol. II. Includes three songs selected and arr. by R. Vaughan Williams. Pub. 1935, Novello.

204. Two English folksongs. Arr. for voice and violin. Ded. Margaret Longman.
1. *Searching for lambs*; 2. *The lawyer*.
Pub. 1935, O.U.P.

205. Six English folksongs. Arr. for voice and piano. Pub. 1935, O.U.P.

206. My soul praise the Lord. Hymn arr. for mixed chorus and unison singing with descant, and organ (or strings and organ). Pub. ?1935, S.P.C.K.; 1947, O.U.P.

207. Five Tudor Portraits. Choral Suite for contralto (or mezzo-soprano), baritone, mixed chorus and orchestra, founded on poems by John Skelton. 1935. Dur. 42′.
1. *The Tunning of Elinor Rumming*. Ballad for contralto, chorus and orchestra.
2. *Pretty Bess*. Intermezzo for baritone, chorus and orchestra.
3. *Epitaph on John Jayberd of Diss*. Burlesca for male chorus and orchestra.
4. *Jane Scroop* (*Her Lament for Philip Sparrow*). Romanza for mezzo-soprano, women's chorus and orchestra.
5. *Jolly Rutterkin*. Scherzo for baritone, chorus and orchestra.
3 fl, pic, 2 ob, ca, 2 cl, 2 bsn, dbsn; 4 hn, 2 tpt, 3 tmb, tuba; timp, 2 pcssn; hp, strings.
fp: 25 September 1936, Norwich Festival, St. Andrew's Hall, Astra Desmond, Roy Henderson, Festival Chorus, London Philharmonic Orchestra, cond. R. Vaughan Williams.
f London p: 27 January 1937, Queen's Hall, Astra Desmond, Roy Henderson, Croydon Philharmonic Society, BBC Chorus, BBC Symphony Orchestra, cond. Sir Adrian Boult.
Pub. 1935, O.U.P.

BIBLIOGRAPHY:
H. C. Colles: Five Tudor Portraits, in *Essays and Lectures*, O.U.P. (London) 1945, p. 104.

Alan Frank: Reincarnating Skelton, *The Listener*, 20 January 1937, p. 141.
Frank Howes: Five Tudor Portraits, *The Listener*, 15 August 1940, p. 249.

208. Little cloister. Hymn tune for unison voices and organ. Pub. 1935, O.U.P.

209. Flourish of trumpets for a folk dance festival. For brass and percussion.
fp: 17 July 1935, Royal Albert Hall, International Folk Dance Festival.
Unpub.

210. Nothing is here for tears. Choral Song (unison or SATB) with piano, organ or orchestra. 1936. Words adapted from Milton. Composed upon the death of King George V.
2 tpt, 3 tmb, tuba; timp, pcssn; organ, strings. Or: 2 fl, 2(1) ob, 2 cl, 2 bsn; 4(2) hn, 2 tpt, 3 tmb (ad lib), tuba (ad lib); timp, pcssn; organ (ad lib); strings. Or: strings and piano.
fp: 26 January 1936, BBC broadcast, BBC Singers, cond. Sir Walford Davies.
Pub. 1936, O.U.P.

211. The Poisoned Kiss (or, The Empress and the Necromancer). Romantic Extravaganza, with spoken dialogue, written by Evelyn Sharp, adapted from a story by Richard Garnett. 1927–9, rev. 1934–5, 1936–7, 1956–7. Dur. *c.* 120′.
2 fl, pic, ob, ca, 2 cl, bsn; 2 hn, 2 tpt, tmb; timp, 2 pcssn; hp (or piano), strings.
fp: 12 May 1936, Cambridge, Arts Theatre, cond. C. B. Rootham; with Mabel [Margaret] Ritchie (Tormentilla), Frederick Woodhouse (Dipsacus), Margaret Field-Hyde (Angelica), Trefor Jones (Amaryllus), Meriel St. Clair (The Empress), Geoffrey Dunn (Gallanthus); producer, Camille Prior.
f London p: 18 May 1936, Sadler's Wells, same cast, cond. R. Vaughan Williams.
Pub. 1936, O.U.P.

BIBLIOGRAPHY:
Scott Goddard: The Poisoned Kiss, *The Listener*, 27 November 1941, p. 737.
Frank Howes: The Poisoned Kiss, *MMR*, June 1936, p. 97.

211a. The Poisoned Kiss: Overture. Dur. 7′.

fp: 8 September 1937, Gloucester, Shire Hall, Three Choirs Festival, London Symphony Orchestra, cond. R. Vaughan Williams.

Pub. O.U.P. (Hire).

211b. Introduction and Scene from 'The Poisoned Kiss'. For tenor, mixed chorus and orchestra. Dur. 12′.

2 fl, pic, ob, 2 cl, bsn; 2 hn; tgle; hp (or piano), strings.

fp: as for No. 211a, with Trefor Jones (tenor).

Unpub. Withdrawn.

212. Dona nobis pacem. Cantata for soprano, baritone, mixed chorus and orchestra. 1936. Text: Walt Whitman, John Bright, and Biblical.

1. *Agnus Dei*; 2. *Beat! beat! Drums!*; 3. *Reconciliation*; 4. *Dirge for two veterans*; 5. (a) *The Angel of Death*, (b) *We looked for peace*, (c) *O man, greatly beloved*, (d) *The glory of this latter house*; (e) *Nation shall not lift up sword against nation*.

3 fl, pic, 2 ob, 2 cl, 2 bsn, dbsn; 4 hn, 4(2) tpt, 5(3) tmb, tuba; timp, pcssn; bells, hp, organ (ad lib), strings. *Or:* strings and piano.

fp: 2 October 1936, Huddersfield, Town Hall, Renée Flynn, Roy Henderson, Huddersfield Choral Society and Halle Orchestra, cond. Albert Coates.

fbp: 13 November 1936, Renée Flynn, Roy Henderson, BBC Chorus and Orchestra, cond. Sir Adrian Boult.

f London p: 5 February 1938, Queen's Hall, Elsie Suddaby, Redvers Llewellyn, Royal Choral Society and London Philharmonic Orchestra, cond. (Sir) Malcolm Sargent.

Pub. 1936, O.U.P.

213. Riders to the Sea. Opera in one act. 1925–32. Text: J. M. Synge. Dur. 37′.

2 fl, pic, ob, ca, bcl, bsn; 2 hn, tpt; timp, GC, sea-machine; strings.

fp: 30 November 1937 (private dress rehearsal), 1 December 1937 (first public performance), Royal College of Music, Palmer Fund for Opera Study, cond. (Sir) Malcolm Sargent; with Olive Hall (Maurya), Janet Smith-Miller (Cathleen), Marjorie Steventon (Nora), Alan Coad (Bartley), Grace Wilkinson (A Woman).

Pub. 1936, O.U.P.

BIBLIOGRAPHY:

F. L. Lunghi: Cavalcate a mare di RVW, *Santa Cecilia*, February 1959, p. 49.

D. Hugh Ottaway: Riders to the Sea, *MT*, August 1952, p. 358.

'Speculum': Riders to the sea, note di passaggio, *La Rassegna musicale*, May–June 1938.

214. Two Hymn-tune Preludes. For small orchestra. 1936. Dur. 6½′.

1. *Eventide*; 2. *Dominus regit me*.

fl, ob, cl, bsn; hn; strings.

fp: 8 September 1936, Hereford Cathedral, Three Choirs Festival, London Symphony Orchestra, cond. R. Vaughan Williams.

Pub. 1960, O.U.P.

215. Flourish for a Coronation. For mixed chorus and orchestra. 1937. Words: Biblical, Chaucer, Agincourt Song. Dur. 13′.

3 fl, 2 ob, 3 cl, alto sax, 2 bsn, dbsn; 8 hn, 6 tpt, 3 tmb, euphonium, tuba; timp, 2 pcssn, glock, bells; 2 hp, organ, piano, strings. *Or:* 2 fl, 2 ob, 2 cl, 2 bsn; 4 hn, 2 tpt, 3 tmb, tuba; timp; strings.

fp: 1 April 1937, Queen's Hall, Royal Philharmonic Society concert, Philharmonic Choir and London Philharmonic Orchestra, cond. Sir Thomas Beecham.

Pub. 1937, O.U.P.

216. Festival Te Deum in F major. Founded on traditional themes, for mixed chorus and organ or orchestra. 1937. Dur. 9′.

3(2) fl, 3(2) ob, 2 cl, bcl (ad lib), 2 bsn, dbsn; 4 hn, 3(2) tpt, 3 tmb, tuba; timp, 2 pcssn; organ, strings.

fp: 12 May 1937, Westminster Abbey, Coronation of King George VI, special choir and orchestra, cond. Sir Adrian Boult.

Pub. 1937, O.U.P.

217. Te Deum. Antonin Dvořák, English adaptation by R. Vaughan Williams. Pub. 1937, Simrock.

218. Music for English Folk Dance Society Masque. 1937.

2 fl, pic, ob, 2 bsn; hn, tpt; timp (ad lib), tgle; strings.

fp: 9 January 1937, Royal Albert Hall, cond. R. Vaughan Williams.

Unpub.

219. England's Pleasant Land. Music for a pageant by various composers, including R. Vaughan Williams. For mixed chorus and military band.

fp: 9 July 1938, Milton Court, Westcott (Surrey), Band of the 2nd Bn. the Duke of Cornwall's Light Infantry, cond. A. Young.
Unpub.

220. Serenade to Music. For 16 solo voices and orchestra. 1938. Text: Shakespeare. Composed for and ded. Sir Henry Wood on the occasion of his jubilee. Dur. 14′.

2 fl, pic, ob, ca, 2 cl, 2 bsn; 4 hn, 2 tpt, 3 tmb, tuba; timp, pcssn; hp, strings. *Or:* strings and piano.

fp: 5 October 1938, Albert Hall, Jubilee Concert of Sir Henry Wood, Isobel Baillie, Elsie Suddaby, Eva Turner, Margaret Balfour, Muriel Brunskill, Astra Desmond, Mary Jarred, Parry Jones, Heddle Nash, Frank Titteron, Walter Widdop, Norman Allin, Robert Easton, Roy Henderson, Harold Williams, BBC Symphony, London Symphony, London Philharmonic and Queen's Hall Orchestras, cond. Sir Henry Wood.
Pub. 1938 (vocal score), 1961 (full score), O.U.P.

220a. Serenade to Music. Version for orchestra.

2 fl, ob, ca, 2 cl, 2 bsn; 4 hn, 2 tpt, 3 tmb, tuba; timp, pcssn; hp, solo violin, strings.

fp: 10 February 1940, Queen's Hall, London Symphony Orchestra, cond. Sir Henry Wood.
Pub. O.U.P. (Hire).

221. All hail the power. Hymn tune 'Miles Lane' by W. Shrubsole arr. for unison (congregation), mixed chorus and organ or orchestra. 1938. Ded. Ivor Atkins.

2 fl, 2(1) ob, 2 cl, 2 bsn, dbsn (ad lib); 4(2) hn, 3(2) tpt, 3 tmb, tuba; timp, pcssn; organ, strings.
Pub. 1938, O.U.P.

222. Double Trio. For string sextet. 1938.

1. *Fantasia*; 2. *Scherzo Ostinato*; 3. *Intermezzo* (*Homage to Henry Hall*); 4. *Rondo*.

fp: 21 January 1939, Wigmore Hall, The Menges Sextet.

fbp: 12 March 1939, The Menges Sextet.

fp (revised version): 12 October 1942, National Gallery, The Menges Sextet.
Unpub. Withdrawn.

222a. Partita for double string orchestra. 1946–8. Rewritten version of preceding. Ded. R. Müller Hartmann. Dur. 21′.

fp: 20 March 1948, BBC broadcast, BBC Symphony Orchestra, cond. Sir Adrian Boult.

fp (concert): 29 July 1948, Royal Albert Hall, Promenade Concert, BBC Symphony Orchestra, cond. R. Vaughan Williams.
Pub. 1948, O.U.P.

223. The Bridal Day. Masque by Ursula Wood (Ursula Vaughan Williams) founded on Epithalamion by Edmund Spenser. For baritone, speaker, dancers, mimers, mixed chorus and instrumental ensemble. 1938–9, rev. 1952–3.

fl, pic, piano, 2 v, va, c, db. *Or:* flute and piano.

fp: 5 June 1953, BBC Television, Cecil Day Lewis (narrator), Denis Dowling (baritone), Michael Mullinar (piano), Chorus and the Wigmore Ensemble, cond. Stanford Robinson; producer, Christian Simpson; choreography, David Paltenghi; settings, John Clements.
Pub. 1956, O.U.P.

223a. Epithalamion. Cantata founded on preceding. For baritone, mixed chorus and small orchestra. 1957. Dur. 37′.

fl, pic, piano, strings.

fp: 30 September 1957, Royal Festival Hall, Gordon Clinton, Goldsmiths' Choral Union Cantata Singers and Royal Philharmonic Orchestra, cond. Richard Austin.
Pub. 1957, O.U.P.

224. Services in D minor. For unison voices, mixed choir and organ. 1939. Ded. Dr. C. S. Lang and his singers at Christ's Hospital.

1. *Morning Service*; 2. *Communion Service*; 3. *Evening Service*.
Pub. 1939, O.U.P.

225. Five Variants of 'Dives and Lazarus'. For strings and harp (two harps if possible). 1939. Dur. 13′.

fp: 10 June 1939, New York, World Fair concert, Carnegie Hall, New York Philharmonic Symphony Orchestra, cond. Sir Adrian Boult.

fEp: 1 November 1939, Bristol, Colston Hall, BBC Symphony Orchestra, cond. Sir Adrian Boult.

Pub. 1940, O.U.P.

226. Suite for pipes. For treble, alto, tenor and bass pipes. 1938 or 1939. Dur. 11'.

1. *Intrada*; 2. *Minuet and Trio*; 3. *Valse*; 4. *Finale* (*Jig*).

fp: August 1939, Chichester, Pipers' Guild Summer School, Pipers' Guild Quartet.

Pub. 1947, O.U.P.

227. The willow whistle (M. E. Fuller). For voice and pipe. ?1938 or 1939. Unpub.

228. A Hymn of Freedom (Canon G. W. Briggs). Written in this time of war, 1939. For unison voices with piano or organ. Pub. 20 December 1939, in *Daily Telegraph*; O.U.P. Later incorporated into *Five Wartime Hymns*.

229. Six Choral Songs—To Be Sung in Time of War (Shelley). For unison voices with piano or orchestra. 1940.

1. *A Song of Courage*; 2. *A Song of Liberty*; 3. *A Song of Healing*; 4. *A Song of Victory*; 5. *A Song of Pity, Peace and Love*; 6. *A Song of the New Age*.

2 fl, 2 ob, 2 cl, 2 bsn, dbsn; 4 hn, 2 tpt, 3 tmb, tuba; timp, pcssn, hp, organ; strings.

fp: 20 December 1940, BBC broadcast, BBC Chorus and BBC Symphony Orchestra, cond. Leslie Woodgate.

Pub. 1940, O.U.P.

230. Valiant for Truth (John Bunyan). Motet for mixed chorus a cappella (or with organ or piano). 1940.

fp: 20 June 1942, St. Michael's Church (Cornhill), St. Michael's Singers, cond. Harold Darke.

Pub. 1941, O.U.P.

231. 49th Parallel. 1940–1. Music for the Ortus Films production, produced and directed by Michael Powell; with Eric Portman, Leslie Howard, Anton Walbrook, Glynis Johns, Laurence Olivier, Raymond Massey; music performed by the London Symphony Orchestra, cond. Muir Mathieson.

2 fl, ob, ca, 2 cl, 2 bsn, dbsn; 4 hn, 2 tpt, 3 tmb, tuba; timp, pcssn; hp, strings.

fp: 8 October 1941, Odeon (Leicester Square).

Unpub.

231a. 49th Parallel: Prelude. Dur. 2'.

2 fl, 2 ob, 2 cl, 2 bsn; 4 hn, 2 tpt, 3 tmb, tuba; timp, cym; hp, strings.

Pub. 1960, O.U.P. Also arr. string orch. by Roy Douglas.

231b. The New Commonwealth (Harold Child). For unison voices with piano or orchestra. Music adapted from preceding.

2 fl, 2 ob, 2 cl, 3 bsn; 4 hn, 3 tpt, 3 tmb, tuba; timp, pcssn; hp, organ, strings. *Or:* strings and piano.

Pub. 1943, O.U.P.

232. Household Music: Three Preludes on Welsh Hymn Tunes. For string quartet (or alternative instruments). 1940–1. Dur. 17'.

1. *Crug-y-bar* (*Fantasia*); 2. *St. Denio* (*Scherzo*); 3. *Aberystwyth* (*Eight variations*).

fp: 4 October 1941, Wigmore Hall, Blech Quartet.

Pub. 1943, O.U.P.

233. England, My England (W. E. Henley). Choral Song for baritone, double choir, unison voices and orchestra or piano. 1941.

2 fl, 2 ob, 2 cl, 3 bsn; 4 hn, 2 tpt, 3 tmb, tuba; timp, pcssn; organ, strings.

fp: 16 November 1941, BBC broadcast, Dennis Noble, BBC Chorus, BBC Symphony Orchestra, cond. Sir Adrian Boult.

Pub. 1941, O.U.P.

234. A Call to the Free Nations (Canon G. W. Briggs). Hymn for choral or unison singing. 1941. Pub. O.U.P. as No. 2 of *Five Wartime Hymns*.

235. Coastal Command. 1942. Music for the Crown Film Unit production, produced by Ian Dalrymple; music performed by the R.A.F. Symphony Orchestra, cond. Muir Mathieson.

fp: 16 October 1942, Plaza Cinema, London.

Unpub.

235a. Coastal Command: Suite. Arr. Muir Mathieson. Dur. 12'.

Vaughan Williams, Ralph

2 fl, 2 ob, ca, 2 cl, 2 bsn; 4 hn, 2 tpt, 3 tmb, tuba; side dm, tgle, cym, ten dm, GC, gong, timp; hp, strings.

fp: 17 September 1942, Manchester, BBC concert, BBC Northern Orchestra, cond. Muir Mathieson.

Pub. O.U.P. (Hire).

236. The Airmen's Hymn (2nd Earl of Lytton). Unison song with piano or organ. Pub. 1942, O.U.P.

237. Nine Carols for male voices. For TTBB a cappella. Pub. 1942, O.U.P.

238. The Pilgrim's Progress. Incidental music for a radio adaptation. 1942.

fl, pic, ob, cl, bsn, dbsn; 2 hn, 2 tpt, 3 tmb, tuba; timp, pcssn; hp, strings.

fp: 5 September 1943, BBC broadcast, Margaret Godley, Margaret Rolfe, Bradbridge White, Stanley Riley, BBC Chorus, BBC Symphony Orchestra, cond. Sir Adrian Boult.

Unpub.

239. The Blessing of the Swords. From 'Les Huguenots' (Meyerbeer), arr. for mixed chorus and orchestra. Pub. 1942, O.U.P.

240. A Winter Piece (For Genia). For piano. New Year's Day, 1943. Unpub.

241. Symphony (No. 5) in D major. 1938–1943. Ded. Jean Sibelius. Dur. 37'.

1. *Preludio* (*Moderato*); 2. *Scherzo* (*Presto*); 3. *Romanza* (*Lento*); 4. *Passacaglia* (*Moderato*).

2 fl, pic, ob, ca, 2 cl, 2 bsn; 2 hn, 2 tpt, 3 tmb; timp; strings.

fp: 24 June 1943, Royal Albert Hall, Promenade Concert, London Philharmonic Orchestra, cond. R. Vaughan Williams.

Pub. 1946, O.U.P.

BIBLIOGRAPHY:
A. E. F. Dickinson: VW's Fifth Symphony, *MR*, February 1945, p. 1.
Roy Douglas: VW and his Fifth Symphony, *Record Times*, January 1963, p. 2.
Hubert Foss: VW's D major Symphony, *Halle*, August 1950, p. 12.
D. Hugh Ottaway: The Fifth and Sixth Symphonies of VW, *Canon*, October 1952, p. 121.

632

— VW: Symphony in D and The Pilgrim's Progress, a comparative note, *MT*, October 1953, p. 456.
— VW 5—a new analysis, *MT*, May 1964, p. 354.

242. The People's Land. 1941–2. Incidental music (founded on traditional melodies) for a film produced for the British Council by Strand Films, produced and directed by Donald Taylor; music played by a section of the London Symphony Orchestra, cond. Muir Mathieson. Unpub.

243. The Flemish Farm. 1943. Music for a Two Cities film, produced by Filippo del Giudice, written and directed by Jeffrey Dell; music played by the London Symphony Orchestra, cond. Muir Mathieson.

fp: 12 August 1943, Leicester Square Theatre.

Unpub.

243a. Suite: Story of a Flemish Farm. Dur. 26'.

2 fl, 2 ob, ca, 2 cl, 2 bsn, dbsn; 4 hn, 2 tpt, 3 tmb, tuba; timp, side dm, tgle, cym, GC, glock, large gong; hp, strings.

fp: 31 July 1945, Royal Albert Hall, Promenade Concert, London Symphony Orchestra, cond. R. Vaughan Williams.

Pub. O.U.P. (Hire).

244. Fantasia on 'Linden Lea'. For oboe, clarinet and bassoon. 1942–3. Unpub.

245. A Wedding Tune for Ann, 27 October 1943. For organ. Pub. 1964, O.U.P. as No. 1 of *A Vaughan Williams Organ Album* (ed. Christopher Morris).

246. Concerto in A minor for oboe and strings. 1944. Ded. Leon Goossens. Dur. 20'.

1. *Rondo Pastorale* (*Allegro moderato*); 2. *Minuet and Musette* (*Allegro moderato*); 3. *Finale: Scherzo* (*Presto*).

fp: 30 September 1944, Liverpool, Philharmonic Hall, Leon Goossens and the Liverpool Philharmonic Orchestra, cond. (Sir) Malcolm Sargent.

f London p: 4 May 1945, Wigmore Hall, Leon Goossens and the Bromley and Chislehurst Orchestra, cond. Marjorie Whyte.

Pub. 1947, O.U.P.

247. String Quartet (No. 2) in A minor (For Jean on her Birthday). 1942–4. Ded. Jean Stewart (Mrs. George Hadley). Dur. 20′.

1. *Prelude* (*Allegro appassionato*); 2. *Romance* (*Largo*); 3. *Scherzo* (*Allegro*); 4. *Epilogue. Greetings from Joan to Jean* (*Andante sostenuto*).

fp: 12 October 1944, National Gallery, Menges Quartet (Isolde Menges, Lorraine du Val, Jean Stewart, Ivor James).

Pub. 1947, O.U.P.

248. Richard II. Incidental music for a broadcast performance of Shakespeare's play, but unused. 1944. Unpub.

249. Thanksgiving for Victory. Later renamed *A Song of Thanksgiving*. For soprano, speaker, mixed chorus and orchestra. 1944. Dur. 15′.

Reduced instrumentation by Roy Douglas. 2 fl, 2 ob, 2 cl, bcl (ad lib), 2 bsn, dbsn (ad lib); 4(2) hn, 3(2) tpt, 3 tmb, tuba (ad lib); timp, side dm, tgle, cym, GC; hp or piano (ad lib), organ (ad lib), strings.

fp: 13 May 1945, BBC broadcast of recording made on 5 November 1944, Elsie Suddaby, Valentine Dyall, BBC Chorus, choir of children from the Thomas Coram Schools, George Thalben-Ball (organ), BBC Symphony Orchestra, cond. Sir Adrian Boult.

fp (concert): 14 September 1945, Royal Albert Hall, Promenade Concert, Elsie Suddaby, Valentine Dyall, BBC Choral Society, Croydon Philharmonic Society, choir of children from the Thomas Coram Schools, BBC Symphony Orchestra, cond. Sir Adrian Boult.

Pub. 1945, O.U.P.

250. Stricken Peninsula. 1944. Music for a Ministry of Information film made for the Department of Psychological Warfare, produced and directed by Hans Nieter; music performed by the London Symphony Orchestra, cond. Muir Mathieson. Unpub.

251. Two Carols. Traditional melodies arr. for SATB a cappella. Pub. 1945, O.U.P.

252. Chant for Psalm 67, Deus Misereatur. 1945. Composed for St. Martin's Church, Dorking, and fp there on 14 October 1945. Unpub.

253. Introduction and Fugue. For two pianos. 1946. Ded. Phyllis and Cyril.

fp: 23 March 1946, Wigmore Hall, Cyril Smith and Phyllis Sellick.

fbp: 23 April 1946, Cyril Smith and Phyllis Sellick.

Pub. 1947, O.U.P.

254. The Loves of Joanna Godden. 1946. Music for an Ealing Studios film, produced by Michael Balcon and directed by Charles Frend; music performed by the Philharmonia Orchestra, cond. Ernest Irving.

2 fl, 2 ob, ca, 2 cl, 2 bsn; 4 hn, 2 tpt, 3 tmb, tuba; timp, pcssn; hp, strings; women's chorus (small).

fp: 16 June 1947, New Gallery Cinema. Unpub.

255. The Souls of the Righteous. Motet for treble (or soprano), tenor, baritone and mixed chorus. 1947. Dur. 3½′.

Composed for and fp: 10 July 1947, Westminster Abbey, dedication of the Battle of Britain Chapel.

fp (concert): 30 April 1948, Wigmore Hall, Tudor Singers, cond. Harry Stubbs.

Pub. 1947, O.U.P.

256. The Voice out of the Whirlwind. Motet for mixed chorus and organ. 1947. Adapted from 'Galliard of the Sons of the Morning' from *Job*.

fp: 22 November 1947, Church of St. Sepulchre (Holborn Viaduct), St. Cecilia's Day Festival Service, cond. J. Dykes Bower, with William McKie (organ).

Pub. 1947, O.U.P.

256a. The Voice out of the Whirlwind. Version with orchestra.

2 fl, pic, 2 ob, 2 cl, 2 bsn, dbsn (ad lib); 4 hn, 3 tpt, 3 tmb, tuba; timp, pcssn; hp, strings.

fp: 16 June 1951, Dorking (Dorking Halls), Leith Hill Festival Choir and Surrey Philharmonic Orchestra, cond. R. Vaughan Williams.

257. Symphony (No. 6) in E minor. 1944–7. Ded. Michael Mullinar. Dur. 37′.

1. *Allegro*; 2. *Moderato*; 3. *Scherzo* (*Allegro vivace*); 4. *Epilogue* (*Moderato*).

3 fl, pic, 2 ob, ca, 2 cl, ten sax, bcl, 2 bsn,

dbsn; 4 hn, 4(3) tpt, 3 tmb, tuba; timp, side dm, GC, tgle, cym, xyl; hp, strings.

fp: 21 April 1948, Royal Albert Hall, Royal Philharmonic Society concert, BBC Symphony Orchestra, cond. Sir Adrian Boult.

Pub. 1948, O.U.P. Revised edition, 1950.

BIBLIOGRAPHY:

Deryck Cooke: Symphony No. 6 in E minor by VW, in *The Language of Music*, O.U.P. (London) 1959/Oxford Paperbacks No. 44 (1962), p. 252.

Martin Cooper: Sixth Symphony by VW, *MQ*, July 1948, p. 424.

A. E. F. Dickinson: Toward the unknown region, an introduction to VW's Sixth Symphony, *MR*, 1948, p. 275.

— A challenging symphony, *The Listener*, 27 January 1949, p. 156.

Scott Goddard: VW's Sixth Symphony, *Halle*, May 1948, p. 1.

Dyneley Hussey: RVW, his new symphony, *Britain Today*, No. 147, July 1948, p. 26.

D. Hugh Ottaway: The Fifth and Sixth Symphonies of VW, *Canon*, October 1952, p. 121.

258. The lake in the mountains. For piano. 1947. Ded. Phyllis Sellick. Pub. 1947, O.U.P.

259. A Wedding Canon (2 in 1 infinite). 'For Nancy, 30 May 1947, with love from Uncle Ralph.' Unpub.

260. Prayer to the Father of Heaven (John Skelton). Motet for mixed chorus a cappella. 1948. Ded. to the memory of Hubert Parry. Dur. 4'.

fp: 12 May 1948, Oxford Festival, Sheldonian Theatre, Oxford Bach Choir (Cantata Section), cond. Thomas Armstrong.

Pub. 1948, O.U.P.

261. Scott of the Antarctic. 1948. Music for the Ealing Studios film, produced by Michael Balcon and directed by Charles Frend; music performed by the Philharmonia Orchestra, cond. Ernest Irving.

fp: 29 November 1948, Empire (Leicester Square), Royal Film Performance.

Unpub.

262. Hymn for St. Margaret. January or February 1948. Words: Ursula Wood (Ursula Vaughan Williams). Pub. 1950, O.U.P.

263. Folk Songs of the Four Seasons. Cantata, based on traditional folksongs, for women's voices (SSAA) and orchestra. 1949. Dur. 45'.

1. *Prologue*; 2. *Spring*; 3. *Summer*; 4. *Autumn*; 5. *Winter*.

2 fl, 2(1) ob, 2 cl, 2(1) bsn; 4 hn, 2 tpt, 3 tmb, tuba; timp, pcssn; hp, celesta, organ, strings. *Or:* 2 fl, ob, 2 cl, bsn; 2 hn, 2 tpt; timp; hp, organ (ad lib), strings. *Or:* strings and piano.

fp: 15 June 1950, Royal Albert Hall, National Singing Festival of National Federation of Women's Institutes, London Symphony Orchestra, cond. Sir Adrian Boult.

Pub. 1950, O.U.P. *Suite* (arr. for small orchestra by Roy Douglas) pub. 1956 (dur. 13½').

264. An Oxford Elegy. For speaker, small mixed chorus and small orchestra. 1949. Words: Matthew Arnold (from 'The Scholar Gipsy' and 'Thyrsis'). Dur. 25'.

fl, ob, ca, 2 cl, bsn; 2 hn; strings.

fp: 20 November 1949, Dorking (The White Gates), Steuart Wilson (speaker), Tudor Singers, Schwiller String Quartet, Michael Mullinar (piano), cond. R. Vaughan Williams.

fp (public): 19 June 1952, Oxford (Queen's College), Sir Steuart Wilson, Eglesfield Musical Society, chamber orchestra, cond. Bernard Rose.

f London p: 22 March 1953, St. Martin-in-the-Fields, Clive Carey, St. Martin's Cantata Choir and orchestra, cond. John Churchill.

Pub. 1952, O.U.P.

265. Fantasia (Quasi Variazione) on the 'Old 104th' Psalm Tune. For piano with mixed chorus and orchestra. 1949. Dur. 15'.

2 fl, pic, 2 ob, 2 cl, 2 bsn; 4 hn, 2 tpt, 3 tmb, tuba; timp, pcssn; organ, strings. *Or:* 2 tpt, 3 tmb, organ, strings. *Or:* strings and organ.

fp: 20 November 1949, Dorking (The White Gates), Michael Mullinar, Tudor Singers, Schwiller String Quartet, cond. R. Vaughan Williams.

fp (public): 6 September 1950, Gloucester Cathedral, Three Choirs Festival, Michael

Mullinar, Festival Chorus and the London Symphony Orchestra, cond. R. Vaughan Williams.

f London p: 15 September 1950, Royal Albert Hall, Promenade Concert, Michael Mullinar, Royal Choral Society and BBC Symphony Orchestra, cond. Sir Malcolm Sargent.

Pub. 1950, O.U.P.

266. Dim Little Island. 1949. Music for a Wessex Film Productions film for the Central Office of Information, produced and directed by Humphrey Jennings. Unpub.

267. Concerto grosso. For string orchestra. 1950. Dur. 14'.

1. *Intrada*; 2. *Burlesca ostinata*; 3. *Sarabande*; 4. *Scherzo*; 5. *March and reprise*.

fp: 18 November 1950, massed orchestra of the Rural Music Schools Association, cond. Sir Adrian Boult.

Pub. 1950, O.U.P.

268. Bitter Springs. 1950. Music for the Ealing Studios film, produced by Michael Balcon and directed by Ralph Smart; music played by the Philharmonia Orchestra, cond. Ernest Irving.

2 fl, 2 ob, 2 cl, bcl, 2 bsn; 2 hn, 2 tpt, 3 tmb, tuba; pcssn; hp, piano, strings.

fp: 10 July 1950, Gaumont (Haymarket). Unpub.

269. The Sons of Light. Cantata for mixed chorus and orchestra. 1950. Words: Ursula Wood (Ursula Vaughan Williams). Ded. Bernard Shore. Dur. 25'.

1. *Darkness and Light*; 2. *The Song of the Zodiac*; 3. *The Messengers of Speech*.

2 fl, 2 ob, ca, 2 cl, 2 bsn, dbsn; 4 hn, 3 tpt, 3 tmb, tuba; timp, pcssn; xyl, glock, celesta, hp, strings. Or: 2 fl, 2(1) ob, 3(2) cl, 2(1) bsn; 2 hn, 3(2) tpt, 3(2) tmb, tuba (or euphonium), 3(2) sax; timp, celesta, pcssn; piano, strings.

fp: 6 May 1951, Royal Albert Hall, massed choir from the Schools' Music Association and London Philharmonic Orchestra, cond. Sir Adrian Boult.

Pub. 1951, O.U.P. Also version with strings and piano arr. Arnold Foster.

269a. Sun, Moon, Stars, and Man. Cycle of four songs for unison voices and strings

and/or piano. 1950. Words: Ursula Vaughan Williams. Based on sections of 'The Sons of Light'.

1. *Horses of the Sun*; 2. *The Rising of the Moon*; 3. *The Procession of the Stars*; 4. *The Song of the Sons of Light*.

fp: 11 March 1955, Birmingham Town Hall, choir from secondary schools in Birmingham North District, City of Birmingham Symphony Orchestra, cond. Desmond MacMahon.

Pub. 1954, O.U.P.

270. Solemn Music for the Masque of Charterhouse (Final Scene). For wind and drums. 1950.

fp: 12 July 1950, Charterhouse School Choir and Orchestra, cond. J. W. Wilson.

Unpub.

271. The Mayor of Casterbridge. Music for a radio serial based on the novel by Thomas Hardy. Unpub.

272. The Pilgrim's Progress. Morality, in a Prologue, four acts and an Epilogue, after John Bunyan. 1906–51. Dur. 119'.

2 fl, pic, 2 ob, ca, 2 cl, 2 bsn, dbsn (ad lib); 4 hn, 2 tpt, 3 tmb, tuba, euphonium (ad lib); timp, side dm, tenor dm, GC, cym, gong, tgle, xyl, glock, bells; hp, celesta (ad lib), strings.

fp: 26 April 1951, Royal Opera House, Covent Garden, cond. Leonard Hancock; with Inia Te Wiata (John Bunyan), Arnold Matters (Pilgrim), Norman Walker, Rhydderch Davies, Dennis Stephenson, Adele Leigh, Patricia Howard, Vera Hoddinott, Edgar Evans, Elisabeth Abercrombie, Monica Sinclair, Parry Jones, Jean Watson &c.; producer, Nevill Coghill; design, Hal Burton.

Pub. 1952, O.U.P.

BIBLIOGRAPHY:

Deryck Cooke: VW's musical language, *The Listener*, 7 April 1960, p. 639.

A. E. F. Dickinson: The Pilgrim's Progress, *MMR*, February 1952, p. 31.

Hubert Foss: VW and Bunyan, *The Listener*, 26 April 1951, p. 684.

— The Pilgrim's Progress, *Radio Times*, 20 April 1951, p. 9.

— The Pilgrim's Progress by VW, in *Music 1952*, Penguin Books (London) 1952, p. 38.

Dyneley Hussey: The Pilgrim's Progress, *Foyer*, No. 1, autumn 1951, p. 15.

Michael Mullinar: The Pilgrim's Progress, *RCM Magazine*, June 1951, p. 46.

Herbert Murrill: VW's Pilgrim, *M&L*, October 1951, p. 324.

D. Hugh Ottaway: Some aspects of The Pilgrim's Progress, *MO*, August 1951, p. 579.

Cecil Smith: The Pilgrim's Progress, *Opera*, June 1951, p. 373.

P. Treves: Pellegrinaggio di VW, *La Scala*, 15 June 1951.

272a. Seven Songs from 'The Pilgrim's Progress'. For voice and piano. Dur. 21′.

1. *Watchful's Song*. Ded. Bryan Drake.
2. *The Song of the Pilgrim* (Bunyan). Ded. Douglas Robinson and the members of the chorus at Covent Garden.
3. *The Pilgrim's Psalm*. Ded. Arnold Matters.
4. *The Song of the Leaves of Life and the Water of Life*. Ded. Elisabeth Abercrombie and Monica Sinclair.
5. *The Song of Vanity Fair* (Ursula Vaughan Williams). Ded. 'to whoever shall first sing it'.
6. *The Woodcutter's Song* (Bunyan). Ded. Iris Kells.
7. *The Bird's Song*. Ded. Adele Leigh.
Pub. 1952, O.U.P.

272b. Pilgrim's Journey. Cantata, devised in 1962 by Christopher Morris and Roy Douglas, from 'The Pilgrim's Progress'. Pub. 1962, O.U.P.

273. Flourish for three trumpets. 1951.
fp: 19 March 1951, Stafford (Borough Hall), cond. Maude Smith.
Composed for Staffordshire schools, unpub.

274. Three Shakespeare Songs. For mixed chorus a cappella. 1951. Ded. C. Armstrong Gibbs. Dur. 7′.
1. *Full fathom five*; 2. *The cloud-capp'd towers*; 3. *Over hill, over dale*.
fp: 23 June 1951, Royal Festival Hall, British Federation of Music Festivals National Competitive Festival, cond. C. Armstrong Gibbs.
Pub. 1951, O.U.P.

275. Romance in D flat. For harmonica, string orchestra and piano. 1951. Ded. Larry Adler. Dur. 6′.
fp: 3 May 1952, New York, Town Hall, Larry Adler and Little Symphony Orchestra, cond. Daniel Saidenberg.
fEp: 16 June 1952, Liverpool Stadium, Larry Adler and Liverpool Philharmonic Orchestra, cond. Hugo Rignold.
f London p: 6 September 1952, Royal Albert Hall, Promenade Concert, Larry Adler and BBC Symphony Orchestra, cond. Sir Malcolm Sargent.
Pub. 1953, O.U.P.

276. In the Spring (William Barnes). For voice and piano. 1952. Ded. members of the Barnes Society. Pub. 1952, O.U.P.

277. Sinfonia Antartica. For orchestra with soprano soloist and women's chorus. 1949–52. Ded. Ernest Irving. Dur. 39′.
1. *Prelude* (*Andante maestoso*); 2. *Scherzo* (*Moderato—poco animando*); 3. *Landscape*; (*Lento*); 4. *Intermezzo* (*Andante sostenuto*); 5. *Epilogue* (*Alla marcia moderato*).
3 fl, pic, 2 ob, ca, 2 cl, bcl, 2 bsn, dbsn; 4 hn, 3 tpt, 3 tmb, tuba; timp, tgle, cym, side dm, GC, gong, bells, glock, xyl, vib, wind machine; hp, celesta, piano, organ (ad lib), strings.
fp: 14 January 1953, Manchester, Free Trade Hall, Margaret Ritchie, Halle Choir and Orchestra, cond. Sir John Barbirolli.
f London p: 21 January 1953, Royal Festival Hall, same artistes.
Pub. 1953, O.U.P.

BIBLIOGRAPHY:

F. Blanks: VW's Sinfonia Antartica, *Canon*, March 1953, p. 324.

Mosco Carner: Eine neue Sinfonie von RVW, *SM*, March 1953, p. 143.

Dyneley Hussey: Sinfonia Antartica, *Britain Today*, No. 204, April 1953, p. 31.

T. Heinitz: First performance of Sinfonia Antartica, *SR*, 28 February 1953, p. 64.

Michael Kennedy: A symphony of heroism, *Halle*, February 1954, p. 7.

Colin Mason: VW's Sinfonia Antartica, *MT*, March 1953, p. 128.

G. Montagu: Sinfonia Antartica, *London Musical Events*, March 1953, p. 128.

D. Hugh Ottaway: Sinfonia Antartica, early reflexions, *MO*, March 1953, p. 337.

Andrew Porter: Sinfonia Antartica, *London Musical Events*, May 1954, p. 30.

Desmond Shawe-Taylor: VW on ice, *New Statesman*, 24 January 1953, p. 91.

Ralph Vaughan Williams: Sinfonia Antartica, *Halle*, January 1953, p. 2.

— Sinfonia Antartica, *M&M*, January 1953, p. 7.

John Weissmann: The new VW, *MR*, 1953, p. 148.

278. O taste and see. Motet for mixed choir a cappella, with an organ introduction. 1952. Dur. 1¾'.

fp: 2 June 1953, Westminster Abbey, Coronation of Queen Elizabeth II, cond. Sir William McKie.

Pub. 1953, O.U.P.

279. Le Paradis. French folksong arr. for voice and harp or piano. 1952.

fp: 17 November 1952, French Institute (Kensington), Sophie Wyss and Maria Korchinska.

Unpub.

280. Silence and music (Ursula Vaughan Williams). For mixed chorus a cappella. 1953. Ded. to the memory of Charles Villiers Stanford, and his Blue Bird. Dur. 5'.

fp: 1 June 1953, Royal Festival Hall, Cambridge University Madrigal Society and the Golden Age Singers, cond. Boris Ord.

Pub. 1953, O.U.P. in *A Garland for the Queen*.

281. The Old Hundredth Psalm Tune. For mixed choir, congregation, orchestra and organ. February 1953. Dur. 5½'.

3 fl, 3 ob, 3 cl, 3 bsn; 4 hn, 3 tpt, 3 tmb, tuba; timp, pcssn; organ, strings. *Extra 'fanfare'*: 4 tpt, 3 tmb, side dm.

fp: 2 June 1953, Westminster Abbey, Coronation of Elizabeth II, Coronation Choir and Orchestra with trumpeters of Royal Military School of Music, Kneller Hall, cond. Sir William McKie.

fp (concert): 27 October 1957, Manchester, Free Trade Hall, Halle Choir and Orchestra, cond. Sir John Barbirolli.

Pub. 1953, O.U.P.

282. Prelude on an old carol tune. For small orchestra. 1953. Founded on incidental music for 'The Mayor of Casterbridge'. Dur. 8'.

2 fl, ob, 2 cl, bsn; 2 hn, 2 tpt, 2 tmb; timp; strings.

fp: 31 July 1953, King's Lynn Festival, St. Nicholas's Chapel, Boyd Neel Orchestra, cond. R. Vaughan Williams; broadcast by the BBC.

Pub. 1953, O.U.P.

283. Te Deum and Benedictus. Set to well-known metrical psalm tunes for unison or mixed voices with organ (or harmonium, or piano). Pub. 1954, O.U.P.

284. Concerto in F minor for bass tuba and orchestra. 1954. Ded. London Symphony Orchestra. Dur. 13'.

1. *Allegro moderato*; 2. *Romanza (Andante sostenuto)*; 3. *Finale (Rondo alla tedesca)*.

2 fl, pic, ob, 2 cl, bsn; 2 hn, 2 tpt, 2 tmb; timp, side dm, tgle, GC, cym; strings.

fp: 13 June 1954, Royal Festival Hall, London Symphony Orchestra Jubilee Concert, Philip Catelinet and the London Symphony Orchestra, cond. Sir John Barbirolli.

fbp: 5 January 1955, Philip Catelinet and the BBC Northern Orchestra, cond. John Hopkins.

Pub. 1955, O.U.P.

285. This Day (Hodie). Christmas Cantata for soprano, tenor, baritone, mixed chorus, boys' voices, organ (ad lib) and orchestra. 1953–4. Words: Biblical, and various authors. Ded. Herbert Howells. Dur. 55½'.

1. *Prologue*; 2. *Narration*; 3. *Song* (Milton); 4. *Narration*; 5. *Choral* (Miles Coverdale, after Martin Luther); 6. *Narration*; 7. *The Oxen* (Thomas Hardy); 8. *Narration*; 9. *Pastoral* (George Herbert); 10. *Narration*; 11. *Lullaby* (William Ballet); 12. *Hymn* (William Drummond); 13. *Narration*; 14. *The March of the Three Kings* (Ursula Vaughan Williams); 15. *Choral* (Anon. and Ursula Vaughan Williams); 16. *Epilogue*.

3(2) fl, pic, 2(1) ob, ca, 2 cl, 2 bsn, dbsn (ad lib); 4(2) hn, 3(2) tpt, 3 tmb, tuba; timp, pcssn; celesta, hp (ad lib), piano, organ (ad lib), strings.

fp: 8 September 1954, Worcester Cathedral,

Three Choirs Festival, Nancy Evans, Eric Greene, Gordon Clinton, Festival Chorus and London Symphony Orchestra, cond. R. Vaughan Williams.

f London p: 19 January 1955, Royal Festival Hall, Nancy Evans, Eric Greene, Gordon Clinton, BBC Chorus & Choral Society, boys of Watford Grammar School and BBC Symphony Orchestra, cond. Sir Malcolm Sargent.

Pub. 1954, O.U.P.

286. Violin Sonata in A minor. 1954. Ded. Frederick Grinke. Dur. 23'.

1. *Fantasia (Allegro giusto)*; 2. *Scherzo (Allegro furioso ma non troppo)*; 3. *Tema con Variazione (Andante—Allegro)*.

fp: 12 October 1954, BBC broadcast, Frederick Grinke and Michael Mullinar.

fp (concert): 14 November 1955, Rochester (N.Y.), Civic Music Association, Josef Szigeti and Carlo Bussotti.

f Ep (concert): 20 December 1955, Wigmore Hall, I.C.A. concert, Frederick Grinke and Michael Mullinar.

BIBLIOGRAPHY:

D. Hugh Ottaway: VW's Violin Sonata, *MO*, December 1954, p. 165.

R. Sabin: VW violin sonata issued, *Musical America*, 1 January 1957, p. 45.

287. Heart's music (Thomas Campion). For mixed chorus a cappella. 1954. Ded. Wilfrid Dykes Bower and the St. Thomas's Hospital Musical Society.

fp: 25 November 1954, Church of St. Sepulchre (Holborn Viaduct), St. Thomas's Hospital Choir, cond. Wilfrid Dykes Bower.

Pub. 1955, O.U.P.

288. Menelaus on the beach at Pharos (Ursula Vaughan Williams). For medium voice and piano. Summer 1954. See No. 305.

fp: 14 November 1954, New York, Cornell University, Keith Falkner and Christabel Falkner.

fEp: 26 May 1955, Wigmore Hall, Keith Falkner and Michael Mullinar.

Pub. 1960, O.U.P.

289. Three Gaelic Songs. Arr. for mixed voices a cappella. 21–26 October 1954, Santa Barbara, California. Pub. 1963, O.U.P.

290. Song for a Spring Festival (Ursula Vaughan Williams). For mixed chorus. 1954. For the exclusive use of the Leith Hill Musical Festival.

fp: 15 April 1955, Dorking, Leith Hill Musical Festival, cond. R. Vaughan Williams.

Privately printed by O.U.P.: not for sale.

291. Prelude on three Welsh Hymn Tunes. For brass band. 1954. Dur. 9'.

fp: 12 March 1955, BBC broadcast, International Staff Band of the Salvation Army, cond. Bernard Adams.

Pub. 1955, Salvationist Publishing and Supplies.

292. Symphony No. 8 in D minor. 1953–5. Ded. John Barbirolli. Dur. 28'.

1. *Fantasia (Variazioni senza Tema)*; 2. *Scherzo alla marcia (per stromenti a fiato)*; 3. *Cavatina (per stromenti ad arco)*; 4. *Toccata*.

2 fl, pic, 2 ob, 2 cl, 2(3) bsn; 2 hn, 2 tpt, 3 tmb; timp, side dm, tgle, cym, GC, vib, xyl, glock, tubular bells, 3 tuned gongs; celesta, 2(1) hp, strings.

fp: 2 May 1956, Manchester, Free Trade Hall, Halle Orchestra, cond. Sir John Barbirolli.

f London p: 14 May 1956, Royal Festival Hall, Halle Orchestra, cond. Sir John Barbirolli.

Pub. 1956, O.U.P.

BIBLIOGRAPHY:

Arthur Jacobs: VW's Eighth Symphony, *MO*, June 1956, p. 533.

Michael Kennedy: VW's Eighth Symphony, *Halle*, April 1956, p. 5.

D. Hugh Ottaway: VW's Eighth Symphony, *M&L*, July 1957, p. 213.

Ralph Vaughan Williams: The new VW Symphony, *M&M*, May 1956, p. 8.

293. The England of Elizabeth. 1955. Music for a British Transport Commission film, produced by Ian Ferguson and directed by John Taylor; executive producer, Edgar Anstey; music played by the Sinfonia of London, cond. John Hollingsworth.

2 fl, pic, ob, ca, 2 cl, bsn; 2 hn, 2 tpt, 3 tmb; timp, pcssn; hp, celesta, piano, strings.

fp: March 1957, Leicester Square Theatre.

Unpub. *Three Portraits* (concert suite arr.

Muir Mathieson) pub. 1964, O.U.P.; *Two Shakespeare Sketches* (arr. for concert use by Muir Mathieson) pub. 1964, O.U.P.

294. A Vision of Aeroplanes. Motet for mixed chorus and organ. 1955. Words: from Ezekiel. Ded. Harold Darke and his St. Michael's Singers. Dur. 15'.

fp: 4 June 1956, St. Michael's Church (Cornhill), St. Michael's Singers, cond. Harold Darke; with John Birch (organ).

fbp: 29 October 1956, Edgbaston. St. George's Church, BBC Midland Chorus, cond. John Lowe; with Arnold Richardson (organ).

Pub. 1956, O.U.P.

295. A Choral Flourish. For mixed chorus with introduction for organ or two trumpets. 1956. Words: Biblical. Ded. Alan Kirby.

fp: 3 November 1956, Royal Festival Hall, twenty-first anniversary of National Federation of Music Societies, Royal Choral Society, Bach Choir, Croydon Philharmonic Society, St. Michael's Singers, cond. Reginald Jacques.

Pub. 1956, O.U.P.

296. Two Organ Preludes. Founded on Welsh folksongs. 1956.

1. *Romanza* (*The White Rock*); 2. *Toccata* (*St. David's Day*).

Pub. 1956, O.U.P.

297. God bless the master of this house. From the Sussex Mummers' Carol, arr. for mixed chorus a cappella. Pub. 1956, O.U.P.

298. Schmücke dich, o liebe Seele. J. S. Bach, arr. for cello and strings. 1956. Unpub.

299. Fen and Flood. Cantata by Patrick Hadley, arr. for soprano, baritone, mixed chorus. Pub. 1956, O.U.P.

300. Variations for brass band. 1957. Dur. 12'.

Andante maestoso; 1. *Poco tranquillo*; 2. *Tranquillo cantabile*; 3. *Allegro*; 4. *Allegro* (*Canon*); 5. *Moderato sostenuto*; 6. *Tempo di Valse*; 7. *Andante sostenuto* (*Arabesque*); 8. *Alla Polacca*; 9. *Adagio*; 10. *Allegro moderato* (*Fugato*); 11. *Chorale*.

fp: 26 October 1957, Royal Albert Hall, National Brass Band Championship of Great Britain.

Pub. 1957, Boosey & Hawkes.

300a. Variations for orchestra. Version of preceding arr. Gordon Jacob, with revision by Frank Wright. Dur. 12'.

2 fl, pic, 2 ob, 2 cl, 2 bsn; 4 hn, 2 tpt, 3 tmb, tuba; timp, 2 pcssn; strings.

fp: 8 January 1960, Birmingham, Town Hall, City of Birmingham Orchestra, cond. Sir Adrian Boult.

f London p: 5 May 1960, Royal Festival Hall, London Philharmonic Orchestra, cond. Sir Adrian Boult.

Pub. O.U.P. (Hire).

301. Flourish for Glorious John. For orchestra. 1957. Dur. 3'.

2 fl, pic, 2 ob, ca, 2 cl, bcl, 2 bsn, dbsn; 4 hn, 3 tpt, 3 tmb, tuba; timp, side dm, GC, cym, glock, tubular bells; hp, organ, piano, strings.

fp: 16 October 1957, Manchester, Free Trade Hall, Hallé Orchestra, cond. Sir John Barbirolli.

Unpub.

302. Symphony No. 9 in E minor. 1956–7, rev. 21 March–2 April 1958. Ded. Royal Philharmonic Society. Dur. 36'.

1. *Moderato maestoso—Tranquillo*; 2. *Andante sostenuto*; 3. *Scherzo* (*Allegro pesante*); 4. *Andante tranquillo*.

3 fl, pic, 2 ob, ca, 2 cl, bcl, 2 bsn, dbsn, 3 sax; 4 hn, flugel hn, 2 tpt, 3 tmb, tuba; timp, glock, xyl, side dm, GC, tenor dm, cym, tgle, gong (deep), tamtam, bells (deep); 2 hp, celesta, strings.

fp: 2 April 1958, Royal Festival Hall, Royal Philharmonic Society concert, Royal Philharmonic Orchestra, cond. Sir Malcolm Sargent.

Pub. 1958, O.U.P.

BIBLIOGRAPHY:

Richard Austin: VW's Ninth, *RCM Magazine*, 1958, No. 2, p. 45.

Michael Kennedy: The Ninth Symphony, *Hallé*, October 1958, p. 3.

Ralph Vaughan Williams: The music of my new Ninth Symphony, *M&M*, April 1958, p. 12.

303. Ten Blake Songs (William Blake). For voice and oboe. Christmastide 1957. Ded. Wilfred Brown and Janet Craxton. Dur. 19'.

Vaughan Williams, Ralph

1. *Infant joy*; 2. *A poison tree*; 3. *The piper*; 4. *London*; 5. *The lamb*; 6. *The shepherd*; 7. *Ah! sunflower*; 8. *Cruelty has a human heart*; 9. *The divine image*; 10. *Eternity*.

fp (concert): 8 October 1958, BBC broadcast, Wilfred Brown and Janet Craxton.

Pub. 1958, O.U.P.

NB. Originally composed for the film *The Vision of William Blake*, produced and directed by Guy Brenton, in which they were performed by the same artists, Nos. 2 & 3 being omitted.

304. Three Vocalises. For soprano and clarinet. 1958. Ded. Margaret Ritchie. Dur. 5'.

1. *Prelude*; 2. *Scherzo*; 3. *Quasi menuetto*.

fp: 8 October 1958, Manchester, Free Trade Hall, Margaret Ritchie and Keith Puddy.

fbp: 22 December 1958, Margaret Ritchie and Gervase de Peyer.

Pub. 1960, O.U.P.

305. Four last Songs (Ursula Vaughan Williams). For medium voice and piano. 1954–8. Dur. 12'.

1. *Procris*. 1958.
2. *Tired*. 1956.
3. *Hands, eyes and heart*. ?1956.
4. *Menelaus*. 1954.

fp (Nos. 1, 2, 4): 27 November 1959, Arts Council, Macnaghten concert, John Carol Case and Daphne Ibbott.

fp (complete): 3 August 1960, BBC broadcast, Pamela Bowden and Ernest Lush.

Pub. 1960, O.U.P.

306. The First Nowell. Nativity Play for soloists, mixed chorus and small orchestra, composed and arr. from traditional tunes by R. Vaughan Williams, with additions after the composer's death by Roy Douglas. Libretto: Simona Pakenham, adapted from medieval pageants. Dur. 50' (stage version), 30' (concert version).

2 fl, ob, 2 cl, bsn; 2 hn, 2 tpt, ten tmb, bs tmb; timp; hp, strings.

fp: 19 December 1958, Theatre Royal, Drury Lane, cond. John Churchill.

Pub. 1959, O.U.P.

307. Romance. For viola and piano. Date unknown.

fp: 19 January 1962, Arts Council,

Macnaghten concert, Bernard Shore and Eric Gritton.

Pub. 1962, O.U.P.

308. Cello Concerto. Unfinished.

309. Thomas the Rhymer. Opera in three acts. Libretto: Ursula Vaughan Williams. Unfinished.

310. A Yacre of Land. Sixteen folksongs from the manuscript collection of R. Vaughan Williams, ed. Imogen Holst and Ursula Vaughan Williams. Arr. for unison voices and piano or for unacc. part-singing by Imogen Holst. Pub. 1961, O.U.P.

Writings by Ralph Vaughan Williams

A School of English music, *Vocalist*, April 1902, p. 8.

The soporific finale, *Vocalist*, April 1902, p. 31.

Palestrina and Beethoven, *Vocalist*, May 1902, p. 36.

Good taste, *Vocalist*, May 1902, p. 38; repr. in *Heirs and Rebels*.

Bach and Schumann, *Vocalist*, June 1902, p. 72; repr. in *Heirs and Rebels*.

The words of Wagner's music-dramas, *Vocalist*, June 1902, p. 94; extract repr. in *Heirs and Rebels*.

Brahms and Tchaikovsky, *Vocalist*, October 1902, p. 198.

A sermon to vocalists, *Vocalist*, November 1902, p. 227.

Ein Heldenleben, *Vocalist*, January 1903, p. 295.

Conducting, in *Grove*, 2nd edn., Macmillan (London) 1904–10, p. 581; repr. in *Heirs and Rebels*.

Fugue, in *–do–*, p. 114.

Preface (The Music, *The English Hymnal*, Henry Frowde (London) 1906; extract repr. in *Heirs and Rebels*.

Preface, Journal of Folk Song Society, Vol. II, No. 8 (1906), p. 141.

The Romantic in Music, VIII: Some thoughts on Brahms, *Music Student*, April 1910, p. 116.

Who wants the English composer?, *RCM Magazine*, Christmas Term 1912, p. 11; repr. in Foss's *RVW* and in *Dansk Musiktidsskrift*, November 1958, p. 80.

English folk songs, *Music Student*, 1912,

March p. 247, April p. 283, May p. 317, June p. 347, July p. 387, August p. 413; repr. Joseph Williams (London) 1912, and in Young's *VW*.

Influence of folk song on chamber music, *Chamber Music*, May 1914, p. 69.

British music, *Music Student*, 1914, September, p. 5, October, p. 25, November, p. 47, December, p. 63.

Appreciation, in *George Butterworth*, p. 92.

Dance tunes, *Music Student*, August 1919, p. 453.

The letter and the spirit, *M&L*, April 1920, p. 87.

Gustav Holst, *M&L*, July and October 1920.

Gervase Elwes, *MN&H*, 22 January 1921, p. 107.

Music for music's sake (Lecture to British Music Society), *MN&H*, 3 February 1923, p. 106.

Charles Villiers Stanford, by some of his pupils, *M&L*, July 1924, p. 195.

How to sing a folk song, *Midland Musician*, April 1926, p. 127.

Folk song, *Midland Musician*, January 1926, p. 8.

Parry, *Midland Musician*, 1926, p. 275.

The late Mr. Frank Kidson, *Journal of the English Folk Dance Society*, 1927, p. 51.

Lucy Broadwood, an appreciation, *Journal of the Folk Song Society*, September 1927, p. 44.

Folk song (part of an article), in *Encyclopaedia Britannica*, 14th edn. (1929), p. 447.

Folk song in chamber music, in *Cobbett's Cyclopedic Survey of Chamber Music*, O.U.P. (1929), Vol. I, p. 410.

Introduction, *English Music* (Sir William Henry Hadow), Longmans, Green (London) 1931, p. vii.

Elizabethan music and the modern world, *MMR*, December 1933, p. 217.

National music, O.U.P. (London) 1934.

Introductory talk to Holst memorial concert, BBC 1934; repr. in *The Orchestra Speaks* (Bernard Shore), Longmans, Green (London) 1938.

Gustav Holst, man and musician, *RCM Magazine*, December 1934, p. 78.

What have we learnt from Elgar? *M&L*, January 1935, p. 13.

Gervase Elwes, in *Gervase Elwes: The story of his life* (Winefride and Richard Elwes), Grayson & Grayson (London) 1935, p. 294.

Cecil James Sharp, in *Dictionary of National Biography*, 1922–30, O.U.P. (1937), p. 761.

Ivor Gurney: the musician, *M&L*, January 1938, p. 12.

A note on Gustav Holst, in *Gustav Hols* (Imogen Holst), O.U.P. (London) 1938, p. vii.

Henry Wood, *London Mercury*, October 1938, p. 497.

A. H. Fox Strangways, AET. LXXX (contribution), *M&L*, October 1939, p. 349.

Making your own music (broadcast talk), BBC 1939; *M&L*, October 1939, p. 349.

The composer in wartime, *The Listener*, 16 May 1940, p. 989.

Let us remember... Early days, *English Dance and Song*, February 1942, p. 27.

Film music, *RCM Magazine*, February 1944, p. 5.

The pianoforte duet, *Crescendo*, No. 10, December 1947, p. 13.

A minim's rest, in *Essays mainly on the nineteenth century presented to Sir Humphrey Milford*, O.U.P. (London) 1948, p. 113.

Lucy Broadwood, in *Journal of the English Folk Dance and Song Society*, December 1948, p. 136.

Gustav Theodore Holst, in *Dictionary of National Biography*, 1931–40, O.U.P. (1949), p. 441.

First performances (Preface to prospectus of Promenade Concerts season), BBC, 1949.

Musical autobiography, in *RVW: a Study* (Hubert Foss), Harrap (London) 1950, p. 18.

Bach the great bourgeois (broadcast talk), *The Listener*, 3 August 1950, p. 170; *Musical America*, 1 December 1953, p. 8.

Verdi, a symposium (contribution), *Opera*, February 1951, p. 111.

Choral singing, in programme of Royal Choral Society concert, 9 June 1951.

Art and organization, in *Music and the Amateur: A Report*, National Council of Social Service Incorporated 1951, p. 3.

Doyen sums up, *Time*, 7 May 1951, p. 51.

The Stanford centenary (broadcast talk), BBC 1952.

Carthusian music in the 'eighties, *The Carthusian*, December 1952, p. 1.

Vaughan Williams, Ralph

Some thoughts on Beethoven's Choral Symphony with writings on other musical subjects, O.U.P. (London) 1953.
Sinfonia Antartica, *Halle*, January 1953, p. 2.
Sinfonia Antartica, *M&M*, January 1953, p. 7.
Address, *Journal of the International Folk Music Council*, January 1953, p. 7.
Preface, *International catalogue of recorded folk music*, O.U.P. (London) 1954.
Cecil Sharp, an appreciation, in *English folk song: some conclusions* (Cecil Sharp), 3rd edn., Methuen (London) 1954, p.v.
Preface, *London Symphony* (Hubert Foss & Noel Goodwin), Naldrett Press (London) 1954.
Arnold Bax (contribution), *M&L*, January 1954, p. 13.
Ernest Irving, *M&L*, January 1954, p. 17.
Gustav Holst: a great composer, *The Listener*, 3 June 1954, p. 965.
The making of music, *Etude*, 1955, July, p. 11, August, p. 14; Cornell University Press (New York) 1955.
Reminiscences of fifty years, in *The Leith Hill Musical Festival 1905–1955*, Pullingers (Epsom) 1955, p. 35.
Where craft ends and art begins, *Saturday Review*, 26 March 1955, p. 37.
Sibelius, *RCM Magazine*, 1955, No. 3, p. 58.
The teaching of Parry and Stanford, BBC 1956; repr. in *Heirs and Rebels*.
The new VW Symphony, *M&M*, May 1956, p. 8.
Preface, *Folksong-Plainsong: A study in origins and musical relationships* (George Bennett Chambers), Merlin Press (London) 1956, p.v.
Introduction, *The art of singing* (Arthur Cranmer), Dennis Dobson (London) 1957.
Message from VW, *Halle*, October 1957, p. 12.
Hands off the Third, *M&M*, October 1957, p. 15.
The English Folk Dance and Song Society, *Ethnomusicology*, September 1958, p. 108.
The Diamond Jubilee of the Folk Song Society, *Journal of the English Folk Dance and Song Society*, December 1958, p. 123.
The music of my new Ninth Symphony, *M&M*, April 1958, p. 12.
Heirs and Rebels, O.U.P. (London) 1959.

GENERAL BIBLIOGRAPHY
Edgar L. Bainton: RVW, some thoughts to share, *Canon*, October 1952, p. 101.
Sir John Barbirolli: RVW, a memoir, *M&M*, October 1958, p. 15.
— VW, a tribute, *Halle*, October 1958, p. 1.
Stanley A. Bayliss: A national composer, *Musical Mirror*, September 1924, p. 167.
— RVW, some notes on his music, *Musical Mirror*, September 1924, p. 247.
— Obsession and originality, *Sackbut*, March 1930, p. 216.
— The prose of VW, *Chesterian*, No. 100, January–February 1932.
— The operas of RVW, *MO*, August 1937, p. 950.
Eric Blom: VW, in *The Book of Modern Composers*, Knopf (New York) 1950 (2nd, enlarged edn.), p. 291.
J. D. Bergsagel: The national aspects of RVW, *Dissertation Abstracts*, September 1957, p. 2026.
Rutland Boughton: Tribute to VW, *Composer*, No. 3, October 1959, p. 3.
(Sir) Adrian Boult: VW as conductor, *Midland Musician*, January 1926, p. 8.
Å. Brandel: En introduktion till VW' Symfonier, *Musikrevy*, 1954, p. 82.
Havergal Brian: The music of RVW, *MO*, 1940, May, p. 345, June, p. 391.
Donald Brook: RVW, in *Composers' Gallery*, Rockliff (London) 1946, p. 112.
David Brown: VW's symphonies, some judgments reviewed, *MMR*, March–April 1960, p. 44.
M. A. Burtch: VW's operatic works, *MO*, February 1955, p. 275.
M.-D. Calvocoressi: VW and Ravel, in *Musicians Gallery*, Faber (London) 1933, p. 832.
Richard Capell: Elgar and VW, *Sackbut*, September 1924, p. 40.
Neville Cardus: Measure of VW, *Saturday Review*, 31 July 1954, p. 45.
— RVW, in *Talking of Music*, Collins (London) 1957, p. 83.
— VW—'his music will not suffer brief life', *Musical America*, September 1958, p. 10.
Joan Chissell: Writings on RVW, *RCM Magazine*, 1954, No. 1, p. 10.
— Octogenarian master, *The Listener*, 8 November 1956, p. 773.

E. Chapman: The music of VW, *London Musical Events*, October 1958, p. 23.

J. W. B. Chapman: VW and Somervell, *The Gramophone*, February 1926, p. 418.

H. C. Colles: The music of VW, *Chesterian*, No. 21, February 1922, p. 129.

— VW's progress, in *Essays and Lectures*, O.U.P. (London) 1945, p. 95.

Martin Cooper: RVW, *The Spectator*, 10 October 1952, p. 463.

David Cox: VW, in *Chamber Music*, Pelican Books (London) 1957, p. 338.

— RVW, in *The Symphony*, Vol. 2, Pelican Books (London) 1967, p. 114.

C. L. Cudworth: RVW, *Music*, October 1952, p. 9.

Gerald Cumberland: Dr. VW, in *Set Down in Malice*, Grant Richards (London) 1919, p. 255.

James Day: VW, Dent (London) 1961.

Norman Demuth: RVW, in *Musical Trends in the 20th Century*, Rockliff (London) 1952, p. 142.

Edward J. Dent: RVW, *MT*, October 1952, p. 443.

A. E. F. Dickinson: A bibliography of the works by RVW, *The Dominant*, July 1928, p. 36.

— An introduction to the music of RVW, O.U.P. (London) 1928.

— The VW tradition, *MMR*, 1939, September, p. 203, October, p. 237.

— Five VW symphonies, *The Listener*, 24 June 1943, p. 765.

— RVW, in *The Music Masters*, Vol. 4, Cassell (London) 1954, p. 387.

— RVW, *Tempo*, No. 49, autumn 1958, p. 33.

— RVW, *MMR*, November–December 1958, p. 204.

— RVW, *MQ*, January 1959, p. 1.

— The legacy of RVW, *MR*, November 1958, p. 290.

— VW's musical editorship, *Hymn Society Bulletin*, winter 1959, p. 188.

— VW, Faber (London) 1963.

O. Downes: English visitor, *New York Times*, 31 October 1954, Section 2, p. 7.

S. Hylton Edwards: A tribute to RVW, *The Dalhousie Review*, 1958–9, p. 486.

Katharine Eggar: RVW, some reflections on his work, *Music Student*, June 1920, p. 515.

H. F. Ellingford: Bach and VW, *Organ*, 1931, July, p. 14, October, p. 85.

Rupert O. Erlebach: VW and his three symphonies, *MMR*, 1922, June, p. 127, July, p. 151.

Edwin Evans: RVW, *MT*, 1920, April p. 232, May, p. 302, June, p. 371.

David Ewen: VW, a personal note, in *The Book of Modern Composers*, Knopf (New York) 1950 (2nd, enlarged edn.), p. 283.

M. Field: RVW, *Nuestra musica*, August 1951, p. 190.

Gerald Finzi: VW, the roots and the tree, *Philharmonic Post*, September–October 1952, p. 64.

Hubert Foss: VW's symphonic manner, *The Listener*, 5 March 1942, p. 317.

— VW and the stage, *The Listener*, 27 October 1949, p. 740.

— VW and the orchestra, *Penguin Music Magazine*, No. 9, July 1949, p. 29.

— RVW, a study, Harrap (London) 1950.

— The style of VW, *The Listener*, 9 October 1952, p. 612.

Alan Frank: Contemporary portraits, No. 8— RVW, *Music Teacher*, November 1951, p. 499.

— RVW, the man and his music, *M&M*, May 1956, p. 11.

Hans Gal (ed.): RVW, in *The Musicians World* (Great Composers in their Letters), Thames & Hudson (London) 1965, p. 423.

Peter Garvie: RVW, *Canadian Musical Journal*, autumn 1958, p. 48.

— RVW, *Canadian Musical Journal*, winter 1959, p. 36.

J. Gilfedder: VW, *Canon*, April 1954, p. 361.

Scott Goddard: The operas of VW, *The Listener*, 27 October 1938, p. 917.

— The music of VW, *World Review*, January 1949, p. 40.

— RVW, O.M., in *British Music of Our Time*, Pelican Books (London) 1946, p. 83.

— Profile, RVW, *Crescendo*, No. 21, March 1949, p. 12; No. 45, February 1952, p. 99.

— RVW, in *The Symphony*, Pelican Books (London) 1949, p. 395.

— VW at eighty, *M&M*, October 1952, p. 5.

— RVW, *Chesterian*, No. 196, autumn 1958, p. 57.

Vaughan Williams, Ralph

Harvey Grace: VW and national music, *The Listener*, 10 April 1935, p. 623.

Sydney Grew: VW, *Musical Herald*, April 1913, p. 99.

— RVW, in *Our Favourite Musicians from Stanford to Holbrooke*, Peter Davies (London) 1924 (2nd edn.), p. 159.

— VW, *Midland Musician*, January 1926, p. 5.

Donald J. Grout; VW, in *A History of Western Music*, Dent (London) 1962, p. 618.

Inglis Gundry: The triumph of VW, *Music Parade*, 1952, No. 12, p. 15.

Carl Willim Hansen: Lidt om RVW, *Dansk Musiktidsskrift*, September 1940, p. 133.

Tom Heinitz: Oldsters in bloom, *Saturday Review*, 30 June 1956, p. 47.

Robin Hawthorne: A note on the music of VW, *MR*, 1948, p. 269.

Peter Heyworth: RVW, *Canon*, November 1957, p. 97.

Everett Helm: VW observes 80th birthday, *Musical America*, October 1952, p. 23.

— RVW zum 80. Geburtstag, *Melos*, November 1952, p. 313.

— RVW, Ende einer Ära, *NZfM*, February 1959, p. 64.

Basil Hogarth: RVW, *The Gramophone*, July 1936, p. 53.

Joseph Holbrooke: RVW, in *Contemporary British Composers*, Cecil Palmer (London) 1925, p. 94.

Herbert Howells: VW, *The Score*, No. 7, December 1952, p. 55.

Frank Howes: Toward the unknown region, *Radio Times*, 9 February 1934, p. 373.

— The later works of VW, O.U.P. (London) 1937.

— The dramatic works of RVW, O.U.P. (London) 1937.

— RVW, *Amateur Musician*, January–March 1938, p. 127.

— The music of RVW, O.U.P. (London) 1954.

— RVW, at 83 he is still composing, *Canon*, September 1955, p. 44.

— VW and Walton, *Musica*, July–August (Nos. 7–8) 1958, p. 405.

- Caminhos da musica inglesa: VW e Walton, *Arte musical*, October 1959, p. 179.

A. Eaglefield Hull: VW and his music, *MO*, 1918, October, p. 29, November, p. 90, December p. 154.

Robert H. Hull: VW, a study of the man and his work, *Radio Times*, 24 January 1930, p. 203.

— The symphonies of VW, *MO*, 1934, January, p. 309, February, p. 405.

John Huntley: British film composers, 3: RVW, *Music Parade*, 1948, No. 8, p. 7.

Dyneley Hussey: An English composer, *Britain Today*, No. 198, October 1952, p. 37.

— VW on record, *Britain Today*, No. 222, October 1954, p. 32.

A. Jablonski: VW, *Hi Fi Music at Home*, November–December 1956, p. 39.

Arthur Jacobs: VW, some documentary notes, *Musical Information Record*, No. 6, 1952, p. 23.

S. G. Joseph: Grand young man of British music, *Etude*, January 1955, p. 9.

Maud Karpeles: RVW, O.M., *Journal of the English Folk Dance and Song Society*, December 1958, p. 121.

— RVW, O.M., *Journal of the International Folk Music Council*, 1959, p. 3.

Sir Gerald Kelly: Painting VW, *RCM Magazine*, 1955, No. 3, p. 61.

Michael Kennedy: VW at eighty, *Halle*, October 1952, p. 10.

— VW and the St. Matthew Passion, *Halle*, March 1956, p. 5.

— A tribute to VW, *Halle*, October 1957, p. 4.

— VW at eighty-five, *MT*, October 1957, p. 545.

— Sibelius and VW, *Halle*, No. 117, 1960–1, p. 10.

— VW, Whitman and Parry, *The Listener*, 12 November 1964, p. 778.

— The works of RVW, O.U.P. (London) 1964.

— Early VW, more facts, *MT*, May 1966, p. 404.

William Kimmel: VW's melodic style, *MQ*, October 1941, p. 491.

— VW's choice of words, *M&L*, April 1938, p. 132.

Alexander Knorr: In memoriam RVW, *Musica*, October 1958, p. 623.

Constant Lambert: VW makes us feel at home, *Radio Times*, 11 December 1931, p. 835.

Douglas Lilburn: VW, *Landfall*, March 1951, p. 57.

Per Lindfors: VW, *Rosier i Radio*, 1943, No. 39, p. 22.

Heinrich Lindlar: RVW der Sinfoniker, *NZfM*, August 1953, p. 457.

Watson Lyle: Dr. VW, a personal impression, *MN&H*, 14 October 1922, p. 340.

J. Lyons: The seven symphonies of VW, *American Record Guide*, August 1954, p. 387.

Joseph Machlis, RVW, in *Introduction to Contemporary Music*, Norton (USA) 1961, Dent (London), p. 293.

Elizabeth Maconchy: RVW, *Crescendo*, No. 124, December 1962, p. 74.

Colin Mason: VW, *The Spectator*, 11 October 1957, p. 481.

Jan M. Mařik: RVW, *Slovenska Hudba*, March 1958, p. 517.

Jeffery Mark: VW and Holst, *Modern Music*, January 1924, p. 24.

J. McKay Martin: VW and the amateur tradition, *Making Music*, No. 21, spring 1953, p. 6.

Wilfrid (W. H.) Mellers: Elgar and VW, in *Romanticism and the 20th Century*, Rockliff (London) 1957, p. 166; in *Man and his Music*, Barrie & Rockliff (London) 1962, p. 966.

— Two generations of English music, *Scrutiny*, autumn 1944, p. 261.

Donald Mitchell: Revaluations: VW, *MO*, 1955, April, p. 409, May, p. 471.

Michael Mullinar: Dr. VW as teacher, *Midland Musician*, January 1926, p. 8.

Oliver Neighbour: RVW, *The Score*, No. 24, November 1958, p. 7.

Ernest Newman: An English and universal music, *New York Times Magazine*, 12 October 1952, p. 20.

(D.) Hugh Ottaway: Two works of VW, *MO*, January 1950, p. 205.

— The symphonies of VW, *MO*, April 1950, p. 391.

— The operas of VW, *MO*, January 1951, p. 141.

— VW and the European background, *Halle*, July 1951.

— The last symphonies of VW, *Halle*, April 1952, p. 8.

— The fifth and sixth symphonies of VW, *Canon*, October 1952, p. 121.

— VW's symphonies, *Disc*, 1952, No. 20, p. 148; 1953, No. 21, p. 7, No. 22, p. 56.

— VW's symphonies, a complete recording, *MO*, January 1955, p. 213.

— VW and the symphonic epilogue, *MO*, December 1955, p. 145.

Simona Pakenham: RVW, a discovery of his music, Macmillan (London) 1957.

Elsie Payne: VW's orchestral colourings, *MMR*, January 1954, p. 3.

— VW and folksong, *MR*, May 1954, p. 103.

Guido Pannain: RVW, *La Rassegna musicale*, 1931, p. 317.

— RVW, in *Modern Composers*, Dent (London) 1932, p. 165.

— RVW, *La Rassegna musicale*, 1945, p. 255.

D. R. Peart: VW and the British radical tradition, *Canon*, October 1952, p. 111.

Hans F. Redlich: RVW 85 Jahre, *Musica*, November 1957, p. 659.

C. B. Rees: Impressions: Dr. RVW, O.M., *London Musical Events*, April 1951, p. 20.

— Dr. RVW, *London Musical Events*, October 1957, p. 26.

— Tea with a great man, *London Musical Events*, March 1958, p. 20.

— Tribute to a great Englishman, *London Musical Events*, October 1958, p. 21.

E. C. Rose: VW, an appreciation, *Sackbut*, July 1926, p. 320.

Edmund Rubbra: VW, some technical characteristics, *MMR*, February 1934, p. 27.

— The later VW, *M&L*, January 1937, p. 1.

— The symphonies of VW, *The Listener*, 25 January 1945, p. 109.

Adolfo Salazar: Dos ingleses, VW y G. von Holst, in *Sinfonía y ballet*, Editorial Mundo Latino (Madrid) 1929, p. 158.

H. C. Schonberg: RVW, *New York Times*, 31 August 1958, Section 2, p. 7.

E. E. Schwarz: The symphonies of RVW, an analysis of their stylistic elements, *Dissertation Abstracts*, February 1963, p. 2938.

Martin Shaw: RVW, O.M., *English Church Music*, No. 28, 1958, p. 73.

Frank H. Shera: The music of VW, *The Listener*, 17 June 1936, p. 1177.

Bernard Shore: VW, in *Sixteen Symphonise*, Longmans, Green (London) 1949, p. 283.

Barry Still: RVW, *Musica Sacra*, 1959, p. 114.

Dennis Stoll: VW, *Philharmonic Post*, July 1941, p. 3.

C. Stuart: VW, *Musikvärlden*, 1949, p. 105.

H. A. Stuckey: The music of Dr. VW, *MO*, May 1914, p. 625.

Norman Suckling: The impact of VW, *The Listener*, 9 October 1947, p. 648.

H. Taubman: A composer nears eighty, *New York Times*, 28 September 1952, Section 2, p. 7.

Ronald Taylor: VW and English national music, *The Cambridge Journal*, July 1953, p. 615.

Sir Richard Terry: 'Dona nobis pacem', *The Listener*, 4 November 1936, p. 879.

Francis Toye: Studies in English music, VI: VW and the folk music movement, *The Listener*, 24 June 1931, p. 1057.

Ursula Vaughan Williams: Choral music of RVW, *Musical Events*, February 1965, p. 6.

John Warrack: VW and opera, *Opera*, November 1958, p. 698.

— RVW, *Crescendo*, No. 74, February 1956, p. 110.

R. Weagly: VW and his contribution to music of the church, *Diapason*, 1 September 1954, p. 14.

R. Wienhorst: The church music of RVW, *Journal of Church Music*, July–August 1961, p. 2; *American Organist*, November 1961, p. 18.

Pamela J. Willetts: Recent British Museum acquisitions, *Music Teacher*, May 1961, p. 287.

— The RVW collection, *British Museum Quarterly*, August 1961, p. 3.

Sir Steuart Wilson: RVW, O.M., *Foyer*, No. 1, autumn 1951, p. 12.

— RVW, *M&L*, January 1959, p. 1.

Percy M. Young: Holst and VW, in *Pageant of England's music*, Heffer (Cambridge) 1939.

— VW, Dobson (London) 1953.

— VW, in *More Music Makers*, Dobson (London) 1955, p. 147.

— RVW, in *Symphony*, Phoenix House (London) 1957, p. 52.

— VW and Holst: in *A History of British Music*, Ernest Benn (London) 1967, p. 547.

MISCELLANEOUS OR UNSIGNED

The music of VW: songs and song writing, *The Times*, 16 February 1918, p. 9.

Three symphonies: VW's progress: influence of Walt Whitman, *The Times*, 4 February 1922, p. 8.

Dr. RVW on Sir R. Terry: resignation from Westminster Cathedral, *The Times*, 4 April 1924, p. 13.

Old master, *Time*, 3 May 1948, p. 48.

VW's symphonies, *The Times*, 11 February 1949, p. 7.

Bunyan and VW, *The Times*, 27 April 1951, p. 8.

The voice of England in music, *M&M*, May 1956, p. 7.

VW, *Röster i Radio*, 1957, No. 10, p. 11.

RVW, *Slovenska Hudba*, March 1958, p. 111.

England loves a master, *Musical America*, September 1958, p. 4.

Parish-pump composer, *Time*, 8 September 1958, p. 71.

ANTON WEBERN (1883–1945)

Anton von Webern—the 'von' was dropped in 1918—was born in Vienna on 3 December 1883, the son of a mining engineer. After infancy in Vienna, he spent much of his early life from the age of six at Graz in Styria and Klagenfurt in Carinthia, but returned to Vienna in 1902 to study music at the University. His musicological work there under Guido Adler led to the award of a D.Phil. in 1906 for a thesis on the *Choralis Constantinus* of Heinrich Isaac (1450–1517). Meanwhile in 1904 Webern had met Arnold Schoenberg and started to study composition with him. Webern's friendships with Schoenberg and with Alban Berg, Schoenberg's other outstanding pupil, were to be of great importance in his life. Most of the rest of that life was seemingly unspectacular. His public career was that of a teacher of composition and conductor, the latter at theatres in Ischl, Teplitz, Danzig, Stettin and Prague from 1908 to 1918, but thereafter mainly in Vienna, which he made his home (Mödling-bei-Wien, 1918–32; Maria Enzerdorf, 1932–45). He married his cousin Wilhelmine Mörtl in 1911, served as an officer cadet in the Austrian Army for a year during the First World War before being released because of poor eyesight, helped with the running of Schoenberg's

Society for Private Musical Performances from 1918 to 1922, conducted the Vienna Workers Symphony Orchestra and Choral Union from 1922 to 1934, and visited London four times between 1929 and 1935 to conduct for the BBC. When the Nazis seized power in Austria in 1938, Webern's music was proscribed as 'cultural Bolshevism'. He was debarred from holding any official post and during the Second World War had to take on editorial and proof-reading work for his publishers, Universal-Edition, to support himself and his family. After his son had been killed in action at the Yugoslav front in the spring of 1945, Webern hurriedly left Vienna and took refuge in the village of Mittersill in the Tyrol. He stayed on there during the first months of the post-war Occupation, and it was at Mittersill on 15 September 1945, during a scuffle which followed the arrest of a son-in-law of his for black-market activities, that Webern was accidentally shot dead by Raymond Bell, an American Army cook.

CATALOGUE OF WORKS

1. Zwei Stücke. For cello and piano. 1899.
1. *Langsam*; 2. *Langsam*.
Unpub.

2. Hochsommernacht (Martin Greif). For vocal duet and piano.

3. String Quartet in A minor.

4. Rondo. For string quartet.

5. Two Songs (Ferdinand Avenarius). For voice and piano. 1900–1.
1. *Wolkennacht*; 2. *Wehmut*.

6. Siegfrieds Schwert (L. Uhland). Ballad for voice and orchestra. September 1903. Poem: Uhland.

7. Drei Gedichte. For voice and piano. 1899–1903.
1. *Vorfrühling* (Ferdinand Avenarius). 12 January 1899, Klagenfurt. Dur. 1′ 15″.
2. *Nachtgebet der Braut* (Richard Dehmel). 1903, Vienna. Dur. 2′ 30″.
3. *Fromm* (Gustav Falke). 11 September 1902, Preglhof. Dur. 1′ 50″.
fp: May 1962, Seattle, Esther LaBerge and Rudolph Ganz.

Pub. 1965, Carl Fischer (ed. Rudolph Ganz); Boosey & Hawkes.

8. Vorfrühling (Ferdinand Avenarius). For voice and piano. Second setting. Unknown date.

9. Acht frühe Lieder. For voice and piano. 1901–4.
1. *Tief von fern* (Richard Dehmel). 21 April 1901, Klagenfurt. Dur. 1′ 5″.
2. *Aufblick* (Richard Dehmel). 1903, Preglhof. Dur. 2′ 25″.
3. *Blumengruss* (Goethe). 1903, Vienna. Dur. 1′ 12″.
4. *Bild der Liebe* (Martin Greif). 11 September 1904, Preglhof. Dur. 1′ 20″.
5. *Sommerabend* (Wilhelm Weigand). 7 September 1903, Preglhof. Dur. 2′ 32″.
6. *Heiter* (Friedrich Nietzsche). 1904. Dur. 1′ 7″.
7. *Der Tod* (Matthias Claudius). 1904, Vienna. Dur. 1′ 8″.
8. *Heimgang in der Frühe* (Detlev von Liliencron). 21 November 1901. Dur. 3′ 57″.
fp: May 1962, Seattle, Esther LaBerge and Rudolph Ganz.
Pub. 1961, 1965, Carl Fischer (ed. Rudolph Ganz); Boosey & Hawkes.

10. Im Sommerwind. Idyll for large orchestra after a poem by Bruno Wille. 16 September 1904, Preglhof. Dur. *c.* 12′.
3 fl, 2 ob, ca, 4 cl, bcl, 2 bsn; 6 hn, 2 tpt; timp, tgle, cym; 2 hp, strings.
fp: 25 May 1962, Seattle, Philadelphia Orchestra, cond. Eugene Ormandy.
Pub. 1962, 1966, Carl Fischer; Boosey & Hawkes.

11. Drei Lieder (Ferdinand Avenarius). For voice and piano. 1903–4.
1. *Gefunden*. 5 April 1904. Dur. 1′ 32″.
2. *Gebet*. 1903, Preglhof. Dur. 1′ 42″.
3. *Freunde*. 6 January 1904. Dur. 2′ 45″.
fp: May 1962, Seattle, Esther LaBerge and Rudolph Ganz.

12. Liebeslied (Hans Böhm). For voice and piano. 1904.

13. String Quartet. August 1905. In one movement. Dur. *c.* 15′.
fp: 26 May 1962, Seattle, University of Washington String Quartet.

Pub. 1961, 1965, Carl Fischer (ed. James Beale); Boosey & Hawkes (min. score No. 787).

14. Langsamer Satz. For string quartet. 1905. Dur. c. 8'.
fp: 27 May 1962, Seattle, University of Washington String Quartet.
Pub. 1961, 1965, Carl Fischer (ed. James Beale); Boosey & Hawkes (min. score No. 788).

15. Satz. For piano. c. 1905–6.

16. Sonatensatz. For piano. c. 1906. Rondo.

17. Piano Quintet. 1906. Pub. 1953, Boelke-Bomart (ed. Jacques Louis Monod).

18. Fünf Dehmel Lieder (Richard Dehmel). For voice and piano. 1906–8.
  1. *Ideale Landschaft.* 1906, Vienna, Ostern. Dur. 1' 40".
  2. *Am Ufer.* 1908, Vienna. Dur. 1' 15".
  3. *Himmelfahrt.* 1908. Dur. 3'.
  4. *Nächtliche Scheu.* 1907. Dur. 1' 50".
  5. *Helle Nacht,* 1908. Dur. 2' 35".
fp: May 1962, Seattle, Grace-Lynne Martin and Leonard Stein.
Pub. 1962, 1966, Carl Fischer (ed. Leonard Stein); Boosey & Hawkes.

19. Alladine und Palomides. Opera, after the play by Maurice Maeterlinck. 1908. Sketches only.

20. Passacaglia Op. 1. For orchestra. 1908.
2 fl, pic, 2 ob, ca, 2 cl, bcl, 2 bsn, cbsn; 4 hn, 3 tpt, 3 tmb, bs tuba; timp, GC, cym, tgle, tamtam; hp, strings.
fEp: 22 August 1931, Queen's Hall, Promenade Concert, BBC Symphony Orchestra, cond. Sir Henry Wood.
Pub. 1922, Universal-Edition. (Version for strings, harmonium and piano, unpub.)

21. Entflieht auf Leichten Kähnen Op. 2. Double Canon for chorus a cappella. 1908. Text: Stefan George.
?fEbp: 25 November 1946, BBC Singers, cond. Cyril Gell.
Pub. 1921, Universal-Edition.

22. Fünf Lieder aus 'Der siebente Ring' Op. 3 (Stefan George). For voice and piano. 1907–8.

1. *Dies ist ein Lied für dich allein*; 2. *Im Windesweben war meine Frage nur Träumerei*; 3. *An Bachesranft die einzigen Frühen die Hasel blühen*; 3. *Im Morgentaun trittst du hervor*; 5. *Kahl reckt der Baum im Winterdunst sein frierend Leben.*
fEbp (No. 5): 11 November 1934, Ruzena Herlinger.
?fEbp (complete): 15 October 1947, Elisabeth Höngen and Frederick Stone.
Pub. 1921, Universal-Edition.

BIBLIOGRAPHY:
Rolf Urs Ringger: Zur Wort-Ton-Beziehung beim frühen AW—Analyse von Op. 3 No. 1, *SM*, November–December 1963, p. 330.

23. Fünf Lieder nach Stefan George Op. 4. For voice and piano. 1908–9. Ded. Werner Reinhart.
  1. *Eingang*; 2. *Noch zwingt mich Treue über dir zu wachen*; 3. *Heil und Dank dir die den Segen brachte*; 4. *So ich traurig bin weiss ich nur ein Ding*; 5. *Ihr tratet zu dem Herde wo alle Glut verstarb.*
fEbp (No. 1): 11 November 1934, Ruzena Herlinger.
Pub. 1923, Universal-Edition. No. 5 orig. pub. 1912 in *Blaue Reiter.*

24. Vier Lieder nach Stefan George. For voice and piano. 1908–9.
  1. *Erwachen aus dem tiefsten Traumesschosse*; 2. *Kunfttag I*; 3. *Trauer I*; 4. *Das lockere Saatgefilde lechzet krank.*

25. Fünf Sätze Op. 5. For string quartet. 1909.
  1. *Heftig bewegt*; 2. *Sehr langsam*; 3. *Sehr bewegt*; 4. *Sehr langsam*; 5. *In zarter Bewegung.*
fFp: 14/16 December 1922, Paris, Concerts Wiener/*Revue Musicale* concert in Théâtre du Vieux-Colombier, Pro Arte Quartet.
fEp: 30 October 1927, BBC concert of modern chamber music, Vienna Quartet (Rudolf Kolisch, Felix Khuner, Eugen Lehner and Benar Heifetz).
Pub. 1922, Universal-Edition.

25a. Fünf Sätze Op. 5. Version for string orchestra. 1929.

fEp: 8 May 1931, BBC broadcast, BBC Orchestra, cond. Anton Webern.

Pub. 1930, Universal-Edition.

26. Sechs Stücke Op. 4. For large orchestra. 1909–10.

1. *Etwas bewegt*; 2. *Bewegt*; 3. *Zart bewegt*; 4. *Langsam*; 5. *Sehr langsam*; 6. *Zart bewebt*.

4 fl, pic, alto fl, 2 ob, 2 ca, E-flat cl, 2 cl, 2 bcl, 2 bsn, cbsn; 6 hn, 6 tpt, 6 tmb, bs tuba; timp, GC, ten dm, cym, tgle, Ruthe, tamtam, glock, bells; celesta, 2 hp, strings.

Pub. 1914, privately; 1961, Universal-Edition.

26a. Sechs Stücke. Revised version, 1928.

1. *Langsam* (Dur. 55″); 2. *Bewegt* (Dur. 1′ 10″); 3. *Mässig* (Dur. 50″); 4. *Sehr mässig* (Dur. 3′ 15″); 5. *Sehr langsam* (Dur. 1′ 50″); 6. *Langsam* (Dur. 1′ 15″).

2 fl, pic, 2 ob, 2 cl, bcl, 2 bsn, dbsn; 4 hn, 4 tpt, 4 tmb, bs tuba; timp, glock, cym, tgle, side dm, GC, tamtam, low bells; celesta, hp, strings.

?fEbp: 15 March 1958, London Symphony Orchestra, cond. Walter Goehr.

Pub. 1956, Universal-Edition. (Arr. for chamber orch., unpub.)

BIBLIOGRAPHY:

Wolf Isensee: A. Schoenbergs Op. 16, A. Bergs Op. 6 und A. Weberns Op. 6— Ein Vergleich, Hamburg, 1959.

Arnold Schoenberg: Foreword to Webern's Six Bagatelle Op. 6, *Die Reihe*, No. 2.

27. Vier Stücke Op. 7. For violin and piano. 1910.

1. *Sehr langsam*; 2. *Rasch*; 3. *Sehr langsam*; 4. *Bewegt*.

?fEbp: 20 March 1958, Yfrah Neaman and Howard Ferguson.

Pub. 1922, Universal-Edition.

28. Zwei Lieder Op. 8 (Rainer Maria Rilke). For voice and eight instruments. 1910.

1. *Du, der ich's nicht sage*; 2. *Du machst mich allein*.

cl, hn, tpt, celesta, hp, v, va, c.

?fEbp: 15 March 1958, Richard Standen and the London Symphony Orchestra, cond. Walter Goehr.

Pub. 1926, Universal-Edition.

29. Sechs Bagatellen Op. 9. For string quartet. 1913.

1. *Mässig* (Dur. 30″); 2. *Leicht bewegt* (Dur. 21″); 3. *Ziemlich fliessend* (Dur. 16″); 4. *Sehr langsam* (Dur. 35″); 5. *Äusserst langsam* (Dur. 1′ 10″); 6. *Fliessend* (Dur. 17″).

Pub. 1924, Universal-Edition.

BIBLIOGRAPHY:

R.-Aloys Mooser: 6 Bagatelles Op. 9, in *Aspects de la musique contemporaine*, Editions Labor et Fidès (Geneva) 1957, p. 168.

Henri Pousser: AW's organic chromaticism— 1st Bagatelle Op. 9, in *Die Reihe*, No. 2, p. 51.

30. Fünf Stücke Op. 10. For orchestra. 1911–13.

1. *Urbild* (Sehr ruhig und zart). Dur. 28″.

2. *Verwandlung* (Lebhaft und zart bewegt). Dur. 14″.

3. *Rückkehr* (Sehr langsam und ässerst ruhig). Dur. 1′ 45″.

4. *Erinnerung* (Fliessend, äusserst zart). Dur. 19″.

5. *Seele* (Sehr fliessend). Dur. 47″.

fl, pic, E-flat cl, cl, bcl; hn, tpt, tmb; hmnm, celesta, mandoline, guitar, hp; glock, xyl, cowbells, bells, tgle, cym, small dm, GC; string quartet.

fFp: 28 March 1929, Paris, Théâtre des Champs-Elysées, cond. Walter Straram.

fEp: 2 December 1929, BBC broadcast, 'Special Orchestra', cond. Anton Webern.

Pub. 1923 (with titles), 1951 (without titles), Universal-Edition.

BIBLIOGRAPHY:

Erwin Stein: AW, Fünf Stücke für Orchester, *Pult und Taktstock*, 1926, p. 109.

31. Vier Stücke. For orchestra. c. 1910–13.

Numbered by Webern: *III.* (*Bewegt*); *IV.* (*Sehr bewegte Viertel*); *V.* (*Langsame Viertel*); *VI.* (*Langsam, sostenuto*).

Unpub.

32. O sanftes Glühn der Berge. Song with orchestra. 1913.

Instrumentation as for No. 30.

Unpub.

33. Drei kleine Stücke Op. 11. For cello and piano. 27 May 1914. Ded. to the composer's father.

1. *Mässige* (Dur. 53″); 2. *Sehr bewegt* (Dur. 13″); 3. *Äusserst ruhig* (Dur. 45″).
Pub. 1924, Universal-Edition.

34. Cello Sonata. 1914. Draft only.

35. Vier Lieder Op. 12. For voice and piano 1915–17.
1. *Der Tag is vergangen* (Folksong). 1915.
2. *Die geheimnisvolle Flöte* (Li-Tai-Po, from Hans Bethge's 'Chinesische Flöte'). 1917.
3. *Schien mir's, als ich sah die Sonne* (from August Strindberg's 'Gespenstersonate'). 1915.
4. *Gleich und gleich* (Goethe). 1917.
Pub. 1925, Universal-Edition.

36. Vier Lieder Op. 13. For voice and orchestra. 1914–18. Ded. Dr. Norbert Schwarzmann. Dur. 7′.
1. *Wiese im Park* (Karl Kraus). 1917. Dur. 2½′.
fl, cl, bcl; hn, tpt, tmb; celesta, hp, glock, v, va, c, db.
2. *Die Einsame* (Wang-Seng-Yu, from Hans Bethge's 'Chinesische Flöte'). 1914. Dur. 1½′.
pic, cl, bcl; hn, tpt, tmb; celesta, hp, glock, v, va, c, db.
3. *In der Fremde* (Li-Tai-Po, from Hans Bethge's 'Chinesische Flöte'). 1917. Dur. 1′.
pic, cl, bcl; tpt; celesta, hp, v, va, c.
4. *Ein Winterabend* (Georg Trakl). 1918. Dur. 2′.
cl, bcl; tpt, tmb; celesta, hp, v, va, c, db.
?fEbp: 15 March 1958, Helga Pilarczyk and the London Symphony Orchestra, cond. Walter Goehr.
Pub. 1926, 1954, 1956, Universal-Edition. English version, Eric Smith.

37. Zwei Lieder. For voice and orchestra. 1914. Instrumentation comparable to No. 36.
1. *Leise Düfte*; 2. *Nun wird es wieder Lenz.*
Unpub.

38. Sechs Lieder Op. 14 (Georg Trakl). For voice, clarinet, bass clarinet, violin and cello. 1917–21.
1. *Die Sonne.* 1921.
2. *Abendland I.* 1919.
3. *Abendland II.* 1919.
4. *Abendland III.* 1917.
5. *Nachts.* 1919.
6. *Gesang einer gefangenen Amsel.* 1919.

fEp (broadcast): 3 November 1960, BBC's Maida Vale Studios, invited audience concert, Dorothy Dorow and English Chamber Orchestra, cond. Bruno Maderna.
Pub. 1924, Universal-Edition.

39. Fünf geistliche Lieder Op. 15. For voice and instrumental ensemble. 1917–22.
fl, cl/bcl, tpt, hp, v/va.
1. *Das Kreuz, das muss'ter tragen* (1921); 2. *Morgenlied* (1922) (from 'Das Knaben Wunderhorn'); 3. *In Gottes Namen aufstehn* (1921); 4. *Mein Weg geht jetzt vorüber, o Welt* (1922); 5. *Fahr hin, o Seel', zu deinem Gott* (1917).
Pub. 1924, Universal-Edition.

BIBLIOGRAPHY:
Hans-Elmar Bach: Betrachtungen zum geistlichen Liedschaffen AWs, *Katholische Kirchenmusik*, 1963, No. 3.
Heins-Klaus Metzger: Analysis of the sacred song Op. 15 No. 4, *Die Reihe*, No. 2 (Eng. edn., p. 75).
Rudolf Stephan: Über einige geistliche Kompositionen AvWs, *Musik und Kirche*, 1954, p. 152.

40. O Mutter, Dank! So fühl' ich deine Hand. For voice and orchestra. 1919. Sketches only.

41. Fünf Canons Op. 16 (Latin texts). For high soprano, clarinet and bass clarinet. 1923–1924.
1. *Christus factus est pro nobis*; 2. *Dormi Jesu* (from 'Das Knaben Wunderhorn'); 3. *Crux fidelis*; 4. *Asperges me*; 5. *Crucem tuam adoramus.*
?fEbp: 4 January 1954, Emelie Hooke, Georgina Dobréc (cl), Wilfred Hambleton (bcl).
Pub. 1928, Universal-Edition.

42. Drei Volkstexte Op. 17. For voice, violin/viola, clarinet and bass clarinet. 1924.
1. *Armer Sünder, du* (Dur. 40″); 2. *Liebste Jungfrau* (Dur. 50″); 3. *Heiland, unsre Missetaten* (Dur. 40″).
Pub. 1955, Universal-Edition. English version, Eric Smith.

43. Stück. For piano. 1924. Pub. 1966, Universal-Edition.

43a. Kinderstück. For piano. 1924. Unpub.

44. Drei Lieder Op. 18. For voice, E-flat clarinet and guitar. 1925.
1. *Schatzerl klein, musst nit traurig sein*;
2. *Erlösung* (from 'Das Knaben Wunderhorn');
3. *Ave, Regina coelorum*.
Pub. 1927, Universal-Edition.

45. Satz. For string trio. 1925. *Ruhig fliessend*. Pub. 1966, Universal-Edition.

46. String Trio. 1925. *Ruhig*. Sketches only.

47. Zwei Lieder Op. 19. For mixed chorus, celesta, guitar, violin, clarinet and bass clarinet. 1926. Text: from Goethe's 'Chinesische-Deutsche Jahres- und Tageszeiten'. Ded. David Josef Bach.
1. *Weiss wie Lilien, reine Kerzen*; 2. *Ziehn die Schafe von der Wiese*.
?fEbp: 20 March 1958, BBC Singers and instrumental ensemble, cond. Walter Goehr.
Pub. 1928, Universal-Edition.

48. String Trio Op. 20. Summer 1927.
1. *Sehr langsam*; 2. *Sehr getragen und ausdrucksvoll*.
fp: 12 September 1928, Siena, Salone Chigi Saracini, ISCM Festival, Kolisch (violin), Lehner (viola), Heifetz (cello).
fEp: 15 October 1928, 2LO broadcast, Arts Theatre, members of the Vienna String Quartet (Rudolf Kolisch, Eugen Lehner and Benar Heifetz).
fEp (concert): 14 December 1938, Aeolian Hall, Washbourne Trio (Kathleen Washbourne, Winifred Copperwheat, William Pleeth).
Pub. 1927, Universal-Edition.

49. Auf Bergen in der reinsten Höhe. Chorus. Autumn 1926. Sketches only.

50. Symphony Op. 21. 1928. Ded. to the composer's daughter Christine. Dur. 10'.
1. *Ruhig schreitend*; 2. *Variationen*.
cl, bcl; 2 hn; hp, 2 v, va, c.
fp: 8 December 1929, New York, League of Composers, cond. Alexander Smallens.
fEp: 27 July 1931, Queen's Hall, ISCM concert, BBC Orchestra, cond. Hermann Scherchen.
Pub. 1929, Universal-Edition.

BIBLIOGRAPHY:
Walter F. Goebel: AWs Sinfonie, *Melos*, November 1961, p. 359.

R.-Alloys Mooser: Symphonie Op. 21, in *Aspects de la musique contemporaine*, Editions Labor et Fidès (Geneva) 1957, p. 103.
Willi Reich: Alban Berg und AvW in ihren neuen Werke, *Der Auftakt*, 1930, Nos. 5–6, p. 134.

51. Quartet Op. 22. For violin, clarinet, tenor saxophone and piano. 1930. Ded. Adolf Loos on his sixtieth birthday.
1. *Sehr mässig*; 2. *Sehr schwungvoll*.
?fEbp: 20 March 1958, instrumental ensemble, cond. Walter Goehr.
Pub. 1932, Universal-Edition.

BIBLIOGRAPHY:
Arnold Elston: Some rhythmic practices in contemporary music, *MQ*, July 1956, p. 325.
H. Grüss: Zu Weberns Quartett Op. 22, *Beiträge zur Musikwissenschaft*, 1966, Nos. 3–4, p. 241.

52. Drei Gesänge Op. 23 (Hildegard Jone: from 'Viae inviae'). For voice and piano. 1934.
1. *Das dunkle Herz, das in sich lauscht*; 2. *Es stürzt aus Höhen Frische, die uns leben macht*; 3. *Herr Jesu mein, Du trittst mit jedem Morgen ins Haus*.
fp: 5 September 1935, Prague, ISCM Festival.
Pub. 1936, Universal-Edition.

53. Concerto Op. 24. For 9 instruments. 1934. Ded. Arnold Schoenberg on his sixtieth birthday. Dur. 9'.
1. *Etwas lebhaft*; 2. *Sehr langsam*; 3. *Sehr rasch*.
fl, ob, cl; hn, tpt, tmb; v, va; p.
fEbp: 11 February 1947, chamber ensemble of the French National Orchestra, cond. René Leibowitz.
fEp: 23 February 1958, Park Lane House, Thurloe Ensemble, cond. Edward Downes.
Pub. 1948, Universal-Edition.

BIBLIOGRAPHY:
Bené Leibowitz: Qu'cst-ce que la musique de douze sons: Le concerto pour neuf instruments Op. 24 d'AW, Liège, 1948.
Leopold Spinner: Analysis of a period, *Die Reihe*, No. 2 (Eng. edn., p. 46).
Paul Stefan: Ein Klavierkonzert von Webern, *Anbruch*, June 1934, p. 132.

Webern, Anton

Karlheinz Stockhausen: Das Konzert für 9 Instrumente Op. 24, *Melos*, December 1953, p. 343.

54. Drei Lieder Op. 25 (Hildegard Jone). For voice and piano. 1934–5.
1. *Wie bin ich froh!* (Dur. 1′); 2. *Des Herzens Purpurvogel fliegt durch die Nacht* (Dur. 1′ 30″); 3. *Sterne, Ihr silbernen Bienen der Nacht* (Dur. 1′ 15″).
Pub. 1956, Universal-Edition. English version, Eric Smith.

55. Das Augenlicht Op. 26 (Hildegard Jone). For mixed chorus and orchestra. 1935. Ded. to the composer's daughter Amalie Waller. Dur. 10′.
fl, ob, cl, alto sax; hn, tpt, tmb; timp, glock, xyl, cym; celesta, hp, mandoline; 8 v, 4 va, 4 c.
fEp: 17 June 1938, Queen's Hall, ISCM Festival, BBC Singers and BBC Orchestra, cond. Hermann Scherchen.
Pub. 1938, Universal-Edition (piano score by Ludwig Zenk); 1956, Universal-Edition (English version by Eric Smith). Also min. score.

56. Variationen Op. 27. For piano. 1936. Ded. Eduard Steuermann. Dur. 10′.
1. *Sehr mässig*; 2. *Sehr schnell*; 3. *Ruhig fliessend.*
Pub. 1937, Universal-Edition.

BIBLIOGRAPHY:
Friedhelm Döhl: Webern's opus 27, *Melos*, December 1963, p. 400.
Armin Klammer: Webern's Piano Variations Op. 27, 3rd movement, in *Die Reihe*, No. 2 (Eng. edn., p. 81).
David Lewin: A metrical problem in Webern's Op. 27, *Journal of Music Theory*, 1962, No. 1, p. 124.
Wilbur Lee Ogdon: A Webern analysis, *Journal of Music Theory*, 1962, No. 1, p. 133.
Peter Westergaard: Webern and 'Total Organisation': an analysis of the second movement of the Piano Variations Op. 27, *PNM*, spring 1963, p. 107.

57. String Quartet Op. 28. 1937–8. Ded. Elizabeth Sprague Coolidge.
1. *Mässig*; 2. *Gemächlich*; 3. *Sehr fliessend.*

fp: 22 September 1938, Pittsburgh, Coolidge Festival.
Pub. 1939, Hawkes; 1955, Universal-Edition.

BIBLIOGRAPHY:
Herbert Eimert: Interval proportions, *Die Reihe*, No. 2 (Eng. edn., p. 93).
Erwin Stein: Webern's new Quartet, *Tempo*, No. 4, July 1939.

58. Erste Kantate Op. 29. For soprano, mixed chorus and orchestra. 1938–9. Text: Hildegard Jone. Dur. 20′.
1. *Zündender Lichtblitz des Lebens schlug ein*; 2. *Kleiner Flügel, Ahornsamen schwebst im Winde!*; 3. *Tönen die seligen Saiten Apollo.*
fl, ob, cl, bcl; hn, tpt, tmb; timp, GC, cym, tgle, glock, tamtam; celesta, hp, mandoline, strings.
fbp: 11 February 1947, BBC broadcast, Emelie Hooke, BBC Singers and Boyd Neel Orchestra, cond. Walter Goehr.
Pub. 1954 (vocal score), 1957, Universal-Edition. English version by Eric Smith.

BIBLIOGRAPHY:
Hildegard Jone: A Cantata, *Die Reihe*, No. 2 (Eng. edn., p. 7).
György Ligeti: Über die Harmonik in Weberns erster Kantate, *Darmstadter Beiträge*, 1960, No. 3, p. 49.

59. Variationen Op. 30. For orchestra. 1940. Ded. Werner Reinhart. Dur. 10′.
fl, ob, cl, bcl; hn, tpt, tmb, bs tuba; timp; celesta, hp, strings.
fp: February 1943, Winterthur, cond. Hermann Scherchen.
Pub. 1956, Universal-Edition.

BIBLIOGRAPHY:
R.-Aloys Mooser: Variationen pour orchestre Op. 30, in *Aspects de la musique contemporaine*, Editions Labor et Fidès (Geneva) 1957, p. 229.

60. Zweite Kantate Op. 31. For soprano, bass, mixed chorus and orchestra. 1941–3. Text: Hildegard Jone. Dur. 16′.
1. *Schweigt auch die Welt*. Bass and orchestra.
2. *Sehr tiefverhalten innerst Leben*. Bass and orchestra.

3. *Schöpfen aus Brunnen des Himmels.* Soprano, female chorus and orchestra.

4. *Leichteste Bürden der Bäume.* Soprano and orchestra.

5. *Freundselig ist das Wort.* Soprano, mixed chorus, viola solo and orchestra.

6. *Gelokkert aus dem Schosse.* Chorus and orchestra.

fl, pic, ob, ca, cl, bcl, alto sax, bsn; hn, tpt, tmb, bs tuba; bells, glock, celesta; hp, strings.

fp: 23 June 1950, Brussels, ISCM Festival.

fEbp: 5 August 1950, Ilona Steingruber, Otto Wiener, Chorus and Orchestra of INR, Flemish Service, cond. Herbert Häfner.

Pub. 1956, Universal-Edition. English version by Eric Smith.

BIBLIOGRAPHY:

Niccolò Castiglioni: Sul rapporto tra parola e musica nella II Cantata di Webern, *Incontri Musicali*, August 1959 (No. 3), p. 112.

Leopold Spinner: AWs Kantate Nr. 2, opus 31, *SM*, September–October 1961, p. 303.

ARRANGEMENTS BY WEBERN

J. S. BACH

Ricercare a 6 voce.

fEbp: 25 April 1935, BBC Orchestra, cond. Anton Webern.

Pub. 1935, Universal-Edition.

FRANZ LISZT

Arbeitchor. Arr. for bass, mixed chorus and orchestra.

ARNOLD SCHOENBERG

Sechs Orchester-Lieder Op. 8 Nos. 2 & 6. Arr. for voice and piano.

Kammersymphonie Op. 9. Arr. for flute (or violin), clarinet (or viola), violin, cello and piano. 1922.

Fünf Orchester Stücke Op. 16. Arr. for two pianos.

Gurrelieder: Vorspiel. Arr. for two pianos eight hands. 1910.

FRANZ SCHUBERT

Deutsche Tänze vom Oktober 1824. Arr. for orchestra. Dur. 9'.

2 fl, 2 ob, 2 cl, 2 bsn; 2 hn; strings.

fEbp: 23 April 1933, BBC Orchestra, cond. Anton Webern.

Pub. 1931, Universal-Edition.

Rosamunde: Romanze. Arr. for voice and orchestra.

2 fl, 2 ob, 2 cl, 2 bsn; 2 hn; strings.

Ihr Bild. Arr. for voice and orchestra.

Instrumentation as preceding.

Die Winterreise: Der Wegweiser. Arr. for voice and orchestra.

Instrumentation as preceding.

Du bist die Ruh'. Arr. for voice and orchestra.

Instrumentation as preceding.

Tränenregen. Arr. for voice and orchestra.

Instrumentation as preceding.

Movements from Piano Sonatas. Arr. for orchestra.

1. *Sonata in A minor* Op. 42. Second movement.

2. *Sonata in E flat major* Op. 122. Third movement.

3. *Sonata in B major* Op. 147. Part of second and third movements.

HUGO WOLF

Lebe wohl. Arr. for voice and orchestra.

2 fl, 2 ob, 2 cl, 2 bsn; 2 hn; strings.

Der Knabe und das Immelein. For voice and orchestra.

Instrumentation as preceding.

Denk es, o Seele! Arr. for voice and orchestra. 16 April 1903, Preglhof.

2 fl, 2 ob, 2 cl, 2 bsn; 2 hn, 2 tpt, 3 tmb; pcssn; hp, strings.

WRITINGS BY WEBERN

Heinrich Isaac. Choralis Constantinus 2. Teil, bearbeitet von AvW, *Denkmäler der Tonkunst in Österreich*, Vol. XV, No. 1, 1909.

Über AS, *Rheinische Musik- und Theater-Zeitung*, 1912, pp. 99, 118.

Schoenbergs Musik, in *Arnold Schoenberg*, Munich, 1912, p. 22.

— Der Lehrer (contribution), in –do–, p. 85.

Der Weg zur Komposition in zwölf Tönen, 1932.

Webern, Anton

Der Weg zur neuen Musik, 1933; 1960, Universal-Edition (together with preceding, ed. Willi Reich); transl. Leo Black, 1963.

Das Musikleben des Westers im neuen Reich, *AMZ*, December 1933.

Der Schönbergschüler, '*23*', No. 14, 1934.

Aus Schoenbergs Schriften, in *AS zum 60. Geburtstag*, Universal-Edition 1934.

Homage to Arnold Schoenberg, *Die Reihe*, No. 2 (Eng. edn., p. 9).

Letters, in *–do–*, p. 13.

Was ist Musik?, *Melos*, October 1958.

Letters from Webern and Schoenberg to Roberto Gerhard, *Score*, No. 24, November 1958, p. 36.

Briefe an Hildegard Jone und Josef Humplik (ed. Josef Polnauer), Universal-Edition (Vienna) 1959.

Briefe an zwei Freunde, *Melos*, December 1959.

Nachwort mit Briefen Weberns an W. Reich, Vienna, 1960.

Towards a new music, *The Score*, January 1961, p. 29.

Bekännelse till Arnold Schoenberg, *Nutida musik*, Vol. 6 (1962–3), No. 7, p. 18.

GENERAL BIBLIOGRAPHY

Theodor Wiesengrund Adorno: Berg and Webern, Schoenberg's heirs, *Modern Music*, January–February 1931.

— AW, *Vortrag Südwestfunk*, 21 April 1932; *SM*, 15 November 1932, p. 679; *Der Auftakt*, 1936, p. 159.

— AW, *Anbruch*, June–July 1926, p. 280.

— Meister und Jünger, '*23*', No. 14, 1934.

— AvW, in *Klangfiguren*, Berlin, 1959, p. 157.

Kees Bak: Over de 'Miskenning' von AW, *Mens en melodie*, 1958, p. 299.

Gerth-Wolfgang Baruch: AvW, *Melos*, December 1953, p. 337.

James Beale: Weberns musikalischer Nachlass, *Melos*, October 1964, p. 297.

Jane Guthrie Beale: An archive for Webern, *Music Magazine*, February 1962, p. 13.

André Boucourechliev: Vous entendez demain . . ., *Preuves*, No. 145, March 1963, p. 69.

Pierre Boulez: The Threshold, *Die Reihe*, No. 2 (Eng. edn., p. 40).

— Hommage à Webern, *Domaine musical*, 1954, p. 123.

— Webern, in *Encyclopédie de la musique*, Vol. III, Fasquelle (Paris) 1961, p. 907.

E. Bour: Webern ou pas Webern?, *Musica* (Chaix), No. 76, July 1960, p. 14.

M. K. Bradshaw: Tonal structure in the early works of AW, *Dissertation Abstracts*, August 1963, p. 763.

Cesar Bresgen: AW in Mittersill, *ÖM*, May 1961, p. 226.

— In memoriam AW, *Musikerziehung*, November 1965, p. 66.

A. J. Broekema: A stylistic analysis and comparison of the solo vocal works of Arnold Schoenberg, Alban Berg and AW, *Dissertation Abstracts*, November 1962, p. 1730.

Ida Cappelli: Webern rückt in die erste Reihe auf, *Melos*, December 1962, p. 377.

— Webern a l'Espressionismo, *Musica Università*, September 1964.

Mosco Carner: Webern and the Avant-Garde, *The Listener*, 9 August 1962, p. 225.

E. Casey: Webern, architect of silence, *Music Journal*, September 1961, p. 52.

Paul Collaer: Arnold Schoenberg, AW, Alban Berg, in *La Musique moderne*, Elsevier (Brussels) 1955, p. 35; Eng. transl. Sally Abeles in *A History of Modern Music*, World Publishing Co. (Cleveland) 1961, p. 58.

N. Costarelli: La lezione di AW, *Santa Cecilia*, February 1959, p. 66.

Robert Craft: More Webern, *Saturday Review*, 26 January 1952, p. 56.

— Discoveries and convictions, *Counterpoint*, February 1953, p. 16.

— AW, *Score*, No. 13, September 1955, p. 9.

Luigi Dallapiccola: Incontro con AW, *Il Mondo* (Florence), 3 November 1945; Begegnung mit AW, *Melos*, April 1965, p. 115.

Norman Demuth: AvW, in *Musical Trends in the 20th Century*, Rockliff (London) 1952, p. 233.

B. Dimov: Webern und die Tradition, *ÖM*, August 1965, p. 411.

Friedhelm Döhl: Die Welt der Dichtung in Weberns Musik, *Melos*, March 1964, p. 88.

Friedrich Deutsch Dorian: Webern als Lehrer, *Melos*, April 1960, p. 101.

Leonard Duck: Schoenberg and Webern, *Halle*, No. 117, 1960–1, p. 19.

Herbert Eimert: AW, *Die Reihe*, No. 2.

Ludwig Erhardt: W strone Weberna, *Ruch Muzyczny*, 1961, No. 11, p. 18.

R. Eyer: Evolution of a composer—complete works of Webern, *Musical America*, July 1957, p. 28.

Michel Fano: Pouvoirs transmis, in *La Musique et ses problèmes contemporaines* (Cahiers de la Compagnie Madeleine Renaud-Jean-Louis Barrault), Juillard (Paris) 1954, p. 38.

Louis-René des Forêts: Stravinsky et Webern au domaine musicale, *Nouvelle nouvelle revue française*, No. 49, 1957, p. 160.

Wolfgang Fortner: AW und unsere Zeit, *Neue Zürcher Zeitung*, 1958; *Melos*, November 1960, p. 325.

Roberto Gerhard: Letters of Webern and Schoenberg, *Score*, No. 24, November 1958, p. 36.

— Some lectures by Webern, *Score*, No. 28, January 1961, p. 25.

Bengt Hambraeus: Spel med tolv toner: En studie kring AvWs esoteriska polyfoni, *Ord och bild*, 1952, p. 593.

— Spel med punkter och klangfärger, *Röster i Radio*, 1955, No. 46, p. 6.

Iain Hamilton: Alban Berg and AW, in *European Music in the Twentieth Century*, Routledge & Kegan Paul (London) 1957.

Christopher Hampton: AW and the consciousness of time, *MR*, February 1959, p. 45.

Peter S. Hansen: Berg and Webern, in *An Introduction to Twentieth Century Music*, Allyn & Bacon (Boston) 1961, p. 376.

Everett Helm: Darmstadt, Baden-Baden and twelve-tone music, *Saturday Review*, 30 July 1955, p. 35.

Friedrich Herzfeld: AWs Tod, *NZfM*, March 1958, p. 147.

André Hodeir: AW, in *Since Debussy* (transl. Noel Burch), Secker & Warburg (London) 1961, p. 69.

Heinrich Jalowetz: AW wird 50. Jahre alt, *Anbruch*, November–December 1933, p. 135.

Hildegard Jone & J. Humplik: Dem Freunde '*23*', No. 14, 1934.

Otto Ketting: AW, persona non grata in Nederland, *Mens en melodie*, August 1958.

Eberhard Klemm: Symmetrien in Chorsatz von AW, *Deutsche Jahrbuch der Musikwissen-schaft für 1966*, Edition Peters (Leipzig) 1967, p. 107.

Peter Kolman: AW, der Schöpfer der Neuen Musik, *Slovenska hudba*, Vol. VII, No. 10.

Walter Kolneder: Klangtechnik und Motivbildung bei Webern, *Annales Universitatis Saraviensis*, Philosophie-Letters LX, January 1960, p. 27.

— Stilporträt AW, in *Stilporträts der Neuen Musik*, Berlin, 1961.

— AW, Einführung in Werk und Stil, P. J. Tonger (Rodenkirchen am Rhein) 1961; AW, an introduction to his works (transl. Humphrey Searle), Faber (London) 1968.

Bjarne Kortsen: AWs samlede værke rpå plater, *Dansk Musiktidsskrift*, March 1959, p. 40.

— AW i brev og foredrag, *Dansk Musiktidsskrift*, 1961, No. 2, p. 47.

— Some remarks on the instrumentation of AW, Oslo, 1963.

Ernst Krenek: Freiheit und Verantwortung, '*23*', No. 14, February 1934.

— The same stone which the builders refused is become the headstone of the corner, *Die Reihe*, No. 2 (Eng. edn., p. 12).

— Der ganze Webern in drei Sunden, *Melos*, 1957, p. 304.

René Leibowitz: Le silence d'AW, *Labyrinthe*, 15 November 1945.

— AW, *L'Arche*, 1945, No. 11.

— Innovation and tradition in modern music, 2: The tragic art of AW, *Horizon*, May 1947, p. 282.

— Les œuvres posthumes d'AW, in *Significations des musiciens contemporains*, Liège, 1949.

— AW, in *Schoenberg et son école*, Paris, 1947, p. 191.

György Ligeti: Die Komposition mit Reihen und ihre Konsequenzen bei AW, *ÖM*, June–July 1961, p. 297.

— Weberns Melodik, *Melos*, April 1966, p. 116.

— Einführung in die Musik von AW, Universal-Edition (Vienna) in preparation.

Heinrich Lindlar: Musik der Einsamkeit: Zum 75. Geburtstag AvWs, *Deutsche Zeitung* (Cologne), 29 November 1958.

Karl Linke: AvW und Alban Berg, *Das Musikfestliche Wien* (Vienna), June 1912; in Willi Reich's *Alban Berg*, Zürich, 1959.

Edward Arthur Lippmann: Webern, the complete music recorded, *MQ*, 1958, p. 416.

W. C. McKenzie: The music of AW, *Dissertation Abstracts*, September 1960, p. 640.

Armand Machabey: Notes sur la musique allemande contemporaine, V: Webern, *Le Ménestrel*, 14 November 1930, p. 477.

Joseph Machlis: AW, in *Introduction to Contemporary Music*, Norton (New York), Dent (London), p. 383.

— Three works by Webern, in *–do–*, p. 388.

R. Maren: Music of AW, *Reporter*, 30 May 1957, p. 38.

Colin Mason: Webern's late chamber music, *M&L*, July 1957, p. 232.

Hans-Klaus Metzger: Webern and Schoenberg, *Die Reihe*, No. 2 (Eng. edn., p. 42).

Hans Moldenhauer: The last evening of AW's life, *New York Times*, 25 December 1960, Section 2, p. 11.

— Rich Webern legacy contains unknown compositions, *New York Times*, 17 September 1961.

— Wealth of Webern manuscripts now at University of Washington, *Music of the West Magazine*, November 1961, p. 11.

— The death of AW, a drama in documents, Philosophical Library (New York) 1962.

— Das Webern-Archiv in Amerika, *ÖM*, August 1965.

— In quest of Webern, *Saturday Review*, 27 August 1966, p. 47.

— A Webern pilgrimage, *MT*, February 1968, p. 122.

— Webern's projected Op. 32, *MT*, August 1970, p. 789.

— Webern's death, *MT*, September 1970, p. 877.

Giorgio Moschetti: Postromanticismo ed espressionismo nelle prime opere di AW, *Il Convegno musicale*, No. 1, January–March 1964.

Jeremy Noble: Third International Webern festival, *High Fidelity*, January 1967.

Michael Parsons: Webern's late works, *The Listener*, 25 August 1966, p. 286.

Luigi Pestalozza: Storicità di AW, *La Rassegna musicale*, 1958, p. 303.

Michel Philippot: AW, *Cahiers musicaux*, No. 5.

Paul A. Pisk: Seattle—Auch von Webern gibt es noch Uraufführungen, *Melos*, July–August 1962, p. 252.

— AW, profile of a composer, *Texas Quarterly*, winter 1962, p. 114.

Henri Pousseur: Webern und die Theorie, *Darmstädter Beitrage zur Neuen Musik*, 1958, No. 1, p. 38.

— Webern's organic chromaticism, *Die Reihe*, No. 2 (Eng. edn., p. 51).

— Da Schoenberg a Webern, una mutazione, *Incontri musicali*, No. 1.

Malcolm Rayment: AW, the complete music recorded, *Gramophone Record Review*, July 1960, p. 509.

Willi Reich: AvW, *De Muziek*, 1929, p. 249.

— Alban Berg und AvW in ihren neuesten Werken, *Der Auftakt*, 1930, p. 132.

— AvW, *Die Musik*, August 1930, p. 812.

— AvW, *Der Auftakt*, November–December 1933, p. 164.

— Weberns Musik, '*23*', No. 14, February 1934.

— Weberns Vorträge, in *–do–*.

— Per la morte di AW, *Il Mondo* (Florence), 2 February 1946.

— AW, the man and his music, *Tempo*, No. 14, March 1946.

— 'Meister des dreifachen Pianissimo'—Zum Tode von AW, *SM*, January 1946.

— Aus unbekannten Briefen von Alban Berg an AW, *SM*, February 1953, p. 49.

— Das Gesamtwerk AWs auf Schallplatten, *SM*, September–October 1960, p. 320.

— AW—Weg und Gestalt—Selbstzeugnisse und Worte der Freunde (ed. Willi Reich), Verlag der Arche (Zürich) 1961.

— AW über Alban Berg, *NZfM*, April 1963, p. 143.

— Briefe aus Weberns letzten Jahren, *ÖM*, August 1965, p. 407.

— Berg und Webern schreiben an Hermann Scherchen, *Melos*, 1966, p. 225.

Rolf-Urs Ringger: Zur Formstruktur in AWs späten Klavierliedern, *SM*, January–February 1965, p. 20.

— Sprach-musikalische Chiffern in AWs Klavierliedern, *SM*, January 1966, p. 14.

— Reihenelemente in AWs Klavierliedern, *SM*, May–June 1967, p. 144.

George Rochberg: Webern's search for harmonic identity, *Journal of Music Theory*, spring 1962, p. 109.

— Marcel Rubin: Webern und die Folgen, *Musik und Gesellschaft*, August 1960, p. 463; *Das Ton-Magazin*, 1961, p. 41.

Luigi Rognoni: La scuola musicale di Vienna —Espressionismo e dodecafonia, Giulio Einaudi (Turin) 1966.

Eric Salzman: Unheard scores of Webern found, *New York Times*, 4 September 1961, p. 17.

Helmut Schmidt-Garre: Webern als Angry Young Man—Aus alten Zeitungskritiken über AvW, *NZfM*, April 1964, p. 132.

Rudolf Schwarz: Webern und Berg, *Anbruch*, October 1924.

Humphrey Searle: Conversations with Webern, *MT*, October 1940, p. 405.

— Webern's last works, *MMR*, December 1946, p. 231.

— Studying with Webern, *RCM Magazine*, 1958, No. 2, p. 39.

— Mina studier hos Webern, *Nutida musik*, Vol. 2 (1958–9), No. 4, p. 11.

Gerd Sievers: AvW zum Gedenken, *Musica*, 1954, p. 20.

A. de Spitzmuller: 'Le triomphe de la sensibilité', *Contrepoints*, No. 2, February 1946, p. 71.

Peter Stadlen: Webern symposium, *Score*, No. 25, June 1959, p. 65.

— The complete music of AW, *London Musical Events*, September 1959, p. 37.

— The Webern Legend, *MT*, November 1960, p. 695; Die Webern-Legende, *Musica*, 1961, No. 2, p. 66.

— Webern and the twelve-note row, *Daily Telegraph*, 17 October 1970, p. 11.

Erwin Stein: Alban Berg und AvW, *Chesterian*, No. 26, October 1922, p. 33.

— Alban Berg—AvW, *Anbruch*, January 1923, p. 13.

— The art of AW, *Christian Science Monitor*, 22 June 1929.

— AW, *Anbruch*, June–July 1931, p. 107.

— AW, *Cahiers de la musique*, July–August 1937.

— AW, *MT*, January 1946, p. 14.

Rudolf Stephan: AvW, *Deutsche Univ. Zeitung*, 1956, Nos. 13–14.

Heinrich Strobel: So sehe ich Webern, *Melos*, September 1965, p. 285.

Karlheinz Stockhausen: For the 15th of September, 1955, in *Die Reihe*, No. 2 (Eng. edn., p. 37).

— Structure and experiential time, in *–do–*, p. 64.

H. H. Stuckenschmidt: AW, *Ricordiana*, June 1957, No. 6.

— AvW, in *Schöpfer der neuen Musik*, Suhrkamp Verlag (Frankfurt a.M.) 1958, p. 192.

— AvWs Wild, zurechtgerückt zum 75. Geburtstag, *Frankfurter Allg. Zeitung*, 3 December 1958.

Roy Travis: Direct motion in Schoenberg and Webern, *PNM*, spring–summer 1966, p. 85.

Roman Vlad: AvW e la composizione atematica, *La Rassegna musicale*, April–June 1955, p. 98.

J. van Voorthuysen: AWs complete œuvre, *Symphonia*, 1919, p. 81.

J. Vyslouzil: K hudebnimu slohu Antona Weberna, *Hudebni Rozhledy*, 1962, No. 22, p. 938.

T. Wendel: Webern festival, *Musical America*, August 1962, p. 16.

Arnold Whittall: After Webern, Wagner, *MR*, May 1967, p. 135.

Jacques Wildberger: Webern gestern und heute, Melos, April 1960, p. 126.

Friedrich Wildgans: AvW—Zu seinen 75. Geburtstag am 3. Dezember 1958, *ÖM*, November 1958, p. 457.

— Gustav Mahler und AvW, *ÖM*, June 1960, p. 302.

— AW, Calder & Boyards (London), 1966 (transl. Edith Temple Roberts and Humphrey Searle, with an introduction by Humphrey Searle).

Christian Wolff: Movement, *Die Reihe*, No. 2 (Eng. edn., p. 61).

P. Yates: Webern complete, *Saturday Review*, 11 May 1957, p. 39.

L. Zenk & F. Rederer: Mein Lehrer, '*23*', No. 14, 1934.

Winifried Zillig: AW, Aussenseiter und Vorbild, in *Variationen über neue Musik*, Munich, 1959.

MISCELLANEOUS OR UNSIGNED

Œuvres d'AW, *Musical Information Record*, No. 11, winter 1953–4, p. 17.

World of Webern, *Newsweek*, 16 August 1965, p. 77.

Addenda

Much of the following additional information has become available since this book was written in 1968–9.

BARTÓK

p. 18.   **12.** Pub. 1963, Zenemükiadó, in *Der junge Bartók I*.

              14. Pub. 1904, Bárd Ferenc.

              19. The third movement was pub. 1965 in *Documenta Bartókiana II*; the complete work pub. 1970 in Budapest.

              20. Add to Bibliography:

              Colin Mason: Kossuth, *The Listener*, 12 October 1967, p. 478.

              21. The Hungarian title is: Négy zongoradarab. No. 1 of the set was originally pub. 1904, Bárd Ferenc.

p. 19.   **23.** Pub. 1928–29 (Budapest).

              26. E. Tusa should read: Erzsébet Tusa.

              27. The title of this folksong is: Red apple fell in the mud (Piros alma leesett a sárba). Additionally pub. 1970, in *Documenta Bartókiana IV*.

              28. Pub. 1963, Zenemükiadó, in *Der junge Bartók I*.

p. 20.   **31b.** Pub. 1963, Zenemükiadó, in *Der junge Bartók I*.

              32. Pub. 1907, Budapest.

p. 21.   **39.** Add to Bibliography:

              Alexander L. Ringer: The Art of Third Guess—Beethoven to Becker to Bartók, *MQ*, July 1966, p. 304.

p. 24.   **58.** Pub. 1963, Zenemükiadó, in *Der junge Bartók I*.

              59. Full score pub. 1924.

              61. Add to Bibliography:

              Hilda Gervers: BB's 'Öt dal' Op. 15, *MR*, November 1969, p. 291.

              62. Add to Bibliography:

              Peter Meyer: BBs Ady-Lieder Op. 16, Winterthur, 1965.

p. 26.   **70.** Add to Bibliography:

              Jacques Chailley: Essai d'analyse du Mandarin Merveilleux, *Studia Musicologica*, 1966, VIII, 1–4.

p. 32.   **99.** Add to Bibliography:

              Jürgen Uhde: Bartóks Mikrokosmos—Spielanweisungen & Erläuterungen, Regensburg, n.d.

p. 33.   **103.** Add to Bibliography:

              Ove Nordwall: The original version of Bartók's Sonata for solo violin, *Tempo* No. 74, autumn 1965.

Addenda

105. Add to Bibliography:
John S. Weissmann: BBC concert, 27 November, *MR*, February 1947.

p. 34.   BARTÓK'S. WRITINGS See also:
András Szöllösy: Bartók Béla Összegyüjtött Irásai I., Zenemükiadó (Budapest) 1967.

pp. 34–   Add to General Bibliography:
40.   Henri en Jaap Geraeds: BB, Gottmer (Antwerp), 1951.
Everett Helm: BB in Selbstzeugnissen und Bilddokumente, Rowohlt (Hamburg), 1965.
— Bartók's American years, *London Magazine*, December 1965, p. 69.
Richard Petzold: BB, Sein Leben in Bildern, Leipzig, 1958.
Brunello Rondi: Bartók, Rome, 1950.
Bence Szabolcsi and Benjámin Rajeczky: The Handwriting of BB., Budapest, 1961.
Vernon H. Taylor: Contrapuntal techniques in the music of BB, Northwestern University (Evanston, Ill.), 1950.
Roswitha Traimer: BBs Kompositionstechnik—Dargestellt an seinen Sechs Streichquartetten, Bosse (Regensburg), 1956.
Jürgen Uhde: BB, Berlin-Dahlem, 1959.
John S. Weissmann: BB, an Estimate, *MR*, November 1946, p. 221.
— Bartók's String Quartets—supplement to complete recording (DGG), Hamburg, n.d.
— BB, Serbo-Croatian folk songs, *Journal of the English Folk Dance and Song Society*, December 1952, p. 43.
— BB Rumanian folk music (Ed.. Benjamin Suchoff), in *1969 Yearbook of the IFMC*, University of Illinois Press, p. 251.

BUSONI

p. 68.   61e. This version for orchestra is by Frederick Stock (rev. Busoni). fEbp: 2 March 1948, BBC Scottish Orchestra, cond. Ian Whyte. Another version for orchestra, by Denis ApIvor, also exists.
Bibliography:
Ronald Stevenson: Busoni's Great Fugue, *The Listener*, 3 February 1972.

FAURÉ

p. 167.   7. Also transcribed for cello and piano by Cesare Casella as *Lamento*.
p. 169.   28. Add: BIBLIOGRAPHY. Camille Saint-Saëns: Une sonate, *Journal de Musique*, 7 April 1877.
p. 170.   38. Ded. Mlle Alice Boissonnet.
p. 171.   51. Ded. Mlle Alex. Milochewitch.
65. Ded. Mlle Marie Poitevin.
p. 172.   72. Also arr. for violin or cello and piano, ded. Mlle Léonie Lépine.
75. The vocal score was arr. by Roger-Ducasse.
p. 173.   88. Nos. 2, 4, 5 & 6 were transcribed for piano by Gustave Samazeuilh.

91. Add to Bibliography:
Camille Bellaigue: La Bonne Chanson, *Revue des deux mondes*, 15 October 1897.
E. Jacques-Dalcroze: La Bonne Chanson, *Gazette musicale de la Suisse Romande*, 1 November 1894.

p. 174. 99. Ded. Mme Sigismond Bardac.

p. 175. 111. Also arr. by Alberto Bachmann for violin and piano.
112. This was written for W. H. Squire and was afterwards incorporated into the incidental music to *Pelléas et Mélisande*.

p. 176. 126. Ded. Mme Octave Maus.
138. Ded. Camille Saint-Saëns.

p. 177. 144. Ded. Queen Elisabeth of the Belgians.

p. 180. Philippe Fauré-Fremiet: GF. Add: New edition, Editions Albin Michel (Paris), 1957.
Add: Gabriel Faure: GF, Arthaud (Grenoble & Paris), 1945.
Charles Koechlin: GF, Félix Alcan (Paris), 1927. Add: English transl. Leslie Orrey, Dobson (London), 1945.

p. 181. Add: Norman Suckling: GF, Master Musicians series, Dent (London), 1946; new edition, 1951.

HINDEMITH

p. 189. 53. The revised version of No. 1 (Frau Musica) is entitled *In Praise of Music*.

p. 191. 66. Add: fp: 1929, Baden-Baden.

p. 201. 139. Add instrumentation: fl, ob, cl, bcl, bsn, hn, tpt.

p. 205. Add to Writings by Hindemith:
Unterweisung im Tonsatz: English translations of Book I (Theoretical Part) and Book II (Exercises in Two-Part Writing) were published in 1942 and 1941 respectively; Book III (Der dreistimmige Satz) was published in 1970 (German text only).
Add to General Bibliography:
Andres Briner: PH, Atlantis/Schott (Zürich/Mainz), 1971.

JANÁČEK

p. 267. 61. This is possibly identical with 59.

p. 268. 79. fp: 10 February 1894, Brno, cond. Leoš Janáček.

p. 270. 108. This is possibly the same work as 30.
111. This might better have been listed as 82a. In 1904, the composer extracted (?and revised) three pieces from the original set for separate publication.

p. 279. Add: Hans Hollander: LJ, Leben und Werk, Atlantis Verlag (Zürich), 1964.

KODÁLY

p. 288. 78. Add to publication details: revised edition, Geoffrey Russell-Smith, 1968–.

MAHLER

p. 296. Add: 12a. Bruckner: Symphony No. 3. Arr. Gustav Mahler for piano duet. 1880. Pub. Rättig (Vienna).

p. 297. 20. Add to publication: 1967, Universal-Edition/Internationale Gustav-Mahler Gesellschaft.

p. 298. **23.** Add to publication: 1971, Internationale Gustav-Mahler Gesellschaft.

p. 300. **31.** The original publication had the order of the second and third movements reversed (i.e. *2. Andante; 3. Scherzo*). I have followed the order as in the Internationale Gustav-Mahler Gesellschaft edition.

p. 304. **39.** The 1964 publication edited by Erwin Ratz is the Internationale Gustav-Mahler Gesellschaft edition.

Additions to General Bibliography:

p. 305. Kurt Blaukopf: GM oder Der Zeitgenosse der Zukunft, Molden (Vienna), 1969.

p. 312. Bruno Walter: Briefe 1894–1962, Fischer (Frankfurt), 1969.

NIELSEN

p. 352. Add to General Bibliography:

Robert Simpson: A great symphonist, *The Listener*, 14 June 1951.
— Nielsen the European, *The Listener*, 1 January 1953.
— Sibelius and Nielsen, BBC (London), 1965.

POULENC

p. 357. **36.** The authorship should read: Guillaume Apollinaire and Marie Laurencin.

p. 367. **142.** Add to Bibliography:

Denise Bourdet: Les Dialogues des Carmélites à l'Opéra, *Figaro littéraire*, 22 June 1957.
Claude Rostand: Dialogues des Carmélites, *Carrefour*, 6 February 1957.

p. 368. **148.** Add to Bibliography:

Bernard Gavoty: La Voix Humaine, *Journal musical français*, 17 March 1959.
Hélène Jourdan-Morhange: La Voix Humaine, *Les Lettres françaises*, 12 February 1959.
155. Add to Bibliography:

Marc Pincherle: La Dame de Monte Carlo, *Nouvelles littéraires*, 14 December 1961.

p. 369. Add to Writings by Poulenc:

Mes mélodies et leurs poètes, *Les Annales*, 1947.
Feuilles américaines, *La Table ronde*, June 1950.
La musique de piano d'Erik Satie, *RM*, June 1952.
Hommage à Béla Bartók, *RM* (Bartók number), 1955.
Additions to General Bibliography:

p. 369. Martine Cadieu: Duo avec FP, *Les Nouvelles littéraires*, 4 May 1961.
James Harding: The Ox on the Roof, Macdonald (London), 1972.

p. 370. Rollo H. Myers: Hommage à Poulenc, *M&M*, March 1963.

PROKOFIEV

p. 393. Add to General Bibliography:
Eric Roseberry: Prokofiev's piano sonatas, *M&M*, March 1961.

PUCCINI

p. 395. Add: **9a. La sconsolata.** For violin and piano. Pub. ?1883.
Add to General Bibliography:

p. 402.   W. S. Ashbrook: The operas of Puccini, Cassell (London), 1968.

p. 404.   Spike Hughes: Famous Puccini operas, Robert Hale (London), 1959.

RACHMANINOV

p. 408.   **33.** The revised versions of Nos. 3 & 5 are pub. Charles Foley.

p. 410.   **51.** Add: No. 2 rev. 5 February 1940 (*Allegro*), pub. Charles Foley.

p. 414.   **82a.** No. 2 was later published, slightly revised, as No. 6 of **90.** (Etudes Tableaux, Op. 39).

RAVEL

p. 425.   **32.** Add to Bibliography:

Felix Aprahamian: Ravel and Aloysius Bertrand, *The Listener*, 1 December 1966.

ROUSSEL

p. 447.   **49.** Add:

3 fl, pic, 2 ob, ca, 2 cl, bcl, 3 bsn; 4 hn, 4 tpt, 3 tmb, tuba; timp, cym, GC, tgle, tambour, tamtam, tamb de basque, celesta, xyl; hp, strings.

fp: 21 January 1927, Boston, Boston Symphony Orchestra cond. Serge Kussevitzky.

fFp: 21 May 1927, Concerts Kussevitsky.

fEp: 26 October 1928, Queen's Hall, BBC concert, cond. Sir Henry Wood.

Pub. 1927, Durand; incl. reduction for piano four hands by the composer.

SATIE

p. 462.   **63.** Add: fp: 21 February 1920, Paris, Théâtre des Champs-Elysées, cond. Koubitzky.

p. 463.   Additions to Writings by Erik Satie:

Occasional paragraphs and obiter dicta, in *L'Oeil de veau*, February 1912; in *391*, 1924, June, July, etc.

Mémoires d'un amnésique: Ce que je suis (fragment), *Bulletin de la S.I.M.*, 15 April 1912.

Mémoires d'un amnésique: La journée d'un musicien (fragment), *Bulletin de la S.I.M.*, 15 February 1913.

Mémoires d'un amnésique: L'Intelligence et la musicalité chez les animaux, *Bulletin de la S.I.M.*, 1 February 1914.

Eloge des critiques, *Action*, No. 8, August 1921.

Mémoires d'un amnésique: Recoins de ma vie (fragment), *Feuilles libres*, No. 35, January–February 1924.

Additions to General Bibliography:

p. 464.   Jean Cocteau: Le Rappel à l'ordre, Stock, 1926.

James Harding: The Ox on the Roof, Macdonald (London), 1972.

Patrick Gowers: Satie's Rose-Croix music, *PRMA*, 1965–66.

Addenda

SCHOENBERG

p. 474.   **26.** Add to Bibliography:
Eric Roseberry: Schoenberg's 'oratorio for modern man', *The Listener*, 4 November 1965.

p. 478.   **46.** Add: Libretto by the composer.

SIBELIUS

p. 495.   **7.** Should read: *Suite in G minor* For string trio. 1885. Unpub.
11. This work dates from before 1885.

p. 496.   **34.** fbp: 19 September 1965, BBC Northern Orchestra cond. Meredith Davies.

p. 497.   **35 and 35a.** Add to Bibliography:
Nils-Eric Ringbom: De två versionerna av Sibelius' tondikt En Saga, Turku (1856); summary in English.

p. 506.   **107.** Add to Bibliography:
John Rosas: Sibelius' musik till skadespelet Ödlan, Suomen Musiikin Vuosikirja, 1960–61.

Add to General Bibliography:

p. 515.   Fred Blum: JS, an International Bibliography on the occasion of the Centennial Celebrations, Detroit Studies in Music Bibliography, 1965.

p. 517.   Cecil Gray, Sibelius, OUP (London), 1931; second ed., 1934.

p. 518.   Ilmari Krohn: Der Formenbau in der Symphonien von JS, 2 vols., Helsinki, 1945–46.

p. 519.   John Rosas: Otryckta kammarmusik av JS, Acta Academiae Aboensis, 1961.
Robert Simpson. Sibelius and Nielsen, BBC (London), 1965.

p. 520.   Simon Vestdijk: De symfonieen van JS, De Besige (Amsterdam), 1962.
Ralph Wood: Sibelius's use of percussion, *M&L*, January 1942.

STRAUSS

p. 521.   **4a. Waldkonzert** (Vogel). For voice and piano. 1871.
4b. Der weisse Hirsch (Uhland). For voice and piano. 1871.
4c. Der böhmische Musikant (Oskar Pletzsch). For voice and piano. 1871.
4d. Herz mein Herz (Geibel). For voice and piano. 1871.
5a. Moderato. For piano. 1871.
6a. Langsamer Satz. For piano. 1872.
8a. Zwei Etüden. For two horns. 1873.
8b. Fünf kleine Stücke. For piano. 1873.

p. 522.   **16a. Zwei Lieder** (Eichendorff). For voice and piano. 1876.
32a. Aria. 'Op. 15'. For tenor and chorus.
39. This is an orchestral version of No. 5 from **49.**

p. 524.   **74.** This entry should be deleted: it is the same song as **72.**

p. 525.   **80b.** Also version orch. Robert Heger, pub. 1933, Universal-Edition.

p. 529.   **115c and 117a.** Add: Pub. 1933, Universal-Edition.

p. 530.   **121a.** Add: Pub. 1933, Universal-Edition.

p. 533.   **131a.** There is also a version for horn and piano.

p. 535. **146.** In the instrumentation, the 4 sax are ad lib.

p. 539. **158.** Also version for orchestra by the composer.

p. 540. **159a.** Arr. Otto Singer.

  159c. Arr. Arthur Rodzinsky.

p. 543. **164.** The instrumentation given here follows publisher's specification but is not in accord with the full score where orchestration details are as follows:

  4 fl, pic (3 fl, 2 pic), 3 ob, ca, cl in D, 2 cl, bcl, cbs cl, 4 bsn, cbsn; 6 hn, 4 tpt, 4 tmb, ten tuba, bs tuba; 6 timp, tgle, tamb, side dm, xyl, 2 cast, 2 small cym, glock; 4 cel, 4 hp, piano, organ, strings.

STRAVINSKY

p. 567. **1a. Tarantella.** For piano. 14 October 1898. Ded. A. Kudnev. Unpub.

  1b. Storm Cloud (A. S. Pushkin). Romance for voice and piano. 25 January 1902. Unpub.

  1c. Scherzo. For piano. Ded. 'à Monsieur Nicolas Richter—temoignage d'un profond respect de la part de l'auteur'. 1902. Unpub.

  2a. Cantata for the 60th birthday of N. A. Rimsky-Korsakov. For mixed choir and piano. 1904. fp: 6 March 1904, in the apartment of Rimsky-Korsakov, choir consisting of S.N., N.N. and V.N. Rimsky-Korsakov, A. V. Ossovsky, S. S. Mitusov and I. I. Lapshin. Unpub. MS lost.

  2b. Conductor and Tarantula (Kosma Prutkov). For voice and piano. fp: 6 March 1906, in the apartment of Rimsky-Korsakov. Unpub. MS lost.

p. 589. **94.** Add to Bibliography:

  Eric Roseberry: Some thoughts on Stravinsky's Rake's Progress, *The Listener*, 29 November 1969.

p. 594. **119.** Add to Bibliography:

  Eric Roseberry: Stravinsky's Requiem Canticles, *The Listener*, 1 August 1968.

  121. Two Sacred Songs from the 'Spanisches Liederbuch'. May 1968. Ded. Marilyn Horne.

  1. *Herr, was trägst der Boden hier . . .*

  2. *Wunden trägst du . . .*

  3 cl, 2 hn, solo violins 1 & 2, va, c, db.

  fp: 6 September 1968, Los Angeles, County Museum of Art, Christina Krooskos, cond. Robert Craft.

  Pub. 1969, Boosey & Hawkes.

VAUGHAN WILLIAMS

p. 622. Add: **154a. A Cotswold Romance.** Cantata for tenor, soprano, mixed voice chorus and orchestra. Adapted by Maurice Jacobson (in collaboration with the composer) from the opera Hugh the Drover. Words: Harold Child. Dur. 50'.

  2 fl, 2 ob, 2 cl, 2 bsn; 4 hn, 2 tpt, 3 tmb, tuba; timp, cym, GC, side dm, tgle; hp, strings. *Or* strings and piano (or optional augmentation).

  fp: 10 May 1951, Tooting (Central Hall), Olive Groves, James Johnston,

Addenda

South-West London Choral Society and South-West Professional Orchestra, cond. Frank Odell.

Pub. 1951, Curwen.

p. 644. Add to General Bibliography:

Michael Hurd: VW, Faber (London), 1970.